ISBN 978-0-282-50982-8
PIBN 10854257

English
Français
Deutsche
Italiano
Español
Português

www.forgottenbooks.com

Mythology Photography **Fiction**
Fishing Christianity **Art** Cooking
Essays Buddhism Freemasonry
Medicine **Biology** Music **Ancient
Egypt** Evolution Carpentry Physics
Dance Geology **Mathematics** Fitness
Shakespeare **Folklore** Yoga Marketing
Confidence Immortality Biographies
Poetry **Psychology** Witchcraft
Electronics Chemistry History **Law**
Accounting **Philosophy** Anthropology
Alchemy Drama Quantum Mechanics
Atheism Sexual Health **Ancient History**
Entrepreneurship Languages Sport
Paleontology Needlework Islam
Metaphysics Investment Archaeology
Parenting Statistics Criminology
Motivational

First Edition, Second Issue, with the Supplement. With the fine engraved portrait of King James, enthroned in robes of state, by Simon Pass; the engraved title-page by Elstrack, a full-page woodcut of the royal arms, a small engraved portrait of Prince Charles, by Pass, at the head of the dedication; and woodcut initials. Colophons appear on p. 570 and at the end of the Supplement (p. 622).

The volume includes the famous *Counterblast to Tobacco*, the *Daemonologie*, the *Basilicon Doron* and *Discourse of the Powder Treason*. STC 14345.

TAXIS KAI KOSMOS

Schmidtchen

(Continued over)

MES I. Workes First collected edi-
n. Superb engraved title and portrait.
oodcut initials Folio Original ar-
rial binding. Upper joint cracked. A
ry good copy. 1616. £9/9/0

ncludes the famous " Daemonologie " (45 pps)
nd " A Counterblast to Tobacco " which ter-
inates with " A custome loathsome to the eye,
ateful to the nose, harmfull to the braine, dan-
erous to the lungs, and in the blacke stinking
ume thereof neerest resembling the horrible
tigian smoak of the pit that is bottomless "
he verse beneath the portrait (" Crounes have
neir compasse, length of dayes their date . . ")
as often been ascribed to Shakespeare

" The fearefull aboundinge at this time in this countrie, of these detestable slaves of the Devill, the Witches or enchaunters, hath moved me (beloved reader) to despatch in post, this following treatise of mine, not in any wise (as I protest) to serve for a shew of my learning and ingine, but onely (moved of conscience) to preasse thereby, so farre, as I can, to resolve the doubting harts of many; both that such assaults of Sathan are practised, and that the instrumentes thereof, merits most severely to be punished : against the damnable opinions of two principally in our age, whereof the one called Scot an Englishman, is not ashamed, in publike print to deny, that ther can be such a thing as Witch-craft. . . Etc. "—James I in his

OF SHAKESPEARIAN INTEREST.

1071   A MEDITATION upon the 27, 28, 29 verses of the XXVII. Chapter of St. Matthew, or a paterne for a Kings inauguration. Written by the Kings Maistie.

FIRST EDITION. 12mo. *Original vellum.*

London, Printed by John Bill, 1620.   £12 12s

With dedicatory epistle by James I to his son, afterwards Charles I :—"Make it therefore your vade mecum, to prepare you and put you in a habit for that day, which I dare sweare, you will never wish for, (as you gave sufficient proofe by your

careful attendance in my late great sicknesse, out of which it pleased God to deliver me) and I hope I shal never give you cause. But it will be great reliefe to you in the bearing of your burthen, that you bee not taken tardè; but that you foresee the weight of it before hand, and make your selfe able to support the same," etc.

James I goes on to speak about the succession of Kings, one instance quoted being of special interest as it forms an important scene in Shakespeare's play of Henry IV.

" And one of our owne predecessors, Henrie the fourth (called Henry of Bullenbrooke), being in a trance upon his death bed ; his sonne, Henrie the fift, thinking hee had beene dead, a little nimbly carried away the croune that stood by his Father : but the King recovering a little out of his fit missed his crowne, and called for it. And when his sonne brought it backe againe, he told him that if hee had knowne what a crowne was, hee would not have beene so hastie : for he protested that he was never a day without trouble since it was first put upon his head," etc.

The closing lines in the scene in Henry IV, Part II, run :—

" Thy wish was father, Harry, to that thought :
I stay too long by thee, I weary thee.
Dost thou so hunger for my empty chair,
That thou wilt needs invest thee with my honours,
Before thy hour be ripe? O foolish youth!
Thou seek'st the greatness that will overwhelm thee " Etc., etc.

tion.
Woo
mori
very

Incl
and
minɑ
hate
gero
tum·
Stlg·
The
the
has

26

MOST

. . . .
Bill,
First
spine
The
frout
affec
end·i

A
COLLECTION OF
HIS MAIESTIES
WORKES.

BEATI PACIFICI

Crounes haue their compasse, length of dayes their date,
Triumphes their tombes, felicitie see state :
Of more then earth, can earth make none partaker,
But knowledge makes the KING most-like his maker.

Simon Passæus sculp:Lond.   Ioh: Bill excudit.

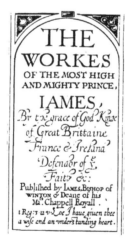

THE
WORKES
OF THE MOST HIGH
AND MIGHTY PRINCE,

IAMES,

By the grace of God Kinge
of Great Brittaine
France & Ireland
Defendor of the
Faith &c:

Published by IAMES, Bishop of
WINTON & Deane of his
Ma. Chappell Royall.

1 Reg: 3 12 v. Loe I haue giuen thee
a wise end an vnderstanding heart.

THE
WORKES OF
THE MOST HIGH
AND MIGHTIE
PRINCE,
IAMES
BY THE GRACE OF
GOD, KING OF GREAT
BRITAINE, FRANCE AND
IRELAND, DEFENDER
of the FAITH, &c.

PVBLISHED BY IAMES, *BISHOP*
of Winton, and Deane of his MAIESTIES
CHAPPEL ROYALL.

---

1. REG. 3. VERS. 12.
Loe, I haue giuen thee a wise and an vnderstanding heart.

LONDON
PRINTED BY ROBERT BARKER AND
IOHN BILL, PRINTERS TO THE KINGS
moſt Excellent MAIESTIE.
ANNO 1616.

¶ *Cum Priuilegio.*

tion
Wo
moi
ver)

Inc
anc
mii
hat
ger
fun
Stij
Th
the
ha:

2(

MOS

. . . .
Bill,
Firs
spin
The
fron
affe
end-

DIEV ET MON DROIT

tion
Wo
mo
ver

Inc
an
mi
hat
ger
fur
Stu
Th
the
ha

2
MOS

. . .
Bill
Fire
spin
The
fron
affe
end-

TO THE THRICE
ILLVSTRIOVS AND
Most Excellent Prince,

CHARLES,

THE ONELY SONNE OF
OVR SOVERAIGNE LORD
The King.

SIR:

 Haue humbly fought leaue of his moft Excellent MAIESTIE, to prefent your *Highneffe* with this *Volume* of his MAIESTIES WORKES. I durft not but make the Suite, and his MAIESTIE could not well deny it. I will not fay, that it had beene a peece of *Iniustice* in the KING to haue denyed you this right : But I dare fay, it had beene a point of Sacriledge in a *Churchman* to haue ftolne from you fuch a por-
tion

tion of your Inheritance, which confifts as much in the
WORKES of his Royall *Vertues*, as in the wealth of his
mighty *Kingdomes*. *Bafilius* wrote *de Infitutione Principis*
to his Sonne *Leo* ; *Conftantinus* to his Sonne *Romanus* ;
Manuell to his Sonne *Iohannes* ; and *Charles* the fift, to
his Sonne *Philip* : The workes of the three former are extant both in *Greeke* and *Latine*. His *Maieftie*, after the
Example of thofe *Emperours*, and fundry other *Kings*,
wrote his ΒΑΣΙΛΙΚΟΝ - ΔΩΡΟΝ to *Prince
Henry*, your *Highneffe* moft worthy *Brother* : His part, by
GOD his Prouidence, is falne to your Lot; and who may
iuftly detaine from you the reft ? The rule in Scripture
is; that if the firft fruits be holy, fo is the whole lumpe; and
to whom the firft was giuen, to him all the reft was due:
To your *Highnes* therefore are thefe offered, as to the trew
Heire and Inheritor of them. And that I may make you
the better accompt of them; May it pleafe your *Highneffe*
to vnderftand, that of thefe *Workes*, fome were out before;
fome other of them neuer faw light before; and others
were almoft loft and gone, or at leaft abufed by falfe copies, to their owne difgrace and his *Maiefties* great difhonour. Now it being the duetie of all *Deanes* in their
Churches, *Diſperfa colligere*; I thought it might fort well
with the nature of my place in the *Chappel*, wherein I haue
had the Honour fo many yeeres to ferue his *Maieftie*,
to gather thefe things that were fcattered, and to bring to
light thofe that too long had lien in darkenes, and to preferue in one body, what might eafily haue bin loft in parts.
In this *Prefentment*, I muft humbly craue of your *Highnes*,
not to be miftaken in the trew meaning and maner of it :
For thefe *Workes* come not to you, as vfually Bookes doe
to men of great *Dignitie*, for *Patronage* and *Protection* ; for
Protection is properly from iniurie ; and that the Royall
Author of them is beft able to right : But to you they
come partly for preferuation, and for that the Difpofition

of

DEDICATORIE.

of Nature hath made you more apt, and more principally for a Patterne, and that not vnfitly; since the *Samplar* is
euer more ancient then the *Exemplification*: And as in the
preseruation, the Sonne hath his aduantage by succeeding; so in the Patterne, the Father by preceding hath his
Prerogatiue. Let these *Workes* therefore, most Gracious
Prince, lie before you as a Patterne; you cannot haue a
better: Neither doeth the Honour of a good Sonne consist in any thing more, then in immitating the good *Presidents* of a good *Father*; as we may very well perceiue by
the Scripture phrase, where the vsuall *Encomium* of good
Kings is, that they walked in the wayes of their Fathers.
Al men see, how like the Patterne GOD and *Nature* haue
framed the outward *Lineaments*: and who knowes your
Highnes wel, knowes also, that the inward *Abilliments* hold
in the like proportion. The *Philosophers* say, that Imitation proceeds from Inclination; And trewly, if your future Imitation be answerable to your forward Inclination, in *Religion, Learning* and *Vertue*; your *Highnesse*
cannot come farre short of your *Patterne*, nor yet of any
of your *Predecessors* that euer went before you:
Which GOD grant together with the length of
many good and happy *Dayes.*

Your HIGHNESSE

Most humbly

IA. WINTON.

THE

tion
Wo
mo
ver

In
an
mi
ha
ge
fur
St
Th
th
ha

2
MOS

. . . .
Bili
Firs
spir
The
fron
affe

THE PREFACE TO
THE READER.

Mongſt the infinite number of great
Volumes wherewith the world ſeemes,
as it were, to bee wayed downe, there
bee few of them that were written at
once, or were at firſt publiſhed together. Writings as they conſiſt of ſundry natures; ſo they will beare a diuers
maner of Edition. To ſet foorth an
Art by pieces, is to ſhew you a body diſmembred; the one is no
more vncomely, then the other is vnproper. To publiſh a Hiſtory before it be at an end, is to turne the Hower-glaſſe before it bee
runne out; neither of both will giue you a trew taſte of the time.
But writings of other Natures, Common places and Controuerſies, Meditations and Commentaries, as they are for the moſt
part, accidentally taken vp, ſo they are as occaſionally ſet out: They
craue no other birth into the world, then they had conceptions in
our braines, ſingly by vs conceiued, and ſingly by themſelues
ſet out.

The different maner of GOD his ſetting foorth of his owne
Workes, may inſtruct vs in this point. His diuine Wiſedome held
one courſe in his Naturall Workes, an other in his Ceremonialls,
Politicalls and Moralls. In his Naturalls he made a maſſe at
once, which ſpeedily he diuerſified into diuers formes. Hee gaue
a kinde of potentiall delineation of all things in that vniuerſall
matter, which preſently hee diſtinguiſhed into diuers Species in
b   perfection:

perfection : But in his Ceremonialls, hee takes another course, he brings not them out of a Masse, but into a Masse : He doeth not out of a Totum produce the parts, but out of the parts make vp the whole. For example; In the Ceremonialls, first he beginnes with Sacrifice, long after he followes with Circumcision, then hee filleth a Tabernacle with them; at last makes them full vp in a Temple. In his Politicalls, hee beginnes with a paternall Gouernment in a family, proceeds to an Election of a Captaine in an Armie, as in Iosuah and the Iudges, perfects it by way of Succession in a setled Kingdome, as in Solomon and his Successors. In his Moralls, hee beginnes with the word out of his owne mouth, proceeds with the Tables written by his owne fingers, followes on with the fiue Bookes penned by Moses, till hee make vp the Canon perfect by a number of succeeding Prophets.

What we haue from GOD in a president, it may wel beseeme vs to practise ; and since his Bookes came out so farre asunder, it is no reproach to any man, though his Workes come not foorth together: for there is a reason for it in vs answerable in some proportion to that of the Workes of GOD, for workes of Nature haue their roote from within vs, and bring with them a radicall kinde of ver- tue, that neuer suffers them to rest, till they haue produced their fruite to perfect forme and perfection : Workes of deliberation and Art, haue their foundation from without vs, and giue vs occasion to worke vpon them, as our phantasies thinke fittest for the present time : Hence proceeds it, that the workes of Nature haue so few errors in them; those of Art so many; They of Nature so constant, they of Arte so variable ; they of Nature so perma- nent, they of Art so soone perish ; they of Nature so well accepted and approued of all, they of Art accepted or reiected, as it pleaseth the seuerall apprehensions of men to conceiue of them.

Now, albeit the workes of men be of Errors so full, of nature so different, subiect to so many Interpretations, published at so diuers times ; Yet hath it bene euer esteemed a matter commendable to collect them together, and incorporate them into one Body, that we may behold at once, what diuers Off-springs haue proceeded from

from one braine, and how various Conceptions the wit of man is able to afford the world. To instance in a few of them beginning a little higher then the writings of ordinarie men. The seruants of Hezekiah are commended in Scripture for collecting together the Sentences of Solomon. Iesus the sonne of Sirach is praised for searching out the Copies of his Grandfathers workes: But principally Ezra is had in great honour for setting in order the whole Bookes of the Old Testament, and deuiding them into Chapters and Verses, which before were caried along in a scroule, by a continuall Series, without any distinction at all. S. Iohn is reported to haue searched out the Copies of the three former Euangelists, and to haue added his owne for the fourth in that order, as now they are extant. And the Primitiue Church was curious to gather together the Epistles of the Holy Apostles; which, they being not able by reason of persecution perfectly to performe in euery place, gaue occasion to after-times, to call the authority of so many of them into question.

But to descend, How are we bound to those, who haue laboured in setting out the Counsells, and Works of the Fathers together? Insomuch, that we thinke our selues as much bound to Eusebius and Hierom, and of later times to Peter Crab and Erasmus, and diuers others, who haue laboured in that kinde, as wee doe almost to the Authors themselues. Traian commended Plutark for gathering the Apothegmes of wise men together. Constantinus the sonne of Leo, collected out of all Histories, both in the East and West, one Corpus Historicum, which they counted an inestimable Treasure. Iustinian by the helpe of Tribonianus did the like in the Lawes. Gratian compiled the Decrees out of the Epistles of Popes, Councells and Fathers. Damascen collected into one body of Diuinitie, the Sentences of the Greeke Fathers; And Peter Lumbard 400. yeeres after him by his example did the like in the Latine Fathers. And how doe wee labour to recouer Bookes that are lost? The Bookes of Origen that amounted to sixe thousand, as Epiphanius witnesseth, were much laboured for by Eusebius and others. The Bookes of Ci-

cero

cero de Repub. *were much fought for by* Cardinall Poole *; and great fummes of money haue bene fpent to recouer the loft* Decades *of* Liuie. *Wherefore fince it hath beene heretofore the practife of all aages, to collect the workes of* Men *of worth, and preferue them from perifhing ; to labour much in recouering thofe that haue bene loft ; to giue to euery childe the owne* Father *; to euery* Booke *the trew* Author *: (for there neuer had bene halfe fo many birds to haue flowen about the world with falfe feathers , if euery* Author *had fet out his owne workes together in his owne time,)* I *hope then it fhall not be now a matter of reproofe in a* Seruant, *to trauaile in the fetting foorth of the* Works *of his* Mafter *; and for giuing you that together , which before yee could hardly get a-funder ; and for preferuing that in a* Maffe *from perifhing, that might eafily be loft in a* Mite.

But while I am collecting workes one way, I heare others fcat-tering wordes as faft an other way , affirming , it had beene better his Maieftie *had neuer written any* Bookes *at all ; and being writ-ten, better they had perifhed with the prefent, like* Proclamations, *then haue remayned to* Pofterity : *For fay thefe* Men *, Little it befitts the* Maiefty *of a* King *to turne* Clerke, *and to make a warre with the penne , that were fitter to be fought with the* Pike *; to fpend the powers of his fo exquifite an vnderftanding vpon pa-per, which had they beene fpent on powder , could not but haue pre-uayled ere this , for the* Conqueft *of a* Kingdome. *For a* King, *fay they, to enter a* Controuerfie *with a* Scholler, *is , as if he fhould fight a* Combate *with a* Kerne *; he doth no more defcend from his* Honour *in the one, then he brings vpon himfelfe* Difgrace *by the other.* And *fince that* Booke-writing *is growen into a* Trade *; It is as difhonorable for a* King *to write* bookes *; as it is for him to be a* Practitioner *in a* Profeffion. If *a* King *will needs write ; Let him write like a* King *; euery* Lyne *a* Law, *euery* Word *a* Pre-cept, *euery* Letter *a* Mandate. In *good trewth, I haue had my eares fo oft dung through with thefe* Obiections *and the like, as I know not whether I conceiued amiffe of my felfe or no, thinking I had more ability to anfwere thefe* Calumnyes, *then I had patience* *to heare them* : *And therefore hauing so fit opportunity, I shall not let to deliuer my opinion* ; Whether it may sorte with the Maieltie of a King, to be a writer of Bookes, or no. *First I could neuer reade, that there was any Law against it ; and where we haue no Law, the best is to follow good Examples : And many Diuines are of opinion, that examples that are not contrary to any Precept, doe binde vs in practise, at least so farre ; that though they doe not inforce vs to the doing, yet they warrant the deede when it is done ; And if Examples will serue the turne, wee haue Examples enough.*

First to beginne with the King of Kings *God himselfe, who as he doth all things for our good ; So doeth he many things for our Imitation. It pleased his Diuine wisedome to bee the first in this Rancke, that we read of, that did euer write. Hee wrote, and the writing was the writing, saith* Moses, *of God ; the maner was after the maner of engrauing ; the matter was in Stone cut into two Tables, and the Tables were the worke of God written on both sides.* Diuines *hold, that the Heart is the principall Seate of the Soule ; which Soule of ours is the immediate worke of God, as these Tables were the immediate worke of his owne fingers. The Stone, the expresse represent of the hardnesse of our heart ; the engrauing the worke of God so deepely impressed, that it can neuer be blotted out ; the writing, the writing of the Law in our hearts ; In two Tables, for our double duty to God and Man ; on both sides to take vp our heart so wholly, that nothing contrary to those Precepts should euer haue any place in our Soules. And certainely from this little* Library, *that God hath erected within vs, is the foundation of all our Learning layd ; So that people Ciuilized doe account themselues depriued of one of the best abilities of nature, if they be not somewhat inabled by writing, to expresse their mindes : And there is no Nation so brutish or Barbarous, that haue not inuented one kinde of Character or other, whereby to conuey to others their inward Conceptions. From these Tables of God, wee may come to the writing of our Blessed* Sauiour, *which we may put in the next place, though not for order yet for Honour.* His Diuine

uine *Maiestie left behinde him no Monument of writing, writ-*
ten by his owne hand in any externall Booke; for he was to induce
and bring in an other maner of the writing of the Law of Loue;
not in Tables of stone; written not with incke and paper, but in the
Tables of our fleshly hearts written by the Spirit of the Liuing
God: Yet did he once with his owne finger, write on the Pauement
of the Temple of Ierusalem. *What he writ, I will not now dif-*
cuffe. S. Ambrofe *faith he wrote this Sentence :* Feſtucam
in oculo fratris cernis, trabem in tuo non vides. Beda
thinkes, he wrote that Sentence that he ſpake : He that is without finne, let him caſt the firſt ſtone at her. Haymo *hath*
a pretty Conceit : He thinketh, he wrote certaine Characters in the
Pauement, which the Accufers beholding might ſee, as in a glaſſe,
their owne wickedneſſe; and ſo bluſhing at it went their wayes.
What euer it was, ſure we are, our Sauiour *would haue falſe accu-*
fations written in duſt, to bee troden vnder foote of them that paſſe
by. But howfoeuer, I ſay, our Bleſſed Sauiour *did leaue behind him*
no writing of his owne hand; Yet we may not deny, but that God
in the old Teſtament *and our* Sauiour *in the New, haue left vs*
many bookes of their owne inditements : For all the Bookes of ho-
ly Scripture were written by inſpiration; and the Prophets and
Apoſtles were but their Amanuenſes, *and writ onely as they*
were led and actuated by the Spirit of God: So that we may not
make the Author of any of thoſe Bookes any other then God
Himſelfe.

The old world before the flood wil afford vs no writings, neither
did that aage require them; for the liues of men of that aage were
liuing Libraries, *and laſted longer then the labors of men doe*
in this aage : Yet S. Iude *doeth inſinuate ſomewhat of the writings*
of Enoch, *who though he were not in Stile a* King, *Yet there is no*
reaſon to contend with him for that Title; for his Dominion would
beare it, ſtanding Heire-Apparent to the greater part of the world.
Origen, Tertullian *and* Auguſtine *report many things out of*
the ſuppoſititous writings that went vnder his name : And Iofephus *and that* Berofus, *that wee haue, tell vs, that hee erected*
two

two pillars, the one of Stone, the other of Bricke, wherein he wrote of the two-fold destructions of the world, the one by Water, the other by Fire : But howsoeuer that be trew, it is very probable, he wrote something of that matter, which though it perished with that world; yet doubtlesse the memory thereof was preserued by Tradition vnto the dayes of the Apostles.

I will not here insist vpon the writings of Moses, *who was not onely a* Priest, *and a* Prophet, *but was, as himselfe records, a-mongst the people a* King, *and was the first that euer receiued authoritie from* G O D *to write in* Diuinitie : *Neither will* I *insist vpon the* Example *of* King Dauid, *in whose* Psalmes *and* Himnes, *are resounded out the praises of* G O D *in all the Churches; for that* I *finde nothing that these men writ, but what they writ as the* Scribes *of* G O D, *acted, as I said euen now, by* G O D *his* Spirit, *and not guided by their owne. Yet I suppose wee may safely collect thus much from them, that if* G O D *had thought it a matter derogatory to the* Maiestie *of a* King *to bee a* Writer, *he would not haue made choice of those, as his chiefe* Instruments *in this kinde, who were principalls in that other* Order. *I would easily beleeue, that such men as haue had the honour to be* G O D *his* Pen-men, *should neuer vouchsafe to write any thing of their owne : for as we hold in a pious opinion, that the blessed* Virgine, *hauing once conceiued by the holy* Ghost, *would neuer after conceiue by man; So surely men, that had deliuered nothing but the conceptions of that* Spirit, *should hardly be drawne euer to set out any of their owne labours. But we see the flat contrary both in* Samuel *and* Solomon, *the one the greatest* Iudge, *the other the most glorious* King, *that euer that* Kingdome *had.* Samuel, *who writ by* G O D's *appointment, the greatest part of those two* Bookes, *that beare his name, writ also by his owne accord, a* Booke *contayning the* Law *of a* King, *or* Institution *of a* Prince, *whereby hee laboured to keepe the* King *as well from declining to* Tyrannie, *as the people from running into* Libertie. Solomon, *besides the* Bookes *of* Scripture, *which remaine, writ many likewise of his owne accord, which are lost : For to say nothing of his* 3000. Para-

bles,

bles, *his* 5000. *Songes, that* ingens opus, *as the* Hebrues *call it, of the nature of all things,* Birds *and* Beasts, Fowles *and* fishes, Trees *and plants, from the* Hyfop *to the* Cedar : *All these were rather workes to manifest humane wisedome, then* Diuine *knowledge; written rather for the recreation of his owne spirit, then for the edification of the* Church : *For I cannot conceiue, but those* Bookes *would rather haue taught vs the learning of* Nature; *(for which* God *hath left vs to the writings of men) then edified vs in the gifts of* Grace ; *for which hee hath giuen vs his owne* Booke. *Neither let any man suggest, that these writings, that are lost, and, as they say, were destroyed in the destruction of the* Temple *by the* Babylonians, *were of the same authoritie, as those that doe remaine : for* I *can hardly be induced to beleeue, that the writings, that were indited by the Spirit of* God, *layed vp in the* Arke, *receiued into the* Canon, *read publikely in the Church, are vtterly perished.* It *is a desperate thing to call, either the prouidence of* God, *or the fidelity of the* Church *in question in this point : For if those, that haue bene, are perished; then, why may not these that remaine as well be lost ? which is contrary to our* Sauiours *affertion, that one* Iota *shall not perish till all bee fulfilled : Therefore* I *rather incline to thinke ; that what euer was Scripture, still is, then that any is lost :* Neither *is this opinion fo curious to hold, as the other is dangerous to beleeue ;* Better *it is euer, to argue our felues of ignorance, then to accufe* God *of improuidence : But if fo much Scripture be lost, as is alleadged, farewell* God *his prouidence, farewell the fidelitie of the* Church, *to whofe care was concredited the* Oracles *of* God. *Let vs come to the writings of* Kings, *where we shall not incurre any danger of this controuerfie ; that were fo farre from being acted by* God *his Spirit; that they were more like those Difciples of* Iohn, *that had not heard whether there were an* Holy-Ghost, *or no ; that knew nothing of* God, *though they felt neuer fo much of his Goodneffe; that neuer beleeued his Omnipotencie, though they had neuer fo much experience of his* Power.

To beginne with the Affyrians, *whofe first* Monarch *was*
Nimrod,

Nimrod, *and his chiefe Citie* Babel : *from his time to* Sardanapalus *the last of that Monarchie, there was no* King *amongst
them, that gaue himselfe to Letters : for as their Kingdome was
founded in Tyrannie , so they laboured to keepe it in Barbaritie ;
neither must we euer looke to see Learning flourish, where Tyrannie beareth the Standerd ; for Learning hath no more a facultie
to bring the minde to vnderstanding , then it hath with it a power,
that workes the will to libertie ; neither of which , can euer consist
with Tyrannie : And therefore it is no wonder, that this aage
affoorded no learned* Kings : *for in that State, which continued
thirteene or foureteene hundred yeeres, yee can scarce reade of a
learned man : Therefore let either* Histories *or* Poets *paint
that out for a Golden aage, as they please, there was neuer any
aage, that hath left so little memory of the Golden tincture of
their Witts.*

After the time of Sardanapalus, *in the dayes of* Phull, Tig-
lath-Philasar *and* Salmanasar , *of whom mention is made in
Scripture, and to whom, as it is thought,* Ionas *preached, and with
whom some of the* Prophets *were conuersant , when as these*
Kings *came into the land of* Israel, *as they did in the dayes of*
Menahem, *who gaue to* Phul-Belochus *a thousand Talents
of Siluer for a Tribute ; And in the dayes of* Hezechiah *came*
Salmanasar *and besieged* Samaria *three yeeres, and caried away
a great part of the people of the Kingdome of* Israel: *From that
time forward, their* Kings *gaue themselues to Letters ; insomuch
as in the dayes of* Nabucodonosor, *who set vp the Monarchy
of the* Babylonians, *within one hundred yeeres of* Salmanasar
King *of the* Assyrians, *learning was in great estimation, and the*
Kings Court *was a Schoole for the best witts of the Kingdome to
be bred in , that they might bee able to stand before the* King *furnished with all learning and vnderstanding. And if* Stories *do
not intollerably deceiue vs ;* Daniel *and his companions instructed
fiue great Monarches , as in the trew knowledge of* G O D *, so in
the vnderstanding of all excellent Arts and Sciences ; Namely*
Nabuchodonosor, Euilmerodack, Baltazar, Darius *of the*

c   Medes,

Medes, *and* Cyrus *of the* Perſians : *And it were no hard mat-*
ter to proue the trewth of this out of Daniel *himſelfe*.

Come to the Perſians, *who conuerſed more with the* Prophets,
as with Ezra, Nehemiah, Zachary, Malachy *and the people*
that were in captiuitie ; we ſhall finde them giuen much to Letters.
Cyrus *the firſt Monarch is recorded to haue written large*
Commentaries *of all his diurnall Actions : amongſt thoſe Books*
are found, ſaith Eſdras, *the* Edicts *of reducing of the* Iewes *to*
their Countrey: He wrote diuers Letters for the ſame purpoſe to all
the chiefe Cities of Aſia ; *ſome whereof, we haue in the* 11. *of* Io-
ſephus, *Chap.the firſt.* *Many things likewiſe are reported to*
haue bene written of Artaxerxes, Darius, *and ſome others of*
thoſe Monarches, as wee may partly conceiue by the Canonicall *Bookes of* Ezra *and* Nehemiah, *and more by the Apocri-*
*phal-*Eſdras, *who reports it to haue bene a cuſtome of thoſe* Kings,
ſo much to delight in learning, and in the ſayings of wiſe men, that
they vſed for an exerciſe in their greateſt Solemnities, to haue ſo-
lemne Orations *made in the preſence of the* King *and State, of*
ſundry purpoſes, which, whoſo performed to the liking of the King,
was rewarded with the higheſt Preferments, that ſo mighty a Mo-
narch could aduance them vnto.

Come we to the Græcians ; *and there we ſhall finde Learning*
in the Tropicke of Cancer *at ſuch a height, as it neuer was before,*
nor euer, that we read of, ſince. And ſurely it is worth the ob-
ſeruing, that when that extarordinary Diuine Light went out, hu-
mane *Learning came in ; and the ende of the* Prophets *was the*
beginning of the Poets: *The laſt of the diuinity of the one, the firſt*
of the Philoſophy of the other: for from the end of the Captiuity till
the Comming of our Sauiour Chriſt, *the ſpace of foure hundreth*
yeares and more, in which there was no Prophet, that euer I reade
of, there were ſo many Orators, Poets *and* Philoſophers *of*
ſuch ſingular giftes in all kindes ; as wee are onely their Schollers
ſince, and can neuer attaine to the Excellency of our Maſter. In
this time Alexander *the Great was as famous for his Learning*
and writings, as he was for his Victories : He wrote to Antipater

of

of all his owne Actions in Asia and in India, *as* Plutark *reports in his Life.* S. Ciprian *in his Tractate of the vanitie of Idoles, saith, that* Alexander *the Great wrote* Insigne Volumen *to his Mother; wherein he signifies vnto her, how it was tolde him by a certaine* Egyptian-Priest, *that all the Gods of the Gentiles had bene but men.* And S. Augustine *also in his twelst Booke* De ciuitate Dei *makes mention of other of the writings of* Alexander *to* Olimpias *his Mother about the Succession of the Monarchies.*

Amongst *the Kings of* Syria, Antiochus *surnamed* Epiphanes, *writ many Bookes, and sent them into* Iudea, *about changing the Rites and Ceremonies of the* Iewes *into the Religion of the* Grecians; *The principall heades of his Bookes may be found in the Bookes of* Machabes *and in* Iosephus. Amongst *the* Romans, *which of their* Emperours *did not aduance his fame by Letters?* Iulius Cæsar, *besides many other things, writ his* Commentaries *after the example of* Cyrus. Octauius, *as* Suetonius *reportes, writ many* Volumes, *The historie of his owne life,* Exhortations *to* Philosophie, Heroick Verses, Epigrams, Tragedies *and diuers other things; of whom I will only relate two* Stories *not impertinent to my purpose. He is reported to haue bene a very diligent searcher out of all such Bookes, as appertayned to the* Roman-Ethnick-Religion. All *the Bookes* Fatidicorum, *of* Fortune-tellers, *that proceeded not from approued Authors both of* Greeke *and* Latin, *he cast in the fire, to the number of two thousand: Onely he reserued the writings of the* Sibills, *but with that choise, as hee burnt all such of them as he thought to bee counterfeit. I relate this* Story *the rather, for that I thinke it were a good Præsident for our* Augustus *to follow, to make a diligent search of all good and profitable Authors;* As *for all* Hereticall Pamphlets, *slanderous* Libells *and impertinent writings, to commit them to* Vulcane: *for one of the maine meanes of corrupting this people in point of* Religion, *proceeds from the free vse of reading of all kinde of writings without any restraint.*

The

The other Storie *of* Auguſtus *is that famous* Inſcription *of his, which he made to be ſet vp in the* Altar *of the* Capitoll *to our* Sauiour Chriſt ; *of which* Nicephorus *makes mention; as alſo* Suidas *in the word* Auguſtus. Cæſar Auguſtus *being proclaimed the firſt* Emperour *of* Rome, *hauing done many great things and achiued great* Glory *and* felicity ; *came to the* Oracle *of* Apollo, *& offering vp a* Heccatomb, *which is of all other the* greateſt Sacrifice; *demaunded of the* Oracle, *who ſhould rule the* Empire *after his deceaſe ; receiuing no anſwere at all , offered vp an other Sacrifice , and asked with all , how it came to paſſe, that the* Oracle *that was wont to vſe ſo many wordes , was now become ſo ſilent ?* The Oracle *after a long pauſe , made this anſwere :*

Me puer Hebræus, Diuos, Deus ipſe gubernans
Cedere ſede iubet, triſtemque redire ſub Orcum :
Aris ergo dehinc tacitus abſcedito noſtris.

The Emperour *receiuing this anſwere, returned to* Rome, *erected in the* Capitoll *the greateſt* Altar *that was there , with this* Inſcription : Ara primogeniti Dei. *Surely, our* Auguſtus, *in whoſe dayes our* Bleſſed Sauiour Chriſt Ieſus *is come to a full and perfeſt aage :* As *hee was borne in the dayes of the other, ſtudying nothing at all to know, who ſhall rule the Scepter after him (for* God *be praiſed, he is much more happie then was* Auguſtus *in a* Bleſſed Poſterity *of his owne) but indeauoring, that* Christ *his* Kingdome, *may euer Reigne in his Kingdome, hath conſulted all the* Oracles *of* God , *and hath found in them, that there is but one onely* Altar *to be erected to the onely* Sonne *of* God, *who is* Bleſſed *for euer ; and therefore hath ſet himſelfe and beſtowed much paines to bid that Man of Sinne, cedere ſede , and redire ſub Orcum , that hath erected ſo many* Altars Athenian-like , *to vnknowne Gods, making more prayers and* Supplications *to ſuppoſed* Saints, *then euer the other did to Gods they knew not.* But to returne, Claudius Cæſar, *that had ſo much wickedneſſe in him, had this*

good

good in him, that hee writte many good Bookes. Suetonius *reports, hee writ so many Bookes in* Greeke *, as that hee erected a Schoole of purpose in* Alexandria *, called after his owne name, and caused his Bookes to be read yeerely in it: He writ in* Latine *likewise* 43. *Bookes, contayning a Historie from the murther of* Cæsar *to his owne time. There would bee no ende of the reporting of the writings of the Heathen* Emperours. *That one example of* Conſtantine *amongſt the Chriſtian* Emperors *shall suffice :* Euſebius *hath written curiouſly his Life, and is not ſparing to report of his Learning; How many* Orations *and diſcourſes he made, exhorting his Subiects and ſeruants to a good and godly life; How many nights hee paſſed without ſleepe in Meditations of* Diuinitie *; His Speeches in the beginning and ende of the* Councell *of* Nice *; That famous* Oration, Ad Sanctorum cœtum, *pronounced in* Latine *by him Selfe, after tranſlated into* Greeke *by diuerſe, doe shew, how much* Glory *hee gayned by* Letters.

From theſe great Monarches abroad, giue mee leaue a little, to deſcend to our owne Kings at home. Alphredus *King of the* Weſt-Saxons, *tranſlated* Paulus Oroſius, S. Gregorie De paſtorali cura, *and his Dialogues into the* Engliſh *tongue: He tranſlated likewiſe* Beda *of the* Actes *of the* Engliſh, *and Boetius de conſolatione* Philoſophiæ, Dauids *Pſalmes, and many other things : Hee writ beſides a Booke of Lawes and* Inſtitutions *againſt wicked Judges : Hee writ the ſayings of* Wiſemen, *and a ſingular Booke of the fortune of* Kings, *a collection of* Chronicles, *and a* Manuel *of* Meditations.

Ethelſtanus *(or* Adelſtan, *as our* Stories *call him) Rex* Anglorum, *as* Baleus *calls him, cauſed to be tranſlated the* Bible *out of* Hebrew *into* Saxon, *and writ himſelfe a Booke of* Aſtrologie *, the* Conſtitutions *of the* Cleargie, *corrected many olde* Lawes, *and made many new.*

King Edgar *writ to the Cleargie of* England *certaine* Conſtitutions *and* Lawes, *and other things.*

Henrie *the firſt, the yongeſt Sonne of the* Conquerour, *was brought*

brought vp in the Vniuerfitie *of* Cambridge; *and excelled fo in the knowledge of all Liberall Arts and Sciences, that to this day he doeth retaine the name of* Beau-Clerke.

Achaius *King of the* Scots, *writ of the Acts of all his Predeceffors. And* Kenethus *King of the* Scots, *writ a huge* Volume *of all the Scottifh* Lawes, *and like an other* Iuftinian, *reduced them into a* Compendium.

Iames *the firft writ diuers Bookes both in* Englifh *and* Latine *Verfe: He writ alfo, as* Baleus *faith,* De vxore futura.

Henrie *the eight writ of the* Inftitution *of a* Chriftian man, *and of the* Inftitution *of youth:* Hee *writ alfo a defence of the* 7. Sacraments *againft* Martin Luther; *for which hee was much magnified of the* Pope, *and all that partie; Infomuch as hee was ftiled with the Title of* Defenfor fidei *for that worke: And trewly it fell out well for the* King, *that hee writ a Booke on the* Popes *fide; for otherwife, he fhould haue them raile on him for his writings as freely, as they reuile him for his Actions. For he writ two Bookes after that; the one* De auctoritate Regia contra Papam; *the other* Sententia de Concilio Mantuano, *as well written for the Stile and Argument, as the other is: But becaufe they feeme to breath an other breath, there is no Trumpet founded in their praife.*

Edward *the fixt, though his dayes were fo fhort, as he could not giue full proofe of thofe fingular parts that were in him; yet hee wrote diuers* Epiftles *and* Orations *both in* Greeke *and* Latine: *He wrote a Treatife* De fide *to the* Duke *of* Somerfet: *He wrote a Hiftory of his owne time, which are all yet extant vnder his owne hand, in the* Kings Library; *as* M[r.] Patrick Young, *his Maiefties learned and Induftrious* Bibliothecarius, *hath fhewed mee; And which is not to bee forgotten, fo diligent a hearer of* Sermons *was that fweet* Prince, *that the notes of the moft of the* Sermons *he heard, are yet to bee feene vnder his owne hand with the* Preachers *name, the time, and the place, and all other circumftances.*

Queene Elizabeth *our late* Soueraigne *of bleffed memory, tranflated*

tranflated the prayers of Queene Katherine *into* Latine, French, *and* Italian : *Shee wrote alfo a Century of* Sentences, *and dedicated them to her Father. I haue heard of her Tranflation of* Saluftius; *but I neuer faw it : And there are yet frefh in our memories the* Orations *fhe made in both the* Vniüerfities *in* Latine; *her entertayning of* Embaffadors *in diuers Languages; her excellent Speaches in the* Parliament, *whereof diuers are extant at this day in* Print. *And to come a little neerer his* Maieftie; *The* Kings Father *tranflated* Valerius Maximus *into* Englifh; *And the* Queene *his* Maiefties Mother, *wrote a Booke of Verfes in* French *of the* Inftitution *of a* Prince, *all with her owne hand, wrought the Couer of it with her needle, and is now of his* Maieftie *efteemed as a moft pretious* Iewell.

Therefore fince wee are compaffed about with fuch a Clowd of Witneffes (*albeit thefe are but a little handfull in comparifon of the infinite multitude, that might be produced;*) *Since we haue the examples of all the Mightie-men of the* World, *euen from the beginning thereof vnto this day; who haue ftriuen as much to get a Name for their writings, as fame for their doings; haue affected as much to be counted* Learned *as* Victorious; *and to be reputed of, as much for their wife Sayings, as for their worthy Deeds; Why fhould it bee thought a thing ftrange in this time, that his* Maieftie, *whom* G O D *hath adorned with as many rare perfections of Nature and Arte, as euer he did any that wee read of,* (*I except fuch as were Diuinely infpired*) *fhould lend the world a few leaues out of the large* Volumes *of his* Learning? *I commend the wifedome of our* Aduerfaries, *who hauing affayed all meanes, the wit of man is able to inuent, to incline his* Maieftie *to like of their partie; and finding by all their* Tricks, *they haue got no ground, would at laft put his* Maieftie *to filence, and gaine thus much of him, at leaft; that fince he will doe nothing for them; yet that he would fay nothing againft them. Therefore they cry out againft his* Maiefties *writing, and vpbrayd him more for that hee doeth write, then they doe for any thing that hee hath written: It is ynough to wonder at, that* Rex fcribit. *Thefe people are wife in their*

their generation, and haue learned by long experience; that as the Kingdome of CHRIST is the Gospel of peace, so it hath bene from the beginning spread more by the Pennes of the Apostles, then by the power of Princes; more propagated by the sweet writings of the ancient Fathers, then it could bee suppressed by the seuere Edicts of Emperours; and of late, their Kingdome hath bene more shaken by a poore Monke, then it hath bene able to recouer by the helpe of Mighty Monarches. Therefore since the writings of poore Schollers haue so raised the Kingdome of CHRIST, and so discouered the Mysterie of Iniquitie; they do well to feare what may follow vpon the Writings of so great a King.

They liue securely from bleeding by his Maiesties Sword; but they are not safe from being blasted by the breath of his Maiesties Bookes. If they could bring it about therefore, to calme and quiet his Maiesties Spirit from working vpon them that way; as they see his Maiesties sweetnesse to bee farre from drawing of their bloods the other way, they would deeme it a greater Conquest, then all the conuersions of the Kings of the East and West-Indies they tell vs so many tales of: For they looke vpon his Maiesties Bookes, as men looke vpon Blasing-Starres, with amazement, fearing they portend some strange thing, and bring with them a certaine Influence to worke great change and alteration in the world: Neither is their expectation herein deceiued; for we haue seene with our eyes, the Operation of his Maiesties Workes in the Consciences of their men so farre, as from their highest Conclaue to their lowest Cells, there haue bene, that haue bene conuerted by them; and that in such number, as wee want rather meanes to maintaine them, then they minds to come to vs. But to conclude this point, that Kings may write; Giue mee leaue to offer you this Meditation.

How many are the wayes that men doe inuent to perpetuate their Memorie! Insomuch, that mortall-men haue made themselues Gods, when they were dead, that they might be adored, as if they were aliue. Wherein, is the Impetus of Nature so strong,

as

asin the affection that propogates to Posteritie? *Wherefore serue*
Pictures, but to continue our features? Why doe men bestow so
much cost in sumptuous Buildings, but to leaue a Monument *of*
their Magnificence? To what end doe we erect Holy-houses
and Hospitalls, but to possesse mens mindes with the Deuotion of
our Soules? And shall wee blesse a King, when wee behold
him in his Posteritie! *Shall wee admire his features, when wee*
contemplate them in his Pictures! *Shall we wonder at his* Magnificence, *when we gaze vpon it in his stately* Edifices! *and may*
wee not as well bee rauished, when wee see his sharpe Wit, his pro-
found Judgement, his infinite Memorie, his Excellent affe-
ctions in his admirable Writings? *Certainely it is a peruersnes*
to esteeme a man least, for that whereby hee liues the longest; to
value him more for the outward worke of his hand, then for the
inward operation of his minde; to esteeme him more for that
which instructs but little, then for that which shall edifie for e-
uer. What now remaines of Cæsar *so famous as his* Commentaries? *What of* Cicero, *as his* Orations? *How comes* Aristotle *to be of more authoritie then* Alexander? Seneca, *then*
Nero? *The Triumphes and Victories of the one are vanished;*
the Vertues of the other remaine in their perfect vigour: And
though all other Monuments *by time consume and come to no-*
thing; yet these by time, gaine strength and get authoritie; and
euer the more ancient, the more Excellent.

Hauing now deliuered my opinion, that I thinke it neither vn-
lawfull nor inconuenient for a King *to write, but that he hath the*
Liberty that other men haue, if hee can get the leysure; to shew
his abilities for the present, to perpetuate his Memory to Posterity; *to aduance his praise before his owne People, and gaine*
Glory from others; but especially to giue Glory *vnto* GOD.

I will craue leaue to descend to an other Consideration: for it
may be, there will not be so much fault found with a King *for wri-*
ting, as for the matter or Subiect whereof he treates: For Persona-
ges *of their eminent Degree and State, must not spend their*
paines on poore purposes; nor write so much to try their witts

on triuiall thinges, as to winne themselues Honor by the Excellency of their subiect. Indeed, if I were worthy to aduise a King, hee should meddle very sparingly, and but vpon important Causes, with Polemicalls : Hee should not often fight but in the field; for put the case a King writ neuer so modestly, that there be not in a whole Booke one word ad hominem, nor any touch of his Aduersary in any personall infirmity; yet I know not how it comes to passe, that in all Controuersies, a solide answere to an argument, is a very sufficient occasion to make an Aduersary wonderfull angrie. And so long as there are diuersity of Opinions, there will neuer want matter for Confutations: And in these Replications the person of a King is more exposed and lyes more open, then the person of a poore Scholler can doe; for as he is a farre greater marke, so he may farre more easily be hit. And though they misse him and can hit vpon nothing iustly to bee reprehended in him; yet they doe thinke it Operæpretium, to make a Scarre in the face of a King: Whereas on the contrary, if a King doe write of Piety or Deuotion, compile a History, giue Precepts of Policy, handle Moralls, or treate of some rare Experiences of Nature; wee doe in these things commend his Iudgement, admire his parts without any euill cogitation against his Person. There can hardly be giuen a more viue Example in this case, then is to be found in the Writings of his Maieftie. When the King had publiſhed his Basilicon-Doron, a Booke so singularly penned; that a Pomegranat is not so full of kernells, as that is of Excellent Counsells: What applause had it in the world? How did it inflame mens minds to a loue and admiration of his Maieftie beyond measure; Insomuch that comming out iust at the time his Maieftie came in, it made the hearts of all his people as one Man, as much to Honour him for Religion and Learning, as to obey him for Title and Authoritie; and gaue vs then a taste, or rather the first fruits, of that we haue since reaped a plentifull Harueft of, by his Maiefties most prudent and Gracious Gouernment ouer vs. The like I may say of his Maiefties Demonologie; a rare peece for many Precepts and Experiments, both in Diuinitie and Naturall Philosophie,

sophie. *In these, there was nothing heard of, but Sunne-shine and faire-weather ; euery countenance sweet and smiling vpon them : But as soone as his* Maiestie *dealt against the* Pope, *tooke the* Cardinall *in hand, made the world see the vsurped power of the one, and Sophistry of the other ; Good Lord, what a stirre we had ; what roaring of the wilde Bulls of* Basan, *what a commotion in euery Countrey ; Insomuch, that I thinke, there is scarce a People, Language or Nation in* Christendome, *out of which his* Maiestie *hath not receiued some answere or other ; either by way of refuting, or at least by rayling : So that, had not the* King *contemned and made himselfe sport and recreation by such kinde of Reuelling, rather then bene mooued to passion ; It could not haue bene but a marueilous perturbation to a* Prince *of so exquisite sense and vnderstanding. But what of all this? Shall wee wish his* Maiestie *had not fought with beasts at* Ephesus, *stopped the roaring of the* Bull, *nor encountered the* Cardinall? *Trewly when I thinke vpon the wonderfull abuses, and Hyperbolicall indignities his* Maiestie *hath receiued from these men ; I am somewhat of that minde : But when on the other side, I consider his* Maiesties *zeale for to maintaine the cause of* GOD *and Right of* Kings ; *his singular dexteritie to doe it ; the blessing of* GOD *that hath followed vpon his so doing of it ; I cannot but change my opinion, and bee of another minde. And the better to induce you to bee of my minde ; I will make vnto you a trew Relation of his* Maiesties *entering into this businesse, and then leaue it to your consideration ; whether there were not a* Diuine *hand, that led his into it, or no. It is the Speach of our Blessed* Sauiour, *that there is nothing hid, that shall not be knowne ; and what is spoken in darkenesse, shall be heard in the Light : This his* Maiestie *as himselfe confesseth, found trew in the comming foorth of one of his* Bookes; *and I thinke it may bee found as trew in the comming foorth of some other of them. For after the* Pope *had put forth his* Breues, *and the* Cardinall *had sent his Letters to the Archpriest ; the one to enioyne the People not to take the* Oath *of Allegiance, affirming they could not take it with safety of their Saluation.*

uation; the other to reproue the *Arch-priest* for that hee had taken it, and to draw him to a penitencie for so foule a *Lapse* : His
Maieſtie *like as became a Prudent and a Religious* Prince,
thought it not meete, that these things should paſſe for current, but
that it was expedient his People should know, that the taking of
this Oath was so farre from endangering their Soules, as that it
intended nothing but ciuill Obedience, and without touching any
point of their conscience, made the State secure of their *Allegi-*
ance. To performe this worke, his Maieſtie thought the Biſhop
of Wincheſter that then was, a very fit man, both for his ſingular Learning, as for that he had long laboured in an Argument
not much of a diuers nature from this : Whereupon his Maieſtie
calling for penne and incke, to giue my L. of Wincheſter directions, how and in what maner to proceed in this Argument, I know
not how it came to paſſe; but it fell out trew, that the Poet ſaith,

      ======= Amphora cœpit
Inſtitui, currente rota, poſt vrceus exit.

For the Kings *Penne ranne so faſt, that in the compaſſe of ſixe*
dayes, his Maieſtie had accompliſhed that, which bee now calleth
his Apologie; *which when my Lord of* Canterburie *that then*
was, and my Lord of Elie *had peruſed, being indeed deliuered by*
his Maieſtie *but as briefe Notes, and in the nature of a Minute*
to bee explicated by the Biſhop *in a larger Volume ; yet they*
thought it so ſufficient an Anſwere both to the Pope *and* Cardi-
nall, as there needed no other: Whereupon his Maieſtie *was per-*
ſwaded, to giue way to the comming of it foorth, but was pleaſed to
conceale his Name : And so haue wee the Apologie *beyond*
his Maieſties *owne purpose or determination.*

    After that the Apologie *was out, his* Maieſtie *diuerſe*
times would bee pleaſed to vtter a Reſolution of his; that if the
Pope *and* Cardinall *would not reſt in his anſwere, and ſit downe*
by it; take the Oath *as it was intended for a point of* Allegiance
and Ciuill Obedience ; Hee would publiſh the Apologie *in*
his owne name with a Preface *to all the* Princes *in* Chriſten-
                      dome;

dome; *wherein hee would publish such a Confession of his Faith,* *perswade the* Princes *so to vindicate their owne Power, discouer* *so much of the* Mysterie *of Iniquitie vnto them; as the* Popes Bulles *should pull in their hornes, and himselfe wish he had neuer medled with this matter.* The Cardinall *contending against the* Apologie, *his* Maiestie *confirmed his* Resolution, *and with the like Celerity, in the compasse of one weeke, wrote his* Monitory-Preface : *for as* Hirtius *said of* Cæsars Comentaries, Qua fœlicitate *they were done, let others iudge; but* Qua celeritate, *I can tell : And being so written, published it and the* Apologie *in his owne* Name; *and made good his word, sent it to the* Emperour *and all the* Kings *and free* Princes *in* Christendome.

Now *hauing made this* Relation, *wherein I haue deliuered nothing but trewth;* Let *me offer vnto you some few things worthy* Consideration.

First, *that vpon the comming foorth of that* Booke, *there were no* States, *that disauowed the* Doctrine *of it in that point of the* Kings *power; And the* Venetians *mainetained it in their writings, and put it in* Execution *; The* Sorbons *maintained it likewise in* France.

Secondly, *their owne writers, that opposed it, so ouerlashed, as they were corrected and castigated of men of their owne* Religion; Becanus *his* Booke *corrected by the* Cardinalles *of* Rome; Bellarmines Booke *burnt in* Paris; Suarez *his* Answere *burnt also in* France. *As for the* Raylers, *I leaue them to* God *his* Iudgment, *whose hand hath bene vpon the most of them.*

Thirdly, *his* Maiesties Confession *of faith, hath bene so generally approued, as it hath conuerted many of their partie : And had it not bene (as I haue bene informed by diuerse) for the* Treatise *of* Antichrist, *many more would easily haue bene induced, to subscribe to all in that* Preface.

Fourthly , Kings *and* Princes *haue by his* Maiesties Premonition, *had a more cleare insight, and a more perfect discouery into the* Iniury *offered them by the* Pope *in the point of their temporall* Power, *then euer they had; Insomuch, as that point was*

neuer

neuer so throughly disputed in Chriftendome, *as it hath bene by the occasion of his* Maiefties *Booke.*

Fiftly and laftly, for the point of Antichrift; *I haue heard many confeffe, that they neuer saw fo much light giuen to that* Myfterie, *neuer defcerned fo much trewth by the vniforme confent of the Text, and ftrength of Interpretation of places, as they haue done by his* Maiefties *Booke.* *So that, though Controuerfies be fitter fubiects for Schollers ordinarily, then for* Kings; *Yet when there was fuch a necefsitie in vndertaking, and fuch a fucceffe being performed; I leaue it to the world to iudge, whether there were not a fpeciall hand of* GOD *in it, or no. Now fince I haue begunne with this point of* Antichrift, *I will make bolde to proceed a little with his* Maiefties Paraphrafe *vpon the* Reuelation, *wherein that* Treatife of Antichrift *is principally grounded.*

His Maiefties *fingular vnderftanding in all points of good Learning is not vnknowne: But yet aboue all other things,* GOD *hath giuen him an vnderftanding Heart in the Interpretation of that* Booke, *beyond the meafure of other men: For this* Paraphrafe, *that leades the way to all the reft of his* Maiefties Workes, *was written by his* Maieftie *before hee was twenty yeeres of aage; and therefore iuftly in this Volume hath the firft place, the reft following in order according to the time of their firft penning.* Anciently Kings *drempt dreames, and saw visions; and* Prophets *expounded them : So with* King Pharaoh *and* Iofeph *in* Egypt; *So with* Nabuchodonofor *and* Daniel *in* Babylon. *In this aage,* Prophets *haue written Visions, and* Kings *haue expounded them.* GOD *raifed vp* Prophets *to deliuer his People from a temporall captiuitie in* Egypt *and* Babylon, *by the Interpretation of the one; And* GOD *hath in this aage ftirred vp* Kings *to deliuer his People from a Spirituall* Egypt *and* Babylon, *by the Interpretation of the other. It is an obferuable thing, that* GOD *neuer made his People any great promife, but he added vnto his promife a famous* Prophecie. *Three great promifes we reade of, that runne through all the Scriptures.*

The

The first of the Messiah *; the second of the land of* Canaan *; the third of the* Kingdome of Heauen *: To these three promises, are reduced all the* Prophecies. *Of the promise of the* Messiah, *prophecied all the* Prophets *from the fall of the first* Adam, *to the comming of the second : Of the promise of the Land of* Canaan, *prophecied* Iacob *and* Ioseph, *and the rest, from the promise made to* Abraham, *to the possessing of it by* Iosuah *and the children of* Israel *: Of the promise of the Kingdome of Heauen, made by our Sauiour* Christ, *prophecied the* Apostles *; principally* S. Paul, *and* S. Iohn *in the Reuelation.* Now *though all were to lay hold on the promises ; yet few were able to vnderstand the* Prophecies. *And surely, though all the people of* God *are to lay hold on the promises of that Glorious Kingdome described in that Booke ; yet few are able to vnderstand the* Prophecies *therein contained, comprehending in them a perfect* History *and* State *of the* Church, *euen from the destruction of* Ierusalem, *till the consummation of the whole world. Yet this I thinke, I may safely say ; That* Kings *haue a kinde of interest in that Booke beyond any other : for as the execution of the most part of the* Prophecies *of that Booke is committed vnto them ; So it may be, that the Interpretation of it, may more happily be made by them : And since they are the principall Instruments, that* God *hath described in that Booke to destroy the Kingdome of* Antichrist, *to consume his State and Citie ; I see not, but it may stand with the Wisedome of* God, *to inspire their hearts to expound it ; into whose handes hee hath put it to excute, vntill the* Lord *shall consume both him and it with the Spirit of his mouth, and shall abolish it with the brightnesse of his comming : For from the day that* S. Iohn *writ the Booke to this present houre ; I doe not thinke that euer any* King *tooke such paines, or was so perfect in the* Reuelation, *as his* Maiestie *is ; which will easily appeare by this* Paraphrase, *by his* Maiesties Meditation *on the* 20. Chap. *and his* Monitorie *Preface. It was my purpose to haue past through all his* Maiesties Books *; to haue expressed the Argument and the occasion of their writing ; But I find by that I haue already*

said,

said, I should be ouer tedious vnto you. This therefore in generall ; They are all worthy of a King, and to be kept to Posterity: For if Ouid *could imagine, that no time should eate out the memory of his* Metamorphoseis, *which were but fictions; I hope no time shall see an end of these Books, that carry in them so much diuine trewth and light. And as in this first worke of the* Paraphrase, *his* Maiestie *hath shewed his* Piety; *So in this last* Pearle *(I meane his Maiesties Speach in the* Starr-Chamber*) his Maiestie hath shewed his* Policy: *The first sheweth, hee vnderstands the Kingdome of* G O D ; *this last, that hee as well apprehends the State of his Kingdomes in this* World : *The first sheweth him to haue a large Portion in that of Heauen; and this last sheweth him to haue a great Power and experience in these Kingdomes hee hath on earth. Therefore, let these men, that delight so much in Detraction and to vilify him, whom* G O D *hath exalted; and to shed his blood, whose Soule* God *hath bound vp in the Bundle of life; Let them, I say, write whateuer the Subtilty of the olde* Serpent *can put into their heads, or the Malice of* Sathan *infuse into their hearts; Let them speake, what the poyson of* Aspes *is able to put into their lippes; they are not all able to make his* Maiestie *to appeare lesse then he is, nor to shew, that euer they had of theirs a King so accomplished. It is trew, that wee haue not had many Kings in this Kingdome of our Profession: But for those we haue had, this Iland of ours neuer saw the like, either for partes of* Nature, *giftes of Learning or Graces of* Piety.*

The little time of life, that God lent to King Edward, *must needs lessen his prayses; But neuer did there appeare beginnings of more rare perfection, then in him.*

The length of Queene Elizabeths *dayes, together with the felicity of her time, was not only a Glory to her owne People, but a wonderment to the World, euen our Aduersaries, as* Moses *said, being Iudges. And praysed be* G O D, *the present time passeth a long with the like felicity and much more Securitie: for let me recount a little, for the Glory of* G O D *and encouragement of his* Maiestie,

Maieſtie, *to goe on in his happie Courſe begunne, the Bleſſings of* GOD *we receiue by him*; *And then let our Aduerſaries tell vs, whether we be a miſerable People or no, as ſome of late haue gone about to perſwade vs.* Neither doe I *ſtand in feare of any mans reprehenſion*; *for* I *will ſpeake nothing but trewth, and I haue my* Preſident *from* GOD *his owne Booke*; *wherein the good Actes of euery good* King *are to their eternall praiſes trewly recounted.*

First to beginne with Religion, *as the Generall to the Armie*: *Of all Gods Bleſſings wee haue it without any alteration or change contynued vnto vs.* His Maieſties *firſt Care was for the Confirmation of the Goſpell*: *for at his* Maieſties *firſt comming in*; *who knowes not the endeauours of men, to haue made a change, either to the* Papiſts, *or to the* Puritanes? His Maieſtie *therefore, to quiet the* State *and Peace of the Church, called a Conference at* Hampton-Court; *where paſſing ouer the one, as being neuer in his heart to giue the leaſt way vnto*; *He ſo tempered the other, as the Harmony hath bene the better euer ſince.*

The Religion *thus ratified*; His Maieſties *next Care was for the Tranſlation of the* Bible, *it being the ground of our Religion*: His Maieſtie *was deſirous his People ſhould haue it in as much perfection, as the Induſtrie and Labors of the beſt Learned were able to afford it them.*

Hauing done *what was neceſſary for the Spirituall part of the Church, his* Maieſtie *tooke into conſideration the Temporal State thereof*: No ſooner came the Parliament, *but finding what ſpoile had bene made of the Lands thereof in the tyme of his* Predeceſſors, *by a libertie they had to take the Landes of the Church for a longer Terme then others could doe*; *Cut himſelfe off from that libertie, and equalled himſelfe to a common perſon in the taking of any State in the Churches Landes.*

When his Maieſtie *had done this in* England, *he looked backe into* Scotland, *and reforming the State of the Church there, as farre as in his* Princely-Wiſedome *he thought conuenient for the time*; *reſtored the* Biſhops *there, as to their Spirituall* Keies;

ſo to their temporall Eſtates, *though it were to the great loſſe and dammage of his owne* Reuennue *and* Crowne.

From Scotland *his* Maieſtie *came to* Ireland, *that forlorne* Kingdome *both for Temporall and Spiritual eſtate, till he looked into it:* There *his* Maieſtie *hath reduced the* Biſhoppricks, *not only to their old* Rents; *but added vnto them many new* Reuennues; *ſo that many places there are anſwerable to the beſt Liuings here:* Neither *hath his* Care *bene onely on theſe high places of the* Church, *but hath deſcended to the loweſt in the ſame, hauing both protected the* Benefices *from being rayſed to any higher* Taxe, *and hindred all courſes, that might giue his Cleargie moleſtation or trouble.*

His Maieſties Bountie *hath not bene wanting to Colledges and* Hoſpitalls, *hauing parted with his owne Tenures, to giue them power of larger Indowments; whereby there hath bene works of more ſumptuouſnes and coſt done in his* Maieſties *time, then there hath bene in any one aage before.*

J may not forget one thing, that ſince his Maieſties *comming to this* Crowne, *he hath neuer put into his Coffers the meane proffitts of any Eccleſiaſticall liuing, but hath bene a* Fidus-Depoſitarius, *and euer giuen them to the next Jncumbent.*

Let me deſcend a little from theſe workes of Piety *to* Peace. Neuer *hath there bene ſo vniuerſall a Peace in* Chriſtendome *ſince the time of our* Sauiour Chriſt, *as in theſe his Dayes: And I dare ſay, as much, if not more, by the procurement of his* Maieſtie, *then by any other earthly meanes in this world.* A Peace *(to let forraigne partes paſſe) ſo entertayned at home; that in his* Maieſties *three* Kingdomes, *apt enough by conſtitution, and not vnaccuſtomed by practiſe to be at variance, there hath bene no Ciuill diſſenſion at all. With* Peace G O D *hath giuen vs* Plentie: *So that, if Peace and Plenty haue not made vs too too wanton, 1 know not what wee want.* Neither *is there any crying out for lacke of* Iuſtice *in our* Courtes; *for neuer was there Iuſtice adminiſtred with more liberty from the* King, *nor more vprightnes from the Judges; And yet in the free diſpenſation of* Iuſtice, Mercie

Mercie *did neuer more triumph. If this bee to bee miserable, I know not what on earth they call Happinesse:* GOD *continue these still vnto vs; and then, let them call Happinesse, what they please.*

But I know wherefore all is miserable; becaufe there is no more Mercy *shewed to their* Catholiks.

I will put it as a Crowne *vpon all his* Maiefties Mercies: *There was neuer* King, *that had fo great a caufe giuen him, that euer tooke fo little bloode, extending his* Mercy *to all, that were not perfonall workers in that* Powder-Plot: *And before that you had hatched that* Monster, *neither was the perfon or purfe of any your reputed* Catholicks *touched. And fince that time, you may doe well to complaine of your* Miferies; *but the* Church *and* Comonwealth *both, doe trauaile and groane vnder the burthen of your difobedience: But the worft I wifh you, is, that at length by his* Maiefties *long* Patience, *you may bee drawne to* Repentance; *for as we are come out from you, left we fhould bee partakers of your plagues; fo we pray for you, that you may come in to vs, that you may be participants of our felicities.*

To Conclude this Preface: GOD *hath giuen vs a* Solomon, *and* GOD *aboue all things gaue* Solomon *Wifedome; Wifedome brought him peace; Peace brought him* Riches; *Riches gaue him* Glory. *His wifedome appeared in his wordes and* Workes: *his Peace, he preferued by the power of his* Army: *His riches he rayfed, as by his* Reuennue, *fo by the* Trade *of his* Nauie: *His* Glory *did accrue from them all.* Now, *as in thefe;* GOD *exalted him beyond all the* Kings *that euer were, or fhould be after him; So had he in other things* Humiliations *not farre behind the proportion of his* Exaltations; *the fearefulleft fall, that the* Scripture *affords an* Example *of; the moft vnchaft life and immoderate exceffe of* Women, *that we read of; the weakeft* Pofterity *for* Wifedome *and* Gouernment, *that we finde in all the* Line *of his* Succeffion. GOD *would haue it fo, that he fhould no more be fet out, as a* Type *of the* Glory *of his owne* Sonne *in the felicity of his* State *one way, then he would haue him propofed as a patterne of* Humane

frailty

frailty an other way. Therefore, though we may not approach him in his Typicall State; yet GODS Name be bleßed, that hath giuen vs to goe farre beyond him in his perfonall Condition: For we haue already, bleßed be GOD, feene the Conftancie and perfeuerance of his Maiefty in his Holy Profeßion, without any Eclipfe or Shaddow of change, longer then we are well able to deduce the whole life and reigne of Solomon. We haue not the Daughter of Pharao an Idolatrous King; nor feare we ftrange women to fteale away his heart from the Seruice of GOD: But a Queene, as of a Royall, fo of a Religious Stocke, profeßing the Gospell of Chrift with him; A Mirrour of trew Modeftie, a Queene of Bounty, both beloued and admired of all his People: A Pofterity that we need not feare for folly in the one Sexe, nor for leuitie in the other; Both which made Solomon fpeake fo much, (as the Iewes fay) in his Prouerbes, of a fooliſh fonne, becaufe his owne was not wife, and of wanton Women, becaufe he feared the vanity of his owne Daughters. But GOD hath left his Maieftie a Sonne, a Prince, as in outward Liniaments, fo in inward Abiliments, (I need fay no more) an Alter-Idem, a fecond-Selfe; A Daughter, a Princeffe of that Piety, fingular vertue and Modeftie, as makes her both beloued at home and admired abroad. I haue done: Only I defire the Readers of thefe Workes, to pray to GOD, that as he hath fo farre aduanced vs, as to beftowe vpon vs, with the Heauenly Treafures of his trewth, the riches of his earthly Iewels in fo Sacred a King, fo admired a Queene, fo hopefull a Prince, fo vertuous a Princes; He would for his Mercies fake, for his Sonnes fake, continue this the Light of his Countenance vpon vs in them and their Pofterity, till the comming of that Kingdome, which neuer fhall haue end. AMEN.

Thine in the Lord,

IA. WINTON.

THE
SEVERALL TREATISES
ACCORDING TO THE TIME,
WHEREIN THEY WERE WRITTEN,
AND THEIR PLACE IN THIS
Collection, &c.

T H E

THE EPISTLE TO THE
WHOLE CHVRCH *MILI-*
TANT, in whatſoeuer part
of the Earth.

O whom could I haue ſo fitly directed (*Chriſtian Readers*) this Paraphraſe *of mine vpon the Re-*uelation, *as vnto you, who are the very and true poſteritie of thoſe Churches, to whom the Booke it ſelfe was dedicated, and for whoſe inſtruction and comfort the ſaid E-piſtle was endited by the Holy Spirit*, and written by that great Theologue I o h n the Apoſtle, *whom our Maſter beloued deerely ? If doubt not but it will ſeeme ſtrange to many, that any of my aage, calling, and litera-ture, ſhould haue medled with ſo obſcure, Theologicall, and high a ſubiect : But let my earneſt deſire (by manifeſting the Trueth,) as well to teach my ſelfe as others, ſerue for excuſe; conſidering alſo that where diuers others in our aage, haue medled with the interpretation of this Booke, preſſing with preoccupied opinions, onely to wreſt and conforme the meaning thereof to their parti-cular and priuate paſſions; If by the contrary proteſt, that all my trauailes tend to ſquare and conforme my opinions to the trew and ſincere meaning thereof : Which cauſes mooued me to vndertake this worke; not thereby to deſpiſe infinite others, who to the glory*

A   *of*

of God, and great comfort of his Church, hath giuen it a great light already, but rather that by oft peruſing and dew conſidering therof, whereto this worke hath led mee, J might be the better acquainted with the meaning of this Booke, which J eſteeme a ſpeciall cannon againſt the Hereticall wall of our common aduerſaries the Papiſts: whom I would wiſh to know, that in this my Paraphraſe vpon it, J haue vſed nothing of my owne coniecture, or of the authoritie of others, but onely haue interpreted it, in that ſenſe which may beſt agree with the methode of the Epiſtle, and not bee contradictorie to it ſelfe: The meaning whereof I expound, partly by it ſelfe, and partly by other parts of the Scriptures, as the worke it ſelfe will beare witneſſe: And therefore this one thing J muſt craue of our Aduerſaries, that they will not refute any part of my Interpretation, till they finde out a more probable themſelues, agreeing with the whole context, & cum ſerie temporum; and where their conſciences beare them witneſſe that J ſpeake the Trueth, that they will yeeld vnto it, and glorifie God therein, and this is all the reward I craue for my paines. But of one thing I muſt forewarne you (Chriſtian Readers) to wit, that yee may vnderſtand, that it is for the making of the Diſcourſe more ſhort and facile, that I haue made I o h n to be the Speaker in all this Paraphraſe; and not that I am ſo preſumptuouſly fooliſh, as to haue meant thereby, that my Paraphraſe is the onely trew and certaine expoſition of this Epiſtle, reiecting all others: For although through ſpeaking in his perſon, I am onely bounded and limitted to vſe one, and not diuers interpretations, of euery ſeuerall place; yet I condemne not others, but rather allow them to interpret it diuerſly, ſo being, it agree with the analogie of faith, with the methode of the Text, & cum ſerie temporum, as I ſaid before: for thoſe three being obſerued, it may fall out that diuers, diuerſly expound one place, and yet all be according to the trueth, and very meaning of the Spirit of God, as may eaſily be proued by the Text it ſelfe: For in the 17. Chapter the Angel expounding to Iohn, the ſeuen heads of the beaſtes that came out of the Sea, hee ſaith the ſeuen heads which thou ſaweſt vpon the beaſt

are

are the seuen Hills, and they are also seuen Kings: Here ye see
one thing is expounded in two very farre different fashions, and
yet both true ; And therefore let wise men take their choice in
these things, obseruing alwayes these rules I haue spoken of ; as spe-
cially for example ; This Hebrew word Arma geddon in the
16. Chapter and sixt Phiale, although I expound it to signifie de-
struction by deceipt , as composed of ערמגדון *Gnarma &*
Geddon which may very well agree with the History, because it is
the name of the place, saith Iohn, *where the wicked being assem-*
bled together by the alluring and deceipt of Satan, and his three
spirits of Diuels to make warre with the faithfull, were all de-
stroyed by God, and so their destruction came, and was procured by
deceipt; Yet others interpret it to signifie destruction by waters,
as composed of היר-מי *&* נ גון *Harma &* Geddon, *which also*
may very well agree with the Historie. For waters indeed in this
Booke signifie oft many people and Nations, as appeareth by the
very Text in the 17. Chapter; And others take it to be an allu-
sion to the destruction that Ioshua *made of Gods enemies vpon the*
hill of Mageddon, *and therefore to bee composed of* הר *Harr,*
which is called a Hill and Mageddon, *which may also very*
well agree with the Historie.

   And as I speake of this, so I speake the like of Gog and Magog *in the 20. Chapter, and of all other ambiguous places in this*
Booke.

   It rests then that what ye finde amisse in this Paraphrase, yee
   impute it to my lacke of yeeres and learning ; and what ye find
   worthy to be allowed in it, that yee attribute the full praise
   thereof to GOD, *to whom onely all praise appertaineth.*

       Fare-well.

     THE

THE ARGVMENT
OF THIS WHOLE
EPISTLE.

HIS Booke or Epiſtle of Reuelation, *was called in doubt, aſwell for the incertaintie of the Author, as alſo for the canonicalneſſe of the Booke it ſelfe, by ſundry of the ancients, and ſpecially by* Euſebe; *For ſoluing whereof I need not to inſiſt, ſince it is both receiued now of all Chriſtians, and alſo diuers of the Neoteriques, in ſpeciall* Beza *in his Preface vpon it, hath handled that matter ſufficiently already; So that this doubt onely reſts now in men, that this* Booke is ſo obſcure and allegorique, that it is in a maner vnprofitable to be taught or interpreted; Whereunto I will ſhortly make anſwere, and then goe forward to ſet downe the methode of the ſame: And therefore to make a deduction from the beginning, let vs vnderſtand in what ſeuerall or principall parts the whole Scriptures may be diuided in; and then which of them this Booke is. How ſoone* Adam *being made perfect in his Creation, and hauing the choiſe of Life and* Death, *Good and* Euill, *did by his horrible defection make choiſe of* Death, *and caſt off* Life, *and by that meanes infected his whole poſteritie with double ſinne, to wit, Originall and Actuall,* God *notwithſtanding had ſuch a Loue to mankinde, as being his moſt Noble workemanſhip, and Creature, made to his owne Likeneſſe and Image, that he ſelected a Church amongſt them, whom firſt becauſe of their weakeneſſe and incredulitie, he with his owne mouth taught, and next inſtructed and raiſed vp notable men amongſt them to be their* Rulers, *whom he endued with ſuch excellent gifts, as not onely their example in life preached, but alſo by* Miracles *they ſtrengthened and confirmed their Faith: But leſt this miniſtrie of men ſhould make them to depend onely vpon their mouthes, forgetting* Him, *and making* Gods *of them, he at length out of his owne mouth gaue them his* Law, *which he cauſed them to put in* Writ, *and retaine ſtill amongſt them; And then leſt they ſhould forget and neglect the ſame, he raiſed vp godly* Rulers, *aſ well Temporall as Spirituall, who by their holy liues and working of* Miracles, *reuiued and ſtrengthened the* Law *in their hearts.*

But

But seeing, that notwithstanding all this , they cast themselues headlong in the gulfe of vices (such is the vnthankefull and repining Nature of Man,) hee raised vp Prophets, as especially Ieremie *and* Daniel, *to accuse them of their sinnes, and by Visions to forewarne them of the times to come , whereby the godly might turne and arme themselues, and the wicked might be made inexcusable. And thus much for the Old Testament. But then God seeing that notwithstanding this, there crept in such a generall corruption amongst them , that scarce one might be found that bowed not his knee to Baal; Hee then by his vnsearchable Wisedome incarnated his E-ternall Sonne and Word* THE LORD IESVS, *who by his death and Passion accomplished the faith of the Fathers; whose Saluation was by the beleeuing in him to come , as also made an open and patent way of Grace to all the world thereafter : And then as vpon a new world , and a new Church, Gods Fatherly care to Mankind was renued , but in a more fauourable forme, because hee looked vpon the Merits of his deare Sonne : Then, first* Christ *with his owne mouth did instruct men, and confirmed his Doctrine by Miracles, and secondly raised vp the Apostles to giue the Law of Faith, confirming it by their liues and Miracles : And last, that notwithstanding this Defection was beginning to creepe in againe, hee inspired one of them, to wit,* IOHN *to write this Booke; that hee might thereby, euen as* Ieremie *and* Daniel *did in the old Law, aswell rebuke them of their sinnes , as by forewarning them, to arme them against the great tentations that were to come after. Then of it selfe it prooues, how profitable this Booke is for this aage ; seeing it is the last Reuelation of Gods will and Prophesie, that euer was, or shall bee in the World : For wee shall haue no more Prophesies nor Miracles hereafter , but must content our selues with the Law and Prophecies already giuen , as* Christ *in his Parable of* La-zarus *and the rich man teacheth. Now as to the Methode, this holy Epistle is di-rected to the seuen Churches of* Asia Minor , *whom hee names and writes to parti-cularly in the first three Chapters of the same , and vnder their Names to all their trew Successors , the whole Church Militant in the World. The whole matter may bee diuided in sixe parts , to wit, The praise or dispraise of euery one of these Churches, according to their merits wherein they merit good or euill, what way they ought to reforme themselues, and this is contained in the three first Chapters : And to make them inexcusable, in case they slide againe , hee shewes the estate of the whole Church Militant in their time; he tells them what it shall be vntill the end of the World , and what it shalbe when it is Triumphant and immortall after the disso-lution : These three last parts are declared by Visions in the rest of the E-pistle, first the present estate of the Church then, and what it should be thereafter vn-to the later day, is summarily declared by the first sixe of the seuen Seales : in the sixt and seuenth Chapters, and afterwards more at large by the seuen Trumpets that came out of the seuenth Seale in the* 8. 9. 10. 11. *Chapters : And because through Tirannie and abuse of the Popedome ,Poperie is the greatest temptation since* Christes *first comming , or that shalbe vnto his last; therefore hee specially insists more at large and cleerly, in the declaration and painting forth of the same, by Vision of the woman in the wildernesse, and of the Beasts that rose out of the sea and the earth ,in the* 12. 13. *and* 14. *Chapters : And then to comfort men that might otherwise despaire, because of the*

greatnesse

Chap. 15. 16.

A 3

Chap. 17. 18.
19.
Chap. 20.

greatneſſe of that temptation , he declares by the next following Viſion of the Phials, what plagues ſhall light vpon the Pope and his followers : Next, he deſcribes him a-gaine, farre clearer then any time before, and likewiſe his ruine, together with the ſor-row of the Earth, and ioy of Heauen therefore : And then to inculcate and ingraue the better the foreſaid Viſions in the hearts and memories of Men , hee in a Viſion makes a ſhort ſumme and recapitulation of them, to wit, of the preſent eſtate of the Church then , and what it ſhould bee thereafter, vnto the Day of Iudgement, to-gether with a ſhort deſcription of the ſaid Day : And laſt he deſcribes by a Viſion, the glorious reward of them, who conſtantly perſiſt in the Trueth , reſiſting all the temptations which he hath foreſpoken, To wit, he deſcribes the bleſſed eſtate of the holy and Eternall Ieruſalem, and Church Triumphant, and ſo with a ſhort and pithie Concluſion makes an end.

A PARA-

A PARAPHRASE VPON
THE REVELATION OF
THE APOSTLE S. IOHN.

CHAP. I.

ARGVMENT.

The Booke, the Writer, and the Inditer ; the end and vse thereof : The dedication of this Epistle to the Churches and Pastors, vnder the vision of the seuen Candlesticks and seuen Starres.

OD THE FATHER hath directed his Sonne and Word, IESVS CHRIST, to send downe an Angel or Minister, to me *Iohn* his seruant, and by him to reueale vnto mee certaine things which are shortly to come to passe, to the effect in time the chosen may be forewarned by me; [2] Who haue borne witnes that the word of God is true, and that IESVS CHRIST is, and was a faithfull witnesse ; and haue made true report of all I saw. [3] Happy are they that read and vnderstand this Prophesie, and conforme themselues thereunto in time, for in very short space it will be fulfilled : [4] I am directed to declare the same, specially to you the *seuen Churches of Asia*, with whom be grace and peace from the Eternall, the Father, and from the Holy Spirit: [5] And IESVS CHRIST, that faithfull witnesse, the first borne of the dead, the Mightie King of the world, and head of his Church; Who for the loue he bare vs, hath made vs innocent by his blood in the worke of Redemption: [6] To him then we, whom hee hath made Spiritual Kings and Priests, in Honour and Holinesse, and ordained to serue and praise his Father, giue all glory and power for euer : so be it. [7] Assure your selues of his comming againe *from Heauen* in all glory, and all eyes shall see him ; Yea the wicked shalbe compelled to acknowledge that it is euen very he, whom

Chrift cruci-
fied.

1.Cor.2.

Iohn banifh-
ed to *Pathmos*
for the trueth,
writeth the
Reuelation.

Verf.10.

Pfal.51.
Efay.4.
Matth.3.
Ierem.1.15.
Efay 17.

Hebr.1.10.
Verf.10.

Ephef.6.
Efay.60.
Matth.7.

Pfal.63.
Pfal. 139.

Chrift is rifen
from death to
life.
Timoth.1.
Hebr.2.

fo they did perfecute : And the whole world fhall haue a feeling before him of their vnthankefulneſſe. So be it. ⁸ I am Eternall, faith the Lord, before whom,all things (which is or was) are prefent , and I am only the worker of all, I who euer Was, and ſtill am, ſhall ſurely come againe according to my promiſe : And as I am Eternall and true, fo I am Almighty, preordinating all things before all beginnings. ⁹ I *Iohn,* your brother in the flefh, and companion with you, afwell in the feruice of *Chriſt,* as in the patient fuffering of the Croſſe, being for that word of God and witneſſing of *Chriſt,* whereof I fpake , fo perfecuted, that for fafety of my life I was conſtrained to flie all alone to the folitarie Ile of *Pathmos.* ¹⁰ Then was I bereft in fpirit vpon the *Sunday,* which is hallowed to the Lord: Then heard I behind me, turne about and take heed , the mighty voyce of the Lord as a Trumpet, becauſe he was to declare the eſtate of the battell of the Church Militant vnto me ; ¹¹ Saying thefe wordes, *I am* A *and* Ω, to wit, *the firſt and the laſt,* write thou in a Booke what thou feeſt, and fend it to the *Seuen Churches in Afia,* the names of which are thefe, *Ephefus,* *Smyrna,* *Pergamos,* *Thyatyra,* *Sardis,* *Philadelphia,* and *Laodicea:* ¹² And when I turned mee to fee the voyce, I did fee *feuen Candlefticks* reprefenting thefe feuen Churches: ¹³ And in the middeſt of them the figure of the *Sonne of man* reprefenting him, clothed with a fide garment for grauitie, and girded about the paps with a girdle of Gold for glory : ¹⁴ His head and haire were white as white Wooll , or Snow for innocencie ; and his eyes were bright like flames of fire, to fignifie his all-feeing knowledge : ¹⁵ His feet were of braſſe, brightly flaming as in a furnace, to declare his ſtanding in Eternity : And his voice like the founding of many waters, reprefenting his Maieſtie in commanding : ¹⁶ And hee had in his Right hand, the fide that the Elect are on, *feuen Starres* for you the *feuen Angels,* that is, Paſtors of the *feuen Churches* : And from his mouth came a two-edged fword, *to wit,* the Sword of the word, which comes onely from him ; and his face was as the Sunne fhining bright, for from his Face comes all light to illuminate blind Man. ¹⁷ And when I thus did fee him, I fell dead at his feet for aſtoniſhment, but he lifted mee vp againe with his right and fauourable hand, and comfortably faid vnto mee, Feare not, be not aſtoniſhed, for *I am the firſt and the laſt.* ¹⁸ Who, as verily as now I liue , was once dead, as thou thy felfe beares witneſſe, and yet now doe liue for euer and euer, and by my death onely I haue ouercome Hell and Death ; and I onely and no other, keepe the Keyes that haue the power of them both. ¹⁹ And now I came to charge thee to write thefe things which thou haſt now feene, becauſe they are afterwards to come to paſſe.

C H A P.

CHAP. II.

ARGVMENT.

Admonition and exhortation to the Churches of Ephesus,
Smyrna, Pergamos and Thyatira.

Rite then this to the Angel, or Paſtour of the Church of *Epheſus*: He that hath the *ſeuen Starres*, or ſeuen Paſtours in his Right hand, or fauourable power, or protection, and who walkes among the *ſeuen Golden Candleſticks*, or watches ouer the ſeuen Churches, euen hee, I ſay, ſayes thus vnto thee: ² I know thy workes, thy trauaile and patience, & that thou ſuffreſt not the wicked to walke with thee, but haſt learned them out, that call themſelues Apoſtles in the Church of *Epheſus*, and are not, and haſt tried them to be lyers: ³ Thou art alſo loaded with a great burden, and yet willingly ſuſtaineſt it, and for the loue of my Name haſt thou trauailed much, and yet wearieſt not: ⁴ But in this I muſt finde fault with thee; that thy former charitie is waxed cold: ⁵ Remember then from whence thou haſt fallen, and repent, turning thy ſelfe to thy firſt workes, otherwiſe I wil turne againſt thee ſoone, and will remoue thy Candleſticke out of the place it is in, *to wit*, the light of the Goſpel, from thy Church, if thou repent not in time: ⁶ But this againe, thou doeſt well to hate the deeds of the *Nicolaitans* which alſo I hate. ⁷ Let all who haue eares, or are willing to be followers of me, heare and take example by this which the Spirit of God ſayes to the ſeuen Churches, or their *ſeuen Paſtours* in the name of them: And to him who is Victor in the battell againſt Satan and the fleſh, I ſhall giue to eate of the *Tree of Life*, which is in the middeſt of the Paradiſe of God, *to wit*, I ſhall make him liue eternally in Heauen. ⁸ To the Angel or Paſtour of the Church of *Smyrna* write thou, This ſayes the firſt and the laſt, who was dead but now liues: ⁹ I know thy workes, thy trouble and pouertie, but thou art rich, *to wit*, in graces; I know alſo what blaſphemies are vſed againſt thee, by them who call themſelues *Iewes*, but are not, but by the contrary are of the Synagogue of Satan. ¹⁰ Feare not when yee ſhall be troubled by the deuil, for he will perſecute and trouble ſome of you in the fleſh, that your conſtancie may be tried, and ye ſhall haue great affliction for the ſpace of tenne dayes, *to wit*, for a certaine ſpace, but be yee faithfull vnto the death, and for your continuance I ſhall giue you the Crowne of life immortall. ¹¹ *Hee that hath an eare, let him heare what the Spirit ſaith to the Churches*; and he that ouercommeth ſhall not be hurt by the ſecond death, which is Hell. ¹² And to the Angel or Paſtour of the Church of *Pergame*, write thou, Thus ſaith he that hath the two edged ſword: ¹³ I know thy workes and where thou dwelleſt, euen where the throne of Satan is, *to wit*, among a great number of wicked; Yet haſt thou not denied thy Faith in me, no not in ſtraighteſt times, when *Antipas* my faithfull Martyr and
witneſſe,

Chap. 1. v. 10.
Pſal. 63.

Chap. 1.

Falſe apoſtles in the Church of *Epheſus*.

Deſtruction to the Church of *Epheſus*, except they repent.
Chap. 1. Ioh. 12. v. 35. Nicolaites.
Pouerbs 15.
Matth. 23.

1. Iohn 2.
1. Iohn 5.
Prou. 3. 5. 18. 21.

Epheſ. 1. 3.

The Church of *Smyrna* afflicted and troubled, yet doeth continew.
Pſal. 91.

Pergame the principall Citie in *Aſtalia*.

Antipas Martyr.

witneſſe, was ſlaine among you, where Satan, *to wit*, many wicked remaine: ¹⁴ Yet haue I ſome few things to lay to your charge, *to wit*, That
yee permit them to remaine amongſt you, who retaine the doctrine of
Balaam , who perſwade men to eate of things immolate to Idols, and to
commit fornication, and filthineſſe in the fleſh : For the very ſame did *Ba-*
laam to Balac, to cauſe the Iſraelites ſtumble. ¹⁵ Thou offendeſt alſo in ſuffering ſome to be amongſt you, who retaine the doctrine of the *Nicolai-*
tans which I hate. ¹⁶ Repent therefore in time, otherwiſe I will come a-
gainſt thee ſoone, and I will fight and ouercome them who are amongſt
you, with the ſword of my mouth, *to wit*, by the force of my word. ¹⁷ He
that hath an eare, let him heare what the Spirit ſaith to the Churches : And
to the Victour ſhall I giue to eate of that ſecret and hidden *Manna*, *to wit*,
of Me the ſpirituall food of the faithfull, of whom that *Manna* which was
hid in the Arke was a figure : And I will alſo giue him a *White ſtone*, or a
Marke of his election and righteouſneſſe through imputation, and in it a
New name written, *to wit*, his name ſhall be written vp in the *Booke of life*,
which no man knoweth but he who receiues it ; for no other may know
the certaintie of ones Election, but onely he who is elected. ¹⁸ And to
the Angel or Paſtour of the Church of *Thyatire*, write, This ſaith the Sonne
of God, whoſe eyes are like flames of fire, and whoſe feet are like to gliſtering braſſe: ¹⁹ I know thy workes, thy charitie, thy almes, and carefull
helping of the weake, thy faith, thy patience, and ſhortly all thy workes ;
but in ſpeciall I praiſe thy great conſtancie and firme continuance, euen ſo,
as thy laſt workes are better then the firſt: ²⁰ Yet ſome few things haue I
to lay to thy charge, *to wit*, that thou ſuffereſt a woman, like to *Iezebel* in
wickedneſſe and Idolatrie, who calls her ſelfe a Propheteſſe, to teach and
ſeduce my ſeruants, to commit fornication and filthineſſe of the fleſh, and
to eate of things immolate vnto Idols : ²¹ Yet gaue I her a time to repent
from her filthineſſe, but ſhe would not. ²² Therefore loe I ſhall caſt her
into a bed, *to wit*, I ſhall deſtroy her in the puddle of her ſinnes, and I ſhall
trouble with great affliction all them who commit adulterie, *to wit*, ſpirituall adulterie with her, if they repent not of their euill workes in time.
²³ And I will kill and deſtroy her ſonnes, *to wit*, all the followers of her
doctrine, that all the Churches and faithfull may know me to be the ſearcher out of the ſecrets of all hearts, and the iuſt renderer and recompencer
of euery man according to his workes. ²⁴ But I ſay vnto the reſt of you
who are at *Thyatire*, who haue not receiued that falſe doctrine, nor know
not the depth nor ſecrets of Satan or wickedneſſe, whereof the other
falſely did purge themſelues, I will not lay any other burthen vpon you,
then that which already conſtantly yee beare : ²⁵ But that which yee
haue, holde it out valiantly vntill my comming againe. ²⁶ For vnto him
who is victour, and beares out to the end that burthen which I lay vpon
him , I will giue power ouer Nations, *to wit*, hee ſhall triumph ouer the
world : ²⁷ And he ſhall rule them with an yron rod, and they ſhall be broken

I. Cor. 10.14.

ken like veſſels of earth, according as I haue receiued the power from my
Father: ²⁸ And I ſhall giue vnto him the *Morning ſtarre*; for as the morning ſtarre ſhines brighter then the reſt, ſo ſhall he ſhine brighter in glory
then his fellowes. ²⁹ *He that hath an eare, let him heare what the Spirit ſayth to
the Churches.*

CHAP. III.

ARGVMENT.

Admonition and exhortation to the Churches of Sardis,
Philadelphia, and Laodicea.

Nd to the Angel or Paſtour of the Church of *Sardis* write | Sardis.
thou, Thus ſayth he who hath the ſeuen Spirits of God, *to
wit*, hee with whom the holy Spirit is vnſeparably ioyned,
and who hath the beſtowing of all the graces of Gods Spirit on the Elect, and hath the *ſeuen Starres, to wit*, who is
the head of you the ſeuen Paſtours, *I know thy workes*, for ye ſay ye liue, and
yet are dead, for your faith is fruitleſſe. ² Be watchfull then, and ſleepe no
longer in negligence and careleſſe ſecuritie, but ſtrengthen againe that
which is dying in you, *to wit*, reuiue your zeale and feruencie which is
waxed cold, and almoſt quenched; for ſurely I haue not found your works
ſo holy, and pure, as they are able to abide a triall before the face of God.
³ Remember then what thou haſt once receiued & heard, that thou maiſt
obſerue the ſame and repent; but if thou watch not as I haue ſaid, I will
come as a thiefe, for the day of triall ſhall come when ye looke leaſt for it,
if ye be not alwayes, and at all times prepared: ⁴ Yet haue yee ſome few
heads and notable perſons in *Sardis*, who haue not defiled their garments,
to wit, corrupted their workes as the reſt haue done, and therefore they
ſhall goe with me being made white, *to wit*, being made innocent by my
merit, for they are worthy thereof: ⁵ And the Victour ſhall be clothed
with a white garment of innocencie by imputation, neither ſhall I wipe
his name out of the Booke of life, but ſhall auow him to be one of mine before my Father and his Angels. ⁶ *He that hath an eare, let him heare what the
Spirit ſayth to the Churches:* ⁷ But to the Angel or Paſtour of the Church of | Philadelphia.
Philadelphia write thou, This ſayth hee who is onely holy and trew, and
who hath the key of *Dauid*, who openeth and no man ſhutteth, who ſhuts | Chap. 22.
and no man openeth, as ſayes *Eſay*; for as *Dauid* was both King and Prophet, and was the figure of me, ſo I, as the veritie and end of that figure, am
onely he, who hath the keyes of abſolute condemning, or abſoluing ſpecially and eternally. ⁸ I know thy workes, and loe, I haue ſet an open doore
before thee, *to wit*, I haue made the way of grace patent vnto thee, which
doore no man can ſhut, becauſe I haue reſerued the ſecret power of election and reprobation onely to my ſelfe; and this fauour will I ſhew you, becauſe

cause yee retaine some good and vertuous things amongst you, and hast kept my Word, and hast not beene ashamed of my Name, nor denyed the same; 9 Loe therefore I will make subiect vnto thee, these who are the *Synagogue of Satan, to wit*, those who call themselues Iewes, and are not, but lye : I shall make them (I say) come and adore before your feete, and they shall be compelled to know that I haue loued thee : 10. And this shall I do vnto thee, because thou hast faithfully returned the tidings of my troubles and sufferings, and therefore shal I deliuer thee also to trie the indwellers of the Earth. 11 Loe, I come shortly, therefore retaine surely to the end, that good which is in thee, lest another doe receiue thy Crowne and reward : 12 For I will make the Victor a pillar in the Temple of my God, *to wit*, a speciall and stedfast instrument in the Church, out of the which he shall neuer againe be cast foorth : for hee who once is elected, is neuer cast off; and I shall write on him, the Name of God, *to wit*, he shal beare the Marke and Seale of an Elect, and the name of the Citie of my God, which is new *Ierusalem, to wit*, the holy and blessed number of Saints and Angels which commeth downe from heauen from my God, *to wit*, is shortly and certeinly to come downe, by the generall compeiring at the latter day : And I shall also write on him mine owne Name, for I shall apply my generall redemption of mankinde to him, in speciall, and so I shall write my new Name vpon him, *to wit*, of Redeemer and Sauiour, which name I haue lately acquired through my passion, death, and rising againe. 13 *Hee that hath an eare, let him heare what the Spirit sayth vnto the Churches.* 14 And to the Angel or Pastour of the Church of *Laodicea*, write thou, *Thus sayth the Amen, to wit*, he that is wholly and perfect holy, and true in all his promises, that faithfull Witnesse, who is the beginning of the workemanship of God, as well because hee is that Word which did create all, and so is their beginning, for that they all receiued their beginning and being from him, as because the vniting of the Manhood with the Godhead in his person is the most excellent, and so the beginning, that is, the chiefe, or first in preeminence of all the workes of God. 15 I know thy workes, sayth hee, *to wit*, that thou art neither hote nor colde, would to God thou wert either hote or cold, *to wit*, either feruent and pure in the trueth, or altogether cold and ignorant, that is, seeing and confessing thine ignorance and slacknesse, that thou mightest be instructed in the same : 16 But thou art lukewarme, and neither hote nor cold, and so inexcusable; and therefore as lukewarme liquor prouokes vomit, so will I spew thee out of my mouth : 17 For thou sayest and thinkest thy selfe to be wealthy, and greatly enriched, and lacke nothing; but thou knowest not thy selfe to be spiritually in miserie and wretchednesse, poore, blinde, and naked of the grace and fauour of God : 18 I would wish thee to buy of me gold purged by the fire, that thou mayst thereby be made truely rich; I meane, I would wish thee to conquer by true repentance and earnest prayer, the Word and trueth of God; (which because it can receiue no filth or spot, and is able to abide the triall, *Dauid*

properly

Laodicea.

Iudgement againſt Laodicea.

properly in his Pſalmes compares to golde purged by the fire) which will
make thee rich in all ſpirituall graces: I would alſo wiſh thee to clothe thy
ſelfe with a white garment, *to wit*, with innocencie and righteouſnes, that
the ſhame of thy nakedneſſe and vncleanneſſe appeare not, and to anoint
thine eyes with an eye-ſalue, that thou mayſt cleerly ſee from whence thou
haſt fallen: ¹⁹ But deſpaire thou not for theſe my ſharpe words, for thoſe
whom I loue, I reproue and fatherly chaſten: Take vp therefore againe
zealouſly the right way to ſaluation, and repent thee earneſtly of thy former iniquities. ²⁰ Loe I ſtand at the doore, and knocke; for I offer my
ſelfe vnto you by my Ambaſſadours, and my word in their mouth, whoſoeuer heareth my voice and openeth the doore, *to wit*, whoſoeuer heareth
my voice, and yeeldeth thereunto due obedience, to him will I come in,
to wit, my holy Spirit ſhall enter into him, and I will ſup and be familiar
with him, as he ſhall doe with me, and reuerence me with loue: ²¹ And
I will make the Victour to ſit with me in my Throne, *to wit*, he ſhalbe partaker of my Glory, euen as I ſit with my Father in his Throne, and am in
my manhood, in which I ouercame, exalted to ſit in glory at his right
hand, equall in power, eternitie and glory with him. ²² *Hee that hath an*
eare, let him heare what the Spirit ſayth to the Churches.

C H A P.   I I I I.

A R G V M E N T.

The rauiſhing of the Writer: The deſcription of the Maieſtie of God in
Heauen, compaſſed about with Angels and Saints, vnder
the figure of Saints and Elders.

Nd when this ſpeech of I E S V S was ended, I looked vp,
and loe, I did ſee a doore opened in Heauen, to the effect
that I might ſee and heare therein, the figuratiue repreſenting of thoſe things that were to come after: And that firſt
voice which ſpake vnto me before, lowd as a trumpet, and
was the voice of I E S V S C H R I S T, ſpake vnto mee, and ſaid,
Mount vp thither, for I am to ſhew thee thoſe things that are to be done here-
after. ² Then was I immediatly bereft in ſpirit; for the eyes of my earthly and groſſe body, could not haue ſeene and comprehended thoſe heauenly and ſpirituall myſteries: And loe, I did ſee a Throne ſet in heauen,
and did ſee one ſit thereon, *to wit*, G O D the Father in all Glory and Maieſtie: ³ And he that ſate thereon, was like in colour to the Iaſper and Sardine ſtones; greene as the Iaſper, to repreſent his euerlaſting flouriſhing
without decay; and fiery redde as the Sardine, to ſignifie his great brightneſſe and conſuming power, who is the trier and ſeparater of the Elect
from the reprobate: and the Rainebow, coloured like the Emerauld,
did compaſſe him round about, to teſtifie thereby, that as after the deluge

Ezech.1.

ned

B　　　　　　　　hee

hee made the Rainebow a Sacrament of the promises made to Noah, so this Rainebow which now I did see compassing his Throne, should serue for a sure Sacrament, that hee will neuer suffer his Elect to perish, but will alwayes, and at all times be compassed, with a great care and watchfulnes ouer them: Greene it was as the Emerauld, to signifie the continuance without ceasing of his care; as the Emerauld comforteth the sight, so is this Sacrament an vnspeakeable comfort vnto the Elect in their trouble-some dayes. 4 And about his Throne were foure and twentie other seats, and I saw foure and twentie Elders or Ecclesiasticall Rulers sitting there-upon, clothed with *white garments*, and hauing *Crownes of Golde* vpon their heads: These are the twelue Patriarkes, and then the twelue Apostles, [who for that they haue beene the speciall teachers both of the olde and new Law, to the saluation, aswell of Iewes as of Gentiles, are set in seates about his Throne for glory, and clothed with white garments for their innocencie and brightnesse] and crowned with crownes of golde in to-ken of their victory ouer Satan and the flesh, and of their glorious reward therefore. 5 And from his Throne went foorth thunder, lightening, and terrible voices, to represent the great seueritie and terriblenes of his Iudge-ments, denounced by the olde Law, and executed on the wicked: And there were seuen lampes of burning fire before his Throne, which is the infinite, mightie, and flaming bright holy Spirit, resembling the loue and light of the new Law of the Gospel of Christ. 6 And there was a sea of glasse like vnto Christall before his Throne, for that as in a glasse he cleere-ly sees euen all the secretest actions and cogitations of all in the world, de-scribed here by the Sea, which is euer before his face; for nothing can be hid from his presence and prescience: And though in lustre and glaunce the world be like the liuely fountaines of waters, which are the faithfull, daily springing and flowing with good workes by fruitfull faith, yet is it indeede without motion or liquor, dead and like glasse, whensoeuer the Lord IEHOVAH doeth thunder his Iudgements vpon it: And in the middest of the Throne, and about the same, were foure beasts; their foure hinder parts were in the midst of it, their shoulders bearing it vp, and their head and wings without and about the same; and these beasts were full of eyes behind and before: These are the holy Cherubims, the highest degree of Angels, foure in number, as well because of their foure qualities to exe-cute his will, (as yee shall heare hereafter) as for that the Lord directs them when it pleaseth him, to all the foure corners of the world, and are as it were his foure windes to blow, that is, to execute either fauour or Iustice, in whatsoeuer place he appointeth them; they are about his Throne, and as it were sustaine the same; testifying thereby, that they are most excel-lent of all others, *& per* αἰϑρωποπαϑείαν, the pillars or footstooles of his glory: Their number of eyes before and behind, signifie their certaine know-ledge of things past, as to come, committed to their charge, together with their continuall vigilancie to execute GODS commandements:

Ezech. 10.12.

7 And

7 And the firſt beaſt was like a Lion, the ſecond like a Calfe, the third was faced like a man, and the fourth was like a flying Eagle; hereby repreſenting their excellent qualities in the execution of the Lords decrees, *to wit*, great power, courage, patience, and ſtrength to trauell, how oft and how much they ſhould be commanded; great wiſedome and a wonderfull ſwiftneſſe in the execution thereof. 8 And euery one of theſe beaſts had ſixe wings in circuit, (Theſe are the ſixe wings *Eſay* ſpeaketh of:) two at their armes, to ſignifie their great celeritie in accompliſhing Gods commandements; two to couer their faces with, to teſtifie that the glory of God is ſo bright, and his Maieſtie ſo great, as the very Angels, his moſt excellent creatures, are not able to behold the ſame; and two at their feete, as well to wipe the filth of the earth off them, after they haue beene here below, (teaching vs thereby, that although they be oft in the world, by the direction of their Creatour, yet cannot the world infect them with her ſinnefulneſſe and corruptions) as alſo to let vs know, that they are ſo farre in glory aboue all men liuing in the earth, as it is impoſſible to vs with corporall eyes, to behold the leaſt part of their glorious brightneſſe without a vaile, euen as it is to them to behold the glory of the Almightie: And within they were all full of eyes, to repreſent their inceſſant looking on God, which commeth from that inward and ineſtimable loue they beare vnto him; which alſo they expreſſed in their continuall ſinging of theſe wordes, *Holy, Holy, Holy*, is that threefold *Lord God Almightie*, who euer was, now is, and ſhall come againe, repleniſhed with all fulneſſe of glory and power: 9 And when theſe Beaſts were giuing all glory, honour, and thankes to him that ſate on the Throne, to him (I ſay) who liues eternally; 10 The foure and twentie Elders, as next in ranke, fell downe vpon their faces before him that ſate on the Throne, and adored Him who liues for euer, and caſt downe their Crownes of golde at his feete, in token that they receiued them onely of him, ſaying, 11 *Thou art onely worthy, O Lord, to be accounted glorious, honourable, and powerfull, for that thou haſt created all things, and for thy will and pleaſure haue they had their being, and were created.* This glance did I ſee of the glory that is in heauen, at the receiuing of my Commiſſion, contained in the following Viſions which I did ſee of the things preſent and to come, in the generall Church militant.

Eſay 6.8.

B 2   CHAP.

CHAP. V.

ARGVMENT.

The defcription of the Booke, wherein was conteined all the Mifteries which were reuealed to this Writer: Chrifts opening of them vnder the figure of a Lion, and of a Lambe: The praifes giuen him by the Saints and Angels therefore, who offer without any Interceffour, euery one his owne thankefgiuing, and praifes to the Mediatour.

Dan.12.4.
Efay 24.11.
Ezck.2.10.

THen firft I did fee in the Right hand of him that fate on the Throne, a Booke, the Booke wherein thefe myfteries are contained; and all the Booke was written vpon, afwell on the backe as within; on the backe was written thefe Vifions that I did fee, and am prefently to declare vnto you; within was written the plaine expofition, and the very proper names of all things which thefe Vifions did reprefent, which are inclofed there, to fignifie that the Lord hath not permitted me to manifeft the fame to the world, for the time thereof is not come yet; which Booke was fealed with feuen Seales; afwell to keepe euery part thereof vnreuealed to any, as alfo to giue the greater certaintie, that thefe things fhall come to paffe, which are prophefied therein. ² And I faw a ftrong Angel proclayming with a loud voice, Who is worthy to open this Booke, and to loofe the Seales thereof? ³ But there could none be found worthy to doe it, neither in heauen nor in earth, nor beneath the earth, no not to looke on it, much leffe to open it: for neither Angel nor deuil either knows or dare meddle with the high myfteries of God, and things future, except fo farre as pleafeth him to commit and reueale vnto them: ⁴ Then wept I very fore that none could be found worthy to open and read that Booke, no not to looke vpon the fame: for I was very forrowfull that I could not haue it reuealed vnto me: ⁵ At laft one of the Elders faid vnto mee, Weepe not, Loe the Lion of the Tribe of *Iuda* hath preuailed, *to wit*, he who is come of *Iuda*, and hath admirable force in his flefh, deriued from the Tribe of *Iuda*, by which he ouercame Sinne, Death, and Hell, and is the roote of *Dauid*, (for *Dauid* was his figure and fore-beer in the flefh) is worthy and onely worthy to open the Booke, and loofe the Seales thereof. ⁶ And then I tooke heed, and behold, I did fee in the middeft of the Throne, and the foure beafts, a fecond perfon of the Trinitie fitting with God, and in the middeft of the Elders, as a man and our brother, a Lambe ftanding like as hee had bene flaine, to fignifie that once indeed hee was flaine, but had rifen againe, and had feuen Hornes and feuen Eyes, reprefenting the innumerable times, mighty and holy Spirit of God, which after his Refurrection he fent out through the whole earth to direct, inftruct, and rule the fame by his prouidence and power: ⁷ This Lambe then came and tooke the Booke out of the Right hand of him that did fit on the Throne: ⁸ And fo foone as he had taken the Booke in his hand, thefe foure beafts, and thefe foure and

twentie

twentie Elders fell vpon their faces before the Lambe, and adored him, and
euery one of them had in his hand Harpes, and golden Phials, full of sweet
odours; these are the prayers of the Saints, which the foure beasts, comprehending all the degrees of Angels, and the foure and twentie Elders
comprehending the whole Church, as well Militant as Triumphant, perceiuing that C H R I S T is to reueale all the tentations which are to fall
vpon the earth and Church, before the latter dayes, doe powre forth, aswel
on the Church triumphants part, thankesgiuing; that by the reuealing or
opening of the Booke, he armeth the Militant Church to resist all the
tentations contained therein, as also on the Church Militants part, to pray
him to hasten the end and dissolution; for the hastening whereof all creatures sigh and grone to their Creator. Euery one of these beasts and Elders, presents their owne praiers vnto him who sits on the Throne, to teach
vs, as he is Mediatour, and therefore our prayers must be offered vnto him
onely, that so there is no Intercessour betweene him and vs, but euery one
of vs must present our owne prayers before him, after the example of the
beasts and Elders : These prayers were inclosed in harpes, to signifie the
sweet and pleasing found, that faithfull prayers make in the eares of God;
they were inclosed in golden Phials, to teach vs that acceptable prayers
must come from an vndefiled heart, and pure as gold; and they themselues
are called *incense*, because their smell is pleasant and sweet like *incense* in
the nostrils of God.   This did the incense at the sacrifice in the old Law | Exod.30.7.
signifie and figurate; and of this *incense* speakes *Dauid* in his Psalmes. 9 And | Psal.141.1.
they, *to wit*, the foure and twenty Elders did sing a new Canticle, for the
matter of their Canticle, *to wit*, the accomplishment of the Mysterie of re-
demption is new, and euer ought to be new and fresh in the hearts of all | Psal.144.
them that would be accompted thankefull: Their song then was this;
Thou art worthy, O Lord, to receiue the Booke, and open the Seales thereof, for thou hast bene slaine, though innocent; and by thy precious Blood
hast redeemed vs to God thy Father, and hast chosen vs out of all Tribes,
tongues, people and nations, aswell *Iewes* as *Gentiles* : ¹⁰ And thou hast
made vs Kings and Priests spiritually to our God : And we shall reigne o-
uer the earth at the last and generall Iudgement, and as Kings, shall be participant of the glory of the holy and new Citie *Ierusalem*. ¹¹ Then I beheld and heard round about the Throne, the beasts, and the Elders, the
voyces of many Angels, to the number of many thousand thousands, *to* | Dan.7.10.
wit, innumerable Legions of them, ¹² Who said all with a loud voice, The
Lambe who was slaine, is worthy to haue all power, riches, wisedome
strength, honour, glory and blessing for euer. ¹³ I also heard all creatures
in Heauen, in earth, and beneath the earth, and in the seas, euen all that are
in them, I heard saying in one voyce vnto him that sits vpon the Throne,
and vnto the *Lambe* be *Blessing*, *Glory*, *Honour* and *Power* for euer, and euer.
And the foure beastes said, Amen, and the foure and twenty Elders fell on
their faces, and adored him that liues for euer, and euer.

CHAP. VI.

ARGVMENT.

The opening of the first sixe Seales : The spreading of the Euangel, signified by the
white horse, in the first seale : The great Persecution by the red horse, in the se-
cond : The number of diuers hereſies by the blacke, in the third : The Popedome
and Tyrannie thereof by the pale, in the fourth : The complaint of the Saints,
and their deliuerance promised : Their blessed estate in the meane time, in the
fift : The day of Iudgement, and the terriblenesse thereof, in the sixt.

Fter this I looked to ſee when the *Lambe* opened the *firſt*
Seale, and loe, I heard one of the foure beaſts, for they were
appointed to aſſiſt me in the time of theſe Viſions, as the
moſt excellent creatures of God ; and his voice was like a
thunder, making me awake, with terrour to take heede to
theſe great and terrible Propheſies, which God was to declare vnto me, and
hee ſaid, *Come and ſee.* ² Then I looked and did ſee a white horſe, and he

Zach. 1. 8.
Zach. 6. 2, 3.

that ſate on him had a bow in his hand, and a Crowne giuen vnto him,
and hee came foorth a Victour to winne and ouercome : This man comming on the white horſe, was the comming and incarnation of our
Bright and Innocent Sauiour, armed with a bow ; for euer ſince his comming till now, and a ſpace hereafter, the dart and arrow of God, *to wit*, the
holy Spirit by the preaching of the Goſpel doeth ſubdue, and bring the
world vnder his ſubiection, and taketh vengeance of his enemies : His
crowne is giuen to him by his Father, in token of his victory ouer the ſecond death, and as King of the Catholike Church to crowne the faith-

Conuerſion
of the Gen-
tiles.

full, and ſo he commeth foorth a Victour ouer Satan, and to ouercome by
once, conuerting a great part of the world to the trew knowledge of God :
This myſterie is already begunne, but is not yet accompliſhed. ³ And
when he opened the ſecond Seale, ⁴ Loe, there came foorth a red horſe, and
there was power giuen to him that ſate on him, to take away peace from
the earth, that euery one might ſlay one another ; and there was giuen him
for that purpoſe a great ſword ; for with the ſpreading of the Euangel and
rooting of the trueth in the hearts of the nations, ſhall a bloody perſecu-

Perſecution
of the body by
the Ciuill
ſword, in the
ſecond Seale.
Continuation
of trew paſtors
after the Mar-
tyres.

tion of Tyrants by the ciuill ſword, be ioyned ; which is meant by the rider on the red horſe : but notwithſtanding the Euangel ſhall ſpread and
flouriſh, for ſuch is the power of God, reſiſting the pride of man, that vnder
the Croſſe, the puritie of the trueth moſt flouriſheth in the Church. ⁵ And
when he opened the third Seale, the third Beaſt ſaid vnto me, *Come and ſee :*
and loe, I did ſee a blacke horſe, and hee that ſate vpon him had balances
in his hand : ⁶ And I heard a voice from among the foure Beaſts, ſaying,
A meaſure of Wheat for one peny, and three meaſures of Barley for one peny,
but wine and oyle harme thou not : for after that this firſt myſterie ſhall be accompliſhed, not onely dearth and famine ſhall enſue the contempt of the
trueth,

trueth, but God ſhall permit Satan to tempt and vexe his Church with a cloud of diuers and dangerous hereſies, which may be meant by the rider on the blacke horſe, for the blackeneſſe and darkeneſſe of them; ſhall obſcure the light of the Goſpel; but yet God, to aſſure vs that hee will neuer forget his owne, ſpeakes from his Throne, comforting vs thereby, that although (as the balances and meaſure ſignifies) good men ſhall beſcant, who are the fine wheat and barley of his harueſt, yet ſome ſhall there be that ſhall not bow their knee to *Baal,* no not in ſtraighter times that ſhall come after; and alwayes giues vs aſſurance, that the word and trueth of God, which is an eternall Oyle, and comfortable Vine, ſhall neuer be deſtroyed, nor any wayes corrupted, in ſpight of all the malice of Satan in his inſtruments. 7 And when hee opened the fourth Seale, the fourth Beaſt ſaid vnto me, *Come and ſee.* 8 Then I beheld, and loe, I did ſee a pale horſe, and the name of him that ſate vpon him was Death: This is the greateſt and heauieſt plague; for after that the perſecutions and hereſies ſhall take an ende, and that infirmitie and coldneſſe haue cropen into the Church; then ſhall God redouble his former plagues, by permitting Satan to erect a tyrannie compoſed of both theſe former plagues; for it ſhall be full of hereſie like the one, and full of ciuill and temporall tyrannie like the other: and therefore becauſe it brings with it al maner of death, both of body and ſoule, the rider is iuſtly called Death, as the fountaine of all the ſorts of the ſame: and the paleneſſe of the horſe is correſpondent in all points to the qualitie of the rider; for as the rider is called Death, ſo the colour of paleneſſe repreſents the ſame: and as the riders qualities are compoſed of hereſies and tyrannie, ſo the colour of pale is compoſed chiefly of blacke and red: And hell followed after him to the vtter damnation of him and his followers: And power was giuen him ouer the fourth part of the earth, *to wit,* the reſt who are not ouercome by the other three riders; for all they who were not marked by the white horſe, nor killed in body by the red, nor killed in ſoule by the blacke, are killed both in body and ſoule by this laſt: And as he hath power of deſtroying thus, giuen him ouer the fourth part of the earth, ſo by foure plagues ſpecially doeth he execute the ſame, *to wit,* by Sword, Hunger, Death, and the Beaſts of the earth: Theſe plagues allude to the plagues, mentioned in the Canticle of *Moſes*; for this tyrannie ſhall begin with perſecution, this perſecution ſhall cauſe a hunger, and great ſcarcitie of the true worſhip of God, this hunger ſhall breed a ſecond and eternall death, and this tyranny ſhall then end with a crueller and bloodier perſecution of the bodies then euer was before; which ſhall be ſo barbarous, that it is compared in this Viſion to the execution, vſed by wilde beaſts vpon offenders, and ſhall ſpare no degree, ſexe nor aage, no more then beaſts doe. 9 But when he opened the fift Seale, I did ſee vnder the Altar, the ſoules of them that were ſlaine for the word of God, and for his Teſtimonie which they maintained: 10 And they cryed with a lowd voice, ſaying, *How long wilt thou delay* (O Lord) ſince thou art holy and

Hereſies ment in the third Seale.

Luke 3.

The Popedom is meant by the pale horſe in the fourth Seale, of hereſie and ciuil tyranny.

Scarcitie of trew Paſtors and worſhipping.
The cruelty of the Popes tyranny.

and trew, to reuenge & iudge our blood vpon them that dwel on the earth; for this laſt perſecution did enter ſo fiercely into the world, and did make ſo great a number of Martyrs, that their ſoules lying vnder the Altar, *to wit,*

Hoſe. 14.3.
Hebr. 13.15.

in the ſafegard of I E S V S C H R I S T (who is the only Altar, whereupon, and by whom it is onely lawfull to vs, to offer the ſacrifice of our hearts and lips, *to wit,* our humble prayers to God the Father) did pray, and their blood did cry to heauen, and craue at the hands of their Father a iuſt reuenge of their torments vpon the wicked, and therewith a haſtening of the generall diſſolution, for the deliuerie of their brethren who did remaine yet aliue. 11 Then white robes were giuen to euery one of them, and it was ſaid vnto them, and they were willed to reſt and haue patience for a ſhort ſpace, vnto the time the number of their fellow ſeruants to God, and brethren companions in the Croſſe, were fulfilled, who were alſo to be ſlaine as they were already: This ſurely ought to be a wonderfull and ineſtimable comfort to all the Church militant, ſince by this Seale wee are aſſured, that both the ſoules of the Martyrs, ſo ſoone as their bodies are killed, ſhall immediatly be rewarded with perpetuall and bright glory in heauen, not going into any other place by the way, which is ſignified by the *White robes*; as alſo that ſo ſoone as their number ſhall be complete, which ſhall be within a ſhort ſpace, God ſhall then craue a full account at their perſecutors hands; and then as the one number ſhall receiue a full and eternall glory in body and ſoule, the other ſhall receiue a full torment in ſoule and body, to the cleere ſhining of his Iuſtice in the one, and his mercy in the other. 12 Then I tooke heed when he opened the ſixt, and loe, there

Matth. 24.29.

was a great earthquake, and the Sunne-beame blacke like ſackecloth made of haire, and the Moone became all bloody: 13 And the Starres fell from the heauens vpon the earth, euen as the figgetree lets her vnripe figges fall, being beaten by a mightie winde: 14 And the heauen went away like a ſcrole that is rolled together, and all the hilles and Iles were remooued from their places: 15 And the Kings of the Earth, the Nobles, the rich men, the Tribunes or commanders of the people, the mighty men, and all the ſlaues, aſwell as free-men, did hide themſelues in cauerns and vnder rockes

Luke 23.30.

of hills: 16 And they ſaid to the hilles and the rocks, Fall vpon vs, and hide vs from the ſight of him that ſits vpon the Throne, and from the wrath of the *Lambe*: 17 For that great day of his wrath is come, and who then may ſtand? This is the accompliſhment of that diſſolution, craued and promiſed in the fift Seale. Theſe terrible things, mentioned in the ſixt Seale, are the alterations and ſignes in the laſt time: the very ſame did our Maſter Chriſt propheſie, when he was walking on this Earth.

C H A P.

CHAP. VII.

ARGVMENT.

A proper and comfortable digreſsion, interieƈted of Gods care ouer the Eleƈt, in the times of greateſt temptations , ſignified by the Viſions of the foure Angels, the Eleƈtion and happie eſtate of the eleƈted.

Vt leſt I, or any other, ſhould doubt of the ſafegard and ſaluation of the Eleƈt, thinking that theſe terrible plagues ſhould haue lighted vpon both good and bad indifferently, he repreſented vnto my ſight foure Angels, ſtanding on the foure corners of the earth , and retayning the foure winds in their hands, and ſtopping them, either to blow vpon the earth, the ſea, or any tree : ² And I did ſee one Angel going vp from the riſing of the Sunne, hauing the Seale of the liuing God , and hee cried with a loud voice to the foure Angels that had power giuen them to harme the earth, and the ſea, ³ Saying ; Harme not the earth nor the ſea, nor the trees, vntill we haue marked the ſeruants of God on the forehead ; Theſe Angels, foure in number, becauſe they ſit vpon the foure corners of the earth, ready to execute Gods iudgements vpon euery part of the World, although they already had ſtayed the winds to blow, *to wit*, the progreſſe of the Euangel vpon the earth, which is the world, vpon the Sea, which is the numbers of people, vpon the Trees, which are the Magiſtrates, Ciuill or Eccleſiaſticall ; Yet one Angel came from the riſing of the Sunne, *to wit*, directed by Christ, who is comfortable like the *Sunne-riſing* to his Eleƈt, and is that *Orient day-ſpring* , and Sunne of Righteouſnes, riſing ouer all the faithfull, which is mentioned in the Scriptures ; Who cries and forbids theſe foure Angels to doe any further temporall harme, while firſt the choſen be ſealed on the forehead, by that Seale which he beares with him for that effeƈt, that theſe Angels might know them, being marked in ſo eminent a place, in the generall deſtruƈtion, and ſo ſpare them, aſſuring vs thereby, that he hath ſuch a care ouer his Eleƈt, as he hath prouided for them before hand, euen as he did for *Noah* and *Loth*, and their families, in the time of the deluge and deſtruƈtion of *Sodome*. ⁴ And I heard the number of them that were ſealed in *Iſrael* , reckoned to be *one hundred fourtie and foure Thouſand* ; for twelue thouſand were ſealed of euery one of the Tribes, which makes iuſtly that number. Out of euery one of the Tribes was a certaine number choſen, to aſſure vs, that a number of euery one of them ſhalbe ſaued : ⁹ And that I might be aſſured that a number, aſwell of the *Gentiles*, as of the *Iewes*, ſhalbe ſaued, Loe, he ſhewed me a number ſo great, as I could not reckon the ſame, and it was compoſed of certaine out of euery Nation, Tribe, people and tongue : And they ſtood before the Throne, and in preſence of the *Lambe*, clothed with white robes, hauing palmes in
their

2.Peter 1.
Luke 1.7.
Malach.4.

their hands, in token of the victorie they obteined of their longfome battaile. ¹⁰ And they cried all with one voice, saying, Our health and our saluation commeth from our God that fits on the Throne, and from his Lambe, *to wit*, their health came from God the Father, by the Mediation of his Sonne. ¹¹ Then all the Angels stood round about the Throne, the Elders, and the foure beastes, and bowed themselues downe vpon their faces, and adored God with thankesgiuing, for his mercy to the chosen, both of Iew and Gentile, and his Iustice vpon all the rest, ¹² Saying, *Amen*, in allowance of the things done, with full confession, that *Blessing, Glory, Wisedome, Thankesgiuing, Honour, Vertue*, and *Power*, belongs only and most iustly to GOD, for euer and euer. ¹³ Then one of the Elders spake vnto me, and said, What are these, and from whence are they come; who are clothed with white robes? ¹⁴ And I answered and said; Thou knowest, my Lord. Then he said vnto me, These are they who are preserued, and come from that great affliction, which was represented to thee in some of the Seales, and they haue washed their garments, and made them white in the blood of the *Lambe*: for they, by vertue of his death, are made righteous by imputation, whose blood is the onely and full purgation of vs, from our sinnes: ¹⁵ And therefore they are before the Throne of GOD, and serue him day and night in his Temple, *to wit*, they, without any intermission, contemplate his Glory, and euer serue him by continuall thankesgiuing, and praising his Name in Heauen, which is his eternall and celestiall Temple: and hee that sits on the Throne shall dwell with them; for they shall neuer be separated from his presence. ¹⁶ And they shall be no more an hungry, or thirstie, nor the Sunne, or any heate shall trouble them: ¹⁷ For the *Lambe* who is in the middest of the Throne, *to wit*, coequall in power with his Father, he shall feed them and guide them to the liuely fountaines of waters, *to wit*, they shall feed of that Spirituall and liuely bread, and drinke of that Spirituall and liuely water, euen himselfe; which Water he promised to the *Samaritane* woman, at the well: And GOD shall wipe all *teares* from their *eyes*; for he shall both by the greatnesse of their present ioyes, put quite out of their memories, all the sorrow of their former troubles; and shall also giue them eternall ioy, which shall neuer be mixed with any kind of trouble or feare: so shall they not be molested with the vehemencie of the Sunne, or any other heate, which signifies great troubles, and sorrow.

Iohn 4.14.

CHAP.

CHAP. VIII.

ARGVMENT.

The opening of the seuenth Seale : The seuen Trumpets comming out of it : The effect of the prayers of the faithfull, signified by the vision of the fire of the Altar : Some persecution, and some heresies, signified by haile mixt with blood and fire, in the first trumpet : The great persecution by the hill of fire, in the second : The number of heresies, by the starres, falling into the fountaines of water, in the third : The vniuersall infirmitie in the Church, in some things by the Sunne, Moone, and starres darkened, in the fourth.

Nd when hee opened the seuenth Seale, there was silence in heauen almost halfe an houre, aswell to let mee know that hee had once already summarily declared the whole things which was to come after, as by silence a while to giue me occasion to meditate vpon that vision which I had seene, to the effect that afterward I might the better vnderstand the more particular rehearsall thereof, which now vnder another vision and forme, was to be declared vnto me by the opening of the seuenth Seale. ² And I saw seuen Angels standing before God, to execute whatsoeuer thing it should please him to command them; and by his direction there were seuen Trumpets giuen vnto them, that by these Trumpets they might with one Maiestie denounce to the world such plagues, as they were by the command of God to powre foorth vpon it. ³ Then another Angel came and stood before the Altar, hauing a golden censer in his hand, and there was much incense giuen vnto him, that he might offer vp the prayers of the Saints vpon the golden Altar, that is before the Throne : ⁴ And the smoke of the incense, which is the prayers of the Saints, mounted vp from the hand of the Angel to the sight of God : ⁵ Then the Angel tooke this new emptied censer, and filled it againe with the fire of the Altar, and did cast it downe on the earth, and there were thundrings, voices, lightenings and earthquakes : By this Angel and his proceedings, we are assured and made certaine, that Christ shall euer be vigilant ouer his owne, and that specially in straightest times hee will heare their prayers, and euer renew them with some light of the Gospel, by the working of his holy Spirit : And to assure vs hereof, the vision of this Angel was showne vnto me immediatly before, that by the seuen Trumpets he is to dilate these visions, showen me in the former Seales : This Angel was Christ, he stood before the Altar : this Altar is likewise himselfe, as I declared before : his standing before it, meaneth, that by his office of Mediatour, hee was to doe as followes : He had a golden censer in his hand, for he keeps the censer wherein are contained the incense which the Saints giue him, *to wit,* their prayers, to be offered vp to God by his mediation, who is that golden and pure Altar, which is euer in the presence of God, and whose requests are no

time

time refufed, and therefore that incenfe and the fmoke thereof, mounts vp to the fight of God, to affure vs that our prayers, being offered in that forme, are euer acceptable: The effect whereof doeth appeare, by the Angels filling againe the cenfer with the fire of the Altar, and cafting it on the earth; wherewith is ioyned the noife ye heard of; for thefe prayers procure, that their Mediatour fhall out of his golden boxe, *to wit*, out of his treafure of power, fend downe the fire of the Altar, *to wit*, the holy Spirit which remaineth with him, to make thunders, voices, lightnings and earthquakes, *to wit*, to giue againe the Law, by renewing the efficacie of the Gofpel, in the hearts of the faithfull, alluding to the giuing of the olde Law, whereof thefe fearefull noifes were the fore-runners: This furely is the care and effect that our Mafter in all troublefome times renewes to ftrengthen our weakeneffe with. ⁶ And then the feuen Angels which had the feuen trumpets prepared themfelues to blow; for although they were before directed, yet were they not permitted to execute their office, no more then the foure Angels, who ftayed the foure windes while Chrift had ftrengthened and armed his owne, as is faid, to affure vs, that euer before any great temptation, hee will make the backes of the elect ready, and able to

1.Cor.10.13.

beare fuch burthens as hee is to lay vpon them. ⁷ Then the firft Angel blew, and there was a great haile, and fire mixed with blood, and this ftorme was caft downe vpon the earth; whereupon followed, that the third part of the trees was withered and burnt vp, and all greene graffe was withered and burnt vp, for the firft plague which hath already begun to worke, fhall be mixed partly of haile, which is herefie, for as haile fhowers by the harme they doe to the corne, makes them to become deare, fo herefie makes the true harueft of the Lord to become fcant: This haile or herefie, and fpirituall perfecution, is ioyned with the fword and perfecution of the flefh, which is fignified by the fire, and the blood: This fiery and two edged triall fhall make the third part, *to wit*, a part, but not the greateft number of trees, *to wit*, of renowmed men; and all greene graffe, *to wit*, all them that are not wel founded and ftrong in the trewth, (this greene graffe

Marke 4.verf. 5,6,7.

is that fort of profeffours, of whom Chrift fpake in the parable of the feed fowen in fandie, and thornie ground;) it fhall make them (I fay) to fall from the trewth, and fo become withered and vnprofitable. ⁸ Then the fecond Angel blew, and there fell as it had beene a great hill, all burning in fire; and this hill was caft into the fea, and the third part of the fea became blood: ⁹ And the third part of the liuing creatures in the fea was flaine, and the third part of the fhips therein did perifh; for after that this former plague fhall haue an end, and yet the world not turne themfelues from their iniquities, then the fecond fhall follow, which is the corporall plague of perfecution, fignified by the red horfe in the fecond Seale, more amply dilated heere: This great heape of fiery perfecution, like a mountaine of fire, fhall make the third part, or a certaine number of people and nations, which is fignified by the feas or many waters, to ouerflow in

blood;

blood; for as it is said of the same in the second Seale, they shall slay one another, for euen among themselues, *to wit*, among the wicked shalbe great bloodshed and warres; for the third, or a certaine number of all sorts of liuing things shall die, *to wit*, no sort of men shall be exempted from this trouble: But especially a number, and not the greatest part of the faithfull shalbe persecuted, which is signified by the ships; for euen as ships on a stormie Sea seeke a hauen, so the faithfull among the wicked of the world, tossed here and there resisting euery waue, striue in despight of many contrarious windes, to attaine to that hauen, where at last casting their Anchor, they are freed from all worldly tempests, and dwell there eternally in a perpetuall calmenesse.   10 Then the third Angel blew, and there fell from heauen a great Starre burning like a torch, and it fell vpon the third part of riuers and fountaines of waters, and the name of the starre was *Wormewood*: and the third part of the riuers and fountaines were turned into *wormewood*, and many men died, for the bitternesse of the waters: This is that same plague which is signified by the *blacke horse* and his rider, *to wit*, a cloud of defections, and Apostatical heresies, here signified by a great starre burning like a torch: for it shall haue a great light, but like the light of a torch; for as the torch and candle-light is false to the eye and makes the colours to appeare otherwise then they are, and is made dimme by the brightnes of the Sunne, so shall this light of false doctrine maske iniquitie for a space, and make it seeme to be the trueth, vnto the time the trew light of God obfuscat and blinde it: These heresies shall be stronger in deceit, then those before: for they shall seduce the very pastours and spirituall Magistrates, which is signified by the Starres falling in a part of the fountaines of waters: for these men are the worldly fountaines, whereout the rest of the faithfull, by the buckets of their eares, draw that spring of heauenly liquor.   11 This starre is called *Wormewood*, for as wormewood is a bitter hearbe, what greater bitternesse can be to the soule of man, then to procure the wrath of the Almightie, through such an horrible fall? and as it turned a part of the pastours, and made them to become of bitter qualitie like it selfe, so their bitternesse did slay with the second death, a great number of men; *to wit*, their disciples and followers. 12 Then the fourth Angel blew, and the third part of the Sunne, the third part of the Moone, and third part of the Starres was stricken, so that the third part of them, *to wit*, of their light was obscured, and the third part of the day, and the third part of the night was obscured, *to wit*, the third part of their light was darkened: For after that one part of the pastours shall make horrible defection, it shall fall out that the whole Church visible, shalbe blinded with some errours, but not yet make a full defection, which is signified by the obscuring of a part of the light of the Sunne, Moone, and starres, *to wit*, of all degrees of spirituall Magistrates; so that by their generall weaknesse in some points, a part of the meaning of the Gospel shal be falsly interpreted, which is meant by the light of the *day*; and of the *night*:

night: for as the cloud by day, and the pillar of fire by night did guide the people of *Ifrael* through the defart, to the land of *Promife*, fo will this light fhining, both day and night in our foules, conduct vs out through the wildernefle of this world, to that fpirituall land of *promife*, where we with our God fhall glorioufly reigne in all Eternitie: This fourth blaft is alfo a part of the third Seale. ¹³ And I faw and heard an other Angel flying through the middeft of heauen, and faying with a lowd voice, *Woe, woe, woe* to the inhabitants of the earth, for the harme that fhalbe done vnto them by the laft three blafts of the Angels Trumpets: for the laft three plagues fhall be exceeding great, which, that I might the better note and take greater heed vnto, God wakens me vp and makes me fee an Angel flying through the middeft of heauen with celeritie, afwell to forewarne the holy Angels and Saints of thefe three plagues, fo farre in greatnefle aboue the reft, as to fignifie by his fwift flying, that they are haftily and within fhort fpace to be put in execution: And the number of Woes, *to wit*, which he cries, are anfwerable to the number of plagues which are hereafter to be declared.

C H A P. IX.

A R G V M E N T.

In the fift Trumpet, the herefies caufe a great blindneſſe and ignorance, whereof commeth the Eccleſiaſticall Papiſticall orders, fignified by the graſhoppers breeding out of the ſmoake, and their power and qualities: Their King and head the Pope, and his ſtyle : In the next Trumpet the beginning of his decay, ſignified by the looſing of the foure Angels at Euphrates: The remedy he uſeth for the ſame by hounding out the Ieſuits, *fignified by the horſe in the Viſion: Their qualities fignified by their breaſt-plates: The Popes and Turkes his gathering to deſtroy the Church, fignified by a great armie of horſe: The Pope is the plague for breaking of the firſt Table : and the Turke for breaking of the ſecond.*

Hen the fift Angel blew, and I faw the ftarre that fell out of heauen vpon earth (for it is to be noted, that all thefe plagues did fall out of heauen vpon the earth, to teach vs, *Quòd nullum malum eſt in ciuitate, quod non faciat Dominus*, by his Iuftice permitting, directing, ordering, and reftrayning it) I did fee it get the key of the bottomleffe pit which was giuen vnto it; for this cloud of herefies fpoken of in the third Trumpet and third Seale, by procefle of time did breed this baftard tyrannie, whereof I fpoke in the fourth Seale, and fo it brought from hell by the opening of the bottomlefle pit, whereof it gate the keyes, *to wit*, by the affiftance, and deuice of Satan, it bred fuch plagues as follow. ² Firft, by opening of the pit, came foorth a great fmoke like the fmoke of a furnace, *to wit*, it did breed fuch a darkenefle and ignorance in the minds of men, as the Sunne and the Aire were obfcured, (*to wit*, the light of the trweth reprefented preſented by the darkening of the Sunne) and ſo in place of liuing vnder, and by the true and cleare aire of the trueth, the world ſhall liue vnder, and by the baſtard and darke aire of falſe doctrine. ᵗ ³ And out of this ſmoake came Graſhoppers vpon the earth : For this great blindneſſe ſhall breed a multitude of diuers Orders of Eccleſiaſticall perſons, as well Monkes and Friers, as others, but all agreeing in one hereticall Religion; Theſe are graſhoppers, becauſe they breed of that filthy ſmoke of hereſies, euen as Graſhoppers breed of corrupted aire; they are euer teaching falſe doctrine with their mouth, which carries with it as great deſtruction to the ſoules of men, as the mouthes of Graſhoppers doe to the greene graſſe and herbs, and the earth ſhalbe ouerloaden with multitudes of them, euen as Graſhoppers ſometimes come in great heapes, and ouercharge the face of a whole countrey: And like power was giuen to them, as hath the earthly Scorpions: for as the Scorpions ſting is not felt ſore at firſt, and is long in working, and impoſſible to be healed, but by the oyle of a dead ſcorpion, ſo the poyſoning of the ſoule cannot be perceiued by the receiuer at the firſt, but is long in operation, for by peece and peece they infect the world with hereſies, and open not all their packe at firſt; and the world ſhall neuer be freed from their hereſies, vnto the vtter deſtruction of theſe falſe teachers themſelues : ⁴ And it was ſaid vnto them, or they were forbidden to harme the graſſe, or any greene thing, or any tree, but onely theſe men that haue not the *marke of God* in their foreheads: for though earthly Graſhoppers when they ſwarme in heapes, doe deſtroy all greene graſſe or trees, yet God ſhall ſo bridle the rage of theſe ſpirituall Graſhoppers, that they ſhall haue no power to peruert the Elect of whatſoeuer degree, or ſort, compared to greene graſſe and fruitful trees; but their power ſhall extend onely vpon them that beare not the marke or Seale of God vpon their forehead, and as withered and vnfruitfull ſticks are ready for the fire: ⁵ But they ſhall haue no power to ſlay them, *to wit*, they ſhall not diſcouer to the world their greateſt blaſphemies at the firſt, as I ſaid before, but they ſhall torment them for the ſpace of fiue monethes, and their torment ſhalbe like the torment that a man ſuffers, being ſtinged by a ſcorpion, *to wit*, they ſhal by peece & peece infect them with ſpirituall poiſon; and as I haue ſaid already, they ſhall not feele the ſmart thereof, while the ſecond death make them to feele the ſame: This torment ſhall endure fiue monethes, that is the time limitted them by God, which alludes to the fiue monethes in Summer when Graſhoppers are; This forme of ſpeech doeth declare the continuing of the Metaphore. ⁶ And in theſe daies men ſhal ſeeke death, and ſhall not finde the ſame, and men ſhall deſire to die, but death ſhall flie from them, for then beginnes the troubleſome times of the later dayes, the miſerie whereof I heard our Maſter, while he was yet on the earth, declare in theſe words that I haue now repeated. ⁷ And the figure of theſe locuſts, was like vnto the horſe prepared for the war, to ſignifie that their forme of practiſe & policie, ſhalbe ſo, worldly wiſe, that they ſhal lacke no-

thing

thing perteyning to the setting forth of their intents, more then a horse of seruice which is curiously barded, seated and prepared, for going forth to the battell. And they had crownes like crownes of gold vpon their heads; for they shall pretend to be holy like the Elders, who for their reward gate Crownes of pure gold set vpon their heads, as you heard before, and so shall outwardly glance in an hypocriticall holinesse; And their faces were like the faces of men, and the faces of men signifie reason, as man is a reasonable creature : the likenesse then of their faces vnto men, signifies that they shall, by curious arguments, pretend reason to maintaine their false doctrine, but it shall be but a counterfait resembling of reason indeed, euen as their crownes are like vnto gold, but are not gold indeed. ⁸ And they haue haire like the haire of women : for as the haire of women is a speciall part of their alluring beautie, so they haue such alluring heresies, whereby they make the way of heauen so easie by their helpe, to whomsoeuer, how wicked soeuer they be, that will vse the same, as they allure them to commit spirituall adulterie with them. And they haue teeth like Lions teeth : for as the Lion is stronger in the mouth, and so may doe greater harme with his teeth then any other beast, so all these that will not be perswaded with their shewes prepared like horses for the warre, with their crownes like crownes of gold, with their faces like the faces of men, nor with their haire like the haire of women, they shall be persecuted by the power of their mouth, *to wit*, by their threatnings and thundering curses. ⁹ And they had breast plates like breastplates of iron, for they shall haue to backe this their authoritie, the assistance of Princes, whose maintayning of them shall appeare vnto the world strong as iron. And the sound of their wings was like the sound of chariots running with many horses vnto the warre : for as the grassehoppers make in the hot time of the yere & the day, a great sound with their wings, so these shalbe made so strong and fearefull by their brestplates like iron, as what they, being in the height of their day shall decree, it shal haue such a maiestie and fearefulnes, as the terrible noise of many horses and chariots hurling to battel : ¹⁰ But they had tailes like the tailes of *Scorpions*, and there were stings in their tailes : for at their first dealing with any, they appeare not harmeful to them that heare them, and beleeue them, but the effect and end of their practise is poison to the soule, and thereafter their tailes are like vnto the tailes of Scorpions, wherein is their sting : And they had power to trouble and harme men the space of fiue moneths : for as I shewed you before, that they should torment men the space of fiue moneths, *to wit*, a certaine space appointed them ; so now I assure you to your comfort, that as grassehoppers last but fiue moneths that are hottest, so these shall be like vnto grassehoppers in that as well as in the rest ; for they shall remaine but for a certaine space prescribed, and then shall be destroyed by the blast of Christs breath. ¹¹ They haue also a King, but to rule ouer them, who is the Angel of the bottomlesse pit, and his name in Hebrew is *Abaddon*, and in Greeke *Apollyon*, for these by
the

the permiſſion of Gods iuſtice, and working of Satan, ſhall haue at the laſt a Monarch to be their head, who ſhall be like vnto themſelues, the angel or meſſenger comming, *to wit*, inſtructed and inſpired by Satan to bee his embaſſadour, and to teach his falſe doctrine to the counterfeit church, as well as the true Paſtours are the Embaſſadours of God to the true Church: He is called *Abaddon* or *Apollyon*, becauſe as hee is both a ſpirituall and ciuill Monarch, ſo he deſtroyes and killes both body and ſoule, as I tolde you in the fourth ſeale, where hee is called *Death*, for the ſame cauſe that hee is called heere *Deſtroyer.* 12 One woe is paſt, and loe two come after, for this which by the fift Trumpet is declared, is the firſt of the three laſt and greateſt plagues, whereunto I wiſhed you to take ſpeciall heed; and therefore take good heed to the other two blaſts of the trumpets that follow. 13 Then the ſixt Angel blewe, and I heard a voice comming from among the foure hornes of the golden Altar that ſtands euer before the eyes of God, ſaying theſe words to the next Angel that had a Trumpet, Looſe theſe foure Angels bound at the great water *Euphrates.* 14 Now the ſummons and warning being giuen by the ſixt blaſt of the trumpet of the ſixt and fearefull plague that was to come; this command of Chriſt (which is the voice here mentioned) comes to the ſixt Angel, commanding him to doe as ye now haue heard: For although the trumpet was alreadie blowen, yet the execution followes not, while Chriſt command and permit it; for theſe foure Angels mentioned here, are the ſame who were ſtanding before vpon the foure airths of the earth, ready to deſtroy the ſame, who were then, as you heard, ſtayed by Chriſt, while firſt he had ſealed his owne; who now being all ſealed, becauſe this is the laſt plague that is to come vpon the world, except that of the conſummation; Chriſt therefore commands them to be looſed, for they were before ſtayed, as it were bound, to the effect they might now put in execution theſe things which they were ready to doe: When they were ſtayed, it is ſaid they were bound at the great riuer *Euphrates*; alluding hereby to the hiſtory of *Balthaſar* in *Daniel*, for as *Euphrates* diuided *Babylon* from the Perſians and the Aſſyrians, which they croſſed when they ſlew *Balthaſar*, ſo this command of ſtay, giuen to theſe Angels by Chriſt, was that great riuer *Euphrates*, beyond the which they were bound, for they had no power to croſſe it, and to plague the world, while firſt all his choſen were ſealed, and that hee had looſed and permitted them, as by this command here is done: 15 And ſo theſe foure Angels were looſed, who were readie at the houre, the day, the moneth, and the yeere, to ſlay the third part of men, *to wit*, they were ready at the very moment preſcribed to them by God, to deſtroy all men, except ſuch as were ſealed, ouer whom they had no power; and ſuch as were reſerued to the deſtruction of the laſt plague, *to wit*, the conſummation; and ſo the third part was left to them to deſtroy. Now followes the plague of the ſixt trumpet. 16 And firſt I ſaw an armie of horſemen, the number whereof were two hundred thouſand thouſand; for I

heard the number reckoned : this double great number signifies, that there shall be raised vp at one time, two great Monarchies and seats of Tyrants; one ruling in the East, and another in the West, who shal cruelly persecute the Church. 17 And in this vision likewise I saw horses, whose riders had breastplates of fire, of Hyacinth and brimstone, and the heads of the horses were like the heads of Lions, and from their mouthes came fire, smoke, and brimstone; noting, that with fiery rage, smokie pride, and pretences, and loathsome and wicked courses, these two Monarches, the one secular, the other Ecclesiasticall, shall conquer and possesse the greatest part of the world: These horses are a part, yet not the least part of the forces of one of these Monarches, in whose description it is most insisted, because he is the *Destroyer*, of whom it is spoken in the fift Trumpet, where hee is named *Abaddon*: These horses and their riders are the last order and sect of his Ecclesiasticall swarme : Their breastplates, *to wit*, their worldly defence is composed of fire, that is, persecution of the body, for they shall haue greater credit at the hands of Princes, then all these grashoppers, spoken of in the fift Seale, and so shall vse their forces to defend themselues therewith: They are composed of the Hyacinth, for as this herbe is darke, and of a smoking colour and bitter to the taste, so shall they be defended and maintained by the craft of their darke and bitter heresies, (which in the third Trumpet are called Wormewood, as here they are called Hyacynth;) and they are composed of brimstone, which signifieth the loathsomnesse and stench of sinne, and the flame and force of hell fire, *to wit*, Satan the authour of the one, and ruler of the other, shall by all maner of craft defend them as his speciall instruments, and the last vermine bred and come vp from the smoke of the bottomlesse pit: And they shall not onely haue power to defend themselues by these three meanes, but they shall also pursue and persecute the faithfull; which is meant by their horses heads like to the heads of Lions, that is, able to deuoure : The meanes whereby they deuoure, are the same whereby they defend themselues, *to wit*, by the power of Princes, to persecute the bodies by false and hereticall bragges and sleights, which are here called Smoake, and by the drifts and frauds of Satan in diuers fashions to deceiue and inflame the soule, which craft of Satan is here resembled to brimstone. 18 By these three plagues, are slaine the third part of men, *to wit*, by fire, smoake, and brimstone, which came out of their mouthes, *to wit*, their malice and strength shall be so great, as they shall vse all meanes wherewith the third part of men shalbe destroyed, although these meanes shall not be vsed by them onely to worke this great destruction with. 19 For their strength is not in their mouthes onely, (as ye haue presently heard) but it is also in their tailes; for their tailes are like the tailes of serpents, hauing stings whereby they doe harme: In this they shall be like vnto the grashoppers. 20 But not the lesse, the wicked shall be so hard hearted, as the rest of them who were not destroyed by the plagues of this trumpet, shall not repent nor desist from the workmanship
of

of their hands, *to wit*, from Idolatry, and adoring of deuils, and of images, of golde, of filuer, of braffe, of ftone, and of wood, who neither can fee, heare, nor goe, (whereof this hereticall Monarch is the punifhment:) ¹¹ Nor yet will they repent them nor defift from breaking the fecond Table, by flaughters, forceries, fornications & thefts, whereof that other Monarch, who onely perfecutes the body, is the reuenge, fcourge, and plague.

CHAP. X.

ARGVMENT.

Iohn heares the explication of thefe myfteries, which was written vpon the backe of the Booke: It is not lawfull to him to manifeft it: By foreknowing things to come, which is fignified by fwallowing the booke, he is mooued to a great ioy in the inftant time, but it turneth in great bitterneffe to him thereafter.

HEN I faw another ftrong Angel comming downe from heauen; hee was clothed with a cloud, and at his head was the raine-bow, and his face was like the Sunne, and his feet like the pillars of fire: This ftrong Angel was Chrift, clothed with a cloude; for in a cloud hee afcended, and in the clouds fhall he come againe at the latter day: Which cloud was a guide to the people of Ifrael by day, while they trauailed through the wilderneffe; and out of that cloud hee powres the raine and dew of his graces in abundance vpon his chofen: His head was clothed with the rainebow, which fignifies his couenant he made with his Elect, as ye heard before: His face was like the Sunne, and his feet like pillars of fire: yee heard thefe two defcribed in the beginning of my Epiftle. ² And he had in his hand an open Booke; this was the Booke of the Euangel, or glad tidings: And he fet his right foote or ftrongeft on the Sea, to make ftable that liquid Element fo vnftable of nature; and his left vpon the earth, which is fooner made firme, by this to fhew the power he hath ouer all things contained in them, who hath no power to paffe the bounds and order which he hath prefcribed vnto them; and therefore the earth is called his *footftoole*, by *Dauid* in his Pfalmes. ³ And he cryed with a mighty voice like a roaring Lyon for they were terrible things and great which hee was to denounce: ⁴ And when he had cryed, the feuen thunders fpake their voices; Thefe were the feuen Spirits of God, who by his direction did fpeake, and I was to haue written what they did fpeake, of purpofe to haue fet it downe with the reft: But I heard a voice from heauen, faying, Seale what the feuen thunders haue fpoken, but write them not: For the holy Spirit hauing declared vnto me by them, the expofition of the fixe trumpets, the voice of God commands me not to manifeft that vnto the world with the reft, but by fealing of it, to keepe it clofe vnto the due time. ⁵ And the Angel, *to wit*, Chrift, whom

whom I faw ftanding on the fea, and on the earth, lifted vp his hand towards heauen, ⁶ And fwore by him that created heauen, the earth, the fea,
and all that is in them, that the time fhould be no longer: ⁷ But in the
dayes of the feuenth Angels voice, when he begins to blow, the myfterie
of God fhould be confummate, according as he tolde to his feruants the
Prophets: This oath he made to affure me, that the world fhould end immediatly after the accomplifhing of thefe things, mentioned in the fixe
Trumpets, and that the feuenth declares the things which are to be done
at the confummation; the forme whereof will be as hee hath declared to
his Prophets. ⁸ Then that voice which I heard, fpake to me from heauen,
to wit, the voice of God the Father, fpake againe vnto me, and faid, Goe
and take that open booke which is in the hand of the Angel, who ftands
on the fea and the earth: ⁹ And fo I went vnto the Angel, and defired him
to giue me the booke: and hee anfwered, Take and fwallow it, and it fhall
bring a bitterneffe vnto thy belly, but in thy mouth it fhall be as fweete as
honie. ¹⁰ Then I tooke the booke, and found that which he faid to me of
it, to be true; for indeed I thought it delightfull vnto me, to know the myfteries of God, by fwallowing the booke, and fo it was fweet in my mouth;
but fo foon as by the digeftion hereof I muft preach it to the world, and for
that caufe become to be hated, contemned, and perfecuted by the wicked,
and fee but a fmall increafe of my great labours, then furely it will be bitter
to my belly, as it was to *Ionas*, and fhall be to all the true preachers thereof
thereafter. ¹¹ Then he faid vnto me, Thou muft prophefie againe before
people, nations, tongues, and many kings for my children in Chrift, *to wit,*
my fucceffours in doctrine, who fhall be in the time of thefe plagues, fhall
haue the fame commiffion to teach ouer againe the fame Euangel, to the faluation of all the beleeuers: thefe fhall haue fuch boldneffe giuen vnto
them, as they fhall conftantly declare their commiffion, not only before the
people, but euen before many kings, and fhall not be afraid of their faces.

CHAP. XI.

ARGVMENT.

Babylon the Popes Empire, is the outward part of the Temple: The trew Church is in
Sancto Sanctorum; but vnder the perfecution of thefe hypocrites for a certaine
fpace: Faithfull Paftours are fent from time to time to witneffe the trewth: They
are perfecuted, condemned, and flaine by Antichrift: God raifeth vp at the laft
ftronger preachers, who fhall defcribe the Popedome, and foretell the deftruction
thereof: In the feuenth Trumpet is the day of Iudgement defcribed.

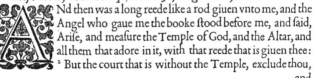
Nd then was a long reede like a rod giuen vnto me, and the
Angel who gaue me the booke ftood before me, and faid,
Arife, and meafure the Temple of God, and the Altar, and
all them that adore in it, with that reede that is giuen thee:
² But the court that is without the Temple, exclude thou,
                                     and

and meafure it not, for it is giuen vnto the Gentiles, who fhall tread down the holy Citie for the fpace of two and fourtie moneths. Now left I fhould defpaire of any profit which my fucceffors could haue made in doctrine in their time, becaufe as it appeareth by the fixt Trumpet, the whole world fhould be fubdued to thefe two Monarchies; Chrift, afwell to affure me fome fhould ftill remaine pure and ynfpotted, as alfo to fhew mee, and by me to forewarne the Church, that this moft dangerous Monarch, called *Apollyon*, fhould corporally fucceede in the Church, and fhould fit in the Temple of God, giues me a reede for that caufe, and commands me to meafure the Temple, for he will faue all them that are of the true Church, for they are the inward parts of the Temple; and the reft by reafon of their hypocrifie, fhalbe accounted of as Gentiles; and this diuifion fhalbe made by my fucceffours in doctrine, (of whom I fpake already) for they by the meafure and triall of the word, fignified by the reede, fhall feparate that holy *Sanctum Sanctorum* from the reft of the outward Temple of God, *to wit*, the hypocriticall and Antichriftian Church, which fhall tread downe and perfecute the true Church, for the fpace of two and fourtie moneths, or three yeeres and an halfe, for it is both one number. This fpace prefcribed by Chrift, alludeth to *Daniels* prophecie of two times, a time, and halfe a time; for as *Daniel* meant thereby the halfe of his propheticall weeke, fo Chrift meanes by this, that the perfecution of this *Deftroyer*, fhall laft the halfe, *to wit*, it fhall reigne about the midft of the laft aage of this whole weeke, which begins at his incarnation and firft comming, and ends at his laft comming againe; which becaufe it is the laft period, it is here compared to a weeke: ³ But I fhall giue that holy towne to two witneffes of mine, who clothed with fackecloth, fhall prophefie the fpace of one thoufand two hundred and threefcore dayes; for thefe my fucceffours he fhall raife vp as witneffes, *to wit*, a fufficient number of them, (*for out of the mouth of two or three witneffes, euery word is confirmed*) to witneffe that their doctrine is falfe, who perfecute the Church which he fhal giue vnto them, for he fhall make them their patrons, to defend and feed them by the power of the true word, and they fhall preach repentance to that counterfeit Church; and therefore they are faid to be *clothed in fackecloth*. And to affure vs to our great comfort, that in all the time of blindneffe, God fhall euer be raifing vp fome of thefe two witneffes againft the hypocriticall *Deftroyer*, and to comfort and confirme his true Church, it is faid, They fhall prophefie the number of dayes that yee haue heard, which is correfpondent iuftly to the moneths before mentioned, *to wit*, they fhall not leaue off to witneffe, all the time of the Antichriftian kingdome. ⁴ Thefe witneffes, are two greene Oliues, who anoint the Elect with that holy oyle; and two Candleftickes (as Chrift faid, to enlighten the world with their brightneffe) who are fet downe, and doe their office, in the prefence of him, who is Lord and ruler of the earth: ⁵ And if any fhal preffe to harme them, fire fhall come out of their mouthes, and deuoure their enemies;
for

for whofoeuer will doe them any hurt, himfelfe muſt be ſlaine ſo, *to wit*, the holy Spirit, who is the fire in their mouth, ſhall accufe and caufe to be deſtroyed with the fecond death, all them that either perfecute them, or will not heare, or obey their doctrine: '⁶ Thefe witneſſes haue power to fhut heauen, that it raine not in the dayes of their prophefie ; and they haue power ouer the waters, to turne them into blood, and to ſtrike the earth with euery kinde of plague, ſo often as they pleafe ; for hee ſhall authorize them and their meſſage, with as fure teſtimonies, as the ſhutting of the heauen, and ſtay of the raine was vnto *Elias*, ſo long as he forefpake it ſhould be ſo ; and as vnto *Moyſes*, the turning of the waters into blood, and the ſtriking of the earth of the land of Egypt, with diuers and fundry plagues : ⁷ But thefe ſhall be witneſſes, by their death as well as by their life : For how ſoone any of them ſhall haue runne that courfe in the earth, which God hath appointed them, they ſhall be perfecuted, ouercome, and ſlaine by that beaſt, the Angel of that bottomleſſe pit, and king of the locuſts, and that great towne & feat of the Monarchy ſhal publikely put them down, as malefactours : ⁸ So as their dead bodies or carkeifes ſhall lie in the ſtreets thereof : And this towne is ſpiritually called *Sodom*, becaufe of the ſpirituall adultery, *to wit*, Idolatrie that it ſhall commit and maintaine ; and ſpiritually Egypt, becaufe it ſhall oppreſſe and intollerably burthen the foules of the chofen, euen as Egypt captiuated the bodies, and burthened the backes of the people of Iſrael, and in that towne alfo was our Lord crucified ; for where Chriſts members are put to death for their Maſters caufe, (as this towne and Kings therof ſhal do) there is Chriſt himfelfe crucified in effect, and his crucifying ſhalbe as wel imputed to them, as to *Iudas* who betrayed him : ⁹ And men of all tribes, peoples, tongues, and nations, ſhall ſee their carkeifes the ſpace of three dayes and a halfe, and they ſhall not be fuffered to be buried in fepulchres : ¹⁰ And the inhabitants of the earth ſhall be glad and reioyce for their ſlaughters, and ſhall ſend gifts one to another, in token of ioy, becaufe they are made quit of thefe two prophets, who tormented the indwellers of the earth ; for the whole world, who are not in *Sancto Sanctorum*, ſhall not onely fuffer, but allow that thefe witneſſes be not onely ſlaine, but alfo be ſo cruelly vfed and contemned, as not to be fuffered to be buried amongſt others : And the whole earth ſhall reioyce at their death ; becaufe that euen as *Achab* blamed *Elias* for troubling of Iſrael, ſo ſhall the world thinke thefe witneſſes troublefome vnto them, becaufe they difcouer vnto them their ſhamefulneſſe, and call them to the repentance thereof. ¹¹ And thus ſhall they be contemned for the ſpace of three dayes and a halfe, *to wit*, of three yeeres and a halfe ; which ſignifies, that during the ſpace of the Antichriſts reigne, they ſhall be thus vfed ; but after the ſpace of three dayes and an halfe, the Spirit of life comming from God, ſhall enter into them, and they ſhall be fet vpon their feete, and a great feare ſhall fall vpon them that did ſee them before : ¹² And they heard a great voice from the heauen, ſaying vnto them, *Come vp hither*, then they afcended vp into heauen, and their enemies faw them doe fo; for although that during the flourifhing of this hereticall and hypocriticall Monarchie, the trew Paftours no fooner appeared, then they were put to death, yet at the laft this Monarchie fhall begin to decay, when the three yeeres, or the three dayes and an halfe thereof fhall be expired: and then fhall the Spirit of life from God, *to wit*, the holy Spirit fent from God, worke mightier in the latter Paftours of thefe dayes, fo as in them fhall the by-paft Martyrs be reuiued, and their doctrine fhall take roote in the hearts of many, and their reafons fhalbe fo pithie, as the Antichriftian fect, and the reft of the world fhall know as perfectly that they fhall preuaile, as if they heard God call them to heauen, to reward them there for their victory: Neither fhall they haue power of their liues, for God fhall mooue the hearts of many to defend them in fuch glory and fafetie, as if they were mounting vp to heauen in a cloud, and they not able to hinder them. ¹³ And then at that time fhall be a great earthquake, *to wit*, great tumults among nations, and the tenth part of the citie fhall fall: This citie is diuided in tenne parts, to fhew it is the fame Monarchie that fhall afterwards be defcribed by a beaft with ten heads: And by the falling of the tenth part thereof, is meant, that diuers nations fhall fhake off the yoke of that Monarchie, and fo a part of the ftrength of that citie fhall decay; and there was flaine in that earthquake, feuen thoufand men, *to wit*, a great number of men fhal be flaine in thefe tumults, and the reft were afraid, and gaue glory vnto the God of *Heauen*, for thefe tumults and iudgements of God, fhall by their terrours reduce fome to the knowledge of the trewth. ¹⁴ The fecond woe is paft, for thefe are the plagues of the fixt Trumpet, and loe, the third woe comes foone; for next followes the declaration of thefe dayes, wherein the confummation fhall be, firft of that Antichriftian kingdome, and next of the whole earth; take therefore good heede vnto the third woe, for it is the laft. ¹⁵ Then the feuenth Angel blew, and there were great voices in heauen, faying, The kingdomes of the world are made the kingdomes of our Lord, and of his Chrift, who fhall reigne for euer and euer. This ioyfull cry was in heauen, becaufe the dayes were come wherein the day of Iudgement fhould be, and fo the power was to be taken from the kings of the earth, who were enemies to the Saints, and Chrift was hereafter to be the great, fole, and immediate King ouer all. ¹⁶ Then the foure and twentie Elders, who fate vpon feats in the fight and prefence of God, for ioy that the faluation of their brethren was at hand, did fall vpon their faces, and adored God, faying, ¹⁷ We thanke thee Lord God Almightie, who is, and who was, and who art prefently to come againe, becaufe now thou art to make thy great power manifeft, and art to begin thy glorious Kingdome. ¹⁸ And the Gentiles waxed wrathfull, for all the wicked now perceiue, that neither their force nor craft can auaile; for thy wrath is now come which none may refift, and the time of the dead is come, for now all the dead are to be iudged, and thou art to reward thy

feruants

feruants the Prophets, and all the Saints, and all that feare thy Name, fmall or great, and thou art to deftroy them that deftroy the earth, by the perfe-cuting of thy Saints, and defiling it with euery fort of vice. ¹⁹ Then the Temple of God was open in heauen, that the Arke of his couenant might be feene, which was within it : God now did fhew the Arke of his coue-nant, to affure all the Saints that he would now haue mind of his promife, and according thereto would prefently fend downe Chrift to Iudge the earth, as was done then in all terrour ; which is fignified by lightning, voi-ces, thunder, and earthquakes, which then were made ; and a great haile, which fignifies the deftruction of the earth, as fhowres of haile of all o-thers, are the moft harmefull and deftroying.

C H A P. XII.

A R G V M E N T.

A new vifion : The deuils malice againſt Chriſt and his Church : The Church by Gods prouidence efcapes his furie : Shee is fecret, and lies hid for a fpace : The deuill raifeth vp herefies and perfecutions to deftroy her ; but all that cannot preuaile ; whereupon he goeth to raife vp her great enemie the Pope.

Ow as this feuenth Seale, wherein thefe feuen Trum-pets were (which ye haue prefently heard declared) was no other thing, but the more ample dilating of the fixe former Seales, (as I did fhew before) fo this vifion which I am next to declare vnto you, is nothing elfe but a clee-rer fetting forth, and fore-warning of thefe times, which are moft perillous for the Church of all them which are to come after, efpe-cially of the three laft woes. ¹ And there was a great figne, and a woon-derfull vifion feene in heauen, *to wit*, a woman clothed with the Sunne, and the Moone was vnder her feete, and fhe had a crowne of twelue ftarres vp-on her head, ² And fhe was great with childe, and fhee was fo neere her childbirth, as fhe was alreadie crying, and was fore pained with the trauell to be deliuered of her childe : ³ And there was alfo another figne, and woonder feene in heauen ; A great red dragon hauing feuen heads, and ten hornes, and vpon his head feuen diamonds: ⁴ And his taile drew the third part of the ftarres of heauen with him, and did caft them downe to the earth: This dragon ftood before the woman, awaiting to deuoure her birth fo foone as fhee was deliuered of it: ⁵ But fhe brought forth a man-childe, who was to rule all nations with a rod of yron, and her fonne was caught vp to God, and his Throne: ⁶ But the woman fled into the wil-derneffe, where fhe hath a place prepared by God, that fhe might be fedde there the fpace of one thoufand two hundred threefcore dayes. ⁷ And there was a great battell ftroken in heauen, for *Michael* and his Angels fought againft the dragon and his angels : ⁸ And the dragon and his angels

gels could not obtaine the victorie, but by the contrary their place was no more found in heauen: ⁹ And so that great dragon, *to wit*, that olde serpent who is called the deuill and Satan, who seduceth the whole face of the earth, was cast downe to the earth, and all his angels were cast downe with him. ¹⁰ And I heard a voice in heauen, saying, Now is wrought the health, the vertue, and the kingdome of our God, and the power of his Christ; for the accuser of our brethren is cast downe, who day and night accused them in the sight of our God: ¹¹ For they that fought with him, haue ouercome him, for the loue they beare vnto the Lambe and his blood, and to the word of his Testimonie, and haue prodigally giuen their liues euen vnto death for that cause: ¹² Therefore reioyce ye heauens, and yee that dwell therein; but woe to the inhabitants of the earth, and the sea, for the deuill is come downe to you, and he is full of great wrath, because he hath but a short space to reigne. ¹³ And when the dragon saw himselfe cast down vpō the earth, he pursued the woman who had borne the manchild: ¹⁴ But there was giuen to the woman two great Eagle wings, that shee might flee from the sight of the serpent into the wildernes, to the place that was there appointed for her to be nourished for a time & times, and halfe a time. ¹⁵ Then the serpent did cast out of his mouth after the woman to ouertake her, a water like a great flood, to carry her away perforce: ¹⁶ But the earth helped the woman, and opened her mouth, and swallowed vp by the way the great flood which the dragon had cast out of his mouth: This part of the Vision was to declare vnto me, that howsoeuer the Church, which is signified here by a woman, (for she is the spouse of CHRIST, who is her head, her husband, and her glory, obeying him with a reuerent loue, and yet weake and infirme like to a woman) how soone, I say, the Church shining in all brightnesse and innocencie, which is represented by her garment of the Sunne, and treading vnder feete, and contemning the world and the vanities thereof, here signified by the Moone, being vnder her feet; a Planet that hath no proper, but a borrowed light, and subiect to all mutabilitie, like the world, and being crowned with the shining glory of the twelue Patriarches and Prophets, and the twelue holy Apostles, succeeding them in the vnitie of doctrine, and therefore are called here a Crowne of twelue starres vpon her head; How soone, I say, that she thus arayed did bring forth CHRIST in the flesh, who is that man-child, who rules the Gentiles with an Iron rod, as *Dauid* saith in his Psalmes: That great red and ancient Dragon, for in our first forefather he vttered his malice, *to wit*, the diuell, who is ruler of infinite numbers of men, which is signified by his seuen heads, and seuen diadems, or Crownes vpon them, and who hath innumerable meanes and instruments to be executors of his malicious will, which is signified by the tenne hornes, alluding to *Daniel*; and who is so mighty in deceipt, that he doeth not onely allure the infidels to follow him, but euen a part of the Pastours, and the visible Church to their destruction, which is signified by his drawing after him with his taile as fol-

lowers

lowers of his intifements, the third part of the Starres of heauen, and caſting them to the earth : This dragon hauing waited to deſtroy her birth,
and for earneſtneſſe gaping for it before it was borne, and not able to preuaile, but by the contrary ſeeing C H R I T s riſing from the dead, and then
his aſcending into heauen, which is ſignified by the Childs pulling vp to
G O D and his Throne, and ſeeing the Church to flouriſh, though vnder
perſecution, which is ſignified by her flying to a place in the wilderneſſe,
which God had prepared for her, where thereafter ſhe muſt lurke for the
ſpace of the dayes ye heard reckoned, *to wit*, the Church ſhalbe vnknowne,
and as it were vnregarded, and no man ſhall know how it ſhalbe ſuſtained;
for G O D ſhall nouriſh it the ſpace of the Antichriſts kingdome, which is
the number of dayes ye heard counted before : The Dragon, I ſay, hauing
found this, that both C H R I S T and his Church did eſcape his hands, and
not onely that, but that himſelfe alſo by the vertue of C H R I S T s renewing of vs, was no more able to accuſe the Saints of God, as he did in time of
the old L aw, ſince now we are made righteous, which is ſignified by the
battell in heauen, where G O D, to declare that none is like vnto him, made
C H R I S T, here called *Michael*, (whoſe name imports, Who is like G O D)
with his Angels, to fight and ouercome the diuel and his angels, and to
caſt them on the earth; Satan, I ſay, finding himſelfe thus debarred from
further accuſing of the Saints, hauing found that he ſhould neuer haue
place to doe that in any time thereafter; as on the one part it reioyced all the
Angels and Saints in heauen, for their bretherens cauſe on the earth, as is
witneſſed by the ſong that the voyce did ſing in Heauen, praiſing God
therefore, and extolling the deed of *Michael* and his Angels, who fought ſo
earneſtly for the Saints on earth, as if they had bene mortall, they would
not haue ſpared their liues in that cauſe for their ſakes, whom C H R I S T had
redeemed with his blood, and of whoſe election he had borne witneſſe to
his Father; ſo on the other part it enraged the Dragon, ſo that he became
the crueller tempter of men vpon the earth, aſwell for that his place of accuſing in heauen was taken away, by the myſterie of the redemption
which is ſignified by this fight, as for that he knew within ſhort ſpace he
was by C H R I S T s ſecond comming, to be caſt downe from the earth into hell, there to be chained in eternall captiuitie and miſery, euen as by the
firſt comming he was caſt from the heauen; which is ſignified by the laſt
part of the Song, ſo as he purſueth the Church with hereſie and ciuil powers, which both are ſignified by the floods of waters which he ſpewed out
of his mouth; after that the Eagle wings were giuen the woman to flie to
that place appointed for her in the wildernes, where ſhe muſt remaine the
number of dayes ye haue heard, *to wit*, after that God had giuen his Church
a ſufficient ſwiftneſſe to eſchew the rage of Satan, and to lurke the ſpace of
Antichriſts raigne, which laſteth three times or three yeeres and a halfe,
that is, a time prefixed by G O D, and vnknowne to men, as ye haue ſundry
times heard already. But ſeeing that all this vaniſheth, as if the earth had
ſwallowed

swallowed and dried vp that flood suddenly. ¹⁷ The Dragon therefore or the diuel, became more wrathfull and enraged then before againſt the woman, or the Church, and went about by ſome other way, to make warre againſt the reſt of the womans ſeed, who kept the Commandements of G o d, and had the teſtimonies of C h r i s t to G o d the Father, that they were choſen and called, for theſe are onely the true poſteritie of the Church, *to wit*, the ſucceſſours in grace, faith, and trewth. ¹⁸ And I ſtood vpon the Sea ſhore, I meane, it ſeemed to me that I ſtood vpon the Sea ſhore, becauſe I did wait to ſee come out of it, which repreſented all peoples and nations, ſuch powers, as Satan would imploy to fight againſt the Church; for the declaring whereof this Viſion was ſhewen vnto me, and whereof theſe two laſt great wonders were but the introduction, that by theſe things paſt, as the roote, I might the better vnderſtand the branches, which are to bud forth thereof as followeth.

C H A P. XIII.

A R G V M E N T.

The Popes ariſing: His deſcription: His riſing cauſed by the ruine of the fourth Monarchie the Romane Empire: The riſing of the falſe and Papiſticall Church; her deſcription; her conformitie with her Monarch the Pope: The great reuerence borne to the Pope by many nations, and not onely to him, but to his Legates: A generall defection ſo great, as there ſhall not be an other viſible Church, but the Popedome: Of the firſt Pope who did take to himſelfe all their blaſphemous and arrogant ſtyles.

Nd then I ſaw a beaſt riſing out of the Sea, *to wit*, from among the number of Nations and peoples; I ſaw a Monarchie choſen and erected vp by this Dragon the deuil, and it had ſeuen heads and tenne hornes, and tenne diadems vpon the tenne hornes : the ſignification of theſe heads and hornes, was declared vnto me by an Angel, as ye ſhall heare in the place conuenient hereafter, and vpon theſe heads was the name of *blaſphemie*: for they by the perſecution of the Saints, and adoring falſe gods, ſhall both by word and deed blaſpheme the name of the Eternall. ² This beaſt or Monarchie, is the fourth King or Monarchie wherof *Daniel* propheſied, *to wit*, euen that Monarchie which preſently reignes, and hath the power of the other three reuiued in it, for it is farre greater then they : And therefore as that Monarchie of the Leopard, gat that name becauſe of the ſwiftnes of the conqueſt : and that of the Lion, becauſe of the mightines and cruelty therof: and that of the Beare, becauſe of the ſtrength and long ſtanding thereof ; ſo this is called like the Leopard, *to wit*, in ſhape; whereof commeth her agilitie : headed like a Lion, becauſe his ſtrength is in the head, as ye heard already : and legged like a beare, becauſe

Chap. 17.

Daniel 7.

in the Beares legges confifts his greateft ftrength, and durableneffe; this proportion fignifies, that this Monarchie is farre greater then all the reft, and all their powers are reuiued in it, as I faid before. ³ And I perceiued that one of the heads of the beaft, had bene deadly wounded, but the wound thereof was healed, and the whole earth followed this beaft with a great wondering; this was to fignifie vnto me, that it was not of this beaft that I was ordained to forewarne you, for the worft of this beaft is almoft paft already, and this Monarchie fhall be within fhort fpace deftroyed, but this beaft or Monarchie is fhewen vnto me, becaufe out of the ruines thereof fhall rife in that fame Seate where it was, that hereticall Monarchie whereof I am to forewarne you, which is fignified by the deadly wound it gat on the head which was healed againe: for as the *Phænix* reuiues of her owne afhes (as prophane ftories make mention) fo out of the afhes of this Empire fhall rife and be reuiued an other, which fhall grow fo mighty, that the whole earth that is without *Sanctum Sanctorum*, fhall with amafement reuerence, obey and follow it, as ye heard prefently declared. ⁴ And they adored the Dragon who gaue power to the Beaft, for they fhall giue themfelues ouer to the workes of darkenes, which is to ferue, and adore the diuel, who raifed vp this beaft to make warre againft the feed of the woman, as ye heard before. And they alfo adored the diuel in his inftrument, by reuerencing that Beaft and Monarchie erected by him: and they faid, Who is like vnto the Beaft, or who may fight with him? for this Monarchie fhall be fo ftrong in worldly power, as the world fhall thinke it fo farre in ftrength aboue all other powers, that it is impoffible to ouercome it, efpecially, that the little ftone which was cut without hands out of the mountaine mentioned by *Daniel*, fhall euer deftroy it, which notwithftanding at the laft fhall bruife it in pieces. ⁵ And there was a mouth giuen vnto it to fpeake great things and blafphemies; It is faid in *Daniel*, that his mouth fhall fpeake in magnificencie, and vtter words againft the Soueraigne, *to wit*, this Monarchie and King thereof, fhall extoll himfelfe farre aboue all liuing creatures, and fhal vfurpe farre higher Styles then euer were heard of before, by the which, and by his falfe doctrine together, he fhall fo derogate from the honour of G O D, and vfurpe fo all power onely proper vnto him, as it fhall bee great wordes againft him, and blafphemie of his Name. And there was power giuen him to doe, *to wit*, G O D fhall permit his Tyrannie to encreafe, and perfecute the Saints the fpace of two and fourtie moneths: This fpace was mentioned vnto me, to let me know thereby, that this Monarchie rifen out of the ruines of the other, is the fame which is meant by that Citie, whereof ye heard alreadie in the fixt Trumpet, which perfecuted the two Witneffes; for the fame fpace is affigned to her there, and confequently it is that fame feate and Monarchie which is meant by the angel of the bottomleffe pit, called *Apollyon* in the fift Trumpet: by the Rider on the pale horfe, called *Death*, in the fourth Seale, and alfo obfcurely meant in the

Chap.12.

Daniel 2.

Daniel 7.11.

Chap.11.

Chap.9.
Chap.6.

the sixt Trumpet by the halfe of that great hoste of horsemen, of the which halfe the armed horse which I saw in the vision, was a part of the power, whose head and Monarchie was the plague for idolatry, as ye heard; which Monarchie, together with the other (of whom yee also heard obscurely in that place, as the plague of the sinnes against the second. Table) *to wit,* this great beast here mentioned, and the other reuealed, a vowed and open enemie of Christs Church, shall both gather their forces to fight against it in that battell of the great day of the Lord, whereof ye shal heare in the owne place : Then this beast, according to the power which was giuen him, opened his mouth in blasphemies against God, and spake iniurious words against his Name, his Tabernacle, *to wit,* his *Sanctum Sanctorum,* which is the Church militant, and them that dwell in heauen ; for his reigne shall be so great, that hee shall not onely blaspheme the Name of God, in such sort as ye heard alreadie, and persecute the members of Christ that shall be on the earth in his dayes, but likewise vpbraid with calumnies the soules of the Saints departed : 7 And for that effect he was permitted by God to make warre against the Saints ; and hee gaue him power to ouercome them corporally, and to rule ouer all tribes, tongues, and nations ; so great shall his Monarchie and power be : 8 And so all the in-dwellers of the earth shal adore him, *to wit,* a great part of them shall reuerence him, whose names are not writen in the booke of life, which is the Lambes that was slaine, which booke was written before the foundation of the world was laide ; for these are alwayes excepted from bowing their knees to *Baal,* who were predestinate by Christ to saluation before all beginnings. 9 He who hath an eare, let him heare and take heede vnto this sentence that followeth, *to wit,* 10 If any man leade in captiuitie, in captiuitie shall he be led againe : if any man slay with the sword, with the sword shall hee be slaine againe : then since ye are assured, that God in his good time shall iustly mete to their tyrannie, the same measure that they shall mete to his Church, let not your hearts in your affliction, through despaire of Gods reuenge, (becaue of his long suffering) swarue from the bold and plaine professing of his trueth ; for in this shall the patience and constant faith of the Saints or the chosen, be tried. 11 And then I saw another beast rise vp vpon the earth, and it had two hornes like vnto the Lambe, but it spake like the dragon, for left this Monarchie should be taken to be a ruler onely ouer the body, and that I might vnderstand the contrary, *to wit,* that he was specially a spirituall tyrant ouer the soules and consciences of men, this other beast was shewen vnto me, which representeth the hereticall kingdome of the grashoppers, whereof *Apollyon* was made King in the fift Trumpet ; and it vseth the coloured authoritie of Christ, by pretending two swords, or two keyes, as receiued from Christ, which is signified by the two hornes like the Lambes, but the end whereof it vseth that authoritie, is to get obedience to that false doctrine which it teacheth, signified by speaking like the dragon or deuil. 12 It is this false and hypocriticall Church then, which doeth exercise all
the

Chap. 9.

Chap. 16.

Chap. 9.

the power of the former beaft, *to wit*, teacheth the Kings of this Monarchy and feat, by what meanes they fhall allure and compell the people to obey their commands; and this Church fhall alfo entife the earth and the inhabitants of the fame, *to wit*, all nations which beleeue the falfe doctrine that it teacheth, to adore this other beaft, whofe deadly wound was healed; for it fhall perfwade them that this hereticall Monarchie ought for confcience fake to be obeyed by all perfons, in whatfoeuer it commandeth, as if it could not erre : ¹³ And to perfwade men thereof, it makes great fignes or wonders, yea euen caufeth fire to fall out of heauen vpon earth in the fight of men ; vpon whom, becaufe they fhall fwarue from the loue of the trewth to beleeue lies, God fhall iuftly by the meanes of this falfe Church, as his inftrument of reuenge, fend a ftrong illufion and deceit, with great efficacie of miracles and woonders, yea as mightie and ftrong as that of *Elias* was, calling for fire from heauen, which here is repeated.   ¹⁴ And all thefe miracles it did in the prefence of the beaft, to make the beaft to be a-dored therefore, by the inhabitants of the earth, and it perfwades them to make an image of the beaft, which was wounded by the fword, and reui-ued againe; for not onely fhall this hereticall Monarchy haue power in his owne perfon to command abfolutely many nations, but euen the nati-ons fhall confent, by the perfwafion of this falfe Church, to obey the abfo-lute command of his Lieutenants, Legats and Embaffadors in euery coun-trey, fo as they fhall not onely be exempted from the lawes of euery coun-trey, wherein they liue, but fhall euen be fellowes and companions in all honours and priuiledges to the princes or kings thereof : And this willing confent of nations vnto this, by the perfwafion of this falfe Church, is fig-nified here, by the making of this image at the Churches perfwafion.   ¹⁵ And power was giuen vnto it, *to wit*, vnto this falfe Church, to quicken this image, and to make it fpeake, and to caufe that all thofe who will not adore this image, fhould be flaine corporally ; for as the confent vnto this authoritie of the image muft be giuen by the nations, and fo they to be the makers thereof, fo the authoritie, which is meant by the quickening of it, and making it fpeake, muft be giuen it by the working of this falfe Church, whofe rage fhall be fo great, as it fhall perfecute any who will not thinke the commands whatfoeuer of this Monarches embaffadours and images, to be an infallible Law, as well as his owne.   ¹⁶ And fo this falfe Church makes that all, fmall or great, rich or poore, bond or free, in fhort, all men of whatfoeuer degree, fhall take the Character or feale of this Mo-narchie into their right hand, or into their forehead, *to wit*, publikely pro-feffe obedience thereto, and affift the maintenance thereof, and downe-throwing of all refifters: ¹⁷ And that none may buy and fell except they haue the Character or the name of the beaft, or the number of his name ; for this defection fhall be fo vniuerfall, and fo receiued by all degrees of men, as it fhall not be poffible to any, neither fhal that hypocriticall church permit any to be partakers of their ciuill focietie, which is meant here by

2.Theff.2.
2.Kings 1.

buying

buying and felling, except they be knowen to be of his fellowfhip in religion, which is meant by the character, and his name, and the number thereof. Then fince you fee that this defection fhall be fo generall, beware of euery one that fhall fay, *Lord, Lord,* thereby to deceiue you, for you fee by this, that falfe prophets fhall for a time fo triumph, as they fhall vaunt themfelues to be the trew Church, becaufe there fhall be no other Church vifible at that time, although there fhall euer be fome that fhall not bow their knee to *Baal*; for the woman fhall not be deuoured by the dragon, but hid and nourifhed in the wildernefſe out of fight for a fpace, as ye heard before. Retaine well in memorie thefe words, for the time fhall come in the latter dayes, that this doctrine, fhall be thornes in the eyes of many. ¹⁸ Now, as to the number of the beaft here is wifedome; let him that is endued with knowledge number it, for the number of the beaft or Monarchie, is the number of the man, *to wit*, of the firft Monarch of this feat, who fhall firft vfurpe all thefe ftyles of blafphemie, and who in the fourth Monarchie fhall reuiue a fpirituall fupremacie and tyrannie; and his number, *to wit*, the date of yeeres that he fhall begin to reigne, in reckoning from the time of this Reuelation, is fixe hundred fixtie and fixe.

margin: 1. Kings. 19. Chap. 12.

margin: Benedictus the 2. Flatine.

C H A P. XIIII.

ARGVMENT.

The happie eftate of the faithfull in the meane time of the Popes Tyrannie: His deftruction: The faithfull onely are all faued.

Ow fo foone as the tyrannicall gouernment of thefe two beafts, *to wit*, the falfe church and their king had bene declared by this laft Vifion vnto me, euen as before, after the denouncing of the fearefulleft plagues, the happy eftate of Chrift and his Church was declared to comfort me, as ye heard before; fo now the plagues that are to be wrought by this fpirituall Tyrannie being declared, the eftate of Chrift and his followers in the meane time is next fet forth as followeth. Then I did looke, and loe I faw the *Lambe* ftanding vpon *Mount Sion*, and with him a hundred fourtie and foure thoufand, hauing the Name of his Father written vpon their foreheads: for in the meane time that this Tyrannie was raging on the earth, this *Lambe* Chrift was ftanding vpon *Mount Sion*, to wit, vpon his holy place, out of which he promifed faluation to the faithfull, as *Dauid* faith, and is accompanied with this great number of faithfull, which number was compofed of twelue thoufand of euery Tribe, as ye heard before; but this number comprehends in this place all the faithfull, afwell of *Gentiles* as of *Iewes*, although it feeme to be vnderftood of the *Iewes* onely, which is done for continuing of the Metaphore, becaufe as *Sanctum Sanctorum*, which was a part of the materiall Temple of *Ierufalem*, did fignifie before

all

all the faithfull, as ye haue heard, so now this number of *Iewes* here, signifies the faithfull, both of *Gentiles* and *Iewes*, as I haue said, who now are descri-bed here making publike profession of Christ, by bearing his marke on their forehead, an eminent part, euen as the wicked beare on their forehead the Character of their king, the angel of the bottomlesse pit: These faith-full followers of Christ did beare now his Marke, to testifie thereby, that they were preserued by it, euen in the very time that this Tyrannie was raging all the fastest. ² And I heard a voyce from heauen like the sound of many waters in greatnesse, and like the roaring of the thunder in ter-riblenesse; And I also heard the voyce of many harpers playing on their harpes, ³ And singing as it were a New-song, before the Throne, and before the foure Beasts, and the Elders, and none could learne that Song, except these hundred foure and fourtie thousand, *to wit*, these who are bought from the earth: for they who were bought and redeemed by the precious Blood of Christ, from among the rest of the world, and so were no more of their number, were onely able to learne and vnderstand these voyces, for vnto them onely it apperteineth: Where first God promised, that he should shortly destroy that Tyrannie, (which voyce of God is here described by resembling it to the sound of many waters, as *Dauid* doeth, and to the roaring of the thunder;) And where next the thankes thereof is giuen by the Saints and Angels in singing the praises of God, as earnest-ly, and cheerefully, as if it were but a New-song, and to represent the har-monie thereof, they sing to the concords of the harpes and instruments in the presence of God sitting in his Maiestie, and compassed about with the foure Beastes, and foure and twentie Elders, of whom ye heard mention made before. ⁴ These attendants on the Lambe, are these who are not defiled with women, *to wit*, not guiltie of spirituall adulterie, for they are Virgines, as Christ called them in the parable of the Lampes: these fol-low the Lambe whithersoeuer he goeth, for they goe not astray from his footsteps, neither to the right, nor the left hand, and those are they who are bought from among men, and are the acceptable first fruits vnto their Father, and his Lambe. ⁵ And in their mouthes was found no guile, for they are inculpable before the Throne of God, because the Lambe hath fully payd their debts for them. ⁶ Then I did see another Angel flying through the middest of heauen, hauing the Eternall Euangel in his hand, that he might preach the same to all the inhabitants of the earth, euen to all nations, tribes, tongues, and peoples: for euen as ye heard before in the sixt Trumpet, of the reuiuing againe of the two Witnesses, who were slaine by this tyrannicall and hereticall Monarchie, so now the same was decla-red vnto me by this Angel, who when this Tyrannie is in the greatest pride, as ye haue heard, flies through the middest of heauen to be publike-ly heard and seene by all, hauing with him these eternall glad tidings to preach them to all the earth, *to wit*, God shall in the end of this Tyrannie, while it is yet triumphing, raise vp and send his Angels or messengers,

who

who shall publikely teach the trewth, and refute the errours of this tyrannie before the eyes of the Sunne and the Moone, to the saluation of a part
of euery countrey, and to double condemnation of the rest through making them inexcusable, who wil not turne in time.   7   And their exhortation shalbe this, which then I heard the Angel say with a lowd voyce;
Feare God, and render him all glory, for the day of his iudgement comes
at hand, adore him therefore who made heauen and earth, and seas, and
fountaines of water, *to wit*, all things, good and euill: and the particular ap-
plications that these Witnesses shall make of this generall doctrine, to the
times of corruption that they shall be in, shall be this that I heard two Angels folowing declare, of whom the first said;   8   It is fallen, It is fallen, *Ba-*
bylon that great City, because she gaue to al nations to drinke of the Vine of
wrath, of her fornication or spiritual adulterie, *to wit*, that great Monarchie
called *Babylon*, because it leades and keepes the soules of men in spirituall
thraldome, euen as the Monarchie of *Babylon* led, and kept the people of
Israel in a corporall captiuitie, that Monarchie, I say, shall be suddenly destroyed: for it is to be noted, that as there is no distinction of times in the
presence of God, but all things are present vnto him, so he and his Angels
calleth oftentimes that thing done, that is shortly and certainly to be done
thereafter, which forme of speach ye wil sundry times heare thus vsed hereafter; That Monarchie, I say then, shall shortly be destroyed, and that iustly, because she hath abused a great part of the earth, by intising them to be
senselesse (as if they were drunken,) and to embrace her errours and ido-
latries or spirituall whoredome: For as men are entised by whores to leaue
their owne spouse, and enter in to them, so shall they perswade the nations
to leaue their societie with their spouse I e s v s   C h r i s t, and onely
settle their saluation vpon her, and for the committing of this spirituall
whoredome, this Monarchie is here called *Shee*, and afterward the great   Chap. 17.
Whore, and the reason that they shall giue why they make this warning,
shall be in these words, which I heard the third Angel proclaime, *to wit*,
9   For whosoeuer shall adore this Beast any longer, or his image, or take
his character on his forehead, or his hand, as ye heard before,   10   He shall
for his iust reward and punishment, drinke of the Wine of the wrath of
God, yea of the pure and immixed wine thereof, powred out in the cup of
his wrath: And he shalbe tormented with fire and brimstone, *to wit*, he
shall be cast into hell, the torments whereof they doe signifie, and that in
the presence of the holy Angels, for they shall beare witnesse against him
in the sight of the *Lambe*: for the *Lambe* shall iudge and condemne him:
11   And the smoake of his torments shall mount vp in all worlds to come,
to wit, he shalbe vnceffantly tormented for euer : For all these that adore
the Beast and his image, and hath the character of his name, shall not haue
rest day nor night, *to wit*, they shalbe perpetually tormented without any
releafe or reliefe.   12   And in these dayes when the Witnesses shalbe making this exhortation, in these things shall the constancie of the Saints or
                                                                    faithfull

faithfull be tried, and by this triall fhall they be knowne and difcerned, that obferue and retaine the Commandements of God, and the faith of Iefus the Sauiour. ¹³ Then I heard a voice from heauen, faying to me, Write, Bleffed are the dead that die for the Lords caufe hereafter, fo fayes the Spirit, for they reft from their trauails, and their workes follow them : This voyce from heauen did by thefe wordes declare vnto me, that thefe Witneffes who fhould make this exhortation that ye haue heard, fhould be perfecuted therefore by that fpirituall *Babylon*; but that thefe fhould be happieft, who loft their liues for fo good a caufe, for the confirmation whereof the holy Spirit fayes, Yea, and fubioynes the reafon, *to wit*, becaufe both they reft from thefe continuall labours and troubles, that they were always fubiect vnto in the earth, and in recompenfe thereof their workes follow them : for as faith is the onely leader of men to heauen, and fo goes before them; fo according to the greatneffe and honour of their calling in earth, if they difcharge it well, they are rewarded in heauen with a meafure of glory conformed thereunto; and fo their workes follow them, to obtaine that meafure in that place wherof they were already affured by the meanes of faith in Chrift onely. For although the Sunne, and the Moone, and the ftarres be all bright lampes and lights of the heauen, yet are they not all alike bright, but the brightneffe of euery one of them is different from the other; Alwayes let vs affure our felues, that although our meafures fhall be vnequall, yet from the greateft to the leaft, all the veffels of mercie fhall enioy in all fulneffe, as much glory as they fhalbe able to containe, and the vnequalitie of the meafure fhalbe, becaufe they are not able euery one of them to containe alike in quantitie; and the like fhalbe done with the meafures of paines to the reprobate in hell. ¹⁴ Then I beheld, and loe I faw a white cloud, and vpon the cloud fate one like a man, hauing on his head a crowne of gold, and in his hand a fharpe fickle : ¹⁵ And an other Angel came out of the temple, & cried with a lowd voice to him that fate vpon the cloud, Thruft in thy fickle to reape, for the houre of thy reaping is come, and the harueft of the earth is withered for ripeneffe, and readineffe to be cut : He who was like the Sunne of man, and was fitting on a white cloud, was Chrift in a bright cloud of glory, crowned with a Crowne of victory; all that was fpoken of him here, was to declare to me, that the laft dayes wherein his comming againe fhalbe, fhall be next following, to the reuealing of *Babylon*, by the reuiuing of the witneffes, as ye heard in the end of the fixt Trumpet; ¹⁶ At what time Chrift fhall gather his harueft of the elect together, as I heard himfelfe fay while he was yet on earth among vs. ¹⁷ Then another Angel came forth of the Temple that is in heauen, and he had an other fharp fickle in his hand: ¹⁸ And an other Angel came from the Altar, who had power ouer the fire, and he cried with a lowd voice to him that had the other fharpe fickle, faying, Put downe thy fharpe fickle, and gather the clufters of the Vine-trees, for the grapes are ripe. ¹⁹ Then the Angel put downe his fickle on the earth, and gathered the Vines of the

earth,

earth, and caſt them in the winepreſſe of the wrath of God : For ſo ſoone
as Chriſt hath gathered his harueſt together, then the reprobate are fully
to be deſtroyed, as is declared here by the Angels command, who came
from the Altar, *to wit*, as directed by Chriſt. This Angel had power ouer
the fire, *to wit*, he had direction to deſtroy, as he commanded, the meſſenger of Gods plagues, who had the ſickle to doe it, who at his command
cut the Vines and caſt them in the great Winepreſſe of Gods wrath, *to wit*,
deſtroyed the reprobate in the abundance of the wrath of God :   ²⁰ And
the Winepreſſe was troden without the Citie, and the blood came out of
the Winepreſſe, euen to the horſe bridles, and ſpred to the bounds of one
thouſand and ſixe hundred furlongs. This is ſurely a great comfort to all
the choſen, that notwithſtanding all the reſt of the world, except ſuch as
are Chriſtes harueſt, whom he hath gathered together in the holy Citie,
the reſt, I ſay, ſhalbe deſtroyed in ſuch a great number, as their blood ſhall
of deepeneſſe come to the horſe bridles, and ouerflow the whole land of
Canaan, whereof the number of furlongs, or eight parts of miles, ye heard,
is the length ; Yet though it ouerflow the whole earth, which is ſignified
by Canaan, it ſhalbe without the holy Citie which is in the middeſt of the
land, *to wit*, although the trew Church ſhalbe in the middeſt of the world,
as *Ieruſalem* was in Canaan, yet that deſtruction ſhall not make a haire of
one of their heads to fall, but it ſhalbe without them, and they fully exempted from it, as the land of *Goſhen* was from the plagues of *Egypt*.

CHAP. XV.

ARGVMENT.

The faithfull praiſeth God for the Popes deſtruction, and their deliuerance :
The plagues which are to light on him and his followers, is to be
declared by the powring forth of the ſeuen Phials.

THen I ſaw another ſigne in heauen, great and wonderfull,
to wit, ſeuen Angels hauing the ſeuen laſt plagues, for by
them is fulfilled the wrath of God ; for the Spirit of God,
hauing already declared vnto me the generall deſtruction
of the whole world, which is without the holy citie, hee
next declared vnto me, vnto my greater comfort, the particular plagues
that are to light vpon ſpirituall Babylon, as a iuſt recompenſe of her ſinnes,
and of the plagues that ſhee is to loade the earth withall ; and theſe are the
ſeuen hinmoſt which are in the hands of the ſeuen Angels, of whom there
is here mention made.   ² And I ſaw as it had beene a glaſſie Sea mixed
with fire, and they that had wonne the victory ouer the beaſt, and ouer
his image, or embaſſadours, and his character and the number of his
name, *to wit*, from that time that the laſt beaſt roſe out of the ruines of the
other, I ſaw theſe victours (I ſay) ſtanding aboue, or vpon this ſea of glaſſe,
and

and they had the harpes of God: For now hauing declared on the one part how vnhappie the state of Babylon shall be by the seuen last plagues, which shall fall vpon it; so on the other part, by these who stand on the sea of glasse mixed with fire, he declared vnto me what should be the blessed estate of the chosen, at that time that these plagues shall fall vpon Babylon, *to wit*, of these victours; for they shall reueale the Antichrist and deface him, they shall then behold the rest of the world, which is here signified by the sea of glasse, and they shall haue the harpes of God, *to wit*, the praises of God in their mouthes, because he hath mixed this glassie sea with fire, *to wit*, hath destroyed and made his iudgements to fall vpon this wicked world, as their song which followes will declare: 3 And they sung the song of *Moses* the seruant of God, & the song of the Lambe: It was called the song of *Moses*, as well because they did sing the praises of Gods iustice vpon this glassie Sea, to the reuenge of the blood of his chosen, as *Moses* sayth in the very last wordes of his Canticle; as because *Moses* praised God for the deliuerance of his people, from the corporall thraldome of Egypt; and the song of the Lambe, because they praised him for doing the like, by relieuing the Church from the thraldome of the spirituall Egypt in the times of the Euangel: and their song was this; Great and wonderfull are thy workes, O Lord God Almightie, iust in punishment, and trew, for the performance of thy promises are thy wayes, O King, and defender of all thy Saints and trew followers: 4 Who will not feare, O Lord, and glorifie thy Name, since thou art onely perfectly holy, for all nations shall come at the latter day, and adore before thee, since thy iudgements are now made manifest, and lighted vpon the earth.   5 And next after this, I saw these particular plagues euery one, (for the which the Saints did thus praise God, as followeth) for I did looke, and I saw the Temple of the Tabernacle of the Testimonie in heauen opened; the like of this ye heard was done in the beginning of the seuenth Trumpet, and for the same cause it was also done here, *to wit*, to shew the Arke of the couenant which was therein, for thereby God did witnesse, that hee was now mindfull of his promise by the sending out of these seuen Angels, and seuen plagues, which were now to be executed.   6 And out of this Temple came seuen Angels, for from the remembrance of his Arke and Couenant proceeded their direction, and they were clothed with pure and white linnen, for innocencie and puritie, and girded about their breasts with gold, for honour and glory.   7 And one of the foure beasts gaue these Angels seuen Phials of golde, full of the wrath of God that liues eternally, and for all worlds to come: These Angels are thus arayed, and these golden and precious Phials of the wrath of God, are giuen them by one of the foure beasts, the most excellent creatures of God, all to teach vs, that as these plagues shall be most bitter to *Babylon* and her followers, so shall they be most sweet to all the chosen for their deliuerance; for they are to light vpon the wicked, and no wayes to harme any of the holy Citie.   8 And the Temple in heauen was filled

with

with the fmoake comming from the Maieftie of God, and from his vertue and power: And there could none go in into the Temple while the feuen plagues of the feuen Angels were fulfilled, to teach vs that no flefh, how guiltlefle foeuer it be, can compeare before God, when in his wrathfull face he is clothed with iuftice, but onely when with a cheerefull countenance, clothed with mercy, he ftretcheth foorth his hands vnto vs.

CHAP. XVI.

ARGVMENT.

By the firft Phyale the Popes followers are plagued with fundry new and vnknowen difeafes: By the fecond Phiale all kinde of plagues, fuch as fword, famine, and peftilence light vpon the nations that acknowledge him: By the third, are diuers Popes raifed vp at one time, who ftriuing for the feats, fight among themfelues, and fo they are iuftly recompenfed for fhedding the blood of the Saints: By the fourth, the reuerence of him begins to waxe colde in the hearts of men: By the fift, his abufes begin to be difcouered: By the fixt, his forces decay, which he perceiuing, houndeth out the Iefuits, to gather all his forces to deftroy the faithfull, with whom God fights to his deftruction: By the feuenth, the latter day is defcribed, and the Popedome rent afunder.

Hen I heard a voice out of the Temple, faying to thefe feuen Angels, Goe powre foorth in great abundance vpon the earth, the feuen Phials of the wrath of God; for now they were to be fhewen, and to be defcribed vnto me. ² Then the firft Angel went to worke, and powred foorth his Phiale on the earth, and there fell a great and grieuous fore vpon all them that had the character of the beaft, or adored his image: Thefe plagues which were fhewed to me, were onely ordained to light on Babylon, (as I faid before) and therefore they mete vnto her with the meafure that fhee fhall meafure others with, *to wit*, they fhall plague her and her followers with the like plagues that fhe fhall plague others with, correfponding afwell in number as in qualitie: they alfo haue allufion to the plagues of Egypt, becaufe fhe is called fpiritually Egypt, (as yee heard in the fixt Trumpet) and fo by this firft plague is fignified, that as fhee perfecuted the faithfull, and killed them, (as is declared in the fixt Trumpet) and as *Mofes* made a fcabbe to come vpon all the Egyptians for *Pharaohs* fake, fo fhall there fall a peftilent and pernicious fore vpon all his followers, *to wit*, they fhall be troubled with diuers new and horrible difeafes. ³ Then the fecond Angel powred foorth his Phiale vpon the fea, and the fea was made by it like the blood of a dead body, and euery liuing thing in the fea died; for as that beaft fhould firft fo trouble the fea, *to wit*, the peoples and nations, with perfecuting all them who wil not adore her, and by her abufe caufe the world to become dead to all good workes and

E   fruitfull

fruitfull faith, as is declared by the vifion where I faw her rife out of the fea; and as _Mofes_ turned the redde fea into a corrupted blood, with drowning the Egyptians, (which is here called the blood of a carrion) by the which all the fifhes therein were poifoned, fo fhal the nations and the peoples, which are the followers and partakers of Babylon, be troubled with warres within and without, and with all kinde of plagues, fuch as peftilence, and famine, and fuch others. ⁴ Then the third Angel powred foorth his phiale vpon the Riuers and fountaines of water, and they became blood; for as this falfe Church and grafhoppers did corporally fucceed to the fountaines of waters, _to wit_, the trew Paftours, (as ye heard in the third Trumpet) and did affift their King _Apollyon_, to perfecute bloodily the liuely fountaines of waters, or trew Paftours, who yet remained vncorrupted, as ye heard in the fixt Trumpet; and as _Moyfes_ made all the riuers and fountaines of waters in Egypt to become blood, fo fhall the teachers and heads of this falfe Church, be diuided among themfelues, yea there fhall be in three or foure diuers places, three or foure diuers perfons, and euery one of them fhall claime to be king of the locufts; which queftion fhall be decided by the cruell and bloodie edge of the fword: And therefore to fhew me how iuftly that great perfecutor of the Saints, is now made to be the perfecutor of himfelfe, diuided in diuers perfons, ⁵ I heard the Angel of the waters, _to wit_, the third Angel, who powred thefe plagues vpon the waters, vfe thefe words; Iuft art thou, O Lord, who is, who was, and holy for that thou haft iudged thefe things; ⁶ Becaufe euen as they, _to wit_, thefe corrupt, filthie, and falfe fountaines of waters, haue fhed the blood of thy Saints and Prophets; fo haft thou now giuen them of blood to drinke, for they are worthy of fuch a reward. ⁷ Then I heard the voice of one from the Sanctuarie, for confirmation hereof, faying; Certainely, O Lord God, trew and iuft are thy Iudgements, for thou haft perfourmed thy promife, and haft iuftly recompenfed them. ⁸ Then the fourth Angel powred foorth his phiale vpon the Sunne, and power was giuen vnto him to afflict men with fire; for euen as the Sunne was darkened in the fourth Trumpet, _to wit_, the fpeciall teachers did begin to fall from the finceritie of the trewth, enticed thereunto, though not by _Apollyon_ himfelfe, (for hee was not yet rifen) yet by the qualities whereof hee is compofed, and therefore is he here punifhed for the fame: And as _Mofes_ troubled by the hote Eafterne winde the land of Egypt by the breeding of grafhoppers, fo fhall the fierie fpirit of God in the mouthes of his witneffes, fo trouble _Babylon_ with the burning funne of Gods trewth, as men fhall be troubled with a great heat, _to wit_, fhe and her followers fhall be tormented and vexed therewith. ⁹ But they blafphemed the name of God who had power ouer thefe plagues, and repented not, that they might giue him glory; for fuch is the nature of the wicked, and fo hardened are their hearts, that the fame fcourges and afflictions which make the godly turne themfelues to God, and fo are the fauour of life vnto them to their eternall
faluation,

saluation, they by the contrary make the wicked to runne from euill vnto worse, and so are the fauour of death vnto them to their iuit and eternall condemnation. ¹⁰ Then the fifth Angel powred forth his phiale euen vpon the very throne of the beast, and his kingdome was made darke, and they, *to wit*, he and his followers gnawed their tongues for dolour : for as this beast did breed and was nourished by the smoake and darkenesse that came foorth of the bottomlesse pit, whereof he is the Angel and messenger, as was declared in the fift Trumpet : And as *Moses* made a great darkenesse to come vpon the land of Egypt , so now after the witnesses reuealing him, which yee heard signified by the heat in the fourth phiale, shall follow, that this kingdome shall become obscure by the light of the trewth , and shall come to be despised by many , whereby he and his followers shall be mooued to a great rage, which I meant by gnawing their tongues for dolour. ¹¹ And they blasphemed the God of heauen for their dolours and griefes, and repented them not of their workes : for as I said before, neither corporall punishments, signified by sores, nor spirituall, signified by dolours, can moue them to repent, but to a greater obstinacie and rage, as ye shall see by their actions , immediatly after the powring foorth of the sixt phiale vpon the great water *Euphrates*. ¹² Then the sixt Angel powred foorth his phiale vpon the great riuer of *Euphrates*, and the waters thereof were dried vp, that the passage of the Kings, comming from the East might be prepared, so as that beast by the meanes of many people (signified by waters) did tyrannize ouer the Church of God ; and as *Moses* by *Aarons* rod made a dry and safe passage through the Red-sea to the people of Israel, so God by this plague dries vp that great water *Euphrates*, which compasseth *Babylon*, during his will, *to wit*, he makes now the power of this Monarchie to decay, and layes it open to inuasion and destruction, as ye shall heare : This water was dried to make passage for the Kings comming from the Sun rising, alluding to *Daniel*, as I shewed in the sixt Trumpet : for euen as the *Persians* and *Medes* came from the East, crossed *Euphrates*, ouercame *Babylon* and slew *Balthasar* King thereof, so immediately after that the Witnesses haue begun to reueale spirituall *Babylon*, as is declared in the fourth phiale, and that thereupon hath followed, that the kingdome thereof is become darke, as is declared in the fift phiale ; then shall follow, that God shall prepare the destruction thereof, by drying *Euphrates* , whereupon shall ensue, that such instruments as God shall appoint, directed by that Sunne rising, *to wit*, Christ (as ye heard in the sixt Seale) shall destroy that King, and sacke that great Citie, to the perpetuall confusion of all her followers, as ye wil heare more clearely declared hereafter. ¹³ And then I saw from the mouth of the dragon, and from the mouth of the beast , and from the mouth of the false prophet, three vncleane spirits come foorth like to froggs ; for this is all the repentance that these three phials shall worke in the heart of *Babylon*, as I said before, *to wit*, for the last remedie, the diuel or dragon shall inuent him a fresh order of

Exod. 14.

Chap 9.

Ecclefiafticall factours and Agents, as the diuels laft brood : Thefe are the
fame that I called horfe, in the vifion in the fixt Trumpet, three in number
to correfpond to their threefold armour, as ye heard in the faid Trumpet,
becaufe there came out of their mouthes three forts of perfecutions and
deftructions ; And themfelues came out of three mouthes, out of the dra-
gons, becaufe the diuel is the inuenter of them, out of the beafts, becaufe
the beaft or King of Locufts commands ouer them, directs and employes
them for the ftanding of his kingdome, as the laft refuge when now he
fees the decay thereof euidently comming on, out of his falfe prophets or
falfe Churches, becaufe it authorifes them for the aforefaid effects : Thefe
vncleane fpirits and teachers of falfe and hereticall doctrines and wicked
policies, refembling frogges, as well for that they are bred of an old, filthy,
and corrupted falfe doctrine, which for a long fpace haue blinded the
world before their comming, as frogges breed of rotten and flimie corruption ; as alfo for that they goe craftily about to vndermine and condemne all Ecclefiafticall orders preceding them, as vnperfect and vnprofitable, becaufe their kingdome is darkeneffe ; But howfoeuer they thus
craftily infinuate themfelues in the fauours of the people, furely their doctrine is nothing elfe, but the very fame filthy puddle of vncleane and wicked herefies and impieties, taught by the grafhoppers before, euen as the
yong frogges grow like the former. ¹⁴ For they are fpirits of diuels, *to
wit*, wicked and craftie like them, doing myracles of deceipt, for they fhall
wonderfully deceiue men ; and they goe to all the Kings of the earth, and
to the whole world, to gather them together to the battell of that day of
God Almightie ; for they fhall haue fuch credit of a great part of the Princes of the earth, as I alfo fhewed you in the fixt Trumpet, as they fhall gather great forces together, as the laft brood of the diuel, as I told you before, to fight againft his Church, who notwithftanding fhall ouercome
them, as will after more clearely be declared. ¹⁵ Happy are they then
that fwarue not, nor defpaire in the meane time, but awake and keepe
their garments cleane and vndefiled from the generall corruption, left o-
therwife they walke naked, not clothed with the garment of righteoufnes,
and fo their fhamefull parts, or naturall inclination to euill be difcouered :
For loe I come as a thiefe, for no man fhall know the houre, nor time of my
comming. ¹⁶ And the place whereunto thefe vncleane fpirits gathered
the Kings to this battell againft Gods Church, in Hebrew is called *Arma-
geddon* : for by deceipt they affembled the Kings and nations to their owne
deftruction. ¹⁷ Then the feuenth Angel powred out his phiale in the
aire, and there came forth a great voyce from the Temple in heauen, euen
from the Throne, faying, It is done. ¹⁸ Then was heard great founds, and
lightnings and thunders, and there was a great earthquake, and fuch in
greatneffe was neuer feene fince men were vpon the face of the earth ; for
euen as the aire was troubled and obfcured by fmoke of hell, out of the
which the king of Locuftes, bred in the firft Seale, and as *Mofes* made haile
in

in great abundance to fall on *Egypt*,which Meteore doeth breed in the aire;
so God hauing stricken the battell against *Babylon*, and her followers, and
hauing ouercome them , as ye heard in the sixt Seale ; now followeth
immediatly the last plague of the consummation by the aire; for in the aire
shall that great noise be heard, which is the fore-runner of that *Great ddy*,
most comfortable to the trew Church, but most terrible to all the rest of
the world,which day is proclaimed by the voice of God from his Temple,
wherein was his Couenant, declaring the consummation in these words
ye heard ; and as the great noise signifies the same, so in speciall doeth the
great earthquake, as Christ himselfe prophesying thereof, doeth declare.
¹⁹ And that Citie was rent in sunder in three parts, and that iustly, because she destroyed the third part of the earth,as ye heard in the sixt Trumpet: and the Cities of the nations fell, because they dranke the cup of her
abominations : And great *Babylon* and her sinnes, came then in memorie
before God ; for then he was to make her drinke the cup full of his wrath,
to her vtter destruction.   ²⁰ And all the Isles fled, and the mountaines
were no more found,for no deepenes of Seas,nor inaccessiblenes of mountaines shall haue power to saue the wicked, from the fearefull and terrible
iudgements of that great and last day : This doeth also signifie the *latter
day*, as ye heard before.   ²¹ And a great haile to the greatnesse of talents
fell vpon men, but they blasphemed God for the plague of haile, for it was
exceeding great; This great haile signifieth also a great destruction at the
latter day, as ye heard in the seuenth Trumpet, but yet the wicked shall be
so stiffenecked, as euen at their last breath, their malice and obstinacie shall
rather encrease then diminish, as is declared here by mens blaspheming of
God for the plague of the haile.

CHAP. XVII.

ARGVMENT.

The Angel expounded to Iohn this vision of the Pope, describes him at
large, and clearely declares the authors, and maner of
his destruction.

Vt because that these plagues, and *Babylon* whereupon they
lighted, did seeme obscure vnto me , therefore one of the
seuen Angels who powred forth their phials ful of plagues,
did say vnto me, Here then, I will shew vnto thee more
plainely the condemnation of this great *Whore*, and what
shee is that sitteth vpon many waters ; ² With whom the Kings of the
earth haue committed spirituall adulterie, and with the wine of whose
whoredome the inhabitants of the earth, *to wit*,a great number of nations,
who are not of the Elect,are made drunke,as you heard before.   ³ Then
he bereft me in Spirit, as I told you in the beginning of this Epistle, to the

wilderness,

wildernes,which signifies the Gentelisme,as saith *Esay*; for she and her followers are Gentiles in effect , as ye heard in the sixt Trumpet : And as our
Master sayes , All these that gather not with vs,they scatter; for no more is
there a middest betwixt God and the diuell,nor betwixt the rewards thereof,heauen and hell ; and as one of these two Masters we must of necessitie
follow, so of the same necessitie to one of these two places must we goe.
And then I saw in the wildernes a woman , euen *Babylon* that *whore* , sitting on a scarlet coloured and bloody beast , euen as shee was sitting before in the likenesse of a man vpon a pale horse, in the fourth Seale : And
this beast was full of blasphemie, and had seuen heads and tenne hornes,as
ye heard before.   4 And the woman was clothed with purple and scarlet
and pretious stones and pearles , and had in her hand a golden Cup ; for
this Monarchie and the Monarch thereof , shall aswell be corporally clothed with these colours, and decked with pretious stones ; as also, these colours which are finest of all others , and these pretious stones signifie,
that this Monarchie and the seat thereof, shalbe most glorious and glaun-
cing to the eyes of the world, as I said before, which shall not onely be the
trew Church by appearance of outward glory, but euen retaine many of
the generall points of religion, which is signified by her golden Cup ; but
this Cup was full of abhominations, and of the vncleannesse of her spirituall whoredomes : For albeit in many points she shal retaine the trewth,
which shall abuse men,and allure them to her, yet shall she mixe and poyson this trewth with her owne abominable and hereticall inuentions, and
traditions , and with the vncleannesse of her spirituall adulterie, whereof
ye haue heard before.   5 And on her forehead was written a mysterie,
Babylon the great, *to wit* , *spirituall Babylon*, as ye heard before,the mother of
the whoredomes and the abhominations of the earth ; for from her shall
proceed the greatest , and in a maner, the onely chiefe abuses and heresies,
coloured and clothed with the shew and title of Christianitie , with the
which these, who shall outwardly say , *Lord , Lord* , shall euer be infected
with, vntill the consummation , and as a mother, she shall not onely breed,
but shalbe the chiefe nourisher and maintainer of them ; And this is called
a mysterie, because although this abuse shall be publike, as is signified by
being written on her forehead, yet none shall consider the abuse thereof,
but onely such, whose eyes it shall please God to illuminate for that effect.
  6 And I saw the woman drunken with the blood of the Saints,and of the
Martyrs, and witnesses of Iesus the Sauiour, *to wit*, she shall greedily and
cruelly shed their blood without all measure, reason or pitie, as yee haue
often heard before : And when I thus saw her, I wondered at her maruei-
loufly, and I could not coniecture the meaning of the seuen heads and ten
hornes that the beast had, on whom she sate.   7 And the Angel who had
now shewen her vnto me, as ye now haue heard, seeing me thus wonder,
sayes vnto me , Marueile not, for I will reueale vnto thee the mysterie of
this woman, and of the beast shee rideth vpon, which hath seuen heads
           and

and ten hornes: ⁸ This beaſt that thou haſt ſeene (or Monarchie) was, (for it is the fourth Monarchie, which is very great and flouriſhing) and is not, for it is now ſo farre decayed, that in a maner it is not, and it is to riſe againe out of the bottomleſſe pit, as yee heard in the fift Trumpet, how ſoone the wound of the head ſhall be healed, whereof ye heard before, and it ſhall goe to perdition, as ye often haue heard already, and the in-dwellers of the earth ſhall wonder, whoſe names are not written in the booke of life, before the foundation of the world was laide ; of this wondering yee heard before ; they ſhall wonder (I ſay) at this beaſt, which was, *to wit*, in great power, and is not, *to wit*, in a maner, as ye preſently heard, and yet is, I meane doeth ſtand, though farre decayed from the former greatneſſe: ⁹ Take good heede vnto this that I declare vnto thee, for herein ſhall the trew wiſedome of men be tried, *to wit*, in knowing by this my deſcription, what particular Empire and Tyrannie I ſpeake of: And the ſeuen heads of this beaſt ſignifie, aſwell ſeuen materiall hilles, whereupon the ſeate of this Monarchie is ſituated, as alſo ſeuen kings, or diuers formes of Magiſtrates that this Empire hath had, and is to haue hereafter ; ¹⁰ Fiue of them haue beene alreadie ; one is preſently, and makes the ſixt, another ſhall follow it, and make the ſeuenth, but it is not yet come ; and when it comes, it ſhall remaine but a very ſhort ſpace. ¹¹ And this beaſt which was, *to wit*, ſo great, and is not, for now it is decaying, as thou preſently haſt heard it, is the eight, and yet one of the ſeuen ; for this beaſt which roſe out of the ruines of the fourth Monarchie, as ye heard before, in reſpect it vſeth an hereticall Tyrannie ouer the conſciences of men, by that new forme of Empire, is different from any of the reſt, and ſo is the eight, and yet becauſe this forme of gouernment ſhall haue the ſame ſeate which the reſt had, and vſe as great Tyrannie, and greater vpon the world, and ſhall vſe the ſame forme in ciuill gouernment, which one of the ſeuen vſed, therefore becauſe it is ſo like them, I call it one of the ſeuen. ¹² And the tenne hornes which thou ſaweſt, ſignifie tenne Kings, *to wit*, the great number of ſubalterne Magiſtrates in all the Prouinces vnder that Monarchy, who haue not yet receiued their kingdome ; for vnder all the diuers ſorts of gouernments that ſhall be in it, except the laſt and hereticall ſort, theſe ſubalterne powers ſhall be but in the ranke of ſubiects, but they ſhall take their kingly power with the beaſt, *to wit*, at the very time that this *Apollyon* ſhall riſe out of the aſhes of the fourth beaſt or Monarchie, the kings of the earth ſhall become his ſlaues and ſubalterne Magiſtrates, whereas the ſubiects were onely the power of that Monarchie before: ſo as the hornes or powers of this beaſt, were but of ſubiects before it was wounded, but after the healing of it, the worldly kings and rulers ſhall become the powers and hornes of it. ¹³ Theſe ſhall haue one counſell, and ſhall giue their ſtrength and power to the beaſt, *to wit*, theſe kings ſhal all willingly yeeld obedience to *Babylon*, and ſhall employ their whole forces for the maintenance of that Monarchie, and the perſecution of the Saints : ¹⁴ For they
                                                                                              ſhall

ſhal fight with the Lambe in his members, albeit all in vaine, for in the end the Lambe ſhall ouercome them, becauſe he is Lord of lords, and King of all kings, and theſe that are with him and followeth him, are called Choſen and Faithfull. ¹⁵ He alſo ſaid vnto me, The waters that thou ſaw this *Whore* ſit vpon, are the peoples, multitudes, nations, and tongues that haue ſubiected themſelues to her Empire: ¹⁶ But as touching theſe ten hornes thou ſaw, thus farre I foretell vnto thee, although that for a time theſe kings ſhall be ſlaues and ſeruants to *Babylon*, and ſhall be her inſtruments to perſecute the Saints, the time ſhall come before the conſummation, that they ſhall hate the *Whore*, who abuſed them ſo ſtrongly and long, and ſhall make her to be alone, for they ſhall withdraw from her their Subiects, the nations that were her ſtrength, and ſhall make her naked, for they ſhall diſcouer the myſterie of her abominations, and ſhall eate her fleſh, and burne her with fire, *to wit*, they ſhall ſpoile her of her riches, power and glory, and ſo deſtroy her. ¹⁷ But doe not thou wonder at this, for God gaue them in their hearts, *to wit*, permitted them to be abuſed by her for a ſpace, that they might doe what pleaſed her, and conſent to all her vnlawfull policies and pretences, and giue their kingdomes vnto this beaſt, vntill the words of God might be accompliſhed, *to wit*, they ſhall ſubmit their very Crownes, and take the right thereof from her, vnto the fulneſſe of times here prophecied: At what time God ſhall raiſe them vp, as ye heard, to deſtroy *Babylon*; for the hearts of the greateſt kings, as well as of the ſmalleſt ſubiects, are in the hands of the Lord, to be his inſtruments, and to turne them as it ſhall pleaſe him to employ them. ¹⁸ And this woman, or *Whore* which thou ſaweſt, is that great citie and ſeate of this Beaſt or Monarchie, which beareth rule ouer the kings of the earth, as thou haſt heard alreadie: But although it be one ſeat, yet diuers and a great number of kings or heads thereof, ſhall ſucceed into it, one to another, all vpholding an hereticall religion, and falſe worſhip of God, and one forme of gouernment, as the fourth Monarchie did, out of the which this did ſpring, as ye haue heard.

CHAP.

CHAP. XVIII.

ARGVMENT.

The sorrow of the earth for the destruction of the Popedome : The profite that worldly men had by his standing : The great riches and wealth of that Church: The Pope by his Pardons makes merchandise of the soules of men : Heauen and the Saints reioyce at his destruction, albeit the earth and the worldlings lament for the same.

Nd then I saw another Angel comming downe from heauen, hauing great power, so that the earth shined with his glory, for so soone as God, by one of the seauen Angels who had the phials, had more plainely described vnto mee this woman sitting on the beast, then he did before, hee now appointeth this other Angel, who is Christ, to declare vnto me, and proclaime to the world (as is signified by his comming downe to the earth for that cause) the iust condemnation of *Babylon* according to her sinnes. ² And hee cryed out with a loude voyce, saying, *It is fallen, It is fallen, Babylon* that great Citie, and it is made the dwelling place of vncleane spirits, and the habitation of all vncleane and hatefull fowles, *to wit*, it shall be destroyed, and that great Citie; the seate of that Monarchie, shall be desolate for euer, euen as it was prophesied of *Ierusalem*; ³ Because all nations haue drunke of the Vine of her whoredome, and the kings of the earth haue committed whoredome with her, and the Merchants of the earth are become rich by the great wealth of her delights, in so great a worldly glory and pompe did that Monarchie shine. ⁴ And I heard another voyce from heauen, *to wit*, the voyce of the holy Spirit, saying, Goe foorth from her my people, *to wit*, all the chosen, lest ye be participants of her sinnes, and of the plagues which are to fall vpon her for them : For if but outwardly ye haunt with her, and seeme to beare with her abominations, yee shall bee accounted guiltie of her sinnes ; for if ye will haue Christ to professe you publikely at the latter day; before his Father and his Angels, and reward both your body and soule with eternall felicitie, yee must not bee ashamed to serue him both in body and soule before men ∴ And this warning I giue you before-hand to make you inexcusable, who will otherwise doe: ⁵ For her sinnes are come to such a height, as they haue touched the heauen, and God is mindfull of them; then not onely haunt not with her, as I haue said, (for it is not enough not to doe euil) but, ⁶ Rayse your selues vp against her, and render the like that she hath done to you, yea pay her with the double of her owne workes, and in the cup which she propined vnto others, render her the double, *to wit*, trouble, and destroy her by all meanes, and in all things, euen as she troubled and destroyed others before ; and according to her pride and wantonnesse, recompence her with torment, woe, and wailing : ⁷ For she sayes in her mind, *I sit a Queene*,

or

or am a ſtabled Monarch, neither am I a widow, or ſhall euer bee deſolate, nor ſhall euer ſee dolour, or taſte deſtruction. 8 And therefore becauſe ſhe thus builds her felicitie vpon her worldly ſtrength, by worldly inſtruments ſhall ſhee bee plagued, with death, with dolour, with hunger, and burnt with fire, *to wit*, after ſuffering all ſorts of torments, ſhee ſhall in the end be vtterly deſtroyed; for ſtrong is the Lord God, who ſhall condemne her. 9 And then ſhall the kings of the earth, who were her hornes, and had committed whoredome and riotouſneſſe with her before, weepe and lament for pittie, when they ſee the ſmoake of her burning; for although ſome of themſelues ſhall be the deſtroyers, as ye heard before, yet ſhall her deſtruction be ſo great, as their hearts ſhall pittie the worke of their hands, when they ſhall ſee the great ſmoake of her deſtruction. 10 And they ſhall ſtand farre off from her torment, *to wit*, her torment ſhall put them in memorie of their guiltineſſe of her ſinnes, which ſhall afray them wonderfully, and ſhall ſay in great admiration, *Alas, Alas*, for that great Citie Babylon, that ſtrong Citie, whoſe iudgement and deſtruction is all come in one howre, and at once. 11 And the Merchants of the earth ſhall weepe and mourne for her, becauſe their merchandiſe wil no more bee bought, for her pompe ſhall make the Merchants rich, by getting readie ſale of all fine wares, 12 Such as gold, ſiluer, precious ſtones, pearles, fine linnen, purple, ſilke, and ſcarlet for her garments, and all kind of veſſels to doe her idolatrous ſeruice, of Iuorie, coſtly wood, braſſe, iron, or marble ſtone; 13 Cynamome, and all kind of odours for her Church, with oyntments, and incenſe for the ſame purpoſe, and the fine flower of wheat, and all kind of victuals and cattell, and ſheepe for her ſumptuous banquets, and horſe, and Chariots, and ſlaues for her triumphes, and proceſſions, and ſoules of men; for ſhee ſhall haue many that ſhall be Merchants vnto her of the ſoules of men, by ſelling for mony, Pardons giuen by that Monarch, which ſhall bee thought to haue power to ſaue, redeeme and free mens ſoules: but ye ſhal heare more ſhortly of this hereafter. 14 And the fruits of the deſire of thy ſoule, O *Babylon*, ſhall goe from thee, *to wit*, thy ioyes and delights ſhall all turne to ſorrow, and all fat and faire things are gone from thee, *to wit*, thou ſhalt leaue all profit and pleaſure, neither ſhalt thou euer find them any more, for thou ſhalt be deſtroyed for euer. 15 And ſo the Merchants of theſe ſtuffes, being made rich by the buying and ſelling of them, they ſhall ſtand afarre off from thy torments, and weepe, and waile, 16 ſaying, *Alas, Alas;* for that great Citie that was clothed with fine linnen, purple, and ſcarlet, and was of ſo gliſtering a pompe, as was gilded with gold, and decked with pretious ſtones and pearles: 17 For loe now how in one houre all her riches and pompe is euaniſhed, and all the gouernours and owners of ſhips, and all the multitudes of men in the ſhips, and all the Marriners in them, and all theſe who gaine their liuing vpon the ſea, ſhal ſtand afarre off for feare, 18 And cry, ſeeing the ſmoke of her burning, ſaying with a great admiration, Who was like in power or

ſhining

shining glorie to this Citie? ⁱ⁹ And for pittie of her decay, and sorow for wanting by that meanes, the carrying to her from all other countries all sorts of merchandise, they shall cast dust and ashes vpon their heades, and say, *Alas, Alas* for that great Citie, wherein was made rich all these that had shippes vpon the sea, by the prices and trade shee made vs haue, and now she is made desolate in one houre: ²⁰ But although the earthly men bee sorrowfull for her fall, as yee haue heard, becaufe they want their earthly commodities and pleasures thereby, which she whose religion was earthly, *to wit,* founded vpon mens traditions and inuentions, and maintained by earthly pompe and power, did make them enioy ; yet reioyce yee heauens for her fall, and ye holy Apostles and Prophets be glad thereof; for God, in punishing her hath reuenged your cause. ²¹ Then for confirmation of this Prophesie of her destruction, I sawe a strong Angel take a great stone like a millstone, and cast it in the sea, saying, Euen with such a force shall Babylon that great Citie be casten downe, and the very place thereof shall no more be found, as *Ieremy* prophesied of corporall Babylon. ²² And the sound of harpers, and musitians, and players on pipes and trumpets shall no more be heard in thee ; for no ioy nor mirth shall any more bee in that Monarchie, or the seate thereof, nor no craftes-man of any craft shall bee found in thee, neither shall the grinding of the mill be heard any more in thee; for that Citie, or seate and Monarchie shall no more bee inhabited : ²³ And the light of a candle shal be no more found in thee, and the voice of the husband and the wife shall no more be heard in thee ; for as it shall not be inhabited any more by the wicked, so neither shall the godly dwell therein; so accursed shall it be, so as the lampes of the fiue virgins shall not burne there, neither shall Christ and his spouse, the true Church any more be there, although that during the standing of that Monarchie, some chosen, though few and secret, were, and at all times shall be, euen within that City, the seate thereof, whose merchants were the great men of the earth, and with whose witchcrafts all nations were seduced. ²⁴ And the blood of the Prophets, and of the Saints was found in her, and of all them that were slaine vpon the earth, *to wit,* this plague of destruction shall iustly fall vpon her, afwell for that she made her messengers or embassadours, who are great in power, (as yee heard before) to bee the sellers of her Pardons, Prayers, Sacraments, Merits, and euen of the sinnes, and soules of men, as ye haue presently heard ; and so by that meanes and the like, bewitched, as it were, and abused many nations ; as also for that shee had cruelly persecuted and murthered the Saints, so as the blood of all the Saints since *Abel,* who willingly sacrificed their liues for the loue of Gods trewth, and for the testimonie of his Sonne, shall be layd vpon her head, and imputed vnto her, in following, fulfilling, and exceeding the rage of former Tyrants, oppressing and persecuting the Church of God.

CHAP. XIX.

ARGVMENT.

The Saints praife God for ioy that the Pope is deftroyed: The glorious forme
of Chriftes fecond comming fet downe at large: The Pope and his
Church is condemned for euer.

Hen according to the voyces fpeaking to the heauen, and
Prophets and Apoftles there, *to wit*, that they fhould re_
ioyce as much for the fall of *Babylon*, as the vnregenerate
men did lament therefore, as ye haue heard; according, I
fay, to this exhortation, I heard the voyce of a great multi-
tude in heauen, faying, *Hallelu-iah*, which is if ye interpret it, *Praife God with*
a lowde voyce, Saluation, honour, glorie, and power is onely with our Lord
God: ² For true and iuft are his Iudgements, and he hath condemned
that great *Whore*, who hath defiled the earth with her whoredome, and he
with his hand hath reuenged vpon her the blood of his feruants: ³ Then
for the fecond time they faid, *Hallelu-iah*; for the fmoake of her deftruction goeth vp in all worlds to come, for fhe fhall neuer rife againe, but
fhalbe burned with a perpetuall fire. ⁴ And likewife for thankefgiuing
for the fame, the foure and twentie Elders fell downe vpon their faces before God, and adored him, and the foure Beafts alfo adored God fitting vpon his Throne, and all the beafts and Elders faid with one voyce, *Amen*,
Hallelu-iah. ⁵ And I heard a voyce come from the Throne, *to wit*, from
one of the foure beaftes that fupported it, faying, Praife our God all ye his
Seruants, and all ye that feare him, fmall and great. ⁶ And then con-
formely to that direction I heard, as it had bene the found or voyce of a
great multitude, and as it had bene the found of many waters, and as the
found of great thunders, *to wit*, the voyce of all the Creatures in heauen,
whofe found in greatnes might be compared to the noife of many waters,
or to the roaring of the thunder, and they faid all in one Voyce, *Hallelu-iah*,
becaufe our Lord God Almightie hath now reigned by deftroying *Baby-*
lon, and her followers. ⁷ Let vs therefore reioyce and be glad, and render
him all glory: for the Marriage of the Lambe is come, *to wit*, the *latter Day*
is at hand, and his wife hath made herfelfe ready for him, *to wit*, his Church
is now purified from among the wicked. ⁸ And it was giuen vnto her
to clothe herfelfe with pure and bright linnen, which is the iuftification of
the Saints; for as fine linnen is a pure bright, white, and pretious ftuffe, fo
are the Saints clothed with that pretious vndefiled, and glorious garment
of righteoufnes through imputation; And this our garment of Iuftification, with the which we fhalbe clothed at the *latter day*, muft onely come
of his righteoufneffe, fo (as ye prefently heard,) it muft be giuen vs by him;
for as of our felues we cannot thinke a good thought, fo can we merit nothing but eternall death, and when we haue done all the good workes we

can, we muſt thinke our ſelues but improfitable ſeruants, as Chriſt himſelfe ſaid.   9   Then the ſame voyce, *to wit*, the voyce of the Angel that
ſhewed me theſe things , ſaid to me, Write and leaue in record to all poſterities : *Happie are they that are called to the Supper of the Lambes marriage*,
whereof thou thy ſelfe heard him ſpeake parabolically ; for thoſe who are
called, ſhall neuer againe be caſt off, but are choſen for euer. ; And he ſaid
vnto me , theſe words of God are trew which I bad thee write, to leaue to
poſteritie, that God himſelfe hath giuen this comfortable promiſe, which I
haue ſpecially willed thee to witneſſe to thy *Brethren* , becauſe it will come
to paſſe in the later dayes, that this whoring and hereticall *Babylon*, ſhall
diſwade all her followers from truſting this promiſe, and ſo driue men to
an vncertaintie of their Election.   10   And I fell downe at this Angels
feete to haue adored him (ſo all fleſh is giuen of it ſelfe, to adore ſome viſible thing which is idolatry, ſuch is the corruption of our fleſh, if it be not
holden vp by grace from aboue,) but he did reproue me, and ſaid, Beware
thou doe it not : For although I be a more excellent creature of God then
thou art, yet am I but thy fellow ſeruant, and ſo one of thy brethren, bearing
the teſtimony of IESVS in heauen , to be his ſeruant and creature, as thou
doeſt in earth : Adore therefore God onely, for no creature muſt either be
prayed to, or adored, nor no mediation can come, but by Chriſt onely,
and thinke mee not a God for propheſying thus vnto thee, (for the witneſſing of Chriſt is the Spirit of propheſie) for that gift is common
to others, aſwell as to mee, and it is the ſame Spirit of propheſie, albeit
not the ſame gift of it that foretells things to come, which giues grace
to all the Elect, to beare trew and conſtant record of Chriſt.   11   Then
I ſaw thereafter the forme of the day of Iudgement ; for I ſaw the Heauens open , and loe, a white horſe came downe from them , (of this
white horſe yee heard in the firſt Seale) and hee that ſate vpon him, *to
wit*, Chriſt, was called *faithfull* and *trew*, for by giuing Iudgement, hee
was now to performe his promiſe ; and hee was alſo called, *Hee that iuſtly
iudgeth, and fighteth,* for hee was preſently to iudge the world, and to condemne perpetually all the reprobate :   12   And his eyes were like the
flames of fire, (as yee heard in the beginning of this Epiſtle) and on his
head were many diademes, for now he was to reigne eternally ouer all the
kingdomes of the earth, as the Elders did ſing in the ſeuenth Trumpet, and
he had a Name written vpon him , which no man did know but himſelfe ;
for the myſterie of his Name of *Redemptor* is ſo profound, as no creature
is able to comprehend it by wiſedome ; and therefore I heard himſelfe ſay,
that no Angel, no not himſelfe in ſo farre as he is man, did foreknow the
day of his laſt comming, which ſhall be the fulfilling of that myſterie.
13   And he was clothed with a garment dipt in blood, wherewith the garments of the ſoules of Martyrs are waſhed, as ye heard in the fift Seale, and
he is named, *The word of God,* as I did ſhew you in the beginning of my
Euangel.   14   And the hoſtes of Angels and Saints in heauen , followed

him vpon white horses clothed in white, and pure linnen, whereof yee heard alreadie: ¹⁵ And from his mouth came foorth a sharpe sword, as ye heard in the beginning of this Epistle, that he might strike the Gentiles therewith; for hee shall rule them with *a rod of yron*, as Dauid sayth, and *he treadeth, to wit*, giueth command and power to tread the lake or sea of the vine of the fury and wrath of God Almightie, as ye heard in the seuenth Trumpet: ¹⁶ And he hath vpon his garment, and vpon his thigh, as the strongest part of his body, this name written, *The King of kings, and Lord of lords.* ¹⁷ And I saw an Angel standing in the Sunne, that there he might be seene publikely of all, and that the Whole world might take heed to that which he was to proclaime; and he cried with a loude voice to all the fowles flying through the middest of heauen, *Come* and gather your selues to the supper of the Lord; ¹⁸ To eate the flesh of Kings, of Tribunes, of mightie men, of horses and of their riders: in short, come eate the flesh of all free-men and slaues, great and small: This was to declare, that the day of Iudgement was come, wherein should that destruction ensue, signified by fowles eating their flesh, (because fowles vse to eate the flesh of dead men vnburied) which should ouerwhelme all sorts of men; excepting always these that were marked, who were sundry times excepted before, as ye heard. ¹⁹ Then I saw that beast, *to wit*, Babylon, together with the kings of the earth who tooke her part, and their armies gathered together, to make warre with him that sate vpon the white horse, and with his armie: ²⁰ But the Beast was taken, together with the false prophet, or false Church, which by her false miracles seduced the nations that did beare the Character of the Beast, and adored his image, as ye heard before, and they were both cast quicke in the lake of fire burning with brimstone: ²¹ And the rest were slaine by the sword which came out of his mouth, that sate vpon the horse, and the fowles were filled with their flesh; for how soone Christ shall come to Iudgement, then shall all the enemies of God be destroyed, and so full victory obtained of this battell, whereof yee heard in the sixt Trumpet, and sixt phiale, and shall heare farther hereafter: And chiefly *Babylon*, and the false Church shall be cast into hell, because they merit double punishment for the abusing of men, although they shall not also want their damnation that followeth them, as is signified by their slaughter with the sword of his mouth, whereof yee heard in the beginning of this Epistle, and by the fowles eating their flesh, as ye presently perceiue.

CHAP.

CHAP. XX.

ARGVMENT.

The summe and recapitulation of all the former visions, to wit, the first estate of the Church in all puritie after Christ: The heresies, and specially the Popedome that followed: The destruction thereof, in their greatest rage: The latter day: The saluation of the Elect, and condemnation of all others.

He Spirit of God hauing now shewen vnto me the estate of the Church militant, with the speciall temptations and troubles of the same, from the death of Christ to the consummation of the world, and their ioyfull deliuerance and victory at that time, by the first sixe Seales ; and next more amply by the seuenth Seale, wherin were the seuen trumpets ; and thirdly, her greatest temptations and troubles, more cleerely and at large, by the vision of the woman, persecuted by the Dragon; and lastly, the cleere and ample description, and damnation of *Babylon*, that great persecuter, the sorrow of the earth, and ioy of heauen therefore: This vision now that ye shall presently heare, was next shewen vnto me, to serue for a summe as it were, and a short recapitulation of the whole Prophecie, so often reiterated before; which is here diuided in three parts : First, the happy estate of Christes Church, though not in the eyes of the world, from his first comming to a long time after, as was declared by the first Seale: Next, the grieuous troubles and temptations, vnto the which shee shall be subiect thereafter, as was declared by the third and fourth Seale; and by the third, fourth, fift, and sixt blastes of the Trumpets : And thirdly, the destruction of all her enemies, her ioyfull deliuerance, and the consummation, as was declared by the sixt Seale, the seuenth Trumpet, the seuenth phiale, and the comming downe of the white horse, which in my last words before these, yee heard described : But specially in this vision is declared, the punishment at the latter day of the deuill himselfe, before the destruction onely of his instruments, being mentioned, as ye formerly heard.　The vision then was this ; ¹ I saw an Angel come downe from heauen, and he had the key of the bottomlesse pit, and a great chaine in his hand : ² And hee tooke the dragon, *to wit*, the ancient serpent, who is the deuill and Satan, *to wit*, the Tempter, and bound him for the space of a thousand yeres : ³ And did cast him in the bottomlesse pit, and closed him in there, that it should not be opened, that he might come foorth and seduce the nations, till the space of a thousand yeeres were completed and past, for thereafter he must be loosed for a short space.　⁴ Then I saw seats, and persons sitting vpon them, and iudgment or power of iudging was giuen vnto them: And I also saw the soules of them who were beheaded, or otherwise put to death, for the testimonie of Christ, and the word of God, and adored not the Beast, nor tooke his image, neither his character on their foreheads,

F 2　　　　　　　　　　　　　nor

nor on their hands : Thefe fhal liue and reigne with Chrift,the fpace of the
thoufand yeres ye heard :   ⁵ But the reft of the dead fhal not reuiue,till the
fpace of thefe yeres be complete : This is the firft refurrectiō.   ⁶ Blefled and
holy is he that is partaker of the firft refurrection; for ouer fuch the fecond
death fhal haue no power,but they fhalbe Priefts of God and Chrift,& fhal
reigne with him for euer. This is the firft part of the diuifion,wherof I prefently told you, *to wit*, Chrift by his paffion did bind the deuill,who before
was raging in the world,and clofed him in hell by the remouing of the vaile
of blindnes from the whole earth, which remained fo the fpace of a thoufand yeres,*to wit*,a long fpace,& all that time the deuil remained bound and
caften into hell by Chrift,who only hath power of it ; fo as in all that fpace,
the nations were not feduced : for the efficacie of herefies was not yet cropen in,and the Saints and Church vifible fhal fo increafe,albeit in the midft
of perfecution all this time,and fo retaine the purity of the trewth, as by the
glory of their conftancie, and patience in the time of their perfecution,they
fhall as it were reigne ouer the earth, and by their Martyrdome be Iudges
therof; for it is called Chrifts reigning and the Saints vpon the earth,when
his word, and trew profeffours thereof,fhine vifibly therein, as I haue faid :
and thefe were they who adored not the beaft,*to wit*,they are the elect,who
were predeftinate before all beginnings,to be preferued from all infections
and herefies, which is generally reprefented by this part of them, that the
beaft or *Babylon* fhal raife and maintaine, as the greateft and moft perillous
that euer fhall be raifed by Satan : And the honourable fitting of the Saints
and foules of Martyrs was fhewed to me, to affure me, that how foone the
foule of any faithfull man is parted from the body, it afcendeth immediatly
vnto heauen,there abiding in all glory,the reioyning againe of his glorified
body at the latter day, coniunctly to poffeffe all glory in heauen eternally ;
like as by the contrary, the reprobate foule, how foone it parteth from the
body of the wicked, goes down immediatly to hell, there abiding in all torment,the knitting again with his curfed body at the latter day,there iointly
to be fubiect to eternall paine ; neither is there any refting place by the way
for any of them : and the reft of the dead,*to wit*,all the wicked,fhal not be reuiued while this fpace be complete; for the wicked fhall neither during this
fpace,nor at any time thereafter,tafte of the regeneration, which is the firft
refurrection,and fecond birth,as Chrift faid to *Nicodemus* : and therfore, as
I faid already, *Blefled and happy are they who are partakers of the firft refurrection,*
for the fecond death, *to wit*, hell,fhall haue no power of them, but they fhall
be Priefts of God and Chrift,and reigne with him thefe thoufand yeeres,*to*
wit, they fhal eternally in heauen offer vp that *Euchariſticall Sacrifice* of praife
to God, and fo be ioyned in fellowfhip with the chofen, which were vpon
the earth in that aforefaid time. This firft part of this vifion is begun alreadie ; now followeth the next part.   ⁷ And when thefe happy dayes are
expired, then fhal the deuill be loofed out of his prifon :   ⁸ And he fhal go
forth with greater liberty to feduce the nations which are in the four airths

of

of the earth, *to wit*, he shal not only, after the spreding of many heresies, cause a general blindnes & defection, but also make a great persecution vpon the faithful Church, by gathering *Gog* and *Magog* to battell against them, whose number is like the sand of the sea, *to wit*, after innumerable troubles, at last he shall gather to the great day of the battell of the Lord (of the which ye heard in the sixt Trumpet, and sixt phiale, and last immediately before this Vision) *Gog* and *Magog, to wit*, two great seates of Monarchies and Tyrannies ouer the Church, who both at one time shall rise in the latter dayes, and both at another time shalbe destroyed by the blast of Christes breath, as ye shall heare; whereof the one is the auowed, and professed enemie of GOD, and his CHRIST, but the other is *Babylon*, the hypocriticall and most dangerous aduersary: Of these two ye heard in the sixt Trumpet; and so these two, although pride, and enuie, shall still keepe a rooted malice betwixt them, yet they shall both with innumerable forces, make warre against the trew Church, as *Herod* and *Pilate* did band themselues against Christ, notwithstanding the particular dislikes which were betwixt them: It is these and their forces that must fight against the Saints at *Arma-geddon*, as ye heard in the sixt phiale, and the speciall drawers on of this battell shalbe the three frogs, who are the last vermin, bred of the smoake of the bottomlesse pit, as ye also heard in the said phiale. 9 These great forces then went vp vpon the earth; for the diuel raised them out of the bottomlesse pit, and they spread themselues vpon the breadth of the earth, so great was their number, and compassed the Tents or dwellings of the Saints, and the holy Citie; for they were prepared to inuade the trew Church on all sides, and by all meanes, but the fire came downe from heauen and deuoured them; for God by his Almighty power, euen when their power was greatest, and nothing so like, as an apparant rooting out of all the faithfull, *in rebus desperatis*, did miraculously confound all the aduersaries of his Church: And now comes in the third and last part of this Vision, *to wit*, the description of the Consummation: 10 For I did see the diuel, who seduced these wicked, cast into a lake of fire and brimstone, *to wit*, in hell, out of the which he shall neuer come againe, where also the *beast*, and the false prophet were, as ye heard before; Here now I saw the diuel punished eternally, to my greater comfort, for troubling the Church, where before I saw onely his instruments punished, as I said in the beginning of this Vision: and he and his instruments shall be tormented there day and night, *to wit*, incessantly for euer and euer. 11 Then I saw a great white Throne, and one sitting thereupon in all glory and brightnesse, *to wit*, IESVS CHRIST, now comming from heauen, to iudge the earth: and from his sight fled the earth and the heauen, and their place was not found; for the whole earth, and much of the heauen shall be destroyed and renewed at his last comming. 12 And I saw all the dead, great and small, standing in GOD his sight; for then is the resurrection of the dead, who at that time must be iudged: And the bookes were opened,

      to wit,

to wit, the counfels, and fecrets of all mens hearts; and another booke, *to wit*, the booke of *Life* was opened, to the effect that all thofe whofe names were written into it, *to wit*, predeftinated and elected for faluation before all beginnings, might there be felected for eternall Glory: And the dead were iudged out of thefe things which were written in the bookes, according to their workes; for as God is a Spirit, fo iudgeth he the thoughts of man, and fo by faith onely iuftifies him, which notwithftanding is done according to his workes, becaufe they, as the fruits of faith, cannot be feparated from it, and beare witneffe of the fame to men in the earth. ¹³ And the Sea gaue vp all the dead fhe had; for all the dead muft then rife, as I haue fhewed already; And death and hell gaue vp all they had, for not onely the bodies, but euen the foules of the wicked fhalbe iudged there, and euery one was iudged according to his workes, as I prefently did fhew you. ¹⁴ And hell and death were caften in the Lake of fire, which is the fecond death, *to wit*, hell and death fhall then be clofed vp for euer within themfelues, and fhall neuer againe come forth to trouble the Saints; for death, which is the laft enemie, fhallbe abolifhed from holy *Ierufalem* for euer. ¹⁵ And whofoeuers name is not found written in the booke of *Life*, is caften into the Lake of fire, for not onely the publike euill doers, but euen whofoeuer is not predeftinate for faluation, fhall at that time be caften into hell, for there is no midway; but whofoeuer gathereth not with Chrift, he fcattereth, as I fhew before.

C H A P. XXI.

A R G V M E N T.

A large and glorious defcription of the Church Triumphant in Heauen: and of all the members of that holy and Eternall Ierufalem.

Ow the Spirit of God hauing by this laft vifion made a fumme and recapitulation of all the former, as yee haue heard, he, by this following and laft vifion, declareth, and glorioufly defcribeth the reward of all them, who conftantly perfeuere vnto the end, in the trew feruice of God, notwithftanding all the affaults of Sathan, which ye haue heard dilated: the reward was then, to be eternall inheritours of holy Ierufalem, as yee fhall prefently heare. ¹ For I faw a new heauen and a new earth: it is ouer this new heauen and new earth that the faithfull fhould reigne kings, and priefts for euer, as yee heard before: And the firft heauen, and the firft earth went away, neither was the fea any more; for all fhall be burnt with fire at the confummation, which fire fhall renew them, and take away their corruption and mutablitie, releeuing them from the feruitude of death, to the liberty of the glory of the fonnes of God; who notwithftanding fhall not dwel there but in heauen. ² And euen I *Iohn* faw the holy new City
Ierufalem,

Ierusalem comming downe from heauen, made ready of God like a bride, that is decked for her bridegroome: For this holy Church triumphant shal come downe in all shining glorie to meete Christ her husband, when hee shall haue iudged the world, (as ye haue heard before) to bee incorporated and ioyned with him for euer. 3 And I heard a mighty voyce from heauen, saying, for confirmation of this happy coniunction ; Loe the Tabernacle of God, and his dwelling place is with men, and hee will now dwell with them for euer, and they shall be his people, and he shall be a God with them, and their God: 4 And God shall wipe all teares from their eyes; for they shall feele no more any sorow, as ye haue often heard before, and death shall be no more, neither shal any sorow, crying, or dolour euer be in that Church triumphant; for the first are gone away, and all these things then shall haue an end. 5 And then hee that sate vpon the Throne, *to wit*, God the Father, said, Loe, I make new or renew all things, and he said vnto me, Write, and leaue in record what thou hast seene : for surely these words are faithfull and trew, and shall come certainely to passe. 6 And he also said vnto me, It is done, for when these things shall come to passe, then is the full accomplishment of all things, I am A and Ω, *to wit*, the beginning, and the ending of all things : For as I made the Creation, so shall I cause the Consummation. And I shall giue to him that thirsteth, of the fountaine of water of life, freely, or for nothing, *to wit*, he will grant saluation to all them who cal vpon him for it, and that for nothing; for it cometh of his free mercie, and not of any merit in vs : How foolish then are they to be accompted, who contemning that saluation which they may obtaine for the crauing, buie with their siluer a counterfeit saluation from Babylon, as ye heard before ? 7 And he that ouercommeth Satan and his owne flesh shall possesse all, *to wit*, he shall be a full inheritour of Gods kingdome, and I shall be a God to him, and he shall be a sonne to me: 8 But for all them who are fearefull and vnbeleeuing, not hauing a sure confidence and trust in my promises, and for execrable men, and murtherers, and fornicators, and sorcerers, and idolaters, and all lyers, for all these sorts of men, I say, there is place appointed in that lake, which burneth with fire and brimstone, which is the second death. 9 Then there came vnto me one of these seuen Angels, which had the seuen phials ful of the seuen last plagues, and he sayd vnto me, *Come* and I will shew vnto thee the Bride, which is the Wife of the Lambe : for this Angel was directed to shewe mee the glorie of this holy Hierusalem, the Church triumphant, not to satisfie my curiosity therewith, but that I might leaue in record to all posterities to come, not as a hearer onely, but as an *Oculatus testis*, what glorious, and eternall reward did abide all the faithfull. 10 And so he tooke me vp in the Spirit to a high and great Mountaine; for it became well, that so glorious a sight should be shewen vpon so eminent a place, and there hee did shew mee a great Citie, *to wit*, that holy *Ierusalem*, comming downe from heauen, and from God, as ye heard before. 11 And it had the glory of God in it, and

the

the light or brightneſſe of it, was like vnto the glittering of a moſt pretious ſtone, yea euen like the greene *Iaſper* in flouriſhing eternitie, and like the cleare *Criſtall* in ſhining brightneſſe; ¹² And this Citie had a great and high wall, to hold out all them who had not the marke of the *Lambe*, as ye ſhall heare after, and to protect the Citizens from all blaſtes of troubles, for all teares will then bee wipte from their eyes, as ye heard before; And this Citie had alſo twelue gates, and in them twelue Angels, and their names were written vpon them, which were the names of the twelue Tribes of the ſonnes of *Iſrael*. ¹³ And there were three gates towards the Eaſt, three towards the Weſt, three towards the South, and three towards the North, to ſignifie that out of all parts and places of the world, and whatſoeuer thy vocation be, if thou call to God with an vpright heart, thou ſhalt find that the entrance into the Citie, is equally diſtributed about the ſame. ¹⁴ And the wall of the Citie had twelue foundations, whereupon were written the twelue names of the Apoſtles of the *Lambe*: Theſe twelue Angels of the twelue gates, and twelue foundations of the wall, are the foure and twentie Elders, of whom ye heard in the beginning of this my Epiſtle; the twelue Angels of the twelue gates, are the twelue Patriarkes, who were the firſt teachers of the way, and ſo the guides to this holy *Ieruſalem*; for by the Law which they repreſent, we muſt firſt beginne to know the trewth, and to know our ſelues: and the twelue foundations are we, the twelue Apoſtles, for vpon our doctrine is that wall founded which hedgeth in the Saints in an eternall ſecuritie, and debarreth all others. ¹⁵ And the Angel who ſpake with me, had a golden reed in his hand, to meaſure therewith the Citie, and the gates, and the walles of the ſame, thereby to ſignifie the iuſt proportion and ſymmetrie, that ſhall be among all the parts of this holy Citie. ¹⁶ And this Citie was foureſquare, becauſe of the gates towards the foure parts of the earth, to receiue indifferently the commers out of any of them, as yee heard before; And it was alike long and broad, to ſignifie the infinite bounds thereof: and hee meaſured the Citie with his reed, and it came to twelue thouſand furlongs: this number alſo expreſſeth the great bounds of this Citie; for it is here vſed for a number of perfection, as ſundry times before: And this Citie was alike in length, breadth and height, for all the parts of it were alike large. ¹⁷ And the Angel did meaſure the wall of it, and it was an hundred and foure and fourtie cubites of height: this number is correſpondent to the number of Saints, who were ſtanding with the *Lambe* on *Mount Sion*, as ye heard before; and the meaſure wherewith this was meaſured, was the meaſure of the man, which is the meaſure of the Angel; This Citie is meaſured with the meaſure of C H R I S T, God and man, to teach vs that he is onely the Architectour of this Spirituall Citie, which he meaſureth by his cubites, and not by the cubites of any man. ¹⁸ And the fabricke of the wall of the Citie, was compoſed of *Iaſper*, to ſignifie that the wall thereof ſhall ſtand eternally: and the Citie it ſelfe was of pure
gold,

gold, and like to cleere glasse, whereon no filth will remaine.   ¹⁹ And the twelue foundations of the Citie were decked with all kind of precious stones : the first foundation was of Iasper, the second of Saphire, the third of Chalcedonie, the fourth of Emerald ,   ²⁰ The fift of a Sardonix, the sixt of a Sardius, the seuenth of a Chrysolite, the eight of a Berill, the ninth of a Topaze, the tenth of a Chrysophrasus, the eleuenth of an Hyacinth, the twelfth of an Amethist : These twelue sundry stones, one for euery one of the foundations, signifie, that we, the twelue Apostles, who are these twelue foundations (as ye heard) shall euery one receiue a diuers reward and crowne of glory, according to the greatnesse and excellencie of our labours in the earth : these twelue precious stones allude also to the twelue precious stones in *Aarons* breftplate.   ²¹ And the twelue gates were of twelue pearles, and euery gate of a sundry pearle ; (this signifies the like of the Patriarches) and the Market place of the Citie was of pure golde, and like the glistering glasse, signifying thereby, as by an euident token, that seeing the Market place (which is the commonest place of euery towne) of this spirituall City, is of so fine and bright stuffe, that no base, and vncleane thing shall be in any part thereof :   ²² And I saw no Temple in it, for the Lord God Almightie, euen the Lambe, is the Temple of it, for no other shall be there wherein God must be praised, but the person of Christ, in whom all the faithfull shall be incorporated, as I said before. ²³ And this Citie shall neede no Sunne nor Moone to shine in it, for the glory of God hath made it bright, and the Lambe is the lampe thereof; for as it is no corporall paradise nor dwelling place on earth, which is heere spoken of, so is no part of the glory thereof earthly , but celestiall and spirituall :   ²⁴ And the Gentiles which are saued, shall walke in that light, and the kings of the earth shall bring their glory vnto that citie ; for all the faithfull kings shall resigne all their worldly glory in that citie, and receiue a new and incorruptible glory from the Lambe, who is the light thereof :   ²⁵ And the gates thereof shall not be shut in the day time; for there shall neuer be any suspicion of trouble there, for which cause worldly cities often shut their gates, and the night shall neuer be there , but an eternall brightnesse through all.   ²⁶ And the honour and the glory of the nations shall be brought into her, for all their worldly glory shalbe nothing in respect of the glory of this City.   ²⁷ And there shall nothing enter into this Citie that defileth or is defiled, nor no man that committeth any abominable deed, or that speakes lies, but onely these shall haue entrance into this holy City, whose names are written in the Lambe his booke of Life, as ye heard before.

CHAP.

CHAP. XXII.

ARGVMENT.

*The rest of the same description : Mans pronenesse of his owne nature to idola-
trie : The Writer tells his name, that no man may doubt who was the writer of
this Booke, and who endited the same : The faithfull ought to wish the comming of the latter day : The curse vpon them who adde or take from this
Booke, and vse it not aright.*

Hen to the effect that I might know that the inhabitants
of this holy Citie, were as well eternall, as the walles and
glory of the same, this Angel did shew vnto me the cleere
and pure flood of the water of life, whereof Christ promised to giue the *Samaritane* to drinke, as I said before : and
it was cleere like cryftall, and it flowed from the Throne of God, and the
Lambe : This Riuer alludeth to that spring of *Ezechiel,*which came foorth
from vnder the Temple floore ; and it also alludeth to the Riuers of earthly Paradise : ² And in the middest of the market place, and on either side
of this Riuer, did grow the Tree of Life, hauing twelue maner of fruits,
euery moneth bearing once, and bearing leaues for the health of the Gentiles : This Tree, and this water of Life, are the heauenly meat and drinke,
meant by Christ, when the Capernaites were scandalized with his doctrine, as ye read in the Euangel written by me ; and of this Tree and water were those of *Ezechiel,* and in earthly paradise the figures : the number
of the fruits thereof answereth to the number of the tribes of Israel, who
through eating the fruits thereof by faith, obtained saluation ; as likewise
the varietie and plentie of ioyes to all the faithfull there; and as it bare
fruit to the Iewes for food, that is, to satisfie them, so it did beare leaues to
the Gentiles, who being healed by these leaues of all spirituall diseases, were
not onely preserued, but also prepared and got appetite thereby, to eat and
turne into nutriment, or spirituall strength and contentation, the fruites
thereof : This tree grew on euery side of the water of Life, to signifie that
they are both but one thing and inseparable, both proceeding from the
mightie and mercifull Throne of God, and his Lambe, and they were both
in the middest of the Market place, to signifie by their being in so common a place, that as they are the support, strength and comfort of the
Church triumphant, or holy Citie, so all the in-dwellers therein haue the
like free accesse thereunto, and are all alike participant thereof : ³ And
no accursed thing shall be any more, for then shall hell and death be confined, and restrained within themselues for euer, as ye heard in the former
vision : for the seat and throne of God and his Lambe, shall remaine in this
holy Citie for euer ; and all his seruants shall be there, seruing him eternally by thankesgiuing and praises : ⁴ And they shall see his face, and be e-
uer reioycing at his presence, hauing his name written vpon their foreheads,

heads, as yee haue often heard. [5] And no night nor darkenesse shall be
there at all, neither haue they need of lampes, nor of light of the Sunne,
nor any materiall light, for the Lord God makes them bright, as yee
haue heard alreadie: and they shall reigne there in all glory for euer and
euer. [6] Then the Angel, after all these things had beene reuealed vnto me, sayde vnto me for the confirmation of them, All the wordes of
this Prophecie are trew and faithfull, and the same Lord GOD who
inspired from time to time his holy Prophets to forewarne his Church
of things to come, hee also sent his Angel vnto mee, that by me hee
might reueale vnto his seruants these things that are shortly to come
to passe. [7] Loe, I come shortly, sayth the *Lord*, happy is hee therefore that obserueth and obeyeth the wordes of the Prophecie in this
Booke. [8] And I *Iohn* am, he who haue heard and seene these things: I
declare you my name the oftener, lest the authority of the Booke should be
called in doubt, through the vncertaintie of the Writer: And when I had
heard and seene these things, I fell at the Angels feet that shewed me them,
with mind to haue adored him: [9] But he said vnto me, *See thou doe it not*,
I am thy fellow-seruant, and one of thy *Brethren* the Prophets, although I
be an Angel, and one of them which keepeth and obeyeth the words of
this *Booke*: adore thou therefore God, to whom all worship onely appertaineth. By this my reiterated fall and offence, notwithstanding that lately
before I had committed the same, and was reproqued for it, and warned to
forbeare it, as ye heard before, I am taught, and by my example the whole
Church, of the great infirmitie of all mankind, and specially in that so great
an offence of the adoring of creatures, whereof God is so iealous, as he saith
in his Lawe: and vpon consideration of man his infirmitie in this point,
not I, but the Spirit of God by me, in the very last words of one of my E-
pistles, saith, *Deare children, beware of Idoles*: and in this I insist so much not
without a cause; For I know that *Babylon* in the latter dayes, shall specially poison her followers with this spirituall adulterie or idolatrie, as ye haue
heard mention made in this Booke. [10] And the Angel said vnto me, Seale
not the words of the Prophecie of this Booke, for the time is at hand. Yee
heard before, how I was commanded to seale that which the seuen Thunders spake, because it was not lawfull for me to reueale the same: but now
on the contrarie I am commanded to write, and forbidden to seale these
Prophecies, because I am appointed to reueale the same, in respect that the
time of their accomplishment is at hand. [11] And hee also said vnto mee,
Despaire thou not of the effect of this Prophecie, although it profite nothing the wicked, but to make them the more inexcusable: For God hath
fore-signified, that he who doeth harme, notwithstanding this Prophecie
shall yet continue his wrongs; and hee who is filthie, shall yet notwithstanding this remaine filthie; euen as on the other part, it shall confirme
and encrease the iust man in his iustnesse, and the holy man in his holines:
for it is not the words of Prophecie spoken, but the Spirit which is coope-
                                                                    rant

rant with it, which makes the feed of faith to take root in any mans heart. ¹² *Loe I come* fpeedily, faith the Lord IESVS, and bring my reward with me, to render to euery man according to his workes, as ye haue heard before. ¹³ I am A and Ω, the beginning and the end; the firft and the laft, as ye haue heard already. ¹⁴ Happie are they who obey and keepe Chriftes commandements, that they may haue right and part in the tree of life; (for by obeying they fhall be made Citizens of that holy Citie, of the which that is the food) and that they may enter at the gates to that Citie : for the gates fhall be readie and open to receiue them : ¹⁵ But without this Citie, as debarred thence, fhall bee *Dogges, to wit,* all prophane liuers, fornicators, forcerers, murtherers, and idolaters, and all who loue, and make lies;and fhortly all, who continue in any kind of knowen finne without repentance. ¹⁶ I I E S V S, faith the Lord, fent my *Angel* to reueale thefe things to *Iohn,* that they might be teftified to you the feuen Churches : I am the root and off-fpring of *Dauid,* and I am the bright morning Starre, *to wit,* the fountaine of all your glorie. ¹⁷ And the *Spirit,* and the Bride faith, *Come,* to wit, *the Church* ; for they for their deliuerance wifh his fecond comming to be haftened, and Chrift, for the loue he beareth them, hath graunted them their requeft : and he that heares it, let him fay, *Come,* for it becommeth all the faithfull to wifh it : And he that thirfteth let him *come, to wit,* he that would drinke of the water of life,let him craue earneftly the diffolution and latter day : And let any who will, receiue the water of life freely and for nothing, as ye heard before. ¹⁸ And I proteft vnto all that fhall heare the words of the Prophefie of this Booke, that if any man adde vnto it any thing, God fhall make all the plagues in this Booke to fall on him. ¹⁹ And if any man take away any thing from the words of the Booke of this Prophefie,God fhal take his part away out of the book of life, and out of the holy Citie, and out of thefe bleffings that are written in this Booke : For whofoeuer in coping or tranflating this Booke, adulterateth any waies the Originall, or in interpreting of it, wittingly ftrayes from the trew meaning of it, and from the analogie of Faith, to follow the fantafticall inuention of man, or his owne preoccupied opinions ; he I fay, that doeth any of thefe, fhalbe accurfed as a peruerter of the trewth of God and his Scriptures. ²⁰ And now I will conclude with this comfort vnto you, *to wit,* He, euen *Chrift,* that teftifies thefe things that ye haue heard : he I fay, doeth fay, *Surely I come* fhortly. Euen fo *come* Lord IESVS to haften our deliuerance. ²¹ The *Grace* of our Lord I E S V S C H R I S T be with you all, and all your fucceffours in trew doctrine, by the which both yee and they may be fo ftrengthened in the trewth, that by your refifting all the temptations contained in this Booke, and conftantly perfeuering to the end, yee may at laft receiue that immortall Crowne of glorie mentioned in the laft Vifion. *AM E N.*

A FRVITFVLL MEDI-TATION,

CONTAINING A PLAINE
AND EASIE EXPOSITION, OR
laying open of the VII. VIII. IX. and X. Verses
of the 20.Chapter of the REVELATION,
in forme and maner of a Sermon.

THE TEXT.

7 *And when the thousand yeeres are expired, or ended, Satan shall be loosed out of his prison.*

8 *And shall goe out to deceiue the people, which are in the foure quarters of the earth, euen Gog and Magog, to gather them together to battaile, whose number are as the sand of the Sea.*

9 *And they went vp to the plaine of the earth, which compassed the tents of the Saints about, and the beloued Citie: but fire came downe from God out of the heauen, and deuoured them.*

10 *And the diuel that deceiued them, was cast into a lake of fire and brimstone, where that beast and that false prophet are, and shalbe tormented euen day and night for euermore.*

THE MEDITATION.

S of all Bookes the holy Scripture is most
necessary for the instruction of a Christian,
and of all the Scriptures; the Booke of the
REVELATION is most meete for this
our last aage, as a Prophesie of the latter
times: so haue I selected or chosen out this
place thereof, as most proper for the action
we haue in hand presently. For after the A-
postle IOHN had prophesied of the latter
times, in the nineteenth Chapter afore-go-
ing, he now in this twentieth Chapter gathered vp a summe of the whole,
wherein are expressed three heads or principall points.

1. First, the happie estate of the Church, from Christs dayes, to the
dayes of the defection or falling away of the Antichrist, in the first sixe
verses of this 20.Chapter.

The necessitie of the knowledge of the Reuelation.

A summe of the 20. Chap. of the Reuelation.

G   2 Next,

2 Next, the defection or falling away it selfe, in this place that I haue in hand, *to wit*, the seuenth, eight, ninth, and tenth verses.

3 Thirdly, the generall punishment of the wicked in the great day of Iudgement, from the tenth verse vnto the end of the Chapter.

The meaning of this present text.

The Apostle his meaning in this place then is this, That after that Satan then had bene bound a thousand yeeres, which did appeare by his discourse afore-going, of the Saints triumphing in the earth, hee shall at last breake forth againe loose, and for a space rage in the earth more then euer before: but yet shall in the end be ouercome and confounded for euer.

The order obserued in handling this text.

It resteth now, knowing the summe, that we come to the exposition or meaning of the Verses; and first expound or lay open by way of a Paraphrase the hardnesse of the words, next declare the meaning of them, and thirdly note what we should learne of all.

THE FIRST PART.

S touching the wordes in them for order sake, wee may note: [1] First Satan his loosing: [2] next his doing, after he is loosed: [3] and last his vnhappie successe.

Satan in his instruments is loosed to trouble the Church.

Then for the first, by Satan is meant not onely the Dragon, enemie to Christ and his Church, but also with him all the instruments in whom he ruleth, and by whom he ruleth, and by whom he vttereth his cruell and crafty intentions, specially the Antichrist and his Clergie, ioyned with the Dragon before in the 16. Chap. verse 17. and called the beast, and the false prophet. For as Christ and his Church are called after one Name, Christ, by reason of their most strait and neere vnion, and heauenly effects flowing there from, 1.*Cor.* 12.12. So Satan and his sinagogue are here rightly called Satan, by reason of their vnion, and cursed effects flowing therefrom. These thousand yeeres, are but a number certaine for an vncertaine, which phrase or maner of speaking, is often vsed by the Spirit of God in the Scriptures, meaning a great number of yeeres.

The thousand yeeres.

The prison whereout Satan is loosed.

Moreouer, the prison whereout he is loosed, is the hels, which by the Spirit of God are called his prison, for two causes: [1] One, because during the time of this world, at times appointed by God, he is debarred from walking on the earth, and sent thither, greatly to his torment, as was testified or witnessed by the miracle at *Genezareth* among the *Gadarens*, *Matth.* 8.28. [2] Next, because that after the consummation or end of the world, he shall be perpetually or for euer imprisoned therein, as is written in the same Chapter, ver. 10. Finally, he is loosed by interruption or hindering, and for the most part, to the iudgement of men, abolition or ouerthrow of the sincere preaching of the Gospel, the true vse of the Sacraments, which are seales and pledges of the promises contained therein, and lawfull exercise of Christian discipline, whereby both Word and Sacraments are maintained in purity, called in the first verse the great chaine, whereby the diuell

2.Pet.2.4. Iud.ver.6.

The loosing of Satan.

uell is bound and fignified by the white horfe, gouerned by the Lambe. *Chap.6. verfe* 2. So the meaning of all this 7. verfe is this : The diuel, hauing bene bound, and his power in his inftruments hauing bene reftrained for a long fpace, by the preaching of the Gofpel, at the laft he is loofed out of hell by the raifing vp of fo many new errors and notable euill inftruments, efpecially the Antichrift and his Clergie, who not onely infect the earth a new, but rule alfo ouer the whole, through the decreafe of trew doctrine, and the number of the faithfull following it, and the dayly increafe of errours, and nations following them, and beleeuing lies hating the trewth, and taking pleafure in vnrighteoufnes, 2. *Theff.* 2.11,12. And thus farre for Satan his loofing.

Now to the next, his doing after he is loofed. Firft he goeth out to feduce or beguile the nations that are into the foure corners of the earth, and they become his, though in certaine degrees his tyrannie and trauaile appeareth, and burfteth out in fome more then in others : For as all that doe good, are infpired of God thereto, and doe vtter the fame in certaine degrees, according vnto the meafure of grace granted vnto them : fo all that doe euill, are infpired by Satan, and doe vtter the fame in diuers degrees, according as that vncleane fpirit taketh poffeffion in them, and by diuers obiects and meanes, allureth them to doe his will, fome by ambition, fome by enuie, fome by malice, and fome by feare, and fo forth : and this is the firft worke.

Satan firft deceaueth, then allures to follow him, and in the end maketh all his to take armour againft the Church.

Secondly, he gathereth *Gog* and *Magog* to battell, in number like the fand of the Sea, and fo he and his inclined to battell and bloodfhed, haue mightie armies, and in number many, inflamed with crueltie. The fpecial heads and rulers of their armies, or rather rankes of their confederats, to goe to battel and to fight, are twaine, here named *Gog* and *Magog*; *Gog* in Hebrew is called Hid, and *Magog* Reuealed, to fignifie that in two forts of men chiefly Satan fhall vtter himfelfe, *to wit*, hypocrites, and auowed or open enemies to God : It is faid then that Satan fhall in the latter times rule a new ouer the world, who fhall ftirre vp the nations vnder the banners of thefe two enemies to God, the hypocriticall and open, to fpread themfelues in great multitudes vpon the earth.

Gog and Magog.

Thirdly, they fhall afcend vpon the plaine of the earth, prefumptuoufly and proudly, bragging of their number and force, and thinking none fhall be able to refift their rage : They fhall compaffe and befiege the campes of the Saints, and beloued Citie, that is, the handfull of the faithfull beloued of the Lord, againft whome, trufting in their vntellable number, like the fand of the fea, they fhall make a cruell and vnceffable warre.

The elect are called Saints and beloued, becaufe they are in the loue of God felected and feuered out, and by grace engraffed in Chrift, in whom they are counted and found iuftified, fanctified, worthy of loue and endleffe glorie : Their faithfull fellowfhip is compared to Tents, and to a Citie beloued, to fignifie their continuall warfare in the earth againft Satan

The Elect are the Saints and beloued Citie of God.

G 2 and

and finne, with all his inftruments : their mutual amitie, and friendly coniunction in loue among themfelues, and ioyning together to maintaine the
good caufe that their God hath clad them with : but chiefly to fignifie the
mightie and al-fufficient protection or defence in profperity. and aduerfity,
flowing from God for their iuft aide againft all powers that can purfue,
whereby they alfo become faire as the Moone, pure as the Sunne, terrible
as an armie with banners, *Cant.* 1.6,9. Yea as a defenced Citie, and yron pillar : and wals of Braffe againft the whole earth, *Ierem.* 1.18.

The fumme of Satan his doing after he is loofed.

The fumme then of Satan his doing after he is loofed, is this : hee fhall
deceiue the nations : he fhall gather an infinite number of hypocrites and
open enemies together, inflamed with crueltie, and thefe fhall in pridefull
prefumption fiercely bend themfelues againft the chofen of God, and his
trewth profeffed by them. But what at laft fhall the fucceffe be? furely moft

The vnhappy fucceffe of Satan.

vnhappy : for fire fhall come downe from heauen and deuoure them, and
the diuell that deceiued them, and all his inftruments, chiefly the Beaft and
falfe Prophet fhall be caft in a lake of fire and brimftone, and fhall bee tormented day and night inceffantly for euer and euer : that is, how greatly
foeuer their brags be, how neere foeuer they fhall appeare to be to obtaine
their purpofe, God from heauen, as the pallace and throne, wherefrom hee
giueth proofe of his mercie towards his owne, and of his iuftice toward
his enemies, fhall fend plagues and deftruction, as well ordinary, as extraordinarie vpon them : Ordinarie, by reuealing their wickedneffe by the
thundring mouthes of trew paftors, which is oft called fire in the Scriptures : Extraordinarie, by all corporall plagues to their vtter deftruction,
and vntellable torment for euer in the hels. Thus farre for the expofition
or paraphrafe of the words.

THE SECOND PART.

The puritie of the Gofpel induring, ftayeth the Antechrift his rifing.

Ow followeth the interpretation of the fentence according to the order vfed in the firft part. And firft we muft
know what time thefe thoufand or many yeres was in, and
when, and how Satan was loofed. This time is to be found
in the fixt Chapter, in the opening of the firft three feales
of the fecret booke of God his prouidence by the Lambe, *to wit*, the time
when the white, red, and blacke horfes had their courfe in the world : And
to fpeake more plainely, the Diuell his power did lurke, which is called
his binding, and the Gofpel did flourifh in a reafonable puritie many hundreth yeeres after Chrift, as the Ecclefiafticall hiftories beare witneffe : For
in greaft puritie the Gofpel did continue long, which is fignified by the
courfe of the white horfe, albeit the profeffors were vnder the croffe fignified by the red horfe, and troubled wonderfully by heretickes, fignified by
the blacke horfe, by wormewood that fell in the Fountaines of waters in
the third trumpet, and by waters that the dragon fpewed out of his mouth,
in the vifion of the Dragon and the woman, *chap.* 12. This time did endure

from

from Chriſt a ſpace after *Auguſtine* his dayes, when the bloodie Sword of perſecution ceaſing, the whole Church began to be defiled with diuers hereſies, which comming vnto a mature and ripe heape, did produce or bring foorth the Antechriſt, ſignified by the pale horſe in the fourth ſeale, by the king of the Locuſts in the fift trumpet, by *Babylon* in the 11. and 18. Chapter, by the ſecond Beaſt riſing out of the ſea in the 13. Chapter, and by the woman clad with ſcarlet in the 17. chapter. The ariſings of the hereſies, and the Antichriſt breeding of their ſmoake, is in this place called the looſing of Satan.

    Now followeth after this his looſing, what he doeth: He deceiueth the nations vniuerſally: he gathereth *Gog* and *Magog* with vntellable armies to fight, he climeth vpon the plaine of the earth, he compaſſeth the tents of the Saints, and the beloued Citie about: Theſe are his doings.

    Now becauſe theſe actions are moſt liuely declared in other places of the ſame booke, I will ſhortly alleadge them to make the matter cleere by conference of places, expounding euery one another. It is ſaid in the ninth chapter, that the Antichriſt ſhall ſend out his locuſts or Eccleſiaſticall orders, by faire allurements to entice the world, to yeeld to his and their abominable hereſies, and ſhall preuaile ouer the moſt part. It is ſaid in the 11. chapter, that he ſhall perſecute the Saints, kill the two witneſſes, and ſhall reioyce with the kings of the earth, for their killing, as hauing beene the onely lets to his full glory. It is ſaid in the 13. chapter, that he ſhall blaſpheme God in vſurping his power, that by the aduice and aſſiſtance of the falſe Prophet, or falſe Church, hee ſhall ſend out his Images or Embaſſadours through the world, perſecuting and deſtroying them that will not obey him and them, and acknowledge his ſupremacie; yea, none ſhall be ſuffered to buy or ſell, or vſe ciuill ſocietie, that acknowledgeth not his ſupreme power and dignity. It is ſaid in the 16. chapter, that God plaguing him for theſe foreſaid abuſes, he ſhall be ſo farre from repentance, as by the contrarie he ſhall finde out a new ſort of vermin, that is, a new Eccleſiaſticall order, which are called their frogges, who ſhall mooue and entice the Princes of the earth to ioyne with him, and make warre againſt the faithfull, preſſing vtterly to deſtroy them: and of that battell, and the end therof doeth this place make mention.

    Now ſhortly ioyne all theſe together, and ſo obtaine the meaning. There ſhall ariſe an Antichriſt and enemie to God and his Church: hee ſhall bee head of a falſe and hypocriticall Church: hee ſhall claime a ſupreme power in earth: he ſhall vſurpe the power of God: he ſhall deceiue men with abuſing locuſts: he ſhall perſecute the faithfull: none ſhall bee found that dare openly reſiſt him: In the end, feeling his kingdome decay, and the trew Church beginning to proſper, he ſhall by a new ſort of deceiuing ſpirits, gather together the Kings of the earth in great multitudes like the ſands of the Sea, and by ioyning or at leaſt ſuffering of that other great open enemy, he ſhall with theſe numbers compaſſe the campes of the faithfull,

The Goſpel being hid, the Antichriſt beginneth to breed & tend to his height.

    beſiege

befiege the beloued Citie, make warre againft the Saints: but victorie fhal he not haue, and fhame and confufion fhalbe his, and all his partakers end.

Now whether the Pope beareth thefe markes or not, let any indifferent man iudge; I thinke furely it expounds it felfe: Doeth he not vfurpe Chrift his office, calling himfelfe vniuerfall Bifhop and head of the Church? Play-eth he not the part of *Apollyon*, and *Abaddon* the king of the Locufts and de-ftroyer, or fonne of perdition, in chopping and changing of foules be-twixt heauen, hell, and his fantafticke or imagined purgatorie at his plea-fure? Blafphemeth he not, in denying vs to be faued by the imputation of Chrift his righteoufneffe? Moreouer, hath hee not fent forth and abufed the world with innumerable orders of locufts and fhauelings? Hath hee not fo fully ruled ouer the world thefe many hundreth yeeres, as to the fire went hee, whofoeuer hee was, that durft deny any part of his vfurped fu-premacie? And hath he not of late dayes, feeing his kingdome going to decay, fent out the Iefuites, his laft and moft pernicious vermin, to ftirre vp the Princes of the earth his flaues, to gather and league themfelues to-gether for his defence, and rooting out of all them that profeffe Chrift truely? And whereas the open enemie of God, the Turke was vnder bloo-dy warres with him euer before, is there not of late a truce among them, that the faithfull may be the more eafily rooted out? And are not the ar-mies prefently affembled, yea vpon the very point of their execution in *France* againft the Saints there? In *Flanders* for the like; and in *Germa-nie*, by whom already the Bifhop of *Collein* is difplaced? And what is pre-pared and come forward againft this Ile? Doe we not daily heare, and by all appearance and likelihood fhall fhortly fee? Now may we iudge if this be not the time, whereof this place that I haue made choice doeth meane, and fo the due time for the reuealing of this Prophecie. Thus farre for the interpretation of the fentence or meaning.

THE THIRD PART.

NOw I come to the laft part, what we may learne of this place, which I will fhortly touch in few points, and fo make an end.

And firft of the deuill his loofing by the rifing of An-tichrift, for the iuft punifhment of the vnthankefull world hating the trewth, and delighting in lies, and manifefting of his owne chofen that ftucke to the trewth; we haue two things to note: One for inftruction, that the iuftice of God in refpect of man his falling wilfully from the trewth, (as *Paul* faith) iuftly did fend to the world the great abufer with efficacie of lies; as well to tyrannize fpiritually ouer the con-fcience by herefie, as corporally ouer their bodies by the ciuill fword. And therefore we muft feare to fall from the trewth reuealed and profeffed by vs, that we may be free from the like punifhment. The other for our com-fort, that this tyrannie of the Antichrift, fifting out the chaffe from the corne,

corne, as our Maſter ſayth, ſhall tend to the double condemnation of the fallers backe, and to the double crowne of glory, to the perſeuerers or ſtan_ders out to the end. Bleſſed therefore are they that perſeuere or ſtand out to the end, for they ſhall be ſaued.

Next, of the number of nations in the foure quarters of the earth deccied, and companies gathered together to fight like the ſand of the ſea, Wee are taught, that the defection or falling away vnder the Antichriſt, was generall, and ſo no viſible Church was there: whereof two things doe follow : One, the Church may be corrupted and erre : another, the Church may lurke, and be vnknowen for a certaine ſpace. :

. Thirdly, of that that Satan is not content onely to deceiue, except hee alſo gather to the battell his inſtruments ; we are informed of the implaca_ble or vnappeaſeable malice, borne by Satan in his inſtruments againſt God in his members, who neuer ceaſeth like a roaring Lyon (as *Peter* ſayth) to goe about aſſailing to deuoure. This his malice is notably laid foorth in the 12. and 13. Chap. of this Booke : For it is ſaid, that when he had ſpew_ed out great riuers of waters, that is, infinite hereſies and lies to ſwallow vp the woman, and notwithſtanding ſhee was deliuered therefro, yet a_gaine hee raiſed vp a beaſt out of the ſea, the bloody Romane Empiⁱe by the ſword, to deuoure her, and her ſeed ; and that being wounded deadly, yet hee raiſeth another beaſt foorth of the earth, which is the Antichriſt, by hereſie and ſword ioyned together to ſerue his turne : So the deuill, ſeeing that no miſt of hereſies can obſcure or darken the Goſpel in the hearts of the faithfull ; and that the cruell ſword of perſecutors cannot ſtay the proſperous ſucceſſe of Chriſt his kingdome, hee raiſeth vp the Antichriſt with both his ſwords, to the effect that as one of them ſayth, That which *Peter* his keyes could not, *Paul* his ſword ſhould : And ſo hath hee done at this time ; For ſeeing the true Church will not be abuſed with the abſurd hereſies, for laſt refuge, now rooted out muſt they be by the ciuill Sword.

Fourthly, of their great numbers, able to compaſſe about the tents of the Saints, and to beſiege the holy Cities, wee are enformed that the wicked are euer the greateſt part of the world: And therfore our Maſter ſayth, *Many are called, few choſen*: And againe, *Wide is the way that leadeth to deſtruction, and many enter thereat : but narrow is the way that leadeth to life, and few enter there-at.* Alſo hee calleth them the world, and the Deuill the prince of the ſame.

Fiftly, the agreeance of *Gog* and *Magog*, the Turke the open enemy, and the Pope the couered enemie, to this perſecution, declareth the rooted ha_tred of the wicked againſt the faithfull : who though they be otherwiſe in enmitie among themſelues, yet agree in this reſpect, *in odium tertij*, as did *Herod* and *Pilate*.

Sixtly, the compaſſing of the Saints, and beſieging of the beloued City, declareth vnto vs a certaine note of a falſe Church, to be perſecution : for they come to ſeeke the faithfull ; the faithfull are thoſe that are ſought: The wicked are the beſiegers ; the faithfull the beſieged.

Seuenthly,

Backe ſliders ſhall periſh : conſtant chri-ſtians ſhall be crowned.
Matth. 10.22.

2
The defecti-on or falling away vnder Antichriſt, ſhall be vni-uerſall.

3
Satan his chil-dren both de-ceiue, and per-ſecute.

4
The wicked in number euer ouerpaſſe the godly.

5
The wicked at variance a-mong them-ſelues, can wel agree in one againſt Chriſt

6
The falſe Church euer perſecuteth.

7
Scripture by
Scripture
ſhould be ex-
pounded.
2.King. 1.
10,11.

Seuenthly, in the forme of language, and phraſe or maner of ſpeaking, of fire comming downe from heauen here vſed, and taken out of the Booke of the Kings, where, at *Elias* his prayers, with fire from heauen were deſtroyed *Achazias* his ſouldiers : as the greateſt part of all the words, verſes, and ſentences of this booke are taken and borrowed of other parts of the Scripture, we are taught to vſe onely Scripture for interpretation of Scripture, if we would be ſure, and neuer ſwarue from the analogie of faith in expounding, ſeeing it repeateth ſo oft the owne phraſes, and thereby expoundeth them.

8

Eightly, of the laſt part of the confuſion of the wicked, euen at the top of their height and wheele, we haue two things to note : One that God although he ſuffereth the wicked to run on while their cup be full, yet in the end he ſtriketh them, firſt in this world, and next in the world to come; to the deliuerance of his Church in this world, and the perpetuall glory of the ſame in the world to come :   The other note is, that after the great perſecution and the deſtruction of the purſuers, ſhall the day of Iudgement follow : For ſo declareth the 11.verſe of this ſame Chapter; but in how ſhort ſpace it ſhall follow, that is onely knowne vnto God; Onely this farre are we certaine, that in the laſt eſtate, without any moe generall mutations, the world ſhall remaine till the conſummation and end of the ſame.

To conclude then with exhortation : It is al our duties in this Iſle at this time, to do two things : One, to conſider our eſtate : An other to conforme our actions according thereunto : Our eſtate is, we are threefold beſieged: Firſt, ſpiritually by the hereſies of the antichriſt: Secondly, corporally & generally, as members of that Church, the which in the whole they perſecute: Thirdly, corporally and particularly by this preſent armie. Our actions then conformed to our eſtate are theſe : Firſt, to call for helpe at God his hands: Next, to aſſure vs of the ſame, ſeeing we haue a ſufficient warrant, his conſtant promiſe expreſſed in his word : Thirdly, ſince with good conſcience we may, being in the tents of the Saints, & beloued City, ſtand in our defence, encourage one another to vſe lawfull reſiſtance, and concurre or ioyne one with another as warriors in one Campe, and citizens of one beloued City, for maintenance of the good cauſe God hath clad vs with, and in defence of our liberties, natiue countrey, and liues: For ſince we ſee God hath promiſed not only in the world to come, but alſo in this world, to giue vs victory ouer them, let vs in aſſurance hereof ſtrongly truſt in our God, ceaſe to miſtruſt his promiſe, and fall through incredulitie or vnbeliefe: For then are we worthy of double puniſhment : For the ſtronger they waxe, and the neerer they come to their light, the faſter approcheth their wracke, and the day of our deliuery: For kind, and louing, true, and conſtant, carefull, and watchfull, mighty, and reuenging is he that promiſeth it : To whom be praiſe and glory for euer. AMEN.

All men
ſhould be law-
fully armed
ſpiritually and
bodily to fight
againſt the
Antichriſt,
and his vphol-
ders,

A MEDITATION VPON THE
xxv. xxvj. xxvij. xxviij. and xxix. verſes of the xv.
Chap. of the firſt Booke of the Chronicles of the Kings :

Written by the moſt Chriſtian King, and ſincere Profeſſour
of the trewth, I A M E S by the grace of God, King of England,
France, Scotland, and Ireland, Defender of the Faith.

THE TEXT.

25 *So Dauid and the Elders of Iſrael and the Captaines of thouſands went to bring*
vp the Arke of the Couenant of the Lord, from the houſe of Obed-Edom
with ioy.

26 *And becauſe that God helped the Leuites that bare the Arke of the Couenant of*
the Lord, they offered ſeuen Bullockes and ſeuen Rammes.

27 *And Dauid had on him a linnen garment, as all the Leuites that bare the Arke,*
and the ſingers and Chenaniah that had the chiefe charge of the ſingers : and
vpon Dauid was a linnen Ephod.

28 *Thus all Iſrael brought vp the Arke of the Lords Couenant with ſhouting and*
ſound of Cornet, and with Trumpets, and with Cymbales, making a ſound with
Violes and with harpes.

29 *And when the Arke of the Couenant of the Lord came into the Citie of Dauid,*
Michal the daughter of Saul looked out at a window, and ſaw King Dauid
dauncing and playing, and ſhee deſpiſed him in her heart.

THE MEDITATION.

S of late when greateſt appearance of perill was
by that forreine and godleſſe fleete, I tooke occaſion by a Text ſelected for the purpoſe, to exhort
you to remaine conſtant, reſting aſſured of a happy deliuerance : So now by the great mercies of
God, my ſpeeches hauing taken an euident effect,
I could doe no leſſe of my carefull duety, then out
of this place cited, teach you what reſteth on
your part to be done; not of any opinion I haue
of my abilitie to inſtruct you, but that theſe meditations of mine, may after my death remaine to the poſteritie, as a certaine teſtimony of my vpright and honeſt meaning in this ſo great and weightie a cauſe. Now I
come

come to the matter. *Dauid* that godly King, you fee, hath no fooner obtained victory ouer Gods, and his enemies the Philiftines, but his firft action which followes, is with concurrence of his whole eftates, to tranflate
the Arke of the Lords couenant to his houfe in great triumph and gladneffe, accompanied with the found of muficall inftruments: And being fo
brought to the Kings houfe, he himfelfe dances and reioyces before it:
which thing *Michal* the daughter of *Saul* and his wife perceiuing, fhe contemned and laughed at her husband in her minde. This is the fumme.

THE METHOD.

For better vnderftanding whereof, thefe heades are to be opened vp in order, and applied. And firft what caufes mooued
Dauid to doe this worke. Secondly, what perfons concurred
with *Dauid* in doing of this worke. Thirdly, what was the a-
ction it felfe, and forme of doing vfed in the fame. Fourthly, the perfon of
Michal. And fiftly, her action.

THE FIRST PART.

Zeale in Da-
uid and expe-
rièce of Gods
kindneffe to-
wards him,
mooued Dauid
to honour
God.

S to the firft part; The caufes moouing *Dauid*, paffing
all others, I note two: One internall, the other, external:
the internall was a feruent and zealous mind in *Dauid*
fully difpofed to extoll the glorie of God that had called him to be King, as he faith himfelfe. The zeale of
thy houfe it eats me vp, *Pfal.* 69.9. But more largely expreffed in the 132. *Pfalme*, compofed at the fame time
while this worke was a doing. The externall was a notable victorie newly
obtained by the power of God ouer and againft the Philiftines, olde and
pernitious enemies to the people of God, expreffed in the laft part of the 14.
chapter preceding. By this victorie or caufe external, the internal caufes
and zeale in *Dauid* is fo doubly inflamed, that all things fet afide, in this
worke onely he will be occupied. Thefe are the two weightie caufes mo-
uing him. Wherof we may learne, firft that the chiefe vertue which fhould
be in a chriftian Prince, and which the Spirit of God alwayes chiefly praifes in him, is a feruencie and conftant zeale to promote the glorie of God,
that hath honoured him. Next, that where this zeale is vnfained, God
leaues neuer that perfon, without continuall powring of his bleffings on
him, thereby to ftirre vp into him a double meafure of zeale and thankfulneffe towards God. Thirdly, that the Church of God neuer wanted ene-

The Church
euer troubled
by men, hath
a ioyfull end.

mies and notable victories ouer them, to affure them at all times of the conftant kindnes of God towards them; euen, when as by the croffe, as a bitter medicine, he cureth their infirmities, faueth them from groffe finnes,
and trieth their faith: For we find plainely in the Scriptures, that no fooner

ner God himſelfe chooſed Iſrael to be his people; but aſſoone, & euer ther-
after as long as they remained his, the diuell ſo enuied their proſperity, as
hee hounded out his inſtruments the nations, at all times to trouble and
warre againſt them, yet to the comfort of his Church afflicted, and wrack
of the afflicters in the end. This firſt was practiſed by *Pharao* in Egypt ⋅
and after their deliuerance, firſt by the Ammonites, and then by the Phi-
liſtines continually thereafter, vntill the riſing of the Monarchies, who
euery one did exerciſe themſelues in the ſame labour. But to note here the
rage of all prophane Princes and nations which exerciſed their crueltie vpon the Church of God, were ſuperfluous and tedious, in reſpect of that
which I haue ſet downe in my former meditation: Wherefore I onely goe
forward then in this. As this was the continuall behauiour of the Nations
towards Iſrael; So it was moſt eſpecially in the time of *Dauid*, and among
the reſt at this time here cited; at what time hauing newly inuaded Iſrael,
and beeing driuen backe, they would yet aſſemble againe in great multitudes to warre againſt the people of God, and not content to defend their
owne countries as the Iſraelites did, would needes come out of the ſame to
purſue them, and ſo ſpread themſelues in the valley: But *Dauid* by Gods direction, brings foorth the people againſt them, who fights, and according
to Gods promiſes, ouercomes them, onely by the hand of God, and not by
their power, as the place it ſelfe moſt plainely doeth ſhew: So the Church
of God may be troubled, but in trouble it cannot periſh; and the end of
their trouble is the very wracke and deſtruction of Gods enemies.

THE SECOND PART.

Ow followes ſecondly the perſons who did concurre
with *Dauid* in this action: The Spirit noteth three
rankes of them. In the firſt are the Elders of Iſrael : In
the next, are the captaines ouer thouſands : In the third,
are the Prieſts and Leuites, of whom ſummarily I will
ſpeake. Theſe Elders were ſubſtituted vnder *Dauid* in
the kingdome, and as his hands in all parts of the countrey miniſtring iuſtice and iudgement to the Kings ſubiects : And they were of two ſorts,
maieſtrates in walled townes, who in the gates of the cities executed iudgement; and chiefe in Tribes, and fathers of families, who in the countrey did
iudge and miniſter iudgement as the Scripture reports: They were not vnlike to two of the eſtates of our kingdome, the Baron and the Burgeſſe.
The Captaines ouer thouſands were godly and valiant men, who vnder
the King did rule in time of warre, had the cuſtodie of the Kings perſon,
and fought his battailes : Theſe were neceſſarie officers for *Dauid*, who
was appointed by God in his time (as wee are taught out of Gods owne
words, ſpeaking by *Nathan* to *Dauid*) to fight Gods battailes, to ſubdue the
enemies of his Church, and to procure by ſo doing, a peaceable kingdome
for

Three rankes
of perſons
concurre with
Dauid in this
worke.

for *Solomon* his fonne, who fhould in peace, as a figure of Chrift the Prince of peace, build the Lords Temple. Thefe are fpoken of here, to teach vs, firft, that their calling is lawfull : next, that in their calling, they fhould be earneft to honour God : and thirdly, that thefe Captaines chiefly were lawfully called, and lawfully walked therein, as we haue plaine declaration out of *Dauids* owne mouth, expreffed well in the whole 101. *Pfalme*, feeing none were admitted in his feruice or houfhold, but fuch as vnfainedly feared God. And without all queftion, godly and zealous *Dauid* would neuer haue committed the guard of his perfon, nor the fighting of Gods battailes to the enemies of God, or men of warre, of whofe godlineffe and vertue he neuer had proofe : See then their names and praife, 1. *Chron.* 11.26. The third ranke of Priefts and Leuites are fet downe in the fame chapter, verf. 4,5,6,7,8,9,10,11. So men of all eftates were prefent in this godly worke. This is to be marked well of Princes, and of all thofe of any high calling or degree that hath to doe in Gods caufe. *Dauid* doth nothing in matters appertaining to God without the prefence and fpeciall concurrence of Gods Minifters, appointed to be fpirituall rulers in his Church : and at the firft meant to conuey the fame Arke to Ierufalem, finding their abfence and want of their counfell hurtfull : now in this chapter, verf. 12,13. he faith to them, *Ye are the chiefe Fathers of the Leuites, fanctifie your felues and your brethren, and bring vp the Arke of the Lord God of Ifrael vnto the place that I haue prepared for it. For becaufe ye were not there at the firft, the Lord our God made a breach among vs : for we fought him not in due order.* And thus farre for the fecond part concerning perfons : Wherein we may learne, firft, that a godly king findes, as his heart wifheth, godly eftates concurring with him. Next a godly king of his godly forefight in choofing good vnder-rulers, reapeth this profit and pleafure, that as hee goeth before, fo they with zealous hearts doe follow.

THE THIRD PART.

He fumme of this ioyfull conuoy may be digefted in three actions, which are thefe : The tranfporting of the Arke; the harmony of muficall inftruments ; and *Dauids* dancing and reioycing before it. He built a Tabernacle for the Arke in mount *Sion*, & tranfported it thereunto, to fignify his thankfulnes for the many victories God had put in his hands : and this tranfporting was the occafion of all this folemnitie and reioycing that followed thereupon. As to the Arke it felfe, we know it was built by *Moyfes* at the

comand of God, in the wildernes of *Sinai* : This Arke was made of *Shittim* wood, which admits no corruption : It was of moft comely fhape and forme, two cubits and a halfe in length, a cubit and a halfe in height, and a cubit and a halfe in breadth, ouerlaid within and without with pure beaten gold, and was not only a figure of *Iefus Chrift* our perfect Sauiour, in whom

all

all the promises of God, are yea and Amen, *2.Corinth.* 1. 20. and in whom as a sure Arke, all abundance of Gods blessings are placed, that out of his fulnesse we may all receiue grace vpon grace, *Iohn* 1. 16. seeing he is made vnto vs of God, wisedome, righteousnesse, sanctification and redemption, 1. *Corinth.* 1. 30. but also a sure pledge of Gods continuall presence in Christ with his people, to blesse them with all maner of blessings. And to signifie this purpose more particularly, within the Arke was placed the Tables of the Couenant, and Law written by God, (for which cause also it was called the Arke of the Couenant) *Rom.* 10. 4. to teach them in Christ promised, the perfection of the whole Law to be found, for all that beleeue in him. Aboue the Arke was a couer or lid called The Mercie Seate, and aboue the lid the figures of two Cherubins, couering with their wings the Mercie Seat : betwixt the which two, the liuing God did louingly speake to the instruction and comfort of his people, to assure them that all Gods mercifull dealings with man (either in communicating his knowledge to them : or in sending his Angels ministring Spirits for their comfort,) hath the ground and foundation in CHRIST IESVS eternally. This Arke then being a sure Sacrament of Gods fauour towards them, and a Couenant of IESVS CHRIST, wherein corporally Gods mercifull promises did insue; followes the third part, the forme of doing vsed therein by these persons. Generally, the action was to bring vp the Arke of the Couenant of the Lord, from the house of *Obed Edom* with ioy, and to be placed in the Tabernacle built for it by the King in Mount *Sion.* The forme of doing vsed by euery person, is : The Priests offer Bullocks and Rammes, becausse that God blessed the worke; The King clad in a linnen garment, dances and playes before the Arke : *Chenaniah* the chiefe of the singers with his fellowes, praises God with Psalmes, and all the estates in Israel, bring the Arke of the Couenant with showting, sound of Cornet, Trumpet, cymbals, violes, and harpes, and place it in the citie of Dauid. Briefly then, *Dauid* vpon his victories doeth transport to his house the same, to testifie hereby his care to receiue Gods fauour towards him and his people : Not thinking it enough to haue once or twise proofe thereof; but also to procure a continuance by the presence of his holy Arke, esteeming this the worthiest trophee or triumph, he could make or erect for his notable victories : A triumph indeed farre surpassing the Egyptian Piramides, the Grecian trophees, or yet the Romane triumphall chariots. As to the harmonie and musicall instruments that accompanied this holy Arke, I trust no man is ignorant of the custome that was among the Iewes, in praising God with all kind of instruments, as *Dauids* Psalmes innumerable times beare witnesse. But in case some would demand wherefore the Church of God should more extraordinarily reioyce at one time, then at another, seeing we are assured that all Gods actions towards vs, are for our weale, either spiritually or corporally, suppose wee cannot at euery time comprehend it : I answere, that although I must confesse that sentence to bee most

marginal note: Heb. 1. 14.
Ioh. 1. 4, 11.

H ortho-

orthodoxe, yet muſt I alſo confeſſe, that whenſoeuer it ſhall pleaſe God to manifeſt by outward ſignes to the world, as at one time more then another the great loue to his Church, by ſome notable worke for their deliuerance; We are then of duty bound in the higheſt degree to praiſe God, as well for confirming of the weake ones amongſt vs, as for ſtopping of the mouthes, and daſhing of the proud wicked without vs, to make the glory of his Name, as farre as in vs lieth, to reſound: The manifold examples of the Saints of God through the whole Scriptures prooue this more then euidently, beſides the examples of the prayers of ſundry of the godly, who for the glory of his Name, more then for their particular weale, haue prayed him to giue publike teſtimonie of his loue towards them: So did *Moſes, Ioſhua, Dauid, Elias, Elizeus,* and innumerable others of the Prophets and ſeruants of God. As to the dancing of *Dauid:* dancing, playing, and ſuch like actions we know are of themſelues indifferent, and good or euil according to their vſe, and the intention of the vſer; and therefore being vſed at this time with a comely zeale, for the ſetting foorth of Gods glory, are not onely to be borne with and excuſed, but euen moſt highly to be prayſed and commended, although that *Michal* diſprayſed the ſame. Moreouer, it is to be marked that *Dauid* in this doing, did nothing without the ſpecial motion of the ſpirit of God, as an extraordinarie worke, which ſo fully poſſeſſed his ſoule at this preſent, that forgetfull, as it were, of the actions of his bodie; hee gaue his whole perſon ouer to be gouerned as it pleaſed him, always ſeeking in all, the honour and glorie of his God, without reſpect to himſelfe: And thus farre for the third part: Whereof wee haue to note firſt in the Arke: The ground of all true and ancient religion, and the body of the whole ſeruice of God that brings ſaluation, is to bee ſituate in Ieſus Chriſt onely, as is plainely ſet downe, *Act.*4.12. *Ioh.*14.6. 1.*Cor.*2.11. 1.*Ioh.*1.7. Next, that they which will be ſaued by this Arke, muſt beare this Arke in their heart by faith, in their mouth by open confeſſion, *Rom.*1. and in their actions confirming their whole doing in their calling to his will, *Matth.*7.21,22,23. Thirdly, that they who are ſincerely ioyned with Chriſt, reioyce in the bearing of Chriſt, and count it their higheſt ioy to be occupied continually in his bearing.

Chriſt is the ground of all true Religion.

THE FOVRTH PART.

Michals hypocriſie.

AS to the perſon of *Michal,* ſhee was *Sauls* daughter, and *Dauids* wife, a woman appearandly euill brought vp by a moſt wicked father; which the Spirit of God will ſignifie, by calling her *Sauls* daughter, as ſhe was in hypocriſie his daughter in deed, as well as by nature: yet ſhee was ioyned with the body of the Church viſible, which is ſignified by the ſtile giuen her, when ſhe was called *Dauids* wife: And ſo ſhe was outwardly a perſon ioyned by mariage in ſocietie with the Church, yet in effect a lurking hypocrite

crite within the bowels of the same. Such kinde of folkes (hypocrites I meane) are a *malum neceſſarium* inſeparably and continually ioyned with the trew Church, neuer to be ſifted while the Maſter of the Harueſt come with the fanne in his hand.

THE FIFT PART.

HEr doings are, being quiet in her lodging, al the time of her huſbands great and publike reioycing with the people not comming out; for not being able, as appeareth, to counterfeit finely euough a diſſimulate ioyfull countenance: And therefore looking out at a window, ſhee ſpies her husband dancing before the Arke, incontinent interprets ſhee this indifferent action *in malam partem*, as not being touched with a true feeling of the cauſe of his ioy, and ſo deſpiſes ſhe his doing in her minde, as onely proceeding of a laſciuious wantonneſſe. A marueilous caſe; ſhee that before of naturall loue to her husband did preſerue him, although to her owne great perill, from the hands of her owne father *Saul*, cannot now abide to ſee him vſe aright that indifferent action, which ſhe her ſelfe (I doubt not) did oft through licentiouſnes abuſe. By this we may note the nature of the hypocrites, and interiour enemies of the Church, who although in their particulars not concerning Religion, there will be none in ſhew more friendly to the godly then they; yet how ſoone matters of Religion or concerning the honour of God, comes in hand, O then are they no longer able to containe or bridle their paſſions, euen as here *Michal* defended her husband, euen in the particulars betwixt him and her owne father; but his dancing before the Arke to the honour of God, ſhe could no wiſe abide.

    Now thus farre being ſaid for the methodicall opening vp of the Text; It reſts onely to examine how pertinently this place doeth appertaine to vs and our preſent eſtate: And firſt as to the perſons, the people of God and the nations their enemies, together with their pridefull purſuite of *Dauid*, and Gods moſt notable deliuerance. Is there not now a ſincere profeſſion of the trewth amongſt vs in this Iſle, oppugned by the nations about, haters of the holy word? And doe we not alſo as Iſrael, profeſſe one onely God, and are ruled by his pure word onely? on the other part, are they not as Philiſtines, adorers of legions of gods, and ruled by the fooliſh traditions of men? Haue they not as the Philiſtines, beene continually the purſuers, and we as Iſrael the defenders of our natiue ſoile and countrey? next, haue they not now at the laſt euen like the Philiſtines, come out of their owne ſoiles to purſue vs, and ſpread themſelues to that effect vpon the great valley of our ſeas, preſumptuouſly threatning the deſtruction and wracke of vs? But thirdly, had not our victory beene farre more notable then that of Iſrael, and hath not the one beene as well wrought by the

Michals doings.

The application of the purpoſe to vs.

hand

hand of God, as the other? For as God by fhaking the tops of the mulbery trees with his mightie windes, put the Philiftines to flight, hath hee not euen in like maner by brangling with his mightie windes their timber ca-ftles, fcattered and fhaken them afunder to the wracke of a great part, and confufion of the whole? Now that we may refemble Ifrael as well in the reft of this action, what triumph refts vs to make for the crowning of this bleffed comedy? Euen to bring amongft vs the Arke with all reioycing. What is the Arke of Chriftians vnder grace, but the Lord Iefus Chrift, whom with ioy wee bring amongft vs, when as receiuing with finceritie and gladneffe the new Teftament in the blood of Chrift our Sauiour, in our heart we beleeue his promifes, and in word and deede wee beare wit-neffe thereto before the whole world, and walke fo in the light as it be-comes the fonnes of the fame? this is the worthieft triumph of our victo-ry that we can make. And although there will doubtleffe be many *Michals* amongft vs, let vs reioyce and praife God for the difcouerie of them, affu-ring our felues they were neuer of vs, accounting all them to be againft vs, that either reioyce at the profperitie of our enemies, or reioyce not with vs at our miraculous deliuerance: For all they that gather not with vs, they fcatter. And let vs alfo diligently and warily trie out thefe craftie *Michals*: for it is in that refpect that Chrift recommends vnto vs the wifedome of Serpents, not thereby to deceiue and betray others (no, God forbid) but to arme vs againft the deceit and treafon of hypocrites that goe about to trap vs. And left that thefe great benefits which God hath beftowed vpon vs, be turned through our vnthankfulneffe into a greater curfe, in feruing for teftimonies at the latter day againft vs, to the procuring of our double ftripes; let vs now to conclude, bring in the Arke amongft vs in two re-fpects before mentioned, feeing we haue already receiued the Gofpel; firft by conftant remaining in the puritie of the trewth, which is our moft cer-teine couenant of faluation in the only merits of our Sauior: And next, let vs
fo reforme our defiled liues, as becomes regenerate Chriftians, to the
great glory of our God, the vtter defacing of our aduerfaries
the wicked, and our vnfpeakeable comfort both
here and alfo for euer. A M E N.

His

His Maiesties owne Sonnet.

THe nations banded gainſt the Lord of might
Prepar'd a force, and ſet them to the way :
Mars dreſt himſelfe in ſuch an awfull plight,
The like whereof was neuer ſeene they ſay:
They forward came in monſtrous aray,
Both Sea and land beſet vs euery where:
Bragges threatned vs a ruinous decay,
What came of that ? the iſſue did declare.
The windes began to toſſe them here and there,
The Seas begun in foming waues to ſwell :
The number that eſcap'd, it fell them faire:
The reſt were ſwallowed vp in gulfes of hell :
But how were all theſe things miraculous done?
God laught at them out of his heauenly throne.

Idem Latinè.

INSANO tumidæ gentes coiere tumultu,
Auſa, inſigne nefas, bello vltro ciere tonantem,
Mars ſeſe accinxit, metuenda tot agmina nunquam,
Viſa ferunt, properare truces miro ordine turmæ,
Noſque mari & terra ſæuo claſere duello,
Exitium diraque minantes ſtrage ruinam;
Irrita ſed triſti lugent conamina fine :
Nam laceras iecit ventus ludibria puppes,
Et merſit rapidis turgeſcens montibus æquor.
Fœlix communi qui euaſit clade ſuperſtes,
Dum reliquos miſero, deglutit abyſſus hiatu.
Qui vis tanta cadit ? quis totque ſtupenda peregit ?
Vanos Ioua ſacro conatus riſit Olympo.

Per Metellanum Cancellarium.

H 3

DAEMONOLOGIE,
IN FORME OF A
DIALOGVE,

Diuided into three Bookes,

WRITTEN BY THE HIGH
AND MIGHTIE PRINCE,
I A M E S by the Grace of G o d King of
England, Scotland, France and Ireland,
Defender of the Faith, &c.

¶ THE PREFACE TO
THE READER.

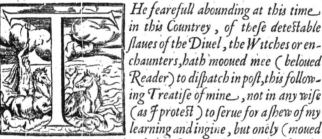

*He fearefull abounding at this time
in this Countrey, of these detestable
slaues of the Diuel, the Witches or enchaunters, hath mooued mee (beloued
Reader) to dispatch in post, this following Treatise of mine, not in any wise
(as I protest) to serue for a shew of my
learning and ingine, but onely (moued
of conscience) to preasse thereby, so farre as I can, to resolue the
doubting hearts of many; both that such assaults of Satan are most
certainely practised, and that the instruments thereof, merits most
seuerely to be punished: against the damnable opinions of two principally in our aage, whereof the one called Scot, an Englishman,
is not ashamed in publike Print to deny, that there can be such a
thing*

thing as *Witch-craft*: and so maintaines the old errour of the *Sad-*
duces in denying of spirits ; The other called *Wierus*, a *German*
Physition, sets out a publike *Apologie* for all these craftsfolkes,
whereby, procuring for their impunitie, he plainely bewrayes himselfe to haue bene one of that profeßion.   *And* for to make this
Treatise the more pleasant and facill, *J* haue put it in forme of a
Dialogue, which I haue diuided into three *Bookes* : The first
speaking of *Magie* in generall, and *Necromancie* in speciall:
The second, of *Sorcerie* and *Witch-craft* : and the third, containes
a discourse of all these kinds of spirits, and Spectres that appeares
and troubles persons; together with a conclusion of the whole
worke.   *My* intention in this labour, is onely to prooue two
things, as I haue already said : The one, that such diuelish artes
haue bene and are : The other, what exact triall and seuere punishment they merit: and therefore reason I, *What* kinde of things
are poßible to be performed in these *Arts*, aud by what naturall
causes they may be, not that I touch euery particular thing of the
Diuels power, for that were infinite : but onely to speake schola-
stickely, (since this cannot be spoken in our language) *J* reason vpon *genus* leauing species, and differentia to bee comprehended
therein :   *As* for example, speaking of the power of *Magiciens*,
in the first booke and sixt *Chapter*, *I* say, that they can suddenly
cause be brought vnto them, all kinds of daintie dishes, by their
familiar spirit; since as a thiefe he delights to steale, and as a spirit he can subtilly and suddenly ynough transport the same. *Now*
vnder this *genus*, may be comprehended all particulars, depending thereupon ; such as the bringing *Wine* out of a wall (as wee
haue heard oft to haue bene practised) and such others ; which
particulars, are sufficiently prooued by the reasons of the generall.
And such like in the second booke of *Witch-craft* in speciall, and
fift *Chapter*, *J* say, and proue by diuers *Arguments*, that *Witches*
can by the power of their master, cure or cast on diseases : *Now*
by these same reasons, that proues their power by the *Diuell* of diseases in generall, is aswell proued their power in special; as of weak-
ning the nature of some men, to make them vnable for women, and
making

making it to abound in others, more then the ordinary course of nature would permit: And such like in all other particular sicknesses.
But one thing I will pray thee to obserue in all these places, where
I reason vpon the diuels power, which is the different ends and
scopes, that God as the first cause, and the diuell as his instrument
and second cause, shoots at in all these actions of the diuel, (as Gods
hang-man:) For where the diuels intention in them is euer to perish, either the soule, or the body, or both of them, that he is so permitted to deale with; God by the contrary, drawes euer out of that
euill, glory to himselfe, either by the wracke of the wicked in his iustice, or by the triall of the patient, and amendment of the faithful,
being wakened vp with that rod of correction. Hauing thus declared vnto thee then, my full intention in this Treatise, thou wilt easily excuse, I doubt not, aswel my pretermitting, to declare the whole
particular rites and secrets of these vnlawfull arts; as also their in-
finit and wonderfull practises, as being neither of them pertinent to
my purpose : the reason whereof, is giuen in the hinder end of the
first Chapter of the third booke: and who likes to be curious in these
things, he may reade, if he will heare of their practises, Bodinus
Dæmonomanie, collected with greater diligence, then written
with iudgement, together with their confessions, that haue bene at
this time apprehended. If he would know what hath bene the opinion of the Ancients, concerning their power, he shall see it well described by Hyperius & Hemmingius, two late Germane writers; Besides innumerable other neotericke Theologues, that write
largely vpon that subject : And if he would know what are the
particular rites, and curiosities of these blacke Arts (which is both
vnnecessary and perillous) he will finde it in the fourth Booke of
Cornelius Agrippa, and in Wierus, whom-of I spake. And
so wishing my paines in this Treatise (beloued Reader) to be effectuall, in arming all them that reade the same, against these a-
boue mentioned errours, and recommending my good
will to thy friendly acceptation, I bid thee
heartily fare-well.

IAMES R.

DAEMONOLOGIE, IN
FORME OF A DIALOGVE.

First Booke.

ARGVMENT.
The exord of the whole. The defcription of
Magie in fpeciall.

Chap. I. Argvment.
Proued by the Scripture, that thefe vnlawfull arts in genere, *haue*
bene and may be put in praʃtife.

PHILOMATHES and EPISTEMON
reafon the matter.

PHILOMATHES.

 Am furely very glad to haue met with you this day : for I am of opinion, that ye can better refolue me of fome thing, whereof I ftand in great doubt, nor any other whomwith I could haue met.

EPI. In what I can, that ye like to fpeir at me, I will willingly and freely tell my opinion, and if I proue it not fufficiently, I am heartily content that a better reafon carry it away then.

PHI. What thinke ye of thefe ftrange newes, which now onely furnifhes purpofe to all men at their meeting : I meane of thefe Witches ?

EPI. Surely they are wonderfull : And I thinke fo cleare and plaine confeffions in that purpofe, haue neuer fallen out in any aage or countrey.

PHI. No queftion if they be true, but thereof the Doctours doubts.

EPI. What part of it doubt ye of ?

PHI.

.. PHI. Euen of all, for ought I can yet perceiue : and namely, that there is such a thing as Witch-craft or Witches, and I would pray you to resolue me thereof if ye may : for I haue reasoned with sundrie in that matter, and yet could neuer be satisfied therein.

EPI. I shall with good will doe the best I can : But I thinke it the difficiller, since ye deny the thing it selfe in generall : for as it is said in the Logicke schooles, *Contra negantem principia non est disputandum.* Alwaies for that part, that Witch-craft, and Witches haue beene ; and are, the former part is clearely prooued by the Scriptures, and the last by daily experience and confessions.

PHI. I know ye wil alleadge me *Sauls Pythonisse* : but that as appeares will not make much for you.

EPI. Not onely that place, but diuers others : But I maruell why that should not make much for me ?

PHI. The reasons are these, first yee may consider, that *Saul* beeing troubled in spirit, and hauing fasted long before, as the text testifieth, and being come to a woman that was bruted to haue such knowledge, and that to enquire so important newes, he hauing so guilty a conscience for his hainous offences, and specially, for that same ynlawfull curiositie, and horrible defection : and then the woman crying out vpon the suddaine in great admiration, for the vncouth sight that she alledged to haue seene, discouering him to be the King, though disguised, and denied by him before : it was no wonder, I say, that his senses being thus distracted, hee could not perceaue her faining of her voice, he being himselfe in another chalmer, and seeing nothing. Next, what could be, or was raised ? The spirit of *Samuel?* prophane, and against all Theologie : the deuill in his likenesse ? as vnappeirant, that either God would permit him to come in the shape of his Saints, (for then could neuer the Prophets in those dayes haue beene sure, what spirit spake to them in their visions) or then that he could fore-tell what was to come thereafter ; for Prophecie proceedeth onely of GOD : and the diuell hath no knowledge of things to come. ·

EPI. Yet if ye will marke the words of the text, yee will finde clearely, that *Saul* saw that apparition : for giuing you that *Saul* was in another chalmer, at the making of the circles and coniurations, needfull for that purpose (as none of that craft wil permit any others to behold at that time) yet it is euident by the text, that how soone that once that vncleane spirit was fully risen, she called in vpon *Saul* : For it is said in the text, that *Saul knew him to be Samuel,* which could not haue beene, by the hearing tell onely of an olde man with a mantill, since there was many moe old men dead in *Israel* nor *Samuel* : And the common weid of that whole countrey was mantils. As to the next, that it was not the spirit of *Samuel,* I grant : In the prouing whereof ye need not to insist, since all Christians of whatsoeuer religion agrees vpon that : and none but either mere ignorants, or Necromanciers, or Witches doubts thereof. And that the deuill is permitted at

some-

sometimes to put himfelfe in the likeneffe of the Saints, it is plaine in the Scriptures, where it is faid, that *Satan can transforme himfelfe into an Angel of light.* Neither could that bring any inconuenience with the vifions of the Prophets, fince it is moft certaine, that God will not permit him fo to deceiue his owne : but onely fuch, as firft wilfully deceiue them-felues, by running vnto him, whom God then fuffers to fall in their owne fnares, and iuftly permits them to be illuded with great efficacie of deceit, becaufe they would not beleeue the trueth (as *Paul* fayth.) And as to the diuels foretelling of things to come, it is true that he knowes not all things future; but yet that hee knowes part, the tragicall euent of this hiftorie declares it, (which the wit of woman could neuer haue fore-fpoken) not that hee hath any prefcience, which is onely proper to God; or yet knowes any thing by looking vpon God, as in a mirrour (as the good Angels doe) hee being for euer debarred from the fauourable prefence and countenance of his Creatour; but onely by one of thefe two meanes : either, as being worldly wife, and taught by a continuall experience, euer fince the Creation, iudges by likelyhood of things to come, according to the like that hath paffed before, and the naturall caufes, in refpect of the viciffitude of all things worldly : or elfe by Gods imploying of him in a turne, and fo forefeene thereof, as appeares to haue beene in this, whereof we finde the very like in *Micheas* propheticke difcourfe to king *Achab*. But to prooue this my firft propofition, that there can be fuch a thing as Witch-craft and Witches, there are many moe places in the Scriptures then this, as I faid before. As firft in the Lawe of G o d, it is plainely prohibited : But certaine it is, that the Law of God fpeakes nothing in vaine, neither doeth it lay curfes, or enioyne punifhments vpon fhadowes, condemning that to be ill, which is not in effence or being, as we call it. Secondly, it is plaine, where wicked *Pharaohs* Wife-men imitated a number of *Mofes* miracles, to harden the tyrants heart thereby. Thirdly, faid not *Samuel* to *Saul*, that *difobedience is as the finne of Witch-craft* ? To compare it to a thing that were not, it were too too abfurd. Fourthly, was not *Simon Magus* a man of that craft ? And fiftly, what was fhe that had the fpirit of *Python* ? befide innumerable other places that were irkefome to recite.

1.Cor.11.14.

1.King.22.

Exod.22.

Exod.7.&2.

1.Sam.15.

Acts 8.
Acts 16.

CHAP.

CHAP. II. ARGV.

What kind of sinne the practisers of these vnlawfull arts commit. The diuision of these arts : And what are the meanes that allure any to practise them.

PHILOMATHES.

Vt I thinke it very ſtrange, that God ſhould permit any man-kind (ſince they beare his owne Image) to fall in ſo groſſe and filthie a defection.

E p i. Although man in his Creation was made to the i- | Gene.1. mage of the Creator, yet through his fall hauing once loſt it, it is but reſtored againe in a part by grace onely to the elect : So all the reſt falling away from God, are giuen ouer into the hands of the diuell that enemy, to beare his image; and being once ſo giuen ouer, the greateſt and the groſſeſt impietie is the pleaſanteſt, and moſt delightfull vnto them.

P h i. But may it not ſuffice him to haue indirectly the rule, and procure the perdition of ſo many ſoules by alluring them to vices, and to the following of their owne appetites, ſuppoſe hee abuſe not ſo many ſimple ſoules, in making them directly acknowledge him for their maſter?

E p i. No ſurely, for he vſes euery man, whom of he hath the rule, according to their complexion and knowledge : and ſo, whom hee findes moſt ſimple, he plainelieſt diſcouers himſelfe vnto them : For he being the enemie of mans ſaluation, vſes all the meanes hee can to intrappe them ſo farre in his ſnares, as it may bee vnable to them thereafter (ſuppoſe they would) to rid themſelues out of the ſame.

P h i. Then this ſinne is a ſinne againſt the holy Ghoſt.

E p i. It is in ſome, but not in all.

P h i. How that? Are not all theſe that runne directly to the diuell in one Categorie?

E p i. God forbid, for the ſinne againſt the holy Ghoſt hath two branches : The one, a falling backe from the whole ſeruice of God, and a refuſall of all his precepts : The other is the doing of the firſt with knowledge, knowing that they doe wrong againſt their owne conſcience, and the te- | Hebr.6.10. ſtimonie of the holy Spirit, hauing once had a taſte of the ſweetnes of Gods mercies : Now in the firſt of theſe two, all ſorts of Necromancers, Enchanters or Witches, are comprehended, but in the laſt; none but ſuch as erre with this knowledge that I haue ſpoken of.

P h i. Then it appeares that there are more ſorts nor one, that are directly profeſſours of his ſeruice : and if ſo be, I pray you tell me how many and what are they?

E p i. There are principally two ſorts, whereunto all the parts of that vnhappy Art are redacted; whereof the one is called *Magie* or *Necromancie*, the other *Sorcerie* or *Witch-craft.*

P h i. What I pray you? and how many are the meanes, whereby the diuell allures perſons in any of theſe ſnares?

I   E p i.

EPI. Euen by thefe three paffions that are within our felues : Curiofitie in great ingines : thirft of reuenge, for fome tortes deepely apprehended, or greedy appetite of geare, caufed through great pouertie. As to the firft of thefe, Curiofitie, it is onely the inticement of *Magicians* or *Necromanciers* : and the other two are the allurers of the *Sorcerers* or *Witches* ; for that old and craftie ferpent being a Spirit, he eafily fpies our affections, and fo conformes himfelfe thereto, to deceiue vs to our wracke.

CHAP. III. ARGV.

The fignifications and etymologies of the words of Magie *and* Necromancie. *The difference betwixt* Necromancie *and* Witchcraft : *What are the entreßis, and beginnings, that bring any to the knowledge thereof.*

PHILOMATHES.

 Would gladly firft heare, what thing it is that ye call *Magie* or *Necromancie*.

EPI. This word *Magi* in the Perfian tongue, imports as much as to be a contemplatour or Interpretour of Diuine and heauenly fciences, which being firft vfed among the *Chaldees*, through their ignorance of the true diuinitie, was efteemed and reputed amongft them, as a principall vertue : And therfore, was named vniuftly with an honourable ftile, which name the *Greekes* imitated, generally importing all thefe kindes of vnlawfull artes : And this word *Necromancie* is a Greeke word, compounded of Νεκρος and φαντεια, which is to fay, the prophecie by the dead. This laft name is giuen, to this blacke and vnlawfull fcience, by the figure *Synecdoche*, becaufe it is a principall part of that arte, to ferue themfelues with dead carcafes in their diuinations.

PHI. What difference is there betwixt this arte, and Witch-craft ?

EPI. Surely, the difference vulgare put betwixt them, is very merry, and in a maner true ; for they fay, that the Witches are feruants onely, and flaues to the diuel ; but the Necromanciers are his Mafters and commanders.

PHI. How can that be true, that any men being fpecially addicted to his feruice, can be his commanders ?

EPI. Yea they may be ; but it is onely *fecundum quid* : For it is not by any power that they can haue ouer him, but *ex pacto* allanerlie ; whereby he obliges himfelfe in fome trifles to them, that he may on the other part obteine the fruition of their body and foule, which is the onely thing he huntes for.

PHI. A very in-æquitable contract forfooth : But I pray you difcourfe vnto me, what is the effect and fecrets of that arte.

EPI. That is an ouer large field ye giue me : yet I fhall doe my goodwill, the moft fummarly that I can, to runne through the principall points thereof. As there are two forts of folkes, that may be entifed to this art, *to wit,*

wit, learned or vnlearned : so is there two meanes, which are the first stee-
rers vp and feeders of their curiositie, thereby to make them to giue themselues ouer to the same : Which two meanes, I call the diuels schoole, and
his rudiments. The learned haue their curiositie wakened vp, and fed by
that which I cal his schole : this is the *Astrologie* iudiciar, For diuers men hauing attained to a great perfection in learning, and yet remayning ouer-
bare (alas) of the Spirit of regeneration and fruits thereof, finding all naturall things common, aswell to the stupide pedants, as vnto them, they assay to vendicate vnto them a greater name, by not onely knowing the
course of things heauenly, but likewise to clime to the knowledge of things
to come thereby: Which, at the first face appearing lawfull vnto them, in
respect the ground thereof seemeth to proceed of naturall causes onely,
they are so allured thereby, that finding their practise to proue trew in sundry things, they study to know the cause thereof, and so mounting from
degree to degree, vpon the slipperie and vncertaine scale of curiositie; they
are at last entised, that where lawfull artes or sciences faile, to satisfie their
restlesse minds, euen to seeke to that blacke and vnlawfull science of *Magie*:
Where, finding at the first, that such diuers formes of circles and coniurations rightly ioyned thereunto, will raise such diuers formes of spirits, to
resolue them of their doubts, and attributing the doing thereof, to the
power inseparably tied, or inherent in the circles, and many wordes of
God, confusedly wrapped in; they blindly glory of themselues, as if they
had by their quicknesse of ingine, made a conquest of *Plutoes* dominion,
and were become Emperours ouer the *Stygian* habitacles: Where, in the
meane time (miserable wretches) they are become in very deed, bond-
slaues to their mortall enemie : and their knowledge, for all that they presume thereof, is nothing increased, except in knowing euill, and the hor-
rors of hell for punishment thereof, as *Adams* was by the eating of the
forbidden tree.

Gene.3.

Chap. IIII. Argv.

The description of the rudiments and Schoole, which are the entresses to the arte of
Magie : And in speciall the differences betwixt Astronomie *and* Astrolo-
gie: Diuision of Astrologie *in diuers parts.*

Philomathes.

Vt I pray you likewise forget not to tell what are the diuels rudiments.

E pi. His rudiments, I call first in generall, all that
which is called vulgarly the vertue of word, herbe, and
stone, which is vsed by vnlawfull charmes, without naturall causes ; as likewise all kinde of practicques, freites,
or other like extraordinary actions, which cannot abide the trew touch of
naturall reason.

Phi. I would haue you to make that plainer, by some particular examples; for your propofition is very generall.

Ep i. I meane either by fuch kinde of Charmes as commonly daft
wiues vfe, for healing of forfpoken goods, for preferuing them from euill
eyes, by knitting roun trees, or fundrieft kinde of hearbes, to the haire or
tailes of the goods : by curing the worme, by ftemming of blood, by healing of Horfe-crookes, by turning of the riddle, or doing of fuch like innumerable things by words, without applying any thing, meete to the part
offended, as Mediciners doe : Or elfe by flaying married folkes, to haue
naturally adoe with other (by knitting fo many knots vpon a point at the
time of their marriage,) And fuch like things, which men vfe to practife in
their merrineffe : For fra vnlearned men (being naturally curious, and
lacking the trew knowledge of God) finde thefe practifes to proue trew, as
fundrie of them will doe, by the power of the diuell for deceiuing men,
and not by any inherent vertue in thefe vaine words and freites; and being
defirous to winne a reputation to themfelues in fuch like turnes, they either (if they be of the fhamefafter fort) feeke to be learned by fome that
are experimented in that Arte, (not knowing it to be euill at the firft) or
elfe being of the groffer fort, runne directly to the diuel for ambition or
defire of gaine, and plainely contract with him thereupon.

Phi. But me thinkes thefe meanes which ye call the Schoole and
rudiments of the diuel, are things lawfull, and haue bene approoued for
fuch in all times and aages : as in fpeciall, this fcience of *Aftrologie*, which is
one of the fpeciall members of the *Mathematiques*.

Ep i. There are two things which the learned haue obferued from the
beginning, in the fcience of the heauenly Creatures, the Planets, Starres,
and fuch like : The one is their courfe and ordinarie motions, which for
that caufe is called *Aftronomia*, Which word is a compound of ἡμας and ἀςιφη, that
is to fay, the law of the Starres : And this Art indeed is one of the members
of the *Mathematiques*, and not onely lawfull, but moft neceffary and commendable: The other is called *Aftrologia*, being compounded of ἀςιφη and λόγε,
which is to fay, the word and preaching of the Starres : Which is diuided
into two parts : The firft, by knowing thereby the powers of fimples, and
fickneffes, the courfe of the feafons and the weather, being ruled by their
influence; which part depending vpon the former, although it bee not of
it felfe a part of *Mathematiques*: yet it is not vnlawfull, being moderately v-
fed, fuppofe not fo neceffarie and commendable as the former. The fecond part is to truft fo much to their influences, as thereby to foretell what
common-weales fhall flourifh or decay : what perfons fhall be fortunate or
vnfortunate : what fide fhall winne in any battell : what man fhal obtaine
victorie at fingular combate : what way, and of what aage fhall men die :
what horfe fhall winne at match-running : and diuers fuch like incredible
things, wherein *Cardanus, Cornelius Agrippa*, and diuers others haue more
curioufly then profitably written at large. Of this roote laft fpoken of,

springs innumerable branches;ſuch as the knowledge by the natiuities; the *Cheiromancie*, *Geomancie*, *Hydromancie*, *Arithmancie*, *Phyſiognomie*, and a thouſand others, which were much practiſed, and holden in great reue-rence by the Gentiles of old: And this laſt part of *Aſtrologie* whereof I haue ſpoken,which is the root of their branches,was called by them *pars fortunæ*. This part now is vtterly vnlawfull to be truſted in, or practiſed amongſt Chriſtians, as leaning to no ground of naturall reaſon : and it is this part which I called before the Diuels ſchoole.

P _H I. But yet many of the learned are of the contrarie opinion.

E P I. I grant,yet I could giue my reaſons to fortifie and maintaine my opinion, if to enter into this diſputation it would not draw me quite off the ground of our diſcourſe, beſides the miſ-ſpending of the whole day thereupon · One word onely I will anſwere to them,and that in the Scrip-tures (which muſt be an infallible ground to all true Chriſtians,) That in the Prophet *Ieremie* it is plainely forbidden, to beleeue or hearken vnto them that propheſie and fore-ſpeake by the courſe of the Planets and Stars.

C H A P. V. A R G V.

How farre the vſing of Charmes is lawfull or vnlawfull. The deſcription of the formes of Circles and Coniurations. And what cauſeth the Magicians *them-ſelues to be wearie thereof.*

P H I L O M A T H E S.

E L, ye haue ſaid farre inough in that argument. But how prooue yee now that theſe Charmes or vnnaturall pra-ctiques are vnlawfull · For ſo many honeſt and merry men and women haue publikely practiſed ſome of them, that I think if ye would accuſe them all of Witch-craft, ye would affirme more nor ye will be beleeued in.

E P I. I ſee if you had taken good tent(to the nature of that word,wher-by I named it,) ye would not haue beene in this doubt, nor miſtaken mee ſo farre as ye haue done : For although, as none can be ſcholers in a ſchoole, and not be ſubiect to the maſter thereof: ſo none can ſtudie and put in pra-ctiſe (for ſtudie the alone, and knowledge,is more perillous nor offenſiue; and it is the practiſe onely that makes the greatneſſe of the offence;) the Circles and Art of *Magie*, without committing an horrible defection from God : And yet as they that reade and learne their rudiments, are not the more ſubiect to any ſchoole-maſter, if it pleaſe not their parents to put them to the ſchoole thereafter : So they who ignorantly prooue theſe pra-ctiques, which I call the Diuels rudiments, vnknowing them to be baits, caſt out by him, for trapping ſuch as God will permit to fall into his hands, this kinde of folkes I ſay, no doubt, are to be iudged the beſt of, in reſpect they vſe no inuocation nor helpe of him (by their knowledge at leaſt) in

I 3 theſe

these turnes, and so haue neuer entred themselues into Satans seruice; Yet
to speake trewly for mine owne part (I speake but for my selfe) I desire not
to make so neere riding : For in my opinion our enemie is ouer craftie, and
wee ouer weake (except the greater grace of God) to assay such hazards,
wherein he preases to trap vs.

PHI. Ye haue reason forsooth : for as the common prouerbe sayth;
They that sup keile with the deuill, haue need of long spoones : But now I
pray you goe forward in the describing of this arte of *Magie.*

EPI. Fra they become once vnto this perfection in euill, in hauing any
knowledge (whether learned or vnlearned) of this blacke arte; they then
begin to be wearie of the raising of their Maister, by coniured circles, being both so difficile and perillous, and so come plainely to a contract with
him, wherein is specially contained formes and effects.

PHI. But I pray you or euer you goe further, discourse me somewhat of
their circles and coniurations; and what should be the cause of their wearying thereof: For it should seeme that that forme should be lesse fearefull
yet, then the direct haunting and societie, with that foule and vncleane
Spirite.

EPI. I thinke yee take me to be a Witch my selfe, or at the least would
faine sweare your selfe prentise to that craft: Alwayes as I may, I shal shortly satisfie you, in that kinde of coniurations, which are contained in such
bookes, which I call the Deuils Schoole: There are foure principall parts:
the persons of the coniurers ; the action of the coniuration ; the words and
rites vsed to that effect ; and the Spirits that are coniured. Ye must first remember to lay the ground, that I tolde you before, which is , that it is no
power inherent in the circles, or in the holinesse of the names of God blas-
phemously vsed; nor in whatsoeuer rites or ceremonies at that time vsed,
that either can raise any infernall spirit, or yet limitate him perforce within or without these circles. For it is he onely, the father of all lies, who hauing first of all prescribed that forme of doing, feining himselfe to be
commanded and restrained thereby, will be loth to passe the boundes of
these iniunctions ; as wel thereby to make them glory in the impiring ouer
him (as I said before:) as likewise to make himselfe so to be trusted in these
little things, that he may haue the better commoditie thereafter, to deceiue
them in the end with a tricke once for all ; I meane the euerlasting perdition of their soule and body. Then laying this ground, as I haue said, these
coniurations must haue fewe or moe in number of the persons coniurers
(alwayes passing the singular number) according to the qualitie of the circle, and forme of apparition. Two principall things cannot well in that
errand be wanted : holy-water (whereby the deuill mockes the *Papists)*
and some present of a liuing thing vnto him. There are likewise certaine
seasons, dayes and houres, that they obserue in this purpose : These things
being all ready and prepared, circles are made triangular, quadrangular,
round, double or single, according to the forme of apparition that they
craue.

craue. But to fpeake of the diuers formes of the circles, of the innumerable charaƈters and croffes that are within and without, and out-through the fame, of the diuers formes of apparitions, that that craftie fpirit illudes them with, and of all fuch particulars in that aƈtion, I remit it to ouermany that haue bufied their heads in defcribing of the fame ; as being but curious, and altogether vnprofitable. And this farre onely I touch, that when the coniured Spirit appeares, which will not be while after many circumftances, long prayers, and much muttring and murmuring of the coniurers ; like a *Papift* Prieft, difpatching a hunting *Maffe* : how foone I fay, he appeares, if they haue miffed one iote of all their rites ; or if any of their feet once flyde ouer the circle through terrour of his fearefull apparition, hee payes himfelfe at that time in his owne hand, of that due debt which they ought him ; and otherwife would haue delayed longer to haue payed him : I meane, hee carries them with him body and foule. If this be not now a iuft caufe to make them weary of thefe formes of coniuration, I leaue it to you to iudge vpon ; confidering the long fomneffe of the labour, the precife keeping of dayes and houres (as I haue faid) the terribleneffe of apparition, and the prefent perill that they ftand in, in miffing the leaft circumftance or freite, that they ought to obferue : And on the other part, the deuill is glad to mooue them to a plaine and fquare dealing with him, as I faid before.

CHAP. VI. ARGV.

The Deuils contraƈt with the Magicians : *The diuifion thereof in two parts : What is the difference betwixt Gods miracles and the Deuils.*

PHILOMATHES.

Ndeed there is caufe enough, but rather to leaue him at all, then to runne more plainely to him, if they were wife hee dealt with : But goe forward now, I pray you, to thefe turnes, fra they become once deacons in this craft.

EPI. From time that they once plainely begin to contraƈt with him : The effeƈt of their contraƈt confifts in two things : in formes and effeƈts, as I began to tell already, were it not ye interrupted me: (for although the contraƈt be mutual; I fpeake firft of that part, wherein the diuel obliges himfelfe to them) By formes, I meane in what fhape or fafhion he fhall come vnto them, when they call vpon him ; And by effeƈts, I vnderftand, in what fpeciall forts or feruices he binds himfelfe to bee fubieƈt vnto them. The qualitie of thefe formes and effeƈts, is leffe or greater, according to the skill and art of the *Magician* : For as to the formes, to fome of the bafer fort of them he obliges himfelfe to appeare at their calling vpon him, by fuch a proper name which he fhewes vnto them, either in likenes of a Dog, a Cat, an Ape, or fuch-like other beaft ; or elfe to anfwere by a

voice

voice onely. The effects, are to anfwere to fuch demands, as concerne curing of difeafes, their owne particular menagerie, or fuch other bafe things
as they require of him. But to the moft curious fort, in the formes hee will
oblige himfelfe, to enter into a dead bodie, and there out of to giue fuch
anfweres, of the euent of battels, of matters concerning the eftate of commonwealths, and fuch like other great queftions : yea, to fome he will bee
a continuall attender, in forme of a Page: Hee will permit himfelfe to bee
coniured, for the fpace of fo many yeeres, either in a tablet or a ring, or fuch
like thing, which they may eafily cary about with them : Hee giues them
power to fell fuch wares to others, whereof fome will be dearer, and fome
better cheape, according to the lying or true fpeaking of the Spirit that is
coniured therein : Not but that in very deed, all deuils muft be lyars ; but
fo they abufe the fimplicitie of thefe wretches, that become their fcholers,
that they make them beleeue, that at the fall of *Lucifer*, fome Spirits fell in
the aire, fome in the fire, fome in the water, fome in the land, in which E-
lements they ftill remaine. Whereupon they build, that fuch as fell in the
fire, or in the aire, are trewer then they, who fell in the water, or in the
land, which are all but meere trattles, and forged by the authour of
all deceite. For they fell not by weight, as a folide fubftance, to fticke
in any one part; but the principall part of their fall, confifting in quality, by the falling from the grace of God, wherein they were created, they
continued ftil thereafter, and fhall doe while the latter day, in wandring
through the world, as Gods hang-men, to execute fuch turnes as hee
employes them in : And when any of them are not occupied in that, returne they muft to their prifon in hell (as it is plaine in the miracle that
Matth.8. CHRIST wrought at *Gennezareth*) therein at the latter day to be all en-
clofed for euer : and as they deceiue their Schollers in this, fo doe they, in
imprinting in them the opinion, that there are fo many Princes, Dukes,
and Kings amongft them, euery one commanding fewer or moe Legions,
and impiring in diuers artes, and quarters of the earth : For though that I
will not deny that there be a forme of order amongft the Angels in Heauen, and confequently, was amongft them before their fall ; yet, either that
they bruike the fame fenfine ; or that God will permit vs to know by damned diuels, fuch heauenly myfteries of his, which he would not reueale to
vs, neither by Scripture nor Prophets, I thinke no Chriftian will once
thinke it. But by the contrary of all fuch myfteries, as he hath clofed vp
with his Seale of fecrecie ; it becommeth vs to be contented with an
humble ignorance, they being things not neceffary for our faluation. But
to returne to the purpofe, as thefe formes, wherein Satan obliges himfelfe
to the greateft of the *Magicians*, are wonderfull curious ; fo are the effects
correfpondent vnto the fame : For he will oblige himfelfe to teach them
artes and fciences, which he may eafily doe, being fo learned a knaue as he
is, to carry them newes from any part of the world, which the agilitie of
a Spirit may eafily performe : to reueale to them the fecrets of any perfons,

fo

so being they be once spoken, for the thought none knowes but G O D; except so farre as ye may ghesse by their countenance, as one who is doubtlesly learned enough in the *Physiognomie* : Yea, hee will make his Schollers to creepe in credite with Princes, by fore-telling them many great things; part true, part false : For if all were false, hee would tyne credite at all handes; but alwayes doubtsome, as his Oracles were. And he will also make them to please Princes, by faire banquets and daintie dishes, carried in short space fra the farthest part of the world : For no man doubts but he is a thiefe, and his agilitie (as I spake before) makes him to come with such speed. Such like, he wil guard his Schollers with faire armies of horsemen and footmen in appearance, Castles and forts, Which all are but impressions in the aire, easily gathered by a Spirit, drawing so neere to that substance himselfe : As in like maner he will learne them many Iuglarie trickes at Cardes, dice, and such like, to deceiue mens senses thereby, and such innumerable false practiques, which are proued by ouer-many in this aage; as they who are acquainted with that *Italian* called SCOTO. yet liuing, can report : And yet are all these things but deluding of the senses, and no wayes true in substance; as were the false miracles wrought by King *Pharaos* Magicians, for counterfeiting *Moyses* : For that is the difference betwixt G O D s miracles and the diuels, G O D is a creatour, what he makes appeare in myracle, it is so in effect : As *Moyses* Rod being casten downe, was no doubt turned into a naturall Serpent : where as the diuel (as Gods Ape) counterfetting that by his *Magicians*, made their wandes to appeare so, onely to mens outward senses : as kythed in effect by their being deuoured by the other; For it is no wonder, that the diuel may delude our senses, since we see by common proofe, that simple Iugglars wil make an hundreth things seeme both to our eyes and eares otherwayes then they are. Now as to the *Magicians* part of the contract, it is in a word that thing which I said before, the diuel hunts for in all men.

P H I. Surely ye haue said much to mee in this art, if all that you haue said be as trew as wonderfull.

E P I. For the trewth in these actions, it wil be easily confirmed, to any that pleases to take paine vpon the reading of diuers authenticke histories, and the enquiring of daily experiences. And as for the trewth of their possibilitie, that they may be, and in what maner, I trust I haue alledged nothing whereunto I haue not ioyned such probable reasons, as I leaue to your discretion, to weigh and consider : One word onely I omitted, concerning the forme of making of this contract, which is either written with the *Magicians* owne blood : or else being agreed vpon (in termes his scholemaster) touches him in some part, though peraduenture no marke remain, as it doeth with all Witches.

CHAP.

Chap. VII. Arg.

The reason why the art of Magie *is vnlawfull: What punishment they merit,*
And who may be accounted guilty of that crime.

Philomathes.

Vrely, ye haue made this art to appeare very monstrous and
deteftable. But what I pray you fhal be faid to fuch as maintaine this arte to bee lawfull, for as euill as you haue
made it?

Ep 1. I fay, they fauour of the panne themfelues, or at
leaft little better ; and yet I would be glad to heare their reafons.

Phi. There are two principally, that euer I heard vfed ; befide that
which is founded vpon the common Prouerbe (that the *Necromancers*
command the deuill, which ye haue already refuted.) The one is grounded
vpon a receiued cuftome: The other vpon an authoritie, which fome think
infallible. Vpon cuftome, we fee that diuerfe Chriftian Princes and Magiftrates feuere punifhers of Witches, will not onely ouer-fee *Magicians* to
liue within their dominions ; but euen fometimes delight to fee them
prooue fome of their practicques. The other reafon is, that *Moyfes* beeing
brought vp (as it is exprefly faid in the Scriptures) *in all the fciences of the E-*
gyptians; whereof no doubt, this was one of the principals ; and hee notwithftanding of this art, pleafing God, as he did, confequently that art profeffed by fo godly a man, could not be vnlawfull.

Ep 1. As to the firft of your reafons, grounded vpon cuftome: I fay, an
euill cuftome can neuer be accepted for a good law , for the ouer great ignorance of the word in fome Princes and Magiftrates , and the contempt
thereof in others, mooues them to finne heauily againft their office in that
point. As to the other reafon, which feemes to be of greater weight, if it
were formed in a Syllogifme ; it behooued to be in many termes, and full of
fallacies (to fpeake in termes of *Logicque:*) for firft, that that generall propofition, affirming *Moyfes* to be taught *in all the fciences of the Egyptians*, fhould
conclude that he was taught in *Magie,* I fee no neceffitie: For we muft vnderftand, that the Spirit of God there, fpeaking of fciences, vnderftands
them that are lawfull ; for except they be lawfull, they are but *abufiuè* called
fciences, and are but ignorances, indeed : *Nam homo pictus, non est homo.* Secondly, giuing that he had beene taught in it, there is great difference betwixt knowledge and practifing of a thing, as I faid before: For God knoweth all things, being alwaies good, and of our finne and our infirmitie proceedeth our ignorance. Thirdly, giuing that he had both ftudied and practifed the fame (which is more then monftrous to bee beleeued by any
Chriftian) yet we know well inough , that before that euer the Spirit of
God began to call *Moyfes,* he was fled out of Egypt, being fourtie yeeres of
aage, for the flaughter of an Egyptian, and in his good father *Iethroes* land,

firft

firſt called at the fierie buſh, hauing remained there other fourtie yeeres in exile: ſo that ſuppoſe hee had beene the wickeddeſt man in the world before, he then became a changed and regenerate man, and very little of olde *Moyſes* remained in him. *Abraham* was an Idolater in *Vr* of *Chaldæa*, before he was called: And *Paul* beeing called *Saul*, was a moſt ſharpe perſecutour of the Saints of God, while that name was changed.

P H I. What puniſhment then thinke ye merit theſe *Magicians* and *Necromancers*?

E P I. The like no doubt, that *Sorcerers* and *Witches* merit; and rather ſo much greater, as their errour proceeds of the greater knowledge, and ſo drawes neerer to the ſinne againſt the holy Ghoſt. And as I ſay of them, ſo ſay I the like of all ſuch as conſult, enquire, entertaine, and ouerſee them, which is ſeene by the miſerable ends of many that aske counſell of them: For the deuill hath neuer better tidings to tell to any, then hee told to *Saul*: neither is it lawfull to vſe ſo vnlawful inſtruments, were it neuer for ſo good a purpoſe: For that axiome in Theologie is moſt certaine and infallible, *Nunquam faciendum eſt malum, vt bonum inde eueniat.*

Actes 3.

THE

THE SECOND·BOOKE
OF DÆMONOLOGIE.

ARGVMENT.
*The defcription of Sorcerie and Witchcraft
in ſpeciall.*

CHAP. I. ARGVMENT.
*Proued by the Scripture, that ſuch a thing can be: And the reaſons refuted of all
ſuch as would call it but an imagination and Melancholicque humour.*

PHILOMATHES.

OW, ſince ye haue ſatisfied mee now ſo fully,
concerning *Magie* or *Necromancie*, I wil pray you
to doe the like in *Sorcerie* or *Witchcraft*.

E P I. That field is likewiſe very large, and
although in the mouthes and pennes of many,
yet few knowe the trewth thereof, ſo well as
they beleeue themſelues, as I ſhall ſo ſhortly as I
can, make you (God willing) as eaſily to perceiue.

PH I. But I pray you before ye goe further,
let mee interrupt you here with a ſhort digreſ-
ſion, which is, that many can ſcarcely beleeue that there is ſuch a thing
as *Witchcraft* : Whoſe reaſons I will ſhortly alleage vnto you, that yee
may ſatisfie mee as well in that, as yee haue done in the reſt. For firſt,
whereas the Scripture ſeemes to prooue *Witchcraft* to bee, by diuers examples, and ſpecially by ſundrie of the ſame, which ye haue alleaged ; it is
thought by ſome, that theſe places ſpeake of *Magicians* and *Necromancers*
onely, and not of *Witches* : As in ſpeciall, theſe wiſe men of *Pharaohs*, that
counterfeited *Moyſes* myracles, were *Magicians* ſay they, and not *Witches* : As
likewiſe that *Pythoniſſe* that *Saul* conſulted with : And ſo was *Simon Magus*
in the new Teſtament, as that very ſtile imports. Secondly, where ye would
oppone the dayly practicque, and confeſſion of ſo many, that is thought
likewiſe to be but very Melancholicque imaginations of ſimple rauing
creatures. Thirdly, if *Witches* had ſuch power of Witching of folkes to
death, (as they ſay they haue) there had bene none left aliue long ſince in
the world but they ; at the leaſt, no good or godly perſon of whatſoeuer
eſtate, could haue eſcaped their diuelrie.

E P I.

, E P I. Your three reasons, as I take, are grounded: the first of them *nega-tiue* vpon the Scripture: The second *affirmatiue* vpó Phisick: And the third vpon the certaine proofe of experience. As to your first, it is most trew indeede, that all these wise men of *Pharaoh* were *Magicians* of arte: As like-wise it appeares well, that the *Pythonisse*, with whom *Saul* consulted, was of that same profession: and so was *Simon Magus*. But ye omitted to speake of the Lawe of God, wherein are all *Magicians*, Diuiners, Enchanters, Sorcerers, Witches, and whatsoeuer of that kind that consult with the de-uill, plainely prohibited, and alike threatned against. And besides that, she who had the Spirit of *Python*, in the Actes, whose Spirit was put to silence by the Apostle, could be no other thing but a very Sorcerer or Witch, if ye admit the vulgar distinction, to be in a maner trew, whereof I spake in the beginning of our conference: For that spirit whereby she conquested such gaine to her Masters, was not at her raising or commanding, as shee pleased to appoint, but spake by her tongue, as well publikely as priuately: where-by she seemed to draw nearer to the sort of *Demoniakes* or possessed, if that coniunction betwixt them, had not beene of her owne consent; as it ap-peared by her, not being tormented therewith, and by her conquesting of such gaine to her Masters (as I haue alreadie said.) As to your second reason grounded vpon Physicke, in attributing their confessions or appre-hensions, to a naturall melancholique humour, any that please physically to consider vpon the naturall humour of melancholly, according to all the Physicians, that euer writ thereupon, they shall find that that will be ouer-short a cloake to couer their knauery with: For as the humour of Melan-cholly in the selfe is blacke, heauie and terrene, so are the symptomes there-of, in any persons that are subiect thereunto, leannesse, palenesse, desire of solitude; and if they come to the highest degree thereof, meere folly and *Manie*: whereas by the contrary, a great number of them that euer haue beene conuict or confessours of Witchcraft, as may be presently seene by many that haue at this time confessed; they are by the contrary, I say, some of them rich and worldly wise, some of them fat or corpulent in their bo-dies, and most part of them altogether giuen ouer to the pleasures of the flesh, continuall haunting of companie, and all kinde of merrinesse, both lawfull and vnlawful, which are things directly contrary to the symptomes of melancholly, whereof I spake; and further experience daily prooues, how loth they are to confesse without torture, which witnesseth their guiltinesse; whereby the contrary, the Melancholiques neuer spare to be-wray themselues, by their continuall discourses, feeding thereby their hu-mor in that which they thinke no crime. As to your third reason, it scarse-ly merits an answere: for if the deuill their master were not bridled, as the Scriptures teach vs, suppose there were no men nor women to bee his instruments, he could finde wayes enough without any helpe of others to wracke all mankinde; whereunto he employes his whole study, and *goeth about like a roaring Lyon* (as *Peter* sayth) to that effect, but the limits of his

Acts 16.

K　　　　　　　　　　power

power were fet downe before the foundations of the world were laide, which he hath not power in the leaſt iote to tranſgreſſe. But beſide all this, there is ouer great a certaintie to prooue that they are, by the daily experience of the harmes that they doe, both to men, and whatſoeuer thing men poſſeſſe, whom God will permit them to be the inſtruments, ſo to trouble or viſite, as in my diſcourſe of that arte, ye ſhall heare clearely prooued.

The Etymologie and ſignification of that word Sorcerie : *The firſt entreſſe and prentiſhip of them that giue themſelues to that craft.*

PHILOMATHES.

Ome on then I pray you, and returne where ye left.

EPI. This word of *Sorcerie* is a Latine word, which is taken from caſting of the lot, and therefore he that vſeth it, is called *Sortiarius à ſorte* : As to the word of *Witchcraft*, it is nothing but a proper name giuen in our language : The cauſe wherefore they were called *Sortiarij*, proceeded of their practiques, ſeeming to come of lot or chance, ſuch as the turning of the riddle, the knowing of the forme of prayers, or ſuch like tokens, if a perſon diſeaſed would liue or die : And in generall, that name was giuen them for vſing of ſuch charmes, and freits, as that Craft teacheth them. Many points of their craft and practicques are common betwixt the *Magicians* and them : for they ſerue both one Maſter, although in diuers faſhions. And as I deuided the *Necromancers* into two ſortes, learned and vnlearned; ſo muſt I deny them in other two, rich and of better accompt; poore and of baſer degree. Theſe two degrees now of perſons, that practiſe this Craft, anſwere to the paſſions in them, which (I tolde you before) the Diuell vſed as meanes to entice them to his ſeruice : for ſuch of them as are in great miſerie and pouertie, he allures to follow him, by promiſing vnto them great riches, and worldly commoditie: Such as though rich, yet burne in a deſperate deſire of reuenge, he allures them by promiſes, to get their turne ſatisfied to their hearts contentment. It is to be noted now, that that olde and craftie enemie of ours, aſſailes none, though touched with any of theſe two extremities, except he firſt finde an entreſſe ready for him, either by the great ignorance of the perſon he deales with, ioyned with an euill life, or elſe by their careleſneſſe and contempt of God : And finding them in an vtter deſpaire, for one of theſe two former cauſes that I haue ſpoken of, he prepares the way by feeding them craftely in their humour, and filling them further and further with deſpaire, while hee finde the time proper to diſcouer himſelfe vnto them : At which time, either vpon their walking ſolitarie in the fieldes, or elſe lying panſing in their bed; but alwaies without the company of any other, hee either by a voyce, or in likeneſſe
of

of a man inquires of them, what troubles them, and promiseth them, a
suddaine and certaine way of remedie, vpon condition on the other part,
that they follow his aduise, and doe such things as he will require of them:
Their mindes being prepared before-hand, as I haue alreadie spoken, they
easily agreed vnto that demand of his, and syne sets an other tryist, where
they may meete againe: At which time, before hee proceede any further
with them, hee first perswades them to addict themselues to his seruice,
which being easily obtained, he then discouers what he is vnto them, makes
them to renounce their God and Baptisme directly, and giues them his
marke vpon some secret place of their bodie, which remaines soare vnhea-
led, while his next meeting with them, and thereafter euer insensible, howsoeuer it be nipped or pricked by any, as is daily prooued, to giue them a
proofe thereby, that as in that doing, he could hurt and heale them; so all
their ill and well doing thereafter, must depend vpon him: And besides
that, the intolerable dolour that they feele in that place, where he hath marked them, serues to waken them, and not to let them rest, while their next
meeting againe: fearing lest otherwaies they might either forget him, being as new Prentises, and not well enough founded yet, in that fiendly fol-
lie: or else remembring of that horrible promise they made him at their last
meeting, they might skunner at the same, and preasse to call it backe. At
their third meeting, he makes a shew to be carefull to performe his promises, either by teaching them waies how to get themselues reuenged, if they
be of that sort: or else by teaching them lessons, how by most vile and vnlawfull meanes, they may obtaine gaine, and wordly commoditie, if they
be of the other sort.

CHAP. III. ARGV.

The Witches *actions diuided into two parts: The actions proper to their owne
perfons: Their actions toward others: The forme of their conuentions, and a-
doring of their Mafter.*

PHILOMATHES.

Ee haue said now enough of their initiating in that order, It
rests then that yee discourse vpon their practises, fra they be
passed Prentises: for I would faine heare what is possible to
them to performe in very deed. Although they serue a common Master with the *Necromancers*, (as I haue before said)
yet serue they him in another forme: For as the meanes are diuers, which
allure them to these vnlawful Arts of seruing the deuill; so by diuers waies
vse they their practises, answering to these meanes, which first the deuill
vsed as instruments in them, though all tending to one end, *to wit,* the en-
larging of Satans tyrannie, and crossing of the propagation of the Kingdome of CHRIST, so farre as lyeth in the possibilitie, either of the one or

other fort, or of the deuill their mafter: For where the _Magicians_, as allured by curiofitie; in the moft part of their practifes, feeke principally the fatif-fying of the fame, and to winne to themfelues a popular honour and efti-mation; thefe Witches on the other part, being inticed, either for the defire of reuenge, or of worldly riches, their whole practifes are either to hurt men and their goods, or what they poffeffe, for fatisfying of their cruell mindes in the former, or elfe by the wracke in whatfoeuer fort, of any whom God will permit them to haue power of, to fatisfie their greedie defire in the laft point.

E p i. In two parts their actions may be diuided; the actions of their owne perfons, and the actions proceeding from them towards any other: And this diuifion being well vnderftood, will eafily refolue you, what is poffible to them to doe: For although all that they confeffe is no lie vp-on their part, yet doubtlefly, in my opinion, a part of it is not indeede, ac-cording as they take it to be: And in this I meane by the actions of their owne perfons: For as I faid before, fpeaking of _Magie_, that the diuell il-ludes the fenfes of thefe fchollers of his, in many things, fo fay I the like of thefe Witches.

P h i. Then I pray you firft to fpeake of that part of their owne per-fons, and fyne ye may come next to their actions towards others.

E p i. To the effect that they may performe fuch feruices of their falfe Mafter, as he employes them in, the deuill as Gods Ape, counterfeits in his feruants this feruice and forme of adoration, that God prefcribed and made his feruants to practife: For as the feruants of God publikely vfe to con-veene for feruing of him, fo makes he them in great numbers to conveene (though publikely they dare not) for his feruice. As none conveenes to the adoration and worfhipping of God, except they be marked with his Seale, the Sacrament of Baptifme: So none ferues Satan, and conveenes to the a-doring of him, that are not marked with that marke, whereof I alreadie fpake. As the Minifter fent by God teacheth plainely at the time of their publike conuentions, how to ferue him in fpirit and trewth; fo that vnclean fpirit, in his owne perfon teacheth his difciples at the time of their conuee-ning, how to worke all kind of mifchiefe, and craues coumpt of all their horrible and deteftable proceedings paffed, for aduancement of his feruice: Yea that hee may the more viuely counterfeit and fcorne God, he oft times makes his flaues to conueene in thefe very places, which are deftinate and ordained for the conveening of the feruants of God (I meane by Churches) But this farre, which I haue yet faid, I not onely take it to be trew in their opinions, but euen fo to be indeed: For the forme that he vfed in counter-faiting God amongft the Gentiles, makes me fo to thinke: As God fpake by his Oracles, fpake he not fo by his? As God had afwell bloodie Sacrifices, as others without blood, had not he the like? As God had Churches fan-ctified to his feruice, with Altars, Priefts, Sacrifices, Ceremonies and Pray-ers; had he not the like polluted to his feruice? As God gaue refponfes by

Vrim

Vrim and _Thummim,_ gaue he not his refponfes by the intralles of beafts, by the finging of fowles, and by their actions in the aire? As God by vifions, dreames, and extafies reuealed what was to come, and what was his will vnto his feruants; vfed hee not the like meanes to forewarne his flaues of things to come? Yea euen as God loued cleaneneffe, hated vice and impuritie, and appointed punifhments therefore; vfed he not the like (though falfly I grant, and but in efchewing the leffe inconuenience, to draw them vpon a greater) yet diffimuled he not, I fay, fo farre as to appoint his priefts to keepe their bodies cleane and vndefiled, before their asking refponfes of him? And fained he not God, to be a protectour of euery vertue, and a iuft reuenger of the contrarie? This reafon then mooues mee, that as he is that fame diuell, and as crafty now as he was then, fo will he not fpare as pertly in thefe actions that I haue fpoken of, concerning the Witches perfons: but further, Witches oft times confeffe, not only his conueening in the Church with them, but his occupying of the Pulpit; Yea, their forme of adoration, to be the kiffing of his hinder parts: Which though it feeme ridiculous, yet may it likewife be trew, feeing we reade that in _Calicute,_ he appearing in forme of a Goat-bucke, hath publikely that vn-honeft homage done vnto him, by euery one of the people: So ambitious is he, and greedy of honour (which procured his fall) that he will euen imitate God in that part, where it is faid, that _Moyfes_ could fee but the _hinder parts of God, for the brightneffe of his glory_ : And yet that fpeech is fpoken but ἀνθρωπαθῶς. | Exod. 33.

CHAP. IIII. ARGV.

What are the wayes poffible, whereby the Witches may tranfport themfelues to places farre diftant : And what are impoffible and meere illufions of Satan : And the reafons thereof.

PHILOMATHES.

Vt by what way fay they, or thinke yee it poffible they can come to thefe vnlawfull conuentions?

EPI. There is the thing which I efteeme their fenfes to be deluded in, and though they lie not in confeffing of it, becaufe they thinke it to be trew, yet not to be fo in fubftance or effect : for they fay, that by diuers meanes they may conueene, either to the adoring of their Mafter, or to the putting in practife any feruice of his, committed vnto their charge : one way is naturall, which is naturall riding, going, or failing, at what houre their mafter comes and aduertifes them : and this way may be eafily beleeued : another way is fome-what more ftrange, and yet it is poffible to bee trew: which is, by being caried by the force of the fpirit which is their conducter, either aboue the earth, or aboue the Sea fwiftly, to the place where they are to meete : which I am perfwaded to bee likewife poffible, in refpect that as _Habakkuk_ was carried by the Angel in that forme, to the den where _Daniel_ lay ; fo thinke I, the diuell will be readie to imitate God,

as

Apocrypha of Bel and the Dragon.

as well in that as in other things : which is much more poſſible to him to doe, being a Spirit, then to a mighty wind, being but a naturall Meteore, to tranſport from one place to another, a ſolide body, as is commonly and daily ſeene in practiſe : But in this violent forme they cannot be caried, but a ſhort bounds, agreeing with the ſpace that they may retaine their breath : for if it were longer, their breath could not remaine vnextinguiſhed, their body being caried in ſuch a violent and forcible maner; as by example : If one fall off a ſmall height, his life is but in perill, according to the hard or ſoft lighting : but if one fall from an high and ſtay rocke, his breath will be forcibly baniſhed from the body, before he can win to the earth, as is oft ſeene by experience : And in this tranſporting they ſay themſelues, that they are inuiſible to any other, except amongſt themſelues, which may alſo be poſſible in my opinion : For if the deuill may forme what kinde of impreſſions he pleaſes in the aire, (as I haue ſaid be ore, ſpeaking of *Magie*) why may hee not farre eaſilier thicken and obſcure ſo the aire, that is next about them, by contracting it ſtraite together, that the beames of any o-ther mans eyes cannot pierce thorow the ſame, to ſee them ? But the third way of their comming to their conuentions, is that, wherein I thinke them deluded : for ſome of them ſay, that being transformed in the likeneſſe of a little beaſt or foule, they will come and pierce through whatſoeuer houſe or Church, though all ordinarie paſſages be cloſed, by whatſoeuer open the aire may enter in at : And ſome ſay, that their bodies lying ſtill, as in an extaſie, their ſpirits will be rauiſhed out of their bodies, and caried to ſuch places; and for verifying thereof, will giue euident tokens, as well by witneſſes that haue ſeene their body lying ſenceleſſe in the meane time, as by naming perſons whom-with they met, and giuing tokens what pur-poſe was amongſt them, whom otherwiſe they could not haue knowen : for this forme of iourneying, they affirme to vſe moſt, when they are tranſ-ported from one countrey to another.

     P H I.   Surely I long to heare your owne opinion of this : for they are like old wiues trattles about the fire. The reaſons that mooue me to thinke that theſe are meere illuſions, are theſe : Firſt, for them that are transformed in likeneſſe of beaſts or foules, can enter through ſo narrow paſſages, al-though I may eaſily beleeue that the diuell could by his workmanſhip vp-on the aire, make them appeare to be in ſuch formes, either to themſelues, or to others : yet how he can contract a ſolide body within ſo little roome, I thinke it is directly contrary to it ſelfe ; for to be made ſo little, and yet not diminiſhed ; to be ſo ſtraitly drawen together, and yet feele no paine, I thinke it is ſo contrary to the qualitie of a naturall bodie, and ſo like to the little tranſubſtantiate god in the Papiſts Maſſe, that I can neuer beleeue it : So to haue a quantitie, is ſo proper to a ſolide body, that as all Philoſo-phers conclude, it cannot be any more without one, then a ſpirit can haue

Acts 12.

one : For, when *Peter* came out of the priſon, and the doores all locked ; it was not by any cotracting of his body in ſo little roome, but by the giuing

place

place of the doore, though vnefpied by the Gaylors : And yet is there no comparifon, when this is done, betwixt the power of God, and of the diuel. As to their forme of extafie and fpirituall tranfporting, it is certaine the foules going out of the body, is the onely definition of naturall death : and who are once dead, God forbid we fhould thinke that it fhould lie in the power of all the diuels in hell, to reftore them to their life againe; although he can put his owne fpirit in a dead body, which the *Necromancers* commonly practife, as ye haue heard : For that is the office properly belonging to God; and befides that, the foule once parting from the body, cannot wander any longer in the world, but to the owne refting place muft it goe immediately, abiding the coniunction of the body againe, at the latter day. And what Chrift or the Prophets did miraculoufly in this cafe , it can in no Chriftian mans opinion, be made common with the diuel. As for any tokens that they giue for prouing of this, it is very poffible to the diuels craft, to perfwade them to thefe meanes : for he being a fpirit, may he not fo rauifh their thoughts, and dull their fenfes, that their body lying as dead, he may obiect to their fpirits, as it were in a dreame, and (as the Poets write of *Morpheus*) reprefent fuch formes of perfons, of places, and other circumftances, as he pleafes to illude them with ? Yea, that he may deceiue them with the greater efficacie ; may he not at that fame inftant by fellow angels of his, illude fuch other perfons fo in that fame fafhion, whom-with hee makes them to beleeue that they mette; that all their reports and tokens, though feuerally examined, may euery one agree with another ? And that whatfoeuer actions, either in hurting men or beafts, or whatfoeuer other thing that they falfly imagine, at that time to haue done, may by himfelfe or his marrowes, at that fame time be done indeed ; fo as if they would giue for a token of their being rauifhed at the death of fuch a perfon within fo fhort fpace thereafter, whom they beleeue to haue poifoned, or witched at that inftant, might he not at that fame houre; haue fmitten that fame perfon, by the permiffion of G o D, to the farther deceiuing of them, and to mooue others to beleeue them ? And this is furely the likelyeft way, and moft according to reafon, which my iudgement can finde out in this, and whatfoeuer other vnnaturall points of their confeffion : And by thefe meanes fhall we faile furely , betwixt *Charybdis* and *Scylla*, in efchewing the not beleeuing of them altogether on the one part, left that draw vs to the errour, that there is no *Witches* : and on the other part in beleeuing of it, make vs to efchew the falling into innumerable abfurdities, both monftroufly againft all Theologie diuine, and Philofophie humane.

.CHAP.

Chap. V. Argv.

Witches actions towards others: Why there are more women of that craft then
men: What things are possible to them to effectuate by the power of their ma-
ster: The reasons thereof: What is the surest remedy of the harmes done by them.

Philomathes.

 Orsooth your opinion in this, seemes to cary most reason with it; and since ye haue ended then the actions belonging properly to their owne persons, say forward now to their actions vsed towards others.

E p i. In their actions vsed towards others, three things ought to be considered: First, the maner of their consulting thereupon: Next, their part as instruments: And last, their masters part, who puts the same in execution. As to their consultations thereupon, they vse them oftest in the Churches, where they conueene for adoring, at what time their master enquiring at them what they would be at, euery one of them propones vnto him, what wicked turne they would haue done, either for obtaining of riches, or for reuenging them vpon any whom they haue malice at; who granting their demaund, as no doubt willingly he will, since it is to doe euill, hee teacheth them the meanes whereby they may doe the same: As for little trifling turnes that women haue adoe with, he causeth them to ioynt dead corpses, and to make powders thereof, mixing such other things there amongst, as he giues vnto them.

P h i. But before ye goe further, permit me, I pray you, to interrupt you one word, which ye haue put me in memorie of, by speaking of Women; What can be the cause that there are twentie women giuen to that craft, where there is one man?

E p i. The reason is easie, for as that sexe is frailer then man is, so is it easier to be intrapped in these grosse snares of the diuell, as was ouer-well prooued to be trew, by the Serpents deceiuing of *Eua* at the beginning, which makes him the homelier with that sexe sensine.

P h i. Returne now where ye left.

E p i. To some others at these times he teacheth, how to make pictures of waxe or clay, that by the roasting thereof, the persons that they beare the name of, may be continually melted or dried away by continuall sickenesse: To some he giues such stones or pouders, as will helpe to cure or cast on diseases: And to some hee teacheth kindes of vncouth poysons, which Mediciners vnderstand not (for he is farre cunninger then man, in the knowledge of all the occult proprieties of nature) not that any of these meanes which he teacheth them (except the poysons which are composed of things naturall,) can of themselues helpe any thing to these turnes, that they are employed in, but onely being G o d s ape, as well in that, as in all other things; Euen as God by his Sacraments which are earthly of themselues, felues, workes a heauenly effect, though no wayes by any cooperation in them: And as Chrift by clay and fpettle wrought together, *opened the eyes of* | Iohn 9. *the blinde man*, fuppofe there was no vertue in that which he outwardly ap-plied, fo the diuel will haue his outward meanes to be fhewes as it were of his doing, which hath no part or cooperation in his turnes with him, how farre that euer the ignorants be abufed in the contrarie. And as to the ef-fects of thefe two former parts; *to wit*, the confultations and the outward meanes, they are fo wonderfull, as I dare not alleadge any of them, without ioyning a fufficient reafon of the poffibilitie thereof; For leauing all the fmall trifles among wiues, and to fpeake of the principall points of their craft, for the common trifles thereof, they can doe without conuerting well enough by themfelues, thefe principall points, I fay, are thefe; They can make men or women to loue or hate other, which may be very pof-fible to the diuel to effectuate, feeing he being a fubtile fpirit, knowes well enough how to perfwade the corrupted affection of them whom God wil permit him fo to deale with: They can lay the fickneffe of one vpon an-other, which likewife is very poffible vnto him: For fince by Gods per-miffion, he laide fickneffe vpon *Iob*, why may he not farre eafilier lay it vpon any other; For as an old practitian, hee knowes well enough what humour domines moft in any of vs, and as a fpirit he can fubtillie waken vp the fame, making it peccant, or to abound; as hee thinkes meet for trou-bling of vs, when God will fo permit him: And for the taking off of it, no doubt he will be glad to relieue fuch of prefent paine, as he may thinke by thefe meanes to perfwade to be catched in his euerlafting fnares and fet-ters. They can bewitch and take the life of men or women, by roafting of the Pictures, as I fpake of before, which likewife is verie poffible to their mafter to performe: for although (as I faid before) that inftrument of waxe haue no vertue in that turne doing, yet may he not very well, euen by the fame meafure, that his coniured flaues melts that waxe at the fire, may hee not, I fay, at thefe fame times, fubtily, as a fpirit, fo weaken and fcatter the fpirits of life of the patient, as may make him on the one part, for faintneffe, to fweat out the humour of his bodie, and on the other part, for the not concurrence of thefe fpirits, which caufes his digeftion, fo debilitate his ftomacke, that this humour radicall continually, fweating out on the one part, and no new good fucke being put in the place thereof, for lacke of di-geftion on the other, he at laft fhall vanifh away, euen as his picture will doe at the fire? And that knauifh and cunning workeman, by troubling him, onely at fometimes, makes a proportion, fo neere betwixt the work-ing of the one and the other, that both fhall end as it were at one time. They can raife ftormes and tempefts in the aire, either vpon Sea or land, though not vniuerfally, but in fuch a particular place and prefcribed bounds, as GOD will permit them fo to trouble: Which likewife is very eafie to be difcerned from any other naturall tempefts that are Meteores, in refpect of the fudden and violent raifing thereof, together with the

fhort

Ephef.2.

fhort induring of the fame. And this is likewife very poffible to their mafter to doe, hee hauing fuch affinitie with the aire,as being a fpirit,and hauing fuch power of the forming and moouing thereof, as yee haue heard
me alreadie declare : For in the Scripture,that ftile of *the Prince of the aire*,
is giuen vnto him. They can make folkes to become Phrenticque or Ma-
niacque, which likewife is very poffible to their mafter to doe, fince they
are but naturall ficknefles : and fo he may lay on thefe kindes,as well as any
others. They can make fpirits, either to follow and trouble perfons, or
haunt certaine houfes, and affray oftentimes the inhabitants, as hath bene
knowne to bee done by our *Witches* at this time. And likewife they can
make fome to bee poffeffed with fpirits, and fo to become very Dæmoniacques: and this laft fort is very poffible likewife to the diuel their mafter
to doe,fince he may eafily fend his owne angels to trouble in what forme
he pleafes,any whom God will permit him fo to vfe.

P H I.   But will God permit thefe wicked inftruments by the power of
the deuill their mafter, to trouble by any of thefe meanes, any that beleeue
in him?

E P I.   No doubt,for there are three kindes of folkes whom God will
permit fo to be tempted or troubled; the wicked for their horrible finnes,
to punifh them in the like meafure ; the godly that are fleeping in any great
finnes or infirmities,and weaknefle in faith; to waken them vp the fafter
by fuch an vncouth forme: and euen fome of the beft, that their patience
may be tried before the world,as *Iobs* was : For why may not God vfe any
kinde of extraordinary punifhment,when it pleafes him ; as well as the ordinarie rods of ficknefle or other aduerfities?

P H I.   Who then may be free from thefe deuilifh practifes? . .

E P I.   No man ought to prefume fo farre as to promife any impunitie
to himfelfe : for God hath before all beginnings, præordinated, as well the
particular forts of plagues, as of benefites for euery man, which in the
owne time he ordaines them to be vifited with, and yet ought we not to be
the more afraide for that, of any thing that the diuell and his wicked inftruments can doe againft vs : for we daily fight againft the diuell in a hundreth other wayes : And therefore, as a valiant captaine affraies no more
being at the combate, nor ftayes from his purpofe for the rummifhing
fhot of a Canon, nor the fmall clacke of a Piftolet , fuppofe he be not certaine what may light vpon him ; Euen fo ought we boldly to goe forward
in fighting againft the diuell without any greater terrour, for thefe his ra-
reft weapons,nor for the ordinary whereof we haue daily the proofe.

P H I.   Is it not lawfull then, by the helpe of fome other Witch, to cure
the difeafe that is caften on by that craft?

E P I.   No wayes lawfull ; for I gaue you the reafon thereof in that axiome of Theologie, which was the laft words I fpake of *Magie*.

P H I.   How then may thefe difeafes be lawfully cured?

E P I.   Only by earneft prayer vnto God, by amendment of their liues,

and

and by sharpe pursuing euery one, according to his calling of these instruments of Satan, whose punishment to the death will be a salutarie sacrifice
for the patient. And this is not onely the lawfull way, but likewise the
most sure: For by the deuils meanes, *can neuer the deuill be casten out,* as Christ   Marke 3.
sayth. And when such a cure is vsed, it may well serue for a short time, but
at the last, it will doubtlesly tend to the vtter perdition of the patient, both
in body and soule.

CHAP. VI. ARGV.

What sort of folkes are least or most subiect to receiue harme by Witchcraft : What
power they haue to harme the Magistrate, and vpon what respects they haue any
power in prison : And to what end may or will the deuill appeare to them therein :
Vpon what respects the deuill appeares in sundry shapes to sundry of them at
any time.

PHILOMATHES.

Vt who dare take vpon him to punish them, if no man can
be sure to be free from their vnnaturall inuasions?

EPI. Wee ought not the more of that restraine from
vertue, that the way wherby we clime thereunto be straight
and perillous: But besides that, as there is no kinde of persons so subiect to receiue harme of them, as these that are of infirme and
weake faith (which is the best buckler against such inuasions :) so haue
they so small power ouer none, as ouer such as zealously and earnestly pursue them, without sparing for any wordly respect.

PHI. Then they are like the Pest, which smites these sickarest, that
flies it farthest, and apprehends deepliest the perill thereof.

EPI. It is euen so with them: for neither is it able to them to vse any
false cure vpon a patient, except the patient first beleeue in their power,
and so hazard the tinsell of his owne soule, nor yet can they haue lesse power to hurt any, nor such as contemne most their doings, so being it comes
of faith, and not of any vaine arrogancie in themselues.

PHI. But what is their power against the Magistrate?

EPI. Lesse or greater, according as he deales with them : for if hee be
slothfull towards them, God is very able to make them instruments to waken and punish his slouth: but if he be the contrary, hee according to the
iust Law of God, and allowable law of all nations, will be diligent in examining and punishing of them : God will not permit their master to trouble or hinder so good a worke.

PHI. But fra they be once in hands and firmance, haue they any further power in their craft?

EPI. That is according to the forme of their detention : If they be
but apprehended and deteined by any priuate person, vpon other priuate
respects, their power no doubt either in escaping, or in doing hurt, is no
lesse

lesse nor euer it `as before : But if on the other part, their apprehending and detention be by the lawfull Magistrate, vpon the iust respects of their guiltinesse in that craft, their power is then no greater then before that e-uer they medled with their master : For where God begins iustly to strike by his lawfull Lieutenants, it is not in the deuils power to defraud or be-reaue him of the office, or effect of his powerfull and reuenging Scepter.

PHI. But will neuer their Master come to visite them, fra they be once apprehended and put in firmance ?

EPI. That is according to the estate that these miserable wretches are in : For if they be obstinate in still denying, he will not spare, when hee findes time to speake with them, either if he finde them in any comfort, to fill them more and more with the vaine hope of some manner of reliefe ; or else if he finde them in a deepe despaire, by all meanes to augment the same, and to perswade them by some extraordinarie meanes to put them-selues downe, which very commonly they doe : But if they bee penitent and confesse, God will not permit him to trouble them any more with his presence and allurements.

PHI. It is not good vsing his counsell I see then : But I would earnest-ly know when he appeares to them in prison, what formes vses hee then to take?

EPI. Diuers formes, euen as hee vses to doe at other times vnto them : For as I told you, speaking of *Magie,* he appeares to that kind of craftes-men ordinarily in a forme, according as they agree vpon it among themselues ; Or if they be but prentises, according to the qualitie of their circles or con-iurations : Yet to these capped creatures, he appeares as hee pleases, and as he findes meetest for their humors : For euen at their publicke conuenti-ons, hee appeares to diuers of them in diuers formes, as we haue found by the difference of their confessions in that point : For he deluding them with vaine impressions in the aire, makes himselfe to seeme more terrible to the grosser sort, that they may thereby be mooued to feare and reuerence him the more : and lesse monstrous and vncouth like againe to the craftier sort, lest otherwise they might sturre and skunner at his vglinesse.

PHI. How can he then be felt ; as they confesse they haue done him, if his body be but of aire ?

EPI. I heare little of that amongst their confessions, yet may hee make himselfe palpable, either by assuming any dead bodie, and vsing the mini-sterie thereof, or else by deluding as well their sence of feeling as seeing ; which is not impossible to him to doe, since all our senses, as wee are so weake, and euen by ordinarie sicknesses will be oftentimes deluded.

PHI. But I would speere one word further yet, concerning his appea-ring to them in prison, which is this : May any other that chances to be pre-sent at that time in the prison, see him as well as they ?

EPI. Sometimes they will, and sometimes not, as it pleases God.

CHAP.

CHAP. VII. ARG.

*Two formes of the diuels visible conuersing in the earth, with the reasons where-
fore the one of them was commonest in the time of* Papistrie, *and the other
sensine. Those that deny the power of the diuell, denie the power of God, and are
guilty of the errour of the* Sadduces.

PHILOMATHES.

Ath the Diuell then power to appeare to any other, except
to such as are his sworne disciples; especially since all Oracles, and such like kinds of illusions were taken away and
abolished by the comming of CHRIST?

EPI. Although it be true indeede, that the brightnesse
of the Gospel at his comming, scaled the cloudes of all these grosse errours
in the Gentilisme; yet that these abusing spirits, cease not sensine at sometimes to appeare, daily experience teaches vs. Indeed this difference is to be
marked betwixt the formes of Satans conuersing visibly in the world: For
of two different formes thereof, the one of them by the spreading of the
Euangel, and conquest of the white horse, in the sixt Chapter of the Reuelation, is much hindred and become rather there-through: This his appearing to any Christians, troubling of them outwardly, or possessing of them
constrainedly: The other of them is become commoner and more vsed
sensine, I meane by their vnlawfull artes, whereupon our whole purpose
hath beene. This wee finde by experience in this Isle to be true: For as wee
know, moe ghosts and spirits were seene, nor tongue can tell, in the time of
blind *Papistrie* in these countries, where now by the contrarie, a man shall
scarcely all his time heare once of such things; and yet were these vnlawful
artes farre rarer at that time, and neuer were so much heard of, nor so rife
as they are now.

PHI. What should be the cause of that?

EPI. The diuers nature of our sinnes procures at the Iustice of God,
diuers sorts of punishments answering thereunto: and therefore as in the
time of *Papistrie*, our fathers erring grossely, and through ignorance, that
mist of errours ouershadowed the Diuell to walke the more familiarly a-
mongst them; and as it were by barnely and affraying terrours, to mocke
and accuse their barnely errours; by the contrarie, we now being found of
Religion, and in our life rebelling to our profession, God iustly by that
sinne of rebellion, as *Samuel* calleth it, accuseth our life so wilfully fighting
against our profession.

PHI. Since ye are entred now to speake of the appearing of spirits, I
would be glad to heare your opinion in that matter: for many denie that
any such spirits can appeare in these daies, as I haue said.

EPI Doubtlesse who denieth the power of the Diuell, would like-
L   wise

wife denie the power of God , if they could for fhame. For fince the Diuel is the very contrarie oppofite to God, there can bee no better way to know God, then by the contrarie; as by the ones power (though a creature) to admire the power of the great Creatour : by the falfhood of the one to con-fider the trewth of the other : by the iniuftice of the one, to confider the Iu-ftice of the other : And by the cruelty of the one, to confider the merciful-neffe of the other : And fo foorth in all the reft of the effence of God, and qualities of the Diuell. But I feare indeed, there bee ouer many *Sadduces* in this world, that denie all kindes of Spirits : For conuicting of whofe errour, there is caufe inough if there were no more, that God fhould permit at fometimes Spirits vifibly to kyith.

THE

THE THIRD BOOKE
OF DÆMONOLOGIE.

ARGVMENT.

The defcription of all thefe kinds of Spirits that trouble men
or women. The conclufion of the whole Dialogue.

CHAP. I. ARGV.

The diuifion of Spirits in foure principall kindes : The defcription of the firft kinde
of them, called Spectra *&* vmbræ mortuorum : *What is the beft way to*
be free of their trouble.

PHILOMATHES.

Pray you now then goe forward in telling what
ye thinke fabulous, or may be trowed in that cafe.

EPI. That kind of the diuels couerfing in the
earth, may be diuided in foure different kindes,
whereby he affraieth and troubleth the bodies of
men : For of the abufing of the foule, I haue fpoken alreadie. The firft is, where fpirits trouble
fome houfes or folitarie places : The fecond,
where Spirits follow vpon certaine perfons,
and at diuers houres trouble them : The third, when they enter within
them, and poffeffe them : The fourth is thefe kinde of Spirits that are called vulgarly the *Fairie* : Of the three former kinds, ye heard already, how
they may artificially be made by *Witchcraft* to trouble folke ; now it reftes
to fpeake of their naturall comming as it were, and not raifed by *Witch-*
craft. But generally I muft forewarne you of one thing before I enter in
this purpofe : that is, that although in my difcourfing of them, I deuide
them in diuers kinds, ye muft notwithftanding thereof note my phrafe of
fpeaking in that : For doubtleffie they are in effect, but all one kinde of Spirits, who for abufing the more of mankinde, take on thefe fundrie fhapes,
and vfe diuers formes of outward actions, as if fome were of nature better
then other. Now I returne to my purpofe : As to the firft kinde of thefe
fpirits, that were called by the ancients by diuers names, according as their
actions were: For if they were Spirits that haunted fome houfes, by appearing in diuers and horrible formes, and making great dinne, they were

L 2 called

called **Lemures** or *Speƈtra*: If they appeared in likeneſſe of any defunƈt to ſome friends of his, they were called *vmbræ mortuorum*: And ſo innumerable ſtiles they got, according to their aƈtions, as I haue ſaid alreadie; as we ſee by experience, how many ſtiles they haue giuen them in our language in the like maner. Of the appearing of theſe Spirits, we are certified by the Scriptures, where the Prophet *Eſay* 13.and 34.Chap.threatning the deſtruƈtion of *Ieruſalem*, declares, that it ſhall not onely be wracked, but ſhall become ſo great a ſolitude, as it ſhall be the habitacle of Howlets, and of *Zijm* and *Ijm*, which are the proper Hebrew names for theſe Spirits. The cauſe why they haunt ſollitarie places, it is by reaſon, that they may affray and brangle the more the faith of ſuch as them alone hauntes ſuch places: For our nature is ſuch, as in companies we are not ſo ſoone moued to any ſuch kind of feare, as being ſollitarie, which the diuel knowing well enough, he will not therefore aſſaile vs but when wee are weake: And beſides that, God will not permit him ſo to diſhonour the ſocieties and companies of Chriſtians, as in publicque times and places to walke viſiblie amongſt them: On the other part, when he troubles certaine houſes that are dwelt in, it is a ſure token either of groſſe ignorance, or of ſome groſſe and ſlanderous ſinnes amongſt the inhabitants thereof, which God by that extraordinarie rod puniſhes.

Eſay 13.
lere.50.

P H I. But by what way or paſſage can theſe Spirits enter into theſe houſes, ſeeing they alledge that they will enter, doore and window being ſteiked?

E P I. They will chooſe the paſſage for their entreſſe, according to the forme that they are in at that time: For if they haue aſſumed a dead bodie, whereinto they lodge themſelues, they can eaſily enough open without dinne any doore or window, and enter in thereat; And if they enter as a Spirit onely, any place where the aire may come in at, is large enough an entrie for them: For as I ſaid before, a Spirit can occupie no quantitie.

P H I. And will God then permit theſe wicked Spirits to trouble the reſt of a dead bodie, before the reſurreƈtion thereof? Or if hee will ſo, I thinke it ſhould be of the reprobate onely.

E P I. What more is the reſt troubled of a dead bodie, when the diuell caries it out of the graue to ſerue his turne for a ſpace, nor when the **Witches** take it vp and ioynts it, or when as Swine wortes vp the graues? The reſt of them that the Scripture ſpeakes of, is not meaned by a locall remaining continually in one place, but by their reſting from their trauailes and miſeries of this world, while their latter coniunƈtion againe with the ſoule at that time; to receiue full glorie in both: And that the diuel may vſe as well the miniſtrie of the bodies of the faithfull in theſe caſes, as of the vnfaithfull, there is no inconuenience; for his haunting with their bodies after they are dead, can no-waies defile them, in reſpeƈt of the ſoules abſence: And for any diſhonour it can be vnto them, by what reaſon can it be greater, then the hanging, heading, or many ſuch ſhamefull deaths, that good men

men

men will suffer? For there is nothing in the bodies of the faithfull, more worthie of honour, or freer from corruption by nature, nor in these of the vnfaithfull, while time they be purged and glorified in the *latter Day*; as is daily seene by the vilde diseases and corruptions, that the bodies of the faithfull are subiect vnto, as ye will see clearely proued, when I speake of the possessed and Dæmoniacques.

PHI. Yet there are sundry that affirme to haue haunted such places, where these spirits are alledged to be; and could neuer heare nor see any thing.

EPI. I thinke well: for that is onely reserued to the secret knowledge of God, whom he will permit to see such things, and whom not.

PHI. But where these spirits haunt and trouble any houses, what is the best way to banish them?

EPI. By two meanes may onely the remeid of such things be procured: The one is ardent prayer to God, both of these persons that are troubled with them, and of that Church whereof they are: The other is the purging of themselues by amendment of life, from such sinnes, as haue procured that extraordinarie plague.

PHI. And what meane then these kindes of spirits, when they appeare in the shadow of a person newly dead, or to die, to his friends?

EPI. When they appeare vpon that occasion, they are called Wraithes in our language: Amongst the *Gentiles* the diuell vsed that much, to make them beleeue that it was some good spirit that appeared to them then, either to forewarne them of the death of their friend, or else to discouer vnto them the will of the defunct, or what was the way of his slaughter, as it is written in the booke of the histories prodigious: and this way he easily deceiued the *Gentiles*, because they knew not God: and to that same effect is it, that he now appeares in that maner to some ignorant Christians: for hee dares not so illude any that knoweth that, neither can the spirit of the defunct returne to his friend, or yet an Angel vse such formes.

PHI. And are not our war-woolfes one sort of these spirits also, that haunt and trouble some houses or dwelling places?

EPI. There hath indeede beene an olde opinion of such like things; for by the *Greekes* they were called λυκανθρωποι, which signifieth men-wolfes: But to tell you simply my opinion in this, if any such thing hath beene, I take it to haue proceeded but of a naturall super-abundance of Melancholy, which as we reade, that it hath made some thinke themselues pitchers, and some horses, and some one kinde of beast or other, so suppose I that it hath so viciat the imagination and memory of some, as *per lucida interualla*, it hath so highly occupied them, that they haue thought themselues very Woolfes indeed at these times: and so haue counterfeited their actions in going on their hands and feete, preassing to deuoure women and barnes, fighting and snatching with all the towne dogges, and in vsing such like other brutish actions, and so to become beasts by a strong apprehension, as

L 3 *Nebu-*

Daniel 4. *Nebuchad-nezzar* was feuen yeeres: but as to their hauing and hiding of their hard and fchelly fluiches, I take that to be but eiked, by vncertaine report, the author of all lies.

Chap. II. Argv.

The defcription of the next two kindes of Spirits, whereof the one followes outward-
ly, the other poffeffes inwardly the perfons that they trouble: That fince all prophe-
cies and vifions are now ceafed, all fpirits that appeare in thefe formes are euill.

Philomathes.

COme forward now to the reft of thefe kinds of fpirits.

Ep i. As to the next two kindes, that is, either thefe that outwardly trouble and follow fome perfons, or elfe in-wardly poffefle them, I wil conioine them in one, becaufe as well the caufes are alike in the perfons that they are permit-ted to trouble; as alfo the wayes whereby they may be remedied and cured.

Phi. What kinde of perfons are they that vfe to be fo troubled?

Ep i. Two kindes in fpeciall; either fuch as being guiltie of grieuous offences, God punifhes by that horrible kinde of fcourge; or elfe being perfons of the beft nature peraduenture, that ye fhall finde in all the coun-trey about them, God permits them to be troubled in that fort, for the triall of their patience, and wakening vp of their zeale, for admonifhing of the beholders, not to truft ouer-much in themfelues, fince they are made of no better ftuffe, and peraduenture blotted with no fmaller finnes (as Chrift Luke 13. faid, fpeaking of them vpon whom the Tower of *Sylo* fell:) And for gi-uing likewife to the fpectators, matter to praife God, that they meriting no better, are yet fpared from being corrected in that fearefull forme.

Phi. Thefe are good reafons for the part of God, which apparantly mooues him fo to permit the Diuell to trouble fuch perfons: But fince the Diuell hath euer a contrarie refpect in all the actions that God imployes him in, which is I pray you the end and marke he fhootes at in this turne?

Ep i. It is to obtaine one of two things thereby, if he may: The one is the tinfell of their life, by inducing them to fuch perillous places, at fuch time as he either followes or poffefles them, which may procure the fame, and fuch like, fo farre as God will permit him, by tormenting them to weaken their bodie, and caft them into incurable difeafes: The other thing that he preaffes to obtaine by troubling of them, is the tinfell of their foule, by intifing them to miftruft & blafpheme God, either for the intolerable-Iob 1. neffe of their torments, as hee affayed to haue done with *Iob*; or elfe for his promifing vnto them to leaue the troubling of them, in cafe they would fo doe, as is knowen by experience at this fame time by the confeffion of a young one that was fo troubled.

Phi. Since ye haue fpoken now of both thefe kinds of fpirits compre-hending them in one, I muft now goe backe againe in fpeering fome queftions

ſtions of euery one of theſe kindes in ſpeciall. And firſt for theſe that follow certaine perſons, ye know that there are two ſorts of them : One ſorte
that trouble and torment the perſons that they haunt with : Another ſort
that are ſeruiceable vnto them in all kind of their neceſſaries, and omit neuer to forewarne them of any ſuddaine perill that they are to bee in : And
ſo in this caſe, I would vnderſtand whether both theſe ſorts be but wicked
and damned ſpirits, or if the laſt ſort be rather Angels, (as ſhould appeare
by their actions) ſent by God to aſſiſt ſuch as hee ſpecially fauours: For it is
written in the Scriptures, that *God ſends legions of Angels to guard and watch* Gene.32.
ouer his elect.   1.Kings 6.
                                                                                         Pſal.34.

E p i. I know well inough wherefra that errour which ye alledge hath
proceeded; For it was the ignorant Gentiles that were the fountaine thereof, Who for that they knew not God, they forged in their owne imaginations, euery man to be ſtil accompanied with two ſpirits, whereof they called the one *genius bonus*, the other *genius malus* : the Greekes called them
ευδαιμονα and κακοδαιμονα : whereof the former they ſaide, perſwaded him to all
the good hee did; the other entiſed him to all the euill. But praiſed bee
G o d, wee that are Chriſtians, and walke not amongſt the *Cymmerian*
coniectures of man, know well inough, that it is the good Spirit of
G o d onely, who is the fountaine of all goodneſſe, that perſwades vs to
the thinking or doing of any good, and that it is our corrupted fleſh
and Satan, that intiſeth vs to the contrarie: And yet the Diuell for confirming in the heades of ignorant Chriſtians, that errour firſt maintained a-
mong the Gentiles, he whiles among the firſt kind of ſpirits that I ſpeake
of, appeared in time of Papiſtrie and blindneſſe, and haunted diuers houſes, without doing any euill, but doing as it were neceſſarie turnes vp and
downe the houſe: and this ſpirit they called *Browniᵉ* in our language,
who appeared like a rough-man : yea, ſome were ſo blinded, as to beleeue
that their houſe was all their ſonſier, as they called it, that ſuch ſpirits re-
ſorted there.

P h i. But ſince the diuels intention in all his actions, is euer to doe e-
uill, what euill was there in that forme of doing, ſince their actions outwardly were good ?

E p i. Was it not euill inough to deceiue ſimple ignorants, in making
them to take him for an Angel of light, and ſo to account of Gods enemy
as of their particular friend ? where by the contrary, all we that are Chriſtians, ought aſſuredly to know, that ſince the comming of Chriſt in the fleſh,
and eſtabliſhing of his Church by the Apoſtles, al miracles, viſions, prophecies, & appearances of Angels or good ſpirits, are ceaſed; which ſerued only
for the firſt ſowing of faith, and planting of the Church : Where now the
Church being eſtabliſhed, and the white Horſe whereof I ſpake before, hauing made his conqueſt, the Law and Prophets are thought ſufficient to
ſerue vs, or make vs inexcuſable, as Chriſt ſaith in his parable of *Lazarus* and
the rich man.

C h a p.

Chap. III. Argv.

The defcription of a particular fort of that kinde of following Spirits, called Incubi *and* Succubi: *And what is the reafon wherefore thefe kinds of Spirits haunt moft the Northerne and barbarous parts of the world.*

PHILOMATHES.

He next queftion that I would fpeere, is likewife concerning this firft of thefe two kinds of Spirits that ye haue conioyned; and it is this: ye know how it is commonly written and reported, that amongft the reft of the forts of Spirits that follow certaine perfons, there is one more monftrous nor all the reft, in refpect as it is alleaged, they conuerfe naturally with them whom they trouble and haunt with: and therefore I would know in two things your opinion herein: Firft, if fuch a thing can be: and next if it be, whether there be a difference of fexes amongft thefe Spirits or not?

E p i. That abhominable kinde of the diuels abufing of men or women, was called of old, *Incubi* and *Succubi*, according to the difference of the fexes that they conuerfed with. By two meanes this great kinde of abufe might poffibly be performed: The one, when the diuel onely as a Spirit, and ftealing out the fperme of a dead bodie, abufes them that way, they not graithly feeing any fhape, or feeling any thing, but that which hee fo conueyes in that part; as we reade of a Monafterie of Nunnes which were burnt for their being that way abufed: The other meane is, when he borrowes a dead body and fo vifibly, and as it feemes vnto them naturally as a man conuerfes with them. But it is to be noted, that in whatfoeuer way he vfeth it, that fperme feemes intollerably cold to the perfon abufed: For if he fteale out the nature of a quicke perfon, it cannot be fo quickly caried, but it will both tine the ftrength and heate by the way, which it could neuer haue had for lacke of agitation, which in the time of procreation is the procurer and wakener vp of thefe two naturall qualities: And if he occupying the dead bodie as his lodging, expell the fame out thereof in the due time, it muft likewife be cold by the participation with the qualities of the dead body whereout of it comes. And whereas ye enquire if thefe Spirits be diuided in fexes or not, I thinke the rules of Philofophie may eafily refolue a man of the contrary: For it is a fure principle of that Art, that nothing can be diuided in fexes, except fuch liuing bodies as muft haue a naturall feed to genere by: But we know Spirits haue no feed proper to themfelues, nor yet can they gender one with an other.

P h i. How is it then, that they fay fundrie monfters haue bene gotten by that way?

E p i. Thefe tales are nothing but *Aniles fabulæ*: For that they haue no nature of their owne, I haue fhewed you alreadie: And that the cold nature

of

of a dead bodie, can worke nothing in generation, it is more nor plaine, as being alreadie dead of it selfe, as well as the rest of the bodie is, wanting the naturall heate, and such other naturall operation, as is necessarie for working that effect, and in case such a thing were possible (which were vtterly against all the rules of nature) it would breed no monster, but onely such a naturall off-spring, as would haue come betwixt that man or woman and that other abused person, in case they both being aliue had had a doe with other : For the Diuels part therein, is but the naked carrying or expelling of that substance; and so it could participate with no quality of the same. Indeede, it is possible to the craft of the Diuell to make a womans belly to swell after he hath that way abused her, which hee may doe either by stirring vp her owne humour, or by hearbes, as wee see beggers daily doe : And when the time of her deliuery should come to make her thoil great dolours, like vnto that naturall course, and then subtilly to slip in the Mid-wiues hands, stocks, stones, or some monstrous barne brought from some other place: but this is more reported and guessed at by others, nor beleeued by me.

PHI. But what is the cause that this kinde of abuse is thought to bee most common in such wilde parts of the world, as *Lap-land,* and *Fin-land,* or in our North Isles of *Orknay* and *Schet-land?*

EPI. Because where the Diuell findes greatest ignorance and barbaritie, there assailes he grosseliest, as I gaue you the reason wherfore there were moe Witches of women-kinde nor men.

PHI. Can any be so vnhappie as to giue their willing consent to the Diuels vile abusing them in this forme?

EPI. Yea, some of the Witches haue confessed, that he hath perswaded them to giue their willing consent thereunto, that hee may thereby haue them feltred the sikarer in his snares: but as the other compelled sort is to be pitied and prayed for, so is this most highly to be punished and detested.

PHI. Is it not the thing which we call the *Mare,* which takes folkes sleeping in their beds, a kinde of these spirits, whereof ye are speaking?

EPI. No, that is but a naturall sickenesse, which the Mediciners haue giuen that name of *Incubus* vnto, *ab incubando,* because it being a thicke fleume, falling into our breast vpon the heart, while we are sleeping, intercludes so our vitall spirits, and takes all power from vs, as makes vs think that there were some vnnaturall burden or spirit, lying vpon vs, and holding vs downe.

CHAP.

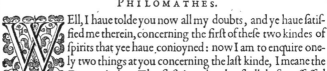

The defcription of the Dæmoniackes and poffeffed: By what reafon the Papifts
may haue power to cure them.

PHILOMATHES.

Ell, I haue tolde you now all my doubts, and ye haue fatif-
fied me therein, concerning the firft of thefe two kindes of
fpirits that yee haue conioyned: now I am to enquire onely two things at you concerning the laft kinde, I meane the
Dæmoniackes. The firft is, whereby fhall thefe poffeffed
folkes be difcerned fra them that are troubled with a naturall Phrenfie or
Manie: The next is, how can it be that they can be remedied by the Papifts
Church, whom we counting as Heretiques, it fhould appeare that one diuell fhould not caft out another, for then would *his kingdome be diuided in it*
felfe, as Chrift faid.

Matth.12.
Marke 3.

EPI. As to your firft queftion; there are diuers fymptomes, whereby
that heauie trouble may be difcerned from a naturall fickeneffe, and fpecially three, omitting the diuers vaine fignes that the Papifts attribute vnto
it: Such as the raging at holy water, their fleeing abacke from the Croffe,
their not abiding the hearing of God named, and innumerable fuch like
vaine things that were alike fafhious and feckles to recite: But to come to
thefe three fymptomes then, whereof I fpake, I account the one of them
to be the incredible ftrength of the poffeffed creature, which will farre exceede the ftrength of fixe of the wighteft and wodeft of any other men
that are not fo troubled: The next is the boldening vp fo farre of the patients breaft and belly, with fuch an vnnaturall fturring and vehement agitation within them, and fuch an ironie hardneffe of his finewes fo ftiffely
bended out, that it were not poffible to pricke out as it were the skinne of
any other perfon fo farre; fo mightily workes the diuell in all the members
and fenfes of his body, hee being locally within the fame, fuppofe of his
foule and affections thereof, hee haue no more power then of any other
mans: The laft is, the fpeaking of fundry languages, which the patient is
knowen, by them that were acquainted with him, neuer to haue learned,
and that with an vncouth and hollow voice, and all the time of his fpeaking, a greater motion being in his breaft then in his mouth: But fra this
laft fymptome is excepted fuch, as are altogether in the time of their poffef-
fing bereft of all their fenfes, being poffeffed with a dumbe and blind fpirit, whereof Chrift relieued one, in the 12. of *Matthew.* And as to your
next demand, it is firft to be doubted if the Papifts, or any not profeffing
the onely true Religion, can relieue any of that trouble: and next, in cafe
they can, vpon what refpect it is poffible vnto them. As to the former, vpon two reafons it is grounded: firft that it is knowen fo many of them to
be counterfeit, which wyle the Clergie inuents for confirming of their

rotten

rotten Religion : The next is, that by experience we finde, that few who are possessed indeed, are fully cured by them; but rather the diuell is content to releafe the bodily hurting of them, for a short space, thereby to obtaine the perpetuall hurt of the foules of so many that by thefe falfe miracles may be induced or confirmed in the profession of that erroneous Religion; euen as I told you before that he doeth in the falfe cures or cafting off of difeases by Witches. As to the other part of the argument in cafe they can, which rather (with reuerence of the learned thinking otherwife) I am induced to beleeue, by reafon of the faithfull report that men found of Religion, haue made according to their fight thereof, I thinke if so be I fay thefe may be the refpects, whereupon the Papifts may haue that power. Chrift gaue a commission and power to his Apoftles to caft out diuels, which they according thereunto put in execution : the rules he bade them obferue in that action, was fafting and prayer ; and the action it felfe to be done in his name. This power of theirs proceeded not then of any vertue in them, but onely in him who directed them ; as was clearely prooued by *Iudas* his hauing as great power in that commission, as any of the reft. It is eafie then to be vnderftood that the cafting out of diuels, is by the vertue of fafting and prayer, and in calling of the Name of God, fuppofe many imperfections be in the perfon that is the inftrument, as Chrift himfelfe teacheth vs of the power that falfe prophets fhall haue to caft out diuels. It is no wonder then, thefe refpects of this action being confidered, that it may be poffible to the Papifts, though erring in fundry points of Religion to accomplifh this, if they vfe the right forme preferibed by Chrift herein : For what the worfe is that action that they erre in other things; more then their Baptifme is the worfe that they erre in the other Sacrament, and haue eiked many vaine freittes to the Baptifme it felfe.

P H I. Surely it is no little wonder that God fhould permit the bodies of any of the faithfull to be fo difhonoured, as to be a dwelling place to that vncleane fpirit.

E P I. There is it which I told right now, would proue and ftrengthen my argument of the diuels entring into the dead bodies of the faithfull : For if he is permitted to enter into their liuing bodies, euen when they are ioyned with the foule; how much more will God permit him to enter into their dead carions, which is no more man, but the filthie and corruptible caife of man? For as Chrift faith, *It is not any thing that enters within man that defiles him, but onely that which proceedes and commeth out of him.*   Marke 7.

CHAP.

Chap. V. Argv.

The defcription of the fourth kinde of Spirits , called the Phairie : *What is poßible therein , and* what *is but illufions. How farre this Dialogue entreates of all thefe things, and to* what *end.*

Philomathes.

Ow I pray you come on to that fourth kinde of Spirits. Epi. That fourth kinde of Spirits, which by the Gentiles was called *Diana,* and her wandering court, and amongft vs was called the *Phairie* (as I told you) or our good neighbours, was one of the forts of illufions that was rifeft in the time of Papiftrie : for although it was holden odious to prophefie by the diuel, yet whom thefe kinde of Spirits caried away, and informed , they were thought to be fonfieft and of beft life. To fpeake of the many vaine trattles founded vpon that illufion, How there was a King and Queene of *Phairie* , of fuch a iolly court and traine as they had, how they had a teynd, and duetie, as it were, of all goods, how they naturally rode and went, eate and dranke, and did all other actions like naturall men and women, I thinke it liker *Virgils Campi Elyfij,* nor any thing that ought to be beleeued by Chriftians, except in generall, that as I fpake fundrie times before, the diuell illuded the fenfes of fundrie fimple creatures, in making them beleeue that they faw and heard fuch things as were nothing fo indeed.

Phi. But how can it be then , that fundrie *Witches* haue gone to death with that confeffion, that they haue bene tranfported with the *Phairie* to fuch a hill, which opening, they went in, and there faw a faire Queene, who being now lighter , gaue them a ftone that had fundrie vertues, which at fundrie times hath bene produced in iudgement?

Epi. I fay that, euen as I faid before of that imaginar rauifhing of the Spirit foorth of the bodie : For may not the diuel obiect to their fantafie, their fenfes being dulled, and as it were afleepe, fuch hilles and houfes within them, fuch gliftering courtes and traines, and whatfoeuer fuch like wherewith he pleafeth to delude them , and in the meane time their bo- dies being fenfeleffe, to conuey in their hand any ftone or fuch like thing, which he makes them to imagine to haue receiued in fuch a place.

Phi. But what fay ye to their foretelling the death of fundrie per- fons, whom they alleage to haue feene in thefe places ? that is, a footh- dreame (as they fay) fince they fee it walking.

Epi. I thinke that either they haue not bene fharpely enough exa- mined, that gaue fo blunt a reafon for their prophefie, or otherwife, I thinke it likewife as poffible that the diuel may prophefie to them when he de- ceiues their imaginations in that fort, as well as when hee plainely fpeakes vnto them at other times : for their prophefying, is but by a kind of vifion,

as

as it were,wherein he commonly counterfeites God among the Ethnicks, as I told you before.

PHI. I would know now whether thefe kinds of Spirits may onely appeare to *Witches*, or if they may alfo appeare to any other.

EPI. They may doe to both; to the innocent fort, either to affray them,or to feeme to be a better fort of folkes nor vncleane Spirits are ; and to the *Witches* to be a colour of fafetie for them, that ignorant Magiftrates may not punifh them for it,as I told euen now : But as the one fort,for being perforce troubled with them ought to be pitied, fo ought the other fort (who may be difcerned by their taking vpon them to prophefie by them,) that fort,I fay, ought as feuerely to be punifhed as any other *Witches*, and rather the more, that they goe diffemblingly to worke.

PHI. And what makes the fpirits haue fo different names from others ?

EPI. Euen the knauerie of that fame diuell ; who as he illudes the *Necromancers* with innumerable feined names for him and his angels,as in fpeciall, making *Satan*, *Beelzebub*, and *Lucifer*, to bee three fundry fpirits, where wee finde the two former, but diuers names giuen to the Prince of all the rebelling Angels by the Scripture ; as by Chrift, the Prince of all the diuels is called *Beelzebub* in that place, which I alleaged againft the power of any hereticque to caft out diuels. By *Iohn* in the Reuelation, the old tempter is called *Satan the Prince of all the euill Angels* : And the laft, to wit, *Lucifer*, is but by allegorie taken from *the day Starre* (fo named in diuers places of the Scriptures) becaufe of his excellencie (I meane the Prince of them) in his creation before his fall ; euen fo I fay hee deceiues the Witches, by attributing to himfelfe diuers names ; as if euery diuers fhape that he transformes himfelfe in, were a diuers kinde of fpirit.

PHI. But I haue heard many moe ftrange tales of this *Phairie*, nor ye haue yet told me.

EPI. As well I doe in that, as I did in all the reft of my difcourfe : For becaufe the ground of this conference of ours, proceeded of your fpeering at me at our meeting: if there was fuch a thing as Witches or fpirits: and if they had any power : I therefore haue framed my whole difcourfe, onely to proue that fuch things are and may be, by fuch number of examples as I fhew to be poffible by reafon , and keepe me from dipping any further in playing the part of a Dictionarie, to tell what euer I haue read or heard in that purpofe, which both would exceede faith, and rather would feeme to teach fuch vnlawfull artes, nor to difallow and condemne them, as it is the duetie of all Chriftians to doe.

M   CHAP.

CHAP. VI. ARG.

Of the tryall and punishment of Witches : What sort of accusation ought to be admit-
ted against them : What is the cause of the increasing so farre of their number in
this aage.

PHILOMATHES.

Hen to make an end of our conference, since I see it drawes
late, what forme of punishment thinke yee merite these
Magicians and Witches? For I see that ye account them to
be all alike guiltie.

E P I. They ought to be put to death according to the
Law of God, the ciuill and imperiall Law, and municipall Law of all Christian nations.

P H Y. But what kinde of death I pray you?

E P I. It is commonly vsed by fire, but that is an indifferent thing to be
vsed in euery countrey, according to the Law or custome thereof.

P H I. But ought no sexe, aage nor rancke to be exempted?

E P I. None at all (being so vsed by the lawfull magistrate) for it is the
highest point of Idolatry, wherein no exception is admitted by the law of
God.

P H I. Then barnes may not be spared.

E P I. Yea, not a haire the lesse of my conclusion: For they are not that
capable of reason as to practise such things: And for any being in company
and not reueiling thereof, their lesse and ignorant aage will no doubt excuse them.

P H I. I see ye condemne them all that are of the counsell of such craftes.

E P I. No doubt, for as I said, speaking of *Magie,* the consulters, trusters
in, ouer-seers, interteiners or stirrers vp of these craftes-folkes, are equally
guiltie with themselues that are the practisers.

P H I. Whether may the Prince then, or supreame Magistrate, spare or
ouer-see any that are guilty of that craft, vpon some great respects knowen
to him?

E P I. The Prince or Magistrate for further trials cause, may continue
the punishing of them such a certaine space as he thinkes conuenient: But
in the end to spare the life, and not to strike when God bids strike, and so
feuerely punish in so odious a fault and treason against God, it is not onely
vnlawfull, but doubtlesse no lesse sinne in that Magistrate, nor it was in
Saules sparing of *Agag* ; and so comparable to the sinne of Witch-craft it
selfe, as *Samuel* alledged at that time.

P H I. Surely then, I thinke since this crime ought to be so seuerely punished, Iudges ought to beware to condemne any, but such as they are sure
are guiltie, neither should the clattering report of a carling serue in so
weightie a case.

                                            E P I.

1. Sam. 15.

EP 1. Iudges ought indeede to beware whom they condemne: for it is as great a crime (as *Salomon* faith,) *To condemne the innocent, as to let the guiltie eſcape free* ; neither ought the report of any one infamous perſon, be admitted for a ſufficient proofe, which can ſtand of no law.

PH 1. And what may a number then of guilty perſons confeſſions, worke againſt one that is accuſed?

EP 1. The Aſſiſe muſt ſerue for interpretour of our law in that reſpect: But in my opinion, ſince in a matter of treaſon againſt the Prince, barnes or wiues, or neuer ſo diffamed perſons, may of our law ſerue for ſufficient witneſſes and proofes; I thinke ſurely that by a farre greater reaſon, ſuch witneſſes may be ſufficient in matters of high treaſon againſt God: For who but Witches can be prooues, and ſo witneſſes of the doings of Witches?

PH 1. Indeed, I trow they will be loath to put any honeſt man vpon their counſell: But what if they accuſe folke to haue bene preſent at their Imaginar conuentions in the ſpirit, when their bodies lye ſenceleſſe, as ye haue ſaid?

EP 1. I thinke they are not a haire the leſſe guiltie: For the Diuel durſt neuer haue borrowed their ſhadow or ſimilitude to that turne, if their conſent had not beene at it: And the conſent in theſe turnes is death of the lawe.

PH 1. Then *Samuel* was a Witch: For the diuell reſembled his ſhape, and played his perſon in giuing reſponſe to *Saul.*

EP 1. *Samuel* was dead as well before that; and ſo none could ſlaunder him with medling in that vnlawful arte · For the cauſe why, as I take it, that God will not permit Satan to vſe the ſhapes of ſimilitudes of any innocent perſons at ſuch vnlawfull times, is, that God will not permit that any innocent perſons ſhalbe ſlandered with that vile defection: for then the diuell would finde waies anew, to calumniate the beſt. And this wee haue in proofe by them that are carried with the *Phairie*, who neuer ſee the ſhadowes of any in that Court, but of them that thereafter are tryed to haue beene brethren and ſiſters of that craft: And this was likewiſe prooued by the confeſſion of a young Laſſe, troubled with ſpirits, laid on her by Witchcraft: that although ſhe ſaw the ſhapes of diuers men and women troubling her, and naming the perſons whom theſe ſhadowes repreſent: yet neuer one of them are found to be innocent, but all clearely tryed to bee moſt guiltie, and the moſt part of them confeſſing the ſame. And beſides that, I thinke it hath beene ſeldome heard tell of, that any, whom perſons guiltie of that crime accuſed, as hauing knowen them to be their marrowes by eye-ſight, and not by heare-ſay, but ſuch as were ſo accuſed of Witchcraft, could not be clearely tried vpon them, were at the leaſt publikely knowen to be of a very euill life and reputation: ſo iealous is God I ſay, of the fame of them that are innocent in ſuch cauſes. And beſides that, there are two other good helps that may be vſed for their triall: The one is, the finding of their marke, and the trying the inſenſiblenes therof: The other

Prou. 17.

is their fleeting on the water: for as in a fecret murther, if the dead carkaffe bee at any time thereafter handled by the murtherer, it will gufh out of bloud, as if the bloud were crying to the heauen for reuenge of the murtherer, God hauing appointed that fecret fupernaturall figne, for triall of that fecret vnnaturall crime, fo it appeares that God hath appointed (for a fupernaturall figne of the monftrous impietie of Witches) that the water fhall refufe to receiue them in her bofome, that haue fhaken off them the facred water of Baptifme, and wilfully refufed the benefite thereof: No, not fo much as their eyes are able to fhed teares (threaten and torture them as ye pleafe) while firft they repent (God not permitting them to diffemble their obftinacie in fo horrible a crime) albeit the women-kind efpecially, be able otherwayes to fhed teares at euery light occafion when they will, yea, although it were diffemblingly like the Crocodiles.

P H I. Well, wee haue made this conference to laft as long as leifure would permit: and to conclude then, fince I am to take my leaue of you, I pray God to purge this countrey of thefe diuellifh practifes: for they were neuer fo rife in thefe parts, as they are now.

E P I. I pray God that fo be too. But the caufes are ouer-manifeft, that make them to be fo rife: For the great wickednes of the people on the one part, procures this horrible defection, whereby God iuftly punifheth finne by a greater iniquitie: and on the other part, the confummation of the world, and our deliuerance drawing neere, makes Satan to rage the more in his inftruments, knowing his kingdome to be fo neere an end. And fo farewell for this time.

BAΣI-

ΒΑΣΙΛΙΚΟΝ ΔΩΡΟΝ.

OR

HIS MAIESTIES IN-
STRVCTIONS TO HIS
DEAREST SONNE, *HENRY*
THE PRINCE.

THE ARGVMENT.

SONNET.

GOD giues not Kings the stile of *Gods* in vaine,
For on his Throne his Scepter doe they swey:
And as their subiects ought them to obey,
So Kings should feare and serue their God againe:
If then ye would enioy a happie raigne,
Obserue the Statutes of your heauenly King,
And from his Law, make all your Lawes to spring:
Since his Lieutenant here ye should remaine,
Reward the iust, be stedfast, true, and plaine,
Represse the proud, maintayning aye the right,
Walke alwayes so, as euer in his sight,
Who guardes the godly, plaguing the prophane:
  And so ye shall in Princely vertues shine,
  Resembling right your mightie King Diuine.

M 3   TO

TO HENRY MY DEAREST
SONNE, AND NATVRAL
SVCCESSOVR.

Hom-to can fo rightly appertaine *this Booke of inftructions to a Prince in all the points of his calling, afwell generall, as a Chriftian towards God; as particular, as a King towards his people? Whom-to, I fay, can it fo iuftly appertaine, as vnto you my deareft Sonne? Since I the authour thereof, as your naturall Father, muft be carefull for your godly and vertuous education, as my eldeft Sonne, and the firft fruits of Gods bleffing towards mee in my pofteritie: and as a King muft timoufly prouide for your trayning vp in all the points of a Kings Office; fince yee are my naturall and lawfull fucceffour therein: that being rightly informed hereby, of the waight of your burthen, ye may in time beginne to confider, that being borne to be a king, ye are rather borne to* onus, *then* honos: *not excelling all your people fo farre in ranke and honour, as in daily care and hazardous paines-taking, for the dutifull adminiftration of that great office, that God hath laide vpon your fhoulders. Laying fo a juft fymmetrie and proportion, betwixt the height of your honourable place, and the heauie waight of your great charge: and con-*
fequently,

ſequently, in caſe of failing, which God forbid, of the ſadneſſe of your fall, according to the proportion of that height. I haue therefore for the greater eaſe to your memory, and that yee may at the firſt, caſt vp any part that yee haue to doe with; deuided this Treatiſe in three parts. The firſt teacheth you your duetie towards God as a Chriſtian: the next, your duetie in your Office as a King: and the third informeth you how to behaue your ſelfe in indifferent things, which of them-ſelues are neither right nor wrong, but according as they are rightly or wrong vſed; and yet will ſerue according to your behauiour therein, to augment or empaire your fame and authoritie at the handes of your people. Receiue and welcome this Booke then, as a faithfull Præceptour and counſellour vnto you: which, becauſe my affaires will not permit mee euer to bee preſent with you, I ordaine to bee a reſident faithfull admoniſher of you: And becauſe the houre of death is vncertaine to mee, as vnto all fleſh, I leaue it as my Teſtament and latter will vnto you. Charge-ing you in the preſence of GOD, and by the fatherly authori-tie I haue ouer you, that yee keepe it euer with you, as carefully, as Alexander did the Iliads of Homer. Yee will finde it a iuſt and impartiall counſellour; neither flattering you in any vice, nor importuning you at vnmeete times. It will not come vn-called, neither ſpeake vnſpeered at: and yet conferring with it when yee are at quiet, yee ſhall ſay with Scipio, that yee are nunquam minûs ſolus, quàm cum ſolus. To conclude then, I charge you, as euer yee thinke to deſerue my Fatherly bleſſing, to follow and put in practiſe, as farre as lyeth in you, the præcepts hereafter following. And if yee follow the contrary courſe, I take the Great GOD to record, that this Booke ſhall one day bee a witneſſe betwixt mee and you; and ſhall procure to bee ratified in Heauen, the curſe that in that caſe here I giue vn-to you. For I proteſt before that Great GOD, I had rather not bee a Father, and childleſſe, then bee a Father of wicked chil-dren. But hoping, yea, euen promiſing vnto my ſelfe, that GOD, who in his great bleſſing ſent you vnto mee; ſhall in the
ſame

ſame bleſſing, as hee hath giuen mee a Sonne; ſo make him a
good and a godly Sonne; not repenting him of his Mercie
ſhewed vnto mee, I end, with my earneſt prayer to G O D, to
worke effectually into you, the fruites of that bleſſing,
which here from my heart I beſtow
vpon you.

Your louing Father

I, R.

T O

TO THE READER.

Haritable *Reader*, it is one of the golden Sentences, which *Chriſt our Sauiour vttered to his Apoſtles*, that there is nothing ſo couered, that ſhal not be reuealed, neither ſo hidde, that ſhall not be knowen: and whatſoeuer they haue ſpoken in darkeneſſe, ſhould be heard in the light: and that which they had ſpoken in the eare in ſecret place, ſhould be publikely preached on the tops of the houſes : *And ſince he hath ſaid it, moſt trew muſt it be, ſince the authour thereof is the fountaine and very being of trewth: which ſhould mooue all godly and honeſt men, to be very warie in all their ſecreteſt actions, and whatſoeuer middeſſes they vſe for attaining to their moſt wiſhed ends; leſt otherwiſe how auowable ſoeuer the marke be, whereat they aime, the middeſſes being diſcouered to be ſhamefull whereby they climbe ; it may turne to the diſgrace both of the good worke it ſelfe, and of the authour thereof; ſince the deepeſt of our ſecrets, cannot be hidde from that all-ſeeing eye, and penetrant light, piercing through the bowels of very darkeneſſe it ſelfe.*

But as this is generally trew in the actions of all men, ſo is it more ſpecially trew in the affaires of Kings: for Kings being publike perſons, by reaſon of their office and authority, are as it were ſet (as it was ſaid of old) vpon a publike ſtage, in the ſight of all the people ; where all the beholders eyes are attentiuely bent to looke and pry in the leaſt circumſtance of their ſecreteſt drifts : Which ſhould make Kings the more carefull not to harbour the ſecreteſt thought in their minde, but ſuch as in the owne time they ſhall not be aſhamed openly to auouch ; aſſuring themſelues that Time the mother of Veritie, will in the due ſeaſon bring her owne daughter to perfection.

The trew practiſe hereof, I haue as a King oft found in my owne perſon, though I thanke God, neuer to my ſhame, hauing laide my count, euer to walke as in the eyes of the Almightie, examining euer ſo the ſecreteſt of my drifts, before I gaue them courſe, as how they might ſome day bide the touchſtone of a publike triall. And amongſt the reſt of my ſecret actions, which haue (vnlooked for of me) come to publike knowledge, it hath ſo fared with my ΒΑΣΙΛΙΚΟΝ ΔΩΡΟΝ *directed to my eldeſt ſon; which I wrote for exerciſe of mine owne ingyne, and inſtruction of him, who is appointed by God (I hope) to ſit on my Throne after me: For the purpoſe and matter thereof being onely fit for a King, as teaching him his office ; and the perſon whom-for it was ordained, a Kings heire, whoſe ſecret counſellor and faithfull admoniſher it muſt be, I thought it no wayes conuenient nor comely, that either it ſhould to all be*

proclaimed,

Luk. 12.

proclaimed, which to one onely appertained (and specially being a messenger betwixt two so coniunct persons) or yet that the mould whereupon he should frame his future behauiour, when hee comes both vnto the perfection of his yeeres, and possession of his inheritance, should before the hand be made common to the people, the subiect of his future happy gouernment. And therefore for the more secret and close keeping of them, I onely permitted seuen of them to be printed, the Printer being first sworne for secrecie : and these seuen I dispersed amongst some of my trustiest seruants, to be keeped closely by them, lest in case by the iniquitie or wearing of time, any of them might haue beene lost, yet some of them might haue remained after me, as witnesses to my Sonne, both of the honest integritie of my heart, and of my fatherly affection and naturall care towards him. But since contrary to my intention and expectation, as I haue alreadie said, this Booke is now vented, and set foorth to the publike view of the world, and consequently subiect to euery mans censure, as the current of his af- fection leades him ; I am now forced, as well for resisting to the malice of the chil- dren of enuie, who like waspes sucke venome out of euery wholsome herbe ; as for the satisfaction of the godly honest sort, in any thing that they may mistake therein, both to publish and spread the true copies thereof, for defacing of the false copies that are alreadie spread, as I am enformed ; as likewise by this Preface, to cleare such parts thereof, as in respect of the concised shortnesse of my Style, may be mis-interpre- ted therein.

To come then particularly to the matter of my Booke, there are two speciall great points, which (as I am informed) the malicious sort of men haue detracted therein ; and some of the honest sort haue seemed a little to mistake : whereof the first and greatest is, that some sentences therein should seeme to furnish grounds to men, to doubt of my sinceritie in that Religion; which I haue euer constantly professed : the other is, that in some parts thereof I should seeme to nourish in my minde, a vindi- ctiue resolution against England, or at the least, some principals there, for the Queene my mothers quarrell.

The first calumnie (most grieuous indeed) is grounded vpon the sharpe and bit- ter wordes, that therein are vsed in the description of the humors of Puritanes, and rash-headie Preachers, that thinke it their honour to contend with Kings, and per- turbe whole kingdomes. The other point is onely grounded vpon the strait charge I giue my Sonne, not to beare nor suffer any vnreuerent speeches or bookes against any of his parents or progenitors : wherein I doe alledge my owne experience anent the Queene my mother ; affirming, that I neuer found any that were of perfit aage the time of her reigne here, so stedfastly trew to me in all my troubles, as these that con- stantly kept their allegiance to her in her time. But if the charitable Reader will ad- uisedly consider, both the methode and matter of my Treatise, he will easily iudge, what wrong I haue iustained by the carping at both : For my Booke, suppose very small, being diuided in three seuerall parts ; the first part thereof onely treats of a Kings duety towards God in Religion, wherein I haue so clearely made profession of my Re- ligion, calling it the Religion wherein I was brought vp, and euer made profession of, and wishing him euer to continue in the same, as the onely trew forme of Gods worship ; that I would haue thought my sincere plainnesse in that first part vpon that subiect, should haue ditted the mouth of the most enuious Momus, that euer

hell

hell did hatch, from barking at any other part of my booke vpon that ground, except they would alledge me to be contrarie to my selfe, which in so small a volume would smell of too great weakenesse, and sliprinesse of memory. And the second part of my booke, teaches my Sonne how to vse his Office, in the administration of Iustice and Politicke Gouernment: The third onely containing a Kings outward behauiour in indifferent things; what agreeance and conformitie hee ought to keepe betwixt his outward behauiour in these things, and the vertuous qualities of his minde; and how they should serue for trunsh-men, to interprete the inward disposition of the minde, to the eyes of them that cannot see farther within him, and therefore must onely iudge of him by the outward appearance: So as if there were no more to be looked into, but the very methode and order of the booke, it will sufficiently cleare me of that first and grieuousest imputation, in the point of Religion: since in the first part, where Religion is onely treated of, I speake so plainely. And what in other parts I speake of Puritanes, it is onely of their morall faults, in that part where I speake of Policie: declaring when they contemne the Law and souereigne authoritie, what exemplare punishment they deserue for the same. And now as to the matter it selfe whereupon this scandall is taken, that I may sufficiently satisfie all honest men, and by a iust Apologie raise vp a brasen wall or bulwarke against all the darts of the ennious, I will the more narrowly rip vp the words, whereat they seeme to be somewhat stomacked.

First then, as to the name of Puritanes, I am not ignorant that the Style thereof doeth properly belong onely to that vile sect amongst the Anabaptists, called the Family of loue; because they thinke themselues onely pure, and in a maner without sinne, the onely trwe Church, and onely worthy to be participant of the Sacraments, and all the rest of the world to be but abomination in the sight of God. Of this speciall sect I principally meane, when I speake of Puritans; diuers of them, as Browne, Penry *and others, hauing at sundrie times come into Scotland, to sow their popple amongst vs (and from my heart I wish, that they had left no schollers behinde them, who by their fruits will in the owne time be manifested) and partly indeede, I giue this style to such brain-ficke and headie Preachers their disciples and followers, as refusing to be called of that sect, yet participate too much with their humours, in maintaining the aboue-mentioned errours; not onely agreeing with the generall rule of all Anabaptists, in the contempt of the ciuill Magistrate, and in leaning to their owne dreams and reuelations; but particularly with this sect, in accounting all men profane that sweare not to all their fantasies, in making for euery particular question of the policie of the Church, as great commotion, as if the article of the Trinitie were called in controuersie, in making the scriptures to be ruled by their conscience, and not their conscience by the Scripture; and he that denies the least iote of their grounds,* sit tibi tanquam ethnicus & publicanus, *not worthy to enioy the benefite of breathing, much lesse to participate with them of the Sacraments: and before that any of their grounds be impugned, let King, people, Law and all be trode vnder foote: Such holy warres are to be preferred to an vngodly peace: no, in such cases Christian Princes are not onely to be resisted vnto, but not to be prayed for, for prayer must come of Faith; and it is reuealed to their consciences, that GOD will heare no prayer for such a Prince. Iudge then, Christian Reader, if I wrong this sort of people, in giuing them the stile of that sect, whose errours they imitate: and since they are contented*

to.

to *weare their liuerie, let them not be aſhamed to borrow alſo their name. It is onely of this kinde of men, that in this booke I write ſo ſharply ; and whom I wiſh my Sonne to puniſh , in-caſe they refuſe to obey the Law, and will not ceaſe to ſturre vp a re-bellion:. Whom againſt I haue written the more bitterly, in reſpeƈt of diuers famous libels,and iniurious ſpeaches ſpred by ſome of them, not onely diſhonourably inueƈtiue againſt all Chriſtian Princes, but euen reprochfull to our profeſsion and Religion, in reſpeƈt they are come out vnder coulour thereof: and yet were neuer anſwered but by Papiſts, who generally medle aſwell againſt them, as the religion it ſelfe; whereby the skandale was rather doubled, then taken away. But on the other part, I proteſt vpon mine honour, I meane it not generally of all Preachers, or others, that like bet-ter of the ſingle forme of policie in our Church, then of the many Ceremonies in the Church of England ; that are perſwaded, that their Biſhops ſmell of a Papall ſupre-macie,that the Surpliſe, the cornerd cap, and ſuch like, are the outward badges of Po-piſh errours. No, I am ſo farre from being contentious in theſe things (which for my owne part I euer eſteemed as indifferent) as I doe equally loue and honour the learned and graue men of either of theſe opinions. It can no wayes become me to pro-nounce ſo lightly a ſentence, in ſo old a controuerſie. Wee all (God be praiſed) doe agree in the grounds ; and the bitterneſſe of men vpon ſuch queſtions, doeth but trouble the peace of the Church ; and giues aduantage and entry to the Papiſts by our diuiſion : But towards them, I onely vſe this prouiſion, that where the Law is other-wayes, they may content themſelues ſoberly and quietly with their owne opinions, not reſiſting to the authoritie, nor breaking the Law of the Countrey; neither aboue all, ſturring any rebellion or ſchiſme : but poſſeſsing th'ir ſoules in peace, let them preaſſe by patience, and well grounded reaſons, either to perſwade all the reſt to like of their iudgements ; or where they ſee better grounds on the other part ,not to bee aſhamed peaceably to incline thereunto, laying aſide all præoccupied opinions.

· And that this is the onely meaning of my Booke, and not any coldneſſe or cracke in Religion,that place doeth plainely witneſſe, where, after I haue ſpoken of the faults in our Eccleſiaſticall eſtate,I exhort my ſonne to be beneficiall vnto the good-men of the Miniſtrie ; praiſing God there, that there is preſently a ſufficient number of good men of them in this kingdome : and yet are they all knowne to be againſt the forme of the Engliſh Church. Yea, ſo farre I am in that place from admitting corruption in Religion, as I wiſh him in promoouing them, to vſe ſuch caution, as may preſerue their eſtate from creeping to corruption ; euer vſing that forme through the whole Booke, where euer I ſpeake of bad Preachers, terming them ſome of the Miniſters, and not Miniſters or Miniſtrie in generall. And to conclude this point of Religion, what indifferencie of Religion can Momus call that in mee, where, ſpeaking of my ſonnes marriage (in-caſe it pleaſed God before that time to cut the threed of my life) I plainly forewarne him of the inconuenients that were like to enſew,incaſe he ſhould marry any that be of a different profeſsion in Religion from him : notwithſtanding that the number of Princes profeſsing our Religion be ſo ſmall,as it is hard to foreſee, how he can be that way,meetly matched according to his ranke.

And as for the other point,that by ſome parts in this booke, it ſhould appeare,that I doe nouriſh in my minde, a vindiƈtiue reſolution againſt England, or ſome princi-pals there ; it is ſurely more then wonderfull vnto me, vpon what grounds they can*

haue

haue gathered such conclusions. For as vpon the one part, I neither by name nor de-
scription poynt out England in that part of my discourse; so vpon the other, I plainly
bewray my meaning to be of Scottish-men, where I conclude that purpose in these
termes : That the loue I beare to my Sonne, hath mooued me to be so plaine in this ar- ,,
gument : for so that I discharge my conscience to him in vttering the verity, I care ,,
not what any traitour or treason-allower doe thinke of it. And English-men could not ,,
thereby be meant, since they could be no traitours, where they ought no alleageance. I
am not ignorant of a wise and princely apophthegme, which the same Queene of En-
gland vttered about the time of her owne Coronation. But the drift of that discourse
doth fully cleare my intention, being onely grounded vpon that precept to my Sonne,
that she should not permit any vnreuerent detracting of his prædecessours; bringing
in that purpose of my mother onely for an example of my experience anent Scottish-
men, without vsing any perswasion to him of reuenge. For a Kings giuing of any
fault the dew stile, inferres no reduction of the saulters pardon. No, I am by a degree
nearer of kinne vnto my mother then he is, neither thinke I my selfe, either that vn-
worthie, or that neere my end, that I neede to make such a Dauidicall testament;
since I haue euer thought it the dewtie of a worthie Prince, rather with a pike, then
a penne, to write his iust reuenge : But in this matter I haue no delite to be large,
wishing all men to iudge of my future proiects, according to my by-past actions.

Thus hauing as much insisted in the clearing of these two points, as will (I hope)
giue sufficient satisfaction to all honest men, and leauing the enuious to the foode of
their owne venome; I will heartily pray thee, louing Reader, charitably to conceiue
of my honest intention in this Booke. I know the greatest part of the people of this
whole Isle, haue beene very curious for a sight thereof : some for the loue they beare
me, either being particularly acquainted with me, or by a good report that perhappes
they haue heard of me; and therefore longed to see any thing, that proceeded from that
authour whom they so loued and honoured; since bookes are viue Idees of the authours
minde. Some onely for meere curiositie, that thinke it their honour to know all new
things, were curious to glut their eyes therewith, onely that they might vaunt them
to haue seene it : and some fraughted with causlesse enuie at the Authour, did gree-
dily search out the booke, thinking their stomacke fit ynough, for turning neuer so
wholesome foode into noysome and infectiue humours : So as this their great concur-
rence in curiositie (though proceeding from farre different complexions) hath enfor-
ced the vn-timous diuulgating of this Booke, farre contrarie to my intention, as I
haue alreadie said. To which Hydra of diuersly-enclined spectatours, I haue no targe
to oppone but plainenesse, patience, and sinceritie : plainenesse, for resoluing and satis-
fying of the first sort; patience, for to beare with the shallownesse of the next; and sin-
ceritie, to defie the malice of the third with-all. Though I cannot please all men there-
in, I am contented, so that I onely please the vertuous sort : and though they also finde
not euery thing therein, so fully to answere their expectation, as the argument would
seeme to require; although I would wish them modestly to remember, that God hes
not bestowed all his gifts vpon one, but parted them by a iustice distributiue; and that
many eyes see more then one; and that the varietie of mens mindes is such, that tot
capita tot sensus; yea, and that euen the very faces, that God hath by nature brought
foorth in the world, doe euery one in some of their particular lineaments, differ from

any

any other : yet in trewth it was not my intention in handling of this purpose (as it is easie to perceiue) fully to set downe heere all such grounds, as might out of the best writers haue beene alledged, and out of my owne inuention and experience added, for the perfite institution of a King : but onely to giue some such precepts to my owne Sonne, for the gouernement of this kingdome, as was meetest for him to be instructed in, and best became me to be the informer of.

If I in this Booke haue beene too particularly plaine , impute it to the necessitie of the subiect, not so much being ordained for the institution of a Prince in generall , as I haue said, as containing particular precepts to my Sonne in speciall : whereof he could haue made but a generall vse, if they had not contained the particular diseases of this kingdome, with the best remedies for the same which it became me best as a King, hauing learned both the theoricke and practicke thereof, more plainely to expresse , then any simple schoole-man, that onely knowes matters of kingdomes by contemplation.

But if in some places it seeme too obscure, impute it to the shortnesse thereof, being both for the respect of my selfe, and of my Sonne, constrained there-unto : my owne respect, for fault of leasure, being so continually occupied in the affaires of my office, as my great bu. then, and restlesse fashery is more then knowen , to all that knowes or heares of me : for my Sonnes respect, because I know by my self, that a Prince so long as he is young, wil be so caried away with some sort of delight or other, that he cannot patiently abide the reading of any large volume : and when he comes to a ful maturity of aage, he must be so busied in the actiue part of his charge , as will not be permitted to bestow many houres vpon the cōtemplatiue part therof: So as it was neither fit for him, nor possible for me, to haue made this Treatise any more ample then it is. Indeed I am litle beholden to the curiositie of some, who thinking it too large alreadie (as appears) for lacke of leisure to copy it, drew some notes out of it, for speeds sake ; putting in the one halfe of the purpose, and leauing out the other : not vnlike the man that alledged that part of the Psalme, non est Deus, but left out the preceeding words, Dixit insipiens in corde suo. And of these notes making a little pamphlet (lacking both my methode and halfe of my matter) entituled it, forsooth, the Kings Testament, as if I had eiked a third Testament of my owne to the two that are in the holy Scriptures. It is trew that in a place thereof, for affirmation of the purpose I am speaking of to my Sonne, I bring my selfe in there, as speaking vpon my Testament : for in that sense, euery record in write of a mans opinion in any thing (in respect that papers out-liue their authours) is as it were a Testament of that mans will in that case : and in that sense it is, that in that place I call this Treatise a Testament. But from any particular sentence in a booke, to giue the booke it selfe a title, is as ridiculous , as to style the booke of the Psalmes, the booke of Dixit insipiens, because with these wordes one of them doeth begin.

Well, leauing these new baptizers and blockers of other mens books, to their owne follies, I returne to my purpose, anent the shortnesse of this booke , suspecting that all my excuses for the shortnesse thereof , shall not satisfie some, especially in our neighbour countrey : who thought, that as I haue so narrowly in this Treatise touched all the principall sicknesses in our kingdome, with ouertures for the remedies thereof, as I said before : so looked they to haue found something therein, that should haue touched the sickenesses of their state, in the like sort. But they will easily excuse me thereof, if they

will

will confider the forme I haue vfed in this Treatife ; wherein I onely teach my Son, out of my owne experience, what forme of gouernment is fitteſt for this kingdome : and in one part thereof fpeaking of the borders, I plainely there doe excufe my felfe, that I will fpeake nothing of the ſtate of England, *as a matter wherein I neuer had experience. I know indeed, no kingdome lackes her owne difeafes, and likewife what intereſt I haue in the profperitie of that ſtate : for although I would be filent, my blood and difcent doeth fufficiently proclaime it. But notwithſtanding, fince there is a lawfull Queene there prefently reigning, who hath fo long with fo great wifedome and felicitie gouerned her kingdomes, as (I muſt in trew finceritie confeſſe) the like hath not beene read nor heard of, either in our time, or fince the dayes of the Romane Emperour* Auguſtus *; it could no wayes become me, farre inferiour to her in knowledge and experience, to be a bufie-body in other princes matters, and to fiſh in other folkes waters, as the prouerbe is : No, I hope by the contrary (with Gods grace) euer to keepe that Chriſtian rule, To doe as I would be done to: and I doubt nothing, yea euen in her name I dare promife, by the bypaſt experience of her happy gouernment, as I haue already faid, that no good fubieɛt ſhall be more carefull to enforme her of any corruptions ſtollen in in her ſtate, then ſhee ſhall be zealous for the difcharge of her confcience and honour, to fee the fame purged, and reſtored to the ancient integritie; and further during her time, becomes me leaſt of any to meddle in.*

And thus hauing refolued all the doubts, fo farre as I can imagine, may be moued againſt this Treatife ; it onely reſts to pray thee (charitable Reader) to interprete fauourably this birth of mine, according to the integritie of the author, and not looking for perfeɛtion in the worke it felfe. As for my part, I onely glory thereof in this point, that I truſt no fort of vertue is condemned, nor any degree of vice allowed in it : and that (though it be not perhaps fo gorgeoufly decked, and richly attired as it ought to be) it is at the leaſt rightly proportioned in all the members, without any monſtrous deformitie in any of them : and fpecially that fince it was firſt written in fecret, and is now publiſhed, not of ambition, but of a kinde of neceſsitie ; it muſt be taken of all men, for the trew image of my very minde, and forme of the rule, which I haue prefcribed to my felfe and mine : Which as in all my aɛtions I haue hitherto preaſſed to expreſſe, fo farre as the nature of my charge, and the condition of time would permit me : fo beareth it a difcouery of that which may be looked for at my hand, and whereto euen in my fecret thoughts, I haue engaged my felfe for the time to come: And thus in a firme truſt, that it ſhall pleafe God, who with my being and Crowne, gaue me this minde, to maintaine and augment the fame in me and my poſteritie, to the difcharge of our confcience, the maintenance of our Honour, and weale of our people, I bid thee heartily farewell.

N 2   OF

OF
A KINGS CHRISTIAN
DVETIE TOWARDS
GOD.

THE FIRST BOOKE.

The trew ground of good gouernment.

S he cannot be thought worthy to rule and command others, that cannot rule and dantone his owne proper affections and vnreafonable appetites, fo can hee not be thought worthie to gouerne a Chriftian people, knowing and fearing God, that in his owne perfon and heart, feareth not and loueth not the Diuine Maieftie. Neither can any thing in his gouernment fucceed well with him, (deuife and labour as he lift) as comming from a filthie fpring, if his perfon be vnfanctified: for (as that royal Prophet

Pfal. 127. 1.

faith) *Except the Lord build the houfe, they labour in vaine that build it: except the Lord keepe the City, the keepers watch it in vaine* : in refpect the bleffing of God hath onely power to giue the fucceffe thereunto : and as *Paul* faith, he

1.Cor.3.6.

planteth, *Apollos watereth ; but it is God onely that giueth the increafe.* Therefore (my Sonne) firft of all things, learne to know and loue that God,

Double bond of a Prince to God.

whom-to ye haue a double obligation; firft, for that he made you a man; and next, for that he made you a little GOD to fit on his Throne, and rule ouer other men. Remember, that as in dignitie hee hath erected you aboue others, fo ought ye in thankfulneffe towards him, goe as farre beyond all others. A moate in anothers eye, is a beame into yours : a blemifh in another, is a leproufe byle into you : and a veniall finne (as the Papifts call it) in another, is a great crime into you. Thinke not therefore, that the

The greatneffe of the fault of a Prince.

highneffe of your dignitie, diminifheth your faults (much leffe giueth you a licence to finne) but by the contrary your fault fhall be aggrauated, according to the height of your dignitie; any finne that ye commit, not being a fingle finne procuring but the fall of one; but being an exemplare finne,

finne, and therefore drawing with it the whole multitude to be guiltie of the fame. Remember then, that this gliftering worldly glorie of Kings, is giuen them by God, to teach them to preaffe fo to glifter and fhine before their people, in all workes of fanctification and righteoufneffe, that their perfons as bright lampes of godlineffe and vertue, may, going in and out before their people, giue light to all their fteps. Remember alfo, that by the right knowledge, and feare of God (which is *the beginning of Wifedome*, as *Salomon* faith) ye fhall know all the things neceffarie for the difcharge of your duetie, both as a Chriftian, and as a King; feeing in him, as in a mirrour, the courfe of all earthly things, whereof hee is the fpring and onely moouer.

The trew glorie of Kings.

Prou 9.10.

Now, the onely way to bring you to this knowledge, is diligently to reade his word, and earneftly to pray for the right vnderftanding thereof. *Search the Scriptures*, fayth Chrift, *for they beare teftimonie of me*: and, *the whole Scripture*, faith Paul, *is giuen by infpiration of God, and is profitable to teach, to conuince, to correct, and to inftruct in righteoufneffe; that the man of God may be abfolute, being made perfite vnto all good workes.* And moft properly of any other, belongeth the reading thereof vnto Kings, fince in that part of Scripture, where the godly Kings are firft made mention of, that were ordained to rule ouer the people of God, there is an expreffe and moft notable exhortation and commandement giuen them, to reade and meditate in the Law of God. I ioyne to this, the carefull hearing of the doctrine with attendance and reuerence: for, *faith commeth by hearing*, fayth the fame Apoftle. But aboue all, beware ye wreft not the word to your owne appetite, as ouer many doe, making it like a bell to found as ye pleafe to interprete: but by the contrary, frame all your affections, to follow precifely the rule there fet downe.

The meanes to know God.

Iohn 5.39.

2.Tim.3. 16, 17.

D:ut.17.

Rom.10.17.

The whole Scripture chiefly containeth two things: a command, and a prohibition, to doe fuch things, and to abftaine from the contrary. Obey in both; neither thinke it enough to abftaine from euill, and do no good; nor thinke not that if yee doe many good things, it may ferue you for a cloake to mixe euill turnes therewith. And as in thefe two points, the whole Scripture principally confifteth, fo in two degrees ftandeth the whole feruice of God by man: interiour, or vpward; exteriour, or downward: the firft, by prayer in faith towards God; the next, by workes flowing therefra before the world: which is nothing elfe, but the exercife of Religion towards God, and of equitie towards your neighbour.

Wherein chiefly the whole Scripture confifteth.

Two degrees of the feruice of God.

As for the particular points of Religion, I need not to dilate them; I am no hypocrite, follow my footfteps, and your owne prefent education therein. I thanke God, I was neuer afhamed to giue account of my profeffion, howfoeuer the malicious lying tongues of fome haue traduced me: and if my confcience had not refolued me, that all my Religion prefently profeffed by me and my kingdome, was grounded vpon the plaine wordes of the Scripture, without the which all points of Religion are

A regardable paterne.

fuperfluous,

superfluous, as any thing contrary to the same is abomination, I had neuer outwardly auowed it, for pleasure or awe of any flesh.

And as for the points of equitie towards your neigbour (because that will fall in properly, vpon the second part concerning a Kings office) I leaue it to the owne roume.

Religion.

For the first part then of mans seruice to his God, which is Religion, that is, the worhip of God according to his reuealed will, it is wholly grounded vpon the Scripture, as I haue alreadie said, quickened by faith, and conserued by conscience: For the Scripture, I haue now spoken of it in generall; but that yee may the more readily make choice of any part thereof, for your instruction or comfort, remember shortly this methode.

The methode of Scripture.

The whole Scripture is dyted by Gods Spirit, thereby, as by his liuely word, to instruct and rule the whole Church militant to the end of the world: It is composed of two parts, the Olde and New Testament: The ground of the former is the Lawe, which sheweth our sinne, and containeth iustice: the ground of the other is Christ, who pardoning sinne containeth grace. The summe of the Law is the tenne Commandements, more largely delated in the bookes of *Moses*, interpreted and applied by the Prophets; and by the histories, are the examples shewed of obedience or disobedience thereto, and what *præmium* or *pæna* was accordingly giuen by God: But because no man was able to keepe the Law, nor any part thereof, it pleased God of his infinite wisedome and goodnesse, to incarnate his only Sonne in our nature, for satisfaction of his iustice in his suffering for vs; that since we could not be saued by doing, we might at least, bee saued by beleeuing.

Of the Law.

Of Grace.

The ground therefore of the word of grace, is contained in the foure histories of the birth, life, death, resurrection and ascention of Christ: The larger interpretation and vse thereof, is contained in the Epistles of the Apostles: and the practise in the faithfull or vnfaithfull, with the historie of the infancie and first progresse of the Church is contained in their Actes.

Vse of the Law.

Would ye then know your sinne by the Lawe? reade the bookes of *Moses* containing it. Would ye haue a commentarie thereupon? Reade the Prophets, and likewise the bookes of the *Prouerbes* and *Ecclesiastes*, written by that great patterne of wisedome *Salomon*; which will not only serue you for instruction, how to walke in the obedience of the Lawe of God; but is also so full of golden sentences, and morall precepts, in all things that can concerne your conuersation in the world, as among all the prophane Philosophers and Poets, ye shall not finde so rich a storehouse of precepts of naturall wisedome, agreeing with the will and diuine wisedome of God. Would ye see how good men are rewarded, and wicked punished? looke the historicall parts of these same bookes of *Moses*, together with the histories of *Ioshua*, the *Iudges*, *Ezra*, *Nehemiah*, *Esther*, and *Iob*: but especially the bookes of the *Kings* and *Chronicles*, wherewith ye ought to bee familiarly

acquain-

acquainted: for there ſhall yee ſee your ſelfe, as in a myrrour, in the catalogue either of the good or the euill Kings.

Would yee know the doctrine, life, and death of our Sauiour Chriſt? reade the Euangeliſts. Would ye bee more particularly trained vp in his Schoole? meditate vpon the Epiſtles of the Apoſtles. And would ye be acquainted with the practiſes of that doctrine in the perſons of the primitiue Church? Caſt vp the Apoſtles Actes. And as to the Apocryphe bookes, I omit them, becauſe I am no Papiſt, as I ſaid before; and indeed ſome of them are no wayes like the dytement of the Spirit of God. *Vſe of the Goſpel.*

But when ye reade the Scripture, reade it with a ſanctified and chaſte heart: admire reuerently ſuch obſcure places as ye vnderſtand not, blaming onely your owne capacitie: read with delight the plaine places, and ſtudie carefully to vnderſtand thoſe that are ſomewhat difficile: preaſſe to bee a good textuarie; for the Scripture is euer the beſt interpreter of it ſelfe; but preaſſe not curiouſly to ſeeke out farther then is contained therein; for that were ouer vnmannerly a preſumption, to ſtriue to bee further vpon Gods ſecrets, then he hath will ye be; for what hee thought needfull for vs to know, that hath he reuealed there: And delyte moſt in reading ſuch parts of the Scripture, as may beſt ſerue for your inſtruction in your calling; reiecting fooliſh curioſities vpon genealogies and contentions, *which are but vaine, and profite not,* as *Paul* ſaith. *How to reade the Scripture.* *Tit. 3. 9.*

Now, as to Faith, which is the nouriſher and quickner of Religion, as I haue alreadie ſaid, It is a ſure perſwaſion and apprehenſion of the promiſes of God, applying them to your ſoule: and therefore may it iuſtly be called, the golden chaine that linketh the faithfull ſoule to Chriſt: And becauſe it groweth not in our garden, but *is the free gift of God,* as the ſame Apoſtle ſaith, it muſt be nouriſhed by prayer, Which is nothing elſe, but a friendly talking with God. *Faith the nouriſher of Religion.* *Philip. 1. 29.*

As for teaching you the forme of your prayers, the Pſalmes of *Dauid* are the meeteſt ſchoole-maſter that ye can be acquainted with (next the prayer of our Sauiour, which is the onely rule of prayer) whereout of, as of moſt rich and pure fountaines, ye may learne all forme of prayer neceſſarie for your comfort at all occaſions: And ſo much the fitter are they for you, then for the common ſort, in reſpect the compoſer thereof was a King: and therefore beſt behoued to know a Kings wants, and what things were meeteſt to be required by a King at Gods hand for remedie thereof. *Prayer, and whence to learne the beſt forme thereof.*

Vſe often to pray when ye are quieteſt, eſpecially forget it not in your bed how oft ſoeuer ye doe it at other times: for publike prayer ſerueth as much for example, as for any particular comfort to the ſupplicant. *Seuerall exerciſe of prayer.*

In your prayer, bee neither ouer ſtrange with God, like the ignorant common ſort, that prayeth nothing but out of bookes, nor yet ouer homely with him, like ſome of the vaine Phariſaicall puritanes, that thinke they rule him vpon their fingers: The former way will breede an vncouth coldneſſe in you towards him, the other will breede in you a contempt of him. *What rule or regard is to be vſed in prayer.*

him. But in your prayer to God speake with all reuerence: for if a subiect will not speake but reuerently to a King, much lesse should any flesh presume to talke with God as with his companion.

Craue in your prayer, not onely things spirituall, but also things temporall, sometimes of greater, and sometimes of lesse consequence; that yee may lay vp in store his grant of these things, for confirmation of your faith, and to be an arles-peny vnto you of his loue. Pray, as yee finde your heart moueth you, *pro re nata*: but see that yee sute no vnlawfull things, as reuenge, lust, or such like: for that prayer can not come of faith : *and whatsoeuer is done without faith, is sinne,* as the Apostle saith.

When ye obtaine your prayer, thanke him ioyfully therefore : if otherwaies, beare patiently, preassing to winne him with importunitie, as the widow did the vnrighteous Iudge: and if notwithstanding thereof yee be not heard, assure your selfe, God foreseeth that which yee aske is not for your weale : and learne in time, so to interprete all the aduersities that God shall send vnto you; so shall yee in the middest of them, not onely be armed with patience, but ioyfully lift vp your eyes from the present trouble, to the happie end that God will turne it to. And when ye finde it once so fall out by proofe, arme your selfe with the experience thereof against the next trouble, assuring your selfe, though yee cannot in time of the showre see through the cloude, yet in the end shall ye find, God sent it for your weale, as ye found in the former.

And as for conscience, which I called the conseruer of Religion, It is nothing else, but the light of knowledge that God hath planted in man, which euer watching ouer all his actions, as it beareth him a ioyfull testimonie when he does right, so choppeth it him with a feeling that hee hath done wrong, when euer he committeth any sinne. And surely, although this conscience be a great torture to the wicked, yet is it as great a comfort to the godly, if we will consider it rightly. For haue wee not a great aduantage, that haue within our selues while wee liue here, a Count-booke and Inuentarie of all the crimes that wee shall bee accused of, either at the houre of our death, or at the Great day of Iudgement; which when wee please (yea though we forget) will chop, and remember vs to looke vpon it; that while we haue leasure and are here, we may remember to amend; and so at the day of our triall, compeare with *new and white garments washed in the blood of the Lambe,* as S.Iohn saith. Aboue all then, my Sonne, labour to keepe sound this conscience, which many prattle of, but ouer few feele : especially be carefull to keepe it free from two diseases, wherewith it vseth oft to be infected; to wit, Leaprosie, and Superstition : the former is the mother of Atheisme, the other of Heresies. By a leaprouse conscience, I meane *a cauterized conscience,* as *Paul* calleth it, being become senselesse of sinne, through sleeping in a carelesse securitie, as King *Dauids* was after his murther and adulterie, euer til he was wakened by the Prophet *Nathans* similitude. And by superstition, I meane, when one restraines himselfe to any
other

What to craue of God.

Rom. 14.13.

How to interpret the issue of prayer.

Conscience the conseruer of Religion.

The inuentarie of our life.

Reu 7.14.

The diseases of conscience.

1. Tim 4.2.

other rule in the feruice of God, then is warranted by the word, the onely trew fquare of Gods feruice.

As for a preferuatiue againft this Leaprofie, remember euer once in the foure and twentie houres, either in the night, or when yee are at greateft quiet, to call your felfe to account of all your laft dayes actions, either wherein ye haue committed things yee fhould not, or omitted the things ye fhould doe, either in your Chriftian or Kingly calling : and in that account, let not your felfe be fmoothed ouer with that flattering φιλαυτία, which is ouerkindly a fickneffe to all mankind : but cenfure your felfe as fharply, as if ye were your owne enemie: *For if ye iudge your felfe, ye fhall not be iudged,* as the Apoftle faith: and then according to your cenfure, reforme your actions as farre as yee may, efchewing euer wilfully and wittingly to contrare your confcience : For a fmall finne wilfully committed, with a deliberate refolution to breake the bridle of confcience therein, is farre more grieuous before God, then a greater finne committed in a fuddaine paffion, when confcience is afleepe. Remember therefore in all your actions, of the great account that yee are one day to make: in all the dayes of your life, euer learning to die, and liuing euery day as it were your laft;

Omnem crede diem tibi diluxiffe fupremum.

And therefore, I would not haue you to pray with the Papifts, to be preferued from fuddaine death, but that God would giue you grace fo to liue, as ye may euery houre of your life be ready for death : fo fhall ye attaine to the vertue of trew fortitude, neuer being afraid for the horrour of death, come when he lift : And efpecially, beware to offend your confcience with vfe of fwearing or lying, fuppofe but in ieft; for othes are but an vfe, and a finne cloathed with no delight nor gaine, and therefore the more inexcufable euen in the fight of men : and lying commeth alfo much of a vile vfe, which banifheth fhame : Therfore beware euen to deny the trewth, which is a fort of lie, that may beft be efchewed by a perfon of your ranke. For if any thing be asked at you that yee thinke not meete to reueale, if yee fay, that queftion is not pertinent for them to aske, who dare examine you further? and vfing fometimes this anfwere both in trew and falfe things that fhall be asked at you, fuch vnmanerly people will neuer be the wifer thereof.

And for keeping your confcience found from that fickeneffe of fuperftition, yee muft neither lay the fafetie of your confcience vpon the credit of your owne conceits, nor yet of other mens humors, how great doctors of Diuinitie that euer they be; but yee muft onely ground it vpon the expreffe Scripture : for confcience not grounded vpon fure knowledge, is either an ignorant fantafie, or an arrogant vanitie. Beware therefore in this cafe with two extremities : the one, to beleeue with the Papifts, the Churches authority, better then your owne knowledge ; the other, to leane with the Anabaptifts, to your owne conceits and dreamed reuelations.

But learne wifely to difcerne betwixt points of faluation and indifferent things,

Preferuatiue againft leprofie of confcience.

1. Cor. 11. 31.

Laft account.

Horat. lib. 1. Epift.

Trew fortitude.

Foolifh vfe of oathes.

Againft fuperftition.

things, betwixt substance and ceremonies; and betwixt the expresse commandement and will of God in his word, and the inuention or ordinance of man; since all that is necessarie for saluation is contained in the Scripture: For in any thing that is expressely commanded or prohibited in the booke of God, ye cannot be ouer precise, euen in the least thing; counting euery sinne, not according to the light estimation and common vse of it in the world, but as the booke of God counteth of it. But as for all other things not contained in the Scripture, spare not to vse or alter them, as the

necessitie of the time shall require. And when any of the spirituall officebearers in the Church, speake vnto you any thing that is well warranted by the word, reuerence and obey them as the heraulds of the most high God: but, if passing that bounds, they vrge you to embrace any of their fantasies in the place of Gods word, or would colour their particulars with a pretended zeale, acknowledge them for no other then vaine men, exceeding the bounds of their calling; and according to your office, grauely and with authoritie redact them in order againe.

To conclude then, both this purpose of conscience, and the first part of this booke, keepe God more sparingly in your mouth, but abundantly in your heart: be precise in effect, but sociall in shew: kythe more by your deedes then by your wordes, the loue of vertue and hatred of vice: and delight more to be godly and vertuous indeed, then to be thought and called so; expecting more for your praise and reward in heauen, then heere: and apply to all your outward actions Chrifts command, to pray and giue your almes secretly: So shal ye on the one part be inwardly garnished with trew Christian humilitie, not outwardly (with the proud Pharisie) glorying in your godlinesse; but saying, as Christ commandeth vs all, when we haue done all that we can, *Inutiles serui sumus*: And on the other part,

yee shall eschew outwardly before the world, the suspition
of filthie proude hypocrisie, and deceit-
full dissimulation.

O F

OF A KINGS DVETIE
IN·HIS OFFICE.

THE SECOND BOOKE.

 VT as ye are clothed with two callings, so must ye be alike carefull for the discharge of them both: that as yee are a good Christian, so yee may be a good King, discharging your Office (as I shewed before) in the points of Iustice and Equitie: which in two sundrie waies ye must doe: the one, in establishing and executing, (which is the life of the Law) good Lawes among your people: the other, by your behauiour in your owne person, and with your seruants, to teach your people by your example: for people are naturally inclined to counterfaite (like apes) their Princes maners, according to the notable saying of *Plato*, expressed by the Poet

―――――― *Componitur orbis*
Regis ad exemplum, nec sic inflectere sensus
Humanos edicta valent, quàm vita regentis.

For the part of making, and executing of Lawes, consider first the trew difference betwixt a lawfull good King, and an vsurping Tyran, and yee shall the more easily vnderstand your duetie herein: for *contraria iuxta se posita magis elucescunt.* The one acknowledgeth himselfe ordained for his people, hauing receiued from God a burthen of gouernment, whereof he must be countable: the other thinketh his people ordeined for him, a prey to his passions and inordinate appetites, as the fruites of his magnanimitie: And therefore, as their ends are directly contrarie, so are their whole actions, as meanes, whereby they preasse to attaine to their endes. A good King, thinking his highest honour to consist in the due discharge of his calling, emploieth all his studie and paines, to procure and maintaine, by the making and execution of good Lawes, the well-fare and peace of his people; and as their naturall father and kindly Master, thinketh his greatest contentment standeth in their prosperitie, and his greatest suretie in hauing their hearts, subiecting his owne priuate affections and appetites to the weale and standing of his Subiects, euer thinking the common interesse his chiefest particular: where by the contrarie, an vsurping Tyran, thinking

Marginal notes:
The Office of a King.
Plato in Polit.
Isocr. in Sym.
Plato in Polit.
Claudian. in 4. consⁱ. Hon.
Difference of a King and a Tyran.
Plato in Polit.
Arist. 5. Polit.
Xen. 8. Cyr.
Cic. lib. 5. de Rep.

Arist.5.Polit.
Tacit.4.hist.

thinking his greateſt honour and felicitie to conſiſt in attaining *per fas, vel nefas*, to his ambitious pretences, thinketh neuer himſelfe ſure, but by the diſſention and factions among his people, and counterfaiting the Saint while he once creepe in credite, will then (by inuerting all good Lawes to ſerue onely for his vnrulie priuate affections) frame the common-weale euer to aduance his particular: building his ſuretie vpon his peoples miſe-rie: and in the end (as a ſtep-father and an vncouth hireling) make vp his owne hand vpon the ruines of the Republicke. And according to their

The iſſue and rewards of a good King.

Cic.6.de Rep.

actions, ſo receiue they their reward: For a good King (after a happie and famous reigne) dieth in peace, lamented by his ſubiects, and admired by his neighbours; and leauing a reuerent renowne behinde him in earth, ob-taineth the Crowne of eternall felicitie in heauen. And although ſome of them (which falleth out very rarelie) may be cut off by the treaſon of ſome vnnaturall ſubiects, yet liueth their fame after them, and ſome notable plague faileth neuer to ouertake the committers in this life, beſides their

The iſſue of Tyrans,
Arist.5.Polit.

Iſocr.in Sym.

infamie to all poſterities hereafter: Whereby the contrarie, a Tyrannes mi-ſerable and infamous life, armeth in end his owne Subiects to become his burreaux: and although that rebellion be euer vnlawfull on their part, yet is the world ſo wearied of him, that his fall is little meaned by the reſt of his Subiects, and but ſmiled at by his neighbours. And beſides the infa-mous memorie he leaueth behind him here, and the endleſſe paine hee ſu-ſtaineth hereafter, it oft falleth out, that the committers not onely eſcape vnpuniſhed, but farther, the fact will remaine as allowed by the Law in di-uers aages thereafter. It is eaſie then for you (my Sonne) to make a choiſe of one of theſe two ſorts of rulers, by following the way of vertue to eſta-bliſh your ſtanding; yea, incaſe ye fell in the high way, yet ſhould it be with the honourable report, and iuſt regrate of all honeſt men.

Anent the making of Lawes.

And therefore to returne to my purpoſe anent the gouernement of your Subiects, by making and putting good Lawes to execution; I remit the making of them to your owne diſcretion, as ye ſhall finde the neceſſi-tie of new-riſing corruptions to require them: for, *ex malis moribus bonæ leges natæ ſunt*: beſides, that in this countrey, wee haue alreadie moe good Lawes then are well execute, and am onely to inſiſt in your forme of go-uernment anent their execution. Onely remember, that as Parliaments haue bene ordained for making of Lawes, ſo ye abuſe not their inſtitution,

The autho-ritie and trew vſe of Parlia-ments.

L.1 2.Tab.

in holding them for any mens particulars: For as a Parliament is the ho-nourableſt and higheſt iudgement in the land (as being the Kings head Court) if it be well vſed, which is by making of good Lawes in it; ſo is it the in-iuſteſt Iudgement-ſeat that may be, being abuſed to mens particu-lars: irreuocable decreits againſt particular parties, being giuen therein vn-der colour of generall Lawes, and oft-times th'Eſtates not knowing them-ſelues whom thereby they hurt. And therefore hold no Parliaments, but for neceſſitie of new Lawes, which would be but ſeldome: for few Lawes and well put in execution, are beſt in a well ruled common-weale. As for

the

the matter of fore-faltures, which alſo are done in Parliament, it is not good rigging with theſe things; but my aduice is, ye fore-fault none but for ſuch odious crimes as may make them vnworthie euer to be reſtored a-gaine: And for ſmaller offences, ye haue other penalties ſharpe enough to be vſed againſt them.

And as for the execution of good Lawes, whereat I left, remember that among the differences that I put betwixt the formes of the gouernment of a good King, and an vſurping Tyran; I ſhew how a Tyran would enter like a Saint while he found himſelfe faſt vnder-foot, and then would ſuffer his vnrulie affections to burſt foorth. Therefore be yee contràre at your firſt entrie to your Kingdome, to that *Quinquennium Neronis*, with his ten-der hearted wiſh, *Vellem neſcirem literas*, in giuing the Law full execution a-gainſt all breakers thereof but exception. For ſince ye come not to your reigne *precariò*, nor by conqueſt, but by right and due diſcent; feare no vp-roares for doing of iuſtice, ſince ye may aſſure your ſelfe, the moſt part of your people will euer naturally fauour Iuſtice: prouiding alwaies, that ye doe it onely for loue to Iuſtice, and not for ſatisfying any particular paſ-ſions of yours, vnder colour thereof: otherwiſe, how iuſtly that euer the offender deſerue it, ye are guiltie of murther before God: For ye muſt con-ſider, that God euer looketh to your inward intention in all your actions.

And when yee haue by the ſeueritie of Iuſtice once ſetled your coun-tries, and made them know that ye can ſtrike, then may ye thereafter all the daies of your life mixe Iuſtice with Mercie, puniſhing or ſparing, as ye ſhall finde the crime to haue bene wilfully or raſhly committed, and according to the by-paſt behauiour of the committer. For if otherwiſe ye kyth your clemencie at the firſt, the offences would ſoone come to ſuch heapes, and the contempt of you grow ſo great, that when ye would fall to puniſh, the number of them to be puniſhed, would exceed the innocent; and yee would be troubled to reſolue whom-at to begin: and againſt your nature would be compelled then to wracke many, whom the chaſtiſemeit of few in the beginning might haue preſerued. But in this, my ouer-deare bought experience may ſerue you for a ſufficient leſſon: For I confeſſe, where I thought (by being gracious at the beginning) to win all mens hearts to a louing and willing obedience, I by the contrary found, the diſ-order of the countrie, and the loſſe of my thankes to be all my reward.

But as this ſeuere Iuſtice of yours vpon all offences would bee but for a time, (as I haue alreadie ſaid) ſo is there ſome horrible crimes that yee are bound in conſcience neuer to forgiue: ſuch as Witch-craft, wilfull mur-ther, Inceſt, (eſpecially within the degrees of conſanguinitie) Sodomie, poi-ſoning, and falſe coine. As for offences againſt your owne perſon and au-thoritie, ſince the fault concerneth your ſelfe, I remit to your owne choiſe to puniſh or pardon therein, as your heart ſerueth you, and according to the circumſtances of the turne, and the qualitie of the committer.

Here would I alſo eike another crime to bee vnpardonable, if I ſhould

Marginal notes

Cic.3 de leg. pro D ſ. & pro S. eſt.

Anent the execution of Lawes.

A iuſt ſeueri-tie to be vſed at the firſt. *Sen. de cl. Ar.7.pol.*

Plato 2. & 10 de Repub. Cic. ad Q. ſr.

A good mix-ture. *Plato in Pol. & 9. de L. Sal. orat. ad Cæſar.*

A deare pre-ſident.

Crimes vn-pardonable.

Treaſon a-gainſt the Prince his perſon, or au-thoritie.

Stayning of
the blood.

Exod. 20.12.

Plat. 4. de
Legib.

not be thought partiall: but the fatherly loue I beare you, will make mee breake the bounds of shame in opening it vnto you. It is then, the false and vnreuerent writing or speaking of malicious men against your Parents and Predecessors: ye know the command in Gods lawe, *Honour your Father and Mother*: and consequently, sen ye are the lawful magistrate, suffer not both your Princes and your Parents to be dishonoured by any; especially, sith the example also toucheth your selfe, in leauing thereby to your successors, the measure of that which they shal mete out againe to you in your like behalfe. I graunt wee haue all our faults, which, priuately betwixt you and God, should serue you for examples to meditate vpon, and mend in your person; but should not be a matter of discourse to others whatsoeuer. And sith ye are come of as honourable Predecessours as any Prince liuing, represse the insolence of such, as vnder pretence to taxe a vice in the person, seeke craftily to staine the race, and to steale the affection of the people from their posteritie: For how can they loue you, that hated them whom-of ye are come? Wherefore destroy men innocent young sucking Wolues and Foxes, but for the hatred they beare to their race? and why wil a coult of a Courser of Naples, giue a greater price in a market, then an Asse-colt, but for loue of the race? It is therefore a thing monstrous, to see a man loue the childe, and hate the Parents: as on the other part, the infaming and making odious of the parent, is the readiest way to bring the sonne in contempt. And for conclusion of this point, I may also alledge my owne experience: For besides the iudgments of God, that with my eyes I haue seene fall vpon all them that were chiefe traitours to my parents, I may iustly affirme, I neuer found yet a constant biding by me in all my straites, by any that were of perfite aage in my parents dayes, but onely by such as constantly bode by them; I meane specially by them that serued the Queene my mother: for so that I discharge my conscience to you, my Sonne, in re-uealing to you the trewth, I care not, what any traitour or treason-allower thinke of it.

Of oppres-
sion.

Arist. 5. polit.
Isocr. de reg.
Cic. in Of. &
ad Q. fr.

The trew glo-
rie of Kings.

A memorable
and worthie
patterne.

Deut. 1.

And although the crime of oppression be not in this ranke of vnpardonable crimes, yet the ouer-common vse of it in this nation, as if it were a vertue, especially by the greatest ranke of subiects in the land, requireth the King to be a sharpe censurer thereof. Be diligent therefore to trie, and awfull to beate downe the hornes of proud oppressours: embrace the quarrell of the poore and distressed, as your owne particular, thinking it your greatest honour to represse the oppressours: care for the pleasure of none, neither spare ye anie paines in your owne person, to see their wrongs redressed: and remember of the honourable stile giuen to my grand-father of worthie memorie, in being called *the poore mans King*. And as the most part of a Kings office, standeth in deciding that question of *Meum* and *Tuum*, among his subiects; so remember when ye sit in iudgement, that the Throne ye sit on is Gods, as *Moyses* saith, and sway neither to the right hand nor to the left; either louing the rich, or pittying the poore. Iustice should
bee

be blinde and friendlesse : it is not there ye should reward your friends, or seeke to crosse your enemies.

Here now speaking of oppressours and of iustice, the purpose leadeth me to speake of Hie-land and Border oppressions. As for the Hie-lands, I shortly comprehend them all in two sorts of people : the one, that dwelleth in our maine land, that are barbarous for the most part, and yet mixed with some shewe of ciuilitie : the other, that dwelleth in the Iles, and are alluterly barbares, without any sort or shew of ciuilitie. For the first sort, put straitly to execution the Lawes made alreadie by me against their Ouer-lords, and the chiefes of their Clannes, and it will be no difficultie to danton them. As for the other sort, follow forth the course that I haue intended, in planting Colonies among them of answerable In-lands subiects, that within short time may reforme and ciuilize the best inclined among them ; rooting out or transporting the barbarous and stubborne sort, and planting ciuilitie in their roomes.

But as for the Borders, because I know, if ye enioy not this whole Ile, according to Gods right and your lineall discent, yee will neuer get leaue to brooke this North and barrenneft part thereof; no, not your owne head whereon the Crowne should stand; I neede not in that case trouble you with them : for then they will be the middeft of the Ile, and so as easily ruled as any part thereof.

And that yee may the readier with wisedome and Iustice gouerne your subiects, by knowing what vices they are naturallie most inclined to, as a good Physician, who must first know what peccant humours his Patient naturallie is most subiect vnto, before he can begin his cure : I shall therefore shortly note vnto you, the principall faults that euery ranke of the people of this countrey is most affected vnto. And as for *England,* I will not speake be-gesse of them, neuer hauing been among them, although I hope in that God, who euer fauoureth the right, before I die, to be as well acquainted with their fashions.

As the whole Subiects of our countrey (by the ancient and fundamentall policie of our Kingdome) are diuided into three eftates, so is euerie eftate hereof generally subiect to some speciall vices; which in a maner by long habitude, are thought rather vertue then vice among them : not that euerie particular man in any of these rankes of men, is subiect vnto them, for there is good and euill of all sorts; but that I meane, I haue found by experience, these vices to haue taken greateft holde with these rankes of men.

And firft, that I prejudge not the Church of her ancient priuiledges, reason would shee should haue the firft place for orders sake, in this catalogue.

The naturall sickenesse that hath euer troubled, and beene the decay of all the Churches, since the beginning of the world, changing the candlesticke from one to another, as *Iohn* saith, hath beene Pride, Ambition, and

O 2   Auarice:

Plat. in polit.
Cic. ad Q. frat.
Arift. 1. Ret.
Plat. in If.

Of the Hie-lands.

Of the Borders.

A neceffarie point in a good gouernment.
Plato in polit.

A confideration of the three eftates.

The difeafes of the church.

Auarice: and now laſt, theſe ſame infirmities wrought the ouerthrow of the Popiſh Church, in this countrey and diuers others. But the reformatioſi of Religion in *Scotland*, being extraordinarily wrought by God, wherin many things were inordinately done by a popular tumult and rebellion, of ſuch as blindly were doing the worke of God, but clogged with their owne paſſions and particular reſpects, as well appeared by the deſtruction of our policie, and not proceeding from the Princes order, as it did in our neighbour countrey of *England*, as likewiſe in *Denmarke*, and ſundry parts of *Germanie*; ſome fierie ſpirited men in the miniſterie, got ſuch a guiding of the people at that time of confuſion, as finding the guſt of gouernment ſweete, they begouth to fantaſie to themſelues a Democraticke forme of gouernment: and hauing (by the iniquitie of time) beene ouerwell baited vpon the wracke, firſt of my Grandmother, and next of mine owne mother, and after vſurping the libertie of the time in my long minoritie, ſetled themſelues ſo faſt vpon that imagined Democracie, as they fed themſelues with the hope to become *Tribuni plebis*: and ſo in a popular gouernment by leading the people by the noſe, to beare the ſway of all the rule. And for this cauſe, there neuer roſe faction in the time of my minoritie, nor trouble ſen-ſyne, but they that were vpon that factious part, were euer carefull to perſwade and allure theſe vnruly ſpirits among the miniſterie, to ſpouſe that quarrell as their owne: where-through I was oftimes calumniated in their populare Sermons, not for any euill or vice in me; but becauſe I was a King, which they thought the higheſt euill. And becauſe they were aſhamed to profeſſe this quarrel, they were buſie to look narrowly in all my actions; and I warrant you a mote in my eye, yea a falſe report, was matter enough for them to worke vpon: and yet for all their cunning, whereby they pretended to diſtinguiſh the lawfulneſſe of the office, froſn the vice of the perſon, ſome of them would ſometimes ſnapper out well groſſely with the trewth of their intentions, informing the people, that all Kings and Princes were naturally enemies to the libertie of the Church, and could neuer patiently beare the yoke of Chriſt: with ſuch ſound doctrine fed they their flockes. And becauſe the learned, graue, and honeſt men of the miniſterie, were euer aſhamed and offended with their temeritie and preſumption, preaſſing by all good meanes by their authoritie and example, to reduce them to a greater moderation; there could be no way found out ſo meete in their conceit, that were turbulent ſpirits among them, for maintaining their plots, as paritie in the Church: whereby the ignorants were emboldened (as bairdes) to crie the learned, godly, and modeſt out of it: paritie the mother of confuſion, and enemie to Vnitie, which is the mother of order: For if by the example thereof, once eſtabliſhed in the Eccleſiaſticall gouernment, the Politicke and ciuill eſtate ſhould be drawn to the like, the great confuſion that thereupon would ariſe may eaſily be diſcerned. Take heede therefore (my Sonne) to ſuch Puritanes, verie peſtes in the Church and Common-weale, whom no deſerts

The occaſion of the Tribunat of ſome Puritanes.

Such were the Demagogi at Athens.

Their formes in the State.

Their razing the ground of the princely rule.

Their pretence of paritie.

ferts can oblige, neither oathes or promifes binde, breathing nothing but
fedition and calumnies, afpiring without meafure, railing without reafon,
and making their owne imaginations (without any warrant of the word)
the fquare of their confcience. I proteft before the great God, and fince I
am here as vpon my Teftament, it is no place for me to lie in, that ye fhall
neuer finde with any Hie-land or Border-theeues greater ingratitude, and
moe lies and vile periuries, then with thefe phanaticke fpirits: And fuffer
not the principals of them to brooke your land, if ye like to fit at reft; except yee would keepe them for trying your patience, as *Socrates* did an e-
uill wife.

> An culli fort of freed-men in the State.

> *Xantippe.*

And for preferuatiue againft their poifon, entertaine and aduance the
godly, learned and modeft men of the minifterie, whom-of (God be praifed) there lacketh not a fufficient number: and by their prouifion to Bifho-
prickes and Benefices (annulling that vile acte of Annexation, if ye finde it
not done to your hand) yee fhall not onely banifh their conceited paritie,
whereof I haue fpoken, and their other imaginarie grounds; which can
neither ftand with the order of the Church, nor the peace of a Common-
weale and well ruled Monarchie: but ye fhall alfo re-eftablifh the olde inftitution of three Eftates in Parliament; which can no otherwife be done.
But in this I hope (if God fpare me dayes) to make you a faire entrie; alwayes where I leaue, follow ye my fteps.

> Preferuatiue againft fuch poifon.

> Parity incompatible with a Monarchie.

And to end my aduice anent the Church eftate, cherifh no man more
then a good Paftor, hate no man more then a proude Puritane; thinking
it one of your faireft ftyles, to be called a louing nourifh-father to the
Church, feeing all the Churches within your dominions planted with
good Paftors, the Schooles (the feminarie of the Church) maintained, the
doctrine and difcipline preferued in puritie, according to Gods word, a
fufficient prouifion for their fuftentation, a comely order in their policie,
pride punifhed, humilitie aduanced, and they fo to reuerence their fuperiours, and their flockes them, as the flourifhing of your Church in pietie, peace, and learning, may be one of the chiefe points of your earthly
glory, being euer alike ware with both the extremities; as well as yee repreffe the vaine Puritane, fo not to fuffer proude Papall Bifhops: but as
fome for their qualities will deferue to bee preferred before others, fo
chaine them with fuch bondes as may preferue that eftate from creeping
to corruption.

> Generall ad-uice in be-halfe of the Church.

The next eftate now that by order commeth in purpofe, according to
their rankes in Parliament, is the Nobilitie, although fecond in ranke,
yet ouer-farre firft in greatneffe and power, either to doe good or euill,
as they are inclined.

> Of the Nobi-litie and their formes.

The naturall fickeneffe that I haue perceiued this eftate fubiect to in my
time, hath beene, a fectleffe arrogant conceit of their greatnes and power;
drinking in with their very nourifh-milke, that their honor ftood in committing three points of iniquitie: to thrall by oppreffion, the meaner fort

O 3   that

that dwelleth neere them, to their seruice and following, although they holde nothing of them : to maintaine their seruants and dependers in any wrong, although they be not answerable to the lawes (for any body will maintaine his man in a right cause) and for anie displeasure, that they apprehend to be done vnto them by their neighbour, to take vp a plaine feide against him; and (without respect to God, King, or common-weale) to bang it out brauely, hee and all his kinne, against him and all his : yea they will thinke the King farre in their common, in-case they agree to grant an assurance to a short day, for keeping of the peace : where, by their naturall dewtie, they are oblished to obey the lawe, and keepe the peace all the daies of their life, vpon the perill of their verie craigges.

Remedie of such euils.
Arist. 5. Polit.

For remeid to these euils in their estate, teach your Nobilitie to keepe your lawes as precisely as the meanest : feare not their orping or beeing discontented, as long as yee rule well; for their pretended reformation of Princes taketh neuer effect, but where euill gouernement precedeth. Ac-

Zeno in Cyr.
Iso. in Eu.
Cis. ad Q. fra.

quaint your selfe so with all the honest men of your Barrons and Gentlemen, and be in your giuing accesse so open and affable to euery ranke of honest persons, as may make them peart without scarring at you, to make their owne suites to you themselues, and not to employ the great Lordes their intercessours; for intercession to Saints is Papistrie: so shall ye bring to a measure their monstrous backes. And for their barbarous feides, put the lawes to due execution made by mee there-anent; beginning euer rathest at him that yee loue best, and is most oblished vnto you; to make him an example to the rest. For yee shall make all your reformations to beginne at your elbow, and so by degrees to flow to the extremities of the land. And rest not, vntill yee roote out these barbarous feides; that their effects may bee as well smoared downe, as their barbarous name is vnknowen to anie other nation : For if this Treatise were written either in French or Latine, I could not get them named vnto you but by circumlocution. And for your easier abolishing of them, put sharpelie to execution my lawes made against Gunnes and traiterous Pistolets; thinking in your heart, tearming in your speech, and vsing by your punishments, all such as weare and vse them, as brigands and cut-throates.

On the other part, eschew the other extremitie, in lightlying and contemning your Nobilitie. Remember howe that errour brake the King my

Plat. in 1. Al.
in pol. & 5.
de l. Arist. 2.
œcon.

Zeno in Cyr.

grand-fathers heart. But consider that vertue followeth oftest noble blood : the worthinesse of their antecessors craueth a reuerent regard to be had vnto them : honour them therfore that are obedient to the law among them, as Peeres and Fathers of your land : the more frequently that your Court can bee garnished with them; thinke it the more your honour; acquainting and employing them in all your greatest affaires; sen it is, they must be your armes and executers of your lawes : and so vse your selfe louinglie to the obedient, and rigoroufly to the stubborne, as may make the greatest of them to thinke, that the chiefest point of their honour, standeth

deth in ſtriuing with the meaneſt of the land in humilitie towards you, and
obedience to your Lawes: beating euer in their eares, that one of the principall points of ſeruice that ye craue of them, is, in their perſons to practiſe,
and by their power to procure due obedience to the Law; without the
which, no ſeruice they can make, can be agreeable vnto you.

But the greateſt hinderance to the execution of our Lawes in this countrie, are theſe heritable Shireſdomes and Regalities, which being in the
hands of the great men, do wracke the whole countrie: For which I know
no preſent remedie, but by taking the ſharper account of them in their
Offices; vſing all puniſhment againſt the ſlouthfull, that the Law will permit: and euer as they vaike, for any offences committed by them, diſpone
them neuer heritably againe: preaſſing, with time, to draw it to the laudable cuſtome of England: which ye may the eaſilier doe, being King of
both, as I hope in God ye ſhall.

And as to the third and laſt eſtate, which is our Burghes (for the ſmall
Barrones are but an inferiour part of the Nobilitie and of their eſtate) they
are compoſed of two ſorts of men; Merchants and Crafteſ-men: either of
theſe ſorts being ſubiect to their owne infirmities.

The Merchants thinke the whole common-weale ordeined for making
them vp; and accounting it their lawfull gaine and trade, to enrich themſelues vpon the loſſe of all the reſt of the people, they tranſport from vs
things neceſſarie; bringing backe ſometimes vnneceſſary things, and at o-
ther times nothing at all. They buy for vs the worſt wares, and ſell them
at the deareſt prices: and albeit the victuals fall or riſe of their prices, according to the aboundance or ſkantneſſe thereof; yet the prices of their
wares euer riſe, but neuer fall: being as conſtant in that their euill cuſtome,
as if it were a ſetled Law for them. They are alſo the ſpeciall cauſe of the
corruption of the coyne, tranſporting all our owne, and bringing in forraine, vpon what price they pleaſe to ſet on it: For order putting to them,
put the good Lawes in execution that are already made anent theſe abuſes;
but eſpecially doe three things: Eſtabliſh honeſt, diligent, but few Search-
ers, for many hands make ſlight worke; and haue an honeſt and diligent
Theſaurer to take count of them: Permit and allure forraine Merchants
to trade here: ſo ſhall ye haue beſt and beſt cheape wares, not buying them
at the third hand: And ſet euery yeere downe a certaine price of all things;
conſidering firſt, how it is in other countries: and the price being ſet reaſonably downe, if the Merchants will not bring them home on the price,
cry forrainers free to bring them.

And becauſe I haue made mention here of the coyne, make your money
of fine Gold and Siluer; cauſing the people be payed with ſubſtance, and
not abuſed with number: ſo ſhall ye enrich the common-weale, and haue
a great treaſure laid vp in ſtore, if ye fall in warres or in any ſtraites: For the
making it baſer, will breed your commoditie; but it is not to bee vſed, but
at a great neceſſitie.

And

Of Shireſ-
domes and
Regalities.

Ar. 2. pol.

Laudable cuſ-
tome of Eng-
land.

The third
eſtate.

The formes
of Merchants.

Pl. 2. de Rep. 8.
& 11. de leg.

Aduice anent
the coyne.

Of craftſmen.
Plat. 11. de leg.

A good poli-
cie of En-
gland.

Plat. 9. de leg.

A generall
fault in the
people.

Sal. in Iug.

Arist. 5. pol.
Iſoc. in paneg.

Hor. de art.
poet.

And the Crafteſ-men thinke, we ſhould be content with their worke, how bad and deare ſoeuer it be: and if they in any thing be controlled, vp goeth the blew-blanket: But for their part, take example by ENGLAND, how it hath flouriſhed both in wealth and policie, ſince the ſtrangers Crafteſ-men came in among them: Therefore not onely permit, but allure ſtrangers to come heere alſo; taking as ſtrait order for repreſſing the mutining of ours at them, as was done in ENGLAND, at their firſt in-bringing there.

But vnto one fault is all the common people of this Kingdome ſubiect, as well burgh as land; which is, to iudge and ſpeake raſhly of their Prince, ſetting the Common-weale vpon foure props; as wee call it; euer wearying of the preſent eſtate, and deſirous of nouelties. For remedie whereof (beſides the execution of Lawes that are to be vſed againſt vnreuerent ſpeakers) I know no better meane, then ſo to rule, as may iuſtly ſtop their mouthes from all ſuch idle and vnreuerent ſpeeches; and ſo to prop the weale of your people, with prouident care for their good gouernment, that iuſtly, Momus himſelfe may haue no ground to grudge at: and yet ſo to temper and mixe your ſeueritie with mildnes, that as the vniuſt railers may be reſtrained with a reuerent awe; ſo the good and louing Subiects, may not onely liue in ſuretie and wealth; but be ſtirred vp and inuited by your benigne courteſies, to open their mouthes in the iuſt praiſe of your ſo well moderated regiment. In reſpect whereof, and therewith alſo the more to allure them to a common amitie among themſelues, certaine dayes in the yeere would be appointed, for delighting the people with publicke ſpectacles of all honeſt games, and exerciſe of armes: as alſo for conueening of neighbours, for entertaining friendſhip and heartlineſſe, by honeſt feaſting and merrineſſe: For I cannot ſee what greater ſuperſtition can be in making playes and lawfull games in Maie, and good cheere at Chriſtmas, then in eating fiſh in Lent, and vpon Fridayes, the Papiſts as well vſing the one as the other: ſo that alwayes the Sabboths be kept holy, and no vnlawfull paſtime be vſed: And as this forme of contenting the peoples mindes, hath beene vſed in all well gouerned Republicks: ſo will it make you to performe in your gouernment that olde good ſentence,

Omne tulit punctum, qui miſcuit vtile dulci.

Ye ſee now (my Sonne) how for the zeale I beare to acquaint you with the plaine and ſingle veritie of all things, I haue not ſpared to be ſomething Satyricke, in touching well quickly the faults in all the eſtates of my kingdome: But I proteſt before God, I doe it with the fatherly loue that I owe to them all; onely hating their vices, whereof there is a good number of honeſt men free in euery eſtate.

And becauſe, for the better reformation of all theſe abuſes among your eſtates, it will be a great helpe vnto you, to be well acquainted with the nature and humours of all your Subiects, and to know particularly the eſtate eftate of euery part of your dominions; I would therefore counfell you, once in the yeere to vifite the principall parts of the countrey, ye fhal be in for the time : and becaufe I hope ye fhall be King of moe countries then this; once in the three yeeres to vifite all your Kingdomes; not lipening to Vice-royes, but hearing your felfe their complaints; and hauing ordinarie Councels and iuftice-feates in euerie Kingdome, of their owne countrie-men: and the principall matters euer to be decided by your felfe when ye come in thofe parts.

lat.in pol. & M in.
Tacit.7. an.
Mart.

Ye haue alfo to confider, that yee muft not onely bee carefull to keepe your fubiects, from receiuing anie wrong of others within; but alfo yee muft be careful to keepe them from the wrong of any forraine Prince with-out · fen the fword is giuen you by God not onely to reuenge vpon your owne fubiects, the wrongs committed amongft themfelues; but further, to reuenge and free them of forraine iniuries done vnto them: And therefore warres vpon iuft quarrels are lawful: but aboue all, let not the wrong caufe be on your fide.

Protection from forraine iniuries.
Xeno. 8. Cyr.
Arifi. 5 pol.
Polib. 6.
Dian. Hal. de Romul.

Vfe all other Princes, as your brethren, honeftly and kindely : Keepe precifely your promife vnto them, although to your hurt : Striue with euerie one of them in courtefie and thankefulneffe : and as with all men, fo efpecially with them, bee plaine and trewthfull ; keeping euer that Chri-ftian rule, *to doe as yee would be done to* : efpecially in counting rebellion a-gainft any other Prince, a crime againft your owne felfe, becaufe of the preparatiue. Supplie not therefore, nor truft not other Princes rebels; but pittie and fuccour all lawfull Princes in their troubles. But if any of them will not abftaine; notwithftanding what-foeuer your good deferts, to wrong you or your fubiects, craue redreffe at leafure; heare and doe all reafon : and if no offer that is lawfull or honourable, can make him to ab-ftaine, nor repaire his wrong doing; then for laft refuge, commit the iuft-neffe of your caufe to God, giuing firft honeftly vp with him, and in a pub-licke and honourable forme.

What formes to be vfed with other Princes.
Ifoc. in Plat. & Parag.

Arifi. ad A.
Varr. 11. de V. P. R.
Cic. 2. Of.
Liu. lib. 4.

Liu. lib. 1.
Cic. eod.

But omitting now to teach you the forme of making warres, becaufe that arte is largely treated of by many, and is better learned by practife then fpeculation; I will onely fet downe to you heere a few precepts therein. Let firft the iuftneffe of your caufe be your greateft ftrength; and then omitte not to vfe all lawfull meanes for backing of the fame. Confult therefore with no Necromancier nor falfe Prophet, vpon the fucceffe of your warres, remembring on king *Saules* miferable end : but keepe your land cleane of all South-fayers, according to the commaund in the Law of God, dilated by *Ieremie*. Neither commit your quarrell to bee tried by a Duell: for befide that generally all Duell appeareth to bee vnlawful, committing the quarrell, as it were, to a lot; whereof there is no warrant in the Scripture, fince the abrogating of the olde Lawe : it is fpecially mofte vn-lawfull in the perfon of a King; who being a publicke perfon hath no power therefore to difpofe of himfelfe, in refpect, that to his pre-feruation

Of warre.

Prop. 4. Eleg.
Lucan. 7.
Varro 11. de V. P. R.

1. Sam. 31.
Deut. 18.

Plutar. in Sert. & Aid.

seruation or fall, the safetie or wracke of the whole common-weale is necessarily coupled, as the body is to the head.

Luke 14.

Before ye take on warre, play the wise Kings part described by Christ;
fore-seeing how ye may beare it out with all necessarie prouision: especially remember, that money is *Neruus belli.* Choose old experimented Captaines, and yong able souldiers. Be extreamely strait and seuere in martiall
Discipline, as well for keeping of order, which is as requisite as hardinesse
in the warres, and punishing of slouth, which at a time may put the whole
armie in hazard; as likewise for repressing of mutinies, which in warres
are wonderfull dangerous. And looke to the *Spaniard,* whose great successe
in all his warres, hath onely come through straitnesse of Discipline and order: for such errours may be committed in the warres, as cannot be gotten
mended againe.

Thuc. 2 Sal in
lug.
Cic. pro l. Man.
Demost. olyn. 2.
Liu. li. 30.
Veget. 1.
Cas. 1. & 3. de
bel. cimli.
Prol. in Thras.

Be in your owne person walkrife, diligent and painefull; vsing the aduice of such as are skilfullest in the craft, as ye must also doe in all other. Be
homely with your souldiers as your companions, for winning their hearts;
and extreamly liberall, for then is no time of sparing. Be cold and foreseeing in deuising, constant in your resolutions, and forward and quicke in
your executions. Fortifie well your Campe, and assaile not rashly without
an aduantage: neither feare not lightly your enemie. Be curious in deuising stratagems, but alwayes honestly: for of any thing they worke greatest effects in the warres, if secrecie be ioyned to inuention. And once or
twise in your owne person hazard your selfe fairely; but, hauing acquired
so the fame of courage and magnanimitie, make not a daily souldier of your
selfe, exposing rashly your person to euery perill: but conserue your selfe
thereafter for the weale of your people, for whose sake yee must more care
for your selfe, then for your owne.

Cas. 1. de bello
ciui.
Li. l. 7.
Xen. 1. & 5.
Cyr. & de dis-
cip. mi.
Xen. in Ages.

Pol. l. 5.

Xen. 1. Cyr.
Thuc. 5.

Isoc. ad Phil.
Pla 9. de leg.
Liu. l. 28. & 31.
Tac. 2. his.
Plut. de fort.

And as I haue counselled you to be slow in taking on a warre, so aduise
I you to be slow in peace-making. Before ye agree, looke that the ground
of your warres be satisfied in your peace; and that ye see a good suretie for
you and your people: otherwaies a honourable and iust warre is more tollerable, then a dishonourable and dis-aduantageous peace.

Of Peace.
Isocr. in Arch.
Polib. 3.
Cic. 1. Of. & 7.
Phil.
Tac. 4. hist.

But it is not enough to a good King, by the scepter of good Lawes well
execute to gouerne, and by force of armes to protect his people; if he ioyne
not therewith his vertuous life in his owne person, and in the person of his
Court and company; by good example alluring his Subiects to the loue of
vertue, and hatred of vice. And therefore (my Sonne) sith all people are
naturally inclined to follow their Princes example (as I shewed you before)
let it not be said, that ye command others to keepe the contrary course to
that, which in your owne person ye practise, making so your wordes and
deedes to fight together: but by the contrary, let your owne life be a law-
booke and a mirrour to your people; that therein they may read the practise of their owne Lawes; and therein they may see, by your image, what
life they should leade.

A Kings life
must be ex-
emplare.
Pl. in pol. & 4.
de leg.

And

And this example in your owne life and perſon, I likewiſe diuide in two parts: The firſt, in the gouernment of your Court and followers, in all godlineſſe and vertue: the next, in hauing your owne minde decked and enriched ſo with all vertuous qualities, that therewith yee may worthily rule your people: For it is not ynough that ye haue and retaine (as priſoners) within your ſelfe neuer ſo many good qualities and vertues, except ye employ them, and ſet them on worke, for the weale of them that are committed to your charge: *Virtutis enim laus omnis in aɛtione conſiſtit.* *Plat. in Thek. & Euth. Ariſt. i. Eth. Cic. in Offic.*

Firſt then, as to the gouernment of your Court and followers, King *Dauid* ſets downe the beſt precepts, that any wiſe and Chriſtian King can practiſe in that point: For as yee ought to haue a great care for the ruling well of all your Subiects, ſo ought yee to haue a double care for the ruling well of your owne ſeruants; ſince vnto them yee are both a Politicke and Oeconomicke gouernour. And as euery one of the people will delite to follow the example of any of the Courteours, as well in euill as in good: ſo what crime ſo horrible can there be committed and ouer-ſeene in a Courteour, that will not be an exemplare excuſe for any other boldly to commit the like? And therfore in two points haue ye to take good heed anent your Court and houſhold: firſt, in chooſing them wiſely; next, in carefully ruling them whom ye haue choſen. *Of the Court. Pſal. 101.*

Cic. ad Q. frat.

It is an olde and trew ſaying, That a kindly Auer will neuer become a good horſe: for albeit good education and company be great helpes to Nature, and education be therefore moſt iuſtly called *altera natura*, yet is it euill to get out of the fleſh, that is bred in the bone, as the olde prouerbe ſayth. Be very ware then in making choice of your ſeruants and companie; —— *Nam* *Plat. 5. de Leg. Ariſt. 2. œcon.*

Turpius eiicitur, quàm non admittitur hoſpes: and many reſpects may lawfully let an admiſſion, that will not be ſufficient cauſes of depriuation. *Ouid. 5. de Triſt.*

All your ſeruants and Court muſt be compoſed partly of minors, ſuch as young Lords, to be brought vp in your company, or Pages and ſuch like; and partly of men of perfit aage, for ſeruing you in ſuch roumes, as ought to be filled with men of wiſedome and diſcretion. For the firſt ſort, ye can doe no more, but chooſe them within aage, that are come of a good and vertuous kinde, *In fide parentum*, as Baptiſme is vſed: For though *anima non venit ex traduce*, but is immediatly created by God, and infuſed from aboue; yet it is moſt certaine, that vertue or vice will oftentimes, with the heritage, be transferred from the parents to the poſteritie, and runne on a blood (as the Prouerbe is) the ſickeneſſe of the minde becomming as kindly to ſome races, as theſe ſickeneſſes of the body, that infect in the ſeede: Eſpecially chooſe ſuch minors as are come of a trew and honeſt race, and haue not had the houſe whereof they are deſcended, infected with falſhood. *Of the choiſe of ſeruants.*

Ariſt. 1. & 5. polit.

Cic. ad Q. frat.

Witneſſe the experience of the late houſe of Gowrie. Plat. 6. de Leg. Ariſt. 2. œcon. & 1. pol.*

And as for the other ſort of your companie and ſeruants, that ought

to

to be of perfit aage ; firſt ſee that they be of a good fame and without blemiſh, otherwiſe, what can the people thinke, but that yee haue choſen a
company vnto you, according to your owne humour, and ſo haue preferred theſe men, for the loue of their vices and crimes, that ye knew them to
be guiltie of? For the people that ſee you not within, cannot iudge of you,
but according to the outward appearance of your actions and companie,
which onely is ſubiect to their ſight: And next, ſee that they be indued
with ſuch honeſt qualities, as are meete for ſuch offices, as ye ordaine them
to ſerue in ; that your iudgement may be knowen in imploying euery man
according to his giftes : And ſhortly, follow good king *Dauids* counſell in
the choiſe of your ſeruants, by ſetting your eyes vpon the faithfull and vpright of the land to dwell with you.

　　But here I muſt not forget to remember, and according to my fatherly
authoritie, to charge you to preferre ſpecially to your ſeruice, ſo many as
haue trewly ſerued me, and are able for it : the reſt, honourably to reward
them, preferring their poſteritie before others, as kindlieſt : ſo ſhall ye not
onely be beſt ſerued, (for if the haters of your parents cannot loue you, as I
ſhewed before, it followeth of neceſſitie their louers muſt loue you) but
further, ye ſhall kyth your thankefull memorie of your father, and procure
the bleſſing of theſe olde ſeruants, in not miſſing their olde maſter in you ;
which otherwiſe would be turned in a prayer for me, and a curſe for you.
Vſe them therefore when God ſhall call me, as the teſtimonies of your affection towards me ; truſting and aduancing thoſe fartheſt, whom I found
faithfulleſt : which ye muſt not diſcerne by their rewards at my hand (for
rewards, as they are called *Bona fortunæ,* ſo are they ſubiect vnto fortune)
but according to the truſt I gaue them ; hauing oft-times had better heart
then hap to the rewarding of ſundry : And on the other part, as I wiſh you
to kyth your conſtant loue towards them that I loued, ſo deſire I you to
kyth in the ſame meaſure, your conſtant hatred to them that I hated : I
meane, bring not home, nor reſtore not ſuch, as ye finde ſtanding baniſhed or fore-faulted by me. The contrary would kyth in you ouer great
a contempt of me, and lightneſſe in your owne nature: for how can they
be trew to the Sonne, that were falſe to the Father?

　　But to returne to the purpoſe anent the choiſe of your ſeruants, yee ſhall
by this wiſe forme of doing, eſchew the inconuenients, that in my minoritie I fell in, anent the choiſe of my ſeruants : For by them that had
the command where I was brought vp, were my ſeruants put vnto mee;
not chooſing them that were meeteſt to ſerue me, but whom they thought
meeteſt to ſerue their turne about me, as kythed well in many of them at
the firſt rebellion raiſed againſt mee, which compelled mee to make a
great alteration among my ſeruants. And yet the example of that corruption made mee to be long troubled there-after with ſolliciters, recommending ſeruants vnto me, more for ſeruing in effect, their friends that
put them in, then their maſter that admitted them. Let my example then
　　　　　　　　　　　　　　　　　　　　　　　　　　　　　　teach

teach you to follow the rules here set downe , choosing your seruants for your owne vse,and not for the vse of others : And since ye must bee *communis parens* to all your people, so choose your seruants indifferently out of all quarters ; not respecting other mens appetites,but their owne qualities: For as ye must command all, so reason would, ye should be serued out of al, as ye please to make choice.

Arist. 2. pol.

But specially take good heed to the choice of your seruants, that ye preferre to the offices of the Crowne and estate: for in other offices yee haue onely to take heede to your owne weale ; but these concerne likewise the weale of your people; for the which they must bee answerable to God. Choose then for all these Offices, men of knowen wisedome, honestie, and good conscience; well practised in the points of the craft, that yee ordaine them for, and free of all factions and partialities; but specially free of that filthie vice of Flatterie, the pest of all Princes,and wracke of Republicks: For since in the first part of this Treatise, I fore-warned you to be at warre with your owne inward flatterer πάθια, how much more should yée be at war with outward flatterers, who are nothing so sib to you, as your selfe is; by the selling of such counterfeit wares,onely preassing to ground their greatnesse vpon your ruines? And therefore bee carefull to preferre none, as yee will bee answerable to God,but onely for their worthinesse : But specially choose honest, diligent, meane , but responsall men, to bee your receiuers in money matters : meane I say, that ye may when yee please, take a sharpe account of their intromission, without perill of their breeding any trouble to your estate : for this ouersight hath beene the greatest cause of my mis-thriuing in money matters. Especially, put neuer a forrainer, in any principall office of estate : for that will neuer faile to stirre vp sedition and enuie in the country-mens hearts, both against you and him : But (as I saide before) if God prouide you with moe countries then this; choose the borne-men of euery countrey, to bee your chiefe counsellers therein.

Of the officers of the Crowne. *Plat. de repub. Cic. ad Q. frat. Isoc. in Panath. ad Nic. & de pace. T Iuc 6. Plutar. in pol.*

Plat. in Phedr. & Menex. Arist. 5 pol. Isoc. in Sym. Tacit. 3. hist. Curt. 8.

Of publicke receiuers.

A speciall principle in policie. *Arist. 5. pol. Cic. ad Q. frat.*

And for conclusion of my aduice anent the choice of your seruants, delight to be serued with men of the noblest blood that may bee had : for besides that their seruice shall breed you great good-will and least enuie, contrarie to that of start-vps ; ye shall oft finde vertue follow noble races, as I haue said before speaking of the Nobilitie.

Plat. in 1. Al. in pol. & 5. de legib. Arist. 2. æcon.

Now, as to the other point, anent your gouerning of your seruants when yee haue chosen them; make your Court and companie to bee a patterne of godlinesse and all honest vertues, to all the rest of the people. Bee a daily watch-man ouer your seruants, that they obey your lawes precisely : For how can your lawes bee kept in the countrey , if they be broken at your eare? Punishing the breach thereof in a Courteour, more seuerely, then in the person of any other of your subiects : and aboue all, suffer none of them (by abusing their credite with you) to oppresse or wrong any of your subiects. Be homely or strange with them,as ye thinke

Gouernment of the Court. *Isocr. in Areop.*

Idem in Panath.

Arist. 2. pol.

P   their

Tacit. 1.hist.

Val. lib. 2.
Curt. 4.

Demost.8 phil.
Sal. in Cat.
Liu. 22.

Tacit. eod. &
1. An.

The ground-
stone of good
gouernment.
Ar. 5. polit.
Tacit. in Ag.
Dion li. 52.
Xens. in Ages.
Isoc. in Sym.
et ad Ph.
Id. de permu-
tat.
Cic. ad Q. frat.

1. King. 10.

Of Mariage.

Gen. 2.23.

Preparation
to mariage.

their behauiour deserueth, and their nature may beare with. Thinke a quarrellous man a pest in your companie. Bee carefull euer to preferre the gentilest natured and trustiest, to the inwardest Offices about you, especially in your chalmer. Suffer none about you to meddle in any mens particulars, but like the Turkes Ianisares, let them know no father but you, nor particular but yours. And if any wil meddle in their kinne or friends quarrels, giue them their leaue: for since ye must be of no surname nor kinne, but equall to all honest men; it becommeth you not to bee followed with partiall or factious seruants. Teach obedience to your seruants, and not to thinke themselues ouer-wise: and, as when any of them deserueth it, ye must not spare to put them away, so, without a seene cause, change none of them. Pay them, as all others your subiects, with *præmium* or *pæna* as they deserue, which is the very ground-stone of good gouernement. Employ euery man as ye thinke him qualified, but vse not one in all things, lest he waxe proude, and be enuied of his fellowes. Loue them best, that are plainnest with you, and disguise not the trewth for all their kinne: suffer none to be euill tongued, nor backbiters of them they hate: command a hartly and brotherly loue among all them that serue you. And shortly, maintaine peace in your Court, bannish enuie, cherish modestie, bannish deboshed insolence, foster humilitie, and represse pride: setting downe such a comely and honourable order in all the points of your seruice; that when strangers shall visite your Court, they may with the Queene of *Sheba*, admire your wisedome in the glorie of your house, and comely order among your seruants.

But the principall blessing that yee can get of good companie, will stand in your marrying of a godly and vertuous wife: for shee must bee nearer vnto you, then any other companie, being *Flesh of your flesh, and bone of your bone*, as *Adam* saide of *Heuah*. And becaufe I know not but God may call mee, before ye be readie for Mariage; I will shortly set downe to you heere my aduice therein.

First of all confider, that Mariage is the greatest earthly felicitie or miferie, that can come to a man, according as it pleafeth God to blesse or curse the same. Since then without the blessing of GOD, yee cannot looke for a happie succesfe in Mariage, yee must bee carefull both in your preparation for it, and in the choice and vfage of your wife, to procure the same. By your preparation, I meane, that yee must keepe your bodie cleane and vnpolluted, till yee giue it to your wife; whom-to onely it belongeth. For how can ye iuftly craue to bee ioyned with a pure virgine, if your bodie be polluted? why fhould the one halfe bee cleane, and the other defiled? And although I know, fornication is thought but a light and a veniall finne, by the most part of the world, yet remember well what I faid to you in my first Booke anent confcience, and count euery finne and breach of Gods law, not according as the vaine world efteemeth of it, but as God the Iudge and maker of the lawe accounteth of the fame

Heare

Heare God commanding by the mouth of *Paul*, to *abstaine from fornication*, declaring that the *fornicator shall not inherite the Kingdome of heauen*: and by the mouth of *Iohn*, reckoning out fornication amongst other grieuous sinnes, that debarre the committers amongst *dogs and swine*, *from entry in that spirituall and heauenly Ierusalem*. And consider, if a man shall once take vpon him, to count that light, which God calleth heauie; and veniall that, which God calleth grieuous; beginning first to measure any one sinne by the rule of his lust and appetites, and not of his conscience; what shall let him to doe so with the next, that his affections shall stirre him to, the like reason seruing for all : and so to goe forward till he place his whole corrupted affections in Gods roome ? And then what shall come of him; but, as a man giuen ouer to his owne filthy affections, shall perish into them ? And because wee are all of that nature, that sibbest examples touch vs neerest, consider the difference of succeffe that God granted in the Mariages of the King my grand-father, and me your owne father : the reward of his incontinencie, (proceeding from his euill education) being the suddaine death at one time of two pleasant yong Princes; and a daughter onely borne to succeed to him, whom hee had neuer the hap, so much as once to see or blesse before his death : leauing a double curse behinde him to the land, both a Woman of sexe, and a new borne babe of aage to raigne ouer them. And as for the blessing God hath bestowed on mee, in granting me both a greater continencie, and the fruits following there-upon, your selfe, and sib folkes to you, are (praise be to God) sufficient witnesses : which, I hope the same God of his infinite mercie, shall continue and increase, without repentance to me and my posteritie. Be not ashamed then, to keepe cleane your body, which is the Temple of the holy Spirit, notwithstanding all vaine allurements to the contrary, discerning trewly and wisely of euery vertue and vice, according to the trew qualities therof, and not according to the vaine conceits of men.

As for your choise in Mariage, respect chiefly the three causes, wherefore Mariage was first ordeined by God ; and then ioyne three accessories, so farre as they may be obtained, not derogating to the principalles.

The three causes it was ordeined for, are, for staying of lust, for procreation of children, and that man should by his Wife, get a helper like himselfe. Deferre not then to Marie till your aage : for it is ordeined for quenching the lust of your youth : Especially a King must tymouslie Marie for the weale of his people. Neither Marie yee, for any accessory cause or worldly respects, a woman vnable, either through aage, nature, or accident, for procreation of children : for in a King that were a double fault, afwell against his owne weale, as against the weale of his people. Neither also Marie one of knowne euill conditions, or vicious education : for the woman is ordeined to be a helper, and not a hinderer to man.

The three accessories, which as I haue said, ought also to be respected, without derogating to the principall causes, are beautie, riches, and friend-

P 2   ship

Marginal notes:
1. Cor. 6. 10.
Reuel. 11. 15.
The dangerous effects of lust.
A domesticke example.
1. Cor. 6. 19.
Mariage ordained for three causes. *Arist.* 7. *pol.*
Id. eod.
Accessory causes of mariage. *Æg. Ro.* 2. *de reg. pr.*

ſhip by alliance,which are all bleſſings of God. For beautie increaſeth your loue to your Wife, contenting you the better with her, without caring for others: and riches and great alliance, doe both make her the abler to be a helper vnto you. But if ouer great reſpect being had to theſe acceſſories, the principall cauſes bee ouer-ſeene (which is ouer oft practiſed in the world) as of themſelues they are a bleſſing being well vſed ; ſo the abuſe of them will turne them in a curſe. For what can all theſe worldly reſpects auaile,when a man ſhall finde himſelfe coupled with a diuel,to be one fleſh with him, and the halfe marrow in his bed ? Then (though too late) ſhall he finde that beautie without bountie,wealth without wiſdome, and great friendſhip without grace and honeſtie ; are but faire ſhewes, and the deceitfull maſques of infinite miſeries.

But haue ye reſpect,my Sonne,to theſe three ſpeciall cauſes in your Mariage, which flow from the firſt inſtitution thereof, & cætera omnia adijcientur vobis. And therefore I would ratheſt haue you to Marie one that were fully of your owne Religion ; her ranke and other qualities being agreeable to your eſtate. For although that to my great regrate, the number of any Princes of power and account, profeſſing our Religion, bee but very ſmall ; and that therefore this aduice ſeemes to be the more ſtrait and difficile: yet ye haue deeply to weigh, and conſider vpon theſe doubts,how ye and your wife can bee of one fleſh ; and keepe vnitie betwixt you, being members of two oppoſite Churches: diſagreement in Religion bringeth euer with it, diſagreement in maners ; and the diſſention betwixt your Preachers and hers, wil breed and foſter a diſſention among your ſubiects, taking their example from your family ; beſides the perill of the euill education of your children. Neither pride you that ye wil be able to frame and make her as ye pleaſe: that deceiued Salomon the wiſeſt King that euer was; the grace of Perſeuerance,not being a flowre that groweth in our garden.

Remember alſo that Mariage is one of the greateſt actions that a man doeth in all his time, eſpecially in taking of his firſt Wife : and if hee Marie firſt baſely beneath his ranke , he will euer be the leſſe accounted of thereafter. And laſtly,remember to chooſe your Wife as I aduiſed you to chooſe your ſeruants : that ſhe be of a whole and cleane race, not ſubiect to the hereditary ſickneſſes,either of the ſoule or the body : For if a man wil be careful to breed horſes and dogs of good kinds,how much more careful ſhould he be,for the breed of his owne loines? So ſhal ye in your Mariage haue reſpect to your conſcience,honour,and naturall weale in your ſucceſſours.

When yee are Maried, keepe inuiolably your promiſe made to God in your Mariage ; which ſtandeth all in doing of one thing, and abſtayning from another : to treat her in all things as your wife,and the halfe of your ſelfe ; and to make your body (which then is no more yours, but properly hers) common with none other. I truſt I need not to inſiſt here to diſſwade you from the filthy vice of adulterie : remember onely what ſolemne promiſe yee make to God at your Mariage: and ſince it is onely by the

Matth.13.
A ſpecial caution in mariage.

For keeping the blood pure.
Pla. 5. de Rep.
Cic. 2. de Diu.
Ariſt. de gen.
An.
Lucr. 4.

Pl. 11. de leg.
Iſ. in Sym.

the force of that promise that your children succeed to you, which otherwayes they could not doe; æquitie and reason would, ye should keepe your
part thereof. God is euer a seuere auenger of all periuries; and it is no oath
made in iest, that giueth power to children to succeed to great kingdomes.
Haue the King my grand-fathers example before your eyes, who by his
adulterie, bred the wracke of his lawfull daughter and heire; in begetting
that bastard, who vnnaturally-rebelled, and procured the ruine of his owne
Souerane and sister. And what good her posteritie hath gotten sensyne, of
some of that vnlawfull generation, *Bothuell* his treacherous attempts can
beare witnesse. Keepe præcisely then your promise made at Mariage, as ye
would wish to be partaker of the blessing therein.

Cic. 2. de leg.

And for your behauiour to your Wife, the Scripture can best giue you
counsell therein · Treat her as your owne flesh, command her as her Lord,
cherish her as your helper, rule her as your pupill, and please her in all
things reasonable; but teach her not to be curious in things that belong
her not: Ye are the head, shee is your body; It is your office to command,
and hers to obey; but yet with such a sweet harmonie, as shee should be as
ready to obey, as ye to command; as willing to follow, as ye to go before;
your loue being wholly knit vnto her, and all her affections louingly bent
to follow your will.

Arist. 8. Æth. & 1 Pol. Xen. & Arist. in æco.

And to conclude, keepe specially three rules with your Wife: first, suffer
her neuer to meddle with the Politicke gouernment of the Common-
weale, but holde her at the Oeconomicke rule of the house; and yet all to,
be subiect to your direction: keepe carefully good and chaste company a-
bout her, for women are the frailest sexe; and be neuer both angry at
once, but when ye see her in passion, ye should with reason danton yours:
for both when yee are setled, ye are meetest to iudge of her errours; and
when she is come to her selfe, she may be best made to apprehend her offence, and reuerence your rebuke.

Arist. 1 rhet. Plu. in Menon. Ægid R. de reg pr. Plu. 5. de Rep. & 7. de leg.

If God send you successeion, be carefull for their vertuous education:
loue them as ye ought, but let them know as much of it, as the gentlenesse
of their nature will deserue; contayning them euer in a reuerent loue and
feare of you. And in case it please God to prouide you to all these three
Kingdomes, make your eldest sonne *Isaac*, leauing him all your kingdomes; and prouide the rest with priuate possessions: Otherwayes by
deuiding your kingdomes, yee shall leaue the seed of diuision and discord
among your posteritie; as befell to this Ile, by the diuision and assigne-
ment thereof, to the three sonnes of *Brutus, Locrine, Albanact,* and *Camber.*
But if God giue you not successeion, defraud neuer the nearest by right,
what-soeuer conceit yee haue of the person: For Kingdomes are euer at
Gods disposition, and in that case we are but liue-rentars, lying no more in
the Kings, nor peoples hands to dispossesse the righteous heire.

A Kings be-
hauiour to-
wards his
children.
Plu. in T hes.
4. & 5 de Rep.
& 6. & 7. de l.
Arist. 7. pol.
A caution
foreshewing
future diui-
sion.

Polid. 1.
Crownes
come not in
commerce.

And as your company should be a paterne to the rest of the people, so
should your person be a lampe and mirrour to your company · giuing light

Plu. in Pol.
Cic. ad Q. frat.

P 3

to

to your feruants to walke in the path of vertue, and reprefenting vnto them fuch worthie qualities, as they fhould preaffe to imitate.

I need not to trouble you with the particular difcourfe of the foure Cardinall vertues, it is fo troden a path: but I will fhortly fay vnto you; make one of them, which is Temperance, Queene of all the reft within you. I meane not by the vulgar interpretation of Temperance, which one-ly confifts in *guftu & tactu*, by the moderating of thefe two fenfes: but, I meane of that wife moderation, that firft commaunding your felfe, fhall as a Queene, command all the affections and paffions of your minde, and as a Phifician, wifely mixe all your actions according thereto. Therefore, not onely in all your affections and paffions, but euen in your moft vertu-ous actions, make euer moderation to be the chiefe ruler: For although holineffe be the firft and moft requifite qualitie of a Chriftian, as procee-ding from a feeling feare and trew knowledge of God: yet yee remember how in the conclufion of my firft booke, I aduifed you to moderate al your outward actions flowing there-fra. The like fay I now of Iuftice, which is the greateft vertue that properly belongeth to a Kings office.

Vfe Iuftice, but with fuch moderation, as it turne not in Tyrannie: o-therwaies *fummum Ius*, is *fumma iniuria*. As for example: if a man of a knowen honeft life, be inuaded by brigands or theeues for his purfe, and in his owne defence flay one of them, they beeing both moe in number, and alfo knowen to bee deboſhed and infolent liuers; whereby the con-trarie, hee was fingle alone, beeing a man of found reputation: yet becaufe they were not at the horne, or there was no eye-witneffe prefent that could verifie their firft inuading of him, fhall hee therefore lofe his head? And likewife, by the law-burrowes in our lawes, men are prohibited vnder great pecuniall paines, from any wayes inuading or molefting their neigh-bours perfon or bounds: if then his horfe breake the halter, and paftour in his neighbours medow, fhall he pay two or three thoufand pounds for the wantonneffe of his horfe, or the weakneffe of his halter? Surely no: for lawes are ordained as rules of vertuous and fociall liuing, and not to bee fnares to trap your good fubiects: and therefore the lawe muft be interpre-ted according to the meaning, and not to the literall fenfe thereof: *Nam ra-tio eft anima legis*.

And as I faid of Iuftice, fo fay I of Clemencie, Magnanimitie, Liberali-tie, Conftancie, Humilitie, and all other Princely vertues; *Nam in medio ftat virtus*. And it is but the craft of the Diuell that falfly coloureth the two vices that are on either fide thereof, with the borrowed titles of it, albeit in very deede they haue no affinitie therewith and the two ex-tremities themfelues, although they feeme contrarie, yet growing to the height, runne euer both in one: For *in infinitis omnia concurrunt*; and what difference is betwixt extreame tyrannie, delighting to deftroy all mankinde; and extreame flackeneffe of punifhment, permitting euery man to tyrannize ouer his companion? Or what differeth extreame

prodiga-

The right vfe of tempe-rance.
*Arift. 5. pol.
Pol. 6.
Cic. 1. off. 2.
de inuen. &
in Par.*

In holineffe.

Iniuftice.
*Pla. 4. de Leg.
Arift. 1. mag.
mor.
Cic. 2. off. pro
Rab. & ad Q.
frat.
Seneca de cl.*

*Arift. 5. eth.
& 1. rhet.
Cicer. pro Cæc.*

The falfe fem-blance of ex-tremities.

Their co-incidence.

prodigalitie, by wasting of all to possesse nothing; from extreame nig-gardnesse, by hoarding vp all to enioy nothing; like the Asse that carying victuall on her backe, is like to starue for hunger, and will bee glad of thrissels for her part? And what is betwixt the pride of a glorious *Nebu-chadnezzar*, and the preposterous humilitie of one of the proud Puritanes, claiming to their Paritie, and crying, Wee are all but vile wormes, and yet will iudge and giue Law to their King, but will be iudged nor control-led by none? Surely there is more pride vnder such a ones blacke bonnet, then vnder *Alexander* the great his Diademe, as was said of *Diogenes* in the like case.

But aboue all vertues, study to know well your owne craft, which is to rule your people. And when I say this, I bid you know all crafts: For except ye know euery one; how can yee controll euery one, which is your proper office? Therefore besides your education, it is necessarie yee delight in reading, and seeking the knowledge of all lawfull things; but with these two restrictions: first, that yee choose idle houres for it, not interrupting therewith the discharge of your office: and next, that yee studie not for knowledge nakedly, but that your principall ende be, to make you able thereby to vse your office; practising according to your knowledge in all the points of your calling: not like these vaine Astrolo-gians, that studie night and day on the course of the starres, onely that they may, for satisfying their curiositie, know their course. But since all Artes and sciences are linked euery one with other, their greatest prin-ciples agreeing in one (which mooued the Poets to faine the nine Muses to be all sisters) studie them, that out of their harmonie, ye may sucke the knowledge of all faculties; and consequently be on the counsell of all crafts, that yee may be able to containe them all in order, as I haue alreadie said: For knowledge and learning is a light burthen, the weight whereof will neuer presse your shoulders.

First of all then, study to be well seene in the Scriptures, as I remem-bred you in the first booke; as well for the knowledge of your owne sal-uation, as that ye may be able to containe your Church in their calling, as *Custos vtriusque Tabulæ*. For the ruling them well, is no small point of your office; taking specially heede, that they vague not from their text in the Pulpit: and if euer ye would haue peace in your land, suffer them not to meddle in that place with the estate or policie; but punish seuerely the first that presumeth to it. Doe nothing towards them without a good ground and warrant, but reason not much with them: for I haue ouer-much surfeited them with that, and it is not their fashion to yeeld. And suf-fer no conuentions nor meetings among Church-men, but by your know-ledge and permission.

Next the Scriptures, studie well your owne Lawes: for how can ye dis-cerne by the thing yee know not? But preasse to draw all your Lawes and processes; to be as short and plaine as ye can: assure your selfe the long-somnesse

The right ex-tention of a kings craft.

Plat. in pol. 5. de Rep. & E-pist. 7. Cic. ad Q. frat. & de or.

Id. 1. de fin.

Id. 1. Offic.

The Scrip-ture. Deut. 17.

Of the Lawes municipall.

Plat.4. de Rep.
& 6. de Leg.
Arist.1. rhet.

Cic 1. de Orat.
Sen. in Lud.
Resort to the
Session.

somnesse both of rights and processes, breedeth their vnsure loosenesse and obscuritie, the shortest being euer both the surest and plainest forme, and the longsomnesse seruing onely for the enriching of the Aduocates and Clerkes, with the spoile of the whole countrey : And therefore delite to haunt your Session, and spie carefully their proceedings; taking good heede, if any briberie may be tried among them, which cannot ouer seuerely be punished. Spare not to goe there, for gracing that farre any that yee fauour, by your presence to procure them expedition of Iustice; although that should be specially done, for the poore that cannot waite on, or are debarred by mightier parties. But when yee are there, remember

Plat. in pol.
Arist.1. Rhet.
Cic. ad Q. frat.
Plut. in Is.

the throne is Gods and not yours, that ye sit in, and let no fauour, nor whatsoeuer respects mooue you from the right. Ye sit not there, as I shewe before, for rewarding of friends or seruants, nor for crossing of contemners, but onely for doing of Iustice. Learne also wisely to discerne betwixt Iustice and equitie; and for pitie of the poore, rob not the rich, because he may better spare it, but giue the little man the larger coat if it be his; eschewing the errour of young *Cyrus* therein : For Iustice, by the Law, giueth euery man his owne; and equitie in things arbitrall, giueth euery one that which is meetest for him.

Xen.1.Cyr.

But specially
to the secret
Counsell.

Be an ordinarie sitter in your secret Counsell : that iudicature is onely ordained for matters of estate, and repressing of insolent oppressions. Make that iudgement as compendious and plaine as ye can; and suffer no Aduocates to be heard there with their dilatours, but let euery partie tell his owne tale himselfe : and wearie not to heare the complaints of the oppressed, *aut ne Rex fis.* Remit euery thing to the ordinary iudicature, for eschewing of confusion : but let it be your owne craft, to take a sharpe account of euery man in his office.

Cic. ad Q. frat.
Tac.1. hist.
Plut. in Demet.

Reading of
histories.

And next the Lawes, I would haue you to be well versed in authentick histories, and in the Chronicles of all nations, but specially in our owne histories (*Ne fis peregrinus domi*) the example, whereof most neerely concernes you : I meane not of such infamous inuectiues, as *Buchanans* or *Knoxes* Chronicles : and if any of these infamous libels remaine vntill your dayes, vse the Law vpon the keepers thereof : For in that point I would

Plat. in Menon.

haue you a Pythagorist, to thinke that the very spirits of these archibelloufes of rebellion, haue made transition in them that hoardes their

Arist.1 Rhet.
Polit.1.
Plut. in Timo.
Cic.2.de Or.

bookes, or maintaines their opinions; punishing them, euen as it were their authours risen againe. But by reading of authenticke histories and Chronicles, yee shall learne experience by Theoricke, applying the by-

Eccles.1.

past things to the present estate, *quia nihil nouum sub sole* : such is the continuall volubilitie of things earthly, according to the roundnesse of the world, and reuolution of the heauenly circles : which is expressed by

Ezech.1.

the wheeles in *Ezechiels* visions, and counterfeited by the Poets *in rota Fortunæ.* And likewise by the knowledge of histories, yee shall knowe how to behaue your selfe to all Embassadours and strangers; being able

to

to difcourfe with them vpon the eftate of their owne countrey. And a-
mong al prophane hiftories, I muft not omit moft fpecially to recommend
vnto you, the Commentaries of *Cæfar*; both for the fweete flowing of
the ftile, as alfo for the worthineffe of the matter it felfe: For I haue euer
beene of that opinion, that of all the Ethnick Emperors, or great Captaines
that euer were, he hath fartheft excelled, both in his practife, and in his precepts in martiall affaires.

As for the ftudie of other liberall artes and fciences, I would haue you
reafonably verfed in them, but not preaffing to bee a paffe-mafter in any
of them : for that cannot but diftract you from the points of your calling,
as I fhewed you before: and when, by the enemie winning the towne, yee
fhall bee interrupted in your demonftration, as *Archimedes* was; your people (I thinke) will looke very bluntly vpon it. I graunt it is meete yee haue
fome entrance, fpecially in the Mathematickes; for the knowledge of the
arte militarie, in fituation of Campes, ordering of battels, making Forti-
fications, placing of batteries, or fuch like. And let not this your knowledge be dead without fruites, as Saint *Iames* fpeaketh of Faith: but let it appeare in your daily conuerfation, and in all the actions of your life.

Embrace trew magnanimitie, not in beeing vindictiue, which the corrupted iudgements of the world thinke to be trew Magnanimitie; but by
the contrarie, in thinking your offendour not worthie of your wrath,
empyring ouer your owne paffion, and triumphing in the commaunding
your felfe to forgiue: husbanding the effects of your courage and wrath,
to be rightly employed vpon repelling of iniuries within, by reuenge taking vpon the oppreffours; and in reuenging iniuries without, by iuft
warres vpon forraine enemies. And fo, where ye finde a notable iniurie,
fpare not to giue courfe to the torrents of your wrath. *The wrath of a King,*
is like to the roaring of a Lyon.

Fofter trew Humilitie, in banniſhing pride, not onely towards God
(confidering yee differ not in ſtuffe, but in vfe, and that onely by his ordinance, from the bafeft of your people) but alfo towards your Parents. And
if it fall out that my Wife ſhall out-liue me, as euer ye thinke to purchafe my
bleffing, honour your mother: fet *Beerſheba* in a throne on your right
hand: offend her for nothing, much leffe wrong her: remember her

Quæ longa decem tulerit faſtidia menfes;

and that your fleſh and blood is made of hers: and beginne not, like
the young lordes and lairdes, your firft warres vpon your Mother; but
preaffe earneftly to deferue her bleffing. Neither deceiue your felfe with
many that fay, they care not for their Parents curfe, fo they deferue it not.
O inuert not the order of nature, by iudging your fuperiours, chiefly in
your owne particular! But affure your felfe, the bleffing or curfe of the
Parents, hath almoft euer a Propheticke power ioyned with it: and if
there were no more, honour your Parents, for the lengthning of your owne
dayes,

Margin notes:

Of the arts liberall.
Sen. ep. 84.

Liu. l. 24.
Plut. in Marc.

Of Mathema-
tickes.
Pl. 7. de leg.
Arift. 1. Meta.
Iam. 2. 17.

Of magna-
nimitie.
Arift. 4. eth.
Sen. de cl.

Cic. 1. off.
Virg. 6. Æn.

Prou. 20.

Of humilitie.

Plat. 4. de Leg.
Xen. 2. de dict.
& fact. Sot.

Exod. 20.

Exod. 10.
Xen. 1. & 3.
Cyr.

dayes, as GOD in his Law promiſeth. Honour alſo them that are *in loco Parentum* vnto you, ſuch as your gouernours, vp-bringers, and Præcep-tours: be thankefull vnto them and reward them, which is your dewtie and honour.

Cic. ad Q. frat.

But on the other part, let not this trew humilitie ſtay your high indig-nation to appeare, when any great oppreſſours ſhall præſume to come in your preſence; then frowne as ye ought: And in-caſe they vſe a colour of Law in oppreſſing their poore ones, as ouer-many doe; that which ye can-

Arift. 5. pol.

not mend by Law, mend by the withdrawing of your countenance from them: and once in the yeere croſſe them, when their erands come in your

Matth. 18.

way, recompencing the oppreſſour, according to Chriſts parable of the two debtours.

Of Conftan-cie.
Arift. 4. eib.
Thuc. 3, 6.
Cic. 1. Of. &
ad Q. f.
Brut. ad Cic.

Keepe trew Conſtancie, not onely in your kindeneſſe towards honeſt men; but being alſo *inuicti animi* againſt all aduerſities: not with that Stoicke inſenſible ſtupiditie, wherewith many in our dayes, preaſſing to winne honour, in imitating that ancient ſect, by their inconſtant behaui-our in their owne liues, belie their profeſſion. But although ye are not a ſtocke, not to feele calamities; yet let not the feeling of them, ſo ouer-rule and doazen your reaſon, as may ſtay you from taking and vſing the beſt re-ſolution for remedie, that can be found out.

Of Libera-litie.
Cic. 1. & 2. Of.
Sal. in Iug.
Sen. 4. de ben.

Vſe trew Liberalitie in rewarding the good, and beſtowing frankly for your honour and weale: but with that proportionall diſcretion, that eue-ry man may be ſerued according to his meaſure, wherein reſpect muſt be had to his ranke, deſerts, and neceſſitie: And prouide how to haue, but caſt not away without cauſe. In ſpeciall, empaire not by your Liberalitie the ordinarie rents of your crowne; whereby the eſtate Royall of you, and your ſucceſſours, muſt be maintained, *ne exhaurias fontem liberalitatis*: for that would euer be kept *ſacroſanctum & extra commercium*: otherwaies, your Liberalitie would decline to Prodigalitie, in helping others with your, and your ſucceſſours hurt. And aboue all, enrich not your ſelfe with ex-

Iſoc. epiſt. 7.
Xen. 8. Cyr.
Phil. Com. 10.

actions vpon your ſubiects; but thinke the riches of your people your beſt treaſure, by the ſinnes of offenders, where no præuention can auaile, making iuſtly your commoditie. And in-caſe neceſſitie of warres, or o-ther extraordinaries compell you to lift Subſidies, doe it as rarely as ye can: employing it onely to the vſe it was ordained for; and vſing your ſelfe in

Arift. 5. pol.

that caſe, as *fidus depoſitarius* to your people.

Anent repor-ters.
Iſocr. ad Ph. in
Panath. & de
per.
Cic. ad Q. fr.
Plut. de curioſ.

And principally, exerciſe trew Wiſedome; in diſcerning wiſely be-twixt trew and falſe reports: Firſt, conſidering the nature of the perſon reporter; Next, what entreſſe he can haue in the weale or euill of him, of whom hee maketh the report; Thirdly, the likely-hood of the purpoſe it ſelfe; And laſt, the nature and by-paſt life of the dilated perſon: and where yee finde a tratler, away with him. And although it bee true, that a Prince can neuer without ſecrecie doe great things, yet it is better oft-times to try reports, then by credulitie to foſter ſuſpicion vpon an honeſt

man.

man. For since suspition is the Tyrants sickenesse, as the fruites of an e‑ *Isot. de pat.*
uill Conscience, *potiùs in alteram partem peccato* : I meane, in not mistrusting *Cic.3.Off.*
one, whom‑to no such vnhonestie was knowne before. But as for such
as haue slipped before, former experience may iustly breed præuention by
fore‑sight.

And to conclude my aduice anent your behauiour in your person ;
consider that G O D is the authour of all vertue, hauing imprinted in
mens mindes by the very light of nature, the loue of all morall vertues ; as *Cicer.3.Tusc.*
was seene by the vertuous liues of the old *Romanes* : and preasse then to
shine as farre before your people, in all vertue and honestie ; as in great‑
nesse of ranke : that the vse therof in all your actions, may turne, with
time, to a naturall habitude in you ; and as by their hearing
of your Lawes,so by their sight of your person,both
their eyes and their eares,may leade and allure
them to the loue of vertue,and ha‑
tred of vice.

O F

OF A KINGS BEHAVI-
OVR IN INDIFFERENT
THINGS.

THE THIRD BOOKE.

C.ph.8.3. de
leg.Ouid.ad
Lim.
Quin.4.decl.

I T is a trew old faying, That a King is as one fet on a ftage, whofe fmalleft actions and geftures, all the people gazingly doe behold : and there-fore although a King be neuer fo præcife in the difcharging of his Office, the people, who feeth but the outward part, will euer iudge of the fub-ftance, by the circumftances ; and according to the outward appearance , if his behauiour bee light or diffolute, will conceiue præ-occupied conceits of the Kings inward intention : which although with time, (the trier of all trewth,) it will euanifh, by the euidence of the contrary effects, yet *interim patitur iuftus*; and præiudged conceits will, in the meane time, breed contempt, the mother of rebellion and diforder. And befides that, it is certaine , that all the indifferent actions and behauiour of a man, haue a certaine holding and dependance, either vpon vertue or vice, accor-ding as they are vfed or ruled : for there is not a middes betwixt them, no more then betwixt their rewards, heauen and hell.

Arift.5.pol.
Indifferent
actions and
their depen-
dancie.
Plato in Phil.
& 9.de leg.

Be carefull then, my Sonne, fo to frame all your indifferent actions and outward behauiour, as they may ferue for the furtherance and forth-fet-ting of your inward vertuous difpofition.

Two forts of
them.

The whole indifferent actions of a man, I deuide in two forts : in his be-hauiour in things neceffary, as food, fleeping, raiment, fpeaking, writing, and gefture ; and in things not neceffary, though conuenient and lawfull, as paftimes or exercifes, and vfing of company for recreation.

Firft fort, and
how they be
indifferent.

As to the indifferent things neceffary, although that of themfelues they cannot bee wanted , and fo in that cafe are not indifferent ; as likewife in-cafe they bee not vfed with moderation , declining fo to the extremitie, which is vice; yet the qualitie and forme of vfing them, may fmell of ver-tue or vice, and be great furtherers to any of them.

To beginne then at the things neceffarie; one of the publickeft indif-ferent actions of a King, and that manieft, efpecially ftrangers, will narrowly

rowly take heed to; is his maner of refection at his Table, and his behauiour thereat. Therefore, as Kings vfe oft to eate publickly, it is meete and honourable that ye alfo doe fo, as well to efchew the opinion that yee loue not to haunt companie; which is one of the markes of a Tyrant; as likewife, that your delight to eate priuatlie, be not thought to be for priuate fatiffying of your gluttonie; which ye would be afhamed fhould bee publicklie feene. Let your Table bee honourably ferued; but ferue your appetite with few difhes, as yong *Cyrus* did : which both is holefommeft, and freeft from the vice of delicacie, which is a degree of gluttonie. And vfe moft to eate of reafonablie-groffe, and common-meates; afwell for making your bodie ftrong and durable for trauell at all occafions, either in peace or in warre: as that yee may bee the heartlier receiued by your meane Subiects in their houfes, when their cheare may fuffice you: which otherwayes would be imputed to you for pride and daintineffe, and breed coldneffe and difdaine in them. Let all your food bee fimple, without compofition or fauces; which are more like medecines then meate. The vfing of them was counted amongft the ancient *Romanes* a filthie vice of delicacie; becaufe they ferue onely for pleafing of the tafte, and not for fatisfying of the neceffitie of nature; abhorring *Apicius* their owne citizen, for his vice of delicacie and monfterous gluttonie. Like as both the *Grecians* and *Romanes* had in deteftation the very name of *Philoxenus*, for his filthie wifh of a Crane-craig. And therefore was that fentence vfed amongft them, againft thefe artificiall falfe appetites, *optimum condimentum fames*. But beware with vfing exceffe of meat and drinke; and chiefly, beware of drunkenneffe, which is a beaftlie vice, namely in a King : but fpecially beware with it, becaufe it is one of thofe vices that increafeth with aage. In the forme of your meate-eating, bee neither vnciuill, like a groffe Cynicke; nor affectatlie mignarde, like a daintie dame; but eate in a manlie, round, and honeft fafhion. It is no wayes comely to difpatch affaires, or to be penfiue at meate : but keepe then an open and cheerefull countenance, caufing to reade pleafant hiftories vnto you, that profite may be mixed with pleafure: and when ye are not difpofed, entertaine pleafant, quicke, but honeft difcourfes.

And becaufe meat prouoketh fleeping, be alfo moderate in your fleepe; for it goeth much by vfe : and remember that if your whole life were deuided in foure parts, three of them would be found to be confumed on meat, drinke, fleepe, and vnneceffarie occupations.

But albeit ordinarie times would commonly bee kept in meate and fleepe; yet vfe your felfe fome-times fo, that any time in the foure and twentie houres may bee alike to you for any of them; that thereby your diet may be accommodate to your affaires, and not your affaires to your diet : not therefore vfing your felfe to ouer great foftneffe and delicacie in your fleepe, more then in your meate; and fpecially in cafe yee haue adoe with the warres.

Q　　　　　Let

Marginal notes:
Formes at the Table.
Xen. in Cyr.
Xen. 1. Cyr.
Plut. in Apoth.
Sen. ep. 96.
Sen. de confol. ad Alb.
Iuuen. fat. 2.
Arift. 4 eth.
Xen. de dict. & fact. Socr.
Laert. in Socr.
Cic. 5. Tuf.
Plat. 6. de Leg.
Plin. l. 14.
Cic. 1. Off.
Of fleepe.
Pla. 7. de leg.
Beft forme of diet.
Pla. 6. de leg.

Formes in the
Chalmer.

Val. 2.
Cur. 4.

Pla. 6. de leg.

Dreames not
to be taken
heede to.

Rom. 14.
Titus 1.
Of apparell.
Isocr. de reg.

Cic. 1. Offic.

Plat. de rege.

Let not your Chalmer be throng and common in the time of your rest,
aswell for comelinesse as for eschewing of carrying reports out of the same.
Let them that haue the credite to serue in your Chalmer, be trustie and secret; for a King will haue need to vse secrecie in many things: but yet behaue your selfe so in your greatest secrets, as yee neede not bee ashamed,
suppose they were all proclaimed at the mercate crosse: But specially see
that those of your Chalmer be of a sound fame, and without blemish.

Take no heede to any of your dreames, for all prophecies, visions, and
propheticke dreames are accomplished and ceased in Christ: And therefore take no heede to freets either in dreames, or any other things; for that
errour proceedeth of ignorance, and is vnworthy of a Christian, who
should be assured, *Omnia esse pura puris*, as *Paul* sayth; all dayes and meates
being alike to Christians.

Next followeth to speake of raiment, the on-putting whereof is the
ordinarie action that followeth next to sleepe. Be also moderate in your
raiment, neither ouer superfluous, like a deboshed waster; nor yet ouer
base, like a miserable wretch; not artificially trimmed and decked, like a
Courtizane, nor yet ouer sluggishly clothed, like a countrey clowne; not
ouer lightly like a Candie souldier, or a vaine young Courtier; nor yet o-
uer grauely, like a Minister: but in your garments be proper, cleanely,
comely and honest, wearing your clothes in a carelesse, yet comely forme:
keeping in them a midde forme, *inter Togatos & Paludatos*, betwixt the
grauitie of the one, and lightnesse of the other: thereby to signifie, that
by your calling yee are mixed of both the professions; *Togatus*, as a Iudge
making and pronouncing the Law; *Paludatus*, by the power of the sword:
as your office is likewise mixed, betwixt the Ecclesiasticall and ciuill e-
state: For a King is not *merè laicus*, as both the Papists and Anabaptists
would haue him, to the which error also the Puritanes incline ouer farre.
But to returne to the purpose of garments, they ought to be vsed according to their first institution by God, which was for three causes: first to
hide our nakednesse and shame; next and consequently, to make vs more
comely; and thirdly, to preserue vs from the iniuries of heate and colde.
If to hide our nakednesse and shamefull parts, then these naturall parts ordained to be hid, should not be represented by any vndecent formes in the
cloathes: and if they should helpe our comelinesse, they should not then
by their painted preened fashion, serue for baites to filthie lecherie, as false
haire and fairding does amongst vnchast women: and if they should
preserue vs from the iniuries of heate and colde, men should not, like senselesse stones, contemne God, in lightlying the seasons, glorying to con-
quere honour on heate and colde. And although it be praise-worthy and
necessarie in a Prince, to be *patiens algoris & æstus*, when he shall haue adoe
with warres vpon the fields; yet I thinke it meeter that ye goe both cloathed and armed, then naked to the battell, except you would make you
light for away-running: and yet for cowards, *metus addit alas*. And shortly

ii

in your cloathes keepe a proportion, aſwell with the ſeaſons of the yeere, as of your aage: in the faſhions of them being careleſſe, vſing them according to the common forme of the time, ſome-times richlier, ſome-times meanlier cloathed, as occaſion ſerueth, without keeping any preciſe rule therein: For if your mind be found occupied vpon them, it wil be thought idle otherwaies, and ye ſhall bee accounted in the number of one of theſe *compti iuuenes*, which wil make your ſpirit and iudgment to be leſſe thought of. But ſpecially eſchew to be effeminate in your cloathes, in perfuming, preening, or ſuch like: and faile neuer in time of warres to bee galliardeſt and braueſt, both in cloathes and countenance. And make not a foole of your ſelfe in diſguiſing or wearing long haire or nailes, which are but excrements of nature, and bewray ſuch miſuſers of them, to bee either of a vindictiue, or a vaine light naturall. Eſpecially, make no vowes in ſuch vaine and outward things, as concerne either meate or cloathes.

Let your ſelfe and all your Court weare no ordinarie armour with your cloathes, but ſuch as is knightly and honourable ; I meane rapier-ſwordes, and daggers: For tuilyeſome weapons in the Court, betokens confuſion in the countrey. And therefore banniſh not onely from your Court, all traiterous offenſiue weapons, forbidden by the Lawes, as guns and ſuch like (whereof I ſpake alreadie) but alſo all traiterous defenſiue armes, as ſecrets, plate-ſleeues, and ſuch like vnſeene armour: For, beſides that the wearers thereof, may be preſuppoſed to haue a ſecret euill intention, they want both the vſes that defenſiue armour is ordained for ; which is, to be able to holde out violence, and by their outward glaunſing in their enemies eyes, to ſtrike a terrour in their hearts: Where by the contrary, they can ſerue for neither, being not onely vnable to reſiſt, but dangerous for ſhots, and giuing no outward ſhowe againſt the enemie ; beeing onely ordained, for betraying vnder truſt, whereof honeſt men ſhould be aſhamed to beare the outward badge, not reſembling the thing they are not. And for anſwere againſt theſe arguments, I know none but the olde Scots faſhion; which if it be wrong, is no more to be allowed for ancientneſſe, then the olde Maſſe is, which alſo our forefathers vſed.

The next thing that yee haue to take heed to, is your ſpeaking and language; whereunto I ioyne your geſture, ſince action is one of the chiefeſt qualities, that is required in an oratour : for as the tongue ſpeaketh to the eares, ſo doeth the geſture ſpeake to the eyes of the auditour. In both your ſpeaking and your geſture, vſe a naturall and plaine forme, not fairded with artifice : for (as the French-men ſay) *Rien contre-faict fin*: but eſchew all affectate formes in both.

In your language be plaine, honeſt, naturall, comely, cleane, ſhort, and ſententious, eſchewing both the extremities, aſwell in not vſing any ruſticall corrupt leide, as booke-language, and pen and inke-horne termes :

Cic. 1. Off.

Ar. ad Alex.

What ordinarie armour to be worne at Court.

Of language and geſture.
Ariſt. 3. ad Theod.
Cic. in orat. ad Q. frat. & ad Bren.

Cic. 1. Offic.

Id. eod.

and leaſt of all mignard and effœminate tearmes. But let the greateſt part of your eloquence conſiſt in a naturall, cleare, and ſenſible forme of the deliuerie of your minde, builded euer vpon certaine and good grounds; tempering it with grauitie, quickeneſſe, or merineſſe, according to the ſubieċt, and occaſion of the time; not taunting in Theologie, nor alleadging and prophaning the Scripture in drinking purpoſes, as ouer many doe.

Vſe alſo the like forme in your geſture; neither looking ſillily, like a ſtupide pedant; nor vnſetledly, with an vncouth morgue, like a new-come-ouer Cavalier : but let your behaviour be naturall, graue, and according to the faſhion of the countrey. Be not ouer-ſparing in your courteſies, for that will be imputed to inciuilitie and arrogancie : nor yet ouer prodigall in iowking or nodding at euery ſtep : for that forme of being popular, becommeth better aſpiring *Abſalons*, then lawfull Kings: framing euer your geſture according to your preſent aċtions : looking grauely and with a maieſtie when yee ſit in iudgement, or giue audience to Embaſſadours; homely, when ye are in priuate with your owne ſeruants; merily, when ye are at any paſtime or merrie diſcourſe; and let your countenance ſmell of courage and magnanimitie when ye are at the warres. And remember (I ſay ouer againe) to be plaine and ſenſible in your language : for beſides that it is the tongues office, to be the meſſenger of the mind, it may be thought a point of imbecillitie of ſpirit in a King, to ſpeake obſcurely, much more vntrewly; as if he ſtood in awe of any in vttering his thoughts.

Remember alſo, to put a difference betwixt your forme of language in reaſoning, and your pronouncing of ſentences, or declaratour of your wil in iudgement, or any other waies in the points of your office: For in the former caſe, yee muſt reaſon pleaſantly and patiently, not like a king, but like a priuate man and a ſcholer; otherwaies, your impatience of contradiċtion will be interpreted to be for lacke of reaſon on your part. Where in the points of your office, ye ſhould ripely aduiſe indeede; before yee giue foorth your ſentence : but fra it be giuen foorth, the ſuffering of any contradiċtion diminiſheth the maieſtie of your authoritie, and maketh the proceſſes endleſſe. The like forme would alſo bee obſerued by all your inferiour Iudges and Magiſtrates.

Now as to your writing, which is nothing elſe, but a forme of en-regiſtrate ſpeech; vſe a plaine, ſhort, but ſtately ſtile, both in your Proclamations and miſſiues, eſpecially to forraine Princes. And if your engine ſpur you to write any workes, either in verſe or in proſe, I cannot but allow you to praċtiſe it : but take no longſome workes in hand, for diſtraċting you from your calling.

Flatter not your ſelfe in your labours, but before they bee ſet foorth, let them firſt bee priuily cenſured by ſome of the beſt skilled men in that craft, that in theſe workes yee meddle with. And becauſe your writes will remaine as true piċtures of your minde, to all poſterities; let them beè free
of

Cic. ad Q. frat. & ad Brut.

Idem. 1. Off.

Phil. ad Alex. Cic. 2. Off.

Ariſt. 4. eth. Cic. ad At.

Iſoc. de reg & in Euagr.

Cic. 3. Off.

Id. 1. Off. Formes in reaſoning.

In iudgment. *Iſoc. ad Nic. Cic. ad Q frat.*

Of writing, and what ſtile fitteth a Prince.

Cic. 1. Off.

of all vncomelineſſe and vn-honeſtie: and according to *Horace* his counſell
——— *Nonumq; premantur in annum.*
I meane both your verſe and your proſe; letting firſt that furie and heate,
wherewith they were written, coole at leaſure; and then as an vncouth
iudge and cenſour, reuiſing them ouer againe, before they bee publiſhed,
——— *quia neſcit ʋox miſſa reuerti.*
If yee would write worthily, chooſe ſubiects worthie of you, that bee
not full of vanitie, but of vertue; eſchewing obſcuritie, and delighting
euer to bee plaine and ſenſible. And if yee write in verſe, remember
that it is not the principall part of a Poeme to rime right, and flowe well
with many pretie wordes: but the chiefe commendation of a Poeme is,
that when the verſe ſhall bee ſhaken ſundrie in proſe, it ſhall bee found ſo
rich in quicke inuentions, and poeticke flowers, and in faire and pertinent compariſons; as it ſhall retaine the luſtre of a Poeme, although in
proſe. And I would alſo aduiſe you to write in your owne language: for
there is nothing left to be ſaide in Greeke and Latine alreadie; and y new of
poore ſchollers would match you in theſe languages; and beſides that,
it beſt becommeth a King to purifie and make famous his owne tongue;
wherein he may goe before all his ſubiects; as it ſetteth him well to doe in
all honeſt and lawfull things.
 And amongſt all vnneceſſarie things that are lawfull and expedient,
I thinke exerciſes of the bodie moſt commendable to be vſed by a young
Prince, in ſuch honeſt games or paſtimes; as may further abilitie and
maintaine health: For albeit I graunt it to be moſt requiſite for a King to
exerciſe his engine, which ſurely with idleneſſe will ruſte and become
blunt; yet certainely bodily exerciſes and games are very commendable;
as well for banniſhing of idleneſſe (the mother of all vice) as for making
his bodie able and durable for trauell, which is very neceſſarie for a King.
But from this count I debarre all rough and violent exerciſes, as the foote-
ball; meeter for laming, then making able the vſers thereof: as likewiſe
ſuch tumbling trickes as only ſerue for Comœdians and Balladines, to win
their bread with. But the exerciſes that I would haue you to vſe (although
but moderately; not making a craft of them) are running, leaping, wra-
ſtling, fencing, dancing, and playing at the caitch or tenniſe, archerie, palle
maillé, and ſuch like other faire and pleaſant field-games. And the honou-
rableſt and moſt commendable games that yee can vſe, are on horſe-
backe: for it becommeth a Prince beſt of any man, to be a faire and good
horſe-man. Vſe therefore to ride and danton great and couragious horſes;
that I may ſay of you, as *Philip* ſaid of great *Alexander* his ſonne, Μακεδ όνιαν ἐκ χωρει,
And ſpecially vſe ſuch games on horſe-backe, as may teach you to handle
your armes thereon; ſuch as the tilt, the ring, and low-riding for handling
of your ſword.
 I cannot omit heere the hunting, namely with running hounds; which
is the moſt honourable and nobleſt ſorte thereof : for it is a theeuiſh forme

De arte Poe-tica.

Idem eod.

Ar. de art. Poet.

Of the exer-ciſe of the bo-die.
Xen. 1. Cyr.

Plat. 6. de leg.
Ar. 7. & 8. pol.
Cic. 1. Off.

Pl. eod.

Xen. in Cyr.
Iſ. de ing.

Plut. in Alex.

Of hunting.

of

In Cyn.1.Cyr.
& de rep.Lac.
Cic.1.Offic.

Cyropædia.

Of hawking.

Arist.10.Eth.

Of house-
games.

Arist.8.pol.

Dan. de luf. al.

Cic.1.Offic.

of hunting to shoote with gunnes and bowes; and greyhound hunting is not so martiall a game : But because I would not be thought a partiall praiser of this sport, I remit you to *Xenophon*, an olde and famous writer, who had no minde of flattering you or me in this purpose : and who also setteth downe a faire paterne, for the education of a yong king, vnder the supposed name of *Cyrus*.

As for hawking I condemne it not, but I must praise it more sparingly, because it neither resembleth the warres so neere as hunting doeth, in making a man hardie, and skilfully ridden in all grounds, and is more vncertaine and subiect to mischances; and (which is worst of all) is therethrough an extreme stirrer vp of passions : But in vsing either of these games, obserue that moderation, that ye slip not therewith the houres appointed for your affaires, which ye ought euer precisely to keepe; remembring that these games are but ordained for you, in enabling you for your office, for the which ye are ordained.

And as for sitting house-pastimes, wherewith men by driuing time, spurre a free and fast ynough running horse (as the prouerbe is) although they are not profitable for the exercise either of minde or body, yet can I not vtterly condemne them; since they may at times supply the roome, which being emptie, would be patent to pernicious idlenesse, *quia nihil potest esse vacuum.* I will not therefore agree with the curiositie of some learned men in our aage, in forbidding cardes, dice, and other such like games of hazard; although otherwayes surely I reuerence them as notable and godly men : For they are deceiued therein, in founding their argument vpon a mistaken ground, which is, that the playing at such games, is a kind of casting of lot, and therefore vnlawfull; wherein they deceiue themselues : For the casting of lot was vsed for triall of the trewth in any obscure thing, that otherwayes could not be gotten cleared; and therefore was a sort of prophecie : whereby the contrary, no man goeth to any of these playes, to cleare any obscure trewth, but onely to gage so much of his owne money, as hee pleaseth, vpon the hazard of the running of the cardes or dice, aswell as he would doe vpon the speede of a horse or a dog, or any such like gaigeour : And so, if they be vnlawfull, all gaigeours vpon vncertainties must likewayes be condemned : Not that thereby I take the defence of vaine carders and dicers, that waste their moyen, and their time (whereof fewe consider the pretiousnesse) vpon prodigall and continuall playing : no, I would rather allow it to be discharged, where such corruption cannot be eschewed. But only I cannot condemne you at some times, when ye haue no other thing adoe (as a good King will be seldome) and are wearie of reading, or euill disposed in your person, and when it is foule and stormie weather; then, I say, may ye lawfully play at the cardes or tables : For as to dicing, I thinke it becommeth best deboshed souldiers to play at, on the head of their drums, being onely ruled by hazard, and subiect to knauish cogging. And as for the chesse, I thinke it ouer fond,

becaufe

becaufe it is ouer-wife and Philofophicke a folly : For where all fuch light playes, are ordained to free mens heades for a time, from the fafhious thoughts on their affaires ; it by the contrarie filleth and troubleth mens heades, with as many fafhious toyes of the play, as before it was filled with thoughts on his affaires.

But in your playing, I would haue you to keepe three rules : firft, or ye play, confider yee doe it onely for your recreation, and refolue to hazard the loffe of all that ye play : and next, for that caufe play no more then yee care to caft among Pages : and laft, play alwaies faire play precifely, that ye come not in vfe of tricking and lying in ieaft : otherwife, if yee cannot keepe thefe rules, my counfell is that yee allutterly abftaine from thefe playes : For neither a madde paffion for loffe, nor falfhood vfed for defire of gaine, can be called a play.

Rules in playing.

Now, it is not onely lawfull, but neceffarie, that yee haue companie meete for euery thing yee take on hand, afwell in your games and exercifes, as in your graue and earneft affaires : But learne to diftinguifh time according to the occafion, choofing your companie accordingly. Conferre not with hunters at your counfell, nor in your counfell affaires : nor difpatch not affaires at hunting or other games. And haue the like refpect to the feafons of your aage, vfing your fortes of recreation and companie therefore, agreeing thereunto : For it becommeth beft, as kindlieft, euery aage to fmell of their owne qualitie, infolence and vnlawful things beeing alwaies efchewed : and not that a colt fhould draw the plough, and an olde horfe run away with the harrowes. But take heede fpecially, that your companie for recreation, be chofen of honeft perfons, not defamed or vicious, mixing filthie talke with merrineffe,

What choife of companie.

Ifoc. de reg.
Cic. 1. Off.

Ar. 2. ad Theod.

Corrumpunt bonos mores colloquia praua.
And chiefly abftaine from haunting before your mariage, the idle companie of dames, which are nothing elfe, but *irritamenta libidinis.* Bee warre likewaies to abufe your felfe, in making your fporters your counfellers : and delight not to keepe ordinarily in your companie, Comœdians or Balladines : for the Tyrans delighted moft in them, glorying to bee both authors and actors of Comœdies and Tragedies themfelues : Wherupon the anfwere that the poet *Philoxenus* difdainefully gaue to the Tyran of *Syracufe* there-anent, is now come in a prouerbe, *reduc me in latomias.* And all the rufe that *Nero* made of himfelfe when he died, was *Qualis artifex pereo?* meaning of his skill in menftrally, and playing of Tragœdies : as indeede his whole life and death, was all but one Tragœdie.

Men.

Pl. 3. de rep.
Ar. 7. & 8. pol.
Sen. 1. ep. Dyon.

Suidas.
Suet. in Ner.

Delight not alfo to bee in your owne perfon a player vpon inftruments, efpecially on fuch as commonly men winne their liuing with : nor yet to be fine of any mechanicke craft : *Leur efprit s'enfuit au bout des doigts,* faith *Du Bartas* : whofe workes, as they are all moft worthie to bee read by any Prince, or other good Chriftian, fo would I efpecially wifh you to bee well verfed in them. But fpare not fome-times by merie company,

1. Sep.

to

to be free from importunitie ; for ye ſhould be euer mooued with reaſon, which is the onely qualitie whereby men differ from beaſts ; and not with importunitie : For the which cauſe (as alſo for augmenting your Maieſtie) ye ſhall not be ſo facile of acceſſe-giuing at all times, as I haue beene; and yet not altogether retired or locked vp, like, the Kings of *Perſia*: appointing alſo certaine houres for publicke audience.

And ſince my truſt is, that God hath ordained you for moe Kingdomes then this (as I haue oft alreadie ſaid) preaſſe by the outward behauiour as well of your owne perſon, as of your court, in all indifferent things, to allure piece and piece, the reſt of your kingdomes, to follow the faſhions of that kingdome of yours, that yee finde moſt ciuill, eaſieſt to be ruled, and moſt obedient to the Lawes : for theſe outward and indifferent things will ſerue greatly for allurements to the people, to embrace and follow vertue. But beware of thrawing or conſtraining them thereto ; letting it bee brought on with time, and at leiſure; ſpecially by ſo mixing through alliance and daily conuerſation, the inhabitants of euery kingdom with other, as may with time make them to grow and welde all in one : Which may eaſily be done betwixt theſe two nations, being both but one Ile of *Britaine*, and alreadie ioyned in vnitie of Religion and language. So that euen as in the times of our anceſtours, the long warres and many bloodie battels betwixt theſe two countreys, bred a naturall and hereditarie hatred in euery of them, againſt the other : the vniting and welding of them hereafter in one, by all ſort of friendſhip, commerce, and alliance, will by the contrary produce and maintaine a naturall and inſeparable vnitie of loue amongſt them. As we haue already (praiſe be to God) a great experience of the good beginning hereof, and of the quenching of the olde hate in the hearts of both the people ; procured by the meanes of this long and happy amitie, betweene the Queene my deareſt ſiſter and me ; which during the whole time of both our Reignes, hath euer beene inuiolably obſerued.

And for concluſion of this my whole Treatiſe, remember my Sonne, by your trew and conſtant depending vpon God, to looke for a bleſſing to all your actions in your office : by the outward vſing thereof, to teſtifie the inward vprightneſſe of your heart; and by your behauiour in all indifferent things, to ſet foorth the viue image of your vertuous diſpoſition ; and in reſpect of the greatneſſe and weight of your burthen, to be patient in hearing, keeping your heart free from præoccupation, ripe in concluding, and conſtant in your reſolution : For better it is to bide at your reſolution, although there were ſome defect in it, then by daily changing, to effectuate nothing : taking the paterne thereof from the microcoſme of your owne body ; wherein ye haue two eyes, ſignifying great foreſight and prouidence, with a narrow looking in all things ; and alſo two eares, ſignifying patient hearing, and that of both the parties : but ye haue but one tongue, for pronouncing a plaine, ſenſible, and vniforme ſentence ; and but one head, and one heart, for keeping a conſtant & vniforme reſolution,

according

Curt.8.

Liu.35.
Xen.in Ageſ.
Cic. ad Q frat.

A ſpeciall good rule in gouernment.

The fruitfull effects of the vnion.

Alreadie kything in the happy amitie.

Concluſion in forme of abridge of the whole Treatiſe.

Thuc. 6.
Dion.52.

according to your apprehenfion : hauing two hands and two feete, with many fingers and toes for quicke execution, in employing all inftruments meet for effectuating your deliberations.

But forget not to digeft euer your paffion , before ye determine vpon a-ny thing, fince *Ira furor breuis eft* : vttering onely your anger according to the Apoftles rule, *Irafcimini, fed ne peccetis* : taking pleafure, not only to reward, but to aduance the good, which is a chiefe point of a Kings glory (but make none ouer-great, but according as the power of the countrey may beare) and punifhing the euill; but euery man according to his owne of-fence : not punifhing nor blaming the father for the fonne, nor the brother for the brother ; much leffe generally to hate a whole race for the fault of one: for *noxa caput fequitur.*

And aboue all, let the meafure of your loue to euery one, be according to the meafure of his vertue ; letting your fauour to be no longer tyed to any, then the continuance of his vertuous difpofition fhall deferue : not admit-ting the excufe vpon a iuft reuenge, to procure ouerfight to an iniurie: For the firft iniurie is committed againft the partie ; but the parties reuenging thereof at his owne hand, is a wrong committed againft you, in vfurping your office, whom to onely the fword belongeth, for reuenging of all the iniuries committed againft any of your people.

Thus hoping in the goodnes of God, that your naturall inclination fhall haue a happy fympathie with thefe precepts, making the wife-mans fchole-mafter, which is the example of others, to bee your teacher, according to that old verfe, *Fœlix quem faciunt aliena pericula cautum;* efchewing fo the ouer-late repentance by your owne experience, which is the fchoole-mafter of fooles ; I wil for end of all, require you my Sonne, as euer ye thinke to deferue my fatherly bleffing, to keepe continually before the eyes of your minde, the greatneffe of your charge : making the faithfull and due difcharge thereof, the principal butt ye fhoot at in all your actions: counting it euer the principall, and all your other actions but as acceffories, to be emploied as middefles for the furthering of that principall. And be-ing content to let others excell in other things, let it be your chiefeft earth-ly glory, to excell in your owne craft : according to the worthy counfel and charge of *Anchifes* to his pofteritie, in that fublime and heroicall Poet, wherein alfo my dicton is included ;

> *Excudent alij fpirantia mollius æra,*
> *(redo equidem, & viuos ducent de marmore vultus,*
> *Orabunt caufas melius, cœlique meatus*
> *Defcribent radio, & furgentia fydera dicent.*
> *Tu, regere imperio populos, Romane, memento*
> *(Hæ tibi erunt artes) pacique imponere morem,*
> " *Parcere fubiectis, & debellare fuperbos.*

Margin notes:
Hor.lib.1.epift.
Ephef.4.
Arift.5.pol.
Dion.52.
Plat.9.de leg.
Plat.in pol.
Cic.5.de rep.
Virg 6.Æn.

THE TREW LAW OF
FREE MONARCHIES:
OR
THE RECIPROCK AND
MVTVALL DVETIE BETWIXT
A FREE KING, AND HIS
naturall Subiects.

AN ADVERTISEMENT
TO THE READER.

Ccept, *I pray you (my deare countrey-men) as thankefully this Pamphlet that I offer vnto you, as louingly it is written for your weale. I would be loath both to be faschious, and fedlesse: And therefore, if it be not senten-tious, at least it is short. It may be yee misse many things that yee looke for in* it: *But for excuse thereof, consider rightly that I onely lay downe herein the trew grounds, to teach you the right-way, without wasting time vpon refuting the aduersaries. And yet I trust, if ye will take narrow tent, ye shall finde most of their great gunnes payed home againe, either with contrary conclusions, or tacite ob-iections, suppose in a dairned forme, and indiredly: For my in-tention*

tention is to instruct, and not irritat, if I may eschew it. The profite I would wish you to make of it, is, as well so to frame all your actions according to these grounds, as may confirme you in the course of honest and obedient Subiects to your King in all times comming, as also, when ye shall fall in purpose with any that shall praise or excuse the by-past rebellions that brake foorth either in this countrey, or in any other, ye shall herewith bee armed against their Sirene songs, laying their particular examples to the square of these grounds. Whereby yee shall soundly keepe the course of righteous Iudgement, decerning wisely of euery action onely according to the qualitie thereof, and not according to your pre-iudged conceits of the committers: So shall ye, by reaping profit to your selues, turne my paine into pleasure. But least the whole Pamphlet runne out at the gaping mouth of this Preface, if it were any more enlarged, I end, with committing you to God, and me to your charitable censures.

C. Φιλόπατρις.

THE

THE TREW LAW OF
FREE MONARCHIES:
OR
The Reciprock and mutuall duetie betwixt a
free King and his naturall Subiects.

AS there is not a thing so necessarie to be knowne by the people of any land, next the knowledge of their God, as the right knowledge of their alleageance, according to the forme of gouernement established among them, especially in a *Monarchie* (which forme of gouernment, as resembling the Diuinitie, approcheth neareft to perfection, as all the learned and wife men from the beginning haue agreed vpon; Vnitie being the perfection of all things,) So hath the ignorance, and (which is worfe) the feduced opinion of the multitude blinded by them, who thinke themfelues able to teach and inftruct the ignorants, procured the wracke and ouerthrow of fundry flourifhing Common-wealths; and heaped heauy calamities, threatning vtter deftruction vpon others. And the fmiling fucceffe, that vnlawfull rebellions haue oftentimes had againft Princes in aages paft (such hath bene the mifery, and iniquitie of the time) hath by way of practife ftrengthned many in their errour: albeit there cannot bé a more deceiueable argument; then to iudge ay the iuftneffe of the caufe by the euent thereof; as hereafter fhalbe proued more at length. And among others, no Common-wealth, that euer hath bene fince the beginning, hath had greater need of the trew knowledge of this ground, then this our fo long difordered, and diftracted Common-wealth hath: the misknowledge hereof being the onely fpring, from whence haue flowed fo many endleffe calamities, miferies, and confufions, as is better felt by many, then the caufe thereof well knowne, and deeply confidered. The naturall zeale therefore, that I beare to this my natiue countrie, with the great pittie I haue to fee the fo-long difturbance thereof for lacke of the trew knowledge of this ground (as I haue faid before) hath compelled me at laft to breake filence, to difcharge my

R   con-

conſcience to you my deare country men herein,that knowing the ground from whence theſe your many endleſſe troubles haue proceeded,as well as ye haue already too-long taſted the bitter fruites thereof,ye may by know-ledge, and eſchewing of the cauſe eſcape,and diuert the lamentable effects that euer neceſſarily follow thereupon. I haue choſen then onely to ſet downe in this ſhort Treatiſe, the trew grounds of the mutuall duetie, and alleageance betwixt a free and abſolute *Monarche*, and his people; not to trouble your patience with anſwering the contrary propoſitions, which ſome haue not bene aſhamed to ſet downe in writ, to the poyſoning of in-finite number of ſimple ſoules, and their owne perpetuall, and well deſer-ued infamie · For by anſwering them,I could not haue eſchewed whiles to pick,and byte wel ſaltly their perſons; which would rather haue bred con-tentiouſneſſe among the readers (as they had liked or miſliked) then found inſtruction of the trewth : Which I proteſt to him that is the ſearcher of all hearts,is the onely marke that I ſhoot at herein.

Firſt then,I will ſet downe the trew grounds,whereupon I am to build, out of the Scriptures, ſince *Monarchie* is the trew paterne of Diuinitie, as I haue already ſaid : next,from the fundamental Lawes of our owne King-dome, which neareſt muſt concerne vs : thirdly, from the law of Nature, by diuers ſimilitudes drawne out of the ſame : and will conclude ſyne by anſwering the moſt waighty and appearing incommodities that can be obiected.

The Princes duetie to his Subiects is ſo clearely ſet downe in many pla-ces of the Scriptures, and ſo openly confeſſed by all the good Princes, ac-cording to their oath in their Coronation,as not needing to be long there-in, I ſhall as ſhortly as I can runne through it.

Pſal.82.6.

Pſal. 101.
Pſal. 101.
2.King. 18.
2.Chron.29.
2.King.22.
and 23. 2.
chro.24.& 35.
Pſal.72.
1.King 3.

Rom.13.

1.Sam.8.

Ierem.29.

Kings are called Gods by the propheticall King *Dauid* , becauſe they ſit vpon G o d his Throne in the earth, and haue the count of their admini-ſtration to giue vnto him.   Their office is,*To miniſter Iuſtice and Iudgement to the people,* as the ſame *Dauid* ſaith : *To aduance the good , and puniſh the euill, as* he likewiſe ſaith : *To eſtabliſh good Lawes to his people , and procure obedience to the ſame* , as diuers good Kings of *Iudah* did : *To procure the peace of the people,* as the ſame *Dauid* ſaith : *To decide all controuerſies that can ariſe among them,* as *Salomon* did : *To be the Miniſter of God for the weale of them that doe well, and as the miniſter of God , to take vengeance vpon them that doe euill,* as S. *Paul* ſaith. And finally,*As a good Paſtour, to goe out and in before his people* as is ſaid in the firſt of *Samuel* : *That through the Princes proſperitie, the peoples peace may be pro-cured,*as *Ieremie* ſaith.

And therefore in the Coronation of our owne Kings, as well as of eue-ry Chriſtian *Monarche* they giue their Oath,firſt to maintaine the Religion preſently profeſſed within their countrie,according to their lawes,where-by it is eſtabliſhed,and to puniſh all thoſe that ſhould preſſe to alter, or di-ſturbe the profeſſion thereof; And next to maintaine all the lowable and good Lawes made by their predeceſſours: to ſee them put in execution,

and

and the breakers and violaters thereof, to be puniſhed, according to the tenour of the ſame: And laſtly, to maintaine the whole countrey, and euery
ſtate therein, in all their ancient Priuiledges and Liberties, as well againſt
all forreine enemies, as among themſelues: And ſhortly to procure the
weale and flouriſhing of his people, not onely in maintaining and putting
to execution the olde lowable lawes of the countrey, and by eſtabliſhing
of new (as neceſſitie and euill maners will require) but by all other meanes
poſſible to fore-ſee and preuent all dangers, that are likely to fall vpon
them, and to maintaine concord, wealth, and ciuilitie among them, as a
louing Father, and careful watchman, caring for them more then for himſelfe, knowing himſelfe to be ordained for them, and they not for him;
and therefore countable to that great God, who placed him as his lieutenant ouer them, vpon the perill of his ſoule to procure the weale of both
ſoules and bodies, as farre as in him lieth, of all them that are committed to
his charge. And this oath in the Coronation is the cleareſt, ciuill, and fundamentall Law, whereby the Kings office is properly defined.

By the Law of Nature the King becomes a naturall Father to all his Lieges at his Coronation: And as the Father of his fatherly duty is bound to
care for the nouriſhing, education, and vertuous gouernment of his children; euen ſo is the king bound to care for all his ſubiects. As all the toile
and paine that the father can take for his children, will be thought light
and well beſtowed by him, ſo that the effect thereof redound to their profite and weale; ſo ought the Prince to doe towards his people. As the kindly father ought to foreſee all inconuenients and dangers that may ariſe towards his children, and though with the hazard of his owne perſon preſſe
to preuent the ſame; ſo ought the King towards his people. As the fathers
wrath and correction vpon any of his children that offendeth, ought to be
by a fatherly chaſtiſement ſeaſoned with pitie, as long as there is any hope
of amendment in them; ſo ought the King towards any of his Lieges that
offend in that meaſure. And ſhortly, as the Fathers chiefe ioy ought to be
in procuring his childrens welfare, reioycing at their weale, ſorrowing and
pitying at their euill, to hazard for their ſafetie, trauell for their reſt, wake
for their ſleepe; and in a word, to thinke that his earthly felicitie and life
ſtandeth and liueth more in them, nor in himſelfe; ſo ought a good
Prince thinke of his people.

As to the other branch of this mutuall and reciprock band, is the duety and alleageance that the Lieges owe to their King: the ground whereof, I take out of the words of *Samuel*, dited by Gods Spirit, when God had
giuen him commandement to heare the peoples voice in chooſing and
annointing them a King. And becauſe that place of Scripture being well
vnderſtood, is ſo pertinent for our purpoſe, I haue inſert herein the very
words of the Text.

9   NOw therefore hearken to their *voice*: howbeit yet teſtifie *vnto* them, and ſhew them the maner of the *King*, that ſhall raigne ouer them.

10   So Samuel tolde all the *wordes* of the Lord *vnto* the people that asked a *King* of him.

11   *And he said,* This ſhall be the maner of the *King* that ſhall raigne ouer you: he *will* take your ſonnes, and appoint them to his Charets, and to be his horſemen, and ſome ſhall runne before his Charet.

12   *Also,* hee *will* make them his captaines ouer thouſands, and captaines ouer fifties, and to eare his ground, and to reape his harueſt, and to make inſtruments of *warre*, and the things that ſerue for his charets:

13   *Hee* *will* alſo take your daughters, and make them *Apothicaries,* and *Cookes,* and *Bakers.*

14   *And* hee *will* take your fields, and your *vineyards,* and your beſt *Oliue* trees, and giue them to his ſeruants.

15   *And he will* take the tenth of your ſeed, and of your *Vineyards,* and giue it to his Eunuches, and to his ſeruants.

16   *And he will* take your men-ſeruants, and your maid-ſeruants, and the chiefe of your yong men, and your aſſes, and put them to his *worke.*

17   *He* *will* take the tenth of your ſheepe: and ye ſhall be his ſeruants.

18   *And ye* ſhall cry out at that day, becauſe of your *King,* whom ye haue choſen you: and the Lord God *will* not heare you at that day.

19   *But the people would* not heare the *voice* of Samuel, but did ſay: Nay, but there ſhalbe a *King* ouer *vs.*

20   *And we alſo will* be like all other *Nations,* and our *King* ſhall iudge *vs,* and goe out before *vs,* and fight our battels.

    That theſe words, and diſcourſes of *Samuel* were dited by Gods Spirit, it needs no further probation, but that it is a place of Scripture; ſince the whole Scripture is dited by that inſpiration, as *Paul* ſaith: which ground no good Chriſtian will, or dare denie. Whereupon it muſt neceſſarily follow, that theſe ſpeeches proceeded not from any ambition in *Samuel,* as one loath to quite the reines that he ſo long had ruled, and therefore deſirous, by making odious the gouernment of a King, to diſſwade the people from their farther importunate crauing of one: For, as the text proueth it plainly, he then conueened them to giue them a reſolute grant of their demand, as God by his owne mouth commanded him, ſaying,

    Hearken to the voice of the people.

And to preſſe to diſſwade them frō that, which he then came to grant vnto them, were a thing very impertinent in a wiſe man; much more in the Prophet of the moſt high God. And likewiſe, it well appeared in all the courſe of his life after, that his ſo long refuſing of their ſute before came not of any ambition in him: which he well proued in praying, & as it were importuning God for the weale of *Saul.* Yea, after God had declared his reprobation vnto him, yet he deſiſted not, while God himſelfe was wrath at his praying,

ing, and difcharged his fathers fuit in that errand. And that thefe words of *Samuel* were not vttered as a prophecie of *Saul* their firft Kings defection, it well appeareth, as well becaufe we heare no mention made in the Scripture of any his tyrannie and oppreffion, (which, if it had beene, would not haue been left vnpainted out therein, as well as his other faults were, as in a trew mirrour of all the Kings behauiours, whom it defcribeth) as likewife in refpect that *Saul* was chofen by God for his vertue, and meet qualities to gouerne his people: whereas his defection fprung after-hand from the corruption of his owne nature, & not through any default in God, whom they that thinke fo, would make as a ftep-father to his people, in making wilfully a choife of the vnmeeteft for gouerning them, fince the election of that King lay abfolutely and immediatly in Gods hand. But by the contrary it is plaine, and euident, that this fpeech of *Samuel* to the people, was to prepare their hearts before the hand to the due obedience of that King, which God was to giue vnto them; and therefore opened vp vnto them, what might be the intollerable qualities that might fall in fome of their kings, thereby preparing them to patience, not to refift to Gods ordinance: but as he would haue faid; Since God hath granted your importunate fuit in giuing you a king, as yee haue elfe committed an errour in fhaking off Gods yoke, and ouer-haftie feeking of a King; fo beware yee fall not into the next, in cafting off alfo rafhly that yoke, which God at your earneft fuite hath laid vpon you, how hard that euer it feeme to be: For as ye could not haue obtained one without the permiffion and ordinance of God, fo may yee no more, fro hee be once fet ouer you, fhake him off without the fame warrant. And therefore in time arme your felues with patience and humilitie, fince he that hath the only power to make him, hath the onely power to vnmake him, and ye onely to obey, bearing with thefe ftraits that I now forefhew you, as with the finger of God, which lieth not in you to take off.

And will ye confider the very wordes of the text in order, as they are fet downe, it fhall plainely declare the obedience that the people owe to their King in all refpects.

Firft, God commandeth *Samuel* to doe two things: the one, to grant the people their fuit in giuing them a king; the other, to forewarne them, what fome kings will doe vnto them, that they may not thereafter in their grudging and murmuring fay, when they fhal feele the fnares here fore-fpoken; We would neuer haue had a king of God, in cafe when we craued him, hee had let vs know how wee would haue beene vfed by him, as now we finde but ouer-late. And this is meant by thefe words:

Now therefore hearken vnto their voice: howbeit yet teftifie vnto them, and fhew them the maner of the King that fhall rule ouer them.

And next, *Samuel* in execution of this commandement of God, hee likewife doeth two things.

Firft, hee declares vnto them, what points of iuftice and equitie their king will breake in his behauiour vnto them: And next he putteth them

out of hope, that wearie as they will, they fhall not haue leaue to fhake off
that yoke, which God through their importunitie hath laide vpon them.
The points of equitie that the King fhall breake vnto them, are expreffed
in thefe words:

  11 *He will take your fonnes, and appoint them to his Charets, and to be his horfe-*
    men, and fome fhall run before his Charet.

  12 *Alfo he will make them his captaines ouer thoufands, and captaines ouer fifties,*
    and to eare his ground, and to reape his harueft, and to make inftruments of
    warre, and the things that ferue for his charets.

  13 *He will alfo take your daughters, and make them Apothecaries, and Cookes,*
    and Bakers.

The points of Iuftice, that hee fhall breake vnto them, are expreffed in
thefe wordes:

  14 *Hee will take your fields, and your vineyards, and your beft Oliue trees, and*
    giue them to his feruants.

  15 *And he will take the tenth of your feede, and of your vineyards, and giue it to*
    his Eunuches and to his feruants: and alfo the tenth of your fheepe.

As if he would fay; The beft and nobleft of your blood fhall be compelled in flauifh and feruile offices to ferue him: And not content of his
owne patrimonie, will make vp a rent to his owne vfe out of your beft
lands, vineyards, orchards, and ftore of cattell: So as inuerting the Law of
nature, and office of a King, your perfons and the perfons of your pofteritie, together with your lands, and all that ye poffeffe fhal ferue his priuate
vfe, and inordinate appetite.

And as vnto the next point (which is his fore-warning them, that, weary
as they will, they fhall not haue leaue to fhake off the yoke, which God thorow their importunity hath laid vpon them) it is expreffed in thefe words:

  18 *And yee fhall crie out at that day, becaufe of your King whom yee haue chofen*
    you: and the Lord will not heare you at that day.

As he would fay; When ye fhall finde thefe things in proofe that now I
fore-warne you of, although you fhall grudge and murmure, yet it fhal not
be lawful to you to caft it off, in refpect it is not only the ordinance of God,
but alfo your felues haue chofen him vnto you, thereby renouncing for e-
uer all priuiledges, by your willing confent out of your hands, whereby in
any time hereafter ye would claime, and call backe vnto your felues againe
that power, which God fhall not permit you to doe. And for further taking
away of all excufe, and retraction of this their contract, after their confent
to vnder-lie this yoke with all the burthens that hee hath declared vnto
them, he craues their anfwere, and confent to his propofition: which appeareth by their anfwere, as it is expreffed in thefe words:

  19 *Nay, but there fhalbe a King ouer vs.*   20 *And we alfo will be like all other*
    nations: and our king fhall iudge vs, and goe out before vs and fight our battels.

As if they would haue faid; All your fpeeches and hard conditions fhall
not skarre vs, but we will take the good and euill of it vpon vs, and we will
                                                  be

be content to beare whatſoeuer burthen it ſhal pleaſe our King to lay vpon vs, aſwell as other nations doe. And for the good we will get of him in fighting our battels, we will more patiently beare any burthen that ſhall pleaſe him to lay on vs.

Now then, ſince the erection of this Kingdome and Monarchie among the Iewes, and the law thereof may, and ought to bee a paterne to all Chriſtian and well founded Monarchies, as beeing founded by God himſelfe, who by his Oracle, and out of his owne mouth gaue the law thereof; what liberty can broiling ſpirits, and rebellious minds claime iuſtly to againſt any Chriſtian Monarchie; ſince they can claime to no greater libertie on their part, nor the people of God might haue done, and no greater tyranny was euer executed by any Prince or tyrant, whom they can obiect, nor was here fore-warned to the people of God, (and yet all rebellion countermanded vnto them) if tyrannizing ouer mens perſons, ſonnes, daughters and ſeruants, redacting noble houſes, and men, and women of noble blood, to ſlauiſh and ſeruile offices; and extortion, and ſpoile of their lands and goods to the princes owne priuate vſe and commoditie, and of his courteours, and ſeruants, may be called a tyrannie?

And that this propoſition grounded vpon the Scripture, may the more clearely appeare to be trew by the practiſe oft prooued in the ſame booke, we neuer reade, that euer the Prophets perſwaded the people to rebell a-gainſt the Prince, how wicked ſoeuer he was.

When *Samuel* by Gods command pronounced to the ſame king *Saul,* that his kingdome was rent from him, and giuen to another (which in ef-fect was a degrading of him) yet his next action following that, was peace-ably to turne home, and with floods of teares to pray to God to haue ſome compaſſion vpon him.

1. Sam. 15.

And *David,* notwithſtanding hee was inaugurate in that ſame degraded Kings roome, not onely (when he was cruelly perſecuted, for no offence; but good ſeruice done vnto him) would not preſume, hauing him in his power, skantly, but with great reuerence, to touch the garment of the an-noynted of the Lord, and in his words bleſſed him: but likewiſe, when one came to him vanting himſelfe vntrewly to haue ſlaine *Saul,* hee, without forme of proces, or triall of his guilt, cauſed onely for guiltineſſe of his tongue, put him to ſodaine death.

1. Sam. 2 4.
2. Sam. 1.

And although there was neuer a more monſtrous perſecutor, and tyrant nor *Achab* was : yet all the rebellion, that *Elias* euer raiſed againſt him, was to flie to the wildernes : where for fault of ſuſtentation, he was fed with the Corbies. And I thinke no man will doubt but *Samuel, Dauid,* and *Elias,* had as great power to perſwade the people, if they had liked to haue employed their credite to vproares & rebellions againſt theſe wicked kings, as any of our ſeditious preachers in theſe daies of whatſoeuer religion, either in this countrey or in France, had, that buſied themſelues moſt to ſtir vp rebellion vnder cloake of religion. This farre the only loue of veritie, I proteſt, without

out hatred at their persons, haue mooued me to be somewhat satyricke.

11. And if any will leane to the extraordinarie examples of degrading or killing of kings in the Scriptures, thereby to cloake the peoples rebellion, as by the deed of *Iehu*, and such like extraordinaries: I answere, besides that they want the like warrant that they had, if extraordinarie examples of the Scripture shall bee drawne in daily practise; murther vnder traist as in the persons of *Ahud*, and *Iael*; theft, as in the persons of the *Israelites* comming out of *Egypt*; lying to their parents to the hurt of their brother, as in the person of *Iacob*, shall all be counted as lawfull and allowable vertues, as rebellion against Princes. And to conclude, the practise through the whole Scripture prooueth the peoples obedience giuen to that sentence in the law of God:

Thou shalt not rayle vpon the Iudges, neither speake euill of the ruler of thy people.

To end then the ground of my proposition taken out of the Scripture, let two speciall, and notable examples, one vnder the law, another vnder the Euangel, conclude this part of my alleageance. Vnder the lawe, *Ieremie* threatneth the people of God with vtter destruction for rebellion to *Nabuchadnezar* the king of Babel: who although he was an idolatrous persecuter, a forraine King, a Tyrant, and vsurper of their liberties; yet in respect they had once receiued and acknowledged him for their king, he not only commandeth them to obey him, but euen to pray for his prosperitie, adioyning the reason to it; because in his prosperitie stood their peace.

And vnder the Euangel, that king, whom *Paul* bids the *Romanes obey* and serue *for conscience sake*, was *Nero* that bloody tyrant; an infamie to his aage, and a monster to the world, being also an idolatrous persecuter, as the King of *Babel* was. If then Idolatrie and defection from God, tyranny ouer their people, and persecution of the Saints, for their profession sake, hindred not the Spirit of God to command his people vnder all highest paine to giue them all due and heartie obedience for conscience sake, giuing to *Cæsar* that which was *Cæsars*, and to God that which was Gods, as Christ saith; and that this practise throughout the booke of God agreeth with this lawe, which he made in the erection of that Monarchie (as is at length before deduced) what shamelesse presumption is it to any Christian people now adayes to claime to that vnlawfull libertie, which God refused to his owne peculiar and chosen people? Shortly then to take vp in two or three sentences, grounded vpon all these arguments, out of the lawe of God, the duetie, and alleageance of the people to their lawfull king, their obedience, I say, ought to be to him, as to Gods Lieutenant in earth, obeying his commands in all things, except directly against God, as the commands of Gods Minister, acknowledging him a Iudge set by G O D ouer them, hauing power to iudge them, but to be iudged onely by G O D, whom to onely hee must giue count of his iudgement; fearing him as their Iudge; louing him as their father; praying for him as their protectour; for his continuance, if

hee

Ier. 27.

Iere. 29.

Iere. 13.

he be good, for his amendement, if he be wicked; following and obeying his lawfull commaunds, efchewing and flying his fury in his vnlawfull, without refiftance, but by fobbes and teares to God, according to that fentence vfed in the primitiue Church in the time of the perfecution.

Preces, & Lachrymæ funt arma Ecclefiæ.

Now, as for the defcribing the alleageance, that the lieges owe to their natiue King, out of the fundamentall and ciuill Lawe, efpecially of this countrey, as I promifed, the ground muft firft be fet downe of the firft maner of eftablifhing the Lawes and forme of gouernement among vs ; that the ground being firft right laide, we may thereafter build rightly thereupon. Although it be trew (according to the affirmation of thofe that pryde themfelues to be the fcourges of Tyrants) that in the firft beginning of Kings rifing among Gentiles, in the time of the firft aage, diuers commonwealths and focieties of men choofed out one among themfelues, who for his vertues and valour, being more eminent then the reft, was chofen out by them, and fet vp in that roome, to maintaine the weakeft in their right, to throw downe oppreffours, and to fofter and continue the focietie among men; which could not otherwife, but by vertue of that vnitie be wel done : yet thefe examples are nothing pertinent to vs ; becaufe our Kingdome and diuers other Monarchies are not in that cafe, but had their beginning in a farre contrary fafhion.

For as our Chronicles beare witneffe, this Ile, and efpecially our part of it, being fcantly inhabited, but by very few, and they as barbarous and fcant of ciuilitie, as number, there comes our firft King *Fergus*, with a great number with him, out of *Ireland*, which was long inhabited before vs, and making himfelfe mafter of the countrey, by his owne friendfhip, and force, as well of the *Ireland-men* that came with him, as of the countrey-men that willingly fell to him, hee made himfelfe King and Lord, as well of the whole landes, as of the whole inhabitants within the fame. Thereafter he and his fucceffours, a long while after their being Kinges, made and eftablifhed their lawes from time to time, and as the occafion required : So the trewth is directly contrarie in our ftate to the falfe affirmation of fuch feditious writers, as would perfwade vs, that the Lawes and ftate of our countrey were eftablifhed before the admitting of a king : where by the contrarie ye fee it plainely prooued, that a wife king comming in among barbares, firft eftablifhed the eftate and forme of gouernement, and thereafter made lawes by himfelfe, and his fucceffours according thereto.

The kings therefore in Scotland were before any eftates or rankes of men within the fame, before any Parliaments were holden, or lawes made: and by them was the land diftributed (which at the firft was whole theirs) ftates erected and decerned, and formes of gouernement deuifed and eftablifhed: And fo it followes of neceffitie, that the kings were the authors and makers of the Lawes, and not the Lawes of the kings. And to prooue this my affertion more clearly, it is euident by the rolles of our Chancellery

(which

(which containe our eldeſt and fundamentall Lawes) that the King is *Dominus omnium bonorum*, and *Dominus directus totius Dominij*, the whole ſubiects being but his vaſſals, and from him holding all their lands as their ouer-lord, who according to good ſeruices done vnto him, chaungeth their holdings from tacke to few, from ward to blanch, erecteth new Baronies, and vniteth olde, without aduice or authoritie of either Parliament, or any other ſubalterin iudiciall ſeate: So as if wrong might bee admitted in play (albeit I grant wrong ſhould be wrong in all perſons) the King might haue a better colour for his pleaſure, without further reaſon, to take the land from his lieges, as ouer-lord of the whole, and doe with it as pleaſeth him, ſince all that they hold is of him, then, as fooliſh writers ſay, the people might vnmake the king, and put an other in his roome: But either of them as vnlawful, and againſt the ordinance of God, ought to be alike odious to be thought, much leſſe put in practiſe.

And according to theſe fundamentall Lawes already alledged, we daily ſee that in the Parliament (which is nothing elſe but the head Court of the king and his vaſſals) the lawes are but craued by his ſubiects, and onely made by him at their rogation, and with their aduice: For albeit the king make daily ſtatutes and ordinances, enioyning ſuch paines thereto as hee thinkes meet, without any aduice of Parliament or eſtates; yet it lies in the power of no Parliament, to make any kinde of Lawe or Statute, without his Scepter be to it, for giuing it the force of a Law: And although diuers changes haue beene in other countries of the blood Royall, and kingly houſe, the kingdome being reft by conqueſt from one to another, as in our neighbour countrey in *England*, (which was neuer in ours) yet the ſame ground of the kings right ouer all the land, and ſubiects thereof remaineth alike in all other free Monarchies, as well as in this: For when the Baſtard of *Normandie* came into *England*, and made himſelfe king, was it not by force, and with a mighty army? Where he gaue the Law, and tooke none, changed the Lawes, inuerted the order of gouernement, ſet downe the ſtrangers his followers in many of the old poſſeſſours roomes, as at this day well appeareth a great part of the Gentlemen in *England*, beeing come of the *Norman* blood, and their old Lawes, which to this day they are ruled by, are written in his language, and not in theirs: And yet his ſucceſſours haue with great happineſſe enioyed the Crowne to this day; Whereof the like was alſo done by all them that conqueſted them before.

And for concluſion of this point, that the king is ouer-lord ouer the whole lands, it is likewiſe daily proued by the Law of our hoordes, of want of Heires, and of Baſtardies: For if a hoord be found vnder the earth, becauſe it is no more in the keeping or vſe of any perſon, it of the law pertains to the king. If a perſon, inheritour of any lands or goods, dye without any ſort of heires, all his landes and goods returne to the king. And if a baſtard die vnrehabled without heires of his bodie (which rehabling onely lyes in the kings hands) all that hee hath likewiſe returnes to the king.

And

And as ye see it manifest, that the King is ouer-Lord of the whole land : so is he Maſter ouer euery perſon that inhabiteth the ſame, hauing power ouer the life and death of euery one of them: For although a iuſt Prince will not take the life of any of his ſubiects without a cleare law ; yet the ſame lawes whereby he taketh them, are made by himſelfe , or his predeceſſours; and ſo the power flowes alwaies from him ſelfe; as by daily experience we ſee, good and iuſt Princes will from time to time make new lawes and ſtatutes, adioyning the penalties to the breakers thereof, which before the law was made, had beene no crime to the ſubiect to haue committed. Not that I de-ny the old definition of a King, and of a law; which makes the king to bee a ſpeaking law, and the Law a dumbe king : for certainely a king that go-uernes not by his lawe, can neither be countable to God for his admini-ſtration, nor haue a happy and eſtabliſhed raigne: For albeit it be trew that I haue at length prooued, that the King is aboue the law, as both the author and giuer of ſtrength thereto ; yet a good king will not onely delight to rule his ſubiects by the lawe, but euen will conforme himſelfe in his owne actions thereuneto , alwaies keeping that ground, that the health of the common-wealth be his chiefe lawe : And where he ſees the lawe doubt-ſome or rigorous, hee may interpret or mitigate the ſame, left otherwiſe *Summum ius* bee *ſumma iniuria* : And therefore generall lawes , made publikely in Parliament, may vpon knowen reſpects to the King by his authoritie bee mitigated, and ſuſpended vpon cauſes onely knowen to him.

As likewiſe , although I haue ſaid, a good king will frame all his actions to be according to the Law ; yet is hee not bound thereto but of his good will, and for good example-giuing to his ſubiects : For as in the law of ab-ſtaining from eating of fleſh in *Lenton*, the king will, for examples ſake, make his owne houſe to obſerue the Law ; yet no man will thinke he needs to take a licence to eate fleſh. And although by our Lawes, the bearing and wearing of hag-buts, and piſtolets be forbidden, yet no man can find any fault in the King, for cauſing his traine vſe them in any raide vpon the Bor-derers, or other malefactours or rebellious ſubiects. So as I haue alreadie ſaid, a good King, although hee be aboue the Law, will ſubiect and frame his actions thereto, for examples ſake to his ſubiects, and of his owne free-will, but not as ſubiect or bound thereto.

Since I haue ſo clearely prooued then out of the fundamentall lawes and practiſe of this country, what right & power a king hath ouer his land and ſubiects, it is eaſie to be vnderſtood, what allegeance & obedience his lieges owe vnto him ; I meane alwaies of ſuch free Monarchies as our king is, and not of electiue kings, and much leſſe of ſuch ſort of gouernors, as the dukes of *Venice* are, whoſe Ariſtocratick and limited gouernment, is nothing like to free Monarchies ; although the malice of ſome writers hath not beene aſhamed to mis-know any difference to be betwixt them. And if it be not lawfull to any particular Lordes tenants or vaſſals, vpon whatſoeuer

pretext,

pretext, to controll and difplace their Mafter, and ouer-lord (as is clearer
nor the Sunne by all Lawes of the world) how much leffe may the fubiects
and vaffals of the great ouer-lord the K I N G controll or difplace him? And
fince in all inferiour iudgements in the land, the people may not vpon any
refpects difplace their Magiftrates, although but fubaltern : for the people
of a borough, cannot difplace their Prouoft before the time of their election : nor in Ecclefiafticall policie the flocke can vpon any pretence difplace the Paftor, nor iudge of him : yea euen the poore Schoolemafter cannot be difplaced by his fchollers : If thefe, I fay (whereof fome are but inferiour, fubaltern, and temporall Magiftrates, and none of them equall in any
fort to the dignitie of a King) cannot be difplaced for any occafion or pretext by them that are ruled by them : how much leffe is it lawfull vpon any
pretext to controll or difplace the great Prouoft, and great Schoole-mafter
of the whole land : except by inuerting the order of all Law and reafon, the
commanded may be made to command their commander, the iudged to
iudge their Iudge, and they that are gouerned, to gouerne their time about
their Lord and gouernour.

   And the agreement of the Law of nature, in this our ground with the
Lawes and conftitutions of God, and man, already alledged, will by two
fimilitudes eafily appeare. The King towards his people is rightly compared to a father of children, and to a head of a body compofed of diuers
members : For as fathers, the good Princes, and Magiftrates of the people
of God acknowledged themfelues to their fubiects. And for all other well
ruled Common-wealths, the ftile of *Pater patriæ* was euer, and is commonly vfed to Kings. And the proper office of a King towards his Subiects,
agrees very wel with the office of the head towards the body, and all members thereof : For from the head, being the feate of Iudgement, proceedeth
the care and forefight of guiding, and preuenting all euill that may come
to the body, or any part thereof. The head cares for the body, fo doeth the
King for his people. As the difcourfe and direction flowes from the head,
and the execution according thereunto belongs to the reft of the members, euery one according to their office : fo is it betwixt a wife Prince, and
his people. As the iudgement comming from the head may not onely imploy the members, euery one in their owne office, as long as they are able
for it; but likewife in cafe any of them be affected with any infirmitie muft
care and prouide for their remedy, in-cafe it be curable, and if otherwife,
gar cut them off for feare of infecting of the reft : euen fo is it betwixt the
Prince, and his people. And as there is euer hope of curing any difeafed
member by the direction of the head, as long as it is whole; but by the contrary, if it be troubled, all the members are partakers of that paine, fo is it betwixt the Prince and his people.

   And now firft for the fathers part (whofe naturall loue to his children
I defcribed in the firft part of this my difcourfe; fpeaking of the dutie that
Kings owe to their Subiects) confider, I pray you what duetie his children
owe

owe to him, & whether vpó any pretext whatſoeuer, it wil not be thought
monſtrous and vnnaturall to his ſons, to riſe vp againſt him, to control him
at their appetite, and when they thinke good to ſley him, or to cut him off,
and adopt to themſelues any other they pleaſe in his roome: Or can any
pretence of wickednes or rigor on his part be a iuſt excuſe for his children
to put hand into him? And although wee ſee by the courſe of nature, that
loue vſeth to deſcend more then to aſcend, in caſe it were trew, that the father hated and wronged the children neuer ſo much, will any man, endued
with the leaſt ſponke of reaſon, thinke it lawfull for them to meet him with
the line? Yea, ſuppoſe the father were furiouſly following his ſonnes with
a drawen ſword, is it lawfull for them to turne and ſtrike againe, or make
any reſiſtance but by flight? I thinke ſurely, if there were no more but the
example of bruit beaſts & vnreaſonable creatures, it may ſerue well enough
to qualifie and proue this my argnment. We reade often the pietie that the
Storkes haue to their olde and decayed parents: And generally wee know,
that there are many ſorts of beaſts and fowles, that with violence and many
bloody ſtrokes will beat and baniſh their yong ones from them, how ſoone
they perceiue them to be able to ſend themſelues; but wee neuer read or
heard of any reſiſtance on their part, except among the vipers; which
prooues ſuch perſons, as ought to be reaſonable creatures, and yet vnnaturally follow this example, to be endued with their viperous nature.

And for the ſimilitude of the head and the body, it may very well fall out
that the head will be forced to garre cut off ſome rotten member (as I haue
already ſaid) to keepe the reſt of the body in integritie: but what ſtate the
body can be in, if the head, for any infirmitie that can fall to it, be cut off,
I leaue it to the readers iudgement.

So as (to conclude this part) if the children may vpon any pretext that
can be imagined, lawfully riſe vp againſt their Father, cut him off, & chooſe
any other whom they pleaſe in his roome; and if the body for the weale of
it, may for any infirmitie that can be in the head, ſtrike it off, then I cannot
deny that the people may rebell, controll, and diſplace, or cut off their king
at their owne pleaſure, and vpon reſpects moouing them. And whether
theſe ſimilitudes repreſent better the office of a King, or the offices of Maſters or Deacons of crafts, or Doctors in Phyſicke (which iolly compariſons are vſed by ſuch writers as maintaine the contrary propoſition) I leaue
it alſo to the readers diſcretion.

And in caſe any doubts might ariſe in any part of this treatiſe, I wil (according to my promiſe) with the ſolution of foure principall and moſt
weightie doubts, that the aduerſaries may obiect, conclude this diſcourſe.
And firſt it is caſten vp by diuers, that employ their pennes vpon Apolo-
gies for rebellions and treaſons, that euery man is borne to carry ſuch a naturall zeale and duety to his common-wealth, as to his mother; that ſeeing
it ſo rent and deadly wounded, as whiles it will be by wicked and tyrannous Kings, good Citizens will be forced, for the naturall zeale and duety

S   they

they owe to their owne natiue countrey, to put their hand to worke for freeing their common-wealth from fuch a peſt.

Whereunto I giue two anſweres: Firſt, it is a ſure Axiome in *Theologie*, that euill ſhould not be done, that good may come of it: The wickednesse therefore of the King can neuer make them that are ordained to be iudged by him, to become his Iudges. And if it be not lawfull to a priuate man to reuenge his priuate iniury vpon his priuate aduerſary (ſince God hath one-ly giuen the ſword to the Magiſtrate) how much leſſe is it lawfull to the people, or any part of them (who all are but priuate men, the authoritie being alwayes with the Magiſtrate, as I haue already proued) to take vpon them the vſe of the ſword, whom to it belongs not, againſt the publicke Magiſtrate, whom to onely it belongeth.

Next, in place of relieuing the common-wealth out of diſtreſſe(which is their onely excuſe and colour) they ſhall heape double diſtreſſe and deſola-tion vpon it; and ſo their rebellion ſhall procure the contrary effects that they pretend it for: For a king cannot be imagined to be ſo vnruly and ty-rannous, but the common-wealth will be kept in better order, notwith-ſtanding thereof, by him, then it can be by his way-taking. For firſt, all ſudden mutations are perillous in common-wealths, hope being thereby giuen to all bare men to ſet vp themſelues, and flie with other mens fea-thers, the reines being looſed to all the inſolencies that diſordered people can commit by hope of impunitie, becauſe of the looſeneſſe of all things.

And next, it is certaine that a king can neuer be ſo monſtrouſly vicious, but hee will generally fauour iuſtice, and maintaine ſome order, except in the particulars, wherein his inordinate luſtes and paſſions cary him away; where by the contrary, no King being, nothing is vnlawfull to none: And ſo the olde opinion of the Philoſophers prooues trew, That better it is to liue in a Common-wealth, where nothing is lawfull, then where all things are lawfull to all men; the Common-wealth at that time reſembling an vndanted young horſe that hath caſten his rider: For as the diuine Poet D v B a r t a s ſayth, *Better it were to ſuffer ſome diſorder in the eſtate, and ſome ſpots in the Common-wealth, then in pretending to reforme, vtterly to ouer-throw the Republicke.*

The ſecond obiection they ground vpon the curſe that hangs ouer the common-wealth, where a wicked king reigneth: and, ſay they, there can-not be a more acceptable deed in the ſight of God, nor more dutiful to their common-weale, then to free the countrey of ſuch a curſe, and vindicate to them their libertie, which is naturall to all creatures to craue.

Whereunto for anſwere, I grant indeed, that a wicked king is ſent by God for a curſe to his people, and a plague for their ſinnes: but that it is lawfull to them to ſhake off that curſe at their owne hand, which God hath laid on them, that I deny, and may ſo do iuſtly. Will any deny that the king of *Babel* was a curſe to the people of God, as was plainly fore-ſpoken and threatned vnto them in the prophecie of their captiuitie? And what was *Nero* to
the

the Chriftian Church in his time? And yet *Ieremy* and *Paul* (as yee haue elfe heard) commanded them not onely to obey them, but heartily to pray for their welfare.

It is certaine then (as I haue already by the Law of God fufficiently pro-ued) that patience, earneft prayers to God, and amendment of their liues, are the onely lawful meanes to moue God to relieue them of that heauie curfe. As for vindicating to themfelues their owne libertie, what lawfull power haue they to reuoke to themfelues againe thofe priuiledges, which by their owne confent before were fo fully put out of their hands? for if a Prince cannot iuftly bring backe againe to himfelf the priuiledges once beftowed by him or his predeceffors vpon any ftate or ranke of his fubieĉts; how much leffe may the fubieĉts reaue out of the princes hand that fuperioritie, which he and his Predeceffors haue fo long brooked ouer them?

But the vnhappy iniquitie of the time, which hath oft times giuen ouer good fucceffe to their treafonable attempts, furnifheth them the ground of their third obieĉtion: For, fay they, the fortunate fucceffe that God hath fo oft giuen to fuch enterprifes, prooueth plainely by the praĉtife, that God fauoured the iuftneffe of their quarrell.

To the which I anfwere, that it is trew indeed, that all the fucceffe of bat-tels, as well as other worldly things, lyeth onely in Gods hand: And there-fore it is that in the Scripture he takes to himfelfe the ftyle of God of Hofts. But vpon that generall to conclude, that hee euer giues victory to the iuft quarrell, would prooue the *Philiĉtims,* and diuers other neighbour enemies of the people of God to haue oft times had the iuft quarrel againft the peo-ple of God, in refpeĉt of the many victories they obtained againft them. And by that fame argument they had alfo iuft quarrell againft the Arke of God: For they wan it in the field, and kept it long prifoner in their coun-trey. As likewife by all good Writers, as well Theologues, as other, the Duels and fingular combats are difallowed; which are onely made vpon pretence, that G o D will kith thereby the iuftice of the quarrell: For wee muft confider that the innocent partie is not innocent before God: And therefore God will make oft times them that haue the wrong fide reuenge iuftly his quarrell; and when he hath done, caft his fcourge in the fire; as he oft times did to his owne people, ftirring vp and ftrengthening their enemies, while they were humbled in his fight, and then deliuered them in their hands. So God, as the great Iudge may iuftly punifh his Deputie, and for his rebellion againft him, ftir vp his rebels to meet him with the like: And when it is done, the part of the inftrument is no better then the diuels part is in tempting and torturing fuch as God committeth to him as his hangman to doe: Therefore, as I faid in the beginning, it is oft times a very deceiueable argument, to iudge of the caufe by the euent.

And the laft obieĉtion is grounded vpon the mutuall paĉtion and ad-ftipulation (as they call it) betwixt the King and his people, at the time of his coronation: For there, fay they, there is a mutuall paĉtion, and contraĉt

S 2   bound

bound vp, and fworne betwixt the king, and the people: Whereupon it followeth, that if the one part of the contract or the Indent bee broken vpon the Kings fide, the people are no longer bound to keepe their part of it, but are thereby freed of their oath: For (fay they) a contract betwixt two parties, of all Law frees the one partie, if the other breake vnto him.

As to this contract alledged made at the coronation of a King, although I deny any fuch contract to bee made then, efpecially containing fuch a claufe irritant as they alledge; yet I confeffe, that a king at his coronation, or at the entry to his kingdome, willingly promifeth to his people, to difcharge honorably and trewly the office giuen him by God ouer them: But prefuming that thereafter he breake his promife vnto them neuer fo inexcufable; the queftion is, who fhould bee iudge of the breake, giuing vnto them, this contract were made vnto them neuer fo ficker, according to their alleageance. I thinke no man that hath but the fmalleft entrance into the ciuill Law, will doubt that of all Law, either ciuil or municipal of any nation, a contract cannot be thought broken by the one partie, and fo the other likewife to be freed therefro, except that firft a lawfull triall and cognition be had by the ordinary Iudge of the breakers thereof: Or elfe euery man may be both party and Iudge in his owne caufe, which is abfurd once to be thought. Now in this contract (I fay) betwixt the king and his people, God is doubtles the only Iudge, both becaufe to him onely the king muft make count of his adminiftration (as is oft faid before) as likewife by the oath in the coronation, God is made iudge and reuenger of the breakers: For in his prefence, as only iudge of oaths, all oaths ought to be made. Then fince God is the onely Iudge betwixt the two parties contractors, the cognition and reuenge muft onely appertaine to him : It followes therefore of neceffitie, that God muft firft giue fentence vpon the King that breaketh, before the people can thinke themfelues freed of their oath. What iuftice then is it, that the partie fhall be both iudge and partie, vfurping vpon himfelfe the office of God, may by this argument eafily appeare : And fhall it lie in the hands of headleffe multitude, when they pleafe to weary off fubiection, to caft off the yoake of gouernement that God hath laid vpon them, to iudge and punifh him, whom-by they fhould be iudged and punifhed; and in that cafe, wherein by their violence they kythe themfelues to be moft paffionate parties, to vfe the office of an vngracious Iudge or Arbiter? Nay, to fpeake trewly of that cafe, as it ftands betwixt the king and his people, none of them ought to iudge of the others breake : For confidering rightly the two parties at the time of their mutuall promife, the king is the one party, and the whole people in one body are the other party. And therfore fince it is certaine, that a king, in cafe fo it fhould fal out, that his people in one body had rebelled againft him, hee fhould not in that cafe, as thinking himfelfe free of his promife and oath; become an vtter enemy, and practife the wreake of his whole people and natiue country : although he ought iuftly to punifh the principall authours and bellowes of that vniuerfall rebellion:

lion : how much leſſe then ought the people (that are alwaies ſubiect vnto him, and naked of all authoritie on their part) preſſe to iudge and ouer-throw him ? otherwiſe the people, as the one partie contracters, ſhall no ſooner challenge the king as breaker, but hee aſſoone ſhall iudge them as breakers : ſo as the victors making the tyners the traitors (as our prouerbe is) the partie ſhall aye become both iudge and partie in his owne particular, as I haue alreadie ſaid.

And it is here likewiſe to be noted, that the duty and alleageance, which the people ſweareth to their prince, is not only bound to themſelues, but likewiſe to their lawfull heires and poſterity, the lineall ſucceſſiô of crowns being begun among the people of God, and happily continued in diuers chriſtian common-wealths : So as no obiection either of hereſie, or what-ſoeuer priuate ſtatute or law may free the people from their oath-giuing to their king, and his ſucceſſion, eſtabliſhed by the old fundamentall lawes of the kingdome : For, as hee is their heritable ouer-lord, and ſo by birth, not by any right in the coronation, commeth to his crowne ; it is a like vnlaw-ful (the crowne euer ſtanding full) to diſplace him that ſucceedeth thereto, as to eiect the former : For at the very moment of the expiring of the king reigning, the neareſt and lawful heire entreth in his place : And ſo to refuſe him, or intrude another, is not to holde out vncomming in, but to expell and put out their righteous King. And I truſt at this time whole *France* ac-knowledgeth the ſuperſtitious rebellion of the liguers, who vpon pretence of hereſie, by force of armes held ſo long out, to the great deſolation of their whole countrey, their natiue and righteous king from poſſeſſing of his owne crowne and naturall kingdome.

Not that by all this former diſcourſe of mine, and Apologie for kings, I meane that whatſoeuer errors and intollerable abominations a ſouereigne prince commit, hee ought to eſcape all puniſhment, as if thereby the world were only ordained for kings, & they without controlment to turne it vp-ſide down at their pleaſure : but by the contrary, by remitting them to God (who is their onely ordinary Iudge) I remit them to the ſoreſt and ſharpeſt ſchoolemaſter that can be deuiſed for them : for the further a king is prefer-red by God aboue all other ranks & degrees of men, and the higher that his ſeat is aboue theirs, the greater is his obligation to his maker. And therfore in caſe he forget himſelfe (his vnthankfulnes being in the ſame meaſure of height) the ſadder and ſharper will his correction be ; and according to the greatnes of the height he is in, the weight of his fall wil recôpenſe the ſame : for the further that any perſon is obliged to God, his offence becomes and growes ſo much the greater, then it would be in any other. *Ioues* thunder-claps light oftner and ſorer vpon the high & ſtately oakes, then on the low and ſupple willow trees : and the higheſt bench is ſliddrieſt to ſit vpon. Neither is it euer heard that any king forgets himſelfe towards God, or in his vocation ; but God with the greatneſſe of the plague reuengeth the greatnes of his ingratitude : Neither thinke I by the force and argument

of

of this my difcourfe fo to perfwade the people, that none will hereafter be raifed vp, and rebell againft wicked Princes. But remitting to the iuftice and prouidence of God to ftirre vp fuch fcourges as pleafeth him, for punifhment of wicked kings (who made the very vermine and filthy duft of the earth to bridle the infolencie of proud *Pharaoh*) my onely purpofe and intention in this treatife is to perfwade, as farre as lieth in me, by thefe fure and infallible grounds, all fuch good Chriftian readers, as beare not onely the naked name of a Chriftian, but kith the fruites thereof in their daily forme of life, to keepe their hearts and hands free from fuch monftrous and vnnaturall rebellions, whenfoeuer the wickedneffe of a Prince fhall procure the fame at Gods hands: that, when it fhall pleafe God to caft fuch fcourges of princes, and inftruments of his fury in the fire, ye may ftand vp with cleane handes, and vnfpotted confciences, hauing prooued your felues in all your actions trew Chriftians toward God, and dutifull fubiects towards your King, hauing remitted the iudgement and punifhment of all his wrongs to him, whom to onely of right it appertaineth.

But crauing at God, and hoping that God fhall continue his bleffing with vs, in not fending fuch fearefull defolation, I heartily wifh our kings behauiour fo to be, and continue among vs, as our God in earth, and louing Father, endued with fuch properties as I defcribed a King in the firft part of this Treatife. And that ye (my deare countreymen, and charitable readers) may preffe by all meanes to procure the profperitie and welfare of your King; that as hee muft on the one part thinke all his earthly felicitie and happineffe grounded vpon your weale, caring more for himfelfe for your fake then for his owne, thinking himfelfe onely ordained for your weale; fuch holy and happy emulation may arife betwixt him and you, as his care for your quietnes, and your care for his honour and preferuation, may in all your actions daily ftriue together, that the Land may thinke themfelues bleffed with fuch a King, and the king may thinke himfelfe moft happy in ruling ouer. fo louing and obedient fubiects.

FINIS.

A COVN-

A COVNTERBLASTE
TO *TOBACCO*.

TO THE READER.

*S euery humane body (deare Countrey men) how wholefome foeuer, is notwithstanding fubiect, or at least naturally inclined to fome forts of difeafes, or infirmities : fo is there no Commonwealth, or Body-politicke, how well gouerned, or peaceable foeuer it be, that lackes the owne popular errors, and naturally inclined corruptions: and therefore is it no wonder, although this our Countrey and Common-wealth, though peaceable, though wealthy, though long flourifhing in both, be amongst the rest, fubiect to the owne naturall infirmities. We are of all Nations the people most louing, and most reuerently obedient to our Prince, yet are we (as time hath often borne witneffe) too eafie to be feduced to make Rebellion vpon very flight grounds. Our fortunate and oft proued valour in warres abroad, our heartie and reuerent obedience to our Princes at home, hath bred vs a long, and a thrice happie peace : Our peace hath bred wealth : And peace and wealth hath brought forth a generall fluggifhneffe, which makes vs wallow in all forts of idle delights, and foft delicacies, the first*

feedes

seeds of the subuersion of all great Monarchies. Our Cleargie ar
become negligent and lazie, Our Nobilitie and Gentrie pro
digall, and sold to their priuate delights, Our Lawyers couetous
Our Common people prodigall and curious; and generally all sort
of people more carefull for their priuate ends, then for their mothe
the Common-wealth.

For remedie whereof, it is the Kings part (as the proper Phi
sician of his Politicke-bodie) to purge it of all those diseases, b
Medicines meete for the same: as by a certaine milde, an
yet iust forme of gouernment, to maintaine the Publicke quiet
nesse, and preuent all occasions of Commotion: by the examp
of his owne Person and Court, to make vs all ashamed of our slug
gish delicacie, and to stirre vs vp to the practise againe of all ho
nest exercises, and Martiall shadowes of Warre; As like
wise by his, and his Courts moderatenesse in Apparell, to make v
ashamed of our prodigalitie: By his quicke admonitions an
carefull ouerseeing of the Cleargie, to waken them vp againe, t
be more diligent in their Offices: By the sharpe triall, and se
uere punishment of the partiall, couetous and bribing Lawyers, t
reforme their corruptions: And generally by the example of h
owne Person, and by the due execution of good Lawes, to reform
and abolish, piece and piece, these olde and euill grounded abuses
For this will not be Opus vnius diei, but as euery one of these di
eases, must from the King receiue the owne cure proper for it,
are there some sorts of abuses in Common-wealths, that thoug
they bee of so base and contemptible a condition, as they are to
low for the Law to looke on, and to meane for a King to interpon
his authoritie, or bend his eye vpon; yet are they corruptions, a
well as the greatest of them. So is an Ant an Animal, aswe
as an Elephant: so is a Wrenne Auis, aswell as a Swanne, an
so is a small dint of the Tooth-ake, a disease aswell as the feare
full Plague is. But for these base sorts of corruption in Com
mon-wealths, not onely the King, or any inferiour Magistrate, bu
Quilibet è populo may serue to be a Phisician, by discouerin
and impugning the error, and by perswading reformation thereo

A

And surely in my opinion, there cannot bee a more base, and yet hurtfull, corruption in a Countrey, then is the vile vse (or rather abuse) of taking Tobacco *in this Kingdome, which hath mooued mee, shortly to discouer the abuses thereof in this following little Pamphlet.*

If any thinke it a light Argument, so is it but a toy that is bestowed vpon it. And since the Subiect is but of Smoke, I thinke the fume of an idle braine, may serue for a sufficient batterie against so fumous and feeble an enemie. If my grounds bee found trew, it is all I looke for; but if they cary the force of perswasion with them, it is all I can wish, and more then I can expect. My onely care is, that you, my deare Countrey-men, may rightly conceiue euen by this smallest trifle, of the sinceritie of my meaning in greater matters, neuer to spare any paine, that may tend to the procuring of your weale and prosperitie.

(∵)

A COVN-

A COVNTERBLASTE
TO TOBACCO.

That the manifold abuſes of this vile cuſtome of *Tobacco* taking, may the better be
eſpied,it is fit, that firſt you enter into conſideration both of the firſt originall thereof,
and likewiſe of the reaſons of the firſt entry
thereof into this Countrey. For certainely
as ſuch cuſtomes, that haue their firſt inſtitution either from a godly, neceſſary,or honourable ground, and are firſt brought in,
by the meanes of ſome worthy, vertuous,
and great Perſonage,are euer,and moſt iuſtly, holden in great and reuerent
eſtimation and account, by all wiſe, vertuous, and temperate ſpirits: So
ſhould it by the contrary, iuſtly bring a great diſgrace into that ſort of cuſtomes, which hauing their originall from baſe corruption and barbaritie,
doe in like ſort, make their firſt entry into a Countrey,by an inconſiderate
and childiſh affectation of Noueltie, as is the trew caſe of the firſt inuention of *Tobacco* taking,and of the firſt entry thereof among vs.For *Tobacco* being a common herbe, which (though vnder diuers names) growes almoſt
euery where, was firſt found out by ſome of the barbarous *Indians*, to be a
Preſeruatiue or Antidote againſt the Pocks,a filthy diſeaſe,wherunto theſe
barbarous people are (as all men know) very much ſubiect, what through
the vncleanely and aduſt conſtitution of their bodies, and what through
the intemperate heate of their Climate: ſo that as from them was firſt
brought into Chriſtendome, that moſt deteſtable diſeaſe; ſo from them
likewiſe was brought this vſe of *Tobacco*, as a ſtinking and vnſauourie Antidote,for ſo corrupted and execrable a maladie, the ſtinking ſuffumigation whereof they yet vſe againſt that diſeaſe, making ſo one canker or venime to eate out another.

And now good Countrey-men, let vs (I pray you) conſider, what honour or policy can mooue vs to imitate the barbarous and beaſtly maners
of the wilde,godleſſe, and ſlauiſh *Indians*, eſpecially in ſo vile and ſtinking a
cuſtome? Shall we that diſdaine to imitate the maners of our neighbour

France

France (hauing the ſtile of the firſt Chriſtian Kingdome) and that cannot endure the ſpirit of the *Spaniards* (their King being now comparable in largeneſſe of Dominions, to the great Emperour of *Turkie*) Shall wee, I ſay, that haue bene ſo long ciuill and wealthy in Peace, famous and inuincible in Warre, fortunate in both, we that haue bene euer able to aide any of our neighbours (but neuer deafed any of their eares with any of our ſupplications for aſſiſtance) ſhall wee, I ſay, without bluſhing abaſe our ſelues ſo farre, as to imitate theſe beaſtly *Indians*, ſlaues to the *Spaniards*, refuſe to the world, and as yet aliens from the holy Couenant of God ? Why doe we not as well imitate them in walking naked as they doe ? in preferring glaſſes, feathers, and ſuch toyes, to gold and precious ſtones, as they doe ? yea why doe we not denie God and adore the diuel, as they doe ?

Now to the corrupted baſeneſſe of the firſt vſe of this *Tobacco*, doeth very well agree the fooliſh and groundleſſe firſt entry thereof into this Kingdome. It is not ſo long ſince the firſt entry of this abuſe amongſt vs here, as this preſent aage cannot yet very well remember, both the firſt Authour, and the forme of the firſt introduction of it amongſt vs. It was neither brought in by King, great Conquerour, nor learned doctour of Phiſicke.

With the report of a great diſcouery for a Conqueſt, ſome two or three Sauage men, were brought in, together with this Sauage cuſtome. But the pitie is, the poore wilde barbarous men died, but that vile barbarous cuſtome is yet aliue, yea in freſh vigor : ſo as it ſeemes a miracle to me, how a cuſtome ſpringing from ſo vile a ground, and brought in by a father ſo generally hated, ſhould be welcomed vpon ſo ſlender a warrant. For if they that firſt put it in practiſe here, had remembred for what reſpect it was vſed by them from whence it came, I am ſure they would haue bene loath, to haue taken ſo farre the imputation of that diſeaſe vpon them as they did, by vſing the cure thereof: For *Sanis non eſt opus medico*, and counterpoiſons are neuer vſed, but where poiſon is thought to precede.

But ſince it is trew, that diuers cuſtomes ſlightly grounded, and with no better warrant entred in a Common-wealth, may yet in the vſe of them thereafter, prooue both neceſſary and profitable; it is therefore next to bee examined, if there be not a full Sympathie and true Proportion, betweene the baſe ground and fooliſh entrie, and the loathſome and hurtfull vſe of this ſtinking Antidote.

I am now therefore heartily to pray you to conſider, firſt vpon what falſe and erroneous grounds you haue firſt built the generall good liking thereof; and next, what ſinnes towards God, and fooliſh vanities before the world you commit, in the deteſtable vſe of it.

As for theſe deceitfull grounds, that haue ſpecially moued you to take a good and great conceit thereof, I ſhall content my ſelfe to examine here onely foure of the principals of them; two founded vpon the Theoricke of a deceiueable apparance of reaſon, and two of them vpon the miſtaken practicke of generall experience.

Firſt,

Firſt, it is thought by you a ſure Aphoriſme in the Phyſickes, That the braines of all men, beeing naturally cold and wet, all drie and hote things ſhould be good for them; of which nature this ſtinking ſuffumigation is, and therefore of good vſe to them. Of this argument, both the propoſition and aſſumption are falſe, and ſo the concluſion cannot but be voyd of it ſelfe. For as to the Propoſition, That becauſe the braines are colde and moiſt, therefore things that are hote and dry are beſt for them, it is an inept conſequence: For man beeing compounded of the foure Complexions, (whoſe fathers are the foure Elements)although there be a mixture of them all in all the parts of his body, yet muſt the diuers parts of our *Microcoſme* or little world within our ſelues, be diuerſly more inclined, ſome to one, ſome to another complexion, according to the diuerſitie of their vſes, that of theſe diſcords a perfect harmonie may be made vp for the maintenance of the whole body.

The application then of a thing of a contrary nature, to any of theſe parts, is to interrupt them of their due function, and by conſequence hurtfull to the health of the whole bodie. As if a man, becauſe the Liuer is hote (as the fountaine of blood) and as it were an ouen to the ſtomacke, would therefore apply and weare cloſe vpon his Liuer and ſtomacke a cake of lead; he might within a very ſhort time (I hope) bee ſuſteined very good cheape at an Ordinarie, beſide the clearing of his conſcience from that deadly ſinne of gluttonie. And as if, becauſe the Heart is full of vitall ſpirits, and in perpetuall motion, a man would therefore lay a heauie pound ſtone on his breaſt,for ſtaying and holding downe that wanton palpitation,I doubt not but his breaſt would be more bruiſed with the weight therof,then the heart would be comforted with ſuch a diſagreeable and contrarious cure. And euen ſo is it with the braines:For if a man,becauſe the braines are cold and humide,would therefore vſe inwardly by ſmells, or outwardly by application, things of hot and dry qualitie , all the gaine that he could make thereof would onely be to put himſelfe in a great forwardnes for running mad,by ouerwatching himſelfe,the coldneſſe and moiſtneſſe of our braine being the onely ordinary meanes that procure our ſleepe and reſt. Indeed I doe not deny,but when it falls out that any of theſe,or any part of our bodie growes to be diſtempered, and to tend to an extremitie, beyond the compaſſe of Natures temperate mixture, that in that caſe cures of contrary qualities,to the intemperate inclination of that part,being wiſely prepared and diſcreetly miniſtred, may be both neceſſary and helpfull for ſtrengthning and aſſiſting Nature in the expulſion of her enemies : for this is the trew definition of all profitable Phiſicke.

But firſt theſe Cures ought not to be vſed, but where there is need of them,the contrary whereof, is daily practiſed in this generall vſe of *Tobacco* by all ſorts and complexions of people.

And next, I denie the Minor of this argument, as I haue already ſaid,in regard that this *Tobacco*, is not ſimply of a dry and hote qualitie ; but rather

hath

hath a certain venemous facultie ioyned with the heat therof, which makes
it haue an Antipathy againſt nature, as by the hateful ſmel therof doth well
appeare. For the noſe being the proper Organ and conuoy of the ſenſe of
ſmelling to the braines, which are the only fountaine of that ſenſe, doth euer
ſerue vs for an infallible witneſſe, whether that odour which we ſmell, be
healthfull or hurtfull to the braine, (except when it fals out that the ſenſe it
ſelfe is corrupted and abuſed through ſome infirmitie, and diſtemper in the
braine.) And that the ſuffumigation thereof cannot haue a drying quality,
it needs no further probation, then that it is a ſmoke, all ſmoke and vapour,
being of it ſelfe humide, as drawing neere to the nature of the aire, and eaſie
to be reſolued againe into water, whereof there needs no other proofe but
the Meteors, which being bred of nothing elſe but of the vapors and exha-
lations ſucked vp by the Sun out of the earth, the ſea, and waters, yet are the
ſame ſmoakie vapors turned and transformed into raines, ſnowes, deawes,
hoare froſts, and ſuch like waterie Meteors, as by the contrary the rainie
cloudes are often transformed and euaporated in bluſtering windes.

The ſecond Argument grounded on a ſhew of reaſon is, That this filthy
ſmoake, aſwell through the heat and ſtrength thereof, as by a naturall force
and quality, is able and fit to purge both the head and ſtomack of rhewmes
and diſtillations, as experience teacheth, by the ſpitting & auoiding fleame,
immediatly after the taking of it. But the fallacie of this Argument may eaſily appeare, by my late preceding deſcription of the Meteors: For euen as
the ſmoakie vapours ſucked vp by the Sunne, and ſtayed in the loweſt and
cold Region of the aire, are there contracted into clouds, and turned into
raine and ſuch other watery Meteors: So this ſtinking ſmoake being ſucked vp by the noſe, & impriſoned in the cold and moyſt braines, is by their
cold and wet facultie, turned and caſt forth againe in waterie diſtillations,
and ſo are you made free and purged of nothing, but that wherewith you
wilfully burdened your ſelues : and therefore are you no wiſer in taking *To-*
bacco for purging you of diſtillations, then if for preuenting the Cholicke
you would take all kind of windie meats and drinkes ; and for preuenting
of the Stone, you would take all kinde of meates and drinkes that would
breed grauell in the kidneys, and then when you were forced to auoide
much winde out of your ſtomacke, and much grauell in your Vrine, that
you ſhould attribute the thanke therof to ſuch nouriſhments, as bred thoſe
within you, that behooued either to be expelled by the force of Nature, or
you to haue *buſt at the broad ſide*, as the Prouerbe is.

As for the other two reaſons founded vpon experience, the firſt of which
is, That the whole people would not haue taken ſo generall a good liking
thereof, if they had not by experience found it very ſoueraigne and good
for them: For anſwere thereunto, how eaſily the mindes of any people,
wherewith God hath repleniſhed this world may be drawen to the fooliſh
affectation of any noueltie, I leaue it to the diſcreet iudgement of any man
that is reaſonable.

Doe we not daily fee,that a man can no fooner bring ouer from beyond the feas any new forme of apparell, but that he cannot be thought a man of fpirit,that would not prefently imitate the fame? And fo from hand to hand it fpreads, till it be practifed by all, not for any commodity that is in it, but only becaufe it is come to be the fafhion. For fuch is the force of that naturall felfe-loue in euery one of vs,and fuch is the corruption of enuy bred in the breft of euery one, as we cannot be content vnleffe wee imitate euery thing that our fellowes doe,and fo prooue our felues capable of euery thing whereof they are capable,like Apes,counterfeiting the maners of others,to our owne deftruction.For let one or two of the greateft Mafters of Mathematicks in any of the two famous Vniuerfities, but conftantly affirme any cleare day,that they fee fome ftrange apparition in the skies ; they wil I warrant you be feconded by the greateft part of the ftudents in that profeffion : So loth will they be,to be thought inferior to their fellowes,either in depth of knowledge or fharpnes of fight : And therfore the generall good liking and imbracing of this foolifh cuftome,doth but only proceed from that affectation of noueltie,and popular errour,whereof I haue already fpoken.

The other argument drawn from a miftaken experience,is but the more particular probation of this generall,becaufe it is alledged to be found trew by proofe , that by the taking of *Tobacco* diuers and very many doe finde themfelues cured of diuers difeafes ; as on the other part,no man euer receiued harme thereby. In this argument there is firft a great miftaking, and next a monftrous abfurditie : For is it not a very great miftaking,to take *non caufam pro caufa*, as they fay in the Logickes ? becaufe peraduenture when a ficke man hath had his difeafe at the height, hee hath at that inftant taken *Tobacco*, and afterward his difeafe taking the naturall courfe of declining, and confequently the Patient of recouering his health, O then the *Tobacco* forfooth,was the worker of that miracle.Befide that,it is a thing wel known to all Phyficians, that the apprehenfion and conceit of the patient, hath by wakening and vniting the vitall fpirits,and fo ftrengthening nature,a great power and vertue , to cure diuers difeafes. For an euident proofe of miftaking in the like cafe, I pray you what foolifh boy, what filly wench, what olde doting wife, or ignorant countrey clowne, is not a Phyfician for the toothach,for the cholicke,and diuers fuch common difeafes ? Yea, will not euery man you meet withall,teach you a fundry cure for the fame,& fweare by that meane either himfelfe, or fome of his neereft kinfemen and friends was cured? And yet I hope no man is fo foolifh as to beleeue them. And all thefe toyes do only proceed frō the miftaking *Non caufam pro caufa*,as I haue already faid, and fo if a man chance to recouer one of any difeafe, after hee hath taken *Tobacco*,that muft haue the thanks of all. But by the contrary, if a man fmoke himfelfe to death with it (and many haue done) O then fome other difeafe muft beare the blame for that fault. So doe old harlots thanke their harlotrie for their many yeeres, that cuftome being healthfull (fay they) *ad purgandos Renes*, but neuer haue mind how many die of the Pockes

in the flower of their youth. And so doe olde drunkards thinke they pro-
long their dayes, by their swinelike diet, but neuer remember how many
die drowned in drinke before they be halfe olde.

And what greater absurditie can there be, then to say that one cure shall
serue for diuers, nay, cōtrarious sorts of diseases? It is an vndoubted ground
among all Physicians, that there is almost no sort either of nourishment
or medicine, that hath not some thing in it disagreeable to some part of
mans bodie; because as I haue alreadie said, the nature of the temperature
of euery part, is so different from another, that according to the olde prouerbe, That which is good for the head, is euill for the necke and the shoulders: For euen as a strong enemy, that inuades a town or fortresse, although
in his siege thereof, he do belay and compasse it round about, yet he makes
his breach and entry, at some one or fewe speciall parts thereof, which hee
hath tried and found to be weakest and least able to resist; so sickenes doth
make her particular assault, vpon such part or parts of our body, as are weakest and easiest to be ouercome by that sort of disease, which then doth assaile vs, although all the rest of the body by Sympathie feele it selfe to be as
it were belayed, and besieged by the affliction of that speciall part, the griefe
and smart thereof being by the sense of feeling dispersed through all the
rest of our members. And therefore the skilfull Physician presses by such
cures to purge and strengthen that part which is afflicted, as are only fit for
that sort of disease, and doe best agree with the nature of that infirme part;
which being abused to a disease of another nature, would proue as hurtfull
for the one, as helpfull for the other. Yea, not onely will a skilfull and wary
Physician be carefull to vse no cure but that which is fit for that sort of disease, but he will also consider all other circumstances, & make the remedies
sutable therunto; as the temperature of the clime, where the Patient is, the
constitution of the Planets, the time of the Moone, the season of the yeere,
the aage and complexion of the Patient, and the present state of his body, in
strength or weaknes: For one cure must not euer be vsed for the selfesame
disease, but according to the varying of any of the foresaid circumstances,
that sort of remedy must be vsed which is fittest for the same. Where by the
contrary in this case, such is the miraculous omnipotencie of our strong ta-
sted *Tobacco*, as it cures al sorts of diseases (which neuer any drugge could do
before) in all persons, and at all times. It cures all maner of distillations, either in the head or stomacke (if you beleeue their Axiomes) although in
very deed it doe both corrupt the braine, and by causing ouer quicke dige-
stion, fill the stomacke full of crudities. It cures the gowt in the feet, and
(which is miraculous) in that very instant when the smoke thereof, as light,
flies vp into the head, the vertue therof, as heauy, runs down to the litle toe.
It helps all sorts of agues. It makes a man sober that was drunk. It refreshes
a weary man, and yet makes a man hungry. Being taken when they goe to
bed, it makes one sleepe soundly, and yet being taken when a man is sleepie
and drowsie, it will, as they say, awake his braine, and quicken his vnder-

ſtanding. As for curing of the Pockes, it ſerues for that vſe but among the pockie Indian ſlaues. Here in *England* it is refined, and will not deigne to cure here any other then cleanly and gentlemanly diſeaſes. O omnipotent power of *Tobacco*! And if it could by the ſmoake thereof chaſe out deuils, as the ſmoake of *Tobias* fiſh did (which I am ſure could ſmell no ſtronglier) it would ſerue for a precious Relicke, both for the ſuperſtitious Prieſts, and the inſolent Puritanes, to caſt out deuils withall.

Admitting then, and not confeſſing, that the vſe thereof were healthful for ſome ſorts of diſeaſes; ſhould it be vſed for all ſickneſſes? ſhould it be v-ſed by all men? ſhould it be vſed at all times? yea ſhould it be vſed by able, yong, ſtrong, healthful men? Medicine hath that vertue, that it neuer leaues a man in that ſtate wherein it finds him: it makes a ſicke man whole, but a whole man ſicke: And as Medicine helps nature being taken at times of ne-ceſſitie, ſo being euer and continually vſed, it doeth but weaken, weary, and weare nature. What ſpeake I of Medicine? Nay let a man euery houre of the day, or as oft as many in this countrey vſe to take *Tobacco*, let a man I ſay, but take as oft the belt ſorts of nouriſhments in meate and drinke that can be deuiſed, he ſhall with the continuall vſe thereof weaken both his head and his ſtomacke: all his members ſhall become feeble, his ſpirits dull, and in the end, as a drowſie lazie belly-god, he ſhall euaniſh in a Lethargie.

And from this weakeneſſe it proceeds, that many in this kingdome haue had ſuch a continuall vſe of taking this vnſauorie ſmoake, as now they are not able to forbeare the ſame, no more then an old drunkard can abide to be long ſober, without falling into an incurable weakneſſe and euill conſtitu-tion: for their continuall cuſtome hath made to them, *habitum, alteram na-turam*: ſo to thoſe that from their birth haue beene continually nouriſhed vpon poiſon and things venemous, wholſome meats are only poiſonable.

Thus hauing, as I truſt, ſufficiently anſwered the moſt principall argu-ments that are vſed in defence of this vile cuſtome, it reſts only to informe you what ſinnes and vanities you commit in the filthy abuſe thereof. Firſt, are you not guiltie of ſinnefull and ſhamefull luſt? (for luſt may be as well in any of the ſenſes as in feeling) that although you be troubled with no diſ-eaſe, but in perfect health, yet can you neither be merry at an Ordinary, nor laſciuious in the Stewes, if you lacke *Tobacco* to prouoke your appetite to a-ny of thoſe ſorts of recreation, luſting after it as the children of Iſrael did in the wilderneſſe after Quailes? Secondly it is, as you vſe or rather abuſe it, a branch of the ſinne of drunkennes, which is the root of all ſinnes: for as the only delight that drunkards take in wine is in the ſtrength of the taſte, and the force of the fume therof that mounts vp to the braine: for no drunkards loue any weake, or ſweet drinke: ſo are not thoſe (I meane the ſtrong heate and the fume) the onely qualities that make *Tobacco* ſo delectable to all the louers of it? And as no man likes ſtrong heady drinke the firſt day (becauſe *nemo repentè fit turpiſſimus*) but by cuſtome is piece and piece allured, while in the ende, a drunkard will haue as great a thirſt to be drunke, as a ſober

man

man to quench his thirſt with a draught when he hath need of it : So is not this the very caſe of all the great takers of *Tobacco* ? which therefore they themſelues doe attribute to a bewitching qualitie in it. Thirdly, is it not the greateſt ſinne of all, that you the people of all ſorts of this kingdome, who are created and ordeined by God, to beſtow both your perſons and goods, for the maintenance both of the honour and ſafety of your King and Common-wealth, ſhould diſable your ſelues in both? In your perſons ha-uing by this continuall vile cuſtome brought your ſelues to this ſhamefull imbecilitie , that you are not able to ride or walke the iourney of a Iewes Sabboth, but you muſt haue a reekie cole brought you from the next poore houſe to kindle your *Tobacco* with ? whereas he cannot be thought able for any ſeruice in the warres, that cannot endure oftentimes the want of meat, drinke, and ſleepe , much more then muſt he endure the want of *Tobacco*. In the times of the many glorious and victorious battailes fought by this Nation, there was no word of *Tobacco* : but now if it were time of warres, and that you were to make ſome ſudden *Caualcado* vpon your enemies, if a-ny of you ſhould ſeeke leiſure to ſtay behinde his fellow for taking of *To-bacco*, for my part I ſhould neuer be ſory for any euill chance that might be-fall him. To take a cuſtome in any thing that cannot be left againe, is moſt harmeful to the people of any land. *Mollicies* and delicacie were the wracke and ouerthrow, firſt of the *Perſian* , and next of the *Romane* Empire. And this very cuſtome of taking *Tobacco* (whereof our preſent purpoſe is) is euen at this day accounted ſo effeminate among the *Indians* themſelues, as in the market they will offer no price for a ſlaue to be ſold, whom they find to be a great *Tobacco* taker.

Now how you are by this cuſtome diſabled in your goods, let the Gen-try of this land beare witneſſe, ſome of them beſtowing three, ſome foure hundred pounds a yeere vpon this precious ſtinke, which I am ſure might be beſtowed vpon many farre better vſes. I read indeed of a knauiſh Cour-tier, who for abuſing the fauour of the Emperor *Alexander Seuerus* his ma-ſter, by taking bribes to intercede, for ſundry perſons in his maſters eare, (for who he neuer once opened his mouth) was iuſtly choked with ſmoke, with this doome, *Fumo pereat, qui fumum vendidit* : but of ſo many ſmoke-buyers, as are at this preſent in this kingdome, I neuer read nor heard.

And for the vanities committed in this filthy cuſtome, is it not both great vanitie and vncleanneſſe, that at the table, a place of reſpect, of clean-lineſſe, of modeſtie , men ſhould not be aſhamed, to ſit toſſing of *Tobacco pipes*, and puffing of the ſmoke of *Tobacco* one to another, making the filthy ſmoke and ſtinke thereof, to exhale athwart the diſhes, and infect the aire, when very often, men that abhorre it are at their repaſt ? Surely ſmoke be-comes a kitchin farre better then a dining chamber, and yet it makes a kit-chin alſo oftentimes in the inward parts of men , ſoyling and infecting them, with an vnctuous and oily kind of ſoote, as hath bene found in ſome great *Tobacco* takers, that after their death were opened. And not only meat time, but no other time nor action is exempted from the publike vſe of this vnciuill tricke : ſo as if the wiues of *Diepe* liſt to conteſt with this Nation for good maners, their worſt maners would in all reaſon be found at leaſt not ſo diſhoneſt (as ours are) in this point. The publike vſe where-of, at all times, and in all places, hath now ſo farre preuailed, as diuers men very found both in iudgement and complexion, haue beene at laſt forced to take it alſo without deſire, partly becauſe they were aſhamed to ſeeme ſingular, (like the two Philoſophers that were forced to ducke themſelues in that raine water, and ſo become fooles as well as the reſt of the people) and partly to be as one that was content to eate Garlick (which he did not loue) that he might not be troubled with the ſmell of it, in the breath of his fellowes. And is it not a great vanitie, that a man cannot heartily welcome his friend now, but ſtraight they muſt be in hand with *Tobacco* : No it is become in place of a cure, a point of good fellowſhip, and hee that will re-fuſe to take a pipe of *Tobacco* among his fellowes, (though by his owne e-lection hee would rather feele the ſauour of a Sinke) is accounted peeuiſh and no good company, euen as they doe with tipling in the colde Eaſterne countreys. Yea the Miſtreſſe cannot in a more manerly kind, entertaine her ſeruant, then by giuing him out of her faire hand a pipe of *Tobacco*. But here-in is not only a great vanity, but a great contempt of Gods good giftes, that the ſweetneſſe of mans breath, being a good gift of God, ſhould be wilfully corrupted by this ſtinking ſmoke, wherin I muſt côfeſſe, it hath too ſtrong a vertue; and ſo that which is an ornament of nature, & can neither by any artifice be at the firſt acquired, nor once loſt be recouered againe, ſhalbe fil-thily corrupted with an incurable ſtinke, which vile qualitie is as directly contrary to that wrong opinion which is holden of the wholeſomneſſe therof, as the venime of putrifaction is contrary to the vertue Preſeruatiue.

Moreouer, which is a great iniquitie, and againſt all humanitie, the huſ-band ſhal not be aſhamed, to reduce therby his delicate, wholſom, & cleane complexioned wife to that extremity, that either ſhe muſt alſo corrupt her ſweet breath therwith, or els reſolue to liue in a perpetual ſtinking torment.

Haue you not reaſon then to be aſhamed, and to forbeare this filthie no-ueltie, ſo baſely grounded, ſo fooliſhly receiued, and ſo groſſely miſtaken in the right vſe thereof? In your abuſe thereof ſinning againſt God, harming your ſelues both in perſons and goods, and raking alſo thereby the markes and notes of vanitie vpon you; by the cuſtome thereof making your ſelues to be wondered at by all forreine ciuill Nations, and by all ſtrangers that come among you, to be ſcorned and contemned : A cuſtome loathſome to the eye, hatefull to the noſe, harmefull to the braine, dangerous to the lungs, and in the blacke ſtinking fume thereof, neereſt re-ſembling the horrible Stigian ſmoake of the pit that is bottomleſſe.

A DISCOVRSE OF THE
MANER OF THE DISCO-
VERIE OF THE POWDER-
TREASON,

IOYNED WITH THE
EXAMINATION OF SOME
OF THE PRISONERS.

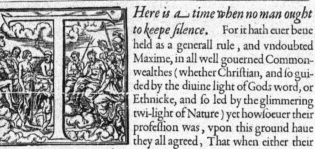

Here is a time when no man ought to keepe silence. For it hath euer bene held as a generall rule, and vndoubted Maxime, in all well gouerned Common-wealthes (whether Chriftian, and fo guided by the diuine light of Gods word, or Ethnicke, and fo led by the glimmering twi-light of Nature) yet howfoeuer their profeffion was, vpon this ground haue they all agreed, That when either their Religion, their King, or their countrey was in any extreme hazard, no good countreyman ought then to withhold either his tongue or his hand, according to his calling and facultie, from ayding to repell the iniurie, repreffe the violence, and auenge the guilt vpon the authors thereof. But if euer any people had fuch an occafion miniftred vnto them, It is furely this people now, nay this whole Ifle, and all the reft belonging to this great and glorious Monarchie. For if in any heathenifh republique, no priuate man could thinke his life more happily and glorioufly beftowed, then in the defence of any one of thefe three, That is, either *pro Aris, pro Focis,* or *pro Patre patriæ*; And that the endangering of any one of thefe, would at once ftirre the whole body of the Common-wealth, not any more as diuided members, but as a folide and indiuiduall lumpe : How much more ought we the trewly Chriftian people that inhabite this vnited and trewly happie happy Ifle, vnder the wings of our gracious and religious Monarch? Nay, how infinitely greater caufe haue we to feele and reffent our felues of the fmart of that wound, not onely intended and execrated (not confecrated) for the vtter extinguifhing of our trew Chriftian profeffion, nor ioyntly therwith onely for the cutting off of our Head and father Politike, *Sed vt nefas iftud & facrilegiofum parricidium omnibus modis abfolutum reddi pofsit?* And that nothing might be wanting for making this facrilegious parricide a patterne of mifchiefe, and a crime (nay, a mother or ftorehoufe of all crimes) without example, they fhould haue ioyned the deftruction of the bodie to the head, fo as *Grex cum Rege, Ara cum focis, Lares cum Penatibus*, fhould all at one thunderclap haue beene fent to heauen together: The King our head, the Queene our fertile mother, and thofe young and hopefull Oliue plants, not theirs but ours: Our reuerend Clergie, our honourable Nobilitie, the faithfull Councellors, the graue Iudges, the greateft part of the worthy Knights and Gentry, afwell as of the wifeft Burgeffes; The whole Clerkes of the Crowne, Counfaile, Signet, Seales, or of any other principall Iudgement feate. All the learned Lawyers, together with an infinite number of the Common people: Nay, their furious rage fhould not onely haue lighted vpon reafonable and fenfible creatures without diftinction either of degree, fexe or aage; But euen the infenfible ftockes and ftones fhould not haue bin free of their fury. The hal of Iuftice; The houfe of Parliament; The Church vfed for the Coronation of our Kings; The Monuments of our former Princes; The Crowne and other markes of Royaltie; Al the Records, afwell of Parliament, as of euery particular mans right, with a great number of Charters and fuch like, fhould all haue bene comprehended vnder that fearefull *Chaos*. And fo the earth as it were opened, fhould haue fent foorth of the bottome of the *Stygian* lake fuch fulphured fmoke, furious flames, and fearefull thunder, as fhould haue by their diabolicall *Domefday* deftroyed and defaced, in the twinkling of an eye, not onely our prefent liuing Princes and people, but euen our infenfible Monuments referued for future aages. So as not only our felues that are mortall, but the immortall Monuments of our ancient Princes and Nobility, that haue beene fo precioufly preferued from aage to aage, as the remaining *Trophees* of their eternal glory, and haue fo long triumphed ouer enuious time, fhould now haue beene all confumed together; and fo not onely we, but the memory of vs and ours, fhould haue beene thus extinguifhed in an inftant. The trew horror therefore of this deteftable deuice, hath ftirred mee vp to bethinke my felfe, wherein I may beft difcharge my confcience in a caufe fo generall and common, if it were to bring but one ftone to the building, or rather with the Widow one mite to the common boxe. But fince to fo hatefull and vnheard-of inuention, there can be no greater enemy then the felfe, the fimple trewth thereof being once publikely knowen; and that there needes no ftronger argument to bring fuch a plot in vniuerfal deteftatió, then the certainty that fo monftrous a thing could once be deuifed, nay cócluded vpon,

wrought

wrought in, in full readinesse, and within twelue houres of the execution : My threefold zeale to those blessings, whereof they would haue so violently made vs all widowes, hath made me resolue to set downe here the trew Narration of that monstrous and vnnaturall intended Tragedie, hauing better occasion by the meanes of my seruice and continuall attendance in Court, to know the trewth thereof, then others that peraduenture haue it onely by relation at the third or fourth hand. So that whereas those worse then *Catilines*, thought to haue extirped vs and our memories ; Their infamous memory shall by these meanes remaine to the end of the world, vpon the one part : and vpon the other, Gods great and merciful deliuerance of his Anoynted and vs all, shall remaine in neuer-dying Records. And God graunt that it may be in marble tables of Thankefulnesse engrauen in our hearts.

WHile this Land and whole Monarchie flourished in a most happie and plentifull PEACE, as well at home as abroad, sustained and conducted by these two maine Pillars of all good Gouernement, PIETIE and IVSTICE, no forreine grudge, nor inward whispering of discontentment any way appearing; The King being vpon his returne from his hunting exercise at *Royston*, vpon occasion of the drawing neere of the Parliament time, which had beene twise prorogued already, partly in regard of the season of the yeere, and partly of the Terme; As the winds are euer stillest immediatly before a storme; and as the Sunne blenks often hottest to foretell a following showre: So at that time of greatest calme did this secretly-hatched thunder beginne to cast foorth the first flashes, and flaming lightnings of the approching tempest. For the Saturday of the weeke immediatly preceding the Kings returne, which was vpon a Thursday (being but tenne dayes before the Parliament) The Lord *Mountegle*, sonne and heire to the Lord *Morley*, being in his owne lodging ready to goe to supper at seuen of the clocke at night, one of his foot-men (whom he had sent of an errand ouer the street) was met by an vnknowen man of a reasonable tall personage, who deliuered him a Letter, charging him to put it in my Lord his masters hands : which my Lord no sooner receiued, but that hauing broken it vp, and perceiuing the same to bee of an vnknowen and somewhat vnlegible hand, and without either date or subscription; did call one of his men vnto him for helping him to reade it. But no sooner did he conceiue the strange contents thereof, although hee was somewhat perplexed what construction to make of it (as whether of a matter of consequence, as indeed it was, or whether some foolish deuised Pasquil by some of his enemies, to skarre him from his attendance at the Parliament) yet did he as a most dutifull and loyall Subiect, conclude not to conceale it, what euer might come of it. Whereupon, notwithstanding the latenesse and darknesse of the night in that season of the yeere, he presently repaired to his Maiesties Pallace at *Whitehall*, and there deliuered the same

A letter deliuered to the Lord *Mountegle.*

to

Reuealed to the Earle of *Salisbury*.

to the Earle of *Salisbury* his Maiefties principall Secretarie. Whereupon the faid Earle of *Salisbury* hauing read the Letter, and heard the maner of the comming of it to his hands, did greatly encourage and commend my Lord for his difcretion, telling him plainly, that whatfoeuer the purpofe of the Letter might proue hereafter, yet did this accident put him in mind of diuers aduertifements he had receiued from beyond the Seas, wherewith he had acquainted afwell the King himfelfe, as diuers of his Priuie Coun-fellors, concerning fome bufineffe the Papifts were in, both at home and abroad, making preparations for fome combination amongft them againft this Parliament time, for enabling them to deliuer at that time to the King

Purpofe of the Papifts for de-liuering a pe-tition to his Maieftie, to craue tolera-tion of Reli-gion.

fome petition for toleration of Religion: which fhould bee deliuered in fome fuch order and fo well backed; as the King fhould be loth to refufe their requefts; like the fturdie beggars crauing almes with one open hand, but carying a ftone in the other, in cafe of refufall. And therefore did the Earle of *Salisbury* conclude with the Lord *Mountegle*, that he would in re-gard of the Kings abfence impart the fame Letter to fome more of his Ma-iefties Councell; whereof my L.*Mountegle* liked well: onely adding this requeft by way of proteftation, That whatfoeuer the euent hereof might proue, it fhould not be imputed to him, as proceeding from too light and too fuddaine an apprehenfion, that he deliuered this Letter, being onely mooued thereunto for demonftration of his ready deuotion, and care for preferuation of his Maieftie and the State. And thus did the Earle of *Sa-*

The Lord *Chamberlaine* made priuie to the Letter by the Earle of *Salisbury*.

lisbury prefently acquaint the Lord *Chamberlaine* with the faid letter. Where-upon they two in prefence of the Lord *Mountegle*, calling to mind the for-mer intelligence already mentioned, which feemed to haue fome relation with this Letter; The tender care which they euer caried to the preferua-tion of his Maiefties perfon, made them apprehend, that fome perillous at-tempt did thereby appeare to be intended againft the fame, which did the more neerly concerne the faid L.*Chamberlaine* to haue a care of, in regard that it doth belong to the charge of his Office to ouerfee as well all places of Af-fembly where his Maiefty is to repaire, as his Highneffe owne priuate hou-fes. And therfore did the faid two Counfailors conclude, That they fhould ioyne vnto themfelues three more of the Councell, to wit, the Lord *Admi-ral*, the Earles of *Worcefter* and *Northampton*, to be alfo particularly acquain-ted with this accident, who hauing all of them concurred together to the re-examination of the Contents of the faid Letter, they did conclude, That how flight a matter it might at the firft appeare to bee, yet was it not abfolutely to be contemned, in refpect of the care which it behooued them to haue of the preferuation of his Maiefties perfon: But yet refolued for

Thought meet by the Councellors to acquaint the King with the Letter.

two reafons, firft to acquaint the King himfelfe with the fame before they proceeded to any further inquifition in the matter, afwell for the expecta-tion and experience they had of his Maiefties fortunate Iudgement in clea-ring and foluing of obfcure riddles and doubtful myfteries; as alfo becaufe the more time would in the meane while be giuen for the Practife to ripen,

                                if

if any was, whereby the Difcouery might be the more cleere and euident, and the ground of proceeding thereupon more fafe, iuft, and eafie. And fo according to their determination did the fayd Earle of *Salisbury* repaire to the King in his Gallery vpon Friday, being *Athallow* day, in the afternoone, which was the day after his Maiefties arriuall, and none but himfelfe being prefent with his Highneffe at that time, where without any other fpeach or iudgement giuing of the Letter, but onely relating fimply the forme of the deliuery thereof, he prefented it to his Maieftie. The contents whereof follow. Vpon Alhal-low day the Earle of Salis-burie shewed the Letter to the King.

MY *Lord, Out of the loue I beare to fome of your friends, I haue a care of your preferuation. Therefore I would aduife you, as you tender your life, to de-uife fome excufe to fhift off your attendance at this Parliament. For God and man haue concurred to punifh the wickedneffe of this Time. And thinke not flightly of this Aduertifement, but retire your felfe into your Countrey, where you may expect the euent in fafety. For though there be no apparance of any ftirre, yet I fay, they fhal receiue a terrible Blow this Parliament; and yet they fhall not fee who hurts them. This counfell is not to be contemned, becaufe it may doe you good, and can doe you no harme; for the danger is paft fo foone as you haue burnt the Letter. And I hope God will giue you the grace to make good Vfe of it: To whofe holy protection I com-mend you.*

The King no fooner read the Letter, but after a little paufe, and then reading it ouer againe, he deliuered his iudgement of it in fuch fort, as hee thought it was not to be contemned, for that the Style of it feemed to bee more quicke and pithie, then is vfuall to be in any Pafquil or libel (the fu-perfluities of idle braines:) But the Earle of *Salisbury* perceiuing the King to apprehend it deepelier then he looked for, knowing his nature, told him that he thought by one fentence in it, that it was like to be written by fome foole or madman, reading to him this fentence in it, *For the danger is paft as foone as you haue burnt the Letter*; which hee faid, was likely to bee the faying of a foole : for if the danger was paft fo foone as the Letter was burnt, then the warning behooued to bee of little auayle, when the burning of the Letter might make the danger to be efchewed. But the King by the contra-ry confidering the former fentence in the Letter, *That they fhould receiue a terrible Blow at this Parliament, and yet fhould not fee who hurt them*, Ioyning it to the fentence immediatly following, already alledged, did therupon coni-ecture, That the danger mentioned, fhould bee fome fuddaine danger by blowing vp of Powder : For no other Infurrection, Rebellion, or what-foeuer other priuate and defperate Attempt could bee committed or at-tempted in time of Parliament, and the Authours thereof vnfeene, except onely it were by a blowing vp of Powder, which might bee performed by one bafe knaue in a darke corner; whereupon he was moued to inter-prete and conftrue the latter Sentence in the Letter (alledged by the Earle of *Salisburie*) againft all ordinarie fence and conftruction in Grammar, His Maiefties iudgement of the Letter.

as

as if by thefe words, *For the danger is past as soone as you haue burned the Let-ter* , fhould be clofely vnderftood the fuddaintie and quickeneffe of the danger, which fhould be as quickly perfourmed and at an end, as that pa-per fhould be of bleafing vp in the fire; turning that word of *as soone,* to the fenfe of, *as quickly*: And therefore wifhed, that before his going to the Par-

His Maiefties opinion for fearching of the vnder roumes of the Parliament Houfe.

liament, the vnder roumes of the Parliament houfe might be well and nar-rowly fearched. But the Earle of *Salisbury* wondering at this his Maiefties Commentary, which he knew to be fo farre contrary to his ordinary and naturall difpofition , who did rather euer finne vpon the other fide; in not apprehending nor trufting due Aduertifements of Practifes and Perils when hee was trewly enformed of them, whereby hee had many times drawen himfelfe into many defperate dangers · and interpreting rightly this extraordinary Caution at this time to proceede from the vigilant care hee had of the whole State, more then of his owne Perfon, which could not but haue all perifhed together, if this defignement had fucceeded : Hee thought good to diffemble ftill vnto the King, that there had beene any iuft caufe of fuch apprehenfion · And ending the purpofe with fome mer-rie ieaft vpon this Subiect, as his cuftome is, tooke his leaue for that time.

But though he feemed fo to neglect it to his Maieftie; yet his cuftomable and watchfull care of the King and the State ftill boyling within him, And hauing with the bleffed Virgine *Marie* laid vp in his heart the Kings fo ftrange iudgement and conftruction of it; He could not be at reft til he ac-quainted the forefaid Lords what had paffed betweene the King and him in priuat : Wherupon they were all fo earneft to renew againe the memory of the fame purpofe to his Maieftie, as it was agreed that he fhould the next day, being Saturday, repaire to his Highneffe : which hee did in the fame priuie Gallery, and renewed the memory thereof, the L. *Chamberlaine* then

The determi-nation to fearch the Parliament houfe and the roumes vnder it.

being prefent with the King. At what time it was determined, that the faid Lord *Chamberlaine* fhould, according to his cuftome and Office , view all the Parliament Houfes, both aboue and below, and confider what likeli-hood or appearance of any fuch danger might poffibly be gathered by the fight of them : But yet, as well for ftaying of idle rumours, as for beeing the more able to difcerne any myfterie, the nearer that things were in readineffe, his iourney thither was ordeined to bee deferred till the afternoone before the fitting downe of the Parliament, which was vp-on the Munday following. At what time hee (according to this conclu-fion) went to the Parliament houfe accompanied with my Lord *Mountegle,* beeing in zeale to the Kings feruice earneft and curious to fee the euent of that accident whereof hee had the fortune to be the firft difcouerer : where,

Wood and Coale found by the Lord *Chamberlaine* in the Vault.

hauing viewed all the lower roumes, hee found in the Vault vnder the vp-per Houfe great ftore and prouifion of Billets, Faggots, and Coales : And enquiring of *Whyneard* Keeper of the Wardrobe, to what vfe hee had put thofe lower roumes and cellars : he told him, That *Thomas Percie* had hi-red

red both the Houfe, and part of the Cellar or Vault vnder the fame, and that the Wood and Coale therein was the faid Gentlemansowne prouifion: Whereupon the Lord *Chamberlaine*, cafting his eye afide, perceiued a fellow ftanding in a corner there, calling himfelf the faid *Percies* man, and keeper of that houfe for him, but indeed was *Guido Fawkes*, the owner of that hand which fhould haue acted that monftrous Tragedie.

Guido Fawkes bearing the name of *Percies* man.

The Lord *Chamberlaine* looking vpon all things with a heedfull indeed, yet in outward appearance with but a careleffe and rackleffe eye (as became fo wife and diligent a minifter) hee prefently addreffed himfelfe to the King in the faid priuie Gallery, wherein the prefence of the Lord *Treafurer*, the Lord *Admirall*, the Earles of *Worcefter*, *Northampton*, and *Salisbury*, hee made his report, what hee had feene and obferued there; noting that *Mountegle* had told him, That he no fooner heard *Thomas Percy* named to be the poffeffour of that houfe, but confidering both his backwardnes in Religion, and the old dearneffe in friendfhip betweene himfelfe and the faid *Percy*, hee did greatly fufpect the matter, and that the Letter fhould come from him. The faid Lord *Chamberlaine* alfo tolde, That he did not wonder a little at the extraordinary great prouifion of wood and coale in that houfe, where *Thomas Percié* had fo feldome occafion to remaine; As likewife it gaue him in his minde that his man looked like a very tall and defperate fellow.

The Lord *Chamberlaines* report and iudgement of what he had obferued in the fearch.

This could not but encreafe the Kings former apprehenfion and iealoufie: whereupon hee infifted (as before) that the Houfe was narrowly to bee fearched, and that thofe Billets and Coales would be fearched to the bottome, it beeing moft fufpicious that they were layed there onely for couering of the powder. Of this fame minde alfo were all the Counfailours then prefent: But vpon the fafhion of making of the fearch was it long debated: For vpon the one fide they were all fo iealous of the Kings fafety, that they all agreed, that there could not be too much caution vfed for preuenting his danger. And yet vpon the other part they were all extreme loath and daintie, that in cafe this Letter fhould proue to bee nothing but the euaporation of an idle braine; then a curious fearch beeing made, and nothing found, fhould not onely turne to the generall fcandall of the King and the State, as being fo fufpicious of euery light and friuolous toy, but likewife lay an ill fauoured imputation vpon the Earle of *Northumberland* one of his Maiefties greateft Subiects and Counfailors, this *Tho. Percie* being his kinfman, and moft confident familiar. And the rather were they curious vpon this point, knowing how far the King detefted to be thought fufpitious or iealous of any of his good Subiects, though of the meaneft degree. And therefore though they all agreed vpon the maine ground, which was to prouide for the fecuritie of the Kings Perfon, yet did they much differ in the circumftances, by which this action might be beft caried with leaft dinne and occafion of flaunder. But the King himfelfe ftill perfifting that there were diuers fhrewd appearances, and that

Difputation about the manner of the further fearch.

V   a narrow

a narrow search of those places could preiudge no man that was innocent, hee at last plainely resolued them, That either must all the partes of those roumes bee narrowly searched, and no possibilitie of danger left vnexamined, or else hee and they all must resolue not to meddle in it at all, but plainly to goe the next day to the Parliament, and leaue the successe to Fortune, which he beleeued they would be loth to take vpon their consciences : for in such a case as this, an halfe doing was worse then no doing at all. Whereupon it was at last concluded, That nothing should bee left vnsearched in those Houses : And yet for the better colour and stay of rumour, in case nothing were found, it was thought meet, that vpon a pretence of *Whyneards* missing some of the Kings stuffe or Hangings which he had in keeping, all those roumes should be narrowly ripped for them. And to this purpose was Sir *Thomas Kneuet* (a Gentleman of his Maiesties priuie Chamber) employed, being a Iustice of Peace in *Westminster*, and one, of whose ancient fidelitie both the late Queene and our now Soueraigne haue had large proofe: who according to the trust committed vnto him, went about the midnight next after, to the Parliament house, accompanied with such a small number as was fit for that errand. But before his entry in the house, finding *Thomas Percies* alleaged man standing without the doores, his cloathes and bootes on at so dead a time of the night, he resolued to apprehend him, as hee did, and thereafter went forward to the searching of the house, where after he had caused to be ouerturned some of the Billets and Coales, he first found one of the small Barrels of Powder, and after all the rest, to the number of thirty sixe Barrels, great and small : And thereafter searching the fellow, whom he had taken, found three matches, and all other instruments fit for blowing vp the Powder, readie vpon him, which made him instantly confesse his owne guiltinesse, declaring also vnto him, That if hee had happened to be within the house when hee tooke him, as he was immediatly before (at the ending of his worke) hee would not haue failed to haue blowen him vp, house and all.

Thus after Sir *Thomas* had caused the wretch to bee surely bound, and well guarded by the company hee had brought with him, hee himselfe returned backe to the Kings Palace, and gaue warning of his successe to the Lord Chamberlaine, and Earle of Salisburie, who immediatly warning the rest of the Councell that lay in the house, as soone as they could get themselues ready, came, with their fellow Counsellers, to the Kings Bedchamber, being at that time neere foure of the clocke in the morning. And at the first entry of the Kings Chamber doore, the Lord Chamberlaine, being not any longer able to conceale his ioy for the preuenting of so great a danger, told the King in a confused haste, that all was found and discouered, and the Traitor in hands and fast bound.

Then, order beeing first taken for sending for the rest of the Councell that lay in the Towne, The prisoner himselfe was brought into the house, where in respect of the strangenes of the accident, no man was stayed from
the

Agreed that the search should be vnder colour of seeking for Wardrobe stuffe missed by *Whynniard.*

Fawkes found at midnight without the house.

Vpon Sir *Thomas Kneuets* returne the Councel warned.

the fight or fpeaking with him. And within a while after, the Council did examine him; Who feeming to put on a *Romane* refolution, did both to the Councill, and to euery other perfon that fpake with him that day, appeare fo conftant and fetled vpon his grounds, as wee all thought wee had found fome new *Mutius Scæuola* borne in England. For notwithftanding the horrour of the fact, the guilt of his confcience, his fudden furprifing, the terrour which fhould haue bene ftroken in him by comming into the prefence of fo graue a Councill, and the reftleffe and confufed queftions that euery man all that day did vexe him with; Yet was his countenance fo farre from being deiected, as he often fmiled in fcornefull maner, not onely auowing the Fact, but repenting onely, with the faid *Scæuola*, his failing in the execution thereof, whereof (he faid) the diuel and not God, was the difcouerer: Anfwering quickly to euery mans obiection, fcoffing at any idle queftions which were propounded vnto him, and iefting with fuch as he thought had no authoritie to examine him. All that day could the Councill get nothing out of him touching his Complices, refufing to anfwere to any fuch queftions which hee thought might difcouer the plot, and laying all the blame vpon himfelfe; Whereunto he faid hee was mooued onely for Religion and confcience fake; denying the King to be his lawfull Soueraigne, or the Anoynted of God, in refpect he was an hereticke, and giuing himfelfe no other name then *Iohn Iohnfon*, feruant to *Thomas Percie*. But the next morning being caried to the Tower, hee did not there remaine aboue two or three dayes, being twife or thrife in that fpace reexamined, and the Racke only offered and fhewed vnto him, when the maske of his Romane fortitude did vifibly beginne to weare and flide off his face; And then did hee beginne to confeffe part of the trewth, and thereafter to open the whole matter, as doeth appeare by his depofitions immediatly following.

THE TREW COPIE OF THE DECLARATION OF *GVIDO FAWKES,* TAKEN IN THE PRESENCE OF THE Counfellers, whofe names are vnder written.

 Confeffe, that a practife in generall was firft broken vnto me, againft his Maieftie for reliefe of the Catholique caufe, and not inuented or propounded by my felfe. And this was firft propounded vnto mee about Eafter laft was twelue moneth beyond the Seas, in the Low-Countreys of the Archdukes obeifance, by *Thomas Winter*, who came thereupon with mee into England, and there wee imparted our purpofe to three other Gentlemen more, namely, *Robert Catesby*, *Thomas Percie*, and *Iohn Wright*, who all fiue confulting together of the meanes how to execute the fame, and taking a vow among our felues for fecrecie ; *Catesby* propounded to haue it performed by Gunpowder, and by making a Myne vnder the vpper Houfe of Parliament : which place wee made choice of the rather, becaufe Religion hauing bene vniuftly fuppreffed there, it was fitteft that Iuftice and punifhment fhould be executed there.

This being refolued amongft vs, *Thomas Percy* hired an houfe at Weftminfter for that purpofe, neere adioyning to the Parliament Houfe, and there we begun to make our Myne about the 11.of December 1604.

The fiue that firft entred into the worke, were *Thomas Percy, Robert Catesby, Thomas Winter, Iohn Wright,* and my felfe : and foone after wee tooke another vnto vs, *Chriftopher Wright,* hauing fworne him alfo, and taken the Sacrament for fecrecie.

When we came to the very foundation of the wall of the Houfe, which was about three yards thicke, and found it a matter of great difficultie, wee tooke vnto vs another Gentleman, *Robert Winter*, in like maner with oath and Sacrament as aforefaid.

It was about Chriftmas when we brought our Myne vnto the Wal, and about Candlemas we had wrought the Wall halfe through : And whileft they were in working, I ftood as Sentinell to defcrie any man that came neere, whereof I gaue them warning, and fo they ceafed vntill I gaue notice againe to proceed.

All we feuen lay in the Houfe, and had fhot and powder, being refolued to die in that place before we fhould yeeld or be taken.

As they were working vpon the wall, they heard a rufhing in a cellar of remoouing of coales, whereupon we feared wee had bene difcouered : and they fent mee to goe to the cellar, who finding that the coales were a felling, and that the cellar was to be let, viewing the commoditie thereof for our purpofe, *Percy* went and hired the fame for yeerely rent.

Wee had before this prouided and brought into the Houfe twentie barrels of powder, which we remooued into the cellar, and couered the fame with billets and faggots, which were prouided for that purpofe.

About Eafter, the Parliament being prorogued till October next, wee difperfed our felues, and I retired into the Low countreys by aduice and direction of the reft, afwell to acquaint *Owen* with the particulars of the plot, as alfo left by my longer ftay I might haue growne fufpicious, and fo haue come in queftion.

In the meane time *Percy* hauing the key of the cellar, layd in more powder and wood into it. I returned about the beginning of September next, and then receiuing the key againe of *Percy*, wee brought in more powder and billets to couer the fame againe, and fo I went for a time into the countrey till the 30.of October.

It was

It was further resolued amongst vs, that the same day that this acte should haue bene performed, some other of our confederates should haue surprised the person of the Lady E L I Z A B E T H the Kings eldest daughter, who was kept in Warwickshire at the Lord *Haringtons* house, and presently haue proclaimed her Queene, hauing a proiect of a Proclamation ready for that purpose, wherein wee made no mention of altering of Religion, nor would haue auowed the deed to be ours, vntill we should haue had power ynough to make our partie good, and then wee would haue auowed both.

Concerning duke C H A R L E S the Kings second sonne, we had sundry consultations how to seize on his person : But because wee found no meanes how to compasse it (the duke being kept neere London, where we had not forces ynough) wee resolued to serue our turne with the Lady E L I Z A B E T H.

THE NAMES OF OTHER
PRINCIPALL PERSONS, THAT
WERE MADE PRIVIE AFTER-
wards to this horrible conspiracie.

⎰	*Euerard Digby* knight.	⎱ ⎰	*Francis Tresham.* ⎱
	Ambrose Rookwood.		*Iohn Grant.* *Robert Keyes.*

Commiß.

⎰	Notingham.	⎱ ⎰	Northampton. Salisbury.
	Worcester.		Marre. Dunbar.
	Suffolke. Deuonshire.		Popham.

Edw.Cooke.   *William Waad.*

ANd in regard that before this discourse could be ready to goe to the Presse, *Thomas Winter* being apprehended, and brought to the Tower, made a confession in substance agreeing with this former of *Fawkes*, onely larger in some circumstances : I haue thought good to insert the same likewise in this place, for the further clearing of the matter, and greater benefit of the Reader.

THOMAS

THOMAS WINTERS CON-
FESSION, TAKEN THE XXIII. OF NO-
VEMBER 1605. IN THE PRESENCE OF
the Counfellors, whofe names are vnder-written.

My moſt Honourable Lords,

 Ot out of hope to obtaine pardon: for, fpeaking of my temporall part, I may fay, The fault is greater then can bee forgiuen; nor affecting hereby the title of a good Subiect: for I muft redeeme my countrey from as great a danger, as I haue hazarded the bringing of her into, before I can pur-chafe any fuch opinion; Onely at your Honours command I will briefly fet downe mine owne accufation, and how farre I haue proceeded in this bufineffe; which I fhall the faithfullier doe, fince I fee fuch courfes are not pleafing to Almightie God, and that all, or the moft materiall parts haue bene already confeffed.

I remained with my brother in the countrey, from Alhallontyde vntill the beginning of Lent, in the yeere of our Lord 1603. the firft yeere of the Kings reigne: about which time mafter *Catesby* fent thither, intreating me to come to London, where hee and other my friends would be glad to fee me. I defired him to excufe me: for I found my felfe not very well difpo-fed; and (which had happened neuer to mee before) returned the meffen-ger without my company. Shortly I receiued another letter, in any wife to come. At the fecond fummons I prefently came vp, and found him with mafter *Iohn Wright* at Lambeth, where he brake with me, how neceffary it was not to forfake our countrey (for he knew I had then a refolution to goe ouer) but to deliuer her from the feruitude in which fhee remained, or at leaft to affift her with our vttermoft endeuours. I anfwered, That I had of-ten hazarded my life vpon farre lighter termes, and now would not refufe any good occafion, wherein I might doe feruice to the Catholicke caufe; but for my felfe I knew no meane probable to fucceed. He faid that he had bethought him of a way at one inftant to deliuer vs from all our bonds, and without any forraine helpe to replant againe the Catholicke Religion; and with all told mee in a word, It was to blow vp the Parliament houfe with Gunpowder; for, faid he, in that place haue they done vs all the mif-chiefe, and perchance God hath deffeigned that place for their punifh-ment. I wondered at the ftrangeneffe of the conceipt, and told him that trew it was, this ftrake at the root, and would breed a confufion fit to beget new alterations; But if it fhould not take effect (as moft of this nature mif-
caried)

caried) the scandall would be so great which Catholicke Religion might
hereby sustaine, as not onely our enemies, but our friends also would with
good reason condemne vs. He told me, The nature of the disease required
so sharpe a remedie, and asked me if I would giue my consent. I told him,
yes, in this or what els soeuer; if he resolued vpon it, I would venture my
life. But I proposed many difficulties, As want of an house, and of one to
cary the Myne, noyse in the working, and such like. His answere was,
Let vs giue an attempt, and where it faileth, passe no further. But first,
quoth hee, Because wee will leaue no peaceable and quiet way vntryed,
you shall goe ouer, and informe the Constable of the state of the Catholickes here in England, intreating him to sollicite his Maiestie at his comming hither, that the penall Lawes may be recalled, and wee admitted into the rancke of his other Subiects; withall, you may bring ouer some confident Gentleman, such as you shall vnderstand best able for his businesse,
and named vnto mee maister *Fawkes*. Shortly after, I passed the Sea, and
found the Constable at *Bergen* neere *Dunkirke*, where, by helpe of maister *O-
wen* I deliuered my message; Whose answere was, that hee had strict command from his Master, to doe all good Offices for the Catholickes, and for
his owne part hee thought himselfe bound in conscience so to doe, and
that no good occasion should be omitted; but spake to him nothing of
this matter.

Returning to *Dunkirck* with maister *Owen*, wee had speach whether hee
thought the Constable would faithfully helpe vs, or no. He said he beleeued nothing lesse, and that they sought onely their owne ends, holding
small account of Catholicks. I told him that there were many Gentlemen
in *England*, who would not forsake their countrey vntill they had tried the
vttermost, & rather venture their liues, then forsake her in this miserie. And
to adde one more to our number, as a fit man both for counsel and execution of whatsoeuer we should resolue, wished for maister *Fawkes*, whom I had
heard good commendations of: hee told mee the Gentleman deserued no
lesse, but was at *Brussels*, and that if he came not, as happily he might, before
my departure, he would send him shortly after into *England*. I went soone
after to *Ostend*, where sir *William Stanley* as then was not, but came two daies
after. I remained with him three or foure daies, in which time I asked him,
if the Catholicks in *England* should do any thing to helpe themselues, whether he thought the Archduke would second them? He answered, No, for
all those parts were so desirous of peace with *England*, as they would endure no speach of other enterprise: neither were it fit, said hee, to set any
proiect afoot, now the Peace is vpon concluding. I told him there was
no such resolution, and so fell to discourse of other matters, vntill I came
to speake of maister *Fawkes*, whose company I wished ouer into *England*.
I asked of his sufficiencie in the warres, and told him wee should need
such as hee, if occasion required; hee gaue very good commendations of
him. And as wee were thus discoursing, and I ready to depart for *New-*
port,

port, and taking my leaue of Sir *William,* Master *Fawkes* came into our companie, newly returned, and saluted vs. This is the Gentleman, said Sir *William,* that you wished for, and so we embraced againe. I told him some good friends of his wished his companie in *England,* and that if hee pleased to come to *Dunkircke,* wee would haue further conference, whither I was then going : so taking my leaue of them both, I departed. About two dayes after came Master *Fawkes* to *Dunkirck,* where I told him that we were vpon a resolution to doe somewhat in *England,* if the Peace with *Spaine* helped vs not, but had as yet resolued vpon nothing ; such or the like talke wee passed at *Graueling,* where I lay for a winde, and when it serued came both in one Passage to *Greenwich,* neere which place wee tooke a paire of Oares, and so came vp to *London,* and came to Master *Catesby* whom wee found in his lodging ; hee welcommed vs into *England,* and asked mee what newes from the Constable. I told him, good words, but I feared the deedes would not answere : This was the beginning of Easter Terme, and about the middest of the same Terme, (whether sent for by Master *Catesby,* or vpon some businesse of his owne) vp came Master *Thomas Percy.* The first word hee spake (after hee came into our company) was, Shall we alwayes (Gentlemen) talke, and neuer doe any thing ? Master *Catesby* took him aside, and had speach about somewhat to be done, so as first we might all take an oath of secrecie, which wee resolued within two or three dayes to doe : so as there we met behind *S. Clements,* Master *Catesby,* Master *Percy,* Master *Wright,* Master *Guy Fawkes,* and my selfe; and hauing vpon a Primer giuen each other the oath of secrecie, in a chamber where no other bodie was, wee went after into the next roome and heard Masse, and receiued the blessed Sacrament vpon the same. Then did Master *Catesby* disclose to Master *Percy,* and I together with *Iacke Wright,* tell to Master *Fawkes* the businesse for which wee tooke this oath, which they both approued. And then was M. *Percy* sent to take the house, which M. *Catesby* in mine absence, had learned did belong to one *Ferris,* which with some difficultie in the end he obtained, and became, as *Ferris* before was, Tenant to *Whynniard.* M. *Fawkes* vnderwent the name of M. *Percies* man, calling himselfe *Iohnson,* because his face was the most vnknowen, and receiued the keyes of the house, vntill wee heard that the Parliament was adiourned to the seuenth of Februarie : At which time we all departed seuerall wayes into the countrey, to meete againe at the beginning of Michaelmas Terme. Before this time also it was thought conuenient to haue a house that might answere to M. *Percies,* where we might make prouision of powder and wood for the Mine, which beeing there made ready, should in a night be conueyed by boate to the house by the Parliament, because wee were loath to foile that with often going in and out. There was none that we could deuise so fit as *Lambeth,* where Master *Catesby* often lay, and to bee keeper thereof (by M. *Catesbies* choice) we receiued into the number, *Keyes,* as a trustie honest man : this was about a moneth before Michaelmas.

Some

Some fortnight after towards the beginning of the Terme, M. *Fawkes* and I came to M. *Catesby* at *Morecrofts*, where we agreed that now was time to beginne and set things in order for the Mine.. So as Master *Fawkes* went to *London*, and the next day sent for me to come over to him : when I came, the cause was, for that the Scottish Lords were appointed to sit in conference of the Vnion in Master *Percies* house. This hindered our beginning vntill a fortnight before Christmas, by which time both Master *Percie* and Master *Wright* were come to *London*, and wee against their comming had prouided a good part of the powder : so as wee all fiue entred with tooles fit to beginne our worke, hauing prouided our selues of Baked-meates, the lesse to need sending abroad. We entred late in the night, and were neuer seene saue onely Master *Percies* man, vntill Christmas Eue, In which time we wrought vnder a little Entry to the wall of the Parliament house, and vnderpropped it, as we went, with wood.

Whilest we were together, we began to fashion our businesse, and discoursed what we should doe after this deed was done. The first question was how we might surprize the next heire, the Prince haply would bee at the Parliament with the King his Father, how should wee then bee able to seaze on the Duke ? This burthen Master *Percie* vndertooke, that by his acquaintance, hee, with another Gentleman would enter the Chamber without suspition, and hauing some doozen others at seuerall doores to expect his comming, and two or three on horsebacke at the Court gate to receiue him, hee would vndertake (the blow beeing giuen, vntill which hee would attend in the Dukes Chamber) to carrie him safe away : for hee supposed most of the Court would bee absent, and suchas were there not suspecting, or vnprouided for any such matter. For the Lady E L I Z A-B E T H, it were easie to surprize her in the Countrey, by drawing friends together at an hunting neere the Lord *Haringtons*, and Ashbie, M. *Catesbies* house, being not farre off was a fit place for preparation.

The next was for money and horses, which if wee could prouide in any reasonable measure (hauing the Heire apparant) and the first knowledge by foure or fiue dayes, was oddes sufficient.

Then what Lords we should saue from the Parliament, which was first agreed in generall as many as we could that were Catholickes, or so disposed : but after we descended to speake of particulars.

Next, what forraine Princes wee should acquaint with this before, or ioyne with after. For this point wee agreed, that first wee could not enioyne Princes to that secrecie, nor oblige them by oath, so to be secure of their promise : besides, we knew not whether they will approue the proiect or dislike it : And if they doe allow thereof, to prepare before, might beget suspition ; and not to prouide vntill the businesse were acted, the same letter that caried newes of the thing done, might as well intreate their helpe and furtherance. *Spaine* is too slow in his preparations to hope any good from in the first extremities, and *France* too neere and too dangerous,

port, and taking my leaue of Sir *William*, Master awke
panie, newly returned, and saluted vs. This the
William, that you wished for, and so we embrac'd a
good friends of his wished his companie in *Erl*
sed to come to *Dunkircke*, wee would haue furthe
was then going : so taking my leaue of them be
dayes after came Master *Fawkes* to *Dunkirck*, wh
vpon a resolution to doe somewhat in *Englan*
helped vs not, but had as yet resolued vpon
talke wee passed at *Graueling*, where I lay for
came both in one Passage to *Greenwich*, neer
paire of Oares, and so came vp to *London*, and
wee found in his lodging; hee welcommed
what newes from the Constable. I told hir
deedes would not answere: This was the
about the middest of the same Terme,
Catesby, or vpon some businesse of his own
The first word hee spake (after hee came i
alwayes (Gentlemen) talke, and ne   c
him aside, and had speach about so
all take an oath of secrecie, which w
to doe: so as there we met behind *S*.
Master *Wright*, Master *Guy Fawkes*, an
giuen each other the oath of secrecie,
was, wee went after into the next ro
the blessed Sacrament vpon the same.
Master *Percy*, and I together with *Iack*
businesse for which wee tooke this oa
then was M. *Percy* sent to take the h
sence, had learned did belong to one *I*
the end he obtained, and became, as *F*
M. *Fawkes* vnderwent the name of *N*
because his face was the mo
house, vntill wee heard that th
of Februarie: At which time we a
trey, to meete againe at the beginn
time also it was thought conuenie
to M. *Percies*, where we might mak
Mine, which beeing there made
boate to the house by the Parliam
with often going in and out. Th
Lambeth, whe   *Catesby* o
Cateshi
n

s I heard M: *Catesby*
d pounds; M.*Percy*
e of *Northumberlands*
to prouide many gal-

ght ſome new Powder,
into the Cellar, and ſet it
vas the Parliament anew
ll went downe vntil ſome
M. *Fawkes* to an houſe by
ne to them, and M. *Catesby*
ce came to the Parliament:
t not to be there. Then muſt
the water, and prouiſion of
aue the Duke alone.
t, in came one to my chamber,
o my L. *Mountegle* to this effect,
m the Parliament, becauſe a blow
eſently caried to my L. of *Salisbury*.
s, and told it M. *Catesby*, aſſuring
; and wiſhing him in any caſe to
d ſee further as yet, and reſolued
teſting if the part belonged to

eturned at night, of which we

fter *Catesby*, Maſter *Treſham*
his Letter ſhould be ſent
after *Treſham* forſware

incolnes Inne walkes:
ſbury ſhould vſe to the
e ſame to M. *Catesby*,
aue M. *Percy* come
Percy being dealt

as M. *Catesby* re-
Percy went to
the next mor-
ger *Wright* to
ountegle, ſay-
call vp my
Goe backe
hortly hee
returned

rous, who with the ſhipping of *Holland*, we feared of all the world might make away with vs.

But while we were in the middle of theſe diſcourſes, we heard that the Parliament ſhould bee anew adiourned vntill after Michaelmas, vpon which tidings we broke off both diſcourſe and working vntill after Chriſt-mas. About Candlemas we brought ouer in a boate the powder, which we had prouided at Lambeth, and laide it in M. *Percies* houſe, becauſe wee were willing to haue all our danger in one place.

We wrought alſo another fortnight in the Mine againſt the ſtone wall, which was very hard to beate thorow; at which time we called in *Kit Wright*, and neare to Eaſter, as we wrought the third time, opportunitie was giuen to hire the Cellar, in which we reſolued to lay the powder, and leaue the Mine.

Now by reaſon that the charge of maintaining vs all ſo long together, beſides the number of ſeuerall houſes, which for ſeuerall vſes had beene hi-red, and buying of powder &c. had layen heauie on M. *Catesby* alone to ſupport; it was neceſſarie for him to call in ſome others to eaſe his charge, and to that ende deſired leaue, that hee, with M. *Percy*, and a third, whom they ſhould call, might acquaint whom they thought fit and willing to the buſineſſe: for many, ſaid hee, may be content that I ſhould know, who would not therefore that all the company ſhould be acquainted with their names: to this we all agreed.

After this Maſter *Fawkes* laid into the Cellar (which hee had newly ta-ken) a thouſand of Billets, and fiue hundred of Faggots, and with that co-uered the Powder, becauſe we might haue the Houſe free, to ſuffer any one to enter that would. Maſter *Catesby* wiſhed vs to conſider, whether it were not now neceſſary to ſend M. *Fawkes* ouer, both to abſent himſelfe for a time, as alſo to acquaint Sir *William Stanley* and M. *Owen* with this matter. Wee agreed that he ſhould (prouided that hee gaue it them with the ſame othe that wee had taken it before) *videlicet*, to keepe it ſecret from all the world. The reaſon why we deſired Sir *William Stanley* ſhould be acquain-ted herewith was, to haue him with vs ſo ſoone as he could: And for M. *Owen*, hee might holde good correſpondencie after with forreine Princes. So M. *Fawkes* departed about Eaſter for *Flanders*, and returned the latter end of Auguſt. He tolde me that when he arriued at *Bruſſels*, Sir *William Stanley* was not returned from *Spaine*, ſo as hee vttered the matter onely to *Owen*, who ſeemed well pleaſed with the buſineſſe, but tolde him that ſure-ly Sir *William* would not be acquainted with any plot, as hauing buſineſſe now afoot in the Court of *England*; but he himſelfe would be alwayes rea-die to tell it him, and ſend him away ſo ſoone as it were done.

About this time did M. *Percy* and M. *Catesby* meete at the *Bathe*, where they agreed that the company being yet but few, M. *Catesby* ſhould haue the others authoritie to call in whom hee thought beſt; By which autho-ritie hee called in after, Sir *Euerard Digby*, though at what time I know not, and

and laſt of all M. *Francis Treſham.* The firſt promiſed, as I heard M: *Catesby* ſay, fifteene hundred pounds; the ſecond two thouſand pounds; M. *Percy* himſelfe promiſed all that hee could get of the Earle of *Northumberlands* rents, which was about foure thouſand pounds, and to prouide many galloping horſes to the number of ten.

Meane while M. *Fawkes* and my ſelfe alone bought ſome new Powder, as ſuſpecting the firſt to be danke, and conueyed it into the Cellar, and ſet it in order, as wee reſolued it ſhould ſtand. Then was the Parliament anew prorogued vntill the fift of Nouember, ſo as we all went downe vntil ſome ten dayes before, when M. *Catesby* came vp with M. *Fawkes* to an houſe by *Enfield Chaſe* called *White-webbes,* whither I came to them, and M. *Catesby* willed me to enquire whether the yong Prince came to the Parliament: I tolde him that I heard that his Grace thought not to be there. Then muſt wee haue our Horſes laid M. *Catesby* beyond the water, and prouiſion of more company to ſurpriſe the Prince, and leaue the Duke alone.

Two dayes after being Sunday at night, in came one to my chamber, and told me that a letter had beene giuen to my L. *Mountegle* to this effect, That he wiſhed his Lordſhips abſence from the Parliament, becauſe a blow would there be giuen; which letter he preſently caried to my L. of *Salisbury.*

On the morrow I went to *White-webbes,* and told it M. *Catesby,* aſſuring him withall that the matter was diſcloſed; and wiſhing him in any caſe to forſake his Countrey. He told me he would ſee further as yet, and reſolued to ſend M. *Fawkes* to trie the vttermoſt, proteſting if the part belonged to himſelfe, he would trie the ſame aduenture.

On Wedneſday Maſter *Fawkes* went and returned at night, of which we were very glad.

Thurſday I came to London, and Friday Maſter *Catesby,* Maſter *Treſham* and I met at *Barnet,* where wee queſtioned how this Letter ſhould be ſent to my L. *Mountegle,* but could not conceiue, for Maſter *Treſham* forſware it, whom we onely ſuſpected.

On Saturday night I met M. *Treſham* againe in Lincolnes Inne walkes: wherein he tolde ſuch ſpeeches, that my Lord of *Salisbury* ſhould vſe to the King, as I gaue it loſt the ſecond time, and repeated the ſame to M. *Catesby,* who hereupon was reſolued to be gone, but ſtayed to haue M. *Percy* come vp, whoſe conſent herein wee wanted. On Sunday M. *Percy* being dealt with to that end, would needs abide the vttermoſt triall.

This ſuſpicion of all hands put vs into ſuch confuſion, as M. *Catesby* reſolued to goe downe into the countrey the Munday that M. *Percy* went to *Syon,* and M. *Percy* reſolued to follow the ſame night, or early the next morning. About fiue of the clocke being Tueſday, came the yonger *Wright* to my Chamber, and tolde me that a Nobleman called the L. *Mountegle,* ſaying, Ariſe, and come along to *Eſſex* houſe, for I am going to call vp my L. of *Northumberland,* ſaying withall, The matter is diſcouered. Goe backe M. *Wright* (quoth I) and learne what you can about *Eſſex* gate. Shortly hee
returned

returned and faid, Surely all is loft: for *Lepton* is got on horfebacke at *Effex* doore, and as he parted, he asked if their Lordfhips would haue any more with him : and being anfwered No, is rode faft vp Fleetftreete as hee can ride. Goe you then (quoth I) to M. *Percy*, for fure it is for him they feeke, and bid him be gone, I will ftay and fee the vttermoft. Then I went to the Court gates, and found them ftraitly guarded, fo as no body could enter. From thence I went downe towards the Parliament houfe, and in the middle of Kings-ftreet, found the Guard ftanding that would not let me paffe. And as I returned I heard one fay, There is a Treafon difcouered, in which the King and the Lords fhould haue beene blowen vp. So then I was fully fatisfied that all was knowen, and went to the Stable where my gelding ftood, and rode into the countrey. Mafter *Catesby* had appointed our meeting at *Dunchurch*, but I could not ouertake them vntill I came to my brothers, which was Wednefday night. On Thurfday wee tooke the Armour at my Lord *Windfores*, and went that night to one *Stephen Littletons* houfe, where the next day (being Friday) as I was early abroad to difcouer, my man came to me, and faid, that an heauie mifchance had feuered all the company, for that M. *Catesby,* M. *Rookwood*, and M. *Grant,* were burned with Gunpowder, vpon which fight the reft difperfed. Mafter *Littleton* wifhed me to flie, and fo would hee: I told him I would firft fee the body of my friend and bury him, whatfoeuer befell me. When I came, I found M. *Catesby* reafonable well, Mafter *Percy*, both the *Wrights*, M. *Rookwood*, and Mafter *Grant.* I asked them what they refolued to doe: they anfwered, We meane here to die. I faid againe, I would take fuch part as they did. About eleuen of the clocke came the company to befet the houfe, and as I walked into the court, I was fhot into the fhoulder, which loft me the vfe of mine arme: the next fhot was the elder *Wright* ftricken dead, after him the yonger M. *Wright*, and fourthly *Ambrofe Rookwood* fhot. Then faid M. *Catesby* to me, (ftanding before the doore they were to enter) Stand by me *Tom*, and we will die together. Sir (quoth I) I haue loft the vfe of my right arme, and I feare that will caufe me to be taken. So as wee ftood clofe together, M. *Catesby*, M. *Percy*, and my felfe, they two were fhot (as farre as I could gueffe with one Bullet) and then the company entred vpon me, hurt me in the Belly with a Pike, and gaue me other wounds, vntill one came behinde, and caught holde of both mine armes.

And fo I remaine yours, &c.

Commiff. {
Notingham , Suffolke, Worcefter ,
Deuonfhire , Northampton , Salisburie ,
Marr , Dunbar ,
Popham.

Ed. *Coke.*   W. *Waad.*

The

The names of thofe that were firft in the Treafon, and laboured in the Mine.

Robert Catesby.
Robert Winter. } *Efquires.*

Thomas Percy.
Thomas Winter.
John Wright. } *Gentlemen.*
Chriftopher Wright.
Guido Fawkes.

And *Bates,* *Catesbyes man.*

Thofe that were made acquainted with it, though not perfonally labouring in the Mine, nor in the Cellar.

Euerard Digby. } *Knight.*

Ambrofe Rookewood.
Francis Trefham. } *Efquires.*

John Grant. } *Gent.*
Robert Keyes.

Vt here let vs leaue *Fawkes* in a lodging fit for fuch a gueft, and taking time to aduife vpon his confcience; and turne our felues to that part of the Hiftorie, which concernes the fortune of the reft of his partakers in that abominable Treafon. The newes was no fooner fpred abroad that morning, which was vpon a Tuefday, the 5. of *Nouember,* and the firft day defigned for that Seffion of Parliament; The newes (I fay) of this fo ftrange and vnlooked for accident, was no fooner diuulged, but fome of thofe Confpiratours, namely *Winter,* and the two brothers of *Wrights* thought it high time for them to haften out of the towne (for *Catesby* was gone the night before, and *Percy* at foure of the clocke in the morning the fame day of the Difcouerie) and all of them held their courfe, with more hafte then good fpeed to *Warwick* Shire toward *Couentry,* where the next day morning being *Wednefday,* and about the fame houre that *Fawks* was taken in *Weftminfter,* one *Graunt* a gentleman hauing affociated vnto him fome others of his opinion, all violent Papifts and ftrong Recufants, came to a Stable of one *Benocke* a rider of great

X   Horfes,

The taking of the horses out of the stable at Warwicke by *Graunt* and others.

Horses, and hauing violently broken vp the same, caried along with them all the great Horses that were therein, to the number of seuen or eight, belonging to diuers Noblemen and Gentlemen of that Countrey, who had put them into the Riders hands to be made fit for ther seruice. And so both that company of them which fledde out of *London,* as also *Graunt* and his complices met all together at *Dunchurch* at Sir *Euerard Digby* his lodging the Tuesday at night, after the discouerie of this treacherous Attempt:

The hunting match appointed by Sir *Euerard Digby.*

The which *Digby* had likewise for his part appointed a match of hunting to haue beene hunted the next day, which was Wednesday, though his mind was *Nimrod*-like vpon a farre other maner of hunting, more bent vpon the blood of reasonable men then bruite beasts.

Their going into armes after the Plot discouered.

This company and hellish societie thus conuened, finding their purpose discouered, and their treacherie preuented, did resolue to runne a desperate course, and since they could not preuaile by so priuate a Blow, to practise by a publike rebellion, either to attaine to their Intents, or at least to saue themselues in the throng of others. And therefore gathering all the company they could vnto them, and pretending the quarrell of Religion, hauing intercepted such prouision of Armour, Horses, and Powder, as the time could permit, thought by running vp and downe the Countrey both to augment peece and peece their number (dreaming to themselues that they had the vertue of a Snow-ball, which being little at the first, and tumbling downe from a great hill groweth to a great quantitie, by encreasing it selfe with the Snow that it meeteth by the way) and also that they beginning first this braue shewe in one part of the Countrey, should by their Sympathy and example stirre vp and encourage the rest of their Religion in other parts of *England* to rise, as they had done there. But when they

Their number neuer aboue fourescore.

had gathered their force to the greatest, they came not to the number of fourescore, and yet were they troubled all the houres of the day to keepe and containe their own seruants from stealing from them; who (notwithstanding of all their care) daily left them, being farre inferiour to *Gedeons* hoste in number, but farre more in faith or iustnesse of quarrell.

And so after that this Catholicke troupe had wandered a while through Warwicke-shire to Worcester-shire, and from thence to the edge and borders of Stafford-shire, this gallantly armed band had not the honour at the last to be beaten with a Kings Lieutenant or extraordinary Commissioner

Their flight.

sent downe for the purpose, but onely by the ordinary Shiriffe of Worcester-shire were they all beaten, killed, taken and dispersed. Wherein yee haue to note this following circumstance so admirable, and so liuely displaying the greatnesse of Gods iustice, as it could not be concealed without betraying in a maner the glory due to the Almighty for the same.

Although diuers of the Kings Proclamations were posted downe after these Traitors with all the speed possible, declaring the odiousnesse of that bloodie attempt, the necessitie to haue had *Percie* preserued aliue, if it had beene possible, and the assembly together of that rightly-damned crew,

now

now no more darned Confpirators, but open and auowed Rebels: yet the farre diftance of the way (which was aboue an hundred miles) together with the extreme deepeneffe thereof, ioyned alfo with the fhortneffe of the day, was the caufe that the heartie and louing affections of the Kings good Subiects in thofe partes preuented the fpeed of his Proclamations: For vpon the third day after the flying downe of thefe Rebels, which was vpon the Friday next after the difcouerie of their Plot, they were moft of them all furprized by the Shiriffe of Worcefter-fhire at *Holbeach*, about the noone of the day, and that in manner following.

Graunt, of whom I haue made mention before for taking the great horfes, who had not all the preceding time ftirred from his owne houfe till the next morning after the attempt fhould haue bene put in execution, he then laying his accompt without his Hoft (as the prouerbe is) that their Plot had, without failing, receiued the day before their hoped-for fucceffe; Tooke, or rather ftole out thofe horfes (as I faid before) for enabling him, and fo many of that foule-leffe fociety that had ftill remained in the Countrey neere about him, to make a fudden furprize vpon the Kings elder daughter, the Lady ELIZABETH, hauing her refidence nere by that place, whom they thought to haue vfed for the colour of their treacherous defigne (His Maieftie her father, her mother, and male children being all deftroyed aboue.) And to this purpofe alfo had that *Nimrod, Digby*, prouided his hunting match againft that fame time, that numbers of people beeing flocked together vpon the pretence thereof, they might the eafilier haue brought to paffe the fudden furprife of her perfon.

Now the violent taking away of thofe horfes long before day, did feeme to bee fo great a ryot in the eyes of the Common-people, that knew of no greater myftery: And the bold attempting thereof did ingender fuch a fufpition of fome following Rebellion in the hearts of the wifer fort, as both great and fmall beganne to ftirre and arme themfelues, vpon this vnlooked-for accident: Among whom Sir *Fulke Greuill* the Elder, Knight, as became one both fo ancient in yeeres and good reputation, and by his Office, beeing Deputie Lieutenant of Warwicke-fhire, though vnable in his bodie, yet by the zeale and trew feruencie of his mind, did firft apprehend this forefaid Ryot to be nothing but the fparkles and fure *indices* of a following Rebellion; whereupon both ftoutly and honeftly hee tooke order to get into his owne hands, the Munition and Armour of all fuch Gentlemen about him, as were either abfent from their owne houfes, or in doubtfull guard; and alfo fent fuch direction to the Townes about him, as thereupon did follow the ftriking of *Winter* by a poore Smith, who had likewife beene taken by thofe vulgar people, but that he was refcued by the reft of his company, who perceiuing that the Countrey before them had notice of them, haftened away with loffe in their owne fight, fixteene of their followers being taken by the townef-men, and fent prefently to the Shiriffe at Warwicke, and from thence to London.

X 2 But

- But before twelue or fixteene houres paft, *Catesby, Percy*, the *Winters, Wrights, Rookewood* and the reft, bringing then the affurance that their maine Plot was failed and bewrayed, whereupon they had builded the golden mountaines of their glorious hopes : They then tooke their laft defperate refolution to flocke together in a troupe, and wander, as they did, for the reafons aforetold. But as vpon the one part, the zealous ducty to their God and their Souereigne was fo deepely imprinted in the hearts of all the meaneft and pooreft fort of the people (although then knowing of no further myfterie then fuch publike mifbehauiours, as their owne eyes taught them) as notwithstanding of their faire fhewes and pretence of their Catholicke caufe, no creature, man or woman through all the Coun-trey, would once fo much as giue them willingly a cuppe of drinke, or any fort of comfort or fupport, but with execrations detefted them : So on the other part, the Sheriffes of the Shires, where-through they wandered, conuening their people with all fpeed poffible, hunted as hotly after them, as the euilneffe of the way, and the vnprouidedneffe of their people vpon that fudden could permit them. And fo at laft after Sir *Richard Verney*, Shiriffe of Warwicke-fhire, had carefully and ftreightly beene in chafe of them to the confines of his Countie, part of the meaner fort being alfo ap-prehended by him : Sir *Richard Walfh* Shiriffe of Worcefter-fhire did like-wife duetifully and hotely purfue them thorow his Shire; And hauing got-ten fure triall of their taking harbour at the houfe aboue-named, hee did fend Trumpetters and Meffengers to them, commaunding them in the Kings name to render vnto him, his Maiefties minifter, and knowing no more at that time of their guilt then was publikely vifible, did promife vp-on their duetifull and obedient rendring vnto him, to intercede at the Kings handes for the fparing of their liues: who receiued onely from them this fcornefull anfwere (they being better witneffes to themfelues of their inward euill confciences) *That hee had need of better afsiftance, then of thofe few numbers that were with him, before hee could bee able to command or comp-troll them.*

The prepara-
tion to affault
the houfe. But here fell the wonderous worke of Gods Iuftice, That while this meffage paffed betweene the Shiriffe and them, The Shiriffes and his peo-ples zeale beeiing iuftly kindled and augmented by their arrogant anfwere, and fo they preparing themfelues to giue a furious affault; and the other partie making themfelues readie within the houfe to performe their pro-mife by a defence as refolute; It pleafed God that in the mending of the fire in their chamber, one fmall fparke fhould flie out, and light among leffe then two pound weight of Powder, which was drying a little from the chimney, which being thereby blowen vp, fo maymed the faces of fome of the principall Rebels, and the hands and fides of others of them (blowing vp with it alfo a great bag full of Powder, which notwithstanding neuer tooke fire) as they were not only difabled and difcouraged hereby from any further refiftance, in refpect *Catesby* himfelfe, *Rookwood, Grant*, and diuers

others

others of greateſt account among them, were thereby made vnable for defence: but alſo wonderfully ſtroken with amazement in their guiltie conſciences, calling to memory how God had iuſtly puniſhed them with that ſame Inſtrument, which they ſhould haue vſed for the effectuating of ſo great a ſinne, according to the olde Latine ſaying, *In quo peccamus, in eodem pleĉtimur*; as they preſently (ſee the wonderfull power of Gods Iuſtice vpon guiltie conſciences) did all fall downe vpon their knees, praying GOD to pardon them for their bloody enterpriſe; And thereafter giuing ouer any further debate, opened the gate, ſuffered the Sheriffes people to ruſh in furiouſly among them, and deſperately ſought their owne preſent deſtruĉtion; The three ſpecials of them ioyning backes together, *Catesby, Percy,* and *Winter*, whereof two with one ſhot, *Catesby* and *Percy* were ſlaine, and the third, *VVinter*, taken and ſaued aliue.

Catesby who was the fiſt inuentor of this Treaſon in generall, and of the maner of working the ſame by powder, in ſpeciall, himſelfe now firſt maimed with the blowing vp of powder, and next he and Ps. ey both killed with one ſhot proceeding from powder.

And thus theſe reſolute and high aſpiring Catholikes, who dreamed of no leſſe then the deſtruction of Kings and kingdomes, and promiſed to themſelues no lower eſtate then the gouernment of great and ancient Monarchies, were miſerably defeated, and quite ouerthrowen in an inſtant, falling in the pit which they had prepared for others; and ſo fulfilling that ſentence which his Maieſtie did in a maner propheciē of them in his Oration to the Parliament: ſome preſently ſlaine, others deadly wounded, ſtripped of their clothes, left lying miſerably naked, and ſo dying rather of cold, then of the danger of their wounds; and the reſt that either were whole, or but lightly hurt, taken and led priſoners by the Sheriffe the ordinary miniſter of Iuſtice, to the Gaole, the ordinarie place euen of the baſeſt malefaĉtors, where they remained till their ſending vp to *London*, being met with a huge confluence of people of all ſorts, deſirous to ſee them as the rareſt ſort of Monſters; fooles to laugh at them, women and children to wonder, all the common people to gaze, the wiſer ſort to ſatisfie their curioſity in ſeeing the outward caſes of ſo vnheard of a villeny: & generally all ſorts of people to ſatiate and fill their eyes with the ſight of them, whom in their hearts they ſo farre admired and deteſted: ſeruing ſo for a fearfull and publike ſpeĉtacle of Gods fierce wrath and iuſt indignation.

What hereafter will be done with them, is to be left to the Iuſtice of his Maieſtie and the State: Which as no good Subieĉt needes to doubt will be performed in the owne due time by a publike and an exemplarie puniſhment: So haue we all that are faithfull and humble Subieĉts, great cauſe to pray earneſtly to the Almighty, that it will pleaſe him who hath the hearts of all Princes in his hands, to put it in his Maieſties heart to make ſuch a concluſion of this Tragedie to the Traitors, but Tragicomedie to the King and all his trew Subieĉts; as thereby the glory of God and his trew Religion may be aduanced, the future ſecuritie of the King and his eſtate procured and prouided for, all hollow and vnhoneſt hearts diſcouered & preuented, & this horrible attempt (lacking due epithetes) to be ſo iuſtly auenged, That where they thought by one Catholike indeed & vniuerſall blow to accomplifh the wifh of that Romane tyrant, who wifhed all the bodies in Rome to haue but one necke, and fo by the violent force of Powder to breake vp as with a Pettard our triple locked peacefull gates of *Ianius,* which (God be thanked) they could not compaffe by any other meanes ; they may iuftly be fo recompenfed for their trewly viperous intended parricide, as the fhame and infamie that otherwife would light vpon this whole Nation, for hauing vnfortunately hatched fuch cockatrice egges, may be repaired by the execution of famous and honourable Iuftice vpon the offendors; and fo the kingdome purged of them, may hereafter perpetually flourifh in peace and profperitie, by the happy coniunction of the hearts of all honeft and trew Subiects, with their iuft and religious Soueraigne.

And thus whereas they thought to haue effaced our memories, the memory of them fhall remaine (but to their perpetuall infamie) and wee (as I faid in the beginning) fhall with all thankefulneffe eternally preferue the memory of fo great a benefite. To which let euery good Subiect fay A M E N.

As Aeneas Syluius doth notably write concerning the murther of K. Iames the firft of Scotland, and the following punifhment of the traitours, whereof himfelfe was an eye witneffe. Hift. de Europa, cap. 46.

Triplici

Triplici nodo, triplex cuneus.

OR
AN APOLOGIE FOR
THE OATH OF
ALLEGIANCE.

AGAINST THE TWO BREVES
OF POPE PAVLVS QVINTVS, AND THE
late Letter of Cardinall BELLARMINE to G.
BLACKVVEL the Arch-prieſt.

Hat a monſtrous, rare, nay neuer heard-of Treacherous attempt, was plotted within theſe few yeeres here in England, for the deſtruction of Mee, my Bed-fellow, and our poſteritie, the whole houſe of Parliament, and a great number of good Subiects of all ſorts and degrees; is ſo famous already through the whole world by the infamie thereof, as it is needleſſe to bee repeated or publiſhed any more; the horrour of the ſinne it ſelfe doeth ſo lowdly proclaime it. For if thoſe * crying ſinnes, * Gen.4 10. (whereof mention is made in the Scripture) haue that epithet giuen them for their publique infamie, and for procuring as it were with a lowd cry from heauen a iuſt vengeance and recompenſe, and yet thoſe ſinnes are both old and too common, neither the world, nor any one Countrey being euer at any time cleane voyd of them: If thoſe ſinnes (I ſay) are ſaid in the Scripture to cry ſo lowd; What then muſt this ſinne doe, plotted without cauſe, infinite in crueltie, and ſingular from all examples? What proceeded hereupon is likewiſe notorious to the whole world; our Iuſtice onely taking hold vpon the offenders, and that in as honourable and publique a forme of Triall, as euer was vſed in this Kingdome.

2. For

2. For although the onely reason they gaue for plotting so heinous an attempt, was the zeale they caried to the Romish Religion; yet were neuer any other of that profession the worse vsed for that cause, as by our gracious Proclamation immediatly after the discouery of the said fact doeth plainly appeare: onely at the next sitting downe againe of the Parliament, there were Lawes made, setting downe some such orders as were thought fit for preuenting the like mischiefe in time to come. Amongst which a forme of O A T H was framed to be taken by my Subiects, whereby they should make a cleare profession of their resolution, faithfully to persist in their obedience vnto mee, according to their naturall allegiance; To the end that I might hereby make a separation, not onely betweene all my good Subiects in generall, and vnfaithfull Traitors, that intended to withdraw themselues from my obedience; But specially to make a separation betweene so many of my Subiects, who although they were otherwise Popishly affected, yet retained in their hearts the print of their naturall duetie to their Soueraigne; and those who being caried away with the like fanaticall zeale that the Powder-Traitors were, could not conteine themselues within the bounds of their naturall Allegiance, but thought diuersitie of religion a safe pretext for all kinde of treasons, and rebellions against their Soueraigne. Which godly and wise intent, God did blesse with successe accordingly: For very many of my Subiects that were Popishly affected, aswell Priests, as Layicks, did freely take the same Oath: whereby they both gaue me occasion to thinke the better of their fidelitie, and likewise freed themselues of that heauie slander, that although they were fellow professors of one Religion with the powder-Traitors, yet were they not ioyned with them in treasonable courses against their Soueraigne; whereby all quietly minded Papists were put out of despaire, and I gaue a good proofe that I intended no persecution against them for conscience cause, but onely desired to be secured of them for ciuill obedience, which for conscience cause they were bound to performe.

3. But the diuel could not haue deuised a more malicious tricke for interrupting this so calme and clement a course, then fell out by the sending hither, and publishing a *Breue* of the Popes, countermanding all them of his profession to take this Oath; Thereby sowing new seeds of ielousie betweene me and my Popish Subiects, by stirring them vp to disobey that lawfull commandement of their Soueraigne, which was ordeined to bee taken of them as a pledge of their fidelitie; And so by their refusall of so iust a charge, to giue mee so great and iust a ground for punishment of them, without touching any matter of conscience: throwing themselues needlesly into one of these desperate straits; either with the losse of their liues and goods to renounce their Allegiance to their naturall Soueraigne; or else to procure the condemnation of their soules by renouncing the Catholicke faith, as he alleadgeth.

4. And on the other part, although disparitie of Religion (the Pope being

being head of the contrary part) can permit no intelligence nor intercourse of meſſengers betweene meeand the Pope: yet there being no denounced warre betweene vs,he hath by this action broken the rules of common ciuilitie and iuſtice betweene Chriſtian Princes,in thus condemning me vnheard, both by accounting me a perſecutor, which cannot be but implied by exhorting the Papiſts to endure Martyrdome; as likewiſe by ſo ſtraitly commanding all thoſe of his profeſſion in England, to refuſe the taking of this Oath;thereby refuſing to profeſſe their naturall obedience to me their Soueraigne. For if he thinke himſelfe my lawfull Iudge, wherefore hath he condemned me vnheard? And, if he haue nothing to doe with me and my gouernment (as indeed he hath not) why doeth he *mittere falcem in alienam meſſem*, to meddle betweene me and my Subiects,eſpecially in matters that meerely and onely concerne ciuill obedience ? And yet could *Pius Quintus* in his greateſt fury and auowed quarrell againſt the late Queene, doe no more iniurie vnto her; then hee hath in this caſe offered vnto mee, without ſo much as a pretended or an alleadged cauſe. For what difference there is, betweene the commanding Subiects to rebell, and looſing them from their Oath of Allegiance as *Pius Quintus* did; and the commanding of Subiects not to obey in making profeſſion of their Oath of their dutifull Allegiance, as this Pope hath now done: no man can eaſily diſcerne.

5. But to draw neere vnto his *Breue*, wherein certainely hee hath taken more paines then he needed, by ſetting downe in the ſaid *Breue* the whole body of the Oath at length; whereas the onely naming of the Title thereof might as well haue ſerued, for any anſwere hee hath made thereunto (making *Vna litura,* that is, the flat and generall condemnation of the whole Oath to ſerue for all his refutation.) Therein hauing as well in this reſpect as in the former, dealt both vndiſcreetly with me, and iniuriouſly with his owne Catholickes. With mee; in not refuting particularly what ſpeciall words he quarrelled in that Oath; which if hee had done, it might haue beene that for the fatherly care I haue not to put any of my Subiects to a needleſſe extremitie, I might haue beene contented in ſome ſort to haue reformed or interpreted thoſe wordes. With his owne Catholickes : for either if I had ſo done, they had beene thereby fully eaſed in that buſineſſe; or at leaſt if I would not haue condeſcended to haue altered any thing in the ſaide Oath, yet would thereby ſome appearance or ſhadow of excuſe haue beene left vnto them for refuſing the ſame· not as ſeeming thereby to ſwarue from their Obedience and Allegiance vnto mee, but onely beeing ſtayed from taking the ſame vpon the ſcrupulous tenderneſſe of their conſciences, in regard of thoſe particular words which the Pope had noted and condemned therein.

And now let vs heare the words of his thunder.

POPE

POPE PAVLVS THE FIFT,

to the E N G L I S H Catholickes.

The Pope his firſt Breue.

Elbeloued Sonnes, Salutation and Apoſtolicall Benediction. *The tribulations and calamities, which yee haue
continually ſuſtained for the keeping of the Catholike Faith,
haue alwayes afflicted vs with great griefe of minde. But
for as much as we vnderſtand that at this time all things are
more grieuous, our affliction hereby is wonderfully increaſed.
For wee haue heard how you are compelled, by moſt grieuous
puniſhments ſet before you, to goe to the Churches of Heretikes, to frequent their aſſemblies, to be preſent at their Sermons. Truely wee doe vndoubtedly beleeue, that
they which with ſo great conſtancie and fortitude, haue hitherto indured moſt cruell
perſecutions and almoſt infinite miſeries, that they may walke without ſpot in the
Law of the Lord; will neuer ſuffer themſelues to be defiled with the communion of
thoſe that haue forſaken the diuine Law. Yet notwithſtanding, being compelled by the
zeale of our Paſtorall Office, and by our Fatherly care which we doe continually take
for the ſaluation of your ſoules, we are inforced to admoniſh and deſire you, that by
no meanes you come vnto the Churches of the Heretickes, or heare their Sermons, or
communicate with them in their Rites, leſt you incurre the wrath of God: For theſe
things may ye not doe without indamaging the worſhip of God, and your owne ſaluation. As likewiſe you cannot, without moſt euident and grieuous wronging of Gods
Honour, bind your ſelues by the Oath, which in like maner we haue heard with very
great griefe of our heart is adminiſtred vnto you, of the tenor vnder-written. viz.*

The Oath.

A. B. doe trewly and ſincerely acknowledge, profeſſe, teſtifie
and declare in my conſcience before God and the world,
That our Soueraigne Lord King I A M E S, is lawfull King
of this Realme, and of all other his Maieſties Dominions and
Countreyes: And that the *Pope* neither of himſelfe, nor by
any authority of the Church or Sea of *Rome*, or by any other meanes with
any other, hath any power or authoritie to depoſe the King, or to diſpoſe
of any of his Maieſties Kingdomes or Dominions, or to authorize any
forreigne Prince to inuade or annoy him or his Countreys, or to diſcharge
any of his Subiects of their Allegiance and obedience to his Maieſtie, or
to giue Licence or leaue to any of them to beare Armes, raiſe tumults, or to
offer any violence or hurt to his Maieſties Royall Perſon, State or Gouernment, or to any of his Maieſties ſubiects within his Maieſties Dominions.
Alſo I doe ſweare from my heart, that, notwithſtanding any declaration or
ſentence of Excommunication, or depriuation made or granted, or to be
made

made or granted, by the *Pope* or his succeffors, or by any Authoritie deriued, or pretended to be denued from him or his Sea, againft the faid King, his heires or fucceffors, or any abfolution of the faid fubiects from their obedience ; I will beare faith and trew Allegiance to his Maieftie, his heires and fucceffors , and him and them will defend to the vttermoft of my power, againft all confpiracies and attempts whatfoeuer, which fhalbe made againft his or their Perfons, their Crowne and dignitie, by reafon or colour of any fuch fentence, or declaration, or otherwife, and will doe my beft endeuour to difclofe and make knowne vnto his Maieftie, his heires and fucceffors, all Treafons and traiterous confpiracies, which I fhall know or heare of, to be againft him or any of them. And I doe further fweare, That I doe from my heart abhorre, deteft and abiure as impious and Hereticall, this damnable doctrine and pofition, That Princes which be excommunicated or depriued by the *Pope*, may be depofed or murthered by their Subiects or any other whatfoeuer. And I doe beleeue, and in confcience am refolued, that neither the *Pope* nor any perfon whatfoeuer, hath power to abfolue me of this Oath, or any part therof; which I acknowledge by good and full authoritie to bee lawfully miniftred vnto mee, and doe renounce all Pardons and Difpenfations to the contrarie. And all thefe things I doe plainely and fincerely acknowledge and fweare, according to thefe expreffe words by mee fpoken, and according to the plaine and common fenfe and vnderftanding of the fame words, without any Equiuocation, or mentall euafion, or fecret referuation whatfoeuer. And I do make this Recognition and acknowledgment heartily, willingly, and trewly, vpon the trew faith of a Chriftian. So helpe me G O D.

Which things fince they are thus ; it muft euidently appeare vnto you by the words themfelues, That fuch an Oath cannot be taken without hurting of the Catholike Faith, and the faluation of your foules; feeing it conteines many things which are flat contrary to Faith and faluation. Wherefore wee doe admonifh you, that you doe vtterly abftaine from taking this and the like Oathes: which thing wee doe the more earneftly require of you, becaufe wee haue experience of the conftancie of your faith, which is tried like gold in the fire of perpetuall tribulation. Wee doe well know, that you will cheerefully vnder-goe all kinde of cruell torments whatfoeuer, yea and conftantly endure death it felfe, rather then you will in any thing offend the Maieftie of G O D. *And this our confidence is confirmed by thofe things, which are dayly reported vnto vs, of the fingular vertue, valour, and fortitude which in thefe laft times doeth no leffe fhine in your* Martyrs, *then it did in the firft beginning of the Church. Stand therefore, your loynes being girt about with veritie, and hauing on the breft-plate of righteoufneffe, taking the fhield of Faith, be ye ftrong in the Lord, and in the power of his might ; And let nothing hinder you. Hee which will crowne you, and doeth in Heauen behold your conflicts, will finifh the good worke which hee hath begun in you. You know how hee hath promifed his difciples, that hee will neuer leaue them Orphanes: for hee is faithfull which hath promifed. Hold faft therefore his correction, that is, being rooted and grounded in Charitie, whatfoeuer ye doe,*

whatfoeuer

whatsoeuer ye indeuour, doe it with one accord, in simplicitie of heart, in meekenesse of spirit, without murmuring or doubting. For by this doe all men know that we are the disciples of CHRIST, *if we haue loue one to another. Which charitie, as it is very greatly to be desired of all faithfull Christians; So certainely is it altogether necessary for you, most blessed sonnes. For by this your charitie, the power of the diuel is weakened, who doeth so much assaile you, since that power of his is especially vpheld by the contentions and disagreement of our sonnes. Wee exhort you therefore by the bowels of our Lord* IESVS CHRIST, *by whose loue we are taken out of the iawes of eternall death; That aboue all things, you would haue mutuall charitie among you. Surely Pope Clement the eight of happy memory, hath giuen you most profitable precepts of practising brotherly charitie one to another, in his Letters in forme of a Breue, to our welbeloued sonne* M. George *Arch-priest of the Kingdome of England, dated the 5. day of the moneth of October* 1602. *Put them therefore diligently in practise, and be not hindered by any difficultie or doubtfulnesse. We command you that ye doe exactly obserue the words of those letters, and that yee take and vnderstand them simply as they sound, and as they lie; all power to interpret them otherwise, being taken away. In the meane while, we will neuer cease to pray to the Father of Mercies, that he would with pitie behold your afflictions and your paines; And that he would keepe and defend you with his continuall protection: whom wee doe gently greet with our Apostolicall Benediction. Dated at* Rome *at* S.Marke, *vnder the Signet of the Fisherman, the tenth of the Calends of October,* 1606. *the second yeere of our* Popedome.

THE ANSWERE TO
THE FIRST *BREVE.*

 Irst, the *Pope* expresseth herein his sorrow, for that persecution which the Catholiques sustaine for the faiths sake. Wherein, besides the maine vntrewth whereby I am so iniuriously vsed, I must euer auow and maintaine, as the trewth is according to mine owne knowledge, that the late Queene of famous memory, neuer punished any Papist for Religion, but that their owne punishment was euer extorted out of her hands against her will, by their owne misbehauiour, which both the time and circumstances of her actions will manifestly make proofe of. For before *Pius Quintus* his excommunication giuing her ouer for a prey, and setting her Subiects at libertie to rebell, it is well knowne she neuer medled with the blood or hard punishment of any Catholique, nor made any rigorous Lawes against them. And since that time, who list to compare with an indifferent eye, the manifold intended inuasions against her whole Kingdome,

dome, the forreine practifes, the internall publike rebellions, the priuate plots and machinations, poyfonings, murthers, and all forts of deuifes, *& quid non?* daily fet abroach; and all thefe wares continually foftered and fomented from *Rome*; together with the continuall corrupting of her Subiects, as well by temporall bribes, as by faire and fpecious promifes of eternall felicitie; and nothing but booke vpon booke publikely fet foorth by her fugitiues, for approbation of fo holy defignes: who lift, I fay, with an indifferent eye, to looke on the one part, vpon thofe infinite and intollerable temptations, and on the other part vpon the iuft, yet moderate punifhment of a part of thefe hainous offendors; fhall eafily fee that that bleffed defunct L A D I E was as free from perfecution, as they fhall free thefe hellifh Inftruments from the honour of martyrdome.

5. But now hauing facrificed (if I may fo fay) to the *Manes* of my late Predeceffour, I may next with Saint P A V L iuftly vindicate mine owne fame, from thofe innumerable calumnies fpread againft me, in teftifying the trewth of my behauiour toward the Papifts: wherein I may trewly affirme, That whatfoeuer was her iuft and mercifull Gouernement ouer the Papifts in her time, my Gouernement ouer them fince hath fo farre exceeded hers, in Mercie and Clemencie, as not onely the Papifts themfelues grewe to that height of pride; in confidence of my mildneffe, as they did directly expect, and affuredly promife to themfelues libertie of Confcience, and equalitie with other of my Subiects in all things; but euen a number of the beft and faithfullieft of my fayde Subiects, were caft in great feare and amazement of my courfe and proceedings, euer prognofticating and iuftly fufpecting that fowre fruite to come of it, which fhewed it felfe clearely in the Powder-Treafon. How many did I honour with Knighthood, of knowen and open Recufants? How indifferently did I giue audience, and acceffe to both fides, beftowing equally all fauours and honours on both profeffions? How free and continuall acceffe, had all rankes and degrees of Papifts in my Court and company? And aboue all, how frankely and freely did I free Recufants of their ordinarie paiments? Befides, it is euident what ftrait order was giuen out of my owne mouth to the Iudges, to fpare the execution of all Priefts, (notwithftanding their conuiction,) ioyning thereunto a gracious Proclamation, whereby all Priefts, that were at libertie, and not taken, might goe out of the countrey by fuch a day: my generall Pardon hauing beene extended to all conuicted Prieftes in prifon: whereupon they were fet at libertie as good Subiects: and all Priefts that were taken after, fent ouer and fet at libertie there. But time and paper will faile me to make enumeration of all the benefits and fauours that I beftowed in generall and particular vpon Papifts: in recounting whereof, euery fcrape of my penne would ferue but for a blot of the Popes ingratitude and iniuftice, in meating me with fo hard a meafure for the fame. So

Y   as

* *Magno cum animi mœrore, &c.*

as I thinke I haue sufficiently, or at least with good reason wiped the * *teares* from the Popes eyes, for complaining vpon such persecution, who if hee had beene but politickely wise, although hee had had no respect to Iustice and Veritie, would haue in this complaint of his, made a difference betweene my present time, and the time of the late Queene : And so by his commending of my moderation, in regard of former times, might haue had hope to haue mooued me to haue continued in the same clement course: For it is a trew saying, that alledged kindnesse vpon noble mindes, doeth euer worke much. And for the maine vntrewth of any persecution in my time, it can neuer bee prooued, that any were, or are put to death since I came to the Crowne for cause of Conscience; except that now this discharge giuen by the Pope to all Catholiques to take their Oath of Allegiance to me, be the cause of the due punishment of many : which if it fall out to be, let the blood light vpon the Popes head, who is the onely cause thereof.

As for the next point contained in his *Breue* concerning his discharge of all Papists to come to our Church, or frequent our rites and ceremonies, I am not to meddle at this time with that matter, because my errand now onely is to publish to the world the Iniurie and Iniustice done vnto me, in discharging my subiects to make profession of their obedience vnto mee. Now as to the point where the Oath is quarrelled, it is set

The intendement of this discourse.

downe in fewe, but very weighty wordes ; to wit, *That it ought to be cleare vnto all Catholiques, that this Oath cannot bee taken with safetie of the Catholique Faith, and of their soules health, since it containeth many things that are plainely and directly contrarie to their faith and saluation.* To this, the old saying fathered vpon the Philosopher, may very fitly bee applied, *Multa dicit, sed pauca probat*; nay indeed, *Nihil omnino probat*: For how the profession of the naturall Allegiance of Subiects to their Prince can be directly opposite to the faith and saluation of soules, is so farre beyond my simple reading in Diuinitie, as I must thinke it a strange and new Assertion, to proceede out of the mouth of that pretended generall Pastor of all Christian soules. I reade indeede, and not in one, or two, or three places of Scripture, that Subiects are bound to obey their Princes for conscience sake, whether they were good or wicked Princes. So said the people to [1] *Ioshua, As wee*

1 Iosh.1.17.
2 Iere. 27.12.

obeyed Moses in all things, so will wee obey thee. So the [2] Prophet commanded the people to obey the King of Babel, saying, *Put your neckes vnder the yoke of the King of Babel, and serue him and his people, that yee may liue.* So were the children of Israel, vnto [3] *Pharaoh*, desiring him to let them goe : so to [4] *Cyrus*, obtaining leaue of him to returne to build the Temple: and in a word, the Apostle willed all men [5] *to bee subiect to the higher powers for conscience sake.* Agreeable to the Scriptures did the Fathers teach. [6] *Augustine* speaking of *Iulian*, saith, *Iulian was an vnbeleeuing Emperour : was hee not an Apostata, an Oppressour, and an Idolater? Christian Souldiers serued that vnbeleeuing Emperour : when they came to the cause of* CHRIST, *they would acknowledge*

3 Exod.5.1.
4 Ezra 1.3.

5 Rom.13.5.

6 *August. in Psalm.* 124.

no

no Lord, but him that is in heauen. When hee would haue them to worship Idoles and to sacrifice, they preferred G O D *before him: But when hee said, Goe forth to fight, inuade such a nation, they presently obeyed. They distinguished their eternall Lord from their temporall, and yet were they subiect euen vnto their temporall Lord, for his sake that was their eternall Lord and Master.* [1] Tertullian sayth, *A Christian is enemie to no man, much lesse to the Prince, whom hee knoweth to bee appointed of God; and so of necessitie must loue, reuerence and honour him, and wish him safe with the whole Romane Empire, so long as the world shall last: for so long shall it endure. Wee honour therefore the Emperour in such sort, as is lawfull for vs, and expedient for him, as a man, the next vnto God, and obtaining from God whatsoeuer hee hath, and onely inferiour vnto God. This the Emperour himselfe would: for so is hee greater then all, while hee is inferiour onely to the trew God.* [2] Iustine Martyr; *Wee onely adore the Lord, and in all other things cheerefully performe seruice to you, professing that you are Emperours and Princes of men.* [3] Ambrose; *I may lament, weepe, and sigh: My teares are my weapons against their armes, souldiers, and the Gothes also: such are the weapons of a Priest: Otherwise neither ought I, neither can I resist.* [4] Optatus; *Ouer the Emperour, there is none but onely God, that made the Emperour.* And [5] Gregory writing to *Mauritius* about a certaine Law, that a Souldier should not be receiued into a Monasterie, *nondum expleta militia, The Almightie God,* sayth hee, *holdes him guiltie, that is not vpright to the most excellent Emperour in all things that hee doeth or speaketh.* And then calling himselfe the vnworthy seruant of his Godlinesse, goeth on in the whole Epistle to shewe the iniustice of that Lawe, as hee pretendeth: and in the end concludes his Epistle with these wordes; *I being subiect to your command, haue caused the same Law to be sent through diuers parts of your Dominions: and because the Law it selfe doeth not agree to the Law of the Almightie God, I haue signified the same by my Letters to your most excellent Lordship: so that on both parts I haue payed what I ought; because I haue yeelded obedience to the Emperour, and haue not holden my peace, in what I thought for God.* Now how great a contrarietie there is, betwixt this ancient Popes action in obeying an Emperour by the publication of his Decree, which in his owne conscience hee thought vnlawfull, and this present Popes prohibition to a Kings Subiects from obedience vnto him in things most lawfull and meere temporall; I remit it to the Readers indifferencie. And answerably to the Fathers, spake the Councels in their Decrees. As the Councell of [6] *Arles,* submitting the whole Councell to the Emperour in these wordes; *These things wee haue decreed to be presented to our Lord the Emperour, beseeching his Clemencie, that if wee haue done lesse then wee ought, it may be supplyed by his wisedome: if any thing otherwise then reason requireth, it may be corrected by his iudgement: if any thing be found fault with by vs with reason, it may bee perfected by his aide with* G O D s *fauourable assistance.*

But why should I speake of *Charles* the great, to whome not one Councell, but sixe seuerall Councels, *Frankeford, Arles, Tours, Chalons, Ments*

Y 2 and

[1] *Tertull. ad Scap.*

[2] *Iust. Martyr. Apol. 2. ad Ant. Imperat.*

[3] *Amb. in orat. cont. Auxentii, de basilicis tradendis. habetur lib. 5. epist. Ambr.*

[4] *Optat. contra Parmen. lib. 3.*

[5] *Greg. Mag. Epist. lib. 2. indict. 11. Epist. 61.*

[6] *Concil. Arelatense sub Carolo Mag. Can. 26.*

and *Rhemes* did wholy fubmit themfelues? and not rather fpeake of all the generall Councels, that of *Nice*, *Conftantinople*, *Ephefus*, *Chalcedon*, and the foure other commonly fo reputed; which did fubmit themfelues to the Emperours wifedome and piety in all things? Infomuch as that of *Ephefus* repeated it foure feuerall times, *That they were fummoned by the Emperours Oracle, becke, charge and commaund, and betooke themfelues to his Godlineffe:*

¹ *Vide Epifto-lam generalu Conc. Ephef. ad Auguft.*

¹ *befeeching him, that the Decrees made againft* Neftorius *and his followers, might by his power haue their full force and validitie,* as appeareth manifeftly in the Epiftle of the generall Councell of *Ephefus* written *ad Auguftos.* I alfo reade

* Iohn 18 36.
³ Matt. 22.21.

that Chrift faid, *His* ² *kingdome was not of this world,* bidding, *Giue to* ³ *Cefar what was Cefars, and to God what was Gods.* And I euer held it for an infallible Maxime in Diuinitie, That temporall obedience to a temporall Magiftrate, did nothing repugne to matters of faith or faluation of foules: But that euer temporall obedience was againft faith and faluation of foules, as in this *Breue* is alledged, was neuer before heard nor read of in the Chriftian Church. And therefore I would haue wifhed the *Pope*, before hee had fet downe this commandement to all Papifts here, That, fince in him is the power by the infabillity of his fpirit, to make new Articles of Faith when euer it fhall pleafe him; he had firft fet it downe for an Article of Faith, before he had commanded all Catholikes to beleeue and obey it. I will then conclude the anfwere to this point in a *Dilemma.*

Queftion.

Either it is lawfull to obey the Soueraigne in temporall things, or not.

1.

If it be lawfull (as I neuer heard nor read it doubted of) then why is the *Pope* fo vniuft, and fo cruell towards his owne Catholikes, as to command them to difobey their Soueraignes lawfull commandement?

2.

If it be vnlawfull, why hath hee neither expreffed any one caufe or rea-fon thereof, nor yet will giue them leaue (nay rather hee fhould command and perfwade them in plaine termes) not to liue vnder a King whom vnto they ought no obedience?

Anfwere to the Popes ex-hortation.

And as for the vehement exhortation vnto them to perfeuere in con-ftancie, and to fuffer Martyrdome and all tribulation for this caufe; it re-quireth no other anfwere then onely this, That if the ground be good whereupon hee hath commaunded them to ftand, then exhortation to conftancie is neceffarie: but if the ground be vniuft and naught (as indeed it is, and I haue in part already proued) then this exhortation of his can worke no other effect, then to make him guilty of the blood of fo many of his fheepe, whom hee doeth thus wilfully caft away; not onely to the needleffe loffe of their liues, and ruine of their families, but euen to the laying on of a perpetuall flander vpon all Papifts; as if no zealous Papift could be a trew fubiect to his Prince, and that the profeffion of that Religi-on, and the Temporall obedience to the Ciuill Magiftrate, were two things repugnant and incompatible in themfelues. But euill information, and

Fama vires ac-quirit eundo.

vntrew reports (which being caried fo farre as betweene this and *Rome,*

cannot

cannot but increafe by the way) might haue.abufed the *Pope*, and made him difpatch this *Breue* fo rafhly : For that great Citie, Queene of the World, and as themfelues confeffe, [1] myftically *Babylon*, cannot but be fo full of all forts of Intelligencies. Befides, all complainers (as the Catholikes here are) be naturally giuen to exaggerate their owne griefes, and multiply thereupon : So that it is no wonder, that euen a iuft Iudge fitting there, fhould vpon wrong information, giue an vnrighteous fentence; as fome of their owne partie doe not fticke to confeffe, That *Pius Quintus* was too rafhly caried vpon wrong information, to pronounce his thunder of Excommunication vpon the late Queene. And it may be, the like excufe fhall hereafter be made for the two *Breues*, which [2] *Clemens Octauus* fent to E N G L A N D immediatly before her death, for debarring me of the Crowne, or any other that either would profeffe, or any wayes tolerate the profeffours of our Religion; contrary to his manifold vowes and proteftations, *fimul & eodem tempore*, and as it were, deliuered *vno & eodem fpiritu*, to diuers of my minifters abroad, profeffing fuch kindneffe, and fhewing fuch forwardneffe to aduance me to this Crowne. Nay, the moft part of Catholikes here, finding this *Breue* when it came to their handes to bee fo farre againft Diuinitie, Policie, or naturall fenfe, were firmely perfwaded that it was but a counterfeit Libell, deuifed in hatred of the Pope; or at the fartheft, a thing haftily done vpon wrong information, as was before faid. Of which opinion were not onely the fimpler fort of Papifts, but euen fome amongft them of beft account, both for learning and experience; whereof the Archprieft himfelfe was one: But for foluing of this obiection, the Pope himfelfe hath taken new paines by fending foorth a fecond *Breue*, onely for giuing faith and confirmation to the former; That whereas before, his finne might haue beene thought to haue proceeded from rafhneffe and mif-information, he will now wilfully and willingly double the fame; whereof the Copy followeth.

[1] *Eufebius, Oecumenius* and *Leo* hold, that by *Babylon*, in 1. Pet. 5. 13. *Rome* is meant, as the *Rhemifts* themfelues confeffe.

[2] See the Relation of the whole proceedings againft the Traitours, *Garnet* and his confederates.

The Catholikes opinion of the *Breue*.

Y 3   TO

TO OVR BELOVED SONNES
the Englifh Catholikes, *Paulus P.P. V^{tus}.*

The fecond Breue.

Eloued fonnes, Salutation and Apoftolicall Benediction. *It is reported vnto vs, that there are found certaine amongſt you, who when as we haue ſufficiently declared by our Letters, dated the laſt yeere on the tenth of the Calends of October in the forme of a* Breue, *that yee cannot with ſafe Conſcience take the Oath, which was then required of you; and when as wee haue further ſtraitly commanded you, that by no meanes yee ſhould take it : yet there are ſome, I ſay, among you, which dare now affirme, that ſuch Letters concerning the forbidding of the Oath, were not written of our owne accord, or of our owne proper will, but rather for the reſpect and at the inſtigation of other men. And for that cauſe the ſame men doe goe about to perſwade you, that our commands in the ſaid Letters are not to be regarded. Surely this newes did trouble vs; and that ſo much the more, becauſe hauing had experience of your obedience (moſt dearely beloued ſonnes) who to the end ye might obey this holy Sea, haue godlily and valiantly contemned your riches, wealth, honour, libertie, yea and life it ſelfe; wee ſhould neuer haue ſuſpected that the trewth of our Apoſtolike Letters could once be called into queſtion among you, that by this pretence ye might exempt your ſelues from our Commandements. But we doe herein perceiue the ſubtiltie and craft of the enemie of mans ſaluation, and we doe attribute this your backwardneſſe rather to him, then to your owne will. And for this cauſe, wee haue thought good to write the ſecond time vnto you, and to ſigni-fie vnto you againe, That our Apoſtolike Letters dated the laſt yeere on the tenth of the Calends of October, concerning the prohibition of the Oath, were written not on-ly vpon our proper motion, and of our certaine knowledge, but alſo after long and weightie deliberation vſed concerning all thoſe things, which are contained in them; and that for that cauſe ye are bound fully to obſerue them, reiecting all interpreta-tion perſwading to the contrary. And this is our meere, pure, and perfect will, being alwayes carefull of your ſaluation, and alwayes minding thoſe things, which are moſt profitable vnto you. And we doe pray without ceaſing, that hee that hath appointed our lowlineſſe to the keeping of the flocke of Chriſt, would inlighten our thoughts and our counſels : whom we doe alſo continually deſire, that he would increaſe in you (our beloued Sonnes) faith, conſtancie, and mutuall charitie and peace one to another. All whom, we doe moſt louingly bleſſe with all charitable affection.*

Dated at Rome *at Saint* Markes *vnder the Signet of the* Fiſherman, *the x. of the Calends of September,* 1607. *the third yeere of our* Popedome.

THE

THE ANSWERE TO THE
ſecond Breve.

Ow for this *Breue*, I may iuſtly reflect his owne phraſe vpon him, in tearming it to be *The craft of the Deuill*. For if the Deuill had ſtudied a thouſand yeeres, for to finde out a miſchiefe for our Catholikes heere, hee hath found it in this: that now when many Catholikes haue taken their Oath, and ſome Prieſts alſo; yea, the Arch-prieſt himſelfe, without compunction or ſticking, they ſhall not now onely be bound to refuſe the profeſſion of their naturall Allegiance to their Soueraigne, which might yet haue beene ſome way coloured vpon diuers ſcruples conceiued vpon the words of the Oath; but they muſt now renounce and forſweare their profeſſion of obedience alreadie ſworne, and ſo muſt as it were at the third inſtance forſweare their former two Oathes, firſt cloſely ſworne, by their birth in their naturall Allegiance; and next, clearely confirmed by this Oath, which doeth nothing but expreſſe the ſame: ſo as no man can now holde the faith, or procure the ſaluation of his ſoule in ENGLAND, that muſt not abiure and renounce his borne and ſworne Allegiance to his naturall Soueraigne.

And yet it is not ſufficient to ratifie the laſt yeeres *Breue*, by a new one come forth this yeere; but (that not onely euery yeere, but euery moneth may produce a new monſter) the great and famous Writer of the Controuerſies, the late vn-Ieſuited Cardinall *Bellarmine*, muſt adde his talent to this good worke, by blowing the bellowes of ſedition, and ſharpening the ſpurre to rebellion, by ſending ſuch a Letter of his to the Archprieſt here, as it is a wonder how paſſion, and an ambitious deſire of maintaining that Monarchie, ſhould charme the wits of ſo famouſly learned a man.

The Copy whereof here followeth.

TO

TO THE VERY REVEREND

Mᵣ *GEORGE BLACKWELL*, ARCH-PRIEST
of the ENGLISH : ROBERT BELLARMINE
Cardinall of the holy Church of *Rome*, Greeting.

Euerend Sir , and brother in CHRIST ; *It is almoſt fourtie
yeeres ſince we did ſee one the other* : *but yet I haue neuer bene vnmindfull of our ancient acquaintance, neither haue I ceaſed ſeeing I
could doe you no other good*, *to commend your labouring moſt pain-
fully in the Lords Vineyard, in my prayers to God. And I doubt not,
but that I haue liued all this while in your memory, and haue had ſome place in your
prayers at the Lords Altar. So therfore euen vnto this time we haue abidden, as* S.
Iohn ſpeaketh , *in the mutuall loue one of the other*, *not by word or letter*, *but in
deed and trewth. But a late meſſage which was brought vnto vs within theſe few
dayes, of your bonds and impriſonment, hath inforced mee to breake off this ſilence ;
which meſſage, although it ſeemed heauie in regard of the loſſe which that Church
hath receiued, by their being thus depriued of the comfort of your paſtorall funſtion
amongſt them , yet withall it ſeemed ioyous, becauſe you drew neere vnto the glory of*
Martyrdome, *then the which gift of God there is none more happy* ; *That you, who
haue fedde your flocke ſo many yeeres with the word and doſtrine , ſhould now feed
it more gloriouſly by the example of your patience . But another heauie tidings did
not a little diſquiet and almoſt take away this ioy*, *which immediatly followed, of the
aduerſaries aſſault, and peraduenture of the ſlip and fall of your conſtancie in refuſing an vnlawfull Oath. Neither trewly (moſt deare brother) could that Oath
therefore bee lawfull, becauſe it was offered in ſort tempered and modified* : *for you
know that thoſe kinde of modifications are nothing elſe , but ſlights and ſubtilties of*
Satan, *that the Catholique faith touching the Primacie of the Sea Apoſtolike , might
either ſecretly or openly be ſhot at* ; *for the which faith ſo many worthy Martyrs e-
uen in that very* England *it ſelfe , haue reſiſted vnto blood. For moſt certaine it is,
that in whatſoeuer words the Oath is conceiued by the aduerſaries of the faith in that
Kingdome, it tends to this end , that the Authoritie of the head of the Church in* England, *may bee transferred from the ſucceſſour of* S.Peter , *to the ſucceſſour of King*
Henry the eight : *For that which is pretended of the danger of the Kings life ,
if the high Prieſt ſhould haue the ſame power in* England , *which hee hath in all o-
ther Chriſtian Kingdomes , it is altogether idle, as all that haue any vnderſtanding,
may eaſily perceiue. For it was neuer heard of from the Churches infancie vntill
this day, that euer any Pope did command, that any Prince , though an Heretike,
though an Ethnike, though a perſecutour, ſhould be murdered* ; *or did approue of the
faſt, when it was done by any other. And why, I pray you, doeth onely the King of*
England *feare that , which none of all other the Princes in Chriſtendome either
doeth feare, or euer did feare* ?

But,

But, as I said, these vaine pretexts are but the traps and stratagemes of Satan: Of which kinde I could produce, not a fewe out of ancient Stories, if I went about to write a Booke, and not an Epistle. One onely for example sake, I will call to your memory. S. Gregorius Nazianzenus *in his first Oration against* Iulian the Emperour, *reporteth, That hee, the more easily to beguile the simple Christians, did insert the Images of the false gods into the pictures of the Emperour, which the Romanes did vse to bow downe vnto with a ciuill kinde of reuerence: so that no man could doe reuerence to the Emperours picture, but withall hee must adore the Images of the false gods; whereupon it came to passe that many were deceiued.* And if there were any that found out the Emperours craft, and refused to worship his picture, those were most grieuously punished, as men that had contemned the Emperour in his Image. Some such like thing, me thinkes, I see in the Oath that is offered to you; which is so craftily composed, that no man can detest Treason against the King, and make profession of his Ciuill subiection, but he must bee constrained perfidiously to denie the Primacie of the Apostolicke Sea. But the seruants of Christ, and especially the chiefe Priests of the Lord, ought to lee so farre from taking an vnlawfull Oath, where they may indamage the Faith, that they ought to beware that they giue not the least suspicion of dissimulation that they haue taken it, least they might seeme to haue left any example of preuarication to faithfull people. Which thing that worthy Eleazar did most notably performe, who would neither eate swines flesh, nor so much as faine to haue eaten it; although hee sawe the great torments that did hang ouer his head; least, as himselfe speaketh in the second Booke of the Machabees, many young men might bee brought through that simulation, to preuaricate with the Lawe. Neither did Basil the Great by his example, which is more fit for our purpose, cary himselfe lesse worthily toward Valens the Emperour. For as Theodoret writeth in his Historie, when the Deputy of that hereticall Emperour did perswade Saint Basil, that hee would not resist the Emperour for a little subtiltie of a few points of doctrine; that most holy and prudent man made answere, That it was not to be indured, that the least syllable of Gods word should bee corrupted, but rather all kind of torment was to be embraced, for the maintenance of the Trewth thereof. Now I suppose, that there wants not amongst you, who say that they are but subtilties of Opinions that are contained in the Oath that is offered to the Catholikes, and that you are not to striue against the Kings Authoritie for such a little matter. But there are not wanting also amongst you holy men like vnto Basil the Great, which will openly auow, that the very least syllable of Gods diuine Trewth is not to bee corrupted, though many torments were to bee endured, and death it selfe set before you: Amongst whom it is meete, that you should bee one, or rather the Standard bearer, and Generall to the rest. And whatsoeuer hath beene the cause, that your (constancie hath quailed, whether it bee the suddainenesse of your apprehension, or the bitternesse of your persecution, or the imbecilitie of your old aage: yet wee trust in the goodnesse of God, and in your owne long continued vertue, that it will come to passe, that as you seeme in some part to haue imitated the fall of Peter and Marcellinus, so you shall happily imitate their valour in recouering your strength, and maintaining the Trewth: For if you will diligently weigh the whole matter with your selfe, trewly you shall see, it is no small

matter

matter that is called in queſtion by this Oath, but one of the principall heads of our Faith, and foundations of Catholique Religion. For heare what your Apoſtle Saint Gregorie *the Great hath written in his* 24. *Epiſtle of his* 11. *Booke.* Let not the reuerence due to the Apoſtolique Sea, be troubled by any mans preſumption; for then the ſtate of the members doeth remaine entire, when the Head of the Faith is not bruiſed by any iniurie: *Therefore by* Saint Gregories *teſtimonie, when they are buſie about diſturbing or diminiſhing, or taking away of the Primacie of the Apoſtolique Sea; then are they buſie about cutting off the very head of the faith, and diſſoluing of the ſtate of the whole body, and of all the members.* Which ſelfe ſame thing S. Leo doth *confirme in his third Sermon of his Aſſumption to the Popedom, when he ſaith,* Our Lord had a ſpecial care of *Peter,* & praied properly for *Peters* faith, as though the ſtate of others were more ſtable, when their Princes mind was not to be ouercome. *Whereupon himſelfe in his Epiſtle to the biſhops of the prouince of Vienna, doth not doubt to affirme,* that he is not partaker of the diuine Myſterie, that dare depart from the ſolidity of *Peter; who alſo ſaith,* That who thinketh the Primacy to be denied to that Sea, he can in no ſort leſſen the authority of it; but by being puft vp with the ſpirit of his owne pride, doth caſt himſelfe headlong into hel. *Theſe and many other of this kind, I am very ſure are moſt familiar to you: who beſides many other books, haue diligently read ouer the viſible Monarchy of your owne* Sanders, *a moſt diligent writer, and one who hath worthily deſerued of the Church of* England. *Neither can you be ignorant, that theſe moſt holy and learned men,* Iohn *biſhop of* Rocheſter, *and* Tho. Moore, *within our memory, for this one moſt weighty head of doctrine, led the way to* Martyrdome *to many others, to the exceeding glory of the Engliſh nation. But I would put you in remembrance that you ſhould take heart, and conſidering the weightines of the cauſe, not to truſt too much to your owne iudgement, neither be wiſe aboue that is meet to be wiſe: and if peraduenture your fall haue proceeded not vpon want of conſideration, but through humane infirmity, & for feare of puniſhment and impriſonment, yet do not preferre a temporall liberty to the liberty of the glory of the Sonnes of God: neither for eſcaping a light & momentanie tribulation, loſe an eternal weight of glory, which tribulation it ſelfe doeth worke in you. You haue fought a good fight a long time, you haue wel-neere finiſhed your courſe; ſo many yeeres haue you kept the faith: do not therefore loſe the reward of ſuch labors; do not depriue your ſelfe of that crowne of righteouſnes, which ſo long agone is prepared for you; Do not make the faces of ſo many yours both brethren and children aſhamed. Vpon you at this time are fixed the eyes of all the Church: yea alſo, you are made a ſpectacle to the world, to Angels, to men; Do not ſo carry your ſelfe in this your laſt act, that you leaue nothing but laments to your friends, and ioy to your enemies. But rather on the contrary, which we aſſuredly hope, and for which we continually powre forth prayers to God, diſplay gloriouſly the banner of faith, and make to reioyce the Church, which you haue made heauy; ſo ſhall you not onely merite pardon at Gods hands, but a Crowne. Farewell. Quite you like a man, and let your heart be ſtrengthened. From* Rome *the* 28. *day of September* 1607.

Your very Reuerendſhips brother and ſeruant in Chriſt,
Robert Bellarmine Cardinall.

THE

THE ANSWERE TO THE
CARDINALS LETTER.

Nd now that I am to enter into the field against him by refuting his Letter, I must first vse this protestation; That no
desire of vaine-glory by matching with so learned a man,
maketh me to vndertake this taske; but onely the care and
conscience I haue, that such smooth *Circes* charmes and
guilded pilles, as full of exterior eloquence, as of inward vntrewths, may
not haue that publike passage through the world without an answere:
whereby my reputation might vniustly be darkened, by such cloudie and
foggie mists of vntrewths and false imputations, the hearts of vnstayed and
simple men be misse-led, and the trewth it selfe smothered.

But before I come to the particular answere of this Letter, I must here
desire the world to wonder with me, at the committing of so grosse an errour by so learned a man·as that he should haue pained himselfe to haue
set downe so elaborate a Letter, for the refutation of a quite mistaken question: For it appeareth, that our English Fugitiues, of whose inward societie with him he so greatly vaunteth, haue so fast hammered in his head the
Oath of Supremacie, which hath euer bene so great a scarre vnto them, as
he thinking by his Letter to haue refuted the last Oath, hath in place thereof onely paied the Oath of Supremacie, which was most in his head; as a
man that being earnestly caried in his thoughts vpon another matter, then
he is presently in doing, will often name the matter or person he is thinking of, in place of the other thing he hath at that time in hand.

A great mista-king of the state of the Question, and case in hand.

For as the Oath of Supremacie was deuised for putting a difference betweene Papists, and them of our profession: so was this Oath, which hee
would seeme to impugne, ordained for making a difference betweene the
ciuilly obedient Papists, and the peruerse disciples of the Powder-Treason.
Yet doeth all his Letter runne vpon an Inuectiue against the compulsion
of Catholiques to deny the authoritie of *S. Peters* successors, and in place
thereof to acknowledge the Successors of King *Henry the eight*: For in K.
Henry the eights time, was the Oath of Supremacie first made: By him were
Thomas Moore and *Roffensis* put to death, partly for refusing of it: From his
time till now, haue all the Princes of this land professing this Religion,
successiuely in effect maintained the same: and in that Oath onely is contained the Kings absolute power, to be Iudge ouer all persons, aswell Ciuill
as Ecclesiastical, excluding al forraigne powers and Potentates to be Iudges
within his dominions; whereas this last made Oath containeth no such
matter,

The diffe-rence be-tweene the Oath of Su-premacie, and this of Allegi-ance.

matter, onely medling with the ciuill obedience of Subiects to their Soueraigne, in meere temporall caufes.

And that it may the better appeare, that whereas by name hee feemeth
to condemne the laft Oath; yet indeed his whole Letter runneth vpon nothing, but vpon the condemnation of the Oath of Supremacie: I haue
here thought good to fet downe the faid Oath, leauing it then to the difcretion of euery indifferent reader to iudge, whether he doth not in fubftance
onely anfwere to the Oath of Supremacie, but that hee giues the child a
wrong name.

I A B. doe vtterly teſtifie and declare in my confcience, that the Kings Highneſſe
is the onely Supreame Gouernour of this Realme, and all other his Highneſſe Do-
minions and Countries, afwell in all Spirituall, or Eccleſiaſticall things or caufes,
as Temporall: And that no forraine Prince, Perfon, Prelate, State or Potentate,
hath or ought to haue any Iurifdiɛtion, Power, Superioritie, Preeminence or Authori-
tie Eccleſiaſticall or Spirituall within this Realme. And therefore I doe vtterly re-
nounce and forfake all forraine Iurifdiɛtions, Powers, Superiorities and Autho-
rities; and doe promife that from hencefoorth I fhall beare faith and trew Allegi-
ance to the Kings Highneſſe, his Heires and lawfull Succeſſours: and to my power
fhall afsiſt and defend all Iurifdiɛtions, Priuiledges, Preeminences and Authorities
granted or belonging to the Kings Highneſſe, his Heires and Succeſſours, or vnited
and annexed to the Imperiall Crowne of the Realme: So helpe me God; and by the
Contents of this booke.

And that the iniuftice, as well as the error of his groffe miftaking in this
point, may yet be more clearely difcouered; I haue alfo thought good to infert here immediatly after the Oath of Supremacie, the contrary conclufions to all the points and Articles, whereof this other late Oath doeth confift: whereby it may appeare, what vnreafonable and rebellious points hee
would driue my Subiects vnto, by refufing the whole body of that Oath, as
it is conceiued: For he that fhall refufe to take this Oath, muft of neceffitie
hold all, or fome of thefe propofitions following.

1.   That I King I A M E s, am not the lawfull King of this Kingdome, and
of all other my Dominions.

2.   That the *Pope* by his owne authoritie may depofe me: If not by his owne
authoritie, yet by fome other authoritie of the Church, or of the Sea of
Rome: If not by fome other authoritie of the Church and Sea of *Rome*,
yet by other meanes with others helpe, he may depofe me.

3.   That the *Pope* may difpofe of my Kingdomes and Dominions.

4.   That the *Pope* may giue authoritie to fome forreine Prince to inuade my
Dominions.

5.   That the *Pope* may difcharge my Subiects of their Allegiance and Obedience to me.

6.   That the *Pope* may giue licence to one, or more of my Subiects to beare
armes againft me.

That

That the *Pope* may giue leaue to my Subiects to offer violence to my Perſon, or to my gouernement, or to ſome of my Subiects. — 7.

That if the *Pope* ſhall by Sentence excommunicate or depoſe mee, my Subiects are not to beare Faith and Allegiance to me. — 8.

If the *Pope* ſhall by Sentence excommunicate or depoſe me, my Subiects are not bound to defend with all their power my Perſon and Crowne. — 9.

If the *Pope* ſhall giue out any Sentence of Excommunication or Depriuation againſt me, my Subiects by reaſon of that Sentence, are not bound to reueale all Conſpiracies and Treaſons againſt mee, which ſhall come to their hearing and knowledge. — 10.

That it is not hereticall and deteſtable to hold, that Princes being excommunicated by the *Pope*, may be either depoſed or killed by their Subiects, or any other. — 11.

That the *Pope* hath power to abſolue my Subiects from this Oath, or from ſome part thereof. — 12.

That this Oath is not adminiſtred to my Subiects, by a full and lawfull authoritie. — 13.

That this Oath is to be taken with Equiuocation, mentall euaſion, or ſecret reſeruation; and not with the heart and good will, ſincerely in the trew faith of a Chriſtian man. — 14.

Theſe are the trew and naturall branches of the body of this Oath. The affirmatiue of all which negatiues, doe neither concerne in any caſe the *Popes* Supremacie in Spirituall cauſes: nor yet were euer concluded, and defined by any complete generall Councell to belong to the *Popes* authoritie; and their owne ſchoole Doctors are at irreconciliable oddes and iarres about them.

Touching the pretended Councell of Lateran. See Plat. *In vita Innocen. III.*

And that the world may yet farther ſee ours and the whole States ſetting downe of this Oath, did not proceed from any new inuention of our owne, but as it is warranted by the word of GOD: ſo doeth it take the example from an Oath of Allegiance decreed a thouſand yeeres agone, which a famous Councell then, together with diuers other Councels, were ſo farre from condemning (as the *Pope* now hath done this Oath) as I haue thought good to ſet downe their owne wordes here in that purpoſe: whereby it may appeare that I craue nothing now of my Subiects in this Oath, which was not expreſly and carefully commaunded then, by the Councels to be obeyed without exception of perſons. Nay not in the very particular point of *Equiuocatiō*, which I in this Oath was ſo carefull to haue eſchewed: but you ſhall here ſee the ſaid Councels in their Decrees, as carefull to prouide for the eſchewing of the ſame; ſo as almoſt euery point of that action, & this of ours ſhalbe found to haue relation & agreeance one with the other, ſaue onely in this, that thoſe old Councels were careful and ſtrait in cōmanding the taking of the ſame: whereas by the contrary, he that now vanteth himſelfe to be head of al Councels, is as carefull & ſtrait in the prohibition of all men from the taking of this Oath of Allegiance.

The Oath of Allegiance confirmed by the authoritie of ancient Councels.

The ancient Councels prouided for Equiuocation. The difference betweene the ancient Councels, and the Pope counſelling of the Catholiques.

Z — The

The words of the Councell be these:

Heare our Sentence.

Concil. Tolet.
4.can.47. Anno
633.

Whosoeuer of vs, or of all the people thorowout all Spaine, *shall goe about by any meanes of conspiracie or practise, to violate the Oath of his fidelitie, which he hath taken for the preseruation of his Countrey, or of the Kings life; or who shall attempt to put violent handes vpon the King; or to depriue him of his kingly power; or that by tyrannicall presumption would vsurpe the Soueraigntie of the Kingdome: Let him bee accursed in the sight of God the Father, and of his Angels; and let him bee made and declared a stranger from the Catholique Church, which hee hath prophaned by his periurie; and an aliant from the companie of all Christian people, together with all the complices of his impietie; because it behooueth all those that bee guiltie of the like offence, to vnder-lie the like punishment.* Which sentence is three seuerall times together, and almost in the same wordes, repeated in the same Canon. After this, *the Synode desired, That this Sentence of theirs now this third time rehearsed, might bee confirmed by the voyce and consent of all that were present. Then the whole Clergie and people answered, Whosoeuer shall cary himselfe presumptuously against this your definitiue sentence, let them be Anathema maranatha, that is, let them bee vtterly destroyed at the Lords comming; and let them and their complices haue their portion with Iudas Iscarioth. Amen.*

¹ Concil. Tolet.
5.Can.7. anno
636.

And in the fifth ¹ Councell, there it is decreed, That this Acte touching the Oath of Allegiance, shall bee repeated in euery Councell of the Bishops of Spaine. The Decree is in these wordes: *In consideration that the mindes of men are easily inclined to euill and forgetfulnesse, therefore this most holy Synode hath ordained; and doeth enact, That in euery Councell of the Bishops* of Spaine, *the Decree of the generall* ² *Councell which was made for the safetie of our Princes, shall bee with an audible voyce proclaimed and pronounced, after the conclusion of all other things in the Synode: That so it beeing often sounded into their eares, at least by continuall remembrance, the mindes of wicked men beeing terrified, might bee reformed, which by obliuion and facilitie [to euill] are brought to preuaricate.*

² Synod. Tolet.
4.vniuersalis,
& magna Synodus dicta,
Synod.Tolet.
5.cap.2.

And in the sixt ³ Councell, *Wee doe protest before God, and all the orders of Angels, in the presence of the Prophets and Apostles, and all the companie of Martyrs, and before all the Catholique Church, and assemblies of the Christians; That no man shall goe about to seeke the destruction of the King: No man shall touch the life of the Prince: No man shall depriue him of the Kingdome: No man by any tyrannicall presumption shall vsurpe to himselfe the Soueraigntie of the Kingdome: No man by any Machination shall in his aduersitie associate to himselfe any packe of Conspirators against him: And that if any of vs shall be presumptuous by rashnesse in any of these cases; let him be stricken with the anatheme of God, and reputed as condemned in eternall iudgement without any hope of recouery.*

³ Concil.Tolet.
6.Can.18.
Anno 638.

And in the tenth ⁴ Councell (to omit diuers others held also at *Toledo*) it is said: *That if any religious man, euen from the Bishop to the lowest Order of the Church-men or Monkes, shall bee found to haue violated the generall Oathes made*

⁴ Concil. Tolet.
10.Can.2.
Æra 694.

made for the preseruation of the Kings Person, or of the Nation and Countrey with a prophane minde; foorthwith let him bee depriued of all dignitie, and excluded from all place and Honour. The occasion of the Decrees made for this Oath, was, That the Christians were suspected for want of fidelitie to their Kings; and did either equiuocate in taking their Oath, or make no conscience to keepe it, when they had giuen it; as may appeare by sundry speeches in the [1] Councell, saying, *There is a generall report, that there is that perfidiousnesse in the mindes of many people of diuers Nations, that they make no conscience to keepe the Oath and fidelitie that they haue sworne vnto their Kings: but doe dissemble a profession of fidelitie in their mouthes, when they hold an vn-pious perfidiousnesse in their mindes.* And [2] againe, *They sweare to their Kings, and yet doe they preuaricate in the fidelitie which they haue promised: Neither doe they feare the Volume of Gods iudgement, by the which the curse of God is brought vpon them, with great threatning of punishments, which doe sweare lyingly in the Name of God.* To the like effect spake they in the Councell of [3] *Aquisgran: If any of the Bishops, or other Church-man of inferiour degree, hereafter thorow feare or couetousnesse, or any other perswasion, shall make defection from our Lord the Orthodoxe Emperour* Lodowicke, *or shall violate the Oath of fidelitie made vnto him, or shall with their peruerse intention adhere to his enemies; let him by this Canonicall and Synodall sentence bee depriued of whatsoeuer place hee is possessed of.*

> [1] *Concil. Tolet. 4. cap. 74.*
>
> [2] *Concil. Tolet. 4. cap. 74.*
>
> [3] *Concil. Aquisgran. sub Ludo. Pio. & Greg. 4. Can. 12. anno 836.*

And now to come to a particular answere of his Letter. First, as concerning the sweet memory hee hath of his old acquaintance with the Arch-priest; it may indeed be pleasing for him to recount: but sure I am, his acquaintance with him and the rest of his societie, our Fugitiues (whereof he also vanteth himselfe in his Preface to the Reader in his Booke of Controuersies) hath prooued sowre to vs and our State: For some of such Priests and Iesuits, as were the greatest Traitors and fomenters of the greatest conspiracies against the late Queene, gaue vp Father *Rob: Bellarmine* for one of their greatest authorities and oracles: And therfore I do not enuy the great honour he can winne, by his vaunt of his inward familiaritie with an other Princes traitors & fugitiues; whom vnto if he teach no better maners then hitherto he hath done, I thinke his fellowship are litle beholding vnto him.

> *Campian and Hart.* See the conference in the Tower.

And for desiring him to remember him in his prayers at the Altar of the Lord: if the Arch-Priests prayers prooue no more profitable to his soule, then *Bellarmines* counsell is like to proue profitable, both to the soule and bodie of *Blackwell* (if he would follow it) the authour of this Letter might very well be without his prayers.

Now the first messenger that I can finde which brought ioyfull newes of the Arch-Priest to *Bellarmine*, was hee that brought the newes of the Arch-Priests taking, and first appearance of Martyrdome. A great signe surely of the Cardinals mortification, that hee was so reioyced to heare of the apprehension, imprisonment and appearance of putting to death of so old and deare a friend of his. But yet apparantly he should first haue beene

sure,

The Cardinals charitie.

sure, that hee was onely to bee punished for cause of Religion, before hee had so triumphed vpon the expectation of his Martyrdome. For first, by what rule of charitie was it lawfull for him to iudge mee a persecutour, before proofe had beene made of it by the said Arch-Priests condemnation and death? What could hee know, that the said Arch-Priest was not taken vpon suspicion of his guiltinesse in the Powder-Treason? What certaine information had hee then receiued vpon the particulars, whereupon hee was to bee accused? And last of all, by what inspiration could he foretell whereupon hee was to bee accused? For at that time there was yet nothing layed to his charge. And if charitie should not bee suspicious, what warrant had hee absolutely to condemne mee of vsing persecution and tyrannie, which could not bee but implyed vpon mee, if *Blackwel* was to bee a Martyr? But surely it may iustly be sayd of *Bellarmine*, in this case, that our Sauiour C H R I S T saith of all worldly and carnall men,

[1] Mat.5.43.

who thinke it enough to loue their [1] friends, and hate their enemies; the limits of the Cardinals charitie extending no farther, then to them of his owne profession. For what euer hee added in superfluous charitie to *Blackwel*, in reioycing in the speculation of his future Martyrdome; hee detracted as much vniustly and vncharitably from me, in accounting of me thereby as of a bloody Persecutour. And whereas this ioy of his was interrupted by the next messenger, that brought the newes of the saide Arch-Priest his failing in his constancie, by taking of this Oath; he needed neuer to haue beene troubled, either with his former ioy or his second sorrow, both beeing alike falsly grounded. For as it was neuer my intention to lay any thing vnto the said Arch-Priests charge, as I haue neuer done to any for cause of conscience; so was *Blackwels* constancie neuer brangled by taking of this Oath; It beeing a thing which he euer thought lawfull before his apprehension, and whereunto hee perswaded all Catholiques to giue obedience; like as after his apprehension, hee neuer made doubt or stop in it; but at the first offering it vnto him, did freely take it, as a thing most lawfull; neither meanes of threatening, or flatterie being euer vsed vnto him, as himselfe can yet beare witnesse.

And as for the temperature and modification of this Oath, except that a reasonable and lawfull matter is there set downe in reasonable and temperate wordes, agreeing thereunto; I know not what he can meane, by quarrelling it for that fault: For no temperatnesse nor modifications in words therein, can iustly be called the Deuils craft; when the thing it selfe is so plaine, and so plainely interpreted to all them that take it; as the onely troublesome thing in it all, bee the wordes vsed in the end thereof, for eschewing *Æquiuocation* and *Mentall reseruation*. Which new Catholike doctrine, may farre iustlier bee called the Deuils craft, then any plaine and temperate wordes, in so plaine and cleare a matter. But what shall we say of these strange countrey clownes, whom of with the *Satyre* we may iustly complaine, that they blow both hote & cold out of one mouth? For *Luther* and

and all our bold and free-ſpeaking Writers are mightily railed vpon by them, as hote-brained fellowes, and ſpeakers by the Deuils inſtinct : and now if we ſpeake moderately and temperately of them, it muſt be tearmed the Deuils craft: And therefore wee may iuſtly complaine with CHRIST, that when we [1] mourne, they wil not lament : and when we pipe, they wil not dance. But neither *Iohn Baptiſt* his ſeueritie, nor CHRIST his meekeneſſe and lenitie can pleaſe them, who build but to their owne Monarchie vpon the ground of their owne Traditions ; and not to CHRIST vpon the ground of his word and infallible trewth.

But what can bee meant by alleadging, that the craft of the Deuill herein, is onely vſed for ſubuerſion of the Catholique Faith, and euerſion of Saint *Peters* Primacie ; had neede bee commented anew by *Bellarmine* himſelfe : For in all this Letter of his, neuer one word is vſed, to prooue that by any part of this Oath the Primacie of Saint *Peter* is any way medled with, except Maſter *Bellarmine* his bare alleadging ; which without proouing it by more cleare demonſtration, can neuer ſatisfie the conſcience of any reaſonable man. For (for ought that I know) heauen and earth are no farther aſunder, then the profeſſion of a temporall obedience to a temporall King, is different from any thing belonging to the Catholique Faith, or Supremacie of Saint *Peter*: For as for the Catholique Faith; can there be one word found in all that Oath, tending or ſounding to matter of Religion ? Doeth he that taketh it, promiſe there to beleeue, or not to beleeue any article of Religion ? Or doeth hee ſo much as name a trew or falſe Church there ? And as for Saint *Peters* Primacie ; I know no Apoſtles name that is therein named, except the name of IAMES ; it being my Chriſten name : though it pleaſe him not to deigne to name me in all the Letter ; albeit, the contents thereof concerne mee in the higheſt degree. Neither is there any mention at all made therein, either *diſertis verbis*, or by any other indirect meanes, either of the Hierarchie of the Church, of Saint *Peters* ſucceſſion, of the Sea Apoſtolike, or of any ſuch matter : but that the Author of our Letter doeth brauely make mention of Saint *Peters* ſucceſſion, bringing it in compariſon with the ſucceſſion of *Henry* the eight. Of which vnapt and vnmannerly ſimilitude, I wonder he ſhould not be much aſhamed: For as to King *Henries* Succeſſour (which hee meaneth by mee) as I, I ſay, neuer did, nor will preſume to create any Article of Faith, or to bee Iudge thereof, but to ſubmit my exemplarie obedience vnto them, in as great humilitie as the meaneſt of the land : ſo if the Pope could bee as well able to prooue his either Perſonall or Doctrinall Succeſſion from Saint *Peter*, as I am able to prooue my lineall deſcent from the Kings of *England* and *Scotland*, there had neuer beene ſo long adoe, nor ſo much ſturre kept about this queſtion in Chriſtendome ; neither had [2] Maſter *Bellarmine* himſelfe needed to haue beſtowed ſo many ſheetes of paper *De ſummo Pontifice*, in his great bookes of Controuerſies : And when all is done, to conclude with a morall certitude, and a *piè credendum* ; bringing in the [3] Popes, that are

Z 3

[1] Mat. 11.17.

No deciſion of any point of Religion in the Oath of Allegiance.

[2] Bellar. de Rom Pont. li. 4. cap. 6.
Ibid. l. 2. ca. 12.
[3] Idem ibid. lib. 2. cap. 14.

are parties in this caufe, to be his witneffes : and yet their hiftoricall narration muft bee no article of Faith. And I am without vanterie fure, that I
doe farre more neerely imitate the worthie actions of my Predeceffours,
then the *Popes* in our aage can be well proued to be *fimiles Petro*, efpecially
in curfing of Kings, and fetting free their Subiects from their Allegiance
vnto them.

But now wee come to his ftrongeft argument, which is, That he would
alledge vpon mee a Panicke terrour, as if I were poffeffed with a needleffe
feare : For, faith the Cardinall, *from the beginning of the Churches firft infancie, euen to this day, where was it euer heard, that euer a* Pope *either commanded to bee killed, or allowed the flaughter of any* Prince *whatfoeuer, whether hee
were an Hereticke, an Ethnicke, or Perfecutour ?* But firft, wherefore doeth he
here wilfully, and of purpofe omit the reft of the points mentioned in
that Oath, for depofing, degrading, ftirring vp of armes, or rebelling
againft them, which are as well mentioned in that Oath, as the killing of
them ? as beeing all of one confequence againft a King, no Subiect beeing
fo fcrupulous, as that hee will attempt the one, and leaue the other vn-
performed if hee can. And yet furely I cannot blame him for paffing it
ouer, fince he could not otherwife haue efchewed the direct belying of
himfelfe in tearmes, which hee now doeth but in fubftance and effect : For
[1] as for the *Popes* depofing and degrading of Kings, hee maketh fo braue
vaunts and bragges of it in his former bookes, as he could neuer with ciuill
honeftie haue denied it here.

But to returne to the *Popes* allowing of killing of Kings, I know not
with what face hee can fet fo ftout a deniall vpon it againft his owne
knowledge. How many Emperours did the *Pope* raife warre againft in
their owne bowels ? Who as they were ouercome in battaile, were fubiect
to haue beene killed therein, which I hope the *Pope* could not but haue allowed, when he was fo farre inraged at [2] *Henry* the fifth for giuing buriall
to his fathers dead corpes, after the [3] *Pope* had ftirred him vp to rebell a-
gainft his father, and procured his ruine. But leauing thefe olde Hiftories
to *Bellarmines* owne bookes, that doe moft authentically cite them, as I
haue already faid, let vs turne our eyes vpon our owne time, and therein remember what a Panegyricke [4] Oration was made by the *Pope*, in praife
and approbation of the Frier and his fact, that murthered king *Henry* the
third of *France*, who was fo farre from either being Hereticke, Ethnicke, or
Perfecutor in their account, that the faid *Popes* owne wordes in that Oration are, *That a trew Frier hath killed a counterfeit Frier.* And befides that vehement Oration and congratulation for that fact, how neere it fcaped, that
the faid Frier was not canonized for that glorious act, is better knowen to
Bellarmine and his followers, then to vs here.

But fure I am, if fome Cardinals had not beene more wife and circum-
fpect in that errand, then the *Pope* himfelfe was, the *Popes* owne Kalender
of his Saints would haue fufficiently proued *Bellarmin* a lier in this cafe. And

to

Marginal notes:

The Cardinals weightieft Argument.

[1] *Bellarm. de Rom. Pont. lib. 5. cap. 8. et lib. 3. cap. 16.*

[2] *Gotfrid. Viterb. Helmod. Cufpinian.*
[3] *Pafchal. 2.*

[4] See the Oration of *Sixtus Quintus*, made in the Confiftory vpon the death of *Henry* the 3.

to draw yet neerer vnto our selues; how many practises and attempts were made against the late Queenes life, which were directly enioyned to those Traitours by their Confessors, and plainly authorized by the *Popes* allowance? For verification whereof, there needs no more proofe, then that neuer *Pope* either then or since, called any Church-man in question for medling in any those treasonable conspiracies; nay, the Cardinals owne S. *Sanderus* mentioned in his Letter, could well verifie this trewth, if hee were aliue; and who will looke his bookes, will finde them filled with no other doctrine then this. And what difference there is betweene the killing, or allowing the slaughter of Kings, and the stirring vp and approbation of practises to kill them; I remit to *Bellarmines* owne iudgement. It may then very clearely appeare, how strangely this Authors passion hath made him forget himselfe, by implicating himselfe in so strong a contradiction against his owne knowledge and conscience, against the witnesse of his former bookes, and against the practise of our owne times. But who can wonder at this contradiction of himselfe in this point, when his owne great Volumes are so filled with contradictions? which when either he, or any other shall euer bee able to reconcile, I will then beleeue that hee may easily reconcile this impudent strong deniall of his in his Letter, of any *Popes* medling against Kings, with his owne former bookes, as I haue already said.

And that I may not seeme to imitate him in affirming boldly that which I no wayes prooue; I will therefore send the Reader to looke for witnesses of his contradictions, in such places here mentioned in his owne booke. In his bookes of [1] Iustification, there he affirmeth, *That for the vncertaintie of our owne proper righteousnesse, and for auoiding of vaine-glory, it is most sure and safe, to repose our whole confidence in the alone mercy and goodnesse of God;* [2] Which proposition of his, is directly contrary to the discourse, and current of all his fiue bookes *de Iustificatione,* wherein the same is contained.

God doeth not encline a man to euill, either [3] *naturally or morally.*

Presently after, hee affirmeth the contrary, *That God doeth not encline to euill naturally, but* [4] *morally.*

All the Fathers teach constantly, *That* [5] *Bishops doe succeed the Apostles, and Priests the seuentie disciples.*

Elsewhere he affirmeth the contrary, *That* [6] *Bishops doe not properly succeede the Apostles.*

That [7] *Iudas did not beleeue.*

Contrary, *That* [8] *Iudas was iust and certainly good.*

The keeping of the [9] *Law according to the substance of the worke, doeth require that the Commandement be so kept, that sinne be not committed, and the man be not guiltie for hauing not kept the Commandement.*

Contrary, [10] *It is to be knowen, that it is not all one, to doe a good morall worke, and to keepe the Commandement according to the substance of the worke: For the Commandement may be kept according to the substance of the worke, euen with sinne;* as if

[1] *Bellar. de Iustif. lib. 5. cap. 7.*

[2] Contrary to all his fiue bookes *de Iustificatione.*

[3] *Bellar. de amiss. gra. & stat. pecca. lib. 2. c. 13.*

[4] *Ibidem paulo post.*

[5] *Bellar. de clericis, lib. 1. c. 14.*

[6] *Bellar. de Pont. l. 4. c. 25.*

[7] *Bellar. de Pont. lib. 1. c. 12.*

[8] *Bellar. de Iustif. lib. 3. c. 14.*

[9] *Bellar. de gra. & lib. arbit. lib. 5. cap. 5.*

[10] *Eodem lib. cap. 9.*

as if one should restore to his friend the thing committed to him of trust, to the end that theeues might afterward take it from him.

... [1] *Peter did not loose that faith, whereby the heart beleeueth vnto iustification.*

Contrary, [2] Peters *sinne was deadly.*

[3] *Antichrist shall be a Magician, and after the maner of other Magicians shall secretly worship the diuel.*

[4] Contrary, *He shall not admit of idolatrie : he shall hate idoles, and reedifie the Temple.*

By the words of [5] *Consecration the trew and solemne oblation is made.*

Contrary, *The sacrifice doeth not consist in the words : but in the* [6] *oblation of the thing it selfe.*

[7] *That the end of the world cannot be knowne.*

[8] Contrary , *After the death of* Antichrist , *there shall bee but fiue and fourtie dayes till the end of the world.*

[9] *That the tenne Kings shall burne the scarlet Whore, that is* Rome.

[10] Contrary, Antichrist *shall hate* Rome, *and fight against it, and burne it.*

[11] *The name of vniuersall Bishop may be vnderstood two wayes; one way, that he which is said to be vniuersall Bishop, may bee thought to be the onely Bishop of all Christian Cities; so that all others are not indeed Bishops, but onely Vicars to him, who is called vniuersall Bishop : in which sense, the* Pope *is not vniuersall Bishop.*

Contrary, *All ordinary* [12] *iurisdiction of Bishops doeth descend immediatly from the* Pope ; *and is in him , and from him is deriued to others.* Which few places I haue onely selected amongst many the like, that the discreet and iudicious Reader may discerne *ex vngue Leonem:* For when euer he is pressed with a weighty obiection, hee neuer careth, nor remembreth how his solution and answere to that, may make him gainesay his owne doctrine in some other places , so it serue him for a shift to put off the present storme withall.

But now to returne to our matter againe : Since Popes , sayeth hee, *haue neuer at any time medled against Kings, wherefore, I pray you , should onely the King of* E N G L A N D *be afraid of that, whereof neuer Christian King is, or was afraid ?* Was neuer Christian Emperour or King afraid of the *Popes?* How then were these miserable Emperours tost and turmoiled, and in the end vtterly ruined by the *Popes* : for proofe whereof I haue already cited *Bellarmines* owne bookes ? Was not the [13] Emperour afraid, who [14] waited barefooted in the frost and snow three dayes at the *Popes* gate, before he could get entrie ? Was not the [15] Emperour also afraid, [16] who was driuen to lie agroofe on his belly, and suffer another *Pope* to tread vpon his necke ? And was not another [17] Emperour afraid, [18] who was constrained in like maner to endure a third *Pope* to beat off from his head the Imperiall Crowne with his foot ? Was not [19] *Philip* afraid, being made Emperour against *Pope Innocentius* the thirds good liking, when he brake out into these words, *Either the Pope shall take the Crowne from* Philip , *or* Philip *shall take the Miter from the Pope ?* whereupon the *Pope* stirred vp *Ottho* against him, who caused

[1] Bellar. de Pont. lib 4 c.3.
[2] Bell. de Iust. lib.3.cap.14.
[3] Bell. de Rom Pontif. lib 3. cap.14.
[4] Ibid. ex sentent. Hypol. & Cyrii & cap. 12. eiusdem libri.
[5] Bell. lib.1. de missa. cap. 17.
[6] Bellar. de miss. lib.2.cap. 12.
[7] Bellar. de anim. Christ. lib.4. cap.5.
[8] Bellar. de Pont. lib.3. cap.17.
[9] Bellar. de Pont. lib.3. cap. 13.
[10] Bellar. ibid.
[11] Bellar. de Pont. lib.2. cap. 31.
[12] Bellar. de Pont. lib.2. cap. 24.

[13] Henry 4.
[14] Abbas Vrspergen. Lamb Scaff. Anno 1077. Plat. in vit. Greg.7
[15] Fredetick Barbarossa.
[16] Nauclcr. gener. 40 Iacob. Bergom. in Sup. plem. chron. Alfonf. Clacon. in vit. Alex.3.
[17] Henry 6
[18] R. Houeden in Rich. 1 Ranulph in Polycronico. lib.7.
[19] Abbas Vrspr. ad Ann. 1191 Nauc. een. 40. Cuspin. in Philippo.

caufed him to be flaine; and prefently went to *Rome*, and was crowned Emperour by the *Pope*, though afterward the *Pope* [1] depofed him too. Was not the Emperour [2] *Fredericke* afraid, when *Innocentius* the fourth excommunicated him, depriued him of his crowne, abfolued Princes of their Oath of fidelitie to him, and in *Apulia* corrupted one to giue him poifon? whereof the Emperour recouering, hee hired his baftard fonne *Manfredus* to poifon him; whereof he died. What did [3] *Alexander* the third write to the *Soldan?* That if he would liue quietly, hee fhould by fome flight murther the [4] Emperour; and to that end fent him the Emperours picture. And did not [5] *Alexander* the fixt take of the Turke *Baiazetes* two hundred thoufand crownes to kill his brother *Gemen*; or as fome call him, *Sifimus*, whom he helde captiue at *Rome?* Did hee not accept of the conditions to poyfon the man, and had his pay? Was not our [6] *Henry* the fecond afraid after the flaughter of *Thomas Becket*; that befides his going bare-footed in Pilgrimage, was whipped vp and down the Chapter-houfe like a fchoole-boy, and glad to efcape fo to? Had not this French King his great grand-father King *Iohn* reafon to be afraid, when the [7] *Pope* gaue away his king-dome of *Nauarre* to the King of *Spaine*, whereof he yet poffeffeth the beft halfe? Had not this King, his Succeffour reafon to be afraid, when he was forced to begge fo fubmiffiuely the relaxation of his Excommunication, as he was content likewife to fuffer his Ambaffadour to be whipped at *Rome* for penance? And had not the late Queene reafon to looke to her felfe, when fhe was excommunicated by *Pius Quintus*; her Subiects loofed from their fidelitie and Allegiance toward her, her Kingdome of *Ireland* giuen to the King of *Spaine*, and that famous fugitiue diuine, honoured with the like degree of a redde Hat as *Bellarmine* is, was not afhamed to publifh in Print an [8] Apologie for *Stanleys* treafon, maintaining, that by reafon of her excommunication and herefie, it was not onely lawfull for any of her Subiects, but euen they were bound in confcience to depriue her of any ftrength, which lay in their power to doe? And whether it were armies, townes, or fortreffes of hers which they had in their hands, they were ob-liged to put them in the King of *Spaine* her enemies hands, fhee no more being the right owner of any thing? But albeit it be trew, that wife men are mooued by the examples of others dangers to vfe prouidence and cau-tion, according to the olde Prouerbe, *Tum tua res agitur, paries cùm proximus ardet*: yet was I much neerlier fummoned to vfe this caution, by the pra-ctife of it in mine owne perfon.

Firft, by the fending foorth of thefe Bulles whereof I made mention al-ready, for debarring me from entrie vnto this Crowne, and Kingdome. And next after my entrie, and full poffeffion thereof, by the horrible Pow-der-treafon, which fhould haue bereft both me and mine, both of crowne and life. And howfoeuer the Pope will feeme to cleare himfelfe of any al-lowance of the faid Powder-treafon; yet can it not be denied, that his prin-cipall minifters here, and his chiefe *Mancipia* the Iefuites, were the plaine
practifers

[1] *Abbas Vrſper.*

[2] *Math. Pariſ. in Hen. 3. Petr. de Vineis, Epiſt.li.1. & 2. Cuſpin in Frider. 2.*

[3] *Vita Frede-rici Germanicè conſcripta.*

[4] *Fredericke Barbaroſſa.*

[5] *Paul. Ioulius, Hiſt.lib.2. Cuſpinian. in Baiazet.11. Guicciard.lib.2,*

[6] *Houeden, pag.308. Matth. Pariſ. in Henric 2. Walſingā, in Hypodig. Neu-ſtriæ. Ioan. Capgraue.*

[7] *Gomecius de rebus geſt.Fran. Ximenij Archi-epiſ,Tolet.lib.5.*

[8] *Card.Allens Anſwere to Stan. letter, Anno 1587.*

practisers thereof: for which the principall of them hath died confessing it, and other haue fled the Countrey for the crime; yea, some of them gone into *Italy*: and yet neither these that fled out of this Countrey for it, nor yet *Baldwine*, who though he then remained in the Low-countreys, was of counsell in it, were euer called to account for it by the Pope; much lesse punished for medling in so scandalous and enormous businesse. And now what needs so great wonder and exclamation, that *the only King of* England *feareth*: And *what other Christian King doeth, or euer did feare but hee*? As if by the force of his rhetoricke he could make me and my good Subiects to mistrust our senses, deny the Sunne to shine at midday, and not with the serpent to stop our eares to his charming, but to the plaine and visible veritie it selfe. And yet for all this wonder, he can neuer prooue mee to be troubled with such a Panicke terrour. Haue I euer importuned the Pope with any request for my securitie? Or haue I either troubled other Christian Princes my friends and allies, to intreat for me at the Popes hand? Or yet haue I begged from them any aide or assistance for my farther securitie? No. All this wondred-at feare of mine, stretcheth no further, then wisely to make distinction betweene the sheepe and goats in my owne pasture. For since, what euer the Popes part hath beene in the Powder-treason; yet certaine it is, that all these caitife monsters did to their death maintaine, that onely zeale of Religion mooued them to that horrible attempt: yea, some of them at their death, would not craue pardon at God or King for their offence; exhorting other of their followers to the like constancie. Had not wee then, and our Parliament great reason, by this Oath to set a marke of distinction betweene good Subiects, and bad? Yea, betweene Papists, though peraduenture zealous in their religion, yet otherwise ciuilly honest and good Subiects, and such terrible firebrands of hell, as would maintaine the like maximes, which these Powder-men did? Nay, could there be a more gracious part in a King, suppose I say it, towards Subiects of a contrary Religion, then by making them to take this Oath, to publish their honest fidelitie in temporal things to me their Soueraigne, and thereby to wipe off that imputation and great slander which was laide vpon the whole professours of that Religion, by the furious enterprise of these Powder-men?

And whereas for illustration of this strong argument of his, hee hath brought in for a similitude the historie of [1] *Iulian* the *Apostata* his dealing with the Christians, when as he straited them either to commit idolatrie, or to come within the compasse of treason: I would wish the authour to remember, that although a similitude may be permitted *claudicare vno pede*; yet this was a very ill chosen similitude, which is lame both of feete and hands, and euery member of the body: For I shall in fewe wordes prooue, that it agreeth in no one point saue one, with our purpose, which is, that *Iulian* was an Emperour, and I a King. First, *Iulian* was an *Apostata*, one that had renounced the whole Christian faith, which he had once professed,

profeſſed, and became an Ethnike againe, or rather an Atheiſt : whereas I am a Chriſtian, who neuer changed that Religion, that I dranke in with my milke : nor euer, I thanke G o D, was aſhamed of my profeſſion. *Iulian* dealt againſt Chriſtians onely for the profeſſion of C H R I S T E S cauſe : I deale in this cauſe with my Subiects, onely to make a diſtinction betweene trew Subiects, and falſe-hearted traitours. *Iulians* end was the ouerthrow of the Chriſtians : my onely end is, to maintaine Chriſtianitie in a peaceable gouernement. *Iulians* drift was to make them commit Idolatrie : my purpoſe is, to cauſe my Subiects to make open profeſſion of their naturall Allegiance, and ciuill Obedience. *Iulians* meanes whereby he went about it, was by craft, and inſnaring them before they were aware : my courſe in this is plaine, cleare, and voyd of all obſcuritie ; neuer refuſing leaue to any that are required to take this Oath, to ſtudy it at leiſure, and giuing them all the interpretation of it they can craue. But the greateſt diſſimilitude of all, is in this : that *Iulian* preſſed them to commit idolatrie to Idoles and Images : but as well I, as all the Subiects of my profeſſion are ſo farre from guilt in this point ; as wee are counted heretiques by you, becauſe we will not commit idolatrie. So as in the maine point of all, is the greateſt contrarietie. For, *Iulian* perſecuted the Chriſtians becauſe they would not commit idolatrie ; and ye count me a perſecutour, becauſe I will not admit idolatrie : So as to conclude this point, this old ſentence may well be applied to *Bellarmine*, in vſing ſo vnapt a ſimilitude,

Perdere quos vult Iupiter, hos dementat.

And therefore his vncharitable concluſion doeth not rightly follow : *That it ſeemeth vnto him, that ſome ſuch thing ſhould be ſubtilly or fraudulently included in this Oath* ; as if no man can deteſt Treaſon againſt the King, or profeſſe ciuill ſubiection, except hee renounce the Primacie of the Apoſtolique Sea. But how he hath ſuckt this apprehenſion out at his fingers ends, I cannot imagine : for ſure I am, as I haue oft ſaid, hee neuer goeth about to prooue it : and to anſwere an improbable imagination, is to fight againſt a vaniſhing ſhadow. It cannot be denied indeed, that many ſeruants of C H R I S T, as well Prieſts, as others, haue endured conſtantly all ſorts of torments, and death, for the profeſſion of C H R I S T : and therefore to all ſuch his examples, as hee bringeth in for verifying the ſame, I need not to giue him any other anſwere, ſaue onely to remember him, that he playeth the part of a ſophiſter in all theſe his examples of the conſtancie of Martyrs ; euer taking *Controuerſum pro confeſſo*, as if this our caſe were of the ſame nature.

But yet that the Reader may the better diſcouer, not onely how vnaptly his ſimilitudes are applied, but likewiſe how diſhoneſtly hee vſeth himſelfe in all his citations : I haue thought good to ſet downe the very places themſelues cited by him, together with a ſhort deduction of the trew ſtate of thoſe particular caſes : whereby, how little theſe examples can touch our caſe ; nay, by the contrary, how rightly their trew ſenſe may bee

vſed,

[1] 2.Maccab. chap.6.ver.18.

An anſwere to the Card. example of *Eleazar*.

vſed, as our owne weapons to be throwen backe vpon him that alledgeth them, ſhall eaſily appeare. And firſt, for [1] *Eleazar* : If the Arch-prieſt his ground of refuſing the Oath, were as good as *Eleazars* was, to forbeare to eate the ſwines fleſh, it might not vnfitly be applied by the Cardinal to this purpoſe : For as *Eleazar* was a principall Scribe, ſo is he a principall Prieſt : As *Eleazars* example had a great force in it, to animate the yonger Scribes to keepe the Lawe, or in his colourable eating it, to haue taught them to diſſemble : ſo hath the Arch-prieſts, either to make the inferiour Prieſts to take the Oath, or to refuſe it : but the ground failing, the building cannot ſtand : For what example is there in all the Scripture, in which diſobedience to the Oath of the King, or want of Allegiance is allowed ? If the Cardinall would remember, that when the Church maketh a Lawe (ſuppoſe to forbid fleſh on certaine dayes) he that refuſeth to obey it, incurreth the iuſt cenſure of the Church : If a man then ought to die rather then to breake the leaſt of Gods Ceremoniall Lawes, and to pine and ſtarue his body, rather then to violate the Church his poſitiue Law : will he not giue leaue to a man to redeeme his ſoule from ſinne, and to keepe his body from puniſhment, by keeping a Kings politike Law, and by giuing good example in his Perſon, raiſe vp a good opinion in me of like Allegiance in the inferiour of his order ? This application, as I take it, would haue better fitted this example.

[2] 1.Sam.14. 25.

But let mee remember the Cardinall of another [2] Oath inioyned by a King to his people, whereby he indangered his owne life, and hazarded the ſafetie of the whole armie, when hee made the people ſweare in the morning, not to taſte of any meate vntill night : which Oath he exacted ſo ſtrictly, that his eldeſt ſonne, and heire apparant, *Ionathan*, for breaking of it, by taſting a little hony of the top of his rodde, though he heard not when the King gaue that Oath, had well-nigh died for it. And ſhall an Oath giuen vpon ſo vrgent an occaſion as this was, for the apparant ſafetie of me and my poſteritie, forbidding my people to drinke ſo deeply in the bitter cup of Antichriſtian fornications, but that they may keepe ſo much hony in their hearts, as may argue them ſtill eſpouſed to me their Soueraigne in the maine knot of trew Allegiance ; ſhall this Law, I ſay, by him bee condemned to hell for *a ſtratageme of Sathan* ? I ſay no more, but Gods lot in the Oath of *Sauls*, and *Bellarmines* verdict vpon this Oath of ours, ſeeme not to be caſt out of one lap.

[3] *Theodoret.* lib.4.cap.19. An anſwere to the Card. example of S. Baſil.

Now to this example of [3] *Baſill*, which is (as he ſayth) ſo fit for his purpoſe : Firſt, I muſt obſerue, that if the Cardinall would leaue a common and ordinarie tricke of his in all his Citations, which is to take what makes for him, and leaue out what makes againſt him; and cite the Authours ſenſe, as well as his Sentence, we ſhould not be ſo much troubled with anſwering the Ancients which he alledgeth. To inſtance it in this very place : if he had continued his allegation one line further, hee ſhould haue found this place out of *Theodoret*, of more force to haue mooued *Blackwell* to take

take the Oath, then to haue diſſwaded him from it : For in the very next words it followeth , *Imperatoris quidem amicitiam magni ſe pendere, cum pietaat; quâ remotâ, perniciofam eſſe dicere.* But that it may appeare, whether of vs haue greateſt right to this place, I will in few words ſhew the Authours drift.

The Emperour *Valens* being an Arrian, at the perſwaſion of his wife, when he had depriued all the Churches of their Paſtours, came to *Cæſarea*, where [1] S. *Baſil* was then Biſhop, who, as the hiſtorie reporteth, was accounted the *Light of the world.* Before hee came, hee ſent his [2] deputie to worke it, that S. *Baſil* ſhould hold fellowſhip with *Eudoxius* (which [3] *Eudoxius* was biſhop of *Conſtantinople*, and the principall of the Arrian faction) or if he would not, that hee ſhould put him to baniſhment. Now when the Emperours Deputie came to *Cæſarea*, he ſent for *Baſil*, intreated him honourably, ſpake pleaſingly vnto him, deſired he would giue way to the time, neither that he would hazard the good of ſo many Churches *tenui exquiſitione dogmatis* : promiſed him the Emperours fauour , and himſelfe to be mediatour for his good. But S. *Baſill* anſwered, *Theſe intiſing ſpeeches were fit to bee vſed to children , that vſe to gape after ſuch things : but for them that were throughly inſtructed in Gods word, they could neuer ſuffer any ſyllable thereof to be corrupted : Nay, if need required, they would for the maintenance thereof refuſe no kind of death. Indeed the loue of the Emperour ought to bee greatly eſteemed with pietie; but pietie taken away, it was pernicious.*

This is the trewth of the hiſtorie. Now compare the caſe of *Baſill* with the Arch-prieſts: *Baſill* was ſollicited to become an Arrian: the Arch-prieſt not once touched for any article of faith. *Baſill* would haue obeyed the Emperour, but that the word of GOD forbade him : this man is willed to obey, becauſe the word of GOD commandeth him. *Baſill* highly eſteemed the Emperours fauour, if it might haue ſtood with pietie : the Arch-prieſt is exhorted to reiect it , though it ſtand with trew godlineſſe in deed, to embrace it. But that he may lay load vpon the Arch-prieſt, it is not ſufficient to exhort him to courage and conſtancie by *Eleazarus* and *Baſils* examples; but he muſt be vtterly caſt downe with the comparing his fall to S. *Peter*, and *Marcellinus* : which two mens caſes were the moſt fearefull, conſidering their perſons and places, that are to be found, or read of, either in all the bookes of diuine Scripture ; or the volumes of Eccleſiaſticall hiſtories ; the one denying the onely trew GOD, the other our Lord and Sauiour IESVS CHRIST ; the one ſacrificing to Idoles, with the prophane heathen: the other forſwearing his Lord and Maſter, with the hard-hearted *Iewes.* Vnleſſe the Cardinall would driue the Arch-prieſt to ſome horrour of conſcience, and pit of deſpaire, I know not what he can meane by this compariſon : For ſure I am, all that are not intoxicated with their cup, cannot but wonder to heare of an Oath of Allegiance to a naturall Soueraigne, to be likened to an *Apoſtats* denying of God, and forſwearing of his Sauiour.

But to let paſſe the *Diſdiapaſon* of the caſes (as his ill-fauoured coupling

A a S. *Peter*

[1] *Theodoret. lib. 4 cap. 19.*

[2] *Modeſtus* as *Nazianzen* vpõ the death of *Baſill* calleth him in his oration.

[3] Looke cap. 12. *eiuſdem libri.*

The Cardinall aſſimilating of the Archpr. caſe to S. *Peters*, and *Marcellinus*, conſidered.

¹ Looke Pla-
tina in vita
Marcellini.
² Concil.Tom.
I.pag.222.
Looke Bro-
nius,Ann.302.
num.96.

S. *Peter* the head of their Church, with an apoſtate Pope) I marueile hee would remember this example of ¹ *Marcellinus*, ſince his brother Cardinall *Baronius*, and the late Edition of the Councels by ² *Binnius* ſeeme to call the credit of the whole hiſtorie into queſtion, ſaying, *That it might plainely be refuted, and that it is probably to be ſhewed, that the ſtory is but obreptious*, but that he would not ſwarue from the common receiued opinion.

See Tom.1.
Concil.in Act.
Concil.Sinuess.

And if a man might haue leaue to coniecture; ſo would his Cardinal-ſhip too, if it were not for one or two ſentences in that Councell of *Si-nueſſa*, which ſerued for his purpoſe; namely, that *Prima ſedes à nemine iudicatur*: And, *Iudica cauſam tuam*: *noſtrâ ſententiâ non condemnaberis*. But to what purpoſe a great Councell (as he termes it) of three hundred Biſhops and others, ſhould meete together, who before they met, knew they could doe nothing; when they were there, did nothing, but like Cuckowes, ſing ouer and ouer the ſame ſong: that, *Prima ſedes à nemine iudicatur*; and ſo af-ter three dayes ſitting (a long time indeed for a great and graue Councell) brake ſo bluntly vp: and yet, that there ſhould be ſeuentie two witneſſes brought againſt him, and that they ſhould ſubſcribe his excommunicati-on, and that at his owne mouth hee tooke the *Anathema maranatha*: how theſe vntoward contradictions ſhall be made to agree, I muſt ſend the Car-dinall to *Venice*, to *Padre Paulo*, who in his ³ Apologie againſt the Cardi-nals oppoſitions, hath handled them very learnedly.

³ Apol.Pat.
Paul.aduerſus
oppoſit.Card.
Bellar.
An anſwere
to the place
alledged out
of S. Gregory.
⁴ Greg.lib.11.
cap.42.
⁵ Beda Eccleſ.
Hiſt.gen.Ang.
lib.1 cap.25.

But from one Pope, let vs paſſe to another: (for, what a principall arti-cle of Faith and Religion this Oath is, I haue alreadie ſufficiently proued.) Why hee called S. ⁴ *Gregory* our Apoſtle, I know not, vnleſſe perhaps it be, for that hee ſent ⁵ *Auguſtine* the Monke and others with him into England, to conuert vs to the faith of Chriſt, wherein I wiſh the *Popes* his ſucceſ-ſours would follow his patterne: For albeit hee ſent them by diuine reue-lation (as hee ſaid) into England vnto King *Ethelbert*; yet when they came, they exerciſed no part of their function, but by the Kings leaue and

⁶ Beda Eccleſi.
Hiſt.gen.Ang.
lib.1.cap.4.

permiſſion. So did King ⁶ *Lucius* ſend to *Eleutherius* his predeceſſour, and hee ſent him diuers Biſhops, who were all placed by the Kings au-thoritie. Theſe conuerted men to the faith, and taught them to obey the King. And if the *Popes* in theſe dayes would but inſiſt in theſe ſteppes of their fore-fathers; then would they not entertaine Princes fugitiues a-broad, nor ſend them home, not onely without my leaue, but directly againſt the Lawes, with plots of treaſon and doctrine of rebellion, to draw Subiects from their obedience to me their naturall King: nor be ſo cruell to their owne *Mancipia*, as returning them with theſe wares, put either a State in iealouſie of them; or them in hazard of their owne liues. Now to our Apoſtle (ſince the Cardinall will haue him ſo called) I perſwade my ſelfe I ſhould doe a good ſeruice to the Church in this my labour, if I could but reape this one fruit of it, to moue the Cardinall to deale faithfully with the Fathers, & neuer to alledge their opinions againſt their own pur-

⁷ Greg.lib.11.
cap 42.

poſe: For, this letter of *Gregorius* was written to *Iohn* Biſhop of ⁷ *Palermo* in
Sicily,

Sicily, to whom he granted *vfum pallij*, to be worne in fuch times, and in fuch order as the Prieſts in the Ile of *Sicily*, and his predeceſſors were wont to vſe: and withall giueth him a caueat, *That the reuerence to the Apoſtolike Sea, be not diſturbed by the preſumption of any: for then the ſtate of the members doeth remaine found, when the head of the Faith is not bruiſed by any iniury, and the authoritie of the Canons alwayes remaine ſafe and ſound.*

Now let vs examine the words. The Epiſtle was written to a Biſhop, eſpecially to grant him the vſe of the Pall; a ceremonie and matter indiffe-rent. As it appeareth, the Biſhop of *Rome* tooke it well at his hands, that he would not preſume to take it vpon him without leaue from the Apoſto-like Sea, giuing him that admonition which followeth in the wordes al-ledged out of him: which doctrine we are ſo farre from impugning, that we altogether approoue and allow of the fame, that whatſoeuer ceremony for order is thought meet by the Chriſtian Magiſtrate, and the Church, the fame ought inuiolably to be kept: and where the head and gouernour in matters of that nature are not obeyed, the members of that Church muſt needs run to helliſh confuſion: But that *Gregory* by that terme, *caput fidei*, held himſelfe the head of our faith, and the head of all religion, cannot ſtand with the courſe of his doctrine and writings: For firſt, when an [1] other would haue had this ſtile to be called *Vniuerſalis Epiſcopus*, hee ſaid, [2] *I doe confidently auouch, that whoſoeuer calleth himſelfe, or deſireth to be called Vniuer-ſall Biſhop, in this aduancing of himſelfe, is the fore-runner of the Antichriſt*: which notwithſtanding was a ſtile farre inferiour to that of *Caput fidei*. And when it was offered to himſelfe, the wordes of S. *Gregory* be theſe, refuſing that Title: [3] *None of my predeceſſours* [Biſhops of Rome,] *euer conſented to vſe this prophane name* [of vniuerſall Biſhop.] *None of my predeceſſours euer tooke vpon him this name of ſingularitie, neither conſented to vſe it, Wee the Biſhops of* Rome *doe not ſeeke, nor yet accept this glorious title, being offered vnto vs.* And now, I pray you, would he that refuſed to be called Vniuerſall Biſhop, be ſtiled *Caput fidei*, vnleſſe it were in that ſenſe, as I haue expreſſed? which ſenſe if he will not admit, giue me leaue to ſay that of *Gregorie*, which him-ſelfe ſayth of [4] *Lyra, Minus cautè locutus eſt*: or which he elſewhere ſayth of *Chryſoſtome*, [5] *Locutus eſt per exceſſum.* To redeeme therefore our Apoſtle out of his hands, and to let him remaine ours, and not his in this caſe; it is very trew that he ſayth in that ſenſe he ſpake it. When yee goe about to di-ſturbe, diminiſh, or take away the authoritie or ſupremacie of the Church, which reſteth on the head of the King, within his dominions, ye cut off the head and chiefe gouernour thereof, and diſturbe the ſtate and members of the whole body. And for a concluſion of this point, I pray him to think, that we are ſo well perſwaded of the good minde of our Apoſtle S. *Gregory* to vs, that wee deſire no other thing to be ſuggeſted to the Pope and his Cardinals, then our Apoſtle S. *Gregory* deſired [6] *Sabinian* to ſuggeſt vnto the Emperour and the State in his time. His words be theſe: *One thing there is, of which I would haue you ſhortly to ſuggeſt to your moſt noble Lord and*

Maſter:

[1] Iohn of Con-ſtantinople. See *Greg.lib.4. Epſl 32.*
[2] *Lib. 6. Epiſt.* 30.

[3] *Greg.l.b.4. epiſt.32. & 36.*

[4] *Bellar.de Rom.Pont.lib.* 2.cap 10.
[5] *Idem lib.2. de Miſſa,cap.10.*

[6] *Greg.l.b.7. Epiſt.1.*

Master : That if I his seruant would haue had my hand in slaying of the Lombards, at this day the Nation of the Lombards had neither had King, nor Dukes, nor Earles, and had beene diuided asunder in vtter confusion : but because I feare God, I dread to haue my hand in the blood of any man.

And thus hauing answered to S. *Gregory*, I come to another Pope, his Apostle, S. *Leo*. And that hee may see, I haue not in the former citations, quarelled him like a Sophister for contention sake, but for finding out of

the trewth, I doe grant, that the authorities out of 1 *Leo*, are rightly alledged all three, the wordes trewly set downe, together with his trew intent and purpose : but withall, let me tell him, and I appeale vnto his owne conscience, whether I speake not trewly, that what *Tullie* said to 2 *Hortensius*, when he did immoderately praise eloquence, that hee would haue lift her

vp to Heauen, that himselfe might haue gone vp with her; So his S. *Leo* lift vp S. *Peter* with praises to the skie, that he being his 3 heire, might haue gone vp with him : For his S. *Leo* was a great Oratour, who by the power of his eloquence redeemed *Rome* from fire, when both 4 *Attilas* and *Gensericus* would haue burnt it.

Some fruites of this rhetoricke hee bestowed vpon S. *Peter*, saying, *The Lord 5 did take Peter into the fellowship of the indiuisible vnitie* : which wordes being coupled to the sentence alledged by the Cardinall (*that he hath no part in the diuine Mysterie, that dare depart from the soliditie of Peter*) should haue giuen him, I thinke, such a skarre, as hee should neuer haue dared to haue taken any aduantage by the wordes immediatly preceding, for the benefite of the Church of *Rome*, and the head thereof; since those which immediatly follow, are so much derogatorie to the diuine Maiestie. And a-

gaine, *My 6 writings be strengthened by the authoritie and merit of my Lord, most blessed S. Peter. We 7 beseech you to keepe the things decreed by vs through the inspiration of God, and the Apostle most blessed S. Peter. If 8 any thing be well done, or decreed by vs ; If any thing be obtained of Gods mercy by daily prayers, it is to be ascribed to S. Peters workes and merits, whose power doeth liue, and authoritie*

excell in his owne Sea. Hee 9 was so plentifully watered of the very fountaine of all graces, that whereas he receiued many things alone, yet nothing passeth ouer to any other, but hee was partaker of it. And in a word, hee was so desirous to ex-

toll Saint Peter, that a messenger from him was an 10 *embassage from* Saint Peter : 11 *any thing done in his presence, was in* S. Peters *presence*. Neither did he vse all this Rhetoricke without purpose : for at that time the Patriarch of *Constantinople* contended with him for Primacie. And in the Councell

of 12 *Chalcedon*, the Bishops, sixe hundred and more, gaue equall authoritie to the Patriarch of that Sea, and would not admit any Priuiledge to the Sea of *Rome* aboue him ; but went against him. And yet he that gaue so much to *Peter*, tooke nothing from *Cæsar*; but gaue him both his Titles and

due, giuing the power of calling a Councell to the Emperour; as it may appeare by these one or two places following of many. *If it may please your* 13 *godlinesse to vouchsafe at our supplication to condiscend, that you will comman*

a Coun

a Councell of Bishops to be holden within Italy. And writing vnto the Bishop of Conftantinople: *Becaufe the moft clement* [1] *Emperour, carefull of the peace of the Church, will haue a Councell to be holden; albeit it euidently appeare, the matter to be handled doeth in no cafe ftand in neede of a Councell.* And againe, *Albeit* [2] *my occafions will not permit me to be prefent vpon the day of the Councell of Bishops, which your godlineffe hath appointed.* So as by this it may well appeare, that hee that gaue fo much to *Peter*, gaue alfo to *Cæfar* his due and prerogatiue. But yet he playeth not faire play in this, that euen in all thefe his wrong applied arguments and examples, hee produceth no other witneffes, but the parties themfelues; bringing euer the *Popes* fentences for approbation of their owne authoritie.

Now indeed for one word of his in the middeft of his examples, I cannot but greatly commend him; that is, that Martyrs ought to endure all forts of tortures and death, before they fuffer one fyllable to be corrupted of the Law of God. Which leffon, if hee and all the reft of his owne profeffion would apply to themfelues, then would not the Sacrament be adminiftred *fub vnâ fpecie*, directly contrary to Chrifts inftitution, the practife of the Apoftles and of the whole Primitiue Church for many hundred yeeres: then would not the priuate Maffes be in place of the Lordes Supper: then would not the words of the [3] Canon of the Maffe be oppofed to the words of S. *Paul* and S. *Luke*, as our Aduerfarie himfelfe confeffeth, and cannot reconcile them: nor then would not fo many hundreths other traditions of men be fet vp in their Church, not onely as equall, but euen preferred to the word of God. But fure in this point I feare I haue miftaken him: for I thinke hee doeth not meane by his *Diuina Dogmata*, the word of the God of heauen, but onely the Canons and Lawes of his *Dominus Deus Papa*: otherwife all his Primacie of the Apoftolike Sea would not be fo much fticken vpon, hauing fo flender ground in the word of God.

And for the great feare he hath, that the fuddennes of the apprehenfion, the bitterneffe of the perfecution, the weakneffe of his aage, and other fuch infirmities might haue been the caufe of the Arch-priefts fall; in this, I haue already fufficiently anfwered him; hauing declared, as the trewth is, and as the faid *Blackwell* himfelfe will yet teftifie, that he tooke this Oath freely of himfelfe, without any inducement thereunto, either *Precibus* or *Minis*.

But amongft all his citations, hee muft not forget holy *Sanderus* and his *vifibilis Monarchia*, whofe perfon and actions I did alreadie a little touch. And furely who will with vnpartiall eyes reade his bookes, they may well thinke, that hee hath deferued well of his Englifh Romane-Church; but they can neuer thinke, but that hee deferued very ill of his Englifh Soueraigne and State: Witneffe his owne books; whereout I haue made choice to fet downe heere thefe fewe fentences following, as flowers pickt out of fo worthy a garland. [4] *Elizabeth Queene of* E N G L A N D, *doeth exercife the Prieftly acte of teaching and preaching the Gofpel in* E N G L A N D, *with no leffe authority then Chrift himfelfe, or Mofes euer did. The fupremacie of a* [5] *woman in*

Aa 3   Church

Margin notes:
[1] *Epift. 18. Flau.*
[2] *Epift. 17. Theodofio.*
[3] *Bellar. de facra Eucharift. lib. 4. cap 14.*
Some of Sanders his worthy fayings remembred.
[4] *Sand. de vifib. Monar. lib. 6. cap. 4.*
[5] *Sand. de claue Dauid. li. 6. c. 1.*

¹ *Sand. de vi-sib. Monar. lib. 2 cap. 4.*

² *Ibidem.*

³ *Ibidem.*

⁴ *Ibidem.*

⁵ *Sand. de clau. Dauid. l. 5.s. 2.*

⁶ *Ibidem.*

⁷ *Sand. de clau. Dauid. li. 5. c. 4.*

The Cardinals paire of Martyrs weighed.

⁸ Called *Elizabeth Barton.* See the Act of Parliament.

Church matters is from no other, then from the Deuill. And of all things in generall thus he speaketh, *The* ¹ *King that will not inthrall himselfe to the Popes authoritie, he ought not to be tolerated; but his Subiects ought to giue all diligence, that another may be chosen in his place assoone as may be. A King that is an* ² *Heretike, ought to be remooued from the Kingdome that hee holdeth ouer Christians; and the Bishops ought to endeauour to set vp another, assoone as possibly they can.* Wee doe constantly ³ *affirme, that all Christian Kings are so farre vnder Bishops and Priests in all matters appertaining to faith, that if they shall continue in a fault against Christian Religion, after one or two admonitions, obstinately, for that cause they may and ought to be deposed by the Bishops from their temporall authoritie they holde ouer Christians.* ⁴ *Bishops are set ouer temporall kingdomes, if those kingdomes doe submit themselues to the faith of Christ.* We doe iustly ⁵ *affirme, that all Secular power, whether Regall, or any other, is of men.* The ⁶ *anoynting which is powred vpon the head of the King by the Priest, doeth declare that hee is inferiour to the Priest. It is altogether against the will of* ⁷ *Christ, that Christian kings should haue supremacie in the Church.*

And whereas for the crowne and conclusion of all his examples, he reckoneth his two English Martyrs, *Moore* and *Roffensis*, who died for that one most weightie head of doctrine, as he alledgeth, refusing the Oath of Supremacie; I must tell him, that he hath not been well informed in some materiall points, which doe very neerely concerne his two said Martyrs: For it is cleare and apparantly to be prooued by diuers Records, that they were both of them committed to the Tower about a yeere before either of them was called in question vpon their liues, for the *Popes* Supremacie; And that partly for their backwardnesse in the point of the establishment of the Kings succession, whereunto the whole Realme had subscribed, and partly for that one of them, to wit, *Fisher,* had had his hand in the matter of the holy ⁸ maide of *Kent*; hee being for his concealement of that false prophets abuse, found guiltie of misprision of Treason. And as these were the principall causes of their imprisonment (the King resting secure of his Supremacie, as the Realme stood then affected, but especially troubled for setling the Crowne vpon the issue of his second mariage) so was it easily to be conceiued, that being thereupon discontented, their humors were thereby made apt to draw them by degrees, to further opposition against the King and his authoritie, as indeede it fell out: For in the time of their being in prison, the Kings lawfull authoritie in cases Ecclesiasticall being published and promulged, as well by a generall decree of the Clergie in their Synode, as by an Acte of Parliament made thereupon; they behaued themselues so peeuishly therein, as the olde coales of the Kings anger being thereby raked vp of new, they were againe brought in question; as well for this one most weighty head of doctrine of the *Pope* his supremacy, as for the matter of the Kings mariage and succession, as by the confession of one of themselues, euen *Thomas Moore,* is euident: For being condemned, he vsed these words at the barre before the Lords, *Non ignoro cur me morti*

Histor. aliquot Martyrum nostri seculi, Anno 1550.

morti adiudicaueritis ; videlicet ob id , quòd nunquam voluerim assentiri in negotio matrimonij Regis. That is, *I am not ignorant why you haue adiudged mee to death: to wit, for that I would neuer consent in the businesse of the new mariage of the King.* By which his owne confession it is plaine, that this great martyr himselfe tooke the cause of his owne death, to be onely for his being refractary to the King in this said matter of Marriage and Succession ; which is but a very fleshly cause of Martyrdome, as I conceiue.

And as for *Roffensis* his fellow Martyr (who could haue bene content to haue taken the Oath of the Kings Supremacie, with a certaine modification, which *Moore* refused) as his imprisonment was neither onely, nor principally for the cause of Supremacie, so died hee but a halting and a singular Martyr or witnesse for that most weighty head of doctrine; the whole Church of *England* going at that time, in one current and streame as it were against him in that Argument, diuers of them being of farre greater reputation for learning and sound iudgement, then euer he was. So as in this point we may well arme our selues with the Cardinals owne reason, where he giueth amongst other notes of the trew Church, *Vniuersalitie* for one, wee hauing the generall and Catholique conclusion of the whole Church of *England*, on our side in this case, as appeareth by their booke set out by the whole Conuocation of *England*, called, *The Institution of a Christian man*; the same matter being likewise very learnedly handled by diuers particular learned men of our Church, as by *Steuen Gardiner* in his booke *De vera obedientia*, with a Preface of Bishop *Boners* adioyning to it, *De summo & absoluto Regis Imperio*, published by M. *Bekinsaw*, *De vera differentia Regiæ Potestatis & Ecclesiastica*, Bishop *Tonstals* Sermon, Bishop *Longlands* Sermon, the letter of *Tonstall* to Cardinall *Poole*, and diuers other both in English and Latine. And if the bitternesse of *Fishers* discontentment had not bene fed with his dayly ambitious expectation of the Cardinals hat, which came so neere as *Calis* before he lost his head to fill it with, I haue great reason to doubt, if he would haue constantly perseuered in induring his Martyrdome for that one most waighty head of doctrine.

And surely these two Captaines and ringleaders to Martyrdome were but ill followed by the rest of their countreymen : for I can neuer reade of any after them, being of any great accompt, and that not many, that euer sealed that weighty head of doctrine with their blood in *England*. So as the trew causes of their first falling in trouble (whereof I haue already made mention) being rightly considered vpon the one part ; and vpon the other the scant number of witnesses, that with their blood sealed it (a point so greatly accompted of by our Cardinal) there can but smal glory redound thereby to our English nation, these onely two, *Enoch* and *Elias*, seruing for witnesses against our Antichristian doctrine.

And I am sure the Supremacie of Kings may, & wil euer be better maintained by the word of God (which must euer be the trew rule to discerne all waighty heads of doctrine by) to be the trew and proper office of Christian

Kings

The Supremacy of Kings sufficiently warranted by the Scriptures.

[1] 2.Chron.
19.4.
[2] 2.Sam.5.6.
[3] 1.Chron.
13.11.
[4] 2.Sam.6.16
[5] 1 Chron.
28.6.
[6] 2.Chron.6.
[7] 2.King. 22.
11.
[8] Nehe.9.38.
Dauid.
Salomon.
[9] 2.King.18.4
[10] 1.King. 15.
12. 2.king.
13.4.
[11] 2.Chron.
17.8,
[12] 1.King.2.27
[13] 2.Sam.7.14
[14] Psal.82.6.
& exod.22.8.
[15] 1.Sam.24.
11.
[16] 1.Chro.9.8.
[17] 2. Chro.6.
15.
[18] 2.Sam.14.
20.
[19] 1.Sam.13.
14.
[20] 1.Sam.21.
17.
[21] Isa. 49.23.
[22] Rom.13.5.
[23] 1.Tim.2.2.
[24] Rom.13.4.
[25] 1.Pet.2.13.
[26] Rom.13.7.
[27] Mat.22.21.
[28] Iohn 18.36.
[29] Luk. 12.14.
[30] Luk.22.25.

Kings in their owne dominions, then he will be euer able to maintaine his annihilating Kings, and their authorities, together with his bafe and vnreuerend fpeaches of them, wherewith both his former great Volumes, and his late Bookes againft *Venice* are filled. In the old Teftament, Kings were directly [1] Gouernours oüer the Church within their Dominions, [2] purged their corruptions; reformed their abuſes, brought the [3] Arke to her reſting place, the King [4] dancing before it; [5] built the Temple; [6] dedicated the ſame, aſſiſting in their owne perſons to the ſanctification thereof; [7] made the Booke of the Law new-found, to bee read to the people; [8] renewed the Couenant betweene God and his people; [9] bruiſed the braſen ſerpent in pieces, which was ſet vp by the expreſſe commandement of God, and was a figure of Chriſt; deſtroyed [10] all Idoles, and falſe gods; made [11] a publike reformation, by a Commiſſion of Secular men and Prieſts mixed for that purpoſe; depoſed [12] the high Prieſt, and ſet vp another in his place: and generally, ordered euery thing belonging to the Church-gouernment, their Titles and Prerogatiues giuen them by God, agreeing to theſe their actions. They are called *the* [13] *Sonnes of the moſt High*, nay, *Gods* [14] *themſelues; The* [15] *Lords anoynted, Sitting* [16] *in Gods throne; His* [17] *ſeruants; The Angels* [18] *of God; According to his* [19] *hearts deſire; The light* [20] *of Iſrael; The* [21] *nurſing fathers of the Church*, with innumerable ſuch ſtiles of honour, wherwith the old Teſtament is filled; whereof our aduerſary can pretend no ignorance. And as to the new Teſtament, *Euery ſoule is* commaunded *to be ſubiect vnto them, euen for* [22] *conſcience ſake.* All men [23] muſt be prayed for; *but eſpecially Kings, and thoſe that are in Authoritie, that vnder them we may leade a godly, peaceable, and an honeſt life.*

The [24] *Magiſtrate is the miniſter of God, to doe vengeance on him that doëth euill, and reward him that doeth well. Ye muſt obey all higher powers, but* [25] *eſpecially Princes, and thoſe that are ſupereminent. Giue euery man his due, feare* [26] *to whom feare belongeth, and honour to whome honour. Giue* [27] *vnto Cæſar what is Cæſars, and to God what is Gods.* [28] *Regnum meum non eſt huius mundi.* [29] *Quis me conſtituit Iudicem ſuper vos?* [30] *Reges gentium dominantur eorum, vos autem non ſic.* If theſe examples, ſentences, titles, and prerogatiues, and innumerable other in the Olde and New Teſtament doe not warrant Chriſtian Kings, within their owne dominions, to gouerne their Church, as well as the reſt of their people, in being *Cuſtodes vtriuſque Tabulæ*, not by making new Articles of Faith, (which is the Popes office, as I ſaid before) but by commanding obedience to be giuen to the word of God, by reforming the religion according to his preſcribed will, by aſſiſting the ſpirituall power with the temporall ſword, by reforming of corruptions, by procuring due obedience to the Church, by iudging, and cutting off all friuolous queſtions

[31] Euſeb. lib. 3.
de vita Conſtantini.

and ſchiſmes, as [31] *Conſtantine* did; and finally, by making *decorum* to be obſerued in euery thing, and eſtabliſhing orders to bee obſerued in all indifferent things for that purpoſe, which is the onely intent of our Oath of Supremacie: If this Office of a King, I ſay, doe not agree with the power
giuen

giuen him by Gods word, let any indifferent man voyd of paſſion, iudge. But how theſe honourable offices, ſtyles, and prerogatiues giuen by God to Kings in the Old and New Teſtament, as I haue now cited, can agree with the braue ſtyles and titles that *Bellarmine* giueth them, I can hardly conceiue.

1   That *Kings are rather ſlaues then Lords.*

2   That *they are not onely ſubiects to Popes, to Biſhops, to Prieſts, but euen to Deacons.*

3   That *an Emperour muſt content himſelfe to drinke, not onely after a Biſhop, but after a Biſhops Chaplen.*

4   That *Kings haue not their Authoritie nor Office immediatly from God, nor his Law, but onely from the Law of Nations.*

5   That *Popes haue degraded many Emperours, but neuer Emperour degraded the Pope; nay, euen* Biſhops *, that are but the Popes vaſſals, may depoſe Kings, and abrogate their lawes.*

6   That *Church-men are ſo farre aboue Kings, as the ſoule is aboue the body.*

7   That *Kings may be depoſed by their people, for diuers reſpects.*

8   But *Popes can by no meanes be depoſed : for no fleſh hath power to iudge of them.*

9   That *obedience due to the Pope, is for conſcience ſake.*

10   But *the obedience due to Kings, is onely for certaine reſpects of order and policie.*

11   That *theſe very Church-men that are borne, and inhabite in Soueraigne Princes countreys, are notwithſtanding not their Subiects, and cannot bee iudged by them, although they may iudge them.*

12   And, that *the obedience that Church-men giue to Princes, euen in the meaneſt and meere temporall things, is not by way of any neceſſarie ſubiection, but onely out of diſcretion, and for obſeruation of good order and cuſtome.*

Theſe contrarieties betweene the Booke of God, and *Bellarmines* bookes, haue I heere ſet in oppoſition each to other, *Vt ex contrariis iuxta ſe poſitis, veritas magis eluceſcere poſſit.* And thus farre I dare boldly affirme, that whoſoeuer will indifferently weigh theſe irreconciliable contradictions here ſet downe, will eaſily confeſſe, that CHRIST is no more contrarie to Belial, light to darkneſſe, and heauen to hell, then *Bellarmines* eſtimation of Kings, is to Gods.

Now as to the concluſion of his letter, which is onely filled with ſtrong and pithie exhortations, to perſwade and confirme *Blackwell* to the patient and conſtant induring of martyrdome, I haue nothing to anſwere, ſaue by way of regrate ; that ſo many good ſentences drawen out of the Scripture, ſo well and ſo handſomely packed vp together, ſhould be ſo ill and vntrewly applied : But an euill cauſe is neuer the better for ſo good a cloake ; and an ill matter neuer amended by good wordes : And therefore I may iuſtly turne ouer that craft of the diuell vpon himſelfe, in vſing ſo holy-like an exhortation to ſo euill a purpoſe. Onely I could haue wiſhed him, that hee had

had a little better obserued his *decorum* herein, in not letting slippe two or three prophane words amongst so many godly mortified Scripture sentences. For in all the Scripture, especially in the New Testament, I neuer read of *Pontifex Maximus*. And the Pope must be content in that style to succeed according to the Law and institution of *Numa Pompilius*, and not to *S. Peter*, who neuer heard nor dreamed of such an Office.

And for his *Caput fidei*, which I remembred before, the Apostles (I am sure) neuer gaue that style to any, but to CHRIST: So as these styles, whereof some were neuer found in Scripture, and some were neuer applyed but to CHRIST in that sense, as hee applieth it, had beene better to haue beene left out of so holy and mortified a letter.

To conclude then this present Discourse, I heartily wish all indifferent readers of the *Breues* and Letter, not to iudge by the speciousnesse of the wordes, but by the weight of the matter; not looking to that which is strongly alledged, but iudiciously to consider what is iustly prooued: And for all my owne good and naturall Subiects, that their hearts may remaine established in the trewth; that these forraine inticements may not seduce them from their natall and naturall duetie; and that all, aswell strangers, as naturall subiects, to whose eyes this Discourse shall come, may wisely and vnpartially iudge of the Veritie, as it is nakedly here set downe, for clearing these mists and cloudes of calumnies, which were iniustly heaped vpon me; for which end onely I heartily pray the courteous Reader to be perswaded, that I tooke occasion to publish this Discourse.

A PRE-

A PREMONITION

TO ALL MOST MIGHTIE

MONARCHES,

KINGS, FREE PRINCES,

AND STATES OF

CHRISTENDOME.

TO

TO THE MOST SACRED
AND INVINCIBLE PRINCE,
RODOLPHE THE II. by
Gods *Clemencie Elect Emperour*
of the ROMANES;

KING OF GERMANIE, HVN-
GARIE, *BOHEME*, *DALMATIE*,
CROATIE, SCLAVONIE, &c.

ARCH-DVKE OF AVSTRIA, DVKE
OF BVRGVNDIE, STIRIA, CARINTHIA,
CARNIOLA, and WIRTEMBERG, &c.
Earle of TYROLIS, &c.

AND TO ALL OTHER
RIGHT HIGH AND
MIGHTIE KINGS;

And Right Excellent free Princes and States
of CHRISTENDOME:

Our louing BRETHREN, COSINS, ALLIES,
CONFEDERATES and FRIENDS:

IAMES by the Grace of GOD, King of GREAT
BRITAINE, FRANCE and IRELAND; Profeſſour,
Maintainer and Defender of the Trew, Chriſtian, Catholique and
Apoſtolique FAITH, Profeſſed by the ancient and Primitiue
CHVRCH, and ſealed with the blood of ſo many Holy Biſhops,
and other faithfull crowned with the glory of MARTYRDOME;

WISHETH euerlaſting felicitie in CHRIST
our SAVIOVR.

TO

T O Y O V M O S T
SACRED AND INVINCI-
BLE EMPEROVR; RIGHT
HIGH AND MIGHTIE
KINGS; RIGHT EXCEL-
LENT FREE PRINCES
AND STATES, MY LO-
VING BRETHREN AND COSINS:

To you, I say, as of right belongeth, doe I confecrate
and direct this Warning of mine, or rather *Preamble* to my reprinted *Apologie for the Oath of Allegiance*. For the caufe is generall, and concerneth the
Authoritie and priuiledge of Kings in generall, and all fupereminent Temporall powers. And if in whatfoeuer Societie, or Corporation of men, either in Corporations of Cities, or in the Corporation of any mechanicke
craft or handie-worke, euery man is carefull to maintaine the priuiledges
of that Societie whereunto he is fworne; nay, they will rather clufter all in
one, making it a common caufe, expofing themfelues to all forts of perill,
then fuffer the leaft breach in their Liberties; If thofe of the bafer fort of
people, I fay, be fo curious and zealous for the preferuation of their common priuiledges and liberties, as if the meaneft amongft them be touched
in any fuch point, they thinke it concerneth them all: Then what fhould
wee doe in fuch a cafe, whom GOD hath placed in the higheft thrones
vpon earth, made his Lieutenants and Vice-gerents, and euen feated vs
vpon his owne Throne to execute his Iudgements? The confideration
hereof hath now mooued mee to expone a Cafe vnto you, which doeth
not fo neerely touch mee in my particular, as it doeth open a breach a-
gainft our Authoritie, (I fpeake in the plurall of all Kings) and priuiledge
in generall. And fince not onely all rankes and forts of people in all Nations doe inuiolably obferue this *Maxime*, but euen the Ciuil Law, by which
the greateft part of Chriftendome is gouerned, doeth giue them an intereft, *qui fouent confimilem caufam*; How much more then haue yee intereft in
this caufe, not beeing *fimilis* or *par caufa* to yours, but *eadem* with yours?

B b   and

and indeed yee all *fouetis*, or at least *fouere debetis eandem caufam mecum.* And fince this caufe is common to vs all; both the Ciuill Lawes, and the municipall Lawes of all Nations, permit and warne them, that haue a common intereft, to concurre in one for the defence of their common caufe; yea, common fenfe teacheth vs with the Poet, *Ecquid*

 Ad te pòst paulò ventura pericula fentis?
 Nam tua res agitur paries cùm proximus ardet.

Awake then while it is time, and fuffer not, by your longer fleepe, the ftrings of your Authoritie to be cut *in fingulis*, and one and one to your generall ruine, which by your vnited forces, would rather make a ftrong rope for the enemie to hang himfelfe in, with *Achitophel*, then that hee fhould euer bee able to breake it. As for this *Apologie* of mine, it is trew, that I thought good to fet it firft out without putting my name vnto it; but neuer fo, as I thought to denie it, remembring well mine owne words, but taken out of the Scripture, in the beginning of the Preface to the Reader, in my ΒΑΣΙΛΙΚΟΝ ΔΩΡΟΝ, *that nothing is fo hid, which fhall not bee opened, &c*: promifing there, which with GOD his grace I fhall euer performe, neuer to doe that in fecret, which I fhall need to be afhamed of, when it fhall come to be proclaimed in publique.

In deed I thought it fit, for two refpects, that this my *Apologie* fhould firft vifite the world without hauing my name written in the forehead thereof. Firft becaufe of the *matter*, and next of the *perfons* that I medled with. The *matter*, it being a *Treatife*, which I was to write, conteining reafons and difcourfes in *Diuinitie*, for the defence of the *Oath of Alleagiance*, and refutation of the condemners thereof; I thought it not comely for one of my place, to put my name to bookes concerning Scholafticke *Difputations*; whofe calling is to fet forth *Decrees* in the Imperatiue mood: for I thinke my felfe as good a man as the Pope, by his reuerence, for whom thefe my *Anfwerers* make the like excufe; for that his *Breues* are fo fummary without yeelding any reafon vnto them. My next reafon was the refpect of the *perfons* whom with I medled: Wherein, although I fhortly anfwered the Popes *Breues*; yet the point I moft laboured, being the refutation of *Bellarmines* Letter, I was neuer the man, I confeffe, that could thinke a *Cardinall* a meet match for a *King*: efpecially, hauing many hundreth thoufands of my fubiects of as good birth as hee. As for his Church dignitie, his *Cardinalfhip* I meane, I know not how to ranke or value it, either by the warrant of God his word, or by the ordinance of *Emperours* or *Kings*; it being indeed onely a new *Papall* erection, tolerated by the fleeping conniuence of our *Predeceffours* (I meane ftill by the plurall of *Kings*.) But notwithftanding of this my forbearing to put my name vnto it, fome *Embaffadours* of fome of you (my louing *Brethren* and *Coufins*) whome this caufe did neerelieft concerne, can witneffe, that I made Prefents of fome of thofe bookes, at their firft printing, vnto them, and that auowedly in my owne name. As alfo the Englifh

Para-

Paragraphist, or rather peruerſe Pamphleter *Parſons*, ſince all his deſcription muſt runne vpon a *P.* hath trewly obſerued, that my Armes are affixed in the frontiſpice thereof, which vſeth not to bee in bookes of other mens doing; whereby his malice in pretending his ignorance, that hee might pay mee the ſoundlier, is the more inexcuſable. But now that I finde my ſparing to put my name vnto it hath not procured my ſparing by theſe anſwerers, who haue neither ſpared my Perſon directly in naming me, nor indirectly by railing vpon the Author of the Booke: it is now high time for me no longer to conceale nor diſauow my ſelfe, as if I were aſhamed of my owne deed. And therefore that ye may the better vnderſtand the nature of the cauſe, I will begin at the firſt ground thereof.

The neuer enough wondered at and abhorred P O VV D E R-T R E A-ſ O N (though the repetition thereof grieueth, I know, the gentle hearted Ieſuite *Parſons*) this Treaſon, I ſay, being not onely intended againſt mee and my Poſteritie, but euen againſt the whole houſe of Parliament, plotted onely by Papiſts, and they onely led thereto by a prepoſterous zeale for the aduancement of their Religion; ſome of them continuing ſo obſtinate, that euen at their death they would not acknowledge their fault; but in their laſt words, immediatly before the expiring of their breath, refuſed to condemne themſelues and craue pardon for their deed, except the *Romiſh* Church ſhould firſt condemne it; And ſoone after, it being diſcouered, that a great number of my Popiſh Subiects of all rankes and ſexes, both men and women, as well within as without the Countrey; had a confuſed notion and an obſcure knowledge, that ſome great thing was to bee done in that Parliament for the weale of the Church; although, for ſecrecies cauſe, they were not acquainted with the particulars; certaine formes of prayer hauing likewiſe beene ſet downe and vſed for the good ſucceſſe of that great errand; adding heereunto, that diuers times, and from diuers Prieſtes, the Archtraitours themſelues receiued the Sacrament for confirmation of their heart, and obſeruation of ſecrecie; Some of the principall Ieſuites likewiſe being found guiltie of the foreknowledge of the Treaſon it ſelfe; of which number ſome fled from their triall, others were apprehended (as holy *Garnet* himſelfe and *Owldcorne* were) and iuſtly executed vpon their owne plaine confeſſion of their guilt: If this Treaſon now, clad with theſe circumſtances, did not miniſter a iuſt occaſion to that Parliament houſe, whome they thought to haue deſtroyed, courageouſly and zealouſly at their next ſitting downe, to vſe all meanes of triall, whether any more of that minde were yet left in the Countrey; I leaue it to you to iudge, whom God hath appointed his higheſt Depute Iudges vpon earth: And amongſt other things for this purpoſe, This *Oath of Allegiance*, ſo vniuſtly impugned, was then deuiſed and enacted. And in caſe any ſharper Lawes were then made againſt the Papiſts, that were not obedient to the former Lawes of the Countrey; if ye will conſider the *Time*, *Place* and *Perſons*, it will be thought no wonder,

ſeeing

seeing that occasion did so iustly exasperate them to make seuerer Lawes, then otherwise they would haue done. The *Time*, I say, being the very next sitting downe of the Parliament, after the discouerie of that abominable Treason : the *Place* being the same, where they should all haue bene blowne vp, and so bringing it freshly to their memorie againe : the *Persons* being the very Parliament men whom they thought to haue destroyed. And yet so farre hath both my heart and gouernment bene from any bitternes, as almost neuer one of those sharpe additions to the former Lawes haue euer yet bene put in execution.

And that ye may yet know further, for the more conuincing these Libellers of wilfull malice, who impudently affirme, That this *Oath of Allegiance* was deuised for deceiuing and intrapping of Papists in points of Conscience ; The trewth is, that the Lower house of Parliament at the first framing of this Oath, made it to containe, That the Pope had no power to excommunicate me; which I caused them to reforme, onely making it to conclude, That no excommunication of the Popes, can warrant my Subiects to practise against my Person or State; denying the deposition of Kings to be in the Popes lawfull power; as indeed I take any such temporall violence, to be farre without the limits of such a Spirituall censure as Excommunication is. So carefull was I that nothing should be contained in this Oath, except the profession of natural Allegiance, and ciuil and temporall obedience, with a promise to resist to all contrary vnciuill violence.

This Oath now grounded vpon so great and iust an occasion, set forth in so reasonable termes, and ordained onely for making of a trew distinction betweene Papists of quiet disposition, and in all other things good subiects, and such other Papists as in their hearts maintained the like violent bloody *Maximes*, that the Powder-Traitours did : This Oath, I say, being published and put in practise, bred such euill blood in the Popes head and his Cleargie, as *Breue* after *Breue* commeth forth, *vt vndam vnda sequitur*; prohibiting all Catholikes from taking the same, as a thing cleane contrary to the Catholike faith ; and that the taking thereof cannot stand with the saluation of their soules.

There commeth likewise a letter of Cardinall *Bellarmines* to *Blackwell* to the same purpose; but discoursing more at length vpon the said Oath. Whereupon, after I had entred in consideration of their vniust impugning that so iust and lawfull an Oath; and fearing that by their vntrew calumnies and Sophistrie the hearts of a number of the most simple and ignorant of my people should bee misse-led, vnder that faire and deceitfull cloake of Conscience ; I thought good to set foorth an *Apologie* for the said Oath : wherein I prooued, that as this Oath contained nothin but matter of ciuill and temporall Obedience, due by Subiects to thei Soueraigne Prince; so this quarrelling therewith was nothing but a lat vsurpation of Popes (against the warrant of all Scriptures, ancient Coun cels and Fathers) vpon the Temporall power of Kings, wherewith onel

m

my *Apologie* doeth meddle. But the publishing of this Booke of mine hath brought such two Answerers, or rather Railers vpon mee, as all the world may wonder at: For my Booke being first written in English, an English Oath being the subiect thereof, and the vse of it properly belonging to my Subiects of *England*; and immediatly thereafter being translated into Latine, vpon a desire that some had of further publishing it abroad; it commeth home to mee now answered in both the Languages. And, I thinke, if it had bene set foorth in all the tongues that were at the confusion of *Babel*, it would haue bene returned answered in them all againe. Thus may a man see how busie a Bishop the Diuell is, and how hee omitteth no diligence for venting of his poysoned wares. But herein their malice doeth clearely appeare, that they pay mee so quickly with a double answere; and yet haue neuer answered their owne Arch-priest, who hath written a booke for the maintenance of the same Oath, and of the temporall authoritie of Kings, alledging a cloud of their owne Scholemen against them.

As for the English *Answerer*, my vnnaturall and fugitiue Subiect, I will neither defile my pen, nor your sacred eyes or eares with the describing of him, who ashames, nay, abhorres not to raile, nay, to rage and spew foorth blasphemies against the late Queene of famous memory. A Subiect to raile against his naturall Soueraigne by birth; A man to raile against a Lady by sexe; A holy man (in outward profession) to insult vpon the dead; nay to take *Radamanthus* office ouer his head, and to sit downe and play the Iudge in hell, And all his quarrell is, that either her Successour, or any of her seruants should speake honourably of her. Cursed be he that curseth the Anointed of God: and destroyed mought he be with the destruction of *Korah*, that hath sinned in the contradiction of *Korah*. Without mought such dogs and swine be cast forth, I say, out of the Spirituall *Ierusalem*.

As for my Latine *Answerer*, I haue nothing to say to his person; hee is not my Subiect; hee standeth or falleth vnto his owne Lord: But sure I am, they two haue casten lotts vpon my Booke, since they could not diuide it: the one of them, my fugitiue, to raile vpon my late Predecessour, (but a rope is the fittest answere for such an Historian;) the other, a stranger, thinketh he may be boldest both to pay my person and my Booke, as indeed he doeth; which how iustly either in matter or maner, wee are now to examine.

But first, who should be the trew Authour of this booke, I can but guesse. Hee calleth himselfe *Mattheus Tortus*, Cardinall *Bellarmins* Chaplaine. A [1] throwne Euangelist indeed, full of throward Diuinitie; an obscure Authour, vtterly vnknowne to mee, being yet little knowne to the world for any other of his workes: and therefore must be a very desperate fellow in beginning his *apprentisage*, not onely to refute, but to raile vpon a King. But who will consider the carriage of the whole booke, shall finde that hee writeth with such authoritie, or at the least *tam elato stylo*,

[1] Being a proper word to expresse the trew meaning of *Tortus*.

Bb 3   so

¹ *P.46.*

² *P.53.*

Pag.69.

ſo little ſparing either Kings in generall, or my perſon in particular; and with ſuch a greatneſſe, ¹ *Habemus enim exemplaria Breuium illorum in manibus*, and ² *Decernimus*: as it ſhall appeare, or at leaſt bee very probable, that it is the Maſters, and not the mans labour; eſpecially in one place, where hee quarrelleth mee for caſting vp his *moralis certitudo* and *piè credi* vnto him; hee there groſſely forgetting himſelfe, ſaith, *malâ fide nobiſcum agit*, thereby making this Authour to be one perſon with *Bellarmine*. But let it bee the worke of a *Tortus* indeed, and not of a perſonated Cardinall; yet muſt it bee the Cardinals deed, ſince Maſter *Tortus* is the Cardinals man, and doeth it in his Maſters defence. The errand then being the Cardinals, and done by his owne man, it cannot but bee accounted as his owne deed; eſpecially ſince the Engliſh Anſwerer doeth foure times promiſe, that *Bellarmine*, or one by his appointment, ſhall ſufficiently anſwere it.

And now to come to his matter and maner of Anſwere: Surely if there were no more but his vnmanerly maner, it is enough to diſgrace the whole matter thereof. For firſt, to ſhew his pride, in his Printers preface of the *Politan* edition of this *elegans libellus*, hee muſt equall the Cardinals greatneſſe with mine in euery thing. For though hee confeſſeth this Maſter *Tortus* to bee an obſcure man; yet being the Cardinals Chapleine, he is ſufficient enough forſooth to anſwere an Engliſh booke, that lacketh the name of an Authour; as if a perſonated obſcure name for Authour of a Cardinals booke, were a meete match for anſwering a K I N G S Booke, that lacketh the name of an Authour; and a Cardinals Chapleine to meete with the Deane of the Kings Chappell, whom *Parſons* with the Cardinall, haue (as it ſeemeth) agreed vpon to intitle to bee the Authour of my *Apologie*. And not onely in the Preface, but alſo through the whole booke doeth hee keepe this comparatiue greatneſſe. Hee muſt bee as ſhort in his anſwere, as I am in my Booke, hee muſt refute all that I haue ſaid againſt the Popes ſecond *Breue*, with equall breuitie, and vpon one page almoſt, as I haue done mine: and becauſe I haue ſet downe the ſubſtance of the Oath in foureteene Articles; in iuſt as many Articles muſt he ſet downe that Acte of Parliament of mine, wherein the Oath is contained: And yet, had hee contented himſelfe with his owne pride, by the demonſtration of his owne greatneſſe, without further wronging of mee, it had bene the more tollerable. But what cauſe gaue I him to farce his whole booke with iniuries, both againſt my Perſon and Booke? For whereas in all my *Apologie* I haue neuer giuen him a foule word, and eſpecially neuer gaue him the Lye: hee by the contrary giueth mee nine times the Lye in expreſſe termes, and ſeuen times chargeth mee with falſehood, which phraſe is equiualent with a Lye. And as for all other wordes of reproch, as *nugæ, conuitia, temeritas, vanitas, impudentia, blaſphemiæ, ſermonis barbaries, cum eadem fœlicitate ſcribendi, cauillationes, applicatio inepta, fingere hiſtorias, audacia quæ in hominem ſanæ mentis cadere non poteſt,*

poteſt, vel ſenſu communi caret, imperitia & leuitas, omnem omnino pudorem & conſcientiam exuiſſe, malâ fide nobiſcum agit, vt lectoribus per fas & nefas imponat : of ſuch like reproches, I ſay, I doubt if there bee a page in all his Booke free, except where hee idlely ſets downe the Popes *Breues*, and his owne *Letter*. And in caſe this might onely ſeeme to touch the vn-knowen Authour of the Booke, whome notwithſtanding he knew well enough, as I ſhew before; hee ſpareth not my Perſon with my owne name : ſometimes ſaying, that *Pope* Clement *thought mee to bee inclined to their Religion* : Sometimes, that I *was a Puritane in Scotland, and a perſe-cutour of Proteſtants.* In one place hee concludeth, *Quia Iacobus non eſt Catholicus, hoc ipſo Hæreticus eſt.* In another place, *Ex Chriſtiano Calui-niſtam fecerunt.* In another place hee ſayeth, *Neque omnino verum eſt, Iacobum nunquam deſeruiſſe Religionem quam primò ſuſceperat.* And in another place, after that hee hath compared and ranked mee with *Iu-lian* the Apoſtate, hee concludeth, *Cùm Catholicus not ſit, neque Chriſtia-nus eſt.* If this now bee mannerly dealing with a King, I leaue it to you to iudge, who cannot but reſent ſuch indignities done to one of your qualitie.

Pag.47.
Pag.98.
Pag.87.
Pag.98.
Ibid.
Pag.97.

And as for the Matter of his Booke, it well fittes indeede the Manner thereof : for hee neuer anſwereth directly to the maine queſtion in my Booke. For whereas my *Apologie* handleth onely two points, as I told you before; One, to prooue that the *Oath of Allegiance* doeth onely meddle with the ciuill and temporall Obedience, due by Subiects to their naturall So-ueraignes : The other, that this late vſurpation of Popes ouer the tempo-rall power of Princes, is againſt the rule of all Scriptures, auncient Coun-cels and Fathers: hee neuer improoues the firſt, but by a falſe inference; that the Oath denyeth the Popes power of Excommunication directly, ſince it denieth his authoritie in depoſing of Kings. And for the ſecond point, he bringeth no proofe to the contrary, but, *Paſce oues meas*: and, *Tibi dabo claues regni Cælorum*: and, That no Catholike euer doubted of it. So as I may trewly ſay of him, that hee either vnderſtandeth not, or at leaſt will not ſeeme to vnderſtand my Booke, in neuer directly anſwering the maine queſtion, as I haue alreadie ſaide; and ſo may I iuſtly turne o-uer vpon himſelfe that doome of ignorance, which in the beginning of his Booke hee raſhly pronounceth vpon mee; ſaying, that I neither vnder-ſtand the Popes *Breues*, his *Letter*, nor the Oath it ſelfe: And as hee deligh-teth to repeate ouer and ouer, I know not how oft, and triumpheth in this wrong inference of his; That to deny the Popes power to depoſe Kings, is to denie the Popes Primacie, and his ſpirituall power of Excommuni-cation : So doeth hee, vpon that ground of *Paſce oues meas*, giue the Pope ſo ample a power ouer Kings, to throne or dethrone them at his pleaſure (and yet onely ſubiecting Chriſtian Kings to that ſlauerie) as I doubt not but in your owne Honours yee will reſent you of ſuch indignities; the ra-ther ſince it concernes ſo many of you as profeſſe the Romiſh religion, farre

more

more then me: For since he accounteth me an heretike, and like *Iulian* the Apostate; I am consequently *extra caulam,* and none of the Popes flocke, and so am in the case of Ethnicke Princes, ouer whom he confesseth the Pope hath no power. But yee are in the Popes folde; and you, that great Pastour may leade as sheepe to the slaughter, when it shall please him. And as the Asses eares must be hornes, if the Lion list so to interprete it; so must yee be remooued as scabbed sheepe from the flocke, if so the Pope thinke you to be, though your skinne be indeed neuer so sound.

Thus hath he set such a new goodly interpretation vpon the wordes of CHRIST, *Pasce oues meas,* as if it were as much to say, as, depose Christian Kings ; and that *Quodcunque solueris* gaue the Pope power to dispense with all sorts of Oathes, Vowes, Penalties, Censures and Lawes, euen with the naturall obedience of Subiects to their Souereigne Lords; much ¹ like to that new coyned glosse that his brother [1] *Baronius* made vpon the wordes in Saint *Peters* vision, *Surge Petre, occide & manduca* ; That is (said he to the Pope) Goe kill and confound the *Venetians.*

And because I haue in my Booke (by citing a place in his controuersies) discouered him to be a small friend to Kings, he is much commoued : For whereas in his said Controuersies, speaking *de Clericis,* he is so bolde as to affirme, that Church-men are exempted from the power of earthly Kings; and that they ought them no subiection euen in temporall matters, but onely *vi rationis* and in their owne discretion, for the preseruation of peace and good order; because, I say, citing this place of his in my Booke, I tell with admiration, that hee freeth all Church-men from any subiection to Kings, euen those that are their borne Subiects : hee is angry with this phrase, and sayth it is an addition for breeding enuie vnto him, and raising of hatred against him : For, sayth hee, although *Bellarmine* affirmed generally, that Church-men were not subiect to earthly Kings; yet did hee not insert that particular clause [*though they were borne and dwelling in their Dominions*] as if the words of Church-men and earthly Kings in generall imported not as much : for Layickes as well as Church-men are subiect to none but to their naturall Soueraigne : And yet doeth hee not sticke to confesse, that he meant it, though it was not fit (he sayth) to be expressed.

And thus quarrels hee me for reuealing his Printed secret. But whose hatred did hee feare in this? was it not yours? Who haue interest, but KINGS, in withdrawing of due subiection from KINGS? And when the greatest Monarches amongst you will remember, that almost the third part of your Subiects and of your Territories, is Church-men, and Church-liuings ; I hope, yee will then consider and weigh, what a feather hee pulles out of your wings, when hee denudeth you of so many Subiects and their possessions, in the Popes fauour : nay, what briars and thornes are left within the heart of your dominions, when so populous and potent a partie shall haue their birth, education and liuelihood in
                     your

your Countries, and yet owe you no fubiection, nor acknowledge you for their SOVERAIGNES? So as where the Church-men of old were content with their tythe of euery mans goods; the Pope now will haue little leffe then the third part of euery Kings *Subiects* and *Dominions*. And as in this place, fo throughout all the reft of his booke, hee doeth nothing but amplifie the Popes power ouer Kings, and exaggerate my vnreafonable rigour for prefling this Oath; which hee will needs haue to bee nothing but a renewed Oath of *Supremacie* in more fubtill and craftie termes, onely to robbe the Pope of his *Primacie* and fpirituall power: making his temporall power and authoritie ouer Princes, to be one of the chiefe Articles of the Catholike Faith.

But that it may the better appeare vnto you, that all my labour and intention in this errand, was onely to meddle with that due temporall Obedience which my Subiects owe vnto mee; and not to intrap or inthrall their Confciences, : Yee fhall firft fee how farre other Godly   d *Kings* were from acknowledging the Popes temporall *Supremacie* ouer them; nay, haue created, controlled and depofed Popes : and next, what a number of my *Predeceffors* in this Kingdome haue at all occafions, euen in the times of the greateft Greatneffe of Popes, refifted and plainely withftood them in this point.

And firft, all Chriftian *Emperours* were for a long time fo farre from acknowledging the Popes Superioritie ouer them, as by the contrary the Popes acknowledged themfelues for their *Vaffals*, reuerencing and obeying the *Emperours* as their *Lords*, for proofe whereof, I remit you to my *Apologie*.

And for the creating of Popes; the *Emperours* were in fo long and continuall poffeffion thereof, as I will vfe for my firft witneffe a Pope himfelfe; who (in a [1] *Synode* of an hundreth fiftie and three *Bifhops* and *Abbots*) did ordeine, That the Emperour CHARLES the Great fhould haue the Right of choofing the Pope, and ordeining the Apoftolicall Seate, and the Dignitie of the *Romane* Principalitie : nay, farther hee ordeined; That all *Archbifhops* and *Bifhops* fhould receiue their Inueftiture from the *Emperour*, or elfe bee of no auaile; And, that a Bifhop wanting it, fhould not bee confecrate, pronouncing an *Anathema* againft all that fhould difobey this Sentence.

And that the *Emperours* affent to the Popes Election was a thing ordinary for a long time, [2] *Platina*, and a number of the Popes owne writers beare witneffe : And [3] *Bellarmine* himfelfe, in his booke of Controuerfies, cannot get it handfomely denied. Nay, the Popes were euen forced then to pay a certaine fumme of money to the *Emperours* for their Confirmation : And this lafted almoft feuen hundreth yeeres after CHRIST; witneffe [4] *Sigebert* and [5] *Luitprandus*, with other Popifh Hiftorians.

And

[1] *Sigebert. ad ann. 773. Walthram. Naumburg. lib. de Epifc. inue-ftitura. Mart. Polon. ad ann. 780. Theod. à Niem de tr-nitieg & Iurib. Imperij & dift. 63. C. Hadrian.*

[2] *See Platin. in vit. Pelag. 2. Gregor. 1. & Seuerini.*
[3] *Lib. de Clericis.*
[4] *In Chron. ad ann. 680.*
[5] *In vit. Aga-thon. & Anaft. in vit. einfd A-gath & Honm. Contract. ad ann. 678. edit. pofter. & dift. 63. c. Agatho.*

[1] *Luitpr Hist. lib 6, c 1, 10, 11. Rheg. in ad an. 963. & Platin. in vit. Ioan. 13.*
[2] *Marianus Scot. Sigeb. Abbas Vrsp. ad ann. 1046 & Plat in vit. Greg. 6.*

[3] *Waltram. Naumburg. in lib. de inuest. Episc. Vix a circa an. 1110.*

[4] *See Annales Franciæ Nicolai Gillij in Phil. Pulcl. ro.*

[5] *Anno 1268. ex Arrestis Senatus Parisiens.*
[6] *Ioan. Maierius, lib. de Scismat & Concil.*

And for *Emperours* depofing of Popes, there are likewife diuers examples. The Emperour [1] *Ottho* depofed Pope *Iohn* the twelfth of that name, for diuers crimes and vices; efpecially of Lecherie. The Emperour [2] *Henry* the third in a fhort time depofed three Popes; *Benedict* the ninth, *Siluefter* the third, and *Gregorie* the fixt, as well for the finne of Auarice, as for abufing their extraordinarie authoritie againft Kings and Princes.

And as for K I N G S that haue denied this Temporall Superioritie of Popes; Firft, wee haue the vnamine teftimonie of diuers famous H I-S T O R I O G R A P H E R S for the generall of many C H R I S T I A N Kingdomes. As [3] *Waltbram* teftifieth, *That the Bifhops of Spaine*, *Scotland*, *England*, *Hungarie*, *from ancient inftitution till this moderne noueltie*, *had their Inueftiture by* K I N G S , *with peaceable inioyning of their Temporalties wholly and entirely; and whofoeuer* (fayeth hee) *is peaceably folicitous, let him perufe the liues of the Ancients, and reade the Hiftories, and hee fhall vnderftand thus much.* And for verification of this generall Affertion; wee will firft beginne at the practife of the K I N G S of France, though not named by *Waltbram* in this his enumeration of Kingdomes: amongft whom my firft witneffe fhall bee that vulgarly knowne letter of [4] *Philip le Bel* King of France, to Pope *Boniface* the eighth, the beginning whereof, after a fcornefull falutation, is, *Sciat tua maxima fatuitas , nos in temporalibus nemini fubeffe.*

And likewife after that [5] *Lewes* the ninth, furnamed *Sanctus*, had by a publique inftrument (called *Pragmatica fanctio*) forbidden all the exactions of the Popes Court within his Realme: Pope *Pius* [6] the fecond, in the beginning of *Lewes* the eleuenth his time, greatly miffeliking this Decree fo long before made, fent his Legate to the faide King *Lewes*, with Letters-patents, vrging his promife which hee had made when hee was Dolphin of France, to repeale that Sanction if euer hee came to bee King. The King referreth the Legate ouer with his Letters-patents to the Councell of Paris: where the matter being propounded, was impugned by *Iohannes Romanus*, the Kings Atturney; with whofe opinion the Vniuerfitie of Paris concurring, an Appeale was made from the attempts of the Pope to the next generall Councell; the Cardinall departing with indignation.

But that the King of France and Church thereof haue euer ftoken to their *Gallican* immunitie , in denying the Pope any Temporall power ouer them, and in refifting the Popes as oft as euer they preft to meddle with their Temporall power, euen in the donation of Benefices; the Hiftories are fo full of them, as the onely examples thereof would make vp a bigge Volume by it felfe. And fo farre were the *Sorbonifts* for the Kings and French Churches priuiledge in this point, as they were wont to maintaine ; That if the Pope fell a quarrelling the King for that caufe, the

the *Gallican* Church might elect a *Patriarch* of their owne, renouncing any obedience to the Pope. And *Gerſon* was ſo farre from giuing the Pope that temporall authority ouer Kings (who otherwiſe was a deuoute *Roman* Catholike) as hee wrote a Booke *de Auferibilitate Papæ*; not onely from the power ouer Kings, but euen ouer the Church.

And now pretermitting all further examples of forraigne Kings actions, I will onely content me at this time with ſome of my owne Predeceſſors examples of this kingdome of England; that it may thereby the more clearely appeare, that euen in thoſe times when the world was fulleſt of darkened blindnes and ignorance, the Kings of England haue oftentimes, not onely repined, but euen ſtrongly reſiſted and withſtood this temporall vſurpation and encrochment of ambitious Popes.

And I will firſt begin at [1] King *Henry* the firſt of that name, after the Conqueſt; who after he was crowned gaue the Biſhopricke of *Wincheſter* to *William Gifford*, and forthwith inueſted him into all the poſſeſſions belonging to the Biſhopricke, contrary to the Canons of the new Synod. [2] *King Henry* alſo gaue the Archbiſhopricke of *Canterbury* to *Radulph* Biſhop of *London*; and gaue him inueſtiture by a Ring and a Croſiers ſtaffe.

Alſo Pope [3] *Calixtus* held a Councell at RHEMES, whither King *Henry* had appointed certaine Biſhops of ENGLAND and NORMANDIE to goe; *Thurſtan* alſo, elected Archbiſhop of YORKE, got leaue of the King to goe thither, giuing his faith that hee would not receiue Conſecration of the Pope; And comming to the Synode, by his liberall gifts (as the faſhion is) wanne the ROMANES fauour, and by their meanes obtained to bee conſecrated at the Popes hand: Which aſſoone as the King of ENGLAND knewe, hee forbade him to come within his Dominions.

Moreouer King *Edward* the firſt prohibited the *Abbot* of [4] *Waltham* and *Deane* of *Pauls*, to collect a tenth of euery mans goods for a ſupply to the holy Land, which the Pope by three *Bulles* had committed to their charge; and the ſaid Deane of *Pauls* compeering before the King and his *Councell*, promiſed for the reuerence he did beare vnto the King, not to meddle any more in that matter, without the Kings good leaue and permiſſion. Here (I hope) a Church-man diſobeyed the *Pope* for obedience to his *Prince* euen in Church matters: but this new *Ieſuited* Diuinitie was not then knowen in the world.

The ſame *Edward I.* impleaded the Deane of the Chappell of *Vuluerhampton*, becauſe the ſaid Deane had, againſt the priuiledges of the Kingdome, giuen a Prebend of the ſame Chappell to one at the Popes command: whereupon the ſaid Deane compeered, and put himſelfe in the Kings will for his offence.

The ſaid *Edward I.* depriued alſo the *Biſhop* of *Durham* of all his liberties, for diſobeying a prohibition of the Kings. So as it appeareth, the Kings

in

[1] *Matth. Paris, in Henr. 1. anno 1100.*

[2] *Idem ibid. anno 1113.*

[3] *Idem ibid. anno 1119.*

[4] *Ex Archiuis Regni.*

in thoſe dayes thought the Church-men their *Subiects*, though now we be taught other Seraphicall doctrine.

For further proofe whereof *Iohn* of *Ibſtocke* was committed to the goale by the ſayde King, for hauing a ſuite in the Court of *Rome* ſeuen yeeres for the Rectorie of *Newchurch*.

And *Edward* II. following the footſteps of his Father; after giuing out a Summons againſt the Abbot of *Walden*, for citing the Abbot of Saint *Albons* and others in the Court of *Rome*, gaue out letters for his apprehenſion.

And likewiſe, becauſe a certaine Prebend of *Banburie* had drawen one *Beuercoat* by a Plea to *Rome* without the Kings Dominions, therefore were letters of Caption ſent foorth againſt the ſaid Prebend.

And *Edward* III. following likewiſe the example of his Predeceſſours; Becauſe a Parſon of *Liche* had ſummoned the Prior of S. *Oſwalds* before the Pope at *Auinion*; for hauing before the Iudges in *England* recouered the arrerage of a penſion; directed a Precept, for ſeaſing vpon all the goods both Spirituall and Temporall of the ſaid Parſon, becauſe hee had done this in preiudice of the King and Crowne. The ſaide King alſo made one *Haywoden* to bee declared culpable and worthie to bee puniſhed, for procuring the Popes *Bulles* againſt a Iudgement that was giuen by the Kings Iudges.

And likewiſe; Becauſe one entred vpon the Priorie of *Barnewell* by the *Popes Bul*, the ſaid Intrant was committed to the Tower of *London*, there to remaine during the Kings pleaſure.

So as my Predeceſſors (ye ſee) of this Kingdome, euen when the *Popes* triumphed in their greatneſſe, ſpared not to puniſh any of their Subiects, that would preferre the *Popes* Obedience to theirs, euen in Church-matters: So farre were they then from either acknowledging the *Pope* for their temporall Superiour, or yet from doubting that their owne Churchmen were not their Subiects. And now I will cloſe vp all theſe examples with an Act of *Parliament* in King *Richard* II. his time ; whereby it was prohibited, That none ſhould procure a Benefice from *Rome*, vnder paine to be put out of the Kings protection. And thus may yee ſee, that what thoſe Kings ſucceſſiuely one to another by foure generations haue acted in priuate, the ſame was alſo maintained by a publike Law.

By theſe few examples now (I hope) I haue ſufficiently cleered my ſelfe from the imputation, that any ambition or deſire of Noueltie in mee ſhould haue ſtirred mee, either to robbe the *Pope* of any thing due vnto him, or to aſſume vnto my ſelfe any farther authoritie, then that which other Chriſtian *Emperours* and *Kings* through the world, and my owne Predeceſſours of *England* in eſpeciall, haue long agone maintained. Neither is it enough to ſay (as *Parſons* doeth in his Anſwere to the Lord *Coke*) That farre more Kings of this Countrey haue giuen many more examples of acknowledging, or not reſiſting the *Popes* vſurped Authoritie; ſome

perchance

perchance lacking the occafion; and fome the abilitie of refifting them : for euen by the Ciuill Law, in the cafe of violent intrufion and long and wrongfull poffeffion againft mee, it is enough if I prooue that I haue made lawfull interruption vpon conuenient occafions.

But the Cardinall thinkes the Oath, not onely vnlawfull for the fub-ftance therof, but alfo in regard of the Perfon whom vnto it is to be fworne: For (faith he) *The King is not a Catholique*; And in two or three other places of his booke, he ftickethn not to call me by my name very broadly, an Here-tike, as I haue already told. But yet before I be publikely declared an Here-tike; by the Popes owne Law my people ought not to refufe their Obedi-ence vnto me. And (I truft) if I were but a fubiect, and accufed by the Pope in his *Conclaue* before his Cardinals, hee would haue hard prouing mee an Heretike, if he iudged me by their owne ancient Orders.

For firft, I am no *Apoftate*, as the Cardinal would make me; not onely ha-uing euer bene brought vp in that Religion which I prefently profeffe, but euen my Father and Grandfather on that fide profeffing the fame: and fo cannot be properly an Heretike, by their owne doctrine, fince I neuer was of their Church. And as for the Queene my Mother of worthy memo-rie; although fhe continued in that Religion wherein fhee was nourifhed, yet was fhe fo farre from being fuperftitious or *Iefuited* therein, that at my Baptifme (although I was baptized by a Popifh Archbifhop) fhe fent him word to forbeare to vfe the fpettle in my Baptifme; which was obeyed, be-ing indeed a filthy and an apifh tricke, rather in fcorne then imitation of CHRIST. And her owne very words were, *That fhe would not haue a pockie prieft to fpet in her childs mouth*. As alfo the Font wherein I was Chriftened, was fent from the late Queene here of famous memory, who was my God-mother; and what her Religion was, *Pius V.* was not ignorant. And for further proofe, that that renowmed Queene my Mother was not fuperfti-tious; as in all her Letters (whereof I receiued many) fhe neuer made men-tion of Religion, nor laboured to perfwade me in it; fo at her laft words, fhe commanded her Mafter-houfhold, a Scottifh Gentleman my feruant and yet aliue, fhe commanded him (I fay) to tell me; That although fhe was of another Religion then that wherein I was brought vp; yet fhe would not preffe me to change, except my owne Confcience forced mee to it : For fo that I led a good life, and were carefull to doe Iuftice and gouerne well; fhe doubted not but I would be in a good cafe with the profeffion of my owne Religion. Thus am I no *Apoftate*, nor yet a deborder from that Religion which one part of my Parents profeffed, and an other part gaue mee good allowance of. Neither can my Baptifme in the rites of their Religion make mee an *Apoftate*, or Heretike in refpect of my prefent profeffion, fince we all agree in the fubftance thereof, being all Baptized *In the Name of the Father, the Sonne, and the holy Ghoft* : vpon which head there is no variance amongft vs.

And now for the point of Heretike; I will neuer bee afhamed to render an accompt of my profeſſion, and of that hope that is in me, as the Apoſtle preſcribeth. I am ſuch a CATHOLIKE CHRISTIAN, as beleeueth the three *Creeds*; That of the Apoſtles, that of the Councell of *Nice*, and that of *Athanaſius*; the two latter being Paraphraſes to the former: And I beleeue them in that ſenſe, as the ancient Fathers and Councels that made them did vnderſtand them : To which three *Creeds* all the Miniſters of England doe ſubſcribe at their Ordination. And I alſo acknowledge for Orthodoxe all thoſe other formes of *Creedes,* that either were deuiſed by Councels or particular Fathers, againſt ſuch particular Hereſies as moſt reigned in their times.

I reuerence and admit the foure firſt generall Councels as Catholique and Orthodoxe: And the ſaid foure generall Councels are acknowledged by our Acts of Parliament, and receiued for Orthodoxe by our Church.

As for the Fathers; I reuerence them as much and more then the Ieſuites doe, and as much as themſelues euer craued. For what euer the Fathers for the firſt fiue hundreth yeeres did with an vnanime conſent agree vpon, to be beleeued as a neceſſary point of ſaluation, I either will beleeue it alſo, or at leaſt will be humbly ſilent; not taking vpon mee to condemne the ſame : But for euery priuate Fathers opinion, it bindes not my conſcience more then *Bellarmines*; euery one of the Fathers vſually contradicting others. I will therefore in that caſe follow [1] *S. Auguſtines* rule in iudging of their opinions, as I finde them agree with the Scriptures : what I finde agreeable thereunto I will gladly imbrace; what is otherwiſe I will (with their reuerence) reiect.

As for the Scriptures; no man doubteth I will beleeue them: But euen for the *Apocrypha*; I hold them in the ſame accompt that the Ancients did: They are ſtill printed and bound with our Bibles, and publikely read in our Churches : I reuerence them as the writings of holy and good men : but ſince they are not found in the *Canon,* wee accompt them to bee *ſecunda lectionis* , or [2] *ordinis* (which is *Bellarmines* owne diſtinction) and therefore not ſufficient whereupon alone to ground any article of Faith, except it be confirmed by ſome other place of Canonicall Scripture; Concluding this point with *Ruffinus* (who is no Noueliſt, I hope) That the Apocryphall books were by the Fathers permitted to be read; not for confirmation of Doctrine, but onely for inſtruction of the people.

As for the Saints departed, I honour their memory, and in honour of them doe we in our Church obſerue the dayes of ſo many of them, as the Scripture doeth canonize for Saints; but I am loath to beleeue all the tales of the *Legended ſaints.*

And firſt for the bleſſed Virgin MARIE, I yeeld her that which the Angel *Gabriel* pronounced of her, and which in her *Canticle* ſhee prophecied of herſelfe : that is, That [3] ſhe is bleſſed amongſt women, and [4] That all generations ſhall call her bleſſed. I reuerence her as the Mother of CHRIST, whom of our Sauiour tooke his fleſh, and ſo the Mother

of

[1] *Lib. 2. cont. Creſconium. cap. 32.*

[2] *Lib. 1. de verb. Dei. c. 4.*

[3] Luk. 1. 28.
[4] Ibid. ver. 48.

of G O D, fince the Diuinitie and Humanitie of C H R I S T are infepa-
rable. And I freely confeffe, that fhee is in glory both aboue Angels
and men, her owne Sonne (that is both G O D and man) onely excepted.
But I dare not mocke her and blafpheme againft G O D, calling her not
onely *Diua* but *Dea*, and praying her to command and controule her
Sonne, who is her G O D; and her S A V I O V R: Nor yet not I thinke,
that fhee hath no other thing to doe in heauen, then to heare euery idle
mans fuite, and bufie her felfe in their errands; whiles requefting, whiles
commanding her Sonne, whiles comming downe to kiffe and make
loue with Prieftes, and whiles difputing and brawling with Deuils. In
heauen fhee is in eternall glory and ioy, neuer to bee interrupted with any
worldly bufineffe; and there I leaue her with her bleffed Sonne our S A-
V I O V R and hers in eternall felicitie.

As for *Prayer to Saints*; C H R I S T (I am fure) hath commanded vs
to Come all to him that are loaden with finne, and hee will relieue vs:
and *Saint Paul* hath forbidden vs to worfhip Angels; or to vfe any fuch
voluntary worfhip, that hath a fhew of humilitie in that it fpareth not the
flefh. But what warrant wee haue to haue recourfe vnto thefe *Dij Pe-*
nates or *Tutelares*, thefe Courtiers of G O D, I know not; I remit that to
thefe Philofophicall Neoterike Diuines. It fatisfieth mee to pray to
G O D through C H R I S T as I am commanded, which I am fure muft be
the fafeft way; and I am fure the fafeft way is the beft way in points of faluation. But if the Romifh Church hath coined new Articles of Faith,
neuer heard of in the firft 500. yeeres after C H R I S T, I hope I fhall neuer bee condemned for an Heretike, for not being a Nouelift. Such are
the *priuate Maffes*, where the Prieft playeth the part both of the Prieft and
of the people; And fuch are the *Amputation of the one halfe of the Sacra-*
ment from the people, *The Tranfubftantiation, Eleuation for Adoration*, and
Circumportation in Proceffion of the Sacrament; *the workes of Supererro-*
gation, rightly named *Thefaurus Ecclefiæ*; *the Baptifing of Bels*, and a thoufand other trickes: But aboue all, *the worfhipping of Images.* If my faith
bee weake in thefe, I confeffe I had rather beleeue too little then too much:
And yet fince I beleeue as much as the Scriptures doe warrant, the Creeds
doe perfwade, and the ancient Councels decreed, I may well be a Schifma-
tike from *Rome*, but I am fure I am no Heretike.

For *Reliques of Saints*; If I had any fuch that I were affured were
members of their bodies, I would honourably bury them, and not giue
them the reward of condemned mens members, which are onely ordeined
to bee depriued of buriall: But for worfhipping either them or *Images*, I
muft account it damnable Idolatrie.

I am no *Iconomachus*, I quarrell not the making of Images, either for publike decoration, or for mens priuate vfes: But that they fhould bee worfhipped, bee prayed to, or any holineffe attributed vnto them, was neuer
knowen of the Ancients: And the Scriptures are fo directly, vehemently

Cc 2   and

Matt.11.28.

Colof.2.8,23.

and punctually against it, as I wonder what braine of man, or suggestion of Sathan durst offer it to Christians; and all must bee salued with nice Philosophicall distinctions: As, *Idolum nihil est* : and, They worship (for_sooth) the Images of things *in being*, and the Image of the trew G O D. But the Scripture forbiddeth to worship the Image of any thing that G O D created. It was not a *nihil* then that God forbade onely to be worshipped, neither was the brasen Serpent, nor the body of *Moses* a *nihil*; and yet the one was destroyed, and the other hidden for eschewing of Idolatrie. Yea, the Image of G O D himselfe is not onely expresly forbidden to bee wor_shipped, but euen to bee made. The reason is giuen, That no eye euer saw G O D; and how can we paint his face, when *Moses* (the man that euer was most familiar with G O D) neuer sawe but his backe parts ? Surely, since he cannot be drawen to the *viue*, it is a thankelesse labour to marre it with a false representation ; which no Prince, nor scarce any other man will bee contented with in their owne pictures. Let them therefore that maintaine this doctrine, answere it to C H R I S T at the latter day, when he shall accuse them of Idolatrie; And then I doubt if hee will bee payed with such nice sophisticall Distinctions.

But C H R I S T s Crosse must haue a particular priuiledge-(say they) and bee worshipped *ratione contactus*. But first wee must know what kinde of touching of C H R I S T s body drew a vertue from it ; whether euery touching, or onely touching by faith? That euery touching of his body drew not vertue from it, is more then manifest. When [1] the woman in the bloody fluxe touched him, shee was healed of her faith: But *Peter* then told him that a crowd and throng of many people then touched him; and yet none of them receiued any benefite or vertue from him. *Iudas* touched him many and many a time, besides his last kisse; so did the vil-laines that buffeted and crucified him; and yet I may safely pronounce them accursed, that would bestow any worship vpon their reliques : yea wee cannot denie but the land of *Canaan* it selfe (whereupon our Lord did dayly tread) is so visibly accursed, beeing gouerned by faithlesse *Turkes*, full of innumerable sects of hereticall Christians, and the very fer-tilitie thereof so farre degenerated into a pitifull sterilitie, as hee must bee accursed that accounteth it blessed. Nay, when a certaine [2] woman blessed the belly that bare C H R I S T, and the breastes that gaue him sucke; Nay, rather (saith hee) *Blessed are those that heare the Word of God, and keepe it.* Except then they could first prooue that C H R I S T had resolued to blesse that tree of the Crosse whereupon hee was nailed; they can neuer proue that his touching it could giue it any vertue. And put the case it had a vertue of doing miracles, as *Peters* shadow had; yet doeth it not fol-low, that it is lawful to worship it, which *Peter* would neuer accept of. Sure-ly the Prophets that in so many places curse those that worship Images, that haue eyes and see not, that haue eares and heare not, would much more haue cursed them that worship a piece of a sticke, that hath not so much

as

[1] Luke 8.

[2] Luk. 11.28.

as any refemblance or reprefentation of eyes or eares.

As for Purgatorie and all the * trafh depending thereupon, it is not worth the talking of; *Bellarmine* cannot finde any ground for it in all the Scriptures. Onely I would pray him to tell me; If that faire greene Meadow that is in Purgatorie, haue a brooke running thorow it; that in cafe I come there, I may haue hawking vpon it. But as for me; I am fure there is a Heauen and a Hell, *præmium & pæna*, for the Elect and reprobate: How many other roomes there be, I am not on God his counfell. *Multæ funt manfiones in domo Patris mei*, faith C H R I S T, who is the trew Purgatorie for our finnes: But how many chambers and anti-chambers the diuell hath, they can beft tell that goe to him: But in cafe there were more places for foules to goe to then we know of, yet let vs content vs with that which in his Word he hath reuealed vnto vs, and not inquire further into his fecrets. Heauen and Hell are there reuealed to be the eternall home of all mankinde: let vs indeauour to winne the one and efchew the other; and there is an end.

Now in all this difcourfe haue I yet left out the maine Article of the Romifh faith; and that is the *Head of the Church* or *Peters Primacie*; for who denieth this, denieth *fidem Catholicam*, faith *Bellarmine*. That Bifhops ought to be in the Church, I euer maintained it, as an Apoftolique inftitution, and fo the ordinance of God; contrary to the *Puritanes*, and likewife to [1] *Bellarmine*; who denies that Bifhops haue their Iurifdiction immediatly from God (But it is no wonder he takes the *Puritanes* part, fince *Iefuits* are nothing but *Puritan-papifts*.) And as I euer maintained the ftate of Bifhops, and the Ecclefiafticall Hierarchie for order fake; fo was I euer an enemie to the confufed Anarchie or paritie of the *Puritanes*, as well appeareth in my ΒΑΣΙΛΙΚΟΝ ΔΩΡΟΝ. Heauen is gouerned by order, and all the good Angels there; nay, Hell it felfe could not fubfift without fome order; And the very deuils are diuided into Legions, and haue their chiefetaines: how can any focietie then vpon earth, fubfift without order and degrees? And therefore I cannot enough wonder with what brafen face this Anfwerer could fay, *That I was a Puritane in Scotland, and an enemie to Proteftants*: I that was perfecuted by *Puritanes* there, not from my birth onely, but euen fince foure moneths before my birth? I that in the yeere of God 84. erected Bifhops, and deprefled all their popular Paritie, I then being not 18. yeeres of aage? I that in my faid Booke to my Sonne, doe fpeake tenne times more bitterly of them nor of the Papifts; hauing in my fecond Edition thereof, affixed along Apologetike Preface, onely in *odium Puritanorum?* and I that for the fpace of fixe yeeres before my comming into England, laboured nothing fo much as to depreffe their Paritie, and re-erect Bifhops againe? Nay, if the dayly Commentaries of my life and actions in Scotland, were written (as *Iulius Cæfars* were) there would fcarcely a moneth paffe in all my life, fince my entring into the 13. yeere of my aage, wherein fome accident or other would not conuince the Cardinall of a Lye in this point.

(margin notes)
* *Iubilees, Indulgences, fatisfactions for the dead, &c.*
Lib. 2. de Purgat. cap. 7.

Iohn 14.

[1] *Bell. lib. 4. de Rom. Pont. cap. 25.*

Page 98.

And furely I giue a faire commendation to the Puritanes in that place of my booke, Where I affirme that I haue found greater honeftie with the high-land and border theeues, then with that fort of people. But leauing him to his owne impudence, I returne to my purpofe.

Of *Bifhops* and Church Hierarchie I very well allowe (as I faid before) and likewife of Ranks and Degrees amongft *Bifhops. Patriarches* (I know) were in the time of the Primitiue Church, and I likewife reuerence that Inftitution for order fake: and amongft them was a contention for the firft place. And for my felfe (if that were yet the queftion) I would with all my heart giue my confent that the *Bifhop* of *Rome* fhould haue the firft Seate: I being a welterne King would goe with the *Patriarch* of the Welt. And for his temporall Principalitie ouer the Signory of *Rome*, I doe not quarrell it neither; let him in God his Name be *Primus Epifcopus inter om-nes Epifcopos*, and *Princeps Epifcoporum*; fo it be no otherwife but as *Peter* was *Princeps Apoftolorum*. But as I well allow of the Hierarchie of the Church for diftinction of orders (for fo I vnderftand it) fo I vtterly deny that there is an earthly *Monarch* thereof, whofe word muft be a Law, and who cannot erre in his Sentence, by an infallibilitie of Spirit. Becaufe earthly Kingdomes muft haue earthly *Monarches*; it doeth not follow, that the Church muft haue a vifible *Monarch* too: for the world hath not O N E earthly temporall *Monarch*. C H R I S T is his Churches *Monarch*, and the holy Ghoft his Deputie: *Reges gentium dominantur eorum, vos au-tem non fic.* C H R I S T did not promife before his afcenfion, to leaue *Peter* with them to direct and iuftruct them in all things; but he promifed to fend the holy Ghoft vnto them for that end.

Luke 22.25.

Iohn 14.26.

And as for thefe two before cited places, vvhereby *Bellarmine* maketh the Pope to triumph ouer Kings: I meane *Pafce oues*, and *Tibi dabo claues*: the Cardinall knowes well enough, that the fame words of *Tibi dabo*, are in another place fpoken by *Chrift* in the plurall number. And he likewife knowes what reafon the Ancients doe giue, why *Chrift* bade *Pater pafcere oues*: and alfo what a cloude of witneffes there is, both of Ancients, and euen of late Popifh writers, yea diuers Cardinals, that do all agree that both thefe fpeeches vfed to *Peter*, were meant to all the Apoftles reprefented in his perfon: Otherwife how could *Paul* direct the Church of *Corinth* to excommunicate the inceftuous perfon *cum fpiritu fuo*, whereas he fhould then haue fayd, *cum fpiritu Petri?* And how could all the Apoftles haue otherwife vfed all their cenfures, onely in *Chrifts* Name, and neuer a word of his Vicar? *Peter* (wee reade) did in all the Apoftles meetings fit amongft them as one of their number: And when chofen men were fent to *Antiochia* from that great Apoftolike *Councel* at *Ierufalem* (*Acts* 15.) The text faith, It feemed good to the Apoftles and Elders with the whole Church, to fend chofen men, but no mention made of the Head thereof; and fo in their Letters no mention is made of *Peter*, but onely of the Apoftles, Elders and Brethren. And it is a wonder, why *Paul* rebuketh the Church of

Matth.18.18.

1.Cor.5.4.

Act.15.12,23.

Corinth for making exception of Perfons, becaufe fome followed *Paul,* fome *Apollos,* fome *Cephas,* if *Peter* was their vifible Head! for then thofe that followed not *Peter* or *Cephas,* renounced the Catholike faith. But it appeareth well that *Paul* knew little of our new doctrine, fince he handleth *Peter* fo rudely, as he not onely compareth but preferreth himfelfe vnto him. But our Cardinall proues *Peters* fuperioritie, by *Pauls* going to vifite him. Indeed *Paul* faith, hee went to *Ierufalem* to vifite *Peter,* and conferre with him; but he fhould haue added, and to kiffe his feet.

To conclude then, The trweth is that *Peter* was both in aage, and in the time of C H R I S T S calling him, one of the firft of the Apoftles; In order the principall of the firft twelue, and one of the three whom C H R I S T for order fake preferred to all the reft. And no further did the Bifhop of *Rome* claime for three hundred yeeres after C H R I S T: Subiect they were to the generall Councels, and euen but of late did the Councell of *Conftance* depofe three Popes, and fet vp the fourth. And vntill Phocas dayes (that murthered his mafter) were they fubiect to Emperours. But how they are now come to be *Chrifts* Vicars, nay, Gods on earth, triple-crowned, Kings of heauen, earth and hell, Iudges of all the world, and none to iudge them; Heads of the faith, Abfolute deciders of all Controuerfies by the infallibility of their fpirit, hauing all power both Spirituall and Temporall in their hands; the high Bifhops, Monarches of the whole earth, Superiours to all Emperours and Kings; yea, Supreme Vice-gods, who whether they will or not cannot erre: how they are now come (I fay) to the toppe of greatneffe, I know not: but fure I am, Wee that are K I N G s haue greateft neede to looke vnto it. As for me, *Paul* and *Peter* I know, but thefe men I know not: And yet to doubt of this, is to denie the Catholique faith; Nay, the world it felfe muft be turned vpfide downe, and the order of Nature inuerted (making the left hand to haue the place before the Right, and the laft named to bee the firft in honour) that this primacie may bee maintained.

Thus haue I now made a free Confeffion of my Faith: And (I hope) I haue fully cleared my felfe from being an Apoftate; and as farre from being an Heretike, as one may bee that beleeueth the Scriptures, and the three Creedes, and acknowledgeth the foure firft generall Councels. If I bee loath to beleeue too much, efpecially of Nouelties, men of greater knowledge may well pitie my weakeneffe; but I am fure none will condemne me for an Heretike, faue fuch as make the Pope their God; and thinke him fuch a fpeaking Scripture, as they can define Herefie no otherwife, but to bee whatfoeuer Opinion is maintained againft the Popes definition of faith. And I will fincerely promife, that when euer any point of the Religion I profeffe, fhalbe proued to be new, and not Ancient, Catholike, and Apoftolike (I meane for matter of Faith) I will as foone renounce it; clofing vp this head with the *Maxime* of *Vincentius Lirinenfis,* that I will neuer refufe to imbrace any opinion in Diuinity neceffary to

faluation

1. Cor. 1. 12.

Galat. 2.
Galat. 1. 18.

Bellar. de Rom. Pont. li. 1. cap. 17.

Libello aduerfus harefes.

ſaluation, which the whole Catholike Church With an vnanime conſent, haue conſtantly taught and beleeued euen from the Apoſtles dayes, for the ſpace of many aages thereafter without any interruption. But in the Cardinals opinion, I haue ſhewed my ſelfe an Heretike (I am ſure) in playing with the name of *Babylon,* and the Towne vpon *ſeuen hilles* ; as if I would inſinuate *Rome* at this preſent to be ſpiritually *Babylon.* And yet that *Rome* is called *Babylon,* both in *Saint Peters* Epiſtle, and in the *Apocalyps,* our Anſwerer freely confeſſeth. As for the definition of the *Antichriſt,* I will not vrge ſo obſcure a point, as a matter of Faith to bee neceſſarily beleeued of all Chriſtians; but what I thinke herein, I will ſimply declare.

That there muſt be an *Antichriſt,* and in his time a generall Defection; wee all agree. But the *Time, Seat,* and *Perſon* of this *Antichriſt,* are the chiefe Queſtions whereupon wee differ: and for that we muſt ſearch the Scriptures for our reſolution. As for my opinion; I thinke S. *Paul* in the 2. to the *Theſſalonians* doeth vtter more clearely that which *Saint Iohn* ſpeaketh more myſtically of the *Antichriſt.*

Firſt, that in that place hee meaneth the *Antichriſt,* it is plaine, ſince hee faith, *There muſt bee firſt a Defection*; and that in the *Antichriſts* time onely that eclipſe of Defection muſt fall vpon the Church, all the *Romiſh Catholikes* are ſtrong enough: otherwiſe their Church muſt be daily ſubiect to erre, which is cleane contrary to their maine doctrine. Then deſcribing him (hee ſaith) that *The man of Sinne, Filius perditionis, ſhall exalt himſelfe aboue all that is called God.* But who theſe be whom of the *Pſalmiſt* faith *Dixi vos Dij eſtis, Bellarmine* can tell. In old Diuinitie it was wont to bee *Kings; Bellarmine* will adde *Churchmen*; Let it bee both. It is well enough knowen, who now exalteth himſelfe aboue both the ſwords.

And after that S. *Paul* hath thus deſcribed the *Perſon,* he next deſcribeth the *Seat,* and telleth that *He ſhall ſit in the Temple of God,* that is, the boſome of the Church ; yea, in the very heart thereof. Now where this Apoſtolike Seat is, I leaue to bee gueſſed : And likewiſe who it is that ſitting there, ſheweth himſelfe to be GOD; pardoning ſinnes, redeeming ſoules, and defining Faith, controlling and iudging all men, and to be iudged of none.

Anent the *Time,* S. *Paul* is plaineſt of all : For hee calleth the *Theſſalonians* to memorie, *That when hee was with them, hee told them theſe things*; and therefore *they know* (faith hee) *what the impediment was, and who did withhold that the man of Sinne was not reuealed,* although *the myſterie of iniquitie was already working.* That the Romane Emperours in *Saint Pauls* time needed no reuealing to the Chriſtians to bee men of Sinne or ſinfull men, no childe doubteth: but the reuelation hee ſpeaketh of was a *myſterie,* a *ſecret*; It ſhould therefore ſeeme that hee durſt not publiſh in his Epiſtle what that impediment was. It may be he meant by the tranſlating of the Seat of the *Romane* Empire, and that the tranſlation thereof ſhould leaue a roume for the man of *Sinne* to ſit downe in. And that he meant not *that man of Sinne* of theſe Ethnicke Emperours in his time, his introduction to

this

1.Pet.5.13.
2.Theſ.2.
Verſe 3.
Verſe 3,4.
Pſal.82.6.
2.Theſſ.2.4.
Verſe 5.
Verſe 6.
Verſe 7.

this difcourfe maketh it more then manifeft. For he faith (fearing they fhould be deceiued, thinking the day of the Lords fecond comming to bee at hand) he hath therefore thought good to forewarne them that this generall Defection muft firft come: Whereby it well appeareth that hee could not meane by the prefent time but by a future, and that a good long time; otherwife he proued ill his argument, that the Lords comming was not at hand. Neither can the forme of the Deftruction of this man of *Sinne* agree with that maner of fpoile, that the *Gothes* and *Vandals* made of * *Ethnick Rome* : For our Apoftle faith, [1] *That this wicked man fhull bee confumed by the Spirit of the Lords mouth, and abolifhed by his comming.* Now I would thinke that the word of God and the Preaching thereof, fhould be meant *by the Spirit of the Lords mouth,* which fhould peece and peece confume and diminifh the power of that man of Sinne, till the brightnes of the Lords fecond comming fhould vtterly abolifh him. And by his expreffing the meanes of his working, he doeth likewife (in my opinion) explane his meaning very much: For he faith, *It fhall be by a ftrong delufion, by lying wonders, &c.* Well, what Church it is that vanteth them of their innumerable miracles, and yet moft of them contrary to their owne doctrine ; *Bellarmine* can beft tell you with his hungry Mare, that turned her taile to her prouender and kneeled to the Sacrament: And yet (I am fure) he will be afhamed to fay, that the holy Sacrament is ordained to be worfhipped by *Oues & Boues, & cætera pecora campi.*

Thus haue I prooued out of *S. Paul* now, that the time of the Antichrifts comming, and the generall Defection was not to be till long after the time that he wrote in ; That his Seat was to be in the Temple and Church of God ; and, That his Action (which can beft point at his Perfon) fhould be to *Exalt himfelfe aboue all that were called Gods.* S. *Iohn* indeed doth more amply, though myftically defcribe this Antichrift, which vnder the figure of a monftrous Beaft, with feuen heads and ten hornes, he fets forth in the xiij. chap. and then interpreteth in the xvij. where hee calles her a *Whore fitting vpon many waters,* and *riding vpon the fayd monftrous Beaft* ; concluding that chapter with calling that Woman, *that great City which reigneth ouer the Kings of the earth.* And both in that Chapter, and in the beginning of the next he calles that great Citie, *Babylon.*

So as to continue herein my formerly purpofed Methode, of the Time, Seat, and Perfon of Antichrift ; this place doth clearely and vndenyably declare that *Rome* is, or fhalbe the Seat of that Antichrift. For firft, no Papift now denieth that by *Babylon* here *Rome* is directly meant ; and that this Woman is the Antichrift, doeth clearely appeare by the time of his working (defcribed by 42. monethis in the xiij. Chap.) which doeth iuftly agree with that three yeeres and a halfes time, which all the Papifts giue to the Reigne of Antichrift. Befides that, the Beaft it felfe with feuen heads and tenne hornes, hauing one of her heads wounded and healed againe, is defcribed iuft alike in the xiij. and xvij. Chap. being in the former prooued

to

* For fo doeth *Tortus* call *Rome* when it was fpoiled by them, though it was Chriftian many yeres before.

[1] Verfe 8.

Verfe. 8. 9.

Bellar. lib. 3. de Eucharift. cap. 8

Reuel. 17. v. 1. Verf. 3.

Verf 18.

Verf. 5.

Cap. 18. v. 1.

Verf. 5.

to be the *Antichrist* by the time of her reigne; and in the latter *Rome* by the name of *Babylon*, by the confeſſion of all the Papiſts; So as one point is now cleare, that *Rome* is the *Seat* of the *Antichriſt*.

    Neither will that place in the eleuenth Chapter ſerue to ſhift off this point, and proue the *Antichriſts Seat* to bee in *Ieruſalem*; where it is ſaide; *That the Corpſes of the Witneſſes ſhall lie in the great City*, *ſpiritually Sodome and Egypt*, *where our Lord alſo was crucified.* For the word *ſpiritually* is applied both to *Sodome*, *Egypt* and *Ieruſalem* in that place; And when hee hath named *Sodome* and *Egypt*, hee doeth not ſubioyne *Ieruſalem* with a ſingle *vbi*; but with an *vbi &*, as if hee would ſay; and this *Antichriſts* abomination ſhall bee ſo great, as his Seate ſhall bee as full of Spirituall whoredomes and Idolatries, as *Sodome* and *Egypt* was; nay, and ſo bloody in the perſecution of the Saints, as our Lord ſhall be crucified againe in his members. And who hath ſo meanely read the Scriptures (if he haue euer read them at all) that knoweth it not to be a common phraſe in them, to call C H R I S T perſecuted and ſlaine, when his Saints are ſo vſed? So did C H R I S T ſay, ſpeaking of the latter day; and in the ſame ſtyle did hee ſpeake to S. *Paul* at his conuerſion. And that *Babylon*, or *Rome* (ſince *Bellarmine* is contented it bee ſo called) is that great Citie where our Lord was crucified, the laſt verſe of the xviij. Chap. doeth alſo clearely proue it: For there it is ſaid, That *in that City was found the blood of the Prophets, and of the Saints, and of all that were ſlaine vpon the earth*; and I hope C H R I S T was one of them that were ſlaine vpon the earth. And beſides that it may well bee ſaid that hee was ſlaine in that great Citie *Babylon*, ſince by the *Romane* authoritie hee was put to death, vnder a *Romane* Iudge, and for a *Romane* quarrell: for he could not be a friend to *Cæſar*, that was not his enemie.

    This point now being cleared of the *Antichriſts Seate*, as I haue already ſayd, we are next to find out the *Time* when the *Antichriſt* ſhall reigne, if it be not already come. In the xiij. Chapter S. *Iohn* ſaith, that this Beaſt with the ſeuen heads and tenne hornes, *had one of his heads wounded and healed againe*; and interpreting that in the xvij. he ſaith, that *theſe ſeuen heads are alſo ſeuen Kings, whereof fiue are fallen, one is, and an other is not yet come, and when hee commeth hee ſhall continue a ſhort ſpace. And the Beaſt that was and is not, is the eight, and yet one of the ſeuen.* By which Beaſt hee meaneth the *Antichriſt*, who was not then come, I meane in the Apoſtles dayes, but was to come after. So as betweene the time of the Apoſtles and the ende of the worlde, muſt the *Time* of the *Antichriſts* comming be; and with this the Papiſts doe alſo agree. Whereby it appeareth that *Babylon*, which is *Rome*, ſhall bee the *Seate* of the *Antichriſt*; but not that *Ethnicke Rome* which was in the Apoſtles dayes (for *Iohn* himſelfe profeſſeth that hee is to write of nothing, but that which is to come after his time.) Nor yet that turning *Chriſtian Rome* while ſhee was in the conuerting, which immediatly followed the Apoſtles time, glorious by the Martyrdome of ſo many godly

                                           Biſhops:

Marginal notes:

Chap. 11.8.

Matt. 25.40.
Acts 9.4.

Reuel. 18.24.

Cha. 13.3.
Chap. 17.10.

Verſe 11.

Reuel. 1.1.
& chap. 4.1.

Bishops: But that *Antichristian Rome*,when as the Antichrist shal set downe his seat there, after that by the working of that Mysterie of iniquitie, *Christian Rome* shall become to be corrupted; and so that deadly wound, which the *Gothes* and *Vandales* gaue Rome, shall bee cured in that Head or King, the *Antichrist*, who thereafter shall arise and reigne for a long space.

   But here it may bee obiected, that the *Antichrist* cannot reigne a long space; since S. *Iohn* saith in two or three sundry places, that the *Antichrist* shall worke but the space of three yeeres and a halfe. Surely who will but a little acquaint himselfe with the phrases and Stile of S. *Iohn* in his *Apocalyps*, shall finde that he doth ordinarily set downe *numerum certum pro incerto.* So doeth hee in his twelue thousand of euery Tribe that will bee safe; so doeth he in his Armie of two hundred thousand, that were sent to kill the third part of the men; and so doeth he in diuers other places. And therefore who will but remember that in all his Visions in the said Booke, hee directly imitates the fashions of the Prophet *Ezekiels, Daniels,* and *Zacharies* Visions (borrowing their phrases that prophecied before CHRIST, to vtter his Prophecies in, that was to speake of the last dayes) shall finde it very probable that in these three dayes and a halfe, hee imitated *Daniels* Weekes, accounting for his Weeke the time betweene CHRISTS first and second comming, and making *Antichrist* to triumph the halfe of that time or spirituall Weeke. For as to that literall interpretation (as all the Papists make it) of three yeeres and a halfe, and that time to fall out directly the very last dayes, saue fiue and fourtie, before CHRIST his second comming, it is directly repugnant to the whole New TESTAMENT. For CHRIST saith, That in the latter dayes men shall be feasting, marrying, and at all such worldly businesse, when the last houre shall come in a clap vpon them; One shall be at the Mill; One vpon the top of the house, and so foorth. CHRIST telleth a Parable of the fiue foolish Virgins, to shew the vnlooked-for comming of this houre; Nay, hee saith, the Sonne of man, nor the Angels in heauen know not this time. S. *Peter* biddeth vs WATCH AND PRAY, euer awaiting vpon that houre. And S. *Iohn* in this same *Apocalyps* doeth [1] twise tell vs, that CHRIST will come as a thiefe in the night; And so doeth CHRIST say in the [2] *Euangel.* Whereas if the *Antichrist* shall reigne three yeeres and a halfe before the Latter day, and that there shall bee but iust fourtie fiue dayes of time after his destruction; then shall not the iust day and houre of the Latter day, bee vnknowne to them that shall be aliue in the world, at the time of *Antichrists* destruction. For first according to the Papists doctrine, all the world shall know him to be the *Antichrist*, both by the two Witnesses doctrine, and his sudden destruction; And consequently they cannot be ignorant, that the Latter day shall come iust fourtie fiue dayes after: and so CHRIST shall not come as a thiefe, nor the world bee taken at vnawares; contrary to all the Scriptures before alleadged, and many more. And thus haue we proued Rome to be the Seat of the *Antichrist*, and the second halfe of that spirituall

Margin notes:
Chap.7.
Chap.9.16, 18.

Matth.24.41.
Matth.25.

[1] Reuel.3.3. and 16.15.
[2] Matth.24. 44.

rituall Weeke betweene the first and second comming of C H R I S T, to be the time of his Reigne: For in the first halfe thereof the mysterie of iniquitie began to worke; but the man of Sinne was not yet reuealed.

. But who these Witnesses should be, is a great question. The generall conceit of the Papists is, that it must bee *Enoch* and *Elias.* And heerein is *Bellarmine* so strong, as hee thinketh him in a great errour (if not an Heretike) that doubteth of it. But the vanitie of the Iewish fable I will in few words discouer.

Bellar. de Rom.
Pont. lib.3.
cap.6.

The Cardinall, in his booke of Controuersies, bringeth foure places of Scripture for probation of this idle dreame: two in the. Old Testament, *Malachie* and *Ecclesiasticus*, and two in the New, C H R I S T in *Matthew* (hee might haue added *Marke* too) and *Iohn* in the xj. of the *Apocalyps.* First, for the generall of all those places, I dare boldly affirme, That there is not a word in them, nor in all the rest of the Scriptures that saith, that either *Enoch* or *Elias* shall returne to fight against *Antichrist,* and shall bee slaine by him, nor any such like matter. Next as to euery place in particular, to begin with *Malachie,* I know not who can better interpret him then C H R I S T, who twise in *Matthew*, Chap.xj. and xvij. and once in *Marke,* tels both the multitude, and his owne Disciples, that *Iohn Baptist* was

Matt.11.14.
and 17.12.
Mar.9.13.

that promised *Elias.* And heerein doeth *Bellarmine* deale most vnfaithfully with C H R I S T: for in his demonstration that *Antichrist* is not yet come, because *Enoch* and *Elias* are not yet returned; hee for his probation thereof, citeth these wordes of C H R I S T in the xvij of *Matthew,* *Elias shall indeed come, and restore all things*; but omits his very next wordes interpreting the same, *That hee is already come,* in the person of *Iohn Baptist.* Nay, whereby hee taketh vpon him to answere *Biblianders* obiection, that C H R I S T did by *Iohn* the *Baptist,* vnderstand the prophecie of *Elias* comming to be accomplished, he picketh out the words, *Qui habet aures, audiat*, in the xj. of *Matthew*, immediatly following that purpose of *Elias,* making of them a great mysterie: and neuer taketh knowledge, that in the xvij. by himselfe before alleaged, C H R I S T doeth interpret *Malachie* in the same maner without any subioyning of these words, *Qui habet aures, audiat*; adioyning shamelesly hereunto a foule Paraphrase of his owne, telling vs what C H R I S T would haue said; nay, in my conscience, he meant what C H R I S T should and ought to haue said, if he had bene a good Catholike, setting downe there a glosse of *Orleance* that destroyes the Text. Thus ye see: how shamefully he abuseth C H R I S T s words, who in three sundry places (as I haue said) interpreteth the second comming of *Elias* to be meant by *Iohn* the *Baptist.* He likewise cauils most dishonestly vpon that word *Venturus.* For C H R I S T vseth that word but in the repeating their opinion: but interpreting it that he was already come, in the *person of Iohn Baptist.* As if hee had said, The prophecie is indeed trew that *Elias* shall

Matt.17.11.

come; but I say vnto you, that *Elias iam venit,* meaning of *Iohn Baptist* and so he first repeats the words of the prophecie in the future time, as the

Prophe

Prophet fpake them; and next fheweth them to be now accomplifhed in the perfon of *Iohn*, in the prefent time. Neither can thefe words of *Malachie* [*Dies magnus & horribilis*] falfifie CHRISTS Commentarie vpon him. For if that day whereupon the Sauiour of the world fuffered, when the [1] Sunne was totally obfcured from the fixt houre to the ninth; the Vaile of the Temple rent afunder from the top to the bottome; and the earth did quake, the ftones were clouen, the graues did open themfelues, and the dead arofe: If that day (I fay) was not a great and horrible day, I know not what to call a horrible day. Which day no doubt had deftroyed the whole nation of the *Iewes* without exception by a iuft *Anatheme*, if the faid *Iohn* the fore-runner had not firft conuerted many by the doctrine of *Repentance* and by *Baptifme*. But why fhould I prefume any more to interprete *Malachie*, fince it is fufficient that CHRIST himfelfe hath interpreted him fo? And fince *Ipfe dixit*; nay, *ter dixit, per quem facta funt omnia*, what mortall man dare interprete him otherwife; nay, directly contrary?

Now for that place of *Ecclefiafticus*; as the fon of *Sirach* onely borroweth it from *Malachie* (as appeareth by thefe words of his, of *conuerting the fonnes hearts to their fathers*, which are *Malachies* own words) fo doth CHRISTS Comentary ferue as well to interprete the one as the other : it being no fhame for that mortal *Iefus*, to be commented & interpreted by the immortall and trew IESVS, though to the fhame & confufion of the *Iefuits* herefies herein.

But *Enoch* muft be ioyned to *Elias* in this errand, onely to beare vp the couples, as I thinke. For no place of Scripture fpeaketh of his returning againe, onely it is faid in *Ecclefiafticus* the 44.that *Enoch* pleafed GOD, and was tranflated to *Paradife*, *vt daret Gentibus fapientiam*, or *pœnitentiam*; fince they will haue it fo. And what is this to fay? marry that *Enoch* fhall returne againe to this world, and fight againft the *Antichrift*. A prettie large Comment indeed, but no right Commentary vpon that Text. When *Bellarmine* was talking of *Elias*; he infifted, That *Elias* muft come to conuert the *Iewes* principally, *reftituere tribus Iacob*. But when he fpeaketh here of *Enoch*, he muft *dare Gentibus pœnitentiam*, and not a word of *Iewes*. Belike they fhall come for fundry errands, and not both for one : Or like *Paul* and *Peter*, the one fhall be Apoftle for the *Iewes*, and the other for the *Gentiles*. What need fuch wilde racked Commentaries for fuch three wordes? Will not the fenfe ftand well and clearely enough, that *Enoch* pleafed GOD, and was tranflated to *Paradife*; that by the example of his reward, the Nations might repent and imitate his Holy footfteps? For what could more mightily perfwade the Nations to repent; then by letting them fee that holy Man carried quicke vp to Heauen, for reward of his vprightneffe; whereas all the reft of the people died and went to corruption? And where Scripture faileth, the Cardinall muft helpe himfelfe with the Fathers, to prooue both that *Enoch* and *Elias* are yet aliue, and that they fhall hereafter die; but with the like felicitie, as in his alledging of Scriptures; to vfe his owne words of mee in his [2] pamphlet : For which purpofe

D d   he

Malach.4.5.
Matth.27.

[1] This obfcuring of the Sunne was fo extraordinary and feare full, that *Dionyfius*, onely led by the light of Nature and humane learning, cried out at the fight thereof, *Aut Deus patitur; aut vices patientis dolet.* *Mala.4.6.*

Ecclus.48.8.

Mala.4.6.

Ecclus.44.16.

[2] *Pag.27.*

he citeth fiue Fathers; *Irenæus*, *Tertullian*, *Epiphanius*, *Hierome* and *Augustine*. Vpon this they all agree in deed, that *Enoch* and *Elias* are ftill aliue both, which no Chriftian (I hope) will denie: For *Abraham*, *Isaac*, and *Iacob* are all

Matt. 22,32.

ftill aliue, as C H R I S T telleth vs; for God is *Deus viuentium, non mortuorum*. Much more then are *Enoch* and *Elias* aliue, who neuer tafted of death after the maner of other men. But as to the next point, that they fhould die here-after, his firft two witneffes, *Irenæus* and *Tertullian* fay the direct contrary:

Lib. 5.

For *Irenæus* faith, that they fhall remaine in *Paradife*, till the confummation, *confpicantes incorruptionem*. Now to remaine there till the confummation, and to fee incorruption, is directly contrary to their returning to the world

Lib cont. Iu-dæos, cap. 2.

againe and fuffering of death. *Tertullian* likewife agreeing hereunto, faith moft clearely, That *Enoch* hath neuer tafted of death, *vt æternitatis candidatus*: now he is ill priuiledged with eternitie, if he muft die againe. As for his places cited out of the other three Fathers, they all confirme that firft point, That they are ftil aliue: but that they muft die again, they make no mention.

But he fpeaking of the *Ancient Fathers*, let mee take this occafion to fore-warne you concerning them : That though they miftake and vnderftand not rightly many myfteries in the *Apocalyps*, it is no wonder: For the booke thereof, was ftill fealed in their dayes. And though *the myfterie of iniquitie*

2. Theff. 2.

was already working, yet was not *the man of Sinne* yet reuealed. And it is a certaine rule in all darke prophecies ; That they are neuer clearely vnder-ftood, till they be accomplifhed.

And thus hauing anfwered his two places, in the Old *Teftament*, by his third in the New *Teftament*, conteining *Chrifts* owne words : which being *luce clariora*, I need fpeake no more of them. I am now to fpeake of the fourth place of Scripture, which is in the xj. of the *Apocalyps* : For the two

Reuelat. 11.

Witneffes (forfooth) there mentioned, muft be *Enoch* and *Elias*. But how this can ftand with any point of Diuinitie or likelihood of reafon, that thefe two glorified Bodies fhall come downe out of heauen or Paradife, (make it what you will) preach, and fight againft the *Antichrift*, bee flaine by him af-ter many thoufand yeeres exempted from the naturall courfe of death, rife againe the third day in imitation of C H R I S T, and then (hauing wrought many wonders) to goe vp againe to Heauen, making an ordinary Pofte be-twixt Heauen and Earth : how this (I fay) can agree either with Diuinitie or good Reafon, I confeffe it paffeth my capacitie. And efpecially that they muft be clad in Sackcloth, whofe bodies (I hope) haue bene fo long agone free from finne, as I thinke they fhall neede no more fuch maceration for finne: For they muft be now either in Heauen or *Paradife*: If in heauen, (as doubtleffe they are) their bodies muft bee glorified ; for no corruptible

Reuel. 21.27.

thing can enter there ; and confequently they can no more bee fubiect to the fenfible things of this world, efpecially to death: But if they be in earth-ly *Paradife*, we muft firft know where it is.

Bellarmine indeed in his Controuerfies is much troubled to finde out

Lib de Grat. primi hominis.

the place where *Paradife* is , and whether it bee in the earth, or in the ayre. But

But thefe are all vanities. The Scriptures tell vs; that *Paradife* and the garden of *Eden* therein, was a certaine place vpon the earth, which G O D chofe out to fet *Adam* into, and hauing thereafter for his finne banifhed him from the fame, it is a blafphemie to thinke that any of *Adams* pofteritie came euer there againe. For in *Adam* were all his pofteritie accurfed, and banifhed from the earthly *Paradife*: like as all the earth in generall, and *Paradife* in fpeciall were accurfed in him; the fecond *Adam* hauing by grace, called a certaine number of them to bee Coheritours, with him of the heauenly *Paradife* and *Ierufalem*. And doubtlefly, the earthly *Paradife* was defaced at the Flood, if not before: and fo loft all that exquifite fertilitie and pleafantneffe, wherein it once furpaffed all the reft of the earth. And that it fhould be lifted vp in the ayre, is like one of the dreames of the *Alcoran*. Surely no fuch miracle is mentioned in the Scriptures, and hath no ground but from the curious fancies of fome boyling braines, who cannot be content, *Sapere ad fobrietatem.* Gen.2: 5

. In heauen then for certaine are *Enoch* and *Elias*: for *Enoch* (faith the Text) walked with G O D, and was taken vp, and *Elias* was feene caried vp to heauen in a fierie chariot. And that they who haue beene the In-dwellers of Heauen thefe many thoufand yeeres, and are freed from the Lawes of mortalitie; that thefe glorious and incorruptible bodies (I fay) fhall come in the world againe, preach and worke miracles, and fighting againft the *Antichrift* be flaine by him, whom naturall death could not before take hold of: as it is a fabulous inuention, fo is it quite contrary to the nature of fuch fanctified creatures. Efpecially I wonder, why *Enoch* fhould bee thought to bee one of thefe two Witneffes for C H R I S T: For it was *Mofes* and *Elias* that were with C H R I S T, at the tranffiguration; fignifying the Law and the Prophets: which would be the fitteft witneffes for conuincing of *Antichrift*. But why they haue exempted *Mofes*, and put *Enochs* head in the yoake, I cannot conceiue. So as I haue too much laboured in the refuting of this foolifh, and indeed childifh fable; which I am fo farre from beleeuing in any fort, as I proteft in G O D s prefence, I cannot hold any learned Diuine (in our aage now) to be a Chriftian, that will beleeue it; but worthy to bee ranked with the Scribes and Pharifes, that raued and dreamed vpon the comming againe of *Elias*, though C H R I S T told them the contrary. As for fome of the Ancients that miftooke this matter, I doe not cenfure them fo hardly; for the reafon that I haue already alleaged concerning them. Rom.12.3.
Gen 5.24.
2.King.2.10,
11.

And hauing now refuted that idle fable; that thofe two Witneffes were *Enoch* and *Elias*: it falleth mee next to gueffe, what in my opinion fhould bee meant by them. I confeffe, it is farre eafier to refute fuch a groundleffe fable as this is, contrary to all grounds of Diuinitie and Reafon; then to fet downe a trew interpretation of fo high and darke a Miftery. And therefore as I will not prefume to bind any other man to my opinion herein, if his owne reafon leade him not thereunto; fo fhall I propone fuch probable coniectures, as (I hope) fhall be free from Herefie, or vnlawfull curiofitie.

In two diuers fashions may the Mysterie of these Witnesses be lawfully and probably interpreted, in my opinion. Whereof the one is, that by these two Witnesses should be meant the Old and New Testaments: For as the *Antichrist* cannot chuse but bee an aduersary to the Word of GOD aboue all things; so will hee omit no endeuour to disgrace, corrupt, suppresse and destroy the same.   And now whether this Booke of the two Testaments, or two Witnesses of CHRIST, haue suffered any violence by the *Babylonian Monarchie* or not; I need say nothing; *Res ipsa loquitur.* I will not weary you with recounting those Common Places vsed for disgracing it: as calling it a *Nose of waxe, a dead Letter, a leaden Rule,* a hundreth such like phrases of reproch. But how farre the Traditions of men, and authoritie of the Church are preferred to these Witnesses, doeth sufficiently appeare in the *Babylonian* doctrine.   And if there were no more but that little booke, with that prettie Inscription, *De l'Insuffisance de l'Escriture Sainte;* it is enough to proue it.

And as to the corrupting therof; the corruptions of the old Latine translation must not be corrected, though it bid *euertere domum* in stead of *euerrere,* for seeking of a penie; and though it say of *Iohn, Sic eum volo manere donec veniam,* in place of *Si,* though it be knowne a plaine Lie, and that the very next words of the Text disproue the same. Nay, so farre must wee be from correcting it, as that the Vulgar Translation must be preferred by Catholikes, to the Bible in the owne Originall tongue. And is it a small corrupting of Scriptures to make all, or the most part of the *Apocrypha* of equall faith with the *Canonicall* Scriptures, contrary to the Fathers opinions and Decrees of ancient Councels? And what blasphemous corrupting of Scripture is it, to turne *Dominus* into *Domina* throughout the whole Psalmes? And thus our Ladies Psalter was lately reprinted in *Paris.* Is not this to confound CHRISTs person with hers? And as for suppressing of the Scriptures; how many hundreth yeeres were the people kept in such blindenes, as these Witnesses were almost vnknowne? for the Layicks durst not, being forbidden, and the most part of the Cleargie, either would or could not meddle with them.

Thus were these two Witnesses of CHRIST, (whom of himselfe saith, *Scrutamini Scripturas, illæ enim testimonium perhibent de me)* These [1]two Oliues bringing peace to all the beleeuers, euen peace of Conscience: These [2]two Candlesticks standing in the sight of GOD, and giuing light to the Nations; represented by Candlesticks euen in the very order of the *Roman Masse:* Thus were these two Witnesses (I say) disgraced, corrupted and suppressed (nay, so suppressed and silenced, as he was brent for an Heretike that durst presume to looke vpon them) kept close in a strange tongue, that they might not be vnderstood, *Legends* and lying wonders supplying their place in the Pulpits. And so did their *Bodies lie in the streets of the great Citie, spiritually Sodome,* for spiritual fornication which is idolatrie; *spiritually Egypt,* for bringing the Saints of God in bodage of humane traditions [*Quare oneramini*

ramini

Cardinall Peron.

Luke 15.8.
Iohn 21.22, 23.

Made by Bonuentura Docter Seraphicus.

Iohn 5.39.
¹ Reuel. 11.4.
² Ibid.

See Expositio Missæ, annexed to Ordo Romanus, set forth by G. Cassander.

Verse 8.

Coloss 2.20.

ramini ritibus.] So did *their bodies* (I fay) *lie* 3 *.dayes and a halfe* ; that is, the halfe of that fpirituall Weeke betweene CHRIST his firft and fecond comming ; and as dead carkafes indeed did the Scriptures then lye without a monument, being layed open to all contempt, cared for almoft by none, vnderftood by as few; nay, no man durft call for them for feare of punifhment, as I haue already faid. And thus lying dead, as it were, without life or vigour (as the Law of GOD did till it was reuiued in *Iofias* time) The *Inhabitants of the earth,* that is, worldly men *reioyced and fent gifts to other,* for ioy that their flefhly libertie was now no more awed, nor curbed by that two edged fword, for they were now fure, that do what they would, their purfe would procure them pardons from *Babylon. Omnia venalia Roma* ; fo as men needed no more to looke vp to heauen, but downe to their purfes to finde Pardons. Nay, what needed any more fuing to heauen, or taking it by violence and feruencie of zeale; when the Pardons came and offered themfelues at euery mans doores? And diuers fpirituall men vanted themfelues, that *they neither vnderftood Old Teftament nor New.*

Thus were thefe 2 *Witneffes* vfed in the fecond halfe of this *fpiritual weeke*; who in the firft halfe therof *were clad in fackcloth*; that is, preached repentance to all nations, for the fpace of 500. or 600. yeres after *Chrift:* God making his *Word* or *Witnes* fo triumph, riding vpó the *white horfe* in the time of the *Primitiue* Church, as that they ouercame al that oppofed themfelues vnto it, beating downe euery high thing, as *Paul* faith; excluding fró heauen al that beleeue not therein: as ftrongly with the fpiritual fire thereof, conuincing the ftif-necked pride of vnbeleeuers, as euer *Mofes* or *Elias* did, by the plagues of *Egypt* and famine, cóuince the rebellious *Egyptians* and ftif-necked *Ifraelites.*

Neither fhall it be enough to difgrace, corrupt and fuppreffe them ; but *Killed muft they be* at the laft. To which purpofe commeth forth *Cenfura generalis, vt mucrone cenforio iugulare eas pofsit*; and cutteth their throats indeed: For the author ordaineth al tranflations, but their owne to be burnt, which is yet cómonly practifed: nay he profeffeth, he commeth not to correct but to deftroy them, controlling and calling euery place of Scripture *Heretical,* that difagreeth fró their Traditions (with almoft as many foule words and railing epithetes, as the *Cardinal* beftoweth on my *Apologie*) not ruling, nor interpreting Scripture by Scripture, but making their Traditiós to be fuch a touchftone for it, as he condemneth of *Herefie*, not onely thofe places of Scripture that he citeth, but layeth the fame general condemnation vpon al other the like places wherefoeuer they be written in the Scriptures. And yet (praifed be God) we beginne now with our eyes, as our predeceffors haue done in fome aages before, to fee thefe *Witneffes* rife againe, and fhine in their former glory: GOD, as it were, *fetting them vp againe vpon their feete,* and *raifing them to the Heauens* in a triumphall cloud of glory, like *Elias* his fiery chariot. Which exalting of the Gofpel againe, hath bred fuch *an earthquake* and alteration amóngft many Nations; as *a tenth part,* or a good portion of thefe that were in fubiection to *that Great Citie,*

Verfe 8.

2.Chro.34. 14. *Verfe* 10.

Verfe 3. Reuel.6.2.

1.Cor.10.4.

Reuel.11.7. * Printed at Venice. Anno 1561.

Verfe 11. 12.

13.

to wit, *Babylon*, are fallen from her ; *seuen thousand*, that is, many thousands hauing *bene killed* vpon the occasion of that great alteration; and many other conuerted to the feare of G O D, *and giuing glory to the God of heauen.* This now is one of the wayes, by which (I thinke) this place of Scripture may be lawfully and probably interpreted.

The other is more common, and seemeth more literally to agree with the Text. And this is to interpret, not the *word of God*, but the *Preachers thereof* to bee meant by these *Witnesses.* Few they were that first began to

Deut.19.15.

reueale the man of *Sinne,* and discouer his corruptions; and therefore well described by the number of *two Witnesses* : *Nam in ore duorum aut trium testium stabit omne verbum.* And in no greater number were they that began this worke, then the greatnesse of the errand did necessarily require. They

Reuel.11.3.

prophesied in sackecloth, for they preached repentance. That diuers of them were put to cruell deaths, is notorious to the world : And likewise that

¹ *Sanguis Martyrum est semen Ecclesiæ.* Verse 11.

(in the persons of their Successours in doctrine) ¹ *they rose againe*; and that in such power and efficacie, as is more then miraculous : For where it is

Actes 2.41.

accounted in the Scriptures a miraculous worke of G O D wrought by his holy Spirit, When the Apostle *Saint Peter* conuerted about three thousand in one day; these *Witnesses* I speake of, by the force of the same Spirit, conuerted many mightie Nations in few yeeres, who still continue praising G O D, that hee hath deliuered vs from the tyrannie of Antichrist, that reigneth ouer that great Citie; and with a full crie proclaiming, *Goe*

Reuel.18.4.

out of her my people, lest yee bee partaker of her sinnes and of her plagues. Let therefore these Miracle-mongers that surfeit the world, and raise the price of paper daily, with setting foorth old, though new gilded Miracles and Legends of lies; Let such (I say) consider of this great and wonderfull Miracle indeed, and to their shame, compare it with their paultry wares. Thus hauing in two fashions deliuered my coniecture, what I take to bee meant by these two *Witnesses* in the xj. of the *Apocalyps,* there beeing no great difference betweene them : In the one, taking it to bee the Word of G O D it selfe; In the other, the Word of God too, but in the mouthes of his Preachers : It resteth now that I come to the *third* point of the description of *Antichrist;* which is anent his *Person.*

That by the Whore of Babylon that rideth vpon the Beast, is meant a Seate of an Empire, and a successiue number of men sitting thereupon, and not any one man; doeth well appeare by the forme of the description

Cap.xvij.
Verse 18.

of the *Antichrist* thorowout all the said Booke. For in the last verse of the xvij. Chapter, the *Woman* is expounded to bee, *That great Citie that reigneth ouer the Kings of the earth* ; which cannot signifie the onely Person of one

Verse.9.

man, but a successiue number of men (as I haue already said) whose Seat that great Citie must be : like as in the same Chapter, *The seuen heads of the Beast* are two wayes expounded. First, they are called *seuen Hils,* which is

Verse 13.

plaine; and next they are called *seuen Kings,* which cannot bee meant by the Kings *that shall giue their power to the Beast,* and bee subiect vnto her,

which

which is immediatly after expreſſed by *the tenne hornes*: But rather appea_
reth to be thoſe ſeuen formes of gouernment of that Seat: fiue of which
had already beene and fallen; As *Kings*, *Conſuls*, *Dictators*, *Decemuiri* and
Tribuni militum. The ſixt was in the time of *S. Iohn* his writing of this
booke, which was the *Gouernement of the Emperour.* The ſeuenth which
was not yet come, and was to laſt but for a ſhort ſpace, was the [1] *Eccleſiaſticall gouernment by Biſhops*, which was not come vpon the tranſlation of
the Empire from *Rome* to *Conſtantinople*; though their gouernment was
in a manner ſubſtitute to the Emperours: For though that forme of Gouernement laſted about the ſpace of 276. yeeres; yet was it but ſhort in
compariſon of the long time of the reigne of the *Antichriſt* (not yet expired) which ſucceeded immediatly thereunto. And the eight, which is
the *Beaſt that was and is not, and is to goe to perdition*, is the A N T I C H R I S T:
the eight forme of Gouernment indeed by his abſoluteneſſe, and yet the
ſeuenth, becauſe hee ſeemeth but to ſucceed to the Biſhop in an Eccleſiaſticall forme of Gouernement, though by his greatneſſe hee ſhall make *Ba-
bylons* Empire in glory, like to that magnificence wherein that great Citie triumphed, when it moſt flouriſhed: which in *Saint Iohns* time was
much decayed, by the factions of the great men, the mutinies of the armies, and the vnworthines of the Emperours. And ſo that flouriſhing ſtate
of that great Citie or Beaſt, which it was in before *S. Iohns* time, and being
much [2] decayed was but *in a maner* in his time, ſhould be reſtored vnto it
againe by *Antichriſt*: who as he aſcendeth out of *the bottomleſſe pit*, ſo muſt
he goe *to Deſtruction*. And likewiſe by that great lamentation that is made
for the deſtruction of *Babylon* in the eighteenth Chapter, both by the
Kings, and by the Merchants of the earth; where it is thrice repeated for
aggrauating the pitie of her deſolation, that *That great Citie fell in an houre*:
By that great lamentation (I ſay) it well appeareth, That the raigne of *Antichriſt* muſt continue longer then three yeeres and a halfe, or any one mans
time: For the Kings that had committed fornication with her, *& in deli-
cijs vixerant*; behoued to haue had a longer time for contracting of that
great acquaintance: And the *Merchants of the earth* ſet her forth and deſcribe
her at great length, as the very ſtaple of all their riches; which could not be
ſo ſoone gathered as in one mans time. And to conclude now this deſcription of the *Antichriſt*; I will ſet downe vnto you all that is ſpoken of him in
the *Apocalyps* in a ſhort methode, for the further explaining of theſe three
points that I haue already handled.

 The *Antichriſt* is foure times (in my opinion) deſcribed by *Iohn* in the
Apocalyps, in foure ſundry viſions; and a ſhort *Compendium* of him repeated againe in the xx. Chapter. He is firſt deſcribed by a *pale Horſe* in the
viſion of the Seales in the ſixt Chapter: For after that C H R I S T had
triumphed vpon a *white Horſe* in the firſt Seale, by the propagation of the
Goſpel; and that the *red Horſe* in the ſecond Seale, is as buſie in perſecution,
as C H R I S T is in ouercomming by the conſtancie of his Martyrs; and
                     that

Verſe 5.

Verſe 8.

ᵗ Or them, after other Tranſlations, whereby is ioyntly vnderſtood the ſaid pale horſe, together with his rider and conuoy, Death and Hell.

Verſe 9.

Verſe 10.

Verſe 12.

The ſecond deſcription.

Reu. Chap. 9. Verſe 1.

Verſe 2.

Verſe 3.

Verſe 11.

Matth. 5. 14.

Verſe 13. Verſe 20.

Lib de Cultu Adoratio. lib. 3 diſp. 1. cap 5. Verſ. 21.

that famine and other plagues ſignified by the *blacke Horſe* in the third Seale, haue ſucceeded to theſe former perſecutions : Then commeth forth the *Antichriſt* vpon a *pale horſe* in the 4. Seale, hauing Death for his rider, and Hell for his conuoy ; which rider fitted well his colour of paleneſſe : *and he had power giuen* ᵗ *him ouer the fourth part of the earth* (which is *Europe*) *to kill with the ſword,* and vſe great perſecution ; as *Ethnick Rome* did, figured by the *red horſe*: and to kill *with* ſpirituall *hunger* or famine of the trew word of God; as the *black horſe* did by corporal famine & *with death,* whereby ſpiritual death is meant. For the *Antichriſt,* ſignified by this *pale horſe,* ſhal afflict the Church both by perſecution and temporal death; as alſo by alluring the Nations to idolatry, and ſo to ſpirituall death : and by the *beaſt of the earth* ſhall he procure their ſpiritual death; for he ſhall ſend out the *Locuſts* (ouer whom he is King) mentioned in the 9. Chap. of this booke; and the 3 *frogs,* mentioned in the 16. of the ſame; for intiſing of al Kings and nations to drinke of the cup of her abominations. That that deſcription now of *Antichriſt* endeth there, it is more then plaine : for at the opening of the firſt Seale, the ſoules and blood of the murthered Saints cry for vengeance and haſting of iudgment ; which in the ſixt Seale is granted vnto them by CHRISTs comming at the Latter day ; ſignified by *heauens departing away, like a ſcroll when it is rolled*: with a number of other ſentences to the ſame purpoſe.

But becauſe this might ſeeme a ſhort and obſcure deſcription of the *Antichriſt,* he deſcribeth him much more largely and ſpecifikely, eſpecially in the viſion of the *Trumpets* in the 9. Chapter. For there he ſaith, at the blowing of the *fift Trumpet,* Hereſies being firſt ſpread abroad in three of the foure former blaſts; to wit, in the firſt, third, and fourth blaſt (for I take temporall perſecution to be onely ſignified by the ſecond blaſt) he then *ſaw a ſtarre fall from Heauen, to whom was giuen the key of the bottomles pit* ; *which being opened by him, with the ſmoke thereof came foorth a number of Locuſts,* whom hee largely deſcribeth, both by their craft & their ſtrength ; and then telleth the name of this their king, who brought them out of the bottomles pit, which is, *Deſtroyer.* By this *ſtarre fallen from heauen,* being ſignified, as I take it, ſome perſon of great dignitie in the Church, whoſe duetie being to giue light to the word (as CHRIST ſaith) doth contrary thereunto fall away like *Lucifer,* and ſet vp a kingdome, by the ſending forth of that nòiſome packe of craftie cruell vermine , deſcribed by *Locuſts* · and ſo is the *Seat* of the *Antichriſt* begun to be erected, whoſe *doctrine* is at length declared in the ſecond *woe,* after the blaſt of the ſixt *Trumpet* ; where it is ſaid, That the *remnant of men which were not killed by the plagues , repented not of the workes of their hands, that they ſhould not worſhip diuels, and idols of gold, and of ſiluer & of braſſe, and of ſtone, and of wood, which neither can ſee, heare, nor goe.* (As for *worſhipping of diuels*; looke your great Ieſuited doctour , *Vaſques* : and as for *all the reſt,* it is the maine doctrine of the *Roman Church.*) And then it is ſubioyned in this Text, that they repented not of *their murther , their ſorcerie , their fornications, nor their theft.*

By

By *their murther*, their perfecution is meant, and bloody maffacres. For *their Sorcery* confider of their *Agnus Dei*, that will flocken fire; of the hallowed fhirts, and diuers forts of Reliques; and alfo of Prayers, that will preferue men from the violence of fhot, of fire, of fword, of thunder, and fuch like dangers; And iudge, if this be not very like to Sorcerie and incantation of charmes.

By *their Fornication* is meant both their fpirituall fornication of Idolatry, and alfo their corporall fornication; which doth the more abound amongft them, as well by reafon of the reftraint of their Churchmen from marriage, as alfo becaufe of the many Orders of idle Monaftike liues amongft them, as well for men as women: And continuall experience prooueth, that idleneffe is euer the greateft fpurre to lecherie. And they are guiltie of *Theft*, in ftealing from G O D the titles and greatnes of power due to him, and beftowing it vpon their head, the *Antichrift*: As alfo by heaping vp their treafure with their iuggling wares and merchandife of the foules of men, by *Iubiles*, *Pardons*, *Reliques* and fuch like ftrong delufions.

That he endeth this defcription of *Antichrift* in the fame ninth. Chapter may likewife well appeare, by the Oath that that *Mightie Angell* fweareth in the fixt verfe of the tenth Chapter: And after the blaft of the fixt *Trumpet*, that *time fhall bee no more*, and that when the feuenth Angell fhall blow his *Trumpet*, *the myfterie of* G O D *fhalbe finifhed, as he had declared it to his feruants the Prophets*. Onely in the eleuenth Chapter he defcribeth the meanes whereby the *Antichrift* was ouercome, whofe raigne he had before defcribed in the ix. Chapter; and telleth vs that the *two witneffes*, after that they haue beene perfecuted by the *Antichrift* fhall in the end procure his deftruction. And in cafe any fhould thinke, that the *Antichrift* is onely fpoken of in the xj. Chapter, and that the Beaft fpoken of in the xiij. and xvij. Chapters doth onely fignifie *Ethnicke Rome*; there needeth no other refutation of that conceit, then to remember them, that the *Antichrift* is neuer named in all that xj. Chapter, but where he is called in the feuenth verfe thereof *the Beaft that commeth foorth of the bottomeles pit*: which by the defcription of the place he commeth out of, prooueth it to be the fame Beaft which hath the fame originall in the xvij. Chapter, and in the very fame words; fo as it is euer but the fame *Antichrift* repeated, and diuerfly defcribed in diuers vifions.

Now in the xij. and xiij. Chapters and fo foorth till the xvij. he maketh a more large and ample propheticall defcription of the ftate of the Church, and reigne of the *Antichrift*: For in the xij. Chap. he figureth the Church by a *Woman* flying from the *Dragon* (the Deuill) to the wilderneffe; And when the Dragon feeth hee cannot otherwife ouer-reach her, hee *fpeweth foorth waters like floods to carry her away*; which fignifieth many Nations, that were let loofe to perfecute and vexe the Church. And in the xiij. Chapter, out of that *Sea* of Nations that perfecuted her, arifeth that *great Citie*
(Queene

Cap.10.vet.6.

Verfe 7.

Cap.11.

Verfe 3.

Cap.11.

Verfe 7.

The third defcription.

Chap xij.
Verfe 6.

Verfe 15.

Chap.xiij.

verſe 1.
Verſe 2.
(Queene of all the Nations, and head of that perſecution) figured by *a Beaſt with ſeuen heads and tenne hornes*, like a *Leopard*; as well for the colour becauſe it was full of ſpots, that is, defiled with corruptions; as alſo vſing a baſtard forme of gouernement, in ſhew ſpirituall, but in deed temporall ouer the Kings of the earth; like the Leopard that is a baſtard beaſt betwixt a Lion and a Parde: hauing *feete like a Beare*, to ſignifie his great ſtrength; and *the mouth of a Lion*, to ſhew his rauenous and cruell diſpoſition.

Verſe 3.

Verſe 6.
Verſe 7.
This Beaſt who had *his power from the Dragon*, and had gotten a *deadly wound in one of his heads*, or formes of gouernment (by the *Gothes and Vandals*) and yet *was healed againe; opened his mouth to blaſphemies, and made warre againſt the Saints*: nay, all the world muſt worſhip him; which worſhip *Ethnicke Rome* neuer craued of any, being contented to call their neighbour Kings *Amici & ſocij populi Romani*. And whether worſhip or adoration, euen with that ſame title, he vſed to *Popes* at their creation, our *Cardinall* can beſt tell you.

Verſe 11.
But then commeth *another beaſt vp out of the earth*, hauing indeed a more firme and ſetled originall: for ſhe doeth viſibly and outwardly ſucceed to the trew Church, and therefore *ſhe hath two hornes like the Lambe*, in outward ſhew repreſenting the ſpouſe of CHRIST, and pretending CHRIST to be her defence: But ſhe *ſpeaketh like the Dragon*, teaching damnable and deuiliſh doctrine. And this *Apoſtatike* (I ſhould ſay *Apoſtolike*) *Church*, after that ſhe hath made her great power manifeſt to the world, by *doing*
Verſe 12.
all that the firſt Beaſt could doe, In conſpectu eius; that is, by ſhewing the greatneſſe of her power, to be nothing inferiour to the greatneſſe of the former *Ethnicke Empire*: ſhe then is mooued with ſo great a deſire to aduance this Beaſt, now become *Antichriſt*, as ſhe *cauſeth the earth and all that dwell therein, to worſhip this former Beaſt* or Roman Monarch; transferring ſo, as it were, her owne power in his perſon. Yea, euen Emperours and Kings ſhall be faine to kiſſe his feet. And for this purpoſe ſhall ſhee worke great Miracles, wherein ſhe greatly prides her ſelfe, deceiuing men with lying wonders and efficacie of lyes, as S. *Paul* ſaith. And amongſt the reſt of
2. Theſ. 2. 9.
Verſe 13.
Verſe 15.
her wonders, ſhe muſt bring *Fire out of heauen, Fulmen excommunications*, which can dethrone Princes: So that all that will not *worſhip the image of the Beaſt*, that is, his vnlimited Supremacie, *muſt be killed* and burnt as Heretikes. Yea, ſo peremptory will this Beaſt or falſe Prophet be (ſo called in the xvj. Chapter of this booke) for the aduauncement of the other Beaſt
Verſe 17.
Verſe 16.
or *Antichriſt*; as all ſorts and rankes of people muſt *receiue the marke or name of that Beaſt in their right hand, or in their forehead; without the which it ſhould be lawfull to none to buy, or ſell*: by the *Marke in the forehead*, ſignifying their outward profeſſion and acknowledgement of their ſubiection vnto her; and by the *Marke in their right hand*, ſignifying their actuall implicite obedience vnto her, who they thinke cannot erre, though ſhe ſhould command them to rebell againſt their naturall princes; like that *Cæca obedientia* whereunto

whereunto all the *Iesuits* are sworne: and like those *Romish* Priests in this Countrey, that haue renounced and forsworne againe that *Oath of Allegiance*, grounded vpon their naturall Oath; which though at their taking it, they confessed they did it out of conscience, and as obliged thereunto by their naturall duetie; yet now must they forsweare it againe, for obedience to the *Popes* command; to whose will their conscience and reason must be blindly captiuated. And who euer denied this absolute power, might *neither buy nor sell*; for no man was bound to keepe any faith, or obserue any ciuill contracts with Heretikes: yea, to æquiuocate and commit periury towards them, is a lawfull thing in a Catholike.

Now as to the Mysterie anent the *Number* of his name; whether it shalbe vnderstood by the number composed of the Letters in that Greeke word ΛΑΤΕΙΝΟΣ; which word well sutes with the *Romish* Church, *Romish* Faith, and *Latine* Seruice: Or whether in respect that in the Text it is called *the number of the man*, ye will take it for the number or date of the yeere of GOD, wherein that first man liued, that first tooke the title of the *Antichrist* vpon him; I leaue it to the Readers choice. By that *first Man*, I meane *Bonifacius tertius*, who first called himselfe *Vniuersall Bishop*; which S. *Gregorie*, that liued till within three yeeres of his time, [1] foretold would be the style of the *Antichrist*, or his *Præcursor*: for though he died threescore yeeres before the 666. of CHRIST; yet was that Title but fully setled vpon his Successors, sixtie yeeres after his time. Or if ye list to count it from *Pompey* his spoiling of the Temple, to this same Mans time; it will goe very neere to make iust vp the said *number 666*.

Now the raigne of the *Antichrist* being thus prophetically described in the xiij. Chapter, his fall is prophecied in the xiiij. First by the ioyfull and triumphall *New song* of the Saints in heauen: And next by the proclamation of three Angels; whereof the first hauing *an euerlasting Gospel in his hand to preach to all Nations* (the trew armour indeed wherewith the *Witnesses* fought against the *Antichrist*;) The first Angel, I say, proclaimed *Feare and glory to* GOD, since *the houre of his Iudgement was come*. And the second proclaimed *the fall of Babylon*, which is the destruction of the *Antichrist*. And the third prohibited vnder great paines, euen the paine of eternall damnation, that none should *worship the Beast*, or receiue *his Marke*. But though that in the rest of this Chapter the Latter day be againe prophecied, as a thing that shall come shortly after the reuealing of the man of *Sinne*: yet in the xv. Chap. he telleth of *seuen plagues*, vnder the name of *Vials*, that shall first fall vpon the *Antichrist* and his kingdome; which, being particularly set downe in the xvj. Chapter, he reckoneth among the rest. In the *fift viall*, the plague of darkenesse; yea, such darkenesse as the kingdome of *Antichrist* shall be obscured. Wherby at the powring foorth of the *sixt Viall*, the *way of the Kings of the East shall be prepared*; the man of *Sinne* being begun to be reuealed, and so all impediments remooued that might let the inuasion of that Monarchie: euen as that great riuer *Euphrates* that runneth by the

Verse 17.

Irenæus aduersus Hæres. lib. 5.

[1] *Epist. lib. 6. cap. 30.*

Chap. xiiij. Verse 3.

Verse 6.

Verse 7.
Verse 8.

Verse 9.

Chap. xv. Verse 1.

Chap. xvj.

Verse 10.

Verse 12.

Dan.5.3. the literall *Babylon*, guarded it from the Kings of the *East*, the *Medes* and *Persians*, the time of the *Babylonian* Monarchie, till by the drying thereof, or, vnexpected passage made through it by *Cyrus*, *Babylon* was wonne, and *Baltasar* destroyed, and his Monarchie ouerthrowne; euen while hee was sitting in that literall *Babylon*, corporally drunken and quaffing in the vessels ordained for G O D s Seruice; and so sitting as it were in the Temple of G O D, and abusing the holy Mysteries thereof.

Verse 13. For remedy whereof, at the powring forth of the *sixt Viall*, *three vncleane spirits, like frogs, shall then come foorth out of the mouth of the Dragon, that beast, and of the false prophet*; which I take to be as much to say, as that how soone as the kingdome of *Antichrist* shall be so obscured, with such a grosse and a palpable ignorance, as learning shall be almost lost out of the world, and that few of the very Priests themselues shall be able to reade Latine, much lesse to vnderstand it; and so a plaine way made for the Destruction of *Babylon*: Then shall a new sect of Spirits arise for the defence of that falling Throne, called *three* in number, by reason of their three-fold direction; being raised and inspired by the Dragon Sathan, authorized and maintained by the Beast the *Antichrist*, and instructed by the false prophet the Apostatike Church; that hath the hornes like the Lambe, but speaketh like the Dragon. These Spirits indeed, thus sent foorth by this three-fold authoritie for the defence of their Triple-crowned Monarch, are well likened to frogges; for they are *Amphibions*, and can liue in either Element, earth or water: for though they be Churchmen by profession, yet Verse 14. can they vse the trade of politique Statesmen; going to the Kings of the earth, to gather them to the battell of that Great day of G O D Almightie. What Massacres haue by their perswasion bene wrought through many parts of Christendome, and how euilly Kings haue sped that haue bene counselled by them; all the vnpartiall Histories of our time doe beare record. And whatsoeuer King or State will not receiue them, and follow their aduise, rooted out must that King or State be, euen with Gunpowder ere it faile. And these *frogges* had reason indeed to labour to become learned, thereby to dissipate that grosse mist of ignorance, wherewith the Verse 17. reigne of *Antichrist* was plagued before their comming forth. Then doeth this Chapter conclude with the last plague that is powred out of the se-Verse 19. uenth *Viall* vpon the *Antichrist*, which is the day of Iudgement: for then *Babylon* (saith he) *came in remembrance before God.*

The fourth description. Chap.17. Verse 3. But in the 17. Chapter is the former Vision interpreted and expounded; and there is the *Antichrist* represented by a *Woman*, *sitting vpon that many-headed Beast*; because as C H R I S T his trew Spouse and Church is represented by a *Woman* in the twelfth Chapter, so here is the Head of his a-dulterous spouse or false Church represented also by a woman, but *hauing* Verse 4. *a cup full of abominations in her hand*: as her selfe is called a *Whoore*, for her Verse 1. spirituall adulterie, hauing seduced the *Kings of the earth* to be partakers Verse 2. of her Spirituall fornication: And yet wonderfull gorgious and glorious

was

was fhe in outward fhew; but *drunken with the blood of the Saints*, by a violent perfecution of them. And that fhee may the better bee knowen, hee writeth her name vpon her forehead agreeable to her qualities : A *Myfterie*, that *great Babylon ; the Mother of whoredomes and abominations of the earth.* A *Myfterie* is a name that belongeth vnto her two maner of wayes: One, as fhee taketh it to her felfe; another, as fhee deferueth indeed. To her felfe fhee taketh it, in calling her felfe the vifible Head of the myfticall Body of C H R I S T, in profeffing her felfe to bee the difpenfer of the myfteries of G O D, and by her onely muft they bee expounded : This great God in earth and Head of the Faith, being a *Myftes* by his profeffion; that is, a Prieft. And if the obferuation of one be trew, that hee had of old the word *Myfterie* written on his Myter; then is this Prophecie very plainely accomplifhed. Now that indeed fhee deferues that name, the reft of her Title doeth beare witneffe that fheweth her to bee *the Mother of all the whoredomes and abominations of the earth* : and fo is fhe vnder the pretext of holineffe, a *Myftery* indeed of all iniquitie and abominations; vnder the maske of pretended feeding of Soules, deuouring Kingdomes, and making *Chriftendome* fwimme in blood.

Now after that this fcarlet or bloody Beaft and her Rider are defcribed, by their fhape, garments, name and qualities : the Angel doeth next interprete this vifion vnto *Iohn*, expounding vnto him what is fignified both by the *Beaft* and her *Rider*; telling him, the feuen heads of the Beaft are *feuen Hilles*, meaning by the fituation of that Citie or feat of *Empire*; and that they are alfo *feuen Kings* or formes of gouernment in the faid Citie, whereof I haue told you my conceit already. As for the *ten Hornes*, which hee fheweth to be *tenne Kings*, *that fhall at one houre receiue their power and kingdome with the Beaft*, I take that number of *ten* to be *Numerus certus pro incerto*; euen as the number of feuen heads and ten hornes vpon the Dragon the Deuill, cannot but be an vncertaine number. And that hee alfo imitates in thofe ten hornes, the ten hornes of the feuen headed Beaft in the feuenth of *Daniel* : and therefore I take thefe ten *Kings* to fignifie, all the Chriftian *Kings*, and free *Princes* and *States* in generall, euen you whom to I confecrate thefe my Labours, and that of vs all he prophefieth, that although our firft becomming abfolute and free Princes, fhould be in one houre with the Beaft ; (for great Chriftian Kingdomes and Monarches did but rife, and receiue their libertie by the ruines of the *Ethnicke Romane Empire*, and at the deftrudion thereof) and at the very time of the beginning of the planting of the *Antichrift* there; and that we fhould for a long time continue to worfhip the Beaft, hauing *one* Catholike or common confenting *minde* in obeying her, *yeelding our power and authoritie vnto her*, and kiffing her feete, drinking with her in her cup of Idolatrie , and *fighting with the Lambe*, in the perfecution of his Saints , at her command that gouerneth fo many Nations and people : yet notwithftanding all this, wee fhall in the time appointed by G O D, hauing thus fought with the

E e   Lambe,

Verfe 6.

Verfe 5.

Verfe 5.

Verfe 9.

Verfe 12.

Verfe 13.

Verfe 14.

Verfe 16.

Verſe 16.

Lambe,but *being ouercome by him,* that is, conuerted by his Word; wee ſhall then (I ſay) *hate the Whore, and make her deſolate, and make her naked,* by diſco-uering her hypocriſie and falſe pretence of zeale; and ſhall *eate her fleſh, and burne her with fire.* And thus *ſhall the way of the Kings of the Eaſt bee pre-*

Reuel.16.12.

pared, as ye heard in the ſixteenth Chapter. And then doeth hee ſubioyne the reaſon of this ſtrange change in vs: for (ſaith hee) G O D *hath put it*

Verſe 17.

in their hearts to fulfill his will, and with one conſent to giue their Kingdomes to the Beaſt, till the words of G O D *be fulfilled,* according to that ſentence of *Solomon;*

Prou.21.1.

That *the hearts of Kings are in the handes of* G O D , *to bee turned at his pleaſure.* And hauing thus interpreted the Beaſt or Empire; hee in a word ex-pounds, that by *the Woman* that rode vpon her, or Monarch that gouerned

Verſe 18.

her, was meant *that great Citie that reigned ouer the Kings of the earth* : by the Seate of the Empire pointing out the qualitie of the perſons that ſhould ſit and domine there.

Chap.18.

Then is the greatneſſe of her fall, and the great lamentation that both the Kings and Merchants of the earth ſhall make for the ſame, proclai-

Verſe 9.10.

med by an other Angel in the eighteenth Chapter. The *Kings* lamenting her fall, becauſe they *liued in pleaſure with her;* which no Kings could doe with *Ethnicke Rome,* who conquered them by her ſword: for ſhee ho-noured them with Titles, and diſpenſed with their luſtes and vnlawfull

Verſe 11, 15,16,17, 18.

marriages. And the *Merchants of the earth, and all Shipmaſters, and traffikers vpon the Sea,* ſhall lament the fall of that great Citie, which *neuer had a fellow,* for the loſſe of their riches and traffique, which they enioyed by her

Verſe 12, 13.

meanes. And there he deſcribeth all ſorts of *rich wares,* whereof that great Citie was the Staple: for indeed ſhee hath a neceſſary vſe for all ſuch rich and glorious wares, as well for ornaments to her Churches and princely Prelates, as for garments and ornaments to her woodden Saints; for the *bleſſed Virgin* muſt be dayly clothed and decked in the neweſt and moſt cu-rious faſhion, though it ſhould reſemble the habit of a *Curtizane.* And of

Verſe 13.

all thoſe rich wares, the moſt precious is laſt named, which is *the Soules of men:* for ſo much beſtowed vpon Maſſes, and ſo much doted to this or that Cloyſter of Monkes or Friers, but moſt of all now to that irregular and in-comprehenſible order of *Ieſuites;* ſhal both redeeme *his* owne Soule, and all his parents to the hundreth generation, from broyling in the fire of *Purga-tory.* And (I hope) it is no ſmall merchandiſe of Soules, when men are ſo highly deluded by the hopes and promiſe of Saluation, as to make a Frier

[1] Henry 3. K. of France.
[2] Henry 4.

murther his [1] *Soueraigne;* a yong knaue attempt the murther of his next [2] *Succeſſour;* many one to conſpire and attempt the like againſt the late *Queene;* and in my time, to attempt the deſtruction of a whole *Kingdome* and *State* by a blaſt of Powder: and hereby to play bankerupt with both the ſoules mentioned in the Scriptures, *Animus & Anima.*

But notwithſtanding of this their great Lamentation, they are comman-

Verſe 4.

ded by a voyce from heauen to doe two things : One, *to flee from Ba-bylon, leſt they bee partakers of her ſinnes,* and conſequently of her *puniſhment*
Which

Which warning I pray God that yee all, my *Beloued Brethren* and *Coufins,* would take heed vnto in time, humbly befeeching him to open your eyes for this purpofe. The other command is, to *reward her as fhee hath re-warded you ; yea, euen to the double.* For as fhe did flie but with your feathers, borrowing as well her Titles of greatnefle and formes of honouring her from you; as alfo enioying all her Temporall liuing by your liberalities; fo if euery man doe but take his owne againe, fhe will ftand vp * naked ; and the reafon is giuen, becaufe of her pride : For *fhee glorifieth herfelfe liuing in pleafure,* and *in her heart faith, fhee fitteth as a Queene* (outward profperitie being one of their notes of a trew Church) and is *no Widow*; for her Spoufe C H R I·S T is bound to her by an inuiolable knot (for he hath fworne neuer to forfake her) *and fhe fhall fee no mourning* : for fhe cannot erre, nor the gates of Hell fhall not preuaile againft her.

~ But though the earth and worldly men lament thus for the fall of *Babylon* in this eighteenth Chapter, yet in the nineteenth, Heauen and all the Angels and Saints therein doe fing a triumphall *Cantique* for ioy of her fall, praifing God for the fall of that *great Whore* : Great indeed, for our * Cardinall confeffeth, that it is hard to defcribe what the Pope is, fuch is his greatnefle. And in the end of that Chapter is the obftinacie of that *Whore* defcribed, who euen *fought to the vttermoft againft him that fate on the white Horfe, and his armie*; till the *Beaft* or *Antichrift was taken, and the falfe Prophet,* or falfe Church with him, who *by Miracles,* and *lying wonders deceiued them that receiued the marke of the Beaft* ; and *both were caft quicke into the burning lake of fire and brimftone* ; *vnde nulla redemptio.* Like as in the ende of the former Chapter, to defcribe the fulnefle of the *Antichriftes* fall (not like to that reparable wound that Ethnicke *Rome* gate) it is firft compared to a *Milftone caft into the fea,* that can neuer rife and fleete againe : And next it is expreffed by a number of ioyfull things that fhall neuer bee heard there againe, where nothing fhall inhabite but defolation. But that the patience and conftancie of Saints on earth, and God his Elected may the better bee ftrengthened and confirmed; their perfecution in the latter dayes, is fhortly prophefied and repeated againe, after that *Satan hath beene bound,* or his furie reftrained, by the worlds enioying of peace for a *thoufand yeeres,* or a great indefinite time; their perfecuters being named *Gog* and *Magog,* the fecret and reuealed enemies of C H R I S T. Whether this be meant of the Pope and the Turke, or not; (who both began to rife to their greatnefle about one time) I leaue to bee gueffed ; alwayes their vtter confufion is there affuredly promifed : and it is faid; that the *Dragon, the Beaft,* and *the falfe Prophet,* fhall all three bee *caft in that lake of fire and brimftone, to be tormented for euer.* And thereafter is the latter day defcribed againe (*which muft be haftened for the Elects fake*) and then for the further comfort of the Elect, and that they may the more conftantly and patiently endure thefe temporall and finite troubles, limited but to a *fhort* fpace ; in the laft two Chapters are the ioyes of the eternall *Ierufalem* largely defcribed.

Margin notes:
- Verfe 6.
- * *Cornicula Aefopica.*
- Verfe 7.
- Cap. xix.
- Verfe 1.
- Verfe 2.
- * *Bellar. in Ref. ad Gerfon, confid. 11.*
- Verfe 19.
- Verfe 20.
- Cap 18.21.
- Ibidem.
- Verf. 22, 32.
- Cap. xx.
- Verfe 2.
- Verfe 8.
- Verfe 9.
- Verfe 10.
- Verfe 11, 12, 13.
- Matth. 24. 2 2.
- Cap. xxj. xxij.

Thus hath the *Cardinals* fhameleffe wrefting of thofe two places of Scripture, *Pafce oues meas*, and *Tibi dabo claues*, for proouing of the Popes fupreame Temporall authoritie ouer Princes ; animated mee to prooue the Pope to bee THE ANTICHRIST, out of this forefaid booke of Scripture; fo to pay him in his owne money againe. And this opinion no Pope can euer make me to recant; except they firft renounce any further medling with Princes, in any thing belonging to their Temporall Iurifdiction. And my onely wifh fhall bee , that if any man fhall haue a fancie to refute this my coniecture of the *Antichrift*; that hee anfwere mee orderly to euery point of my difcourfe ; not contenting him to difprooue my opinion,except hee fet downe fome other Methode after his forme for interpretation of that Booke of the *Apocalyps*, which may not contradict no part of the Text, nor conteine no abfurdities : Otherwife, it is an eafie thing for *Momus* to picke quarrels in another mans tale, and tell it worfe himfelfe; it being a more eafie practife to finde faults, then amend them.

Hauing now made this digreffion anent the *Antichrift*, which I am fure I can better faften vpon the Pope, then *Bellarmine* can doe his pretended Temporall Superioritie ouer Kings : I will returne againe to fpeake of this Anfwerer; who (as I haue already told you) fo fitteth his matter with his manner of anfwering, that as his Style is nothing but a Satyre and heape full of iniurious and reprochfull fpeaches, as well againft my Perfon, as my Booke; fo is his matter as full of lyes and falfities indeed, as hee vniuftly layeth to my charge : For three lies hee maketh againft the Oath of Alleagiance, conteined and maintained in my Booke; befides that ordinary repeated lie againft my Booke,of his omitting to anfwere my lyes,trattles,iniurious fpeaches and blafphemies. One groffe lye he maketh euen of the Popes firft *Breue*. One lye of the Puritanes, whom he would gladly haue to be of his partie. And one alfo of the Powder-Traitours, anent the occafion that mooued them to vndertake that treafonable practife. Three lies hee makes of that Acte of Parliament wherein this Oath of Alleagiance is conteined. Hee alfo maketh one notable lie againft his owne Catholike Writers. And two, of the caufes for which two *Iefuites* haue beene put to death in *England.*And he either falfifies, denies or wrefts fiue fundry Hiftories and a printed Pamphlet : befides that impudent lye that hee maketh of my Perfon; that I was a Puritane in *Scotland*, which I haue already refuted. And for the better filling vp of his booke with fuch good ftuffe; hee hath alfo fiue fo ftrange and new principles of Diuinitie therein,as they are either new, or at leaft allowed by very few of his owne Religion. All which lyes, with diuers others, and fiue ftrange, and (as I thinke) erroneous points of Doctrine, with fundry falfifications of Hiftories; are fet downe in a Table by themfelues in the end of this my Epiftle,hauing their Refutation annexed to euery one of them.

But as for the particular anfwering of his booke; it is both vnnecef-

fary

fary and vncomely for me to make a Reply. Vnneceffary, becaufe (as I haue already told you) my Booke is neuer yet anfwered, fo farre as belongeth to the maine queftion anent the Oath of Alleagiance: the picking of aduantages vpon the wrong placing of the figures in the citations, or fuch errors in the Print by cafuall addition, or omiffion of words that make nothing to the Argument; being the greateft weapons wherewith hee affaults my Booke. And vncomely it muft needs be (in my opinion) for a *King* to fall in altercation with a *Cardinal*, at leaft with one no more nobly defcended then he is: That Ecclefiafticall dignitie, though by the floath of Princes (as I faid before) it now come to that height of vfurped honour, yet being in the trew originall and foundation thereof nothing elfe, but the title of the Priefts and Deacons of the Parifh Churches in the towne of *Rome ;* at the firft, the ftile of *Cardinals* being generally giuen to all Priefts and Deacons of any Cathedral Church, though the multitude of fuch *Cardinal* Priefts and Deacons reforting to *Rome,* was the caufe that after bred the reftraining of that title of *Cardinall* Priefts and Deacons, onely to the Parifh priefts and Deacons of *Rome.* And fince that it is *S. Gregorie,* who in his Epiftles fixe hundreth yeeres after C H R I S T, maketh the firft mention of *Cardinals* (and fo thefe now *Electours* of the Apoftolike Sea, beeing long and many hundreth yeeres vnknowen or vnheard of, after the Apoftolik aage; and yet doeth hee fpeake of them but in this fence as I haue now defcribed) I hope the *Cardinall,* who calleth him the *Apoftle* of *England,* cannot blame mee that am King thereof, to ackowledge the *Cardinall* in no other degree of honour, then our faid Apoftle did. But how they fhould now become to bee fo ftrangely exalted aboue their firft originall inftitution, that from Parifh-priefts and Deacons (Priefts inferiours) they fhould now come to bee Princes and Peeres to Kings; and from a degree vnder Bifhops (as both [1] *Bellarmine* and [2] *Onuphrius* confeffe) to bee now the Popes fole Electours, fupplying with him the place of a Generall Councell; whereby the conuening of Generall Councels is now vtterly antiquated and abolifhed; nay, out of their number onely, the Pope to be elected; who claimeth the abfolute Superioritie ouer all Kings: how this their ftrange vfurped exaltation (I fay) fhould thus creepe in and bee fuffered, it belongeth to all them in our place and calling to looke vnto it; who being G O D his Lieutenants in earth, haue good reafon to bee iealous of fuch vpftart Princes, meane in their originall, come to that height by their owne creation, and now accounting themfelues Kings fellowes. But the fpeciall harme they do vs, is by their defrauding vs of our common & Chriftian intereft in General Councels; they hauing (as I faid) vtterly abolifhed the fame, by rolling it vp, & making as it were a Monopoly thereof, in their Conclaue with the Pope. Whereas, if euer there were a poffibilitie to be expected of reducing all Chriftians to an vniformitie of Religio, it muftcome by the means of a Generall Councel: the place of their meeting being chofen fo indifferent, as all Chriftian Princes, either in their owne Perfons, or their Deputie

[1] *Lib. de Clericis, cap. 16.*
[2] *Lib de Epifco. patibus, Titulis & Diaconijs Cardinalium.*

Com-

Commiſſioners, and all Church-men of Chriſtian profeſſion that beleeue and profeſſe all the ancient grounds of the trew, ancient, Catholike, and A-poſtolike Faith, might haue *tutum acceſſum* thereunto; All the incendiaries and Noueliſt fire-brands on either ſide being debarred from the ſame, as well *Ieſuites* as *Puritanes.*

And therefore hauing reſolued not to paine my ſelfe with making a Re-plie for theſe reaſons heere ſpecified, grounded as well vpon the conſi-deration of the matter, as of the peſſon of the Anſwerer; I haue thought good to content my ſelfe with the reprinting of my *Apologie* : hauing in a manner corrected nothing but the Copiers or Printers faults therein, and prefixed this my Epiſtle of Dedication and Warning thereunto; that I may yet ſee, if any thing will be iuſtly ſaid againſt it : Not doubting but enow of my Subiects will replie vpon theſe Libellers, and anſwere them ſufficiently; wiſhing Y o v deepely to conſider, and weigh your com-mon intereſt in this Cauſe. For neither in all my *Apologie*, nor in his pre-tended Refutation thereof, is there any queſtion made anent the Popes power ouer mee in particular, for the excommunicating or depoſing of mee : For in my particular; the Cardinall doeth mee that grace, that hee ſaith, The Pope thought it not expedient at this time to excommunicate mee by name; our queſtion being onely generall, Whether the Pope may lawfully pretend any temporall power ouer Kings, or no?

That no Church-men can by his rule bee ſubiect to any Temporall Prince, I haue already ſhewed you; And what Obedience any of you may looke for of any of them *de facto,* hee plainely forewarneth you of, by the example of *Gregory* the Great his obedience to the Emperour *Mauritius*: not being aſhamed to ſlaunder that great Perſonages Chriſtian humilitie and Obedience to the Emperour, with the title of a conſtrained and for-ced obedience, becauſe hee might, or durſt doe no otherwiſe. Whereby he not onely wrongs the ſaid *Gregory* in particular, but euen doeth by that meanes lay on an heauie ſlaunder and reproach vpon the Chriſtian humi-litie and patience of the whole Primitiue Church, eſpecially in the time of perſecution : if the whole glory of their Martyrdome and Chriſtian patience ſhall bee thus blotted with that vile gloſſe of their coacted and conſtrained ſuffering, becauſe they could or durſt doe no otherwiſe; like the patience and obedience of the Iewes or Turkiſh ſlaues in our time, Rom.13.5.
1.Pet.2.13. cleane contrary to *Saint Paul* and *Saint Peters* doctrine of obedience for conſcience ſake; and as contrary to *Tertullians Apologie* for Chriſtians, and all the proteſtations of the ancient Fathers in that caſe. But it was good lucke for the ancient Chriſtians in the dayes of Ethnicke Emperours, that this prophane and new conceit was then vnknowen among them : o-therwiſe they would haue beene vtterly deſtroyed and rooted out in that time, and no man to haue pitied them, as moſt dangerous members in a Common-wealth; who would no longer be obedient, then till they were furniſhed with ſufficient abilitie and power to reſiſt and rebell.

Thus

Thus may ye see, how vpon the one part our *Cardinall* will haue all Kings and Monarchs to bee the *Popes Vassals*; and yet will not on the other side, allow the meanest of the *Pope* his vassals, to be subiect to any Christian Prince. But he not thinking it enough to make the *Pope* our Superior, hath in a late Treatise of his (called the *Recognition of his bookes of Controuersies*) made the people and Subiects of euery one of vs, our Superiors. For hauing taken occasion to reuisite againe his bookes of Controuersies, and to correct or explaine what he findeth amisse or mistaketh in them; in imitation of S. *Augustine* his retractions (for so he saith in his *Preface*) he doth in place of retracting any of his former errours, or any matter of substance; not retract, but *recant* indeed, I meane sing ouer againe, and obstinatly confirme a number of the grossest of them: Among the which, the exempting of all Church-men from subiection to any Temporall Prince, and the setting vp not onely of the *Pope*, but euen of the People aboue their naturall King; are two of his maine points.

As for the exemption of the Clerickes; he is so greedy there to proue that point, as he denieth *Cæsar* to haue beene *Pauls* lawfull Iudge: contrary to the expresse Text, and *Pauls* plaine Appellation, and acknowledging him his Iudge; besides his many times claiming to the Roman priuiledges, and auowing himselfe a Roman by freedome; and therefore of necessitie a Subiect to the Roman Emperour. But it is a wonder that these *Romane Catholikes*, who vaunt themselues of the ancientie both of their doctrine and Church, and reproch vs so bitterly of our Nouelties, should not be ashamed to make such a new inept glosse as this vpon S. *Pauls* Text; which as it is directly contrary to the Apostles wordes, so is it without any warrant, either of any ancient *Councell*, or of so much as any one particular *Father* that euer interprets that place in this sort: Neither was it euer doubted by any Christian in the Primitiue Church, that the Apostles, or any other degree of Christians, were subiect to the Emperour.

And as for the setting vp of the People aboue their owne naturall King, he bringeth in that principle of Sedition, that he may thereby proue, that Kings haue not their power and authoritie immediatly from God, as the Pope hath his: For euery King (saith he) is made and chosen by his people; nay, they doe but so transferre their power in the Kings person, as they doe notwithstanding retaine their habituall power in their owne hands, which vpon certaine occasions they may actually take to themselues againe. This, I am sure, is an excellent ground in Diuinitie for all Rebels and rebellious people, who are hereby allowed to rebell against their Princes; and assume libertie vnto themselues, when in their discretions they shall thinke it conuenient.

And amongst his other Testimonies for probation, that all Kings are made and created by the People; he alledgeth the Creation of three Kings in the Scripture, *Saul*, *Dauid* and *Ieroboam*; and though hee bee compelled by the expresse words of the Text, to confesse, that God by his

Acts.15.10.

Acts 22.28.

Prophet

1.Sam.10.1
1.Sam.16.
12.13.

Actes 1.

Cyprian.lib.
1.Epist.4.

1 King.12.10.

Prophet *Samuel* annointed both [1] *Saul* and [2] *Dauid*; yet will he, by the post-consent of the people, proue that those Kings were not immediatly made by God, but mediatly by the people; though he repeat thrise that word of *Lott*, by the casting whereof he confesseth that *Saul* was chosen. And if the Election by *Lott* be not an immediate Election from God; then was not *Matthias*, who was so chosen and made an Apostle, immediatly cho-sen by GOD: and consequenly, he that sitteth in the Apostolike Sea can-not for shame claime to be immediatly chosen by God, if *Matthias* (that was one of the twelue Apostles, supplying *Iudas* his place) was not so cho-sen. But as it were a blasphemous impietie, to doubt that *Matthias* was immediatly chosen by GOD, and yet was hee chosen by the casting of Lots, as *Saul* was: so is it well enough knowen to some of you (my louing *Brethren*) by what holy Spirit or casting of Lots the *Popes* vse to be elected; the Colledge of *Cardinals*, his electors, hauing beene diuided in two mightie factions euer since long before my time; and in place of casting of Lotts, great fat pensions beeing cast into some of their greedy mouthes for the election of the *Pope*, according to the partiall humours of Princes. But I doe most of all wonder at the weakenesse of his memorie: for in this place he maketh the post-consent of the people to be the thing that made both these Kings, notwithstanding of their preceding inauguration and anoyntment by the Prophet at GODs commandement; forgetting that in the beginning of this same little booke of his, answering one that alled-geth a sentence of S. *Cyprian*, to prooue that the Bishops were iudged by the people in *Cyprians* time, he there confesseth, that by these words, the *consent of the people* to the Bishops Election must be onely vnderstood. Nor will he there any wayes be mooued to graunt, that the peoples power, in consenting to or refusing the Election of a Bishop, should be so vnder-stood, as that thereby they haue *power to elect B.shops*: And yet do these words of *Cyprian* seeme to bee farre stronger, for granting the peoples power to elect Churchmen, then any words that he alledgeth out of the Scripture are for the peoples power in electing a King. For the very words of *Cyprian* by himselfe there cited, are, That *the very peopl. haue prin-cipally the power, either to chuse such Priests as are worthy, or to refuse such as are vnworthie*: And, I hope, hee can neuer prooue by the Scripture, that it had beene lawfull to the people of Israel, or that it was left in their choise, to haue admitted or refused *Saul* or *Dauid* at their pleasure, after that the Prophet had anoynted them, and persented them vnto them.

Thus ye see how little he careth (euen in so little a volume) to contra-dict himselfe, so it may make for his purpose; making the *consent* of the people to signifie their *power of Election* in the making of Kings: though in the making of Bishops, by the peoples *consent*, their *approbation* of a deed done by others must onely be vnderstood. And as for his example of *Iero-boams* election to bee King; hee knoweth well enough, that *Ieroboam* was made King in a popular mutinous tumult and rebellion; onely
permitted

permitted by God, and that in his wrath, both againſt theſe two Kings and their people. But if he will needs helpe himſelfe, againſt all rules of Diuinitie, with ſuch an extraordinary example for proofe of a generall Rule; why is it not as lawfull for vs Kings to oppoſe hereunto the example of *Iehu* his Inauguration to the Kingdome; who vpon the Prophets priuat anointment of him, and that in moſt ſecret manner, tooke preſently the Kings office vpon him, without euer crauing any ſort of approbation from the people? *2.King.9.2,3.*

And thus may ye now clearely ſee, how deepe the claime of the Babylonian Monarch toucheth vs in all our common intereſt: for (as I haue already told) the *Pope*, nor any of his Vaſſals, I meane Church-men, muſt be ſubiect to no Kings nor Princes: and yet all Kings and their Vaſſals muſt not onely be ſubiect to the Pope, but euen to their owne people. And now, what a large libertie is by this doctrine left to Church-men, to hatch or foſter any treaſonable attempts againſt Princes; I leaue it to your conſiderations, ſince do what they will, they are accountable to none of vs : nay, all their treaſonable practiſes muſt be accounted workes of pietie, and they (being iuſtly puniſhed for the ſame) muſt be preſently inrolled in the liſt of Martyrs and Saints; like as our new printed Martyrologie hath put *Garnet* and *Ouldcorne* in the Regiſter of Engliſh *Martyrs* abroad, that were hanged at home for *Treaſon* againſt the Crowne and whole State of *England* : ſo as I may iuſtly with *Iſaiah*, pronounce a *Woe to them that ſpeake good of euill, and euill of good; which put light for darkeneſſe, and darkeneſſe for light; which iuſtifie the wicked for a reward, and take away the righteouſnes of the righteous from him.* *Iſai 5.20.* *Verſe 23.* For euen as in the time of the greateſt blindneſſe in Popery, though a man ſhould find his wife or his daughter lying a bed in her Confeſſors armes; yet was it not lawfull for him ſo much as to ſuſpect that the Frier had any errand there, but to Confeſſe and inſtruct her: Euen ſo, though *Ieſuites* practiſing in Treaſon be ſufficiently verified, and that themſelues cannot but confeſſe it; yet muſt they be accounted to ſuffer *Martyrdome* for the Faith, and their blood worke miracles, and frame a *ſtramineum argumentum* vpon ſtrawes; when their heads are ſtanding aloft, withered by the Sunne and the winde, a publike ſpectacle for the eternall commemoration of their treacherie. Yea, one of the reaſons, that is giuen in the Printers Epiſtle of the *Colonian* edition of the Cardinall or his Chaplains pamphlet, why he doth the more willingly print it, is; becauſe that the innocencie of that moſt holy and conſtant man *Henry Garnet*, is declared and ſet forth in that booke; againſt whom, ſome (*he knew not who*) had ſcattered a falſe rumour of his guiltineſſe of the Engliſh treaſon.

But, Lord, what an impudencie or wilfull ignorance is this, that he, who was ſo publikely and ſolemnely conuicted and executed, vpon his owne ſo cleare, vnforced and often repeated confeſſion, of his knowledge and concealing of that horrible Treaſon, ſhould now be ſaid to haue a certaine rumor ſpred vpon him of his guiltineſſe, by *I know not who?* with ſo many attributes

attributes of godlineſſe, conſtancie and innocencie beſtowed vpon him,
as if publike Sentences and Executions of Iuſtice, were rumors of *I know
not who*. Indeed, I muſt confeſſe, the booke it ſelfe ſheweth a great affection to performe, what is thus promiſed in the Preface thereof: for in two
or three places therein, is there moſt honorable lying mention made of
that ſtraw-Saint; wherein, though he confeſſe that *Garnet* was vpon the
foreknowledge of the Powder-Treaſon, yet in regard it was (as he ſaith)
onely vnder the Seale of Confeſſion, he ſticketh not to praiſe him for his
concealing thereof, and would gladly giue him the crowne of glory for
the ſame: not being aſhamed to proclaime it as a principall head of Catholique doctrine; *That the ſecret of Sacramentall confeſsion ought not to be reuealed,
not for the eſchewing of whatſoeuer euill*. But how damnable this doctrine is,
and how dangerouſly preiudiciall to all Princes and States; I leaue it to
you to iudge, whom all it moſt highly concerneth. For although it bee
trew, that when the Schoolemen came to be Doctors in the Church, and to
marre the old grounds in Diuinitie by ſowing in among them their Philo-
ſophicall diſtinctions; though they (I ſay) do maintaine, That whatſoeuer
thing is told a Confeſſor vnder the vaile of confeſſion, how dangerous ſoeuer the matter be, yet he is bound to conceale the parties name: yet doe
none of them, I meane of the old Schoolemen, deny; that if a matter be reuealed vnto them, the concealing whereof may breed a great or publike
danger; but that in that caſe the Confeſſor may diſcloſe the matter, though
not the perſon, and by ſome indirect means make it come to light, that the
danger thereof may be preuented. But that no treaſon nor deuiliſh plot,
though it ſhould tend to the ruine or exterminion of a whole Kingdome,
muſt be reuealed, if it be told vnder Confeſſion, no not the matter ſo farre
indirectly diſcloſed, as may giue occaſion for preuenting the danger thereof: though it agree with the conceit of ſome three or foure new *Ieſuited*
Doctors, it is ſuch a new and dangerous head of doctrine, as no King nor
State can liue in ſecuritie where that Poſition is maintained.

    And now, that I may as well prooue him a lyar *in facto*, in his narration
of this particular Hiſtory; as I haue ſhewed him to be *in iure*, by this his
damnable and falſe ground in Diuinity: I will trewly informe you of
Garnets caſe, which is farre otherwiſe then this Anſwerer alleadgeth. For
firſt, it can neuer be accounted a thing vnder Confeſſion, which he that
reueals it doth not diſcouer with a remorſe, accounting it a ſinne whereof
hee repenteth him; but by the contrary, diſcouers it as a good motion,
and is therein not diſſuaded by his Confeſſor, nor any penance enioyned him for the ſame: and in this forme was this Treaſon reuealed to *Garnet*, as himſelfe confeſſed. And next, though he ſtood long vpon it, that
it was reuealed vnto him vnder the vaile of Confeſſion, in reſpect it was
done in that time, while as the partie was making his Confeſſion vnto him; Yet at the laſt hee did freely confeſſe, that the party reuealed it
vnto him as they were walking, and not in the time of Confeſſion: But
                                           (he

(he faid) he deliuered it vnto him vnder the greateſt Seale that might bee, and ſo he tooke that he meant by the Seale of Confeſſion; And it had (as he thought) a relation to Confeſſion; in regard that hee was that parties Confeſſor, and had taken his Confeſſioh ſometimes before, and was to take it againe within few dayes thereafter. He alſo ſaid, that he pretended to the partie, that he would not conceale it from his Superior. And further it is to be noted, that he confeſſed, that two diuers perſons conferred with him anent this Treaſon; and that when the one of them which was (a-tesby, conferred with him thereupon, it was in the other parties preſence and hearing: and what a Confeſſion can this be in the hearing of a third perſon? And how farre his laſt words (whereof our Anſwerer ſo much vaunts him) did diſproue it to haue bene vnder Confeſſion, the Earle of Northamptons booke doeth beare witneſſe.

Now as to the other parties name, that reuealed the Powder-Treaſon vnto him, it was _Greenewell_ the _Ieſuite_; and ſo a _Ieſuite_ reuealed to a _Ieſuite_ this Treaſonable plot, the _Ieſuite_ reuealer not ſhewing any remorſe, and the _Ieſuite_ whom-to it was reuealed not ſo much as enioyning him any pe-nance for the ſame. And that ye may know that more _Ieſuits_ were alſo vp-on the partie, _Owldcorne_ the other Powder-Martyr, after the miſgiuing and diſcouery of that Treaſon, preached conſolatory doctrine to his Catho-lique auditorie; exhorting them not to faint for the miſgiuing of this en-terpriſe, nor to thinke the worſe thereof that it ſucceeded not; alleadging diuers Preſidents of ſuch godly enterpriſes that miſgaue in like maner: eſpecially, one of S. _Lewes_ King of France, who in his ſecond iourney to the _Holy-land_ died by the way, the greateſt part of his armie being deſtroyed by the plague; his firſt iourney hauing likewiſe miſgiuen him by the _Sol-dans_ taking of him: exhorting them thereupon not to giue ouer, but ſtill to hope that GOD would bleſſe their enterpriſe at ſome other time, though this did faile.

Thus ſee ye now, with what boldneſſe and impudencie hee hath belied the publiquely knowne veritie in this errand; both in auowing generally that no _Ieſuite_ was any wayes guiltie of that Treaſon, for ſo he affirmeth in his booke; and alſo that _Garnet_ knew nothing thereof, but vnder the Seale of Confeſſion. But if this were the firſt lye of the affaires of this State, which my fugitiue Prieſts and Ieſuits haue coyned and ſpread abroad, I could charme them of it, as the prouerbe is. But as well the walles of di-uers Monaſteries and _Ieſuites_ Colledges abroad, are filled with the pain-ting of ſuch lying Hiſtories, as alſo the bookes of our ſaid fugitiues are far-ced with ſuch ſort of ſhameleſſe ſtuffe; ſuch are the innumerable ſorts of torments and cruell deathes, that they record their Martyrs to haue ſuffred here, ſome torne at foure Horſes; ſome ſowed in Beares ſkinnes, and then killed with Dogges; nay, women haue not bene ſpared (they ſay) and a thouſand other ſtrange fictions; the vanities of all which I will in two words diſcouer vnto you.

Firſt,

First, as for the cause of their punishment, I doe constantly maintaine that which I haue said in my *Apologie*: That no man, either in my time, or in the late *Queenes*, euer died here for his conscience. For let him be neuer so deuout a Papist, nay, though he professe the same neuer so constantly, his life is in no danger by the Law, if hee breake not out into some outward acte expresly against the words of the Law; or plot not some vnlawfull or dangerous practise or attempt; Priests and Popish Church-men onely excepted, that receiue Orders beyond the Seas; who for the manifold treasonable practises that they haue kindled and plotted in this countrey, are discharged to come home againe vnder paine of Treason, after their receiuing of the said Orders abroad; and yet, without some other guilt in them then their bare home-comming, haue none of them bene euer put to death. And next, for the cruell torments and strange sorts of death that they say so many of them haue bene put vnto; if there were no more but the Law and continually obserued custome of England, these many hundred yeeres, in all criminall matters, it will sufficiently serue to refute all these monstrous lies: for no tortures are euer vsed here, but the Manacles or the Racke, and these neuer but in cases of high Treason; and all sorts of Traitours die but one maner of death here, whether they be Papist or Protestant Traitors; Queene *Maries* time onely excepted. For then indeede no sorts of cruell deathes were spared vnexecuted vpon men, women and children professing our Religion: yea, euen against the Lawes of God and Nature, women with childe were put to cruell death for their profession; and a liuing childe falling out of the mothers belly, was throwen in the same fire againe that consumed the mother. But these tyrannous persecutions were done by the Bishops of that time, vnder the warrant of the Popes authoritie; and therefore were not subiect to that constant order and formes of execution, which as they are heere established by our Lawes and customes, so are they accordingly obserued in the punishment of all criminals: For all Priestes and Popish Traitours here receiue their Iudgements in the temporall Courts, and so doe neuer exceed those formes of execution which are prescribed by the Law, or approued by continuall custome. One thing is also to bee marked in this case that strangers are neuer called in question here for their religion, which is farre otherwise (I hope) in any place where the *Inquisition* domines.

But hauing now too much wearied you with this long discourse, whereby I haue made you plainely see, that the wrong done vnto mee in particular first by the *Popes Breues*, and then by these Libellers, doth as deepely interest you all in generall, that are *Kings*, free *Princes*, or *States* as it doth me in particular: I will now conclude, with my humble prayers to God, that he will waken vs vp all out of that Lethargike slumber of Securitie, wherein our Predecessors and wee haue lien so long; and that wee may first grauely consider, what we are bound in conscience to doe for the
planting

planting and spreading of the trew worship of God, according to his reuealed will, in all our Dominions; therein hearing the voice of our onely
Pastor (*for his Sheepe will know his Voyce*, as himselfe sayeth) and not
following the vaine, corrupt and changeable traditions of men. And
next, that we may prouidently looke to the securitie of our owne States,
and not suffer this incroching *Babylonian Monarch* to winne still ground
vpon vs.. And if G o d hath so mercifully dealt with vs, that are his
Lieutenants vpon earth, as that he hath ioyned his cause with our interest,
the spirituall libertie of the Gospell with our temporall freedome: with
what zeale and courage may wee then imbrace this worke: for our labours
herein being assured, to receiue at the last the eternall and inestimable
reward of felicitie in the kingdome of Heauen; and in the meane time to
procure vnto our selues a temporall securitie, in our temporall Kingdomes in this world.

And markers: Iohn 10.17.

As for so many of you as are alreadie perswaded of that Trewth which
I professe, though differing among your selues in some particular points;
I thinke little perswasion should moue you to this holy and wise Resolution: Our Greatnesse, nor our number, praised bee G o d, being not so
contemptible, but that wee may shew good example to our neighbors;
since almost the halfe of all Christian people and of all sorts and degrees,
are of our profession; I meane, all gone out of *Babylon*, euen from Kings
and free Princes, to the meanest sort of People. But aboue all (my louing *Brethren* and *Cosins*) keepe fast the vnity of Faith among your selues;
Reiect ¹ questions of Genealogies and ² *Aniles fabulas*, as *Paul* saith; Let
not the foolish heate of your Preachers for idle Controuersies or indifferent things, teare asunder that Mysticall Body, whereof ye are a part, since
the very coat of him whose members wee are was without a seame: And
let not our diuision breed a slander of our faith, and be a word of reproch
in the mouthes of our aduersaries, who make *Vnitie* to be one of the speciall
notes of the trew Church.

¹ 1.Tim.1.4.
² Ibid c.4.7.

And as for you (my louing *Brethren* and *Cosins*) whom it hath not yet
pleased G o d to illuminate with the light of his trewth; I can but humbly
pray with *Elizeus*, that it would please G o d to open your eyes, that
yee might see what innumerable and inuincible armies of Angels are euer
prepared and ready to defend the trewth of G o d: and with S. *Paul* I
wish, that ye were as I am in this case; especially that yee would search the
Scriptures, and ground your Faith vpon your owne certaine knowledge,
and not vpon the report of others; since euery *Man must bee safe by his owne
faith.* But, leauing this to G o d his mercifull prouidence in his due time,
I haue good reason to remember you, to maintaine the ancient liberties of
your Crownes and Common-wealthes, not suffering any vnder G o d to
set himselfe vp aboue you; and therein to imitate your owne noble *predecessors*, who (euen in the dayes of greatest blindnesse) did diuers times coura-
giously oppose themselues to the incroaching ambition of Popes. Yea,

Actes.26.29.

Abac.2.4.

some

fome of your Kingdomes haue in all aages maintained, and without any interruption enioyed your libertie, againſt the moſt ambitious Popes. And ſome haue of very late had an euident proofe of the Popes ambitious aſpiring ouer your Temporall power, wherein ye haue conſtantly maintained and defended your lawfull freedome, to your immortall honour. And therefore I heartily wiſh you all, to doe in this caſe the Office of godly and iuſt Kings and earthly Iudges : which conſiſteth not onely in not wronging or inuading the Liberties of any other perſon (for to that will I neuer preſſe to perſwade you) but alſo in defending and maintaining theſe lawfull Liberties wherewith G o d hath indued you : For yee, whom G o d hath ordained to protect your people from iniuries, ſhould be aſhamed to ſuffer your ſelues to be wronged by any. And thus, aſſuring my ſelfe, that ye will with a ſetled Iudgement, free of preiudice, weigh the reaſons of this my *Diſcourſe*, and accept my plainneſſe in good part, gracing this my *Apologie* with your fauours, and yet no longer then till it ſhall be iuſtly and worthily refuted ; I end, with my earneſt prayers to the A l m i g h t i e for your proſperities, and that after your happie Temporall Raignes in earth, ye may liue and raigne in Heauen with him for euer.

A CA-

A CATALOGVE OF
THE LYES OF *TORTVS*,
TOGETHER WITH A BRIEFE
Confutation of them.

TORTVS.   Edit. Politan. pag. 9.

N the Oath of *Allegiance the Popes power to excom-
municate euen Hereticall Kings, is expresly denied.*

CONFVTATION.

The point touching the Popes power in excommunicating Kings, is neither treated of, nor
defined in the Oath of Allegiance, but was purposely declined.   See the *wordes of the Oath*, and
the *Præmonition. pag.* 292.

TORTVS.   pag. 10.

2   For all Catholike *writers doe collect from the wordes of Christ,* Whatsoeuer
thou shalt loose vpon earth, *shall be loosed in heauen, that there appertaineth
to the Popes authoritie, not onely a power to absolue from sinnes, but also from penalties, Censures, Lawes, Vowes, and Oathes.*

CONFVTATION.

That all Roman-Catholike writers doe not concurre with this Libeller, in thus collecting from CHRISTS wordes, *Matth.* 16. To omit other
reasons, it may appeare by this that many of them doe write, that what
CHRIST promised *there,* that hee did actually exhibite to his Disciples,
Iohn 20. when hee said, *Whose sinnes ye remit, they shall be remitted,* thereby restraining this power of loosing formerly promised, vnto loosing from
sinnes, not mentioning any absolution from Lawes, Vowes and Oathes in
this place. So doe *Theophylact, Anselme, Hugo Cardin. & Ferus in Matt.* 16. So
doe the principall Schoolemen, *Alexand. Hales in Summa. part.* 4. *q.* 79. *memb.*
5. *& 6. art.* 3. *Thom. in* 4. *dist.* 24. *q.* 3. *art.* 2. *Scotus in* 4. *dist.* 19. *art.* 1.   Pope

Hadrian.

*Hadrian.6.in 4.dist q.2. de clauib.pag.302.edit.Parisien. anno 1530.*who also al-leadgeth for this interpretation,*Augustine* and the *interlinear Glosse.*

TORTVS. Pag. 18.

3   *I abhorre all Parricide, I detest all conspiracies : yet it cannot be denied but oc-casions of despaire were giuen* [*to the Powder-plotters.*]

CONFVTATION.

That it was not any iust occasion of despaire giuen to the Powder-Traitours, as this Libeller would beare vs in hand, but the instructions which they had from the Iesuits, that caused them to attempt this bloody designe : See the *Premonition, pag.291. & 335.* and the booke intituled, *The proceedings against the late Traitours.*

TORTVS. Pap.26.

4   *For not onely the Catholiques, but also the Caluinist puritanes detest the ta-king of this Oath.*

CONFVTATION.

The Puritanes doe not decline the Oath of Supremacie, but daily doe take it, neither euer refused it. And the same Supremacie is defended by *Cal-uin* himselfe, *Instit. lib.4. cap. 20.*

TORTVS. Pag.28.

5   *First of all the Pope writeth not, that he was grieued at the calamities which the Catholikes did suffer for the keeping of the Orthodox faith in the time of the late Queene, or in the beginning of King* Iames *his reigne in England, but for the cala-mities which they suffer at this present time.*

CONFVTATION.

The onely recitall of the wordes of the Breue will sufficiently confute this Lye. For thus writeth the Pope, *The tribulations and calamities which ye haue continually susteined for the keeping of the Catholique faith, haue alway affli-Eted vs with great griefe of minde. But forasmuch as we vnderstand, that at this time all things are more grieuous,our affli.Etion hereby is wonderfully increased.*

TORTVS. Pag.28.

6   *In the first article* [*of the Statute*] *the Lawes of Queene* Elizabeth *are con-firmed.*

CONFVTATION.

There is no mention at all made of confirming the Lawes of Queene *Elizabeth,*in the first article of that Statute.

TORTVS. Pag.29.

7   *In the 10.Article* [*of the said Statute*] *it is added that if the* [*Catholicks*] *re-fuse the third time to take the Oath being tendered vnto them, they shall incurre the danger of loosing their liues.*

CONFVTATION.

There is no mention in this whole Statute either of offering the Oath the third time, or any indangering of their liues.

TORTVS. Pag.30.

8 *In the 12. Article, it is enacted, that whosoeuer goeth out of the land to serue in the warres vnder forreine Princes, they shall first of all take this Oath, or els be accounted for Traitours.*

CONFVTATION.

It is no where said in that Statute, that they which shall thus serue in the warres vnder forraine Princes, before they haue taken this Oath, shall be accounted for Traitors, but onely for Felons.

TORTVS. Pag.35.

9 *Wee haue already declared, that the* [Popes] *Apostolique power in binding and loosing is denied in that* [Oath of Alleageance.]

CONFVTATION.

There is no Assertory sentence in that Oath, nor any word but onely conditionall, touching the power of the Pope in binding and loosing.

TORTVS. Pag.37.

10 *The* Popes *themselues, euen will they, nill they, were constrained to subiect themselues to* Nero *and* Diocletian.

CONFVTATION.

That Christians without exception, not vpon constraint but willingly and for conscience sake, did subiect themselues to the Ethnicke Emperors, it may appeare by our *Apologie, pag.*255,256. and the *Apologetickes* of the ancient Fathers.

TORTVS. Pag.47.

11 *In which words* [*of the* Breues *of* Clement *the* 8.] *not onely* Iames *King of* Scotland, *was not excluded, but included rather.*

CONFVTATION.

If the *Breues* [of *Clement*] did not exclude mee from the Kingdome, but rather did include me, why did *Garnet* burne them? why would he not reserue them that I might haue seene them, that so hee might haue obteined more fauour at my hands for him and his Catholikes?

TORTVS. Pag.60.

12 *Of those* 14. Articles [*conteined in the Oath of Alleagiance*] *eleuen of them concerne the Primacie of the Pope in matters Spirituall.*

CONFVTATION.

No one Article of that Oath doeth meddle with the *Primacie* of the *Pope* in matter Spirituall: for to what end should that haue bene, since we haue an expresse Oath elsewhere against the *Popes Primacie* in matters Spirituall?

TOR-

TORTVS. Pag.64.

13 *Amongst other calumnies this is mentioned, that* Bellarmine *was priuie to sundry conspiracies against* Q.Elizabeth,*if not the author.*

CONFVTATION.

It is no where said [in the *Apologie*] that *Bellarmine* was either the Authour, or priuie to any conspiracies against Queene *Elizabeth*; but that he was their principall instructer and teacher, who corrupted their iudgement with such dangerous positions and principles, that it was an easie matter to reduce the generals into particulars, and to apply the dictates which hee gaue out of his chaire, as opporunitie serued, to their seuerall designes.

TORTVS. Pag.64.

14 *For he* [Bellarmine] *knoweth, that* Campian *onely conspired against Hereticall impietie.*

CONFVTATION.

That the trew and proper cause of *Campians* execution, was not for his conspiring against Hereticall impietie, but for conspiring against Queene *Elizabeth* and the State of this Kingdome, it was most euident by the iudiciall proceedings against him.

TORTVS. Pag 65.

15 *Why was* H.Garnet, *a man incomparable for learning in all kindes, and holinesse of life, put to death, but because he would not reueale that which he could not doe with a safe conscience.*

CONFVTATION.

That *Garnet* came to the knowledge of this horrible Plot not onely in confession as this Libeller would haue it, but by other meanes, neither by the relation of one alone, but by diuers, so as hee might with safe conscience haue disclosed it; See the *Premonition, pag.*334,335, &c. and the Earle of *Northamptons* booke.

TORTVS. Pag.71.

16 *Pope* Sixtus 5. *neither commanded the French King to bee murthered, neither approoued that fact, as it was done by a priuate person.*

CONFVTATION.

The falsehood of this doeth easily appeare by the Oration of *Sixtus* 5.

TORTVS. Pag.91.

17 *That which is added concerning* Stanley *his Treason, is neither faithfully nor trewly related: for the Apologer (as his maner is) doeth miserably depraue it, by adding many lyes.*

CONFVTATION.

That which the *Apologie* relateth concerning *Stanley* his Treason,is word for word recited out of Cardinall *Allens* Apologie for *Stanleys* treason: as it is to be seene there.

TOR-

TORTVS. Pag.93.

18. *It is very certaine that* H. Garnet *at his arraignement, did alwayes con-stantly auouch, that neither hee nor any Iesuite either were authors, or compartners, or aduisers, or consenting any way* [*to the Powder-Treason.*] And a little after. *The same thing hee protested at his death in a large speach, in the presence of innumerable people.*

CONFVTATION.

The booke of the proceedings againſt the late Traitours, and our *Premonition, pag.* 334,335,&c. doe clearely prooue the contrary of this to bee trew.

TORTVS. Pag.97.

19. *King* Iames *since he is no Catholike, neither is he a Chriſtian.*

CONFVTATION.

Contrary : I am a trew Catholike, a profeſſor of the trewly ancient, Catholike, and Apoſtolike Faith : and therefore am a trew Chriſtian. See the confeſſion of my faith in the *Premonition, pag.*302.303, &c.

TORTVS. Pag.98.

20. *And if the reports of them which knew him moſt inwardly, be trew, when hee was in* Scotland, *he was a Puritane, and an enemie to Proteſtants :* Now in England *he profeſſeth himſelfe a Proteſtant, and an enemie to the Puritans.*

CONFVTATION.

Contrary ; and what a Puritane I was in *Scotland :* See my ΒΑΣΙΛΙΚΟΝ ΔΩΡΟΝ and this my *Premonition, pag.*305,306.

HIS FALSIFICATIONS IN
HIS ALLEDGING OF HISTORIES,
together with a briefe declaration of
their falſhood

THE WORDS OF TORTVS. Pag.70.

1. *T was certaine that he* [Henry 4. *the Emperour.*] *died a natu-rall death.*

CONFVTATION.

It was not certaine : ſince ſundry Hiſtorians write otherwiſe, that he died vpó his impriſonment by his ſonne *Henry* 5. either with the noyſomneſſe and loathſomneſſe of the priſon, or being pined to death by hunger. Read *Faſciculus temporum* at the yeere 1094. *Laziardus epitom. vniuerſal. Hiſtor. c.* 198. *Paulus Langius in Chronico Citizenſi* at the yeere 1105. and *Iacobus Wimphelingus epitome Rerum Germanic. c.*28.

TOR-

TORTVS. Pag. 83.

2 Henry 4. *The Emperour feared indeed, but not any corporall death, but the cenſure of Excommunication, from the which that he might procure abſolutiin, of his owne accord; he did thus demiſſely humble himſelfe* [before Gregory 7.]

CONFVTATION.

That *Henry* 4. thus deiected himſelfe before the Pope, it was neither of his owne accord, neither vpon any feare of the Popes Excommunication, which [in this particular] hee eſteemed of no force, but vpon feare of the loſſe of his Kingdome and life, as the records of antiquitie doe euidently teſtiſie. See *Lambertus Schaſnaburg* at the yeere 1077. *Abbas Vrſpergen.* at the yeere 1075. The Author of the life of *Henry* 4. *Bruno* in his Hiſtory of the Saxon warre. *Laziard. in epitom. vniuerſal. Hiſtor. c.* 193. *Cuſpinian. in Henr.* 4. *Sigonius de Regno Italiæ lib.* 9.

TORTVS. Pag. 83.

3 *The trewth of the Hiſtory* [of Alexander 3. *treading vpon the necke of* Fredericke Barbaroſſa *with his foot*] *may be iuſtly doubted of.*

CONFVTATION.

But no Hiſtorian doubteth of it ; and many do auouch it, as *Hieronym. Bard. in victor. Naual. ex Beſſarion. Chronico apud Baron. ad an.*1177.*num.*5. *Gerſon de poteſtate Eccleſiæ conſd.* 11. *Iacob Bergom. in ſupplem. Chronic. ad an.*1160. *Nauclerus Gener.* 40. *Petrus iuſtinian lib.* 2. *Rerum Venetar. Papirius Maſſon. lib.* 5. *de Epiſcop. vrbis.* who alledgeth for this *Gennadius* Patriarch of *Conſtantinople.* Beſides *Alphonſus Cicconius de vit. Pontif. in Alex. and.* 3. and *Azorius* the Ieſuite: *Inſtit. Moral. part. lib.* 5. *c.* 43.

TORTVS. Pag. 83.

4 What other thing feared *Fredérick Barbaroſſa* but excommunication?

CONFVTATION.

That *Frederick* feared onely Pope *Alexander* his Excommunication, no ancient Hiſtorian doth teſtiſie. But many do write, that this ſubmiſſion of his was principally for feare of looſing his Empire and Dominions. See for this, *Martin. Polon. ad an.*1166. *Platina in vita Alexan.* 3. *Laziard. in epitom. Hiſtoriæ vniuerſal. c.* 212. *Naucler. Generat* 40. *Iacobus Wimphelingus in epitom. Rerum Germanic. c.* 32.

TORTVS. Pag. 88.

5 *Adde heereunto, that* Cuſpinian. [*in relating the hiſtory of the Turkes brother who was poyſoned by* Alexander 6.] *hath not the conſent of other writers to witn.ſſe the trewth of this Hiſtory.*

CONFVTATION.

The ſame Hiſtory, which is reported by *Cuſpinian*, is recorded alſo by ſundry other famous Hiſtorians. See *Francis Guicciardin. lib.* 2. *Hiſtor. Ital. Paulus Iouius lib.* 2. *Hiſt. ſui temporis. Sabellic. Enneaed.* 10. *lib.* 9. *Continuator Palmerij,* at the yeere. 1494.

THE

THE NOVEL DOCTRINES,
WITH A BRIEFE DECLARATION
of their Noueltie.

NOVEL DOCTRINE. Pag. 9.

1 *T is agreed vpon amongst all, that the Pope may lawfully depose Hereticall Princes, and free their Subiects from yeelding obedience vnto them.*

CONFVTATION.

Nay, *all* are so farre from consenting in this point, that it may much more trewly be auouched; that *none* entertained that conceit before *Hildebrand*: since he was the first brocher of this new doctrine neuer before heard of, as many learned men of that aage, and the aage next following (to omit others of succeeding aages) haue expresly testified. See for this point, the Epistle of the whole Clergie of *Liege* to Pope *Paschal* the second. See the iudgement of many Bishops of those times, recorded by *Auentine* in his historie, *lib.5.fol.579.* Also the speech vttered by *Conrade* bishop of *Vtretcht*, in the said fifth booke of *Auentine, fol.582.* And another by *Eberhardus* Archbishop of *Saltzburge. Ibid. lib.7.p.684.* Also the iudgement of the Archbishop of *Triers, in constitut. Imperialib. à M. Haimensfeldio editis.prg.47.* The Epistle of Walthram Bishop of *Megburgh* which is extant in *Dodechine* his Appendix to the Chronicle of *Marianus Scotus,* at the yeere 1090. *Benno* in the life of *Hildebrand.* The author of the booke *De vnitate Ecclesiae*, or *the Apologie* for *Henry* the fourth. *Sigebert* in his Chronicle, at the yeere 1088. *Godfrey* of *Viterbio* in his History entituled *Pantheon, part.17. Ottho Frisingensis, lib.6.c.35. & prafat. in lib.7. Frederick Barbarossa. lib.6. Gunther. Ligurin. de gestis Frederici.* and *lib.1.c.10.* of *Raduicus de gestis eiusdem Frederici. Vincentius in speculo historiali lib.15.c.84.* with sundry others.

NOVEL DOCTRINE. Pag. 51.

2 *In our supernaturall birth in Baptisme wee are to conceiue of a secret and implied oath, which we take at our new birth, to yeeld obedience to the spirituall Prince, which is Christes Vicar.*

CONFVTATION.

It is to bee wondred at, whence this fellow had this strange new Diuinitie, which surely was first framed in his owne fantasticall braine. Else let him make vs a Catalogue of his Authors, that hold and teach, that all Christians, whether infants or of aage, are by vertue of an oath taken in their Baptisme, bound to yeeld absolute obedience to CHRISTS Vicar the Pope, or baptized in any but in CHRIST.

NOVEL

NOVEL DOCTRINE. Pag.94.

3 *But since that Catholike doctrine doth not permit for the auoidance of any mischiefe whatsoeuer,to discouer the secret of Sacramentall confession,he* [Garnet] *rather chose to suffer most bitter death,then to violate the seale of so great a Sacrament.*

CONFVTATION.

That the secret of Sacramentall confession is by no meanes to bee disclosed, no not indirectly,or in generall, so the person confessing bee concealed, for auoydance and preuention of no mischiefe, how great soeuer: Besides that it is a position most dangerous to all Princes and Commonwealths,as I shew in my *Præmonition,pag.*333,334. It is also a Nouell Assertion, not heard of till of late dayes in the Christian world: Since the common opinion euen of the Schoolemen and Canonists both old and new, is vnto the contrary; witnesse these Authors following: *Alexander Hales part.*4.*qu.*78.*mem.*2.*art.*2. *Thom.*4. *dist.*21.*qu.*3. *art.* 1.*ad* 1.*Scotus in* 4.*dist.*21. *qu.*2. *Hadrian.*6.*in* 4. *dist. vbi de Sacramen. Confes. edit. Paris.* 1530. *pag.*289. *Dominic. Sot.in* 4. *dist.*18.*q.*4.*art.*5. *Francis. de victor.summ. de Sacram. n.*189. *Nauar. in Enchirid. c.* 8. *Ioseph. Angles in Florib.part.*1. *pag.*247. *edit. Antuerp. Petrus Soto lect.* 11. *de confes.* The Iesuites also accord hereunto, *Suarez. Tom.*4.*disp.in* 3 *part. Thom.disp.*33. § 3. *Gregor.de Valentia. Tom.*4. *disp.*7. *q.*13. *punct.*3. who saith the common opinion of the Schoolemen is so.

NOVEL DOCTRINE. Pag.102.

4 *I dare boldly auow, that the Catholikes haue better reason to refuse the Oath* [of *Allegeance*] *then Eleazar had to refuse the eating of Swines flesh.*

CONFVTATION.

This assertion implieth a strange doctrine indeede,that the Popes *Breues* are to be preferred before Moses Law: And that Papists are more bound to obey the Popes decree, then the Iewes were to obey the Law of God pronounced by Moses.

NOVEL DOCTRINE. Pag.135.

5 *Churchmen are exempted from the Iurisdiction of secular Princes,and therefore are no subiects to Kings : yet ought they to obserue their Lawes concerning matters temporall, not by vertue of any Law, but by enforcement of reason, that is to say, not for that they are their Subiects, but because reason will giue it, that such Lawes are to be kept for the publike good,and the quiet of the Common-wealth.*

CONFVTATION.

How trew friends the Cardinall and his Chaplen are to Kings that would haue so many Subiects exempted from their power: See my *Præmonition,Pag.*296,297. Also,Pag.330.331.&c. But as for this and the like new *Aphorismes,* I would haue these cunning Merchants to ceafe to vent such stuffe for ancient and Catholike wares in the Christian world, till they haue disprooued their owne *Venetians,* who charge them with Noueltie and forgerie in this point.

* *
*

A DE

A DECLARATION

CONCERNING THE

PROCEEDINGS WITH

The States
GENERALL,

OF THE UNITED PRO-
VINCES OF THE LOW
COVNTREYS,

Jn the cause of D. CONRADVS
VORSTIVS.

TO

TO THE HONOVR
OF OVR LORD AND
SAVIOVR *JESVS CHRIST,*
THE ETERNALL SONNE
OF THE ETERNALL
FATHER,

·THE ONELY ΘΕΑΝΘΡΩΠΟΣ,
MEDIATOVR, AND RECONCILER
OF MANKIND,

IN SIGNE OF THANKFVLNES,

HIS MOST HVMBLE, AND
MOST OBLIGED SERVANT,
IAMES BY THE GRACE OF GOD,
KING OF GREAT BRITAINE,
FRANCE AND IRELAND,
Defender of the FAITH,

Doeth DEDICATE, and CONSECRATE
this his DECLARATION.

That

Hat it is one of the principall parts of that duetie which appertaines vnto a Chriſtian King, to protect the trew Church within his owne Dominions, and to extirpate hereſies, is a Maxime without all controuerſie; in which reſpect thoſe honourable Titles of *Cuſtos & Vindex vtriuſquè Tabulæ, Keeper and Auenger of both the Tables of the Law,* and *Nutritius Ecclefia, Nurſin Father of the Church,* doe rightly belong vnto euery Emperour, King, and Chriſtian Monarch. But what intereſt a Chriſtian King may iuſtly pretend to meddle *in alienâ Repub. within another State or Common wealth* in matters of this nature (where Strangers are not allowed to be too curious) is the point in queſtion, and whereof we meane at this time to treate.

For our zeale to the glory of God, being the onely motiue that induced vs (as he who is the ſearcher of the heart and reines can witneſſe) to make ſundry Inſtances and Requeſts vnto the States Generall of the *Vnited Prouinces* for the baniſhment of a wretched *Heretique,* or rather *Athieſt,* out of their Dominions, named D. *Conradus Vorſtius,* hath bene ſo ill interpreted, or rather wreſted to a peruerſe ſence, by a ſort of people, whoſe corrupted ſtomacke turnes all good nouriſhment into bad and pernitious humors, (as if it had bene ſome vanitie and deſire of vaine glory in vs, or elſe an Ambition to encroach by little and little vpon the libertie of their State, which had caried vs headlong into the buſineſſe) As both to cleare our owne honour from the darke miſts of theſe falſe and ſcandalous imputations, as alſo to make it trewly appeare vnto the Chriſtian world, in what ſort wee haue proceeded herein; Wee haue thought good to publiſh this preſent Declaration, containing as well the diſcourſe of our whole Negotiation hitherto with the States in this cauſe, as alſo the reaſons which haue mooued vs to take it ſo to heart, and to perſeuere therein as we haue done, and will doe (God willing) vntill it pleaſe him, to bring it to ſome good and happy end.

In Autumne laſt, about the end of Auguſt, being in our hunting Progreſſe, there came to our hands two bookes of the ſaid *Vorſtius,* the one intituled *Tractatus Theologicus de Deo,* dedicated to the Lantgraue of *Heſſen,*

G g

ſen, imprinted in the yeere 1610. the other his *Exegeſis Apologetica* vpon
that booke, dedicated to the States, and printed in the yeere 1611. Which
books, aſſoone as we had receiued, and (not without much horror and deteſtation) caſt our eye onely vpon ſome of the principall Articles of his diſputations conteined in the firſt booke, and his Commentary thereupon in
the ſecond, God is our witneſſe, that the zeale of his glory did ſo tranſport
vs, as (to ſay with S. *Paul*) We ſtayed not one houre, but diſpatched a Letter preſently to our Ambaſſadour reſident with the States, to this purpoſe following.

Ruſtie and welbeloued, &c.   *You ſhall repaire to the* States
Generall, *with all poſſible diligence in our name, telling them,
that wee doubt not, but that their Ambaſſadours which were
with vs about two yeeres ſince, did informe them of a forewarning, that we wiſhed the ſaid Ambaſſadours to make vnto them in
our name, to beware in time, of ſeditious and hereticall Preachers, and not to ſuffer
any ſuch to creepe into their State. Our principall meaning was of* Arminius,
*who though himſelfe were lately dead, yet had hee left too many of his diſciples
behinde him. Now according to that care which wee continually haue of the weale
of their State, wee haue thought good to ſend vnto them a new aduertiſement
vpon the like occaſion, which is this: That there is lately come to our handes
a piece of worke of one* Vorſtius, *a Diuine in thoſe parts, wherein hee hath
publiſhed ſuch monſtrous blaſphemie and horrible Atheiſme, as out of the care that a
Chriſtian Prince, and Defender of the Faith, (as we haue euer bene) ought to haue of
the good of the Church, wee hold not onely ſuch a ſcandalous booke worthy to bee
burnt, but euen the Authour himſelfe to bee moſt ſeuerely puniſhed. This notwithſtanding wee are informed, that the States are ſo farre from beeing ſenſible
of ſo great a ſcandall to the Church, as that the moſt part of them haue already
yeelded him their free conſents and voyces, for the obteining of the place of Diuinitie Reader in the Vniuerſitie of* Leyden, *which the aboue-named* Arminius *of
little better ſtuffe, lately enioyed: and though himſelfe be dead, hath left his ſting yet
liuing among them. Hauing therefore vnderſtood, that the time of Election will
be about* Michaelmas *next, and holding our ſelues bound in honour and conſcience,
as a Chriſtian Prince, and one who hath vouchſafed the States our Royall fauour
and ſupport in reſpect of their Religion, to preuent ſo great a miſchiefe ſo farre as
we are able: Wee will and require you to let them vnderſtand, how infinitely wee
ſhall bee diſpleaſed if ſuch a Monſter receiue aduancement in the Church. And
if it bee alleadged, that hee hath recanted his Atheiſticall opinions, and that thereupon he may be capable of the place, you ſhall tell them, that wee thinke his Recan-
tation ſo ſlender a ſatisfaction for ſo fowle an offence, as that wee hold him rather
worthy of puniſhment, or at leaſt to be debarred from all promotion: Wherein though
wee*

Wee aſſure our ſelfe, that they will of their owne diſcretions eſchew ſuch a viper, who may make a fearefull rent not onely in their Eccleſiaſticall, but alſo in their Politique State, yet notwithſtanding all this, if they will continue their reſolution to preferre him, you ſhall then make a proteſtation to them in our name, That wee will not faile to make knowen to the world publikely in print, how much wee deteſt ſuch abominable Hereſies, and all allowers and tolerators of them: And becauſe the States ſhall know vpon what reaſons we haue grounded this our Admonition, you ſhall receiue herewith a * Catalogue of his damnable Poſitions, of which no one page of the booke is free.

Giuen vnder our Signet, &c.

* This Cata-logue is here purpoſely omit-ted for auoy-ding a needleſſe repetition, ſee-ing the princi-pall points ther-of are contei-ned in a little Collection an-nexed at the end of our ſe-cond letter written to Wynwood.

For obſeruing, that ſo prodigious a Monſter began to liue among them, We could do no leſſe (conſidering the infinite obligations which wee owe vnto God) then to make Our zeale appeare againſt ſuch an enemie to the Eſſence of the Deity. Beſides, the charitie, which Wee beare to the ſaid States Our neighbors and Confederates, profeſſing the ſame Religion that we do, did enforce Vs to admoniſh them, to eſchew and preuent in time ſo dangerous a contagion, which diſperſing it ſelfe, might infect, not onely the bodie of their State, but all Chriſtendome alſo; the danger where-of was ſo much greater to our Dominions then to many others, by how much the *Prouinces* of the ſaid States are neerer vnto Vs in their ſituation.

Our Ambaſſadour therefore hauing ſufficiently acquitted himſelfe of that which Wee gaue him in charge, by exhorting them in Our Name, timely to preuent the danger which might enſue by enterteyning ſuch a gueſt as VORSTIVS, (which at that time they might eaſily haue done, ſeeing he was not yet ſetled at *Leyden*, neither was he lodged in the houſe appointed for the publique Reader, nor were his wife and family yet ar-riued, and therefore much more eaſie for them to haue rid him out of their countrey, ſending him backe to the place from whence he came, according to the old Prouerbe,

Turpiùs eijcitur, quàm non admittitur hoſpes.

It is more honeſt to refuſe a gueſt, then when you haue once receiued him, to thruſt him out of doores.) Yet notwithſtanding all the diligence that Our Ambaſſadour could vſe, and the oportunity which at that time was offered them to diſcharge him, all the anſwere he could procure from them, was but this, that,

Whereas a Propoſition was made on the behalfe of his Maieſtie of Great Bri-taine, *in the aſſembly of the Lords States Generall of the* Vnited Prouinces *by* Sir Ralph Winwood *his Maieſties Ambaſſadour and Councellour in the Coun-cel of State in thoſe countreys, exhibited in writing the* 21. *of the moneth precedent* (*the ſubſtance thereof being firſt amply debated by the Deputies of the States of* Holland *and* Weſt-Frizeland, *and thereupon mature deliberation had*) *The ſaid*

G g 2 Lords

Lords States Generall in anſwere to the ſaid Propoſition, haue moſt humbly re-
queſted, and by theſe preſents doe humbly requeſt his Maieſtie to beleeue, that as, for
preſeruation of the libertie, rights and priuiledges of the Low-Countreys, againſt
the vniuſt, tyrannicall and bloody courſes contrary thereunto, practiſed for many
yeeres vpon the conſciences, bodies and fortunes of the good Inhabitants of all qualities of theſe Countreys by the Spaniards and their Adherents, they haue bene conſtrained after a long patience, many Remonſtrances, Requeſts and other ſubmiſſiue
proceedings vſed in vaine, to take armes for their neceſſary defence, (when they ſaw
no other remedy,) as alſo to craue the aſſiſtance of his Maieſtie particularly, and of
other Kings, Princes and Common wealths, by whoſe fauor, but principally by
his Maieſties they haue ſince continually ſuſteined for many yeeres, with an exceeding
great conſtancie and moderation as well in proſperitie as in aduerſity, a heauie, chargeable and bloody warre, many terrible and cruell encounters, notable Battailes both
by land and ſea, matchleſſe Sieges of a number of Townes, Ruines, and deuaſtation of
Cities and Countreys, and other difficulties incident to the warre: So doe their Lordſhips alwayes confeſſe, that in ſpecie the chiefe and principall reaſon which hath moued them at firſt to entertaine, and ſince to maintaine the ſaid reſolution, hath beene
the foreſaid tyrannie exerciſed vpon the conſciences, bodies, and goods of their people,
by introduction of the Inquiſition and conſtraint in matter of Religion: For which
reſpects their Obligation to his Maieſtie is greatly increaſed, in that after ſo many de-
monſtrations of affection, fauours, and aſſiſtances in the purſuite of their iuſt cauſe,
his Maieſtie is yet pleaſed, like a louing Father, to aſſure vnto them the continuance
of the ſame Royall affection and aſſiſtance, by taking care that the trew Chriſtian
reformed Religion bee purely and ſincerely taught within their Countreys, aſwell
in Churches as in Schooles; For which the Lords States Generall doe moſt humbly
thanke his Maieſtie, and will for their parts by all lawfull meanes, endeauour ſo to
ſecond his ſincere and Chriſtian intention in this particular, as his Maieſtie ſhall receiue all good contentment.

　　As concerning the buſineſſe of Doct. Vorſtius, principally handled in the foreſaid Propoſition, the Lords States Generall (to make the matter more plaine)
haue informed themſelues, Firſt that the Curators of the Vniuerſitie of Leyden
(according to their duetie, and the ancient cuſtome euer ſince the foundation of that
Vniuerſitie,) hauing diligently made inquirie for ſome Doctor to bee choſen into
the place of Diuinitie Profeſſor there, at that time voyd, after mature deliberation were giuen to vnderſtand, that at Steinford within the Dominions of the
Counts of Tecklenbourg, Bentem, &c. (who were of the firſt Counts that in
Germanie had caſt off the yoke of the Papacie, Idolatrie, and impure religion, and
imbraced the reformed Religion, which to this day they maintaine) there did remaine one Doct. Conradus Vorſtius, who had continued in that place about fifteene yeeres a Profeſſor of trew Religion, and a Miniſter; and that the ſaide
Conradus Vorſtius for his learning and other good parts was much ſought after by Prince Maurice, Lantgraue of Heſſen, with intent to make him Diuinitie Profeſſor in ſome Vniuerſitie of his Countrey. Moreouer, that hee had
ſufficiently, and to the great contentment; euen of thoſe that are now become
his greateſt aduerſaries, ſhewed with a Chriſtian moderation his learning and puritie

ritie in the holy knowledge of Diuinity, againſt the renowned Ieſuite Bellarmine: *And that the ſayd* Conradus Vorſtius *was thereupon ſent for by the* Curators *aforeſayde, about the beginning of* Iuly, 1610. *which meſſage beeing ſeconded by letters of recommendation from his* Excellencie, *and from the deputy Councelors for the* States *of* Holland *and* Weſtfrizeland, *vnto the ſayd Counts of* Tecklenburg, *did accordingly take effeƈt. In the moneth of Auguſt following, the ſaid Eleƈtion and Calling was countermined by certaine perſons, to whoſe office or diſpoſition the buſineſſe did nothing at all belong: which being perceiued, and the ſayd* Vorſtius *charged with ſome vnſoundneſſe of doƈtrine, the* Curators *did thereupon thinke fit, with the good liking of* Vorſtius *himſelfe, that as well in the Vniuerſitie of* Leyden, *as at the* Haɡe, *he ſhould appeare in his owne iuſtification to anſwere all accuſers and accuſations whatſoeuer. At which time there was not any one that did offer to charge him. In the moneth of* May *following, ſixe* Miniſters *did vndertake to prooue, that* VORSTIVS *had publiſhed falſe and vnſound doƈtrine, who afterward beeing heard in full aſſembly of the* States *of* Holland *and* Weſtfrizeland, *(in the preſence of the* Curators, *and ſixe other* Miniſters*) on the one part, and* Vorſtius *in his owne defence on the other part; and that which could bee ſaid on either ſide to the ſeuerall points in their ſeuerall refutations reſpeƈtiuely: The ſaid Lords* States *hauing grauely deliberated vpon the allegations as well of the one part as of the other, as alſo heard the opinions of the ſaid* Miniſters *(after the maner and cuſtome of the ſayd aſſembly)could not ſee any reaſon, why the execution of that which was done by the* Curators *lawfully, and according to order, ought to bee hindred or impeached. In* Auguſt *following there being ſent ouer hither certaine other* Articles, *wherewith* Vorſtius *was charged, and diſperſed in little printed Pamphlets amongſt the people, the ſayd Lords* States *entred into a new conſultation, and there reſolued, that* Vorſtius *(according both to Gods Law, the Law of Nature, and the law written; as alſo according to the laudable vſe and cuſtomes of their country,) ſhould be heard againſt his new accuſers, concerning thoſe* Articles *there layed to his charge. And moreouer, it was generally declared by the* States *of* Holland *and* Weſtfrizeland *there aſſembled, (as euery one of them likewiſe in his owne particular, and the* Curators *and* Bourgmaſters *of* Leyden *for their parts did ſpecially declare:) That there was neuer any intention to permit other Religion to bee taught in the Vniuerſity of* Leyden, *then the Chriſtian Religion reformed and grounded vpon the word of God: And beſides, that if the ſayd* Vorſtius *ſhould bee found guilty in any of the aforeſayd points whereof hee was accuſed, that they would not admit him to the place of Profeſſour. The Deputies of the ſayd Lords* States *of* Holland *and* Weſtfrizeland *further declaring, that they doe aſſuredly beleeue, that if his Maieſty of* Great Britaine *were well informed of the trew circumſtances of this buſineſſe, and of their ſincere intention therein, hee would (according to his high wiſedome, prudence, and benignitie) conceiue fauourably of them, and their proceedings: whereof the Lords* States Generall *are no leſſe confident; and the rather, for that the ſaid Deputies haue aſſured them, that the Lords* States *of* Holland *and* Weſtfrizeland *their Superiors would proceede in this buſineſſe (as in all others) with all due reuerence, care, and reſpeƈt vnto his Maieſties ſerious admonition, as becommeth them.*

And

And the Lords States Generall, doe request the said Lord Ambassadour to recommend this their Answere vnto his Maiestie with fauour.
　　　Giuen at the Hage, in the Assembly of the said Lords States Generall.
　　　　　1. October. 1611.

BVt before wee had receiued this answere from the States, some of *Vorstius* books were brought ouer into *England*, and (as it was reported) not without the knowledge and direction of the Authour. And about the same time one *Bertius*, a scholler of the late *Arminius*, (who was the first in our aage that infected *Leyden* with Heresie) was so impudent, as to send a Letter vnto the Archbishop of *Canterbury*, with a Booke intituled, *De Apostasia Sanctorum*. And not thinking it sufficient to auow the sending of such a booke, (the title whereof onely, were enough to make it worthy the fire) hee was moreouer so shamelesse, as to maintaine in his Letter to the Archbishop, that the doctrine conteined in his booke, was agreeable with the doctrine of the Church of *England*. Let the Church of CHRIST then iudge, whether it was not high time for vs to bestirre our selues, when as this Gangrene had not onely taken holde amongst our neerest neighbours; so as *Non solùm paries proximus iam ardebat* : not onely the next house was on fire, but did also begin to creepe into the bowels of our owne Kindome; For which cause hauing first giuen order, that the said bookes of *Vorstius* should be publikely burnt, as well in *Pauls* Church-yard, as in both the Vniuersities of this Kingdome, wee thought good to renew our former request vnto the States, for the banishment of *Vorstius*, by a Letter which wee caused our Ambassadour to deliuer vnto them from vs at their Assembly in the *Hage*, the fifth of Nouember; whereunto they had referred vs in their former answere, the tenor of which Letter was as followeth :

Igh and mightie Lords , *Hauing vnderstood by your answere to that Proposition which was made vnto you in our name by our Ambassadour there resident , That at your Assembly to bee holden in Nouember next , you are resolued then to giue order concerning the businesse of that wretched* D. Vorstius, *Wee haue thought good (notwithstanding the declaration which our Ambassadour hath already made vnto you in our name touching that particular,) to put you againe in remembrance thereof by this Letter , and thereby freely to discharge our selues , both in point of our duetie towards God , and of that sincere friendship which wee beare towards you.*
　　First We assure Our selues that you are sufficiently perswaded that no worldly respect could moue Vs to haue thus importuned you in an affaire of this nature, being drawen into it onely through Our zeale to the glory of God ; and the care which Wee haue that all occasion of such great scandals as this is, vnto the trew reformed Church
　　　　　　　　　　　　　　　　　　　　　　　　　　of

of God, might bee in due time foreſeene and preuented. Wee are therefore to let you vnderſtand, that Wee doe not a little wonder, that you haue not onely ſought to pro-uide an habitation in ſo eminent a place amongſt you, for ſuch a corrupted perſon as this Vorſtius *is, but that you haue alſo afforded him your licenſe and proteƐion to print that Apologie which he hath dedicated vnto you; A booke wherein he doeth moſt impudently maintaine the execrable blaſphemies, which in his former hee had diſgorged; The which wee are now able to affirme out of our owne know-ledge, hauing ſince that Letter which wee wrote vnto our Ambaſſadour, read ouer and ouer againe with our owne eyes (not without extreme miſlike and horrour) both his bookes, the firſt dedicated to the Lantgraue of* Heſſen, *and the other to you. We had well hoped, that the corrupt ſeed which that enemie of God* Arminius *did ſowe amongſt you ſome few yeeres ſince (whoſe diſciples and followers are yet too bold and frequent within your Dominions) had giuen you a ſufficient warning, af-terwards to take heed of ſuch infeƐed perſons, ſeeing your owne Countrey-men al-ready diuided into FaƐions vpon this occaſion, a matter ſo oppoſite to vnitie (which is indeed the onely prop and ſafetie of your State next vnder God) as of neceſſitie it muſt by little and little bring you to vtter ruine, if wiſely you doe not prouide a-gainſt it, and that in time.*

It is trew that it was Our hard hap not to heare of this Arminius *before he was dead, and that all the Reformed Churches of* Germanie *had with open mouth com-plained of him. But aſſoone as Wee vnderſtood of that diſtraƐion in your State, which after his death he left behind him, We did not faile (taking the opportunitie when your laſt extraordinary Ambaſſadors were here with Vs) to vſe ſome ſuch ſpeeches vnto them concerning this matter, as We thought fitteſt for the good of your State, and which we doubt not but they haue faithfully reported vnto you; For what need We make any queſtion of the arrogancie of theſe Heretiques, or rather Atheiſti-call SeƐaries amongſt you, when one of them at this preſent remaining in your towne of* Leyden, *hath not onely preſumed to publiſh of late a blaſphemous Booke of the Apoſtaſie of the Saints, but hath beſides beene ſo impudent, as to ſend the other day a copie thereof, as a goodly preſent, to Our Arch-Biſhop of* Canterbury, *together with a letter, wherein he is not aſhamed (as alſo in his Booke) to lie ſo groſſely, as to auowe, that his Hereſies conteined in the ſaid Booke, are agreeable with the Religion and profeſſion of Our Church of* England. *For theſe reſpeƐs therefore haue Wee cauſe enough very heartily to requeſt you, to roote out with ſpeed thoſe Hereſies and Schiſmes, which are beginning to bud foorth amongſt you, which if you ſuffer to haue the reines any longer, you cannot expeƐ any other iſſue thereof, then the curſe of God, infamy throughout all the reformed Churches, and a perpetuall rent and diſtraƐion in the whole body of your State. But if peraduenture this wretched* Vorſtius *ſhould denie or equiuocate vpon thoſe blaſphemous poynts of Hereſie and Atheiſme, which already hee hath broached, that perhaps may mooue you to ſpare his perſon, and not cauſe him to bee burned (which neuer any Heretique better deſerued, and wherein we will leaue him to your owne (chriſtian wiſedome) but to ſuffer him vpon any de-fence or abnegation, which hee ſhall offer to make, ſtill to continue and to teach a-mongſt you, is a thing ſo abominable, as we aſſure our ſelues it will not once enter in-to any of your thoughts: For admit hee would proue himſelfe innocent (which neuer-*

theleſſe

theleſſe he cannot doe) in moſt of thoſe points wherewith hee is charged; yet were it but the ſcandall of his perſon , which will ſtill remaine , it were cauſe more then enough for you to remooue him out of your Dominions. You know what is written of Cæſars wife, that it was not ſufficient for her to be innocent , but ſhe muſt alſo bee free from all occaſion of ſuſpicion : how much more then ought you to bee warie and cautious in a matter of ſo great importance as this , which concerneth the glory of God , the ſaluation of your ſoules, the ſoules of your people , and the ſafetie of your State; and not to ſuffer ſo dangerous a ſparke to lie kindling amongſt you ? For a man may eaſily coniecture, that feare and the horrour of his owne actions will make him boldly denie that poyſon which boyleth at his heart : For what will not hee denie , that denieth the Eternitie and Omnipotencie of God ? And howbeit hee were innocent (as we haue ſaid before) the Church of God is not ſo ill furniſhed with men of ſufficiencie for that place, as that you need bee vnprouided of ſome other , who ſhall not be ſubiect to that ſcandall , wherewith hee is ſo tainted, as it muſt bee a long penance, and many yeeres of probation , that muſt weare it away. But eſpecially ought you to bee very carefull, not to hazard the corruption of your youth in ſo famous an Vniuerſitie by the doctrine of ſo ſcandalous a perſon, who (it is to bee feared) when hee findeth himſelfe once well ſetled there , will returne againe to his ancient vomite.

We will therefore conclude with this requeſt vnto you, that you will aſſure your ſelues, that the affection onely which wee beare vnto your State , hath enforced vs to vſe this libertie towards you, not doubting for our part, but that, as this which wee haue written vnto you proceedes from the ſinceritie of our conſcience, ſo our good God will bee pleaſed to giue you a due apprehenſion thereof , and that your reſolution in a matter of ſo great conſequence, may tend to his glory, to your owne honour and ſafetie, to the extirpation of theſe ſpringing Atheiſmes and Hereſies, and to the ſatisfaction, not onely of vs, but of all the reformed Churches, who haue bene hitherto extremely ſcandalized therewith : But if on the contrary part, we faile of that wee expect at your hands (which God forbid) and that you ſuffer hereafter ſuch peſtilent Heretiques to neſtle among you, who dare take vpon them that licentious libertie, to fetch againe from Hell the ancient Hereſies long ſince condemned , or elſe to inuent new of their owne braine , contrary to the beliefe of the trew Catholike Church, wee ſhall then bee conſtrained (to our great griefe) publikely to proteſt againſt theſe abominations : and (as God hath honoured vs with the Title of Defender of the Faith) not onely to depart and ſeparate our ſelues from the vnion of ſuch falſe and heretical Churches, but alſo to exhort all other reformed Churches to ioyne with vs in a common Councel, how to extinguiſh and remand to hell theſe abominable Hereſies, that now newly begin to put foorth againe. And furthermore for our owne particular, we ſhall be enforced ſtrictly to inhibit the youth of our Dominions from repairing to ſo infected a place, as is the Vniuerſitie of Leyden. Sed meliora ſperamus & ominamur, We hope and expect for better, aſſuring our ſelues in the mercie of our good God, that as he hath a long time preſerued you from your temporall enemies, and at this time is beginning to eſtabliſh your Eſtate to the contentment of all your friends, (but eſpecially to ours , who haue neuer beene wanting to aſsiſt you vpon all occaſions) that the ſame God will not leaue you for a prey to your ſpirituall aduerſaries,

who

who gape at nothing but your vtter deſtruction. And in this confidence wee will recommend you and the proſperitie of your affaires to the protection of God, remaining as we haue euer beene,

Your good friend IAMES R.

Giuen at our Pallace of Weſtminſter the 6.of October. 1611.

Wee writ likewiſe at the ſame time, another Letter to our Ambaſſadour, for his direction in the whole buſineſſe; the Copie whereof is this which followeth:

TRuſtie and welbeloued. *Perceiuing by the States their anſwere to your Propoſition deliuered to them in our name, concerning the matter of* Vorſtius, *that they haue taken time for their proceeding with him; and hauing ſome reaſon to thinke that his fauourers amongſt them are ſtronger then were to bee wiſhed, Wee haue thought good to renew our Admonition vnto them in this matter, by a Letter of our owne, written at good length, and in earneſt maner, which you ſhall heerewith receiue, and at the time of their meeting for this purpoſe, preſent vnto them in our name: Inſiſting with them with all the earneſtneſſe you can, both for the remoouing of this blaſphemous Monſter, as alſo that they may now at leaſt take ſome ſuch ſolid order, as this licentious libertie of diſputing or arguing ſuch vnprofitable queſtions (whereby new opinions may bee dayly ſet abroach againſt the grounds of Diuinitie) may hereafter bee reſtrained as well at* Leyden, *as in all the reſt of their Dominions. And for the better ſtrengthening of this motion, wee doe herewith ſend you a Note of ſome of the moſt ſpeciall Atheiſticall points, wherewith his booke is full farced. But if contrary to our expectation, all our labour cannot mooue them to giue ſatisfaction, not to vs, but to the whole Church of God in this caſe; Then are you (if no better may be) to renew our Proteſtation vnto them, which wee ſent you in our former Letter, aſſuring them, that our firſt labour ſhall be to publiſh to the world their defection from the Faith, and trew Church of Chriſt: Wee meane the defection of them, whom they maintaine and harbour in their boſomes: though wee purpoſely omitted this point in our Letter vnto them for being too harſh, except all other remedies were deſperate. But we both wiſh and hope for better.*

Theobaldes. 6. October. 1611.

BVt before our Ambaſſadour had opportunitie to deliuer our Letter to the States, there were not onely certaine people more cunning then zealous, who cauſed a rumour to bee ſpread amongſt the States, that we were become exceeding cold in the buſineſſe, nay that wee had almoſt quite giuen it ouer; but alſo in the meane time, the ſaid *Vorſtius* was ſetled at *Leyden*, lodged in the qualitie of a publike Reader, and his
wife,

wife, & his familie there arriued, as he himſelfe witneſſeth in his Booke called *Chriſtiana, & modeſta reſpōſio.* For his own words in his preface are theſe,
*Quum igitur Diuinâ vocatione ſic ferente in eâ vrbe ac Prouinciâ ſedem fixerim,
cunq; domo totâ nunc habitem, quæ ſupremam in terrâ iuriſdiĉtionem veſtram agnoſ-*
‟ *cit, &c.* That is to ſay, Since therefore (God ſo diſpoſing of me,) I haue ſet-
‟ led my ſelfe, and with my whole family do now inhabite in that City and
‟ prouince, which acknowledgeth your ſupreme authority on earth, &c.
Our Ambaſſador therefore hauing on the one ſide conſideration of that
falſe report which was ſpred abroad of our coldnes in the buſines, and on
the other ſide obſeruing how *Vorſtius* was eſtabliſhed at *Leyden* after our
firſt Admonition and requeſt made vnto the *States*, but before their Aſſembly on the fift of Nouember, hee then reſolued firſt to preſent vnto
them our Letter, making likewiſe himſelfe a remonſtrance to the ſame purpoſe, which We haue here ſet downe, together with an extraĉt of certaine
paſſages, collećted out of the ſaid Bookes of *Vorſtius*, which We ſent vnto
our Ambaſſadour, and was by him then ſhewed vnto the *States*, that they
might diſcerne the Lyon by his pawe.

M*Y Lords : If euer the King of Great Britaine my Maſter hath merited any
thing of this State, (and how much he hath merited in reſpeĉt of his great
fauours, and Royall aſſiſtances, your Lordſhips acknowledging them with
all gratitude can beſt witneſſe, and beſt iudge) he hath ſurely merited at this preſent
hauing by his Letters full of zeale and pietie, which he hath written vnto you, ende-
uoured to procure the eſtabliſhment of that Religion onely within your Prouinces,
which the Reformed Churches of Great Britaine, France and Germanie, by a mutuall conſent, haue generally embraced. For what is it to his Maieſtie, whether D.
Vorſtius be admitted Profeſſor in the Vniuerſitie of Leyden, or not ? or whether the
doĉtrine of Arminius bee preached in your Churches ? ſauing that as a Chriſtian
Prince, he deſires the aduancement of the Goſpel, and as your beſt friend and allye, the
ſtrengthening of your Commonwealth, whoſe firſt foundations were cymented with
the blood of his ſubieĉts, and which in his iudgement can no way ſubſiſt, if wittingly
and willingly you ſuffer the Reformed Religion to be either by the praĉtiſes of your
Doĉtors ſophiſticated, or by their malice depraued.
   If therefore Religion be as it were the Palladium of your Common wealth, and
that to preſerue the one in her glory and perfeĉtion, bee to maintaine the other in her
puritie, let your ſelues then be iudge, in how great a danger the State muſt needs bee
at this preſent, ſo long as you permit the Schiſmes of Arminius to haue ſuch vogue
as now they haue in the principall Townes of Holland, and if you ſuffer Vorſtius to
be receiued Diuinitie Profeſſour in the Vniuerſitie of Leyden (the Seminarie of
your Church) who in ſcorne of the Holy word of G O D, hath after his owne fancie,
deuiſed a new Seĉt, patched together of ſeuerall pieces of all ſorts of ancient and moderne Hereſies. The foole ſaid in his heart, There is no God : but hee that
with open mouth, of ſet purpoſe, and of prepenſed malice, hath let his penne runne at
randome, to diſgorge ſo many blaſphemies againſt the Sacred Maieſtie of G O D,*
this

this fellow ſhall weare the garland of all that euer yet were heard of, ſince by the meanes of the Goſpel, the light of Chriſtian Religion hath ſhined vnto the world. ¶ *If any man doubt of it, for a proofe, ſee here what his Maieſtie with his owne hand hath collected out of his writings.*

OVT OF HIS ANNOTATIONS.

Pag 210.

Æterùm, nihil vetat Deo etiam corpus aſcribere, ſi vocabulum corporis in ſignificatione latiore ſumamus.

But there is nothing forbids vs to ſay, that God hath a Body, ſo as we take a body in the largeſt ſignification.

Pag. 211.

Non ſatis igitur circumſpectè loquuntur, qui Deum vt eſſentiâ, ſic etiam volun-tate prorſus immutabilem eſſe affirmant.

They therefore doe not ſpeake circumſpectly enough, who ſay, that God is altogether as vnchangeable in his will, as he is in his eſſence.

Pag 232.

Nuſquam ſcriptum legimus Dei ſubſtantiam ſimpliciter immenſam eſſe, immò non pauca ſunt, quæ contrarium ſenſum habere videntur.

We finde it no where written, That the ſubſtance of God is ſimply im-menſe: nay, there are many places, which ſeeme to cary a contrary mea-ning.

Pag. 237.

Magnitudo nulla actu infinita eſt: ergo nec Deus.

No Magnitude is actually infinite, and therefore God is not actually infinite.

Pag. 308.

Et ſanè ſi omnia, & ſingula rerum euenta, præciſè & ab æterno definita fuiſſent, nihil opus eſſet continua rerum inſpectione, & procuratione, quæ tamen Deo paſsim tribuitur.

And ſurely, if all and euery euent of things were preciſely ſet downe, and from eternitie, there needed not then that continuall inſpection and pro-curation, which neuertheleſſe is euery where attributed vnto God.

Pag. 441.

Pleniùs tamen reſpondere videntur, qui certam quidem in genere vniuerſalem Dei ſcientiam eſſe docent; Sed ita tamen, vt plures certitudinis cauſas in viſione præſentium, ac præteritorum, quàm in viſione futurorum contingentium agnoſcant.

They therefore, who teach that there is in God a certaine vniuerſall knowledge *in genere*, doe ſeeme to anſwere more fully; but ſo as they doe confeſſe likewiſe that there bee more cauſes of certaintie in the viſion of things preſent, then in the viſion of things future contingent.

Pag. 271.

Omnia etiam decreta quæ ſemel apud ſe præciſè definiuit, vno modo & actu, poſt factam definitionem accuratiſsimè nouit: ſed de alijs omnibus, & ſingulis, quæcunque ſunt & fiunt, ſeorſim, & per ſe conſideratis, hoc affirmari non poteſt; quippe quæ non modò

modò ſuccesſiuè in tempore, verumetiam contingenter, & ſæpe conditionaliter exiſtunt.

All things which GOD hath once decreed, and preciſely determined, *vno modo & aɛtu,* he doth after ſuch his determination exaɛtly know them: But this cannot be affirmed of all and euery other thing, which are, or come to paſſe, being conſidered ſeuerally and by themſelues, becauſe they haue their exiſtence, not onely ſucceſſiuely in time, but alſo contingently, and oftentimes conditionally.

OVT OF HIS APOLOGIE.

Pag 38.

Ater peculiarem quandam entitatem, ſeu quaſi limitatam, & reſtriɛtam eſſentiam habere putandus eſt.

It is to be vnderſtood that the Father hath a certaine peculiar being, or as it were a limitted and bounded eſſence.

Pag.43.

Vnde porrò non difficulter efficitur, etiam interna quædam accidentia in Deo, hoc eſt, in ipſâ (vt ſic dicere liceat) proæreticâ Dei mente, ac voluntate, reuerâ exiſtere.

From whence it is eaſily prooued, that there are really certaine internall accidents in God, that is to ſay, (if it be lawfull to vſe ſuch a word) in the very fore-electing minde and will of God.

In the 16. Chapter, he doeth dangerouſly diſſent from the receiued opinion of Diuines, concerning the Vbiquitie of Gods preſence.

In the 19. Chapter, pag. 99. he doth attribute vnto God, Magnitude and Quantitie.

Theſe are in part the opinions of that great Diuine, whom they haue choſen to domineere in the Chaire at Leyden: *In oppoſition whereunto, I meane not to ſay any thing elſe, then that which the* Romane Oratour *did once pronounce in the like caſe:* Mala eſt & impia conſuetudo contra Deum diſputandi, ſiuè ſeriò id fit, ſiuè ſimulatè: *It is an euill and a wicked cuſtome* (ſaith hee) *to diſpute againſt God, whether it be in earneſt, or in ieſt.*

Now my Lords, I addreſſe my ſelfe vnto your Lordſhips, and according vnto the charge which I haue receiued from the King my Maſter, I coniure you by the amitie that is betwixt his Kingdomes and your Prouinces, (the which on his part will continue alwayes inuiolable) to awaken your ſpirits, and to haue a carefull eye at this Aſſembly of Holland, *(which is already begunne)* ne quid Reſpublica detrimenti capiat, *That the Common wealth take no harme: which vndoubtedly, at one time or other, will be turned vpſide downe, if you ſuffer ſuch a dangerous contagion to harbour ſo neere you, and not remoue it out of your Prouinces aſſoone as poſſibly you may. The diſciples of* Socinus *(with whoſe doɛtrine he hath bene ſuckled in his childhood)*
doe

doe ſeeke him for their Maſter, and are ready to embrace him. Let him goe, hee is a Bird of their owne feather : Et dignum ſanè patellâ operculum; *A couer fit for ſuch a diſh.*

On the other ſide, the Students in Diuinitie at Leyden *to the number of 56. by a ductiful Remonſtrance preſented vnto the States of* Holland *the 16. of October the laſt yeere, did moſt humbly beſeech the ſaid States, not to vſe their authoritie in compelling them to receiue a Profeſſor, who both by the atteſtations of the Diuinitie Colledges at* Baſil *and* Heydelberg, *as alſo by manifeſt euidence out of his owne writings, is conuinced of an infinite number of Hereſies.*

Theſe reaſons therefore, namely, the proofes of ſo many enormous and horrible Hereſies maintained in his Bookes, the inſtance of his Maieſtie grounded vpon the welfare and honour of this Countrey, the requeſts either of all, or of the moſt part of your Prouinces, the petitions of all the Miniſters (excepting thoſe onely which are of Arminius *Sect) ſhould me thinkes preuaile ſo farre with my Lords the States of* Holland, *and (we hope) will ſo farre preuaile, as they will at the laſt apply themſelues to the performance of that, which both the ſinceritie of* Religion, *and the ſeruice of their Countrey requireth at their hands. Furthermore, I haue commandement from his Maieſtie to mooue you in his Name, to ſet downe ſome certaine Reglement in matters of* Religion *throughout your Prouinces, that this licentious freedome of diſputation, may by that meanes be reſtrained, which breeds nothing but Factions, and part-taking ; and that you would abſolutely take away the libertie of Prophecying, which* Vorſtius *doeth ſo much recommend vnto you in the dedicatorie Epiſtle of his* Anti-Bellarmine, *the Booke whereof his Patrons doe boaſt ſo much.*

To conclude, his Maieſtie doeth exhort you, ſeeing you haue heretofore taken Armes for the libertie of your conſciences, and haue ſo much endured in a violent and bloody warre, the ſpace of fourtie yeeres, for the profeſſion of the Goſpel, that now hauing gotten the vpper hand of your miſeries, you would not ſuffer the followers of Arminius, *to make your actions an example for them to proclaime throughout the world, that wicked doctrine of the* Apoſtaſie of the Saints.

To bee ſhort, the account which his Maieſtie doeth make of your amitie appeares ſufficiently by the Treaties which hee hath made with your Lordſhips, by the ſuccours which your Prouinces haue receiued from his crownes, by the deluge of blood, which his ſubiects haue ſpent in your warres. Religion is the onely ſowder of this Amitie: For his Maieſtie being, by the Grace of G O D, *Defender of the Faith, (by which Title hee doeth more value himſelfe, then by the Title of King of* Great Britaine) *doeth hold himſelfe obliged to defend all thoſe, who profeſſe the ſame Faith and* Religion *with him. But if once your zeale begin to grow colde therein, his Maieſtie will then ſtraightwayes imagine, that your friendſhip towards him and his ſubiects will likewiſe freeze by little and little. Thus much I had in charge to adde vnto that which his Maieſtie in his owne letters hath written vnto you. You may bee pleaſed to conſider of it, as the importance of the cauſe doeth require, and to reſolue thereupon, that which your wiſedomes ſhall thinke fitteſt for the honour and ſeruice of your Countrey.*

But our Ambaſſadour hauing, after a delay for the ſpace of diuers

Hh   weekes,

weekes, receiued this cold and ambiguous anſwere vnto our Letter and Propoſition, that is to ſay, That, *The Lords States Generall hauing ſeriouſly deliberated vpon the Propoſition which was made vnto them by our Ambaſſadour the fift of Nouember, as alſo vpon our Letters of the ſixt of October deliuered vnto them at the ſame time, did very humbly giue vs thankes for the continuance of our Royall affection toward the welfare of their Countreys, and the preſeruation of the trew reformed Chriſtian Religion therein; And that the ſaid States Generall, as alſo the States of* Holland *and* Weſtfrizeland *in their ſeuerall aſſemblies reſpectiuely, hauing entred into conſultation (with all due reuerence and regard vnto vs) concerning thoſe Articles wherewith* Doctor Conradus Vorſtius *was charged, the Curators of the Vniuerſitie of* Leyden *did thereupon take occaſion to make an order prouiſionall, that the ſaid* Vorſtius *ſhould not bee admitted to the exerciſe of his place, which was accordingly performed; So as vpon the matter, hee was then in the Citie of* Leyden, *but as an inhabitant or Citizen. And that in caſe the ſaid* Vorſtius *ſhould not bee able to cleare himſelfe from thoſe accuſations which were layd to his charge, before, or in the next Aſſembly of the States of* Holland *and* Weſtfrizeland *(which was to bee holden in* February *following) the Lords States Generall did then aſſure themſelues, that the States of* Holland *and* Weſtfrizeland *would decide the matter with good contentment. And therefore foraſmuch as at that time there could be no more done in the cauſe, without great inconuenience and diſtaſte to the principall Townes of the ſaid Prouinces, our Ambaſſadour was required to recommend thus much in the beſt manner he could vnto vs, and with the moſt aduantage to the ſeruice of their Countrey.*

Vpon the coldneſſe therefore of this Anſwere, (which hee feared would giue vs no ſatisfaction) hee thought it was now high time to conſider what the laſt remedy might bee, whereof vſe was to bee made for the aduancement of this buſineſſe: and perceiuing that hee had already performed all the reſt of our commandements, excepting onely to Proteſt in caſe of refuſall, and eſteeming ſuch a cold anſwere, accompanied with ſo many delayes, to be no leſſe in effect then an abſolute refuſall, hee thereupon reſolued to make this Proteſtation in their publique aſſemblie, which hereafter followeth.

M Y *Lords; The Hiſtoriographers, who haue diligently looked into the Antiquities of* France, *doe obſerue, that the Aduocates there in times paſt, were accuſtomed to begin their pleadings with ſome Latine Sentence taken out of the holy Scriptures:* I *ſhall at this time follow their example, and my Sentence ſhall be this:* Si peccauerit in te frater tuus, argue eum inter te & ipſum ſolum; ſi audiuerit te, lucratus es fratrem tuum; ſi non audiuerit te, adhibe vnum atque alterum, vt in ore duorum vel trium ſtet omne verbum: ſi non audiuerit eos, dic Eccleſiæ. *If thy brother treſpaſſe againſt thee, goe and tell him his fault betweene him and thee alone; if he heare thee, thou haſt wonne thy brother; but if bee heare thee not, take yet with thee one or two, that by the mouth of two or three*

three witneſſes euery word may bee confirmed: and if hee refuſe to heare them, tell it
vnto the Church.

There is not any one of you (as I ſuppoſe) in this Aſſemblie, that will not acknow-
ledge the brotherly loue wherewith the King my Maſter hath alwayes affected the
good of your Prouinces, and the fatherly care which hee hath euer had to procure the
eſtabliſhment of your State. In which reſpect, his Maieſtie hauing vnderſtood, that
my Lords the States of Holland *were determined to call vnto the place of Diuinitie*
Profeſſour in the Vniuerſitie of Leyden, *one Doctor Conradus Vorſtius, a per-*
ſon attainted by many witneſſes, iuris & facti, *of a number of Hereſies (the ſhame*
whereof would light vpon the Church of God, and conſequently vpon his Maieſties
perſon and Crownes) is therewith exceedingly offended: And for the more timely pre-
uention of an infinitie of euils, which neceſſarily would thereupon enſue, did giue mee
in charge by expreſſe Letters to exhort you (which I did the 21. of September laſt) to
waſh your hands from that man, and not to ſuffer him to come within your Countrey.
To this exhortation, your anſwere was, that in the carriage of this buſineſſe, all due
obſeruance and regard ſhould be had vnto his Maieſtie. Neuertheleſſe ſo it is, that
his Maieſtie hath receiued ſo little reſpect heerein, as that in ſtead of debarring
Vorſtius *from comming into the Countrey (which euen by the lawes of friendſhip*
his Maieſtie might haue required) the proceedings haue beene cleane contrary; for he
is ſuffered to come vnto Leyden, *hath beene receiued there with all honour, hath*
there taken vp his habitation, where he is treated and lodged in the qualitie of a
publique Profeſſour. His Maieſtie then perceiuing, that his firſt motion had ſo
little preuailed, thought good to write himſelfe a Letter vnto you, to the ſame pur-
poſe, full of zeale and affection, perſwading you by many reaſons there ſet downe
at length, not to ſtaine your owne honour, and the honour of the reformed Chur-
ches, by calling vnto you that wretched and wicked Atheiſt. Theſe Letters
were preſented in this Aſſembly the fifth of Nouember, *a great number of the De-*
puties of the Townes of Holland *being then preſent; At which time (as I was*
commanded by his Maieſtie) I vſed ſome ſpeach my ſelfe to the ſame effect. Some
ſixe weekes after, I receiued an Anſwere to my Propoſition, but an Anſwere confu-
ſed, ambiguous and wholly impertinent, by which I haue reaſon to conceiue, that
there is no meaning at all to ſend Vorſtius *away, who is at this preſent in* Leyden,
receiued and acknowledged, reſpected and treated as publique Profeſſour, whether
it be to grace that Vniuerſitie in ſtead of the deceaſed Ioſeph Scaliger, *I cannot tell,*
or whether it bee to giue him meanes to doe more miſchiefe in ſecret, which perhaps
for ſhame hee durſt not in publique: For theſe reaſons, according vnto that charge,
which I haue receiued from the King my Maſter, I doe in his name, and on his be-
halfe Proteſt in this Aſſembly, againſt the wrong, iniurie, and ſcandall done vnto
the reformed Religion by the receiuing and reteining of Conradus Vorſtius *in the*
Vniuerſitie of Leyden, *and againſt the violence offered vnto that Alliance which is*
betwixt his Maieſtie and your Prouinces; the which beeing founded vpon the pre-
ſeruation and maintenance of the reformed Religion, you haue not letted (ſo much
as in you lies) abſolutely to violate in the proceeding of this cauſe. Of which enor-
mous indignities committed againſt the Church of GOD *and againſt his Maieſties*
perſon, in preferring the preſence of Vorſtius, *before his Amitie and Alliance, the*

King

King my Maſter holds himſelfe bound to bee ſenſible, and if reparation thereof bee not made, and that ſpeedily, (which cannot be by any other meanes then by ſending Vor-ſtius away) his Maieſtie will make it appeare vnto the world by ſome ſuch Decla-ration, as he will cauſe to be printed and publiſhed how much he deteſts the Atheiſmes and Hæreſies of Vorſtius, *and all thoſe that maintaine, fauour and cheriſh them. This is my charge, which if I had failed to performe, I had failed in my duetie, both towards the Seruice of* GOD, *which is now in queſtion, as alſo toward the honour of the King my Maſter, who will alwayes bee ready to maintaine the puritie of the reformed Religion, though it were with the profuſion of his owne blood, the blood of his children, and ſubiects.*

This Proteſtation being made, the States after ſome deliberation, framed vs an anſwere in theſe termes : *That howſoeuer His Maieſtie of* GREAT BRITAINE *had not yet receiued that contentment which Hee might expect in this buſineſſe of* Vorſtius, *neuertheleſſe, they did not doubt, but that at the Aſſembly of the States of* Holland *in February next, His Maieſtie ſhould receiue entire ſatiſ-faction.* Which anſwere gaue ſome life to our hope, that at the ſaid aſſem-bly of the States, to bee holden the fifteenth day of the next moneth of Februarie, GOD will vouchſafe ſo to open the eyes of thoſe of *Holland*, as that they may be able to diſcerne, what a Cockatrice egge they hatch with-in their boſome, and that (ſeeing the ſmooth ſpeaches of *Vorſtius* doe but verifie the old Prouerbe, *Latet anguis in herbâ*, There lurkes a ſnake in the graſſe,) they will at that aſſembly reſolue to purge their Territories from the poiſon of his Hereſie. We mention *Holland*, becauſe the other Pro-uinces, namely *Frizeland* and *Zeland*, and ſome part of *Holland* likewiſe, are already ſo diſtaſted with his Hereſies, as of themſelues they haue deſired *Holland* to baniſh him out of the Countrey.

And certainely wee are no leſſe ſorie, then amazed, that the **Curators** of *Leyden*, (as appeareth by a long letter which they haue written to the States Ambaſſador reſident with vs) can haue their vnderſtanding ſo ſtupified, as to haue made choice of the perſon of *Vorſtius* for a man well qualified to appeaſe the Schiſmes and troubles of their Church and Vniuerſitie, and as an apt inſtrument of peace. For to ſhew their blindneſſe in this, they need no other anſwere, then, *Exitus acta probat*, The iſſue tries the action. Seeing to our great griefe it cannot bee denied, but that there hath bene more diſtraction of ſpirits, and a greater diuiſion in their State ſince the comming of *Vorſtius*, then was for many yeeres before witneſſe ſo many Bookes and Accuſations written againſt him, and his anſweres thereunto: witneſſe alſo the proteſtation of a great number of Profeſſors of *Leyden* againſt him, and many of the principall members, as well Prouinces as Townes of the Vnited body of that State, who haue accuſed him as before we haue ſaid. So as if for that purpoſe onely, they brought him vnto their Vniuerſitie, they muſt needes acknowledge it hath had a very vnhappie ſucceſſe.

Hauing

Auing now finiſhed the difcourfe of our whole procee-ding in this caufe, from the beginning vntill this prefent, It remaineth that we fet downe the reafons which perfwa-ded vs to ingage our felues in *aliená republicâ* in a bufineffe of this nature. But wee haue done that already, although but fummarily, and by the way : For in that place where wee make men-tion of the bookes of *Vorſtius* which were brought into our Kingdome, wee yeeld three Reafons , which mooued vs to take this caufe to heart : Firſt, the zeale of Gods glory, to whom we are fo much bound: Secondly, charity towards our next neighbours and Allies: and Thirdly , the iuſt reafon we had to feare the like infection within our owne Dominions.

As concerning the Glory of God ; If the fubiect of *Vorſtius* his Herefies had not bene grounded vpon Queſtions of a higher qualitie then touching the number and nature of the Sacraments , the points of Iuſtification, of Merits, of Purgatorie, of the vifible head of the Church, or any fuch mat-ters,as are in controuerfie at this day betwixt the Papiſts and vs ; Nay more, If hee had medled onely with the nature and workes of G O D *ad extra*, (as the Schoolemen fpeake,) If (wee fay) hee had foared no higher pitch (al-though wee ſhould haue bene very fory to fee fuch Herefies begin to take roote amongſt our Allies and ancient confederates ;) Neuertheleffe, wee doe freely profeffe, that in that cafe wee ſhould neuer haue troubled our felues with the bufineffe in fuch faſhion, and with that feruencie as hither-to we haue done. But this *Vorſtius* mounting aloft like an *Anti-S.Iohn* with the wings of the Eagle, vp to the Heauens, and to the Throne of G O D,di-fputing of his Sacred and ineffable Effence , *Quæ tremenda & admiranda eſt, ſed non ſcrutanda* , Which is to be trembled at, and admired, but not to be fearched into ; confounding *infinitie*, (one of the proper attributes of GoD,) and *immenſitie* , (fometime applied to creatures,) the *eſſence* and *ſubſtance*, with the *hypoſtaſis*, difputing of a firſt and fecond *creation, immediate* and *me-diate*, making G O D to be *quale* and *quantum*, changing *eternitie*, into *euiter-nitie*, teaching *eternitie* to confiſt of a number of aages , and in the end as a fworne enemie not onely to Diuinitie, but euen to all Philofophie, both humane and naturall,denying God to be *Actus purus*,and void of qualities, but hauing in fome fort(with horror be it fpoken) *aliquid diuerſitatis aut mul-tiplicitatis in ſe ipſo,etiam principium cuiuſdam mutabilitatis*; That is to fay, Some kind of diuerfitie or multiplicitie in himfelfe,yea euen a beginning of a cer-taine mutabilitie : Let the world then iudge whether we had not occafion herevpon, to be mooued, not onely as one that maketh profeffion of the re-formed Religion,but as a Chriſtian at large; yea, euen as a *Theiſt*, or a man that acknowledgeth a G O D, or as a *Platonique* Philofopher at the leaſt.

Secondly,

Secondly, for the Charitie which we owe to our neighbours and Allies; the Charitie of euery Chriſtian ought to extend to all men, but *eſpecially towards them that be of the Houſhold of faith.* The States then being not onely our confederates, but the principall bond of our coniunction being our vniformitie in the trew Religion, we had reaſon to admoniſh them, not to permit ſuch dangerous Hereſies to ſpring, and take roote amongſt them, which being once ſuffered, could produce no other effects; then the danger of their ſoules, a rent betwixt them and all other Chriſtian Churches, and at the laſt a rupture and diuiſion in their Temporall State, which (next vnder God) can be maintained by nothing but Vnitie. To which reſolution we were the rather induced by the example of diuers other Prouinces vnder the dominion of the ſaid States, who did accuſe *Vorſtius*, and perſwaded *Holland* to ſend him away out of their countrey, as before we haue declared.

It is trew, that if *Vorſtius* had beene a natiue of *Holland*, as *Iohn of Leyden* was, it had beene ſufficient for vs to haue giuen them a generall warning of the danger, and then to haue referred it vnto themſelues, to take ſuch courſe therein, as to them ſhould ſeeme conuenient: But this *Vorſtius* being a ſtranger, and ſent for out of another Countrey to inſtruct their youth, hee can challenge no ſuch priuiledge by reaſon of his birth, but that the States may lawfully diſcharge him, whenſoeuer they pleaſe. And for his profeſſion, it is (without doubt) leſſe dangerous, to ſuffer a thouſand Lay Heretiques to liue in a Common wealth (for that is but matter of policie, ſo long as they offend not in their ſpeach, and ſeduce not others,) then to haue ſo much as one Doctour that may poiſon the youth: For, *Quo ſemel eſt imbuta recens ſeruabit odorem Teſta diu*; The veſſell will taſte a long time after of that liquor wherewith it is firſt ſeaſoned; And what ſhall become of the litle brookes, if their Fountaine be corrupted?

And from hence is deriued our third reaſon which perſwaded vs to meddle in this buſineſſe. For if generally the youth of thoſe Countreys our neereſt neighbours ſhould happen to be infected, in what danger then were wee? eſpecially ſeeing ſo many of the yonger ſort of our Subiects doe repaire for learning ſake to the Vniuerſitie of *Leyden*: an Vniuerſitie of long time famous, but ſo much the more renowned, for that, within our remembrance, it hath beene adorned with thoſe two excellent perſonages *Scaliger* and *Iunius.* It is furthermore to bee noted, that the ſpirituall infection of *Hereſie*, is ſo much more dangerous, then the bodily infection of the plague, by how much the ſoule is more noble then the body, which cauſed the *Apoſtle* S. *Iohn*, when, entring into a Bath, he met there by chance *Cerinthus* the Heretique, to turne backe againe vpon the ſuddain, for feare of infection. Now if that great *Apoſtle* the beloued of Chriſt did ſo much feare the infection of *Hereſie*, as himſelfe hath giuen vs a warning in one of his Epiſtles, *Ne dicas illi, Aue*; Bid him not God ſpeed: haue not we then much more cauſe to feare the corruption of the youth of our owne Kingdomes?   Bu

But we very well know, that ſome will ſay *Vorſtius* is not rightly vnder-ſtood; that ſome conſequences are violently wreſted out of his words, contrary to the intention of the Author; that thoſe things which he pro-pounds ſcholaſtically by way of queſtion, ſhould not bee taken for his owne reſolution; and admit pearaduenture hee may haue ſpoken in ſome phraſes *minùs cautè*, not warily enough, yet that is but *Logomachie*, con-tention about words, and ought not to bee imputed vnto him for *Hereſie*; and beſies that, in his laſt works he hath ſufficiently purged himſelfe from all calumnies, and renounced all manner of *Hereſies*.

To the firſt Obiection wee anſwere, that we neuer accuſed him by con-ſequences, but that we find his owne words and ſentences full of *Hereſies*.

To the ſecond, concerning his queſtions or diſquiſitions (as he termeth them) wee ſay, that in doubtfull matters, and where a man may reſolue either one way or other, without danger of making ſhipwracke of Faith, it is not onely tolerable, but very commendable to propound queſtions or arguments, at leaſtwiſe in Schooles : But to deuiſe new queſtions vpon the principall Articles of our Faith, to enter not onely into the ſecret Ca-binet of G o d, but to intrude our ſelues into his Eſſence, to prie into his moſt inward parts, and like the Phyſicians of *Pantagruel*, to viſite with torch-light all the moſt hidden places in the Eſſence of G o d, wee may boldy pronounce, *Omnia hæc ad deſtructionem, planè nihil ad ædificationem*; All theſe things tend to deſtruction, and nothing ſurely to edification. S. *Auguſtine* ſpeaketh againſt the curioſitie of thoſe people, who would needs know what G o d did before hee made the Fabrique of the world. The Iewes during their integritie, did beare another maner of reuerenee to the Diuinitie, who thought themſelues dead, if once they ſhould ſee G o d. And their great Law-giuer *Moyſes* could obtaine no more (not-withſtanding his humble and inſtant requeſt) then to ſee the hinder parts of G o d. So as to call into queſtion, or to make doubts of theſe high points of the Eſſence of G o d, of the *Trinitie*, of the *hypoſtaticall* Vnion in the perſon of C h r i s t, or to ſpeake of them in other termes then the Church of God hath vniformely eſtabliſhed, and in all aages ſucceſſiuely approued, as it is conteined in all the Orthodox Creeds, and declared in the foure firſt Councels, is by no meanes lawfull: And to make any queſtion or diſquiſition vpon theſe high myſteries, is as much in effect, as to make a contrary concluſion; and ſuch a diſquiſition deſerues the puniſhment of the Inquiſion. *Non eſt bonum ludere cum Sanctis, multò minùs ergo cum Deo*; It is not good to ieſt with Saints, much leſſe therefore with G o d: and one of the firſt verſes which our little children are taught, is this : *Mitte arcana Dei, cælùmque inquirere quid ſit*; Let the ſecrets of God alone, and be not too curious to enquire into heauen. For what difference is there I pray you, to ſay, It may be that ſuch a Lady is a whore; or that there be probable arguments to perſwade vs that ſhe is ſuch a one; or to ſay abſo-lutely that ſhee is a wHore? And (wee imagine) *Vorſtius* would not hold

him

him for his friend, that ſhould ſay it were a matter very diſputable whether *Vorſtius* were a damnable Heretique, and ſhould goe quicke to Hell, yea or no: not that he did beleeue him to bee ſuch a one, but that there were many arguments probable enough to perſwade a man to take him for no leſſe. The nature of man, through the tranſgreſſion of our firſt parents hath loſt free-will, and reteineth not now any ſhadow thereof, ſauing an inclination to euill, thoſe onely excepted whom God of his meere grace hath ſanctified and purged from this originall Leproſie; Inſomuch as it is a very perillous thing to ſet abroach theſe new and dangerous queſtions, although they bee accompanied with good anſweres: For the greateſt part of the world, following the footſteps of our firſt Parents, are naturally enclined to chooſe the euill, and to leaue that which is good, and therefore the Diuine Poet *Du Bartas*, ſpeaking of the deſtruction of *Sodome*, and loath to name the ſinne for which it was deſtroyed, ſaith thus;

> *De peur qu' en offençant des ſain-cts l'oreille tendre,*
> *Ie ne les ſemble plus enſeigner, que reprendre.*

For feare that in offending of good peoples tender eare,
I rather ſeeme to teach them, then to wiſh them to forbeare.

And there is a report (I know not how trew it is) that *Bellarmines* bookes of Controuerſies, are not very well receiued in *Italy*, becauſe his obiectionsare too ſtrong, and his anſweres too weake. In which qualitie, as alſo in one other, whereof we will ſpeake anon, *Vorſtius* hath a certaine tincture of *Bellarmine*.

To the third obiection, where it is alleadged, that perhaps hee hath not bene warie ynough in ſome of his phraſes of ſpeach, and that it is but contention for wordes. To that we anſwere, as before we haue ſaid, That it is in no ſort lawfull to ſpeake of thoſe great Myſteries of the *Eſſence* of God, of the *Trinitie*, of the *Hypoſtaticall* vnion of natures in the Perſon of *Chriſt*, or any ſuch high points, vnleſſe wee vſe the ſame phraſes and maner of ſpeech, which the Church of G o d hath alwayes vſed in ſpeaking of the ſaid Myſteries. They that will talke of *Chanaan*, muſt vſe the language of *Chanaan*. And the ſonnes of *Aaron* were ſeuerely puniſhed, for preſuming to bring ſtrange fire vnto the Altar. By the difference of leſſe then one letter, betweene *Siboleth* and *Shiboleth*, the ten Tribes of Iſrael could diſcerne their friends from their foes, and that by the pronuntiation onely: And the like difference of one little letter betwixt *homoouſion*, and *homoiouſion*, ſerued to make a diſtinction betwixt the enemies of *Chriſt* in the Eaſt Church, and the Church *Orthodoxall*.

As concerning the fourth and laſt excuſe; namely, that *Vorſtius* hath in his laſt Bookes ſufficiently purged himſelfe from theſe calumnies, and renounced all Hereſies: Our anſwere is, That we would very heartily requeſt the States in their next Aſſembly, ſeriouſly and aduiſedly to conſider and obſerue the ſtyle which he vſeth in his writings and excuſes, and then

                                       ſhall

ſhall they be able to iudge what kind of ſpirit it is that guideth his penne.

For, to beginne with the Preface of his Booke, intituled his *Chriſtian and modeſt Anſwere,* he makes there ſo light reckoning of his queſtions before-mentioned, as if it were but about the tale of *Tobies* dogge. For in the ſe-cond page of his ſaid Preface, theſe be his wordes : *Omnis homo eſt mendax, immò vanitate ipſâ vanior, ſolus verò Deus eſt verax, &c. Quod cùm in omnibus magni momenti negotijs, tum maximè in ſanctiſſimâ fidei cauſâ humiliter nobis ſem-per agnoſcendum eſt : ne videlicet quidquam quod primâ fronte nobis nouum, immò falſum, & abſurdum videatur, facilè damnemus, nec contra quicquid vulgò recep-tum eſt, (in rebus præſertim abſtruſis ac perplexis, nec tamen ad ſalutem ſcitu neceſſa-rijs) & quidem cum opinione præciſæ neceſſitatis, ſtatim approbemus. In his talibus, ſi quis Regem, aut Principem, alioqui pientiſſimum, immò Reges, & Principes eiuſ-modi complures, (addo & Epiſcopos, ſeu Doctores Eccleſiæ, non diſsimiles) aliquan-tulum errare dixerit, nihil opinor aduerſus Regiam Maieſtatem, nihil aduerſus Prin-cipum, aut Epiſcoporum dignitatem reuerâ peccauerit, modò ſemper rationes ſuorum dictorum modeſtè reddere paratus ſit.* That is to ſay, Euery man is a lyer, yea, more vaine then vanity it ſelfe, God onely is trew, &c. Which ſeeing wee ought euer humbly to acknowledge in all great and weighty cauſes, moſt of all ought we to confeſſe it in the moſt holy cauſe of our Faith : inſomuch as we ſhould not therefore eaſily condemne euery thing which at the firſt ſeemes ſtrange, yea falſe and abſurd vnto our eares, nor on the contrary ſide, ought wee foorth-with to approoue, and that with an opinion of preciſe neceſſitie, whatſoeuer is commonly receyued, eſpecially in mat-ters abſtruſe and intricate, whereof the knowledge is not neceſſarie to ſaluation. In ſuch poynts as theſe, if any man ſhall ſay, that ſuch a King, or Prince, howſoeuer otherwiſe moſt godly and religious, yea that ma-ny ſuch Kings, and Princes (nay, I will not except Biſhops, or the like Doctors of the Church) haue in ſome ſort erred; I am of opinion, hee ſhall not giue any iuſt cauſe of offence, either to the Maieſtie of Kings, or to the dignitie of Princes and Biſhops, ſo as hee bee alwaies ready modeſtly to yeeld a reaſon for that which hee ſhall affirme. In which words, hee maintaineth two Principles : Firſt, that euery man is a ly-ar, aſwell in matter of Faith, as in any thing elſe; and next, that wee muſt not euer eſteeme the vulgar opinion, and that which is generally re-ceiued in matter of Faith to be the treweſt, nor alwayes condemne euery opinion for abſurd, which at the firſt ſeemes vnto vs vncouth, and new. Now we pray you obſerue, that this man is not accuſed of ſmall ſcapes, and therefore beeing not charged with leſſer *peccadillos,* then thoſe which be-fore wee haue mentioned, it neceſſarily followes, that in his excuſe hee muſt vnderſtand the ſame points whereof he is accuſed. And wee hope by the mercy of GOD, that no Chriſtian (wee ſpeake in this particular, as well for the Papiſts, as for our ſelues) ſhall euer be found to erre in any of thoſe maine points : at the leaſt wee will anſwere, (by the grace of God,) for one of thoſe Kings whom he names in general. And as for his new o-
pinions,

pinions, which he would ſo gladly vent abroad, the ancient Faith needes not be changed like an old garment, either in ſubſtance, or faſhion.

Furthermore, in the third page of his Preface, hee vſeth theſe words, *Sed neque plures vno aliquo ſemper hîc ditiores ſunt. Nemo igitur vnus ſibi arro-*
" *get omnia. Nec numero plures vni alicui, ſingulare quidquam inuideant.* Nei-
" ther are many men alwayes richer [*in knowledge.*] then ſome one man. Let
" not therefore any one man arrogate all things to himſelfe. Nor let the
" greater multitude enuie a particular man, for hauing ſome ſingularitie more then his fellowes. The trew principle and foundation of the error of the *Anabaptiſts*, taking away by this meanes, all maner of gouernment from the Church: For hauing firſt ouerthrowen the Monarchicall power of the Pope, he ſweepes away next all manner of power both Ariſtocraticall and Democraticall from the Church, cleane contrary to the Apoſtles inſtitution, which ordeineth, that *the ſpirits of the Prophets ſhould bee ſubiect to the Prophets.* For if one particular man may take vpon him ſuch a ſingularitie as this, how ſhall he bee ſubiect to Generall, Nationall, and Synodicall Councels? For ſtraight will he ſay vnto them; Sirs, yee haue no authoritie to iudge mee, for I haue a ſingular gift aboue you all. And in the fift Page, theſe are his words · *Planiſsimè enim perſuaſus ſum, Sereniſ-ſimo Regi nunquam in animo fuiſſe, nunquam in animo fore, alienæ conſcientiæ (quod ne Apoſtoli quidem ſibi vnquam arrogârunt) ſiue directè, ſiue indirectè, ſiue per ſe-ipſum, ſiue per alios vllatenùs dominari, vel fidem noſtram vlli humanæ authori-*
" *tati alligare velle.* For I am abſolutely perſwaded, that it was neuer his Ma-
" ieſties meaning, nor euer will bee, either directly, or indirectly, by him-
" ſelfe, or by others, in any ſort to ouer-rúle another mans conſcience,
" (which euen the Apoſtles neuer challenged to themſelues) nor did, or
" will his Maieſtie euer ſeeke to tie our Faith to any humane authoritie. Whereby hee is plainely diſcouered, to bee reſolued not to bee ſubiect in any ſort to the iudgement of the Church, in thoſe matters whereof hee is accuſed. For hee knowes too well, that the ancient Church hath eſtabliſhed vpon neceſſary conſequences drawen from the holy Scripture, both a forme of beliefe, and a forme of ſpeach concerning the holy Myſteries aforeſaid: And this is the reaſon why hee will not in theſe points ſubmit himſelfe to the iudgement of any mortall man; But vpon this occaſion in the ſeuenth page of his Preface, maintaines his Chriſtian libertie in this maner: *Qui quidem humanas deciſiones à Diuinis myſterijs ſcrupuloſè ſe-gregem; & præſertim in audaces Scholarum hypotheſes, pro Chriſtiana libertate*
" *interdum diligentiùs inquiram;* I, who curiouſly make a ſeparation betwixt
" the iudgements of men and the Diuine myſteries, and eſpecially accor-
" ding to Chriſtian libertie, doe ſometimes more narrowly looke into the
" bold ſupoſitions of the Schoolemen. As if the Schoole Diuines had bene too ventrous, to explaine and to defend the Articles aforeſaid, already ſo eſtabliſhed by the Church: But we may trewly wiſh in that point, as *Bel-larmine* did touching *Caluin: Vtinam ſemper ſic erraſſent Scholaſtici;* Would
God

God the Scholemen had alwayes so erred: For in the maine grounds of Christian Religion; they are worthy of all commendation. Reade *Aquinas* against the *Gentiles.* But in matters of controuersie, where they were to flatter the Pope in his resolutions, and to auow the new ordinances and traditions of their Church; there they yeelded (alas) vnto the iniquitie of the time, and the mysterie of iniquitie, which was euen then in working, got likewise the vpper hand ouer them. And as for this Christian libertie, which he doeth vrge so much, certainely he doeth it with no other intention, but onely vnder this faire pretext, to haue the better meanes, and with more safetie to abuse the world: For Christian libertie is neuer meant in the holy Scripture, but onely in matters indifferent, or when it is taken for our deliuerance from the thraldome of the Law, or from the burden of humane traditions, and in that sense S. *Paul* speaketh in his Epistle to the *Colossians*, *Quare oneramini ritibus?* Why are ye burdened with traditions? But to abuse Christian libertie, in presuming to propound a new doctrine into the world, in point of the highest and holiest mysteries of G O D, is most audacious rashnesse, and an impudent arrogancie: Concerning which S. *Paul* saith, *Though an Angel from heauen, preach vnto you otherwise then that which we haue preached vnto you, let him bee accursed.* And *Saint Iohn* likewise commandeth vs, that wee should not so much as say, *God speed* to that man, which shall bring vs any other doctrine, as wee haue obserued before.

Now to shew that he is a forger of new opinions; by which he would faine make himselfe singular, see but his wordes immediately preceding those which a little before wee mentioned, where hee boasteth, and is wonderfully in loue with a new name which he hath taken vpon himselfe, that is to say, *Purus putus Euangelicus*, A mainly pure Gospeller; although indeed the word *pure* was neuer yet taken in a good part. For amongst the ancient *Heretiques*, there was a Sect that called themselues *Cathari*, and there was also another Sect among the *Anabaptists*, that were called *Purines*, from whence the *Precisians* of our Kingdomes, who out of selfe-will and fancie refuse to conforme themselues to the Orders of our Church, haue borrowed their name. And for the word *Gospeller*, although it hath beene assumed in diuers places by some of our Religion, yet hath it this ill fortune, that it is more vsually receiued in those parts of *Hungary* and *Bohme*, where there are such infinite diuersities of Sects (agreeing in nothing but in their Vnion against the *Pope*) then in any other place. The holy Scripture it selfe in the *Actes of the Apostles*, mentioneth the name of *Christians*: and the ancient *Primitiue* Church did attribute vnto the faithfull, the names of *Catholique* and *Orthodox*. So as for such a fellow as *Vorstius*, to affect new Titles for his Religion, it hath surely no good relish: his intention without doubt being no other, then by this meanes to make a distinction, and in time a rupture betwixt himselfe, and the *Orthodox* professors of our Religion. And for proofe that hee is stedfastly resolued to persist

in

in all theſe nouelties, and not to retract any thing of that which he hath written, ſee what hee ſaith in the laſt page ſaue one of his ſaid Preface. *Opinor enim ipſe (vt magni illius Eraſmi verba hîc æmuler) in libris meis nihil reperiri, quo deterior quiſpiam reddi poſsit.* For I am of opinion (to vſe the words of that great *Eraſmus*) that there is nothing to be found in my Bookes, that can make any man the worſe that reads them.

As for his Booke which followes this Preface, it verifies the Prouerbe, *Dignum patellâ operculum*, A couer fit for ſuch a diſh. For it is ſo full of diſtinctions, and ſophiſticall euaſions, ſo ſtuft with *As it weres*, *in ſome ſorts*, *in my ſence*, and ſuch words as theſe, as euen in that poynt hee hath alſo a tincture of *Bellarmine*. But God is *Vnity* it ſelfe, and *Veritie* is *One*, and naked, and in our vſuall manner of ſpeech, we call it *the ſimple Verity*, but neuer was it yet called, *the double veritie*.

Wee haue thought good to ſet downe here two places of his ſayd Booke, that thereby the Reader may iudge of the reſt; whereof one is in the twelfth page, in theſe words, *Argumenta quæ adferuntur à Patribus, vel à recentioribus Theologis pro æterna Chriſti generatione, aut fallacia ſunt, aut friuola.* The arguments which are vſed both by the Fathers and by the moderne Diuines, for the eternall generation of *Chriſt*, are either ſophiſticall or friuolous. Theſe words (as he ſaith) he is charged to haue vſed, and he cannot bethinke him of any other euaſion, but to adde the word *Quædam*, ſome arguments, &c. Now wee ſhall deſire thee (good Reader) here to obſerue, that this man condemning ſome arguments which the Fathers had gathered out of the holy Scripture, to prooue the eternall generation of Chriſt, as deceitfull and friuolous, hee will bee ſure howſoeuer not to alleadge any other arguments, either out of the Fathers, or of his owne brayne, which ſhall be ſtronger then thoſe which he hath reiected. And in the ſame faſhion he behaues himſelfe throughout his whole Booke: for we ſhew you this but for a ſcantling. In the other place, he directly denies that euer he affirmed in his other Booke, that *Feare* and *Deſperation* were incident to God: his wordes are theſe in the eighth page, *Nam metum & deſperationem ne quidem vſpiàm nominaui.* For I did neuer ſo much as name *Feare* and *Deſperation*, in any place. And yet neuertheleſſe, let any man looke vpon his other Booke, *pag.*114. and *pag.*450. and hee ſhall find two ſeuerall Diſcourſes of a good length, concerning theſe two points. Herein hauing no other ſhift, he betakes himſelfe to an abſolute and flat Negatiue. But to the intent, that the Reader may iudge of his maner of ſpeaking through his whole laſt Booke intituled, *A Chriſtian and modeſt Anſwere*, and how he playes the Sophiſter therein; we haue ſet downe diuers of his phraſes (in manner of a Table) which we haue cauſed to be extracted out of his ſaid Booke.

Tract.Theol. de Deo.

¶ 1. *Eſtr*

¶ 1. *Eſtne Deus eſſentialiter immenſus, & vbiq́; preſens?*

NVſquam diſertè ſcriptum eſt, ſubſtantiam Dei ſimpliciter, ſeu quouis modo, immenſam & infinitam eſſe. *Et non pauca in S.Literis occurrunt, quæ contrarium, non dico clarè aſſerunt, ſed tamen aſſerere videntur.* Interim aliud eſt videri, aliud reuerâ eſſe. *Reſpondeo tamen ex ſenſu meo.*

Quoad Theſin, ſeu rem ipſam eſt.

Tametſi non quoad ² ſpecialem modum, ſeu ³ hypotheſin ſcholaſticam.

4 Quæ tamen falſa non eſt, verùm aliquatenùs hactenus infirmiùs aſſerta, & ſic aliquatenùs dubia.

Pag.16.lin. 16.
Pag.16.lin. 23.
Pag.22.ſin. 23.
Pag.4.l.19.
Pag.22.l. 26.
Pag.23.l.1.

Is God eſſentially immenſe, and euery where preſent?

It is in no place clearly ſet downe, that the ſubſtance of God is ſimply, and euery way immenſe, and infinite. And there be many places in the holy Scripture, which (I doe not ſay, clearely affirme) yet ſeeme to affirme the contrary. In the meane time, it is one thing to ſeeme, and another thing to be indeed. Yet in mine owne ſenſe I anſwere thus:

Simply, and poſitiuely it is.

Howſoeuer, not in that ſpeciall maner and ſort as the Scholemen hold.

Which opinion, neuertheleſſe, I doe not ſay is falſe, but I ſay it hath hitherto bene ſomewhat weakely proued, & therefore in ſome ſort doubtful.

¶ 2. *Eſtne in Deo quantitas?*

Eſt, ſed ¹ non phyſica.

Verùm ² hyperphyſica.

Attamen ³ nobis planè imperceptibilis, & merè ſpiritualis.

Pag.2.L.18.
Pag.23.l. 12.
Pag.2.l.19.

Is there Quantitie in God?

There is, but not a naturall Quantitie:

But a ſupernaturall.

Neuertheleſſe, not poſſible to be perceiued by vs, but meerely ſpirituall.

¶ 3. *Eſtne Deus infinitus?*

¹ Omnia Entia certam & definitam eſſentiam habent, id quod Deo ipſi aliquatenus aptare licet. ² Deum quolibet ſenſu rectè infinitum dici non poſſe, quum infinitudo illa quæ definitioni certæ oponitur in Deum reuerâ non cadat.

Pag.3.l.16.
Pag.3.l.18.

Is God infinite?

Euery thing that hath a being hath a certaine and definite Eſſence, which may be applied in ſome kinde vnto God. That God cannot rightly in euery ſence be ſaid to be infinite, ſeeing that infiniteneſſe which is oppoſite to certaine definiteneſſe, cannot indeed be attributed vnto God.

¶ 4. *Eſtne Deus in aliquo loco?*

Eſt, ſed non ¹ phyſico;

Verùm in ſpatio abſtractiſsimè ſumpto, quod Deus ſuo diuino modo adimplet.

Pag.3.l.22, 23.

Ii   Is

Is God in a place?

He is, but not in a naturall place;

But *in ſpatio abſtractiſsimè ſumpto*, which God after his Diuine maner doeth fill.

¶ 5. *Eſtne Deus corporeus ?*

¹ Pag.3.l.34.
² Pag.15.l.6.
³ Pag.4.l.3.
⁴ Pag.15.l. 14.
⁵ Pag.15.l. 10.& 3.

¹ *Propriè loquendo minimè corporeus eſt.*

² *Sed tamen nihil abſurdi erit, ſi Deo (impropriè loquendo) corpus aſcribamus,* ³ *nempè quatenus vocabulum Corporis impropriè & latiſsimè pro verâ ſubſtantiâ* ⁴ *non prorſus abſurdè ſumitur ,* ⁵ *iuxta latam ſignificationem, quæ figurata, & impropria, ſeu mauis catachreſtica eſt.*

Hath God a body ?

If we will ſpeake properly, he hath none.

Yet is it no abſurditie, ſpeaking improperly, to aſcribe a body vnto God, that is to ſay, as the word Body is taken improperly and generally, (and yet not very abſurdly) for a trew ſubſtance, in a large ſignification which is figuratiue, and improper, or (if you will) abuſiue.

¶ 6. *Eſtne Deus compoſitus è materiâ & formâ ?*

¹ Pag.5.l.3.

¹ *Nullo modo, propriè loquendo. Eſt tamen in ſenſu quodam improprio, vel, ſi mauis, per καταχρησιν quandam, per quam vocabulum Corporis, item quaſi materiæ & formæ, ſeu quaſi compoſitionis ex genere & differentiâ, aliquando eidem attribui poſſe non immeritò alicui videatur.*

Is God compounded of matter and forme ?

By no meanes, ſpeaking properly : Although it bee trew in a certaine improper ſence, or (if you pleaſe) by a certaine *Catachreſis*, by the which the word *Body*, and as it were *materia & forma*, or as it were a Compoſition *ex genere & differentia*, may ſometimes ſeeme to ſome (and not without cauſe) to be fitly attributed to God.

¶ 7. *Eſtne Deus immutabilis, vt eſſentiâ, ſic voluntate ?*

¹ Pag.15.l. 15.

Non eſt ¹ *vt eſſentiâ, ſic voluntate; Id eſt, non eſt æqualiter.*

Is God vnchangeable *in his* Will, *as he is in his* Eſſence?

He is not vnchangeable in his will, as he is in his Eſſence. That is, not alike vnchangeable in the one, as he is in the other.

¶ 8. *Eſtne Deus ſubiectus accidentibus?*

¹ Pag 7.l.8.
² Pag.7.l.9.

¹ *Non vllis veris.*

² *Tametſi per liberam voluntatem quædam accidentia latisſimè ſic dicta, tum ad ſe, tum in ſe recipit Deus.*

Is God ſubiect to accidents ?

Not to any trew accidents.

Although God doeth by his Free will take to himſelfe, and into himſelfe, certaine accidents, ſo called in the largeſt ſenſe.

¶ 9. *An Deus per discursum conijcit de futuris?*

Interdum, [1] *aliquatenus,* [2] *discursum quendam instituit, & quasi de incertis conij-*
cit, [3] *sed improprie & metaphorice, citraque omnem imperfectionem.*
[4] *Conijcit autem non coniecturâ qualis hominum esse solet, sed planè diuinâ.*

[1] Pag.7.l.14.
[2] Pag.8.l.9.
[3] Pag.7.l.22.
[4] Pag.8.l.1.

Doeth *God* coniecture *of things to come by* difcourfe?

Sometimes in fome fort, he frameth to himfelfe a certaine difcourfe, and
doeth (as it were) coniecture of things vncertaine, but improperly and me-
taphorically, and without all imperfection.

And he doeth coniecture not in fuch fort as men doe, but after a meerely diuine maner.

¶ 10. *Affectus amoris, odij, &c. Deone propriè attribuuntur?*

Propriè, sed [1] *vt pro veritate potiùs, quàm pro vsitatâ nobisque notâ proprietate*
accipiendum sit.
[2] *Nulli affectus cum humanâ infirmitate coniuncti propriè Deo attribuuntur;*
verè tamen, & suo modo propriè, hoc est, pro suæ, non pro naturæ nostræ proprietate.

[1] Pag.8.l.16.
[2] Pag.9.l.1.

The affections *of* loue, hatred, *&c.* be they properly attributed
vnto God or not?

Yes, but fo as ye take it rather for a veritie, then for that property which
is vulgarly vnderftood and knowne vnto vs.

No affections accompanied with humane infirmitie are properly attributed vnto God: yet trewly, and in his owne kinde properly, that is to fay,
as they are proper to his nature, and not to ours.

¶ 11. *Pater, habetne peculiarem quandam, seu quasi restrictam*
essentiam?

[1] *Vox essentiæ, perinde vt Entis, amplissimam significationem habet, & sic nihil*
omninò vetat vtramque non minùs ad personas diuinas, quàm ad ipsam Deitatis na-
turam in sano sensu referri.

[1] Pag.22.l.13.

Hath the Father a certaine peculiar, or *(as it were)* limited Effence?
The word *Effence*, as well as *Ens*, hath a very large fignification, and we
may apply both of them fafely, in a good fence, as well to the Diuine perfons, as to the nature of the Deitie it felfe.

¶ 12. *Suntne Patrum argumenta friuola, pro æternâ*
Christi generatione?

Siquidem [1] *vnica vox* [*quædam*] *ab initio inferatur, argumenta à Patribus ha-*
ctenus aptata, aut fallacia, aut friuola sunt.

[1] Pag.14.l.3.

Be thofe arguments which the *Fathers* haue vfed to proue the
Eternall generation *of Chrift,* friuolous or no?

If this one word [*quædam*, fome,] were added to the beginning of that
pofition, it were then trew, that the arguments which the Fathers haue at
any time applied to prooue the Eternall generation of *Chrift*, are either deceitfull, or friuolous.

¶ 13. *Eftne*

Pag. 18.l.
19, 20.

Pag. 18. l.
29.

¶ [13] *Eſtne in Deo viſio præſentium, & præteritorum magis certa,*
quàm futurorum præuiſio?

[1] *Nota modeſtiam meam in verbo* [*videntur,*] *opinionem duntaxat probabi-*
lem hîc afferri, non autem dogmaticam aſſertionem.

Futura [2] *contingentia (comparatiuè loquendo) etiam coram Deo dici poſſunt mi-*
nus certa quàm præterita, & præſentia.

Whether doeth God ſee things paſt *and* preſent, *more certainely*
then things to come?

Note here my modeſtie in this word [*videntur*] for in this place I deliuer onely a probable opinion, and not a dogmaticall aſſertion.

Things future contingent (ſpeaking comparatiuely) may be ſaid to bee
leſſe certaine, euen vnto God, then things paſt, and preſent.

By this may the Reader manifeſtly diſcerne, that there is nothing which
a man, ſpeaking in this faſhion ſhall not be able to maintaine, and by this
meanes eaſily prooue *quidlibet ex quolibet.* And certainely his manner
of excuſes and euaſions are framed iuſt after the mould of the ancient Heretiques, and namely of *Arrius,* and *Paulus Samoſatenus,* when they ſaw
themſelues pinched with the Arguments of the *Orthodoxe* Church, and
had no power to reſiſt. The ſame alſo doeth more plainely appeare by an
other little booke which he hath publiſhed, intituled, *Theologicall poſitions,*
which booke he hath made of purpoſe to blinde the world withall ; becauſe they are indeed but the ſame *Theſes* or *Poſitions,* vpon which he hath
diſputed in his firſt wicked booke, that beareth the title *Of God and his*
Attributes. For in the *Theſes* themſelues there is but little harme, but in
his diſputations thereupon are couched all the horrible Hereſies : And
therefore in this booke hath hee publiſhed onely his *Theſes* which are iu-
ſtifiable, and left out his diſputations vpon the *Theſes,* wherein all the
poiſon is conteined. It is moreouer ſomewhat ſuſpicious in ſuch a tainted
perſon as he is, that in an Appendix which hee hath placed at the end of
his *Theſes,* he taketh occaſion to name a number of Heretiques who are
aduerſaries to the doctrine of his *Theſes,* and thoſe eſpecially who haue erred concerning the Diuinitie, Humanitie, Perſon, or Office of Chriſt,
as the *Ebionites, Cerinthians, Arrians, Praxians, Sabellians, Marcionites, Mani-*
chees, Docites, Apollinariſts, Mennonites, Swenkfeldians, Neſtorians, Monothelites,
Eutychians, Monophyſites, Iewes, Millenaries, Papiſts. Amongſt which rabble
he doeth not once make mention of *Paulus Samoſatenus,* nor of *Photinius,*
who ſucceeded him as well in his Biſhopricke as in his errour : Yet neuertheleſſe it is reported, that *Vorſtius* in his heart is not very farre from their
erronious opinion.

Now in the Preface of this little booke hee hath taken vpon him very
ſuccinctly to make anſwere to fiue Articles which he confeſſeth were layd
to his charge, by which anſwere, in our opinion, hee diſcouers himſelfe
very plainely.

The

The first point is, That hee was once accused (as himselfe saith) of the *Samosatenian* Heresie, because he had sometime both written and receiued letters from diuers of that Sect; which he confesseth he did indeed in his youth, to this end, that by that meanes hee might the more easily come by some of their bookes, but that afterward hee did forbeare all correspondencie with them. First of all then, we would be glad to know why hee forgot the Heresie of *Samosatenus* in his *Appendix*, where he names so many others, and yet confesseth in the Preface of his said booke, that he himselfe was accused of that errour. Secondly, to what end had hee in his youth so great traffique with these Heretiques? was it to enable him the better to confute them? We heare him not say so much, as indeed it was neuer his end. Surely this fellow would be an excellent cleanser of a Pesthouse, for he feares no infection: *Picem contrectare non timet*, he dares handle any pitch: And yet for all that, the Prouerbe is trew; *Qui ambulat in Sole, colorabitur*; He that walketh in the Sun-shine, shall bee Sun-burnt. It followes then, seeing his intention was not to arme himselfe against them, that it must be of necessitie to make himselfe worthy of their Schoole, the which hee almost confesseth in the last words of his Answere to that point, where he saith thus; *Non enim (quod multi solent) alienis sensibus sic fidendum putaui, aut temerè quidquam in causa Fidei damnandum* : For I doe not thinke it fit (as many others doe) to relie in these cases vpon other mens constructions, or rashly to condemne any thing which concernes matter of Faith.

To the second Article of his Accusation, hee confesseth that hee gaue some of his *Samosatenian* bookes vnto his schollers; Surely, a goodly gift: But the caution was prettie which he gaue withall vnto them when he deliuered them the bookes; which was that they ought to reade them with iudgement, not rashly reiecting the doctrine commonly receiued. What an Epithite is heere for our holy *Orthodoxe* Faith, to terme it no otherwise then the doctrine commonly receiued? And as for his caution, not rashly to forsake the old doctrine, it is no more then the Turkes would giue vnto any Christian, that should suddenly offer to become a Mahometist. Nay what Christian did euer sollicite a Pagan, or Heretique to bee conuerted, but with this caution? Who would perswade a man to receiue the holy Sacrament rashly? S. *Paul* commands euery man to examine himselfe diligently, before hee come to that holy Table. But on the other side, an *Orthodoxe* Christian would in this case haue said to his schollers: If you will » reade these wicked bookes, reade them with horrour and detestation, and » with an intent to arme your selues against such wiles and subtilties of Sa- » than, and withall pray vnto G O D to keepe you constant in the holy Ca- » tholique and *Orthodoxe* Faith, that these Heresies may haue no power » once to mooue you, trusting in his mercy, and not in your owne strength. »

To the third Article, he confesseth that his schollers did publish bookes of the *Socinian* Heresie; and his excuse is, that it was without his knowledge:

ledge:

ledge : But howſoeuer , he condemnes them not for hauing done it · onely
this he ſaith , That they declared vpon their oathes , they did not fauour
the Hereſie.

To the fourth point , he confeſſeth that about ten yeeres ſince, he wrote
a booke *De Filiatione Chriſti* , (for which Title onely , an Authour , ſo ſuſpected as he , is worthy of the fagot ,) and all his excuſe is , That he wrote
an Epitome vpon *Bellarmine.* Wee doubt not but hee did it for his recreation. Forſooth , a prety conceit. Yet it appeares not by his wordes , that
he deteſts the ſubiect of that Booke : but ſaith , That no man can thereby
coniecture what his opinion is of that argument , no more then they can
vpon his Epitome of *Bellarmine* , which was likewiſe his worke. For to
condemne it , had beene contrary to that which hee auowed in his other
booke , neuer to repent himſelfe of any thing that he hath once written , as
already we haue obſerued.

As for the fift and laſt point , he will neither confeſſe , nor deny the accu-
ſation : onely hee ſaith , That a certaine booke intituled *Dominicus Lopez* ,
which is (as we haue heard) a very blaſphemous Treatiſe, was ſuppreſſed by
him *pacis ergò* , for peace ſake; but he is ſo farre from condemning it , as
that he alleadgeth , the booke hath bene maintained by others , which in
time ſhall appeare. Two things are here to bee obſerued ; Firſt , that hee
ſuppreſſed it *pacis ergò* , for quietneſſe ſake ; Not therefore for the wickedneſſe of the ſubiect , The next, that in his due time : the trewth thereof ſhall
appeare. In which laſt point onely , we will willingly ioyne with him ,
beſeeching our good G O D , for his C H R I S T S ſake , that hee will bee
pleaſed to diſcouer the trewth of this mans intentions , as well for his owne
Glory , as to purge the ſcandall , and to auoyd the danger which may enſue
vnto Chriſtendome, by the darnell of Hereſies which he hath ſowne.

It is therefore to bee noted , That to all theſe fiue Articles his anſweres
are ſo ſilly and weake , as in three of them we haue found him *planè confi-
tentem reum* , plainely pleading guiltie ; blanching it onely with ſome poore
excuſes. And to the other two points his anſwers are doubtfull ; yet neither condemning the act of his ſchollers , nor the laſt wicked booke called
Dominicus Lopez.

Hauing now therefore briefly laied open the ſubtilties, friuolous diſtinctions , and excuſes of the ſaid *Vorſtius* , we will conclude this point with
this proteſtation ; That if he had bene our owne Subiect , we would haue
bid him *Excrea* , ſpit out : and forced him to haue produced , and confeſſed
thoſe wicked Hereſies , that are rooted in his heart. And in caſe he ſhould
ſtand vpon his Negatiue , we would enioyne him to ſay (according to the
ancient cuſtome of the Primitiue Church in the like caſes of Heretiques) I
renounce and from my ſoule deteſt them : Anathema ; Maranatha vpon ſuch and
ſuch Hereſies ; And not to ſay, *For peace ſake I cauſed this booke to be ſuppreſſed,
And theſe bookes are to bee read with great iudgement and diſcretion.* S. *Hierome*
liketh not that any man ſhould take it patiently, to be ſuſpected of Hereſie.

And

And now to make an end of this Diſcourſe, we doe very heartily deſire all good Chriſtians in generall, and My Lords the States in particular (to whom the managing of this affaire doeth moſt ſpecially belong) to conſider but two things: Firſt what kinde of people they be that ſlander vs, and our ſincere intention in this cauſe: And next, what priuate intereſt wee can poſſibly haue (in reſpect of any worldly honour or aduancement) herein to engage our ſelues in ſuch ſort as we haue done.

Concerning the firſt point, There are but three ſorts of people, that ſeeke to calumniate vs vpon this occaſion: That is to ſay; either ſuch as are infected with the ſame, or the like Hereſies, wherewith *Vorſius* is tainted, *& ideo fouent conſimilem cauſam*, and therefore doe maintaine the like cauſe: or elſe ſuch as be of the Romane Religion, who in this confuſion, and libertie of prophefying would thruſt in for a part; conceiuing it more reaſonable, that their doctrine ſhould be tolerated by thoſe of our Religion, then the doctrine of *Vorſius*: or elſe ſuch, as for reaſon of State enuie peraduenture the good amitie and correſpondencie which is betwixt vs, and the Vnited Prouinces.

Touching our owne intereſt, the whole courſe of our life doeth ſufficiently witneſſe, that we haue alwayes bene contented with that portion which G O D hath put into our hands, without ſeeking to inuade the poſſeſſions of any other. Beſides, in two of our boukes, as well in our ΒΑΣΙΛΙΚΟΝ ΔΩΡΟΝ, as in the Preface to our *Apologie*, we haue ſhewed the ſame inclination. For in the firſt booke, ſpeaking of warre, we ſay that a King ought not to make any inuaſion vpon anothers Dominions, vntill Iuſtice be firſt denied him. And in the other booke, hauing ſhewed the vſurpation of the Pope, aboue all the Kings and Princes of Chriſtendome, our concluſion is, that we will neuer goe about to perſwade them to aſſault him within his Dominions, but onely to reſume, and preſerue their owne iuſt Priuiledges from his violent intruſion. So as (thankes be to G O D) both our *Theorique* and *Practique* agree well together, to cleare vs from this vniuſt and ſlanderous imputation. And as for the States in particular, it is very vnlikely that we (who haue all our life time held ſo ſtrict an amitie with them, as for their defence wee haue bene contented to expoſe the liues of many of our Subiects of both Nations,) would now practiſe againſt their State, and that vpon ſo poore a ſubiect as *Vorſius*: eſpecially, that ſo damnable a thing could euer enter into our heart, as vnder the vaile and pretext of the glory of G O D, to plot the aduancement of our owne priuate deſeignes.

The reaſons which induced vs to meddle in this buſineſſe, we haue already declared. We leaue it now to his owne proper Iudges to conſider what a nurſling they foſter in their boſome: A ſtranger, bred in the *Socinian Hereſie* (as it is ſaid;) often times accuſed of *Hereſie* by the Churches of *Germanie*; one that hath written ſo wicked and ſcandalous bookes; maintaining and ſeriouſly proteſting in the preface of his *Apologie* to the States,

for

for the libertie of prophecying; and twice or thrice infifting vpon that libertie in the Preface of his *Modeſt Anſwere* (a dangerous and pernitious libertie, or rather licentioufneſſe, opening a gap to all rupture, Schiſme, and confuſion in the Church;) yea hauing had ſome diſciples that be Heretiques themſelues, and others that accuſe him of Hereſie. And though there were no other cauſe then the ſilly and idle ſhifts wherewith hee ſeekes to defend himſelfe in his laſt bookes, it were enough to conuince him, either to haue maintained a bad cauſe, and in that reſpect worthy of a farre greater puniſhment then to be put by his place of *Profeſſour*; or at the leaſt to be a perſon vnworthy of the name of a *Profeſſour* in ſo famous an Vniuerſitie; for hauing ſo weakely maintained a cauſe that is iuſt. For our part, G O D is our witneſſe, we haue no quarrell againſt his perſon; he is a Stranger, borne farre from our dominions: he is a *Germane*, and it is well knowen, that all *Germanie* are our friends, and the moſt part of the great Princes there, be either neerely allied vnto vs, or our Confederates: he doth outwardly profeſſe the ſame Religion which we do: he hath written againſt *Bellarmine*: and hath not mentioned vs, either in ſpeach or writing (for any thing we know) but with all the honour and reſpect that may be. G O D knowes, the worſt that we do wiſh him is, that he may ſincerely returne into the high beaten path-way of the *Catholique* and *Orthodoxall* Faith.

And for my Lords the States (ſeeing wee haue diſcharged our conſcience) we will now referre the managing of the whole Action vnto their owne diſcretions. For wee are ſo farre from preſcribing them any rule herein, as we ſhall be very well contented (ſo as the buſineſſe be well done) that there be euen no mention at all made of our interceſſion, in their publique Acts or Records. Their maner of proceeding, we leaue abſolutely to their owne Wiſedomes. *Modò prædicetur Chriſtus*, ſo as C H R I S T bee preached, let them vſe their owne formes in the Name of G O D. For we deſire that G O D ſhould ſo iudge vs at the laſt Day, as we affect not in this Action any worldly glory, beſeeching the Creatour ſo to open their eyes, to illuminate their vnderſtandings, direct their reſolutions, and, aboue all, to kindle their zeale, ſanctifie their affections, & at the laſt ſo to bleſſe their Actions and their proceedings in this cauſe, as the iſſue thereof may tend to his Glory, to the comfort and ſolace of the Faithfull, to the honour of our Religion, to the confuſion and extirpation (at the leaſt, profligation) of Hereſies, and, in particular, to the corroboration of the Vnion of the ſayd Prouinces.

A RE-

A REMONSTRANCE
FOR THE RIGHT OF
KINGS, AND THE
INDEPENDANCE OF
THEIR CROVVNES,

AGAINST AN ORATION OF
THE MOST ILLVSTRIOVS CARD.
OF PERRON, PRONOVNCED IN THE
Chamber of the third Eſtate.

IAN. 15. 1615.

THE PREFACE.

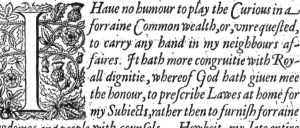

*Haue no humour to play the Curious in a_
forraine Common wealth, or, vnrequeſted,
to carry any hand in my neighbours affaires. Jt hath more congruitie with Royall dignitie, whereof God hath giuen mee
the honour, to preſcribe Lawes at home for
my Subiects, rather then to furniſh forraine
Kingdomes and people with counſels. Howbeit, my late entire
affection to K. Henry IV. of happy memorie, my moſt honoured brother, and my exceeding ſorrow for the moſt deteſtable parricide acted vpon the ſacred perſon of a King, ſo complete in all
heroicall and Princely vertues; as alſo the remembrance of my*
owne

owne dangers, incurred by the practife of confpiracies flowing from the fame fource, hath wrought mee to fympathize with my friends in their grieuous occurrents : no doubt fo much more dangerous, as they are leffe apprehended and felt of Kings themfelues, euen when the danger hangeth ouer their owne heads.   Upon whom, in cafe the power and vertue of my aduertifements be not able ef-fectually to worke, at leaft many millions of children and people yet vnborne, fhall beare me witneffe, that in thefe dangers of the higheft nature and ftraine, I haue not bene defectiue : and that neither the fubuerfions of States, nor the murthers of Kings, which may vnhappily betide hereafter, fhall haue fo free paffage in the world for want of timely aduertifement before.   For touching my particular, my reft is vp, that one of the maynes for which God hath aduanced me vpon the loftie ftage of the fupreme Throne, is, that my words vttered from fo eminent a place for Gods honour, moft fhamefully traduced and vilified in his owne Deputies and Lieutenants, might with greater facilitie be conceiued.

Now touching France, *faire was the hope which I conceiued of the States affembled in Parliament at* Paris : *That calling to minde the murthers of their Noble Kings, and the warres of the League which followed the Popes fulminations, as when a great ftorme of haile powreth downe after a Thunder-cracke, and a world of writings addreffed to iuftifie the parricides, and the de-thronings of kings, they would haue ioyned heads, hearts, & hand, together, to hammer out fome apt and wholefome remedy againft fo many fearefull attempts and practifes.   To my hope was added no little ioy, when I was giuen to vnderftand the third* Eftate *had preferred an Article or Bill, the tenor and fubftance whereof was concerning the meanes whereby the people might bee vnwit-ched of this pernicious opinion ;* That Popes *may* toffe th French King *his* Throne *like a tennis ball, and that killing of* Kings is *an* acte meritorious to the purchafe of th crowne of Martyrdome. *But in fine, the proiect was encoun-tred with fucceffe cleane coutrary to Expectation. For this Ar-ticle of the third Eftate, like a figh of libertie breathing her laft*

ferue

ferued onely fo much the more to inthrall the Crowne , and to make the bondage more grieuous and fenfible then before . Euen as thofe medicines which worke no eafe to the patient , doe leaue the difeafe in much worfe tearmes : fo this remedy inuented and tendred by the third Eftate , did onely exafperate the prefent malady of the State ; for fo much as the operation and vertue of the wholefome remedy was ouermatched with peccant humours, then ftirred by the force of thwarting and croffing oppofition. Yea much better had it bene , the matter had not bene ftirred at all, then after it was once on foot and in motion, to giue the Trewth leaue to lye gafping and fprawling vnder the violence of a forraine faction. For the opinion by which the Crownes of Kings are made fubiect vnto the Popes will and power, was then auowed in a moft Honourable Affembly , by the auerment of a Prelate in great authoritie , and of no leffe learning: He did not plead the caufe as a priuate perfon, but as one by reprefentation that ftood for the whole body of the Clergie ; was there applauded , and feconded with approbation of the Nobilitie ; no refolution taken to the contrary, or in barre to his plea . After praifes and thankes from the Pope , followed the printing of his eloquent harangue or Oration , made in full Parliament : a fet difcourfe , maintaining Kings to be depofeable by the Pope, if he fpeake the word. The faid Oration was not onely Printed with the Kings priuiledge, but was likewife addreffed to mee by the Author and Orator himfelfe ; who prefuppofed the reading thereof would forfooth driue me to fay, Lord Cardinall, in this high fubiect your Honour hath fatisfied me to the full. *All this poyfed in the ballance of equall iudgement, why may not I trewly and freely affirme, the faid Eftates affembled in Parliament , haue fet Royall Maieftie vpon a doubtfull chance , or left it refting vpon vncertaine tearmes : and that now if the doctrine there maintained by the Clergie fhould beare any pawme , it may lawfully be doubted, who is King in France ? For I make no queftion, hee is but a titular King that raigneth onely at an others difcretion , and whofe Princely head the Pope hath power to bare of his Regall Crowne.*

In

In temporall matters, how can one be Soueraigne, that may be fleeced of all his Temporalties by any superiour power ? But let men at a neere sight marke the pith and marrow of the Article proposed by the third Estate, and they shall soone perceiue the skilfull Architects thereof aymed onely to make their King a trew and reall King, to bee recognised for Soueraigne within his owne Realme, and that killing their King might no longer passe the muster of workes acceptable to God.

But by the vehement instance and strong current of the Clergie and Nobles, this was borne downe as a pernicious Article, as a cause of Schisme, as a gate which openeth to all sorts of Heresies : yea, there it was maintained tooth and naile, that in case the doctrine of this Article might goe for currant doctrine, it must follow, that for many aages past in sequence, the Church hath beene the kingdome of Antichrist, and the synagogue of Satan. The Pope vpon so good issue of the cause, had reason, I trow, to addresse his Letters of triumph vnto the Nobilitie and Clergie, who had so farre aprrooued themselues faithfull to his Holinesse; and to vaunt withall, that hee had nipped Christian Kings in the Crowne, that hee had giuen them checke with mate, through the magnanimous resolution of this courageous Nobilitie, by whose braue making head, the third Estate had beene so valiantly forced to giue ground. In a scornefull reproach hee qualified the Deputies of the third Estate, nebulones ex fœce plebis, a sort or a number of knaues, the very dregges of the base vulgar, a packe of people, presuming to personate well affected Subiects, and men of deepe vnderstanding, and to reade their masters a learned Lecture. Now it is no wonder, that, in so goood an office and loyall cariage towards their King, the third Estate hath outgone the Clergie. For the Clergie denie themselues to haue any ranke among the Subiects of the King : they stand for a Soueraigne out of the Kingdome, to whom, as to the Lord Paramount they owe suite and seruice : they are bound to aduance that Monarchie, to the bodie whereof they properly apperteine as parts or members, as elsewhere I haue

written

I haue receiued aduertisement from diuers parts, that in the Popes letters to the Nobitie these wordes were extant, howsoeuer they haue bin left out in the impression, & rased out of the copies of the said letters.

written more at large. But for the Nobilitie, the Kings right arme, to proſtitute and ſet as it were to ſale the dignitie of their King, as if the arme ſhould giue a thruſt vnto the head; I ſay for the Nobilitie to hold and maintaine euen in Parliament, their King is liable to depoſition by any forreine power or Potentate, may it not paſſe among the ſtrangeſt miracles and rareſt wonders of the world? For that once granted, this conſequence is good and neceſſarie; That in caſe the King, once lawfully depoſed, ſhall ſtand vpon the defenſiue, and hold out for his right, he may then lawfully be murthered. Let mee then here freely profeſſe my o-pinion, and this it is: That now the French Nobilitie may ſeeme to haue ſome reaſon to diſrobe themſelues of their titles, and to transferre them by reſignation vnto the third Eſtate. For that body of that third Eſtate alone hath caried a right noble heart: in as much as the could neither be tickled with promiſes, nor ter-rified by threatnings, from reſolute ſtanding to thoſe fundamen-tall points and reaſons of State, which moſt concerne the honour of their King, and the ſecuritie of his perſon.

Of all the Clergie, the man that hath moſt abandoned, or ſet his honour to ſale, the man to whom France is leaſt obliged, is the Lord Cardinall of Perron: a man otherwiſe inferiour to few in matter of learning, and in the grace of a ſweete ſtyle. This man in two ſuerall Orations, whereof the one was pronounced be-fore the Nobilitie, the other had audience before the third Eſtate, hath ſet his beſt wits on worke, to draw that doctrine into all ha-tred and infamie, which teacheth Kings to be indepoſeable by the Pope. To this purpoſe bee termes the ſame doctrine, a breeder of Schiſmes, a gate that openeth to make way, and to giue en-trance vnto all hereſies; in briefe, a doctrine to bee held in ſo high a degree of deteſtation, that rather then he and his fellow-Bi-ſhops will yeeld to the ſigning thereof, they will bee contented like Martyrs to burne at a ſtake. At which reſolution, or obſtina-cie rather in his opinion, I am in a manner amaſed, more then I can be mooued for the like brauado in many other: foraſmuch as hee was many yeeres together, a follower of the late King, euen when

Kk

the

the King followed a contrary Religion, and was depofed by the
Pope: as alfo becaufe not long before, in a certaine Affemblie holden at the Iacobins in Paris, hee withftood the Popes Nuntio to
his face, when the faid Nuntio laboured to make this doctrine,
touching the Popes temporall Soueraigntie, paff: for an Article of
Faith. But in both Orations, hee fingeth a contrary fong, and
from his owne mouth paffeth fentence of condemnation againft his
former courfe and profeffion. I fuppofe, not without follide iudge-
men; as one that heerein hath well accommodated himfelfe to the
times : For as in the reigne of the late King, hee durft not
offer to broach this doctrine (fuch was his fore-wit;) fo now he is
bold to proclaime and publifh it in Parliament vnder the reigne
of the faid Kings fonne; whofe tender yeeres and late fucceffion
to the Crowne, doe make him lie the more open to iniuries, and the
more facill to be circumuented : Such is now his afterwifedome.

Of thefe two Orations, that made in prefence of the Nobilitie
he hath, for feare of incurring the Popes difpleafure, cauteloufly
fuppreffed. For therein he hath beene fomewhat prodigall in affirming this doctrine maintained by the Clergie, to bee but problematicall; and in taking vpon him to auouch, that Catholikes of my
Kingdome are bound to yeeld me the honour of obedience: Whereas on the other fide, he is not ignorant, how this doctrine of depofing
Princes and Kings, the Pope holdeth for meerely neceffarie, and
approoueth not by any meanes Alleagiance to bee performed vnto mee by the Catholikes of my Kingdome. Yea if credit may be
giuen vnto the abridgement of his other Oration publifhed, wherein he paralells the Popes power in receiuing honours in the name
of the Church, with the power of the Venetian Duke in receiuing
honours in the name of that moft renowned Rebublike; no marueile that when this Oration was difpatched to the preffe, he commanded the fame to be gelded of this claufe and other like, for feare
of giuing his Holineffe any offenfiue diftafte.

His pleafure therefore was, and content withall, that his Oration imparted to the third Eftate, fhould be put in Print, and of
his courtefie he vouchfafed to addreffe vnto me a copie of the fame.
Which

Which after I had perufed, I foorthwith well perceiued, what and how great difcrepance there is betweene one man that perorateth from the ingenuous and ſincere diſpoſition of a ſound heart, and an other that flaunteth in flouriſhing ſpeech with inward checkes of his owne conſcience: For euery where he contradicts himſelfe, and ſeemes to be afraid leſt men ſhould picke out his right meaning.

First, he grants this Queſtion is not hitherto decided by the holy Scriptures, or by the Decrees of the ancient Church, or by the analogie of other Eccleſiaſticall proceedings : and neuertheleſſe hee confidently doeth affirme ; that whoſoeuer maintaine this doctrine to be wicked and abbominable, that Popes haue no power to put Kings by their ſupreame Thrones, they teach men to beleeue, there hath not bene any Church for many aages paſt, and that indeed the Church is the very Synagogue of Antichriſt.

In 11. ſeuerall paſſages the L. Card. ſeemeth to ſpeake againſt his owne conſcience. Pag. 85.

Secondly, he exhorts his hearers to hold this doctrine at leaſt for problematicall, and not neceſſary : and yet herein he calls them to all humble ſubmiſſion vnto the iudgement of the Pope and Clergie, by whom the cauſe hath bene already put out of all queſtion, as out of all hunger and cold.

Thirdly, he doeth auerre, in caſe this Article be authorized, it makes the Pope in good conſequence to bee the Antichriſt : and yet he grants that many of the French are tolerated by the Pope to diſſent in this point from his Holineſſe ; prouid. d, their doctrine be not propoſed as neceſſary, and materiall to faith ; As if the Pope in any ſort gaue toleration to hold any doctrine contrary to his owne, and moſt of all that doctrine which by conſequence inferres himſelfe to be the Antichriſt.

Pag. 99.

Fourthly, he proteſteth forwardneſſe to vndergoe the flames of Martyrdome, rather then to figne this doctrine, which teacheth Kings Crownes to ſit faſter on their heads, then to be ſtirred by any Papal power whatſoeuer : and yet ſaith withall, the Pope winketh at the French, by his toleration to hold this dogmaticall point for problematicall. And by this meanes, the Martyrdome that hee affecteth in this cauſe, will prooue but a problematicall Martyrdome, whereof queſtion might grow very well, whether it were to

be

be muStered with grieuous crimes, or with phreneticall paßions of the braine, or with deserued punishments.

Fiftly, he denounceth Anathema, dischargeth maledictions like haile-shot, againSt parricides of Kings: and yet elsewhere hee layes himselfe open to speake of Kings onely so long as they stand Kings. But who doeth not know that a King deposed is no longer King? And so that limme of Satan, which murthered Henry the III. then vn-king'd by the Pope, did not Stabbe a King to death.

Sixtly, he doeth not allow a King to be made away by murder: and yet he thinks it not much out of the way, to take away al meanes whereby he might be able to stand in defence of his life.

Pag. 95. 97. Seuenthly, hee abhorreth killing of Kings by appoSted throat-cutting, for feare leSt body and soule should perish in the same inStant: and yet he doth not mislike their killing in a pitcht field, and to haue them Slaughtered in a set battaile: For he presuppoSeth, no doubt out of his charitable mind, that by this meanes the soule of a poore King so diSpatched out of the way, shall inStantly flie vp to heauen.

Eightly, he saith a King deposed, retaineth Stil a certaine internal habitude and politike impreßion, by vertue and efficacie whereof he may, being once reformed and become a new man, be reStored to the lawfull vse and practise of Regalitie. Whereby hee would beare vs in hand, that when a forraine Prince hath inuaded and rauenoußy seised the kingdome into his hands, he will not onely take pittie of his predeceßour to saue his life, but will also proue so kind-hearted, vpon sight of his repentance, to reStore his kingdome with-out fraud or guile.

Ninthly, he saith euery where in his Discourse, that he dealeth not in the cause, otherwise then as a problematicall difcourser, and without any refolution one way or other: and yet with might and maine hee contends for the opinion, that leaues the States and Crownes of Kings controulable by the Pope: refutes obiections, propounds the authoritie of Popes and Councils, by name the La-teran Councill vnder Innocent. III. as also the confent of the Church. And to croffe the Churches iudgement, is, in his opinion

to

to bring in *schisme*, and to leaue the world without a Church for many hundred yeeres together: which (to my vnderstanding) is to speake with resolution, and without all hesitation.

Tenthly, he acknowledgeth none other cause of sufficient validitie for the deposing of a King, besides heresie, apostasie, and infidelitie: neuerthelesse that Popes haue power to displace Kings for heresie and apostasie, hee proueth by examples of Kings whom the Pope hath curbed with deposition, not for heresie, but for matrimoniall causes, for ciuill pretences, and for lacke of capacitie.

Eleuenthly, hee alledgeth euery where passages, as well of holy Scripture, as of the Fathers and moderne histories; but so impertinent, and with so little trewth, as hereafter wee shall cause to appeare, that for a man of his deepe learning and knowledge, it seemeth not possible so to speake out of his iudgement.

Lastly, whereas all this hath bene hudled and heaped together into one masse, to currie with the Pope: yet hee suffereth diuers points to fall from his lips, which may well distast his Holinesse in the highest degree. As by name, where he prefers the authoritie of the Councill before that of the Pope, and makes his iudgement inferiour to the iudgement of the French; as in fit place hereafter shalbe shewed. Againe, where he representeth to his hearers the decrees of Popes and Councils already passed concerning this noble subiect; and yet affirmes that he doth not debate the question, but as a Questionist, and without resolution: As if a Cardinal should be afraid to be positiue, and to speake in peremptory straines, after Popes and Councils haue once decided the Question: Or as if a man should perorate vpon hazard, in a cause for the honour whereof, he would make no difficultie to suffer Martyrdome. Adde hereunto, that his Lordship hath alwayes taken the contrary part heretofore, and this totall must needs arise, that before the third Estate, his lips looked one way, and his conscience another.

All these points, by the discourse which is to follow, and by the ripping vp of his Oration (which by Gods assistance I will vndertake) tending to the reproch of Kings, and the subuersion of kingdomes, I confidently speake it, shalbe made manifest. Yet doe

・ I not

In the Pre-
face to my A-
pologie,

I not conceiue it can any way make for my honour, to enter the lists against a Cardinall: For I am not ignorant how farre a Cardinals Hat, commeth vnder the Crowne and Scepter of a King; For well I wot vnto what sublimitie the Scripture hath exalted Kings, when it styles them Gods; Whereas the dignitie of a Cardinall is but a late vpstart inuention of man; as I haue elsewhere prooued. But I haue imbarqued my selfe in this action, mooued thereunto: First, by the common interest of Kings in the cause it selfe: Then by the L. Cardinall, who speaketh not in this Oration as a priuate person, but as one representing the body of the Clergie and Nobilitie, by whom the cause hath bene wonne, and the garland borne away from the third Estate: Againe, by mine owne particular; because he is pleased to take me vp for a sower of dissention, and a persecutour, vnder whom the Church is hardly able to fetch her breath; yea, for one by whom the Catholikes of my Kingdome are compelled to endure all sorts of punishments; and withal he tearmes this Article of the third Estate, a monster with a fishes taile that came swimming out of England: Last of all, by the present state of France; because France being now reduced to so miserable tearmes, that it is now become a crime for a Frenchman to stand for his King; it is a necessary duetie of her neighbours to speake in her cause, and to make triall whether they can put life into the trewth now dying, and ready to be buried by the power of violence, that it may resound and ring againe from remote regions.

I haue no purpose once to touch many prettie toyes which the ridges of his whole booke are sowen withall: Such are his allegations of Pericles, Agesilaus, Aristotle, Minos, the Druides; the French Ladies, Hannibal, Pindarus, and Poeticall fables: All resembling the red and blew flowers that pester the corne when it standeth in the fields, where they are more noysome to the growing crop, then beautifull to the beholding eye. Such pettie matters, nothing at all beseemed the dignitie of the Assembly, and of the maine subiect, or of the Orator himselfe: For it was no Decorum to enter the Stage with a Pericles in his mouth, but with the sacred Name of God; nor should hee haue marshalled the passage of a Royall Poet,

Poet, after the example of an heathen Oratour.

Neither will I giue any touch to his conceit of the Romane ᵃ Pag. 4. *conquests, which the L. Cardinall bestoweth in the list of Gods graces and temporall blessings, as a recompence of their zeale to the seruice and worship of Idols: As if God were a recompencer of wickednes, or as if the forcible eiecting of Tenants out of their farmes and other possessions, might be reckoned among the blessings of God.*

Nor to that of the Milesian *Virgins, dragged stark-naked* Pag.7. & 8. *after they were dead; which the L. Cardinall drawes into his discourse for an example of the eternall torments denounced by the Lawes Ecclesiasticall, to be inflicted after this life.*

Nor to his exposition of the word Problematicall *; where he* Pag. 13. *giueth to vnderstand that by Problematicall, hee meaneth such things as are of no necessitie to matter of faith; and in case men shall beleeue the contradictory of the said points, they are not bound for such beleefe, to vndergoe the solemne curse of the Church, and the losse of communion: Whereas* Aristotle, *of whom all Schooles* Aristot. 1.top. cap. 4. σαφ πασᾶ κφ σφοδολίσεως, found both one thing, Ανθ πασας γδ φσυταδονεε πσφωσας ποιανες, prouided the word πιντσι or στισμ, do stand before, as, Verum homo sit animal. *haue borrowed their tearmes, hath taught vs that euery proposition is called a* Probleme, *when it is propounded in a formall doubt, though in it proper nature it containes a necessary trewth, concerning the matter therof: As for example, to say in forme of question,* Whether *is there but one God? or,* Whether *is man a creature indued with reason? By which examples it is plaine, that propositions in problematicall forme, doe not forgoe the necessitie of their nature; and that many times the contradictory binds the beleeuers thereof to* Anathema *and losse of communion.*

There is a confused heape or bundle of other like toyes, which my purpose is to passe ouer in silence, that I may now come to cast anchor, as it were in the very bottome and substance of the cause.

A Re-

A REMONSTRANCE

FOR THE RIGHT OF

KINGS, AND THE INDEPEN-

DENCIE OF THEIR CROVVNES.

Against an Oration of the most Illustrious Cardinall
of PERRON, pronounced in the Chamber of
the third Estate.

The 15. of Ianuar. 1615.

HE L.Cardinall euen in the first passage of his Oration, hath laid a firme foundation, *That Ecclesiastics in France are more deepely obliged to the King, then the Nobilitie, and third Estate*: His reason; Becaufe the Clergie doe fweetly enioy their dignities and promotions, with all their infinite wealth, of the Kings meere grace, without all danger, and with faire immunities ; whereas the other two Orders hold their offices by a chargeable and burdenfome title or tenure, euen to the great expence of their blood, and of their fubftance. But fee now, how loofe and weake a frame he hath erected and pinned together, vpon his firme and folide foundation: *Ergo*, the third Eftate is to lay all care to prouide remedies againft appofted cut-throats, vpon the Clergy; and the faid remedies (as he boldly affirms) muft be deriued from the laws of confcience, which may carry an effectuall acting or operatiue efficacie vpon the foule, and not from ciuil or temporall punifhments. Now this confequence limpeth like a lame creple after the premifes · For it is no vfuall and common matter, to fee men that are deepeft in obligation, performe their duties and couenants with moft fidelity. Againe, were it graunted the Clergie had well hitherto demonftrated their carefull watching ouer the life and honour of their Prince; yet is it not for fpirituall punifhments thundred by Ecclefiaftics, to bind the hands of the ciuill Magiftrate, nor to ftop the current of temporall

porall punishments : which ordinarily doe carrie a greater force and
vertue to the bridling of the wicked, then the apprehension of Gods
iudgement.

The third Estate therefore, by whom all the officers of France are properly represented, as to whom the administration of iustice and protection of the Kings rights and Honour doth appertaine, can deserue no blame
in carrying so watchfull an eye, by their wholesome remedie to prouide
for the safetie of the King, and for the dignitie of his Crowne. For if the
Clergie shall not stand to their tackle, but shrinke when it commeth to the
push of their duetie; who shall charge themselues with carefull foresight
and preuention of mischiefes ? Shall not the people ? Now, haue not all the
calamities, which the third Estate haue sought prouidently to preuent;
haue they not all sprung from the Clergie, as from their proper and naturall fountaine ? From whence did the last ciuill warres, wherein a world of
blood was not more profusely then prodigiously and vnnaturally spilt, and
wherein the parricide of King *Henrie III.* was impiously and abominably
committed : from whence did those bloodie warres proceed, but from the
deposing of the said King by the Head of the Church ? Were they not Prelats, Curats, and Confessours; were they not Ecclesiastics, who partly
by seditious preachments, and partly by secret confessions, powred many
a iarre of oyle vpon this flame ? Was not he that killed the forenamed King,
was not he one of the Clergie ? Was not *Guignard* a Iesuite ? Was not *Iohn
Chastel* brought vp in the same schoole ? Did not *Rauaillac* that monster
of men, vpon interrogatories made at his examination; among the rest,
by whom he had beene so diabolically tempted and stirred vp to his most
execrable attempt and act of extreme horror : did not he referre his exami-
ners to the Sermons made the Lent next before, where they might be satisfied concerning the causes of his abominable vndertaking and execution ?
Are not *Bellarmine*, *Eudæmonoiohannes*, *Suarez*, *Becanus*, *Mariana*, with
such other monsters, who teach the doctrine of parricides, vphold the
craft of Ianus-like Equiuocations in Courts of Iustice, and in secret confessions : are they not all Clerics ? are not all their bookes approoued and allowed, as it were by a corporation or grosse companie of Doctors, with
their signes manuel to the said bookes ? What were the heads, the chiefe
promoters, the complices of the powder-conspiracie in my Kingdome ?
were they not Ecclesiastics ? Hath not *Faux* by name, a confederate of the
same damned crew ; hath not he stoutly stood to the gunners part, which
then he was to act in that most dolefull Tragedie, with asseueration of a
conscience well assured and setled, touching the lawfulnesse of his enterprise ? Did he not yeild this reason ? to wit, because he had bin armed with
instruction of musket proofe in the case, before he made passage ouer from
the Low Countries ? Is it not also the generall beleefe of that Order, that
Clerics are exempted from the condition of Subiects to the King ? Nay, is
it not confessed by the L. Cardinall himselfe, that King-killers haue ingaged `Pag. 7.`
                                                                    themselues

themselues to vndertake the deteftable act of parricide vnder a falfe cre-
dence of Religion, as beeing inftructed by their fchoolemafters in Religion? And who were they but Ecclefiafticall perfons? All this prefuppofed
as matter of trewth,I draw this conclufion: Howfoeuer no fmall number
of the French Clergie may perhaps beare the affection of louing Subiects
to their King, and may not fuffer the Clericall character to deface the impreffion of naturall allegiance; yet, for fo much as the Order of Clerics is
dipped in a deeper die, and beareth a worfe tincture of daungerous practifes then the other Orders; the third Eftate had beene greatly wanting to
their excellent prouidence and wifedome, if they fhould haue relinquifhed
and transferred the care of defignements and proiects for the life of their
King, and the fafety of his Crowne, to the Clergie alone. Moreouer, the
Clergie ftandeth bound to referre the iudgement of all matters in controuerfie, to the fentence of the Pope, in this caufe beeing a partie, and one
that pretendeth Crownes to depend vpon his Mitre. What hope then
might the third Eftate conceiue,that his Holineffe would paffe againft his
owne caufe, when his iudgement of the controuerfie had beene fundrie
times before publifhed and teftified to the world? And whereas the plot
or modell of remedies proiected by the third Eftate,and the Kings Officers,
hath not prooued fortable in the euent: was it becaufe the faid remedies
were not good and lawfull? No verily: but becaufe the Clergie refufed to
become contributors of their duty and meanes to the grand feruice. Likewife, for that after the burning of bookes, addreffed to iuftifie rebellious
people, traytors, and parricides of Kings; neuertheleffe the authors of the
faid bookes are winked at, and backt with fauour. Laftly, for that fome
wretched parricides drinke off the cuppe of publike iuftice; whereas to
the firebrands of fedition, the fowers of this abominable doctrine, no man
faith fo much as blacke is their eye.

It fufficiently appeareth, as I fupofe, by the former paffage, that his
Lordfhip exhorting the third Eftate to referre the whole care of this Regall
caufe vnto the Clergie, hath tacked his frame of weake ioynts and renons
to a very worthy but wrong foundation. Howbeit, he laboureth to fortifie his exhortation with a more weake and feeble reafon: For to make
good his proiect he affirmes, that matters and maximes out of all doubt
and queftion, may not be fhuffled together with points in controuerfie.
Now his rules indubitable are two · The firft, It is not lawfull to murther
Kings for any caufe whatfoeuer: This he confirmeth by the example of
Saul (as he faith) depofed from his Throne, whofe life or limbs *Dauid* neuertheleffe durft not once hurt or wrong for his life: Likewife he con-
firmes the fame by a Decree of the Councill held at Conftance: His other
point indubitable; The Kings of France are Soueraignes in all Temporall
Soueraigntie, within the French Kingdome, and hold not by fealtie either
of the Pope,as hauing receiued or obliged their Crownes vpon fuch tenure
and condition, or of any other Prince in the whole world, Which point,
neuer-

Page.3.

Conc. Conftan.
Seff.15.

neuertheleffe he takes not for certaine and indubitable, but onely according
to humane and hiftoricall certaintie. Now a third point he makes to be fo
full of controuerfie, and fo farre within the circle of difputable queftions,
as it may not be drawne into the ranke of clafficall and authenticall points,
for feare of making a certaine point doubtfull, by fhuffling and iumbling
therewith fome point in controuerfie. Now the queftion fo difputable, as
he pretendeth, is this: A Chriftian Prince breakes his oath folemnely taken to God, both to liue and to die in the Catholique Religion: Say this
Prince turnes Arrian, or Mahometan, fals to proclaime open warre, and
to wage battell with Iefus Chrift: Whether may fuch a Prince be declared
to haue loft his Kingdome, and who fhall declare the Subiects of fuch a
Prince to be quit of their oath of allegiance? The L. Cardinall holds the
affirmatiue, and makes no bones to maintaine, that all other parts of the
Catholique Church, yea the French Church, euen from the firft birth of
her Theologicall Schooles, to *Caluins* time and teaching, haue profeffed
that fuch a Prince may bee lawfully remooued from his Throne by the
Pope, and by the Councill: and fuppofe the contrarie doctrine we e the
very Quinteffence or fpirit of trewth, yet might it not in cafe of faith be
vrged and preffed otherwife then by way of problematicall difceptation.
That is the fumme of his Lordfhips ample difcourfe: The refuting whereof I am conftrained to put off, and referre vnto an other place; becaufe he
hath ferued vs with the fame difhes ouer and ouer againe. There we fhall
fee the L. Cardinall maketh way to the difpatching of Kings after depofition: that *Saul* was not depofed, as he hath prefumed: that in the Councill
of Conftance there is nothing to the purpofe of murthering Soueraigne
Princes: that his Lordfhip, fuppofing the French King may be depriued of
his Crowne by a fuperiour power, doth not hold his liege Lord to be So-
ueraine in France: that by the pofition of the French Church from aage to
aage, the Kings of France are not fubiect vnto any cenfure of depofition by
the Pope: that his Holineffe hath no iuft and lawfull pretence to produce,
that any Chriftian King holds of him by fealtie, or is obliged to doe the
Pope homage for his Crowne.

Well then, for the purpofe; he dwelleth onely vpon the third point pretended queftionable, and this hee affirmeth: If any fhall condemne, or
wrappe vnder the folemne curfe, the abettours of the Popes power to vn-
king lawfull and Soueraigne Kings; the fame fhall runne vpon foure dangerous rocks of apparent incongruities and abfurdities.

Firft, he fhall offer to force and entangle the confciences of many deuout
perfons: For he fhall binde them to beleeue and fweare that doctrine, the
contrary whereof is beleeued of the whole Church, and hath bene beleeued by their Predeceffors.

Secondly, he fhall ouerturne from top to bottome the facred authoritie
of holy Church, and fhall fet open a gate vnto all forts of herefie, by allowing Lay-perfons a bold libertie to be iudges in caufes of Religion and
                                                            Faith

Pag. 14.
,,
,,   2
,,
,,

" Faith: For what is that degree of boldnesse, but open vsurping of the
" Prieſthood ; what is it but putting of prophane hands vpon the Arke;
" what is it but laying of vnholy fingers vpon the holy Cenſor for perfumes?

3   "   Thirdly, hee ſhall make way to a Schiſme, not poſſible to bee put by
" and auoyded by any humane prouidence. For this doctrine beeing held
" and profeſſed by all other Catholiques; how can we declare it repugnant
" vnto Gods word; how can wee hold it impious ; how can wee account it
" deteſtable, but wee ſhall renounce communion with the Head and other
" members of the Church ; yea, we ſhall confeſſe the Church in all aages to
" haue bene the Synagogue of Satan, and the ſpouſe of the Deuill?

4   "   Laſtly, by working the eſtabliſhment of this Article, which worketh an
" eſtabliſhment of Kings Crownes; He ſhall not onely worke the intended
" remedy for the danger of Kings, out of all the vertue and efficacie there-
" of, by weakening of doctrine out of all controuerſie, in packing it vp with
" a diſputable queſtion ; but likewiſe in ſtead of ſecuring the life and eſtate
" of Kings, he ſhall draw both into farre greater hazards, by the traine or ſe-
" quence of warres, and other calamities , which vſually waite and attend
" on Schiſmes.

The L. Cardinall ſpends his whole diſcourſe in confirmation of theſe
foure heads, which wee now intend to ſift in order, and demonſtratiuely
to prooue that all the ſaid inconueniences are meere nullities , matters of
imagination, and built vpon falſe preſuppoſitions. But before wee come
to the maine, the reader is to be enformed and aduertiſed, that his Lordſhip
ſetteth a falſe gloſſe vpon the queſtion ; and propounds the caſe not onely
contrary to the trewth of the ſubiect in controuerſie, but alſo to the Popes
owne minde and meaning : For he reſtraines the Popes power to depoſe
Kings, onely to caſes of Hereſie, Apoſtaſie, and perſecuting of the Church;
whereas Popes extend their power to a further diſtance. They depoſe
Princes for infringing , or in any ſort diminiſhing the Priuiledges of Monaſteries: witneſſe *Gregorie* the firſt in the pretended Charter granted to
the Abbey of *S. Medard* at *Soiſſons ;* the ſaid Charter beeing annexed to his
Epiſtles in the rere. The ſame hee teſtifieth in his Epiſtle to *Senator,* by
name the tenth of the eleuenth booke. They depoſe for naturall dulneſſe
and lacke of capacitie, wether in-bred and trew indeed, or onely pretended
and imagined : witneſſe the glorious vaunt of *Gregory* VII. that *Childeric*

Cauſ. 15.
Can Alius.
Qu.6.

King of France was hoyſted out of his Throne by Pope *Zachary,* *Not ſo
much for his wicked life , as for his vnableneſſe to beare the weightie burden of ſo
great a Kingdome.* They depoſe for collating of Benefices and Prebends:
witneſſe the great quarrels and ſore contentions betweene Pope *Innocent*
III. and *Iohn* King of England : as alſo betweene *Philip* the Faire and *Boniface* VIII. They depoſe for adulteries and Matrimoniall ſuites: witnes
Philip I. for the repudiating or caſting off his lawfull wife *Bertha* , and

Paul Aemil.
in Phi'.3.

marrying in her place with *Bertrade* wife to the Earle of Aniou. Finally,
faine would I learne into what Hereſie or degree of Apoſtaſie, either

Henry

Henry IV. or *Frederic Barbaroſſa*, or *Frederic* II. Emperours were fallen, when they were ſmitten with Papall fulminations, euen to the depriuation of their Imperiall Thrones. What? was it for Hereſie or Apoſtaſie, that Pope *Martin* IV. bare ſo hard a hand againſt *Peter* King of Arragon, that he acquitted and releaſed the Aragonnois from their oath of Alleagiance to *Peter* their lawfull King? Was it for Hereſie or Apoſtaſie, for Arrianiſme or Mahumetiſme, that *Lewis* XII. ſo good a King and Father of his Countrey, was put downe by *Iulius* the II? Was it for Hereſie or Apoſtaſie, that *Sixtus* V. vſurped a power againſt *Henrie* III. euen ſo farre as to denounce him vnkingd; the iſſue whereof was the parricide of that good King, and the moſt wofull deſolation of a moſt flouriſhing Kingdome? But his Lordſhip beſt liked to worke vpon that ground, which to the outward ſhew and appearance, is the moſt beautifull cauſe that can be alleaged for the diſhonouring of Kings by the weapon of depoſition : making himſelfe to beleeue that he acted the part of an Orator before perſonages not much acqainted with ancient and moderne hiſtories, and ſuch as little vnderſtood the ſtate of the queſtion then in hand. It had therefore beene a good warrant for his Lordſhip, to haue brought ſome authenticall inſtrument from the Pope, whereby the French might haue beene ſecured, that his Holineſſe renounceth all other cauſes auouchable for the degrading of Kings; and that he will henceforth reſt in the caſe of Hereſie, for the turning of Kings out of their Free-hold : as alſo that his Holineſſe by the ſame or like inſtrument might haue certified his pleaſure, that hee will not hereafter make himſelfe Iudge, whether Kings bee tainted with damnable Hereſie, or free from Hereticall infection. For that were to make himſelfe both Iudge and Plaintiffe, that it might be in his power to call that doctrine Hereticall, which is pure Orthodoxe : and all for this end, to make himſelfe maſter of the Kingdome, and there to ſettle a Succeſſour, who receiuing the Crowne of the Popes free gift and grant, might be tyed thereby to depend altogether vpon his Holineſſe. Hath not Pope *Boniface* VIII. declared in his proud Letters all thoſe to be Heretiques, that dare vndertake to affirme, the collating of Prebends apperteineth to the King? It was that Popes groſſe errour, not in the fact, but in the right. The like crime forſooth was by Popes imputed to the vnhappy Emperour *Henrie* IV. And what was the iſſue of the ſaid imputation? The ſonne is inſtigated thereby to rebell againſt his father, and to impeach the interrement of his dead corps, who neuer in his life had beate his braines to trouble the ſweet waters of Theologicall fountaines. It is recorded by *Auentine*, that Biſhop *Virgilius* was declared Heretique, for teaching the Poſition of Antipodes. The Bull *Exurge*, marching in the rere of the laſt Lateran Councel, ſets downe this Poſition for one of *Luthers* hereſies, *A new life is the beſt repentance.* Among the crimes which the Councel of Conſtance charged Pope *Iohn* XXIII. withall, one was this, that hee denied the immortalitie of the ſoule, and that *ſo much was publiquely,*

Annal. Boio.
Lib. 3.
Inuanen.
Epiſcop.

Optima pœnitentia nona
vita.
Conc. Conſtan. Seſſ. 2.

L l

liquely, manifestly, and notoriously knowen. Now if the Pope shall be caried by the streame of these or the like errours, and in his Hereticall prauitie shall depose a King of the contrary opinion, I shall hardly bee perswaded, the said King is lawfully deposed.

THE FIRST INCONVENI-
ENCE EXAMINED.

THE first inconuenience growing (in the Cardinall his conceit) by entertaining the Article of the third Estate (whereby the Kings of France are declared to be indeposeable by any superiour power spirituall or temporall) is this: *It offereth*
" *force to the conscience, vnder the penaltie of Anathema, to con-*
" *demne a doctrine beleeued and practised in the Church, in the continuall current of*
" *the last eleuen hundred yeeres.* In these words he maketh a secret confession, that in the first fiue hundred yeeres, the same doctrine was neither apprehended by faith, nor approoued by practise. Wherein, to my vnderstanding, the L. Cardinall voluntarily giueth ouer the suite: For the Church in the time of the Apostles, their disciples, and successors, for 500. yeeres together, was no more ignorant what authoritie the Church is to challenge ouer Emperours and Kings, then at any time since in any succeeding aage; in which as pride hath still flowed to the height of a full Sea, so puritie of religion and manners hath kept for the most part at a lowe water-marke. Which point is the rather to be considered, for that during the first 500. yeeres, the Church groned vnder the heauy burthen, both of heathen Emperours, and of hereticall Kings; the Visigot Kings in Spaine, and the Vandals in Affrica. Of whose displeasure the Pope had small reason or cause to stand in any feare, beeing so remote from their dominions, and no way vnder the lee of their Soueraigntie.

But let vs come to see, what aide the L. Cardinall hath amassed and piled together out of latter histories: prouided wee still beare in mind, that our question is not of popular tumults, nor of the rebellion of subiects making insurrections out of their owne discontented spirits and brainesicke humors, nor of lawfull Excommunications, nor of Canonicall censures and reprehensions; but onely of a iuridicall sentence of deposition, pronounced by the Pope, as armed with ordinary and lawfull power to depose, against a Soueraigne Prince.

Now then, The L. Cardinall sets on, and giues the first charge with *Anastasius* the Emperour, whom *Euphemius* Patriarke of Constantinople would neuer acknowledge for Emperour : (that is to say, would neuer consent he should be created Emperour by the helpe of his voice or suffrage) except he would first subscribe to the *Chalcedon* Creed : notwithstanding
the

he great Empreſſe and Senate ſought by violent courſes and practiſes to make him yeeld. And when afterward the ſaid Emperour, contrary to his oath taken, played the relaps by falling into his former hereſie, and became a perſecutor; he was firſt admoniſhed, and then excommunicated by *Symmachus* Biſhop of Rome. To this the L. Cardinall addes, that when the ſaid Emperour was minded to choppe the poiſon of his hereticall aſſertions into the publique formes of diuine ſeruice, then the people of Conſtantinople made an vproare againſt *Anaſtaſius* their Emperour; and one of his Commanders by force of armes, conſtrained him to call backe ceraine Biſhops whom he had ſent into baniſhment before.

In this firſt example the L. Cardinall by his good leaue, neither comes cloſe to the queſtion, nor ſalutes it a farre off. *Euphemius* was not Biſhop of Rome: *Anaſtaſius* was not depoſed by *Euphemius*; the Patriarch onely made no way to the creating of *Anaſtaſius*. The ſuddaine commotion of the baſe multitude makes nothing, the rebellion of a Greeke Commaunder makes leſſe, for the authorizing of the Pope to depoſe a Soueraigne Prince. The Greeke Emperour was excommunicated by Pope *Symmachus*: who knowes whether that be trew or forged? For the Pope himſelfe is the onely witneſſe here produced by the L. Cardinall vpon the point: and who knowes not how falſe, how ſuppoſititious, the writings and Epiſtles of the auncient Popes are iuſtly eſteemed? But graunt it a trewth; yet *Anaſta-*
ius excommunicated by Pope *Symmachus*, is not *Anaſtaſius* depoſed by Pope *Symmachus*. And to make a full anſwere, I ſay further, that excommuniation denounced by a forraine Biſhop, againſt a party not beeing within the limits of his iuriſdiction, or one of his owne flocke, was not any barre to the party from the communion of the Church, but onely a kind of publiſation, that he the ſaid Biſhop in his particular, would hold no further communion with any ſuch party.

For proofe whereof, I produce the Canons of the Councils held at Carthage. In one of the ſaid Canons it is thus prouided and ordained; If any Biſhop ſhall wilfully abſent himſelfe from the vſuall and accuſtomed Synodes, let him not be admitted to the communion of other Churches, but *let him onely vſe the benefit and libertie of his owne Church.* In an other of the ſame Canons thus; * If a Biſhop ſhall inſinuate himſelfe to make a conueiance of his Monaſterie, and the ordering thereof vnto a Monke of any other Cloiſter; let him be cut off, *let him be ſeparated from the communion with other Churches, and content himſelfe to liue in the communion of his owne flocke.* In the ſame ſenſe *Hilarius* Biſhop of Poictiers excommunicated *Liberius* Biſhop of Rome, for ſubſcribing to the Arrian Confeſſion. In the ſame ſenſe, *Iohn* Biſhop of Antioch excommunicated *Caleſtine* of Rome, and *Cyrill* of Alexandria, Biſhops; for proceeding to ſentence againſt *Neſtorius,* without ſtaying his comming to anſwere in his owne cauſe. In the ſame ſenſe likewiſe, *Victor* Biſhop of Rome did cut off all the Biſhops of the Eaſt, not from the communion of their owne flocks, but from communion

with

* *Nomocan.*
*Affric Can.*77.
Ὀφείλει τῆς
τοιούτης τῆς κοι-
νωνία Τῆς ἰδίας
αὐτῇ ἀρκεῖσθαι
ἐκκλησίας.

* *Can.*81.*eiuſd.*
Nomo.
Χωρὶς τῆς λοιπῆς
κοινωνίας χωρι-
ζέσθως τῆς τε
ἰδίᾳ δὲ κοινωνίᾳ
ἀρκεῖσθαι μόνον.

Anathema tibi
a me Liberi.
Faber. in frag.
Hilarij.

with *Victor* and the Romane Church. What refemblance, what agreement, what proportion, betweene this courfe of excommunication, and that way of vniuft fulmination which the Popes of Rome haue vfurped againft Kings, but yet certaine long courfes of time after that auncient courfe?

Examp. 2.

And this may ftand for a full anfwere likewife to the example of *Clotharius*. This ancient King of the French, fearing the cenfures of Pope *Agapetus*, erected the Territorie of Yuetot vnto the title of a Kingdome, by way of fatisfaction for murdering of *Gualter*, Lord of Yuetot. For this example the L. Cardinall hath ranfackt records of 900. yeeres antiquitie and vpward; in which times it were no hard piece of worke to fhew, that Popes would not haue any hand, nor fo much as a finger in the affaires and acts of the French Kings. *Gregorie* of Tours that liued in the fame aage, hath recorded many acts of excefle, and violent iniuries done againft Bifhops by their Kings, and namely againft *Prætextatus* Bifhop of Roan; for any of which iniurious prankes then played, the Bifhop of Rome durft not reprooue the faid Kings with due remonftrance. But fee heere the words of *Gregorie* himfelfe to King *Chilperic*; *If any of vs, O King, fhall fwarue from the path of Iuftice, him haft thou power to punifh: But in cafe thou fhalt at any time tranfgrefse the lines of equitie, who fhall once touch thee with reproofe? To thee wee fpeake, but are neuer heeded and regarded, except it be thy pleafure: and hee thou not pleafed, who fhall challenge thy greatnefse, but hee that iuftly challengeth to bee Iuftice it felfe?* The good Bifhop, notwithftanding thefe humble remonftrances, was but roughly entreated, and packt into exile, being banifhed into the Ifle of Guernfay. But I am not minded to make any deepe fearch or inquifition, into the titles of the Lords of Yuetot; whofe honourable priuiledges and titles are the moft honourable badges and cognizances of their Anceftours, and of fome remarkeable feruice done to the Crowne of France: fo farre I take them to differ from a fatisfaction for finne: And for the purpofe I onely affirme, that were the credit of this hiftorie beyond all exception, yet makes it nothing to the prefent queftion, Wherein the power of depofing, and not of excommunicating fupreme Kings, is debated. And fuppofe the King by Charter granted the faid priuiledges for feare of Excommunication; how is it prooued thereby, that Pope *Agapetus* had lawfull and ordinary power to depriue him of his Crowne? Nay, doubtlefle it was rather a meanes to eleuate and aduance the dignitie of the Crowne of France, and to ftyle the French King, a King of Kings, as one that was able to giue the qualitie of King, to all the reft of the Nobles and Gentry of his Kingdome. Doeth not fome part of the Spanifh Kings greatnefle, confift in creating of his, great?

Examp. 3. *pag.* 22.

In the next place followeth *Gregorie I.* who in the 10. Epiftle of the 11. booke, confirming the priuiledges of the Hofpitall at *Auguftodunum* in *Bourgongne*, prohibiteth all Kings and Prelates whatfoeuer, to infringe or diminifh the faid priuiledges, in whole or in part. His formall and ex-
prefle

preſſe words bee theſe :, *If any King, Prelate, Iudge, or any other Secular per-_ ſon, informed of this our Conſtitution, ſhall preſume to goe or doe contrary thereunto, let him bee caſt downe from his power and dignitie.* I anſwere; the Lord Cardinall heere wrongs himſelfe very much, in taking imprecations for Decrees. Might not euen the meaneſt of the people vſe the ſame tenour of words, and ſay? If any ſhall touch the life, or the moſt ſacred Maieſtie of our Kings, be he Emperour, or be he Pope, let him bee accurſed ; let him fall from his eminent place of authoritie; let him loſe his dignitie ; let him tumble into beggerie, diſeaſes, and all kindes of calamities ? I forbeare to ſhew how eaſie a matter it is for Monkes, to forge titles after their owne humour, and to their owne liking, for the vpholding and maintaining of their priuiledges. As for the purpoſe, the ſame *Gregorie* citeth in the end of his Epiſtles another priuiledge, of the like ſtuffe and ſtampe to the former, granted to the Abbey of *S. Medard* at Soiſſons: It is fenced with a like clauſe to the other, But of how great vntrewth, and of how little weight it is, the very date that it beareth, makes manifeſt proofe: For it runs, Dated the yeere of our Lords Incarnation 593. the 11. Indiction; whereas the 10. Indiction agreeth to the yeere 593. Beſides, it was not *Gregories* maner to date his Epiſtles according to the yeere of the Lord. Againe, the ſaid priuiledge was ſigned by the Biſhops of Alexandria and Carthage, who neuer knew (as may well bee thought) whether any ſuch Abbey of S. *Medard,* or citie of Soiſſons, was euer built in the world. Moreouer, they ſigned in the thickeſt of a crowd as it were of Italian Biſhops. Laſtly, hee that ſhall reade in this *Gregories* Epiſtles, with what ſpirit of reuerence and humilitie he ſpeaketh of Emperours, will hardly beleeue that euer hee armed himſelfe with authoritie to giue or to take away Kingdomes. Hee ſtyles himſelfe *The Emperours vnworthie ſeruant : preſuming to ſpeake vnto his Lord, when he knowes himſelfe to bee but duſt and a very worme: Hee profeſ-ſeth ſubiection vnto the Emperours commands, euen to the publiſhing of a certaine Law of the Emperours, which in his iudgement ſomewhat iarred and iuſtled with Gods Law* ; as elſewhere I haue ſpoken more at large.

* *Epiſt.6. l.3. Ego autem in-dignus pietatis tuæ ſeruus. Ego verò hæc Domino meis loquens, quid ſum niſi puluis & vermis ? Ibid. Ego qui-dem iuſſioni ſubiectus, &c. Epiſt. c 1.l.2.*

The L. Cardinall next bringeth vpon the ſtage *Iuſtinian II.* Hee, being in ſome choller with *Sergius* Biſhop of Rome, becauſe hee would not fauour the erroneous Synode of Conſtantinople, would haue cauſed the Biſhop to bee apprehended by his Conſtable *Zacharias.* But by the Romane *Militia,* (that is, the troupes which the Emperour then had in Italie) *Zacharias* was repulſed and hindered from his deſeigne, euen with opprobrious and reproachfull termes. His Lordſhip muſt haue my ſhallow-neſſe excuſed, if I reach not his intent by this Allegation; wherein I ſee not one word of depoſing from the Empire, or of any ſentence pronounced by the Pope.

Examp.4.

Heere are now 712. yeeres expired after the birth of Ieſus Chriſt : in all which long tract of time, the L. Cardinal hath not light vpon any inſtance, which might make for his purpoſe with neuer ſo little ſhew: For the example

ample of the Emperor *Philippicus* by the Cardinall alledged next in fequence, belongeth to the yeere 713. And thus lies the hiftorie: This Emperour *Philippicus Bardanes*, was a profeffed enemie to the worfhipping of Images, and commanded them to be broken in pieces. In that very time the Romane Empire was ouerthrowen in the Weft, and fore fhaken by the Saracenes in the Eaft. Befides thofe miferies, the Emperour was alfo incumbred with a ciuill and inteftine warre. The greateft part of Italie was then feized by the Lombards, and the Emperour in Italie had nothing left faue onely the Exarchat of Rauenna, and the Dutchie of Rome, then halfe abandoned by reafon of the Emperours want of forces. Pope *Conftantine* gripes this occafion whereon to ground his greatneffe, and to fhake off the yoke of the Emperour his Lord, Vndertakes againft *Philippicus* the caufe of Images : by a Councel declares the Emperour Heretique: Prohibites his refcripts or coine to bee receiued, and to goe current in Rome: Forbids his Imperiall ftatue to bee fet vp in the Temple, according to ancient cuftome: The tumult groweth to a height: The Pope is principall promoter of the tumult: In the heate of the tumult the Exarche of Rauenna lofeth his life. Here fee now the mutinie of a fubiect againft his Prince, to pull from him by force and violence a citie of his Empire. But who feeth in all this any fentence of depofition from the Imperiall dignitie? Nay, the Pope then miffed the cufhion, and was difappointed vtterly of his purpofe : The citie of Rome ftood firme, and continued ftill in their obedience to the Emperour.

About fome 12. yeeres after, the Emperour *Leo Ifauricus* (whom the Lord of Perron calleth *Iconoclaft*) falles to fight it out at fharpe, and to profecute worfhippers of Images with all extremitie. Vpon this occafion, Pope *Gregory* 2. then treading in the fteps of his predeceffor, when he perceiued the citie of Rome to be but weakely prouided of men or munition, and the Emperour to haue his hands full in other places, found fuch meanes to make the citie rife in rebellious armes againft the Emperour, that he made himfelfe in fhort time mafter thereof. Thus farre the Lord Cardinall, whereunto my anfwere for fatisfaction is; that degrading an Emperour from his Imperiall dignitie, and reducing a citie to reuolt againft her Mafter, that a man at laft may carry the piece himfelfe, and make himfelfe Lord thereof, are two feuerall actions of fpeciall difference. If the free-hold of the citie had beene conueied to fome other by the Pope depriuing the Emperour, as proprietarie thereof, this example might haue challenged fome credit at leaft in fhew : but fo to inuade the citie to his owne vfe, and fo to feize on the right and authority of another, what is it but open rebellion, and notorious ambition? For it is farre from Ecclefiafticall cenfure, when the fpirituall Paftor of foules forfooth, pulles the cloake of a poore finner from his backe by violence, or cuts his purfe, and thereby appropriates an other mans goods to his priuate vfe. It is to be obferued withall, that when the Emperours were not of fufficient ftrength, and

Popes

Popes had power to beard and to braue Emperours, then thefe Papall practifes were firft fet on foot. This Emperour notwithftanding, turned
head and peckt againe: his Lieutenant entred Rome, and *Gregorie* 3. fucceffor to this *Gregorie* 2. was glad to honour the fame Emperour with
ftyle and title of his Lord: witneffe two feuerall Epiftles of the faid *Grego-*
rie 3. written to *Boniface*, and fubfcribed in this forme: *Dated the tenth Ca-*
lends of December: In the raigne of our moſt pious and religious Lord, Auguſtus
Leo, crowned of God, the great Emperour, in the tenth yeere of his raigné.

Dat. 10.
Cal. Decem Im-
perante Dom.
piiſſimo Augu-
ſto Leone, à
Deo coronato,
magno Imp.
anno decimo
Imperij eius.
Examp. 7.

The L. Cardinall with no leffe abufe alleadgeth Pope *Zacharie*, by whom
the French, as he affirmeth, were abfolued of the oath of allegiance, wherein they ſtood bound to *Childeric* their King: And for this inftance, he ftandeth vpon the teftimonie of *Paulus Aemilius*, and *du Tillet*, a paire of late
writers. But by authors more neere that aage wherein *Childeric* raigned, it
is more trewly teſtified, that it was a free and voluntarie act of the French,
onely asking the aduife of Pope *Zacharie*, but requiring neither leaue nor
abfolution. *Ado* Bifhop of *Vienna*, in his Chronicles hath it after this manner: *The French, following the Counſell of Embaſſadors, and of Pope* Zachary,
electd Pepin *their King, and eſtabliſhed him in the Kingdome.* Trithemius in
his abridgement of Annals, thus: Childeric, *as one vnfit for gouernement,*
was turnd out of his Kingdome, with common conſent of the Eſtates and Peeres of
the Realme, ſo aduiſed by Zacharie Pope *of Rome.* Godfridus of *Viterbe* in the
17. part of his Chronicle, and *Guauguin* in the life of *Pepin*, affirme the
fame. And was it not an eafie matter to worke *Pepin* by counfell to lay
hold on the Kingdome, when he could not be hindered from faftening on
the Crowne, and had already feizd it in effect, howfoeuer he had not yet attained to the name of King? Moreouer, the rudeneffe of that Nation,
then wanting knowledge and Schooles either of diuinitie, or of Academi-
call fciences, was a kind of fpurre to make them runne for counfell ouer
the mountaines: which neuerthelelle in a caufe of fuch nature, they required not as neceffary, but onely as decent and for fafhion fake. The
Pope alfo for his part was well appaied, by this meanes to draw *Pepin* vnto
his part; as one that ſtood in fome neede of his aide againft the Lombards;
and the more, becaufe his Lord the Emperour of Conftantinople was then
brought fo low, that hee was not able to fend him fufficient aide, for the
defence of his territories againft his enemies. But had *Zacharie* (to deale
plainely) not ſtood vpon the refpect of his owne commodity, more then
vpon the regard of Gods feare; he would neuer haue giuen counfell vnto
the feruant, vnder the pretended colour of his Mafters dull fpirit, fo to
turne rebell againft his Mafter. The Lawes prouide Gardians, or ouer-
feers, for fuch as are not well in their wits; they neuer depriue and fpoile
them of their eftate: they punifh crimes, but not difeafes and infirmities
by nature. Yea, in France it is a very auncient cuftome, when the King is
troubled in his wits to eftablifh a Regent, who for the time of the Kings
difability, may beare the burden of the Kingdomes affaires. So was the
practife

practife of that State in the cafe of *Charles 6.* when hee fell into a phrenfie ; whom the Pope notwithftanding his moft grieuous and fharpe fits, neuer offered to degrade. And to be fhort, what reafon, what equity will beare the children to be punifhed for the fathers debilitie? Yet fuch punifhment was laid vpon *Childerics* whole race and houfe; who by this practife were all difinherited of the Kingdome. But fhall wee now take fome view, of

Pag. 25.

the L. Cardinals excufe for this exemplarie fact? The caufe of *Childerics* depofing,(as the L.Cardinall faith) did neerely concerne and touch Religion: For *Childerics* imbecillity brought all France into danger, to fuffer a moft wofull fhipwracke of Chriftian religion, vpon the barbarous and hoftile inuafion of the Saracens. Admit now this reafon had beene of iuft weight and value, yet confideration fhould haue beene taken, whether fome one or other of that Royall ftemme, and of the Kings owne fucceffors neereft of blood, was not of better capacity to rule and mannage that mighty State. The feare of vncertaine and accidentall mifchiefe, fhould not haue driuen them to flie vnto the certaine mifchiefe of actuall and effectuall depofition. They fhould rather haue fet before their eies the example of *Charles Martel*, this *Pepins* father; who in a farre more eminent danger, when the Saracens had already maftered, and fubdued a great part of France, valiantly encountred, and withall defeated the Saracens ; ruled the Kingdome vnder the title of *Steward* of the Kings houfe, the principall Officer of the Crowne; without affecting or afpiring to the Throne for all that great ftep of aduantage, efpecially when the Saracens were quite broken, and no longer dreadfull to the French Nation.

In our owne Scotland, the fway of the Kingdome was in the hand of *Walles*, during the time of *Brufe* his imprifonment in England, who then was lawfull heire to the Crowne. This *Walles* or *Vallas* had the whole power of the Kingdome at his becke and command. His Edicts and ordinances to this day ftand in full force. By the deadly hatred of *Brufe* his mortall enemie, it may be coniectured, that he might haue bene prouoked and inflamed with defire to truffe the Kingdome in his tallants. And notwithftanding all thefe incitements, he neuer affumed or vfurped other title to himfelfe, then of Gouernour or Adminiftratour of the Kingdome. The reafon: Hee had not beene brought vp in this new doctrine and late difcipline, whereby the Church is endowed with power to giue and to take away Crownes. But now (as the L. Cardinall would beare the world in hand) the ftate of Kings is brought to a very dead lift. The Pope forfooth muft fend his Phyficians, to know by way of infpection or fome other courfe of Art, whether the Kings braine be crackt or found: and in cafe there be found any debilitie of wit and reafon in the King, then the Pope muft remooue and tranflate the Crowne, from the weaker braine to a ftronger: and for the acting of the ftratageme, the name of Religion muft be pretended. Ho, thefe Heretikes begin to crawle in the Kingdome: order muft bee taken they bee not fuffered by their multitudes and fwarmes,

like

like locusts or caterpillers to pester and poison the whole Realme. Or in a case of Matrimony, thus :·Ho, marriage is a Sacrament: touch the Order of Matrimonie, and Relgion is wounded. By this deuice not onely the Kings vices, but likewise his naturall diseases and infirmities are fetcht into the circle of Religion; and the L. Cardinall hath not done himselfe right, in restraining the Popes power to depose Kings, vnto the cases of Heresie, Apostasie, and persecution of the Church.

In the next place followeth *Leo* III. who by setting the Imperial Crowne vpon the head of *Charles*, absolued all the Subiects in the West, of their obedience to the Greeke Emperours, if the L. of Perron might bee credited in this Example. But indeed it is crowded among the rest by a slie tricke, and cleane contrary to the naked trewth of all histories: For it shall neuer be iustified by good historie, that so much as one single person or man (I say not one Countrey, or one people) was then wrought or wonne by the Pope to change his copy and Lord, or from a subiect of the Greeke Emperours, to turne subiect vnto *Charlemaine*. Let me see but one Towne that *Charlemaine* recouered from the Greeke Emperours, by his right and title to his Empire in the West : No, the Greeke Emperours had taken their farewell of the West Empire long before: And therefore to nicke this vpon the tallie of Pope *Leo* his Acts, that he tooke away the West from the Greeke Emperour, it is euen as if one should say, that in this aage the Pope takes the Dukedome of *Milan* from the French Kings, or the citie of Rome from the Emperours of Germanie, becaufe their Predecessours in former aages had beene right Lords and gouernours of them both. It is one of the Popes ordinary and solemne practises to take away, much after the maner of his giuing : For as he giueth what he hath not in his right and power to giue, or bestoweth vpon others what is already their owne ; euen so he taketh away from Kings and Emperors the possessions which they haue not in present hold and possession. After this maner he takes the West from the Greeke Emperors, when they hold nothing in the West, and lay no claime to any citie or towne of the West Empire. And what shall wee call this way of depriuation, but spoiling a naked man of his garments, and killing a man already dead? Trew it is the Imperiall Crowne was then set on *Charlemaines* head by *Leo* the Pope: did *Leo* therefore giue him the Empire? No more then a Bishop that crownes a King, at his Royall and solemne confecration, doeth giue him the Kingdome: For shall the Pope himselfe take the Popedome from the Bishop of *Ostia* as of his gift, becaufe the crowning of the Pope is an Office of long time peculiar to the *Ostian* Bishop? It was the custome of Emperours, to be crowned Kings of Italy by the hands of the Archbishop of *Milan*: did he therefore giue the Kingdome of Italy to the said Emperours? And to returne vnto *Charlemaine*; If the Pope had conueyed the Empire to him by free and gracious donation, the Pope doubtlesse in the solemnitie of his coronation, would neuer haue perfourmed vnto his owne creature, an Emperour of his owne ma-

king,

king the dueties of adoration , as *Ado* that liued in the same aage, hath left it on record : *After the solemne prayses ended* (saith *Ado*) *the chiefe Bi-shop honoured him with adoration, according to the custome of ancient Princes.* The same is likewise put downe by *Auentine*, in the 4. booke of his Annals of *Bauaria*. The like by the President *Fauchet* in his Antiquities : and by Monsieur *Petau* Counsellour in the Court of Parliament at *Paris*,in his Pre-face before the Chronicles of *Eusebius, Hierome*, and *Sigebert*. It was there-fore the people of *Rome*, that called this *Charles* the Great vnto the Im-periall dignitie,and cast on him the title of Emperour. So testifieth *Sige-bert* vpon the yeere 801. *All the Romanes with one generall voice and consent, ring out acclamations of Imperiall praises to the Emperour , they crowne him by the hands of* Leo *the Pope , they giue him the style of* Cæsar *and* Augustus. *Mari-anus Scotus* hath as much in effect : Charles *was then called* Augustus *by the Romanes.* And so *Platina* : *After the solemne seruice,* Leo *declareth and proclai-meth* Charles *Emperour , according to the publike Decree and generall request of the people of* Rome. *Auentine*, and *Sigonius* in his 4. booke of the Kingdome of *Italie* witnesse the same. Neuerthelesse, to gratifie the L. Cardinall; Sup-pose Pope *Leo* dispossessed the Greeke Emperours of the West Empire: What was the cause? what infamous acte had they done? what prophane and irreligious crime had they committed ? *Nicephorus* and *Irene*, who reigned in the Greeke Empire in *Charlemaines* time , were not reputed by the Pope,or taken for Heretikes. How then? The L. Cardinall helpeth at a pinch,and putteth vs in minde, that *Constantine* and *Leo*, predecessours to the said Emperours, had beene poysoned with Heresie, and stained with persecution. Here then behold an Orthodoxe Prince deposed: For what cause? for Heresie forsooth, not in himselfe , but in some of his Predeces-sors long before. An admirable case : For I am of a contrary minde, that he was worthy of double honour , in restoring and setting vp the trewth againe , which vnder his predecessors had endured oppression , and suf-fered persecution. Doubtlesse Pope *Siluester* was greatly ouerseene, and played not well the Pope, when hee winked at *Constantine* the Great, and cast him not downe from his Imperiall Throne, for the strange infidelitie and Paganisme of *Diocletian*, *of Maximian*, and *Maxentius* , whom *Constan-tine* succeeded in the Empire.

From this example the L. of *Perron* passeth to *Fulke* Archbishop of *Reims* : by whom *Charles* the Simple was threatned with Excommunica-tion, and refusing to continue any longer in the fidelity and allegiance of a subiect. To what purpose is this example ? For who can be ignorant,that all aages haue brought forth turbulent and stirring spirits, men altogether forgetfull of respect and obseruance towards their Kings , especially when the world finds them shallow and simple-witted , like vnto this Prince? But in this example, where is there so much as one word of the Pope,or the deposing of Kings?

Here the L. Cardinall chops in the example of *Philip* I.King of France, but

but mangled, and ftrangely difguifed, as hereafter fhall be fhewed.

At laft he leadeth vs to *Gregory* VII. furnamed *Hildebrand*, the fcourge of Emperours, the firebrand of warre, the fcorne of his aage. This Pope, after he had (in the fpirit of pride, and in the very height of all audacioufneffe) thundred the fentence of excommunication and depofition, againft the Emperour *Henry* IIII. after he had enterprifed this act without all precedent example: after he had filled all Europe with blood: this Pope, I fay, funke downe vnder the weight of his affaires, and died as a fugitiue at *Salerne*, ouerwhelmed with difcontent and forrow of heart: Here lying at the point of giuing vp the ghoaft, calling vnto him (as it is in *Sigebert*) a certaine Cardinall whom he much fauoured, *He confeffeth to God, and Saint Peter, and the whole Church, that he had beene greatly defectiue in the Paftorall charge committed to his care; and that by the Deuils inftigation, he had kindled the fire of Gods wrath and hatred againft mankind: Then hee fent his Confeffor to the Emperour, and to the whole Church to pray for his pardon, becaufe hee perceiued that his life was at an end.* Likewife Cardinall *Benno* that liued in the faid *Gregories* time, doth teftifie, *That fo foone as he was rifen out of his Chaire to excommunicate the Emperour from his Cathedrall feate: by the will of God the faid Cathedrall feate, new made of ftrong board or plancke, did cracke and cleaue into many pieces or parts; to manifeft how great and terrible Schifmes had beene fowen againft the Church of Chrift, by an excommunication of fo dangerous confequence, pronounced by the man that had fit Iudge therein.* Now to bring and alleadge the example of fuch a man, who by attempting an act which neuer any man had the heart or face to attempt before, hath condemned all his predeceffors of cowardife, or at leaft of ignorance; what is it elfe, but euen to fend vs to the fchoole of mightie robbers, and to feeke to correct and reforme ancient vertues by late vices? Which *Otho Frifingenfis* calling into his owne priuate confideration, hee durft freely profeffe, *that hee had not reade of any Emperour before this* Henry the IIII. *excommunicated or driuen out of his Imperiall Throne and Kingdome by the chiefe Bifhop of Rome.* But if this quarrell may be tryed and fought out with weapons of examples, I leaue any indifferent reader to iudge what examples ought in the caufe to be of chiefeft authority and weight: whether late examples of Kings depofed by Popes, for the moft part neuer taking the intended effect; or auncient examples of Popes actually and effectually thruft out of their thrones by Emperours and Kings.

The Emperour *Conftantius* expelled *Liberius* Bifhop of Rome out of the citie, banifhed him as farre as *Beroe*, and placed *Fœlix* in his roome. Indeed *Conftantius* was an Arrian, and therein vfed no leffe impious then vniuft proceeding: Neuertheleffe, the auncient Fathers of the Church, doe not blame *Conftantius* for his hard and fharpe dealing with a chiefe Bifhop, ouer whom hee had no lawfull power, but onely as an enemie to the Orthodoxe faith, and one that raged with extreame rigour of perfecution againft innocent beleeuers.

In the raigne of *Valentinian* the I. and yeare of the Lord 367. the contention

*Exam.*11. *An.*1076.

Sigeb.ad an. 1085.

*Otho Frifingenf. in vita Hen.*4. *lib.*4.*cap* 31.

*Theo.lib.*2. *Hift.cap.*16.

*Ammia.lib.*17

tion betweene *Damafus* and *Vrcifinus* competitors for the Bifhopricke, filled the citie of Rome with a bloody fedition, in which were wickedly and

Decret. d.ft.79. cruelly murdered 137. perfons. To meet with fuch turbulent actions, *Ho-*
norius made a law extant in the Decreetalls, the words whereof be thefe; *If*
it fhall happen henceforth by the temeritie of competitors, that any two Bifhops be ele-
Eted to the See, we ftraitly charge and command, that neither of both fhall fit in the faid

Platina.
Sigebertus. *See.* By vertue of this Law, the fame *Honorius* in the yeare 420. expelled
Bonifacius and *Eulalius*, competitors and Antipopes out of Rome, though
not long after he reuoked *Bonifacius*, and fetled him in the Papall See.

Anaftatius.
Platina.
Lib. Pontifi.
Diaconus. *Theodoric* the Goth King of Italy, fent *Iohn* Bifhop of Rome Embaffador
to the Emperour *Iuftinian*, called him home againe, and clapt him vp in
the clofe prifon, where he ftarued to death. By the fame King, *Peter* Bifhop
of Altine was difpatched to Rome, to heare the caufe and examine the
proceffe of Pope *Symmachus*, then indited and accufed of fundry crimes.

King *Theodatus* about the yeare 537. had the feruice of Pope *Agapetus*,
as his Embaffadour to the Emperour *Iuftinian*, vpon a treatie of peace.
Agapetus dying in the time of that feruice, *Syluerius* is made Bifhop by
Theodatus. Not long after, *Syluerius* is driuen out by *Belifarius* the Emperour his Lieutenant, and fent into banifhment. After *Syluerius* next fuc-
ceedeth *Vigilius*, who with currant coine purchafed the Popedome of
Belifarius. The Emperour *Iuftinian* fends for *Vigilius* to Conftantinople,
and receiues him there with great honour. Soone after, the Emperour
takes offence at his freeneffe in fpeaking his mind, commands him to bee
beaten with ftripes in manner to death, and with a roape about his necke
to be drawne through the city like a thiefe, as *Platina* relates the hiftorie.
Nicephorus in his 26. booke, and 17. chapter, comes very neere the fame
relation.

Platina.
Baronius.
Sigebertus. The Emperour *Conftantius*, in the yeere 654. caufed Pope *Martin* to be
bound with chaines, and banifhed him into Cherfonefus, where he ended
his life. The Popes in that aage writing to the Emperours, vfed none but
fubmiffiue tearmes, by way of moft humble fupplications; made profeffion of bowing the knee before their facred Maiefties, and of executing
their commands with entire obedience; payed to the Emperours twenty
pound weight of gold for their Inueftiture; which tribute was afterward

Iuftin. Authent.
123.cap.3. releafed and remitted, by *Conftantine* the *Bearded*, to Pope *Agatho*, in the
yeere 679. as I haue obferued in an other place.

Nay further, euen when the power and riches of the Popes was growne
to great height, by the moft profufe and immenfe munificence of *Charle-*
mayne and Lewis his fonne; the Emperours of the Weft did not relinquifh
and giue ouer the making and vnmaking of Popes, as they faw caufe.
Pope *Adrian* 1. willingly fubmitted his necke to this yoke: and made this
Law to be paffed in a Councill, that in *Charlemayne* fhould reft all right and
power for the Popes election, and for the gouernement of the Papall
See. This Conftitution is incerted in the *Decretals*, Diftinct.63. Can.
                                                          * *Hadri-*

* *Note that in the same Dist. the Can of Greg. 4. beginning with Cùm Hadrianus 1. is false, and supposititious, because Gregorie 4. was Pope long before Hadr. 2. Tria reterrima monstra.*

* *Hadrianus*, and was confirmed by the practife of many yeeres.

In the yeere of the Lord 963. the Emperour *Otho* tooke away the Popedome from *Iohn* 13. and placed *Leo* 8. in his roume. In like maner, *Iohn* 14. *Gregory* 5. and *Siluefter* 2. were feated in the Papall Throne by the *Othos*.

The Emperour *Henrie* 2. in the yeere 1007. depofed three Popes, namely, *Bendict* 9. *Siluefter* 3. and *Gregorie* 6. whom *Platina* doeth not fticke to call, three moft deteftable and vile monfters. This cuftome continued, this practife ftood in force for diuers aages, euen vntill the times of *Gregorie* 7. by whom the whole Weft was toffed and turmoiled with lamentable warres, which plagued the world, and the Empire by name with intolerable troubles and mifchiefes. For after the faid *Gregorian* warres, the Empire fell from bad to worfe, and fo went on to decay, till Emperours at laft were driuen to beg, and receiue the Imperiall Crowne of the Pope.

The Kingdome of *France* met not with fo rude entreatie, but was dealt withall by courfes of a milder temper. *Gregorie* 4. about the yeere of the Lord, 832. was the firft Pope that perfwaded himfelfe to vfe the cenfure of Excommunication againft a King of *France*. This Pope hauing a hand in the troublefome factions of the Realme, was nothing backeward to fide with the fonnes of *Lewis* furnamed the Courteous, by wicked confpiracie entring into a defperate courfe and complot againft *Lewis* their owne father; as witneffeth *Sigebert* in thefe words, *Pope* Gregorie *comming into* France, *ioyned himfelfe to the fonnes againft the Emperour their Father.* But Annals of the very fame times, and hee that furbufhed *Aimonius*, a Religious of S. *Benedicts* Order, doe teftifie, that all the Bifhops of *France* fell vpon this refolution; by no meanes to reft in the Popes pleafure, or to giue any place vnto his defigne: and contrariwife, *In cafe the Pope fhould proceed to Excommunication of their King, hee fhould returne out of* France *to* Rome *an excommunicate perfon himfelfe.* The Chronicle of S. *Denis* hath words in this forme: *The Lord Apoftolicall returned anfwere, that hee was not come into* France *for any other purpofe, but onely to excommunicate the King and his Bifhops, if they would bee in any fort oppofite vnto the fonnes of* Lewis, *or difobedient vnto the will and pleafure of his Holineffe:* The Prelates *enformed heereof, made anfwere, that in this cafe they would neuer yeeld obedience to the Excommunication of the faid Bifhops; becaufe it was contrary to the authoritie and aduife of the ancient Canons.*

Bochel. Decret. Ecclef Gallican. lib. 2. tit. 16.

After thefe times, Pope *Nicolas* 1. depriued King *Lotharius* of Communion (for in thofe times not a word of depofing) to make him repudiate or quit *Valdrada*, and to refume or take againe *Thetberga* his former wife. The Articles framed by the French vpon this point, are to bee found in the writing of *Hincmarus*, Archbifhop of *Reims*, and are of this purport; that in the iudgement of men both learned and wife, it is an ouerruled cafe, that as the King whatfoeuer hee fhall doe, ought not by his owne Bifhops to be excommunicated, euen fo no forreine Bifhop hath power to fit for his Iudge: becaufe the King is to be fubiect onely vnto God, and

his

his Imperiall authoritie, who alone had the all-fufficient power to fettle him in his Kingdome. Moreouer, the Clergie addreffed letters of anfwere vnto the fame Pope, full of ftinging and bitter termes, with fpeaches of great fcorne and contempt, as they are fet downe by *Auentine* in his Annals of *Bauaria*,not forbearing to call him *thiefe, wolfe, and tyrant.*

Annal. Boio. lib.4.

When Pope *Hadrian* tooke vpon him like a Lord, to command *Charles* the Bald vpon paine of interdiction, that hee fhould fuffer the Kingdome of *Lotharius* to bee fully and entirely conueyed and conferred vpon *Lewis* his fonne; the fame *Hincmarus*, a man of great authoritie and eftimation in that aage, fent his letters conteining fundry remonftrances touching that fubiect: Among other matters thus he writeth, *The Ecclefiaftics and Seculars of the Kingdome affembled at* Reims, *haue affirmed and now doe affirme by way of reproach, vpbraiding, and exprobation, that neuer was the like Mandate fent before from the See of* Rome *to any of our predeceffours.* And a little after: *The chiefe Bifhops of the Apoftolike See, or any other Bifhops of the greateft autho-ritie and holineffe, neuer withdrew themfelues from the prefence, from the reuerend falutation, or from the conference of Empererours and Kings, whether Heretikes, or Schifmatikes and Tyrants*: as Conftantius *the Arrian,* Iulianus *the Apoftata,* and Maximus *the Tyrant.* And yet a little after; *Wherefore if the Apoftolike Lord bee minded to feeke peace, let him feeke it fo, that he ftirre no brawles, and breed no quarrels · For we are no fuch babes to beleeue, that we can or euer fhall at-taine to Gods Kingdome, vnleffe wee receiue him for our King in earth, whom God himfelfe recommendeth to vs from heauen.* It is added by *Hincmarus* in the fame place, that by the faid Bifhops and Lords Temporall, fuch threat-ning words were blowen forth, as hee is afraid once to fpeake and vtter. As for the King himfelfe, what reckoning hee made of the Popes man-dates, it appeareth by the Kings owne letters addreffed to Pope *Hadria-nus*,as we may reade euery where in the Epiftles of *Hincmarus.* For there, after King *Charles* hath taxed and challenged the Pope of pride, and hit him in the teeth with a fpirit of vfurpation, hee breaketh out into thefe words: *What Hell hath caft vp this law fo croffe and prepofterous? what infer-nall gulph hath difgorged this law out of the darkeft and obfcureft dennes? a law quite contrary, and altogether repugnant vnto the beaten way fhewed vs in the ho-ly Scriptures, &c.* Yea, he flatly and peremptorily forbids the Pope, except he meane or defire to be recompenfed with difhonour and contempt, to fend any more the like Mandates,either to himfelfe,or to his Bifhops.

Vnder the reigne of *Hugo Capetus* and *Robert* his fonne, a Councell now extant in all mens hands, was held and celebrated at *Reims* by the Kings authoritie· There *Arnulphus* Bifhop of *Orleans*, then Prolocutor and Spea-ker of the Councel,calls the Pope Antichrift,and lets not alfo to paint him forth like a monfter : as well for the deformed and vgly vices of that vn-holy See, which then were in their exaltation, as alfo becaufe the Pope then wonne with prefents, and namely with certaine goodly horfes, then prefented to his Holineffe, tooke part againft the King, with *Arnul-*
phus

phus Bifhop of *Reims*, then difpoffeffed of his Paftorall charge.

When *Philip* 1. had repudiated his wife *Bertha*, daughter to the Earle of *Holland*; and in her place had alfo taken to wife *Bertrade* the wife of *Fulco* Earle of *Aniou* yet being aliue; hee was excommunicated, and his Kingdome interdicted by *Vrbanus* then Pope, (though he was then bearded with an Antipope) as the L. Cardinal here giueth vs to vnderftand. But his Lordfhip hath skipt ouer two principall points recorded in the hiftorie. The firft is, that *Philip* was not depofed by the Pope: whereupon it is to be inferred, that in this paffage there is nothing materiall to make for the Popes power againft a Kings Throne and Scepter. The other point is, that by the cenfures of the Pope, the courfe of obedience due to the King before was not interrupted, nor the King difauowed, refufed, or difclaimed: but on the contrary, that *Iuo* of *Chartres* taking Pope *Vrbanus* part, was punifhed for his prefumption, difpoyled of his eftate, and kept in prifon: whereof he makes complaint himfelfe in his 19.and 20.Epiftles. The L. Cardinall befides, in my vnderftanding, for his Mafters honour, fhould haue made no words of interdicting the whole Kingdome. For when the Pope, to giue a King chaftifement, doeth interdict his Kingdome; hee makes the people to beare the punifhment of the Kings offence: For during the time of interdiction, the Church doores through the whole Kingdome are kept continually fhut and lockt vp: publike feruice is intermitted in all places: bels euery where filent: Sacraments not adminiftred to the people. bodies of the dead fo proftituted and abandoned, that none dares burie the faid bodies in holy ground. More, it is beleeued, that a man dying vnder the curfe of the interdict (without fome fpeciall indulgence or priuiledge) is for euer damned and adiudged to eternall punifhments, as one that dyeth out of the communion of the Church. Put cafe then the interdict holdeth and continueth for many yeares together; alas, how many millions of poore foules are damned, and goe to hell for an others offence? For what can, or what may the faltleffe and innocent people doe withall, if the King will repudiate his wife, and fhe yet liuing, ioyne himfelfe in matrimonie to an other?

The Lord Cardinall after *Philip* the 1. produceth *Philippus Auguftus*, who hauing renounced his wife *Ingeberga* daughter to the King of *Denmarke*, and marrying with *Agnes* daughter to the Duke of *Morauia*, was by Pope *Innocent* the third interdicted himfelfe and his whole Kingdome. But his Lordfhippe was not pleafed to infert withall, what is auerred in the Chronicle of Saint *Denis*: that Pope *Caleftinus* 3. fent forth two Legats at once vpon this errand: *Who being come into the affemblie and generall Council of all the French Prelats, became like dumbe dogs that can not barke, fo as they could not bring the feruice which they had vndertaken to any good paffe, becaufe they ftood in a bodily feare of their owne hydes. Not long after, the Cardinall of Capua was in the like taking: For hee durft not bring the Realme within the limits of the interdict, before hee was got out of the limits of the Kingdome. The King here-*

*Examp.*12.

*Bochel.pag.*320

with incenſed, thruſt all the Prelates that had giuen conſent vnto theſe pro-ceedings out of their Sees, confiſcated their goods, &c. To the ſame effect is that which wee reade in *Matthew Paris.* After the Pope had giuen his Maieſtie to vnderſtand by the Cardinal of *Anagnia,* that his kingdome ſhould be interdicted, vnleſſe he would be reconciled to the King of Eng-land; the King returned the Pope this anſwere, that he was not in any ſort afraid of the Popes ſentence, for as much as it could not be grounded vpon any equitie of the cauſe : and added withall, *that it did no way appertaine vnto the Church of Rome to ſentence Kings, eſpecially the King of France.* And this was done, ſaith *Iohannes Tilius* Regiſter in Court of Parliament of Pa-ris, *by the counſell of the French Barons.*

Moſt notable is the example of *Philip the faire,* and hits the bird in the right eye. In the yeere 1032. the Pope diſpatched the Archbiſhop of *Nar-bona* with *mandates* into France, commanding the King to releaſe the Bi-ſhop of *Apamia* then detained in priſon, for contumelious words tending to the Kings defamation, and ſpoken to the Kings owne head. In very deed this Pope had conceiued a ſecret grudge, and no light diſpleaſure a-gainſt King *Philip* before : namely, becauſe the King had taken vpon him the collation of Benefices, and other Eccleſiaſtical dignities. Vpon which occaſion the Pope ſent letters to the King of this tenour and ſtyle : *Feare God, and keepe his Commandements : Wee would haue thee know, that in Spirituall and Temporall cauſes thou art ſubiect vnto our ſelfe : that collating of Benefices and Prebends, doeth not in any ſort appertaine to thy office and place : that, in caſe as kee-per of the Spiritualties, thou haue the cuſtodie of benefices and Prebends in thy hand when they become voyd, thou ſhalt by ſequeſtration reſerue the fruits of the ſame, to the vſe and benefit of the next Incumbents and ſucceſſors : and in caſe thou haſt heretofore collated any, we ordaine the ſaid collations to be meerely void : and ſo farre as herein thou haſt proceeded to the fact, we reuoke the ſaid collations. We hold them for hereticks whoſoeuer are not of this beliefe.* A Legate comes to Paris, and brings theſe brauing letters : By ſome of the Kings faithfull ſeruants they are violently ſnatched and pulled out of the Legates hands : by the Earle of Artois they are caſt into the fire. The good King anſweres the Pope, and payes him in as good coyne as he had ſent. *Philip by the grace of God King of the French, to Boniface calling and bearing himſelfe the Soueraigne Biſhop, little greeting or none at all. May thy exceeding ſottiſhneſſe vnderſtand, that in Tem-porall cauſes we are not ſubiect vnto any mortall and earthly creature : that collating of Benefices and Prebends, by Regall right appertaineth to our office and place : that appropriating their fruits when they become void, belongeth to our ſelfe alone during their vacancie : that all collations by vs heretofore made, or to bee made hereafter, ſhall ſtand in force : that in the validitie and vertue of the ſaid collations, wee will euer couragiouſly defend and maintaine, all Incumbents and poſſeſſors of Benefices and Prebends ſo by vs collated. We hold them all for ſots and ſenſeleſſe, whoſoeuer are not of this beliefe.* The Pope incenſed herewith, excommunicates the King : but no man dares publiſh that cenſure, or become bearer thereof.

The

The King notwithstanding the said proceedings of the Pope, assembles his Prelates, Barons, and Knights at Paris: askes the whole assembly, of whom they hold their Fees, with al other the Temporalties of the Church. They make answere with one voice, that in the said matters they disclaime the Pope, and know none other Lord beside his Maiestie. Meane while the Pope worketh with Germanie and the Low Countreis, to stirre them vp against France. But *Philip* sendeth *William* of *Nogaret* into Italy. *William* by the direction and aide of *Sciarra Columnensis,* takes the Pope at *Anagnia,* mounts him vpon a leane ill-fauoured iade, caries him prisoner to Rome; where ouercome with choller, anguish, and great indignation, he takes his last leaue of the Popedome and his life. All this notwithstanding, the King presently after, from the successours of *Boniface* receiues very ample and gratious Bulls, in which the memorie of all the former passages and actions is vtterly abolished. Witnesse the Epistle of *Clement* 5. wherein this King is honoured with praises, for a pious and religious Prince, and his Kingdome is restored to the former estate. In that aage the French Nobilitie caried other maner of spirits, then the moderne and present Nobilitie doe: I meane those by whom the L. Cardinal was applauded and assisted in his Oration. Yea, in those former times the Prelates of the Realme stood better affected towards their King, then the L. Cardinal himselfe now standeth: who could finde none otherway to dally with, and to shift off this pregnant example, but by plaine glosing, that heresie and Apostasie was no ground of that question, or subiect of that controuersie. Wherein hee not onely condemnes the Pope, as one that proceeded against *Philip* without a iust cause & good ground; but likewise giues the Pope the Lie, who in his goodly letters but a little aboue recited, hath enrowled *Philip* in the list of heretiques. Hee saith moreouer, that indeed the knot of the question was touching the Popes pretence, in challenging to himselfe the temporall Soueraigntie of France, that is to say, in qualifying himselfe King of France: But indeed and indeed no such matter to be found. His whole pretence was the collating of Benefices, and to pearch aboue the King, to crow ouer his Crowne in Temporall causes. At which pretence his Holinesse yet aimeth, still attributing and challenging to himselfe plenarie power to depose the King. Now if the L. Cardinal shall yet proceed to cauill, that *Boniface* the eighth was taken by the French for an vsurper, and no lawfull Pope, but for one that crept into the Papacie by fraud and symonie; he must be pleased to set downe positiuely who was Pope, seeing that *Boniface* then sate not in the Papall chaire. To conclude, If hee that creepeth and stealeth into the Papacie by symonie, by canuases or labouring of suffrages vnder hand, or by bribery, be not lawfull Pope; I dare be bold to professe, there will hardly be found two lawfull Popes in the three last aages.

Pope *Benedict* in the yeere 1408. being in choller with *Charles* the sixt, because *Charles* had bridled and curbed the gainefull exactions and extorsions

Extrauag. Meruit.

See the treatise of *Charles du Moulin contrà paruas Datas,*

Mm 3

fions of the Popes Court, by which the Realme of France had bene exhaufted of their treafure, fent an excommunicatorie Bull into France, againſt
Charles the King, and all his Princes. The Vniuerſitie of Paris made requeſt or motion that his Bull might be mangled, and Pope *Benediſt* himfelfe, by fome called *Petrus de Luna,* might be declared *heretike*, *fchiſmatike*,
and *perturber of the peace*. The ſaid Bull was mangled and rent in pieces, according to the petition of the Vniuerſitie, by Decree of Court vpon the
tenth of Iune, 1 4 0 8. Tenne dayes after, the Court riſing at eleuen in the
morning, two Bul-bearers of the faid excommunicatorie cenfure vnderwent ignominious puniſhment vpon the Palace or great Hal ſtaires. From
thence were led to the *Louure* in fuch maner as they had bene brought
from thence before : drawne in two tumbrels, clad in coates of painted
linnen, wore paper-mytres on their heads, were proclaimed with found of
Trumpet, and euery where diſgraced with publike deriſion: So litle reckoning was made of the Popes thundering canons in thofe dayes. And what
would they haue done, if the ſaid Buls had imported fentence of depoſition againſt King *Charles?*

The French Church affembled at *Tours* in the yeere 1 5 10. decreed that
Lewis X I I. might with fafe confcience contemne *the abuſiue Bulls, and vniuſt cenſures of Pope* Iulius *the* I I. and by armes might withſtand the Popes
vſurpations, in cafe hee ſhould proceed to excommunicate or depofe the
King. More, by a Councill holden at *Piſa,* this *Lewis* declared the Pope
to bee fallen from the Popedome, and coyned crownes with a ſtampe of
this inſcription, *I will deſtroy the name of Babylon.* To this the L. of *Perron*
makes anfwere, that all this was done by the French, as acknowledging
thefe iars to haue fpruńg not from the fountaine of Religion, but from paffion of ſtate: Wherein he condemneth Pope *Iulius,* for giuing fo great fcope
vnto his publike cenfures, as to ferue his ambition, and not rather to aduance Religion. He fecretly teacheth vs befides, that when the Pope vndertakes to depofe the King of France, then the French are to fit as Iudges
concerning the lawfulneſſe or vnlawfulneſſe of the caufe; and in cafe they
ſhall finde the caufe to be vnlawfull, then to difanull his iudgements, and
to fcoffe at his thunderbolts.

Iohn *d'Albret* King of Nauarre, whofe Realme was giuen by the forefaid Pope to *Ferdinand* King of Arragon, was alfo wrapped and entangled
with ſtriſt bands of depoſition. Now if the French had bene touched
with no better feeling of affeſtion to their King, then the fubieſts of Nauarre were to the Nauarrois; doubtleſſe France had fought a new Lord, by
vertue of the Popes (as the L. Cardinall himfelfe doeth acknowledge and
confeſſe) vniuſt fentence. But behold, to make the ſaid fentence againſt
Iohn d'Albret feeme the leſſe contrary to equitie, the L. Cardinall pretends,
the Popes donation was not indeed the principall caufe, howfoeuer *Ferdinand* himfelfe made it his pretence. But his Lo. giues this for the principall
caufe: that *Iohn d'Albret* had quitted his alliance made with condition, that

in

in cafe the Kings of Nauarre fhould infringe the faid alliance, and breake
the league, then the kingdome of Nauarre fhould returne to the Crowne
of Arragon. This condition, betweene Kings neuer made, and without
all fhew of probabilitie, ferueth to none other purpofe from the Cardinals
mouth, but onely to infinuate and worke a perfwafion in his King, that he
hath no right nor lawfull pretenfion to the Crowne of Nauarre : and
whatfoeuer hee now holdeth in the faid kingdome of Nauarre, is none
of his owne, but by vfurpation and vnlawfull poffeffion. Thus his Lordfhip French-borne, makes himfelfe an Aduocate for the Spanifh King, a-
gainft his owne King, and King of the French : who fhalbe faine, as hee
ought (if this Aduocats plea may take place) to draw his title and ftyle of
King of Nauarre out of his Royall titles, and to acknowledge that all the
great endeuours of his predeceffors to recouer the faid Kingdome, were
difhonourable and vniuft. Is it poffible, that in the very heart and head
Citie of France, a fpirit and tongue fo licentious can be brooked? What,
fhall fo great blafphemie (as it were) of the Kings freehold, bee powred
foorth in fo honourable an affembly, without punifhment or fine? What,
without any contradiction for the Kings right, and on the Kings behalfe?
I may perhaps confeffe the indignitie might bee the better borne, and the
pretence alledged might paffe for a poore excufe, if it ferued his purpofe
neuer fo little. For how doeth all this touch or come neere the queftion? in which the Popes vfurpation in the depofing of Kings, and the refolution of the French in refifting this tyrannicall practife, is the proper
iffue of the caufe: both which points are neuer a whit more of the leffe confequence and importance, howfoeuer *Ferdinand* in his owne iuftification
ftood vpon the forefaid pretence. Thus much is confeffed, and wee aske
no more · Pope *Iulius* tooke the Kingdome from the one, and gaue it vnto
the other : the French thereupon refifted the Pope, and declared him to be
fallen from the Papacie.

This noble fpirit and courage of the French, in maintayning the dignitie and honour of their Kings Crownes, bred thofe ancient cuftomes,
which in the fequence of many aages haue bene obferued and kept in
vfe. This for one : That no Legate of the Pope, nor any of his refcripts
nor *mandates*, are admitted and receiued in France, *without licence from the*
King : and vnleffe the Legate impart his faculties to the Kings Atturney
Generall, to be perufed and verified in Court of Parliament: where they are
to be tyed by certaine modifications and reftrictions, vnto fuch points as
are not derogatorie from the Kings right, from the liberties of the Church,
and from the ordinances of the Kingdome. When Cardinal *Balua*, contrary to this ancient forme, entred France in the yeere 1484. and there without
leaue of the King did execute the office, & fpeed certaine Acts of the Popes
Legate ; the Court vpon motion made by the Kings Atturney Generall,
decreed a Commiffion, to be informed againft him by two Councellors of
the faid Court, and inhibited his further proceeding to vfe any facultie or
power

Pag.16.
Nifi de confen-
fu Regis Chri-
ftianiffimi.

Bochellus.

power of the Popes Legate, vpon paine of beeing proclaimed rebell.

· In the yeere 1 5 6 1. *Iohannes Tanquerellus* Batchelour in Diuinitie, by order of the Court was condemned to make open confeſſion, that hee had *indiſcreetly and raſhly without conſideration* defended this propoſition, *The Pope is the Vicar of Chriſt, a Monarke that hath power both Spirituall and Secular, and he may depriue Princes, which rebell againſt his commandements of their dignities.* Which propoſition, howſoeuer he proteſted that he had propounded the ſame *onely to be argued, and not iudicially to be determined* in the affirmatiue, *Tanquerellus* neuertheleſſe was compelled openly to recant. Here the L. Cardinall anſweres; The hiſtorie of *Tanquerellus* is from the matter, becauſe his propoſition treateth neither of Hereſie nor of Infidelitie: but I anſwere, The ſaid propoſition treateth of both, foraſmuch as it maketh mention of diſobedience to the Pope. For I ſuppoſe hee will not denie, that whoſoeuer ſhall ſtand out in Hereſie, contrary to the Popes monitorie proceedings, he ſhal ſhew but poore and ſimple obedience to the Pope. Moreouer, the caſe is cleare by the former examples, that no Pope will ſuffer his power to caſt downe Kings, to be reſtrained vnto the cauſe of Hereſie and Infidelitie.

In the heate of the laſt warres, raiſed by that holy-prophane League, admonitory Bulls were ſent by Pope *Gregorie* 14. from *Rome*, Anno 1 5 9 1. By theſe Bulls King *Henrie* 4. as an Heretike and relapſe, was declared incapable of the Crowne of *France*, and his Kingdome was expoſed to hauocke and ſpoile. The Court of Parliament being aſſembled at *Tours* the 5.of Auguſt, decreed the ſaid admonitorie Bulls to bee cancelled, torne in pieces, and caſt into a great fire by the hand of the publike executioner. The Arreſt it ſelfe or Decree is of this tenour: *The Court duely pondering and approouing the concluding and vnanſwerable reaſons of the Kings Attourney Generall, hath declared, and by theſe preſent doeth declare, the admonitorie Bulls giuen at* Rome *the* 1.*of March* 1 5 9 1. *to be of no validitie, abuſiue, ſeditious, damnable, full of impietie and impoſtures, contrary to the holy decrees, rights, franchiſes, and liberties of the French Church: doeth ordeine the Copies of the ſaid Bulls, ſealed with the ſeale of* Marſilius Landrianus, *and ſigned* Septilius Lamprius, *to bee rent in pieces by the publike executioner, and by him to be burnt in a great fire to be made for ſuch purpoſe, before the great gates of the common Hall or Palace, &c.* Then, euen then the L. of *Perron* was firme for the better part, and ſtood for his King againſt *Gregorie* the Pope, notwithſtanding the crime of e-reſie pretended againſt *Henrie* his Lord.

All the former examples by vs alledged, are drawen out of the times after Schooles of Diuinitie were eſtabliſhed in *France* For I thought good to bound my ſelfe within thoſe dooles and limits of time, which the L. Cardinal himſelfe hath ſet. Who goeth not ſincerely to worke and in good earneſt, where he telleth vs there be three inſtances (as if wee had no more) obiected againſt Papall power, to remooue Kings out of their chaires of State: by name, *the example of* Philip *the Faire, of* Lewis XII.

and

Indiſcretè ac inconſideratè.

Doctrinaliter tantùm & non iuridicè.

Page 47.

and of Tanquerellus : For in very trewth all the former examples by vs produced, are no leſſe pregnant and euident, howſoeuer the L. Cardinall hath bene pleaſed to conceale them all for feare of hurting his cauſe.

Nay, *France* euen in the dayes of her foreſt ſeruitude, was neuer vnfurniſhed of great Diuines, by whom this vſurped power of the Pope, ouer the Temporalties and Crownes of Kings, hath beene vtterly miſlikèd and condemned.

Robert Earle of *Flanders* was commanded by Pope *Paſchal* 2. to perſecute with fire and ſword the Clergie of *Liege*, who then adhered and ſtood to the cauſe of the Emperour *Henrie* 4. whom the Pope had ignominiouſly depoſed. *Robert* by the Popes order and command, was to handle the Clergie of *Liege* in like ſort as before hee had ſerued the Clergie of *Cambray*, who by the ſaid Earle had beene cruelly ſtript both of goods and life: The Pope promiſed the ſaid Earle and his army pardon of their ſinnes for the ſaid execution. The Clergie of *Liege* addreſſed anſwere to the Pope at large: They cried out vpon the Church of *Rome*, and called her *Babylon*: Told the Pope home, that God had commanded to giue vnto *Cæſar* that which is *Cæſars*: that euery ſoule muſt bee ſubiect vnto the ſuperiour powers: that no man is exempted out of this precept: and that euery oath of alleagiance is to be kept inuiolable; yea, that hereof they themſelues are not ignorant, in as much as they by a new Schiſme, and new traditions, making a ſeparation and rent of the Prieſthood from the Kingdome, doe promiſe to abſolue of periurie, ſuch as haue perfidiouſly forſworne themſelues againſt their King. And whereas by way of deſpight and in opprobrious maner, they were excommunicated by the Pope, they gaue his Holineſſe to vnderſtand, that *Dauids heart had vttered a good matter, but* Paſchals *heart had ſpèwed vp ſordid and railing words, like old bawdes and ſpinſters or webſters of linnen, when they ſcold and brawle one with another.* Finally, they reiected his Papal excommunication, as a ſentence giuen without diſcretion. This was the voyce and free ſpeach of that Clergie, in the life time of their noble Emperour: But after hee was thruſt out of the Empire by the rebellion of his owne ſonne, inſtigated and ſtirred vp thereunto by the Popes perſwaſion and practiſe, and was brought vnto a miſerable death; it is no matter of wonder, that for the ſafegard of their life, the ſaid Clergie were driuen to ſue vnto the Pope for their pardon.

Hildebert Biſhop of *Cœnomanum* vpon the riuer of *Sartre*, liuing vnder the reigne of King *Philip* the firſt, affirmeth in his Epiſtles 40. and 75. that *Kings are to bee admoniſhed and inſtructed, rather then puniſhed: to be dealt with by counſell, rather then by command, by doctrine and inſtruction, rather then by correction: For no ſuch ſword belongeth to the Church, becauſe the ſword of the Church is Eccleſiaſticall diſcipline, and nothing elſe.* *Bernard* writeth to Pope *Eugenius* after this manner: *Whoſoeuer they bee that are of this mind and opinion, ſhall neuer be able to make proofe, that any one of the Apoſtles did euer ſit in qualitie of Iudge or Diuider of lands. I reade where they haue ſtood to bee iudged, but neuer where they*
Bibliotheca Patrum Tom. 3.

De conſider. lib. 1. cap. 6.

ſate

fate downe to giue iudgement. Againe, *Your authoritie ſtretcheth vnto crimes, not vnto poſſeſſions : becauſe you haue receiued the keies of the kingdome of heauen, not in regard of poſſeſſions, but of crimes, to keepe all that pleade by couin or colluſion, and not lawfull poſſeſſors, out of the heauenly kingdome.* A little after : *Theſe baſe things of the earth are iudged by the Kings and Princes of this world : wherefore doe you thruſt your ſickle into an others harueſt ? wherefore doe you incroach and intrude* Lib.2.cap.6. *vpon an others limits ?* Elſewhere. *The Apoſtles are directly forbid to make themſelues Lords and rulers. Goe thou then, and beeing a Lord vſurpe Apoſtleſhip, or beeing an Apoſtle vſurpe Lordſhip. If thou needes wilt haue both, doubtleſſe thou ſhalt haue neither.*

Diſ.24.queſt.3 *Iohannes Maior* Doctor of *Paris : The Soueraigne Biſhop hath no temporall authoritie ouer Kings. The reaſon : Becauſe it followes (the contrarie being once granted) that Kings are the Popes vaſſals.* Now let other men iudge, whether he that hath power to diſpoſſeſſe Kings of all their Temporalties, hath not likewiſe authoritie ouer their Temporalties.

Comment in l.4.Sent.Diſt. 24 fol.214. The ſame Author : *The Pope hath no manner of title ouer the French or Spaniſh Kings in temporall matters.* Where it is further added, That Pope *Innocent* 3. hath beene pleaſed to teſtifie, that Kings of *France* in Temporall cauſes doe acknowledge no ſuperiour : For ſo the Pope excuſed himſelfe to a certaine Lord of Montpellier, who in ſtead of ſuing to the King, had petitioned to the Pope for a diſpenſation for his baſtard. *But perhaps (as he ſpeaketh) it will be alledged out of the gloſſe, that bee acknowledgeth no ſuperiour by fact, and yet ought by right. But I tell you the gloſſe is an Aurelian gloſſe, which marres the text.* Amongſt other arguments, *Maior* brings this for one : *This opinion miniſtreth matter vnto Popes, to take away an others Empire by force and violence : which the Pope ſhall neuer bring to paſſe,* as we reade of Boniface 8. againſt Philip the Faire : *Saith beſides, That from hence proceede warres, in time of which many outragious miſchiefes are done,* and that Gerſon *calls them egregious flatterers by whom ſuch opinion is maintained.* In the ſame place *Maior* denies that *Childeric* was depoſed by Pope *Zacharie : The word, Hee depoſed,* ſaith *Maior, is not ſo to bee vnderſtood, as it is taken at the firſt bluſh or ſight ; but hee depoſed, is thus expounded in the gloſſe, Hee gaue his conſent vnto thoſe by whom he was depoſed.*

De poteſt.Regia & Papali. cap.10. *Iohn* of Paris : *Were it graunted that Chriſt was armed with Temporall power, yet he committed no ſuch power to Peter.* A little after : *The power of Kings is the higheſt power vpon earth : in Temporall cauſes it hath no ſuperiour power aboue it ſelfe, no more then the Pope hath in ſpirituall matters.* This author ſaith indeede, the Pope hath power to excommunicate the King ; but he ſpeaketh not of any power in the Pope to put downe the King from his regall dignity and authority : He onely ſaith, When a Prince is once excommunicated, hee may accidentally or by occaſion be depoſed : becauſe his precedent excommunication, incites the people to diſarme him of all ſecular dignity and power. The ſame Iohn on the other ſide holdeth opinion; that *in the Emperour there is inueſted a power to depoſe the Pope, in caſe the Pope ſhall abuſe his power.*

Almainus

Almainus Doctor of the Sorbonic schoole: *It is essentiall in the Lay-power to inflict ciuill punishment, as death, banishment, and priuation or losse of goods. But according to diuine institution, the power Ecclesiasticall can lay no such punishment vpon delinquents: nay more, not lay in prison, as to some Doctors it seemeth probable: but stretcheth and reacheth onely to spirituall punishment, as namely to excommunication: all other punishments inflicted by the spirituall power, are meerely by the Lawe positiue.* If then Ecclesiasticall power by Gods Lawe hath no authoritie to depriue any priuate man of his goods; how dares the Pope and his flatterers build their power to depriue Kings of their scepters vpon the word of God?

Almain.de potest.Eccl.& Laica.Quest.2. cap.8. De dominio naturæ ciuil & Eccl.5.vlt.pars.

The same author in an other place: *Bee it graunted that* Constantine *had power to giue the Empire vnto the Pope; yet is it not hereupon to bee inferred, that Popes haue authority ouer the Kingdome of* France, *because that Kingdome was neuer subiect vnto* Constantine: *For the King of* France *neuer had any superiour in Temporall matters.* A little after: *It is not in any place to bee found, that God hath giuen the Pope power to make and vnmake Temporall Kings.*

Quest 1.de potest.Eccles.& laik c.12 & 14

He maintaineth elsewhere, that *Zacharie* did not depose *Childeric*, but onely consented to his deposing; *and so deposed him not as by authoritie.* In the same booke, taking vp the words of *Occam*, whom he styles the Doctor: *The Emperour is the Popes Lord in things Temporall, and the Pope calls him Lord, as it is witnessed in the body of the Text.* The Lord Cardinall hath dissembled and concealed these words of Doctor *Almainus*, with many like places: and hath beene pleased to alledge *Almainus* reciting *Occams* authoritie, in stead of quoting *Almainus* himselfe in those passages, where he speaketh as out of his owne opinion, and in his owne words. A notable piece of slie and cunning conueiance: For what heresie may not be fathered and fastened vpon S. *Augustine*, or S. *Hierome*, if they should be deemed to approoue all the passages which they alledge out of other authors? And that is the reason wherefore the L. Cardinall doeth not alledge his testimonies whole and perfect, as they are couched in their proper texts, but clipt and curtaild. Thus he dealeth euen in the first passage or testimonie of *Almainus*; he brings it in mangled and pared: he hides and conceales the words added by *Almainus*, to contradict and crosse the words going before: For *Almainus* makes this addition and supply; *Howsoeuer some other Doctors doe stand for the negatiue, and teach the Pope hath power onely to declare that Kings and Princes are to be deposed.* And so much appeareth by this reason; because this ample and Soueraigne power of the Pope, might giue him occasion to be puft vp with great pride, and the same fulnesse of power might prooue extreamely hurtfull to the subiects, &c.

Quest.1.c.8.& sic non deposuit autoritatiue.

Qua.3.c 2. Quest.11.can. Sacerd.

The same *Almainus* brings in *Occams* opinion in expresse tearmes deciding the question, and there ioynes his owne opinion with *Occams*. The Doctors opinion, saith *Almainus*, doeth simply carrie the most probabilitie; that a Pope hath no power, neither by excommunication, nor by any other meanes, to depose a Prince from his Imperiall and Royall dignitie. And a little before, hauing maintained

Quest.2.de potest.Eccl & Laic.cap.12.

In cap.9 10. & 11.

tained the Greeke Empire was neuer tranfported by the Pope to the Germaines, and that when the Pope crownes the Emperour, he doeth not giue him the Empire, no more then the Archbifhop of Reims when he crownes the King of France, doth giue him the kingdom; he drawes this conclufion according to *Occams* opinion : *I denie that an Emperour is bound by oath to promife the Pope allegiance. On the other fide, if the Pope hold any Temporall poffeffions , hee is bound to fweare allegiance vnto the Emperour, and to pay him tribute.* The faid *Occam* alledged by *Almainus* doeth further auerre, that *Iuftinian* was acknowledged by the Pope for his fuperiour in Temporall caufes : for as much as diuers Lawes which the Pope is bound to keepe and obferue, were enacted by *Iuftinian*; as by name the Law of prefcription for an hundred yeeres : which Law ftandeth yet in force againft the Bifhop of Rome. And to the end that all men may clearely fee, how great diftance there is betweene *Occams* opinion and the L. Cardinals, who towards the end of his Oration, exhorts his hearers at no hand to diffent from the Pope ; take you here a view of *Occams* owne words, as they are alledged by *Almainus* : *The* Queft.1.cap. 14. *Doctour affoyles the arguments of Pope* Innocent, *by which the Pope would prooue out of thefe words of* CHRIST, *Whatfoeuer thou fhalt binde, &c. that fulneffe of power in Temporall matters, belongeth to the Soueraigne Bifhop*: For Innocent *faith, Whatfoeuer, excepteth nothing* : But Occam *affoyles* Innocents *authoritie, as not onely falfe, but alfo hereticall; and faith withall, that many things are fpoken by* Innocent, *which by his leaue fauour and fmell of herefie, &c.*

Pag.40. The L. Cardinall with leffe fidelitie alledgeth two places out of *Thomas* his Summe. The firft, in the fecond of his fecond, Queft. 10. Art.10. in the body of the Article; In which place (let it bee narrowly examined) *Thomas* will eafily bee found to fpeake, not of the fubiection of beleeuing Subiects vnder Infidel Kings, as the Lord Cardinall pretendeth, but of beleeuing feruants that liue vnder Mafters, whether Iewes or Infidels : As when a Iew keepeth feruants which profeffe *Iefus Chrift* ; or as when fome of the faithfull kept in *Cæfars* houfe; who are not confidered by *Thomas* as they were fubiects of the Empire, but as they were feruants of the family. The other place is taken out of Queft.11. and 2. Art. in the body of the article: where no fuch matter as the L. Cardinal alledgeth can be found.

Pag.44. With like fidelitie he taketh *Gerfon* in hand : who indeed in his booke of Ecclefiafticall power, and 12. Confider. doeth affirme, *When the abufe of Secular power redoundeth to manifeft impugning of the faith, and blafpheming of the Creator; then fhall it not bee amiffe to haue recourfe vnto the laft branch of this* 12. *Confider. where, in fuch cafe as aforefaid, a certaine regitiue, directiue, regulatiue, and ordinatiue authoritie is committed to the Ecclefiafticall power.* His very words: which make no mention at all of depofing, or of any compulfiue power ouer Soueraigne Princes: For that forme of rule and gouernment whereof *Gerfon* fpeaketh, is exercifed by Ecclefiafticall cenfures and excommunications; not by loffe of goods, of Kingdomes, or of Empires. This place then is wrefted by the L. Cardinall to a contrary fenfe. Neither fhould his
Lord-

Lordſhip haue omitted, that *Gerſon*, in the queſtion of Kings ſubiection in Temporall matters , or of the dependance of their Crownes vpon the Popes power, excepteth alwayes the King of France: witneſſe that which *Gerſon* a little before the place alleadged by the Cardinall, hath plainely affirmed: *Now ſince Peters time , ſaith* Gerſon *, all Imperiall, Regall, and Secular power is not immediatly to draw vertue and ſtrength from the Soueraigne Biſhop: as in this maner the moſt Chriſtian King of France hath no Superiour, nor acknow-ledgeth any ſuch vpon the face of the earth.* Now here need no great ſharpe-neſſe of wit for the ſearching out of this deepe myſterie; that if the Pope hath power to giue or take away Crownes for any cauſe or any preten-ded occaſion whatſoeuer, the Crowne of France muſt needs depend vpon the Pope.

But for as much as we are now hit in with *Gerſon*, we will examine the L.Cardinals allegations towards the end of his Oration, taken out of *Ger-ſons* famous Oration made before *Charles* the 6. for the Vniuerſitie of Pa-ris : where he brings in *Gerſon* to affirme, *That killing a Tyrant is a ſacrifice ac-ceptable to God.* But *Gerſon* (let it be diligently noted) there ſpeaketh not in his owne perſon: he there brings in ſedition ſpeaking the words: Of which wordes vttered by ſedition, and other like ſpeeches, you ſhall now heare what iudgement *Gerſon* himſelfe hath giuen. *When ſedition had ſpoken with ſuch a furious voyce, I turned away my face as if I had bene ſmitten with death, to ſhew that I was not able to endure her madneſſe any longer.* And indeed when diſſimulation on the one ſide, and ſedition on the other, had ſugge-ſted the deuiſes of two contrary extremes , hee brings foorth *Diſcretion* as a iudge, keeping the meane betweene both extremes, and vttering thoſe words which the L.Cardinall alledgeth againſt himſelfe. *If the head, (ſaith* Gerſon *) or ſome other member of the ciuill body , ſhould grow to ſo deſperate a paſſe, that it would gulpe and ſwallow downe the deadly poyſon of tyrannie ; euery member in his place, with all power poſsible for him to raiſe by expedient meanes , and ſuch as might preuent a greater inconuenience , ſhould ſet himſelfe againſt ſo madde a purpoſe, and ſo deadly practiſe : For if the head be grieued with ſome light paine , it is not fit for the hand to ſmite the head: no, that were but a fooliſh and a mad part: Nor the hand forthwith to chop off or ſeparate the head from the body, but rather to cure the head with good ſpeach and other meanes, like a skilfull and wiſe Phyſitian : Yea nothing would be more cruel or more voyd of reaſon , then to ſeeke to ſtop the ſtrong and violent ſtreame of tyrannie by ſedition.* Theſe words, me thinke, doe make very ſtrongly and expreſly againſt butchering euen of Tyrannical Kings. And whereas a little after the ſaid paſſage, he teacheth to expell Tyrannie, he hath not a word of expelling the Tyrant, but onely of breaking and ſha-king off the yoke of Tyrannie. Yet for all that, he would not haue the re-medies for the repreſsing of Tyrannie, to be fetcht from the Pope, who pre-meth to degrade Kings, but from *Philoſophers, Lawyers, Diuines, and perſo-nages of good conuerſation.* It appeareth now by all that hath bin ſaid before, that whereas *Gerſon* in the 7. Conſiderat. *againſt Flatterers*, doeth affirme:

When-

Pag.108.109. 119. where the Card. takes Char. 7. for Charl. 6.

*Whenſoeuer the Prince doeth manifeſtly purſue and proſecute his naturall ſubiects, and ſhew himſelfe obſtinately bent with notorious iniuſtice, to vexe them of ſet purpoſe, and with full conſent, ſo farre as to the fact; then this rule and law of Nature doeth take place, It is lawfull to reſiſt and repell force by force; and the ſentence of Se-*neca, *There is no ſacrifice more acceptable to God, then a tyrant offered in ſacrifice;* the words, *doeth take place,* are ſo to be vnderſtood, as he ſpeaketh in another paſſage, to wit, with or amongſt ſeditious perſons. Or elſe the words, *doeth take place,* doe onely ſignifie, *is put in practiſe.* And ſo *Gerſon* there ſpeaketh not as out of his owne iudgement.

His Lordſhip alſo ſhould not haue balked and left out *Sigebertus,* who with more reaſon might haue paſſed for French, then *Thomas* and *Occam,* whom hee putteth vpon vs for French. *Sigebertus* in his Chronicle vpon the yeere 1 0 8 8. ſpeaking of the Emperours depoſing by the Pope, hath words of this tenour : *This Hereſie was not crept out of the ſhell in thoſe dayes, that his Prieſts, who hath ſaid to the King* Apoſtata, *and maketh an hypocrite to rule for the ſinnes of the people, ſhould teach the people they owe no ſubiection vnto wicked Kings, nor any alleagiance, notwithſtanding they haue taken the oath of alleagiance.*

Now after the L.Cardinal hath courſed in this maner through the hiſtories of the laſt aages (which in caſe they all made for his purpoſe, doe lacke the weight of authority) in ſtead of ſearching the will of God in the ſacred Oracles of his word and ſtanding vpon examples of the ancient Church; at laſt, leauing the troupe of his owne allegations, he betakes himſelfe to the ſharpening and rebating of the points of his aduerſaries weapons.

For the purpoſe, he brings in his aduerſaries, the champions of Kings Crownes, & makes them to ſpeake out of his own mouth(for his Lordſhip faith it will be obiected) after this maner: *It may come to paſſe, that Popes either caried with paſſion, or miſled by ſiniſter information, may without iuſt cauſe faſten vpon Kings the imputation of hereſie or apoſtaſie.* Then for King-depoſers he frames this anſwere: *That by hereſie they vnderſtand notorious hereſie, and formerly condemned by ſentence of the Church.* Moreouer, *in caſe the Pope hath erred in the fact, it is the Clergies part adhering to their King, to make remonſtrances vnto the Pope, and to require the cauſe may be referred to the iudgement of a full Councel, the French Church then and there being preſent.* Now in this anſwere, the L. Cardinall is of another mind then *Bellarmine* his brother Cardinall : For hee goes thus farre, That a Prince condemned by vniuſt ſentence of the Pope, ought neuertheleſſe to quit his Kingdome, and that his Paſtors vniuſt ſentence ſhall not redound to his detriment; prouided that hee giue way to the ſaid ſentence, and ſhew himſelfe not refractarie, but ſtay the time in patience, vntill the holy Father ſhall renounce his error, and reuoke his foreſaid vniuſt ſentence. In which caſe theſe two material points are to be preſuppoſed: The one, That he who now hath ſeized the kingdome of the Prince diſplaced, wil forthwith (if the Pope ſhall ſollicit and intercede) returne the Kingdome to the hand of the late poſſeſſor: The other, That in the

Pag. 5 2. & ſequentibus.

Aduerſ. Barclaium.

the *interim* the Prince vniuſtly depoſed, ſhall not need to feare the bloody murderers mercileſſe blade and weapon. But on the other ſide, the Popes power of ſo large a ſize, as *Bellarmine* hath ſhaped, is no whit pleaſing to the L. Cardinals eye. For in caſe the King ſhould be vniuſtly depoſed by the Pope *not well informed*, he is not of the minde the Kingdome ſhould ſtoupe to the Popes beheſts, but will rather haue the Kingdome to deale by remonſtrance, and to referre the cauſe vnto the Council: Wherein he makes the Council to be of more abſolute and ſupreme authority then the Pope; a ſtraine to which the holy father will neuer lend his eare. And yet doubt-leſſe, the Council required in this caſe muſt be vniuerſall; wherein the French, for ſo much as they ſtand firme for the King and his cauſe, can be no Iudges: and in that regard the L. Cardinal requireth onely the preſence of the French Church. Who ſeeth not here into what pickle the French cauſe is brought by this meanes? The Biſhops of *Italie* forſooth, of *Spaine*, of *Sicilie*, of *Germanie*, the ſubiects of Soueraignes many times at profeſ-ſed or priuie enmitie with *France*, ſhall haue the cauſe compremitted and referred to their iudgement, whether the Kindome of *France* ſhall driue out her Kings, and ſhall kindle the flames of ſeditious troubles, in the ve-ry heart and bowels of the Realme. But is it not poſſible, that a King may lacke the loue of his owne ſubiects, and they taking the vantage of that occaſion, may put him to his trumps in his owne Kingdome? Is it not poſſible, that calumniations whereby a credulous Pope hath beene ſedu-ced, may in like maner deceiue ſome part of a credulous people? Is it not poſſible that one part of the people may cleaue to the Popes Faction, another may hold and ſtand out for the Kings rightfull cauſe, and ciuill warres may be kindled by the ſplene of theſe two ſides? Is it not poſſible, that his Holineſſe will not reſt in the remonſtrances of the French, and will no further purſue his cauſe? And whereas now a dayes a Generall Councill cannot be held, except it be called and aſſembled by the Popes authority; is it credible, the Pope will take order for the conuocation of a Council, by whom he ſhall be iudged? And how can the Pope be Preſi-dent in a Councill, where himſelfe is the party impleaded? and to whom the ſifting of his owne ſentence is referred, as it were to Committies, to ex-amine whether it was denounced according to Law, or againſt Iuſtice? But in the meane time, whileſt all theſe remonſtrances and addreſſes of the Council are on foot; behold, the Royall Maieſtie of the King hangeth as it were by looſe gimmals, and muſt ſtay the iudgement of the Council to whom it is referred. Well: what if the Councill ſhould happe to be two or three yeeres in aſſembling, and to continue or hold eighteene yeeres, like the Councill of *Trent*; ſhould not poore *France*, I beſeech you, be reduced to a very bad plight? ſhould ſhe not be in a very wiſe and warme taking? To be ſhort; His Lordſhips whole ſpeach for the vntying of this knot, not onely ſurmounteth poſſibilitie, but is ſtuft with ridiculous toyes. This I make manifeſt by his addition in the ſame paſſage. *If the Pope deceiued* _in fact, shall rashly and vniustly declare the King to be an heretike; then the Popes declaration shall not be seconded with actuall deposition, vnles the Realme shall consent vnto the Kings deposing._ What needes any man to bee instructed in this doctrine? Who doth not knowe, that a King, so long as he is vpheld and maintained in his Kingdome by his people, cannot actually and effectually be deposed from his Throne? Hee that speaketh such language and phrase, in effect saith, and saith no more then this: A King is neuer depriued of his Crowne, so long as he can keepe his Crowne on his head: a King is neuer turned and stript naked, so long as he can keepe his cloathes on his backe: a King is neuer deposed, so long as he can make the stronger partie and side against his enemies: in briefe, a King is King, and shall still remaine King, so long as he can hold the possession of his Kingdome, and sit fast in his Chaire of Estate. Howbeit, let vs here by the way, take notice of these words vttered by his Lordship: _That for the deposing of a King, the consent of the people must be obtained:_ For by these words the people are exalted aboue the King, and are made the Iudges of the Kings deposing.

Can. Si Papa, Dist. 40. Nisi sit à fide deuius.

But here is yet a greater matter: For that Popes may erre in faith, it is acknowledged by Popes themselues: For some of them haue condemned Pope _Honorius_ for a Monothelite: S. _Hierome_, and S. _Hilarius_, and S. _Athanasius_ doe testifie, that Pope _Liberius_ started aside, and subscribed to _Arrianisme_: Pope _Iohn_ 23. was condemned in the Councill of _Constance_, for maintaining there is neither hell nor heauen: Diuerse other Popes haue been tainted with errour in faith. If therefore any Pope hereticall in himselfe, shall depose an Orthodoxe King for heresie; can it be imagined, that he which

Omnia iura in scrinio pectoris.

boasts himselfe to beare all diuine and humane lawes in the priuy coffer or casket of his breast, will stoope to the remonstrances of the French, and vayle to the reasons which they shall propound, though neuer so iustifiable, and of neuer so great validitie? And how can he, that may be infected with damnable heresie (when himselfe is not alwayes free from heresie) be a iudge of heresie in a King? In this question some are of opinion, that as a man, the Pope may fall into error, but not as Pope. Very good: I demand then vpon the matter, wherefore the Pope doth not instruct and reforme the man? or wherefore the man doth not require the Popes instructions? But whether a King be deposed by that man the Pope, or by that Pope the man, is it not all one? is he not deposed? Others affirme, the Pope may erre in a question of the fact, but not in a question of the right. An egregious gullery and imposture: For if he may be ignorant whether Iesus Christ died for our sinnes, doubtles he may also be to seeke, whether we should repose all our trust and assured confidence in the death of Christ. Consider with me the Prophets of olde: They were all inspired and taught of God, to admonish and reproue the Kings of Iudah and Israel: they neither erred in matter of fact, nor in point of right: they were as farre from being blinded and fetcht ouer by deceitfull calumniations, as from beeing seduced by the painted shew of corrupt and false doctrine: As
they

they neuer trode awry in matter of faith ; so they neuer whetted the edge
of their tongue or style against the faultlesse. Had it not beene a trimme
deuice in their times, to say, that as *Esay* and as *Daniel* they might haue
sunke into heresie, but not as Prophets? For doubtlesse in this case, that
Esay would haue taken counsell of the Prophet which was himselfe. To
be short; If Kings are onely so long to be taken for Kings, vntill they shall
be declared heretikes, and shall be deposed by the Pope; they continually
stand in extreame danger, to vndergoe a very heauy and vniust sentence.
Their safest way were to know nothing, and to beleeue by proxie; least, if
they should happen to talke of God, or to thinke of religion, they should be
drawne for heretikes into the Popes Inquisition.

All the examples hitherto produced by the Lord Cardinall on a rowe,
are of a latter date, they lacke weight, are drawne from the time of bondage, and make the Popes themselues witnesses in their owne cause:
They descant not vpon the point of deposition, but onely strike out
and found the notes of excommunication and interdiction, which
make nothing at all to the musicke of the question. And therefore
hee telleth vs (in kindnesse as I take it) more oftentimes then once or
twice, that hee speaketh onely of the fact; as one that doeth acknowledge himselfe to bee out of the right: Hee relates things done, but
neuer what should bee done : which, as the Iudicious know, is to
teach nothing.

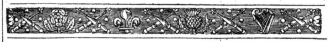

THE SECOND INCON-
VENIENCE EXAMINED.

 HE second Inconuenience like to grow, (as the Lord Cardinall seemeth to be halfe afraid) if the Article of the third
Estate might haue passed with approbation, is couched in
these words : *Lay-men shall by authoritie bee strengthened with*
power, to iudge in matters of Religion; as also to determine the
doctrine comprised in the said Article to haue requisite conformitie with Gods word:
yea they shall haue it in their hands to compell Ecclesiastics by necessitie, to sweare,
preach, and teach the opinion of the one side, as also by Sermons and publike writings to
impugne the other. This inconuenience he aggrauateth with swelling words,
and breaketh out into these vehement exclamations : *O reproach, O scandall, O*
gate set open to a world of heresies. He therefore laboureth both by reasons, and
by autorities of holy Scripture, to make such vsurped power of Laics, a
fowle, shameful, and odious practise. In the whole, his Lordship toyles himselfe in vaine, & maketh suppositions of castles in the aire. For in preferring
this Article, the third Estate haue born themselues not as iudges or vmpires,

Nn 3   but

Pag. 86.

but altogether as petitioners : requesting the said Article might be receiued into the number of the Parliament bookes to bee presented vnto the
King and his Counsell, vnto whom in all humilitie they referred the iudgment of the said Article; conceiuing all good hope the Clergie and Nobilitie would be pleased to ioyne for the furtherance of their humble petition.
They were not so ignorant of State-matters, or so vnmindfull of their
owne places and charges, to beare themselues in hand, that a petition put
vp and preferred by the third Estate, can carry the force of a Law or Statute, so long as the other two Orders withstand the same, and so long as
the King himselfe holds backe his Royall consent. Besides, the said Article
was not propounded as a point of Religious doctrine; but for euer after
to remaine and continue a fundamentall Law of the Common-wealth
and State it selfe, the due care whereof was put into their handes, and committed to their trust. If the King had ratified the said Article with Royall
consent, and had commanded the Clergie to put in execution the contents
thereof; it had bene their duetie to see the Kings will and pleasure fulfilled, as they are subiects bound to giue him aide in all things, which may
any way serue to procure the safetie of his life , and the tranquilitie of his
Kingdome: Which if the Clergie had performed to the vttermost of their
power, they had not shewed obedience as vnderlings, vnto the third Estate,
but vnto the King alone; by whom such command had bene imposed, vpon suggestion of his faithfull subiects, made the more watchfull by the
negligence of the Clergie ; whom they perceiue to be lincked with stri-
cter bandes vnto the Pope, then they are vnto their King. Here then the
Cardinall fights with meere shadowes , and mooues a doubt whereof his
aduersaries haue not so much as once thought in a dreame: But yet, according to his great dexteritie and nimblenesse of spirit, by this deuice
he cunningly takes vpon him to giue the King a lesson with more libertie,
making semblance to direct his masked Oration to the Deputies of the
people, when hee shooteth in effect, and pricketh at his King, the Princes
also and Lords of his Counsell, whom the Cardinall comprifeth vnder the
name of Laics; whose iudgment (it is not vnlikely) was apprehended much
better by the Clergie, then the iudgement of the third Estate. Now these
are the men whom he tearmes intruders into other mens charges, and such
as open a gate for I wot not how many legions of heresies, to rush into
the Church: For if it be proper to the Clergie and their Head, to iudge in
this cause of the Right of Kings ; then the King himselfe, his Princes, and
Nobilitie, are debarred and wiped of all iudgement in the same cause, no
lesse then the representatiue body of the people.

Pag. 62. Well then, the L. Cardinall showres downe like haile sundry places and
testimonies of Scripture, where the people are commanded to haue their
Pastors in singular loue, and to beare them all respects of due obseruance.
Be it so, yet are the said passages of Scripture no barre to the people, for their
vigilant circumspection, to preserue the life and Crowne of their Prince,

against

againſt all the wicked enterpriſes of men ſtirred vp by the Clergie, who haue their Head out of the Kingdome, and hold themſelues to be none of the Kings ſubiects: a thing neuer ſpoken by the ſacrificing Prieſts and Prelates, mentioned in the paſſages alleadged by the Lord Cardinal. He likewiſe produceth two Chriſtian Emperours, *Conſtantine* and *Valentinian* by name; the firſt refuſing to meddle with iudgement in Epiſcopall cauſes: the other forbearing to iudge of ſubtile Queſtions in Diuinity, with proteſtation, that *Hee would neuer bee ſo curious, to diue into the ſtreames, or ſound the bottome of ſo deepe matters.* But who doth not know, that working and prouiding for the Kings indemnitie and ſafetie, is neither Epiſcopall cauſe, nor matter of curious and ſubtile inquiſition? The ſame anſwere meets with all the reſt of the places produced by the L. Cardinal out of the Fathers. And that one for example, out of *Gregory Nazianzenus,* is not cited by the Cardinall with faire dealing. For *Gregory* doeth not boord the Emperour himſelfe, but his Deputy or L. Preſident, on this maner: *For we alſo are in authoritie and place of a Ruler, we haue command aſwell as your ſelfe:* wheras the the L. Cardinal with foule play, turnes the place in theſe termes, *We alſo are Emperours.* Which words can beare no ſuch interpretation, as well becauſe he to whom the Biſhop then ſpake, was not of Imperiall dignitie; as alſo becauſe if the Biſhop himſelfe, a Biſhop of ſo ſmall a citie as *Nazianzum,* had qualified himſelfe Emperour, hee ſhould haue paſſed all the bounds of modeſtie, and had ſhewed himſelfe arrogant aboue meaſure. For as touching ſubiection due to Chriſtian Emperours, hee freely acknowledgeth a little before, *that himſelfe and his people are ſubiect vnto the ſuperiour powers, yea bound to pay them tribute.* The hiſtorie of the ſame *Gregories* life doeth teſtifie, that he was drawen by the *Arrians* before the Conſuls iudgement ſeate, and from thence returned acquitted, without either ſtripes or any other kinde of contumelious entreatie and vſe: yet now at laſt vp ſtarts a Prelate, who dares make this good Father vaunt himſelfe to be an Emperour. It is willingly granted, that Emperours neuer challenged, neuer arrogated, to bee Soueraigne Iudges in controuerſies of doctrine and faith; neuertheleſſe it is clearer then the Sunnes light at high noone, that for moderation at Synods, for determinations and orders eſtabliſhed in Councils, and for the diſcipline of the Church, they haue made a good and a full vſe of their Imperiall authoritie. The firſt Council held at *Conſtantinople,* beares this title or inſcription; *The dedication of the holy Synode to the moſt religious Emperour* Theodoſius *the Great, to whoſe will and pleaſure they haue ſubmitted theſe Canons by them addreſſed and eſtabliſhed in Councill.* And there they alſo beſeech the Emperour, to confirme and approue the ſaid Canons. The like hath bene done by the Council of *Trullo,* by whom the Canons of the fift and ſixt Councils were put foorth and publiſhed. This was not done, becauſe Emperours tooke vpon them to bee infallible Iudges of doctrine; but onely that Emperours might ſee and iudge, whether Biſhops (who feele the pricke of ambition as other men doe) did

pro-

Pag. 62.

Orat. ad ciues timore percul-ſos.

Vide Canones Græcos à Tilio editos.

propound nothing in their Conuocations and Confultations, but moſt of all in their Determinations, to vndermine the Emperours authoritie, to diſturbe the tranquilitie of the Common-wealth, and to croſſe the determinations of precedent Councils. Now to take the cognizance of ſuch matters out of the Kings hand or power; what is it but euen to transforme the King into a ſtanding Image, to wring and wreſt him out of all care of himſelfe and his Kingly Charge, yea to bring him downe to this baſeſt condition, to become onely an executioner, and (which I ſcorne to ſpeake) the vnhappy hangman of the Clergies will, without any further cognizance, not ſo much as of matters which moſt neerely touch himſelfe, and his Royall eſtate?

. I grant it is for Diuinitie Scholes, to iudge how farre the power of the Keyes doth ſtretch: I grant againe, that Clerics both may, and ought alſo to diſplay the colours and enſignes of their cenſures againſt Princes, who violating their publike and ſolemne oath, doe raiſe and make open warre againſt *Ieſus Chriſt*: I grant yet againe, that in this caſe they need not admit Laics to be of their counſell, nor allow them any ſcope or libertie of iudgement. Yet all this makes no barre to Clerics, for extending the power of their keyes, many times a whole degree further then they ought; and when they are pleaſed, to make vſe of their ſaid power, to depriue the people of their goods, or the Prince of his Crowne: all this doeth not hinder Prince or people from taking care for the preſeruation of their owne rights and eſtates, nor from requiring Clerics to ſhew their cards, and produce their Charts, and to make demonſtration by Scripture, that ſuch power as they aſſume and challenge, is giuen them from God. For to leaue the Pope abſolute Iudge in the ſame cauſe, wherein hee is a partie, and (which is the ſtrongeſt rampier and bulwarke, yea the moſt glorious and eminent point of his domination) to arme him with power to vnhorſe Kings out of their ſeates; what is it elſe but euen to draw them into a ſtate of deſpaire for euer winning the day, or preuailing in their honourable and rightful cauſe?

It is moreouer granted, if a King ſhall command any thing directly contrary to Gods word, and tending to the ſubuerting of the Church; that Clerics in this caſe ought not onely to diſpenſe with ſubiects for their obedience, but alſo expreſly to forbid their obedience: For it is alwayes better to obey God then man. Howbeit in all other matters, whereby the glory and maieſtie of God is not impeached or impaired, it is the duety of Clerics to plie the people with wholeſome exhortation to conſtant obedience, and to auert by earneſt diſſwaſions the ſaid people from tumultuous reuolt and ſeditious inſurrection. This practiſe vnder the Pagan Emperours, was held and followed by the ancient Chriſtians; by whoſe godly zeale and patience in bearing the yoke, the Church in times paſt grew and flouriſhed in her happy and plentifull increaſe, farre greater then Poperie ſhall euer purchaſe and attaine vnto by all her cunning deuices and ſleights: as namely by degrading of Kings, by interdicting of Kingdoms, by appo-

ſted

fted murders, and by Diabolicall traines of Gunne-powder-mines.

The places of Scripture alleadged in order by the Cardinal, in fauour of thofe that ftand for the Popes claime of power and authoritie to depofe Kings, are cited with no more fincerity then the former : *They alledge* (thefe are his words) *that* Samuel *depofed King* Saul, *or declared him to bee depofed, becaufe hee had violated the Lawes of the Iewes Religion* : His Lordſhip auoucheth elfewere, that *Saul* was depofed, becaufe he had fought prophanely to vfurpe the holy Prieſthood. Both falfe and contrary to the tenour of trewth in the facred hiftory : For *Saul* was neuer depofed according to the fenfe of the word (I meane, *depofe*) in the prefent queſtion ; to wit, as depofing is taken for defpoiling the King of his royall dignitie, and reducing the King to the condition of a priuate perfon : But *Saul* held the title of King, and continued in poffeffion of his Kingdome, euen to his dying day. Yea, the Scripture ftyles him King, euen to the periodicall and laſt day of his life, by the teſtimony of *Dauid* himfelfe, who both by Gods promife, and by precedent vnction, was then heire apparant as it were to the Crown, in a maner then ready to gird and adorne the temples of his head. For if *Samuel*, by Gods commandement, had then actually remooued *Saul* from his Throne, doubtleffe the whole Church of Ifrael had committed a groffe errour, in taking and honouring *Saul* for their King, after fuch depofition : doubtleffe the Prophet *Samuel* himfelfe, making knowen the Lords Ordinance vnto the people, would haue enioyned them by ſtrict prohibition to call him no longer the King of Ifrael : Doubtleffe, *Dauid* would neuer haue held his hand from the throat of *Saul*, for this refpect and confideration, becaufe he was the Lords Anointed. For if *Saul* had loſt his Kingly authority, from that inftant when *Samuel* gaue him knowledge of his reiection ; then *Dauid*, left otherwife the Body of the Kingdome fhould want a Royall Head, was to beginne his Reigne, and to beare the Royall fcepter in the very fame inftant : which were to charge the holy Scriptures with vntrewth, in as much as the facred hiftorie begins the computation of the yeeres of *Dauids* Reigne, from the day of *Sauls* death. Trew it is, that in the 1. Sam. cap. 15. *Saul* was denounced by Gods owne fentence, a man reiected, and as it were excommunicated out of the Kingdome, that hee fhould not rule and reigne any longer as King ouer Ifrael ; neuertheleffe, the faid fentence was not put in execution, before the day when God, executing vpon *Saul* an exemplarie iudgement, did ftrike him with death. From whence it is manifeft and cleare, that when *Dauid* was annointed King by *Samuel*, that action was onely a promife, and a teſtimony of the choice, which God had made of *Dauid* for fucceffion immediately after *Saul*; and not a prefent eſtabliſhment, inueſtment, or inſtallment of *Dauid* in the Kingdome. Wee reade the like in 1. King. cap. 19. where God commandeth *Elias* the Prophet, to annoint *Hafael* King of *Syria* : For can any man bee fo blinde and ignorant in the facred hiftorie, to beleeue the Prophets of Ifrael eſtabliſhed, or facred the Kings of *Syria* ? For this caufe,

Pag 66.

1. Sam. 13. 20.
& 24. 15. & 2.
Sam. 2. 5.

1. Sam. 26. 11

1. Sam. 16. 13.

1.Sam.1.4.

caufe, when *Dauid* was actually eftablifhed in the Kingdome, hee was an-nointed the fecond time.

In the next place he brings in the Popes champions vfing thefe words;
1.King.12.
Rehoboam was depofed by Abiah the Prophet, from his Royall right ouer the tenne " *Tribes of Ifrael, becaufe his father Salomon had played the Apoſtata, in falling from* " *the Law of God.* This I fay alfo is more, then the trewth of the facred hiftory doeth afoard : For *Abiah* neuer fpake to *Rehoboam* (for ought we reade,)nor brought vnto him any meffage from the Lord; As for the paffage quoted by the L.Cardinal out of 3.*Reg.*chap.11.it hath not reference to the time of *Rehoboams* raigne, but rather indeed to Salomons time : nor doeth it carry the face of a iudicatorie fentence for the Kings depofing, but rather of a Propheticall prediction : For how could *Rehoboam*, before hee was made King, be depriued of the Kingdome? Laft of all, but worft of all ; to al-leadge this paffage for an example of a iuft fentence in matter of depofing a King,is to approoue the difloyall treacherie of a feruant againft his mafter, and the rebellion of *Ieroboam* branded in Scripture with a marke of perpe-tuall infamie for his wickedneffe and impietie.

1.King.19.
He goes on with an other example of no more trewth; *King Achab was* " *depofed by Elias the Prophet, becaufe he imbraced falfe religion, and worſhipped falfe* " *gods.*Falfe too like the former; King *Achab* loft his crowne and his life both together. The Scripture, that fpeaketh not according to mans fancie,but according to the trewth, doeth extend and number the yeeres of *Achabs* raigne,to the time of his death. Predictions of a Kings ruine, are no fen-tences of depofition. *Elias* neuer gaue the fubiects of *Achab* abfolution from their oath of obedience; neuer gaue them the leaft inckling of any fuch abfolution ; neuer fet vp,or placed any other King in *Achabs* throne.

Pag.68.
That of the L.Cardinall a little after, is no leffe vntrew : *That King Vz-* " *ziah was driuen from the conuerfation of the people by Azarias the Prieſt,and there-* " *by the adminiſtration of his Kingdome was left no longer in his power.* Not fo:For
2.Chro.26.
when God had fmitten *Vzziah* with leprofie in his forehead, he withdrew himfelfe,or went out into an houfe apart,for feare of infecting fuch as were whole by his contagious difeafe. The high Prieft fmote him not with any fentence of depofition, or denounced him fufpended from the adminiftra-tion of his Kingdome. No : the dayes of his raigne are numbred in Scrip-ture,to the day of his death. And whereas the Prieft,according to the Law in the 13.of *Leuit.*iudged the King to be vncleane; he gaue fentence againft him,not as againft a criminall perfon, and thereby within the compaffe of depofition; but as againft a difeafed body : For the Law inflicteth punifh-ments,not vpon difeafes, but vpon crimes. Hereupon, whereas it is recor-
Antiq.l.9.
cap.11.
ded by *Iofephus* in his Antiquities,that *Vzziah* led a priuate,and in a maner, a folitarie life ; the faid author doeth not meane , that *Vzziah* was depofed, but onely that he disburdened himfelfe of care to mannage the publique affaires.

Pag.69.
The example of *Mattathias*, by whom the Iewes were ftirred vp to rebel
againft

againſt *Antiochus*, is no better worth: For in that example we finde no ſentence of depoſition, but onely an heartning and commotion of a people
then grieuouſly afflicted and oppreſſed. He that makes himſelfe the ring-
leader of conſpiracie againſt a King, doeth not foorthwith aſſume the perſon, or take vp the office and charge of a Iudge, in forme of Law, and iuri-
dically to depriue a King of his Regall rights, and Royall prerogatiues.
Mattathias was chiefe of that conſpiracie, not in qualitie of Prieſt, but of
cheiftaine, or leader in warre and a man the beſt qualified of all the people.
Things acted by the ſuddaine violence of the baſe vulgar, muſt not ſtand
for Lawes, nor yet for proofes and arguments of ordinarie power, ſuch as
the Pope challengeth to himſelfe, and appropriateth to his triple-Crowne.

Theſe be our ſolide anſweres: we diſclaime the light armour which the
L.Cardinall is pleaſed to furniſh vs withall, forſooth to recreate himſelfe, in
rebating the points of ſuch weapons, as hee hath vouchſafed to put into
our hands. Now it wil be worth our labour to beate by his thruſts, fetcht
from the ordinary miſſion of the New Teſtament, from leproſie, ſtones,
and locks of wooll: A leach no doubt of admirable skill, one that for ſubiecting the Crownes of Kings vnto the Pope, is able to extract arguments
out of ſtones; yea, out of the leproſie, and the drie ſcab, onely forſooth becauſe hereſie is a kind of leproſie, and an heretike hath ſome affinitie with
a leper. But may not his *Quoniam,* bee as fitly applyed to any contagious
and inueterate vice of the minde beſide hereſie? His warning-piece therefore is diſcharged to purpoſe, whereby hee notifies that hee pretendeth to
handle nothing with reſolution: For indeed vpon ſo weake arguments, a
reſolution is but ill-fauouredly and weakely grounded.

His bulwarkes thus beaten downe, let vs now view the ſtrength of our
owne. Firſt, he makes vs to fortifie on this maner: *They that are for the ne-*
gatiue, doe alleadge the authoritie of S. Paul; *Let euery ſoule bee ſubiect vnto the*
higher powers: For whoſoeuer reſiſteth the power, reſiſteth the ordinance of God. And
likewiſe that of S.Peter; *Submit your ſelues, whether it be vnto the King, as vnto*
the ſuperiour, or vnto gouernours, &c. Vpon theſe paſſages, and the like, they in-
ferre, that obedience is due to Kings by the Law of God, and not diſpenſable by any
Spirituall or Temporall authoritie. Thus he brings vs in with our firſt weapon. But here the very chiefe ſinew and ſtrength of our argument, hee
doeth wittingly balke, and of purpoſe conceale: To wit; That all the Emperors of whom the ſaid holy Apoſtles haue made any mention in their diuine Epiſtles, were profeſſed enemies to CHRIST, Pagans, Infidels, fearefull and bloody Tyrants: to whom notwithſtanding *euery ſoule,* and therefore the Biſhop of Rome for one, is commanded to ſubmit himſelfe, and to
profeſſe ſubiection. Thus much *Chryſoſtome* hath expreſly taught in his
Hom.23.vpon the Epiſtle to the Romanes; *The Apoſtle giues this comman-*
dement vnto all: euen to Prieſts alſo, and cloiſtered Monkes not onely to Secular: be
thou an Apoſtle, an Euangeliſt, a Prophet, &c. Beſides, it is here worthy to be
noted, that howſoeuer the Apoſtles rule is generall, and therefore bindeth
all

Page 67.

Page 66.

Page 69.

all the faithfull in equall bands; yet is it particularly, directly, and of purpose addreſſed to the Church of Rome by S. *Paul*, as by one who in the ſpirit of an Apoſtle did foreſee, that rebellion againſt Princes was to riſe and ſpring from the citie of Rome. Now in caſe the Head of that Church by warrant of any priuiledge, contained in the moſt holy Regiſter of Gods holy word, is exempted from the binding power of this generall precept or rule; did it not become his Lordſhip to ſhew by the booke, that it is a booke caſe, and to lay it foorth before that honourable aſſembly, who no doubt expected and waited to heare when it might fall from his learned lips? But in ſtead of any ſuch authenticall and canonicall confirmation, he flieth to a ſleight ſhift, and with a cauill is bold to affirme the foundation, laid by thoſe of our ſide, doeth no way touch the knot of the controuerſie.

« Let vs heare him ſpeake : *It is not in controuerſie, whether obedience be due to*
« *kings by Gods Law, ſo long as they are kings, or acknowledged for Kings, but our point*
« *controuerted, is whether by Gods Law it be required, that hee who hath bene once re-*
« *cogniſed and receiued for King by the body of Eſtates, can at any time be taken and*
« *reputed as no King, that is to ſay, can doe no maner of acte whereby hee may looſe his*
« *right, and ſo ceaſe to be ſaluted King.* This anſwere of the L. Cardinall is the rare deuiſe, euaſion, and ſtarting hole of the *Ieſuites* : In whoſe eares of delicate and tender touch, King-killing ſoundeth very harſh; but forſooth to vn-king a King firſt, and then to giue him the ſtab, that is a point of iuſt and trew deſcant : For to kill a King, once vnking'd by depoſition, is not killing of a King : For the preſent, I haue one of that Ieſuiticall Order in priſon, who hath face enough to ſpeake this language of Aſhdod, and to maintaine this doctrine of the *Ieſuites* Colledges. The L. Cardinall harpes vpon the ſame ſtring; He can like ſubiection and obedience to the King, whileſt he ſitteth King : but his Holineſſe muſt haue all power, and giue order withall, to hoyſt him out of his Royall Seat. I therefore now anſwer, that in very deed the former paſſages of S. *Paul* and S. *Peter* ſhould come nothing neere the queſtion, if the ſtate of the queſtion were ſuch as he brings it, made and forged in his owne ſhop. But certes the ſtate of the queſtion is not, whether a King may doe ſome acte, by reaſon whereof hee may fall from his right, or may not any longer be acknowledged for King : For all our contention is, concerning the Popes power to vn-authorize Princes; wheras in the queſtion framed and fitted by the L. Cardinal, not a word of the Pope. For were it granted and agreed on both ſides, that a King by election might fal from his Kingdom, yet ſtil the knot of the queſtion would hold, whether he can be diſpoſſeſſed of his Regal authoritie, by any power in the Pope, & whether the Pope hath ſuch fulnes of power, to ſtrip a King of thoſe Royall robes, rights, and reuenewes of the Crowne, which were neuer giuen him by the Pope; as alſo by what authoritie of holy Scripture, the Pope is able to beare out himſelfe in this power, and to make it good.

Page 71. But here the L. Card. ſtoutly ſaith in his owne defence by way of reioin-
« der; *As one text hath, Let euery ſoule be ſubiect vnto the higher powers;* in like maner
                                                                                          an

an other text hath, Obey your Prelates, and be subiect vnto your Pastors : for they ,,
watch ouer your soules, as men that shall giue an accompt for your soules. This rea- ,,
son is void of reason, and makes againſt himſelfe: For may not Prelates be
obeyed and honoured, without Kings be depoſed? If Prelates preach the
doctrine of the Coſpell, will they in the pulpit ſtirre vp ſubiects to rebell
againſt Kings? Moreouer, whereas the vniuerſall Church in theſe daies is
diuided into ſo many diſcrepant parts, that now Prelates neither doe nor
can draw all one way; is it not exceeding hard, keeping our obedience towards God, to honour them all at once with due obedience? Nay; is not
here offered vnto me a dart out of the L. Cardinals armorie, to caſt at himſelfe? For as God chargeth all men with obedience to Kings, and yet from
that commaundement of God, the L. Cardinall would not haue it inferred, that Kings haue power to degrade Eccleſiaſticall Prelates : euen ſo
God giueth charge to obey Prelates, yet doeth it not follow from hence,
that Prelates haue power to depoſe Kings. Theſe two degrees of obedience agree well together, and are each of them bounded with peculiar and
proper limits.

But for ſo much as in this point, we haue on our ſide the whole auncient
Church, which, albeit ſhe liued and groned for many aages together vnder
heathen Emperours, heretikes, and perſecuters, did neuer ſo much as whiſ-
per a word about rebelling and falling from their Soueraigne Lords, and
was neuer by any mortall creature freed from the oath of allegiance to the
Emperour; the Cardinall is not vnwilling to graunt, that ancient Chriſtians in thoſe times were bound to performe ſuch fidelity and allegiance, for
as much as the Church (the Cardinall for ſhame durſt not ſay the Pope)
then had not abſolued them of their oath. No doubt a pleaſant dreame, or
a merry conceit rather, to imagine the Biſhop of Rome was armed with
power to take away the Empire of the world from *Nero*, or *Claudius*, or
Domitianus; to whom it was not knowen, whether the citie of Rome had
any Biſhop at all. Is it not a maſter-ieſt, of a ſtraine moſt ridiculous, to preſuppoſe the Grand-maſters and abſolute Lords of the whole world, had a
ſent ſo dull, that they were not able to ſmell out, and to noſe things vnder
their owne noſes? that they ſaw ſo little with other mens eies and their
owne, that within their capitall citie, they could not ſpie that Soueraigne
armed with ordinary and lawfull authority to degrade, and to turne them
out of their renowned Empire? Doubtleſſe the ſaid Emperours, vaſſals belike of the Popes Empire, are to be held excuſed for not acknowledging
and honouring the Pope in quality of their Lord, as became his vaſſals; becauſe they did not know there was any ſuch power in the world, as after-
times haue magnified and adored vnder the qualitie of Pope : For the Biſhops of Rome in thoſe times, were of no greater authoritie, power, and
meanes, then ſome of the Biſhops are in theſe daies within my Kingdomes.

But certes thoſe Popes of that primitiue aage, thought it not expedient in
the ſaid times to draw their ſwords : they exerciſed their power in a more

mild

mild and soft kind of carriage toward thofe miferable Emperours, for three feuerall reafons alledged by the L. Cardinall.

The firft: becaufe the Bifhops then durft not by their cenfures whet and prouoke thofe Emperours, for feare of plunging the Church in a Sea of perfecutions. But if I be not cleane voide of common fenfe, this reafon ferueth to charge not onely the Bifhops of Rome, but all the auncient profeffors of Chrift befides, with deepe diffimulation and hypocrifie: For it is all one as if he had profeffed, that all their obedience to their Soueraignes, was but counterfeit, and extorted, or wrong out of them by force; that all the fubmiffiue fupplications of the auncient Fathers, the affured teftimonies and pledges of their allegiance, humilitie, and patience, were but certaine formes of difguifed fpeech, proceeding not freely from the fuggeftions of fidelity, but faintly and fainedly, or at leaft from the ftrong twitches and violent conuulfions of feare. Whereupon it followes, that all their torments and punifhments, euen to the death, are wrongfully honoured with the title, and crowned with the crowne of Martyrdome; becaufe their patience proceeded not from their owne free choice and election, but was taught by the force of neceffitie, as by compulfion: and whereas they had not mutinoufly and rebellioufly rifen in armes, to affwage the fcorching heat and burning flames of tyrannicall perfecuters, it was not for want of will, but for lacke of power. Which falfe and forged imputation, the Fathers haue cleared themfelues of in their writings. *Tertullian* in his Apologet: *All places are full of Chriftians, the cities, ifles, caftles, burroughs, armies, &c. If we that are fo infinite a power, and multitude of men, had broken from you into fome remote nooke or corner of the world, the cities no doubt had become naked and folitarie: there had beene a dreadfull and horrible filence ouer the face of the whole Empire: the great Emperours had beene driuen to feeke out newe cities, and to d*ifcouer newe nations, ouer whom to beare Soueraigne fway and rule; there had remained more enemies to the State, then fubiects and friends.* Cyprian alfo againft Demetrianus: *None of vs all, howfoeuer we are a people mighty and without number, haue made refiftance againft any of your vniuft and wrongfull actions, executed with all violence; neither haue fought by rebellious armes, or by any other finifter practifes, to crie quittance with you at any time for the righting of our felues.* Certaine it is, that vnder *Iulianus*, the whole Empire in a manner profeffed the Chriftian Religion; yea, that his Leiftenants and great Commanders, as *Iouinianus*, and *Valentinianus* by name, profeffed Chrift: Which two Princes not long after attained to the Imperiall dignitie, but might haue folicited the Pope fooner to degrade *Iulianus* from the Imperiall Throne. For fay that *Iulians* whole army had renounced the Chriftian Religion: (as the L. Cardinall againft all fhew and appearance of trewth would beare vs in hand, and contrary to the generall voice of the faid whole army, making this profeffion with one confent when *Iulian* was dead, *Wee are all Chriftians*:) yet *Italie* then perfifting in the faith of Chrift, and the army of *Iulian* then lying quartered in *Perfia*, the vtmoft limit of the Empire to the Eaft, the Bifhop of
Rome

*Tert. Apol.
cap. 37.
Hefterni fumus
& omnia veftra
impleuimus.*

*Cypr. cont.
Demetr.*

*Socr. lib 3.
cap. 19. Theod.
lib. 4. cap. 1.
Sozom. lib. 6.
cap. 1.*

Rome had fit opporunitie to draw the fword of his authoritie (if hee had then any fuch fword hanging at his Pontificall fide) to make *Iulian* feele the fharpe edge of his weapon, and thereby to pull him downe from the ftately pearch of the Romane Empire. I fay moreouer, that by this generall and fudden profeffion of the whole *Cæfarian* armie, *Wee are all Chriftians*, it is clearely teftified, that if his armie or fouldiers were then addicted to Paganifme, it was wrought by compulfion, and cleane contrary to their fetled perfwafion before : and then it followes, that with greater patience they would haue borne the depofing of *Iulian*, then if hee had fuffered them to vfe the libertie of their confcience. To bee fhort in the matter, S. *Auguftine* makes all whole, and by his teftimony doth euince, that *Iulians* armie perfeuered in the faith of Chrift. *The fouldiers of Chrift ſerued a Heathen Emperour : But when the caufe of Chrift was called in queſtion, they acknowledged none but Chrift in heauen : When the Emperor would haue them to ſerue, and to perfume his idols with frankincenſe, they gaue obedience to God, rather then to the Emperour.* After which words, the very fame words alleadged by the L. Cardinall againft himfelfe doe follow ; *They did then diſtinguiſh betweene the Lord Eternal, and the Lord temporall: neuertheleſſe, they were ſubiect vnto the Lord temporall, for the Lord Eternall.* It was therefore to pay God his duetie of obedience, and not for feare to incenfe the Emperour, or to draw perfecution vpon the Church (as the L. Cardinal would make vs beleeue) that Chriftians of the Primitiue Church, and Bifhops by their cenfures, durft not anger and prouoke their Emperours. But his Lordfhip by his coloured pretences doeth manifeftly prouoke and ftirre vp the people to rebellion, fo foone as they know their own ftrength to beare out a rebellious practife : Whereupon it followes, that in cafe their confpiracie fhall take no good effect, all the blame and fault muft lie, not in their difloyalty and treafon, but in the bad choice of their times for the beft aduantage, and in the want of taking a trew fight of their owne weakeneffe. Let ftirring fpirits be trained vp in fuch practicall precepts, let defperate wits be feafoned with fuch rules of difcipline; and what need we, or how can wee wonder they contriue Powder-confpiracies, and practife the damnable art of parricides?

After *Iulian*, his Lordfhip falles vpon *Valentinian* the younger, who maintaining Arrianifme with great and open violence, might haue bene depofed by the Chriftians from his Empire, and yet (fay wee) they neuer dream'd of any fuch practife. Heere the L. Cardinall maketh anfwere: *The Chriftians mooued with refpect vnto the freſh memory both of the brother and father, as alſo vnto the weake eſtate of the ſonnes young yeeres, abſtainēd from all counſels and courſes of ſharper effect and operation.* To which anfwere I replie: thefe are but friuolous coniectures, deuifed and framed to ticle his owne fancie : For had *Valentinianus* the younger beene the fonne of an *Arrian*, and had then alfo attained to threefcore yeeres of aage, they would neuer haue borne themfelues in other fafhion then they did, towards their Emperour. Then the Cardinall goeth on : The people would not abandon the

Auguſt. in Pſal. 124.

Page 82.

Pag. 82.
»
»

factious and seditious party, but were so firme or obstinate rather for the faction, that *Valentinian* for feare of the tumultuous vproares was constrained to giue way, and was threatened by the souldiers, that except hee would adhere vnto the Catholikes, they would yeeld him no assistance, nor stand for his partie. Now this answere of the L. Cardinall makes nothing to the purpose, concerning the Popes power to pull downe Kings from their stately nest. Let vs take notice of his proper consequence. *Valentinian* was afraid of the popular tumult at *Milan* : the Pope therefore hath power to curbe Hereticall Kings by deposition. Now marke what distance is betweene *Rome* and *Milan*, what difference betweene the people of *Milan*, and the Bishop of *Rome* ; betweene a popular tumult, and a iudicatorie sentence ; betweene fact and right, things done by the people or souldiers of *Milan*, and things to be done according to right and law by the Bishop of *Rome* ; the same distance, the same difference (if not farre greater) is betweene the L. Cardinals antecedent and his consequent, betweene his reason, and the maine cause or argument which we haue in hand. The mad commotion of the people was not heere so much to bee regarded, as the sad instruction of the Pastour, of their good and godly Pastour S. *Ambrose* so farre from hartening the people of *Milan* to rebel, that being Bishop of *Milan*, he offered himselfe to suffer Martydome : *If the Emperour abuse his Imperiall authority,* (for so *Theodoret* hath recited his words) *to tyrannize thereby, heere am I ready to suffer death.* And what resistance he made against his L.Emperor, was onely by way of supplication in these termes ; *Wee beseech thee, O* Augustus, *as humble suppliants ; we offer no resistance : we are not in feare, but we flie to supplication.* Againe, *If my patrimony be your marke, enter vpon my patrimony if my body, I wil goe and meet my torments. Shall I be drag'd to prison or to death ? I will take delight in both.* Item, *in his Oration to* Auxentius; *I can afflict my soule with sorrow, I can lament, I can send forth grieuous groanes: My weapons against either of both, souldiers or Goths, are teares : A Priest hath none other weapons of defence: I neither can resist, nor ought in any other maner to make resistance.*

Epist.lib.5.
Epist.33.

Epist.lib.5.

Iustinian the Emperour in his old aage fell into the heresie of the *Aphthartodocites.* Against *Iustinian*, though few they were that fauoured him in that heresie, the Bishop of *Rome* neuer darted with violence any sentence of excommunication, interdiction, or deposition.

The *Ostrogot* Kings in *Italie*, the *Visigot* in *Spaine*, the *Vandal* in *Africa* were all addicted to the *Arrian* impietie, and some of them cruelly persecuted the trew professours. The *Visigot* and *Vandall* were no neighbours to *Italie*. The Pope thereby had the lesse cause to feare the stings of those waspes, if they had bene angred. The Pope for all that neuer had the humour to wrestle or iustle with any of the said Kings in the cause of deposing them from their Thrones. But especially the times when the *Vandals* in *Affricke*, and the *Goths* in *Italie* by *Belisarius* and *Narses*, professours of the Orthodoxe Faith, were tyred with long warres, and at last were vtterly defeated in bloody battels, are to bee considered. Then were the times

or

or neuer, for the Pope to vnſheath his weapons, and to vncaſe his arrowes of depoſition; then were the times to draw them out of his quiuer, and to ſhoot at all ſuch *Arrian* heads ; then were the times by diſpenſations to re-leaſe their ſubiects of their oathes, by that peremptorie meanes to aide and ſtrengthen the Catholique cauſe: But in that aage the ſaid weapons were not knowne to haue bene hammered in the Pontificall forge.

Gregorie the I. made his boaſts, that he was able to ruine the Lombards, (for many yeeres together ſworne enemies to the Biſhops of Rome) their ſtate preſent, and the hope of all their future proſperitie. But he telleth vs, that by the feare of God before his eyes and in his heart, he was bridled and reſtrained from any ſuch intent ; as elſewhere we haue obſerued : *If I would haue medled with practiſing and procuring the death of the Lombards, the whole na-tion of the Lombards at this day had bene robbed of their Kings, Dukes, Earles, they had bene reduced to the tearmes of extreame confuſion.* He might at leaſt haue depoſed their King, (if the credit of the L. Cardinals iudgement be currant) without polluting or ſtayning his owne conſcience.

In Apol. pro iuram fidel. His owne words lib.7. Epiſt.1.

What can we tearme this aſſertion of the L. Cardinal, but open charging the moſt ancient Biſhops of Rome with crueltie, when they would not ſuccour the Church of CHRIST oppreſſed by tyrants, whoſe oppreſſion they had power to repreſſe by depoſing the oppreſſors. Is it credible, that IESVS CHRIST hath giuen a Commiſſion to S. *Peter* and his ſucceſſors for ſo many aages, without any power to execute their Commiſſion, or to make any vſe thereof by practiſe ? Is it credible, that hee hath giuen them a ſword to bee kept in the ſcabbard, without drawing once in a thouſand yeeres ? Is it credible, that in the times when Popes were moſt deboſhed, a-bandoning themſelues to all ſorts of corrupt and vitious courſes, as is teſti-fied by their owne flatterers and beſt affected ſeruants; is it credible that in thoſe times they began to vnderſtand the vertue & ſtrength of their Com-miſſion? For if either feare or lacke of power, was the cauſe of holding their hands, and voluntarie binding of themſelues to the Peace or good behaui-our: wherefore is not ſome one Pope at leaſt produced, who hath complai-ned that he was hindered from executing the power that CHRIST had conferred vpon his Pontificall See? Wherefore is not ſome one of the an-cient and holy Fathers alledged, by whom the Pope hath bene aduiſed and exhorted to take courage, to ſtand vpon the vigor and ſinewes of his Papall Office, to vnſheath and yncaſe his bolts of thunder againſt vngodly Prin-ces, and grieuous enemies to the Church ? wherefore liuing vnder Chri-ſtian and gracious Emperours, haue they not made knowne the reaſons, why they were hindred from drawing the pretended ſword; left long cu-ſtome of not vſing the ſword ſo many aages, might make it ſo to ruſt in the ſcabbard, that when there ſhould be occaſion to vſe the ſaid ſword, it could not be drawne at all ; and left ſo long cuſtome of not vſing the ſame, ſhould confirme preſcription to their greater preiudice ? . If weakeneſſe be a iuſt let, how is it come to paſſe, that Popes haue enterpriſed to depoſe

Philip the Faire, Lewis the XII. and ELIZABETH my predeceſſor of happy memorie; (to let paſſe others) in whom experience hath well proued, how great inequalitie was betweene their ſtrengths? Yea, for the moſt part from thence grow moſt grieuous troubles and warres, which iuſtly recoile and light vpon his owne head; as happened to *Gregorie* the VII. and *Boniface* the VIII. This no doubt is the reaſon, wherefore the Pope neuer ſets in (for feare of ſuch inconueniences) to blaſt a King with lightning and thunder of depoſition, but when hee perceiues the troubled waters of the Kingdome by ſome ſtrong faction ſetled in his Eſtate, or when the King is confined and bordered by ſome Prince more potent, who thirſteth after the prey, and is euer gaping for ſome occaſion to picke a quarrell. The King ſtanding in ſuch eſtate, is it not as eaſie for the Pope to pull him downe, as it is for a man with one hand to thruſt downe a tottering wall, when the ground ſill is rotten, the ſtuddes vnpind and nodding or bending towards the ground? But if the King ſhall beare downe and breake the faction within the Realme; if hee ſhall get withall the vpper hand of his enemies out of the Kingdome; then the holy Father preſents him with pardons neuer ſued for, neuer asked; and in a fathers indulgence forſooth, giues him leaue ſtill to hold the Kingdome, that hee was not able by all his force to wreſt and wring out of his hand, no more then the club of *Hercules* out of his fiſt. How many worthy Princes, incenſed by the Pope, to conſpire againſt Soueraigne Lords their Maſters, and by open rebellion to worke ſome change in their Eſtates, haue miſcarried in the action, with loſſe of life, or honour, or both? For example; *Rodulphus* Duke of *Sueuia* was eg'd on by the Pope, againſt *Henry* IIII. of that name Emperour. How many maſſacres, how many deſolations of Cities and townes, how many bloody battels enſued thereupon? Let hiſtories bee ſearched, let iuſt accompts be taken, and beſide ſieges layde to Cities, it will appeare by trew computation, that *Henry* the IIII. and *Frederic* the firſt, fought aboue threeſcore battels, in defence of their owne right againſt enemies of the Empire, ſtirred vp to armes by the Pope of Rome. How much Chriſtian blood was then ſpilt in theſe bloody battels, it paſſeth mans wit, penne, or tongue to expreſſe. And to giue a little touch vnto matters at home; doeth not his Holineſſe vnderſtand right well the weakeneſſe of Papiſts in my Kingdome? Doeth not his Holineſſe neuertheleſſe animate my Papiſts to rebellion, and forbid my Papiſts to take the Oath of Allegiance? Doeth not his Holineſſe by this meanes draw (ſo much as in him lyeth) perſecution vpon the backes of my Papiſts as vpon rebels, and expoſe their life as it were vpon the open ſtall, to be ſold at a very eaſie price? All theſe examples, either ioynt or ſeuerall, are manifeſt and euident prooſes, that feare to draw miſchiefe and perſecution vpon the Church, hath not barred the Popes from thundering againſt Emperours and Kings, whenſoeuer they conceiued any hope, by their fulminations to aduance their greatneſſe.

Laſt

Laſt of all; I referre the matter to the moſt poſſeſſed with preiudice, euen the very aduerſaries, whether this doctrine, by which people are trained vp in ſubiection vnto Infidel or hereticall Kings, vntill the ſubiects be of ſufficient ſtrength to mate their Kings, to expell their Kings, and to depoſe them from their Kingdomes, doth not incenſe the Turkiſh Empe-rours and other Infidell Princes, to roote out all the Chriſtians that drawe in their yoke, as people that waite onely for a fit occaſion to rebell, and to take themſelues ingaged for obedience to their Lords, onely by con-ſtraint and feruile feare. Let vs therefore now conclude with *Oʒius*, in that famous Epiſtle ſpeaking to *Conſtantius* an Arrian heretike : *As beé that by ſecret practiſe or open violence would bereaue thee of thy Empire, ſhould violate Gods ordinance : ſo bee thou touched with feare, leaſt, by vſurping authoritie ouer Church matters, thou tumble not headlong into ſome hainous crime.* Where this holy Biſhop hath not vouchſafed to inſert and mention the L. Cardinals ex-ception ; to wit, the right of the Church alwaies excepted and ſaued, when ſhe ſhall be of ſufficient ſtrength to ſhake off the yoke of Emperours. Nei-ther ſpeaks the ſame holy Biſhop of priuate perſons alone, or men of ſome particular condition and calling ; but hee ſetteth downe a generall rule for all degrees, neuer to impeach Imperiall Maieſtie vpon any pretext what-ſoeuer.

Apud Athan. in Epiſt. ad ſolitar. vitam agentes.

. As his Lordſhips firſt reaſon drawne from weakeneſſe is exceeding weake : ſo is that which the L. Cardinall takes vp in the next place : *He tel-leth vs there is very great difference betweene Pagan Emperours, and Chriſtian Prin-ces : Pagan Emperours who neuer did homage to Chriſt, who neuer were by their ſub-iects receiued, with condition to acknowledge perpetuall ſubiection vnto the Empire of Chriſt ; who neuer were bound by oath and mutuall contract betweene Prince and ſubiect. Chriſtian Princes who ſlide backe by Apoſtaſie, degenerate by Arrianiſme, or fall away by Mahometiſme.* Touching the latter of theſe two, (as his Lord-ſhippe ſaith) *If they ſhall as it were take an oath, and make a vowe contrary to their firſt oath and vow made and taken when they were inſtalled, and contrary to the con-dition vnder which they receiued the Scepter of their Fathers ; if they withall ſhall turne perſecutors of the Catholike religion ;* touching theſe I ſay, the L. Cardinal holds, that without queſtion they may bee remooued from their King-domes : He telleth vs not by whom, but euery where he meaneth by the Pope. Touching Kings depoſed by the Pope vnder pretence of ſtupidity, as *Childeric* ; or of matrimoniall cauſes, as *Philip* I. or for collating of benefi-ces, as *Philip* the Faire ; not one word : By that point he eaſily glideth, and ſhuffles it vp in ſilence, for feare of diſtaſting the Pope on the one ſide, or his auditors on the other.

The 2. reaſ. Pag. 77.

Now in alledging this reaſon, his Lordſhip makes all the world a witnes, that in depoſing of Kings, the Pope hath no eye of regard to the benefit and ſecuritie of the Church : For ſuch Princes as neuer ſuckt other milke then that of Infidelitie, and perſecution of Religion, are no leſſe noiſome and pernicious vermin to the Church, then if they had ſucked of the Churches

ches breaſts. And as for the greatneſſe of the ſinne or offence, it ſeemes to me there is very little difference in the matter. For a Prince that neuer did ſweare any religious obedience to *Ieſus Chriſt*, is bound no leſſe to ſuch obedience, then if he had taken a ſolemne oath: As the ſonne that rebelliouſly ſtands vp againſt his father, is in equall degree of ſinne, whether he hath ſworne or not ſworne obedience to his father; becauſe he is bound to ſuch obedience, not by any voluntarie contract or couenant, but by the law of Nature. The commaundement of God to kiſſe the Sonne, whom the Father hath confirmed and ratified King of Kings, doeth equally bind all Kings, as well Pagans as Chriſtians. On the other ſide, who denies, who doubts, that *Conſtantius* Emperour at his firſt ſteppe or entrance into the Empire, did not ſweare and bind himſelfe by ſolemne vowe, to keepe the rules and to maintaine the precepts of the Orthodox faith, or that he did not receiue his fathers Empire vpon ſuch condition? This notwithſtanding, the Biſhop of *Rome* pulled not *Conſtantius* from his Imperiall throne, but *Conſtantius* remooued the Biſhop of *Rome* from his Papall See. And were it ſo, that an oath taken by a King at his conſecration, and after violated, is a ſufficient cauſe for the Pope to depoſe an Apoſtate or hereticall Prince; then by good conſequence the Pope may in like ſort depoſe a King, who beeing neither dead in Apoſtaſie, nor ſicke of Hereſie, doeth neglect onely the due adminiſtration of iuſtice to his loyall ſubiects: For his oath taken at conſecration importeth likewiſe, that he ſhall miniſter iuſtice to his people. A point wherein the holy Father is held ſhort by the L. Cardinall, who dares preſcribe new lawes to the Pope, and preſumes to limit his *fulneſſe of power*, within certaine meeres and head-lands, extending the Popes power only to the depoſing of Chriſtian Kings, when they turne Apoſtats forſaking the Catholike faith; and not ſuch Princes as neuer breathed any thing but pure Paganiſme, and neuer ſerued vnder the colours of Ieſus Chriſt. Meane while his Lordſhip forgets, that King *Attabaliba* was depoſed by the Pope from his Kingdome of *Peru*, and the ſaid Kingdome was conferred vpon the King of *Spaine*, though the ſaid poore King of *Peru*, neuer forſooke his heathen ſuperſtition; and though the turning of him out of his terreſtriall Kingdome was no way to conuert him vnto the faith of Chriſt. Yea his Lordſhip a little after telleth vs himſelfe, that *Be the Turkes*

Pag. 77.

poſſeſsion in the conqueſts that he maketh ouer Chriſtians neuer ſo auncient, yet by no long tract of time whatſoeuer, can he gaine ſo much as a thumbes breadth of preſcription: that is to ſay, the Turke for all that is but a diſſeiſor, one that violently and wilfully keeps an other man from his owne, and by good right may be diſpoſſeſſed of the ſame: whereas notwithſtanding the Turkiſh Emperours neuer fauoured nor ſauoured Chriſtianitie. Let vs runne ouer the examples of Kings whom the Pope hath dared and preſumed to depoſe; and hardly will any one be found, of whom it may be trewly auouched, that he hath taken an oath contrary to his oath of ſubiection to *Ieſus Chriſt*, or that he hath wilfully caſt himſelfe into Apoſtaticall defection.

And

And certes to any man that weighs the matter with due confideration, it wil be found apparantly falfe, that Kings of *France* haue bene receiued of their fubiects at any time, with condition to ferue I e s v s C h r i s t. They were actually Kings before they came forth to the folemnitie of their fa-cring, before they vfed any ftipulation or promife to their fubiects. For in hereditary kingdoms, (nothing more certaine, nothing more vncontrouleable) the Kings death inftantly maketh liuery and feifin of the Royaltie, to his next fucceffour. Nor is it materiall to replie, that a King fucceeding by right of inheritance, takes an oath in the perfon of his predeceffor. For euery oath is perfonall, proper to the perfon by whom it is taken: and to God no liuing creature can fweare, that his owne fonne or his heire fhall proue an honeft man. Well may the father, and with great folemnitie, pro-mife that he will exhort his heire apparant with all his power and the beft of his endeauours, to feare God and to practife piety. If the fathers oath be agreeable to the dueties of godlineffe, the fonne is bound thereby, whether he take an oath, or take none. On the other fide, if the fathers oath come from the puddles of impietie, the fonne is bound thereby to goe the con-trary way. If the fathers oath concerne things of indifferent nature, and fuch as by the variety or change of times, become either pernicious or im-poffible; then it is free for the Kings next fucceffor and heire, prudently to fit and proportion his Lawes vnto the times prefent, and to the beft benefit of the Common-wealth.

When I call thefe things to mind with fome attention, I am out of all doubt, his Lordfhip is very much to feeke, in the right fenfe and nature of his Kings oath taken at his Coronation, to defend the Church, and to per-feuere in the Catholike faith: For what is more vnlike and leffe credible then this conceit, that after *Clouis* had reigned 15. yeeres in the ftate of Pa-ganifme, and then receiued holy Baptifme, he fhould become Chriftian vp-on this condition, That in cafe hee fhould afterward reuolt from the Faith, it fhould then bee in the power of the Church, to turne him out of his Kingdome? But had any fuch conditionall ftipulation beene made by *Clouis*, in very good earneft and trewth; yet would hee neuer haue in-tended, that his depofing fhould bee the acte of the Romane Bifhop, but rather of thofe (whether Peeres or people, or whole body of the State) by whom he had bene aduanced to the Kingdome. Let vs heare the trewth, and this is the trewth: It is farre from the cuftomary vfe in *France*, for their Kings to take any fuch oath, or to vfe any fuch ftipulation with their fub-iects. If any King or Prince wherefoeuer, doth vfe an oath or folemne pro-mife in thefe expreffe termes, *Let me lofe my Kingdome, or my life, be that day my laft both for life and reigne, when I fhall firft reuolt from the Chriftian Religion*: By thefe words he calleth vpon God for vengeance, hee vfeth imprecation a-gainft his owne head: but hee makes not his Crowne to ftoupe by this meanes to any power in the Pope, or in the Church, or in the people.

And touching infcriptions vpon coynes, of which point his Lordfhip
fpea-

speaketh by the way; verely the nature of the money or coine (the ſtamping and minting whereof is one of the marks of the Prince his dignity and Soueraignty) is not changed by bearing the letters of Chriſts Name on the reuerſe or on the front. Such charaćters of Chriſts Name, are aduertiſements and inſtrućtions to the people, that in ſhewing and yeelding obedience vnto the King, they are obedient vnto Chriſt; & thoſe Princes likewiſe, who are ſo wel aduiſed, to haue the moſt ſacred Names inſcribed and printed in their coines, doe take and acknowledge *Ieſus Chriſt* for ſupreme King of Kings. The ſaid holy charaćters are no repreſentation or profeſſion, that any Kings Crowne dependeth vpon the Church, or can be taken away by the Pope. The L. Cardinal indeed ſo beareth vs in hand. But he inuerts the words of *Ieſus Chriſt*, and wrings them out of the right ioynt: For Chriſt without all ambiguitie and circumlocution, by the image and inſcription of the money, doeth directly and expreſſely prooue *Cæſar* to bee free from ſubiećtion, and entirely Soueraigne. Now if ſuch a ſupreme and Soueraigne Prince, at any time ſhall bandie and combine againſt God, and thereby ſhall become a rebellious and perfidious Prince; doubtleſſe for ſuch diſloyaltie he ſhall deſerue, that God would take from him all hope of life eternall: and yet hereby neither Pope nor people hath reaſon to bee puft vp, in their power to depriue him of his temporall Kingdome.

Page 76.
The L. Cardinall ſaith beſides; *The champions of the Popes power to depoſe Kings, doe expound that commandement of S. Paul, whereby euery ſoule is made ſubiećt vnto the ſuperiour powers, to bee a prouiſionall precept or caution accommodated to the times; and to ſtand in force, onely vntll the Church were growen in ſtrength vnto ſuch a ſcantling, that it might be in the power of the faithfull, without ſhaking the pillars of Chriſtian ſtate, to ſtand in the breach, and cautelouſly to prouide that none but Chriſtian Princes might be receiued; according to the Law in Deut: Thou ſhalt make thee a King from among thy brethren.* The reaſon whereupon they ground, is this: *Becauſe Paul ſaith, It is a ſhame for Chriſtians to be iudged vnder vniuſt Infidels, in mattrs or buſineſſe, which they had one againſt another: For which inconuenience,* Iuſtinian *after prouided by Law; when hee ordeined that no Infidel nor Heretike might be admitted to the adminiſtration of iuſtice in the Common-wealth.*

In which words of the Cardinall, the word *Receiued*, is to bee obſerued eſpecially and aboue the reſt: For by chopping in that word, hee doeth nimbly and with a tricke of *Legier-demain*, transforme or change the very ſtate of the queſtion. For the queſtion or iſſue of the cauſe, is not about receiuing, eſtabliſhing, or chooſing a Prince; (as in thoſe Nations where the Kingdome goes by election) but about doing homage to the Prince, when God hath ſetled him in the Kingdome, and hath caſt it vpon a Prince by hereditary ſucceſſion: For that which is writtten, *Thou ſhalt make thee a King*, doeth no way concerne and touch the people of *France* in theſe dayes: becauſe the making of their King hath not of long time been tyed to their election. The paſſage therefore in Deuter. makes nothing to the purpoſe; no more then doth *Iuſtinians* law: For it is our free and voluntary con-

confeſſion, that a Chriſtian Prince is to haue ſpeciall care of the Lawes, and to prouide that no vnbeleeuer be made Lord Chiefe-Iuſtice of the Land, that no Infidel be put in truſt with adminiſtration of Iuſtice to the people. But here the iſſue doeth not direct vs to ſpeake of Delegates, of ſubordinate Magiſtrates, and ſuch as are in Commiſſion from the Prince, but of the ſupreame Prince himſelfe, the Soueraigne Magiſtrate ordained by nature, and confirmed by ſucceſſion. Our queſtion is, whether ſuch a Prince can be vnthroned by the Pope, by whom he was not placed in the Throne; and whether the Pope can deſpoile ſuch a Prince, of that Royaltie which was neuer giuen him by the Pope, vnder any pretended colour and imputation of hereſie, of ſtupiditie, or infringing the priuiledges of Monaſteries, or tranſgreſſing the Lawes and lines of holy Matrimonie.

Now that S. *Pauls* commandement which bindeth euery ſoule in the bands of ſubiection vnto the higher powers, is no precept giuen by way of *prouiſo*, and onely to ſerue the times, but a ſtanding and a perpetuall rule, it is hereby more then manifeſt. S. *Paul* hath grounded this commandement vpon certaine reaſons, not onely conſtant and permanent by their proper nature, but likewiſe neceſſary for euery ſtate, condition, and reuolution of the times. His reaſons; *Becauſe all powers are ordained of God : becauſe reſiſting of powers is reſiſting the ordinance of God : becauſe the Magiſtrate beares the ſword to execute iuſtice : becauſe obedience and ſubiection to the Magiſtrate is neceſſary, not onely for feare of his wrath, or feare of puniſhment, but alſo for conſcience ſake.* It is therefore a caſe grounded vpon conſcience, it is not a Law deuiſed by humane wiſedome; it is not faſhionable to the qualities of the times. Apoſtolicall inſtructions for the right informing of maners, are not changeable according to times and ſeaſons. To vſe the L. Cardinals language, and to follow his fancie in the matter, is to make way for two peſtiferous miſchiefes : Firſt, let it be free and lawfull for Chriſtians, to hold the commanding rules of GOD for prouiſionall cautions, and what followes ? Men are ledde into the broad way of impietie, and the whole Scripture is wiped of all authoritie. Then againe, for the other miſchiefe · The glorious triumphes of moſt bleſſed Martyrs in their vnſpeakable torments and ſufferings, by the L. Cardinals poſition ſhall bee iudged vnworthy to weare the title and Crowne of Martyrdome. How ſo? Becauſe (according to his new fiction) they haue giuen place to the violence and furie of heathen Magiſtrates, not in obedience to the neceſſary and certaine Commandement of God, but rather to a prouiſionall direction, accomodated to the humours of the times. And therfore the L. Cardinal hath vſed none other clay wherewith to dawbe ouer his deuiſe, but plaine falſification of holy Scripture : For he makes the Apoſtle ſay to the Corinthians, *It is a ſhame for Chriſtians to bee iudged vnder vnbeleeuing Magiſtrates;* whereas in that whole context of Paul, there is no ſuch matter. For when the Apoſtle ſaith, *I ſpeake it euen to your ſhame*; he doeth not ſay it is a ſhame for a beleeuer to be iudged vnder an Infidel, but he makes them aſhamed of

their

their vngodly courſe, and vnchriſtian practiſe, that in ſuing and impleading one another, they layd their actions of cōtention in the Courts of vnbeleeuing Iudges. The ſhame was not in bearing that yoke which God had charged their necks withall, but in deuouring and eating vp one an other with Writs of *habeas corpus*, and with other Proceſſes; as alſo in vncouering the ſhame, in laying open the ſhamefull parts and prankes played by Chriſtians, before Infidels, to the great ſcandall of the Church. Here I ſay the L. Cardinall is taken in a tricke of manifeſt falſification. If therefore a King when he falls to play the heretike, deſerueth to be depoſed; why ſhould not a Cardinall when he falls to play the iuggler with holy Scripture, deſerue to be diſrobed?

Meane while the indifferent Reader is to conſider, how greatly this doctrine is preiudicial, and how full of danger, to Chriſtians liuing vnder hereticall or Pagan Princes. For make it once knowne to the Emperour of Turkes, let him once get neuer ſo little a ſmacke of this doctrine; that Chriſtians liuing vnder his Empire doe take Gods commandement, for obedience to Princes whom they count Infidels, to be onely a prouiſional precept for a time, and wait euery houre for all occaſions to ſhake off the yoke of his bondage; doubtleſſe he will neuer ſpare with all ſpeed to roote the whole ſtocke, with all the armes and branches of Chriſtians out of his dominions. Adde hereunto the L. Cardinals former determination; that poſſeſſion kept neuer ſo long by the Turke in his Conqueſts ouer Chriſtians, gaines him not by ſo long tract of time one inch of preſcription; and it will appeare, that his Lordſhip puts the Turkiſh Emperour in minde, and by his inſtruction leades the ſaid Emperour as it were by the hand, to haue no maner of affiance in his Chriſtian ſubiects; and withall to afflict his poore Chriſtians with all ſorts of moſt grieuous and cruell torments. In this regard the poore Chriſtians of Græcia and Syria, muſt needs be very little beholden to his Lordſhip. As for my ſelfe, and my Popiſh Subiects, to whom I am no leſſe then an heretike forſooth am not I by this doctrine of the Cardinall, pricked and whetted againſt my naturall inclination, to turne clemencie into rigour; ſeeing that by his doctrine my ſubiects are made to beleeue, they owe me ſubiection onely by way of *prouiſo*, and with waiting the occaſion to worke my vtter deſtruction and finall ruine; the rather, becauſe Turkes, miſcreants, and heretikes are marſhalled by the Cardinall in the ſame ranke; and heretikes are counted worſe, yea more iuſtly depoſeable, then Turkes and Infidels, as irreligious breakers and violaters of their oath? Who ſeeth not here how great indignitie is offered to me a Chriſtian King, paralleld with Infidels, reputed worſe then a Turke, taken for an vſurper of my Kingdomes, reckoned a Prince, to whom ſubiects owe a forced obedience by way of prouiſion, vntill they ſhall haue meanes to ſhake off the yoke, and to bare my temples of the Crowne, which neuer can be pulled from the ſacred Head, but with loſſe of the head it ſelfe?

Touching

Touching the warres vndertaken by the *French, Englifh*, and *Germaines*, in their expedition for Ierufalem, it appeares by the iffue and euent of the faid warres, that God approoued them not for honourable. That expedition was a deuife and inuention of the Pope, whereby he might come to be infeoffed in the Kingdomes of Chriftian Princes. For then all fuch of the *French, Englifh* or *Germaines*, as vndertooke the Croifade, became the Popes meere vaffals. Then all robbers by the high way fide, adulterers, cut-throats, and bafe bankerupts, were exempted from the Secular and Ciuill power, their caufes were fped in Confiftorian Courts, fo foone as they had gotten the Croffe on their caffocks or coat-armours, and had vowed to ferue in the expedition for the Leuant. Then for the Popes pleafure and at his commaundement, whole countryes were emptied of their Nobles and common fouldiers. Then they made long marches into the Leuant: For what purpofe? Onely to die vpon the points of the *Saracens* pikes, or by the edge of their barbarous courtelaffes, battle-axes, fauchions, and other weapons, without any benefit and aduantage to themfelues or others. Then the Nobles were driuen to fell their goodly Mannors, and auncient demaines to the Church-men, at vnder prifes and low rates; the very roote from which a great part of the Church and Church-mens reuenewes hath fprung and growne to fo great height. Then, to be fhort, his moft boun-tifull Holineffe gaue to any of the riffe-raffe-ranke, that would vndertake this expedition into the Holy land, a free and full pardon for all his finnes, befides a degree of glory aboue the vulgar in the Celeftiall Paradife. Military vertue, I confeffe, is commendable and honourable; prouided it bee employed for iuftice, and that generous nobleneffe of valiant fpirits bee not vnder a colour and fhadow of piety, fetcht ouer with fome cafts or deuifes of Italian cunning.

See the Bull of Innoc.3. at the end of the Later.Conc.

Now let vs obferue the wifedome of the Lord Cardinall through this whole difcourfe. His Lordfhip is pleafed in his Oration, to cite certaine few paffages of Scripture, culls and picks them out for the moft gracefull in fhewe: leaues out of his lift whole troupes of honourable witneffes, vpon whofe teftimonie, the Popes themfelues and their principall adhe-rents doe build his power to depofe Kings, and to giue order for all Tem-porall caufes. Take a fight of their beft and moft honourable witneffes. *Peter* faid to Chrift, *See here two fwords*; and Chrift anfwered, *It is fufficient.* Chrift faid to *Peter, Put vp thy fword into thy fheath.* God faid to *Ieremie, I haue eftablifhed thee ouer Nations and Kingdomes. Paul* faid to the Corinthi-ans, *The fpirituall man difcerneth all things.* Chrift faid to his Apoftles, *What-foeuer yee fhall loofe vpon earth*: by which words the Pope hath power for-footh to loofe the oath of allegiance. *Mofes* faid, *In the beginning God created the heauen and the earth.* Vpon thefe paffages, Pope *Boniface* 8. grapling and tugging with *Philip* the Faire, doth build his Temporall power. Other Popes and Papifts auouch the like authorities. Chrift faid of himfelfe, *All things are giuen to me of my Father, and all power is giuen vnto me in heauen and in earth.*

Ier.1. 1.Cor.2. Extrauag. VnamSanctam,

P p

earth. The Deuils faid, *If thou caſt vs out, ſend vs into this herd of ſwine.* Chriſt faid to his Diſciples, *Yee ſhall finde the colt of an aſſe bound, looſe it and bring it vnto me.* By theſe places the aduerſaries prooue, that Chriſt diſpoſed of Temporall matters; and inferre thereupon, why not Chriſts Vicar as well as Chriſt himſelfe. The places and teſtimonies now following are very ex-preſſe: *In ſtead of thy fathers ſhall be thy children : thou ſhalt make them Princes through all the earth.* • Item, Ieſus Chriſt not onely commaunded *Peter* to feed his lambs; but ſaid alſo to *Peter*, *Ariſe, kill, and eat* : the pleaſant gloſſe, the rare inuention of the L. Cardinall *Baronius*. Chriſt faid to the people, *If I were lift vp from the earth, I will draw all things vnto me.* who lets, what hin-ders this place from fitting the Pope? *Paul* ſaid to the Corinthians, *Know ye not that we ſhall iudge the Angels? how much more then the things that pertaine vn-to this life?* A little after, *Haue not we power to eate?* Theſe are the chiefe paſ-ſages, on which as vpon maine arches, the roofe of Papall Monarchie, con-cerning Temporall cauſes, hath reſted for three or foure aages paſt. And yet his Lordſhip durſt not repoſe any confidence in their firme ſtanding to beare vp the ſaid roofe of Temporall Monarchie, for feare of making his auditors to burſt with laughter. A wiſe part without queſtion, if his Lordſhip had not defiled his lips before, with a more ridiculous argument drawne from the leproſie and drie ſcab.

Let vs now by way of compariſon behold Ieſus Chriſt paying tribute vnto *Cæſar*, and the Pope making *Cæſar* to pay him tribute : Ieſus Chriſt perſwading the Iewes to pay tribute vnto an heathen Emperour, and the Pope diſpenſing with ſubiects for their obedience to Chriſtian Empe-rours : Ieſus Chriſt refuſing to arbitrate a controuerſie of inheritance part-able betweene two priuate parties, and the Pope thruſting in himſelfe without warrant or Commiſſion to bee abſolute Iudge in the depoſing of Kings : Ieſus Chriſt profeſſing that his Kingdome is not of this world, and the Pope eſtabliſhing himſelfe in a terrene Empire. In like manner the Apoſtles forſaking all their goods to followe Chriſt, and the Pope robbing Chriſtians of their goods; the Apoſtles perſecuted by Pagan Emperours, and the Pope now ſetting his foote on the very throate of Chriſtian Empe-rours, then proudly treading Imperiall Crownes vnder his feete. By this compariſon, the L. Cardinals allegation of Scripture in fauour of his Ma-ſter the Pope, is but a kind of puppet-play, to make Ieſus Chriſt a mocking ſtocke, rather then to ſatisfie his auditors with any ſound precepts and wholeſome inſtructions. Hereof he ſeemeth to giue ſome inckling him-ſelfe : For after he hath beene plentifull in citing authorities of Scripture, and of newe Doctors, which make for the Popes power to depoſe Kings; at laſt he comes in with a faire and open confeſſion, that neither by diuine Oracles, nor by honourable antiquitie, this controuerſie hath beene yet determined : and ſo pulls downe in a word with one hand, the frame of worke that he had built and ſet vp before with an other; diſcouering with-all, the reluctation and priuie checkes of his owne conſcience.

There

Pſal.45.

Ioh.12.

Pag.85.

There yet remaineth one obiection, the knot whereof the L. Cardinall in a maner ſweateth to vntie. His words be theſe : *The champions for the ne-* Page 84. *gatiue flie to the analogie of other proceedings and practiſes in the Church : They af-* " *firme that priuate perſons, maſters or owners of goods and poſſeſſions among the* " *common people, are not depriued of their goods for Hereſie; and conſequently that* " *Princes much more ſhould not for the ſame crime bee depriued of their eſtates.* For " anſwere to this reaſon, he brings in the defendants of depoſition, ſpeaking after this maner; *In the Kingdome of* France *the ſtrict execution of lawes decreed* " *in Court againſt Heretikes, is fauourably ſuſpended and ſtopped, for the preſeruation* " *of peace and publike tranquilitie.* He ſaith elſewhere; *Conniuence is vſed towards* " *theſe Heretikes in regard of their multitude, becauſe a notable part of the French Na-* ". *tion and State is made all of Heretikes.* I ſuppoſe that out of ſpeciall charitie, he " would haue thoſe Heretikes of his owne making, forewarned what courteous vſe and entreaty they are to expect; when he affirmeth that execution of the lawes is but ſuſpended: For indeed ſuſpenſions hold but for a time. But in a cauſe of that nature and importance, I dare promiſe my ſelfe, that my moſt honoured brother the King of *France*, will make vſe of other counſell : will rather ſeeke the amitie of his neighbour Princes, and the peace of his Kingdome · will beare in mind the great and faithfull ſeruice of thoſe, who in matter of religion diſſent from his Maieſtie, as of the onely men that haue preſerued and ſaued the Crowne for the King his father, of moſt glorious memorie. I am perſwaded my brother of *France* wil beleeue, that his liege people pretended by the L. Cardinall to bee heretikes, are not halfe ſo bad as my Romane Catholike ſubiects, who by ſecret practiſes vndermine my life, ſerue a forreine Souereigne, are diſcharged by his Bulls of their obedience due to me their naturall Souereigne, are bound (by the maximes and rules publiſhed and maintained in fauour of the Pope, before this full and famous aſſemblie of the Eſtate at *Paris*; if the ſaid maximes be of any weight and authoritie) to hold mee, for no lawfull King, are there taught and inſtructed, that *Pauls* commandemement concerning ſubiection vnto the higher Powers, aduerſe to their profeſſed religion, is onely a prouiſionall precept, framed to the times, and watching for the opportunitie to ſhake off the yoake. All which notwithſtanding, I deale with ſuch Romane-Catholikes by the rules and wayes of Princely clemencie; their heinous and pernicious error, in effect no leſſe then the capitall crime of high treaſon, I vſe to call ſome diſeaſe or diſtemper of the mind. Laſt of all, I beleeue my ſaid brother of *France* will ſet downe in his tables, as in record, how little hee ſtandeth ingaged to the L. Cardinall in this behalfe : For thoſe of the reformed Religion profeſſe and proclaime, that next vnder God, they owe their preſeruation and ſafetie to the wiſedome and benignity of their Kings. But now comes the Cardinall, and he ſeekes to ſteale this perſwaſion out of their hearts : He tells them in open Parliament, and without any going about buſhes, that all their welfare and ſecuritie ſtandeth in their multitude, and in the feare which others conceiue

Note by the way that here the Church of Rome is called a Sect.

to trouble the State, by the ſtrict execution of lawes againſt Heretikes.

He addeth moreouer, that *In caſe a third Sect ſhould peepe out and growe vp in* France, *the profeſſors thereof ſhould ſuffer confiſcation of their goods, with loſſe of life it ſelfe; as hath bene practiſed at* Geneua *againſt* Seruetus, *and in* England *againſt* Arians. My anſwere is this, That puniſhments for heretikes, duely and according to Law conuicted, are ſet downe by decrees of the ciuill Magiſtrate, bearing rule in the countrey where the ſaid heretikes inhabite, and not by any ordinances of the Pope. I ſay withall, the L. Cardinall hath no reaſon to match and parallell the reformed Churches with *Seruetus* and the *Arians* : For thoſe heretikes were powerfully conuicted by Gods word, and lawfully condemned by the ancient Generall Councils, where they were permitted and admitted to plead their owne cauſe in perſon. But as for the trewth profeſſed by me, and thoſe of the reformed Religion, it was neuer yet hiſſed out of the Schooles, nor caſt out of any Council, (like ſome Parliament bills) where both ſides haue bene heard with like indifferencie. Yea, what Council ſoeuer hath bene offered vnto vs in theſe latter times, it hath bene propoſed with certaine preſuppoſitions : as, That his Holineſſe (beeing a partie in the cauſe, and conſequently to come vnder iudgement as it were to the barre vpon his triall) ſhall be the Iudge of Aſſize with Commiſſion of *Oyer* and *Determiner* : it ſhall bee celebrated in a citie of no ſafe acceſſe, without ſafe conduct or conuoy to come or goe at pleaſure, and without danger : it ſhall be aſſembled of ſuch perſons with free ſuffrage and voyce, as vphold this rule, (which they haue already put in practiſe againſt *Iohn Hus* and *Hierome* of *Prage*) that faith giuen, and oath taken to an Heretike, muſt not be obſerued.

Now then to reſume our former matter ; If the Pope hitherto hath neuer preſumed, for pretended hereſie to confiſcate by ſentence, either the lands or the goods of priuate perſons, or common people of the French Nation, wherefore ſhould hee dare to diſpoſſeſſe Kings of their Royall thrones? wherefore takes he more vpon him ouer Kings, then ouer priuate perſons ; wherefore ſhall the ſacred heads of Kings be more churliſhly, vnciuilly, and rigorouſly handled, then the hoods of the meaneſt people? Here the L. Cardinal in ſtead of a direct anſwer, breakes out of the liſts, alledging cleane from the purpoſe examples of heretikes puniſhed, not by the Pope but by the ciuill Magiſtrate of the Countrey : But *Bellarmine* ſpeakes to the point with a more free and open heart : hee is abſolute and reſolute in this opinion, that his Holineſſe hath plenary power to diſpoſe all Temporall eſtates and matters in the whole world ; *I am confident* (ſaith *Bellarmine* *and I ſpeake it with aſſurance, that our Lord* Ieſus Chriſt *in the dayes of his mortalitie, had power to diſpoſe of all Temporall things : yea, to ſtrip Soueraigne Kings and abſolute Lords of their Kingdomes and Seigniories : and without all doubt hath granted and left euen the ſame power vnto his* Vicar, *to make vſe thereof whenſoeuer bee ſhall thinke it neceſſary for the ſaluation of ſoules.* And ſo his Lordſhip ſpeaketh without exception of any thing at all : For who doth not know, that *Ieſus*
Chriſt

Contr. Barclaium, cap. 27.

Chriſt had power to diſpoſe no leſſe of priuate mens poſſeſſions, then of whole Realmes and Kingdomes at his pleaſure, if it had beene his pleaſure to diſplay the enſignes of his power? The ſame fulneſſe of power is likewiſe in the Pope. In good time: belike his Holineſſe is the ſole heire of Chriſt, in whole and in part. The laſt Lateran Council fineth a Laic that ſpeaketh blaſphemie, for the firſt offence (if he be a gentleman) at 2 5. ducats, and at 50. for the ſecond. It preſuppoſeth and taketh it for graunted, that the Church may rifle and ranſacke the purſes of priuate men, and caſt lots for their goods. The Councill of *Trent* diggeth as deepe for the ſame veine of gold and ſiluer. It ordaines; *That Emperours, Kings, Dukes, Princes, and Lords of cities, caſtles, and territories holding of the Church, in caſe they ſhall aſſigne any place within their limits or liberties for the duell betweene two Chriſtians ſhall be de-priued of the ſaid citie, caſtle, or place, where ſuch duell ſhall be performed, they holding the ſaid place of the Church by any kind of tenure: that all other Eſtates held in fee, where the like offence ſhall be committed, ſhall forthwith fall and become forfeited to their immediate and next Lords: that all goods, poſſeſſions, and eſtates, as well of the combatants themſelues, as of their ſeconds ſhall bee confiſcate.* This Councill doeth neceſſarily preſuppoſe, it lieth in the hand and power of the Church, to diſpoſe of all the lands and eſtates, held in fee throughout all Chriſten-dome; (becauſe the Church forſooth can take from one, and giue vnto an other all eſtates held in fee whatſoeuer, as well ſuch as hold of the Church, as of ſecular Lords) and to make ordinances for the confiſcation of all pri-uate perſons goods. By this Canon the Kingdome of *Naples* hath need to looke well vnto it ſelfe For one duell it may fall into the Exchequer of the Romane Church; becauſe that Kingdome payeth a Reliefe to the Church, as a Royaltie or Seignorie that holdeth in fee of the ſaid Church. And in *France* there is not one Lordſhip, not one Mannor, not one farme which the Pope by this meanes cannot ſhift ouer to a new Lord. His Lordſhip therefore had carried himſelfe and the cauſe much better, if in ſtead of ſee-king ſuch idle ſhifts, he had by a more large aſſertion maintained the Popes power to diſpoſe of priuate mens poſſeſſions, with no leſſe right and au-thoritie then of Kingdomes: For what colour of reaſon can bee giuen, for making the Pope Lord of the whole, and not of the parts? for making him Lord of the forreſt in groſſe, and not of the trees in parcell? for ma-king him Lord of the whole houſe, and not of the parlour or the di-ning chamber?

His Lordſhip alleadgeth yet an other reaſon, but of no better weight: *Betweene the power of priuate owners ouer their goods, and the power of Kings ouer their eſtates, there is no little difference: For the goods of priuate perſons are or-dained for their owners, and Princes for the benefit of their Common-wealths.* Heare me now anſwere. If this Cardinal-reaſon hath any force to inferre, that a King may lawfully be depriued of his Kingdome for hereſie, but a priuate perſon cannot for the ſame crime be turned out of his manſion houſe; then it ſhall follow by the ſame reaſon, that a Father for the ſame cauſe may be

Seſſ.9.

Seſſ.25.cap.19.

bee depriued of all power ouer his children, but a priuate owner cannot be depriued of his goods in the like case: because goods are ordeined for the benefit and comfort of their owners, but fathers are ordeined for the good and benefit of their children: But most certain it is, that Kings representing the image of God in earth and Gods place, haue a better and closer seate in their chaires of Estate, then any priuate persons haue in the saddle of their inheritances and patrimonies, which are dayly seene for sleight causes, to flit and to fall into the hands of new Lords: Whereas a Prince being the Head, cannot bee loosed in the proper ioynt, nor dismounted; like a cannon when the carriage thereof is vnlockt, without a sore shaking and a most grieuous dislocation of all the members, yea, without subuerting the whole bodie of the State, whereby priuate persons without number are inwrapped together in the same ruine; euen as the lower shrubs and other brush-wood are crushed in pieces altogether by the fall of a great oake. But suppose his Lordships reason were somewhat ponderous and solide withall, yet a King (which would not bee forgotten) is endowed not onely with the Kingdome, but also with the ancient Desmenes and Crowne-lands, for which none can be so simple to say, The King was ordeined and created King; which neuerthelesse he loseth when hee loseth his Crowne. Admit againe this reason were of some pith, to make mighty Kings more easily deposeable then priuate persons from their patrimonies; yet all this makes nothing for the deriuing and fetching of deposition from the Popes Consistorie. What hee neuer conferred, by what right or power can he claime to take away?

But see heere no doubt a sharpe and subtile difference put by the L. Cardinall betweene a Kingdome, and the goods of priuate persons. *Goods*, as "his Lordship saith, *are without life: they can be constrained by no force, by no ex-* "*ample, by no inducement of their owners to lose eternall life: Subiects by their Prin-* "*ces may.* Now I am of the contrary beliefe, That an hereticall owner, or master of a family, hath greater power and meanes withall, to seduce his owne seruants and children, then a Prince hath to peruert his owne subiects; and yet for the contagion of Heresie, and for corrupt religion, children are not remoued from their parents, nor seruants are taken away from their masters. Histories abound with examples of most flourishing Churches, vnder a Prince of contrary religion. And if things without life or soule are with lesse danger left in an heretikes hands; why then shall not an hereticall King with more facilitie and lesse danger keepe his Crowne, his Royall charge, his lands, his customes, his imposts, &c? For will any man, except he bee out of his wits, affirme these things to haue any life or soule? Or why shall it bee counted folly, to leaue a sword in the hand of a mad Bedlam? Is not a sword also without life and soule? For my part, I should rather be of this minde; that possession of things without reason, is more dangerous and pernicious in the hands of an euill master, then the possession of things endued with life and reason: For things without
life

life lacke both reafon and iudgement, how to exempt and free themfelues from being inftruments in euill and wicked actions, from being emploied to vngodly and abominable vfes. I will not deny, that an hereticall Prince is a plague, a pernicious and mortall fickeneffe to the foules of his fubiects: But a breach made by one mifchiefe, muft not bee filled vp with a greater inconuenience: An errour muft not be fhocked and fhouldered with diffoialtie, nor herefie with periurie, nor impietie with fedition and armed rebellion againft G o d and the King. G o d, who vfeth to try and to fchoole his Church, will neuer forfake his Church; nor hath need to protect his Church by any proditorious and prodigious practifes of perfidious Chriftians: For he makes his Church to be like the burning bufh: In the middeft of the fire and flames of perfecutions, hee will prouide that fhe fhall not be confumed, becaufe hee ftandeth in the midft of his Church. And fuppofe there may be fome iuft caufe for the French, to play the rebels againft their King; yet will it not follow, that fuch rebellious motions are to be raifed by the bellowes of the Romane Bifhop, to whofe Paftorall charge and office it is nothing proper, to intermeddle in the ciuill affaires of forraine Kingdomes.

Here is the fumme and fubftance of the L. Cardinals whole difcourfe, touching his pretence of the fecond inconuenience. Which difcourfe hee hath clofed with a remarkeable confeffion: to wit, that neither by the authoritie of holy Scripture, nor by the the teftimonie and verdict of the Primitiue Church, there hath bene any full decifion of this queftion. In regard whereof he falleth into admiration, that Lay-people haue gone fo farre in audacioufneffe, as to labour that a doubtfull doctrine might for euer paffe currant, and be taken for a new article of faith. *What a fhame, what a reproach is this? how full of fcandall?* for fo his Lordfhip is pleafed to cry out. *This breakes into the feueralls and inclofures of the Church: this lets in whole herds of herefies to grafe in her greene and fweet paftures.* On the other fide, without any fuch Rhetoricall outcries; I fimply affirme: It is a reproach, a fcandall, a crime of rebellion, for a fubiect hauing his full charge and loade of benefits, in the new fpring of his Kings tender aage, his King-fathers blood yet reeking, and vpon the point of an addreffe for a double match with Spaine; in fo honourable an affembly, to feeke the thraldome of his Kings Crowne, to play the captious in cauilling about caufes of his Kings depofing, to giue his former life the Lye with fhame enough in his old aage, and to make himfelfe a common by-word, vnder the name of a *Problematicall Martyr*; one that offers himfelfe to fagot and fire, for a point of doctrine but problematically handled, that is, diftruftfully and onely by way of doubtfull and queftionable difcourfe: yea for a point of doctrine, in which the French (as he pretendeth) are permitted to thwart and croffe his Holines in iudgement, prouided they fpeake in it as in a point, not certaine and neceffary, but onely doubtfull and probable.

THE

THE THIRD INCON-
VENIENCE EXAMINED.

Pag. 87.

He third Inconuenience pretended by the L. Cardinall to grow by admitting this Article of the third Estate, is flourished in these colours: *It would breed and bring foorth an open and vnauoydeable schisme against his Holinesse, and the rest of the whole Ecclesiasticall body: For thereby the doctrine long approued and ratified by the Pope and the rest of the Church, should now be taxed and condemned of impious and most detestable consequence ; yea the Pope and the Church, euen in faith and in points of saluation, should be reputed and beleeued to be erroniously perswaded.* Hereupon his Lordship giues himselfe a large scope of the raines, to frame his elegant amplifications against schismes and schismatikes.

Now to mount so high, and to flie in such place vpon the wings of amplification for this Inconuenience, what is it else but magnifically to report and imagine a mischiefe by many degrees greater then the mischiefe is? The L. Cardinal is in a great errour, if hee make himselfe beleeue, that other nations wil make a rent or separation from the communion of the French, because the French stand to it tooth and naile, that French Crownes are not liable or obnoxious to Papall deposition ; howsoeuer there is no schisme that importeth not separation of communion. The most illustrious Republike of *Venice*, hath imbarked herselfe in this quarrell against his Holinesse, hath played her prize, and caried away the weapons with great honour. Doeth she, notwithstanding her triumph in the cause, forbeare to participate with all her neighbours in the same Sacraments? doeth she liue in schisme with all the rest of the Romane Church? No such matter. When the L. Cardinal himselfe not many yeeres past, maintained the Kings cause, and stood honourably for the Kings right against the Popes Temporall vsurpations, did he then take other Churches to be schismaticall, or the rotten members of *Antichrist* ? Beleeue it who list, I beleeue my Creed. Nay, his Lordship telleth vs himselfe a little after; that his Holinesse giues the French free scope, to maintaine either the affirmatiue or negatiue of this question. And will his Holinesse hold them schismatikes, that dissent from his opinion and iudgement in a subiect or cause esteemed problematicall? Farre be it from his Holinesse. The King of Spaine, reputed the Popes right arme, neuer gaue the Pope cause, by any acte or other declaration, to conceiue that he acknowledged himselfe deposeable by the Pope for heresie, or Tyrannie, or stupiditie. But being well assured the Pope standeth in greater feare of his arme, then hee doeth of the Popes head and

shoulders,

fhoulders, he neuer troubles his owne head about our queftion. More,
when the booke of Cardinall *Baronius* was come foorth, in which booke
the Kingdome of Naples is defcried and publiquely difcredited (like falfe
money) touching the qualitie of a Kingdome, and attributed to the King
of Spaine, not as trew proprietary thereof, but onely as an Eftate held in
fee of the Romane Church ; the King made no bones to condemne and to
banifh the faid booke out of his dominions. The holy Father was contented to put vp his Catholike fonnes proceeding to the Cardinals difgrace, neuer opened his mouth againft the King, neuer declared or noted the King
to be fchifmaticall. He waits perhaps for fome fitter opportunitie; when
the Kingdome of Spaine groaning vnder the burthens of inteftine diffentions and troubles, hee may without any danger to himfelfe giue the Catholike King a Bifhops mate. Yea, the L. Cardinal himfelfe is better feene in
the humors and inclinations of the Chriftian world, then to be grofly perfwaded, that in the Kingdome of Spaine, and in the very heart of Rome it
felfe there be not many, which either make it but a ieaft, or elfe take it in
fowle fcorne, to heare the Popes power ouer the Crownes of Kings once
named : efpecially fince the Venetian Republike hath put his Holineffe to
the worfe in the fame caufe, and caft him in Law.

What needed the L. Cardinall then, by cafting vp fuch mounts and
trenches, by heaping one amplification vpon an other, to make fchifme
looke with fuch a terrible and hideous afpect? Who knowes not how great
an offence, how heinous a crime it is to quarter not I E s v s C H R I S T S
coat, but his body, which is the Church? And what needed fuch terrifying
of the Church with vglineffe of fchifme; whereof there is neither colourable fhew, nor poffibilitie?

The next vgly monfter, after fchifme, fhaped by the L. Cardinall in the
third fuppofed and pretended inconuenience, is herefie. His Lordfhip
faith for the purpofe: *By this Article we are caft headlong into a manifeft herefie,*
as binding vs to confeffe, that for many aages paft, the Catholike Church hath bene
banifhed out of the whole world. For if the champions of the doctrine contrary to this
Article, doe hold an impious and a deteftable opinion ; repugnant vnto Gods word,
then doubtleffe the Pope for fo many hundred yeeres expired, hath not bene the head
of the Church, but an heretike and the Antichrift. He addeth moreouer; That the
Church long agoe hath loft her name of Catholike, and that in France there hath no
Church flourifhed, nor fo much as appeared thefe many and more then many yeeres: for
as much as all the French doctors for many yeres together, haue ftood for the contrary
opinion. We can erect and fet vp no trophey more honorable for heretikes in token of
their victory, then to auow that Chrifts vifible Kingdom is perifhed from the face of
the earth, and that for fo many hundred yeres there hath not bene any Temple of God,
nor any fpoufe of Chrift, but euery where, and all the world ouer, the kingdom of Anti-
chrift, the fynagogue of Satan, the fpoufe of the diuel, hath mightily preuailed and borne
all the fway. Laftly, what ftronger engines can thefe heretikes wifh or defire; for the
battering and the demolifhing of tranfubftantiation, of auricular confeffion, and other
                                                                                    like

Pag. 89.

" *like towers of our* (*Catholike Religion, then if it should bee granted the Church hath*
" *decided the said points without any authoritie?* &c.

Mee thinkes the L. Cardinal in the whole draught and courſe of theſe
words doeth ſeeke not a little to blemiſh the honour of his Church, and
to marke his religion with a blacke coale : For the whole frame of his
Mother-Church is very eaſie to be ſhaken, if by the eſtabliſhing of this Article ſhe ſhall come to finall ruine, and ſhall become the Synagogue of Satan. Likewiſe, Kings are brought into a very miſerable ſtate and condition, if their Souereigntie ſhall not ſtand, if they ſhall not bee without danger of depoſition, but by the totall ruine of the Church, and by holding the
Pope, whom they ſerue, to be Antichriſt. The L. Cardinall himſelfe (let
him be well ſifted) herein doeth not credit his owne words : For doeth
not his Lordſhip tell vs plaine, that neither by Diuine teſtimony, nor by
any ſentence of the ancient Church, the knot of this controuerſie hath
bene vntied? againe, that ſome of the French, by the Popes fauourable indulgence, are licenſed or tolerated to ſay their mind, to deliuer their opinion of this queſtion, though contrary to the iudgement of his Holineſſe;
prouided they hold it onely as problematicall, and not as neceſſary? What?
Can there be any aſſurance for the Pope, that hee is not Antichriſt; for
the Church of *Rome*, that ſhe is not a Synagogue of Satan, when a mans
aſſurance is grounded vpon wauering and wilde vncertainties, without
Canon of Scripture, without conſent or countenance of antiquitie, and
in a cauſe which the Pope by good leaue ſuffereth ſome to toſſe with
winds of problematicall opinion? It hath beene ſhewed before, that by
Gods word, whereof ſmall reckoning perhaps is made, by venerable antiquitie, and by the French Church in thoſe times when the Popes power
was mounted aloft, the doctrine which teacheth depoſing of Kings by
the Pope, hath bene checked and countermanded. What, did the French
in thoſe dayes beleeue the Church was then ſwallowed vp, and no where
viſible or extant in the world? No verely; Thoſe that make the Pope of
Soueraigne authoritie for matters of Faith, are not perſwaded that in this
cauſe they are bound abſolutely to beleeue and credit his doctrine. Why
ſo? Becauſe they take it not for any decree or determination of Faith; but
for a point perteining to the myſteries of State, and a pillar of the Popes
Temporall Monarchie; who hath not receiued any promiſe from God,
that in cauſes of this nature hee ſhall not erre : For they hold, that errour
by no meanes can crawle or ſcramble vp to the Papall See, ſo highly mounted; but grant ambition can ſcale the higheſt walls, and climbe the loftieſt
pinacles of the ſame See. They hold withall, that in caſe of ſo ſpeciall aduantage to the Pope, whereby he is made King of Kings, and as it were
the pay-maſter or diſtributer of Crownes, it is againſt all reaſon that hee
ſhould ſit as Iudge, to carue out Kingdomes for his owne ſhare. To bee
ſhort, let his Lordſhip be aſſured that he meeteth with notorious blocke-
heads, more blunt-witted then a whetſtone, when they are drawen to beleeue

leeue by his perſwaſion, that whoſoeuer beleeues the Pope hath no right nor power to put Kings beſide their Thrones, to giue and take away Crownes, are all excluded and barred out of the heauenly Kingdome.

But now followes a worſe matter: For they whom the Cardinall reproachfully calls heretikes, haue wrought and wonne his Lordſhip (as to mee ſeemeth) to plead their cauſe at the barre, and to betray his owne cauſe to theſe heretikes: For what is it in his Lordſhip, but plaine playing the Præuaricator, when he crieth ſo lowd, that by admitting and eſtabliſhing of this Article, the doctrine of Cake-incarnation and priuie Confeſſion to a Prieſt, is vtterly ſubuerted? Let vs heare his reaſon, and willingly accept the trewth from his lips. The Articles (as his Lordſhip granteth) of Tranſubſtantiation, auricular Confeſſion, and the Popes power to depoſe Kings, are all grounded alike vpon the ſame authoritie. Now he hath acknowledged the Article of the Popes power to depoſe Kings, is not decided by the Scripture, nor by the ancient Church, but within the compaſſe of certaine aages paſt, by the authoritie of Popes and Councils. Then he goes on well, and inferres with good reaſon, that in caſe the point of the Popes power be weakened, then the other two points muſt needs bee ſhaken, and eaſily ouerthrowen: So that hee doeth confeſſe the monſtrous birth of the breaden-God, and the blind Sacrament or vaine fantaſie of auricular confeſſion, are no more conueyed into the Church by pipes from the ſprings of ſacred Scripture, or from the riuers of the ancient Church, then that other point of the Popes power ouer Kings and their Crownes. Very good: For were they indeed deriued from either of thoſe two heads, that is to ſay, were they grounded vpon the foundation of the firſt or ſecond authoritie; then they could neuer bee ſhaken by the downefall of the Popes power to depoſe Kings. I am well aſſured, that for vſing ſo good a reaſon, the world will hold his Lordſhip in ſuſpicion, that he ſtill hath ſome ſmacke of his fathers diſcipline and inſtruction, who in times paſt had the honour to be a Miniſter of the holy Goſpel.

Howbeit he playeth not faire, nor vſeth ſincere dealing in his proceeding againſt ſuch as he calls heretikes; when hee caſts in their diſh, and beares them in hand they frowardly wrangle for the inuiſibilitie of the Church in earth: For indeed the matter is nothing ſo. They freely acknowledge a viſible Church: For howſoeuer the aſſembly of Gods elect, doth make a body not diſcerneable by mans eye; yet we aſſuredly beleeue, and gladly profeſſe, there neuer wanted a viſible Church in the world; yet onely viſible to ſuch as make a part of the ſame. All that are without, ſee no more but men, they doe not ſee the ſaid men to be the trew Church. Wee beleeue moreouer of the vniuerſall Church viſible, that it is compoſed of many particular Churches, whereof ſome are better fined and more cleane from lees and dregs then other: and withall, we denie the pureſt Churches to be alwayes the greateſt and moſt viſible.

THE

THE FOVRTH AND LAST
INCONVENIENCE EXAMINED.

THE Lord Cardinall before he looketh into the laſt Incon-uenience, vſeth a certaine preamble of his owne life paſt, and ſeruices done to the Kings, *Henry* the III. and IIII. Tou-ching the latter of which two Kings, his Lordſhip ſaith in a ſtraine of boaſting, after this manner: *I, by the grace of God, or the grace of God by mee rather, reduced him to the Catholike religion. I ob-tained at Rome his abſolution of Pope Clement 8. I reconciled him to the holy See.* Touching the firſt of theſe points; I ſay the time, the occaſions, and the foreſaid Kings neceſſary affaires doe ſufficiently teſtifie, that he was indu-ced to change his mind, and to alter his religion, vpon the ſtrength of o-ther manner of arguments then Theologicall ſchooles, or the perſwaſions of the L. Cardinals fluent Rhetoricke, doe vſually afford, or could poſſibly ſuggeſt. Moreouer, who doeth not know, that in affaires of ſo high na-ture and conſequence, reſolutions once taken, Princes are to proceede with inſtructions by a formall courſe? As for the Kings abſolution, pretended to bee purchaſed of *Clement* 8. by the L. Cardinals good ſeruice, it had beene the part of ſo great a Cardinall, for the honour of his King, of the Realme, and of his owne place, to haue buried that piece of his notable ſeruice in perpetuall ſilence, and in the darke night of eternall obliuion: For in this matter of reconcilement, it is not vnknowne to the world, how ſhamefully and baſely hee proſtituted the inuiolable dignity of his King, when his Lordſhip repreſenting the perſon of his King, and couching on the ground by way of ſufficient penance, was glad (as I haue noted in the Preface to my Apologie) to haue his venerable ſhoulders gracefully ſaluted with ſtripes, and reuerently worſhipped with baſtonados of a Pontificiall cudgell. Which gracefull, or diſgracefull blemiſh rather, it pleaſed Pope *Clement* of his rare clemencie, to grace yet with a higher degree of ſpirituall graces; in giuing the L. Cardinall then Biſhop of *Eureux*, a certaine quantity of holy graines croſſes, and medals, or little plates of ſiluer, or ſome other mettall, to hang about the necke, or to bee borne about againſt ſome euill: Which treaſures of the Popes grace, whoſoeuer ſhould gracionſly and reuerently kiſſe, they ſhould without faile purchaſe vnto themſelues a pardon for one hundred yeeres. Theſe feate and pretty gugawes for children, were no doubt a ſpeciall comfort vnto the good Kings heart, after his Maieſtie had beene handſomely baſted vpon the L. Biſhops backe. But with what face can his Lordſhip brag, that he preuailed with Pope *Clement* for the Kings abſolution? The late Duke of *Neuers*, not long before had ſolicited his

Holines,

Holines, with all earneſt and humble inſtance to the ſame purpoſe; howſoeuer, the Kings affaires then ſeeming deſperate in the Popes eye, he was
licenſed to depart for *France*, without any due and gracious reſpect vnto his
errand. But ſo ſoone as the Pope receiued intelligence, of the Kings fortunes growing to the full, and the affaires of the League to be in the wane,
and the principall cities, the ſtrongeſt places of garriſon through all *France*
to ſtrike tops and tops gallant, and to hale the King; then the holy Ghoſt in
good time inſpired the holy Father with a holy deſire and tender affection,
to receiue this poore wandring ſheep againe into the flocke of Chriſt, and
boſome of holy Church. His Holineſſe had reaſon: For he feared by his
obſtinate ſeuerity to prouoke the patience of the French, and to driue that
Nation (as they had many times threatned before) then to put in execution
their auncient deſigne; which was, to ſhake off the Pope, and to ſet vp ſome
of their owne tribes or kinreds for Patriarch ouer the French Church. But
let his Lordſhippe vouchſafe to ſearch the ſecret of his owne boſome, and
no doubt he wil not ſticke to acknowledge, that before he ſtirred one foote
out of *France*, he had good aſſurance of the good ſucceſſe and iſſue of his
honourable embaſſage.

Now the hearers thus prepared by his Preface, the L. Cardinall proceedeth in his purpoſe; namely to make proofe, how this Article of the third
Eſtate, wherein doubtfull and queſtionable matters are mingled and confounded with certaine and indubitable principles, doth ſo debilitate and
weaken the ſinewes and vertue of any remedy intended for the danger of
Kings, as it maketh all remedies and receipts preſcribed for that purpoſe,
to become altogether vnprofitable, and without effect. He yeelds this reaſon, (take it forſooth vpon my warrant) a reaſon full of pith and ſubſtance:
The onely remedie againſt parricides, is to thunder the ſolemne curſes of
the Church, and the puniſhments to be inflicted after death: which points,
if they be not grounded vpon infallible authoritie, will neuer be ſetled in
mens perſwaſions with any certaine aſſurance. Now in the ſolemne curſes of the Church, no man can attaine to the ſaid aſſurance, if things not denied be mingled with points not graunted, and not conſented vnto by the
Vniuerſall Church. By a thing not denied and not conteſted, the L. Cardinall meanes prohibiting and condemning of King-killing: and by points
conteſted, he meanes denying of the Popes power to depoſe Kings.

In this whole diſcourſe, I find neither pith of argument, nor courſe of
proofe; but onely a caſt of the L. Cardinalls office by way of counſell:
whereunto I make this anſwere. If there be in this Article of the third E-
ſtate any point, wherein all are not of one mind and the ſame iudgement;
in whom lieth all the blame, from whence riſes the doubt, but from the
Popes and Popiſh paraſites, by whom the certaintie of the ſaid point hath
bin cunningly remooued and conueied away, and muſt be reſtored againe
by publike authority? Now the way to reſtore certainty vnto a point, which
againſt reaſon is called into doubt and queſtion, is to make it vp in one

maſſe,

maſſe,or to tie it vp in the ſame bundle, with other certaine points of the ſame nature.

. Here I am forced to ſummon the conſciences of men,to make ſome ſtand or ſtay vpon this point,and with me to enter into deepe conſideration,how great and vnuanquiſhable force is euer found in the trewth : For theſe two queſtions , Whether Kings may lawfully be made away by aſſaſſins waged and hired for the act ; and Whether the Pope hath lawfull power to chaſe Kings out of their Thrones,are by the L. Cardinals owne confeſſion , in ſo full aſpect of coniunction, that if either bee brought vnder any degree of doubt,the other alſo is fetcht within the ſame compaſſe.In which words he directly pointeth as with a finger to the very trew ſource of the maine miſ-chiefe,and to the baſiliqueand liuer veine,infected with peſtilential blood, inflamed to the deſtruction of Baſilicall Princes by deteſtable parricide:For whoſoeuer ſhall confidently beleeue that Popes are not armed with power to depoſe Kings; will beleeue with no leſſe confidence and aſſurance, it is not lawful by ſudden aſſaults to flie at their throats. For are not all deſperate villaines perſwaded,when they are hired to murder Kings, that in doing ſo damnable a feate,they doe it for a piece of notable and extraordinary ſeruice to the Pope? This maxime therfore is to be held for a principle vnmoouea-ble and indubitable; that,If ſubiects deſire the life of their Kings to bee ſe-cured; they muſt not yeeld the Pope one inch of power, to depriue their Kings of their Thrones and Crownes,by depoſing their Kings.

    The Lord Cardinall teſtifieth no leſſe himſelfe in theſe words : *If thoſe monſters of men, and furies of hell, by whom the life-blood of our two laſt Kings was let out,had euer beene acquainted with Lawes Eccleſiaſticall , they might haue read themſelues adiudged by the Councill of Conſtance to expreſſe damnation.* For in theſe words, the L. Cardinall preferreth a bill of inditement to caſt his Holineſſe ; who,vpon the commencing of the Leaguers warres,in ſtead of giuing order for the publiſhing of the ſaid Eccleſiaſticall Lawes for the re-ſtraining of all parricidicall practiſes and attempts,fell to the terrour of his fulminations,which not long after were ſeconded and ratified by the moſt audatious and bloody murder of King *Henry* III. In like manner,the whole Clergy of *France* are wrapped vp by the L. Cardinals words, and inuolued in the perill of the ſaid inditement: For in ſtead of preaching the ſaid Ec-cleſiaſticall Lawes, by which all King-killing is inhibited ; the Prieſts taught,vented, and publiſhed nothing but rebellion ; and when the people in great deuotion came to powre their confeſſions into the Prieſts eares; then the Prieſts , with a kind of counterbuffe in the ſecond place when their turne was come, and with greater deuotion, powred blood into the eares of the people ; out of which roote grewe the terrour of thoſe cruell warres,and the horrible parricide of that good King.

    But let vs here take ſome neere ſight of theſe Eccleſiaſticall Lawes, whereby ſubiects are inhibited to kill , or deſperately to diſpatch their Kings out of the way. The Lord Cardinall, for full payment of all ſcores

vpon

vpon this reckoning, layeth downe the credit of the Councill at *Conſtance*, which neuertheleſſe affoardeth not one myte of trew and currant payment: The trewth of the hiſtory may bee taken from this briefe relation. *Iohn* Duke of Burgundy, procured *Lewis* Duke of Orleans to be murthered in Paris : To iuſtifie and make good this bloody acte, he produced a certaine petimaſter, one called by the name of *Iohn Petit*. This little *Iohn* cauſed nine propoſitions to be giuen foorth or ſet vp, to bee diſcuſſed in the famous Vniuerſitie of Paris: The ſumme of all to this purpoſe; It is lawfull, iuſt, and honourable, for euery ſubiect or priuate perſon, either by open force and violence, or by deceit and ſecret lying in waite, or by ſome wittie ſtratagem, or by any other way of fact, to kil a Tyrant practiſing againſt his King, and other higher powers; yea the King ought in reaſon, to giue him a penſion or ſtipend, that hath killed any perſon diſloyal to his Prince. The words of *Petits* firſt propoſition be theſe : *It is lawfull for euery ſubiect, with-   out any command or commiſsion from the higher powers, by all the Lawes of nature, of man, and of God himſelfe, to kill or cauſe to be killed any Tyrant, who either by a couetous and greedie deſire, or by fraud, by diuination vpon caſting of Lots, by double and treacherous dealing, doeth plot or practiſe againſt his Kings corporall health, or the health of his higher powers.* In the third propoſition: *It is lawfull for euery ſubiect, honourable and meritorious, to kill the ſaid Tyrant, or cauſe him to be killed as a Traitor, diſloyall and trecherous to his King.* In the ſixt propoſition: *The King is to appoint a ſalarie and recompence for him that hath killed ſuch a Tyrant, or hath cauſed him to bee killed.* Theſe propoſitions of *Iohannes Paruus*, were condemned by the Councill of Conſtance, as impious, and tending to the ſcandall of the Church. Now then, whereas the ſaid Councill no doubt vnderſtood the name or word Tyrant in the ſame ſenſe, wherein it was taken by *Iohannes Paruus*; certaine it is, the Councill was not of any ſuch iudgement or mind, to condemne one that ſhould kill a King or Soueraigne Prince; but one that by treaſon, and without commandement ſhould kill a ſubiect, rebelling and practiſing againſt his King. For *Iohn Petit* had vndertaken to iuſtifie the making away of the Duke of Orleans to be a lawfull acte, and calls that Duke a Tyrant, albeit hee was no Soueraigne Prince; as all the aboue recited words of *Iohn Petit* doe teſtifie, that he ſpeaketh of ſuch a Tyrant, as being in ſtate of ſubiection, rebelleth againſt his free and abſolute Prince : So that whoſoeuer ſhall narrowly ſearch and looke into the mind and meaning of the ſaid Council, ſhal eaſily perceiue, that by their decrees the ſafetie of Kings was not confirmed but weakened, not augmented but diminiſhed; for as much as they inhibited priuate perſons to kill a Subiect, attempting by wicked counſels and practiſes to make away his King.

But be it granted, the Councill of Conſtance is flat and altogether direct againſt King-killers; For I am not vnwilling to be perſwaded, that had the queſtion then touched the murdering of Soueraigne Princes, the ſaid Councill would haue paſſed a ſound and holy decree: But, I ſay, this granted,

Gerſon.

ted, what fheild of defence is hereby reached to Kings, to ward or beat off the thruft of a murderers weapon, and to faue or fecure their life? feeing the L. Cardinall, building vpon the fubtile deuife and fhift of the *Iefuites*, hath taught vs out of their Schooles, that by Kings are vnderftood Kings in *effe*, not yet fallen from the fupreame degree of Soueraigne Royaltie : For being once depofed by the Pope, (fay the *lefuites*) they are no longer Kings, but are fallen from the rights of Soueraigne dignitie; and confequently to make ftrip and waft of their blood, is not forfooth to make ftrip and waft of Royall blood. The *Iefuiticall* mafters, in the file of their words are fo fupple and fo limber, that by leauing ftill in their fpeech fome ftarting hole or other, they are able by the fame, as by a pofterne or backdoore, to make an efcape.

Meane while the Readers are here to note (for well they may) a tricke of monftrous and moft wicked cunning. The L. Cardinall contends for the bridling and hampering of King-killers by the Lawes Ecclefiafticall. Now it might be prefumed, that fo reuerend and learned a Cardinal intending to make vfe of Ecclefiafticall Lawes, by vertue whereof the life of Kings may be fecured, would fill his mouth and garnifh the point with diuine Oracles, that wee might the more gladly and willingly giue him the hearing, when hee fpeakes as one furnifhed with fufficient weight and authoritie of facred Scripture. But behold, in ftead of the authenticall and moft ancient word, hee propounds the decree of a lateborne Councill at Conftance, neither for the Popes tooth, nor any way comming neere the point in controuerfie. And fuppofe it were pertinent vnto the purpofe, the L. Cardinall beareth in his hand a forke of diftinction, with two tines or teeth to beare off, nay to fhift off and to auoid the matter with meere dalliance. The fhorteft and neereft way (in fome fort of refpects) to eftablifh a falfe opinion, is to charge or fet vpon it with falfe and with ridiculous reafons. The like way to worke the ouerthrow of trew doctrine, is to reft or ground it vpon friuolous reafons or authorities of ftubble-weight. For example; if we fhould thus argue for the immortalitie of the foule with *Plato* : The fwan fingeth before her death; *ergo*, the foule is immortall. Or thus with certaine feduced Chriftians : The Pope hath ordained the word of God to be authenticall: *ergo*, all credit muft be giuen to diuine Scripture. Vpon the fpurkies or hookes of fuch ridiculous arguments and friuolous reafons, the L. Cardinall hangs the life and fafetie of Kings.

With like artificiall deuifes hee pretendeth to haue the infamous murders, and appofted cutting of Kings throats in extreame deteftation; and yet by depofing them from their Princely dignities, by degrading them from their fupreame and Soueraigne authorities, hee brings their facred heads to the butchers blocke: For a King depofed by the Pope, (let no man doubt) will not leaue any ftone vnremooued, nor any meanes and wayes vnattempted, nor any forces or powers of men vnleuied or vnhired, to defend himfelfe and his Regall dignitie, to repreffe and bring vnder his rebellious

In Phædone.

bellious people, by the Pope discharged of their alleagiance. In this perplexitie of the publike affaires, in these tempestuous perturbations of the
State, with what perils is the King not besieged and assaulted? His head is
exposed to the chances of warre; his life a faire marke to the insidious practises of a thousand traitours; his Royall person obuious to the dreadfull
storme of angry fortune, to the deadly malice, to the fatall and mortall weapons of his enemies. The reason: He is presupposed to be lawfully and orderly stripped of his Kingdome. Wil he yet hold the sterne of his Royall e-
state? Then is he necessarily taken for a Tyrant, reputed an vsurper, and his
life is exposed to the spoile: For the publike lawes make it lawful and free,
for any priuate person to enterprise against an vsurper of the Kingdome:
Euery man, saith *Tertullian*, *is a souldier, to beare armes against all traitors and pub-*
like enemies. Take from a King the title of lawfull King, you take from
him the warrant of his life, and the weapons whereby he is maintained in
greater securitie, then by his Royall Guard armed with swords and hal-
berds, through whose wards and ranks, a desperate villaine will make himselfe an easie passage, being master of another mans life, because he is prodigall and carelesse of his owne. Such therefore as pretend so much pity
towards Kings, to abhorre the bloody opening of their liuer-veine, and
yet withall, to approoue their hoysting out of the Royall dignity, are iust
in the veine and humour of those that say, Let vs not kill the King, but
let vs disarme the King that he may die a violent death: let vs not depriue
him of life, but of the meanes to defend his life: let vs not strangle the
King and stop his vitall breath, so long as he remaineth King; O that were
impious, O that were horrible and abominable; but let him be deposed,
and then whosoeuer shall runne him through the body with a weapon
vp to the very hilts, shall not beare the guilt of a King-killer. All this
must be vnderstood to be spoken of Kings, who after they are despoiled
of Regalitie, by sentence of deposition giuen by the Pope, are able to arme
themselues, and by valiant armes doe defend their Soueraigne rights.
But in case the King, blasted with Romane lightning, and stricken with
Papall thunder, shall actually and speedily bee smitten downe from his
high Throne of Regality, with present losse of his Kingdome; I beleeue it
is almost impossible for him to warrant his owne life, who was not able to
warrant his owne Kingdome. Let a cat be throwen from a high roofe to
the bottome of a cellour or vault, she lighteth on her feet, and runneth a-
way without taking any harme. A King is not like a cat, howsoeuer a cat
may looke vpon a King: he cannot fall from the loftie pinacle of Royalty,
to light on his feet vpon the hard pauement of a priuate state, without
crushing all his bones in pieces. It hath bene the lot of very few Emperors
and Kings, to outliue their Empire: For men ascend to the loftie Throne
of Kings, with a soft and easie pace, by certaine steps and degrees; there be
no stately staires to come downe, they tumble head and heeles together
when they fall. He that hath once griped anothers Kingdome, thinks him-

In reos Maie-
statis, & pub-
licos hostes om-
nis homo miles
est. Tertul.a-
pol.cap.2.

selfe

felfe in little fafetie,fo long as he fhall of his courtefie fuffer his diffeifed predeceſſour to draw his breath. And fay that fome Princes, after their fall
from their Thrones,haue efcaped both point and edge of the Tyrants weapon; yet haue they wandred like miferable fugitiues in forreine countreys,
or elfe haue bene condemned like captiues to perpetuall imprifonment at
home, a thoufand-fold worfe and more lamentable then death it felfe. *Dio-*
nyfius the Tyrant of *Syracufa,* from a great King in *Sicilie* tur'nd Schoole-
mafter in *Corinth*.It was the onely calling and kind of life,that as he thought
bearing fome refemblance of rule and gouernment, might recreate his
mind, as an image or picture of his former Soueraigntie ouer men. This
Dionyfius was the onely man (to my knowledge) that had a humour to
laugh after the loſſe of a Kingdome, and in the ftate of a Pedant or gouernour of children, merily to ieaft and to fcorne his former ftate and
condition of a King. In this my Kingdome of *England,*fundry Kings haue
feene the walls as it were of their Princely fortreſſe difmantled, razed, and
beaten downe. By name, *Edward* and *Richard*,both I I.and *Henrie* the V I.
all which Kings were moſt cruelly murdered in prifon. In the reigne of
Edward III. by Acte of Parliament, *Whofoeuer fhall imagine,* (that is the very
word of the Statute) *or machinate the Kings death , are declared guiltie of Re-*
bellion and high Treafon. The learned Iudges of the Land, grounding vpon
this Law of *Edward* the third , haue euer fince reputed and iudged them
traitors according to Law, that haue dared onely to whifper or talke foftly
betweene the teeth, of depofing the King : For they count it a cleare cafe,
that no Crowne can be taken from a Kings head, without loſſe of Head
and Crowne together,fooner or later.

Page 95.　The L. Cardinal therefore in this moſt weightie and ferious point doth
meerely dally and flowt after a fort, when hee tells vs, *The Church doeth not*
intermeddle with releafing of fubiects, and knocking off their yrons of obedience, but
onely before the Ecclefiaſticall tribunall feat ; and that befides this double cenfure,of
abfolution to fubiects, and excommunication to the Prince,the Church impofeth none
other penaltie. Vnder pretence of which two cenfures,fo farre is the Church (as the
L. Cardinall pretendeth) *from confenting that any man fo cenfured fhould bee tou-*
ched for his life, that fhe vtterly abhorreth all murder whatfoeuer ; but efpecially all
fudden and vnprepenced murders for feare of cafting away both body and foule; which
often in fudden murders goe both one way. It hath bene made manifeſt before,
that all fuch profcription and fetting forth of Kings to port-fale, hath alwaies for the traine thereof,either fome violent and bloody death,or fome
other mifchiefe more intolerable then death it felfe. What are we the better,that parricides of Kings are neither fet on,nor approued by the Church
in their abominable actions ; when fhee layeth fuch plots, and taketh fuch
courfes , as neceſſarily doe inferre the cutting of their throates ? In the
next place be it noted, that his Lordfhip againſt all reafon , reckons the ab-
foluing of fubiects from the oath of alleagiance, in the ranke of penalties a-
warded and enioyned before the Ecclefiaſticall tribunall feate : For this
penaltie

penaltie is not Ecclefiafticall, but Ciuill, and confequently not triable in Ecclefiafticall Courts, without vfurping vpon the Ciuill Magiftrate. But I wonder with what face the L. Cardinall can fay, The Church neuer confenteth to any practife againſt his life, whom fhe hath once chaftifed with feuere cenfures : For can his Lordſhip be ignorant, what is written by Pope *Vrbanus, Can. Excommunicatorum. Wee take them not in any wiſe to bee man-ſlayers, who in a certaine heat of zeale towards the Catholike Church their Mother, ſhall happen to kill an excommunicate perſon.* More, if the Pope doth not approoue and like the practife of King-killing, wherefore hath not his Holineffe impofed fome feuere cenfure vpon the booke of *Mariana* the Iefuite (by whom parricides are commended, nay highly extolled) when his Holineffe hath beene pleafed to take the paines to cenfure and call in fome other of *Mariana's* bookes? Againe, wherefore did his Holineffe aduife himfelfe to cenfure the Decree of the Court of Parliament in *Paris* againſt *Iohn Chaſtell?* Wherefore did hee fuffer *Garnet* and *Oldcorne* my powder-miners, both by bookes and pictures vendible vnder his nofe in *Rome*, to be inrowled in the Canon of holy Martyrs? And when hee faw two great Kings murdered one after another, wherefore by fome publike declaration did not his Holineffe teftifie to all Chriftendome, his inward fenfe and trew apprehenfion of fo great misfortune, as all *Europe* had iuſt caufe to lament on the behalfe of *France?* Wherefore did not his Holineffe publifh fome Law or Pontificiall Decree, to prouide for the fecuritie of Kings in time to come? Trew it is, that he cenfured *Becanus* his booke: But wherefore? That by a captious and fleight cenfure, he might preuent a more exact and rigorous Decree of the *Sorbone* Schoole : For the Popes checke to *Becanus*, was onely a generall cenfure and touch, without any particular fpecification of matter touching the life of Kings. About fome two moneths after, the faid booke was printed againe, with a dedication to the Popes *Nuntio* in *Germany*; yet without any alteration, faue onely of two articles conteining the abfolute power of the people ouer Kings. In recompence and for a counterchecke whereof, three or foure articles were inferted into the faid booke, touching the Popes power ouer Kings; articles no leffe wicked & iniurious to Regall rights, nay more iniurious then any of the other claufes, whereof iuft caufe of exception and complaint had bene giuen before. If I would collect and heape vp examples of ancient Emperours, (as of *Henrie* IV. whofe dead corps felt the rage and furie of the Pope; or of *Frederic* II. againſt whom the Pope was not afhamed to whet and kindle the Sultane; or of Queene *Elizabeth* our Predeceffour, of glorious memorie, whofe life was diuers times affaulted by priuie murderers, expreffly difpatched from *Rome* for that holy feruice) if I would gather vp other examples of the fame ftampe, which I haue layd forth in my Apologie for the oath of alleagiance; I could make it more cleare then day-light, how farre the L. Cardinals words are difcrepant from the trewth, where his Lordſhip out of moſt rare confidence is bold to auow, *That neuer* any

Can.excom.
Cauſ. 23.
Queſt.6.

any *Pope went fo farre , as to giue confent or counfell for the defperate murdering of Princes.* That which already hath bene alleadged may fuffice to conuince his Lordfhip: I meane,that his Holineffe by depofing of Kings,doeth lead them directly to their graues and tombes.

The Cardinall himfelfe feemeth to take fome notice hereof. *The Church* Pag.95. (as he fpeaketh)*abhorreth fudden and vnprepenfed murders aboue the reft.* Doth not his Lordfhip in this phrafe of fpeech acknowledge, that murders committed by open force, are not fo much difauowed or difclaimed by the Church? A little after he fpeakes not in the teeth, as before, but with full and open mouth; that hee doeth not diflike a King once depofed by the Pope, fhould be purfued with open warre: Whereupon it followes, that in warre the King may be lawfully flaine. No doubt a remarkeable degree of his Lordfhips clemencie. A King fhall bee better entreated and more mildly dealt withal,if he be flaine by the fhot of an harquebufe or caleeuer in the field, then if hee bee ftabd by the ftroke or thruft of a knife in his chamber: or if at a fiege of fome city hee be blowne vp with a myne, then by a myne made,and a traine of gunpowder laid vnder his Palace or Parliament houfe in time of peace. His reafon : Forfooth, becaufe in fudden murders,oftentimes the foule and the body perifh both together. O fingular bountie,and rare clemencie! prouokers , inftigators , ftrong puffers and blowers of parricides , in mercifull compaffion of the foule, become vnmercifull and fhamefull murderers of the body. This deuice may well claime and challenge kinred of *Mariana* the *Iefuites* inuention: For he liketh not at any hand the poifoning of a Tyrant by his meat or drinke ; for feare left he taking the poifon with his owne hand, and fwallowing or gulping it downe in his meate or drinke fo taken , fhould be found *felo de fe,* (as the common Lawyer fpeaketh) or culpable of his owne death. But *Mariana* likes better,to haue a Tyrant poyfoned by his chaire,or by his apparell and robes,after the example of the *Mauritanian* Kings; that being fo poyfoned onely by fent,or by contact , he may not be found guiltie of felfe-fellonie; and the foule of the poore Tyrant in her flight out of the body may be innocent. O hel-hounds,O diabolical wretches,O infernall monfters! Did they onely fufpect and imagine , that either in Kings there is any remainder of Kingly courage , or in their fubiects any fparke left of ancient libertie; they durft as foone eat their nailes , or teare their owne flefh from the bones, as once broach the veffell of this diabolicall deuice. How long then, how long fhall Kings whom the Lord hath called his Anointed, Kings the breathing Images of God vpon earth; Kings that with a wry or frowning looke,are able to crufh thefe earth-wormes in pieces ; how long fhall they fuffer this viperous brood, fcotfree and without punifhment, to fpit in their faces ? how long, the Maieftie of G o d in their perfon and Royall Maieftie , to be fo notorioufly vilified, fo difhonourably trampled vnder foot?

'The L.Cardinall borads vs with a like manifeft ieaft,and notably trifles; firft, firſt, diſtinguiſhing betweene Tyrants by adminiſtration, and Tyrants by vſurpation; then ſhewing that he by no meanes doeth approue thoſe pro-phane and heatheniſh Lawes, whereby ſecret practiſes and conſpiracies againſt a Tyrant by adminiſtration are permitted. His reaſon; *Becauſe after depoſition there is a certaine habitude to Royall dignitie, and as it were a kinde of politicke Character inherent in Kings, by which they are diſcerned from perſons meerely priuate, or the common ſort of people; and the obſtacle, croſſe-barre, or ſparre once remooued and taken out of the way, the ſaid Kings depoſed are at length reinueſted and endowed againe with lawfull vſe of Royall dignitie, and with law-full adminiſtration of the Kingdome.* Is it poſſible that his Lordſhip can ſpeake and vtter theſe words according to the inward perſwaſion of his heart? I beleeue it not. For admit a King caſt out of his Kingdome were ſure to eſ-cape with life; yet being once reduced to a priuate ſtate of life, after hee hath wound or wrought himſelfe out of deadly danger, ſo farre he is from holding or retayning any remainder of dignity or politike impreſſion, that on the contrary he falleth into greater contempt and miſery, then if he had bene a very peaſant by birth, and had neuer held or gouerned the ſterne of Royall eſtate. What fowle is more beautifull then the peacocke? Let her be plumed and bereft of her feathers; what owle, what iacke-daw more ridiculous, more without all pleaſant faſhion? The homely ſowter, the infamous catchpol, the baſe tincker, the rude artificer, the pack-horſe-porter, then liuing in Rome with libertie, when *Valentinian* was detain'd captiue by *Saporas* the Perſian King, was more happie then that Romane Emperour. And in caſe the L. Cardinall himſelfe ſhould bee ſo happie (I ſhould ſay ſo vnfortunate) to be ſtript of all his dignities and Eccleſiaſticall promotions; would it not redound to his Lordſhips wonderfull conſola-tion, that in his greateſt extremity, in the loweſt of his bareneſſe and na-kedneſſe, he ſtill retaineth a certaine habituall right and character of a Car-dinall, whereby to recouer the loſſe of his former dignities and honours? when hee beholds theſe prints and impreſſions of his foreſaid honours; would it not make him the more willing and glad, to forſake the backe of his venerable mule, to vſe his Cardinals foot-cloath no longer, but euer af-ter like a Cardinall in print and character, to walke on foot?

But let vs examine his Lordſhips conſolation of Kings, thruſt out of their kingdomes by the Pope for hereſie. *The obſtacle* (as the L. Cardinall ſpeaketh) *being taken away; that is to ſay, when the King ſhall be reformed; this habituall right and character yet inherent in the perſon of a King, reſtores him to the lawfull adminiſtration of his Kingdome.* I take this to be but a cold com-fort: For here his Lordſhip doeth onely preſuppoſe, and not prooue, that after a King is thruſt out of his Throne, when hee ſhall repent and turne trew Romane Catholike, the other by whom he hath bene caſt out, and by force diſſeiſed, will recall him to the Royall ſeat, and faithfully ſettle him a-gaine in his ancient right, as one that reioyceth for the recouery of ſuch a loſt ſheepe. But I ſhould rather feare, the new King would preſſe and ſtand

vpon

vpon other termes; as a terme of yeeres for a triall, whether the repentance of the King difplaced be trew & found to the coare, or counterfeit, diffembled, and painted holines; for the words, the forrowfull and heauie lookes, the fad and formall geftures, of men pretending repentance, are not alwayes to bee taken, to be refpected, to be credited. Againe, I fhould feare the afflicted King might be charged and borne downe too, that albeit hee hath renounced his former herefie, hee hath ftumbled fince at an other ftone, and runne the fhip of his faith againft fome other rocke of new hereticall prauitie. Or I fhould yet feare, he might be made to beleeue, that herefie maketh a deeper impreffion, and a character more indeleble in the perfon, then is the other politike character of Regal Maieftie. Alas, good Kings! in how hard, in how miferable a ftate doe they ftand? Once depofed, and euer barred of repentance: As if the fcapes and errors of Kings, were all finnes againft the Holy Ghoft, or finnes vnto death, for which it is not lawfull to pray. Falls a priuate perfon? he may be fet vp, and new eftablifhed. Falls a King? is a King depofed? his repentance is euer fruitleffe, euer vnprofitable. Hath a priuate perfon a traine of feruants? He can not be depriued of any one without his priuitie and confent. Hath a King millions of fubiects? He may be depriued by the Pope of a third part, when his Holineffe will haue them turne Clerics or enter Cloifters, without asking the King leaue: and fo of fubiects they may be made non-fubiects.

But I queftion yet further. A King falling into herefie, is depofed by the Pope, his fonne ftands pure Catholike· The Regal feat is empty. Who fhall fucceed in the depofed Kings place? Shall a ftranger be preferred by the Pope? That were to doe the innocent fonne egregious and notorious wrong. Shall the fonne himfelfe? That were a more iniurious part in the fonne againft his father: For if the fonne bee touched with any feare of God, or mooued with any reuerence towards his father, hee will diligently and ferioufly take heed, that hee put not his father by the Kingdome, by whofe meanes he himfelfe is borne to a Kingdome. Nor will hee tread in the fteps of _Henry_ the V. Emperour, who by the Popes inftigation, expelled and chafed his aaged father out of the Imperiall dignitie. Much leffe wil he

Lib.6.cap.4.Si Papa Regem deponæ, ab illis tantum poteris, expelli vel interfici, quibus ipfe id commiferit.

hearken to the voice and aduife of Doctor _Suares_ the Iefuite; who, in his booke written againft my felfe, a booke applauded and approoued of many Doctours, after hee hath like a Doctour of the chaire, pronounced, _That a King depofed by the_ Pope_, cannot bee lawfully expelled or killed, but onely by fuch as the Pope hath charged with fuch execution_: falleth to adde a little after: _If the_ Pope _fhall declare a King to bee an heretike_, _and fallen from the_ Kingdome_, without making further declaration touching execution_; that is to fay, without giuing expreffe charge vnto any to make away the King: _then the lawfull fucceffour being a Catholike, hath power to doe the feate; and if he fhall refufe, or if there fhall be none fuch, then it appertaineth to the comminaltie or body of the_ Kingdome_. A moft deteftable fentence: For in hereditarie Kingdomes, who is the Kings lawfull fucceffour, but his fonne?

The

The fonne then by this doctrine, shall imbrew his hands in his owne fathers blood, so soone as he shall be deposed by the Pope. A matter so much the neerer and more deepely to bee apprehended, becaufe the faid most outragious booke flyeth like a furious maftiffe directly at my throat, and withall instilleth such precepts into the tender difpofition of my fonne, as if hereafter hee shall become a Romane Catholike, so soone as the Pope shall giue me the lift out of my Throne, shall bind him forthwith to make effufion of his owne fathers blood. Such is the religion of thefe reuerend Fathers, the pillars of the Pontificiall Monarchie: In comparifon of whofe religion and holineffe, all the impietie that euer was among the Infidels, and all the barbarous crueltie that euer was among the Canibals, may paffe hencefoorth in the Christian world for pure clemencie and humanitie. Thefe things ought his Lordship to haue pondered, rather then to babble of habitudes and politike characters, which to the common people are like the Bergamafque or the wilde-Irifh forme of fpeach, and paffe their vnderftanding.

All thefe things are nothing in a maner, if we compare them with the laft claufe, which is the clofer, and as it were the vpfhot of his Lordships difcourfe: For therein he laboureth to perfwade concerning this Article, framed to bridle the Popes tyrannicall power ouer Kings, if it should receiue gracious entertainement, and generall approbation; *That it would* »
breed great danger, and worke effects of pernicious confequence vnto Kings. The » *reafon: becaufe it would prooue an introduction to fchifme; and fchifme would* » *ftirre vp ciuil warres, contempt of Kings, diftempered inclinations and motions to* » *intrap their life; and which is worft of all, the fierce wrath of God, inflicting all forts* » *of calamities.* An admirable paradoxe, and able to ftrike men ftone-blind: that his Holineffe muft haue power to depofe Kings, for the better fecurity and fafegard of their life; that when their Crownes are made fubiect vnto anothers will and pleafure, then they are come to the higheft altitude and eleuation of honour; that for the onely warrant of their life, their fupreme and abfolute greatneffe muft be depreffed; that for the longer keeping of their Crownes, another muft plucke the Crowne from their heads. As if it should be faid, Would they not be ftript naked by another? the beft way is, for themfelues to vntruffe, for themfelues to put off all, and to goe naked of their owne accord. Wil they keepe their Souereigntie in fafetie for euer? The beft way is to let another haue their Soueraigne authoritie and fupreme Eftate in his power. But I haue bene euer of this mind, that when my goods are at no mans command or difpofing but mine own, then they are trewly and certainly mine owne. It may be this error is growen vpon me and other Princes for lacke of braines: whereupon it may be feared, or at leaft coniectured, the Pope meanes to fhaue our crownes, and thruft vs into fome cloifter, there to hold ranke in the brotherhood of good King *Childeric.* Forafmuch then as my dull capacitie doeth not ferue mee to reach or comprehend the pith of this admirable reafon, I haue thought good

good to feeke and to vſe the inſtruction of old and learned experience, which teacheth no ſuch matter : by name, that ciuill warres and fearefull perturbations of State in any nation of the world, haue at any time growen from this faithful credulity of ſubiects, that Popes in right haue no power to wreſt and lift Kings out of their dignities and poſſeſſions. On the other ſide, by eſtabliſhing the contrary maximes, to yoke and hamper the people with Pontificiall tyrannie, what rebellious troubles and ſtirres, what extreme deſolations hath *England* bene forced to feare and feele , in the Reigne of my Predeceſſours *Henrie* II. *Iohn* and *Henrie* III? Theſe be the maximes and principles, which vnder the Emperour *Henrie* IV. and *Frederic* the I. made all *Europe* flowe with channels and ſtreames of blood, like a riuer with water, while the Saracens by their incurſions and victories ouerflowed , and in a manner drowned the honour of the Chriſtian name in the Eaſt. Theſe be the maximes and principles, which made way for the warres of the laſt League into *France*; by which the very bowels of that moſt famous and flouriſhing Kingdome were ſet on ſuch a combuſtion, that *France* her ſelfe was brought within two fingers breadth of bondage to another Nation, and the death of her two laſt Kings moſt villenouſly and traiterouſly accompliſhed. The L. Cardinall then giuing theſe diabolicall maximes for meanes to ſecure the life and Eſtate of Kings, ſpeaketh as if he would giue men counſell to dry themſelues in the riuer, when they come as wet as a water ſpaniell out of a pond ; or to warme themſelues by the light of the Moone, when they are ſtark-naked, and well neere frozen to death.

THE CONCLVSION OF THE
LORD OF PERRON EXAMINED.

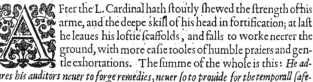 Fter the L. Cardinal hath ſtoutly ſhewed the ſtrength of his arme, and the deepe ſkiſl of his head in fortification; at laſt he leaues his loftie ſcaffolds , and falls to worke neerer the ground, with more eaſie tooles of humble praiers and gentle exhortations. The ſumme of the whole is this: *He adiures his auditors neuer to forge remedies, neuer ſo to prouide for the temporall ſafetie of Kings , as thereby to worke their finall falling from eternall ſaluation: neuer to make any rent or rupture in the vnitie of the Church, in this corrupt aage infected with peſtilent Hereſies, which already hauing made ſo great a breach in the walles of France, will no doubt double their ſtrength by the diſſentions, diuiſions, and ſchiſmes of Catholikes. If this infectious plague ſhall ſtill increaſe and grow to a carbuncle, it can by no meanes poyſon Religion, without bringing Kings to their winding ſheetes and woſull hearſes. The firſt rowlers of that ſtone of offence, aimed at no*

other

other marke, then to make an ignominious and lamentable rent in the Church. Hee thinks the Deputies of the third Estate, had neither head nor first hand in contriuing this Article; but holds it rather a new deuice and subtile inuention, suggested by persons, which beeing already cut off by their owne practises from the body of the Romane Church, haue likewise inueigled and insnared some that beare the name of Catholiks, with some other Ecclesiastics; and vnder a faire pretence and goodly cloake, by name, the seruice of the King, haue surprisd and played vpon their simplicitie. These men (as the Cardinall saith) doe imitate Iulian the Apostata, who to bring the Christians to idolatrous worship of false gods, commaunded the idols of Iupiter and Venus to be intermingled with Imperiall statues, and other Images of Christian Emperours, &c. Then after certaine Rhetoricall flourishes, his Lordship fals to prosecute his former course, and cries out of this Article; A monster hauing the tayle of a fish, as if it came cutting the narrow Seas out of England : For in full effect it is downright the English oath; sauing that indeed the oath of England runneth in a more mild forme, and a more moderate straine. And here he suddenly takes occasion to make some digression: For out of the way, and cleane from the matter, he entreth into some purpose of my praise and commendation : He courteously forsooth is pleased to grace mee with knowledge of learning, and with ciuill vertues : He seemeth chiefly to reioyce in his owne behalfe, and to giue me thanks, that I haue done him the honour to enter the lists of Theologicall dispute against his Lordship. Howbeit he twitches and carpes at me withall, as at one that soweth seeds of dissention and schisme amongst Romane Catholiks : And yet he would seeme to qualifie the matter, and to make all whole againe, by saying, That in so doing I am perswaded I doe no more then my duetie requires. But now (as his Lordship followes the point) it standeth neither with godlinesse, nor with equity, nor with reason, that Acts made, that Statutes, Decrees, and Ordinances ratified for the State and Gouernement of England, should be thrust for binding Laws vpon the Kingdome of France : nor that Catholikes, and much lesse that Ecclesiastics, to the end they may liue in safetie, and freely enioy their priuiledges or immunities in France, should be forced to beleeue, and by oath to seale the same points, which English Catholikes to the end they may purchase libertie onely to breath, nay sorrowfully to sigh rather, are constrained to allow and to aduow besides. And whereas in England there is no small number of Catholikes, that lacke not constant and resolute minds to endure all sorts of punishment, rather then to take that oath of allegiance; will there not be found another manner of number in France, armed with no lsse constancie and Christian resolution ? There will, most honourable Auditors, there will without all doubt : and we all that are of Episcopall dignity will sooner suffer Martyrdome in the cause. Then out of the super-abundance and ouerweight of his Lordships goodnes, he closely coucheth and conuayeth a certaine distastfull opposition betweene mee and his King; with praises and thanks to God, that his King is not delighted, & takes no pleasure to make Martyrs.

All this Artificiall and swelling discourse like vnto puffe-past, if it be viewed at a neere distance, will be found like a bladder full of wind, without any soliditie of substantiall matter. For the Deputies of the third

Estate

Eftate were neuer fo voide of vnderftanding, to beleeue that by prouiding for the life and fafety of their King, they fhould thruft him headlong into eternall damnation. Their braines were neuer fo much blafted, fo farre be-nummed, to dreame the foule of their King cannot mount vp to heauen, except he be difmounted from his Princely Throne vpon earth, whenfoe-uer the Pope fhall hold vp his finger.

And whereas he is bold to pronounce, that heretikes of *France* doe make their benefit and aduantage of this diuifion; that fpeech is grounded vpon this propofition; That profeffors of the Chriftian Religion reformed (which is to fay, purged and cleanfed of all Popifh dregs) are heretikes in fact, and ought fo to bee reputed in right: Which propofition his Lord-fhip will neuer foundly and fufficiently make good, before his Holineffe hath compiled an other Gofpell, or hath forged an other Bible at his Ponti-ficiall anuile. The L. Cardinall vndertooke to reade mee a lecture vpon that argument; but euer fince hath played Mum-budget, and hath put himfelfe to filence, like one at a Non-plus in his enterprife. There be three yeeres already gone and paft, fince his Lordfhip beganne to fhape fome an-fwere to a certaine writing difpatched by mee in few daies: With forming and reforming, with filing and polifhing, with labouring and licking his anfwere ouer and ouer againe, with reiterated extractions and calci-nations, it may be coniectured that all his Lordfhips labour and coft is long fince euaporated and vanifhed in the aire. Howbeit as well the friend-ly conference of a King, (for I will not call it a contention) as alfo the dig-nitie, excellencie, and importance of the matter, long fince deferued, and as long fince required the publifhing of fome or other anfwere. His Lordfhips long filence will neuer be imputed to lacke of capacity, wherewith who knoweth not how abundantly he is furnifhed; but rather to well aduifed agnition of his owne working in building vpon a weake foundation.

But let vs returne vnto thefe heretikes, that make fo great gaine by the difagreement of Catholikes. It is no part of their dutie to aime at fowing of diffentions; but rather to intend and attend their faithfull performance of feruice to their King. If fome be pleafed, and others offended, when fo good and loyall duties are fincerely difcharged; it is for all good fubiects to grieue and to be fory, that when they fpeake for the fafetie of their King & honour of the trewth, it is their hard hap to leaue any at all vnfatis-fied. But fuppofe the faid heretiks were the Authors of this article preferred by the third Eftate: What need they to conceale their names in that regard? What need they to difclaime the credit of fuch a worthy act? Would it not redound to their perpetuall honour, to be the onely fubiects that kept watch ouer the Kings life and Crowne, that ftood centinell, and walked the rounds for the preferuation of his Princely diademe, when all other had no more touch, no more feeling thereof then fo many ftones? And what neede the Deputies for the third Eftate, to receiue inftructions from for-raine Kingdomes, concerning a caufe of that nature; when there was
no want

no want of domesticall examples, and the French histories were plentifull in that argument? What neede they to gape for this reformed doctrine, to come swimming with a fishes tayle out of an Island to the mayne continent, when they had before their eyes the murders of two Kings, with diuerse ciuill warres, and many Arrests of Court, all tending to insinuate and suggest the introduction of the same remedy? Suggestions are needlesse from abroad, when the mischiefe is felt at home. It seemes to me that his Lordship in smoothing and tickling the Deputies for the third Estate, doth no lesse then wring and wrong their great sufficiencie with contumely and outragious abuse; as if they were not furnished with sufficient foresight, and with loyall affection towards their King, for the preseruation of his life and honour, if the remedie were not beaten into their heads by those of the Religion, reputed heretikes.

Touching my selfe, ranged by his Lordship in the same ranke with sowers of dissention; I take my God to witnes, and my owne conscience, that I neuer dream'd of any such vnchristian proiect. It hath beene hitherto my ordinary course to follow honest counsells, and to walke in open waies. I neuer wonted my selfe to holes and corners, to crafty shifts, but euermore to plaine and open designes. I neede not hide mine intentions for feare of any mortall man, that puffeth breath of life out of his nostrils. Nor in any sort doe I purpose, to set *Iulian* the Apostata before mine eyes, as a patterne for me to follow. *Iulian* of a Christian became a Pagan: I professe the same faith of Christ still, which I haue euer professed: *Iulian* went about his designes with crafty conueiances; I neuer with any of his captious and cunning sleights: *Iulian* forced his subiects to infidelitie againstIesus Christ; I labour to induce my subiects vnto such tearmes of loyalty towards my selfe, as Iesus Christ hath prescribed and taught in his word. But how farre I differ from *Iulian*, it is to be seene more at large in my answere to *Bellarmines* Epistles written to *Blackwell*; from whence the Lord Cardinall borrowing this example, it might well haue beseemed his Lordship to borrow likewise my answere from the same place.

Now as it mooues me nothing at all, to be drawne by his Lordship into suspitions of this nature and qualitie: so by the prayses, that he rockes me withall, I will neuer be lulled asleepe. To commend a man for his knowledge, and withall to take from him the feare of God, is to admire a souldier for his goodly head of haire or his curled locks, and withall to call him base coward, faint-hearted and fresh-water souldier. Knowledge, wit, and learning in an hereticke, are of none other vse and seruice, but only to make him the more culpable, & consequently obnoxious to the more grieuous punishments. All vertues turne to vices, when they become the seruants of impietie. The hand-maids which the Soueraigne Lady Wisedome calleth to be of her traine in the. 9. Prouerb. are morall vertues, and humane sciences; which then become pernicious, when they run away from their Soueraigne Lady-Mistris, and put ouer themselues in seruice to the

Deuill.

diuel. What difference is betweene two men, both alike wanting the
knowledge of God; the one furnished with arts and ciuill vertues, the o-
ther brutishly barbarous and of a deformed life, or of prophane maners?
What is the difference betweene these two? I make this the onely difference:
the first goeth to hell with a better grace, and falleth into perdition with
more facilitie, then the second : But hee becommeth exceedingly wicked,
euen threefold and fourefold abominable, if he wast his treasure and stocke
of ciuill vertues in persecuting the Church of CHRIST and if that may be
layd in his dish which was cast in *Cæsars* teeth, that in plaine sobernes and
well-setled temper, he attempts the ruine of the Common-wealth, which
from a drunken sot might receiue perhaps a more easie fall. In briefe, I
scorne all garlands of praises, which are not euer greene; but being dry and
withered for want of sap and radicall moysture, doe flagge about barbarous Princes browes. I defie and renounce those praises, which fit mee no
more then they fit a *Mahumetane* King of *Marocco*. I contest against all
praises which grace me with petie accessories, but rob me of the principall,
that one thing necessary; namely, the feare and knowledge of my GOD:
vnto whose Maiestie alone, I haue deuoted my Scepter, my sword, my
penne, my whole industrie, my whole selfe, with all that is mine in whole
and in part. I doe it, I doe it in all humble acknowledgement of his vn-
speakable mercie and fauour, who hath vouchsafed to deliuer me from the
erroneous way of this aage, to deliuer my Kingdome from the Popes tyrannicall yoke, vnder which it hath lyen in times past most grieuously oppressed: My Kingdom where God is now purely serued, and called vpon in
a tongue which all the vulgar vnderstand: My Kingdome, where the people may now reade the Scriptures without any special priuiledge from the
Apostolike See, and with no lesse libertie then the people of Ephesus, of
Rome, and of Corinth did reade the holy Epistles, written to their Churches by *S. Paul*: My Kingdome, where the people now pay no longer any
tribute by the poll for Papall indulgences, as they did about an hundred
yeeres past, and are no longer compelled to the mart, for pardons beyond
the Seas and mountaines, but haue them now freely offered from God, by
the doctrine of the Gospel preached at home within their owne seuerall
parishes and iurisdictions. If the Churches of my Kingdome, in the L.
Cardinals accompt, bee miserable for these causes and the like; let him
dreame on, and talke his pleasure : for my part I will euer auow, that more
worth is our misery then all his felicitie. For the rest, it shal by Gods grace
be my daily endeauour and serious care, to passe my daies in shaping to my
selfe such a course of life, that without shamefull calumniating of my person, it shall not rest in the tip of any tongue, to touch my life with iust re-
prehension or blame. Nor am I so priuie to mine owne guiltinesse, as to
thinke my state so desperate, so deplorable, as Popes haue made their owne:
For some of them haue bene so open-hearted and so tongue-free, to pronounce that Popes themselues, the key-bearers of Heauen and hell, cannot

be

Aliquot annis post. Apostolicæ sedis nuncius in Angliam ad colligendum S. Petri vectigal missus. Onu-phri. in vit. Paul. 4. Vide & Math. Pa-ris.

be faued.ʳ Two Popes, reckoned among the beſt of the whole bunch or packe, namely, *Adrian* the IV. and *Marcelline* the II. haue both ſung one and the ſame note; that in their vnderſtanding they could not conceiue any reaſon why, or any meanes how thoſe that ſway the Popedome can be partakers of ſaluation; But for my particular, grounding my faith vpon the promiſes of God contained in the Goſpel, I doe confidently and aſſuredly beleeue, that repenting me of my ſinnes, and repoſing my whole truſt in the merits of IESVS·CHRIST, I ſhall obtaine forgiueneſſe of my ſinnes through his Name. Nor doe I feare, that I am now, or ſhall be hereafter caſt out of the Churches lap and boſome; that I now haue or hereafter ſhall haue no right to the Church as a putrified member thereof, ſo long as I do or ſhall cleaue to CHRIST IESVS, the Head of the Church: the appel-lation and name whereof, ſerueth in this corrupt aage, as a cloake to couer a thouſand new inuentions; and now no longer ſignifies the aſſembly of the faithfull, or ſuch as beleeue in IESVS CHRIST according to his word, but a certaine glorious oſtentation and temporall Monarchie, whereof the Pope forſooth is the ſupreame head.

But if the L. Cardinall by aſſured and certaine knowledge (as perhaps he may by common fame) did vnderſtand the horrible conſpiracies that haue bin plotted and contriued, not againſt my perſon and life alone, but alſo a-gainſt my whole ſtocke: if he rightly knew & were inly perſwaded, of how many fowle periuries & wicked treaſons, diuers Eccleſiaſtical perſons haue bene lawfully conuicted: in ſtead of charging me with falſe imputations, that *I ſuffer not my Catholiks to fetch a ſigh, or to draw their breath; and that I thruſt my Catholikes vpon the ſharpe edge of puniſhment in euery kinde*; he would, and might well, rather wonder, how I my ſelfe, after ſo many dangers run, after ſo many proditorious ſnares eſcaped, do yet fetch my owne breath, and yet practiſe Princely clemencie towards the ſaid Catholiks, notorious tráſgreſ-ſors of diuine & humane lawes. If the French king in the heart of his king-dom, ſhould nouriſh and foſter ſuch a neſt of ſtinging hornets and buſie waſps, I meane ſuch a pack of ſubiects, denying his abſolute Soueraignty, as many Romane Catholiks of my Kingdome do mine: It may wel be doub-ted, whether the L. Cardinal would aduiſe his king ſtil to feather the neſt of the ſaid Catholiks, ſtil to keep them warme, ſtil to beare them with an eaſie and gentle hand: It may wel be doubted, whether his Lordſhip would ex-tol their conſtancie, that would haue the courage to ſheath vp their ſwords in his Kings bowels, or blow vp his King with gun-powder, into the nea-ther ſtation of the loweſt regió: It may wel be doubted, whether he would indure that Orator, who (like as himſelfe hath done) ſhould ſtir vp others to ſuffer Martyrdome after ſuch examples, and to imitate parricides & traitors in their conſtancy. The ſcope then of the L. Cardinall, in ſtriking the ſweet ſtrings, and ſounding the pleaſant notes of praiſes, which faine he would fil mine eares withal; is only by his excellent skil in the muſick of Oratory, to bewitch the harts of my ſubiects, to infatuate their minds, to ſettle them in a

reſolu-

Oſiup. de vitis Pontif. in vit. Mar. 2. doeth teſtifie, that Marcel. alſo after Adrian the 4. vſed theſe words: Non video quo modo qui locum hunc altiſſ.te-nent, ſaluari poſſint.

refolution to depriue me of my life. The reafon : Becaufe the plotters and practifers, againft my life, are honoured and rewarded with a glorious name of Martyrs : their conftancie (what els?) is admired, when they fuffer death for treafon. Wheras hitherto during the time of my whole raigne to this day, (I fpeake it in the word of a King, and trewth it felfe fhall make good the Kings word) no man hath loft his life, no man hath indured the Racke, no man hath fuffered corporall punifhment in other kinds,meerely or fimply,or in any degree of refpect, for his confcience in matter of religion ; but for wicked confpiring againft my life, or Eftate, or Royall dignitie ; or els for fome notorious crime, or fome obftinate and wilfull difobedience : Of which traiterous and viperous brood, I commanded one to be hanged by the necke of late in *Scotland* ; a Iefuite of intolerable impudencie, who at his arraignment and publike triall, ftiffely maintained, that I haue robbed the Pope of his right, and haue no manner of right in the poffeffion of my Kingdome. His Lordfhip therefore in offering himfelfe to Martyrdome, after the rare example of Catholiks, as he faith,fuffering all fort of punifhment in my Kingdome, doeth plainely profeffe himfelfe a follower of traytors and parricides. Thefe be the Worthies,thefe the heroicall fpirits, thefe the honourable Captaines and Coronels, whofe vertuous parts neuer fufficiently magnified and prayfed, his Lordfhippe propoundeth for imitation to the *French* Bifhops. O the name of Martyrs, in olde times a facred name! how is it now derided and fcoffed? how is it in thefe daies filthily prophaned? O you the whole quire and holy company of Apoftles, who haue fealed the trewth with your deareft blood! how much are you difparaged? how vnfitly are you paragoned and matched, when traytors,bloody butchers,and King-killers are made your affiftants, and of the fame *Quorum* ; or to fpeake in milder tearmes, when you are coupled with Martyrs that fuffer for maintaining the Temporall rites of the Popes Empire ? with Bifhops that offer themfelues to a Problematicall Martyrdome, for a point decided neither by the authorities of your Spirit-infpired pens, nor by the auncient and venerable teftimonie of the Primitiue Church? for a point which they dare not vndertake to teach, otherwife then by a doubtfull, cold, fearefull way of difcourfe, and altogether without refolution. In good footh, I take the Cardinall for a perfonage of a quicker fpirit and clearer fight, (let his Lordfhip hold mee excufed) then to perfwade my felfe,that in thefe matters his tongue and his heart, his pen and his inward iudgement,haue any concord or correfpondence one with another : For beeing very much againft his minde (as hee doeth confeffe) thruft into the office of an Aduocate to pleade this caufe; he fuffered himfelfe to bee carried (after his engagement) with fome heat, to vtter fome things againft his confcience, murmuring and grumbling the contrary within; and to affirme fome other things with confidence, whereof hee had not beene otherwife informed, then onely by vaine and lying report. Of which ranke is that bold affertion of his Lordfhip ; That many Catholiks

liks in England, rather then they would subscribe to the oath of allegiance in the forme thereof, haue vndergone all sorts of punishment : For in *England* (as we haue trewly giuen the whole Christian world to vnderstand in our Preface to the Apologie) there is but one forme or kind of punishment ordained for all sorts of traytors.

Hath not his Lordship now graced me with goodly testimonialls of prayse and commendation ? Am I not by his prayses proclaimed a Tyrant, as it were inebriated with blood of the Saints , and a famous Enginer of torments for my Catholikes ? To this exhortation for the suffering of Martyrdome, in imitation of my English traytors and parricides, it wee shall adde ; how craftily and subtilly hee makes the Kings of *England* to hold of the Pope by fealty, and their kingdome in bondage to the Pope by Temporall recognizance; it shall easily appeare, that his holy-water of prayses wherewith I am so reuerently besprinkled, is a composition extracted out of a dram of hony and a pound of gall, first steeped in a strong decoction of bitter wormewood, or of the wild gourd called Coloquintida: For after he hath in the beginning of his Oration, spoken of Kings that owe fealtie to the Pope, and are not Soueraignes in the highest degree of Temporall supremacie within their Kingdomes; to explaine his mind and meaning the better, he marshals the Kings of *England* a little after in the same ranke. His words be these; *When King* Iohn *of* England, *not yet bound in any temporall recognizance to the Pope, had expelled his Bishops, &c.* His Lordship means, that King *Iohn* became so bound to the Pope not long after. And what may this meaning be, but in plaine teatmes and broad speach, to call me vsurper and vnlawfull King? For the feudatarie, or he that holdeth a Mannor by fealty , when he doeth not his homage, with all suit and seruice that he owes to the Lord *Paramount*, doeth fall from the propertie of his fee. This reproach of the L. Cardinals, is seconded with an other of *Bellarmines* his brother Cardinall; That *Ireland* was giuen to the Kings of *England* by the Pope. The best is that his most reuerend Lordship hath not shewed, who it was that gaue *Ireland* to the Pope.

And touching *Iohn* King of *England*, thus in briefe stands the whole matter. Betweene *Henry* 2. and the Pope had passed sundry bickerments, about collating of Ecclesiasticall dignities. *Iohn* the sonne, after his fathers death, reneweth, vndertaketh, and pursueth the same quarrell: Driueth certaine *English* Bishops out of the Kingdome, for defending the Popes insolent vsurpation vpon his Royall prerogatiue, and Regall rights: Sheweth such Princely courage and resolution in those times, when all that stood and suffered for the Popes Temporall pretensions against Kings, were enrowled Martyrs or Confessors. The Pope takes the matter in fowle scorne, and great indignation; shuts the King by his excommunicatory Bulls out of the Church; stirres vp his Barons, for other causes the Kings heauy friends, to rise in armes; giues the Kingdome of *England* (like a masterlesse man turned ouer to a new master) to *Philippus Augustus* King of *France*;

Page. 10.

France; bindes *Philip* to make a conquest of *England* by the sword, or else no bargaine, or else no gift; promises *Philip*, in recompence of his trauell and Royall expences in that conquest, full absolution and a generall pardon at large for all his sinnes: to bee short, cuts King *Iohn* out so much worke, and makes him keepe so many yrons in the fire for his worke, that he had none other way, none other meanes to pacifie the Popes high displeasure, to correct or qualifie the malignitie of the Popes cholericke humour, by whom he was then so entangled in the Popes toyles, but by yeelding himselfe to become the Popes vassal, and his Kingdome feudatary, or to hold by fealty of the Papall See. By this meanes his Crowne is made tributary, all his people liable to payment of taxes by the poll for a certaine yeerely tribute, and he is blessed with a pardon for all his sinnes. Whether King *Iohn* was mooued to doe this dishonourable act vpon any deuotion, or inflamed with any zeale of Religion; or inforced by the vnresistable weapons of necessitie, who can be so blind, that he doeth not well see and clearely perceiue? For to purchase his owne freedome from this bondage to the Pope; what could he bee vnwilling to doe, that was willing to bring his Kingdome vnder the yoake of *Amirales Murmelinus* a Mahumetan Prince, then King of *Granado* and *Barbaria*? The Pope after that, sent a Legat into *England*: The King now the Popes vassall, and holding his Crowne of the Pope, like a man that holds his land of another by Knights seruice, or by homage and fealtie, doeth faire homage for his Crowne to the Popes Legat, and layeth downe at his feet a great masse of the purest gold in coyne. The reuerend Legat, in token of his Masters Soueraigntie, with more then vsuall pride falls to kicking and spurning the treasure, no doubt with a paire of most holy feet: Not onely so; but likewise at solemne feasts is easily entreated to take the Kings chaire of Estate. Heere I would faine know the Lord Cardinals opinion; whether these actions of the Pope were iust or vniust, lawfull or vnlawfull, according to right or against all right and reason. If he will say against right; it is then cleare, that against right his Lordship hath made way to this example: if according to right, let him then make it knowen, from whence or from whom this power was deriued and conueyed to the Pope, whereby hee makes himselfe Souereigne Lord of Temporalties in that Kingdome, where neither he nor any of his predecessours euer pretended any right, or layd any claime to Temporall matters before. Are such prankes to be played by the Pontificiall Bishop? Is this an act of Holinesse, to set a Kingdome on fire by the flaming brands of sedition? to dismember and quarter a Kingdome with intestine warres; onely to this end, that a King once reduced to the lowest degree of miserie, might be lifted by his Holinesse out of his Royall prerogatiue, the very soule and life of his Royall Estate? When began this Papall power? In what aage began the Pope to practise this power? What! haue the ancient Canons, (for the Scripture in this question beareth no pawme) haue the Canons of the ancient Church imposed

any

any such satisfaction vpon a sinner, that of a Souereigne and free King, he should become vassall to his ghostly Father; that he should make himselfe together with all his people and subiects tributaries to a Bishop, that shall rifle a whole Nation of their coine, that shall receiue homage of a King, and make a King his vassall? What! Shall not a sinner be quitted of his faults, except his Pastor turne robber, and one that goeth about to get a booty? except hee make his Pastour a Feoffee in his whole Estate, and suffer himselfe vnder a shadow of penance to freeze naked, to be turned out of all his goods and possessions of inheritance? But be it granted, admit his Holinesse robs one Prince of his rights and reuenewes, to conferre the same vpon another: were it not an high degree of tyrannie to finger another mans estate, and to giue that away to a third, which the second hath no right, no lawfull authoritie to giue? Well, if the Pope then shall become his owne caruer in the rights of another; if he shall make his owne coffers to swell with anothers reuenewes, if he shall decke and aray his owne backe in the spoiles of a sinner, with whom in absolution he maketh peace, and taketh truce; what can this be else, but running into further degrees of wickednesse and mischiefe? what can this be else, but heaping of robbery vpon fraud, and impietie vpon robbery? For by such deceitfull, craftie, and cunning practises, the nature of the Pontificiall See, meerely spirituall, is changed into the Kings-bench-Court, meerely temporall: the Bishops chaire is changed into a Monarchs Throne. And not onely so; but besides, the sinners repentance is changed into a snare or pit-fall of cousening deceit; and S. *Peters* net is changed into a casting-net or a flew; to fish for all the wealth of most flourishing Kingdomes. Moreouer, the King (a hard case) is driuen by such wiles and subtilties, to worke impossibilities, to acte more then is lawfull or within the compasse of his power to practise: For the King neither may in right, nor can by power transnature his Crowne, impaire the Maiestie of his Kingdome, or leaue his Royal dignitie lesse free to his heire apparant, or next successor, then he receiued the same of his predecessour: Much lesse, by any dishonourable capitulations, by any vnworthy contracts, degrade his posteritie, bring his people vnder the grieuous burden of tributes and taxes to a forreine Prince: Least of all, make them tributary to a Priest; vnto whom it no way apperteineth to haue any hand in the ciuill affaires of Kings, or to distaine, and vnhallow their Crownes. And therefore when the Pope dispatched his *Nuntio* to *Philippus Augustus*, requesting the King to auert *Lewis* his sonne from laying any claime to the Kingdome of *England*; *Philip* answered the Legat (as we haue it in *Matth.Paris;*) No *King, no Prince can alienate or giue away his Kingdom, but by consent of his Barons, bound by Knights seruice to defend the said Kingdome: and in case the Pope shall stand for the contrary error, his Holines shall giue to Kingdomes a most pernicious example.* By the same Author it is testified, that King *Iohn* became odious to his subiects, for such dishonourable and vnworthy inthralling of his Crowne, and Kingdome. Therefore the Popes right pretended

tended to the Crowne of *England*, which is nothing elfe but a ridiculous vfurpation, hath long agoe vanifhed into fmoake, and required not fo much as the drawing of one fword to fnatch and pull it by violence out of his hands: For the Popes power lying altogether in a certaine wilde and wandring conceit or opinion of men, and being onely an imaginary caftle in the ayre, built by pride, and vnderpropped by fuperftition, is very fpeedily difperfed vpon the firft rifing and appearing of the trewth in her glorious brightneffe. There is none fo very a dolt or block-head to deny, that in cafe this right of the Pope ouer *England*, is grounded vpon Gods word, then his Holineffe may challenge the like right ouer all other Kingdomes: becaufe all other Kingdomes, Crownes, and Scepters are fubiect alike to Gods word: For what priuiledge, what charter, what euidence can *France* fetch out of the Rolles, or any other treafurie of her monuments or records, to fhew that fhe oweth leffe fubiection to God then *England?* Or was this yoke of bondage then brought vpon the Englifh Nation; was it a prerogatiue, whereby they might more eafily come to the libertie of the fonnes of God? Or were the people of *England* perfwaded, that for all their fubftance, wealth, and life beftowed on the Pope, his Holineffe by way of exchange returned them better weight and meafure of fpirituall graces? It is ridiculous, onely to conceiue thefe toyes in thought; and yet with fuch ridiculous, with fuch toyes in conceit, his Lordfhip feeds and entertains his auditors.

Pag. 105.
From this point hee falleth to another bowt and fling at his heretikes, with whom he played no faire play before : " *There is not one Synode of minifters* (as he faith) *which would willingly fubfcribe to this Article, whereunto wee fhould bee bound to fweare.* But herein his Lordfhip fhooteth farre from the marke. This Article is approoued and preached by the Minifters of my Kingdome : It is likewife preached by thofe of *France*, and if need bee (I affure my felfe) will bee figned by all the Minifters of the French Church.

The L. Cardinall proceedeth, (for hee meaneth not fo foone to giue ouer thefe heretikes :) " *All their Confiftories beleeue it as their Creed; that if Catholike Princes at any time fhall offer force vnto their confcience, then they are difpenfed withall for their oath of alleagiance. Hence are thefe modifications and reftrictions, toffed fo much in their mouthes; Prouided the King force vs not in our confcience. Hence are thefe exceptions in the profeffion of their faith; Prouided the Soueraigne power and authoritie of God, bee not in any fort violated or infringed.* I am not able to conceiue what engine can bee framed of thefe materialls, for the bearing of Kings out of their eminent feates, by any lawfull authoritie or power in the Pope: For fay, thofe of the Religion fhould be tainted with fome like errour; how can that be any fhelter of excufe for thofe of the Romifh Church, to vndermine or to digge vp the Thrones of their Kings? But in this allegation of the L. Cardinall, there is nothing at all, which doeth not iumpe iuft and accord to a haire with the Article of the
third

third Eſtate, and with obedience due to the King: For they doe not profeſſe, that in caſe the King ſhall commaund them to doe any act contrarie
to their conſcience, they would flie at his throat, would make any attempt
againſt his life, would refuſe to pay their taxations, or to defend him in the
warres: They make no profeſſion of depoſing the King, or diſcharging
the people from the oath of allegiance tendred to the King: which is the
very point or iſſue of the matter in controuerſie, and the maine miſcheife,
againſt which the third Eſtate hath bin moſt worthily careſull to prouide
a wholeſome remedie by this Article. There is a world of difference betweene the termes of diſobedience, and of depoſition. It is one thing to
diſobey the Kings commaund in matters prohibited by diuine lawes, and
yet in all other matters to performe full ſubiection vnto the King. It is a-
nother thing of a farre higher degree or ſtraine of diſloyaltie, to bare the
King of his Royall robes, throne, and ſcepter, and when he is thus farre diſgraced, to degrade him and to put him from his degree and place of a King.
If the holy Father ſhould charge the L. Cardinal to doe ſome act repugnant in his owne knowledge to the Law of God, I will religiouſly, and
according to the rule of charitie preſume, that his Lordſhip in this caſe
would ſtand out againſt his Holineſſe, and notwithſtanding would ſtill
acknowledge him to be Pope.

His Lordſhip yet proſecutes and followes his former purpoſe: *Hence*
are thoſe armes which they haue oftentimes borne againſt Kings, when Kings practi-
ſed to take away the libertie of their conſcience and Religion. Hence are thoſe turbu-
lent Commotions and ſeditions by them raiſed, as well in the Low-countryes againſt
the King of Spaine, as in Swethland againſt the Catholike King of Polonia. Beſides,
he caſteth *Iunius Brutus, Buchananus, Barclaius,* and *Gerſon* in our teeth. To
what end all this? I ſee not how it can bee auaileable to authorize the depoſing of Kings, eſpecially the Popes power to depoſe. And yet his Lordſhip here doth outface (by his leaue) and beare downe the trewth: For I
could neuer yet learne by any good and trew intelligence, that in France
thoſe of the Religion tooke armes at any time againſt their King: In the
firſt ciuill warres they ſtood onely vpon their guard: they ſtood onely to
their lawfull wards and locks of defence: they armed not, nor tooke the
field before they were purſued with fire and ſword, burnt vp and ſlaughtred.
Beſides, Religion was neither the root nor the rynde of thoſe inteſtine
troubles. The trew ground of the quarrell was this: During the minority of King *Francis* II. the Proteſtants of France were a refuge and ſuccour
to the Princes of the blood, when they were kept from the Kings preſence,
and by the ouer powring power of their enemies, were no better then
plaine driuen and chaſed from the Court. I meane, the Grand-father of
the King now raigning, and the Grand-father of the Prince of *Conde,*
when they had no place of ſafe retreate. In regard of which worthy and
honourable ſeruice, it may ſeeme the French King hath reaſon to haue the
Proteſtants in his gracious remembrance. With other commotion or inſurrection,

rection, the Proteſtants are not iuſtly to be charged. But on the contrary, certaine it is that King *Henry* III. rayſed and ſent forth ſeuerall armies a-gainſt the Proteſtants, to ruine and roote them out of the Kingdome: howbeit, ſo ſoone as they perceiued the ſaid King was brought into dange-rous tearms, they ranne with great ſpeed and ſpeciall fidelitie to the Kings reſcue and ſuccour, in the preſent danger. Certaine it is, that by their good ſeruice the ſaid King was deliuered, from a moſt extreame and imminent perill of his life in the city of Tours. Certaine it is, they neuer abandoned that *Henry* 3. nor his next ſucceſſor *Henry* 4. in all the heat of reuolts and re-bellions, raiſed in the greateſt part of the Kingdome by the Pope, and the more part of the Clergie · but ſtood to the ſaid Kings in all their battels, to beare vp the Crowne then tottering and ready to fall. Certaine it is, that euen the heads and principalls of thoſe by whom the late King deceaſed was purſued with all extremities, at this day doe enioy the fruit of all the good ſeruices done to the King by the ſaid Proteſtants: And they are now diſgraced, kept vnder, expoſed to publike hatred. What, for kindling coales of queſtions and controuerſies about Religion? Forſooth, not ſo: but be-cauſe if they might haue equall and indifferent dealing, if credit might be giuen to their faithfull aduertiſements, the Crowne of their Kings ſhould bee no longer pinned to the Popes flie-flap; in France there ſhould bee no French exempted from ſubiection to the French King; cauſes of benefices or of matrimonie, ſhould bee no longer citable and ſummonable to the Romiſh Court; and the Kingdome ſhould bee no longer tributarie vnder the colour of annats, the firſt fruits of Benefices after the remooue or death of the Incumbent, and other like impoſitions.

But why doe I ſpeake ſo much in the behalfe of the French Proteſtants? The Lord Cardinall himſelfe quittes them of this blame, when he telleth vs this doctrine for the depoſing of Kings by the Popes mace or verge, had credit and authoritie through all France, vntill *Caluins* time. Doth not his Lordſhip vnder-hand confeſſe by theſe words, that Kings had beene al-waies before *Caluins* time, the more diſhonoured, and the worſe ſerued? Item, that Proteſtants, whom his Lordſhip calls heretikes, by the light of holy Scripture made the world then and euer ſince to ſee the right of Kings, oppreſſed ſo long before? As for thoſe of the Low Countries, and the ſubiects of Swethland, I haue little to ſay of their caſe, becauſe it is not within o dinary compaſſe, and indeed ſerueth nothing to the purpoſe. Theſe Nations, beſides the cauſe of Religion, doe ſtand vpon certaine reaſons of State, which I will not here take vpon me like a Iudge to deter-mine or to ſift.

Iunius Brutus, Whom the Lord Cardinall obiecteth, is an author vn-knowne; and perhaps of purpoſe patcht vp by ſome Romaniſt, with a wyly deceit to draw the reformed Religion into hatred with Chriſtian Princes.

Buchanan I reckon and ranke among Poets, not among Diuines, claſſicall

or

or common. If the man hath burſt out here and there into ſome tearmes of
exceſſe, or ſpeach of bad temper ; that muſt be imputed to the violence of
his humour, and heate of his ſpirit, not in any wiſe to the rules and conclu-
ſions of trew Religion, rightly by him conceiued before.

Barclaius alledged by the Cardinall, meddles not with depoſing of
Kings; but deals with diſavowing them for Kings, when they ſhal renounce
the right of Royalty, and of their owne accord giue ouer the Kingdome.
Now he that leaues it in the Kings choice, either to hold or to giue ouer his
Crowne, leaues it not in the Popes power to take away the Kingdome.

Of *Gerſon* obtruded by the Cardinal, we haue ſpoken ſufficiently before,
where it hath beene ſhewed how *Gerſon* is diſguiſed, masked, and peruer-
ted by his Lordſhip. In briefe, I take not vpon me to iuſtifie and make
good all the ſayings of particular authors : We glory (and well we may)
that our religion affordeth no rules of rebellion ; nor any diſpenſation to
ſubiects for the oath of their allegiance ; and that none of our Churches
giue entertainement vnto ſuch monſtrous and abhominable principles
of diſloyaltie.

If any of the French, otherwiſe perſwaded in former times, now hauing *Richerius.*
altered and changed his iudgement, doth contend for the Soueraignty of
Kings againſt Papall vſurpation : He doubtles, for winding himſelfe out of
the Laborinth of an error ſo intricate & pernicious, deſerueth great honour
and ſpeciall praiſe: He is worthy to hold a place of dignity aboue the L. Cardinall ; who hath quitted and betrayed his former iudgement, which was
holy and iuſt: Their motions are contrary, their markes are oppoſite : The
one reclineth from euill to good, the other declineth from good to euill.

At laſt his Lordſhip commeth to the cloſe of his Oration, and bindes vp
his whole harangue with a feate wreath of praiſes, proper to his King. He ”
ſtyles the King the eldeſt Sonne of the Church, a young ſhoot of the lilly; ”
which King Salomon in all his Royaltie was not able to match. He leades ”
vs by the hand into the pleaſant meadowes of Hiſtories, there to learne vp- ”
on the very firſt ſight and view, That ſo long, ſo oft as the Kings of France ”
embraced vnion, and kept good tearmes of concord with Popes and the ”
Apoſtolike See; ſo long as the ſpouſe of the Church was paſtured and fed ”
among the lillies, all ſorts of ſpirituall and temporall graces abundantly ”
ſhowred vpon their Crownes, and vpon their people: On the contrary, ”
when they made any rent or ſeparation from the moſt holy See; then the ”
lillies were pricked and almoſt choaked with ſharpe thornes; they beganne ”
to droope, to ſtoope, and to beare their beautifull heads downe to the ”
very ground, vnder the ſtrong flawes and guſts of boyſtrous windes ”
and tempeſts.

My anſwere to this flouriſhing cloſe and vpſhot, ſhall be no leſſe apert
then apt. It ſauours not of good and faithfull ſeruice, to ſmooth and ſtroake
the Kings head with a ſoft hand of oyled ſpeech, and in the meane time to
take away the Crowne from his head, and to defile it with dirt. But let vs

try the caufe by euidence of Hiſtorie, yea by the voice and verdiċt of experience; to fee whether the glorious beauty of the French lillies hath beene
at any time blaſted, and thereupon hath faded, by ſtarting afide, and making feparation from the holy See. Vnder the raigne of King *Philip* the Faire,
France was bleſſed with peace and profperity, notwithſtanding fome outragious aċts done againſt the Papall See, and contumelious crying quittance by King *Philip* with the Pope. *Lewis* 12. in ranged battell defeated
the armies of Pope *Iulius* 2. and his Confederates: proclaimed the faid Pope
to be fallen from the Popedome: ſtamped certaine coynes and pieces of
gold with a diſhonourable mot, euen to Rome it felfe, *Rome is Babylon*:
yet fo much was *Lewis* loued and honoured of his people, that by a peculiar
title he was called, *the Father of the Country*. Greater bleſſings of God, greater
outward peace and plenty, greater inward peace with fpirituall and celeſti-
all treaſures, were neuer heaped vpon my Great Brittaine, then haue beene
fince my Great Brittaine became Great in the greateſt and chiefeſt refpeċt
of all; to wit, fince my Great Brittaine hath ſhaken off the Popes yoke;
fince ſhe hath refufed to receiue and to entertaine the Popes Legats, employed to colleċt S. *Peters* tribute or *Peter-pence*; fince the Kings of England, my Great Brittaine, haue not beene the Popes vaſſals to doe him homage for their Crowne, and haue no more felt the laſhings, the fcourg-
ings of bafe and beggarly Monkes. Of Holland, Zeland, and Frifeland,
what neede I fpeake? yet a word and no more. Were they not a kinde of
naked and bare people, of fmall value, before God lighted the torch of the
Gofpel, and aduanced it in thofe Nations? were they not an ill fedde
and fcragged people, in comparifon of the ineſtimable wealth and profperity (both in all military aċtions and mechanicall trades, in trafficke as
merchants, in marting as men of warre, in long nauigation for difcouerie)
to which they are now rayfed and mounted by the mercifull bleſſing of
God, fince the darknes of Poperie hath beene fcattered, and the bright
Sunne of the Gofpel hath ſhined in thofe Countryes? Behold the Venetian Republique : Hath ſhee now leſſe beautie, leſſe glory, leſſe peace and
profperitie, fince ſhe lately fell to bicker and contend with the Pope? fince
ſhe hath wrung out of the Popes hand, the one of his two fwords? fince
ſhe hath plumed and ſhaked his Temporall dominion ? On the contrarie; after the French Kings had honoured the Popes, with munificent
graunts and gifts of all the cities and territories, lands and poſſeſſions,
which they now hold in Italy, and the auncient Earledome of *Auignon* in
France for an ouer-plus; were they not rudely recompenced, and homely
handled by their moſt ingratefull fee-farmers and copy-holders? Haue
not Popes forged a donation of *Conſtantine*, of purpofe to blot out all memory of *Pepins* and *Charlemaignes* donation? Haue they not vexed and
troubled the State? haue they not whetted the fonnes of *Lewis* the Courteous againſt their owne Father, whofe life was a patterne and example of
innocencie? Haue they not by their infinite exaċtions, robbed and fcoured
the

the Kingdome of all their treafure? Were not the Kings of France, driuen to ftoppe their violent courfes by the pragmaticall fanction? Did they not fundry times interdict the Kingdome, degrade the Kings, folicite the neighbour-Princes to inuade and lay hold on the Kingdome, and ftirre vp the people againft the King, whereby a gate was opened to a world of troubles and parricides? Did not *Rauaillac* render this reafon for his monftrous and horrible attempt, That King *Henry* had a defigne to warre with God, becaufe he had a defigne to take armes againft his Holineffe, who is God? This makes me to wonder, what mooued the L. Cardinall to marfhall the laft ciuill warres and motions in *France*, in the ranke of examples of vnhappy feparation from the Pope, when the Pope himfelfe was the trumpetor of the fame troublefome motions. If the Pope had bene wronged and offended by the French King, or his people, and the Kingdome of *France* had been fcourged with peftilence, or famine, or fome other calamitie by forraine enemies, it might haue beene taken in probabilitie, as a vengeance of God for fome iniurie done vnto his Vicar: But his Holineffe being the roote, the ground, the mafter-workeman and artificer of all thefe mifchiefes; how can it be faid, that God punifheth any iniurie done to the Pope? but rather that his Holineffe doth reuenge his owne quarrell, and which is worft of all, when his Holineffe hath no iuft caufe of quarrell or offence. Now then; to exhort a Nation (as the L. Cardinall hath done) by the remembrance of former calamities, to curry fauour with the Pope, and to hold a ftrict vnion with his Holineffe, is no exhortation to beare the Pope any refpect of loue, or of reuerence, but rather a rubbing of memory, and a calling to minde of thofe grieuous calamities, whereof the Pope hath been the only occafion. It is alfo a threatning and obtruding of the Popes terrible thunder-bolts, which neuer fcorched nor parched any skinne, (except crauens and meticulous bodies) and haue brought many great fhowres of bleffings vpon my Kingdome.

As for *France*, if fhe hath enioyed profperity in the times of her good agreement with Popes, it is becaufe the Pope feekes the amity of Princes that are in profperitie, haue the meanes to curbe his pretenfions, and to put him to fome plunge. Kings are not in profperity, becaufe the Pope holds amitie with Kings; but his Holineffe vfeth all deuifes, & feeketh all meanes to haue amitie with Kings, becaufe he fees them flourifh & fayle with profperous winds. The fwallow is no caufe, but a companion of the fpring: the Pope is no worker of a Kingdoms felicity, but a wooer of kings when they fit in felicities lap · he is no founder, but a follower of their good fortunes. On the other fide: let a Kingdome fall into fome grieuous difafter or calamitie, let ciuill warres boile in the bowels of the Kingdom; ciuil wars no leffe dangerous to the State, then fearefull and grieuous to the people; who rifeth fooner then the Pope, who rufheth fooner into the troubled ftreames then the Pope, who thrufteth himfelfe fooner into the heate of the quarrell then the Pope, who runneth fooner to raife his gaine by the publike wrack then the

Pope,

Pope, and all vnder colour of a heart wounded and bleeding for the saluation of soules? If the lawfull King happen to be foyled, to be oppressed, and
thereupon the State by his fall to get a new master by the Popes practise;
then the said new master must hold the Kingdome as of the Popes free gift,
and rule or guide the sterne of the State at his becke, and by his instruction.
If the first and right Lord, in despite of all the Popes fulminations and fire-
workes, shall get the honourable day, and vpper hand of his enemies; then
the holy Father with a cheerfull and pleasant grace, yea with fatherly gratulation, opens the rich cabinet of his iewells, I meane the treasurie of his indulgences, and falls now to dandle and cocker the King in his fatherly lap,
whose throat if he could, he would haue cut not long before.

    This pestilent mischiefe hath now a long time taken roote, and is growne
to a great head in the Christian world, through the secret, but iust iudgement of God; by whom Christian Kings haue beene smitten with a spirit
of dizzinesse: Christian Kings, who for many aages past haue liued in ignorance, without any sound instruction, without any trew sense and right
feeling of their owne right and power, whilest vnder a shadow of Religion
and false cloake of pietie, their Kingdomes haue beene ouer-burdened, yea
ouer-borne with tributes, and their Crownes made to stoope euen to miserable bondage. That God in whose hand the hearts of Kings are poised,
and at his pleasure turned as the water-courses; that mighty God alone, in
his good time, is able to rouze them out of so deepe a slumber, and to take
order (their drowzy fits once ouer and shaken off with heroicall spirits)
that Popes hereafter shall play no more vpon their patience, nor presume to
put bits and snaffles in their noble mouthes, to the binding vp of their
power with weake scruples, like mighty buls lead about by litle children
with a small twisted thred. To that God, that King of Kings I deuote my
scepter; at his feet in all humblenes I lay downe my Crowne; to his holy
decrees and commaunds I will euer be a faithfull seruant, and in his battels
a faithfull champion. To conclude; in this iust cause and quarrell, I dare
send the challenge, and will require no second, to maintaine as a defendant
of honour, that my brother-Princes and my selfe, whom God hath aduanced vpon the Throne of Soueraigne Maiestie and supreame dignity, doe
hold the Royall dignitie of his Maiestie alone; to whose seruice,
as a most humble homager and vassall, I consecrate all the
glory, honour, splendor, and lustre of my
earthly Kingdomes.

A SPEACH,

A SPEACH, AS IT WAS,

DELIVERED IN THE VPPER
HOVSE OF THE PARLIAMENT TO
.THE LORDS SPIRITVALL AND
Temporall, and to the Knights, Citizens
and Burgesses there assembled,

ON MVNDAY THE XIX.
DAY OF MARCH 1603. BEING
THE FIRST DAY OF THE
firft Parliament.

IT did no fooner pleafe God to lighten his hand, and relent the violence of his deuouring Angel againft the poore people of this Citie, but as foone did I refolue to call this Parliament, and that for three chiefe and principall reafons: The firft whereof is, (and which of it felfe, although there were no more, is not onely a fufficient, but a moft full and neceffary ground and reafon for conuening of this Affembly) This firft reafon I fay is; That you who are here prefently affembled to reprefent the Body of this whole Kingdome, and of all forts of people within the fame, may with your owne eares heare, and that I out of mine owne mouth may deliuer vnto you the affurance of my due thankefulnes for your fo ioyfull and generall applaufe to the declaring and receiuing of mee in this Seate (which GOD by my Birthright and lineall defcent had in the fulneffe of time prouided for me) and that, immediatly after it pleafed God to call your late Soueraigne of famous memory, full of dayes, but fuller of immortall trophes of Honour, out of this tranfitorie life. Not that I am able to expreſſe by wordes, or vtter by eloquence the viue Image of mine inward thankfulnes, but onely that out of mine owne mouth you may reſt aſſured to expect that meaſure of thankefulnes at my hands, which is according to the infinitenes of your deſerts, and to my inclination and abilitie for requitall of the ſame. Shall I euer? nay, can I euer be able, or rather ſo vnable in memorie, as to forget your vnexpected readineſſe and alacritie, your euer memorable reſolution, and your moſt wonderfull coniunction and harmonie of your hearts in declaring and embracing mee as your vndoubted and lawfull King and Gouernour? Or ſhall it euer bee blotted out of my minde, how at my firſt entrie into this Kingdome, the people of all ſorts rid and ran, nay rather flew to meet mee? their eyes flaming nothing but ſparkles of affection, their mouthes and tongues vttering nothing but ſounds of ioy, their hands, feete, and all the reſt of their members in their geſtures diſcouering a paſſionate longing, and earneſtneſſe to meete and embrace their new Soueraigne. *Quid ergo retribuam?* Shall I allow in my ſelfe, that which I could neuer beare within another? No I muſt plainely and freely confeſſe here in all your audiences, that I did euer naturally ſo farre miſlike a tongue to ſmoothe, and diligent in paying their creditors with lip payment and verball thankes, as I euer ſuſpected that ſort of people meant not to pay their debtors in more ſubſtantiall ſort of coyne. And therefore for expreſſing of my thankefulneſſe, I muſt reſort vnto the other two reaſons of my conuening of this Parliament, by them in action to vtter my thankefulneſſe: Both the ſaid reaſons hauing but one ground, which is the deedes, whereby all the dayes of my life, I am by Gods grace to expreſſe my ſaid thankfulneſſe towards you, but diuided in this, That in the firſt of theſe two, mine actions of thankes, are ſo inſeparably conioyned with my Perſon, as they are in a maner become indiuidually annexed to the ſame: In the other reaſon, mine actions are ſuch, as I may either doe them, or leaue them vndone, although by Gods grace I hope neuer to be weary of the doing of them.

As to the firſt: It is the bleſſings which God hath in my Perſon beſtowed vpon you all, wherein I proteſt, I doe more glorie at the ſame for your weale, then for any particular reſpect of mine owne reputation, or aduantage therein.

1   He firſt then of theſe bleſſings, which God hath ioyntly with my Perſon ſent vnto you, is outward Peace: that is, peace abroad with all forreine neighbours: for I thanke God I may iuſtly ſay, that neuer ſince I was a King, I either receiued wrong of any other Chriſtian Prince or State, or did wrong to any: I haue euer, I praiſe God, yet kept Peace and amitie with all, which hath bene ſo farre tyed to my perſon, as at my comming here you are witneſſes I found the State embarqued in a great and tedious warre, and onely by mine arriuall here, and by the Peace in my Perſon, is now amitie kept, where warre was before, which is no ſmal

bleſſing

bleſſing to a Chriſtian Common-wealth: for by Peace abroad with their neighbours the Townes flouriſh, the Merchants become rich, the Trade doeth encreaſe, and the people of all ſorts of the Land enioy free libertie to exerciſe themſelues in their ſeuerall vocations without perill or diſturbance. Not that I thinke this outward Peace ſo vnſeparably tyed to my Perſon, as I dare aſſuredly promiſe to my ſelfe and to you, the certaine continuance thereof: but thus farre I can very well aſſure you and in the word of a King promiſe vnto you, That I ſhall neuer giue the firſt occaſion of the breach thereof, neither ſhall I euer be moued for any particular or priuate paſſion of mind to interrupt your publique Peace, except I be forced thereunto, either for reparation of the honour of the Kingdom, or elſe by neceſſitie for the weale and preſeruation of the ſame: In which caſe, a ſecure and honourable warre muſt be preferred to an vnſecure and diſhonourable Peace: yet doe I hope by my experience of the by-paſt bleſſings of Peace, which God hath ſo long euer ſince my Birth beſtowed vpon mee, that hee wil not be weary to continue the ſame, nor repent him of his grace towards me, transferring that ſentence of King *Dauids* vpon his by-paſt victories of warre, to mine of Peace, That, *that God who preſerued me from the deuouring iawes of the Beare and of the Lion, and deliuered them into my hands, ſhall alſo now grant me victory ouer that vncircumciſed Philiſtine.*

B Vt although outward Peace be a great bleſſing; yet is it as farre inferiour to peace within; as Ciuill warres are more cruell and vnnaturall then warres abroad. And therefore the ſecond great bleſſing that G o d hath with my Perſon ſent vnto you, is Peace within, and that in a double forme. Firſt, by my deſcent lineally out of the loynes of *Henry* the ſeuenth, is reunited and confirmed in mee the Vnion of the two Princely Roſes of the two Houſes of L A N C A S T E R and Y O R K E, whereof that King of happy memorie was the firſt Vniter, as he was alſo the firſt ground-layer of the other Peace. The lamentable and miſerable euents by the Ciuill and bloody diſſention betwixt theſe two Houſes was ſo great and ſo late, as it need not be renewed vnto your memories: which, as it was firſt ſetled and vnited in him, ſo is it now reunited and confirmed in me, being iuſtly and lineally deſcended, not onely of that happie coniunction, but of both the Branches thereof many times before. But the Vnion of theſe two princely Houſes, is nothing comparable to the Vnion of two ancient and famous Kingdomes, which is the other inward Peace annexed to my Perſon.

And here I muſt craue your patiences for a little ſpace, to giue me leaue to diſcourſe more particularly of the benefits that doe ariſe of that Vnion which is made in my blood, being a matter that moſt properly belongeth to me to ſpeake of, as the head wherein that great Body is vnited. And firſt, if we were to looke no higher then to naturall and Phyſicall reaſons, we may eaſily be perſwaded of the great benefits that by that Vnion do redound

dound to the whole Ifland : for if twentie thoufand men be a ftrong Armie,is not the double thereof, fourtie thoufand, a double the ftronger Armie ? If a Baron enricheth himfelfe with double as many lands as hee had before, is he not double the greater? Nature teacheth vs, that Mountaines are made of Motes,and that at the firft,Kingdomes being diuided,and euery particular Towne or little Countie, as Tyrants or Vfurpers could obtaine the poffeffion, a Segniorie apart, many of thefe little Kingdomes are now in proceffe of time, by the ordinance of God, ioyned into great Monarchies,whereby they are become powerfull within themfelues to defend themfelues from all outward inuafions, and their head and gouernour thereby enabled to redeeme them from forreine affaults, and punifh priuate tranfgreffions within. Do we not yet remember,that this Kingdome was diuided into feuen little Kingdomes,befides Wales? And is it not now the ftronger by their vnion ? And hath not the vnion of Wales to England added a greater ftrength thereto? Which though it was a great Principalitie, was nothing comparable in greatneffe and power to the ancient and famous Kingdome of Scotland. But what fhould we fticke vpon any naturall appearance, when it is manifeft that God by his Almightie prouidence hath preordained it fo to be? Hath not God firft vnited thefe two Kingdomes both in Language, Religion, and fimilitude of maners? Yea, hath hee not made vs all in one Ifland, compaffed with one Sea, and of it felfe by nature fo indiuifible, as almoft thofe that were borderers themfelues on the late Borders, cannot diftinguifh, nor know, or difcerne their owne limits ? Thefe two Countries being feparated neither by Sea, nor great Riuer, Mountaine, nor other ftrength of nature, but onely by little fmall brookes, or demolifhed little walles, fo as rather they were diuided in apprehenfion, then in effect; And now in the end and fulneffe of time vnited,the right and title of both in my Perfon, alike lineally defcended of both the Crownes, whereby it is now become like a little World within it felfe,being intrenched and fortified round about with a naturall, and yet admirable ftrong pond or ditch, whereby all the former feares of this Nation are now quite cut off: The other part of the Ifland being euer before now not onely the place of landing to all ftrangers, that was to make inuafion here,but likewife moued by the enemies of this State by vntimely incurfions,to make inforced diuerfion from their Conquefts, for defending themfelues at home,and keeping fure their backe-doore, as then it was called, which was the greateft hinderance and let that euer my Predeceffors of this Nation gat in difturbing them from their many famous and glorious conquefts abroad : What God hath conioyned then, let no man feparate. I am the Husband, and all the whole Ifle is my lawfull Wife; I am the Head,and it is my Body; I am the Shepherd, and it is my flocke : I hope therefore no man will be fo vnreafonable as to thinke that I that am a Chriftian King vnder the Gofpel, fhould be a Polygamift and husband to two wiues; that I being the Head,fhould haue a diuided and monftrous

Body ;

Body ; or that being the Shepheard to fo faire a Flocke (whofe fold hath
no wall to hedge it but the foure Seas) fhould haue my Flocke parted in two.
But as I am affured, that no honeft Subiect of whatfocuer degree within
my whole dominions, is leffe glad of this ioyfull Vnion then I am ; So may
the friuolous obiection of any that would bee hinderers of this worke,
which God hath in my Perfon already eftablifhed, bee eafily anfwered,
which can be none, except fuch as are either blinded with Ignorance, or
els tranfported with Malice, being vnable to liue in a well gouerned Commonwealth, and onely delighting to fifh in troubled waters. For if they
would ftand vpon their reputation and priuiledges of any of the Kingdomes, I pray you was not both the Kingdomes Monarchies from the beginning, and confequently could euer the Body bee counted without the
Head, which was euer vnfeparably ioyned thereunto ? So that as Honour
and Priuiledges of any of the Kingdomes could not be diuided from their
Soueraigne; So are they now confounded & ioyned in my Perfon, who am
equall and alike kindly Head to you both. When this Kingdome of *Eng-*
land was diuided into fo many little Kingdomes as I told you before ; one of
them behooued to eate vp another, till they were all vnited in one. And
yet can *Wiltfhire* or *Deuonfhire*, which were of the *Weft Saxons*, although
their Kingdome was of longeft durance, and did by Conqueft ouercome
diuers of the reft of the little Kingdomes, make claime to Prioritie of Place
or Honour before *Suffex*, *Effex*, or other Shires which were conquered by
them ? And haue we not the like experience in the Kingdome of *France*, being compofed of diuers Dutchies, and one after another conquered by the
fword ? For euen as little brookes lofe their names by their running and fall
into great Riuers, and the very name and memorie of the great Riuers fwallowed vp in the Ocean · fo by the coniunction of diuers little Kingdomes
in one, are all thefe priuate differences and queftions fwallowed vp. And
fince the fucceffe was happie of the *Saxons* Kingdomes being conquered
by the fpeare of *Bellona*; How much greater reafon haue wee to expect a Mart.
happie iffue of this greater Vnion, which is only faftened and bound vp by
the wedding Ring of *Aftrea* ? And as God hath made *Scotland* the one halfe Loue and
of this Ifle to enioy my Birth, and the firft and moft vnperfect halfe of my Peace.
life, and you heere to enioy the perfect and the laft halfe thereof; fo can I
not thinke that any would be fo iniurious to me, no not in their thoughts
and wifhes, as to cut afunder the one halfe of me from the other. But in this
matter I haue farre enough infifted, refting affured that in your hearts and
mindes you all applaud this my difcourfe.

N Ow although thefe bleffings before rehearfed of Inward and Outward peace, be great : yet feeing that in all good things, a great part 3
of their goodneffe and eftimation is loft, if they haue not apparance of perpetuity or long continuance; fo hath it pleafed Almighty God
to accompany my perfon alfo with that fauour, hauing healthful and hopefull

full Iſſue of my body, whereof ſome are here preſent, for continuance and propagation of that vndoubted right which is in my Perſon, vnder whom I doubt not but it will pleaſe God to proſper and continue for many yeeres this Vnion, and all other bleſſings of Inward and outward Peace, which I haue brought with me. . ·

4   BVt neither Peace outward, nor Peace inward, nor any other bleſ-ſings that can follow thereupon, nor appearance of the perpetuitie thereof, by propagation in the poſteritie, is but a weake pillar and a rotten reed to leane vnto, if God doe not ſtrengthen and by the ſtaffe of his bleſſing make them durable: For in vaine doeth the Watchman watch the Citie, if the Lord be not the principall defence thereof: In vaine doeth the builder build the houſe, if God giue not the ſucceſſe: And in vaine (as *Paul* ſaith) doeth *Paul* plant and *Apollo* water, if God giue not the increaſe: For all worldly bleſſings are but like ſwift paſſing ſhadowes, fading flowers, or chaffe blowen before the wind, if by the profeſſion of trew Religion, and works according thereunto, God be not moued to maintaine and ſettle the Thrones of Princes. And although that ſince mine entry into this King-dome, I haue both by meeting with diuers of the Eccleſiaſticall Eſtate, and likewiſe by diuers Proclamations clearely declared my minde in points of Religion, yet doe I not thinke it amiſſe in this ſo ſolemne an Audience, I ſhould now take occaſion to diſcouer ſomewhat of the ſecrets of my heart in that matter.: For I ſhall neuer (with Gods grace) bee aſhamed to make publike profeſſion thereof at all occaſions, left God ſhould bee aſhamed to profeſſe and allow mee before men and Angels, eſpecially left that at this time men might preſume further vpon the misknowledge of my meaning to trouble this Parliament of ours then were conuenient. At my firſt com-ming, although I found but one Religion, and that which by my ſelfe is profeſſed, publikely allowed, and by the Law maintained: Yet found I ano-ther ſort of Religion, beſides a priuate Sect, lurking within the bowels of this Nation. . The firſt is the trew Religion, which by me is profeſſed, and by the Law is eſtabliſhed: The ſecond is the falſly called Catholikes, but trewly Papiſts: The third, which I call a ſect rather then Religion, is the *Puritanes* and *Noueliſts*, who doe not ſo farre differ from vs in points of Re-ligion, as in their confuſed forme of Policie and Paritie, being euer diſcon-tented with the preſent gouernment, & impatient to ſuffer any ſuperiority, which maketh their ſect vnable to be ſuffred in any wel gouerned Cōmon wealth. But as for my courſe toward them, I remit it to my Proclamations made vpon that Subiect. And now for the Papiſts, I muſt put a difference betwixt mine owne priuate profeſſion of mine owne ſaluation, and my po-litike gouernment of the Realme for the weale and quietnes thereof. As for mine owne profeſſion, you haue me your Head now amongſt you of the ſame Religion that the body is of. As I am no ſtranger to you in blood, no more am I a ſtranger to you in Faith, or in the matters concerning the houſe

of

of God. And although this my profeſſion be according to mine education, wherein (I thanke God) I ſucked the milke of Gods trewth, with the milke of my Nurſe: yet do I here proteſt vnto you, that I would neuer for ſuch a conceit of conſtancy or other preiudicate opinion, haue ſo firmly kept my firſt profeſſion, if I had not found it agreeable to all reaſon, and to the rule of my Conſcience. But I was neuer violent nor vnreaſonable in my pro-feſſion: I acknowledge the Romane Church to be our Mother Church, al-though defiled with ſome infirmities and corruptions, as the Iewes were when they crucified Chriſt: And as I am none enemie to the life of a ſicke man, becauſe I would haue his bodie purged of ill humours; no more am I enemie to their Church, becauſe I would haue them reforme their errors, not wiſhing the downethrowing of the Temple, but that it might be pur-ged and cleanſed from corruption: otherwiſe how can they wiſh vs to en-ter, if their houſe be not firſt made cleane? But as I would be loather to diſ-penſe in the leaſt point of mine owne Conſcience for any worldly reſpect, then the fooliſheſt Preciſian of them all; ſo would I bee as ſory to ſtraight the politique Gouernement of the bodies and mindes of all my Subiectes to my priuate opinions: Nay, my minde was euer ſo free from perſecution, or thralling of my Subiects in matters of Conſcience, as I hope that thoſe of that profeſſion within this Kingdome haue a proofe ſince my comming, that I was ſo farre from encreaſing their burdens with *Rehoboam*, as I haue ſo much as either time, occaſion, or law could permit, lightened them. And euen now at this time haue I bene carefull to reuiſe and conſider deeply vpon the Lawes made againſt them; that ſome ouerture may be proponed to the preſent Parliament for clearing theſe Lawes by reaſon (which is the ſoule of the Law) in caſe they baue bene in times paſt further, or more rigo-rouſly extended by Iudges, then the meaning of the Law was, or might tend to the hurt aſwell of the innocent as of guiltie perſons. And as to the per-ſons of my Subiects which are of that profeſſion, I muſt diuide them into two rankes, Clerickes and Layickes; for the part of the Layicks, certainely I euer thought them farre more excuſable then the other ſort, becauſe that ſort of Religion containeth ſuch an ignorant, doubtfull, and implicit kinde of faith in the Layickes grounded vpon their Church, as except they doe ge-nerally beleeue whatſoeuer their Teachers pleaſe to affirme, they cannot be thought guilty of theſe particular points of hereſies and corruptions, which their Teachers doe ſo wilfully profeſſe. And againe I muſt ſubdiuide the ſame Layickes into two rankes, that is, either quiet and well minded men, peaceable Subiects, who either being old, haue retayned their firſt drunken in liquor vpon a certaine ſhamefaſtneſſe to be thought curious or changea-ble: Or being young men, through euill education haue neuer bene nurſed or brought vp, but vpon ſuch venim in place of wholeſome nutriment. And that ſort of people I would be ſorry to puniſh their bodies for the errour of their minds; the reformation whereof muſt onely come of God and the trew Spirit. But the other ranke of Layicks, who either through Curioſitie,

affectation

affectation of Noueltie, or difcontentment in their priuat humours, haue changed their coates, onely to be factious ftirrers of Sedition, and Perturbers of the common wealth, their backwardneffe in their Religion giueth a ground to me the Magiftrate, to take the better heed to their proceeding, and to correct their obftinacie. But for the part of the Clerickes, I muft directly fay and affirme, that as long as they maintaine one fpeciall point of their doctrine, and another point of their practife, they are no way fufferable to remaine in this Kingdome. Their point of doctrine is that arrogant and ambitious Supremacie of their Head the Pope, whereby he not onely claimes to bee Spirituall head of all Chriftians, but alfo to haue an Imperiall ciuill power ouer all Kings and Emperors, dethroning and decrowning Princes with his foot as pleafeth him, and difpenfing and difpofing of all Kingdomes and Empires at his appetite. The other point which they obferue in continuall practife, is the affaffinates and murthers of Kings, thinking it no finne, but rather a matter of faluation, to doe all actions of rebellion and hoftilitie againft their naturall Soueraigne Lord, if he be once curfed, his fubiects difcharged of their fidelitie, and his Kingdome giuen a prey by that three crowned Monarch, or rather Monfter their Head. And in this point, I haue no occafion to fpeake further here, fauing that I could wifh from my heart, that it would pleafe God to make me one of the members of fuch a generall Chriftian vnion in Religion, as laying wilfulneffe afide on both hands, wee might meete in the middeft, which is the Center and perfection of all things. For if they would leaue, and be afhamed of fuch new and groffe Corruptions of theirs, as themfelues cannot maintaine, nor denie to bee worthy of reformation, I would for mine owne part be content to meete them in the mid-way, fo that all nouelties might be renounced on either fide. For as my faith is the Trew, Ancient, Catholike and Apoftolike faith, grounded vpon the Scriptures and expreffe word of God: fo will I euer yeeld all reuerence to antiquitie in the points of Ecclefiafticall pollicy; and by that meanes fhall I euer with Gods grace keepe my felfe from either being an hereticke in Faith, or fchifmatick in matters of Pollicie. But of one thing would I haue the Papifts of this Land to bee admonifhed, That they prefume not fo much vpon my Lenitie (becaufe I would be loath to be thought a Perfecuter) as thereupon to thinke it lawfull for them dayly to encreafe their number and ftrength in this Kingdome, whereby if not in my time, at leaft in the time of my pofteritie, they might be in hope to erect their Religion againe. No, let them affure themfelues, that as I am a friend to their perfons if they be good fubiects: fo am I a vowed enemie, and doe denounce mortall warre to their errors: And that as I would be fory to bee driuen by their ill behauiour from the protection and conferuation of their bodies and liues; So will I neuer ceafe as farre as I can, to tread downe their errors and wrong opinions. For I could not permit the encreafe and growing of their Religion, without firft betraying of my felfe, and mine owne confcience:

fcience: Secondly, this whole Ifle, afwell the part I am come from, as the part I remaine in, in betraying their Liberties, and reducing them to the former flauifh yoke, which both had caften off, before I came a-mongft them: And thirdly, the libertie of the Crowne in my pofteritie, which I fhould leaue againe vnder a new flauery, hauing found it left free to me by my Predeceffors. And therefore would I wifh all good Subiects that are deceiued with that corruption, firft if they find any beginning of inftinction in themfelues of knowledge and loue to the Trewth, to fofter the fame by all lawfull meanes, and to beware of quenching the fpirit that worketh within them; And if they can find as yet no motion tending that way, to be ftudious to reade and conferre with learned men, and to vfe all fuch meanes as may further their Refolution; affuring themfelues, that as long as they are difconformable in Religion from vs, they cannot bee but halfe my Subiects, bee able to doe but halfe feruice, and I to want the beft halfe of them, which is their foules. And here haue I occafion to fpeake to you my Lords the Bifhops: For as you, my Lord of Durham, faid very learnedly to day in your Sermon, Correction without inftruction, is but a Tyrannie: So ought you, and all the Clergie vnder you, to be more carefull, vigilant, and diligent then you haue bene, to winne Soules to God, afwell by your exemplary life, as doctrine. And fince you fee how carefull they are, fparing neither labour, paines, nor extreme perill of their perfons to diuert, (the Deuill is fo bufie a Bifhop) yee fhould bee the more carefull and wakefull in your charges. Follow the rule prefcribed you by S. *Paul*, *Bee carefull to exhort and to inftruct in feafon, and out of feafon* : and where you haue beene any way fluggifh before, now waken your felues vp againe with a new diligence in this point, remitting the fucceffe to God, who calling them either at the fecond, third, tenth or twelfth houre, as they are alike welcome to him, fo fhall they bee to mee his Lieutenant here.

The third reafon of my conuening of you at this time, which conteineth fuch actions of my thankefulneffe toward you, as I may either doe, or leaue vndone, yet fhall with Gods grace euer preffe to performe all the dayes of my life: It confifts in thefe two points; In making of Lawes at certaine times, which is onely at fuch times as this in Parliament; or in the carefull execution thereof at all other times. As for the making of them, I will thus farre faithfully promife vnto you, That I will euer preferre the weale of the body, and of the whole Common-wealth, in making of good Lawes and conftitutions, to any particular or priuate ends of mine, thinking euer the wealth and weale of the Common-wealth to bee my greateft weale and worldly felicitie: A point wherein a lawfull King doeth directly differ from a Tyrant. But at this time I am onely thus farre to forewarne you in that point, That you beware to feeke the making of too many Lawes, for two efpeciall reafons : Firft, becaufe *In corrup-*

The third reafon of affembling the Parliament.

T t *tifsima*

tiſſima Republica plurimæ leges; and the execution of good Lawes is farre
more profitable in a Common-wealth , then to burden mens memories
with the making of too many of them. And next, becauſe the making
of too many Lawes in one Parliament, will bring in confuſion,for lacke of
leiſure wiſely to deliberate before you conclude : For the Biſhop ſaid well
to day, That to Deliberation would a large time be giuen, but to Execution a greater promptneſſe was required. As for the execution of good
Lawes, it hath bene very wiſely and honourably foreſeene and ordered
by my predeceſſours in this Kingdome , in planting ſuch a number of
Iudges, and all ſorts of Magiſtrates in conuenient places for the execution
of the ſame : And therefore muſt I now turne mee to you that are Iudges
and Magiſtrates vnder mee, as mine Eyes and Eares in this caſe. I can ſay
none otherwiſe to you, then as *Ezekias* the good King of *Iuda* ſaid to their
Iudges, *Remember that the Thrones that you ſit on are Gods, and neither yours nor
mine*: And that as you muſt be anſwerable to mee,ſo muſt both you and
I be anſwerable to God, for the due execution of our Offices. That place
is no place for you to vtter your affections in , you muſt not there hate
your foe nor loue your friend,feare the offence of the greater partie,or pity
the miſerie of the meaner; yee muſt be blinde and not ſee diſtinctions of
perſons, handleſſe, not to receiue bribes ; but keepe that iuſt temper and
mid-courſe in all your proceedings, that like a iuſt ballance ye may neither
ſway to the right nor left hand. Three principall qualities are required
in you ; Knowledge,Courage,and Sinceritie : that you may diſcerne with
knowledge,execute with courage,and doe both in vpright ſinceritie. And
as for my part, I doe vow and proteſt here in the preſence of God, and of
this honourable Audience , I neuer ſhall be wearie, nor omit no occaſion,
wherein I may ſhew my carefulneſſe of the execution of good Lawes.
And as I wiſh you that are Iudges not to be weary in your Office in doing
of it; ſo ſhall I neuer be wearie, with Gods grace , to take account of you,
which is properly my calling.

   And thus hauing tolde you the three cauſes of my conuening of this
Parliament, all three tending onely to vtter my thankefulneſſe, but in diuers formes, the firſt by word, the other two by action; I doe confeſſe
that when I haue done and performed all that in this Speech I haue promiſed, *Inutilis ſeruus ſum* : Inutile, becauſe the meaning of the word *Inutilis* in that place of Scripture is vnderſtood, that in doing all that ſeruice
which wee can to God, it is but our due, and wee doe nothing to God
but that which wee are bound to doe. And in like maner, when I haue
done all that I can for you, I doe nothing but that which I am bound
to doe, and am accomptable to God vpon the contrary : For I doe acknowledge, that the ſpeciall and greateſt point of difference that is betwixt
a rightfull King and an vſurping Tyrant is in this; That whereas the
proude and ambitious Tyrant doeth thinke his Kingdome and people
are

are onely ordeined for fatisfaction of his defires and vnreafonable appetites; The righteous and iuft King doeth by the contrary acknowledge himfelfe to bee ordeined for the procuring of the wealth and profperitie of his people, and that his greateft and principall worldly felicitie muft confift in their profperitie. If you bee rich I cannot bee poore, if you bee happy I cannot but bee fortunate, and I proteft that your welfare fhall euer be my greateft care and contentment : And that I am a Seruant it is moft trew, that as I am Head and Gouernour of all the people in my Dominion who are my naturall vaffals and Subiects, confidering them in numbers and diftinct Rankes; So if wee will take the whole People as one body and Maffe, then as the Head is ordeined for the body and not the Body for the Head; fo muft a righteous King know himfelfe to bee ordeined for his people, and not his people for him : For although a King and people be *Relata*; yet can hee be no King if he want people and Subiects. But there be many people in the world that lacke a Head, wherefore I will neuer bee afhamed to confeffe it my principall Honour to bee the great Seruant of the Common-wealth, and euer thinke the profperitie thereof to be my greateft felicitie, as I haue already faid.

But as it was the whole Body of this Kingdome, with an vniforme affent and harmonie, as I tolde you in the beginning of my Speech, which did fo farre oblige mee in good will and thankefulneffe of requitall by their alacritie and readineffe in declaring and receiuing mee to that place which God had prouided for mee, and not any particular perfons : (for then it had not bene the body) So is my thankefulneffe due to the whole State. For euen as in matter of faults, *Quod à multis peccatur, impunè peccatur* : Euen fo in the matter of vertuous and good deedes, what is done by the willing confent and harmonie of the whole body, no particular perfon can iuftly claime thankes as proper to him for the fame. And therefore I muft heere make a little Apologie for my felfe, in that I could not fatiffie the particular humours of euery perfon, that looked for fome aduancement or reward at my hand fince my entrie into this Kingdome. Three kinde of things were craued of mee : Aduancement to honour, Preferment to place of Credit about my Perfon, and Reward in matters of land or profit. If I had beftowed Honour vpon all, no man could haue beene aduanced to Honour : for the degrees of Honour doe confift in preferring fome aboue their fellowes. If euery man had the like acceffe to my Priuy or Bed-chamber, then no man could haue it, becaufe it cannot containe all. And if I had beftowed Lands and Rewards vpon euery man, the fountaine of my liberalitie would be fo exhaufted and dried, as I would lacke meanes to bee liberall to any man. And yet was I not fo fparing, but I may without vaunting affirme that I haue enlarged my fauour in all the three degrees, towards as many and more then euer King of *England* did in fo fhort a fpace : No, I rather craue your pardon that I haue beene fo bountifull: for if the meanes of the Crowne bee wafted, I behoued then to haue recourfe to you my Subiects, and bee burdenfome to you, which I would bee lotheft to bee of any King aliue. For as it is trew, that as I haue already faid, it was a whole Body which did deferue fo well at my hand, and not euery particular perfon of the people: yet were there fome who by reafon of their Office, credit with the people or otherwife, tooke occafion both before, and at the time of my comming amongft you, to giue proofe of their loue and affection towards me. Not that I am any way in doubt, that if other of my Subiects had beene in their places, and had had the like occafion, but they would haue vttered the like good effects, (fo generall and fo great were the loue and affection of you all towards mee:) But yet this hauing beene performed by fome fpeciall perfons, I could not without vnthankfulneffe but requite them accordingly. And therefore had I iuft occafion to aduance fome in Honour, fome to places of feruice about mee, and by rewarding to enable fome who had deferued well of mee, and were not otherwife able to maintaine the rankes I thought them capable of, and others who although they had not particularly deferued before, yet I found them capable and worthy of place of preferment and credit, and not able to fuftaine thofe places for which I thought them fit, without my helpe. Two efpeciall caufes moued mee to be fo open handed: whereof the one was reafonable and honourable; but the other I will not bee afhamed to confeffe vnto you, proceeded of mine owne infirmitie. That which was iuft and honourable, was: That being fo farre beholding to the body of the whole State, I thought I could not refufe to let runne fome fmall brookes out of the fountaine of my thankefulneffe to the whole, for refrefhing of particular perfons that were members of that multitude: The other which proceeded out of mine owne infirmitie, was the multitude and importunitie of Sutors. But although reafon come by infufion in a maner, yet experience groweth with time and labour: And therefore doe I not doubt, but experience in time comming will both teach the particular Subiects of this Kingdome, not to be fo importune and vndifcreete in crauing: And mee not to be fo eafily and lightly mooued, in granting that which may be harmefull to my Eftate, and confequently to the whole Kingdome.

And thus hauing at length declared vnto you my minde in all the points, for the which I called this Parliament: My conclufion fhall onely now be to excufe my felfe, in cafe you haue not found fuch Eloquence in my Speech, as peraduenture you might haue looked for at my hands. I might, if I lift, alledge the great weight of my Affaires and my continuall bufineffe and diftraction, that I could neuer haue leafure to thinke vpon what I was to fpeake, before I came to the place where I was to fpeake: And I might alfo alledge that my firft fight of this fo famous and Honourable an Affembly, might likewife breede fome impediment. But

leauing

leauing thefe excufes, I will plainely and freely in my maner tell you the trew caufe of it, which is; That it becommeth a King, in my opinion, to vfe no other Eloquence then plainneffe and finceritie.　By plaineneffe I meane, that his Speeches fhould be fo cleare and voyd of all ambiguitie, that they may not be throwne, nor rent afunder in contrary fences like the old Oracles of the Pagan gods.　And by finceritie, I vnderftand that vprightneffe and honeftie which ought to be in a Kings whole Speeches and actions: That as farre as a King is in Honour erected aboue any of his Subiects, fo farre fhould he ftriue in finceritie to be aboue them all, and that his tongue fhould be euer the trew Meffenger of his heart : and this fort of Eloquence may you euer affuredly looke for at my hands.

(***)

Tt 3

A SPEACH IN THE
PARLIAMENT HOVSE,
AS NEERE THE VERY WORDS
As Covld Be Gathered
at the inftant.

Y Lords Spirituall and Temporall, and you the Knights and Burgeffes of this Parliament, It was farre from my thoughts till very lately before my comming to this place, that this Subiect fhould haue bene miniftred vnto mee, whereupon I am now to fpeake. But now it fo falleth out, That whereas in the preceding Seffion of this Parliament, the principall occafion of my Speach was, to thanke and congratulate all you of this Houfe, and in you, all the whole Common-wealth (as being the reprefentatiue body of the State) for your fo willing, and louing receiuing and embracing of mee in that place, which G o d and Nature by defcent of blood, had in his owne time prouided for me : So now my Subiect is, to fpeake of a farre greater Thankefgiuing then before I gaue to you, being to a farre greater perfon, which is to G o d, for the great and miraculous Deliuery he hath at this time granted to me, and to you all, and confequently to the whole body of this Eftate.

I muft therefore begin with this old and moft approued Sentence of Diuinitie, *Mifericordia Dei fupra omnia opera eius.* For Almightie God did not furnifh fo great matter to his glory by the Creation of this great World, as he did by the Redemption of the fame. Neither did his generation of the little world in our old & firft Adam, fo much fet forth the praifes of God in his Iuftice and Mercy, as did our Regeneration in the laft & fecond Adam.

a   And

And now I muſt craue a little pardon of you, That ſince Kings are in the word of G O D it ſelfe called Gods, as being his Lieutenants and Vice-gerents on earth, and ſo adorned and furniſhed with ſome ſparkles of the Diuinitie; to compare ſome of the workes of G O D the great K I N G, towards the whole and generall world, to ſome of his workes towards mee, and this little world of my Dominions, compaſſed and ſeuered by the Sea from the reſt of the earth. For as G O D for the iuſt puniſhment of the firſt great ſinnes in the originall world, when the ſonnes of GOD went in to the daughters of men, and the cup of their iniquities of all ſorts was filled, and heaped vp to the full, did by a generall deluge and ouerflowing of waters, baptize the world to a generall deſtruction, and not to a gene-rall purgation (onely excepted N O A H and his family, who did repent and beleeue the threatnings of G O D s iudgement:) So now when the world ſhall waxe old as a garment, and that all the impieties and ſinnes that can be deuiſed againſt both the firſt and ſecond Table, haue and ſhall bee committed to the full meaſure; G O D is to puniſh the world the ſecond time by fire, to the generall deſtruction and not purgation thereof. Al-though as was done in the former to N O A H and his family by the wa-ters; So ſhall all we that beleeue be likewiſe purged, and not deſtroyed by the fire. In the like ſort, I ſay, I may iuſtly compare theſe two great and fearefull *Domeſ-dayes*, wherewith G O D threatned to deſtroy mee and all you of this little world that haue intereſt in me. For although I confeſſe, as all mankinde, ſo chiefly Kings, as being in the higher places like the high Trees, or ſtayeſt Mountaines, and ſteepeſt Rockes, are moſt ſubiect to the dayly tempeſts of innumerable dangers; and I amongſt all other Kings haue euer bene ſubiect vnto them, not onely euer ſince my birth, but euen as I may iuſtly ſay, before my birth: and while I was yet in my mothers belly: yet haue I bene expoſed to two more ſpeciall and greater dangers then all the reſt.

The firſt of them, in the Kingdome where I was borne, and paſſed the firſt part of my life: And the laſt of them here, which is the greateſt. In the former I ſhould haue bene baptized in blood, and in my deſtruction not onely the Kingdom wherein I then was, but ye alſo by your future in-tereſt, ſhould haue taſted of my ruine: Yet it pleaſed G O D to deliuer mee, as it were from the very brinke of death, from the point of the dagger, and ſo to purge me by my thankefull acknowledgement of ſo great a benefite. But in this, which did ſo lately fall out, and which was a deſtruction pre-pared not for me alone, but for you all that are here preſent, and wherein no ranke, aage, nor ſexe ſhould haue bene ſpared; This was not a crying ſinne of blood, as the former, but it may well bee called a roaring, nay a thundring ſinne of fire and brimſtone, from the which G O D hath ſo mi-raculouſly deliuered vs all. What I can ſpeake of this, I know not: Nay ra-ther, what can I not ſpeake of it? And therefore I muſt for horror ſay with the Poet, *Vox faucibus hæret.*

In

In this great and horrible attempt, whereof the like was neuer either heard or read, I obserue three wonderfull, or rather miraculous euents.

Three miraculous euents be to be obserued in the Attempt.

Irst, in the crueltie of the Plot it selfe, wherein cannot be enough admired the horrible and fearefull crueltie of their deuice, which was not onely for the destruction of my Person, nor of my Wife and posteritie onely, but of the whole body of the State in generall; wherein should neither haue bene spared, or distinction made of yong nor of old, of great nor of small, of man nor of woman: The whole Nobilitie, the whole reuerend Clergie, Bishops, and most part of the good Preachers, the most part of the Knights and Gentrie; yea, and if that any in this Societie were fauourers of their profession, they should all haue gone one way: The whole Iudges of the land, with the most of the Lawyers, and the whole Clerkes: And as the wretch himselfe which is in the Tower, doeth confesse, it was purposely deuised by them, and concluded to be done in this house; That where the cruell Lawes (as they say) were made against their Religion, both place and persons should all be destroyed and blowne vp at once. And then consider therewithall the cruel fourme of that practise: for by three different sorts in generall may mankinde be put to death.

1. The crueltie of the Plot.

Three wayes how mankind may come to death.

The first, by other men, and reasonable creatures, which is least cruell: for then both defence of men against men may be expected, and likewise who knoweth what pitie God may stirre vp in the hearts of the Actors at the very instant? besides the many wayes and meanes, whereby men may escape in such a present furie.

1. By Man.

And the second way more cruell then that, is by *Animal* and vnreasonable creatures: for as they haue lesse pitie then men, so is it a greater horror and more vnnaturall for men to deale with them: But yet with them both resistance may auaile, and also some pitie may be had, as was in the Lions, in whose denne *Daniel* was throwne; or that thankefull Lion, that had the Romane in his mercie.

2. By vnreasonable creatures.

But the third, which is most cruel and vnmercifull of all, is the destruction by insensible and inanimate things, and amongst them all, the most cruell are the two Elements of Water and Fire; and of those two, the fire most raging and mercilesse.

3. By insensible things.

Econdly, how wonderfull it is when you shall thinke vpon the small, or rather no ground, whereupon the practisers were entised to inuent this Tragedie. For if these Conspirators had onely bene bankrupt persons, or discontented vpon occasion of any disgraces done vnto them; this might haue seemed to haue bene but a worke of reuenge. But for my owne part, as I scarcely euer knew any of them, so cannot they alledge so much as a pretended cause of griefe: And the wretch himselfe in hands doeth confesse, That there was no cause moouing him or them,

2. The small ground the Conspirators had to moue them.

them, but meerely and only Religion. And specially that christian men, at least so called, Englishmen, borne within the Countrey, and one of the specials of them my sworne Seruant in an Honourable place, should pra-ctise the destruction of their King, his Posterity, their Countrey and all: Wherein their following obstinacie is so ioyned to their former malice, as the fellow himselfe that is in hand, cannot be moued to discouer any signes or notes of repentance, except onely that he doeth not yet stand to auow, that he repents for not being able to performe his intent.

3
Miraculous
euent, the dif-
couerie.

Hirdly, the discouery hereof is not a little wonderfull, which would bee thought the more miraculous by you all, if you were aswell acquainted with my naturall disposition, as those are who be neere about me: For as I euer did hold Suspition to be the sicknes of a Tyrant, so was I so farre vpon the other extremity, as I rather contemned all aduertisements, or apprehensions of practises. And yet now at this time was I so farre contrary to my selfe, as when the Letter was shewed to me by my Secretary, wherein a generall obscure aduertisement was giuen of some dangerous blow at this time, I did vpon the instant interpret and apprehend some darke phrases therein, contrary to the ordinary Grammer construction of them, (and in an other sort then I am sure any Diuine, or Lawyer in any Vniuersitie would haue taken them) to be meant by this horrible forme of blowing vs vp all by Powder; And thereupon ordered that search to be made, whereby the matter was discouered, and the man apprehended: whereas if I had apprehended or interpreted it to any other sort of danger, no worldly prouision or preuention could haue made vs escape our vtter destruction.

And in that also was there a wonderfull prouidence of God, that when the party himselfe was taken, he was but new come out of his house from working, hauing his Fireworke for kindling ready in his pocket, where-with as he confesseth, if he had bene taken but immediatly before when he was in the House, he was resolued to haue blowen vp himselfe with his Takers.

One thing for mine owne part haue I cause to thanke GOD in, That if GOD for our sinnes had suffered their wicked intents to haue preuailed, it should neuer haue bene spoken nor written in aages succeeding, that I had died ingloriously in an Ale-house, a Stews, or such vile place, but mine end should haue bene with the most Honourable and best company, and in that most Honourable and fittest place for a King to be in, for doing the turnes most proper to his Office. And the more haue We all cause to thanke and magnifie GOD for this his mercifull Deliuery; And specially I for my part, that he hath giuen me yet once leaue, whatsoeuer should come of me hereafter, to assemble you in this Honourable place; And here in this place, where our generall destruction should haue bene, to magnifie and praise him for Our generall deliuery: That I may iustly now say of mine
Enemies

Enemies and yours, as *Dauid* doeth often fay in the Pfalme, *Inciderunt in foueam quam fecerunt.* And fince *Scipio* an Ethnick, led onely by the light of Nature, That day when he was accufed by the *Tribunes* of the people of *Rome* for mifpending and wafting in his *Punick* warres the Cities Treafure, euen vpon the fudden brake out with that diuerfion of them from that matter, calling them to remembrance how that day, was the day of the yeere, wherein God had giuen them fo great a victory againft *Hannibal*, and therefore it was fitter for them all, leauing other matters, to runne to the Temple to praife God for that fo great deliuery, which the people did all follow with one applaufe : How much more caufe haue we that are Chriftians to beftow this time in this place for Thankef-giuing to God for his great Mercy, though we had had no other errant of affembling here at this time? wherein if I haue fpoken more like a Diuine then would feeme to belong to this place, the matter it felfe muft plead for mine excufe : For being here commen to thanke God for a diuine worke of his Mercy, how can I fpeake of this deliuerance of vs from fo hellifh a practife, fo well as in language of Diuinitie, which is the direct oppofite to fo damnable an intention? And therefore may I iuftly end this purpofe, as I did begin it with this Sentence, *The Mercie of God is aboue all his workes.*

It refteth now that I fhould fhortly informe you what is to bee done hereafter vpon the occafion of this horrible and ftrange accident. As for your part that are my faithfull and louing Subiects of all degrees, I know that your hearts are fo burnt vp with zeale in this errant, and your tongues fo ready to vtter your duetifull affections, and your hands and feete fo bent to concurre in the execution thereof, (for which as I neede not to fpurre you, fo can I not but praife you for the fame :) As it may very well be poffible that the zeale of your hearts fhall make fome of you in your fpeaches rafhly to blame fuch as may bee innocent of this attempt; But vpon the other part I wifh you to confider, That I would be forie that any being innocent of this practife, either domefticall or forraine, fhould receiue blame or harme for the fame. For although it cannot be denied, That it was the onely blinde fuperftition of their errors in Religion, that led them to this defperate deuice; yet doth it not follow, That all profeffing that *Romifh* religion were guiltie of the fame. For as it is trew, That no other fect of heretiques, not excepting *Turke*, *Iew*, nor *Pagan*, no not euen thofe of *Calicute*, who adore the deuill, did euer maintaine by the grounds of their religion, That it was lawfull, or rather meritorious (as the *Romifh* Catholickes call it) to murther Princes or people for quarrell of Religion. And although particular men of all profeffions of Religion haue beene fome Theeues, fome Murtherers, fome Traitors, yet euer when they came to their end and iuft punifhment, they confeffed their fault to bee in their nature, and not in their profeffion, (Thefe *Romifh* Catholicks onely excepted :) Yet it is trew on the other fide, that many honeft men blinded peraduenture with fome opinions of Popery, as if they be not found in the queftions of the

Reall

Reall presence, or in the number of the Sacraments, or some such Schoole-question: yet doe they either not know, or at least not beleeue all the trew grounds of Popery, which is in deed *The mysterie of iniquitie.* And therefore doe we iustly confesse, that many Papists, especially our forefathers, laying their onely trust vpon C H R I S T and his Merits at their last breath, may be, and often times are saued, detesting in that point, and thinking the crueltie of Puritanes worthy of fire, that will admit no saluation to any Papist. I therefore thus doe conclude this point, That as vpon the one part manyhonest men, seduced with some errors of Popery, may yet remaine good and faithfull Subiects: So vpon the other part, none of those that trewly know and beleeue the whole grounds, and Schoole conclusions of their doctrine, can euer proue either good Christians, or faithfull Subiects. And for the part of forraine Princes and States, I may so much the more acquite them, and their Ministers of their knowledge and consent to any such villanie, as I may iustly say, that in that point I better know all Christian Kings by my selfe, That no King nor Prince of Honour will euer abase himselfe so much, as to thinke a good thought of so base and dishonourable a Treachery, wishing you therefore, that as God hath giuen me an happie Peace and Amitie, with all other Christian Princes my neighbours (as was euen now very grauely told you by my L. Chancellor) that so you will reuerently iudge and speake of them in this case. And for my part I would wish with those ancient Philosophers, that there were a Christall window in my brest, wherein all my people might see the secretest thoughts of my heart, for then might you all see no alteration in my minde for this accident, further then in these two points. The first, Caution and warinesse in gouernment, to discouer and search out the mysteries of this wickednesse as farre as may be: The other, after due triall, Seueritie of punishment vpon those that shall bee found guilty of so detestable and vnheard of villanie. And now in this matter if I haue troubled your eares with an abrupt speach, vndigested in any good methode or order; you haue to consider that an abrupt, and vnaduised speach doeth best become in the relation of so abrupt and vnorderly an accident.

And although I haue ordained the proroguing of this Parliament vntill after Christmas vpon two necessary respects whereof the first is, that neither I nor my Councell can haue leisure at this time both to take order for the Apprehension and triall of these Conspiratours, and also to wait vpon the dayly affaires of the Parliament, as the Councell must doe: And the other reason is, the necessitie at this time of diuers of your presences in your Shires that haue Charges and Commandements there. For as these wretches thought to haue blowen vp in a maner the whole world of this Island, euery man being now commen vp here, either for publike causes of Parliament, or else for their owne priuate causes in Law, or otherwise: So these Rebels that now wander through the Countrey, could neuer haue gotten so fit a time of safetie in their passage, or whatsoeuer vnlawfull Actions,

ons, as now when the Countrey by the forefaid occafions is in a maner left defolate, and wafte vnto them. Befides that, it may be that I fhall defire you at your next Seffion, to take vpon you the Iudgement of this Crime: For as fo extraordinary a Fact deferues extraordinary Iudgement, So can there not I thinke (following euen their owne Rule) be a fitter Iudgement for them, then that they fhould be meafured with the fame meafure where-with they thought to meafure vs: And that the fame place and perfons, whom they thought to deftroy, fhould be the iuft auengers of their fo vn-naturall a Parricide: Yet not knowing that I will haue occafion to meete with you my felfe in this place at the beginning of the next Seffion of this Paliament, (becaufe if it had not been for deliuering of the Articles agreed vpon by the Commiffioners of the Vnion, which was thought moft con-uenient to be done in my prefence, where both Head and Members of the Parliament were met together, my prefence had not otherwife been requi-fite here at this time.) I haue therefore thought good for conclufion of this Meeting, to difcourfe to you fomewhat anent the trew nature and de-finition of a Parliament, which I will remit to your memories till your next fitting downe, that you may then make vfe of it as occafion fhall bee miniftred.

For albeit it be trew, that at the firft Seffion of my firft Parliament, which was not long after mine Entrie into this Kingdome, It could not become me to informe you of any thing belonging to Law or State heere: (for all knowledge muft either bee infufed or acquired, and feeing the former fort thereof is now with Prophecie ceafed in the world, it could not be poffible for me at my firft Entry here, before Experience had taught it me, to be able to vnderftand the particular myfteries of this State:) yet now that I haue reigned almoft three yeeres amongft you, and haue beene carefull to ob-ferue thofe things that belong to the office of a King, albeit that Time be but a fhort time for experience in others, yet in a King may it be thought a reafonable long time, efpecially in me, who, although I be but in a maner a new King heere, yet haue bene long acquainted with the office of a King in fuch another Kingdome, as doeth neereft of all others agree with the Lawes and cuftomes of this State. Remitting to your confideration to iudge of that which hath beene concluded by the Commiffioners of the Vnion, wherein I am at this time to fignifie vnto you, That as I can beare witneffe to the forefaid Commiffioners, that they haue not agreed nor con-cluded therein any thing, wherein they haue not forefeen as well the weale and commodity of the one Countrey, as of the other; So can they all beare mee record, that I was fo farre from preffing them to agree to any thing, which might bring with it any preiudice to this people; as by the contrary I did euer admonifh them, neuer to conclude vpon any fuch Vnion, as might cary hurt or grudge with it to either of the faid Nations: for the leauing of any fuch thing, could not but be the greateft hinderance that might be to fuch an Action, which God by the lawes of Nature had prouided to be in his owne time, and hath now in effect perfected in my Perſon, to which purpoſe my Lord Chancellour hath better ſpoken, then I am able to relate.

And as to the nature of this high Court of Parliament, It is nothing elſe but the Kings great Councell, which the King doeth aſſemble either vpon occaſion of interpreting, or abrogating old Lawes, or making of new, according as ill maners ſhall deſerue, or for the publike puniſhment of notorious euill doers, or the praiſe and reward of the vertuous and well deſeruers; wherein theſe foure things are to be conſidered.   1

1   Firſt, whereof this Court is compoſed.

2   Secondly, what matters are proper for it.

3   Thirdly, to what end it is ordeined.

4   And fourthly, what are the meanes and wayes whereby this end ſhould bee brought to paſſe.

As for the thing it ſelfe, It is compoſed of a Head and a Body: The Head is the King, the Body are the members of the Parliament. This Body againe is ſubdiuided into two parts; The Vpper and Lower Houſe: The Vpper compounded partly of Nobility, Temporall men, who are heritable Councellors to the high Court of Parliament by the honour of their Creation and Lands: And partly of Biſhops, Spirituall men, who are likewiſe by the vertue of their place and dignitie Councellours, Life Renters, or *Ad vitam* of this Court. The other Houſe is compoſed of Knights for the Shire; and Gentry, and Burgeſſes for the Townes. But becauſe the number would be infinite for all the Gentlemen and Burgeſſes to bee preſent at euery Parliament, Therefore a certaine number is ſelected and choſen out of that great Body, ſeruing onely for that Parliament, where their perſons are the repreſentation of that Body.

Now the matters whereof they are to treate ought therefore to be generall, and rather of ſuch matters as cannot well bee performed without the aſſembling of that generall Body, and no more of theſe generals neither, then neceſſity ſhall require: for as *in Corruptiſſima Republica ſunt plurima leges:* So doeth the life and ſtrength of the Law conſiſt not in heaping vp infinite and confuſed numbers of Lawes, but in the right interpretation and good execution of good and wholeſome Lawes. If this be ſo then, neither is this a place on the one ſide for euery raſh and harebrained fellow to propone new Lawes of his owne inuention: nay rather I could wiſh theſe buſie heads to remember that Law of the Lacedemonians, That whoſoeuer came to propone a new Law to the people, behooued publikely to preſent himſelfe with a rope about his necke, that in caſe the Law were not allowed, he ſhould be hanged therwith. So warie ſhould men be of proponing Nouelties, but moſt of all not to propone any bitter or ſeditious Laws, which can produce nothing but grudges and diſcontentment betweene the Prince and his people. Nor yet is it on the other ſide a conuenient place for priuate men vnder the colour of generall Lawes,

to proto propone nothing but their owne particular gaine, either to the hurt of their priuate neighbours, or to the hurt of the whole State in generall, which many times vnder faire and pleafing Titles, are fmoothly paffed o-uer, and fo by ftealth procure without confideration, that the priuate mea-ning of them tendeth to nothing but either to the wrecke of a particular partie, or elfe vnder colour of publike benefite to pill the poore people, and ferue as it were for a generall Impoft vpon them for filling the purfes of fome priuate perfons.

And as to the end for which the Parliament is ordeined, being only for the aduancement of Gods glory, and the eftablifhment and wealth of the King and his people : It is no place then for particular men to vtter there their priuate conceipts, nor for fatisfaction of their curiofities, and leaft of all to make fhew of their eloquence by tyning the time with long ftudied and eloquent Orations: No, the reuerence of God, their King, and their Countrey being well fetled in their hearts, will make them afhamed of fuch toyes, and remember that they are there as fworne Councellours to their King, to giue their beft aduife for the furtherance of his Seruice, and the florifhing Weale of his Eftate.

And laftly, if you will rightly confider the meanes and wayes how to bring all your labours to a good end, you muft remember, That you are heere affembled by your lawfull King to giue him your beft aduifes, in the matters propofed by him vnto you, being of that nature, which I haue al-ready told, wherein you are grauely to deliberate, and vpon your confcien-ces plainely to determine how farre thofe things propounded doe agree with the weale, both of your King and of your Countrey, whofe weales cannot be feparated. And as for my felfe, the world fhall euer beare mee witneffe, That I neuer fhall propone any thing vnto you, which fhall not as well tend to the weale publike; as to any benefite for me : So fhall I ne-uer oppone my felfe to that, which may tend to the good of the Common-wealth, for the which I am ordeined, as I haue often faid. And as you are to giue your aduife in fuch things as fhall by your King be propofed : So is it on your part your dueties to propone any thing that you can after mature deliberation iudge to be needefull, either for thefe ends already fpoken of, or otherwife for the difcouery of any latent euill in the Kingdome, which peraduenture may not haue commen to the Kings eare. If this then ought to bee your graue maner of proceeding in this place, Men fhould bee afha-med to make fhew of the quickneffe of their wits here, either in taunting, fcoffing, or detracting the Prince or State in any point, or yet in breaking iefts vpon their fellowes, for which the Ordinaries or Ale-houfes are fitter places, then this Honourable and high Court of Parliament.

In conclufion then fince you are to breake vp, for the reafons I haue al-ready told you, I wifh fuch of you as haue any charges in your Countreys, to haften you home for the repreffing of the infolencies of thefe Rebels, and apprehenfion of their perfons, wherin as I heartily pray to the Almightie for your profperous fucceffe : So doe I not doubt, but we fhall fhortly heare the good newes of the fame; And that you fhall haue an happie re-turne, and meeting here to all our comforts.

Here the Lord Chancellor fpake touching the proroguing of the Parliament: And hauing done, his Maieftie rofe againe, and faid,

Since it pleafed God to graunt mee two fuch notable Deliueries vpon one day of the weeke, which was Tuefday, and likewife one day of the Moneth, which was the fifth; Thereby to teach mee, That as it was the fame deuill that ftill perfecuted mee; So it was one and the fame GOD that ftill mightily deliuered mee: I thought it therefore not amiffe, That the one and twentieth day of Ianuary, which fell to be vpon Tuefday, fhould bee the day of meeting of this next Seffion of Parliament, hoping and affuring my felfe, that the fame GOD, who hath now granted me and you all fo notable and gracious a deliuerie, fhall profper all our affaires at that next Seffion, and bring them to an happie conclufion. And now I confider GOD hath well prouided it, that the ending of this Parliament hath bene fo long continued : For as for my owne part, I neuer had any other intention, but onely to feeke fo farre my weale, and profperitie, as might coniunĉtly ftand with the flourifhing State of the whole Commonwealth, as I haue often told you; So on the other part I confeffe, if I had bene in your places at the beginning of this Parliament, (which was fo foone after mine entry into this Kingdome, wherein ye could not poffibly haue fo perfeĉt a knowledge of mine inclination, as experience fince hath taught you,) I could not but haue fufpeĉted, and mif-interpreted diuers things, In the trying whereof, now I hope, by your experience of my behauiour and forme of gouernment, you are well ynough cleared, and refolued.

(****)

A SPEACH

A SPEACH TO BOTH
THE HOVSES OF PARLIA-
MENT, DELIVERED IN THE
GREAT CHAMBER AT
WHITE-HALL,

THE LAST DAY OF
March 1607.

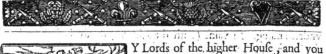

Y Lords of the higher House, and you
Knights and Burgesses of the Lower house,
All men at the beginning of a Feast bring
foorth good Wine first, and after, worse.
This was the saying of the Gouernour of the
Feast at *Cana* in *Galile*, where CHRIST
wrought his first miracle by changing water into Wine. But in this case now whereof I am to speake vnto you, I must follow
that Gouernours rule, and not CHRISTS
example, in giuing you the worst and sowrest Wine last. For all the time
of this long Session of the Parliament you haue bene so fed and cloy'd, (specially you of the Lower house) with such banquets, and choise of delicate
speeches, and your eares so seasoned with the sweetnesse of long precogi-
tate Orations; as this my Speach now in the breaking vp of this Assembly, cannot but appeare vnto your taste as the worst Wine proposed in
the end of the Banquet, since I am onely to deliuer now vnto you matter without curious forme, substance without ceremonie, trewth in all
sinceritie. Yet considering the Person that speaketh, the parties to whom
I speake, the matter whereof I meane to speake; it fits better to vtter mat-

1.   Vu 3   ter,

ter, rather then wordes, in regard of the greatnesse of my place who am to speake to you, the grauitie of you the Auditorie, which is the high Court of Parliament; the weight of the matter, which concernes the securitie and establishment of this whole Empire, and litle world. Studied Orations and much eloquence vpon little matter is fit for the Vniuersities, where not the Subiect which is spoken of, but the triall of his wit that speaketh, is most commendable: but on the contrary, in all great Councels of Parliaments, fewest wordes with most matter doeth become best, where the dispatch of the great errands in hand, and not the praise of the person is most to bee looked vnto: like the garment of a chaste woman, who is onely set forth by her naturall beautie, which is properly her owne: other deckings are but ensignes of an harlot that flies with borrowed feathers. And besides the conueniencie, I am forced hereunto by necessitie, my place calling me to action, and not leauing me to the libertie of contemplation, hauing alwayes my thoughts busied with the publique care of you all, where euery one of you hauing but himselfe, and his owne priuate to thinke of, are at more leisure to make studied speeches. And therefore the matter which I deliuer you confusedly as in a sacke, I leaue it to you when you are in your chambers, and haue better leysure then I can haue, to ranke them in order, euery one in their owne place.

Thus much by way of Preface. But I proceed to the matter: Whereof I might say with S. *Paul*, I could speake in as many tongues as you all, but I had rather speake three wordes to edification, then talke all day without vnderstanding. In vaine (saith the *Psalmist*) doeth the builder build the house, or the watchman watch the Citie, vnlesse the Lord giue his blessing thereunto. And in the New Testament S. *Paul* saith, That hee may plant, *Apollo* may water, but it is God onely that must giue the increase. This I speake, because of the long time which hath bene spent about the Treatie of the Vnion. For my selfe, I protest vnto you all, When I first propounded the Vnion, I then thought there could haue bene no more question of it, then of your declaration and acknowledgement of my right vnto this Crowne, and that as two Twinnes, they would haue growne vp together. The errour was my mistaking; I knew mine owne ende, but not others feares: But now finding many crossings, long disputations, strange questions, and nothing done; I must needs thinke it proceeds either of mistaking of the errand, or else from some iealousie of me the Propounder, that you so adde delay vnto delay, searching out as it were the very bowels of Curiositie, and conclude nothing. Neither can I condemne you for being yet in some iealousie of my intention in this matter, hauing not yet had so great experience of my behauiour and inclination in these few yeeres past, as you may peraduenture haue in a longer time hereafter, and not hauing occasion to consult dayly with my selfe, and heare mine owne opinion in all those particulars which are debated among you.

But

But here I pray you now miftake mee not at the firft, when as I feeme to finde fault with your delayes and curiofitie, as if I would haue you to re-folue in an houres time, that which will take a moneths aduifement : for you all know, that *Rex eft lex loquens*; And you haue oft heard mee fay, That the Kings will and intention being the fpeaking Law, ought to bee *Luce clarius*: and I hope you of the Lower houfe haue the proofe of this my clearenefle by a Bil fent you downe from the Vpper houfe within thefe few dayes, or rather few houres : wherein may very well appeare vnto you the care I haue to put my Subiects in good fecuritie of their poffeffions for all pofterities to come. And therefore that you may clearely vnderftand my meaning in that point, I doe freely confefle you had reafon to aduife at leafure vpon fo great a caufe : for great matters doe euer require great de-liberation before they be well concluded. *Deliberandum eft diu quod ftatu-endum eft femel.* Confultations muft proceed *lento pede*, but the execution of a fentence vpon the refolution would be fpeedie. If you will goe on, it matters not though you goe with leaden feet, fo you make ftill fome pro-greffe, and that there be no let or needleffe delay, and doe not *Nodum in fcirpo quærere.* I am euer for the *Medium* in euery thing. Betweene foolifh rafhnefle and extreame length, there is a middle way. Search all that is rea-fonable, but omit that which is idle, curious and vnneceffary; otherwife there can neuer be a refolution or end in any good worke.

And now from the generall I wil defcend to particulars, and wil onely for the eafe of your memories diuide the matter that I am to fpeake of, in-to foure heads, by opening vnto you, Firft, what I craue : Secondly, in what maner I defire it : Thirdly, what commodities will enfue to both the Kingdomes by it : Fourthly, what the fuppofed inconueniencie may be that giues impediments thereunto.

For the firft, what I craue, I proteft before GOD who knowes my heart, and to you my people before whom it were a fhame to lie, that I claime nothing but with acknowledgement of my Bond to you; that as yee owe to me fubiection and obedience : So my Soueraigntie obligeth mee to yeeld to you loue, gouernment and protection : Neither did I euer wifh any happinefle to my felfe, which was not conioyned with the happinefle of my people. I defire a perfect Vnion of Lawes and perfons, and fuch a Naturalizing as may make one body of both Kingdomes vnder mee your King, That I and my pofteritie (if it fo pleafe God) may rule ouer you to the worlds ende; Such an Vnion as was of the Scots and Pictes in Scot-land, and of the Heptarchie here in England. And for Scotland I auow fuch an Vnion, as if you had got it by Conqueft, but fuch a Conqueft as may be cemented by loue, the onely fure bond of fubiection or friendfhip : that as there is ouer both but *vnus Rex*, fo there may be in both but *vnus Grex & vna Lex* : For no more poffible is it for one King to gouerne two Countreys *Contiguous*, the one a great, the other a leffe, a richer and a poo-rer, the greater drawing like an Adamant the leffer to the Commodities

dities thereof, then for one head to gouerne two bodies, or one man to be husband of two wiues,whereof Chrilt himfelfe faid,*Ab initio non fuit fic.*

But in the generall Vnion you muft obferue two things : for I will difcouer my thoughts plainly vnto you ; I ftudy clearenes, not eloquence, And therefore with the olde Philofopers, I would heartily wifh my breft were a tranfparent glaffe for you all to fee through , that you might looke into my heart, and then would you be fatisfied of my meaning. For when I fpeake of a perfect Vnion, I meane not confufion of all things : you muft not take from Scotland thofe particular Priuiledges that may ftand as well with this Vnion, as in England many particular cuftomes in particular Shires, (as the Cuftomes of Kent, and the Royalties of the Countie Palatine of Chefter) do with the Common Law of the Kingdome : for euery particular Shire almoft, and much more euery Countie, haue fome particular cuftomes that are as it were naturally moft fit for that people. But I meane of fuch a generall Vnion of Lawes as may reduce the whole Iland, that as they liue already vnder one Monarch, fo they may all bee gouerned by one Law : For I muft needs confeffe by that little experience I haue had fince my comming hither, and I thinke I am able to prooue it, that the grounds of the Common Law of England, are the beft of any Law in the world, either Ciuil or Municipall, and the fitteft for this people. But as euery Law would be cleare and full, fo the obfcuritie in fome points of this our written Law, and want of fulneffe in others, the variation of Cafes and mens curiofitie, breeding euery day new queftions, hath enforced the Iudges to iudge in many Cafes here, by Cafes and prefidents, wherein I hope Lawyers themfelues will not denie but that there muft be a great vncertaintie, and I am fure all the reft of you that are Gentlemen of other profeffions were long agoe wearie of it, if you could haue had it amended : For where there is varietie and vncertaintie, although a iuft Iudge may do rightly, yet an ill Iudge may take aduantage to doe wrong ; and then are all honeft men that fucceede him, tied in a maner to his vniuft and partiall conclufions. Wherefore, leaue not the Law to the pleafure of the Iudge, but let your Lawes be looked into : for I defire not the abolifhing of the Lawes, but onely the clearing and the fweeping off the ruft of them, and that by Parliament our Lawes might be cleared and made knowen to all the Subiects. Yea rather it were leffe hurt, that all the approued Cafes were fet downe and allowed by Parliament for ftanding Lawes in all time to come : For although fome of them peraduenture may bee vniuft as fet downe by corrupt Iudges ; yet better it is to haue a certaine Law with fome fpots in it, nor liue vnder fuch an vncertaine and arbitrarie Law, fince as the prouerbe is, It is leffe harme to fuffer an inconuenience then a mifchiefe. And now may you haue faire occafion of amending and polifhing your Lawes, when Scotland is to bee vnited with you vnder them : for who can blame Scotland to fay, If you will take away our owne Lawes, I pray you giue vs a better and cleerer in place thereof.

But

But this is not poſsible to bee done without a fit preparation. Hee that buildeth a Ship, muſt firſt prouide the timber; and as Chriſt himſelfe ſaid, No man will build an houſe, but he will firſt prouide the materials : nor a wiſe King will not make warre againſt another, without he firſt make prouiſion of money : and all great workes muſt haue their preparation : and that was my end in cauſing the Inſtrument of the Vnion to be made. Vnion is a mariage : would he not bee thought abſurd that for furthering of a mariage betweene two friends of his, would make his firſt motion to haue the two parties be laid in bedde together, and performe the other turnes of mariage? muſt there not precede the mutuall ſight and acquaintance of the parties one with another, the conditions of the contract, and Ioincture to be talked of and agreed vpon by their friends, and ſuch other things as in order ought to goe before the ending of ſuch a worke? The vnion is an eternall agreement and reconciliation of many long bloody warres that haue beene betweene theſe two ancient Kingdomes. Is it the readieſt way to agree a priuate quarell betweene two, to bring them at the firſt to ſhake hands, and as it were kiſſe other, and lie vnder one roofe or rather in one bedde together, before that firſt the ground of their quarell be communed vpon, their mindes mitigated, their affections prepared, and all other circumſtances firſt vſed, that ought to be vſed to proceed to ſuch a finall agreement? Euery honeſt man deſireth a perfect Vnion, but they that ſay ſo, and admit no preparation thereto, haue *mel in ore ; fel in corde.* If after your ſo long talke of Vnion in all this long Seſsion of Parliament, yee riſe without agreeing vpon any particular, what will the neighbour Princes iudge, whoſe eyes are all fixed vpon the concluſion of this Action, but that the King is refuſed in his deſire, whereby the Nation ſhould bee taxed, and the King diſgraced? And what an ill preparation is it for the mindes of Scotland toward the Vnion, when they ſhall heare that ill is ſpoken of their whole Nation, but nothing is done nor aduanced in the matter of the Vnion it ſelfe? But this I am glad was but the fault of one, and one is no number : yet haue your neighbours of Scotland this aduantage of you, that none of them haue ſpoken ill of you (nor ſhall as long as I am King) in Parliament, or any ſuch publique place of Iudicature. Conſider therefore well, if the mindes of Scotland had not neede to be well prepared to perſwade their mutuall conſent, ſeeing you here haue all the great aduantage by the Vnion. Is not here the perſonall reſidence of the King, his whole Court and family? Is not here the ſeate of Iuſtice, and the fountaine of Gouernment? muſt they not be ſubiected to the Lawes of England, and ſo with time become but as Cumberland and Northumberland, and thoſe other remote and Northerne Shires? you are to be the husband, they the wife : you conquerours, they as conquered, though not by the ſword, but by the ſweet and ſure bond of loue. Beſides that, they as other Northerne Countreys will be ſeldome ſeene and ſaluted by their King, and that as it were but in a poſting or hunting iourney.

How

How little caufe then they may haue of fuch a change of fo ancient a
Monarchie into the cafe of priuate Shires, iudge rightly herein. And
that you may be the more vpright Iudges, fuppofe your felues the Patients
of whom fuch fentence fhould be giuen. But what preparation is it which
I craue? onely fuch as by the entrance may fhew fomething is done, yet
more is intended. There is a conceipt intertained, and a double iealoufie
poffeffeth many, wherein I am mifiudged.

Firft, that this Vnion will be the *Crifis* to the ouerthrow of England,
and fetting vp of Scotland: England will then bee ouerwhelmed by the
fwarming of the Scots, who if the Vnion were effected, would raigne and
rule all.

The fecond is, my profufe liberalitie to the Scottifh men more then
the Englifh, and that with this Vnion all things fhalbe giuen to them,
and you turned out of all: To you fhall bee left the fweat and labour, to
them fhall bee giuen the fruite and fweet; and that my forbearance is but
till this Vnion may be gained. How agreeable this is to the trewth, Iudge
you; And that not by my wordes, but by my Actions. Doe I craue the
Vnion without exceptions? doe I not offer to binde my felfe and to referue
to you, as in the Inftrument, all places of Iudicature? doe I intend any
thing which ftandeth not with the equall good of both Nations? I could
then haue done it, and not fpoken of it: For all men of vnderftanding
muft agree, that I might difpofe without affent of Parliament, Offices of
Iudicature, and others, both Ecclefiafticall and Temporall: But herein
I did voluntarily offer by my Letters from Royfton to the Commiffioners,
to bind my Prerogatiue.

Some thinke that I will draw the Scottifh Nation hither, talking idlely
of tranfporting of Trees out of a barren ground into a better, and of leane
cattell out of bad pafture into a more fertile foile. Can any man difplant
you, vnleffe you will? or can any man thinke that Scotland is fo ftrong to
pull you out of your houfes? or doe you not thinke I know England hath
more people, Scotland more waft ground? So that there is roumth in Scotland rather to plant your idle people that fwarme in London ftreets, and
other Townes, and difburden you of them, then to bring more vnto you;
And in cafes of Iuftice, if I bee partiall to either fide, let my owne mouth
condemne me, as vnworthy to be your King.

I appeale to your felues, if in fauour or Iuftice I haue beene partiall:
Nay, my intention was euer, you fhould then haue moft caufe to praife
my difcretion, when you faw I had moft power. If hitherto I haue done
nothing to your preiudice, much leffe meane I hereafter. If when I might
haue done it without any breach of promife; Thinke fo of mee, that
much leffe I will doe it, when a Law is to reftraine me. I owe no more to
the Scottifh men then to the Englifh. I was borne there, and fworne here,
and now raigne ouer both. Such particular perfons of the Scottifh Nation, as might claime any extraordinary merit at my handes, I haue already
                                                              reafonably

reafonably rewarded, and I can aſſure you that there is none left, whom for I meane extraordinary to ſtraine my ſelfe further, then in ſuch ordinary benefit as I may equally beſtow without mine owne great hurt, vpon any Subiect of either Nation; In which caſe no Kings handes can euer be fully cloſed. To both I owe Iuſtice and protection, which with Gods grace I ſhall euer equally ballance.

For my Liberalitie, I haue told you of it heretofore: my three firſt yeeres were to me as a Chriſtmas; I could not then be miſerable: ſhould I haue bene ouerſparing to them? they might haue thought *Ioſeph* had forgotten his brethren, or that the King had beene drunke with his new Kingdome. But Suites goe not now ſo cheape as they were wont, neither are there ſo many fees taken in the Hamper and Pettibagge for the great Seale as hath beene. And if I did reſpect the Engliſh when I came firſt, of whom I was receiued with ioy, and came as in a hunting iourney, what might the Scottiſh haue iuſtly ſaid, if I had not in ſome meaſure dealt bountifully with them that ſo long had ſerued me, ſo farre aduentured themſelues with me, and beene ſo faithfull to mee. I haue giuen you now foure yeeres proofe ſince my comming; and what I might haue done more to haue rai-ſed the Scottiſh nation you all know, and the longer I liue, the leſſe cauſe haue I to be acquainted with them, and ſo the leſſe hope of extraordinary fauour towards them: For ſince my comming from them I doe not alrea-die know the one halfe of them by face, moſt of the youth being now riſen vp to bee men, who were but children when I was there, and more are borne ſince my comming thence.

Now for my lands and reuenues of my Crowne which you may thinke I haue diminiſhed, They are not yet ſo farre diminiſhed, but that I thinke no prince of Chriſtendome hath fairer poſſeſſions to his Crowne then yet I haue: and in token of my care to preſerue the ſame to my poſteritie for euer, the intaile of my lands to the Crowne hath beene long agoe offe-red vnto you: and that it is not yet done, is not my fault as you know. My Treaſurer here knoweth my care, and hath already in part declared it, and if I did not hope to treble my Reuenue more then I haue empai-red it, I ſhould neuer reſt quietly in my bed. But notwithſtanding my comming to the Crowne, with that extraordinarie applauſe which you all know, and that I had two Nations to bee the obiects of my libera-litie, which neuer any Prince had here before; will you compare my gifts out of mine inheritance with ſome Princes here that had onely this Nation to reſpect, and whoſe whole time of reigne was litle longer then mine hath bene already? It will be found that their gifts haue farre ſurpaſ-ſed mine, albeit as I haue already ſaid, they had nothing ſo great cauſe of vſing their liberalitie.

For the maner of the Vnion preſently deſired, It ſtandeth in 3. parts: Secondly
The firſt, taking away of hoſtile Lawes: for ſince there can bee now no Warres betwixt you, is it not reaſon hoſtile Lawes ſhould ceaſe?
For,

For, *deficiente cauſa deficit effeƐlus.* The King of England now cannot haue warres with the King of Scotland, therefore this failes of it ſelfe. The ſecond is communitie of Commerce. I am no ſtranger vnto you : for you all know I came from the loynes of your ancient Kings. They of Scotland be my Subiects as you are. But how can I bee naturall Liege Lord to you both, and you ſtrangers one to the other? Shall they which be of one alleagance with you, be no better reſpected of you, nor freer amongſt you, then Frenchmen and Spaniards? Since I am Soueraigne ouer both, you as Subiects to one King, it muſt needes follow that you conuerſe and haue Commerce together. There is a rumour of ſome ill dealings that ſhould be vſed by the Commiſſioners, Merchants of Scotland. They be heere in England, and ſhall remaine till your next meeting, and abide triall, to prooue themſelues either honeſt men or knaues.

3.

   For the third point, of Naturalization, All you agree that they are no Aliens, and yet will not allow them to bee naturall. What kinde of prerogatiue will you make? But for the *Poſt nati,* your owne Lawyers and Iudges at my firſt comming to this Crowne, informed me, there was a difference betweene the *Antè* and the *Poſt nati* of each Kingdome, which cauſed mee to publiſh a Proclamation, that the *Poſt nati* were Naturalized (*Ipſo faƐlo*) by my Acceſſion to this Crowne. I doe not denie but Iudges may erre as men, and therefore I doe not preſſe you here to ſweare to all their reaſons. I onely vrge at this time the conueniencie for both Kingdomes, neither preſſing you to iudge nor to be iudged. But remember alſo it is as poſſible and likely your owne Lawyers may erre as the Iudges : Therefore as I wiſh you to proceede herein ſo farre as may tend to the weale of both Nations; So would I haue you on the other part to beware to diſgrace either my Proclamations or the Iudges, who when the Parliament is done, haue power to trie your lands and liues, for ſo you may diſgrace both your King and your Lawes. For the doing of any acte that may procure leſſe reuerence to the Iudges, cannot but breede a looſeneſſe in the Gouernement, and a diſgrace to the whole Nation. The reaſon that moſt mooues mee for ought I haue yet heard, that there cannot but bee a difference betweene the *Antè nati* and the *Poſt nati,* and that in the fauour of the laſt, is that they muſt bee neerer vnto you being borne vnder the preſent Gouernement and common Allegiance: but in point of conueniencie, there is no queſtion but the *Poſt nati* are more to bee reſpected : For if you would haue a perfect and perpetuall Vnion, that cannot be in the *Antè nati,* who are but few in compariſon of thoſe that ſhall be in all aages ſucceeding, and cannot liue long. But in the *Poſt nati* ſhall the Vnion be continued and liue euer aage after aage, which wanting a difference cannot but leaue a perpetuall marke of ſeparation in the worke of the Vnion: as alſo that argument of iealouſie will be ſo farre remooued in the caſe of the *Poſt nati* which are to reape the benefit in all ſucceeding aages, as by the contrary there will then riſe *Pharaos* which neuer knew *Ioſeph.* The Kings my

Succeſ-

Succeſſours, who beeing borne and bred heere, can neuer haue more occaſion of acquaintance with the Scottiſh Nation in generall, then a-ny other Engliſh King that was before my time. Bee not therefore abu-ſed with the flattering ſpeeches of ſuch as would haue the *Antè nati* preferred, alleadging their merit in my Seruice, and ſuch other reaſons which indeede are but Sophiſmes : For, my rewarding out of my Libe-ralitie of any particular men, hath nothing adoe with the generall acte of the Vnion, which muſt not regard the deſerts of priuate perſons, but the generall weale and conioyning of the Nations. Beſides that, the actuall Naturalizing, which is the onely point that is in your handes, is already graunted to by your ſelues to the moſt part of ſuch particular perſons as can haue any vſe of it heere : and if any other well deſeruing men were to ſue for it hereafter, I doubt not but there would neuer bee queſtion mooued among you for the granting of it. And therefore it is moſt euident, that ſuch diſcourſers haue *mel in ore*, *fel in corde*, as I ſaid before ; carying an outward appearance of loue to the Vnion, but in-deed a contrary reſolution in their hearts. And as for limitations and re-ſtrictions, ſuch as ſhall by me be agreed vpon to be reaſonable and neceſ-ſary after you haue fully debated vpon them, you may aſſure your ſelues I will with indifferencie grant what is requiſite without partiall reſpect of Scotland. I am, as I haue often ſaid, borne and ſworne King ouer both Kingdomes ; onely this farre let me entreat you, in debating the point at your next meeting, That yee be as ready to reſolue doubts as to mooue them, and to be ſatisfied when doubts are cleered.

And as for Commodities that come by the Vnion of theſe Kingdoms, they are great and euident ; Peace, Plentie, Loue, free Intercourſe and common Societie of two great Nations. All forreigne Kings that haue ſent their Ambaſſadours to congratulate with me ſince my comming, haue ſaluted me as Monarch of the whole Iſle, and with much more reſpect of my greatneſſe, then if I were King alone of one of theſe Realmes : and with what comfort doe your ſelues behold Iriſh, Scottiſh, Welſh, and En-gliſh, diuers in Nation, yet all walking as Subiects and ſeruants within my Court, and all liuing vnder the allegiance of your King, beſides the honour and luſtre that the encreaſe of gallant men in the Court of diuers Nations carries in the eyes of all ſtrangers that repaire hither? Thoſe confining places which were the Borders of the two Kingdomes, where heretofore much blood was ſhed, and many of your anceſtours loſt their liues ; yea, that lay waſte and deſolate, and were habitations but for run-nagates, are now become the Nauell or Vmbilick of both Kingdomes, planted and peopled with Ciuilitie and riches : their Churches begin to bee planted, their doores ſtand now open, they feare neither robbing nor ſpoiling : and where there was nothing before heard nor ſeene in thoſe parts but bloodſhed, oppreſſions, complaints and outcries, they now liue euery man peaceably vnder his owne figgetree, and all their former cryes and complaints turned onely into prayers to God for their King, vnder whom they enioy such ease and happy quietnesse. The Marches beyond and on this side Twede, are as fruitfull and as peaceable as most parts of England: If after all this there shall be a Scissure, what inconuenience will follow, iudge you.

And as for the inconueniences that are feared on Englands part, It is alleadged, that the Scots are a populous Nation, they shall be harboured in our nests, they shall be planted and flourish in our good Soile, they shall eate our commons bare, and make vs leane: These are foolish and idle surmises. That which you possesse, they are not to enioy; by Law they cannot, nor by my partialitie they shall not: for set apart conscience and honour, (which if I should set apart indeede, I had rather wish my selfe to bee set apart and out of all being) can any man conclude either out of common reason or good policie, that I will preferre those which perhaps I shall neuer see, or but by poste for a moneth, before those with whom I must alwayes dwell? Can they conquer or ouercome you with swarmes of people, as the Goths and the Vandals did *Italy?* Surely the world knowes they are nothing so populous as you are: and although they haue had the honour and good fortune neuer to be conquered, yet were they euer but vpon the defensiue part, and may in a part thanke their hilles and inaccessible passages that preserued them from an vtter ouerthrow at the handes of all that pretended to conquer them. Or are they so very poore and miserable in their owne habitations, that necessitie should force them all to make incursions among you?

And for my part, when I haue two Nations vnder my gouernment, can you imagine I will respect the lesser, and neglect the greater? would I not thinke it a lesse euill and hazard to mee that the plague were at Northampton or Barwicke, then at London, so neere Westminster, the Seat of my habitation, and of my wife and children? will not a man bee more carefull to quench the fire taken in his neerest neighbours house, then if a whole Towne were a fire farre from him? You know that I am carefull to preserue the woods and game through all England, nay, through all the Isle: yet none of you doubts, but that I would be more offended with any disorder in the Forrest of Waltham, for stealing of a Stagge there, which lieth as it were vnder my nose, and in a maner ioyneth with my garden, then with cutting of timber, or stealing of a Deare in any Forrest of the North parts of Yorkeshire or the Bishopricke. Thinke you that I will preferre them that be absent, lesse powerfull, and farther off to doe me good or hurt, before you, with whom my security and liuing must be, and where I desire to plant my posterity? If I might by any such fauours raise my selfe to a greatnesse, it might bee probable: All I cannot draw, and to lose a whole state here to pleafe a few there, were madnesse. I neede speake no more of this with protestations. Speake but of wit, it is not likely: and to doubt of my intention in this, were more then deuilish.

For

For mine owne part, I offer more then I receiue, and conueniencie I preferre before law, in this point. For, three parts, wherein I might hurt this Nation, by partiality to the Scots, you know doe absolutely lie in my hands and power: for either in difpofition of rents, or whatfoeuer benefit, or in the preferring of them to any dignitie or office, ciuill or Ecclefiafticall, or in calling them to the Parliament, it doeth all fully and onely lie within the compaffe of my Prerogatiue, which are the parts wherein the Scottifh men can receiue either benefite or preferment by the Vnion, and wherein for the care I haue of this people, I am content to binde my felfe with fome reafonable reftrictions.

As for the fourth part, the Naturalizing, which onely lieth in your hands; It is the point wherein they receiue leaft benefit of any: for in that they can obteine nothing, but what they buy by their purfe, or acquire by the felfe fame meanes that you doe. And as for the point of naturalizing, which is the point thought fo fit, and fo precifely belonging to Parliament; not to fpeake of the Common law, wherein as yet I can profeffe no great knowledge, but in the Ciuill law wherein I am a little better verfed, and which in the point of Coniunction of Nations fhould beare a great fway, it being the Law of Nations; I will mainteine two principles in it, which no learned and graue Ciuilian will deny, as being clearely to be proued; both out of the text it felfe in many places, and alfo out of the beft approued Doctours and interpreters of that law; The one, that it is a fpeciall point of the Kings owne Prerogatiue, to make Aliens Citizens, and *donare Ciuitate*; The other, that in any cafe wherein the Law is thought not to be cleare (as fome of your felues doe doubt, that in this cafe of the *poft nati*, the Law of England doth not clearely determine) then in fuch a queftion wherein no pofitiue Law is refolute, *Rex eft Iudex*, for he is *Lex loquens*, and is to fupply the Law, where the Law wants, and if many famous hiftories be to be beleeued, they giue the example for mainteining of this Law in the perfons of the Kings of England and France efpecially, whofe fpeciall Prerogatiue they alleadge it to be. But this I fpeake onely as knowing what belongeth to a King, although in this cafe I preffe no further then that which may agree with your loues, and ftand with the weale and conueniencie of both Nations.

And whereas fome may thinke this Vnion will bring preiudice to fome Townes and Corporations within England; It may bee, a Merchant or two of Briftow, or Yarmouth, may haue an hundred pounds leffe in his packe: But if the Empire gaine, and become the greater, it is no matter: You fee one Corporation is euer againft another, and no priuate Companie can be fet vp, but with fome loffe to another.

For the fuppofed inconueniences rifing from Scotland, they are three. Firft, that there is an euill affection in the Scottifh Nation to the Vnion. Next, the Vnion is incompatible betweene two fuch Nations. Thirdly, that the gaine is fmal or none. If this be fo, to what end do we talke of an Vnion?

Fourth.

For proofe of the firſt point, there is alleadged an auerſeneſſe in the Scottiſh Nation expreſſed in the Inſtrument, both in the preface and body of their Acte; . In the preface, where they declare, That they will remaine an abſolute and free Monarchie; And in the body of the Acte, where they make an exception of the ancient fundamentall Lawes of that Kingdome. And firſt for the generall of their auerſenes , All the maine current in your Lower-houſe ranne this whole Seſſion of Parliament with that opinion , That Scotland was ſo greedy of this Vnion, and apprehended that they ſhould receiue ſo much benefit by it, as they cared not for the ſtrictneſſe of any conditions, ſo they might attaine to the ſubſtance · And yet you now ſay, they are backwards and auerſe from the Vnion. This is a direct contradiction *in adiecto* : For how can they both be beggers and backwards, in one and the ſelfe ſame thing, at the ſame time?

But for anſwere to the particulars, It is an old Schoole point, *Eius eſt explicare, cuius eſt condere.* You cannot interpret their Lawes, nor they yours ; I that made them with their aſſent, can beſt expound them.

And firſt I confeſſe, that the Engliſh Parliaments are ſo long, and the Scottiſh ſo ſhort, that a meane betweene them would doe well : For the ſhortneſſe of their continuing together, was the cauſe of their haſtie miſtaking, by ſetting theſe wordes of exception of fundamentall Lawes in the body of the Acte, which they onely did in preſſing to imitate word by word the Engliſh Inſtrument, wherein the ſame wordes be conteined in your Preface. And as to their meaning and interpretation of that word, I will not onely deliuer it vnto you out of mine owne conceipt, but as it was deliuered vnto mee by the beſt Lawyers of Scotland, both Counſellours and other Lawyers, who were at the making thereof in Scotland, and were Commiſſioners here for performance of the ſame.

Their meaning in the word of Fundamentall Lawes, you ſhall perceiue more fully hereafter, when I handle the obiection of the difference of Lawes : For they intend thereby onely thoſe Lawes whereby confuſion is auoyded, and their Kings deſcent mainteined, and the heritage of the ſucceſſion and Monarchie, which hath bene a Kingdome, to which I am in deſcent, three hundreth yeeres before CHRIST : Not meaning it as you doe, of their Common Law , for they haue none, but that which is called IVS REGIS : and their deſire of continuing a free Monarchie, was onely meant , That all ſuch particular Priuiledges (whereof I ſpake before) ſhould not bee ſo confounded, as for want either of Magiſtrate, Law , or Order, they might fall in ſuch a confuſion, as to become like a naked Prouince, without Law or libertie vnder this Kingdome. I hope you meane not I ſhould ſet Garriſons ouer them, as the Spaniards doe ouer Sicily and Naples, or gouerne them by Commiſſioners , which are ſeldome found ſucceedingly all wiſe and honeſt men.

This I muſt ſay for Scotland, and I may trewly vaunt it; Here I ſit and
gouerne

gouerne it with my Pen, I write and it is done, and by a Clearke of the Councell I gouerne Scotland now, which others could not doe by the fword. And for their auerfenffe in their heart againft the Vnion, It is trew indeede, I proteft they did neuer craue this Vnion of me, nor fought it either in priuate, or the State by letters, nor euer once did any of that Nation preffe mee forward or wifh mee to accelerate that bufineffe. But on the other part, they offered alwayes to obey mee when it fhould come to them, and all honeft men that defire my greatneffe haue beene thus minded, for the perfonall reuerence and regard they beare vnto my Perfon, and any of my reafonable and iuft defires.

I know there are many *Piggots* amongft them, I meane a number of feditious and difcontented particular perfons, as muft be in all Commonwealths, that where they dare, may peraduenture talke lewdly enough: but no Scottifh man euer fpake dishonourably of England in Parliament. For here muft I note vnto you the difference of the two Parliaments in thefe two Kingdomes, for there they muft not fpeake without the Chauncellors leaue, and if any man doe propound or vtter any feditious or vncomely fpeeches, he is ftraight interrupted and filenced by the Chauncellors authoritie: where as here, the libertie for any man to fpeake what hee lift, and as long as he lift, was the onely caufe he was not interrupted.

It hath bin obiected, that there is a great Antipathy of the Lawes and Cuftomes of thefe two Nations. It is much miftaken: for Scotland hath no Common Law as here, but the Law they haue is of three forts.

All the Lawe of Scotland for Tenures, Wards and Liueries, Seigniories and Lands, are drawen out of the Chauncerie of England, and for matters of equitie and in many things elfe, differs from you but in certaine termes: *Iames* the firft, bred here in England, brought the Lawes thither in a written hand. The fecond is Statute lawes, which be their Acts of Parliament, wherein they haue power as you, to make and altar Lawes: and thofe may be looked into by you, for I hope you fhall be no more ftrangers to that Nation. And the principall worke of this Vnion will be, to reconcile the Statute Lawes of both Kingdomes. The third is the Ciuill Law: *Iames* the fift brought it out of France by eftablifhing the Seffion there, according to the forme of the Court of Parliament of Fraunce, which he had feene in the time of his being there: who occupie there the place of Ciuill Iudges in all matters of Plee or controuerfie, yet not to gouerne abfolutely by the Ciuill Law as in Fraunce. For if a man plead that the Law of the Nation is otherwife, it is a barre to the Ciuill, and a good Chauncellor or Prefident, will oftentimes repell and put to filence an Argument that the Lawyers bring out of the Ciuill Law, where they haue a cleare folution in their owne Law. So as the Ciuil Law in Scotland is admitted in no other cafes, but to fupply fuch cafes wherein the Municipall Law is defectiue. Then may you fee it is not fo hard a matter as is thought, to reduce that Countrey to bee vnited with you vnder this Law; which neither are subiect to the Ciuill Lawe, nor yet haue any olde Common Law of their owne, but such as in effect is borrowed from yours. And for their Statute Lawes in Parliament, you may alter and change them as oft as occasion shall require, as you doe here. It hath likewise beene obiected as an other impediment, that in the Parliament of Scotland the King hath not a negatiue voice, but must passe all the Lawes agreed on by the Lords and Commons. Of this I can best resolue you: for I am the eldest Parliament man in Scotland, and haue sit in more Parliaments then any of my Predecessors. I can assure you, that the forme of Parliament there, is nothing inclined to popularitie. About a twentie dayes or such a time before the Parliament, Proclamation is made throughout the Kingdome, to deliuer in to the Kings Clearke of Regifter (whom you heere call the Master of the Rolles) all Bills to be exhibited that Session before a certaine day. Then are they brought vnto the King, and perused and considered by him, and onely such as I allowe of are put into the Chancellors handes to bee propounded to the Parliament, and none others; And if any man in Parliament speake of any other matter then is in this forme first allowed by mee, The Chancellor tells him there is no such Bill allowed by the King.

Besides, when they haue passed them for lawes, they are presented vnto me, and I with my Scepter put into my hand by the Chancellor, must say, *I ratifie and approue all things done in this present Parliament.* And if there bee any thing that I dislike, they rase it out before. If this may bee called a negatiue voyce, then I haue one I am sure in that Parliament.

The last impediment is the French liberties : which is thought so great, as except the Scots forsake Fraunce, England cannot bee vnited to them. If the Scottish Nation would bee so vnwilling to leaue them as is said, it would not lye in their hands : For the League was neuer made betweene the people, as is mistaken, but betwixt the *Princes* onely and their Crownes. The beginning was by a Message from a King of Fraunce, *Charlemaine* I take it (but I cannot certainely remember) vnto a King of Scotland, for a League defensiue and offensiue betweene vs and them against England, Fraunce being at that time in Warres with England.

The like at that time was then desired by England against Fraunce, who also sent their Ambassadours to Scotland. At the first, the Disputation was long maintained in fauour of England, that they being our neerest Neighbours ioyned in one continent, and a strong and powerfull Nation, it was more fitte for the weale and securitie of the State of Scotland, to be in League and Amitie with them, then with a Countrey, though neuer so strong, yet diuided by Sea from vs : especially England lying betwixt vs and them, where we might be sure of a suddaine mischiefe, but behooued to abide the hazard of wind and weather, and other accidents that might hinder our reliefe.

But

But after, when the contrary part of the Argument was maintained: wherein allegation was made, that England euer fought to conquer Scotland, and therefore in regarde of their pretended intereft in the Kingdoome, would neuer keepe any found Amitie with them longer, then they faw their aduantage; whereas France lying more remote and clayming no intereft in the Kingdome, would therefore bee found a more conftant and faithfull friend: It was vnhappily concluded in fauour of the laft partie, through which occafion Scotland gate many mifchiefes after: And it is by the very tenour thereof ordered, to bee renewed and confirmed from King to King fucceffiuely, which accordingly was euer performed by the mediation of their Ambaffadours, and therefore meerely perfonall, and fo was it renewed in the Queene my mothers time, onely betweene the two Kings, and not by affent of Parliament or conuention of the three Eftates, which it could neuer haue wanted if it had beene a League betweene the people. And in my time when it came to be ratified, becaufe it appeared to be in *odium tertii*, it was by me left vnrenewed or confirmed as a thing incompatible to my Perfon, in confideration of my Title to this Crowne. Some Priuiledges indeede in the Merchants fauour for point of Commerce, were renewed and confirmed in my time: wherein for my part of it, there was fcarce three Counfellours more then my Secretarie, to whofe place it belonged, that medled in that matter.

It is trew, that it behooued to be enterteined, as they call it, in the Court of Parliament of *Paris*: but that onely ferues for publication, and not to giue it Authoritie: That Parliament (as you know) being but a Iudiciall Seate of Iudges and Lawyers, and nothing agreeing with the definition or office of our Parliaments in this Ifle. And therefore that any fruites or Priuiledges poffeffed by the League with Fraunce is able now to remaine in Scotland, is impoffible: For ye may be fure, that the French King ftayes onely vpon the fight of the ending of this Vnion, to cut it off himfelfe. Otherwife when this great worke were at an end, I would be forced for the generall care I owe to all my Subiects, to craue of France like Priuiledges to them all as Scotland alreadie enioyes, feeing the perfonall friendfhip remaines as great betweene vs as betweene our Progenitors; and all my Subiects muft be alike deare vnto me: which either hee will neuer grant, and fo all will fall to the ground; or elfe it will turne to the benefite of the whole Ifland: and fo the Scottifh Priuiledges cannot hold longer then my League with France lafteth.

And for another Argument to prooue that this league is only betweene the Kings, and not betweene the people: They which haue Penfions, or are priuie Intelligence giuers in France without my leaue, are in no better cafe by the Law of Scotland, then if they were Penfioners to Spaine.

As for the Scottifh Guard in France, the beginning thereof was, when an Earle of *Boghan* was fent in aide of the French with tenne thoufand men, and there being made Conftable, and hauing obtained a victorie,

was

was murthered with the moſt of the Scottiſh Armie. In recompenſe whereof, and for a future ſecuritie to the Scottiſh Nation, the Scottiſh Guard was ordeined to haue the priuiledge and prerogatiue before all other Guards in guarding the Kings perſon.

And as for the laſt point of this ſubdiuiſion concerning the gaine that England may make by this Vnion, I thinke no wiſe ror honeſt man will aske any ſuch queſtion. For who is ſo ignorant, that doeth not know the gaine will bee great? Doe you not gaine by the Vnion of Wales? And is not Scotland greater then Wales? Shall not your Dominions bee encreaſed of Landes, Seas, and perſons added to your greatneſſe? And are not your Landes and Seas adioyning? For who can ſet downe the limits of the Borders, but as a Mathematicall line or *Idea*? Then will that backe doore bee ſhut, and thoſe portes of *Ianus* be for euer cloſed: you ſhall haue them that were your enemies to moleſt you, a ſure backe to defend you: their bodies ſhall bee your aides, and they muſt bee partners in all your quarrels: Two ſnow-balls put together, make one the greater: Two houſes ioyned, make one the larger: two Caſtle walles made in one, makes one as thicke and ſtrong as both. And doe you not ſee in the Low countreys how auaileable the Engliſh and the Scottiſh are being ioyned together? This is a point ſo plaine, as no man that hath wit or honeſtie, but muſt acknowledge it feelingly.

And where it is obiected that the Scottiſhmen are not tyed to the ſeruice of the King in the warres aboue forty dayes; It is an ignorant miſtaking. For the trewth is, That in reſpect the Kings of Scotland did not ſo abound in Treaſure and money to take vp an Armie vnder pay, as the Kings of England did; Therefore was the Scottiſh Army wont to be rayſed onely by Proclamation, vpon the penaltie of their breach o' alleageance; So as they were all forced to come to the Warre like Snailes who carry their houſe about with them; Euery Nobleman and Gentleman bringing with him their Tents, money, prouiſion for their houſe, victuals of all ſorts, and all other neceſſaries, the King ſupplying them of nothing: Neceſſitie thereupon enforcing a warning to be giuen by the Proclamation of the ſpace of their attendance, without which they could not make their prouiſion accordingly, eſpecially as long as they were within the bounds of Scotland, where it was not lawfull for them to helpe themſelues by the ſpoile or waſting of the Countrey. But neither is there any Law Preſcribing preciſely ſuch a certaine number of dayes, nor yet is it without the limits of the Kings power to keepe them together, as many more dayes as hee liſt, to renew his Proclamations from time to time ſome reaſonable number of dayes, before the expiring of the former, they being euer bound to ſerue and waite vpon him, though it were an hundreth yeere if need were.

Now to conclude, I am glad of this occaſion, that I might *Liberare animam meam*; You are now to recede: when you meete againe, remember
I pray

I pray you, the trewth and sincerity of my meaning, which in seeking
Vnion, is onely to aduance the greatnesse of your Empire seated here in
England; And yet with such caution I wish it, as may stand with the weale
of both States.　What is now desired, hath oft before bene sought when it
could not bee obteined: To refuse it now then, were double iniquitie.
Strengthen your owne felicitie, *London* must bee the Seate of your King,
and Scotland ioyned to this kingdome by a Golden conquest, but cymented with loue, (as I said before) which within will make you strong against
all Ciuill and intestine Rebellion, as without wee will bee compassed and
guarded with our walles of brasse.　Iudge mee charitably, since in this I
seeke your equall good, that so both of you might bee made fearefull to
your Enemies, powerfull in your selues, and auaileable to your friendes.
Studie therefore hereafter to make a good Conclusion, auoyd all delayes,
cut off all vaine questions, that your King may haue his lawfull desire, and
be not disgraced in his iust endes.　And for your securitie in such reasonable points of restrictions, whereunto I am to agree, yee need neuer doubt
of my inclination: For I will not say any thing which I will not promise, nor promise any thing which I will not sweare;
What I sweare I will signe, and what I signe,
I shall with G o D s grace euer
performe.

A SPEACH TO THE
LORDS AND COMMONS
OF THE PARLIAMENT AT
WHITE-HALL,
ON WEDNESDAY THE
XXI. OF MARCH.
ANNO 1609.

 E being now in the middeſt of this ſeaſon appointed for penitence and prayer, it hath ſo fallen out, that theſe two laſt dayes haue bene ſpent in a farre other ſort of exerciſe, I meane in Euchariſticke Sacrifice, and gratulation of thankes, preſented vnto mee by both the parts of this body of Parliament: and therefore to make vp the number of three ; (which is the number of Trinitie, and perfection) I haue thought good to make this the third Day, to be ſpent in this exerciſe.

As ye made mee a faire Preſent indeed in preſenting your thankes and louing dueties vnto mee: So haue I now called you here, to recompence you againe with a great and a rare Preſent, which is a faire and a Chriſtall Mirror; Not ſuch a Mirror wherein you may ſee your owne faces, or ſhadowes; but ſuch a Mirror, or Chriſtall, as through the tranſparantneſſe thereof, you may ſee the heart of your King. The Philoſophers wiſh, That euery mans breaſt were a Chriſtall, where-through his heart might be ſeene, is vulgarly knowne, and I touched it in one of my former Speaches vnto you: But though that were impoſſible in the generall, yet will I now performe this for my part, That as it is a trew Axiome in Diuinitie,

nitie, That *Cor Regis* is *in manu Domini*, So will now fet *Cor Regis in oculis populi*. I know that I can fay nothing at this time, whereof fome of you that are here, haue not at one time or other, heard me fay the like already : Yet as corporall food nourifheth and mainteineth the body, it doeth *Reminifcentia* nourifh and mainteine memory.

I Will reduce to three generall and maine grounds, the principall things that haue bene agitated in this Parliament, and whereof I wil now fpeake.

Firft, the Arrand for which you were called by me; And that was, for fupporting of my ftate, and neceffities.

The fecond is, that which the people are to mooue vnto the King : To reprefent vnto him fuch things, whereby the Subiects are vexed, or wherein the ftate of the Common wealth is to be redreffed: And that is the thing which you call grieuances.

The third ground that hath bene handled amongft you, and not onely in talke amongft you in the Parliament, but euen in many other peoples mouthes, afwell within, as without the Parliament, is of a higher nature then any of the former (though it be but an Incident?) and the reafon is, becaufe it concernes a higher point; And this is a doubt, which hath bene in the heads of fome, of my Intention in two things.

Firft, whether I was refolued in the generall, to continue ftill my gouernment according to the ancient forme of this State, and the Lawes of this Kingdome : Or if I had an intention not to limit my felfe within thofe bounds, but to alter the fame when I thought conuenient, by the abfolute power of a King.

The other branch is anent the Common Law, which fome had a conceit I difliked, and (in refpect that I was borne where another forme of Law was eftablifhed) that I would haue wifhed the Ciuill Law to haue bene put in place of the Common Law for gouernmēt of this people. And the complaint made amongft you of a booke written by doctour *Cowell*, was a part of the occafion of this incident: But as touching my cenfure of that booke, I made it already to bee deliuered vnto you by the Treafurer here fitting, which he did out of my owne directions and notes; and what he faid in my name, that had he directly from me : But what hee fpake of himfelfe therein without my direction, I fhal alwayes make good; for you may be fure I will be loth to make fo honeft a man a lyer, or deceiue your expectations : always within very few dayes my Edict fhall come forth anent that matter, which fhall fully difcouer my meaning.

There was neuer any reafon to mooue men to thinke, that I could like of fuch grounds : For there are two qualities principally, or rather priuations that make Kings fubiect to flatterie; *Credulitie* and *Ignorance* ; and I hope none of them can bee iuftly obiected to mee : For if *Alexander* the great, for all his learning, had bene wife in that point to haue confidered the ſtate of his owne naturall body and diſpoſition, hee would neuer haue thought himſelfe a god. And now to the matter. As it is a Chriſtan duety in euery man, *Reddere rationem fidei*, and not to be aſhamed to giue an account of his profeſſion before men, and Angels, as oft as occaſion ſhall require: So did I euer hold it a neceſſitie of honour in a iuſt and wiſe King, though not to giue an account to his people of his actions, yet clearely to deliuer his heart and intention vnto them vpon euery occaſion. But I muſt inuert my order, and begin firſt with that incident which was laſt in my diuiſion (though higheſt of nature) and ſo goe backward.

He State of MONARCHIE is the ſupremeſt thing vpon earth: For Kings are not onely GODS Lieutenants vpon earth, and ſit vpon GODS throne, but euen by GOD himſelfe they are called Gods. There bee three principall ſimilitudes that illuſtrate the ſtate of MONARCHIE: One taken out of the word of GOD; and the two other out of the grounds of Policie and Philoſophie. In the Scriptures Kings are called Gods, and ſo their power after a certaine relation compared to the Diuine power. Kings are alſo compared to Fathers of families: for a King is trewly *Parens patriæ*, the politique father of his people. And laſtly, Kings are compared to the head of this Microcoſme of the body of man.

Kings are iuſtly called Gods, for that they exerciſe a manner or reſemblance of Diuine power vpon earth: For if you wil conſider the Attributes to God, you ſhall ſee how they agree in the perſon of a King. God hath power to create, or deſtroy, make, or vnmake at his pleaſure, to giue life, or ſend death, to iudge all, and to bee iudged nor accomptable to none: To raiſe low things, and to make high things low at his pleaſure, and to God are both ſoule and body due. And the like power haue Kings: they make and vnmake their ſubiects: they haue power of raiſing, and caſting downe: of life, and of death: Iudges ouer all their ſubiects, and in all cauſes, and yet accomptable to none but God onely. They haue power to exalt low things, and abaſe high things, and make of their ſubiects like men at the Cheſſe; A pawne to take a Biſhop or a Knight, and to cry vp, or downe any of their ſubiects, as they do their money. And to the King is due both the affection of the ſoule, and the ſeruice of the body of his ſubiects: And therefore that reuerend Biſhop here amongſt you, though I heare that by diuers he was miſtaken or not wel vnderſtood, yet did he preach both learnedly and trewly annent this point concerning the power of a King: For what he ſpake of a Kings power in *Abſtracto*, is moſt trew in Diuinitie: For to Emperors, or Kings that are Monarches, their Subiects bodies & goods are due for their defence and maintenance. But if I had bene in his place, I would only haue added two words, which would haue cleared all: For after I had told as a Diuine, what was due by the Subiects to their Kings in generall, I would then haue concluded as an Engliſhman, ſhewing this people,

Yy   That

That as in generall all Subiects were bound to relieue their King; So to exhort them, that as wee liued in a setled state of a Kingdome which was gouerned by his owne fundamentall Lawes and Orders, that according thereunto, they were now (being assembled for this purpose in Parliament) to consider how to helpe such a King as now they had; And that according to the ancient forme, and order established in this Kingdome: putting so, a difference betweene the generall power of a King in Diuinity, and the setled and established State of this Crowne, and Kingdome. And I am sure that the Bishop meant to haue done the same, if hee had not bene straited by time, which in respect of the greatnesse of the presence preaching before me, and such an Auditory, he durst not presume vpon.

As for the Father of a familie, they had of olde vnder the Law of Nature *Patriam potestatem,* which was *Potestatem vitæ & necis,* ouer their children or familie, (I meane such Fathers of families as were the lineall heires of those families whereof Kings did originally come:) For Kings had their first originall from them, who planted and spread themselues in *Colonies* through the world. Now a Father may dispose of his Inheritance to his children, at his pleasure: yea, euen disinherite the eldest vpon iust occasions, and preferre the youngest, according to his liking; make them beggers, or rich at his pleasure; reftraine, or banish out of his presence, as hee findes them giue cause of offence, or restore them in fauour againe with the penitent sinner: So may the King deale with his Subiects.

And lastly, as for the head of the naturall body, the head hath the power of directing all the members of the body to that vse which the iudgement in the head thinkes most conuenient. It may apply sharpe cures, or cut off corrupt members, let blood in what proportion it thinkes fit, and as the body may spare, but yet is all this power ordeined by God *Ad ædificationem, non ad destructionem.* For although God haue power aswell of destruction, as of creation or maintenance; yet will it not agree with the wisedome of God, to exercise his power in the destruction of nature, and ouerturning the whole frame of things, since his creatures were made, that his glory might thereby be the better expressed: So were hee a foolish father that would disinherite or destroy his children without a cause, or leaue off the carefull education of them; And it were an idle head that would in place of phisicke so poyson or phlebotomize the body as might breede a dangerous distemper or destruction thereof.

But now in these our times we are to distinguish betweene the state of Kings in their first originall, and betweene the state of setled Kings and Monarches, that doe at this time gouerne in ciuill Kingdomes: For euen as God, during the time of the olde Testament, spake by Oracles, and wrought by Miracles; yet how soone it pleased him to setle a *Church* which was bought, and redeemed by the blood of his onely Sonne *Christ,* then was there a cessation of both; Hee euer after gouerning his people and Church within the limits of his reueiledwill. So in the first originall of

Kings,

Kings, whereof some had their beginning by Conquest, and some by election of the people, their wills at that time serued for Law; Yet how soone Kingdomes began to be setled in ciuilitie and policie, then did Kings set downe their minds by Lawes, which are properly made by the King onely; but at the rogation of the people, the Kings grant being obteined thereunto. And so the King became to be *Lex loquens*, after a sort, binding himselfe by a double oath to the obseruation of the fundamentall Lawes of his kingdome : *Tacitly*, as by being a King, and so bound to protect aswell the people, as the Lawes of his Kingdome; And *Expresly*, by his oath at his Coronation : So as euery iust King in a setled Kingdome is bound to obserue that paction made to his people by his Lawes, in framing his gouernment agreeable thereunto, according to that paction which God made with *Noe* after the deluge, *Hereafter Seed-time, and Haruest, Cold and Heate, Summer and Winter, and Day and Night shall not cease, so long as the earth remaines.* And therefore a King gouerning in a setled Kingdome, leaues to be a King, and degenerates into a Tyrant, assoone as he leaues off to rule according to his Lawes. In which case the Kings conscience may speake vnto him, as the poore widow said to Philip of Macedon ; Either gouerne according to your Law, *Aut ne Rex sis*. And though no Christian man ought to allow any rebellion of people against their Prince, yet doeth God neuer leaue Kings vnpunished when they transgresse these limits : For in that same Psalme where God saith to Kings, *Vos Dij estis*, hee immediatly thereafter concludes, *But ye shall die like men.* The higher wee are placed, the greater shall our fall be. *Vt casus sic dolor* : the taller the trees be, the more in danger of the winde; and the tempest beats sorest vpon the highest mountaines. Therefore all Kings that are not tyrants, or periured, wil be glad to bound themselues within the limits of their Lawes ; and they that perswade them the contrary, are vipers, and pests, both against them and the Commonwealth. For it is a great difference betweene a Kings gouernment in a setled State, and what Kings in their originall power might doe in *Indiuiduo vago*. As for my part, I thanke God, I haue euer giuen good proofe, that I neuer had intention to the contrary : And I am sure to goe to my graue with that reputation and comfort, that neuer King was in all his time more carefull to haue his Lawes duely obserued, and himselfe to gouerne thereafter, then I.

I conclude then this point touching the power of Kings, with this Axiome of Diuinitie, That as to dispute what God may doe, is Blasphemie; but *quid vult Deus*, that Diuines may lawfully, and doe ordinarily dispute and discusse; for to dispute *A Posse ad Esse* is both against Logicke and Diuinitie: So is it sedition in Subiects, to dispute what a King may do in the height of his power : But iust Kings wil euer be willing to declare what they wil do, if they wil not incurre the curse of God. I wil not be content that my power be disputed vpon: but I shall euer be willing to make the reason appeare of all my doings, and rule my actions according to my Lawes.

The other branch of this incident is concerning the Common Law, being conceiued by some, that I contemned it, and preferred the Ciuill Law thereunto. As I haue already said, Kings Actions (euen in the secretest places) are as the actions of those that are set vpon the Stages, or on the tops of houses : and I hope neuer to speake that in priuate, which I shall not auow in publique, and Print it if need be, (as I said in my BASILICON DORON.) For it is trew, that within these few dayes I spake freely my minde touching the Common Law in my Priuie Chamber, at the time of my dinner, which is come to all your eares; and the same was likewise related vnto you by my Treasurer; and now I will againe repeate and con-firme the same my selfe vnto you. First, as a King I haue least cause of any man to dislike the Common Law : For no Law can bee more fauou-rable and aduantagious for a King, and extendeth further his Prerogatiue, then it doeth : And for a King of England to despise the Common Law, it is to neglect his owne Crowne. It is trew, that I doe greatly esteeme the Ciuill Law, the profession thereof seruing more for generall learning, and being most necessary for matters of Treatie with all forreine Nations : And I thinke that if it should bee taken away, it would make an entrie to Barbarisme in this Kingdome, and would blemish the honour of England : For it is in a maner LEX GENTIVM, and maintaineth In-tercourse with all forreine Nations : but I onely allow it to haue course here, according to those limits of Iurisdiction, which the Common Law it selfe doeth allow it : And therefore though it bee not fit for the generall gouernment of the people here ; it doeth not follow, it should be extinct, no more, then because the Latine tongue is not the Mother or Radi-call Language of any Nation in the world at this time, that therefore the English tongue should onely now be learned in this Kingdome, which were to bring in Barbarisme. My meaning therefore is not, to preferre the Ciuill Law before the Common Law ; but onely that it should not be extinguished, and yet so bounded, (I meane to such Courts and Causes) as haue beene in ancient vse; As the Ecclesiasticall Courts, Court of Ad-miraltie, Court of Requests, and such like, reseruing euer to the Com-mon Law to meddle with the fundamentall Lawes of this Kingdome, either concerning the Kings Prerogatiue, or the possessions of Subiects, in any questions, either betweene the King, and any of them, or amongst themselues, in the points of *Meum & tuum.* For it is trew, that there is no Kingdome in the world, not onely Scotland, but not France, nor Spaine, nor any other Kingdome gouerned meerely by the Ciuill Law, but euery one of them hath their owne municipall Lawes agreeable to their Cu-stomes, as this Kingdome hath the Common Law : Nay, I am so farre from disallowing the Common Law, as I protest, that if it were in my hand to chuse a new Law for this Kingdome, I would not onely preferre it before any other Nationall Law, but euen before the very Iudici-all Law of *Moyses* : and yet I speake no blasphemie in preferring it for

conue-

conueniencie to this Kingdome, and at this time, to the very Law of God: For God gouerned his felected people by thefe three Lawes, *Ceremoniall*, *Morall*, and *Iudiciall* : The *Iudiciall*, being onely fit for a certaine people, and a certaine time, which could not ferue for the general of all other people and times. As for example, If the Law of hanging for Theft, were turned here to reftitution of treble or quadruple, as it was in the Law of *Moyfes*, what would become of all the middle Shires, and all the Irifhrie and Highlanders ? But the maine point is , That if the fundamentall Lawes of any Kingdome fhould be altered , who fhould difcerne what is *Meum & tuum*, or how fhould a King gouerne ? It would be like the *Gregorian* Calender, which deftroyes the old , and yet doeth this new trouble all the debts and Accompts of Traffiques and Merchandizes : Nay by that accompt I can neuer tell mine owne aage; for now is my Birth-day remooued by the fpace of ten dayes neerer me then it was before the change. But vpon the other part, though I haue in one point preferred our Common Law , concerning our vfe, to the very Law of GOD; yet in another refpect I muft fay, both our Law and all Lawes elfe are farre inferiour to that Iudiciall Law of GOD; for no booke nor Law is perfect nor free from corruption, except onely the booke and Law of GOD. And therefore I could wifh fome three things fpecially to be purged & cleared in the Common Law; but alwayes by the aduife of Parliament: For the King with his Parliament here are abfolute, (as I vnderftand) in making or forming of any fort of Lawes.

First I could wifh that it were written in our vulgar Language: for now it is in an old, mixt, and corrupt Language, onely vnderftood by Lawyers: whereas euery Subiect ought to vnderftand the Law vnder which he liues: For fince it is our plea againft the Papifts, that the language in GODs Seruice ought not to be in an vnknowne tongue, according to the rule in the Law of *Moyfes*, That the Law fhould be written in the fringes of the Priefts garment, and fhould be publikely read in the eares of all the people: fo mee thinkes ought our Law to be made as plaine as can be to the people, that the excufe of ignorance may be taken from them , for conforming themfelues thereunto.

Next, our Common Law hath not a fetled Text in all Cafes, being chiefly grounded either vpon old Cuftomes, or elfe vpon the Reports and Cafes of Iudges, which ye call *Refponfa Prudentum*. The like whereof is in all other Lawes: for they are much ruled by Prefidents (faue onely in *Denmarke* and *Norway* , where the letter of the Law refolues all doubts without any trouble to the Iudge,) But though it be trew, that no Text of Law can be fo certaine, wherein the circumftances will not make a variation in the Cafe, (for in this aage, mens wits increafe fo much by ciuilitie, that the circumftances of euery particular cafe varies fo much from the generall Text of Law, as in the Ciuill Law it felfe, there are therefore fo many Doctors that coment vpon the Text, & neuer a one almoft agrees with another; Otherwife there needed no Iudges, but the bare letter of the

Law.)

Law.) Yet could I wiſh that ſome more certaintie were ſet downe in this caſe by Parliament : for ſince the very Reports themſelues are not alwayes ſo binding, but that diuers times Iudges doe diſclaime them, and recede from the iudgment of their predeceſſors; it were good, that vpon a mature deliberation, the expoſition of the Law were ſet downe by Acte of Parliament, and ſuch reports therein confirmed, as were thought fit to ſerue for Law in all times hereafter, and ſo the people ſhould not depend vpon the bare opinions of Iudges, and vncertaine Reports.

And laſtly, there be in the Common Law diuers contrary Reports, and Preſidents : and this corruption doeth likewiſe concerne the Statutes and Acts of Parliament, in reſpect there are diuers croſſe and cuffing Statutes, and ſome ſo penned, as they may be taken in diuers, yea contrary ſences. And therefore would I wiſh both thoſe Statutes and Reports, aſwell in the Parliament as Common Law, to be once maturely reuiewed, and reconciled ; And that not onely all contrarieties ſhould be ſcraped out of our Bookes, but euen that ſuch penall Statutes as were made, but for the vſe of the time (from breach whereof no man can be free) which doe not now agree with the condition of this our time, might likewiſe be left out of our bookes, which vnder a tyrannous or auaritious King could not be endured: And this reformation might (me thinkes) bee made a worthy worke, and well deſerues a Parliament to be ſet of purpoſe for it.

I know now that being vpon this point of the Common Law, you looke to heare my opinion concerning *Prohibitions*; and I am not ignorant that I haue bene thought to be an enemie to all *Prohibitions*, and an vtter ſtayer of them : But I will ſhortly now informe you what hath bene my courſe in proceeding therein. It is trew that in reſpect of diuers honorable Courts, and Iuriſdictions planted in this Kingdome, I haue often wiſhed that euery Court had his owne trew limit, and iuriſdiction clearely ſet downe, and certainly knowne ; which if it be exceeded by any of them, or that any of them encroch one vpon another, then I grant that a *Prohibition* in that caſe is to goe out of the *Kings Bench*, but chieflieſt out of the *Chancery*; for other Benches I am not yet ſo well reſolued of their Iuriſdiction in that point. And for my part, I was neuer againſt *Prohibitions* of this nature, nor the trew vſe of them, which is indeed to keepe euery Riuer within his owne banks and channels. But when I ſaw the ſwelling and ouerflowing of *Prohibitions* in a farre greater abundance then euer before, euery Court ſtriuing to bring in moſt moulture to their owne Mill, by multitudes of Cauſes, which is a diſeaſe very naturall to all Courts and Iuriſdictions in the world; Then dealt I with this Cauſe, and that at two ſeuerall times, once in the middeſt of Winter, and againe in the middeſt of the next following Summer; At euery of which times I ſpent three whole daies in that labour. And then after a large hearing, I told them as *Chriſt* ſaid concerning Mariage, *Ab initio non fuit ſic.* For as God conteins the Sea within his owne bounds and marches (as it is in the *Pſalmes*,) So is it my office to make

euery

euery Court conteine himſelfe within his own limits; And therfore I gaue admonitions to both ſides: To the other Courts, that they ſhould be carefull hereafter euery of them, to conteine themſelues within the bounds of their owne Iuriſdictions; and to the Courts of Common Law, that they ſhould not bee ſo forward, and prodigall in multiplying their *Prohibitions.* Two cautions I willed them to obſerue in graunting their *Prohibitions:* Firſt, that they ſhould be graunted in a right and lawfull forme: And next, that they ſhould not grant them, but vpon a iuſt and reaſonable cauſe. As to the forme, it was, That none ſhould be graunted by any one particular Iudge, or in time of Vacation, or in any other place, but openly in Court: And to this the Iudges themſelues gaue their willing aſſent. And as to the Cauſe, That they ſhould not be granted vpon euery ſleight ſurmiſe, or information of the partie, but alwayes that a due and graue examination ſhould firſt precede. Otherwiſe if *Prohibitions* ſhould raſhly, and headily be granted, then no man is the more ſecure of his owne, though hee hath gotten a Sentence with him: For as good haue no Law, or Sentence, as to haue no execution thereof. A poore Miniſter with much labour and expenſe, hauing exhauſted his poore meanes, and being forced to forbeare his ſtudie, and to become *non reſident* from his flocke, obtaines a *Sentence,* and then when hee loookes to enioy the fruits thereof, he is defrauded of all by a *Prohibition,* according to the parable of Chriſt, That night when hee thinkes himſelfe moſt happy, ſhall his ſoule be taken from him: And ſo is he tortured like *Tantalus,* who when he hath the Apple at his mouth, and that he is gaping and opening his mouth to receiue it, then muſt it be pulled from him by a *Prohibition,* and he not ſuffered to taſte thereof. So as to conclude this point, I put a difference betweene the trew vſe of *Prohibitions,* and the ſuperabounding abuſe thereof: for as a thing which is good, ought not therefore bee abuſed; ſo ought not the lawfull vſe of a good thing be forborne, becauſe of the abuſe thereof.

Now the ſecond generall ground whereof I am to ſpeake, concernes the matter of *Grieuances:* There are two ſpeciall cauſes of the peoples preſenting *Grieuances* to their King in time of Parliament. Firſt, for that the King cannot at other times be ſo well informed of all the *Grieuances* of his people, as in time of Parliament, which is the repreſentatiue body of the whole Realme. Secondly, the Parliament is the higheſt Court of Iuſtice, and therefore the fitteſt place where diuers natures of *Grieuances* may haue their proper remedie, by the eſtabliſhment of good and wholſome Lawes. But though my Speech was before directed to the whole Body of Parliament; yet in this caſe I muſt addreſſe my Speech in ſpeciall to you of the Lower Houſe.

I am now then to recommend vnto your conſiderations the matter and manner of your handling and preſenting of *Grieuances.* As for the manner, though I will not denie, but that yee, repreſenting the Body of the people, ple,

ple, may as it were both *opportune* and *inopportune* (I meane either in Parliament as a Body, or out of Parliament as priuate men) prefent your *Grieuances* vnto mee; yet would I haue you to vfe this caution in your behauiour in this point: which is, that your *Grieuances* be not as it were greedily fought out by you, or taken vp in the ftreetes (as one faid) thereby to fhew a willingneffe that you would haue a fhew made, that there are many abufes in the gouernment, and many caufes of complaint: but that according to your firft inftitution, ye fhould only meddle with fuch *Grieuances*, as your felues doe know had neede of reformation, or had informations thereof in your countreys for which you ferue, and not fo to multiply them, as might make it noifed amongft the people, that all things in the gouernment were amiffe and out of frame: For euen at the beginning of this very Seffion of Parliament, the generall name of *Grieuances* being mentioned among you, fuch a conceipt came in the heads of many, that you had a defire to multiply and make a great mufter of them, as euery one exhibited what his particular fpleene ftirred him vnto. Indeed there fell out an accident vpon this occafion, for which I haue reafon to thanke you of the Lower houfe, I meane for your fire worke; wherein I confeffe you did Honour to me; and right to your felues : For hauing one afternoone found many *Grieuances* clofely prefented in papers, and fo all thruft vp in a facke together, (rather like *Pafquils*, then any lawfull Complaints) farre againft your owne Orders, and diuers of them proceeding from grudging and murmuring fpirits; you, vpon the hearing read two or three of the firft lines of diuers of them, were not content with a publique confent to condemne them, and to difcharge any further reading of them, but you alfo made a publique bonefire of them. In this, I fay, you fhewed your care and ieloufie of my Honour, and I fent you thankes for it by the Chancellour of the Exchequer, a member of your owne Houfe, who by your appointment, that fame night acquainted me with your proceedings; And by him alfo I promifed at that time, that you fhould heare more of my thankes for the fame at the firft occafion; And now I tell you it my felfe, that you may know how kindely I take your duetifull behauiour in this cafe. But fince this was a good effect of an euill caufe, I muft not omit alfo to admonifh you vpon the other part, to take a courfe amongft your felues, to preuent the like accident in all times hereafter: otherwife the Lower houfe may become a place for *Pafquils*, and at another time fuch *Grieuances* may be caft in amongft you, as may conteine Treafon or fcandal againft Me, or my Pofterity. Therfore in this cafe, looke ouer your ancient Orders, & follow them, and fuffer not hereafter any petitions or *Grieuances* to be deliuered obfcurely or in the darke, but openly and auowedly in your Publique houfe, and there to be prefented to the Speaker. And as to the matter of your *Grieuances*, I wifh you here now to vnderftand me rightly. And becaufe I fee many writing and noting, I will craue your pardons, to holde you a little longer by fpeaking the more diftinctly, for feare of miftaking.

First

First then, I am not to finde fault that you informe your selues of the particular iust *Grieuances* of the people; Nay, I must tell you, ye can neither be iust nor faithfull to me, or to your Countreys that trust and imploy you, if you doe it not : For true Plaints proceede not from the persons imployed, but from the Body represented, which is the people. And it may very well bee, that many Directions and Commissions iustly giuen forth by me, may be abused in the Execution thereof, vpon the people : and yet I neuer to receiue information, except it come by your meanes, at such a time as this is; (as in the case of *Stephen* Procter.) But I would wish you to be carefull to auoide three things in the matter of *Grieuances.*

First, that you doe not meddle with the maine points of Gouernment; that is my craft : *tractent fabrilia fabri;* to meddle with that, were to lesson me : I am now an old King; for sixe and thirtie yeeres haue I gouerned in *Scotland* personally, and now haue I accomplished my apprenticeship of seuen yeeres heere; and seuen yeeres is a great time for a Kings experience in Gouernment : Therefore there would not bee too many *Phormios* to teach *Hannibal:* I must not be taught my Office.

Secondly, I would not haue you meddle with such ancient Rights of mine, as I haue receiued from my Predecessors, possessing them, *More Maiorum :* such things I would bee sorie should bee accounted for *Grieuances.* All nouelties are dangerous as well in a politique as in a naturall Body : And therefore I would be loth to be quarrelled in my ancient Rights and possessions : for that were to iudge mee vnworthy of that which my Predecessors had, and left me.

And lastly, I pray you beware to exhibite for *Grieuance* any thing that is established by a setled Law, and whereunto (as you haue already had a proofe) you know I will neuer giue a plausible answere : For it is an vndutifull part in Subiects to presse their King, wherein they know beforehand he will refuse them. Now, if any Law or Statute be not conuenient, let it be amended by Parliament, but in the meane time terme it not a *Grieuance :* for to be grieued with the Law, is to be grieued with the King, who is sworne to bee the Patron and mainteiner thereof. But as all men are flesh, and may erre in the execution of Lawes; So may ye iustly make a *Grieuance* of any abuse of the Law, distinguishing wisely betweene the faults of the person, and the thing it selfe. As for example, Complaints may be made vnto you of the high Commissioners : If so be, trie the abuse, and spare not to complaine vpon it, but say not there shall be no Commission; For that were to abridge the power that is in me : and I will plainely tell you, That something I haue with my selfe resolued annent that point, which I meane euer to keepe, except I see other great cause · which is, That in regard the high Commission is of so high a nature, from which there is no appellation to any other Court, I haue thought good to restraine it onely to the two Archbishops, where before it was common amongst a great part of the Bishops in England. This Law I haue set to my selfe, and therefore you may be affured, that I will neuer finde fault with any man, nor thinke him the more Puritane, that will complaine to me out of Parliament, afwell as in Parliament, of any error in execution thereof, fo that hee prooue it; Otherwife it were but a calumnie. Onely I would bee loath that any man fhould grieue at the Commiffion it felfe, as I haue already faid. Yee haue heard (I am fure) of the paines I tooke both in the caufes of the Admiralty, and of the Prohibitions: If any man therefore will bring me any iuft com-plaints vpon any matters of fo high a nature as this is, yee may affure your felues that I will not fpare my labour in hearing it. In faith you neuer had a more painefull King, or that will be readier in his perfon to determine caufes that are fit for his hearing. And when euer any of you fhall make experience of me in this point, ye may be fure neuer to want acceffe, nor ye fhall neuer come wrong to me, in, or out of Parliament.

And now to conclude this purpofe of *Grieuances*, I haue one generall *grieuance* to commend vnto you, and that in the behalfe of the Countreys from whence ye come. And this is, to pray you to beware that your *Grie-uances* fauour not of particular mens thoughts, but of the generall griefes rifing out of the mindes of the people, and not out of the humor of the propounder. And therefore I would wifh you to take heede carefully, and confider of the partie that propounds the *grieuance*: for ye may (if ye lift) eafily difcerne whether it bee his owne paffion, or the peoples griefe, that makes him to fpeake: for many a man will in your houfe propound a *Grieuance* out of his owne humour, becaufe (peraduenture) he accounts highly of that matter: and yet the countrey that imployes him, may per-haps either be of a contrary minde, or (at leaft) little care for it. As for example, I affure you, I can very well fmell betweene a Petition that mooues from a generall *Grieuance*, or fuch a one as comes from the fpleene of fome particular perfon, either againft Ecclefiafticall gouernment in generall, or the perfon of any one Noble man, or Commiffioner in particular.

Nd now the third point remaines to bee fpoken of; which is the caufe of my calling of this Parliament. And in this I haue done but as I vfe to doe in all my life, which is to leaue mine owne errand hindmoft.

It may bee you did wonder that I did not fpeake vnto you publikely at the beginning of this Seffion of Parliament, to tell you the caufe of your calling, as I did (if I bee rightly remembred) in euery Seffion before. But the trewth is, that becaufe I call you at this time for my particular Errand, I thought it fitter to bee opened vnto you by my Treafurer, who is my publike and moft principall Officer in matters of that nature, then that I fhould doe it my felfe: for I confeffe I am leffe naturally eloquent, and haue greater caufe to diftruft mine elocution in matters of this nature, then in any other thing. I haue made my Treafurer already to giue you a very cleere and trew accompt both of my hauing, and expenfes: A fauour I
confeffe,

confeſſe, that Kings doe ſeldome beſtow vpon their Subiects, in making them ſo particularly acquainted with their ſtate. If I had not more then cauſe, you may be ſure I would be loth to trouble you : But what he hath affirmed in this, vpon the honour of a Gentleman, (whom you neuer had cauſe to diſtruſt for his honeſtie,) that doe I now confirme and auow to be trew in the word and honour of a King ; And therein you are bound to beleeue me. Duetie I may iuſtly claime of you as my Subiects ; and one of the branches of duetie which Subiects owe to their Soueraigne, is Supply: but in what quantitie, and at what time, that muſt come of your loues. I am not now therefore to diſpute of a Kings power, but to tell you what I may iuſtly craue, and expect with your good wills. I was euer againſt all extremes ; and in this caſe I will likewiſe wiſh you to auoyd them on both ſides. For if you faile in the one, I might haue great cauſe to blame you as Parliament men, being called by me for my Errands : And if you fall into the other extreme, by ſupply of my neceſſities without reſpectiue care to auoyd oppreſſion or partialitie in the Leuie, both I and the Countrey will haue cauſe to blame you.

When I thinke vpon the compoſition of this body of Parliament, I doe well conſider that the Vpper houſe is compoſed of the Seculer Nobilitie, who are hereditary Lords of Parliament ; and of Biſhops, that are liue Renter Barons of the ſame : And therefore what is giuen by the Vpper houſe, is giuen onely from the trew body of that Houſe, and out of their owne purpoſes that doe giue it ; whereas the Lower houſe is but the repreſentatiue body of the Commons, and ſo what you giue, you giue it aſwell for others, as for your ſelues : and therefore you haue the more reaſon to eſchew both the extreames. On the one part, ye may the more eaſily be liberall, ſince it comes not all from your ſelues ; and yet vpon the other part, if yee giue more then is fit for good and louing Subiects to yeeld vpon ſuch neceſſary occaſions, yee abuſe the King, and hurt the people ; And ſuch a gift I will neuer accept : For in ſuch a caſe you might deceiue a King, in giuing your flattering conſent to that which you know might moue the people generally to grudge and murmure at it, and ſo ſhould the King find himſelfe deceiued in his *Calcule*, and the people likewiſe grieued in their hearts ; the loue and poſſeſſion of which (I proteſt) I did, and euer will accompt the greateſt earthly ſecuritie (next the fauour of GOD) to any wiſe or iuſt King. For though it was vainely ſaide by one of your Houſe, That yee had need to beware, that by giuing mee too much, your throats were not in danger of cutting at your comming home : yet may ye aſſure your ſelues, that I will euer bee lothe to preſſe you to doe that which may wrong the people, and make you iuſtly to beare the blame thereof. But that yee may the better bee acquainted with my inclination, I will appeale to a number of my Priuie Councell here preſent, if that before the calling of this Parliament, and when I found that the neceſſitie of my eſtate required ſo great a ſupply, they found me more deſirous to obtaine

that

that which I was forced to feeke, then carefull that the people might yeeld me a fupply in fo great a meafure as my neceffities required, without their too great loffe. And you all that are Parliament men, and here prefent of both Houfes can beare me witneffe, if euer I burthened or imployed any of you for any particular Subfidies, or fummes by name, further then my laying open the particular neceffities of my ftate, or yet if euer I fpake to any Priuie Councellour, or any of my learned Councell, to labour voyces for me to this end; I euer detefted the hunting for *Emendicata Suffragia*. A King that will rule and gouerne iuftly, muft haue regard to Confcience, Honour and Iudgement, in all his great Actions, (as your felfe M. Speaker remembred the other day.) And therefore ye may affure your felues, That I euer limit all my great Actions within that compaffe. But as vpon the one fide, I doe not defire you fhould yeeld to that extreame, in giuing me more then (as I faid formerly) vpon fuch neceffary occafions are fit for good and louing Subiects to yeeld; For that were to giue me a purfe with a knife: So on the other fide, I hope you will not make vaine pretences of wants, out of caufeleffe apprehenfions, or idle excufes, neither cloake your owne humours (when your felues are vnwilling) by alledging the pouertie of the people. For although I will be no leffe iuft, as a King, to fuch perfons, then any other: (For my Iuftice with Gods grace, fhalbe alike open to all) yet ye muft thinke I haue no reafon to thanke them, or gratifie them with any fuits or matters of grace, when their errand fhall come in my way; And yet no man can fay, that euer I quarrelled any man for refufing mee a Subfidie, if hee did it in a moderate fafhion, and with good reafons. For him that denies a good Law, I will not fpare to quarrell: But for graunting or denying money, it is but an effect of loue: And therefore for the point of my neceffities, I onely defire that I be not refufed in that which of duety I ought to haue: For I know if it were propounded in the generall amongft you, whether the Kings wants ought to be relieued or not, there is not one of you, that would make queftion of it. And though in a fort this may feeme to be my particular; yet it can not bee diuided from the generall good of the Common wealth; For the King that is *Parens Patriæ*, telles you of his wants. Nay, *Patria ipfa* by him fpeakes vnto you. For if the King want, the State wants, and therefore the ftrengthening of the King is the preferuation and the ftanding of the State; And woe be to him that diuides the weale of the King from the weale of the Kingdome. And as that King is miferable (how rich foeuer he bee) that raines ouer a poore people, (for the hearts and riches of the people, are the Kings greateft treafure;) So is that Kingdome not able to fubfift, how rich and potent foeuer the people be, if their King wants meanes to mainaine his State: for the meanes of your King are the finewes of the kingdome both in warre and peace: for in peace I muft minifter iuftice vnto you, and in warre I muft defend you by Armes: but neither of thefe can I do without fufficient means, which muft come from

your

your Aide and Supply. I confeſſe it is farre againſt my nature to be bur-
thenſome to my people : for it cannot but grieue me to craue of others,
that was borne to be begged of. It is trew, I craue more then euer King
of England did ; but I haue farre greater and iuſter cauſe and reaſon to
craue, then euer King of England had. And though my Treaſurer hath at
length declared the reaſons vnto you of my neceſſities, and of a large ſupply
that he craued for the ſame, wherein he omitted no arguments that can be
vſed for that purpoſe ; yet will I my ſelfe now ſhortly remember you ſome
of the weightieſt reaſons that come in my head, to proue the equitie of
my demaund.

Firſt, ye all know, that by the acceſſion of more Crownes, which in my
Perſon I haue brought vnto you, my charge muſt be the greater in all reaſon : For the greater your King be, both in his dominion and number of
Subiects, he cannot but be forced thereby to be at the more charge, and it is
the more your honour, ſo to haue it.

Next, that poſteritie and iſſue which it hath pleaſed God to ſend me for
your vſe, cannot but bring neceſſarily with it a greater proportion of
charge. You all know that the late Queene of famous memory (notwithſtanding her orbitie) had much giuen vnto her, and more then euer any of
her predeceſſors had before her.

Thirdly, the time of creation of my Sonne doeth now draw neere, which
I chuſe for the greater honour to bee done in this time of Parliament. As
for him I ſay no more ; the ſight of himſelfe here ſpeakes for him.

Fourthly, it is trew I haue ſpent much ; but yet if I had ſpared any of
thoſe things, which cauſed a great part of my expenſe, I ſhould haue diſho-
nored the kingdome, my ſelfe, and the late Queene. Should I haue ſpared the funerall of the late Queene ? or the ſolemnitie of mine and my
wiues entrie into this Kingdome, in ſome honourable ſort? or ſhould I
haue ſpared our entrie into *London*, or our Coronation? And when moſt
of the Monarches, and great Princes in Chriſtendome ſent their Ambaſſadours to congratulate my comming hither, and ſome of them came in
perſon, was I not bound, both for my owne honour, and the honour of
the Kingdome, to giue them good entertainement? But in caſe it might be
obiected by ſome, that it is onely vpon occaſions of warre, that Kings
obtaine great Supplies from their Subiects : notwithſtanding my interne
Peace, I am yet in a kinde of warre, which if it bee without, the more is
your ſafetie : For (as the Treaſurer tolde you at large) I am now forced both
in reſpects of State, and my promiſe, and for the generall cauſe of Religion, to ſend a Supply of forces to *Cleues*, and how long that occaſion
may laſt, or what greater ſupply the neceſſitie of that Errand may draw
mee vnto, no man can yet tell. Beſides that, although I haue put downe
that forme of warlike keeping of *Barwicke* ; yet are all thoſe commaunders
my penſioners that were the late Queenes ſouldiers, And I hope I ſuſtaine
a prettie Seminarie of Souldiers in my Forts within this Kingdome, beſides

the

the two cautionary Townes in the Low-countreys, *Flushing* and *Brill*. And as for *Ireland*, yee all know how vncertaine my charges are euer there, that people being so easily stirred, partly through their barbaritie, and want of ciuilitie, and partly through their corruption in Religion to breake foorth in rebellions. Yee know, how vnlooked for a Rebellion brake foorth there the last yeere, which could not but put mee to extraordinary charges. Besides I doe maintaine there continually an Armie, which is a goodly Seminarie of expert and old Souldiers. And I dare neuer suffer the same to be diminished, till this Plantation take effect, which (no doubt) is the greatest moate that euer came in the Rebels eyes: and it is to be looked for, that if euer they will bee able to make any stirre, they will presse at it by all meanes, for the preuenting and discouraging this Plantation. Now it is trew, that besides all these honourable and necessary occasions of my charge, I haue spent much in liberalitie: but yet I hope you will consider, that what I haue giuen, hath bene giuen amongst you; and so what comes in from you, goes out againe amongst you. But it may be thought that I haue giuen much amongst Scottishmen. Indeed if I had not beene liberall in rewarding some of my old seruants of that Nation, ye could neuer haue had reason to expect my thankefulnesse towards any of you that are more lately become my Subiects, if I had beene ingrate to the old: And yet yee will find, that I haue dealt twice as much amongst Englifh men as I haue done to Scottishmen. And therefore he that in your House was not afhamed to affirme, that the siluer and gold did so abound in *Edenburgh*, was very farre miftaken; but I wifh him no worse punifhment, then that hee fhould onely liue vpon such profit of the money there. But I hope you will neuer miflike me for my liberalitie, since I can looke very few of you this day in the face, that haue not made suits to mee, at leaft for some thing, either of honour or profit. It is trew, a Kings liberalitie muft neuer be dried vp altogether: for then he can neuer maintaine nor oblige his seruants and well deseruing Subiects: But that vaftnesse of my expence is paft, which I vfed the firft two or three yeeres after my comming hither: And, as I oft vfed to say, that Chriftmas and open tide is ended: For at my firft comming here, partly ignorance of this State (which no man can acquire but by time and experience) and partly the forme of my comming being so honourable and miraculous, enforced me to extend my liberalitie so much the more at the beginning. Ye saw I made Knights then by hundreths, and Barons in great numbers: but I hope you find I doe not so now, nor minde not to doe so hereafter. For to conclude this point anent expences, I hold that a Kings expence muft alwayes bee honourable, though not waftefull, and the charges of your King in maintaining thofe ancient honourable formes of liuing that the former Kings of *England* my Predeceffours haue done, and his liuing to bee ruled according to the proportion of his greatnesse, is afwell for the honour of your Kingdome,

as

as of your King. Now this cannot be supplied out of the ayre or liquid e-lements, but must come from the people. And for remouing of that diffi-dence which men may haue, that I minde not to liue in any wastefull sort hereafter, will you but looke vpon my selfe and my posteritie; and if there were no more but that, it will teach you that if I were but a naturall man, I must needs bee carefull of my expences : For as for my owne person, I hope none that knowes me well, can thinke me but as little inclined to any prodigall humours of vnnecessary things, as any other reasonable man of a farre meaner estate. Therefore since (as I haue said) I cannot be helped but from the people; I assure my selfe that you will well allow mee such measure of Supplie, as the people may beare, and support him with more Honourable meanes then others haue had, that (as I may say without vaunting) hath brought you more Honour then euer you had : For I hope there are no good Subiects either within, or out of the Parliament House, that would not be content for setting streight once and setling the Honourable State of their King, to spare so much euery one of them out of their purses, which peraduenture they would in one night throw a-way at Dice or Cards, or bestow vpon a horse for their fancies, that might breake his necke or his legge the next morning : Nay I am sure euery good Subiect would rather chuse to liue more sparingly vpon his owne, then that his Kings State should be in want.

For conclusion then of this purpose, I wish you now to put a speedie end to your businesse. Freenesse in giuing graceth the gift, *Bis dat, qui citò dat*; The longer I want helpe, the greater will my debt still rise : and so must I looke for the greater helpes. And now I would pray you to turne your eyes with mee from home, and looke vpon forreine States. Consider that the eyes of all forreine States are vpon this affaire, and in expectation what the successe thereof will be ; And what can they thinke, if ye depart without relieuing mee in that proportion that may make me able to maintaine my State, but that either ye are vnwilling to helpe mee, thinking me vnworthy thereof, or at least that my State is so desperate, as it cannot be repaired, and so that the Parliament parts in disgrace with the King, and the King in distaste with the Parliament, which cannot but weaken my reputation both at home and abroad ? For of this you may be assured, that forreine Princes care the more one for an other, if they may haue reason to expect that they may bee able to doe them good or harme in Retribution. And ye know, that if a King fall to be contem-ned with his neighbours, that cannot but bring an oppression and warre by them vpon him, and then will it be too late to support the King, when the cure is almost desperate. Things foreseene and preuented, are euer ea-sliest remedied : And therefore I would aduise you now so to settle your businesse, as ye may not take in hand so many things at once, as may both crosse my errand, and euery one of them crosse another. Yee remem-ber the French Prouerbe, *Qui trop embrasse, rien estreint*; We are not in this

Parliament to make our Teftament, as if wee fhould neuer meete againe, and that all things that were to be done in any Parliament, were to be done at this time: and yet for filling vp of your vacant houres, I will recommend to your confideration fuch nature of things, as are to bee fpecially thought vpon in thefe times. Firft I will beginne at GOD: for the beginning with him makes all other actions to bee bleffed: And this I meane by the caufe of Religion. Next I will fpeake of fome things that concerne the Common-wealth. And thirdly, matters of Pleafure and ornament to the Kingdome.

As for Religion, we haue all great caufe to take heed vnto it; Papifts are waxed as proud at this time as euer they were, which makes many to think they haue fome new plot in hand. And although the pooreft fort of them bee (God be thanked) much decreafed, yet doeth the greater fort of them dayly increafe, efpecially among the fœminine Sexe; nay they are waxed fo proud, that fome fay, no man dare prefent them, nor Iudges meddle with them, they are fo backed and vpholden by diuers great Courtiers. It is a furer and better way to remooue the materials of fire before they bee kindled, then to quench the fire when once it is kindled.

Nam leuius ladit quicquid prauidimus ante.

I doe not meane by this to mooue you to make ftronger Lawes then are already made, but fee thofe Lawes may bee well executed that are in force; otherwife they cannot but fall into contempt and become ruftie. I neuer found, that blood and too much feueritie did good in matters of Religion: for, befides that it is a fure rule in Diuinitie, that God neuer loues to plant his Church by violence and bloodfhed; naturall reafon may euen perfwade vs, and dayly experience prooues it trew, That when men are feuerely perfecuted for Religion, the gallantneffe of many mens fpirits, and the wilfulnes of their humors, rather then the iuftneffe of the caufe, makes them to take a pride boldy to endure any torments, or death it felfe, to gaine thereby the reputatiom of Martyrdome, though but in a falfe fhadow.

Some doubts haue beene conceiued anent the vfing of the Oath of Allegiance, and that part of the Acte which ordaines the taking thereof, is thought fo obfcure, that no man can tell who ought to bee preffed therewith. For I my felfe, when vpon a time I called the Iudges before mee at their going to their Circuits, I mooued this queftion vnto them; wherein, as I thought they could not refolutely anfwere me: And therefore if there bee any fcruple touching the miniftring of it, I would wifh it now to bee cleared. And fince I haue with my owne pen brought the Popes quarell vpon mee, and proclaimed publique defiance to *Babylon* in maintaining it; fhould it now fleepe, and fhould I feeme (as it were) to fteale from it againe?

As for Recufants, let them bee all duely prefented without exception: for in times paft there hath beene too great a conniuence, and forbearing

of

of them, especially of great mens wiues, and their kinne and followers. None ought to be spared from being brought vnder the danger of
Law, and then it is my part to vse mercie, as I thinke conuenient. To
winke at faults, and not to suffer them to bee discouered, is no Honour,
nor Mercy in a King, neither is he euer thanked for it; It onely argues
his dulnesse: But to forgiue faults after they are confessed, or tried, is
Mercie. And now I must turne me in this case to you, my Lords the Bishops, and euen exhort you earnestly, to be more carefull, then you haue
bene; that your Officers may more duely present Recusants, then heretofore they haue done, without exception of persons; That although it
must be the worke of G o d that must make their mindes to bee altered,
yet at least by this course they may be stayed from increasing, or insulting
vpon vs.

And that yee all may know the trewth of my heart in this case, I diuide all my Subiects that are Papists, into two rankes: either olde Papists, that were so brought vp in times of Poperie, like old Queene *Mary*
Priests, and those, that though they bee younger in yeeres, yet haue neuer drunke in other milke, but beene still nulled in that blindnesse: Or
else such as doe become Apostats; hauing once beene of our Profession,
and haue forsaken the trewth, either vpon discontent, or practise, or else
vpon a light vaine humour of Noueltie, making no more scruple to seeke
out new formes of Religion, then if it were but a new forme of Garment,
or a new cut or courtsey after the French fashion.

For the former sort, I pitie them; but if they bee good and quiet Subiects, I hate not their persons; and if I were a priuate man, I could well
keepe a ciuill friendship and conuersation with some of them: But as for
those Apostates, who, I know, must be greatest haters of their owne Sect,
I confesse I can neuer shew any fauourable countenance toward them, and
they may all of them be sure without exception, that they shall neuer finde
any more fauour of mee, further then I must needs in Iustice afford them.
And these would I haue the Law to strike seuerelie st vpon, and you care-
fullest to discouer. Yee know there hath beene great stirre kept for begging Concealements these yeeres past; and I pray you, let mee begge this
concealement both of the Bishops, and Iudges, That Papists be no longer concealed.

Next, as concerning the Common wealth, I doe specially recommend
vnto you the framing of some new Statute for preseruation of woods. In
the end of the last Session of Parliament, ye had a Bill amongst you of that
subiect, but because you found some faults therein, you cast out the whole
Bil: But I could haue rather wished that yee had either mended it, or made a
new one; For to cast out the whole Bill because of some faults, was euen as
if a man, that had a new garment brought him, would chuse rather to go naked, then haue his garment made fit for him: But on my cōscience, I cannot

imagine

imagine why you fhould fo lightly haue efteemed a thing, fo neceffary for the Common wealth, if it were not out of a litle frowardneffe amongft you at that time, that what I then recommended earneftly vnto you, it was the worfe liked of. The maintenance of woods is a thing fo neceffary for this Kingdome, as it cannot ftand, nor be a Kingdome without it · For it concernes you both in your *Effe*, *Bene effe*, and in pleafures. Your *Effe*: for without it you want the vfe of one of the moft neceffarie Elements (which is Fire and fewell to dreffe your meate with; for neither can the people liue in thefe colde Countries, if they want fire altogether, nor yet can you dreffe your meate without it; and I thinke you will ill liue like the Cannibals vpon raw flefh: for the education of this people is farre from that. As to your *bene effe*; The decay of woods will neceffarily bring the decay of Shipping, which both is the fecurity of this Kingdome, fince God hath by nature made the Sea to bee the wall of this Iland; and the rather now, fince God hath vnited it all in my Perfon and Crowne; As alfo by the decay of Shipping will you loofe both all your forraine commodities that are fit for this countrey, and the venting of our owne, which is the loffe of Trade, that is a maine pillar of this kingdome. And as for Pleafure, yee know my delight in Hunting and Hawking, and many of your felues are of the fame minde; and all this muft needes decay, by the decay of Woods: Ye haue reafon therefore to prouide a good Law vpon this Subiect.

Now as to the laft point concerning matters of Pleafure, it confifts in the preferuing of Game, which is now almoft vtterly deftroyed through all the Kingdome. And if you offer not now a better Law for this, then was made in the laft Seffion of Parliament, I will neuer thanke you for it: For as for your Law anent Partridge and Phefant, you haue giuen leaue to euery man how poore a Farmour that euer hee bee, to take and deftroy them in his owne ground how he lift. But I pray you, how can the Game bee maintained, if Gentlemen that haue great Lordfhips fhall breed and preferue them there, and fo foone as euer they fhall but flie ouer the hedge and light in a poore fellowes Clofe, they fhall all be deftroyed? Surely I know no remedie for preferuing the Game that breedes in my grounds, except I caft a roofe ouer all the ground, or elfe put veruels to the Partridges feet with my Armes vpon them, as my Hawkes haue: otherwife I know not how they fhall bee knowen to be the Kings Partridges, when they light in a Farmours Clofe.

And by your Lawe againft ftealing of Deere or Conies, after a long difcourfe and prohibition of ftealing them, you conclude in the end with a reftriction, that all this punifhment fhall bee vnderftood to bee vfed againft them that fteale the Game in the night: Which hath much encouraged all the loofer fort of people, that it is no fault to fteale Deere, fo they doe it not like théeues in the night. As was that Law of the *Lacedemonians* againft againſt theft, that did not forbid theft, but onely taught them to doe it cunningly, and without diſcouerie: Whereupon a fooliſh boy ſuffered a Foxe to gnaw his heart through his breaſt. And this doctrine is like that Leſſon of the Cannon Law, *Si non caſtè, tamen cautè.* I knowe you thinke that I ſpeake partially in this caſe like a Hunter; But there is neuer a one of you that heares mee, that cares the leaſt for the ſport, for preſeruation of the Game, but he would be as glad to haue a paſtie of Ve-niſon if you might get it, as the beſt Hunter would : And if the Game be not preſerued, you can eate no Veniſon. As for Partridge and Phe-ſant, I doe not denie that Gentlemen ſhould haue their ſport, and ſpeci-ally vpon their owne ground. But firſt I doe not thinke ſuch Game and pleaſures ſhould be free to baſe people. And next I would euen wiſh that Gentlemen ſhould vſe it in a Gentlemanlike faſhion, and not with Nets, or Gunnes, or ſuch other vngentlemanlike faſhions that ſerue but for vt-ter deſtruction of all Game, nor yet to kill them at vnſeaſonable times, as to kill the Pheſant and Partridges when they are no bigger then Mice, when as for euery one their Hawkes kill, ten will be deſtroyed with their Dogs and Horſe feet; beſides the great and intolerable harme they doe to Corne in that ſeaſon.

And now in the end of all this faſchious Speach, I muſt conclude like a Grey Frier, in ſpeaking for my ſelfe at laſt. At the beginning of this Seſ-ſion of Parliament, when the Treaſourer opened my neceſſities vnto you, then my Purſe onely laboured ; But now that word is ſpread both at home and abroad of the demaunds I haue made vnto you; my Reputation la-boureth aſwell as my Purſe: For if you part without the repairing of my State in ſome reaſonable ſort, what can the world thinke, but that the e-uill will my Subiects beare vnto mee, hath bred a refuſe? And yee can neuer part ſo, without apprehending that I am diſtaſted with your be-hauiour, and yet to be in feare of my diſpleaſure. But I aſſure and promiſe my ſelfe farre otherwiſe.

Hus haue I now performed my promiſe, in preſenting vnto you the Chriſtall of your Kings heart.

Yee know that principally by three wayes yee may wrong a Mirrour.

Frſt, I pray you, looke not vpon my Mirrour with a falſe light: which yee doe, if ye miſtake, or miſ-vnderſtand my Speach, and ſo alter the ſenſe thereof.

But ſecondly, I pray you beware to ſoile it with a foule breath, and vn-cleane hands: I meane, that yee peruert not my words by any corrupt af-fections,

fections, turning them to an ill meaning, like one, who when hee heares the tolling of a Bell, fancies to himselfe, that it speakes those words which are most in his minde.

And lastly, (which is worst of all) beware to let it fall or breake; (for glasse is brittle) which ye doe, if ye lightly esteeme it, and by contemning it, conforme not your selues to my perswasions.

To conclude then: As all these three dayes of *Iubile* haue fallen in the midst of this season of penitence, wherein you haue presented your thanks to me, and I the like againe to you: So doe I wish and hope, that the end of this Parliament will bee such, as wee may all haue cause (both I your Head, and yee the Body) to ioyne in Eucharisticke Thanks and Praises vnto God, for our so good and happie an end.

(*.*)

A SPEACH

A SPEACH IN THE
STARRE-CHAMBER,
THE XX. OF JVNE.
ANNO 1616.

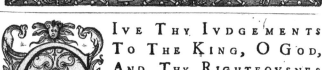

IVE THY IVDGEMENTS
TO THE KING, O GOD,
AND THY RIGHTEOVSNES
TO THE KINGS SONNE.

These be the firſt words of one of the Pſalmes of the Kingly Prophet *Dauid*, whereof the literall ſenſe runnes vpon him, and his ſonne *Salomon*, and the myſticall ſenſe vpon GOD and CHRIST his eternall Sonne: but they are both ſo wouen together, as ſome parts are, and can onely bee properly applied vnto GOD and CHRIST, and other parts vnto *Dauid* and *Salomon*, as this Verſe, *Giue thy Iudgements to the King, O God, and thy Righteouſſe to the Kings Sonne*, cannot be properly ſpoken of any, but of *Dauid* and his ſonne; becauſe it is ſaid, *Giue thy Iudgements, &c.* Now God cannot giue to himſelfe. In another part of the ſame Pſalme, where it is ſaid, that *Righteouſnes ſhall flouriſh, and abundance of Peace, as long as the Moone endureth*, it ſignifieth eternitie, and cannot be properly applied but to GOD and CHRIST: But both ſenſes, aſwell literall as myſticall, ſerue to Kings for imitation, and eſpecially to Chriſtian Kings: for Kings ſit in the Throne of GOD, and they themſelues are called Gods.

And therefore all good Kings in their gouernment, muſt imitate GOD
and

and his Chrift, in being iuft and righteous; *Dauid* and *Salomon*, in being godly and wife: To be wife, is vnderftood, able to difcerne, able to iudge others: To be godly is, that the fountaine be pure whence the ftreames proceed: for what auailes it though all his workes be godly, if they proceed not from godlineffe : To bee righteous, is to a mans felfe: To bee iuft, is towards others. But Iuftice in a King auailes not, vnleffe it be with a cleane heart: for except he bee Righteous afwell as Iuft, he is no good King; and whatfoeuer iuftice he doeth, except he doeth it for Iuftice fake, and out of the pureneffe of his owne heart, neither from priuate ends, vaine-glory, or any other by-refpects of his owne, all fuch Iuftice is vnrighteoufneffe, and no trew Iuftice. From this imitation of G O D and CHRIST, in whofe Throne wee fit, the gouernment of all Commonwealths, and efpecially Monarchies, hath bene from the beginning fetled and eftablifhed. Kings are properly Iudges, and Iudgement properly belongs to them from G O D : for Kings fit in the Throne of G O D; and thence all Iudgement is deriued.

In all well fetled Monarchies, where Law is eftablifhed formerly and orderly, there Iudgement is deferred from the King to his fubordinate Magiftrates; not that the King takes it from himfelfe, but giues it vnto them: So it comes not to them *Priuatiuè*, but *cumulatiuè*, as the Shoolemen fpeake. The ground is ancient, euer fithence that Counfell which *Iethro* gaue to *Mofes* : for after that *Mofes* had gouerned a long time, in his owne perfon, the burthen grew fo great, hauing none to helpe him, as his father in law comming to.vifite him, found him fo cumbred with miniftring of Iuftice, that neither the people were fatisfied, nor he well able to performe it; Therefore by his aduice, Iudges were deputed for eafier queftions, and the greater and more profound were left to *Mofes:* And according to this eftablifhment, all Kings that haue had a formall gouernement, efpecially Chriftian Kings in all aages haue gouerned their people, though after a diuers maner.

This Deputation is after one manner in *France*, after another here, and euen my owne Kingdomes differ in this point of gouernment: for *Scotland* differs both from *France* and *England* herein; but all agree in this, (I fpeake of fuch Kingdomes or States where the formalitie of Law hath place) that the King that fits in Gods Throne, onely deputes fubalterne Iudges, and he deputes not one but a number (for no one fubalterne Iudges mouth makes Law) and their office is to interprete Law, and adminifter Iuftice. But as to the number of them, the forme of gouernement, the maner of interpretation, the diftinction of Benches, the diuerfitie of Courts; thefe varie according to the varietie of gouernment, and inftitution of diuers Kings: So this ground I lay, that the feate of Iudgement is properly Gods, and Kings are Gods Vicegerents ; and by Kings Iudges are deputed vnder them, to beare the burden of gouernement, according to the firft example of *Mofes* by the aduice of *Iethro*, and
fithence

fithence practifed by *Dauid* and *Salomon*, the wifeft Kings that euer were; which is in this Pfalme fo interlaced, that as the firft verfe cannot be applied properly but to *Dauid* and *Salomon*, in the words, *Giue thy Iudgements to the King*, &c. So the other place in the fame Pfalme, *Righteoufnefſe ſhall flouriſh, and abundance of peace ſhall remaine as long as the Moone endureth,* properly fignifieth the eternitie of CHRIST. This I fpeake, to fhew what a neere coniunction there is betweene God and the King vpward, and the King and his Iudges downewards: for the fame coniunction that is betweene God and the King vpward; the fame coniunction is betweene the King and his Iudges downewards.

As Kings borrow their power from God, fo Iudges from Kings: And as Kings are to accompt to God, fo Iudges vnto God and Kings; and both Kings and Iudges by imitation, haue two qualities from God and his Chrift, and two qualities from *Dauid* and his *Salomon*: Iudgement and Righteoufneffe, from God and Chrift: Godlineffe and Wifedome from *Dauid* and *Salomon*. And as no King can difcharge his accompt to God, vnleffe he make confcience not to alter, but to declare and eftablifh the will of God: So Iudges cannot difcharge their accompts to Kings, vnleffe they take the like care, not to take vpon them to make Law, but ioyned together after a deliberate confultation, to declare what the Law is; For as Kings are fubiect vnto Gods Law, fo they to mans Law. It is the Kings Office to protect and fettle the trew interpretation of the Law of God within his Dominions: And it is the Iudges Office to interprete the Law of the King, whereto themfelues are alfo fubiect.

Hauing now perfourmed this ancient Prouerbe, *A Ioue principium;* which though it was fpoken by a Pagan, yet it is good and holy: I am now to come to my particular Errand, for which I am heere this day; wherein I muft handle two parts: Firft, the reafon why I haue not thefe fourteene yeeres, fithence my Coronation vntill now, fatisfied a great many of my louing fubiects, who I know haue had a great expectation, and as it were a longing, like them that are with child, to heare mee fpeake in this place, where my Predeceffors haue often fitten, and efpecially King *Henry* the feuenth, from whom, as diuers wayes before, I am lineally defcended, and that doubly to this Crowne; and as I am neereft defcended of him, fo doe I defire to follow him in his beft actions.

The next part is the reafon, Why I am now come: The caufe that made mee abftaine, was this: When I came into *England*, although I was an old King, paft middle aage, and practifed in gouernment euer fithence I was twelue yeeres olde; yet being heere a ftranger in gouernement, though not in blood, becaufe my breeding was in another Kingdome; I refolued therefore with *Pythagoras* to keepe filence feuen yeeres, and learne my felfe the Lawes of this Kingdome, before I would take vpon mee to teach them vnto others: When this Apprentifhip was ended, then another impediment came, which was in the choice of that caufe, that fhould firft
bring

bring me hither. I expected fome great caufe to make my firft entry vpon : For I thought that hauing abftained fo long, it fhould be a worthy
matter that fhould bring mee hither. Now euery caufe muft be great or
fmall : In fmall caufes I thought it difgracefull to come, hauing beene fo
long abfent : In great caufes, they muft be either betwixt the King and
fome of his Subiects,or betwixt Subiect and Subiect.

In a caufe where my felfe was concerned, I was loath to come, becaufe
men fhould not thinke I did come for my owne priuate, either Prerogatiue or profit ; or for any other by-refpect : And in that cafe I will alwayes
abide the triall of men and Angels, neuer to haue had any particular end,
in that which is the Maine of all things, *Iuſtice.*

In a great caufe alfo betweene partie and partie, great in refpect either
of the queftion, or value of the thing, my comming might feeme, as it
were obliquely, to be in fauour of one partie,and for that caufe this Coun-
fellour, or that Courtier might be thought to mooue me to come hither;
And a meane caufe was not worthy of mee, efpecially for my firft entrance : So,lacke of choice in both refpects kept mee off till now : And
now hauing paffed a double apprentifhip of twice feuen yeeres, I am come
hither to fpeake vnto you. And next as to the reafons of my comming at
this time, they are thefe.

I haue obferued in the time of my whole Reigne here, and my double
Apprentifhip, diuers things fallen out in the Iudicatures here at *Weſtminſter* Hall, that I thought required and vrged a reformation at my
hands; whereupon I refolued with my felfe, that I could not more fitly
begin a reformation, then here to make an open declaration of my meaning. I remember Chrifts faying, *My ſheepe heare my voyce,* and fo I affure
my felfe, my people will moft willingly heare the voyce of me, their owne
Shepheard and King; whereupon I tooke this occafion in mine owne perfon here in this Seate of Iudgement, not iudicially, but declaratorily and
openly to giue thofe directions, which, at other times, by piece-meale,
I haue deliuered to fome of you in diuers leffe publike places; but now
will put it vp in all your audience, where I hope it fhall bee trewly caried, and cannot be miftaken, as it might haue bene when it was fpoken
more priuately : I will for order fake take mee to the methode of the number of Three, the number of perfection, and vpon that number diftri-
bute all I haue to declare to you.

Irft,I am to giue a charge to my felfe : for a King,or Iudge vnder
a King, that firft giues not a good charge to himfelfe, will neuer
be able to giue a good charge to his inferiours ; for as I haue faid,
Good riuers cannot flow but from good fprings; if the fountaine be impure,fo muft the riuers be.

Secondly,to the Iudges: And thirdly,to the Auditory,and the reft of the
inferiour minifters of Iuftice.

Firft,

Firſt, I proteſt to you all, in all your audience, heere ſitting in the ſeate of Iuſtice, belonging vnto G O D, and now by right fallen vnto mee, that I haue reſolued, as Confirmation in Maioritie followeth Baptiſme in minoritie; ſo now after many yeeres, to renew my promiſe and Oath made at my Coronation concerning Iuſtice, and the promiſe therein for maintenance of the Law of the Land. And I proteſt in G O D s preſence, my care hath euer beene to keepe my conſcience cleare in all the points of my Oath, taken at my Coronation, ſo farre as humane frailtie may permit mee, or my knowledge enforme mee, I ſpeake in point of Iuſtice and Law; For Religion, I hope I am reaſonably well knowen already: I meane therefore of Lawe and Iuſtice; and for Law, I meane the Common Law of the Land, according to which the King gouernes, and by which the people are gouerned. For the Common Law, you can all beare mee witneſſe, I neuer preſſed alteration of it in Parliament; but on the contrary, when I endeauoured moſt an Vnion reall, as was already in my perſon, my deſire was to conforme the Lawes of *Scotland* to the Law of *England*, and not the Law of *England* to the Law of *Scotland*; and ſo the prophecie to be trew of my wiſe Grandfather *Henry* the ſeuenth, who foretold that the leſſer Kingdome by marriage, would follow the greater, and not the greater the leſſer; And therefore married his eldeſt daughter *Margaret* to *Iames* the fourth, my great Grandfather.

It was a fooliſh Querke of ſome Iudges, who held that the Parliament of *England*, could not vnite *Scotland* and *England* by the name of *Great Britaine*, but that it would make an alteration of the Lawes, though I am ſince come to that knowledge, that an Acte of Parliament can doe greater wonders: And that old wiſe man the Treaſourer *Burghley* was wont to ſay, Hee knew not what an Acte of Parliament could not doe in *England*; For my intention was alwayes to effect vnion by vniting *Scotland* to *England*, and not *England* to *Scotland*: For I euer meant, being euer reſolued, that this Law ſhould continue in this Kingdome, and two things mooued mee thereunto; One is, that in matter of Policie and State, you ſhall neuer ſee any thing anciently and maturely eſtabliſhed, but by Innouation or alteration it is worſe then it was, I meane not by purging of it from corruptions, and reſtoring it to the ancient integritie; Another reaſon was, I was ſworne to maintaine the Law of the Land, and therefore I had beene periured if I had altered it; And this I ſpeake to root out the conceit and miſapprehenſion, if it be in any heart, that I would change, damnifie, vilifie or ſuppreſſe the Law of this Land: G O D is my Iudge I neuer meant it; And this confirmation I make before you all.

To this I ioyne the point of Iuſtice, which I call *Vnicuique ſuum tribuere*. All my Councell, and Iudges dead and aliue, can, and could beare mee witneſſe, how vnpartiall I haue beene in declaring of Law.

And where it hath concerned mee in my owne inheritance, I haue as willingly submitted my interest to the Lawe, as any my Subiects could doe; and it becomes mee so to doe, to giue example to others: much lesse then will I be partiall to others, where I am not to my selfe. And so resolue your selues, Iustice with mee may bee moderated in point of clemencie: for no Iustice can be without mercie. But in matters of Iustice to giue euery man his owne, to be blinde without eyes of partialitie; This is my full resolution.

I vsed to say when I was in *Scotland*, if any man mooued mee to delay Iustice, that it was against the Office of a King so to doe; But when any made suite to hasten Iustice, I told them I had rather grant fourtie of these suits, then one of the other: This was alwayes my custome and shall be euer, with Gods leaue.

Now what I haue spoken of Law and Iustice, I meane by the Lawe kept in her owne bounds: For I vnderstand the inheritance of the King, and Subiects in this land, must bee determined by the Common Law, &c; and that is, by the Law set downe in our forefathers time, expounded by learned men diuers times after in the declaratory Comments, called *Responsa Prudentum*; Or else by Statute Law set downe by Acte of Parliament, as occasion serues: By this I doe not seclude all other Lawes of *England*, but this is the Law of inheritance in this Kingdome.

There is another Law, of all Lawes free and supreame, which is GODS LAVV: And by this all Common and municipall Lawes must be gouerned· And except they haue dependance vpon this Law, they are vniust and vnlawfull.

When I speake of that Law, I onely giue this touch, That that Law in this Kingdome hath beene too much neglected, and Churchmen too much had in contempt; I must speake trewth, Great men, Lords, Iudges, and people of all degrees from the highest to the lowest, haue too much contemned them: And God will not blesse vs in our owne Lawes, if wee doe not reuerence and obey GODS LAVV; which cannot bee, except the interpreters of it be respected and reuerenced.

And it is a signe of the latter dayes drawing on; euen the contempt of the Church, and of the Gouernours and Teachers thereof now in the Church of ENGLAND, which I say in my Conscience, of any Church that euer I read or knew of, present or past, is most pure, and neerest the Primitiue and Apostolicall Church in Doctrine and Discipline, and is sureliest founded vpon the word of God, of any Church in Christendome.

Next vnto this Law is the Law of Nations, which God forbid should bee barred, and that for two causes: One, because it is a Law to satisfie Strangers, which will not so well hold themselues satisfied with other municipall Lawes: Another, to satisfie our owne Subiects in matters of Piracie, Marriage, Wills, and things of like nature: That Law I

diuide

diuide into Ciuil and Canon; And this Law hath bene so much encroched vpon, sithence my comming to the Crowne, and so had in contempt, that young men are discouraged from studying, and the rest wearie of their liues that doe professe it, and would be glad to seeke any other craft.

So, speaking of the Common Law, I meane the Common Law kept within her owne limits, and not derogating from these other Lawes, which by longer custome haue beene rooted here; first, the Law of GOD and his Church; and next, the Law Ciuill and Canon, which in many cases cannot be wanting.

To conclude this charge which I giue my selfe, I professe to maintaine all the points of mine Oath, especially in Lawes, and of Lawes, especially the Common Law:

And as to maintaine it, so to purge it; for else it cannot bee maintained: and especially to purge it from two corruptions, Incertaintie and Nouel-tie : Incertaintie is found in the Law it selfe, wherein I will bee painefull to cleare it to the people; and this is properly to bee done in Parliament by aduice of the Iudges.

The other corruption is introduced by the Iudges themselues, by Ni-cities that are vsed, where it may be said, *Ab initio non fuit sic.*

Nothing in the world is more likely to be permanent to our eyes then yron or steele, yet the rust corrupts it; if it bee not kept cleane : which sheweth, nothing is permanent here in this world, if it be not purged; So I cannot discharge my conscience in maintaining the Lawes; if I keepe them not cleane from corruption.

And now that I may bee like the Pastor, that first takes the Sacrament himselfe, and then giues it to the people : So I haue first taken my owne charge vpon me, before I giue you your Charge, lest it might be said,

Turpe est doctori, cùm culpa redarguit ipsum.

Now my Lords the Iudges for your parts, the Charge I haue to giue you, consists likewise in three parts.

First in generall, that you doe Iustice vprightly, as you shall an-swere to GOD and mee: For as I haue onely GOD to answere to, and to expect punishment at his hands, if I offend; So you are to answere both to GOD and to mee, and expect punishment at GODs hands and mine, if you be found in fault.

Secondly, to doe Iustice indifferently betweene Subiect and Subiect, betweene King and Subiect, without delay, partialitie, feare or bribery, with stout and vpright hearts, with cleane and vncorrupt hands.

When I bid you doe Iustice boldly, yet I bid you doe it fearefully; fearefully in this, to vtter your owne conceites, and not the trew mea-ning of the Law : And remember you are no makers of Law, but Inter-pretours of Law, according to the trew sence thereof; for your Office is *Ius dicere*, and not *Ius dare* : And that you are so farre from making Law, that euen in the higher house of Parliament, you haue no voyce in making of a Law, but only to giue your aduice when you are required.

And though the Laws be in many places obscure, and not so wel knowen to the multitude as to you; and that there are many parts that come not into ordinary practise, which are knowen to you, because you can finde out the reason thereof by bookes and presidents; yet know this, that your interpretations must be alwayes subiect to common sense and reason.

For I will neuer trust any Interpretation, that agreeth not with my common sense and reason; and trew Logicke: for *Ratio est animæ Legis* in all humane Lawes, without exception; it must not be Sophistrie or straines of wit that must interprete, but either cleare Law, or solide reason.

But in Countreys where the formalitie of Law hath no place, as in *Denmarke*, which I may trewly report, as hauing my selfe beene an eye-witnesse thereof; all their State is gouerned onely by a written Law; there is no Aduocate or Proctour admitted to plead; onely the parties themselues plead their owne cause, and then a man stands vp and reads the Law, and there is an end; for the very Law-booke it selfe is their onely Iudge. Happy were all Kingdomes if they could be so: But heere, curious wits, various conceits, different actions, and varietie of examples breed questions in Law: And therefore when you heare the questions, if they be plaine, there is a plaine way in it selfe; if they be such as are not plaine (for mens inuentions dayly abound) then are you to interprete according to common sense, and draw a good and certaine *Minor* of naturall reason, out of the *Maior* of direct Lawe, and thereupon to make a right and trew *Conclusion*.

For though the Common Law be a mystery and skill best knowen vnto your selues, yet if your interpretation be such, as other men which haue Logicke and common sense vnderstand not the reason, I will neuer trust such an Interpretation.

Remember also you are Iudges; and not a Iudge; and diuided into Benches, which sheweth that what you doe, that you should doe with aduice and deliberation, not hastily and rashly, before you well study the case, and conferre together; debating it duely, not giuing single opinions, *per emendicata suffragia*; and so to giue your Iudgement, as you will answer to God and me.

Now hauing spoken of your Office in generall, I am next to come to the limits wherein you are to bound your selues, which likewise are three. First, Incroach not vpon the Prerogatiue of the Crowne: If there fall out a question that concernes my Prerogatiue or mystery of State, deale not with it, till you consult with the King or his Councell, or both: for they are transcendent matters, and must not be sliberely caried with ouer-rash wilfulnesse; for so may you wound the King through the sides of a priuate person: and this I commend vnto your speciall care, as some of you of late haue done very well, to blunt the sharpe edge and vaine popular humour of some Lawyers at the Barre, that

that thinke they are not eloquent and bold spirited enough, except they meddle with the Kings Prerogatiue: But doe not you suffer this; for certainely if this liberty be suffered, the Kings Prerogatiue, the Crowne,and I, shall bee as much wounded by their pleading, as if you resolued what they disputed: That which concernes the mysterie of the Kings power, is not lawfull to be disputed; for that is to wade into the weakenesse of Princes,and to take away the mysticall reuerence, that belongs vnto them that sit in the Throne of God.

Secondly,That you keepe your selues within your owne Benches, not to inuade other Iurisdictions,which is vnfit,and an vnlawful thing; In this I must inlarge my selfe. Besides the Courts of Common Law, there is the Court of Requests; the Admiraltie Court; the Court of the President and Councell of Walles,the President and Councell of the North; High Commission Courts,euery Bishop in his owne Court.

These Courts ought to keepe their owne limits and boundes of their Commission and Instructions, according to the ancient Presidents: And like as I declare that my pleasure is, that euery of these shall keepe their owne limits and boundes; So the Courts of Common Lawe are not to encroach vpon them,no more then it is my pleasure that they should encroach vpon the Common Law. And this is a thing Regall,and proper to a King, to keepe euery Court within his owne bounds.

In *Westminster* Hall there are foure Courts: Two that handle causes Ciuill,which are the Common-pleas, and the Exchequer: Two that determine causes Criminall, which are the Kings-Bench,and the Starre-Chamber, where now I sit. The Common-Pleas is a part and branch of the Kings-Bench; for it was first all one Court; and then the Common-Pleas being extracted, it was called Common-Pleas; because it medled with the Pleas of Priuate persons,and that which remained, the Kings-Bench. The other of the Courts for ciuill Causes, is the Exchequer, which was ordeined for the Kings Reuenew: That is the principall Institution of that Court,and ought to be their chiefe studie; and as other things come orderly thither by occasion of the former,they may be handled, and Iustice there administred.

Keepe you therefore all in your owne bounds, and for my part, I desire you to giue me no more right in my priuate Prerogatiue, then you giue to any Subiect; and therein I will be acquiescent: As for the absolute Prerogatiue of the Crowne, that is no Subiect for the tongue of a Lawyer, nor is lawfull to be disputed.

It is Athiesme and blasphemie to dispute what God can doe: good Christians content themselues with his will reuealed in his word. so, it is presumption and high contempt in a Subiect, to dispute what a King can doe, or say that a King cannot doe this, or that; but rest in that which is the Kings reuealed will in his Law.

The Kings-Bench is the principall Court for criminall causes, and in some respects it deales with Ciuill causes.

Then is there a Chancerie Court; this is a Court of Equitie, and hath power to deale likewise in Ciuill causes: It is called the dispenser of the Kings Conscience, following alwayes the intention of Law and Iustice; not altering the Law, not making that blacke which other Courts made white, nor *è conuerso*; But in this it exceeds other Courts, mixing Mercie with Iustice, where other Courts proceed onely according to the strict rules of Law: And where the rigour of the Law in many cases will vndoe a Subiect, there the Chancerie tempers the Law with equitie, and so mixeth Mercy with Iustice, as it preserues men from destruction.

And thus (as before I told you) is the Kings Throne established by Mercy and Iustice.

The Chancerie is vndependant of any other Court, and is onely vnder the King: There it is written *Teste meipso*; from that Court there is no Appeale. And as I am bound in my Conscience to maintaine euery Courts Iurisdiction, so especially this, and not suffer it to sustaine wrong; yet so to maintaine it, as to keepe it within the owne limits, and free from corruption. My Chancellour that now is, I found him Keeper of the Seale, the same place in substance, although I gaue him the Stile of Chancellour, and God hath kept him in it till now; and I pray God he may hold it long; and so I hope he will. He will beare mee witnesse, I neuer gaue him other warrant, then to goe on in his Court according to Presidents, warranted by Law in the time of the best gouerning Kings, and most learned Chancellours: These were the limits I gaue vnto him; beyond the same limits he hath promised me he will neuer goe.

And as he hath promised me to take no other Iurisdiction to himselfe, so is it my promise euer to maintaine this Iurisdiction in that Court: Therefore I speake this to vindicate that Court from misconceipt and contempt.

It is the duetie of Iudges to punish those that seeke to depraue the proceedings of any the Kings Courts, and not to encourage them any way: And I must confesse I thought it an odious and inept speach, and it grieued me very much, that it should be said in *Westminster* Hall, that a *Premunire* lay against the Court of the Chancery and Officers there: How can the King grant a *Premunire* against himselfe?

It was a foolish, inept, and presumptuous attempt, and fitter for the time of some vnworthy King: vnderstand mee aright; I meane not, the Chancerie should exceed his limite; but on the other part, the King onely is to correct it, and none else: And therefore I was greatly abused in that attempt: For if any was wronged there, the complaint should haue come to mee. None of you but will confesse you haue a King of reasonable vnderstanding, and willing to reforme; why then should you spare to complaine to me, that being the high way, and not goe the other way, and backe-way, in contempt of our Authoritie?

And

And therefore fitting heere in a feat of Iudgement, I declare and command, that no man hereafter prefume to fue a *Premunire* againft the Chancery, which I may the more eafily doe, becaufe no *Premunire* can bee fued but at my Suit: And I may iuftly barre my felfe at mine owne pleafure.

As all inundations come with ouerflowing the bankes, and neuer come without great inconuenience, and are thought prodigious by Aftrologers in things to come : So is this ouerflowing the bankes of your Iurifdiction in it felfe inconuenient, and may proue prodigious to the State.

Remember therefore, that hereafter you keepe within your limits and Iurifdictions. It is a fpeciall point of my Office to procure and command, that amongft Courts there bee a concordance, and muficall accord ; and it is your parts to obey, and fee this kept : And, as you are to obferue the ancient Lawes and cuftomes of *England*; fo are you to keepe your felues within the bound of direct Law, or Prefidents; and of thofe, not euery fnatched Prefident, carped now here, now there, as it were running by the way; but fuch as haue neuer beene controuerted, but by the contrary, approued by common vfage, in times of beft Kings, and by moft learned Iudges.

The *Starre-Chamber* Court hath bene likewife fhaken of late, and the laft yeere it had receiued a fore blow, if it had not bene affifted and caried by a few voyces; The very name of *Starre-Chamber*, feemeth to procure a reuerence to the Court.

I will not play the Criticke to defcant on the name; It hath a name from heauen, a Starre placed in it; and a Starre is a glorious creature, and feated in a glorious place, next vnto the Angels. The *Starre-Chamber* is alfo glorious in fubftance: for in the compofition, it is of foure forts of perfons: The firft two are Priuie Counfellours and Iudges, the one by wifedome in matters of State; the other, by learning in matters of Law, to direct and order all things both according to Law and State : The other two forts are Peeres of the Realme, and Bifhops: The Peeres are there by reafon of their greatneffe, to giue authority to that Court : The Bifhops becaufe of their learning in Diuinitie, and the intereft they haue in the good gouernment of the Church: And fo, both the learning of both Diuine and humane Law, and experience and practife in Gouernment, are conioyned together in the proceedings of this Court.

There is no Kingdome but hath a Court of Equitie, either by it felfe, as is heere in *England*, or elfe mixed, and incorporate in their Office that are Iudges in the Law, as it is in *Scotland* : But the order of *England* is much more perfect, where they are diuided. And as in cafe of Equitie, where the Law determines not clearely, there the Chancerie doeth determine, hauing Equitie belonging to it, which doeth belong to no other Court : So the *Starre-Chamber* hath that belonging to it, which belongs to no other Court : For in this Court Attempts are punifhable, where other Courts punifh onely facts ; And alfo where the Law punifheth facts eafily,

eafily, as in cafe of Riots or Combates, there the Starre-Chamber punifheth in a higher degree; And alfo all combinations of practifes and confpiracies; And if the King be difhonoured or contemned in his Prerogatiue,
it belongeth moft properly to the Peeres and Iudges of this Court to punifh it : So then this Court being inftituted for fo great caufes, it is great
reafon it fhould haue great honour.

Remember now how I haue taught you brotherly loue one toward
another : For you know well, that as you are Iudges, you are all brethren,
and your Courts are fifters. I pray you therefore, labour to keepe that
fweete harmonie, which is amongft thofe fifters the *Mufes.* What greater
miferie can there bee to the Law, then contempt of the Law? and what
readier way to contempt, then when queftions come, what fhall bee
determined in this Court, and what in that? Whereupon two euils doe
arife; The one, that men come not now to Courts of iuftice, to heare
matters of right pleaded, and Decrees giuen accordingly, but onely out of
a curiofitie, to heare queftions of the Iurifdictions of Courts difpu-
ted, and to fee the euent, what Court is like to preuaile aboue the other;
And the other is, that the Pleas are turned from Court to Court in an endleffe circular motion, as vpon *Ixions* wheele: And this was the reafon why
I found iuft fault with that multitude of Prohibitions : For when a poore
Minifter had with long labour, and great expence of charge and time,
gotten a fentence for his Tithes, then comes a Prohibition, and turnes
him round from Court to Court, and fo makes his caufe immortall and
endleffe : for by this vncertaintie of Iurifdiction amongft Courts, caufes are fcourged from Court to Court, and this makes the fruit of Suits
like *Tantalus* fruite, ftill neere the Suiters lips, but can neuer come to
tafte it. And this in deed is a great delay of Iuftice, and makes caufes endleffe: Therefore the onely way to auoyd this, is for you to keepe your
owne bounds, and nourifh not the people in contempt of other Courts,
but teach them reuerence to Courts in your publique fpeaches, both in
your Benches, and in your Circuits; fo fhall you bring them to a reuerence, both of GOD, and of the King.

Keepe therefore your owne limits towards the King, towards other
Courts, and towards other Lawes, bounding your felues within your
owne Law, and make not new Law. Remember, as I faid before, that
you are Iudges, to declare, and not to make Law: For when you make
a Decree neuer heard of before, you are Law-giuers, and not Law-
tellers.

I haue laboured to gather fome Articles, like an *Index expurgatorius,* of
noueltie new crept into the Law, and I haue it ready to bee confidered
of: Looke to *Plowdens* Cafes, and your old *Refponfa prudentum* ; if you
finde it not there, then (*ab initio non fuit fic*) I muft fay with CHRIST, A-
way with the new polygamie, and maintaine the ancient Law pure and
vndefiled, as it was before.

To

TO the Auditory I haue but little to fay, yet that little will not bee ill beftowed to be faid at this time.

Since I haue now renewed and confirmed my refolution to maintaine my Oath, the Law and Iuftice of the Land ; So doe I expect, that you my Subiects doe fubmit your felues as you ought, to the obferuance of that Law.

And as I haue diuided the two former parts of my Charge; So will I diuide this your fubmiffion into three parts, for orderly diuifions and methode, caufe things better to be remembred.

Firft in generall, that you giue due reuerence to the Law ; and this generall diuides it felfe into three.

Firft, not to fue, but vpon iuft caufe.

Secondly, beeing fued, and Iudgement paffed againft you, Acquiefce in the Iudgement, and doe not tumultuate againft it ; and take example from mee, whom you haue heard here proteft, that when euer any Decree fhall be giuen againft me in my priuate right, betweene me and a Subiect, I will as humbly acquiefce as the meaneft man in the Land. Imitate me in this, for in euery Plea there are two parties, and Iudgement can be but for one, and againft the other; fo one muft alwayes be difpleafed.

Thirdly, doe not complaine and importune mee againft Iudgements; for I hold this Paradoxe to bee a good rule in Gouernment, that it is better for a King to maintaine an vniuft Decree, then to queftion euery Decree and Iudgement, after the giuing of a fentence, for then Suites fhall neuer haue end : Therefore as you come gaping to the Law for Iuftice, fo bee fatisfied and contented when Iudgement is paft againft you, and trouble not mee; but if you finde briberie or corruption, then come boldly : but when I fay boldly, beware of comming to complaine, except you bee very fure to prooue the iuftice of your caufe : Otherwife looke for *Lex Talionis* to bee executed vpon you; for your accufing of an vpright Iudge, deferues double punifhment, in that you feeke to lay infamie vpon a worthy perfon of that reuerent calling.

And be not tild on with your own Lawyers tales, that fay the caufe is iuft for their owne gaine; but beleeue the Iudges that haue no hire but of me.

Secondly, in your Pleas, prefume not to meddle with things againft the Kings Prerogatiue, or Honour : Some Gentlemen of late haue beene too bold this wayes; If you vfe it, the Iudges will punifh you; and if they fuffer it, I muft punifh both them and you. Plead not vpon new Puritanicall ftraines, that make all things popular; but keepe you within the ancient Limits of Pleas.

Thirdly, make not many changes from Court to Court : for hee that changeth Courts, fhewes to miftruft the iuftneffe of the caufe. Goe to the right place, and the Court that is proper for your caufe; change not thence, and fubmit your felues to the Iudgement giuen there.

Thus hauing finifhed the Charge to my felfe, the Iudges and the Auditorie,

torie, I am to craue your pardon if I haue forgotten any thing, or beene inforced to breake my Methode; for you muſt remember, I come not hither with a written Sermon: I haue no Bookes to reade it out of, and a long ſpeach, manifold buſineſſe, and a little leaſure may well pleade pardon for any fault of memorie; and trewly I know not if I haue forgotten any thing or not.

And now haue I deliuered, Firſt my excuſe, why I came not till now: Next, the reaſons why I came now: Thirdly, my charge, and that to my ſelfe, to you my Lords the Iudges, and to the Auditory.

I haue alſo an ordinary charge that I vſe to deliuer to the Iudges before my Councell, when they goe their Circuits; and ſeeing I am come to this place, you ſhall haue that alſo, and ſo I will make the old ſaying trew, *Combe ſeldome, combe ſore*, I meane by my long deteining you at this time, which will bee ſo much the more profitable in this Auditorie; becauſe a number of the Auditorie will be informed here, who may relate it to their fellow Iuſtices in the countrey.

My Lords the Iudges, you know very well, that as you are Iudges with mee when you ſit here; ſo are you Iudges vnder mee, and my Subſtitutes in the Circuits, where you are Iudges Itinerant to doe Iuſtice to my people.

It is an ancient and laudable cuſtome in this Kingdome, that the Iudges goe thorow the Kingdome in Circuits, eaſing the people thereby of great charges, who muſt otherwiſe come from all the remote parts of the Kingdome to *Weſtminſter Hall*, for the finding out and puniſhing of offences paſt, and preuenting the occaſion of offences that may ariſe.

I can giue you no other charge in effect, but onely to remember you againe of the ſame in ſubſtance which I deliuered to you this time Twelue-moneth.

Firſt, Remember that when you goe your Circuits, you goe not onely to puniſh and preuent offences, but you are to take care for the good gouernment in generall of the parts where you trauell, as well as to doe Iuſtice in particular betwixt party and party, in cauſes criminall and ciuill.

You haue charges to giue to Iuſtices of peace, that they doe their dueties when you are abſent, aſwell as preſent: Take an accompt of them, and report their ſeruice to me at your returne.

As none of you will hold it ſufficient to giue a charge, except in taking the accompt, you finde the fruit of it: So I ſay to you, it will not bee ſufficient for you, to heare my charge, if at your returne you bring not an accompt to the harueſt of my ſowing, which cannot be done in generall, but in making to me a particular report what you haue done.

For, a King hath two Offices.

Firſt, to direct things to be done:

Secondly, to take an accompt how they are fulfilled; for what is it the better for me to direct as an Angel, if I take not accompt of your doings.

I know

I know not whether mifunderftanding, or flackneffe bred this, that I had no accompt but in generall, of that I gaue you in particular in charge the laft yeere : Therefore I now charge you againe, that at your next returne, you repaire to my Chancellour, and bring your accompts to him in writing, of thofe things which in particular I haue giuen you in charge: And then when I haue feene your accompts, as occafion fhall ferue, it may bee I will call for fome of you, to be informed of the ftate of that part of the countrey where your Circuit lay.

Of thefe two parts of your feruice, I know the ordinary Legall part of *Nifi prius* is the more profitable to you: But the other part of Iuftice is more neceffary for my feruice. Therefore as CHRIST faid to the Pharifes, *Hoc agite*, as the moft principall : yet I will fay, *Et illud non omittite:* which, that you may the better doe, I haue allowed you a day more in your Circuits, then my Predeceffours haue done.

And this you fhall finde, that euen as a King, (let him be neuer fo godly, wife, righteous, and iuft) yet if the fubalterne Magiftrates doe not their parts vnder him, the Kingdome muft needes fuffer : So let the Iudges bee neuer fo carefull and induftrious, if the Iuftices of Peace vnder them, put not to their helping hands, in vaine is all your labour : For they are the Kings eyes and eares in the countrey. It was an ancient cuftome, that all the Iudges both immediatly before their going to their Circuits, and immediatly vpon their returne, repaired to the Lord Chancellour of *England*, both to receiue what directions it fhould pleafe the King by his mouth to giue vnto them ; as alfo to giue him an accompt of their labours, who was to acquaint the King therewith : And this good ancient cuftome hath likewife beene too much flacked of late; And therefore firft of all, I am to exhort and command you, that you be carefull to giue a good accompt to me and my Chancellour, of the dueties performed by all Iuftices of Peace in your Circuits : Which gouernment by Iuftices, is fo laudable and fo highly efteemed by mee, that I haue made *Scotland* to bee gouerned by Iuftices and Conftables, as *England* is. And let not Gentlemen be afhamed of this Place ; for it is a place of high Honour, and great reputation, to be made a Minifter of the Kings Iuftice, in feruice of the Common-wealth.

Of thefe there are two forts, as there is of all Companies, efpecially where there is a great number ; that is, good and bad Iuftices : For the good, you are to enforme me of them, that I may know them, thanke them, and reward them, as occafion ferues: For I hold a good Iuftice of Peace in his Countrey, to doe mee as good feruice, as hee that waites vpon mee in my Priuie Chamber, and as ready will I be to reward him ; For I accompt him as capable of any Honour, Office, or preferment about my Perfon, or for any place of Councell or State, as well as any Courteour that is neere about mee, or any that haue deferued well of me in foreine employments : Yea, I efteeme the feruice done me by a good Iuftice of of Peace, three hundred miles, yea fixe hundred miles out of my fight, as well as the feruice done me in my prefence: For as God hath giuen me large limits, fo muft I be carefull that my prouidence may reach to the far-theft parts of them: And as Law cannot be honoured, except Honour be giuen to Iudges: fo without due refpect to Iuftices of Peace, what regard will be had of the feruice?

Therefore let none be afhamed of this Office, or be difcouraged in be-ing a Iuftice of Peace, if he ferue worthily in it.

The Chancellour vnder me, makes Iuftices, and puts them out; but nei-ther I, nor he can tell what they are: Therefore wee muft bee informed by you Iudges, who can onely tell, who doe well, and who doe ill; without which, how can the good be cherifhed and maintained, and the reft put out? The good Iuftices are carefull to attend the feruice of the King and countrey, for thanks onely of the King, and loue to their countrey, and for no other refpect.

The bad are either idle Slowbellies, that abide alwayes at home, giuen to a life of eafe and delight, liker Ladies then men; and thinke it is enough to contemplate Iuftice, when as *Virtus in actione confiftit* : contemplatiue Iuftice is no iuftice, and contemplatiue Iuftices are fit to be put out.

Another fort of Iuftices are bufie-bodies, and will haue all men dance af-ter their pipe, and follow their greatneffe, or elfe will not be content; A fort of men, *Qui fe primos omnium effe putant, nec funt tamen*: thefe proud fpirits muft know, that the countrey is ordained to obey and follow God and the King, and not them.

Another fort are they, that goe feldome to the Kings feruice, but when it is to helpe fome of their kindred or alliance; So as when they come, it is to helpe their friends, or hurt their enemies, making Iuftice to ferue for a fha-dow to Faction, and tumultuating the countrey.

Another fort are Gentlemen of great worth in their owne conceit, and cannot be content with the prefent forme of Gouernement, but muft haue a kind of libertie in the people, and muft be gracious Lords, and Redeemers of their libertie; and in euery caufe that concernes Prerogatiue, giue a fnatch againft a Monarchie, through their Puritanicall itching after Popu-laritie: Some of them haue fhewed themfelues too bold of late in the lower houfe of Parliament: And when all is done, if there were not a King, they would be leffe cared for then other men.

And now hauing fpoken of the qualities of the Iuftices of Peace; I am next to fpeake of their number. As I euer held the midway in all things to be the way of Vertue, in efchewing both extremities: So doe I in this: for vpon the one part, a multitude of Iuftices of Peace in the countrey more then is neceffary, breeds but confufion · for although it be an old Prouerbe, that *Many handes make light worke*; yet too many make flight worke; and too great a number of Iuftices of Peace, will make the bufineffe of the coun-trey to be the more neglected, euery one trufting to another, fo as nothing

fhall

fhall bee well done; befides the breeding of great corruption: for where there is a great number, it can hardly bee, but fome will bee corrupted. And vpon the other part, too few Iuftices of Peace, will not be able to vndergoe the burthen of the feruice; And therefore I would neither haue too few, nor too many, but as many in euery countrey, as may, according to the proportion of that countrey, bee neceffary for the performing of the feruice there, and no more.

As to the Charge you are to giue to the Iuftices, I can but repeat what formerly I haue told you; yet in fo good a bufineffe,

Lectio lecta placet, decies repetita placebit.

And as I began with fulfilling the Prouerbe, _A Ioue principium_; fo will I begin this Charge you are to giue to the Iuftices with Church-matters: for GOD will bleffe euery good bufineffe the better, that he and his Church haue the precedence. That which I am now to fpeake, is anent Recufants and Papifts. You neuer returned from any Circuit, but by your accompt made vnto me, I both conceiued great comfort and great griefe: Comfort, when I heard a number of Recufants in fome Circuits to be diminifhed: Griefe to my heart and foule, when I heard a number of Recufants to be in other Circuits increafed.

I proteft vnto you, nothing in the earth can grieue mee fo much, as mens falling away from Religion in my dayes; And nothing fo much ioyes mee, as when that Religion increafeth vnder mee. GOD is my witneffe, I fpeake nothing for vaine-glory; but fpeake it againe; My heart is grieued when I heare Recufants increafe: Therefore I wifh you Iudges, to take it to heart, as I doe, and preuent it as you can; and make me knowen to my people, as I am.

There are three forts of Recufants: The firft are they that for themfelues will bee no Recufants, but their wiues and their families are; and they themfelues doe come to Church, but once or twice in a yeere, inforced by Law, or for fafhion fake; Thefe may be formall to the Law, but more falfe to GOD then the other fort.

The fecond fort are they that are Recufants and haue their confcience miffe-led, and therefore refufe to come to Church, but otherwife liue as peaceable Subiects.

The third fort are practifing Recufants: Thefe force all their feruants to bee Recufants with them; they will fuffer none of their Tenants, but they muft bee Recufants; and their neighbours if they liue by them in peace, muft be Recufants alfo.

Thefe you may finde out as a foxe by the foule fmell, a great way round about his hole; This is a high pride and prefumption, that they for whofe foules I muft anfwere to GOD, and who enioy their liues and liberties vnder mee, will not onely be Recufants themfelues, but infect and draw others after them.

As I haue faid in Parliament houfe, I can loue the perfon of a Papift, being otherwife a good man and honeſtly bred, neuer hauing knowen any other Religion : but the perſon of an Apoſtate Papiſt, I hate. And ſurely for thoſe Polypragmaticke Papiſts, I would you would ſtudie out ſome ſeuere puniſhment for them : for they keepe not infection in their owne hearts onely, but alſo infect others our good Subiects. And that which I ſay for Recuſants, the ſame I ſay for Prieſts : I confeſſe I am loath to hang a Prieſt onely for Religion ſake, and ſaying Maſſe; but if he refuſe the Oath of Alleagiance (which, let the Pope and all the deuils in Hell ſay what they will) yet (as you finde by my booke and by diuers others, is meerely Ciuill) thoſe that ſo refuſe the Oath, and are Polypragmaticke Recuſants; I leaue them to the Law; it is no perſecution, but good Iuſtice.

And thoſe Prieſts alſo, that out of my Grace and Mercy haue beene let goe out of priſons, and baniſhed, vpon condition not to returne; aske mee no queſtions touching theſe, quit me of them, and let mee not heare of them : And to them I ioyne thoſe that breake priſon; for ſuch Prieſts as the priſon will not hold, it is a plaine ſigne nothing will hold them but a halter : Such are no Martyrs that refuſe to ſuffer for their conſcience. *Paul*, notwithſtanding the doores were open, would not come foorth : And *Peter* came not out of the priſon till led by the Angel of God : But theſe will goe forth though with the angel of the Diuell.

I haue giuen order to my Lord of *Canterbury*, and my Lord of *London* for the diſtinction, &c. of the degrees of Prieſts; and when I haue an accompt from them, then will I giue you another charge concerning them.

Another thing that offendeth the Realme, is abundance of Ale-houſes; and therefore to auoyd the giuing occaſion of euill, and to take away the root, and puniſh the example of vice, I would haue the infamous Ale-houſes pulled downe, and a command to all Iuſtices of Peace that this be done.

I may complaine of Ale-houſes, for receipt of Stealers of my Deere; but the countrey may complaine for ſtealing their horſes, oxen, and ſheepe; for murder, cutting of purſes, and ſuch like offences; for theſe are their haunts. Deuouring beaſts, as Lyons and Beares, will not bee where they haue no dennes nor couert; So there would be no theeues, if they had not their receipts, and theſe Ale-houſes as their dennes.

Another ſort, are a kinde of Alehouſes, which are houſes of haunt and receipt for debauſhed rogues and vagabonds, and idle ſturdie fellowes; and theſe are not properly Ale-houſes, but baſe victuallers, ſuch as haue nothing elſe to liue by, but keeping houſes of receipt for ſuch kinde of cuſtomers. I haue diſcouered a ſtrange packe of late, That within tenne or twelue miles of *London*, there are ten or twelue perſons that liue in ſpight of mee, going with Piſtols, and walking vp and downe from harbour to harbour killing my Deere, and ſo ſhift from hold to hold, that they cannot be apprehended.

For Rogues, you haue many good Acts of Parliament: *Edward* the ſixt,
                                                                    though

though hee were a child, yet for this, he in his time gaue better order then many Kings did in their aage : You muſt take order for theſe Beggars and Rogues ; for they ſo ſwarme in euery place, that a man cannot goe in the ſtreetes, nor in the high wayes, nor any where for them.

Looke to your houſes of Correction , and remember that in the chiefe Iuſtice *Pophams* time, there was not a wandering begger to bee found in all *Somerſetſhire,* being his natiue countrey.

Haue a care alſo to ſuppreſſe the building of Cottages vpon Commons, which are as bad as Alehouſes, and the dwellers in them doe commonly ſteale Deere, Conies, ſheepe, oxen, horſes, breake houſes, and doe all maner of villanies. It is trew , ſome ill Iuſtices make gaine of theſe baſe things : take an accompt of the Iuſtices of Peace , that they may know they doe theſe things againſt the will of the King.

I am likewiſe to commend vnto you a thing very neceſſarie , High-wayes and Bridges ; becauſe no Common-weale can bee without paſſage : I proteſt, that as my heart doeth ioy in the erection of Schooles and Hoſpitals, which haue beene more in my time, then in many aages of my predeceſſours ; ſo it grieues mee, and it is wonderfull to ſee the decay of charitie in this ; how ſcant men are in contributing towards the a-mendment of High-wayes and Bridges : Therefore take a care of this, for that is done to day with a penie, that will not bee done hereafter with an hundred pounds, and that will be mended now in a day, which hereaf-ter will not be mended in a yeere ; and that in a yeere, which will not bee done in our time, as we may ſee by *Pauls* Steeple.

Another thing to be cared for, is, the new Buildings here about the Ci-tie of *London* ; concerning which my Proclamations haue gone foorth, and by the chiefe Iuſtice here, and his Predeceſſor *Popham,* it hath bene re-ſolued to be a generall nuſans to the whole Kingdome : And this is that, which is like the Spleene in the body, which in meaſure as it ouergrowes, the body waſtes. For is it poſſible but the Countrey muſt diminiſh, i f *London* doe ſo increaſe, and all ſorts of people doe come to *London* ? and where doeth this increaſe appeare? not in the heart of the Citie, but in the ſuburbes ; not giuing wealth or profit to the Citie, but bringing mi-ſerie and ſurcharge both to Citie and Court ; cauſing dearth and ſcarſitie through the great prouiſion of victuals and fewel, that muſt be for ſuch a multitude of people : And theſe buildings ſerue likewiſe to harbour the worſt ſort of people, as Alehouſes and Cottages doe. I remember, that before Chriſtmas was Twelue-moneth I made a Proclamation for this cauſe , That all Gentlemen of qualitie ſhould depart to their owne coun-treys and houſes, to maintaine Hoſpitalitie amongſt their neighbours ; which was equiuocally taken by ſome, as that it was meant onely for that Chriſtmas : But my will and meaning was , and here I declare that my meaning was, that it ſhould alwayes continue.

One of the greateſt cauſes of all Gentlemens deſire, that haue no calling or errand, to dwell in *London*, is apparently the pride of the women: For if they bee wiues, then their husbands; and if they be maydes, then their fathers muft bring them vp to *London*; becaufe the new fafhion is to bee had no where but in *London*: and here, if they be vnmarried, they marre their marriages, and if they be married, they loofe their reputations, and rob their husbands purfes.. It is the fafhion of *Italy*, efpecially of *Naples*, (which is one of the richeft parts of it) that all the Gentry dwell in the principall Townes, and fo the whole countrey is emptie: Euen fo now in *England*, all the countrey is gotten into *London*; fo as with time, *England* will onely be *London*, and the whole countrey be left wafte : For as wee now doe imitate the French fafhion, in fafhion of Clothes, and Lackeys to follow euery man; So haue wee got vp the Italian fafhion, in liuing miferably in our houfes, and dwelling all in the Citie: but let vs in Gods Name leaue thefe idle forreine toyes, and keepe the old fafhion of *England*: For it was wont to be the honour and reputation of the Englifh Nobilitie and Gentry, to liue in the countrey, and keepe hofpitalitie; for which we were famous aboue all the countreys in the world; which wee may the better doe, hauing a foile abundantly fertile to liue in.

And now out of my owne mouth I declare vnto you, (which being in this place, is equall to a Proclamation, which I intend likewife fhortly hereafter to haue publikely proclaimed,) that the Courtiers, Citizens, and Lawyers, and thofe that belong vnto them, and others as haue Pleas in Terme time, are onely neceffary perfons to remaine about this Citie; others muft get them into the Countrey; For befide the hauing of the countrey defolate, when the Gentrie dwell thus in *London*, diuers other mifchiefes arife vpon it : Firft, if infurrections fhould fall out (as was lately feene by the Leuellers gathering together) what order can bee taken with it, when the countrey is vnfurnifhed of Gentlemen to take order with it? Next, the poore want reliefe for fault of the Gentlemens hofpitalitie at home: Thirdly, my feruice is neglected, and the good gouernment of the countrey for lacke of the principall Gentlemens prefence, that fhould performe it: And laftly, the Gentlemen lofe their owne thrift, for lacke of their owne prefence, in feeing to their owne bufineffe at home. Therefore as euery fifh liues in his owne place, fome in the frefh, fome in the falt, fome in the mud : fo let euery one liue in his owne place, fome at Court, fome in the Citie, fome in the Countrey; fpecially at Feftiuall times, as Chriftmas and Eafter, and the reft.

And for the decreafe of new Buildings heere, I would haue the builders reftrained, and committed to prifon; and if the builders cannot be found, then the workemen to be imprifoned; and not this onely, but likewife the buildings to bee caft downe; I meane fuch buildings as may be ouerthrowen without inconuenience, and therefore that to be done by order and direction.

There may be many other abufes that I know not of; take you care my
Lords

Lords the Iudges of thefe, and of all other; for it is your part to looke vn_
to them. I heare fay, robbery begins to abound more then heretofore,
and that fome of you are too mercifull; I pray you remember, that mercy
is the Kings, not yours, and you are to doe Iuftice where trew caufe is:
And take this for a rule of Policie , That what vice moft abounds in a
Common-wealth, that muft be moft feuerely punifhed, for that is trew
gouernment.

And now I will conclude my Speach with G o d, as I began. Firft,
that in all your behauiours, afwell in your Circuits as in your Benches,
you giue due reuerence to G o d; I meane, let not the Church nor Church_
men bee difgraced in your Charges, nor Papifts nor Puritanes counte-
nanced : Countenance and encourage the good Church-men, and teach
the people by your example to reuerence them : for, if they be good, they
are worthy of double honour for their Office fake; if they be faultie, it is
not your place to admonifh them; they haue another *Forum* to anfwere to
for their misbehauiour.

Next, procure reuerence to the King and the Law, enforme my people
trewly of mee, how zealous I am for Religion, how I defire Law may bee
maintained and flourifh ; that euery Court fhould haue his owne Iurifdiction; that euery Subiect fhould fubmit himfelfe to Law ; So may you
liue a happie people vnder a iuft K I N G, freely enioying the fruite of
P E A C E and I V S T I C E, as fuch a people fhould doe.

Now I confeffe, it is but a *Tandem aliquando*, as they fay in the Schooles,
that I am come hither : Yet though this bee the firft, it fhall not, with the
grace of G o d, bee the laft time of my comming , now my choice is taken away ; for hauing once bene here, a meaner occafion may bring mee
againe : And I hope I haue euer caried my felfe fo, and by G o d s grace
euer will, as none will euer fufpect, that my comming here will be to any
partiall end; for I will euer bee carefull in point of Iuftice, to keepe my
felfe vnfpotted all the dayes of my life. And vpon this my generall proteftation; I hope the world will know, that I came hither this
day to maintaine the Law, and doe Iuftice
according to my Oath.
(***)

IMPRINTED AT
LONDON BY ROBERT
BARKER, AND IOHN BILL,
PRINTERS TO THE KINGS
MOST EXCELLENT
MAIESTIE.

ANNO DOM. 1616.

Cum Priuilegio.

A MEDITATION
VPON THE LORDS
PRAYER:
WRITTEN BY THE KINGS
MAIESTIE,

For the benefit of all his ſubiects, eſpecially of
ſuch as follow the Court.

THE PREFACE.

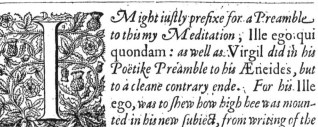

*M ight iuſtly prefixe for a Preamble
to this my Meditation ; Ille ego qui
quondam :* as well as *Virgil did in his
Poëtike Preamble to his* Æneides, *but
to a cleane contrary ende. For his.* Ille
ego, *was to ſhew how high hee was mounted in his new ſubiect, from writing of the
plough, to write now of Princes and their Warres : whereas ʃ
now, cleane contrary, am come from wading in theſe high and
profound Myſteries in the Reuelation, wherein an Elephant
may ſwimme; to meditate vpon the plaine , ſmoothe and eaſie
Lords Prayer, that euery olde wife can either ſay or mumble,
and euery well bred childe can interprete by his Catechiſme :
Hauing left ſo the ſolid meate that men feede vpon, for the milke*

Ccc   *fit*

*The Triall of
Wits wisheth
euery man to
abstaine from
writing any
bookes, as
soone as he is
past fiftie,
cap. 1.

* Reiice ani-
les fabulas.
1. Tim.

fit for babes. But the *reason is* , *f grow in yeeres , and olde men are twice babes, as the* Prouerbe is ; *hauing imitated* Cardinall Bellarmine *heerein, who of late yeeres hath giuen ouer his bickerings in* Polemikes *and* Controuersies, *wherein hee was bred all his life, and betaken himselfe now to set out a short Meditation euery yeere, onely embellishing almost euery one of them with some two or three* *fabulous miracles, wherein hee shall goe alone for my part. But now when I bethinke my selfe, to whom f can most aptly dedicate this little labour of mine , most of it being stollen from the houres ordained for my sleepe : and calling to minde , how carefull I haue euer beene to obserue a* decorum *in the dedication of my bookes.* As my ΒΑΣΙΛΙΚΟΝ ΔΩΡΟΝ *was dedicated to my Sonne* HENRY, *now with God, because it treated of the Office of a King , it now belonging to my only Sonne* CHARLES, *who succeeds to it by right, as well as to all the rest of his brothers goods : and as I dedicated my* Apologie for the Oath of Allegiance *to all free Christian Princes and States , because they had all of them an interest in that argument. other of my bookes which treated of matters belonging to euery qualitie of persons , being therefore indefinitely dedicated to the* Reader *in generall , f cannot surely finde out a person, to whom I can more fitly dedicate this short* Meditation *of mine, then to you,* BVCKINGHAM. *For it is made upon a very short and plaine* Prayer, *and therefore the fitter for a Courtier: For Courtiers , for the most part , are thought neither to haue list nor leisure to say long prayers, liking best* courte Messe & long *disner. But to confesse the trueth now in earnest , it is the fitter for you that it is both short and plaine. That it is short, because when I consider of your continuall attendance vpon my seruice, your dayly imployments in the same, and the vncessant swarme of suitors importunately hanging vpon you, without discretion or distinction of times, I can find but very little time for you to spare vpon meditation: And that it is plaine, it is the fitter for you, since you were not bred a scholler. You may likewise claime a iust interest in it for diuers other respects. First, from the ground of my*

Like S. Chri-
stopher that
neither could
nor would fast
nor pray for
attayning to
the seruice of
Christ, and
therefore was
set to a Por-
ters worke by
the Ermite.

writing

writing it; for diuers times before I medled with it, I told you, and
only you, of some of my conceptions vpon the Lords Prayer, and
you often solicited me to put penne to paper: next, as the person to
whom we pray it, is our heauenly Father, so am I that offer it vnto you, not onely your politike, but also your œconomike Father,
and that in a neerer degree then vnto others. Thirdly, that you
may make good vse of it ; for since I dayly take care to better your
vnderstanding, to enable you the more for my seruice in wordly a-
faires, reason would that Gods part should not be left out, for ti-
mor Domini, &c. initium sapientiæ. And lastly, I must with
ioy acknowledge, that you deserue this gift of mee, in not onely giuing so good example to the rest of the Court, in frequent hearing
the word of God: but in speciall, in so often receiuing the Sacrament, which is a notable demonstration of your charitie in pardoning them that offend you, that being the thing I most labour to recommend to the world, in this Meditation of mine: and how godly
and vertuous all my aduises haue euer been vnto you, I hope you
will faithfully witnesse to the world. Receiue then this New-
yeeres gift from me, as a token of my loue, being begun vpon the
Eue of our Sauiours Natiuitie, and ended farre within the first
moneth of the yeere: praying God, that as you are regene-
rated and borne anew, so you may rise to him, and
bee sanctified in him for euer.
Amen.

This paper-
friend will not
importune
you at vnseaso-
nable houres,
come vncal-
led, nor speake
vnrequired, &
yet wil he nei-
ther flatter, lie,
nor dissemble.

Ccc 2

A MEDITATION
VPON THE LORDS
PRAYER.

F all things, the Seruice of God is the moſt due, neceſſary, and profitable action of a Chriſtian man. Of all Seruices of God, Prayer is the moſt excellent for many reſpects, & of all Prayers, the Lords Prayer is the moſt perfect, vſeful and comfortable. That the Seruice of God is to be preferred to all other actions of a Chriſtian man, no Chriſtian will doubt, the glory of God beeing the proper end of mans creation, whom hee is ordained to glorifie : Firſt, temporally, during the time of his pilgrimage vpon this earth ; and next for euer in his eternall habitation. That Prayer is to be preferred to all other actions of a Chriſtian man, the Commandement giuen vs, the excellencie of the Action, and the infinite fruit wee receiue by the vſe thereof, doeth ſufficiently prooue it. The Commandement, *Pray continually*, wee are commaunded to doe no other thing continually, but to pray : all other things haue fit times ſet for them. Euery thing * hath a time, as *Salomon* ſayes, but prayer is barred at no time, if a mans zeale kindle his heart, and diſpoſe his thoughts vnto it, And the excellencie of the action is manifeſt in that, that, whereas at all other times when wee ſpeake, it is but with men like our ſelues ; wee then by prayer ſpeake with God, and in a manner conferre with him , as halfe Angels for that time, our faith and hope beeing, by the force of Prayer, ſtirred vp and enabled to draw God downe to vs, and make him become ours ; yea, euen to dwell with vs, that we may be his for euer. And as to the infinite fruit wee receiue by the vſe thereof, wee are commanded by our Sauiour , to aske and it ſhall be granted vnto vs, to ſeeke and wee ſhall find, to knocke and it ſhall

                                    bee

*Eccles.3.

bee opened vnto vs. If * wee aske bread, wee ſhall not haue ſtones, if
wee aske fiſhes, wee ſhall not haue ſerpents; and if wee aske egges, wee
ſhall not haue ſcorpions. Hee alſo tels vs, what things ſoeuer wee deſire when wee pray, ſo that wee beleeue wee receiue them, wee ſhall
haue them ; Yea, euen wee are commanded to imitate the importunity of the * widowe in prayer, with aſſurance of the like ſucceſſe. And
if euer this doctrine was needfull in any age, it is moſt in ours : for
now our zeale to prayer is quite dried vp and cooled, and turned to
* pratling, eſpecially in this Iſle, where the *Puritanes* will haue vs hunt
for hearing of Sermons without ceaſing; but as little prayer as yee will,
turning the commandement of the Apoſtle from *Pray continuallie* to
Preach continually, onely obeying another commandement of the ſame
Apoſtle, in preaching and exhorting both in ſeaſon and out of ſeaſon.
Now that the L O R D S P R A Y E R is the moſt excellent and perfect
of all prayers, is agreed vpon by all Chriſtians, euen by the very rebellious *Browniſts* themſelues (though they will neuer ſay it in their owne
prayers) the reaſon is, becauſe it is the only prayer that our Sauiour dicta-
ted out of his own mouth, with a precept to vs of imitation. But that fooliſh ground, whereupon the *Browniſts* diſobey Chriſts precept of imitation, is onely founded vpon their imitation of their fathers, the Engliſh
Puritans, whom they ſtriue to outgoe in zeale, vpon their owne grounds.
For our *Puritanes* will ſay no ſet prayer, forſooth, * that is preſcribed
by their mother the Church, but euery brother muſt conceiue one vpon the ſudden, and therefore the *Browniſts* refuſe to ſay the L O R D S
P R A Y E R, becauſe it is a ſet Prayer, though preſcribed by God himſelfe, ſhifting their diſobedience vpon this æquiuocation, that they are
commanded to pray after this manner, but not in the ſame words, that
is, they may pray, or rather ſing the deſcant of it, as their owne vaine
braines ſhall pleaſe to conceiue it, but not the plaine ſong, they may
pray by a Commentary, but not by a Text. And thus, * *nec agnoſ-
cunt Deum pro Patre, nec Eccleſiam pro Matre*, in ſetting downe rules
vnto them; for in the Text it ſelfe, Saint *Luke* 11. Chriſt himſelfe
preſcribeth, *Quando oratis, dicite*, P A T E R N O S T E R, *&c.* and indeed our
Puritans goe very neere to ioyne with them in blotting out the L O R D S
P R A Y E R. For they * quarell our Church for hauing it twiſe ſaid in our
dayly Common prayer, ſo as they could be content with as little of it as
may bee. But this monſtrous conceit of * conceiued prayers, without
any premeditation, ſpoyleth both *Puritanes* and *Browniſts*. I iuſtly call
it monſtrous, ſince they will haue a thing both conceiued and borne at
once, contrary to nature, which will haue euery thing to lie in the belly
of the mother a certaine time, after the conception, there to grow and
ripen before it bee produced; and this is the vniuerſall courſe of nature,
aſwell in animall as vegetable things, yea, euen in mineralls within the
bowels of the earth; though the *Alchymiſts* in that point agree with the

Puritans

* Luke 6.

* Luke 18.

* In this age
wee content
our ſelues to
talke of the
ſeruice of God
in common
diſcourſe, but
our actions in-
tend nothing
leſſe, euery ig-
norant wo-
man, and or-
dinary craftſ-
man, taking
vpon them to
interpret the
Scriptures, as
Ierome com-
plaines *ad
Paulinum.*

* Set formes
of Common
Prayers haue
euer bin ap-
pointed, and
vſed in all
Churches, in
all ages.
*Conc. Mileuit.
can.* 12. *Nec a-
lie omnino pre-
ces dicantur in
Ecclesia, niſque
à prudentiori-
bus ſueſta tra-
ctata, vel com-
probata in Sy-
nodo fuerint,
&c.*
* *Aug. Symb.
ad catech. lib. 4.*
* The firſt
yeere of my
reigne in Eng-
land at the
conference
kept at Hamp-
ton Court by
my appoint-
ment, one of
the things
quarrelled by
the *Puritans*,
in our Engliſh
Liturgie, was
the repetition
of the Lords
Prayer.
* Abuſing that
place, Mat. 10.
19. *dabitur vo-
bis in illa hora,
&c.*

Puritanes and *Brownifts*: and indeed, our *Puritanes* may iuftly be called *Chymicall* Doctors in Diuinity, with their quinteffence of refined and pure doctrine. And in this, Grace imitates Nature, not producing any perfect worke at the firft, but by degrees. But in cafe men might thinke that I wrong our *Puritans*, in calling them the *Brownifts* fathers; I muft craue leaue of the Reader to digreffe here a little, for his better fatisfacti-on in this point. I told you already, how that vpon our *Puritans* ground of reiecting all fet prayers, they refufe to fay the LORDS PRAYER. And now I am to prooue, how that vpon our *Puritanes* grounds they found their totall feparation from vs. Our *Puritans* are aduerfe to the gouernment of Bifhops, calling it an Antichriftian gouernement, and therefore the *Brownifts*, left the ruines of *Babylon* fhould fall vpon them, will not acknowledge the Bifhops, neither in their name or Title, neither in their Temporall or Spirituall iurifdiction. And our *Puritanes* quarrell with all the Ceremonies of our Church, that agree not with their tafte, be-caufe the Church of *Rome* doth vfe them, who (fay they) haue polluted them, though they were cleane before; abufing thefe words in the Can-

*Thefe words of the Canti-cle were al-leadged in this fence in the Lincolnfhire *Puritans* Peti-tion, prefented by themfelues vnto me.

ticle of *Salomon*; * *nigra fum, fed formofa*; whereupon the *Brownifts* con-clude; that they can no longer remaine in the bofome of that Church, nor fucke her breafts any longer; that is fo polluted with Antichriftian fuperftitions. And this is the true ground of their feparation, for thefe caufes, which make our *Puritane* minifters, *defertores officij fui, & gregis eis commiffi*, feeme to the *Brownifts* a iuft ground for going out of our Church: and becaufe that all our goodly materiall Churches were built in time of Popery, and fo polluted by the hands of Papifts, and with their confecrations and holy water, therefore to the woods and caues muft they goe, like outlawes and rebels, to their Sermons and diuine exercifes,

*Cartwright contra Whit-gift.

iuft building vpon * *Cartwrights* ground, That he that was once a Popifh Prieft, can neuer bee admitted to the Miniftery in a rightly reformed Church. And thus haue I fufficiently prooued, I hope, that our *Puri-taus* are the founders and fathers of the *Brownifts*; the latter onely boldly putting in practife what the former doe teach, but dare not performe. And not only are our *Puritans* founders and fathers to the *Brownifts*, but vpon their foundation and ground are alfo built vp all thefe innumera-ble Sects of newe Herefies, that now fwarme in *Amfterdam*.

For the true vifible Church, when fhee is in profperity, as (GOD bee thanked) fhee is now is this Kingdome, is *ciuitas fuper montem pofita*, fhe is feated vpon the top of a fteepe hill, where her children muft ftay and dwell with her; for one ftep downe may make them flide ouer the preci-pice, where there is no bufh nor ftay to hold them by, till they fall to the bottome of the hill with all their weight, where lies that vnquenchable fiery lake of fire and brimftone. For although a man that had neuer knowen Chrift, being willing to become a Chriftian, muft bee well aduifed what Church he will become a member of, if hee be not already bred

in

in the bosome of the true Church; and therein he must trust to his owne conscience to beare him witnesse, what Church doeth truely preach the word of saluation, according to the reuealed will of God, and doth not mixe, and contradict the points of saluation conteined in the Scripture, with their owne Traditions : For all the points of our saluation are (God be thanked) cleere and plaine in the Scriptures; a lambe may easily wade through that foord, as Saint * *Gregory* saith : Yet then as soone as he hath thus made his choice what Church to liue and die in, *audi eam,* as Christ commands : for his conscience in this must onely serue him for a guide to the right Church , but not to iudge her, but to bee iudged by her. For hee that will haue God to bee his Father, must also haue the true Church to be his Mother, as Saint * *Augustine* saith. Hold fast therefore your profession, as the * Apostle exhorts vs, and be not caried away with the winde of euery doctrine; nor trust not to that priuate spirit or holy ghost which our *Puritans* glory in; for then a little fiery zeale will make thee turne *Separatist*, and then * proceede still on from *Brownist* to some one Sect or other of *Anabaptist*, and from one of these to another, then to become a Iudaized *Traskite*, and in the end a profane *Familist*. Thus yee see; how that letting slippe the hold of the true Church, and, once trusting to the priuate spirit of Reformation, according to our *Puritans* doctrine, it is easie to fall and slide by degrees into the *Chaos*, filthy sinke and *farrago* of all horrible heresies, whereof hell is the iust reward.

And now I returne to my purpose, crauing pardon for this digression, for the zeale I haue to preserue the Church from these foxes, and little foxes, *Heretiques* and *Sectaries*, hath enforced mee, that with the Doue tooke this Oliue branch in my mouth in this Meditation of mine vpon the L O R D S P R A Y E R ; to seeme to play the Rauen that was sent out of the Arke, in flying ouer the sweet Oliue boughes, and lighting on a stinking carrion.

The L O R D s P R A Y E R then beeing my present Meditation, I haue thought good, first to set downe the Prayer it selfe, as it is written by S. *Matthew*, next, I will, with Gods grace, shortly interpret the meaning thereof, and last, I will in very few words draw it into a short summe : which will be the more easily vnderstood when the meaning of the words shall be first explaned. The words then are these; OVR FATHER WHICH ART IN HEAVEN, HALLOVVED BE THY NAME : THY KINGDOM COME : THY WILL BEE DONE IN EARTH, AS IT IS IN HEAVEN : GIVE VS THIS DAY OVR DAYLY BREAD : AND FORGIVE VS OVR DEBTS, AS WE FORGIVE OVR DEBTORS : AND LEAD VS NOT IN- TO TEMPTATION, BVT DELIVER VS FROM EVILL : FOR THINE IS THE KINGDOME, AND THE POVVER, AND THE GLORY, FOR EVER, AMEN.

OVR FATHER : FATHER, is a title of dignity and honour, but OVR FATHER is a title of infinite loue, ioyned with greatnesse. These two first

words,

words,are to put vs in minde, that are but duſt and aſhes, what perſon we
are to ſpeake vnto ; for preparing our reuerence in the higheſt degree;
not like the *Puritans*,to talke homely with God,as our fellow: who therefore loue to ſit *Iack-fellowlike* with Chriſt at the Lords Table , as his brethren and camerades: and yet our reuerence to bee mixed with a ſweete
confidence in his loue;for he is our Father, and we are his adopted children and coheires with Chriſt of his Kingdome. Euery one of vs is commanded to call him Ovr Father, in the plurall number , to ſhew that
holy communion which is among the Saints , and that euery one of vs is
a member of a body of a Church, that is compacted of many members :
contrary to thoſe little ſtart vp ſects in *Amſterdam* , where two or three
make a Church ; and contrary to all thoſe contemners of Antiquitie, that
will haue nothing,but all Babyloniſh till their time.

    Which Art In Heaven : This is the place where the
Throne of his Maieſtie is ſet ; for though hee bee preſent euery where as
well in his infinite eſſence as power, in ſpight both of *Vorſtius* and ſome
of the *Arminians* ; yet is hee onely reſident in heauen , as the Seat of his
Maieſtie,according to that of *Eſay 66. 1. Heauen is my Throne, and earth is
my foot-ſtoole.* And by the nomination heere of heauen,it puts vs in mind
what Father we pray vnto, that it is no earthly man , but onely our heauenly Father, *ſurſum corda*.

    Now wee come to the Petitions,the number whereof by moſt of the
ancient Church was reckoned to bee ſeuen ; diuiding in two Petitions,
Leade vs not into temptation, and deliuer vs from euill : whereas of late dayes
wee haue confounded them in one. But ſurely in mine opinion, the
Fathers had good reaſon to diuide them ; as I ſhall ſhew in the owne
time.

    Hallovved Be Thy Name : This is the firſt Petition,
and this is the affirmatiue of that whereof the contrary is prohibited in
the third Commandement. *Thou ſhalt not take the Name of the Lord thy
God in vaine.* Wee firſt make this Petition , that all men may doe
their homage which they owe vnto God, as wee now doe, before
wee make our ſuites, either for the publike welfare of the Church , or
our owne priuate benefit. For it were an impudent thing for any
Subiect to make a ſute to his Soueraigne Prince ; before hee did his
homage vnto him. The principall ende for which God created man
after his Image, was that hee might ſanctifie his Name ; and this is not
onely the Office of the Militant Church heere ; and of euery one of
them ; but it is alſo the eternall Office of the Church triumphant in
Heauen ; compoſed of Angels and men, who without ceaſing praiſe and
ſanctifie the Name of God for euer. Wee ſanctifie his Name in this
earth, either when wee praiſe God,pray to him with reuerence, or ſpeake
of his wonderfull workes, repent vs of our ſinnes: with confeſſion of
them, edifie our brethren to ſaluation, or beare witneſſe to the trueth

being duely required. Wee are also to obserue that these wordes are not heere set downe in the present time, *Wee hallow thy Name*, but in the sense of the Optatiue moode, *Hallowed be thy Name*; becaufe euery Chriftian man as a feeling member of the body of the Church, ought to pray that Gods Name may bee prayfed, and fanctified by men and Angels: not onely for the prefent, but in all times comming, and after that there fhall be no more time, for euer and euer eternally. And although wee knowe it muft and euer will bee fo, yet wee pray and wifh it, to fhewe and expreffe our harmonie and holy zeale to prayfe God, ioyntly with the reft of the members, both of the Militant and Triumphant Church. But that wee are to pray for in this Petition is, that all the behauiour of the Militant Church may euer hee directed chiefly to that end, that his Name may bee fanctified in all their words and actions. Now that wee doe not wifh God to be hallowed, but his Name; the reafon is eafie, for God is not onely perfectly holy, but hee is euen *ipfa fanctitas, & quicquid eft in Deo eft Deus* : therefore wee pray that his Name may bee hallowed amongft vs here vpon earth, as himfelfe is perfectly holy both in his Name and effence, not that hereby wee can imagine to make him and his Name holy, but that God would giue vs grace to vfe it holily. It is also to bee noted, that not onely in this Prayer, but euen in all other Prayers, wee fpeake to God in the fingular number, *Thou*, whereas, *Wee*, is a ftile of greatneffe amongft men; the reafon is, that God is one, yea, vnitie it felfe : not that Wee acknowledge with the *Iewes*, *Arrians*, and other *Heretikes*, But one perfon in the God-head, blotting out both the Sonne and the Holy Ghoft; but becaufe though there bee three perfons, yet is there but one indiuiduall effence, one in three, and three in one, diftinguifhed, but not diuided, according to the *Athanafian* Creede. And therefore becaufe wee haue onely one to pray vnto, to whom onely all glory appertaines, wee call him *Thou*, *per excellentiam*; keeping out of our Kalender, as well the Heathen gods, as the Popifh Saints; for God-Almighty will haue no fellowes ioyned in worfhip with him, as himfelfe declares in the firft of the ten Commandements, and alfo in *Efay* 42.8. God tells vs, hee will not giue his glory to another.

THY KINGDOME COME, This is the fecond Petition, and it will admit two interpretations, that may both ftand with the Analogie of faith. The firft, that in thefe words we pray for the fecond comming of CHRIST, which is promifed to bee haftened for the elects fake : the reafon is that an end may be put to the miferies of the Church, efpecially in regard of that fearefull defection that is threatned to come in the latter dayes, and whereof wee in our dayes haue the dolefull experience, that *Faith fhall not bee found on the earth, and the *loue of many fhall waxe colde. And whofoeuer will make choyce of this interpretation, muft vnderftand the next Petition in this forme, In the

*Luke 18.8.
*Matt.24.12.

meane

meane time, *Thy will bee done in earth as it is in Heauen.* The other interpretation is, to which I rather incline, that the wordes of *Thy Kingdome
come* are seconded by the next following Petition, *Thy will bee done in
earth, as it is in Heauen.* The reasons perswading mee to like best of
this opinion are two; First, becauseit is C H R I S T S vsuall phrase in
the Gospell by the Kingdome of Heauen to meane the Church Militant; and all the faithfull are bound to pray for the flourishing prosperitie of the Church, and that there may bee peace in Israel. The o-
ther reason is, becausе of the next following Petition; *Thy will bee done,
&c.* that is, that by the meanes of the flourishing of the Church, the
will of G O D may bee done in earth as it is in heauen. And vpon the
other part, although wee bee commaunded when wee shall see the
signes going beefore the latter day, to * lift vp our heads, knowing that
the latter day, the day of our deliuerance is at hand: and although Saint

*Luk.21.28.
*Rom.8.22.

Paul tells vs, that *the * whole creation groaneth and trauaileth in paine*, to bee
renewed; and that Saint *Iohn* after hee had been rauished in spirit, where
besides many other heauenly mysteries, hee saw the glory of the very
Throne of G O D. Albeit (I say) that vpon that glorious sight he burst

*Reuel.22.20

foorth in these words, * *etiam veni Domine Iesu:* yet I can finde no cleare
place of Scripture that commands euery faithfull man to pray continually for the hastening of the Lords comming: and to alleadge these words
in the L O R D S P R A Y E R for it, is *petitio principij,* and to take *controuer-
sum pro confesso.* For though death bee the deliuerer of euery faithfull
man from this prison and body of sinne, to eternall felicity, our Sauiour
by his death and passion hauing killed the sting of death in vs: and al-

*Phil.1.23.

though Saint *Paul,* rauished in a high contemplation wished to bee * dis-
solued, and bee with Christ, yet haue wee no warrant euery man to pray
for the hastening of his owne death; and death is to euery particular
faithfull man the same thing, that the generall transmutation will be at
the latter day to the whole body of the Elect; except that we will after the
generall dissolution, attaine to a greater degree of glory. Now that
wee desire the Kingdome of God to come, is thereby meant, that we desire, that the Church of God may more and more bee spread vpon the
face of the earth; and that the number of the Elect may bee multiplied.
In a word, that hee would send a plentifull haruest, with sufficient store of
labourers.

T H Y W I L B E D O N E I N E A R T H A S I T I S I N H E A V E N.
This third Petition I take to bee a Prayer, to grant vs the meanes of attaining to his Kingdome, as if yee would say, *Thy Kingdome come,*
and to this effect let thy will be done, &c. Saint *Luke* hath it, *as in heauen, so in
earth,* to shew how precisely wee ought to wish that Gods will were done
in earth iust as it is in heauen. God hath two * wills, a reuealed will to-

* Voluntas sig-
ni & bene pla-
citi.

wards vs, and that will is here vnderstood; hee hath also a secret will in his
eternal counsel, wherby all things are gouerned, and in the end made euer

                                                          to

to turne to his glory, oftentimes drawing good effects out of bad caufes, and light out of darkeneſſe, to the fulfilling either of his mercie or
iuſtice;which made S. *Auguſtine* fay, *bonum eſt vt fit malum.*

Wee are then to pray, that his reuealed will may bee obeyed in earth
by his Militant Church, as it is by his Triumphing Church in heauen:
then would this Militant Church vpon earth obſerue better the two Tables of the Law, then now they doe, and then would the Church bee
free of Schiſmes, Hereſies, and all new opinions; but this is neuer to
bee looked for in this world. Wee are onely to wiſh, that God would
multiplie and increaſe his bleſſings vpon her, in that meaſure that hee
ſhall thinke moſt expedient for his glory, and her comfort. For let the
vaine *Chiliaſts* gape for that thouſand yeeres of C H R I S T s kingdome to
bee ſetled vpon earth, and let *Brightmam* bring downe that heauenly
Ieruſalem, and ſettle it in this world, the word of God aſſures vs, that
the later dayes ſhall prooue the worſt,and moſt dangerous dayes. Now
as for the performance of the decrees and ſecret will of God, wee are not
commanded to pray for that, for it is ineuitable; but wee muſt without
murmuring ſubmit our ſelues vnto it, ſaying with our Sauiour, *Matth.*
26.39. *not my will, but thy will bee done.* For the firſt Article of the Apoſtles Creede teacheth vs, that God is Almighty, how euer *Vorſtius* and
the *Arminians* thinke to robbe him of his eternall decree, and ſecret will,
making many things to bee done in this world whether he will or not.

G I V E V s T H I S D A Y O V R D A Y L Y B R E A D. This is
the fourth Petition in order, but the firſt that euery particular man is to
begge for himſelfe, hauing firſt preferred his generall Petitions for the
aduancement of the glory of God, and the felicitie, by conſequence, of
the whole Church Militant in generall. But though euery man in particular is to begge this for himſelfe, yet doe wee begge it for vs, in the
plurall number, and this wee doe to ſhew our charitie, as feeling members of that Bodie, whereof Chriſt is the Head: and ſo in all the reſt of
our petitions following, according to that rule in the New Teſtament,
* *Orate aij pro alijs.* And by this word, O V R, are wee alſo taught neuer ⟨*Iames 5.16.⟩
to pray for our ſelues,without praying alſo for our neighbour. But vpon
this rule of praying one for another,to ground the prayer to the Saints to
pray for vs,is very farre fetched; for then ſhould follow,That ſince we are
commanded to pray one for another, wee ſhould pray for the Saints, as
well as they for vs. Surely wee that are vpon this earth, are commanded to pray one for another; but no mention is made of Saints nor Angels in that precept, nor any where elſe in the word of God: and it is a
good ſure rule in Theologie, in matter of worſhip of God, *Quod dubi-*
tas ne feceris; according to that of Saint *Paul*, Rom.14.5.*Let euery man*
bee fully perſwaded in his minde. Beſides,we doe not make a formall prayer and worſhip one to another, that hee may pray for vs, as the Papiſtes
doe to their Saints. I meddle not with that queſtion, whether the Saints

or

or Angels pray for vs or not; but I am sure wee haue no warrant in the
word of God to pray to them for that end. Now the thing we pray for
in this petition, is *our daily bread*, which this day we begge at Gods hand.
We begge our daily bread, this day, at Gods hand, to shew that from the
poorest begger to the greatest King, no mortall creature is exeemed from
that necessity of daily begging all temporall benefits that we haue neede
of, at Gods hand: for euery houre, yea, euery minute we haue neede of
Gods assistance, both in our Spirituall and Temporall necessities ; and
therefore Saint *Luke* hath it, *day by day*, to expresse our daily necessity so
to pray. And we are to obserue, that not onely in this Petition, which is
the first in order of these foure which euery man prayes for himselfe ; but
also in the other three following, this word *daily*, is to be vnderstood, although it be not expressed : for we haue daily, yea, hourely neede to craue
pardon for our sinnes, to pray that we be not led into temptation, and to
be preserued from all euill. By this word, *Hodie, this day*, is likewise vnderstood the supplying of our temporall necessities through the whole course
of our life ; for in that sence the word, *Hodie*, for the * whole life, is taken
in diuers places of the Scripture.

    This word, *daily*, doth likewise put vs in mind, that we are but Pilgrims
in this world, and therefore are not to make a setled prouision for our
selues here ; according to the rule that our Sauiour gaue to his Apostles,
not to take care for to morrow. Not that hereby all lawfull prouidence
is forbidden to any man, according to his degree, for that were a tempting of God ; but onely that we should not haue a distrustfull or anxious
care, nor preferre the care of prouiding for worldly things, to our care of
laying vp a store of heauenly treasure : laying our speciall trust vpon
Gods blessing of our lawfull and moderate industry , for prouision of
temporall things ; remembring euer, that in vaine we plant or sow, except God giue the increase and blessing vnto it. For our principall care
must euer be for our heauenly habitation, and then God will the better
blesse and prosper our second and moderate care, for prouiding for our
temporall necessities. Let vs care for the principall, and not omit the o-
ther, as Christ said to the Pharises, Matth. 23. 23. By this word, *bread*, that
we pray for, is signified and vnderstood all kind of food, or other temporall necessities. Bread thorow all the Scriptures signifies all sort of foode ;
for it is the most common and necessary sort of food for man. And wee
see euen in these Northren parts of the world where we liue, and where
flesh is most eaten, corne, whereof bread is made, is onely called victuall,
and the word victuall comes *à victu*, becaufe we liue vpon it : and notwithstanding the abundance of flesh that we confume, yet good cheape
yeeres, or deare yeeres, are onely counted so, becaufe of the abundance or
scarcetie of corne in these yeeres. And therefore Christ ordained the
Sacrament in bread, to reprefent thereby our foode in generall vnto
vs ; for his flesh is very meate indeede. All our temporall necessities
                                         are

* Heb. 3. 7.

are alſo comprehended heere vnder the name of bread, to teach vs, that as bread is the commoneſt foode both to rich and poore, ſo wee ought to pray onely for ſuch temporall things as are neceſſary for our *eſſe*, or at fartheſt for our *bene eſſe* ; but not for thoſe things that are *ad luxum & ad ſuperfluitatem.* For commonly wee abuſe them to our owne hurt, and they ſerue vs but for baites to entice vs to ſinne : but if it ſhall pleaſe God, liberally to beſtow likewiſe theſe things vpon vs, wee are bound to bee thankefull for them, vſing them with ſobrietie and without exceſſe, according to our rankes and calling , euer remembring whoſe gift they are. And when we pray for *Bread*, that is, to be ſupplied of all our temporall neceſsities, wee muſt alſo comprehend therein the ſtaffe of bread, that is, to pray that the bleſsing may bee ioyned with the benefit, that it may ſerue vs for the right vſe for which it is ordained : otherwiſe wee ſhall ſtarue of hunger and the bread in our mouthes, wee ſhall die like the *Iſraelites*, with the fleſh of Quailes amongſt our teeth, and we ſhall haue all things for the ſupplying of our worldly neceſsities, and yet want the vſe and comfort of them : like the rich Miſer , who abounding in wealth ſtarues for want, or like the carriage-Moyle that carries a load of Prouender, and yet cannot ſatisfie her hungrie bellie with any part of it. Now that wee pray God to giue it vs, it is eaſie to bee vnderſtood ; for the Lord is the onely proprietarie both of Heauen and Earth , and all that therein is ; and wee are onely Vſu-fructuaries and his Tenants at will , euery one of vs of ſuch little parcels of earth, as it pleaſeth him to beſtowe vpon vs ; *nam * Domini eſt terra & plenitudo eius.*

* Pſal.24.1.

AND FORGIVE VS OVR DEBTS AS VVE FORGIVE OVR DEBTERS. This is the fift Petition, and the moſt important of them all, for euery man in particular ; and therefore we are not to craue that ineſtimable benefite of the pardon of our debts, except vpon that condition, that wee forgiue our debters. Saint *Luke* expreſſeth this condition more clearely : for hee hath it thus, *And forgiue vs our ſinnes ; for wee alſo forgiue euery one that is indebted vnto vs.* So as God cannot bee mooued for any other condition to pardon our ſinnes, but becauſe hee ſees wee haue already pardoned euery one that hath offended vs ; and where euery one is expreſſed, none is excepted : *durus eſt hic ſermo* amongſt them that are thought the braue men of this world. Our ſinnes are called debts in Saint *Matthew*, as an argument *à maiore ad minus* , that if wee would haue God to pardon vs our debts, how can wee refuſe to pardon our debters ; except wee looke for the like * reward that the euill ſeruant got of his maſter ? and in Saint *Luke* they are called ſinnes, to teach vs that if wee would haue our heauenly Father to remitte vnto vs all our innumerable mortall ſinnes ; how much more haue wee reaſon to pardon the offences of our brethren againſt vs, which are but ſlight debts , in compariſon of our grieuous ſinnes againſt God. And in that

* Matth.18.34

D d d   wee

wee pray God to forgiue vs our finnes, wee thereby make a generall implicite confeffion of our finnes: for if wee had committed no finnes,
wee would haue no neede to craue pardon for them. Whereupon it
doth neceffarily follow, that if the doctrine of the Church of *Rome* bee
true, that diuers men can keepe the tenne Commandements, without e-
uer in their life committing any mortall finne; then muft all fuch perfons
bee exeemed from praying the LORDS PRAYER, as not hauing neede of
it, and their diftinction betweene Mortall and Veniall finnes cannot
elide this confequence. For what needes a man craue pardon at GOD
for his Veniall finnes, when hee may haue as many Pardons from the
Pope *, as hee fhall pleafe to beftow his money vpon, both for Mortall
and Veniall finnes; and not onely for finnes already committed, but
euen for finnes to come, which is a farre greater grace then euer God
promifed vs. And I proteft that I haue feene two of thefe Authenticall Bulles with mine eyes: one, when I was very young in *Scotland*, and
it was taken from a *Scottifh* Prieft; and the other I fawe here in *England*,
taken from an Irifh-man, and both of them pa. doning fuch and fuch
finnes, as well by-paft as to come. But I returne to their diftinction
betwixt Mortall and Veniall finnes. For Veniall finnes carrie the
foules but to Purgatorie, according to their doctrine, whereof the
Pope hath the key to open and locke at his pleafure; and yet I hope
no man doubts, but all the Apoftles prayed the LORDS PRAYER;
for their Mafter taught it them in fpeciall, as appeares in Saint *Luke*: and
it is likely that they were as holy, and committed as few Mortall finnes,
as any of the Popes late legended Saints haue done. But we are all commaunded in Saint *Matthew* to pray thus, and where all are commaunded none are excepted, no not the bleffed Virgine her felfe, (whome
all ages fhall call bleffed) though the gray Friers, and *Bellarmine* with
them, labour hard to exeeme her, both from originall and actuall finnes.
And wee ought dayly to make this generall confeffion of our finnes, and
craue pardon for them, becaufe wee dayly commit finnes, * *Septies in die*
cadit iuftus. Heere now are wee taught to confeffe our finnes to GOD,
but I cannot finde, that in any place of the Scriptures a neceffitie is
impofed vpon vs; vnder the payne of damnation, of confeffing the
leaft one of our fecret finnes to a Prieft: nay if the leaft finfull thought
bee omitted, all the charme is fpilt. For as to that place, * *Confitemi-*
ni aly alijs, if yee meane it of the offences made by one againft another
in this world, a Prieft will not bee neceffarie to take the confeffion; or
if yee meane it by confeffion of finnes, wee are not by that commandement reftrained to make it to no other degree of perfons, but to a Prieft:
though I confeffe indeede, a godly difcreete Church-man is the fitteft
friend, that a man can choofe to confeffe his finnes vnto; and by his
helpe to obtaine comfort, and abfolution of his finnes, by the power
of the keyes. Neither will thefe places ferue their turne, *Dic * Ecclefia*,
or,

* This was *fœlix error* in the Church of *Rome*. For the monftrous & vnfupportable abufe of thefe Pardons in *Germany* in the time of *Leo decimus*, awaked *Luther*, by whom fuch a breach was made in the Popes iurifdiction, as could neuer after be made vp againe.

*Prou. 14. 16

*Iames 5. 16.

Matth. 18. 17.

or, *Present* *thy selfe to the high Priest,* or, *Quorum remiseritis peccata.* For the ſirſt of theſe places, *Dic Ecclesiæ,* is onely meant by the offences that one of vs commits againſt another; beſides that the Confeſſion in that caſe muſt bee publike, the offence being firſt made publike, for purging the publike ſcandall, contrary to their priuate whiſpering in a Prieſts eare, who is bound by his profeſſion neuer to reueale it to any creature, no though the concealing of it ſhould endanger a Kings life, and the deſtruction of a whole Kingdome: * nay euen though it ſhould endanger the life of our Sauiour, if hee were come in mortall fleſh into this worlde againe. And the ſecond concerning the comming before the high Prieſt, is likewiſe to bee vnderſtood of a publike action; beſides that their preſenting themſelues before the high Prieſt, was rather done for a publike Thankeſgiuing, and declaration of their obteining of health, or any ſuch benefit, as is manifeſt in that particular caſe of cleanſing of the Leper, to whom CHRIST, gaue * that commandement. And as to the third place, *Quorum remiseritis peccata;* that doeth indeede conteine the power of the Keyes giuen to the Church, not by aſtricting euery particular man, to make a particular enumeration of euery ſin, to a priuate Prieſt by Auricular confeſſion: but onely to ſhew the Churches miniſteriall power in pardoning, *that is,* in declaring ſuch ſinnes to bee pardoned in heauen, as the partie ſhall then ſhew a due contrition for. And yet *Bellarmine* is not aſhamed to ſay, that this conſtrained Auricular confeſſion of theirs, is *Iuris diuini,* and grounded vpon the word of God. For my part, with * *Caluine* I commend Confeſſion, euen priuately to a Churchman, as I ſaid before. And withall my heart I wiſh it were more in cuſtome amongſt vs then it is, as a thing of excellent vſe, eſpecially for preparing men to receiue the Sacrament worthily. But that neceſſity impoſed vpon it by the Romiſh Church, that euery ſecret thought that can be ſtretched towards any ſinne, muſt bee reuealed to a Confeſſor; that neceſſitie, I ſay, I iuſtly condemne, as hauing no warrant at all in the worde of God, though very beneficiall to the Church of *Rome.* Now as to the clauſe irritant in the contract betwixt God and vs, That hee will not pardon our ſinnes, except wee firſt forgiue euerie one that is indebted to vs, I told you alreadie, it is *durus sermo,* and ſpecially to them that are thought to haue high ſpirits: but I am ſure wee ſhall neuer attaine to that height of our heauenly habitation, except wee doe it. Since then this clauſe is *causa fine qua non,* in the point of our eternall felicitie, wee haue all great reaſon ſeriouſly to conſider; Firſt, what we are to win or loſe, in the performing or not performing of this condition ſet vnto vs: and next, whether the performance thereof, may eaſily be done or not, in caſe wee haue a minde to it. For the firſt, the caſe is plaine, for by performing of this condition vpon our part, we gaine the kingdom of Heauen, by obtaining pardon for our ſinnes: and by not performing it, we ſhut with our owne hands the gates of heauen againſt vs; for without

*Matth.8.4.
*Iohn 10.23.

* According to that aſſertion of a Ieſuite, mentioned in reſp. ad Epiſt. Card. Peronij, pag. 28.

*Matth.8.4.

Inſt. lib. 3. cap. 4 ſect. 12.

† Matt. 5. 39.
* Matt. 18. 9.

* *Origen* was iuftly puni-fhed in a point like this, for turning all the plaine places of the Scrip-ture into alle-gories, beeing fo blinded in the literal mif-underftanding of the allego-ry of caftrati-on, as he foo-lifhly gelded himfelfe.
'It is a Tenent, fit for an A-theiftical Ma-chiauell to hold, that Re-ligion daunts a mans cou-rage; and a-bundantly confuted by the conftancy of many thou-fand Martyrs.

* Matth. 11. 28. 30.

remiffion of fins can be no faluation. As to the next queftion, our braue men, at leaft thefe that would be thought fo, tell vs that this is a hard and almoft impoffible condition, and that wee muft put our felues in Chrifts mercy for not performing this, no more then diuers other of his precepts, as, *If one giue thee a boxe vpon the one eare, hold vp the other* ; and *if thine eye offend thee, plucke it out, for better it is, &c.* But thefe two are not to be vnder-ftood as abfolute precepts, as fome of the *Anabaptifts* haue done the firft of them, and fome other *Heretikes* haue done the laft. But they are on-ly meant comparatiuely, as thus : Rather, then that thou fhouldeft thy felfe be the auenger of thine owne wrong, *refiftendo malo, ratione vllâ malâ;* and fo to take the fword out of GODs and his Deputy the Magiftrates hand, it were better or leffe harme for thee to endure a double iniury. Otherwife Fortitude were a vice, which indeed is a high vertue, beeing rightly defined and vnderftood: For *vim vi repellere*, is *iuris naturalis*, and our Sauiour came not to peruert or deftroy Nature, but onely to rectifie and fanctifie it : and I dare fay, there is no vaine fabulous *Romanzo*, that more highly commends Fortitude, and valiant men * for their valour, then the Scripture doth : but all is in the right vfe of it. And fo is likewife to be vnderftood that, of plucking out thine eye ; for if thou cannot keepe thy felfe from giuing offence, by the meanes of one of thine eyes, better it were or leffe harme, to plucke it out and be faued with the loffe of one eye, then bee damned with both. But the meaning of this precept is not to bee vnderftood literally, of the amputation, or deftruction of any of our members; for that were a fort of parricide : but onely, that if wee finde that any of our fences prouoke vs to be tempted, as if the fight of faire and beautifull women prouoke vs to luft, or if any other of our fen-ces tempt vs to any fin, let vs depriue our felues of fuch occafions, which may otherwife be lawfull, rather then hazard to bee led into temptation by them, and fo by depriuing our felues of that fight, which fo much pleafeth vs, wee doe, as it were, plucke out one of our eyes : and by de-priuing our felues from the hearing of that which fo much delights vs, wee cut off in a manner one of our eares ; and the like in the other fences. For when wee depriue our felues of that vfe of any of our fences, which wee moft delight in, we doe in a manner robbe our felues of that fence. And whereas they account this condition in the LORDS PRAYER to bee impoffible to bee performed : I anfwere, It is blafphe-mie to fay, that any of CHRISTS precepts are impoffible to bee per-formed ; for it is to giue himfelfe the lie, who out of his owne mouth told vs, that * his yoke is eafie, and bids vs that are burthened, come to him, and he will eafe vs. For our Sauiour came into this world, that by his merits and paffion, hee might redeem vs from the thraldome of the Law, to the liberty of the fonnes of GOD. Since therefore this conditi-on is of no lower price then the Kingdome of heauen, and that it is not onely poffible, but eafie to bee performed by vs, if wee will earneftly

set

set our mindes to it ; what should wee not doe ; *omnem mouendo lapidem,* for enabling vs to attaine to so great a felicity ; and to eschew so great a misery ? for there is no mid-way in this case. Now the onely way for enabling vs to performe it, is by our earnest prayer to God, that hee will enable vs to doe it, according to that of Saint *Augustine , Da Domine quod iubes, & iube quod vis :* For it is true, that that grace is a flower, that growes not in our owne garden, but we must set our mind to it, as I said already, and not lazily leaue it off; and betake vs to his mercy; because it agrees not with our humour and passions : for wilfully to disobey his precept, is a plaine refusing , and scorne of his mercy, which is but offered vnto vs in case of obedience ; and to refuse obedience because it is against our minde, is like the excuse of the Tobacco-drunkards, who cannot abstaine from that filthy stinking smoake, because, forsooth, they are bewitched with it. And this is an excuse for any sinne, they will not leaue it, because they cannot leaue it ; but the truth is, because they will not leaue it : like a sluggard , who when hee hath lien in bed, and slept more then can doe him good ; yet hee cannot rise, because hee will not rise for lazinesse. But since wee cannot pardon them that haue offended vs, except we haue charity, I will shortly set downe and describe the contrary to it ; which is rancour and reuenge , that so I may make that diuine vertue of charity , the better to shine and appeare in the owne colors, when her contrary is set downe, *ex diametro* opposed vnto her, according to that old and true saying, *Contraria iuxta se posita magis elucescunt.*

The sin of rancor and reuenge proceeds from basenes and want of courage in men, and euen amongst beasts and creeping things, it proceeds of a defect and want of courage in them. Among men these are iustly to be accounted the basest ; that are reprobates and outlawes to their heauenly King ; for these that are disgraced and banished euen out of an earthly Kings Court, are in a lower estate, then these that are highly preferred in it. The first that euer practised it, was *Cain* vpon his brother *Abel,* for not beeing able to auenge himselfe vpon God, who was the agent, for accepting his brothers oblation, & reiecting of his, he exercised his rancour vpon his brother in murthering of him, who was but the patient. But what came of this? He was made an out-law & a runnagate for it, both from the presence of God, & his owne father. O braue *Cain,* thou wast brauely exalted & preferred for this braue and manly act, in giuing the first example of murther & shedding of innocent blood! We read of another after, who not content to practise it, made his vaunt of it, as of a braue and honourable resolution ; and this was *Lamech ,* who made his vaunt of reuenge before his two wiues, to make them afraid of him, as it is thought. But if it be true that some of the *Iewish Rabbines* guesse at, hee killed *Cain,* and so got the curse for his reward ; that God set vpon any that should kill *Cain,* when hee had marked him. How euer it bee, sure I am that both *Cain* and hee were damned , and all their posterity destroyed by the Flood.

But

But of this point I neede to cite no more examples, whereof there bee so many thousands in all ages. And I will come a degree lower, from wicked men to cowards; for though wicked men and Outlawes be inferiour to honest and good men; yet cowards are farre inferiour to them, for they are not accounted in the ranke of men. And it is a knowen and vndeniable truth, that cowards are much more cruell and vindicatiue, then men of courage are : for a coward can neuer enough secure himselfe of his enemy; In so much as when he is lying dead at his feet, he is yet afraid, *qu'il ne luy saute aux yeux*, as the French prouerbe is. But let vs looke a degree lower yet, vpon women, who are weaker vessels then men : the world knowes that the most part of them are cowards, and it is also well knowen, that they are a great deale more vindicatiue and cruell then men. But if wee will yet goe lower, euen to beastes, wee shall finde that the fearefullest beasts are euer the most cruell and vindicatiue. What the Lion is, my *diction* tels you, *Est nobilis ira leonis, &c.* Besides that, the most part of the beasts of reafe, and the noblest sorts of them, prey for hunger and for necessity of food, and not for reuenge. But the Deere that are so naturally cowards, as one chop of a Beagle, will make a herd of great Stagges runne away, I know not how many miles, these cowardly beasts, I fay, who neuer dare fight, but when they are enraged, either with lust, desperate feare, or reuenge : yet are they so cruell after that they haue once gotten the victory, that when life leaues the party whom one of them hath ouercome; yet will hee not leaue him for a long time after, still wounding the dead carkase, and insulting and trampling vpon it. And the better to expresse the reuenging nature of these fearefull creatures, I haue thought it not amisse to set downe heere, what I haue heard by credible report to haue been done by two diuers Stagges in two diuers places. The one of the Stagges was in a little Red Deere Parke of the late Vifcount *Bindon*, which keeping rut in a corner of the Parke with a brace of Hinds, the Keeper chanced in making his walke, to come thorow the bush where these Hinds were, whereupon they ranne away, and the Stagge followed them : but not beeing able to make them stay with him any longer, by reason of their suddaine fright, hee looked backe once or twice very sullenly vpon the Keeper, without pressing to doe any more for that time. But within two dayes after, or thereabout, hee watched the Keeper walking in the Parke, and after hee had worne him by little and little to a strait, at a corner of the Pale he ranne fiercely at the Keeper, broke his bill, and gaue him many wounds, whereof hee dyed within a day or two after, though the Stagge was put from him at that time, by I know not what accident. The other Stagge was one of them that was first put in, in my Lord of Suffolkes Redde-Deere Parke, who, being the first rut time there, mastered onely by one Deere, that was greater and older then hee, and so kept from the Hindes, watched his time the next spring when the other mewed

his

his head, he being ſtill vnmewed, as the younger Deere, and immediatly
thereupon ſet on him in a morning in the ſight of one of the Keepers firſt,
and then of all the reſt: and notwithſtanding that they followed him,
for ſauing the other, both on horſe and foot as faſt as they could, yet neuer left he courſing of his fellow through the Parke, like a Grey-hound
after a Hare, till he killed him with a number of wounds. And this vindicatiue Stagge did I kill with my Hounds, I and all my Huntſmen giuing
him no other ſtile, but, *The murtherer.* And of all beaſts none are more
vnprofitable for the neceſſary vſe of man, then Apes and Monkies, ſeeming onely to be created *in ludibrium naturæ;* ſo as *Galen* carried euer ſome
of them about with him whereſoeuer hee went, onely to make Anota-
mies of them, for their likeneſſe in proportion to man. For in *Galens*
time it was thought an inhumane thing to make Anatomies of men or
women, wherein the Chriſtian world now hath leſſe horrour then the
Ethnickes then had. And that ſort of beaſts are knowen to be ſo naturall
cowards, that they dare neuer purſue any body to bite them, but women
or children, and ſuch as they ſee afraid of them or flying from them; and
yet will they remember an iniury two or three yeeres, and watch an opportunity for reuenging it. And if we will goe yet lower, euen to them
that licke the duſt of the earth, as to Serpents and all ſorts of venimous
Wormes, the Hiſtories are full of their malitious and reuengefull nature: but it is no new thing with them, the ſeede of the woman muſt
bruiſe their heads, and they muſt bite his heele. Nay, will we for concluſion of this point, conſider of the very loweſt of all places, euen
hell it ſelfe; wee ſhall finde that the Inhabitants thereof, the Deuils,
breathe nothing but malice and reuenge. Sathan was a lyer and a murtherer from the beginning, and his firſt worke, after his fall, was to
auenge himſelfe vpon the Image of GOD in Man, by deceiuing him;
ſince his malice could not reach to GOD himſelfe, making choyce of
that malicious beaſt the Serpent for his organe. And now, I hope, I
haue ſufficiently prooued by the low deſcent of this ſinne by degrees,
euen to hell it ſelfe; that as it is a greeuous, ſo is it a baſe ſinne, contrary
to true courage. But ſince we haue now put it in hell, from whence it
firſt came, there let vs leaue it, and ſolace our ſight a little with the contemplation of that diuine Vertue, Charitie, the right oppoſite to that helliſh ſinne and vice.

Charitie is not onely a diuine Vertue, but GOD himſelfe is Charitie, as I ſaide already. Saint *Paul* reckoning the three great * Theologicall Vertues, without which no man can bee ſaued, not onely puts
in Charitie for one, but euen for the moſt excellent of all, without
the which the reſt are nothing. And it is alſo the onely permanent
Vertue of them all, for Faith and Hope remaine onely with the elect,
while they are in this world, but Charitie is euer with them, heere and
hence for euer. Yea euen, will ye looke to God himſelfe, *miſericordia eius*

* 1. Cor. 13.

ſuper

super omnia opera eius, and mercie is a worke of Charitie. *Charitie* dwels with GOD ; and all the Elect, Angels, Saints and men are clad with it, eternally. I know not by what fortune, the *dicton* of P A C I- F I C V S was added to my title, at my comming in *England*; that of the Lyon, expressing true fortitude, hauing beene my *dicton* before: but I am not ashamed of this addition, for King *Salomon* was a figure of CHRIST in that, that he was a King of peace. The greatest gift that our Sauiour gaue his Apostles, immediatly before his Ascension, was, that hee left his Peace, with them ; hee himselfe hauing prayed for his persecutours, and *forgiuen his owne death*, as the Prouerbe is. The footsteppes of his charitie beeing so viuely imprinted in the Disciple whom his Master loued, and who leaned on our Sauiours bosome ; as hee said nothing, wrote nothing, did nothing : yea, in a manner breathed nothing all the dayes of his life, but Loue and Charitie. To the blessed Virgine and him C H R I S T vpon the Crosse recommended their charitable cohabitation together, as Mother and Sonne : his stile in all his writings, is full of Loue and Charitie, his Gospell and Epistles found nothing but Charitie. Yea * Saint *Hierome* maketh mention, that when hee was so old, as he could not preach and scarce walke, he would many times make himselfe bee led to the Preaching place, and there repeating oft these words, *Little Children loue one another*, hee would come backe againe; and being asked why he so often repeated that sentence, his answere was, *This is the new and last Commaundement that our Master left vs, Et si solum fiat, sufficit.* But aboue all the third Chapter of his Gospell deserues to be grauen in letters of Marble, in the hearts of all Christians, especially, the sixteenth verse thereof, *G O D so loued the world, &c.* And here I must record to the eternall memorie and good fame, of my Father in Law the late King of Denmarke, that he not being a Scholler, yet tooke hee the paines to write vp a little * Manuell, with his owne hand, of some of the most comfortable selected Psalmes ; which was his continuall *Vade mecum*, as *Homers* Iliads was to *Alexander* : And at his death he made that part of the third Chapter of Saint *Iohns* Gospell to be read ouer and ouer vnto him. And as hee thus dyed happily, so left he a goodly and prosperous posteritie behinde him. And in the issue of one of his, I hope God shall in his mercy deale with me in one point, as hee did with *Iob* : if in not restoring vnto me so many children as hee hath taken from me, yet in restoring them vnto me in my childrens children; praying God to blesse that worke of mercy, that he hath already begun towards mee, in this point. But to returne to Saint *Iohn*, wee may see at last, euen by his death, how God loued him for his charitie, besides the manifold other proofes, that hee gaue him thereof during his life; for hee died peaceably in his bed, full of daies; and was the notablest Confessour that euer was, albeit no Martyr, as all the rest of the Apostles were. To conclude then my description of this diuine vertue, Charity,

* Hieron. in Epist. Paul. ad Gal.

* This manuel of my Father in law, Sir PETER YOVNG, my old master brought out of Denmarke, and shewed me, and told me also of this forme of his death.

rity, I remit you to that paterne, which that admirable, learned, and eloquent Pen-man of the holy Ghost, hath set forth of her in his thirteenth
of his first to the _Corinthians._

And thus hauing with the Pensill of my penne represented vnto
you, as viuely as I can, in so little compasse, the bright beautie of this
diuine vertue, Charitie: it rests that I set downe her true limits, and
how wee may make our right vse of her, by knowing towards whom
our charitie is to be extended, in what cases, and in what measure, that
so we may be able to performe vpon our part, that condition which God
so exactly requires at our hands. As to the first question, towards
whom; no doubt we ought to extend our Charitie towards all persons,
yea, euen in some sort to beasts: we are in diuers places of the Scripture
commanded to bee * mercifull to our beasts; * _boni tritarantis os non_
obligabis. But wee ought especially to be † charitable to the houshold
of faith, and then wee are more particularly to measure our Charitie
according to those degrees that doe more or lesse concerne vs, as our
Countrey, our Magistrates Spirituall or Temporall, the strangers
within our gates, Widdowes and Orphans, and those of our consan-
guinitie or affinitie, our Wiues, Parents, Brethren or Sisters, or Children, our professed friends, especially those that wee are obliged vnto
in thankfulnesse. And as wee ought to bee charitable to all persons,
so are we bound to extend our Charitie to them in all cases, by giuing
them either Spirituall or Temporall comfort, as they haue neede of it,
assisting them as well with our aduice and counsell, as with our fortunes: but in our assisting them, especially with our fortunes, wee are
to measure it, according to the before mentioned degrees, and our owne
abilities; otherwise, whereas wee were able before to ease the burthens
of others, wee shall then make our selues to become burthensome
to others. And aboue all, wee must pardon all them that haue offended vs, which is the direct point now in hand. But in all these cases
of Charitie, wee are to obserue such a measure, as may preserue vs
from both extreamities; for though wee be to pray for all men, yet are
we not to keepe company with all men, much lesse to be in professed
friendship with euery man. No man ought to be so secure of himselfe,
as not to bee afraide to bee corrupted with euill company: yee know
the saying, _Corrumpunt bonos mores colloquia mala_; and therefore, _Qui_
stat, videat ne cadat, besides the euill name a man gets by haunting infamous companie. It is reported of that holy Apostle of loue, of whom
I lately made large mention, that one day in his age he * went in _Ephe-_
sus, to bathe himselfe in a hot Bath, and seeing _Cerinthus_ the Heretique,
he hasted out of the Bath before hee was bathed, fearing that the Bath
should fall, because _Cerinthus_ the enemy of the truth was in it. And indeede this practise of his agrees well with his doctrine in his Epistle; If
thou meete one that brings not this doctrine, _ne dicas ei, aue_, lest thou be
partaker

* _Prou._11.10.
† 1 Cor.9.9.
* Gal.6.10.

1 Cor.15.33.
1. Cor. 10.12.

* _Irenæus ad-_
uersus hæres.
lib.3. & Euseb.
lib.3.eccl.hist.
cap.25.

Io.ep.1.10.

partaker of his finne. Since then this holy Apoſtle whom his Maſter loued was fo afraide of euill company ; how much more reaſon haue wee to bee fo, confidering how much weaker the beſt of vs are in ſpirituall graces, then hee was? And likewife this condition which is required at our hands, in pardoning them that offend vs, hath alfo the owne limits, which makes the performance thereof the more eafie vnto vs. For our Sauiour commands vs, to forgiue them that offend vs, as oft as they repent them of their offending vs: fo as they are as well tyed to repent, as we to forgiue, albeit our forgiueneſſe muſt not bee precifely tyed to their repentance, *Marke* the 11.25. *When yee ſtand and pray, &c.* So as what part foeuer of the world your debtour bee in, you cannot pray with fruit except you forgiue him. Wee muſt alfo vnderſtand, that our forgiuing them that offend vs, ties not the hands of fuch of vs as are Magiſtrates, to puniſh them that are offenders, according to the nature of their offences; fo that wee doe it for our zeale to Iuſtice onely, and not for feruing of our owne particular endes, or fatisfaction of our paſſions. And priuate men are not by this precept reſtrained, from complaining to the lawfull Magiſtrate, and feeking redreſſe of the iniuries done vnto them, agreeable to the qualities of the offences, according to that rule of our Sauiour, *Dic Ecclefia*: but wee ought fo to loue, and eſteeme euery man more or leſſe, according as their vertues, good name, or particular behauiour towards vs ſhall deferue. Wee are no way likewife barred of our iuſt defence, in cafe wee bee vnlawfully inuaded and affailed; for defence is *iuris naturalis*, and tolerated by the Lawes of all Nations; onely we are to keepe rancor and malice out of our hearts, and our hands from reuenge: for reuenge belongs onely to God, and by

Rom.12.19. deputation from him, to his Lieutenants vpon earth, *Mihi vindictam, ego retribuam.* And I pray you, what life would wee haue in this world, if euery man were his owne Iudge, and auenged his owne iniuries? Sure I am, there would bee no neede of Kings nor Magiſtrates, and I thinke, there would bee no people left to bee gouerned. For then euery man

* πολιτικὸν ζῶα. would bee *homo homini lupus,* whereas, by the contrary, men are created to bee * *animalia gregalia,* and to liue together like fociable creatures. It

Gen.16.12. was a curfe pronounced vpon *Iſmael,* when it was prophecied, that *his hand ſhould bee againſt euery man, and euery mans hand againſt him.* But our braue fpirited men, cannot digeſt wrongs fo eafily, and they are aſhamed to complaine to the Magiſtrates. I anfwere, they muſt then bee aſhamed to obey God, and the King, and confequently to liue vnder their protection, but like Giants and mighty hunters, they muſt wander vp and downe the world, and liue vpon fpoyle. But what vfe is there for fwords then and fword-men? I anfwere, excellent good vfe, for the feruice of God, their King and their countrey, for their owne iuſt defence, and preferuing the weaker fort from iniurie or oppreſſion, in cafe of accidentall

1.Chron.11. neceſſitie. How honourably are the worthies of *Dauid* recorded in the

word

word of God, and what made the Gentiles to deifie *Hercules* ? Reade the ancient oathes of the Orders of Knighthood, in fpeciall, ours of the Order of the *Garter*, and euen the Oath that is ftill giuen to euery ordinary Knight at this day in *Scotland* ; and let vs vpon this occafion confider with pitie the miferable cafe that too many are in , in this Ifland ; who will not receiue the Sacrament, becaufe they haue malice in their hearts ; forgetting Saint *Pauls* two precepts, firft to trie our felues, and then to come. 1.Cor.11.28. But they thinke it enough to prooue themfelues, fo they neuer come, and thinke it neuer time for them to come there, till they be perfect; not remembring that C H R I S T came in this world for the ficke and not for the whole, and that wee come to that Table weake and full of infirmities, to bee ftrengthened with that Spirituall and Heauenly foode ; onely carying with vs there, a will and an earneft defire of amendment. And if they will not purge their hearts of malice, what can their abftaining from the Lords Supper auaile them ? For how fhall they pray the LORDS PRAYER, except they forgiue their debtours? and confequently how fhall they obtaine remiffion of finnes, without which there can bee no faluation ? They muft refolue then, as long as they liue in this ftate, to liue as Outlawes and Aliants from the couenant of God ; and if they die without repentance, to bee certaine of damnation. Truely the beft man liuing hath great neede to pray earneftly to bee preferued from a fodaine death, as it is in our Englifh Letánie, that before his ende hee may haue fpace and grace to purge his heart, and cleare his confcience from all vncleannefle. For wee are all of vs intifed and allured to our owne perdition, by three terrible perfwafiue folicitours, the World, the Flefh, and the Deuill. But if the beft liue ftill in that dangerous warrefare, what cafe then are thefe men in, if they fhall die in that open rebellion, in difobeying the commandement of God, and not being able to pray for the remiffion of their finnes ? and yet is none of them fecure of a minutes repriuall from death. Surely, me thinkes, the apprehenfion of a fodaine death fhould bee a perpetuall torture to their confciences ; and yet the number of them is growne fo great amongft vs heere, as a man cannot difcerne betwixt a Papift and an Atheift, in this point: for many Papifts take the pretext of malice for keeping them out of the penaltie of the law, for not receiuing the Sacrament. And now that I haue beene a great deale longer vpon this Petition then vpon any of the reft, I hope the Reader will eafily excufe mee, fince the remiffion of our finnes is *caufa fine qua non* to euery Chriftian man (as I faide before) as alfo fince this condition annexed vnto it, is fo lightly regarded, and fo little obeyed in our age, yea euen in the Court, & amongft the better fort of men, I meane for qualitie. Following in this the example of CHRIST himfelfe, the Author of this prayer, who in the fame place, where he teacheth it, *Mat.5.* doth immediatly thereafter inlarge himfelfe vpon the interpretation of the condition of this Petition, without preffing to interpret any of the reft.

AND

AND LEADE VS NOT INTO TEMPTATION. The *Arminians* cannot but miſlike the frame of this Petition; for I am ſure, they would haue it, *And ſuffer vs not to bee ledde into temptation.* ; and *Vorſtius* would adde; *as farre, Lord, as is in thy power, for thy power is not infinite.* And vpon the other part, wee are alſo to eſchew the other extremitie of ſome *Puritans*, who by conſequent make God Authour of ſinne, with which errour the Papiſts doe wrongfully charge our religion ; but *medio tutius itur*. Saint * *Auguſtine* is the beſt deçider of this queſtion, to whom I remit mee. In ſo high a point it is fit for euery man, *ſapere ad ſobrietatem* ; which is Saint *Pauls* counſell, Romans 12. Notwithſtanding that himſelfe was rauiſhed to the third heauen, and beſt acquainted with theſe high myſteries ; not to bee ſearched vnto, but to bee adored. And it ſufficeth vs to know that *Adam* by his fall, loſt his free-will, both to himſelfe and all his poſteritie ; ſo as the beſt of vs all hath not one good thought in him, except it come from God ; who drawes by his effectuall grace, out of that attainted and corrupt maſſe, whom hee pleaſeth, for the * worke of his Mercie, leauing the reſt to their owne wayes, which all leade to perdition : ſo as though God * draw all the Elect vnto him, who otherwiſe can neuer winne heauen, yet doeth hee force none to fall from him ; *perditio tua ex te Iſrael.* And therefore God is ſayde *to leade vs into temptation*, when by a ſtrong hand hee preſerues vs not from it ; and ſo was hee ſayde to harden *Pharaos* heart becauſe hee did not ſoften it : Euen as a nurſe, hauing a childe that is but beginning yet to learne to goe, may bee iuſtly ſayde to make the childe fall, if ſhee leaue it alone, knowing that it cannot ſcape a fall without helpe. Now temptations are either bred within vs, or come from externall cauſes; If they breed within vs, earneſt prayer and holy Meditations are often to bee vſed ; cures alſo would bee applyed of contrary qualitie to theſe ſinnes that wee finde budding within vs, for *contraria contrarys curantur* : good bookes likewiſe will bee a great helpe, and ſpecially the good aduice of a ſound Diuine, prouided that hee haue the reputation of a good life. And if our temptations come from externall cauſes ; if any of our ſences bee caught with vnlawfull delights, let vs then (as I ſaid alreadie) depriue our ſences of theſe dangerous obiects. If proſperitie or aduerſitie bring vs in temptation, let vs apply the remedies accordingly : againſt aduerſitie tempting vs to deſpaire, let vs arme our ſelues with patience the beſt wee can, flee ſolitude, and oft ſeeke conſolation from wiſe, godly, honeſt, and intire friends. If wee bee tempted with proſperitie (which commonly is the more dangerous, though the other bee ſharper) let vs conſider by euery little diſeaſe, and other croſſes, our naturall frailtie, often meditate vpon the neceſſitie of death, and bee carefull to reade and heare oft good funerall Sermons, *Puluis es, & in puluerem reuerteris.* And in a word, let vs conſider, that hauing ſo many

                                                 tempters

marginal notes:
* *Aug. de predeſtinatione Sanctorum, de dono perſeuerantiæ, contra Pelagianos; & paſſim alibi in ſuis operibus.*

* Rom. 9. 18.

* Ioh. 6. 44.

Oſe. 13. 9.

Gen. 3. 19.

tempters, and occasions of temptation within and about vs, all the houres of the day ; so as the whole life of a true Christian, is nothing else but a continuall triall of his constancie, in his vnceßant spirituall warre-fare. We haue therefore the greater reason to watch our selues continu-ally, and carefully take heede to all our thoughts and actions : for other-wise it will bee in vaine for vs to pray to God, not to leade vs in tempta tion ; and in the meane time wee shall bee leading our selues into it vpon euery occasion ; like one that will wilfully lie in the mire, and call to ano-ther to helpe him out of it.

BVT DELIVER VS FROM EVILL. This is the last petition, and the seuenth in the account of the ancient Church, as I tolde you before, and the sixt as wee now doe ordinarily reckon it. The Fathers made it the seuenth, diuiding it from , *Leade vs not into temptation*, becaufe wee pray heere to bee deliuered from euill. Now deliuerie presuppoceth a preceding thraldome, or at least an iminent danger ; so as in the former petition wee pray to bee kept out of temptation in times to come ; and in this wee pray to bee deliuered from all euill that already is fallen, or pre-sently hangeth vpon vs ; not onely euill of *temptation, but euill of pu-nishment, or whatsoeuer aduersitie that is laide vpon vs. But our Church makes this a branch of the former Petition, and so a part of the sixt ; in regard it begins with ᾀ, ' *but*, as ye would say, *Lord leade vs not into temp-tation, but keepe vs euer safe from all such euill.* But whether yee account it the seuenth Petition, or a branch of the sixt, either of the wayes is ortho-doxe, and good enough ; (though the older way bee the fuller, as I haue now showen) for the substance is, that we pray to God, not to leade vs in temptation, but to deliuer vs from any euill either present or to come. The Greeke hath it, ᾀπὸ τ μπηρς *from the euill one* ; and these words put vs in minde, what neede we haue of continuall prayer to God, to be preserued from that olde traiterous and restlesse enemie, * *qui circundat terram*, like a roaring Lion seeking whom he may deuoure. And by this Petition thus vnderstood, wee are taught, not to trust to our owne strength, against so strong and fiercely cruell an enemie, but to bee armed with faith, that we may safely sleepe, *sub vmbra alarum tuarum Domine.* The Latine tranflation *à malo*, will beare either any euill thing, or the euill one ; and our vulgar tranflation, *euill*, is generall for eschewing of any euill that may befall vs, whether by the meanes of Satan, or otherwise. And so wee are to pray that God by his mercifull hand would deliuer vs from all euill, either in corporall or spirituall things ; either against our temporall necessities and comforts in this life, or our spirituall graces for our eternall saluation : that we may lie down safe, and rise againe, and not be afraid, though thousands of enemies, both spirituall and temporall, should incompasse vs. Heere now the LORDS PRAYER ends in S. *Luke*, but in S. *Matthew* is subioyned that Epilogue, *For thine is the Kingdome, the power and the glorie for euer. Amen.*

Malum pœna & malum culpa.

1.Pet.5.8.

Psal.91.4.

Who

Who will ferioufly confider the occafion, whereupon our Sauiour
taught the L O R D S P R A Y E R in both the Gofpels, hee fhall finde,
that C H R I S T taught it twice ; firft, priuately to his difciples, at the
fuite of one of them to teach them to pray ; and then he taught the Petitions onely, prefixing that fhort preamble, *Our Father which art in hea-*
uen : and at that time hee expreffed two or three of the Petitions in this
Prayer, more plainely then he did after in his publique Sermon before
the people. For his manner was euer, to expreffe himfelfe more plainly
to his difciples, then hee did to the whole people: and this is the forme
fet downe in the 11. of Saint *Luke*. And after at another time, he taught
it vpon the mountaine, to a multitude of people in the middeft of a
long Sermon that hee made vnto them, and then hee added this fore-
faide Epilogue ; and this forme is contayned in the fixth of *Matthew*, at
which time it feemes he added the Epilogue, to teach the people to pray;
both with the greater confidence and reuerence, fince to him whom
they prayed vnto, belonged *the Kingdome*, *&c.* It is true that this E-
pilogue is wanting in the vulgar Latine Tranflation, euen in Saint *Mat-*
thew : and *Robert Steuen* that learned Printer faith, it is alfo wanting in
fome old greeke exemplar; but that is no matter, it is fufficiently acknowledged to bee Canonicall. Now as to the words of this Epilogue, they
containe the reafon of our praying to our heauenly Father ; for his is the
Kingdome, hee is not onely a King, but the Kingdome *per excellentiam*
is his ; βασιλεια. Euen as, although there fhall bee *multi Antichrifti*, yet is the
great Antichrift, head of the generall defection, called ἀντίχριστος: So as
G O D is the onely K I N G of all *in folidum*, all earthly depute Kings kingdomes being but fmall brookes and riuers deriued from that Sea. And
he is not onely King of all, but power is his onely, fo as he is not only an
infinitely great K I N G (for great Kings may not doe all that they would)
but hee is alfo an infinitely powerfull, and Almightie K I N G. And
not onely is the *Kingdome* his, and the *Power* his, but alfo the *Glorie*
is his ; which maketh the other two excellent: fo as all wordly kingdomes, powers, and honours, (for without honour all world Kingdomes and powers are nothing) are onely droppes borrowed out of
that great and vaft Ocean. But if all this were but temporall, then
might wee doubt of the decay thereof; and therefore to refolue vs of
this doubt alfo ; *For euer*, is fubioyned to the end of thefe fupremely
high titles; to fhew that his Kingdome, his Power, and his Glorie, is
neuer to receiue end, change or diminution. Remembring then, that
in the firft words of this Prayer, we call him *Our Father*, which fettles
our confidence in his loue ; and in the laft words thereof wee acknowledge his infinite power ; with great comfort wee may bee confident,
that hee both may and will heare, and grant thefe our petitions. And to
this Prayer is *Amen* put, as the conclufion of all ; for heereby are wee
ftirred vp, to recollect fhortly to our memory all that which wee haue
                                                                                              faid:

said : adding a faithfull wish, that our petitions may be graunted vnto vs.
Which is a signe that we should know what we say, when we make this
Prayer, contrary to the Papists, who teach ignorant wiues and children,
to mumble, or rather mangle this Prayer in Latine *ad intentionem Ecclesiæ*.
But if Saint *Pauls* rule be true in his 14. of his 1. to the *Corinthians*, those
ignorants can neuer say *Amen*, to their owne prayer which they vnderstand not : but the Church of *Rome* hath not only euil luck to be contrarie to S. *Paul* in this point, but also to Chrifts owne prohibition, in his
Preface to this same Prayer in the sixt of Saint *Matthew*. For there he forbids vaine repetitions, as the Heathen doe, but bids them pray thus. Now
they haue preferred the imitation of the Heathen to C H R I S T's example, witnesse *our Ladies Rosarie*, and witnesse all their prayers vpon Beads,
making vp such a rable of *Paters* and *Aues*, contrary to C H R I S T that
forbids vaine repetitions. and I am sure there cannot be a vainer repetition, then to repeate a * prayer they vnderstand not, and contrary to
Saint *Paul* also, as I said already, and I dare say without any precept or
example of antiquity, for the space of many hundred yeeres after Christ:
and yet these vaine and ignorant repetitions are matters of great merit
with them. And it is also to bee obserued, that although our Sauiour
commaunded vs to make our petitions to G O D in his Name, yet hath
he not made mention of his owne Name in this Prayer, not that I doubt
but that vnder the Name of the F A T H E R in this Prayer, all the Tri-
nity is to be vnderstood ; but it may be that he hath omitted the inserting
of his Name in this Prayer, foreseeing that in the latter dayes, superstition would insert too many intercessours in our prayers, both of he and
she Saihts. And surely the darknesse of this superstition was so grosse
in our Fathers times, as a great Theologue was not ashamed, within
little more then these threescore yeres to preach publikely in S. *Andrewes*;
That the L O R D S P R A Y E R might bee said to our Lady : whereupon grew such a controuersie in the Vniuersitie there, that a Synode
in that same place, was forced to take knowledge of it and decide it. And
what lesse superstition was it in so learned a man as *Bonauenture,* to turne
the meaning of the Psalmes vpon our Lady ? I meane whatsoeuer was
spoken of G O D in them to be meant of our Ladie : and yet was this famous booke of his reprinted at *Paris* within these few yeeres. But since
G O D in his great mercy hath freed vs in this Iland, from that more then
Egyptian darknesse, I cannot wonder inough at the inconstancie of too
many amongst vs in our dayes ; that *like fooles faine of flitting,* as the Scottish Prouerbe is, are so greedy of noüelties ; that forsaking the pure veritie
for painted fables, they will wilfully hoodwinke themselues, and thrust
their heads in the darke againe, refusing the light, which they may liue and
ioy in, if they list: ... ... mod! ...
And thus hauing ended this my Meditation vpon the L O R D S
P R A Y E R, it rests onely that I draw it into a short summe (as I promised)

that

* I read with
mine eies
within these
ten or twelue
yeres, a little
Pamphlet, set
out by an
English prieft,
printed in
some part of
the Arch-
dukes domini-
on, which la-
boured to
maintaine by
many argu-
ments, that
the L O R D S
P R A Y E R, and
other short
prayers, were
more profita-
ble for the
vulgar and ig-
norant sort, to
be said by the
in Latine, al-
though they
vnderstood it
not, then in
their owne
naturall lan-
guage.

that we may the better vnderſtand, and remember what wee pray; and that our prayer may the more viuely and deepely bee imprinted and engrauen in our hearts. And it is ſhortly this: We firſt for a preamble inuocate G O D, by the ſweete name of *Our Father*; thereby to ſettle our confidence in his loue, that he will heare and graunt our petitions, next, to breede the greater reuerence in vs, and to aſſure our ſelues of his all-ſeeing eye, we make mention of the place of the reſidence of his glory, which is Heauen. Then wee make firſt three generall petitions for his glory, before we come to our owne particular ſuites. In the firſt whereof we doe our homage vnto him, in wiſhing his Name to be hallowed, both in Heauen and earth, like as we then doe; then our next generall petition is, that his Kingdome may come, as well, generally and vniuerſally at his ſecond comming, as that the Militant Church may flouriſh in the meane time, and that wee may in Gods appointed time, euery one of vs come to that Kingdome of his. That in the meane time his will may be done in earth as it is in heauen; the effect which the Kingdome of heauen in this earth will produce, which is our third and laſt generall petition for the propagation of his glory, and the felicitie of his Church. And if we pleaſe a little deeplier to meditate vpon theſe three petitions, they may likewiſe put vs in minde of the Trinitie; of G O D the Father, by wiſhing his Name to be ſanctified, whoſe Name no tongue can expreſſe: of G O D the Sonne, by wiſhing his Kingdome to come, for he is King, Prieſt, and Prophet, and of his Kingdome there ſhall neuer bee an end. And we are put in mind of G O D the holy Ghoſt, by praying that his will may be done in earth, as it is Heauen, for he it is that ſanctifies the wils of the elect, and makes them acceptable to God the Father, through Ieſus Chriſt. And our firſt priuate ſuite that followes, is for our daily bread; for except God preſently furniſh, and ſuſtaine vs, with that which our temporall neceſſities doe require; our being in this world will faile before we can performe any part of our ſeruice which he requires at our hands, and a ſuddaine death will preuent our due preparation for our iourney to our true home. Wee next pray for remiſſion of our by-paſt ſinnes, that we may ſtand *recti in curia*, being waſhed in the blood of the Lambe; for elſe our corporall ſuſtenance doth but feede vs to the ſlaughter. And wee ſhew our ſelues capable of this great and ineſtimable bleſſing and benefit, by the profeſſion of our Charity in pardoning our brethren, according to his commaundement. And then the vgly horrour of our by-paſt ſinnes, and our true and ſenſible ſorrow for the ſame, together with the acknowledgement of our owne weakeneſſe, and diſtruſt in our owne ſtrength, makes vs pray that we bee not hereafter led into ſo dangerous temptations: but that he will heereafter deliuer vs from all euill both in body and ſoule; eſpecially from the cruell and craftie aſſaults of that euill one. And as in the preamble we called him our heauenly Father, to ſtirre vp our reuerent confidence in his loue; ſo doe wee

in

in the Epilogue acknowledge his Almightie and eternall glorious power: thereby to affure our felues, that he is as able, as hee is ready to
heare and graunt thefe our petitions ; clofing vp all with A M E N, for
the ftrengthening our wifhes with that fmall meafure of faith that
is in vs, and affurance of the truth of the performance of our
petitions, that our requefts may be graunted. To
which I adde another A M E N, *etiam fiat*
D O M I N E I E S V.

Eee 3

A MEDITATION

Vpon the 27.28.29. Verſes of the XXVII.
Chapter of Saint MATTHEVV.

OR

A PATERNE FOR A KINGS
INAVGVRATION:

Written by the KINGS MAIESTIE.

THE EPISTLE DEDICATORIE.

MY dearest and onely Sonne, *in
the beginning of this ſame yeere, I
wrote a ſhort* Meditation *vpon the*
Lords Prayer, *and I told the reaſon, that now being growen in yeares,
I was weary of* Controuerſies *and to
write of high queſtions, and therefore had choſen now a plaine and*
eaſie ſubieā *to treat of: But of late it hath fallen out, that one
day reading priuatly to my ſelfe the paſsion of* CHRIST, *in the
end of* S. Matthewes *Goſpell, I lighted vpon that part, where
the* Gouernors Souldiers *mocked our* Sauiour, *with putting the
ornaments of a* King *vpon him. Which appeared to me to be ſo
punāually ſet doune, that my head hammered vpon it diuers
times after, and ſpecially the* Croune *of thornes went neuer out
of my mind, remembring the thorny cares, which a* King *(if
he)*

he haue a care of his office) muſt be ſubiect vnto, as (God
knowes) I daily and nightly feele in mine owne perſon. Whereupon I apprehended that it would bee a good paterne to put in-
heritors to kingdomes in minde of their calling, by the forme of
their inauguration ; and ſo reſolued to borrow ſome houres from
my reſt, to write a ſhort Meditation vpon it. But on a time telling Buckingham this my intention, and that I thought you
the fitteſt perſon to whom I could dedicate it, for diuers reaſons following, hee humbly and earneſtly deſired mee, that hee
might haue the honour to be my amanuenſis in this worke. Firſt,
becauſe it would free mee from the paine of writing, by ſparing
the labour both of mine eyes and hand ; and next, that hee might
doe you ſome peece of ſeruice thereby ; proteſting, that his natural obligation to you (next me) is redoubled by the many fauours
that you daily heape vpon him. And indeed, I muſt ingenuouſly
confeſſe to my comfort, that in making your affections to follow and ſecond thus your Fathers, you ſhew what reuerent loue
you carry towards me in your heart ; beſides the worthy example you giue to all other Kings eldeſt Sonnes for imitation, beginning heereby to performe one of the rules ſet doune to my
ſonne HENRY, that is with God, in my ΒΑΣΙΛΙΚΟΝ ΔΩΡΟΝ. And
indeede my graunting of this requeſt to Buckingham hath
much eaſed my labour, conſidering the ſlowneſſe, ilneſſe, and
vncorrectnes of my hand.

    As I dedicated therfore my Meditation vpon the Lords
Prayer to him, in regard aſwell of the neceſſity that Courtiers
haue to pray (conſidering that among great reſort of people they
cannot euer be in good company, beſides the many allurements
they haue to ſinne) as alſo that ſhort Prayers are fitteſt for
them ; for they haue ſeldome leiſure to beſtow long time vpon
praying, as I told him in my Preface: euen ſo I can dedicate this
my Paterne of a Kings inauguration to none ſo fitly, as to you,
my deareſt Sonne, both for the ſubiect and the ſhortneſſe of
it : the ſhortneſſe, ſince you ſpend ſo much time abroad, as you
can beſtow but little vpon the Muſes at home. And yet I will
                                                                    thus

*thus farre excuse you, that I would haue euery age be like it selfe:
to see a yong man old, and an old man yong, is an ill-fauoured
sight.* Youth should bee actiue and laborious, or else (I feare)
dulnesse wil come with age:Imberbisiuuenis, tandem custo-
de remoto, Gaudet equis canibusque & aprici gramine
campi. *but yet vpon the other part, est modus in rebus, and
moderata durant.* And as to the subiect, whom can a paterne for a Kings Inauguration so well fit as a Kings sonne
and heire, beeing written by the King his Father, and the
paterne taken from the King of all Kings?

To your brother (now with G o d) I dedicated my ΒΑΣΙΛΙΚΟΝ
ΔΩΡΟΝ, *wherein I gaue him my aduice anent the gouernement
of* Scotland *in particular :* this is but a short preparatiue for
a Kings Inauguration, and a little forewarning of his great and
heauie burthen. it is soone read and easily caried: make it therefore your vade mecum, to prepare you, and put you in a
habit for that day, which (I dare sweare) you will neuer wish for,
(as you gaue sufficient proofe by your carefull attendance in
my late great sickenesse, out of which it pleased God to deliuer
mee) and I hope I shall neuer giue you cause. But it will bee
a great reliefe to you in the bearing of your burthen, that you
be not taken tardè; but that you foresee the weight of it before hand, and make your selfe able to support the same : nam
leuius lœdit quicquid preuidimus antè; *and it is a good old
Scottish prouerbe,* that a man warned is halfe armed.
Looke not therefore to finde the softnesse of a doune-pillow in a
Croune, but remember that it is a thornie piece of stuffe and
full of continuall cares. And because examples mooue much,
I will remember you, what some kings of olde thought of the
weight of a Diademe.

Antigonus, *one of* Alexanders successors, *told an olde
wife, that was praising vnto him his happinesse in his raigne;
shewing his Diademe, that, if shee knew how many euils that
clout was stuffed with, shee would not take it vp, if shee found
it lying on the ground.* And Seleucus *another of them
spake*

Stob.serm.47.
& Val Max.
lib.7.cap.2.

Plutar.an seni
gerenda sit
Respub.

Cic.l.5.Tuſc.
quæſt.

ſpake many times to the like effect. And Dionyſius, the firſt tyrant of Syracuſe, though hee gouerned like a Tyrant all his life, and therefore onely cared for himſelfe and not for his people ; yet, when Damocles his flatterer recounted vnto him his great magnificence, wealth, power, and all his Kingly maieſtie, affirming, that neuer any man was more happie, thinking therby to pleaſe his humour ; the tyrant asked him (if he thought his life ſo pleaſant) whether he would be contented to trie his fortune a little. And his flatterer anſwering him that hee was contented, hee made him to bee ſet in a golden bed, and in the middeſt of a rich and ſumptuous feaſt, where no ſort of princely magnificence was wanting ; and while Damocles was in the middeſt of his happie eſtate (as hee thought) hee made a naked ſword to bee hanged in a horſe haire perpendicularly ouer his head with the point dounward. Vpon the ſight whereof neither could his meate nor all his glorious royall attyre delight him any more ; but all turned into his humble begging of the Tyrant ; that hee might haue leaue to bee gone : for he was now reſolued that he would be no more happie. And one of our owne predeceſſours, Henrie the fourth (called Henrie of Bullenbrooke) being in a traunce vpon his death-bed ; his Sonne, Henrie the fift, thinking he had beene dead, a little too nimbly carried away the croune that ſtood by his Father : but the King recouering a little out of his fit miſſed his croune, and called for it ; and when his ſonne brought it backe againe, hee tolde him that, if hee had knowen what a croune was, hee would not haue beene ſo haſtie : for hee proteſted that hee was neuer a day without trouble ſince it was firſt put vpon his head. It is true that hee was an vniuſt vſurper of the croune, but after hee gouerned both with iuſtice and valour. For you muſt remember that there bee two ſorts of tyrants ; the one by vſurpation, the other by their forme of gouernment, or rather miſgouernement. As for vſurpation you neede it not : you are like to ſucceede to a reaſonable proportion : and certainely, Conquerours are but ſplendide robbers. And for tyrannous go-

uernement

vernement, I *hope, you haue it not of kinde, nor shall euer learne
it by me. All this* I *speake not to scarre you from cheerefull accepting of that place, when* God *shall bring you vnto it ; but
onely to forewarne you , that you deceiue not your selfe with
vaine hopes. But as* I *wrote in my late Meditation, that a
man should both examine himselfe, and then receiue the blessed*
Sacrament*; but neither examine and not receiue , nor yet receiue and not examine : so I say to you , in this case prepare
your selfe for the worst, and yet bee not discouraged for it,*
sed contrà audentior ito. *Remember that,* difficilia quæ
pulchra, *and that,* via virtutis est ardua. *And for my part
I will pray the Lord of heauen and earth so to blesse you(that
are the sonne and heire of a* King) *with this paterne of the
inauguration of a* King, *written by a* King ; *as you
may in the owne time be worthy of a heauenly and permanent King-
dome.* Amen.

Dat. 29. Decemb. 1619.

ADVERTISEMENT TO
THE READER.

 Vrteous Reader, *I know that in this extreamly short discourse of mine of the* Paterne of a Kings inauguration, *thou wilt bee farre from finding the office of a King fully described therein. And therefore I haue thought good to informe thee hereby, that I onely write this as a ground, whereupon I meane (if God shall spare mee dayes and leisure) to set doune at large (as in the descant) the whole principall points belonging to the office of a King. And if my leisure cannot permit (whereof I despaire) I intend (God willing) to set some other more nimble pen on worke with my instructions. In the meane time, I haue made this as a short forewarning to my Son, that he may in time prepare himselfe for the bargaine, and study his craft; that if it shall please God by course of nature to bring him to it, (which I pray God he may) hee may not make his entry in it like a raw* Spanish Bisogno, *but rather like an olde souldier of a trained band, that needes no prompting nor direction to teach him how to vse his armes. So as mine end in this is rather a warning, then an instruction vnto him.*

And so farewell.

A PATERNE
FOR A KINGS
INAVGVRATION.

S. Matthevv. Chap.27. Verf. 27,28,29.

Then the fouldiers of the Gouernour tooke Iefus into the Com-
mon Hall, and gathered vnto him the whole band of foul-
diers.

And they ftripped him, and put on him a fkarlet Robe.
And when they had platted a crowne of thornes, they put it
vpon his head, and a reed in his right hand, and they bow-
ed the knee before him, and mocked him, faying, HAILE
KING OF THE IEVVES.

Eere haue wee in thefe three Verfes, fet
downe the forme and paterne of the Inauguration of a King, together with a
perfect defcription of the cares and croffes, that a King muft prepare himfelfe to
indure in the due adminiftration of his
office. For the true vnderftanding whereof, two things are to be refpected and had
in confideration, the Perfon and the Paterne : the qualities of the Perfon to bee
applied to our comfort and faluation; the Paterne for our imitation or
example. The Perfon was our SAVIOVR IESVS CHRIST,
who was humbled for our exaltation, tortured for our comfort, defpi-
fed for our glory, and fuffered for our faluation.

What belongs therefore to his Perfon in his paffion, I diftinguifh,
in this my *Meditation*, from that which hee left as a paterne for imitation by all good Kings; the former feruing for the generall foules health
of all Chriftians, the later onely for the inftruction of Kings. But fince
my chiefe end in this difcourfe is to fpeake of the paterne, as properly

Fff   belonging

belonging to my calling; I will onely glaunce flightly at that which
alanerly concernes his Perſon, that part being already ſufficiently handled by a whole armie of Diuines. But heere it may bee obiected that
this wrong and iniurie done by the Gouernours Souldiers to our S A-
V I O V R, cannot fitly be drawne in example, and ſet foorth as a paterne
for the Inauguration of Kings, becauſe they did it but in a mockerie of

Matth. 27.11.

C H R I S T; who hauing beene immediately before accuſed for vſurping
the title of King of the *Iewes*; they thought his perſon and preſence ſo
contemptible, as if it had beene worthy of no better Kingdome, then
that ſcornefull reproach, which then they put vpon him.   To this I
anſwere, that heere I conſider not their wicked and ſcornefull actions, but what vſe it hath pleaſed the *Almightie* and *All-mercifull* God to
draw out of their wickedneſſe, and turne it to his glorie.   For it is ordinarie with *God* to bring light out of darkeneſſe, as hee did at the

Gen.1.23.
Iud.14.14.

Creation, and to extract out of the worſt of things good effects, as was
expreſſed by *Sampſons* riddle.   And therefore I obſerue and diſtinguiſh in this action betwixt the part of *God*, that wrang his glory out of
their corruption without their knowledge; and their peruerſe inclination. For, though the nobler part of man, which is the ſoule, was vtterly corrupted in them, yet *God* inforced their bodies (which is the
vileſt part of man) to doe that homage to his onely Sonne, vnwitting
of their ſoules; which both their ſoules and their bodies ought to haue
performed: euen as hee made *Balaams* Aſſe to inſtruct her maſter. And

Num.21.28.
Num.6.10.
Ioh.11.49.

Balaam himſelfe to bleſſe the people of *Iſrael*, when hee came of intent
to curſe them for filthy lucres ſake, and as hee made *Caiphas* the high
Prieſt to propheſie, though quite contrary to his owne meaning. It
pleaſed therefore the *Almighty* to make thoſe Souldiers worſhip *Chriſt* in
their bodies with the reuerence due to a King, which their wretched
ſoules neuer intended; thereby teaching vs, that we euer ought to worſhip him and his onely Sonne as well with our bodies (as they did) as
with our ſoules, which no Chriſtians denie; ſince he is the Creator and
Redeemer of both.   Theſe therefore, that will refuſe in any place or at
any time to worſhip *Chriſt* aſwell in body as in ſoule, are in that point
inferiour to thoſe prophane ſouldiers: which I wiſh were well obſerued
by our fooliſh ſuperſtitious *Puritanes*, that refuſe to kneele at the receiuing of the bleſſed *Sacrament*. For, if euer at any time *Chriſt* is to bee
worſhipped, it is in time of prayer: and no time can be ſo fit for prayer
and meditation, as is the time of our receiuing the *Sacrament*; and if any
place can be more fit then other for worſhipping of *God* and his *Chriſt*
in, it is the *Church*, where is the ordinary aſſembly and meeting of his
Saints.   And now I returne to ſpeake of the paterne.

                                                          Then

2 _Then the Souldiers of the Gouernour tooke_ I E S V S _into the common Hall_ (S. M A R K. 15, 16. calleth it _Pratorium,_ which was the _common Hall,_ like our _Westminster Hall,_ and serued for administration of Iustice; as the place of greatest resort) _and gathered vnto him the whole band of Souldiers._

Ee see heere the Emperour of the whole world receauing the homage due vnto him, in that place, after that forme, and by that sort of persons; as it pleased him that many of the _Romane_ Emperours (his shadowes and substitutes) should bee soone after his death inaugurated and inuested in the Empire, after that the gouernement of _Rome_ was turned into a Monarchie, and ruled by Emperours. And it is worthy the obseruation (for proouing of the lawfulnesse of Monarchies and how farre that sort of gouernement is to bee preferred to any other). that as _Christ_ himselfe was the Sonne and right heire by lineall descent of King _Dauid_; so was he borne vnder the first _Romane_ Emperour, that euer established the _Romane_ Empire. For, though _Iulius Casar_ was in a manner the first Empe-rour, yet as he wan it by bloud, so ended hee in bloud : and therefore as _God_ would not permit King _Dauid_ to build him a materiall temple, be-cause of his shedding of bloud ; but made him leaue that worke to his sonne _Salomon,_ who was a King of peace : so had it not beene fitting that the Sauiour of the World, the builder of his Church (whose body was likewise the true Temple represented by that of _Salomon_) should haue beene borne but vnder a King of peace, as was _Augustus,_ and in a time of peace, when as the Temple of _Ianus_ was shut, and when as all the World did pay him an vniuersall contribution, as is said in the second of Saint _Lukes Gospel._ Of which happy and peacefull time the _Sibyls_ (though Ethnikes) made notable predictions, painting forth very viuely the blessed Child that then was to bee borne. Now as all publique so-lemnities haue a respect to these three circumstances, of forme, place, and person (whereof I haue already made mention) so in this action were all these three punctually obserued. First, the place, wherein this action was done, was the _common Hall,_ the publique place for admini-stration of Iustice. And although the _Romanes_ did not precisely obserue any one place for the inauguration of their Emperours; yet were all the places, where that action was performed, places of most publique resort of the people, as was this _common Hall._ For it is very fitting that he, that is to be acknowledged the head of all sorts of people, should be inuested in a place where all sorts of people may conuene and concurre to doe him homage. And as to the qualities of the persons that perfor-med this action, they were _Romane_ Souldiers; and not a small number of them, but it was done by the whole band of the Gouernours Souldiers.

And

2. Sam. 7. 5.
2. Sam. 7. 13.
Luk. 2. 1.

And this was iuſt the forme of the election of a number of the *Romane* Emperours: for the *Romane* Emperours were neither elected by the Senate, nor by the people. For although the authoritie till the time of the Emperours was in the Senate and people of *Rome*, yet euer after the riſing of the great factions in *Rome*, betweene *Iulius Cæſar* and *Pompey*, things were brought to that confuſion, that the Senate and people retained but the ſhadow of authority: but in very deede it was the armie that vſurped the power of electing of all the Emperours, beginning at *Claudius*, who next *Caligula* ſucceeded *Tiberius*, who reigned at the time of *Chriſts* death, and ſo continuing ſtill till after *Titus Veſpaſian*, and after *Commodus* almoſt all were thus choſen for the ſpace of many yeares, as all the beſt Writers of the *Romane* hiſtory make mention. Now the *Prætorian cohorts* (who were indeed the very flowre and greateſt ſtrength of the *Roman* armie, had the chiefe ſway in the election of the Emperors. The reſemblance whereof we may at this day ſee in the *Turkiſh* Empire. For the great *Turkes Ianiſaries* are his '*Prætorian cohorts*; and although that Empire be hereditary, yet haue the *Ianiſaries* ſo great power in it (as it was lately ſeene) that by them, after the death of *Achmat* this great Turkes father, this Princes Vncle was ſet vpon the throne and quickly after depoſed by them againe, and this Prince *Oſman* ſet vp in his fathers place. And euen ſo after the long troubles that were in *Moſcouia*, after the death of their Duke or Emperour *Iuan Vaſiliwich* (who was the laſt Prince that gouerned that land in in peace) the **Coſackes*, which are the very *Prætorian cohorts* in that countrey, elected this Duke or Emperour, *Michael Feodorwich*, which now reignes. I know there was many ſorts of *Pretors* in *Rome*, one was *Prætor ciuilis*, who iudged but in ciuill cauſes, and another was *Prætor militaris*, who was indeed the Captaine of the Emperours guards: and of them I now make mention, not that I meane hereby to exclude the power of the reſt of the armie in that action; but the *Prætorian cohorts* being the ſtrength and floure of them (as I ſaid already) the reſt of the armie commonly followed, where they led the ring. Now the kingdome of the *Iewes* being, in the time of *Chriſt*, ſubiect to the Emperour of *Rome*, the Emperours gouernours band of ſouldiers, which had a reſemblance to the Emperours *Prætorian cohorts* (euen as a Viceroy repreſents the perſon of the Emperour or King his maſter) brought *Ieſus* to the *common Hall* or *Prætorium*, and there did inaugurate him as you ſhall hereafter heare. And as to the forme of his inauguration, the ſpirit of GOD, ſets it downe very punctually: Firſt, *they ſtripped him, and put on him a ſcarlet robe*; S. *Marke* and S. *Iohn* cals it a *purple robe*, which is one in ſubſtance, * although they were of diuers ingredients. For the ancient *purple* was of a reddiſh colour, and both ſcarlet and purple were ſo rich and princely dyes of old, as they were onely worne by Kings and Princes, and that chiefely in their princely robes: but now theſe ſorts of dyes are loſt. This purple or ſcarlet dye may alſo admit a metapho-

* The *Coſackes* are a ſort of warlike people dwelling vpon the riuer *Boryſthenes*, whereof a number ſerues the K. of *Poland* in his warres; and others J Duke of *Moſcouia*: and of this latter ſort, I ſpeake here.

Mar. 15. 17.
Io. 19. 2.

*The purple was of J iuyce of a ſhellfiſh, named *Purpura*, and the ſcarlet of the graines of a berry.

metaphoricall allufion to the blood of *Chrift*, that was fhed for vs. For the robes of his flefh were dyed in that true purple and fcarlet dye of his bloud, whofe bloud muft wafh our finnes, that wee may appeare holy and vnfpotted before him in our white robes, wafhed in the bloud of the *Lambe*. They firft *ftripped him* then, for it is thought (and not improbably) that his owne cloathes were after the auncient forme of a Prophets garment; onely his coate, without any feame in it, was to fulfill the prophecie of *Dauid*, that *they fhould caft lots for it*; and did alfo fignifie the indiuifible vnitie of the *Church*, which I pray God the true *Church of Chrift* would now well remember. Now therefore, when they were to declare him a King, they tooke off his Prophets garment and put a royall robe vpon him.

Kings euer vfed to weare robes when they fate in their throne of Maieftie, and euen purple robes: for robes or long gownes are fitteft to fit withall, and fitting is the fitteft pofture for expreffing of grauitie in iudgment; ftanding fignifies too great precipitation, which is chiefly to bee auoyded in iudgement, for no man can ftand long without wearying; walking betokens a wandring lightneffe and diftraction of the fenfes; leaning portends weakneffe, and lying inability. And therefore *God* himfelfe is (*per ἀνθρωπαιθειαν*) defcribed in his word to fit in his Throne, and *Chrift* to fit at his right hand; nay, the foure and twenty Elders haue Thrones fet for them to fit in, for they are euen to be CHRISTS affiftants in iudging of the world. Kings therefore, as GODS Deputieiudges vpon earth, fit in thrones, clad with long robes, not as laikes and fimply *togati* (as inferior fecular Iudges are) but as *mixtæ perfonæ* (as I faid in my ΒΑΣΙΛΙΚΟΝ ΔΩΡΟΝ) being bound to make a reckoning to GOD for their fubiects foules as well as their bodies. Not that they ought to vfurpe any point of the Prieftly office, no more then the Prieft fhould the Kings, for thefe two offices were deuided in *Aarons* Priefthood; but it is the Kings office to ouerfee and compell the *Church* to do her office, to purge all abufes in her, and by his fword (as *vindex vtriufq; tabulæ*) to procure her due reuerence and obedience of all his temporall fubiects. And that royall robes are of *purple*, it is to reprefent thereby as well the continuance and honor of their function, as that their iuftice and equitie fhould be without ftaine or blemifh. For the ancient purple, whereof we haue now but the counterfeit, was of extreame long lafting, and could not be ftayned. And next,

When they had platted a crowne of thornes, they fet it vpon his head.

Eere is fet doune what thing they fet vpon his head, of what ftuffe it was made, and in what manner it was wrought. The thing they fet vpon his head was a *crowne*, in the greeke text called *στέφανον*. Anciently the Kings of the Gentiles wore diademes: it is a greeke compound

Marginal notes:
Efa.63. 1,2,3.
Reuel.19.13.
Pfal.22.18.
Reuel.4.2.
Mar.16.19.
Reuel.4.4.
Saint Paul
1.Cor.6.2.&3.

word of אזר & חגר which is *to binde about*, for it went about the head: but in case one would stretch it to אזר & חגר, which is *the people* (though the greeke language will no way beare it) It wil serue for a good remembrance to a King; for the diademe or croune must put him in mind how he raignes by the loue and acknowledgement of his people. I will not heere play the linguist to contest with a sort of popular tribunes, whether that חגר may in a greeke coniunction of wordes bee sometimes vsed as well for *for*, as *from*: for I admit that sense, that it shall onely bee vnderstood *from the people*. For no question, though all successiue Kings receiue their crounes from GOD onely, yet the people at their inauguration giue a publike acknowledgement of their willing subiection to his person and authority, submitting themselues to the will of GOD, who is the onely giuer of it; which is signified by the putting of the diademe or croune vpon his head.

The *diademe* it selfe was a manner of garland which went about the head made like a wreath of silke ribban, or some such like thing; which signified, that as all such, as wan the prize in any match, had garlands put vpon their heads, in signe of the popular applause for their good seruings; so Kings had diademes put vpon their heads, in signe of the peoples willing consent to bee subiect vnto them, that diademe or garland being a marke of their eminencie aboue all others: not that I meane that the forme of diademes was taken from the garlands (for I take the diademes to bee farre more ancient then the garland) but I onely speake heere of the resemblance betweene them in some cases. Neither will I denie that many Kings of the nations had their diademes or crounes giuen them by the people, who translated and transferred by that act all their power into their Kings; but it followeth not that GOD therefore did not set those Kings vpon their thrones. For although those infidell nations knew not *God*, yet *God, qui disponit omnia suauiter*, put it in the peoples hearts to acknowledge them for their Kings, and willingly to submit themselues vnto them, euen that *God*, who is not onely the searcher and knower, but euen the rule of all hearts. But among the people of *God*, where *God* visibly ruled, the King of his people was immediately chosen by himselfe, and the people onely gaue obedience thereunto (as is more then plaine in the *old Testament*) so as the only difference was, that, what GOD did directly by his word and oracle among his owne people in the election of Kings, he did it onely by his secret working in the hearts of other nations, though themselues knew not from whence those motions came, which GOD by his finger wrought in their hearts. And the latine word *corona* signifies also the same thing that *diadema* did. For the croune is set vpon the Kings head and compasseth it, to shew, that as the croune compasseth the Kings head, so is hee to sit in the middest of his people. His wakerif care is euer to bee imployed for their good, their loue is his greatest safetie, and their prosperitie is his greatest honour

nour

Wisd. 8. 1.

Psal. 7. 9.
Prou. 21. 1.
1. Sam. 9. 16.
1. Sam. 16. 13.

nour and felicitie. For many times among the *Romans*, the word *corona* signified the people, as * *Aliquid etiam coronæ datum.* And Saint *Paul*, 1. *Theſſ.* 2. 19. calls them the *Croune of his reioycing* or glorying.

Cic. De finib. bon. & mal. lib. 4.

As to the ſtuffe wherof this Croune was made, it was made of thornes: and it is vulgarly well knowen that thornes ſignifie ſtinging and pricking cares. That King therefore, who will take his paterne from this heauenly King, muſt not thinke to weare a Croune of gold and precious ſtones only, but it muſt be lyned with *Thornes*, that is, thornie cares: for he muſt remember that hee weares not that croune for himſelfe, but for others; that hee is ordayned for his people, and not his people for him. For he is a great watchman and ſhepheard, as well as Church-men are: and his eye muſt neuer ſlumber nor ſleepe for the care of his flocke, euer remembring that his office, beeing duely executed, will prooue as much *onus* as *honos* vnto him. And as to the forme of making the croune of thornes, it is ſaid, *they platted thornes and made a croune of them.* Now euery man knoweth, that where a number of long things, in forme of lines, ſhall bee platted through other, it makes a troubleſome and intricate worke to finde out all the ends of them, and ſet them aſunder againe, eſpecially to ſet ſtraight and euen againe all the ſeuerall peeces that muſt be bowed in the platting: but aboue all, to ſet ſtraight and aſunder againe thornes that are platted, is a moſt vncomfortable worke. For though any one peece of thorne may be handled in ſome place without hurt, yet no man can touch platted thornes without danger of pricking. As a croune of thornes then repreſents the ſtinging cares of Kings, ſo a croune of platted thornes doth more viuely repreſent the anxious and intricate cares of Kings, who muſt not onely looke to be troubled with a continuall care for the good gouernement of their people, but they muſt euen expect to meete with a number of croſſe and intricate difficulties, which will appeare to bee ſo full of repugnances among themſelues, as they can ſcantly be touched without ſmarting. And euen as a good and skilfull Phyſitian is moſt troubled with that ſort of patient, that hath many implicate diſeaſes vpon him (the fitteſt cure for ſome of them beeing directly noyſome to others, and the antidote to one of his diſeaſes proouing little better then poyſon to another of them) ſo muſt Kings exerciſe their wiſedome in handling ſo wiſely theſe knotty difficulties, and with ſo great a moderation; that too great extremitie in one kinde may not prooue hurtfull in another, but, by a muſicall skill, temper and turne all theſe diſcords into a ſweet harmonie.

And they put a reede in his right hand.

His reede repreſented the Kingly ſcepter, which is the paſtorall rod of a King; and the ſtraightneſſe of the reed, his righteouſneſſe in the adminiſtration of iuſtice, without any partiality, as it is *Pſal.* 45. 7. *The ſcepter of thy kingdome is a right ſcepter.* The ſcepter repreſents the Kings authority;

authority ; for as the royall robes are firſt put on vpon a King, to ſhew the grauitie and dignitie of the perſon that is to bee inaugurated, and as the croune repreſents the loue and willing acknowledgement of his people, ſo the ſcepter is next put in his hand to declare his authoritie who is already found worthy to enioy the ſame by his coronation. The autho

Pſal. 2. 9.

ritie of God himſelfe is expreſſed in the 2. Pſal. by a *rod of yron*, wherewith he is to bruiſe the nations that rebel againſt him, which rod of yron ſignifies his ſcepter. But this ſcepter put in the hand of *Chriſt* was a reede. It is true that the reeds of thoſe countreys, as thoſe of India are, bee a great deale bigger, harder and more ſolid then ours ; but though one may giue a great blow with them, yet are they much more brittle then ſolide timber is, and hard blowes giuen with them will eaſily make them breake: thereby teaching Chriſtian Kings that their ſcepters (which repreſent their authority) ſhould not be too much vſed nor ſtretched, but where neceſſity requires it. For many harde blowes giuen with a reede would make it quickly breake (as I haue ſayd) and wiſe Kings would bee loth to put their prerogatiue vpon the tenter-hookes, except a great neceſſity ſhould require it. For there is a great difference betweene the ſcepter (which repreſents the authority of a King toward all his ſubiects as well good as bad) and the ſword, which is onely ordayned for the puniſhment of the euill. And therefore the ſcepter of a King ſhould bee of a reede, that is, to correct gently : but the ſword, which is ordayned for puniſhment of vice, and purging the land of haynous and crying ſinnes, muſt bee a ſharpe weapon. And alſo the ſcepter of a reede did not onely ſerue for a paterne to other Kings, but it fitted properly the perſon of *Chriſt*, who, being the true King of mercy, came to conuert ſinners

Math. 9. 13.
Math. 11. 30.

and bring them to repentance, but not to deſtroy them ; for as himſelfe ſayth, *his burthen is light and his yoke is eaſie.* But although this ſcepter muſt bee put in the KINGS hand by ſome one of his ſubiects (for *God* will not come himſelfe, nor by an Angell out of heauen deliuer it vnto him, for that were miraculous and is not to bee expected) yet I hope no Chriſtian doubts but that the authority of a King, whereof the ſcep

Prou. 8. 15.

ter is the repreſentation, is onely giuen by *God.* *Per me reges regnant & domini dominantur.* Kings are anoynted of *God* ſitting in his ſeate and therefore called *Gods* : and all ſuperiour powers are of *God*; nay the Pro

Pſal. 82. 6.
Rom. 13. 1.
Iere. 34. 10.
Rom. 13. 4.

phet *Ieremie* cals that Ethnike Emperour, *Nebuchadnezar*, *the ſeruant of God*, and *S. Paul* calls the tyrant *Nero*, in his time, *the miniſter of God.* And that it was put in his right hand, it was becauſe the right hand

Coloſ. 3. 1.
Verſe 1.

ſignifieth both honour and power : Honour, *Chriſt ſits at the right hand of God. Sit thou at my right hand*, *Pſal. 110.* Power, as the hand of action : *And thy right hand ſhall teach thee terrible things*, *Pſal. 45.* and *Pſal. 118. 16.* both are expreſſed, *The right hand of the Lord hath the preeminence, the right hand of the Lord bringeth mighty things to paſſe.*

And

And they bowed the knee before him, and (as Saint *Marke* witnesseth) *they worshipped him.*

Ow though this kneeling and worship was in a mockery done by them; yet may wee learne heere that *God* thought it no Idolatry that his sonne should be kneeled vnto, euen in the time of his greatest humilitie, and entring in his passion. But I haue touched this point already. As for their worshipping him, it is true that both their kneeling and worship were intended as a ciuill homage done to a temporal King. And in that sence the old word of *worship* was wont to be vsed in English, and as yet it is vsed here in the celebration of marriage. This ciuill worship is easily distinguished by them that please from diuine worship: for to reuerence an earthly creature, and do him respect in regard of the eminencie of his place, yea euen to make a request or prayer vnto him, is quite different from a diuine and spirituall worship. For in the former we onely doe reuerence or make our request to these temporall Kings or persons that are subiect to our senses; but we can vse no spirituall worship or prayer that can be auaileable vnto vs without faith. Let the schoole distinctions of δουλεια ὑπερδουλεια and λατρεια deceiue them that list to be deceiued with them: for all prayer in faith is due to *God* onely.

And after their kneeling and worshipping him,

They mocked him, saying, HAILE KING OF THE IEVVES.

S for their mocking him, I haue largely declared that point already: but as to the words which they vsed in saluting him, they are also vsed in the ordinary forme of the Inaugurtion of Kings; that, after all the actions of ceremony are vsed vnto him, the people that are more remote & cannot with their eies see the performance of those actions, may know they are performed by the publike proclaiming of him. And becaufe the rest of this inauguration of *Christ*, is set doune in other places of the *new Testament*, I must here supply it: for I onely set doune, in the beginning, the Text of S. *Matthew*, as being the only place of Scripture which makes the longest and most particular relation of his inauguration. For this action stayed not here, but *Pilate* (who was both iudge and gouernour, vnder the *Romanes* of that par of the country) made him to bee sent forth out of the *common hall*, and shewed to all the people in that kingly attire: and when as the bloudy and malitious *Iewes* cryed out to crucifie him, hee answered againe, *shall I crucifie your King?* And after that, he sent him to *Herod* (who was Tetrarc and Viceroy of the fourth part of *Iewrie*) who put other gorgeous robes vpon him: so as he was not only inaugurated and

Ioh. 19. 4.

Io. 19. 13.

Luc. 23. 11.

and proclaimed King of the *Iewes* by the Gouernours *Roman* Souldiers who reprefented the *Prætorian cohorts*; but hee was alfo fo acknowledged by the iudge and gouernour *Pilate*, and by the Tetrarch *Herod*. But herein was the difference, that all this action performed by *Herod* and his Souldiers, was but a wicked mockery in their intention: whereas by the contrary, *Pilate*, being both iudge and gouernour, meant it not in mockery; but was in a great doubt and wift not what to make of it : as

* Io. 18.33. & 37.

it appeares both by his queftioning of *Chrift*, and alfo that hee brought him forth of the *common hall* and fhewed him to the whole multitude in

Io. 19.5.

his royall robes and his croune vpon his head, faying vnto them, *Behold the Man*; thereby as it were confirming publikely his inauguration done by the Souldiers before. and when the people cryed, *Away with him*, his

Io. 19.15.

anfwere was (as I faid already) *Shall I crucifie your King*? Both which words he fpake to ftrike a terrour into them, or at leaft to mooue them, to commiferation, feeming to mocke him as they did : for both Chrifts anfwere vnto him, and his Wiues meffage vpon a dreame fhe had, put him in a great perplexitie; till the feare he had of offending the Emperor in cafe CHRIST had proued thereafter to haue beene the righteous King of the *Iewes* (which *Herod* the great alfo apprehended at his birth) enforced him to pronounce fo iniuft and deteftable a fentence; fo as, that in his owne heart he meant no ieft in it, is clearely apparant in making his title to be written aboue his head vpon the Croffe, as an honorable infcription, euen fet in that place aboue his head, and to the view of all the world. And to make it the more publike , it was written in

Io. 19.20.

three languages, *Hebrew, Greeke*, and *Latine* : *Hebrew*, as the vulgar language of that people; and *Greeke* and *Latine* as the moft common and publike languages of all *Profelytes* and ftrangers, that fhould come to fee that fpectacle: efpecially, thefe two were the languages of all prophane learning. Euen as in this kingdome it was the ancent cuftome and is ftill obferued to this day, that vpon S. *Georges* day, and at other high feftiuall times, the chiefe *Herald garter* comes in the niddeft of the feaft, and proclaimes my titles in three languages, *Latine French*, and *Englifh* : *Englifh*, becaufe it is the vulgar language of this kngdome ; and *Latine* and *French*, as the two ftrange tongues that manift here do vnderftand. Efpecially the time is to be obferued whe the orde of the *Garter* was firft inftituted by *Edward* the third, who as hee was Sonne to the daughter of *France*, fo at that time the *French* tongue was in a manner the vulgar language of this Nation : and therefce they are proclaimed in three languages heere, that it may bee vderftood by the vulgar fort (as *Pilates* infcription was) and not corealed from them. Now what ground the *Papifts* can haue heerby, to haue not onely their *Maffe* and feruice in an vnknowne tonge, but euen that ignorant people fhall bee taught their prayers in a ftrange tongue which they vnderftand not, I leaue it to the iudgement of the indifferent reader : for, besides that it is directly prohibited by Saint *Paul*, it is flatly contrary to *Pilates* action in this case. For one of the three languages wherein *Christs* title was written vpon the crosse, was *Hebrew*, which was the vulgar language of that Countrie; and the other two were these that were best vnderstood by the strangers and *Proselytes* there. So as it is a flat contradiction betweene *Pilates* act (who by all meanes stroue to make *Christs* title so to be read and vnderstood by all men) and our *Papists*, that will haue their seruice and prayers to bee in an vnknowen tongue, that no ignorant country-man may vnderstand them. But it is ill lucke for the *Church* of *Rome*, that the best warrant they can bring for this their forme of the worship of *God*, is grounded vpon the example of *Pilate*. But to returne to our purpose; though it was the common fashion that great offendors, so executed, had the nature and qualitie of their crimes written aboue their heads; yet in my opinion it is cleare enough (as I said already) that *Pilate* gaue the title to *Christ* in earnest. Not onely for that hee made it so solemnely to be written aboue his head vpon the crosse, but euen after that the high Priest had wittily and maliciously requested him to correct that writing, and in place of IESVS OF NAZARETH KING OF THE IEVVES, to say, IESVS OF NAZARETH THAT CALLETH HIMSELFE KING OF THE IEVVES, he absolutely refused it, in these words, *quod scripsi scripsi*, which was a constant refusall, worthy of a iudge in maintenance of a iust decree. Happy had *Pilate* beene, if base feare had not made him pronounce a worse sentence before. So as, if there were no more but this action of *Pilate* so constant and absolute, it were enough to prooue (according to my first ground in the beginning of this discourse) that though the wicked people (both *Iewes* and *Romanes*) intended nothing in all this worke, but a malicious and blasphemous mockery, yet had *God* his worke to two ends heerein. First, that his onely Sonne might thus be put to the height of derision, that his passion might be fully accomplished for our saluation: and next, that (as I said in the beginning) he, that brings light out of darkenes, might wring from this malitiously blinded people a bodily externall acknowledgement of his Sonnes true title to that kingdome, prophecied of old, that *the scepter should not depart from Iuda, nor a law-giuer from betweene his feete till Shiloh came*: prophecied likewise by *Balaam*, which prophecie (as * some learned writers thinke) instructed the wise Kings of the East, who were guided by the starre, to come and worship *Christ*. This title was likewise the occasion of great trouble to *Herod the greats* minde, whereupon came his murthering of the children; and is so carefully set doune in the genealogie of *Christ*, written by two *Euangelists*; and was not denied by *Christ* himselfe, when *Pilate* asked him the question. And so this forme of *Christs* inauguration was left for a paterne to all Christian Kings thereafter.

Yet amongst all these *insignia regalia*, the *sword* is amissing, the reason is,

1.Cor.14.15.

Io.19.21.

Verse 22.

Gen.49.10.
Num.24.17.
Iust. mart. Epiphan.Basil.,&c.
Mat.2.15.

Matth 2.&
Luk. 3.

is , his firſt comming was to ſuffer for our ſaluation from the ſword c̄ diuine iuſtice; and not to vſe the ſword, to take vengeance vpon euill doers: at his ſecond comming he will come as a iudge,and vſe his ſword vpon the wicked. And therefore he came in the fleſh, as a lambe, not once opening his mouth when hee was led to the ſlaughter: ſuffering without repining the higheſt outrages to the minde, which is, mockery with contempt, a kinde of perſecution; and the greateſt tortures in the body that could bee deuiſed, that the prophecie of *Ieremie* might bee accompliſhed, *non eſt dolor ſicut dolor meus*. He was buffeted, and ſo made a ſlaue, he was ſpit vpon as a worme, and ſo, farre leſſe then any humane creature; *he was beaten with his owne rod*, as the prouerbe is: for after that they had put a reede in his right hand,they pulled it out againe and ſmote him with it: hee was mocked in the higheſt meaſure, both before and after his nayling to the croſſe. and as to the torture of his body, hee was extreamly ſcourged: the croune of platted thornes made innumerable bloudy wounds in his head: and he was nayled both through his hands and feete to the infamous death of the croſſe; that the extremity of his anguiſh in mind, and torture in body, might ſerue as a full ranſome, to ſatisfie his fathers iuſtice for our redemption. He came then at this time as a titularie King of that kingdome, but not to exerciſe any worldly iuriſdiction, *regnum eius non erat huius mundi,* and ſo he taught his Diſciples to follow him, *Reges gentium dominantur eis vos autem non ſic.* He had no vſe of a ſword then, nay, he found fault with Saint *Peters* vſing it, telling him, *Hee that ſtriketh with the ſword ſhall periſh by the ſword;* leauing it belike to thoſe that call themſelues *Peters* ſucceſſors, who come in the ſpirit of *Elias* with fire, adding gun-powder and the ſword vnto it. But our *Sauiour* knew not how to ſet both croune and mitre vpon one head: nor yet was he acquainted with that diſtinction,that a Church-man may vſe the temporall ſword, to procure *bonum ſpirituale.*

But to returne to our purpoſe of *Chriſts* humilitie; it may bee obiected that it is not likely, that our *Sauiour* would in the very middeſt of his paſſion (which was the action of his greateſt humility) giue euen then a glance of his title to a worldly kingdome: for ſuffering of iniuries, eſpecially ſuch baſe abuſes, is directly contrary to the maieſty of a King and the honour of his inauguration. To this I anſwere two wayes. *firſt*, it was neceſſary that *Chriſt* in the time of his paſſion ſhould approue himſelfe to bee lineally deſcended from *Dauid*, yea euen next heire to the croune of the *Iewes*; that he might in the ſight of the world, before his going out of it,fulfill theſe prophecies which I lately made mention of, thereby to prooue himſelfe the true *Meſſias* that was promiſed. And *next*, as hee was both *God* and *Man*, ſo ſhall ye finde that euen from his conception till his very expiring vpon the croſſe,he euer intermixed glances of his glory,in the midſt of his greateſt humilitie.Was it not a glorious thing that the Angel *Gabriel* ſhould be the meſſenger to the bleſſed

                                                                                 Virgin

Iſai.53.7.

Lam.1.12.
Luc.22.65.
Matt.27.30.

Io.18.36.
Matth.20.25.

Matth.26.52.

Luk.1.26.

Virgin of his conception? When *Ioseph* thought to put away his wife, thinking shee had beene vnlawfully with childe by a man, hee was prohibited by an Angel in a dreame. When the blessed *Virgin*, beeing with child, went to the hill countrey to visit her cousin *Elizabeth*, *Iohn* the *Baptist* sprang in the belly of his mother, which was a miraculous kinde of worshipping and congratuling our *Sauiour* in the belly of his blessed mother. He was borne in a poore stable, in a beasts cribb, and amongst beasts, but the Angels sung a glorious hymne of gratulation at his birth. His parents fled to *Egypt* with him, when hee was yet in the cradle; but, immediatly before that, three Kings of the East brought presents to him, and worshipped him. Hee was obedient to his parents during his minority; but, being but twelue yeeres of age, hee disputed publikely in the Temple with the Doctors of their Law, to the admiration of all the hearers. Hee was baptized in *Iordan* by *Iohn Baptist*, as many of the common people were: but at his baptisme the *Holy Ghost* descended vpon his head in the likenesse of a doue, and a voice was heard from his Father, saying, *This is my beloued* SONNE, *in whom I am well pleased.* And hee auowed to the *Scribes* and *Pharisees*, that *Abraham* longed to see his day and did see it, giuing the title to himselfe which *God* vsed in the fiery bush to *Moses*, *I am that I am; for* hee sayd vnto them, *before Abraham was, I am.* Hee fled diuers times from the fury of the *Iewes*, nay, *the sonne of man had not a hole to hide his head in*: and yet hee purged the temple twice, and like a great temporall magistrate scourged and thrust out those that bought and sold in the temple: yea hee rebuked the windes and commanded the seas. And, at his transfiguration, he made his body appeare a glorified body, by dispensation at that time, hauing (as the true *God*) the *Law* and the commentary and application thereof, which is the *Prophets*, to attend vpon him in the persons of *Moses* and *Elias*. He payed tribute, to shew, that neither *Christ* as man, nor S. *Peter* must bee exempted from giuing vnto *Caesar* that which is *Caesars*: but caused *Peter* to angle for it, and take it out of the mouth of a fish, to shew the power of his Godhead. Sometimes hee went vp priuately to the feast at *Ierusalem* for feare of the *Iewes*: but at his last *Passeouer* hee sent some of his Disciples, and by them commanded him, whom hee meant to make his host, to prepare his house for him, *for the Lord meant to keepe his Passeouer there.* He refused to be a King when the people would haue made him one: and yet hee commanded some of his Disciples to vntie an asse, telling her owner *that the Master had neede of her.* And then made a publike entrie vpon her through *Ierusalem* like a temporall King, euen with many solemnities belonging to a Kings riding in state. For his Disciples put their clothes vpon the asse and the colt, as it were to represent the garnishing with foot-clothes, as wel the horse he rode on as his led horse: the people also spread their garments in the way, and others cut downe branches and strawed them; all which is an vsuall forme that princes

people

Matt.1.20.
Luk.1.41.

Luk.2.7.
Cap.2.14.
Matt.2.1.
2.11.
Luk.2.46.

Matt.3.13.

Ioh.8.

Matt.3.17.
.18.

Io.8.58.

Matt.8.20.
Io.2.15.
Matt.8.26.
Matth.17.1.

Matt.17.27.

Io.7.10.

Matth.26.18.
Io.6.15.

Matth.21.3.

people vſe to honour their King with, at ſuch ſolemne times. He had
alſo the acclamation of all the people crying *Hoſanna to the ſonne of Da-*
uid, &c. nay, euen hee himſelfe tooke it vpon him as his due; for when
the chiefe Prieſts and Scribes thinking that hee would not take ſuch
ſtate vpon him, asked if hee heard what the people ſaid, hee anſwered
them out of that of the eight *Pſalme, Out of the mouthes of babes and ſuck-*
lings thou haſt perfeɛted prayſe. And as for his riding vpon an aſſe, it was
not a contemptible thing for Kings and Princes in the Eaſt, eſpecially a-
mong the *Iewes*, to ride vpon aſſes euen in the ſight of the people. Hee
waſhed his diſciples feete, to teach them humility, immediatly before
his laſt *Supper* : and yet a few dayes before that, he highly commended
Mary Magdalen for breaking an alabaſter boxe of oyntments vpon his
feete, and ſuffered her to wipe them with the haire of her head. When
the *Iewes* ſent their officers with *Iudas* to apprehend him; though he ſuffered them at the laſt to carrie him away, yet at the firſt with a flaſh and
caſt of his eye (wherein, no queſtion, the Diuinitie ſparkled when he li-
ſted) he made them all fall backewards, ſo as they could not approch him
againe till hee permitted them. The caſt of his eye made likewiſe S. *Pe-*
ter goe forth and weepe when the cocke crew. And euen vpon the very
croſſe, though the death thereupon was accurſed by the Law, he was exalted, as S. *Paul* ſaith ; and there promiſed the penitent thiefe, he ſhould
be that day with him in *Paradiſe*, hauing that royall inſcription (whereof I haue made mention already) written aboue his head in the three
moſt publike tongues. Yea, euen after that his body was taken off the
croſſe, a principall man amongſt the *Iewes*, *Ioſeph* of *Arimathea*, begged
his bodie of *Pilate* ; and not onely imbaumed it (as kings and Princes bodies vſe to bee) but put it in a new faire ſepulchre, which had been prepared for himſelfe. And thus you ſee, that, through all the courſe of our
Sauiours life in this world, he gaue vpon euery occaſion ſome glances of
his glory ; for the conuerſion or confirming of ſome of his elect, and for
making the wicked and ſtubborne hearted inexcuſable. For *bee thought*
it no robberie to bee equall with God.

   And now to conclude this paterne of a King, I will ſhortly ſumme
vp theſe regall ornaments together with their ſignification, which before I handled. A King hath firſt great cauſe of contentment if the people of all ſorts (eſpecially thoſe to whoſe place it belongs) doe willingly
conueene and concurre to his publike inauguration. A King muſt looke
to haue that action performed in publike, and in a publike place; that the
loue of his people may appeare in that ſolemne action. Two things a
King hath ſpecially to looke vnto at his inauguration ; *firſt*, that his title
to the croune be iuſt, and *next* that he may poſſeſſe it with the loue of his
people. For although a Monarchie or hereditary kingdome cannot iuſtly
be denied to the lawful ſucceſſor, whateuer the affectiós of the people be;
yet it is a great ſigne of the bleſſing of *God*, when he enters in it with the
                                                                willing

Matt. 21.9.

Pſal. 8. v. 2.

Iud. 10.4. &
12.14.
Io. 13.4.

Io. 12.7.

Reuel. 1. 14.
Io. 18.6.

Luk. 23.61.

Phil. 2.9.

Luk. 23.43.

Luk. 23.50.

Philip. 2. 6.

willing applause of his subiects. Now the first ornament, that is to be put vpon him, are his robes, to put him in memory that in his sitting in iudgment he is to vse grauitie, great patience in hearing all parties, & mature deliberation before he pronounce his sentence. And the purple dye of his robe, should put him in memory not to prooue vnwo thy of so ancient a croune and dignitie; and to take great heed to his conscience, that his iudgement may be without blemish or staine of whatsoeuer corrupt affections. For iustice must be blinde, and it is she *that establisheth the thrones* Prou. 16. 12. *of* K I N G S. The setting of the croune vpon his head must put him in mind, that he is euer to walke in the middest of his people, that their loue is his greatest safetie, and their prosperitie his greatest glory and worldly felicitie. But he must not expect a soft and easie croune, but a croune full of thornie cares, yea, of platted and intricate cares: and therefore hee ought to make it his principall studie (next the safetie of his soule) to learne, how to make himselfe able to rid and extricate those many knottie difficulties, that will occurre vnto him; according to my admonition to my sonne H E N R Y in the end of my ΒΑΣΙΛΙΚΟΝ ΔΩΡΟΝ, wherein I apply some verses of *Virgil* to that purpose. And therefore, in all other commendable things he may presse so farre to excell, as his inclination and leisure will permit him; but in the science of gouernmen. hee must presse to be an artf-master. And his Scepter made of a reede, must put him in minde to manage his authoritie boldly, and yet temperately, not stretching his roya'l Prerogatiue but where necessitie shall require it. Temporall Kings must not likewise be barred the sword, though it bee not in this paterne (as I told before) for it is to be drawne for the punishment of the wicked in defence of the good: *for a King carries not his sword* Rom. 3. 14. *for naught.* But it must neither bee blunt: for lawes without execution are without life. nor yet must it be euer drawne: for a King should neuer punish but with a weeping eye. In a word, a Christian King should neuer be without that continuall and euer wakeriffe care; of the account he is one day to giue to *God*, of the good gouernment of his people, & their prosperous estate both in soules and bodies; which is a part of the health of his owne soule. And then he shall neuer need to doubt of that happy and willing acclamation of his people, with an *Aue Cæsar*, or *haile King*, (which was mentioned in this paterne) not onely to begin at his entry to the croune, but euen to accompany him all the daies of his life thereafter; and when they haue bedewed and washed his graue with their teares, his posteritie to bee well-commed by them, as a bright and sunne-shining morning after a darke and gloomie night.

LONDON

Printed by ROBERT BARKER and IOHN
BILL, Printers to the Kings moſt
Exceellent Maieſtie.

ANNO M.DC.XX.

CPSIA information can be obtained
at www.ICGtesting.com
Printed in the USA
BVHW01s1829110318
510295BV00015B/257/P